How Children DEVELOP

ROBERT **SIEGLER**

Carnegie Mellon University

JUDY **DELOACHE**

University of Virginia

NANCY **EISENBERG**

Arizona State University

WORTH PUBLISHERS

How Children Develop
First Edition

Printed in the United States of America
ISBN: 1-57259-249-4
Second printing, 2003

Sponsoring Editor: Marjorie Byers
Developmental Editor: Peter Deane
Production Editor: Vivien Weiss
Executive Marketing Manager: Renée Altier
Associate Managing Editor: Tracey Kuehn
Production Manager: Sarah Segal
Art Director, Cover Designer: Barbara Reingold
Interior Designer: Lissi Sigillo
Layout Designer: Paul Lacy
Photo Editor: Meg Kuhta
Photo Researcher: Deborah Goodsite
Senior Illustration Coordinator: Bill Page
Illustrator: Todd Buck Illustration, Precision Graphics, TSI Graphics, Inc.
Composition: TSI Graphics, Inc.
Printing and Binding: R. R. Donnelly & Sons Company

Library of Congress Control Number: 2002113230

Worth Publishers
41 Madison Avenue
New York, NY 10010
www.worthpublishers.com

ABOUT THE AUTHORS

Robert Siegler is the Teresa Heinz Professor of Cognitive Psychology at Carnegie Mellon University. He is author of the cognitive development textbook *Children's Thinking* and has written or edited several additional books on child development. His books have been translated into Japanese, Korean, Spanish, and French. In the past few years, he has presented keynote addresses at the conventions of the Society for Research in Child Development, the Cognitive Development Society, the International Society for the Study of Behavioral Development, The Jean Piaget Society, the Conference on Human Development, the American Psychological Association, and the American Psychological Society. He also has served as Associate Editor of the journal *Developmental Psychology* and co-edited the cognitive development volume of the 1998 *Handbook of Child Psychology.*

Judy DeLoache is the Lawrence R. Kenan, Jr. Professor of Psychology at the University of Virginia. She has been the editor and co-editor of three editions of *Current Research in Child Development,* a book of readings for use in child development courses. She is also co-editor of the recently published *A World of Babies,* a book on cultural differences in the treatment of infants. She recently served as President of the Developmental Division of the American Psychological Association and as a member of the Executive Boards of the International Society for the Study of Infancy and the Cognitive Development Society. Dr. DeLoache has presented major invited addresses at meetings of the Society for Research in Child Development, the American Psychological Association, the American Psychological Society, Zero-to-Three, the Cognitive Development Society, and the Minnesota Symposium on Child Psychology. Dr. DeLoache has been a Fellow of the Center for Advanced Study in the Behavioral Sciences, and she is the holder of a MERIT award from NIH. She has been recognized several times for outstanding undergraduate teaching.

Nancy Eisenberg is Regent's Professor of Psychology at Arizona State University. She is editor or author of numerous books on prosocial, social, and emotional development, including Volume 3 of *The Handbook of Child Psychology* (Social, Emotional, and Personality Development). She is also the author of *The Caring Child.* Several of her books have been translated into Japanese, Spanish, or Polish. She is currently on the Publications Board of the Society for Research in Child Psychology and recently served as the editor of *Psychological Bulletin.* Dr. Eisenberg was the associate editor of *Merrill-Palmer Quarterly* and *Personality and Social Psychology Bulletin* and served as president of the Western Psychological Association. She has been on the governing board of the Society for Research in Child Development and has served on the council of the American Psychological Association.

This is dedicated to the ones we love

BRIEF CONTENTS

CONTENTS

PREFACE

This is an exciting time to be writing a child development textbook. The past decade has brought new theories, new ways of thinking, new areas of research, and innumerable new findings in the field. We wrote *How Children Develop* to describe this ever improving knowledge of children and to convey the excitement that we feel about the progress that is being made toward understanding the developmental process.

As teachers of child-development courses, we appreciate the challenge that instructors face in trying to present these advances and discoveries, as well as major prior ideas and findings, in a one-semester course. Therefore, rather than aiming at encyclopedic coverage, we have focused on identifying the most important developmental phenomena and describing them in sufficient depth to make them meaningful and memorable to students. In short, our goal has been to write a textbook that makes the child-development course coherent and enjoyable for students and teachers alike.

Classic Themes

The basic premise of the book is that all areas of child development are unified by a small set of enduring themes. These themes can be stated in the form of questions that child-development research tries to answer:

1. How do nature and nurture together shape development?
2. How do children shape their own development?
3. In what ways is development continuous and in what ways is it discontinuous?
4. How does change occur?
5. How does the sociocultural context influence development?
6. How do children become so different from each other?
7. How can research promote children's well-being?

These seven themes provide the core structure of the book. They are introduced and illustrated in Chapter 1, highlighted repeatedly where relevant in the subsequent thirteen content chapters, and utilized in the final chapter as a framework for integrating findings from all areas of development that are relevant to each theme. The continuing coverage of these themes allows us to tell a story with a beginning (introduction of the themes), middle (specific findings relevant to them), and ending (the overview of what students have learned about the themes). We believe that this thematic emphasis and storylike structure will not only help students understand enduring questions about child development but will also leave them with a greater sense of satisfaction and completion at the end of the course.

Contemporary Perspective

The goal of providing a thoroughly contemporary perspective on how children develop has influenced the organization of our book as well as its contents. Whole new areas and perspectives have emerged that barely existed when most of today's child-development textbooks were originally written. Placing these topics in their current context is much easier in a new book.

Consider the case of Piaget's theory and current research relevant to it. Piaget's theory usually is presented in its own chapter, three-quarters of which describes the theory in full detail and the rest of which offers contemporary research that demonstrates problems with the theory. This approach often leaves students wondering why so much time was spent on Piaget's theory if modern research shows it to be wrong in so many ways.

The fact is that the line of research that began thirty years ago as an effort to challenge Piaget's theory has emerged since then as a vital area in its own right—the area of conceptual development. Research on conceptual development provides extensive information on such fascinating topics as children's understanding of human beings, plants and animals, and the physical universe. As with other research areas, most studies in this field are aimed primarily at providing evidence relevant to current claims, not those of Piaget.

We have adapted to this changing intellectual landscape in two ways. First, our chapter "Theories of Cognitive Development" describes the fundamental aspects of Piaget's theory in depth, honoring his legacy by focusing on the contributions of his work that have proven to be the most enduring. Second, we present an entirely new chapter, "Conceptual Development," which addresses the types of issues that inspired Piaget's theory but concentrates on modern perspectives and findings regarding those issues. This approach allows us to tell students about the numerous intriguing proposals and observations that are being made in this field, without the artificiality of classifying the findings as "pro-Piagetian" or "anti-Piagetian."

The opportunity to create a textbook based on current understanding also led us to assign prominent positions to such rapidly emerging areas as brain development, behavioral genetics, nutritional and eating disorders, prenatal learning, infant cognition, acquisition of academic skills, emotional development, prosocial behavior, and friendship patterns. All of these areas have seen major breakthroughs in recent years, and their growing prominence is reflected in the coverage they receive in our book.

Getting Right to the Point

Our desire to offer a contemporary, streamlined approach has led to other departures from the traditional organization. It is our experience that today's students take child-development courses for a variety of practical reasons and are eager to learn about *children*. Traditionally, however, they have to wait for two or three or even four chapters—on the history of the field, on major theories, on research methods, on genetics—before actually getting to the study of children. We want to build on their initial motivation immediately. Rather than opening the book, then, with an extensive examination of the history of the field, we include in Chapter 1 a brief overview of the social and intellectual context in which the scientific study of children arose and then provide historical background wherever it is pertinent in subsequent chapters. Rather than having an early theories chapter that covers all the major cognitive and social theories at once, at a point far removed from the content chapters to which the theories apply, we present a chapter on cognitive developmental theories just before the chapters that focus on specific aspects of cognitive development, as well as a chapter on social developmental theories just before the chapters that focus on specific aspects of social development. Rather than having a separate chapter on genetics, we include basic aspects of genetics as part of Chapter 3

("Biology and Behavior") and then discuss contributions of genetics to individual differences throughout the book. This approach allows us from the first weeks of the course to kindle students' enthusiasm for finding out how children develop.

Features

The most important feature of this book is the exposition, which we have tried to make as clear, compelling, and interesting as possible. Multiple drafts, scrupulous editing, and several rounds of class testing have resulted, we believe, in a presentation that is direct, transparent, and accessible to a broad range of students.

To further enhance the appeal and accessibility of the text, we have included three types of discussion boxes that explore material of special interest. "Applications" boxes focus on how child-development research can be used to promote children's well being. Among the applications covered in these boxes are the Carolina Abecedarian Project, interventions to reduce child abuse, programs for helping rejected children gain acceptance with their peers, and Fast Track interventions to help aggressive children learn how to manage their anger and behavior. "Individual Differences" boxes focus on populations that differ from the norm with regard to the specific topics under consideration or on variations among children in the general population. These boxes cover such topics as intellectual giftedness, adolescent depression, and cultural differences in emotional expression. "A Closer Look" boxes examine important and interesting research in greater depth than would otherwise be possible: the areas examined range from brain-imaging techniques to the developmental impact of homelessness and the issues surrounding children's immersion in the digital world.

We have also incorporated a number of other features intended to improve students' learning. These include boldfacing key terms and providing definitions of them both within the immediate text and in margin glossaries; providing summaries at the end of each major section, as well as overall chapter summaries; and, at the end of each chapter, posing critical thinking questions intended to promote deeper consideration of essential topics.

Supplements

A variety of excellent teaching and learning tools are available to enrich and reinforce the text.

Exploring Child Development Student CD-Rom

This integrative tool brings the excitement of the research lab to the student. Short video clips of classic and contemporary studies add a hands-on dimension to the text presentations. Chapter quizzes and flashcards help students to review. The CD-Rom was prepared by Lisa Huffman, Ball State University; Thomas Ludwig, Hope College; Tanya Renner, Kapiolani Community College; Catherine Robertson, Grossmont College; Stavros Valenti, Hofstra University; and Connie Varnhagen, University of Alberta. It can be packaged on request with the textbook at no additional cost.

Exploring Child Development: A Media Tool Kit for Instructors

An expanded version of the student CD-Rom above, this set for instructors, combines over 100 video clips, animations, and interactive exercises to enhance your child development course. All video material is available on DVD and VHS.

Instructor's Resource Manual

Written by Lynne Baker-Ward, North Carolina State University, this innovative *Instructor's Resource Manual* includes handouts for student projects, reading lists from journal articles, course-planning suggestions, supplementary readings, and a guide to videos and software, in addition to lecture guides, chapter overviews, and learning objectives.

Student Study Guide

The *Student Study Guide,* written by Jill Saxon, includes in each chapter a review of key concepts and multiple-choice and essay questions to help students evaluate their mastery of the material.

Test Bank

To assure seamless coordination between the content that students review and the content on which they are tested, we asked Jill Saxon, who wrote the *Study Guide,* to also write the *Test Bank.* It includes 80 multiple-choice and 20 essay questions for each chapter. Each question is keyed to the textbook by topic, type (factual, definitional or conceptual, or applied), and level of difficulty.

Test Bank on CD-Rom

The *Diploma Test Bank CD-Rom,* on dual platform for Windows and Macintosh, guides instructors through the process of creating a test and allows them to add, edit, and scramble questions; to change formats; and to include pictures, equations, and media links. The CD-Rom is also the access point for *Diploma Online Testing,* which allows you to create and administer examinations on paper, over a network, or over the Internet.

Transparency Set

This set of 100 full-color overhead transparencies includes art, charts, graphs, and tables from *How Children Develop.*

PowerPoint Slides

PowerPoint slides are available in three formats that can be used as is or customized to fit your needs. One set contains simple chapter outlines to help you orient your current slides or to use as a foundation for new slides. Another set includes all the textbook's illustrations and tables. The third set consists of lecture slides from Rona McCall, Regis University, which focus on key themes and terms in the book and include text illustrations and tables. PowerPoint slides are available on CD-Rom or from the course Web site.

Observation Videos

Journey Through Childhood offers students an opportunity to observe children from varied cultures from birth through adolescence, in a variety of settings. Noted experts in child development discuss their work in areas ranging from the biology of early brain development to prosocial behavior in middle childhood. These are available on VHS and DVD.

The Scientific American Frontiers Videos

This series for Developmental Psychology features 17 video clips of 15 minutes each on a wide range of topics, including gene therapy, infant motor skill development, dyslexia, and memory. A guide to using these video series with specific chapters is included in the *Instructor's Resource Manual.*

Companion Web Site

The *Siegler Companion Web Site* at worthpublishers.com/siegler, created by Rona McCall, Regis College, provides students with virtual study aids and instructors with a variety of teaching resources. At no cost and with no password needed, students will find chapter outlines, annotated Web links to expand on each chapter's coverage, online quizzes to test their knowledge, and interactive flashcards. The password-protected instructors' site offers three prebuilt PowerPoint slide sets (one containing outlines and two containing art) for each chapter and an online quiz gradebook.

Online Course Materials

As a service to adopters using WebCT or Blackboard course management systems, Worth provides the electronic instructor and student resources in the appropriate format. Adopters of *How Children Develop* can request a Blackboard or WebCT formatted version of the book's test bank.

Acknowledgments

So many people have contributed directly and indirectly to this textbook that it is impossible to know where to start or where to stop in thanking them. All of us have been given exceptional support by our spouses and significant others—Jerry Clore, Jerry Harris, Grazyna Kochanska, Alice Rysdon—and by our children—Benjamin Clore, Michael Harris, and Todd, Beth, and Aaron Siegler—as well as by our parents, relatives, friends, and other loved ones. Our advisors in college and graduate school, Ann Brown, Les Cohen, Harry Hake, Robert Liebert, Paul Mussen, and Jim Pate, helped launch our careers and taught us how to recognize and appreciate good research. We also have all benefited from collaborators who shared our quest for understanding child development and from a great many exceptionally helpful and generous colleagues, including Karen Adolph, Martha Alibali, Renee Baillargeon, Zhe Chen, Shari Ellis, Richard Fabes, Cindy Fisher, David Klahr, Angel Lillard, Patrick Lemaire, John Opfer, Tracy Spinrad, and David Uttal. Special thanks are due to our assistants, Sally Kaufmann and Theresa Treasure, who helped in innumerable ways in preparing the book.

The book also has been greatly improved by the comments of many conscientious and thoughtful reviewers of drafts of the manuscript: **Mark Alcorn,** University of Northern Colorado; **Linda Acredolo,** University of California, Davis; **Karen Adolph,** New York University; **Martha Alibali,** University of Wisconsin, Madison; **Catherine Best,** Wesleyan University; **Rebecca S. Bigler,** University of Texas; **Susan Bowers,** Northern Illinois University; **Nathan Brody,** Wesleyan University; **Judith Becker Bryant,** University of South Florida; **Susan Calkins,** University of North Carolina, Greensboro; **Tara Callaghan,** St. Francis Xavier University; **Elaine Cassel,** Lord Fairfax Community College; **Keith Crnic,** Pennsylvania State University; **Zoe Ann Davidson,** Alabama A&M University; **Marlene DeVoe,**

St. Cloud State University; **Maryann Fischer,** Indiana University Northwest; **Oney D. Fitzpatrick, Jr.,** Lamar University; **Kathleen Cranley Gallagher,** University of Wisconsin, Madison; **Leilani Greening,** University of Alabama; **Heather A. Holmes-Lonergan,** Metropolitan State College of Denver; **Kathleen V. Hoover-Dempsey,** Vanderbilt University; **Judith Hudson,** Rutgers University; **Lisa Huffman,** Ball State University; **Gavin Huntley-Fenner,** University of California, Irvine; **Scott P. Johnson,** Cornell University; **Roger Kobak,** University of Delaware; **Marta Laupa,** University of Nevada, Las Vegas; **Brett Laursen,** Florida Atlantic University; **Kathryn S. Lemery,** Arizona State University; **Kevin MacDonald,** California State University, Longbeach; **Derek Montgomery,** Bradley University; **Laura Namy,** Emory University; **Rochelle Newman,** University of Iowa; **Jodie Plumert,** University of Iowa; **Joe Price,** San Diego State University; **Amanda Rose,** University of Missouri, Columbia; **Rosemary Rosser,** University of Arizona; **Greg B. Simpson,** University of Kansas; **Mark Strauss,** University of Pittsburgh; **Esther Thelen,** Indiana University; **David Uttal,** Northwestern University; **Marcia L. Weinstein,** Salem State College; **Arlene S. Walker-Andrews,** Rutgers University; **Noel Wescombe,** Whitworth College; **Jacqueline Woolley,** University of Texas. We learned from their expertise and were stimulated by their feedback to think more clearly and deeply about a great many issues.

Our special thanks go to Lynne Baker-Ward, North Carolina State University; Doreen Eichorst, Northern Illinois University; Rona McCall, Regis College; and Georgene Troseth, Vanderbilt University. Thanks also to their students, who tested the manuscript in their child-development courses. We are indebted to them for their perceptive insights as well as their early enthusiasm.

Thanks are particularly due to our friends and collaborators at Worth Publishers. As sponsoring editor and publisher, respectively, Marge Byers and Catherine Woods provided exceptional support and any number of excellent suggestions. They nurtured the project and helped us to realize our vision. Peter Deane, the development editor, is in a class by himself in both skill and dedication. He set a new standard for excellence in editing, far beyond the level that any of us had experienced previously. Our thanks also to our project editors Vivien Weiss and Tracey Kuehn, art director Barbara Reingold, photo editor Meg Kuhta, production manager Sarah Segal, and page designer Paul Lacy, for their excellent work. They have created a book that we hope you and your students will find a pleasure to look at as well as to read. Marketing manager Renée Altier provided outstanding promotional materials to inform professors about the book. Supplements editor Graig Donini coordinated the superb package of ancillary material.

Finally, we want to thank our “book team” of sales representatives and managers. Tom Kling, Julie Hirshman, Kari Ewalt, Greg David, Tom Scotty, Cindy Rabinowitz, Glenn Russell, and Matt Dunning provided a sales perspective, valuable suggestions, and unflagging enthusiasm throughout this project.

How Children DEVELOP

CHAPTER 1

An Introduction to Child Development

PAUL KLEE, *Senecio*, 1922

THEMES

- Nature and Nurture
- The Active Child
- Continuity/Discontinuity
- Mechanisms of Change
- The Sociocultural Context
- Individual Differences
- Research and Children's Welfare

In 1955, a group of child-development researchers embarked on a unique study. Their goal, like that of many developmental researchers, was to find out how biological and environmental factors influence children's intellectual, social, and emotional growth. What made their study unique was that they examined these diverse aspects of development for all 698 children born that year on the Hawaiian island of Kauai and that they continued studying the children and their parents for more than thirty years.

The project's personnel, headed by Emmy Werner, sought and received parental consent to collect many types of data about the children's development. To learn about complications during the prenatal period and the birth process, the researchers examined physicians' records. To learn about family interactions and the children's behavior at home, they arranged for nurses and social workers to observe the families and to interview the children's mothers when the children were 1 year old and again when they were 10 years old. The researchers also arranged interviews with teachers to learn about the children's academic performance and classroom behavior during the elementary school years. In addition, the investigators examined police, family court, and social service records that involved the children, either as victims or perpetrators. Finally, the investigators administered standardized intelligence and personality tests to the children when they were 10 and 18 years old and interviewed them at age 18 and again in their early 30s to find out how they saw their own development.

Results from this study illustrated some of the many ways in which biological and environmental factors combine to influence child development. Children who experienced complications during the prenatal period or at birth that put them at risk for biological reasons were more likely than others to develop physical handicaps, mental illness, and learning difficulties. However, the quality of the home environment appeared to play an even larger role in their development. Parents' income, educational level, and mental health, together with the quality of the relationship between the parents, exerted particularly large influences on their children's subsequent development. By age 2, toddlers who had experienced severe birth problems but who lived in harmonious middle-income families were nearly as advanced in language and motor skills as were children who had not experienced such problems. By the time children were 10-year-olds, prenatal and birth problems were consistently related to impaired psychological development *only* if the children also encountered poor rearing conditions.

What of children who faced both biological and environmental challenges—prenatal or birth complications and adverse family circumstances? The majority of such children developed serious learning or behavior problems by age 10. By age 18, most had acquired a police record, encountered mental health problems, or become pregnant. However, one-third of such at-risk children grew into young adults who, in the words of Werner, "loved well, worked well, and played well" (Werner, 1989, p. 109). These children often were befriended by an adult outside the immediate family—an uncle, aunt, neighbor, teacher, or clergyperson—who helped them navigate through the temptations and dangers in their environment.

Michael was one such resilient child. Born prematurely, with low birth weight, to teenage parents, he spent the first three weeks of his life in a hospital, separated from his mother. By his eighth birthday, Michael's parents were divorced, his mother had permanently deserted the family, and he and his three brothers and sisters were being raised by their father, with the help of their elderly grandparents. Yet by age 18, Michael was successful in school, had high self-esteem, was popular with his peers, and was a caring young man with a positive attitude toward life. The fact that there are many Michaels—children who show great resilience in the face of adversity—is among the most heartening findings of research on child development.

Werner's remarkable study, like most studies of child development, raises at least as many questions as it answers. How, exactly, did the children's biological nature, their family environment, and the environments they encountered outside the family combine to shape their development? Would the same results have emerged if the study had been conducted in a primarily African-American or Latino urban community rather than in the primarily Asian, Native Hawaiian, and northern European rural community studied in Kauai? Was it chance that some children from adverse backgrounds were befriended by adults from outside the immediate family, or did the children's individual characteristics, such as their personality, attract the friendship and help? Can programs be designed that would allow more children to overcome difficult backgrounds?

Reading this chapter will introduce you to these and other basic questions about child development. Once you have read the chapter, you should have a clear sense of why it is worthwhile to study child development, as well as what researchers are trying to learn about the developmental process and what methods they use in this endeavor.

JEFF GREENBERG / PHOTOEDIT

Will this child be resilient enough to overcome his disadvantaged environment? The answer will depend in large part on how many risk factors he faces and on his personal characteristics.

Why Study Child Development?

To us, and to many others, the sheer enjoyment of watching children and trying to understand them is its own justification: What could be more fascinating than the development of a child? But there are also practical and intellectual reasons to study child development. Understanding how children develop can help parents raise their children more effectively, lead society as a whole to adopt wiser policies regarding children's welfare, and answer intriguing questions about human nature.

Raising Children

Being a good parent is not easy. Among its many challenges are the endless questions it raises over the years. When will my baby start to know who I am? Should I stay at home with her, or should I enroll her in day care so that she can get to know other children? If she starts talking earlier than her friends, does that mean that she is gifted? Will she have the same difficulties learning math that I did? How can I get her to be less angry? Why has she become so withdrawn since she became an adolescent, when she was so friendly before?

Child-development research can help answer such questions. For example, one problem that confronts almost all parents is how to help their children manage anger and other negative emotions. Research indicates several effective approaches (Denham, 1998). One is expressing sympathy: when parents respond to their children's distress with sympathy, the children are better able to cope with the situation causing the distress. Another effective approach is helping angry children find positive alternatives to expressing anger. For example, distracting them from the

LAURA DWIGHT

Quite a few children have difficulty controlling their anger. Developmental research has yielded a number of strategies, including the "turtle technique," that can help them cope.

source of their anger and encouraging them to do something they enjoy helps them cope with the negative feelings.

These strategies work not only for parents but also for other people who contribute to raising children, such as day-care personnel and teachers. One demonstration of this was provided by a special curriculum that was devised for use with preschoolers (3- and 4-year-olds) who were angry and out of control (Denham & Burton, 1996). With this curriculum, which lasted thirty-two weeks, preschool teachers helped children recognize their own and other children's emotions, taught them techniques for surmounting their anger, and guided them in resolving conflicts with other children. One approach that children were taught for coping with anger was the "turtle technique": they were told that when they felt themselves becoming angry, they were to move away from other children and retreat into their "turtle shell," where they could think through the situation until they were ready to emerge from the shell.

The curriculum was quite successful. Children who participated in it became more skillful in recognizing and regulating anger when they experienced it and generally less negative. One boy, who had regularly gotten into fights when angry, told the teacher after an argument with another child about a toy, "See, I used my words not my hands" (Denham, 1998, p. 219). Similar programs have proved effective with elementary school children (Greenberg, Kusche, Cook, & Quamma, 1995).

As this example illustrates, knowledge of child-development research can help parents and teachers alike. Throughout this book, we will discuss a wide variety of research efforts that have practical implications for raising children.

Choosing Social Policies

Another reason to learn about child development is to be able to make informed decisions not just about one's own children but also about social-policy questions that affect children in general. Are public resources better spent trying to detect and prevent potential developmental problems, such as overaggressiveness, in young children, or should they be reserved for remedying problems that have become more serious? How much trust should judges and juries place in preschoolers' testimony in child-abuse cases? Should preschool programs that teach academic and social skills be made available to all children from low-income families, and should such programs be followed up beyond the preschool period? How effective are health-education courses aimed at reducing teenage smoking, drinking, and pregnancy, and how can such courses be improved? Child-development research provides information relevant to all of these policy decisions and many others.

Consider the issue of how much preschoolers' testimony in court cases should be trusted. At present, more than 100,000 children testify in legal cases each year (Ceci & Bruck, 1998). Many of these children are very young: more than 40% of children who testify in sexual-abuse trials, for example, are below age 5 (Gray, 1993). The stakes are extremely high in such cases. If juries believe children who falsely testify that they were abused, innocent people may spend years in jail, and their reputations may be ruined forever. If juries do not believe children who accurately report abuse, the perpetrators will go free and may abuse other children. So how can we know when to believe children? More specifically, what kind of questioning is most likely to help children to testify accurately about events that are uncomfortable for them to discuss, and what kind of questioning may lead them to report events that never happened?

Psychological research has helped us answer such questions. In one experiment that was designed to test the accuracy of young children's memory and their susceptibility to biased questioning, 3- to 6-year-olds first played a game similar to "Simon Says" and a month later were interviewed about the experience by a social worker (Ceci, Leichtman, & White, 1999). Before the social worker conducted the interviews, she was given a description of each child's experiences. Unknown to the social worker, the description included inaccurate as well as accurate information. For example, if during the game a child had touched her own stomach and another child's nose, the social worker might be told that the child had touched her own stomach and the other child's toes. After receiving the description, the social worker was given instructions much like those in a court case: "Find out what the child remembers."

As it turned out, in her efforts to determine what the child remembered, the social worker's questioning often reflected the version of events she had been told. If, for example, a child's account of an event was contrary to what the social worker believed to be the case, the social worker tended to question the child repeatedly about the event ("Are you sure you touched his nose? Is it possible you touched some other part of his body?") Faced with such repeated questioning, children fairly often assumed that the answer they had given must have been wrong and subsequently brought their accounts into line with the questioner's expectations. As a result, 34% of 3- and 4-year-olds, and 18% of 5- and 6-year-olds, corroborated at least one of the social worker's incorrect beliefs. Especially alarming, the children became increasingly confident about their inaccurate memories as the social worker continued questioning them. Children were led to "remember" not only plausible events but also unlikely ones that the social worker had been told about. For example, children "recalled" their knee being licked and a marble being inserted in their ear. Thus, an interrogator's beliefs about what happened in a given event can influence how young children answer the interrogator's questions about the event.

Studies such as this have yielded a number of conclusions regarding children's testimony in legal proceedings. The most important finding is that when shielded from leading questions, even 3- to 5-year-olds can be reliable witnesses in legal cases. They often forget details of events, but what they do say is usually accurate (Howe & Courage, 1997; Poole & Lindsay, 1995). At the same time, young children are highly susceptible to leading questions, especially ones asked repeatedly. The younger the children, the more susceptible they are and the more their recall reflects the biases of the interviewer's questions. Therefore, to obtain accurate testimony, especially from young children, questions should be stated in a neutral fashion that does not presuppose the answer, and a question should not be repeated if the child has already answered it (Ceci & Bruck, 1998). Such findings can help courts obtain more accurate testimony from young children. At a broader level, the findings illustrate how knowledge of child development can inform social policies.

In courtrooms such as this one, asking questions that will help children to testify accurately is of the utmost importance.

STACY PICK / STOCK BOSTON

Understanding Human Nature

A third reason to study child development is to better understand human nature. Many of the most intriguing questions regarding human nature concern children. For example, does the process of human learning start only after children are born, or can it occur in the womb? Do infants see the world in basically the same way that adults do, or does it look very different to them? Do children vary in personality and intellect from day one, or are they similar at birth, with differences arising only because they have different experiences? Until recently, people could only speculate about such questions. Now, however, developmental scientists have concepts and methods that enable them to observe, describe, and explain the process of development. As a result, our understanding of children, and of human nature, is growing rapidly.

Consider the question of whether fundamental concepts such as number begin to develop in infancy or whether the development of such concepts requires instruction from parents and teachers. Infants clearly do not know that 5 + 5 = 10, but might they be born with some intuitive understanding of numbers? The evidence indicates that a rudimentary concept of number is present surprisingly early in infancy, perhaps from birth (Starkey, Spelke, & Gelman, 1990; Strauss & Curtis, 1984; van Loosbroek & Smitsman, 1990). In the relevant studies, infants in their first half-year were shown a series of photos, each containing a small number of objects, for example, two or three squares. The objects shown in each photo varied in many ways, such as their size, color, spacing, and brightness, but there was always the same number of objects in a given series of photos. Despite the other differences among the objects, the infants spent less and less time looking at each new photo, suggesting that they were losing interest. Then the infants were shown a photo that was comparable to the others in almost all respects, except that it had a different number of objects, perhaps three rather than two or vice versa. Seeing the new number of objects inspired renewed looking, a sign that the infants discriminated between two and three objects and that the numerical difference interested them. Thus, infants seem to have a rudimentary sense of number long before parents and teachers provide any instruction.

Understanding of numbers begins to develop in infancy, but children must overcome many misunderstandings on the way to a sophisticated understanding.

"Daddy, how many fingers do I hold up for five and a half?"

Child-development research also informs us about more general aspects of human nature, such as whether early and later emotional adjustment are connected. A large body of research indicates that people who as infants had a close and secure attachment to their mothers subsequently tend to be better adjusted than people whose early attachment to their mothers was insecure. For example, babies who were rated by researchers as securely attached to their mothers at 18 months have been found in later childhood to be more socially competent and emotionally healthy than other children (Shulman, Elicker, & Sroufe, 1994). In contrast, infants who were rated as insecurely attached to their mothers have been found to be at heightened risk for behavior problems during childhood (Easterbrooks, Davidson, & Chazan, 1993) and for anxiety disorders when they are teenagers (Warren, Huston, Egeland, & Sroufe, 1997).

Does this mean that people's destiny is forever determined by their early relations with their mothers? No. Even children who spent their infancy and early childhood as orphans in Nazi concentration camps—and who therefore could not have been attached to their mothers—nonetheless often led successful lives as adults (Kagan, 1996; Moskowitz, 1983).

Children are influenced by their early experiences, but some are able to overcome even the most traumatic backgrounds.

review: There are at least three good reasons to learn about child development. The first is to gain information and understanding that can help parents raise their own children successfully. The second is to gain insight into social-policy issues related to children and to help society adopt policies that promote children's well-being. The third is to better understand human nature in general.

Historical Foundations of the Study of Child Development

From ancient Greece to the early years of the twentieth century, a number of profound thinkers observed and wrote about children. Their goals were like those of contemporary researchers: to help people become better parents, to improve children's well-being, and to understand human nature. Unlike contemporary researchers, they usually based their conclusions on unsystematic observations of small numbers of children whom they happened to encounter. Still, the issues they raised were sufficiently important, and their insights sufficiently deep, that their views continue to be of interest.

Early Philosophical Views of Children's Development

Some of the earliest recorded ideas about children's development were those of Plato and Aristotle. These two Greek philosophers, who lived in the fourth century B.C., were particularly interested in how children's nature and the nurture they receive influence development.

Both Plato and Aristotle believed that the long-term welfare of society depended on children's being raised properly. Careful upbringing was essential, because children's nature would otherwise lead to their becoming rebellious and unruly. Plato viewed this as an especially large problem with boys. He wrote:

> Now of all wild things, a boy is the most difficult to handle. Just because he more than any other has a fount of intelligence in him which has not yet "run clear," he is the craftiest, most mischievous, and unruliest of brutes.
>
> (*Laws,* bk. 7, p. 808)

Consistent with this view, Plato emphasized self-control and discipline as the most important goals of education (Borstelmann, 1983).

Aristotle agreed with Plato that discipline was necessary, but he was more concerned with fitting child rearing to the needs of the individual child. He wrote:

> It would seem then that a study of individual character is the best way of making education perfect, for then each has a better chance of receiving the treatment that suits him.
>
> (*Nicomachean Ethics,* bk. 10, chap. 9, p. 1180)

Plato and Aristotle differed more profoundly in their views of how children acquire knowledge. Plato believed that children are born with innate knowledge. For example, he believed that children are born with a concept of "animal" that allows them to recognize that the particular dogs or cats they encounter are animals. In contrast, Aristotle believed that all knowledge comes from experience and that without experience, the mind is merely a potential. He compared the mind of an infant to a writing tablet on which nothing has yet been written.

Roughly 2,000 years later, the English philosopher John Locke (1632–1704) and the French philosopher Jean-Jacques Rousseau (1712–1778) proposed ideas that were related to, but also somewhat different from, those of Plato and Aristotle regarding how parents and the general society can best promote child development. Locke, like Aristotle, viewed the child as a tabula rasa, a blank slate, whose development largely reflects the nurture provided by the child's parents and the broader society. He believed that the most important goal of child rearing is the growth of character. To build children's character, parents need to set good examples of honesty, stability, and gentleness. They need to avoid indulging the child, especially early in life, but once discipline and reason have been instilled,

> authority should be relaxed as fast as their age, discretion, and good behavior could allow it. . . . The sooner you treat him as a man, the sooner he will begin to be one.
>
> (Cited in Borstelmann, 1983, p. 20)

Whereas Locke advocated first instilling discipline and then progressively increasing the child's freedom, Rousseau believed that parents and society should give children maximum freedom from the beginning. Rousseau claimed that children learn primarily from their own spontaneous interactions with objects and other people, rather than through instruction by parents or teachers. He even argued that children should not receive any formal education until about age 12, when they reach "the age of reason" and can judge for themselves the worth of what they read and are told. Before then, they should be allowed the freedom to explore whatever interests them.

Although all these philosophical views raised fundamental questions, they were based more on impressions and general beliefs than on systematic observations that could reveal how children actually develop. Such systematic observations would await a scientific approach.

The Beginnings of Research on Children

A research-based approach to understanding child development began to emerge in the nineteenth century, in part as a result of two converging forces: social reform movements and Charles Darwin's theory of evolution.

During the Industrial Revolution, a great many children in Europe and the United States worked as paid laborers. Some were as young as 5 and 6 years old; many spent as much as twelve hours a day working in factories or mines, often in extremely hazardous circumstances. These harsh conditions concerned a number of social reformers, who began to study the effects of the conditions on the children's development. For example, in 1842, the Earl of Shaftesbury delivered a speech before the British House of Commons in which he summarized a committee's findings regarding conditions in the mines. He noted that the narrow tunnels where the children dug out the coal

> are wrought in a very rude manner. There is very insufficient drainage. The ways are so low that only little boys can work in them, which they do naked, and often in mud and water, dragging sledge-tubs by the girdle and chain. . . . the Rev. W.

> Parlane, of Tranent, says, "Children of amiable temper and conduct, at 7 years of age, often return next season from the collieries greatly corrupted, and as an old teacher says, with most hellish dispositions. . . . Near Huddlesfield the sub-commissioner examined a female child. He says, "I could not have believed that I should have found human nature so degraded."
>
> (Quoted in Kessen, 1965, pp. 46–50)

The Earl of Shaftesbury's effort at social reform was partially successful—a law was passed forbidding employment of girls and of boys under 10. In addition to bringing about the first child labor laws, this and other early social reform movements established a legacy of research conducted for the benefit of children and provided some of the earliest descriptions of the adverse effects that harsh environments can have on child development.

Later in the nineteenth century, Charles Darwin's work on biological evolution inspired a number of scientists to propose that an intensive study of child development might lead to important insights into the nature of the human species. Darwin himself was interested in child development and in 1877 published an article entitled "A Biographical Sketch of an Infant," which presented his careful observations of the motor, sensory, and emotional growth of his own infant son. Darwin's "baby biography"—a systematic description of day-to-day development—represented one of the first methods for studying children.

BETTMAN / CORBIS

During the eighteenth, nineteenth, and early twentieth centuries, many young children worked in coal mines and factories. Their hours were long, and the work was often unhealthy and dangerous. Concern over the well-being of such children led to some of the earliest research in the area of child development.

The Emergence of Child Development as a Discipline

In the late nineteenth and early twentieth centuries, child development began to emerge as a formal field of inquiry. A number of universities established departments of child development, and the first professional journals devoted to the study of child development were founded. Also emerging during this period were the first theories of child development to incorporate research findings. One prominent theory, that of Sigmund Freud, was based in large part on results from experiments with hypnosis and analysis of patients' recollections of their dreams and childhood experiences. On the basis of this evidence, Freud concluded that biological drives, especially sexual ones, were a crucial influence on development. Another prominent theory of the same era, that of John Watson, was based in large part on the results of experiments that examined the effects of reward and punishment on the behavior of rats and other animals. On the basis of this evidence, Watson concluded that children's development is controlled by environmental conditions, especially the rewards and punishments that follow particular behaviors.

By current standards, the research methods on which these theories were based were crude to say the least, and the theories were limited accordingly. Nonetheless, these early scientific theories were better grounded in research evidence than their predecessors, and they inspired more sophisticated thinking about how development occurs.

review: Philosophers such as Plato, Aristotle, Locke, and Rousseau, and early scientific theorists such as Darwin, Freud, and Watson raised many of the deepest issues about child development. These issues included how nature and nurture influence development, how best to raise children, and how knowledge of children's development can be used to advance their welfare. Although the work of these thinkers lacked scientific rigor, it helped set the stage for modern perspectives on these and other fundamental issues.

TABLE 1.1

Basic Questions About Child Development

1. How do nature and nurture together shape development? (Nature and nurture)
2. How do children shape their own development? (The active child)
3. In what ways is development continuous, and in what ways is it discontinuous? (Continuity/Discontinuity)
4. How does change occur? (Mechanisms of developmental change)
5. How does the sociocultural context influence development? (The sociocultural context)
6. How do children become so different from each other? (Individual differences)
7. How can research promote children's well-being? (Research and children's welfare)

Could appropriate nurture have allowed The Three Stooges to become upper-class gentlemen?

THE EVERETT COLLECTION

Enduring Themes in Child Development

The modern study of child development begins with a set of fundamental questions. Everything else—theories, concepts, research methods, data, and so on—is part of the effort to answer these questions. Although experts in the field might choose different particular questions as the most important, there is widespread agreement that the seven questions in Table 1.1 are among the most important. The broad answers that have emerged from attempts to answer these questions form a set of seven themes that we will highlight throughout the book as we examine specific aspects of child development. In this section, we introduce and briefly discuss each question and the theme that corresponds to it.

1 *Nature* and *Nurture:* How Do Nature and Nurture Together Shape Development?

The single most basic question about child development is how nature and nurture interact to shape the developmental process. **Nature** refers to our biological endowment, in particular, the genes we receive from our parents. This genetic inheritance influences everything from our physical appearance, personality, intellectual ability, and mental health to certain of our preferences, such as the propensity for thrill-seeking (Plomin, DeFries, McClearn, & Rutter, 1997). **Nurture** refers to the wide range of environments, both physical and social, that influence our development, including the womb in which we spend the prenatal period, the homes in which we grow up, the schools in which we enroll, the broader communities in which we live, and the many people with whom we interact.

Popular representations of the nature–nurture issue often approach it as an either/or question: "What determines a person's fate, heredity *or* environment?" However, this either/or phrasing of the question is misleading. Human development requires both normal DNA and an environment that allows normal interactions with the physical and social world.

Today, developmentalists recognize that every characteristic that we possess—our intellects, our personalities, our physical appearances, our emotions—is created through the *joint* workings of nature and nurture. Accordingly, rather than asking whether nature or nurture is more important, developmentalists ask how nature *and* nurture work together to shape development. That this is the right question to ask is illustrated by findings on the development of schizophrenia. Schizophrenia is a serious mental illness that is characterized by irrational behavior, hallucinations, delusions, and so on. Although most children of schizophrenic parents do not themselves develop the illness, their probability of developing it is much higher than that of the general population, even when they are adopted as infants and never see their biological parents (Kety et al., 1994). Thus, children's genes influence their likelihood of becoming schizophrenic. The environment is also influential; children who grow up in troubled homes are more likely to become schizophrenic than are other children. Most important, however, is the interaction of genes and environment. A study of adopted children, some of whose biological parents were schizophrenic, indicated that the only children who had any substantial likelihood of becoming schizophrenic were those who had a schizophrenic parent *and* who also were adopted into a troubled family (Tienari et al., 1990). The finding is reminiscent of one with the children of Kauai: only the combination of prenatal or birth trauma and an adverse rearing environment put these children at serious risk.

The interaction of nature and nurture can be seen in greater detail by examining popular stereotypes that depict early adolescence in the United States as a period of "storm and stress." According to these stereotypes, young adolescents, buffeted by the physical and psychological changes associated with puberty, rebel against authority, fight with their parents, and experience unpredictable mood swings, reduced self-esteem, and poor grades. Research has shown that, in fact, these stereotypes do not characterize most young teenagers. However, they do apply to a significant minority of them, perhaps 15% to 30%. For this minority, family conflicts, particularly over issues of control and freedom, increase during early adolescence, and grades, interest in school, motivation to succeed, and self-concepts all deteriorate (Collins, 1997; Grotevant, 1998; Larson & Richards, 1994; Peterson et al., 1993). The key questions are why such problems occur when they do, why they occur with some young adolescents but not others, and how nature and nurture contribute to these problems.

nature our biological endowment; the genes we receive from our parents

nurture the environments, both physical and social, that influence our development

To answer these questions, we must consider not only the physical and psychological changes young adolescents experience, but also the new environments that they encounter (Eccles et al., 1993). One such new environment involves school. Early adolescence is the time when most students in the United States move from elementary school to junior high or middle school. The new school environment differs in many ways from the old one. Teachers see individual students for less time each day, making teacher–student relationships more impersonal. Relative to elementary school teachers, junior high school teachers place greater emphasis on control and discipline, set more stringent grading standards, and are more critical (Eccles, Lord, & Buchanan, 1996). Students, in turn, report feeling less academically competent and less motivated to succeed (Anderman & Midgley, 1997). They also rate their junior high school learning experiences less favorably than their elementary school experiences (Wigfield & Eccles, 1994). Students and teachers agree that seventh graders in junior high have less freedom and decision-making responsibility than do sixth graders in elementary school (Simmons & Blyth, 1987).

The biological changes associated with puberty also contribute to a fair number of teenagers becoming resentful of rules and authority. We might therefore expect that physically mature seventh graders, who are further into puberty than their classmates, would be especially prone to conflict with teachers and other authorities. Because seventh-grade girls generally are more physically mature than seventh-grade boys, we also might expect early-maturing girls to find the transition to junior high especially difficult. This turns out to be the case. Physically mature seventh-grade girls are more likely than less mature classmates to see large discrepancies between how much independence they have in the classroom (e.g., freedom to decide what to do with free time after finishing an assignment early) and how much they think they should have. Early-maturing girls also have higher rates of misconduct in school after they go to junior high school than do less mature girls. Their problems are not limited to school—early-maturing girls also have more conflicts with their parents (Steinberg, 1988)—but the girls often find the school environment especially exasperating.

JOEL GORDON

The highly different development of these 12-year-olds is typical of this age. Different rates of physical maturation can have differing effects on children's psychological development, depending in part on their social environment.

As this example illustrates, to say that either nature or nurture is more important than the other is to oversimplify the developmental process. Just as physical maturation and personal characteristics interact with the school environment and other environmental factors to influence adolescent adjustment, so do nature and nurture work together to produce all developmental outcomes.

One of the main lessons of research on nature–nurture interactions is that the timing of experiences often is crucial. For example, as noted above, the timing of

individual differences 1.1

The Importance of Normal Early Experience

A particularly poignant illustration of the importance of normal early experience comes from cases of children whose early life was spent in horribly inadequate orphanages in Romania in the late 1980s and early 1990s (O'Connor et al., 2000; Rutter et al., 1998). Children in these orphanages had almost no contact with any caretaker; for reasons that remain unknown, the cruel communist dictatorship of that era instructed staff workers not to interact with the children even when they brought them their bottles. Conditions in the orphanages were so bad that the backs of many infants' heads became flattened from the babies' lying on their backs for 18 to 20 hours per day.

Shortly after the collapse of communist rule in Romania, several hundred of these children were brought to Great Britain. The physical, intellectual, and social development of about 150 of these Romanian-born children has been followed through age 6 years (O'Connor et al., 2000; O'Connor & Rutter, 2000). Some of these children were adopted into British families before they were 6 months old, others between 6 and 24 months old, yet others between 24 and 42 months old. A control group of British-born children adopted into British families provided a point of comparison for evaluating whether the Romanian-born children's early deprivation had lasting negative effects.

When the Romanian-born children arrived in Britain, most were severely malnourished, with more than half being in the lowest 3% of children their age in terms of height, weight, and head circumference. Most also showed mental retardation and were socially immature. The parents who adopted them knew of their deprived backgrounds and were highly motivated to provide loving homes that would help the children overcome whatever lingering obstacles the early deprivation posed.

By age 6, the physical development of the Romanian-born children had improved considerably, both in absolute terms and in relation to the British-born control group. However, the Romanian children's early adverse experience continued to influence their development, with the extent of negative influence depending on how long they had been institutionalized. For example, Romanian-born children who were adopted before age 6 months, and who had therefore spent the smallest portion of their early lives in the orphanages, weighed about the same as British-born children when both were 6-year-olds. Romanian-born children adopted between the ages of 6 and 24 months, and who therefore had spent more of their early lives in the orphanages, weighed less; those adopted between the ages of 24 and 42 months weighed even less.

Intellectual development showed a similar pattern. Children from Romania who had been adopted before age 6 months demonstrated levels of intellectual competence at 6 years comparable to that of children in the control group. Those adopted between the ages of 6 and 24 months did somewhat less well. Those adopted between the ages of 24 and 42 months did yet less well.

Social development showed correspondingly adverse effects of the early experience in the orphanages (O'Connor & Rutter, 2000). Almost 20% of the Romanian-born children who were adopted after age 6 months showed extremely abnormal social behavior at age 6 years (versus 3% of the British-born control group). Particularly striking was that they often seemed not to differentiate between their parents and other adults—they would go off with a stranger—and often did not look to their parents for reassurance in anxiety-provoking situations. These children also tended not to form good relations with peers.

The loving family environments provided by the adoptive parents definitely enhanced the children's physical, intellectual, and social development. Still, there may be limits to what can be done to overcome the children's early deprivation. The improvements that were evident at age 6 years had already been evident when the children were examined at age 4 years; the Romanian-born children did not catch up further between ages 4 and 6 (O'Connor & Rutter, 2000). Future research will tell us whether the adoptive parents' continuing efforts to help their children will allow them to catch up completely or whether the early deprivation will continue to exercise negative effects on their development.

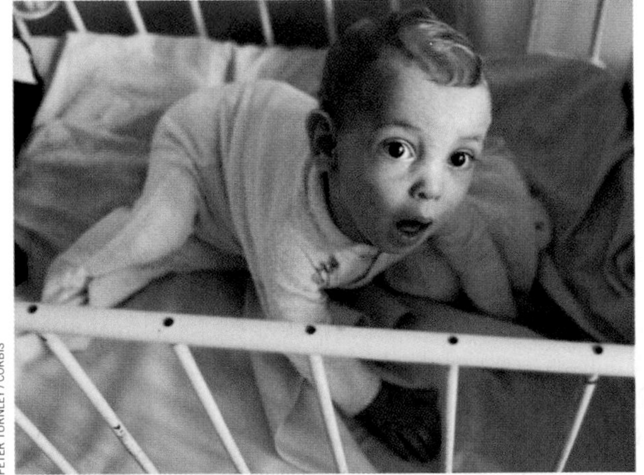

PETER TURNLEY / CORBIS

What will be the long-term consequences of this child's early adverse experience in a Romanian orphanage, now that he has been adopted into a loving home in Great Britain?

puberty influences girls' reactions to junior high school. Many other instances where the timing of experience is vital occur in the first year or two after birth. In particular, as illustrated in Box 1.1, if highly abnormal experiences occur early in life, they often have especially serious and lasting negative effects on development.

2 *The Active Child:* How Do Children Shape Their Own Development?

With all the attention that is paid to the role of nature and nurture in development, it is sometimes easy for people to overlook the ways in which children contribute to their own development. Even in infancy and early childhood, this contribution can be seen in a multitude of ways. Three of the most important contributions during children's first years are their attentional patterns, their use of language, and their play.

Children first begin to shape their own development through their selection of what to pay attention to. Even newborns look toward things that make noise and that move. This preference helps them learn about important parts of the world, such as people and other animals. Infants' attention is also attracted by faces, especially their mother's face: given a choice of looking at their mother's face or a stranger's, infants in their first month already choose to look at Mom (Bushnell, Sai, & Mullen, 1989). This preference is useful to the infant in that it strengthens the mother–infant bond (what new mother wouldn't be happy that her baby sought out her face?).

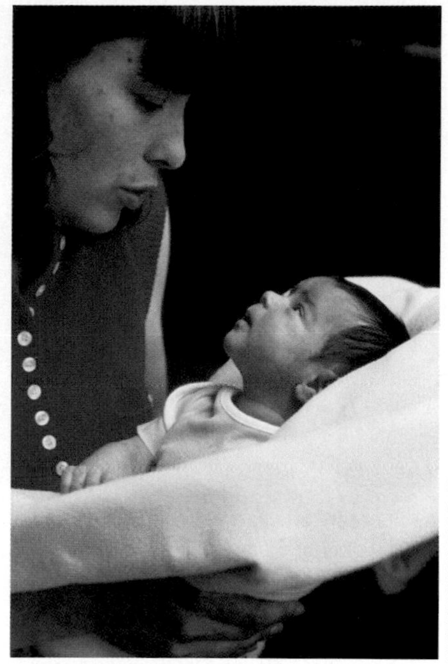

ELIZABETH CREWS / THE IMAGE WORKS

One of the earliest ways children begin to shape their own development is through their choice of where to look. From the first month of life, seeing Mom is a high priority.

Once children begin to speak, usually between 9 and 15 months of age, the contribution of their mental activity to their development becomes evident in their use of language. For example, toddlers (1- and 2-year-olds) often talk when they are alone in a room and no one else is present to reward them or react to what they are saying. Only if children were internally motivated to learn language would they practice talking under these circumstances. Many parents are startled when they hear such "crib speech" and wonder if something is wrong with a baby who would engage in such odd behavior. However, the activity is entirely normal, and the practice probably helps toddlers improve their speech.

Young children's play provides many other examples of how their internally motivated activity contributes to their development. Children play by themselves for the sheer joy of doing so, but they also learn a great deal in the process. Anyone who has seen a baby banging a spoon against different parts of a high chair or intentionally dropping food on the floor would agree that, for the baby, the activity is its own reward. At the same time, the baby is learning about the noises that are made when different objects collide, about the speed at which objects fall, and perhaps about the limits of his or her parents' patience. Children's active contribution to their own development also is evident in the particular play activities they choose. Starting at around age 2, children sometimes engage in sociodramatic play, an activity in which they pretend to be different people in make-believe situations. For example, they may pretend to be superheroes doing battle with monsters. In addition to being inherently enjoyable, these make-believe games teach children valuable lessons, such as how to cope with fears (Howes & Matheson, 1992).

Young children often contribute to their own development through their pretend play, which allows them to explore their interests and concerns.

MIKE FISHER / AP / WIDE WORLD PHOTOS

Children's contribution to their own development increases as they grow older (Scarr & McCartney, 1983). When children are young, their parents largely determine their environments, deciding whether or not they will attend day care, go to parks and playgrounds, play with this child or that, take music lessons, and so on. In contrast, older children and adolescents choose many environments, friends,

DAVID YOUNG-WOLFF / PHOTOEDIT

Adolescents who participate in sports and other extracurricular activities are more likely to complete high school, and less likely to get into trouble, than peers who are not engaged in these activities. This is one more example of how children contribute to their own development.

and activities for themselves. Their choices can exert a large impact on their future. To cite just one example, students who participate in one or more extracurricular activities, such as those of athletic teams and clubs, for at least a year between sixth and tenth grade are more likely to complete high school than are initially similar peers who do not participate in any such activities (Mahoney, 2000). Participants in such extracurricular activities also are less likely to be arrested. The differences in outcomes for participants and nonparticipants are especially great for children from low-income backgrounds who previously were rated as aggressive and unpopular by their classmates. Thus, children contribute to their own development from early in life, and their contributions increase as they grow older.

3 *Continuity/Discontinuity:* In What Ways Is Development Continuous, and in What Ways Is It Discontinuous?

Some scientists envision children's development as a **continuous** process of small changes, like that of a pine tree growing taller and taller. Others see the process as a series of sudden, **discontinuous** changes, like the transition from caterpillar to cocoon to butterfly (Figure 1.1). Determining which view has greater validity has been an enduring goal of research on child development.

Researchers who view development as *discontinuous* start from a common observation: Children of different ages seem *qualitatively different.* A 4-year-old and a 6-year-old, for example, seem to differ not just in how much they know but in the whole way they approach the world.

To appreciate these differences, consider two conversations between Beth, the daughter of one of the authors, and Beth's mother. The first conversation occurred when Beth was a 4-year-old, the second when she was a 6-year-old. Both conver-

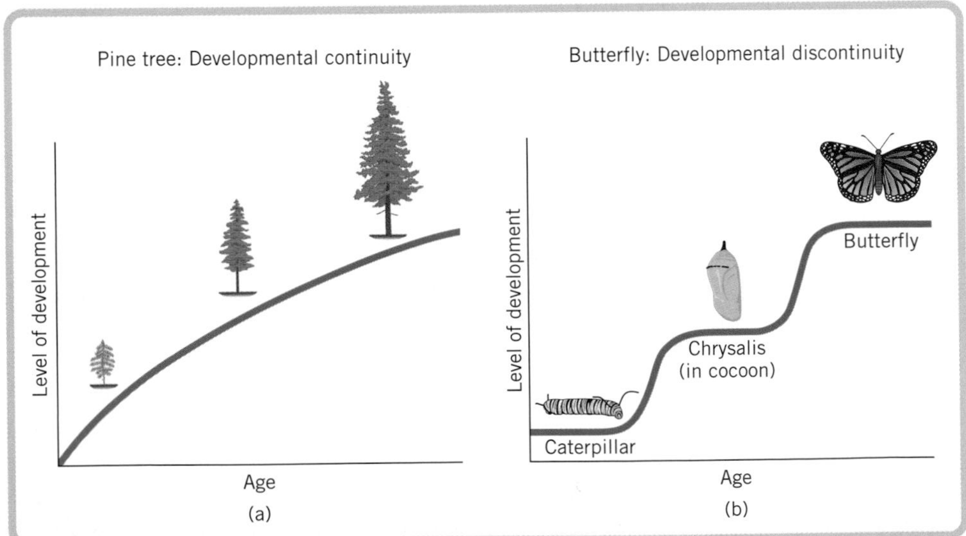

FIGURE 1.1 Continuous and discontinuous development Some researchers see development as a continuous, gradual process, akin to a tree growing taller with each passing year. Others see it as a discontinuous process, involving sudden dramatic changes, such as the transition from caterpillar to cocoon to butterfly. Both views fit some aspects of child development.

continuous development the idea that changes with age occur gradually, in small increments, like that of a pine tree growing taller and taller

discontinuous development the idea that changes with age include occasional large shifts, like the transition from caterpillar to cocoon to butterfly

stage theories approaches that propose that development involves a series of discontinuous, age-related phases sations occurred after Beth watched her mother pour all of the water from a typical drinking glass into a taller, narrower glass. Here is the conversation that occurred when Beth was 4:

Mother: Is there still the same amount of water?
Beth: No.
Mother: Was there more water before, or is there more now?
Beth: There's more now.
Mother: What makes you think so?
Beth: The water is higher; you can see it's more.
Mother: Now I'll pour the water back into the regular glass. Is there the same amount of water as when the water was in the same glass before?
Beth: Yes.
Mother: Now I'll pour all the water again into the tall thin glass. Does the amount of water stay the same?
Beth: No, I already told you, there's more water when it's in the tall glass.

Two years later, when Beth was 6, she responded to the same problem quite differently:

Mother: Is there still the same amount of water?
Beth: Of course.

What differences in Beth's thinking produced these very different reactions? The differences cannot be attributed to her having had further experience with the water-pouring procedure; to the best of her parents' knowledge, she never encountered it in the intervening period. Then why as a 4-year-old would she be so confident that pouring the water into the narrower glass increased the amount, and as a 6-year-old, so confident that it did not?

The water-pouring procedure is actually a classic technique designed to test children's level of thinking. It has been used with thousands of children around the world—almost all of whom have responded in the same fashion as Beth did. Further, such age-related differences in understanding pervade children's thinking. Consider two letters to Mr. Rogers, one sent by a 4-year-old and one by a 5-year-old (Rogers, 1996, pp. 10–11):

Dear Mr. Rogers,
I would like to know how you get in the TV. (Robby, age 4)

Dear Mr. Rogers,
I wish you accidentally stepped out of the TV into my house so I could play with you. (Josiah, age 5)

Clearly, these are not ideas that an older child would entertain. What is it about 4- and 5-year-olds that leads them to believe that a person could get in and out of a TV? And what changes occur that makes such notions laughable to 6- and 7-year-olds?

A common approach to answering these questions comes from **stage theories,** which propose that development occurs in a progression of distinct age-related stages. According to these theories, a child's entry into a new stage involves relatively sudden, qualitative changes from one coherent way of experiencing the world to a different coherent way of experiencing it. Among the best-known stage theories is Jean Piaget's theory of *cognitive development,* that is, the development of thinking and reasoning. This theory holds that between birth and adolescence, children go through four stages, each characterized by distinct intellectual abilities and ways of understanding the world. For example, according to Piaget's theory, 2- to 5-year-olds are in a stage of development in which they can focus on only one

TONY FREEMAN / PHOTOEDIT

Children's behavior on Piaget's conservation-of-liquid problem is often used to exemplify the idea that development is discontinuous. The child first sees equal amounts of liquid in similarly shaped glasses and an empty, differently shaped glass. Then, the child sees the liquid from one glass poured into the differently shaped glass. Finally, the child is asked whether the amount of liquid remains the same or whether one glass has more. Most 5- and 6-year-olds, like this boy, are unshakable in their belief that the glass with the taller liquid column has more liquid. A year or so later, they are unshakable in their belief that the amount of liquid in each glass is the same.

aspect of an event, or one type of information, at a time. By age 6 or 7, children enter a different stage, in which they can simultaneously focus on and coordinate two or more aspects of an event or types of information. Confronted with a problem like the one that Beth's mother presented to her, 4- and 5-year-olds focus on the single dimension of height, and thus perceive the tall, narrow glass as having more water. In contrast, some 6-year-olds and most 7-year-olds consider both relevant dimensions of the problem simultaneously. This allows them to realize that although the column of water in the tall glass is higher, the glass is narrower, and the two differences offset each other. According to stage theories, once children have entered a new stage—as when they become able to consider two aspects of an event or problem simultaneously—they demonstrate their new way of thinking across a broad spectrum of tasks.

In the course of reading this book, you will encounter a number of other stage theories, including Sigmund Freud's theory of psychosexual development, Erik Erikson's theory of psychosocial development, and Lawrence Kohlberg's theory of moral development. Each of these stage theories proposes that children of a given age show broad similarities across many situations and that their behaviors differ sharply at different ages.

Such stage theories have been very influential. In the past twenty years, however, many researchers have concluded that, in most aspects of development, changes are gradual rather than sudden, and that development occurs skill by skill, task by task, rather than in a broadly unified way (Elman et al., 1996; Klahr & MacWhinney, 1998; Rogoff, 1998). This view of development is less dramatic, but a great deal of evidence supports it. One such piece of evidence is the fact that a child often will behave in accord with one stage on one task but in accord with a different stage on another task (Flavell, 1982). This variable level of reasoning makes it difficult to view the child as being "in" either stage.

Much of the difficulty in deciding whether development is continuous or discontinuous is that the same facts can look very different, depending on one's perspective. Consider the seemingly simple question of whether children's height increases continuously or discontinuously. Figure 1.2a shows a boy's height, measured yearly from birth to age 18 (Tanner, 1961). When one looks at the boy's height at each age, development seems smooth and continuous, with growth occurring rapidly early in life and then slowing down.

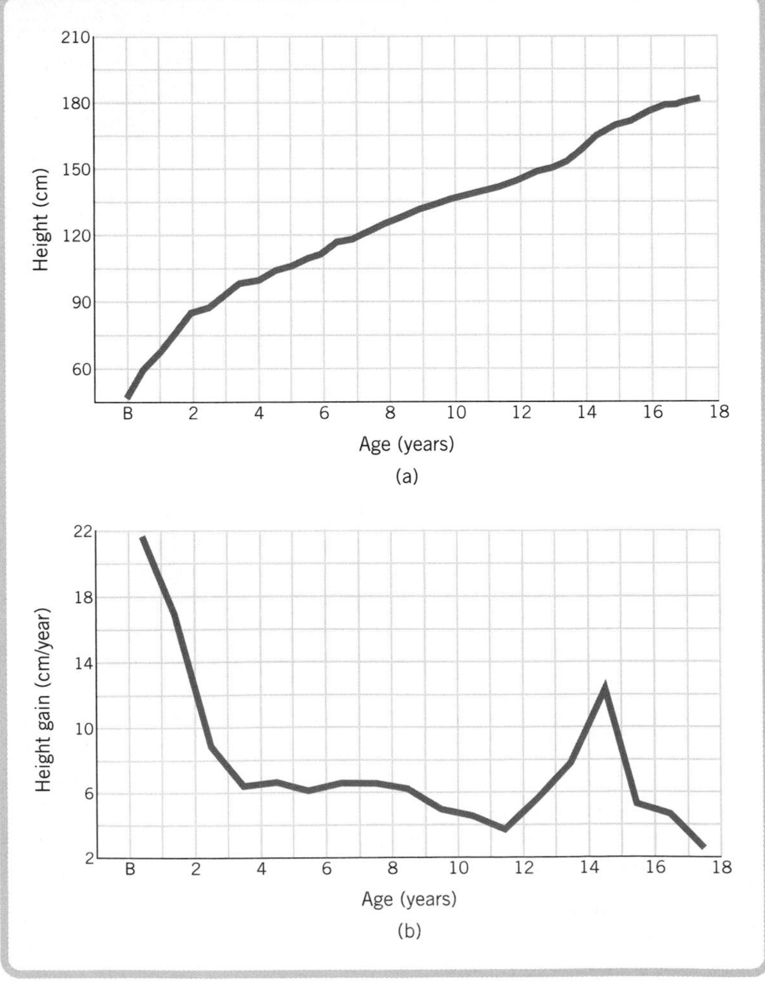

FIGURE 1.2 Continuous and discontinuous growth Depending on how it is viewed, changes in height can be viewed as either continuous or discontinuous. (a) Examining a boy's height at yearly intervals from birth to 18 years makes the growth look gradual and continuous (from Tanner, 1961). (b) Examining changes in the same boy's height from one year to the next over the same period shows rapid growth during the first three years, then slower growth, then a growth spurt in adolescence, then a rapid decrease in growth; viewed this way, growth is discontinuous.

However, when you look at Figure 1.2b, a different picture emerges. This graph illustrates the same boy's growth, but it depicts the amount of growth from one year to the next. The boy grew every year, but he grew most during two periods: from birth to age 3, and from 12 to 15. These are the kinds of data that lead people to talk about discontinuous growth and about a separate stage of adolescence that includes a growth spurt.

Yet another picture of growth is revealed in Figure 1.3. These data illustrate the growth of an infant whose length was measured every day from age 3 months to 7 months. Examination of the infant's growth on a day-by-day basis indicates that there were many days on which he did not grow and a relatively small number of days on which he grew a lot. To be more precise, the infant grew more on the 13 high-growth days combined than he did on the other 115 days combined. The finding was not unique to the particular infant; other infants show similar growth patterns (Lampl, Veldhuis, & Johnson, 1992). Thus, at this very detailed level of analysis, growth seems to be discontinuous—a few days are "growth days," most are not.

So is development fundamentally continuous or fundamentally discontinuous? The most reasonable answer seems to be, "It depends on how you look at it and how often you look." Imagine the difference between the perspective of an uncle who sees his niece every two or three years, and that of the niece's parents who see her every day. The uncle will almost always be struck with the huge changes in his niece since he last saw her. The child will be so different that it will seem that she has progressed to a higher stage of development. In contrast, the parents will most often be struck by the continuity of her development; to them, she usually will just seem to grow up a bit each day. Even parents, however, are sometimes shocked by their child's suddenly seeming much more mature than they had noticed previously. Throughout this book, we will be considering the changes, large and small, sudden and gradual, that have led some researchers to emphasize the continuities in development and others to emphasize the discontinuities.

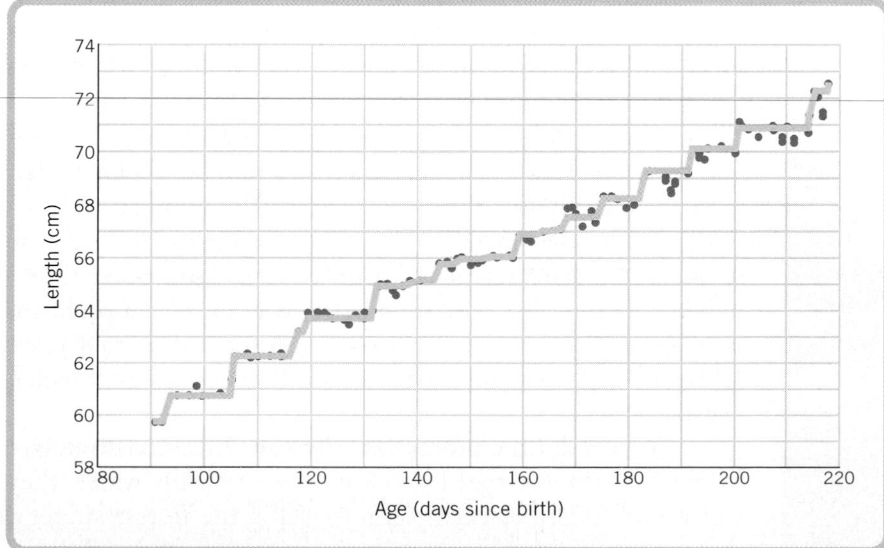

FIGURE 1.3 Continuous and discontinuous infant growth The general trend in an infant's length suggests continuous growth, but examining the changes day by day shows discontinuous bursts of growth on some days (Lampl et al., 1992).

4 Mechanisms of Developmental Change: How Does Change Occur?

Perhaps the deepest mystery about children's development is expressed by the question "How does change occur?" In other words, what are the mechanisms that produce the remarkable changes that all children experience? A very general answer was implicit in the discussion of the theme of *nature and nurture.* The interaction of genes and environments determines both what changes occur and when those changes occur. The challenge comes in specifying more precisely how particular changes occur.

A useful framework for thinking about these issues is suggested by Darwin's theory of evolution. According to evolutionary theory, species originate and change through two main processes: variation and selection. **Variation** refers to differences within and among individuals. **Selection** involves the more frequent survival, and therefore the greater reproduction, of organisms that are well adapted to their environment. Through the joint operation of variation and selection, species that are better adapted to a given environment become more prevalent in that environment over time, while less well adapted species become rarer or disappear altogether.

In an analogous way, psychological variation and selection appear to produce changes within an individual lifetime. Psychological variation involves the diverse ways in which people think, act, and relate to each other. Psychological selection includes increasing reliance, with age and experience, on the most useful of these ways of thinking, acting, and relating. Together, such variation and selection seem to produce a wide variety of positive changes in psychological functioning (Changeux & Dehaene, 1989; Geary & Bjorklund, 2000; Gibson, 1994; Siegler, 1996; Thelen & Smith, 1994).

The ways in which variation and selection produce psychological change can be illustrated in the context of changes in the strategies young children use to solve single-digit addition problems. First, consider the variation in children's strategies. From 4 or 5 years of age onward, children use a variety of strategies to solve simple problems such as 3 + 5 (Bisanz, Morrison, & Dunn, 1995; Geary, 1994). Sometimes they count from 1: on 3 + 5, they would count "1, 2, 3" while putting up three fingers, then count "1, 2, 3, 4, 5" while putting up five fingers, and then count all the raised fingers. Other times, they use retrieval (recalling an answer from memory). Yet other times, they use the counting-on strategy, choosing the larger of the two numbers being added and then counting-on from that point the number of times indicated by the smaller addend. For example, on 3 + 5, the child would start at 5 and count "6, 7, 8." Still other times, when children can't think of a better way to solve a problem, they resort to the strategy of guessing. Almost all 5- to 8-year-olds use at least three of these addition strategies (Siegler, 1996).

One key mechanism of developmental change is variation and selection in the use of strategies. As this 6-year-old acquires more efficient ways of solving addition problems, she will abandon her current strategy of counting on her fingers.

ELLEN B. SENISI / THE IMAGE WORKS

Now consider the process of selection. Addition strategies differ in both the speed and the accuracy with which they solve problems. For example, retrieval is the fastest strategy, but young children cannot apply it accurately on difficult problems. Other strategies, such as counting from 1, are slower and more effortful but can produce correct answers on problems where retrieval cannot. The challenge is to choose among the strategies in ways that enhance both speed and accuracy and that produce increasing reliance on the most effective strategies.

Even preschoolers and early elementary school students choose adaptively among the strategies they know. They use retrieval predominantly on simple problems where it produces fast and accurate answers. On the other hand, they use more time-consuming and effortful strategies on more difficult problems, where such strategies are necessary for accurate performance. Thus, 6-year-olds usually retrieve the answer to 3 + 3 but count from 12 to solve 2 + 12 (Siegler, 1987).

In biological evolution, the organisms best adapted to the environment tend to increase in number over time. Similarly, in cognitive development, the most efficient strategies increase in use as children gain age and experience. Thus, as children generate the correct answer to a problem increasingly often, they come to associate the answer with the problem, which allows them to retrieve it from memory increasingly often.

Evolutionary accounts have proved useful for understanding development in many areas beyond arithmetic (Geary & Bjorklund, 2000). These include development of social relationships (Bowlby, 1969), sex differences (Maccoby, 1998), language (Pinker, 1997), and sports (Pellegrini & Smith, 1998). New variations in these areas often emerge out of the universal tendency for children to play and explore the environment (Geary, 1998; Pellegrini & Smith, 1998). Selection occurs through children's increasing use of those variations that allow them to meet their goals consistently, quickly, and easily (Geary & Bjorklund, 2000; Siegler, 1996).

variation differences in thought and behavior within and among individuals

selection the more frequent survival and reproduction of organisms that are well adapted to their environment

sociocultural context the physical, social, cultural, economic, and historical circumstances that make up any child's environment

5 *The Sociocultural Context:* How Does the Sociocultural Context Influence Development?

Children grow up in a particular set of physical and social environments, in a particular culture, under particular economic circumstances, at a particular point in history. Together, these physical, social, cultural, economic, and historical circumstances constitute the **sociocultural context** of a child's life. This sociocultural context influences every aspect of children's development.

The most obviously important parts of children's sociocultural contexts are the people with whom they interact—parents, grandparents, brothers, sisters, day-care workers, friends, peers, and so on—and the physical environment in which they live—their house, day-care center, school, neighborhood, and so on. Another important but less tangible part of the sociocultural context is the institutions that influence children's lives: school systems, religious institutions, sports leagues, scouting groups, and so on. Yet another important set of influences are the general characteristics of the child's society: its wealth and technological advancement; its values, attitudes, beliefs, and traditions; its laws and political structure; and so on.

Just as people and the physical environment influence children's development, so do the less tangible characteristics of the sociocultural context. For example, the fact that most toddlers and preschoolers growing up in the United States today go to day care or other forms of child care outside their homes reflects a number of sociocultural factors, including the historical era (for most of the twentieth century, far fewer children in the United States attended day-care centers); the economic structure (most women with young children work outside the home); cultural beliefs within the society (for example, that receiving child care outside the home does not harm children); and cultural values (for example, that mothers of young children should be able to work outside of the home if they wish). Attendance at day-care centers, in turn, partly determines which people children meet and what activities they engage in.

OWEN FRANKEN / CORBIS

In many countries, including Denmark, mothers and children sleep together for the first several years of the child's life. This sociocultural pattern is in sharp contrast to the U.S. practice of having infants sleep separately from their parents soon after birth.

One method that developmentalists use to understand the influence of the sociocultural context is to compare the lives of children who grow up in different cultures. Such comparisons often reveal that practices that one culture takes for granted and views as "natural" are different in other cultures, and that practices that are rare or nonexistent in one's own culture are common in, and may have important advantages for, other cultures. The following comparison of young children's sleeping arrangements in different societies illustrates the value of such cross-cultural research.

In most families in the United States, newborn infants sleep in their parents' bedroom, either in a crib or in the same bed. However, when infants are 2 to 6 months old, parents usually move them to another bedroom where they sleep alone (Shweder, Balle-Jensen, & Goldstein, 1995). This seems only natural to most people raised in the United States. From a worldwide perspective, however, such sleeping arrangements are highly unusual. In one survey of 100 cultures, the United States was the only one in which babies slept in different rooms than their parents did (Whiting & Edwards, 1988). In other societies, including industrialized nations such as Italy, Japan, and Korea, babies almost always sleep in the same bed as their mother for the first few years, and older children also sleep in the same room as she does, sometimes in the same bed (e.g., Caudill & Plath, 1966). Where does this leave the father? In some cultures, the father sleeps in the same bed with mother and baby; in others, he sleeps in a separate bed or in a different room; and in yet others, he sleeps in a different house altogether.

How do these differences in sleeping arrangements affect children? To find out, Morelli, Rogoff, Oppenheim, and Goldsmith (1992) interviewed mothers in middle-class U.S. families in Salt Lake City, Utah, and in rural Mayan families in Guatemala. These interviews revealed that by age 6 months, the large majority of U.S. children had begun sleeping in their own separate bedrooms. As the children grew out of infancy, the nightly separation of child and parents became a complex ritual, surrounded by activities intended to comfort the child: telling stories, reading children's books, singing songs, and so on. One mother said, "When my friends hear that it is time for my son to go to bed, they teasingly say, 'See you in an hour'" (Morelli et al., 1992, p. 608). About half of the children were reported as taking a comfort object, such as a blanket or teddy bear, to bed with them.

In contrast, interviews with the Mayan mothers indicated that Mayan children typically sleep in the same bed with their mother until the age of 2 or 3 and continue to sleep in the same room for years thereafter. The children usually go to sleep at the same time as their parents or in someone's arms. None of the Mayan parents reported bedtime rituals; almost none reported their children taking comfort objects, such as dolls or stuffed animals, to bed with them. In addition, none of the Mayan children were said to suck their thumbs when they went to bed, unlike many children in the United States.

Why do sleeping arrangements differ in different cultures? One obvious possibility was that people in other cultures, particularly impoverished ones, lack the space needed for separate bedrooms. However, interviews with the Mayan parents indicated that they did not see space as the crucial consideration. Instead, the key consideration seems to be cultural values. Mayan culture prizes interdependence among people. The Mayan parents expressed the belief that having a young child sleep with the mother is important for developing a good parent–child relationship, for avoiding the child's becoming distressed at being alone, and for revealing to parents any problems the child has.

In contrast, U.S. culture prizes independence and self-reliance. The U.S. mothers expressed the belief that having babies and young children sleep alone promotes these values. The example illustrates both how practices that strike us as natural may differ greatly across cultures and how the simple conventions of everyday life often reflect deeper values.

Contexts of development differ not just between cultures but within any one culture as well. In multicultural societies, many contextual differences are related to ethnicity, race, and **socioeconomic status** (a measure of social class based on income and education, often abbreviated SES). Virtually all aspects of children's lives, from the food they eat to the parental discipline they receive to the games they play, are influenced by these characteristics.

The economic context exerts a particularly large influence on children's lives. In economically advanced societies, including the United States, most children grow up in comfortable circumstances, but millions of other children do not. In 1999, about 17% of U.S. children lived in homes with incomes below the poverty line (around $17,000 at the time for a family of four). In absolute numbers, this is about 12,000,000 children growing up in poverty (U.S. Department of Health and Human Services, 2001). As shown in Table 1.2, poverty rates are especially high in black and Hispanic families and in homes headed by single mothers.

TABLE 1.2

Percentages of U.S. Children Below Age 18 from Several Demographic Groups Growing Up in Families Below Poverty Line in 1999

Group	% in Poverty
Overall U.S. population	17
White, non-Hispanic	9
Black	33
Hispanic	30
Asian or Pacific Islander	12
Married Couples	9
White, non-Hispanic	4
Black	10
Hispanic	19
Asian or Pacific Islander	7
Single parent: Female head of household	37
White	26
Black	47
Hispanic	46
Asian or Pacific Island	26

Source: U.S. Census Bureau, 2001

Children from poor families tend to do less well than other children in many ways (Duncan & Brooks-Gunn, 2000). In infancy, they are more likely to have serious health problems. In childhood, they are more likely to have social/emotional or behavioral problems. Throughout childhood and adolescence, they tend to have smaller vocabularies, lower IQs, and lower math and reading scores on standardized achievement tests. In adolescence, they are more likely to become pregnant or drop out of school (Garbarino, 1992; McLoyd, 1998).

And yet, as we saw in Werner's study of the children of Kauai, described at the beginning of the chapter, many children do overcome the obstacles that poverty presents. Such resilient children tend to have three characteristics (Masten & Coatsworth, 1998). One is positive personal qualities, such as high intelligence, an easygoing personality, and adaptability to change. Another characteristic of resilient children is a close relationship with at least one parent. A third common characteristic is a close relationship with at least one adult other than their parents, such as a grandparent, teacher, coach, or clergyperson. Thus, although poverty poses obstacles to successful development, many children do surmount them.

6 *Individual Differences:* How Do Children Become So Different from One Another?

Anyone who has experience with children is struck by their uniqueness—their differences not only in physical appearance but in everything from activity level and temperament to intelligence, persistence, emotionality, and so on. These differences among children emerge quickly. In the first year, some children are shy, others outgoing (Kagan, 1998). Some children play with objects or look at them for prolonged periods of time; other children shift from activity to activity

socioeconomic status a measure of social class based on income and education

(Rothbart & Bates, 1998). As Mark Twain observed in his autobiography (1966), even children in the same family often differ substantially:

> My mother had a good deal of trouble with me, but I think she enjoyed it. She had none at all with my brother Henry, who was two years younger than I, and I think that the unbroken monotony of his goodness and truthfulness and obedience would have been a burden to her, but for the relief and variety that I furnished in the other direction. (pp. 35–36)

More recently, the distinguished writer John Edgar Wideman devoted an entire book (Wideman, 1995) to the same question of why children within the same family sometimes develop so differently: How was it that he became an eminent novelist whereas his brother became a drug addict and criminal?

Scarr (1992) identified four factors that could lead children from a single family (as well as children from different families) to turn out so different from each other:

1. genetic differences;
2. differences in treatment by parents and others;
3. differing effects on children of similar experiences;
4. children's choices of environments.

The most obvious reason for differences among children is that, except for identical twins, every individual is genetically unique. Even siblings (brothers and sisters), who share 50% of their genes, differ in the other 50%.

A second major source of variation among children is that they are treated differently by parents and other people. The different treatment is often associated with preexisting differences in the children's characteristics. For example, parents tend to provide more sensitive care to easygoing infants than to difficult ones; by the second year, parents of difficult children are often angry with them even when the children have done nothing wrong in the immediate situation (van den Boom & Hoeksma, 1994). Teachers, likewise, react to children's individual characteristics. With pupils who are learning well and are well behaved, teachers tend to provide positive attention and encouragement. With pupils who are doing poorly and are disruptive, they tend to be openly critical and to deny the pupils' requests for special help (Good & Brophy, 1996).

In addition to being shaped by objective differences in the treatment they receive, children also are influenced by their subjective interpretations of the treatment. A classic example occurs when each of a pair of siblings feels that his or her parents favor the other. Siblings also may react differently to events that affect the whole family, such as unemployment of one or both parents. In one study, 69% of negative events, such as parents losing their jobs, elicited fundamentally different reactions from siblings (Beardsall & Dunn, 1989). Some children were extremely concerned at a parent's loss of a job; others were confident that everything would be OK.

Different children, even ones within the same family, often react to the same experience in completely different ways.

RIP GRIFFITH / PHOTO RESEARCHERS, INC.

A fourth major source of differences among children within a family relates to the previously discussed theme of the *active child:* children increasingly choose activities and friends for themselves and thus influence their own subsequent development (recall the differences between children who chose to participate or not participate in extracurricular activities). Children choose niches for themselves; within a family, one child may become "the smart one," another "the popular one," another "the bad boy," and so on (Scarr & McCartney, 1983). A child labeled by family members as "the smart one" may strive to live up to the label; so may a child labeled "the naughty one." Thus, children's genes, their treatment by other people, their subjective reactions to other people's treatment of them, and their choice of environments all contribute to differences among children, even ones in the same family.

7 *Research and Children's Welfare:* How Can Research Promote Children's Well-Being?

Improved understanding of child development often leads to practical benefits. Several examples of such practical benefits have already been described, including the program for helping children deal with their anger and the recommendations regarding how to obtain valid eyewitness testimony from young children.

Another type of benefit that child-development research has yielded is procedures for diagnosing developmental problems early, when they can be corrected most easily and completely. For example, some infants are born with cataracts, areas of cloudiness in the lens of the eye. Some such cataracts are dense, clearly requiring surgery as early in life as possible (Ellemberg, Lewis, Maurer, & Brent, 2000). However, when infants' cataracts are milder, ophthalmologists often cannot tell whether the loss of vision is sufficient to warrant surgery.

Standard techniques for evaluating vision require patients to report what they see; infants, of course, cannot provide such reports. However, a child-development research method known as preferential looking allows their behavior to speak for them. This method builds from research showing that infants who can see the difference between a simple pattern and a solid gray field consistently prefer to look at the pattern. This is true even when the pattern is just a set of vertical stripes. Therefore, to diagnose the effects of infants' cataracts, researchers present the infants with cards on which a gray area and a striped area sit side by side. By varying the spacing of the stripes and the contrast between them and the white areas, a researcher can assess the extent of the visual impairment.

This preferential-looking procedure has proved useful with infants from age 2 months onward (Maurer, Lewis, Brent, & Levin, 1999; Teller et al., 1986). Dobson (1983) described several cases in which she administered the procedure to infants referred to her by ophthalmologists who suspected visual problems. In some cases, the preferential-looking test indicated that the infant's vision was unimpaired, thus alleviating parents' worry and avoiding unnecessary surgery. In other cases, the preferential-looking test revealed serious visual impairments; such findings led to the children's getting corrective surgery very early, when it would be most effective.

Another valuable application of child-development research has been programs for helping children learn more effectively. Among the useful instructional applications has been a program aimed at helping children with a disability known as *specific language impairment* (SLI). These individuals, approximately 5% of the children in the United States, have normal nonverbal intelligence but develop spoken language unusually slowly. Their main difficulty seems to be a weakness in rapid processing of auditory information (meaningful sounds). This difficulty interferes with their understanding of speech, which requires rapid integration of sounds into words and sentences.

A group of researchers (Merzenich, 2001; Tallal et al., 1996) reasoned that this difficulty in rapid processing of auditory information could be remedied by applying the psychological principle of *successive approximation,* according to which acquisition of a difficult skill can be aided by first presenting learners with a simplified version of the task until they succeed with it and then gradually increasing the difficulty of the task until they become skillful enough to succeed on the original, demanding version.

Merzenich, Tallal, and their colleagues applied this principle in an intensive program in which children with SLI played a variety of computer games aimed at increasing the speed at which they could process sounds. For example, in one game, the children heard two similar syllables in different orders (e.g., *buhduh* and *duhbuh*) and were required to identify whether the *buh* came first or second. Initially, the sounds were presented at rates much slower than normal speech, rates at which the children with SLI could succeed at the task. Then the sounds were presented increasingly rapidly, forcing the children to process them faster and faster until the sounds were being presented at, or even beyond, the rate of normal speech.

This application of the psychological principle of successive approximation produced large improvements on the training tasks. More important, by the end of the program, the children performed normally on tests of speech comprehension. As this and the previous example illustrate, child-development research is yielding practical benefits both in diagnosing children's problems and in helping them overcome them.

review:

The modern field of child development is in large part an attempt to answer a small set of fundamental questions about children. These include:

1. What is the relation between nature and nurture?
2. How do children contribute to their own development?
3. Is development best viewed as continuous or discontinuous?
4. What mechanisms produce development?
5. How does the sociocultural context influence development?
6. Why are children so different from one other?
7. How can we use research to improve children's welfare?

Methods for Studying Child Development

As illustrated in the previous section on Enduring Themes in Child Development, modern scientific research has advanced our understanding of fundamental questions about child development well beyond that of the historical figures who first raised the questions. This progress is not due to modern researchers' being smarter or working harder than the great thinkers of the past; rather, it reflects the successful application of the scientific method to the study of child development. In this section, we describe the scientific method and how its application to child development has advanced our understanding.

The Scientific Method

The basic assumption of the **scientific method** is that all beliefs, no matter how probable they seem, may be wrong. Therefore, until beliefs have been tested, they must be viewed as **hypotheses,** that is, as educated guesses rather than truth. If a hypothesis is tested, and evidence repeatedly indicates that it is incorrect, it must be abandoned no matter how reasonable it seems.

Use of the scientific method involves four basic steps:

1. choosing a question to be answered;
2. formulating a hypothesis regarding the question;

3. developing a method for testing the hypothesis;
4. using the data yielded by the method to draw a conclusion regarding the hypothesis.

To illustrate these steps, let us take as the *question* to be answered "What abilities of preschoolers predict which children will become good readers?" A reasonable *hypothesis* might be "Preschoolers who can identify the separate sounds within words will become better readers than those who cannot." A straightforward *method* for testing this hypothesis would be to select a group of preschoolers, test their ability to identify the separate sounds within words, and then, several years later, test the reading skills of the same children. Research using this method has, in fact, shown that preschoolers who are aware of the component sounds within words later read more skillfully, at least through fourth grade, than do their peers who lack this ability (Wagner et al., 1997). These results support the *conclusion* that preschoolers' ability to identify sounds within words predicts their later reading skill.

The first, second, and fourth of these steps are not unique to the scientific method. As we have seen, great thinkers of the past also asked questions, formulated hypotheses, and drew conclusions that were reasonable given the evidence available to them. What distinguishes scientific research from past approaches is the third step, the research methods used to test the hypotheses. These research methods, and the higher-quality evidence that they yield, allow investigators to progress beyond their initial hypotheses so that they can draw firmly grounded conclusions.

scientific method an approach to testing beliefs that involves choosing a question, formulating a hypothesis, testing the hypothesis, and drawing a conclusion

hypotheses educated guesses

reliability the degree to which independent measurements of a given behavior are consistent

interrater reliability the amount of agreement in the observations of different raters who witness the same behavior

The Importance of Appropriate Measurement

Crucial to the scientific method is obtaining measures that are relevant to the hypotheses being tested. A researcher who hypothesized that children would learn more from one curriculum than from another probably would measure the percentage of correct answers children gave following exposure to each curriculum. The reason is that the hypothesis concerns which curriculum will produce greater knowledge, and correct answers are a good measure of knowledge. In contrast, a researcher who hypothesized that infants prefer bright colors to dull ones might present infants with identical shapes in bright and dull colors and measure the amount of time the infants looked at each one. The reason is that the hypothesis concerns infants' preferences, and relative looking time is a good measure of such preferences.

Regardless of the particular measure used, many of the same criteria determine whether a measure is a good one. One key criterion already has been noted—the measure must be directly relevant to the hypothesis. Two other qualities that good measures must possess are reliability and validity.

Reliability

The degree to which independent measurements of a given behavior are consistent is referred to as the **reliability** of the measure. One important type of consistency, **interrater reliability,** indicates the amount of agreement in the observations of different raters who witness the same behavior. Sometimes the observations are qualitative, as when raters classify a child's temperament as "easygoing" or "difficult." Other times the observations are quantitative, as when raters score on a scale of 1 to 10 how upset babies become during a visit to a pediatrician. In both cases, interrater reliability is attained when there is close agreement between the observations of different raters. Without such close agreement, one cannot have confidence in the research findings, because there is no way to tell which (if either) rating was accurate.

test–retest reliability the degree of similarity of a child's performance on two or more occasions

validity the degree to which a test measures what it is intended to measure

internal validity the degree to which effects observed within experiments can be attributed to the variables that the researcher intentionally manipulated

external validity the degree to which results can be generalized beyond the particulars of the research

structured interview a research procedure in which all participants are asked to answer the same questions

clinical interview a procedure in which questions are adjusted in accord with the answers the interviewee provides

A second important type of consistency is **test–retest reliability.** This type of reliability is attained when measures of a child's performance are similar on two or more occasions. Suppose that researchers presented a vocabulary test to the same children on two occasions, one week apart. If the test is reliable, those children who scored highest on the first testing should also score highest on the second, because none of the children's vocabularies would change much over such a short period. As in the example of interrater reliability, a lack of test–retest reliability would make it impossible to know which result (if either) accurately reflected children's knowledge.

Validity The **validity** of a test or experiment refers to the degree to which it measures what it is intended to measure. Returning to the example of the vocabulary test, if some children scored badly on the test because they were nervous, their scores would not be a valid measure of their vocabulary. This would be true even if the test possessed both interrater and test–retest reliability. Thus, even if all observers agreed that on both occasions the nervous children answered few items correctly, the test would not be a valid measure of the children's vocabularies because it would underestimate their knowledge. As this example illustrates, a measure can be reliable without being valid. However, to be valid, a test must be reliable; if two raters assign a child different scores on the vocabulary test, these scores cannot both be valid indicators of the child's knowledge.

Researchers strive for two types of validity: internal and external. **Internal validity** refers to whether effects observed within experiments can be attributed to the conditions that the researcher intentionally manipulated. For example, suppose that a number of depressed adolescents are provided psychotherapy and that three months later, fewer of them are depressed. Can we conclude that the psychotherapy was effective? No, because the mere passage of time might have caused the improvement. Moods fluctuate, and many adolescents who are depressed at any given time will be happier three months later even without psychotherapy. In this example, the passage of time is a source of internal invalidity, because the factor believed to cause the improvement (the psychotherapy) may have had no effect.

External validity, in contrast, concerns the ability to generalize beyond the particulars of the research. Studies of child development almost never are intended to yield conclusions that apply only to the particular children and the exact methods used in the particular study. Rather, the goal is to draw conclusions that apply more generally. Obtaining findings in a single experiment only begins the process of determining the external validity of the findings. Any study is inevitably conducted with a particular set of participants and with a particular set of procedures. Additional studies with participants from different backgrounds and with different particular methods are invariably needed to establish the external validity of the findings.

Thus, the scientific method involves choosing a question to be answered, formulating hypotheses regarding the question, developing methods for testing the hypotheses, and drawing conclusions consistent with the data. Useful measures must be directly relevant to the hypothesis, reliable over raters and time, and internally and externally valid (Table 1.3).

TABLE 1.3

Key Properties of Behavioral Measures

Property	Question of Interest
Relevance to hypotheses	Do the hypotheses predict in a straightforward way what should happen on these measures?
Interrater reliability	Do different raters who observe the same behavior classify or score the same way?
Test–retest reliability	Are the scores or classifications that children receive on the measure stable over time?
Internal validity	Can effects within the experiment be attributed to the variables that the researcher intentionally manipulated?
External validity	How widely can the findings be generalized to different children, measures, and experimental procedures than the ones in the study?

Contexts for Gathering Data About Children

Researchers obtain data about children in three main contexts: interviews, naturalistic observation, and structured observation. In the sections following, we consider how gathering data in each context can help answer different important questions about children.

Interviews

The most obvious way to collect data about children is to go straight to the source and ask the children questions about various aspects of their lives. One type of interview, the **structured interview,** is especially useful when the goal is to collect self-reports on the same topics from all of the people being studied. For example, Valeski and Stipek (2001) asked kindergartners and first-graders questions regarding their feelings about school (How much does your teacher care about you? How do you feel when you're at school?) and also questions about their beliefs about their academic competence (How much do you know about numbers? How good are you at reading?). The children's general attitude toward school and their feelings about their relationship with their teacher proved to be positively related to their beliefs about their competence in math and reading. Children who expressed confidence in their math and reading skills were viewed by teachers as more engaged in classroom activities than other children. Only by asking children questions about their feelings and beliefs could the researchers have learned about them.

A second type of interview, the **clinical interview,** is especially useful for obtaining in-depth information about an individual child. In this approach, the interviewer begins with a set of prepared questions, but if the child says something intriguing, the interviewer can depart from the script to follow up on the child's lead.

Clinical interviews were used to good advantage in studying Bobby, a 10-year-old child who was referred for evaluation because he was believed to be depressed (Schwartz & Johnson, 1985). When the interviewer asked him about school, Bobby said that he did not like it because the other children disliked him and he was bad at sports. As he put it, "I'm not really very good at anything" (p. 214). To explore the source of this sad self-description, the interviewer asked Bobby what he would wish for if three wishes could be granted. Bobby replied, "I would wish that I was the type of boy my mother and father want, I would wish that I could have friends, and I would wish that I wouldn't feel sad so much" (p. 214). Such heartrending comments provide a sense of the subjective experience of this depressed child, one that would be impossible to obtain from methods that were not tailored to the individual.

As with all contexts for collecting data, interviews have both strengths and weaknesses. On the positive side, they yield a great deal of data quite quickly and can provide in-depth information about individual children. On the negative side, answers to interview questions often are biased. Children (like adults) often report past events inaccurately. They avoid disclosing facts that put them in a bad light, distort the way that events happened, and fail to understand their own motivations (Nisbett & Wilson, 1977). In addition, children (again like adults) are not very accurate in predicting how they would act in new situations. These limitations have led increasing numbers of researchers to collect data by observing the behavior of interest for themselves.

naturalistic observation examination of how children behave in their usual environments—schools, playgrounds, homes, and so on

structured observation a procedure that involves presenting an identical situation to each child and recording the child's behavior

Naturalistic Observation

When the primary goal is to describe how children behave in their usual environments—schools, playgrounds, homes, and so on—**naturalistic observation** is the method of choice. In this approach to gathering data, observers try to remain unobtrusively in the background in the chosen setting, so as not to influence the behaviors they are observing.

An outstanding example of naturalistic observation is Gerald Patterson's (1982) comparative study of family dynamics in "troubled" and "typical" families. The troubled families were defined by the presence of at least one child who had been labeled "out of control" and referred for treatment by a school, court, or mental health professional. The typical families were defined by the fact that none of the children in them showed signs of behavioral difficulties. Income levels and children's ages were matched for the troubled and typical families.

To observe the frequency with which children and parents engaged in negative behaviors—teasing, yelling, whining, criticizing, and so on—research assistants repeatedly observed dinnertime interactions in both troubled and typical homes. The research assistant for each family made several home visits before beginning to collect data in order to accustom family members to his or her presence, always sat quietly in the background, and avoided interacting with family members during the observations.

The researchers found that both parents and children in the troubled families acted differently from their counterparts in the typical ones. Parents in the troubled families were more self-absorbed and less responsive to their children than were parents in the typical households. Children in the troubled families responded to parental punishment by becoming more aggressive, whereas children in the typical households responded to such punishment by becoming less aggressive. In the troubled families, interactions often fell into a vicious cycle in which

1. the child acted in a hostile or aggressive manner, for example, by defying a parent's request to clean up his or her room;
2. the parent reacted angrily, for example, by shouting at the child to obey;
3. the child further increased the level of hostility, for example, by yelling back;
4. the parent ratcheted up the aggression yet further, perhaps by spanking the child.

As Patterson's study suggests, naturalistic observations are particularly useful for illuminating social interactions, such as those between children and parents.

Psychologists sometimes observe family interactions around the dinner table, because mealtimes evoke strong emotions in many families.

BILLY E. BARNES / PHOTOEDIT

Although naturalistic observation yields detailed information about certain aspects of children's everyday lives, it also has important limitations. One is that naturally occurring contexts vary on many dimensions, and it is often hard to know which ones influenced the behavior of interest. Thus, while it was clear in the Patterson study that the troubled families' interactions differed from those of the more harmonious families, the interactions and family histories differed in so many ways that it was difficult to identify their specific contributions. A second limitation of naturalistic studies is that many important behaviors only occur occasionally in the everyday environment, which reduces researchers' opportunities to study them. Using structured observation as a context for collecting data provides a means for overcoming both limitations.

Structured Observation

To test specific hypotheses, researchers often design a situation that will elicit behavior relevant to the hypothesis and then observe different children in that situation. In such **structured observations,** the researcher records what every child does in the situation and relates the behavior to characteristics of the child, such as age, gender, or personality, and to the child's behavior in other situations.

In one such study, Kochanska, Coy, and Murray (2001) were interested in how the mother–child relationship influences 2- and 3-year-olds' willingness to comply with their mothers' requests that they forgo appealing activities or participate in unappealing ones. The researchers invited mother–toddler pairs to a laboratory room that included a number of especially attractive toys on a shelf, as well as a great many less attractive toys scattered around the room. Each mother was asked to tell her child that he or she could play with any of the toys *except* the especially attractive ones on the shelf. Raters observed children over the next few minutes and classified them as complying wholeheartedly, grudgingly, or not at all. Then the experimenter asked the mother to leave the room and observed through a one-way mirror whether the child played with the "forbidden" toys in the mother's absence.

The researchers found that the children who earlier complied wholeheartedly with their mother's request not to play with the forbidden toys were less likely to disobey it in her absence than were children who had complied only grudgingly when she was present or who had not complied at all. The children who complied wholeheartedly also were more likely than the others to engage wholeheartedly in the onerous activity of cleaning up the many toys on the floor when their mother subsequently asked them to do so. When retested at 45 months of age, most children showed the same type of compliance as they had as toddlers. Overall, the results indicated that the quality of young children's compliance with their mother's requests is a somewhat stable, general property of the mother–child relationship.

COURTESY OF SUWANNA AND DAVID SIEGLER

Temptation is everywhere.

This type of structured observation offers an important advantage over naturalistic observation. It ensures that all children encounter identical situations, which allow direct comparisons of different children's behavior and make it possible to establish the generality of behavior across different tasks. On the other hand, structured observation does not provide as extensive information about individual children's subjective experience as do interviews, nor can it provide as natural a situation as does naturalistic observation. Thus, the ideal data-gathering situation depends on which qualities are most important for the goals of the study. Table 1.4 summarizes the advantages and disadvantages of interviews, naturalistic observation, and structured observation as contexts for gathering data.

TABLE 1.4

Advantages and Disadvantages of Three Contexts for Gathering Data

Data-Gathering Situation	Key Features	Advantages	Disadvantages
Interview	Children answer questions asked either in person or on a questionnaire.	Can reveal children's subjective experience. Structured interviews are inexpensive means for collecting in-depth data about individuals. Clinical interviews allow flexibility for following up unexpected comments.	Reports are often biased to reflect favorably on interviewee. Memory of interviewee often inaccurate and incomplete. Prediction of future behaviors often is inaccurate.
Naturalistic observation	Activities of children in everyday settings are observed.	Useful for describing behavior in everyday settings. Helps illuminate social interaction processes.	Difficult to know which aspects of situation are most influential. Limited value for studying infrequent behaviors.
Structured observation	Children are brought to laboratory and presented prearranged tasks.	Ensures that all children's behaviors are observed in same context. Allows controlled comparison of children's behavior in different situations.	Context is less natural than in naturalistic observation. Reveals less about subjective experience than interviews.

(a) $r = 1.00$

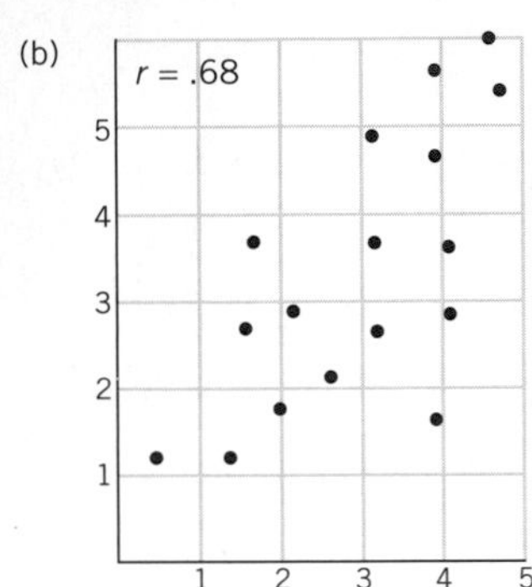

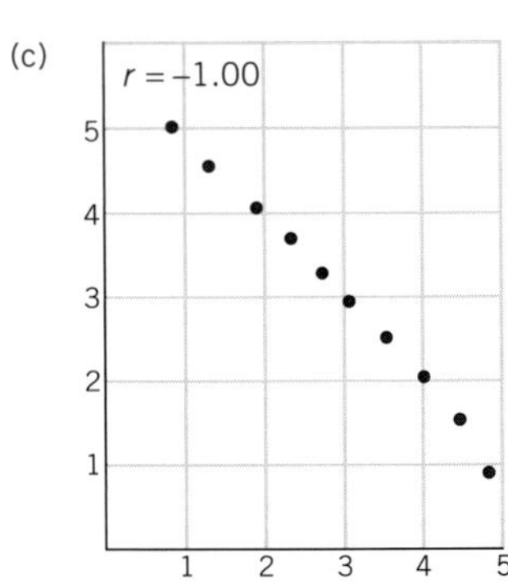

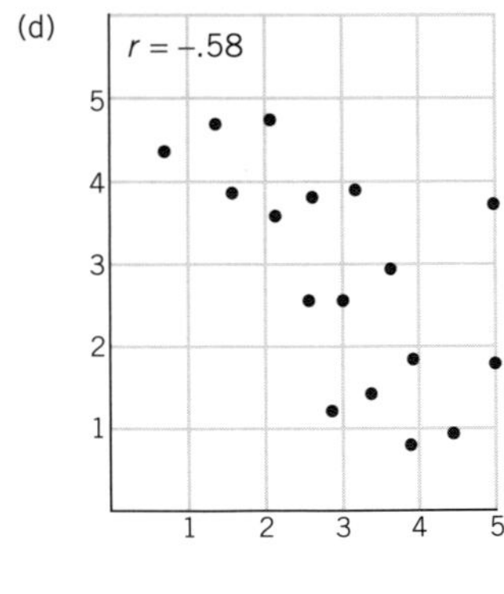

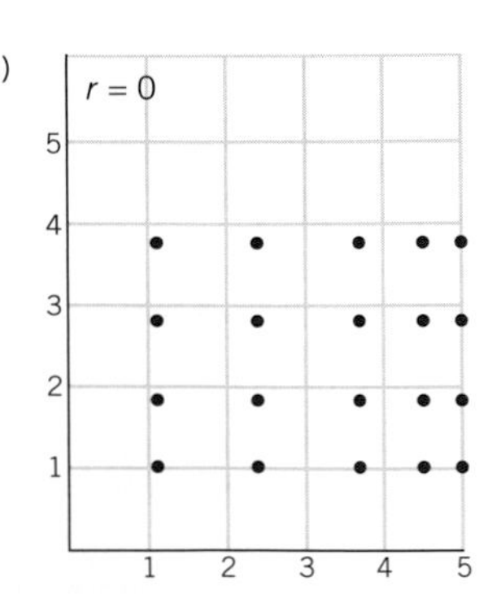

Correlation and Causation

People differ along an infinite number of **variables,** that is, attributes that vary across individuals and situations, such as age, sex, activity level, socioeconomic status, particular experiences, and so on. Among the major goals of child-development research is to determine how these and other major variables are related to each other, both in terms of associations and in terms of cause–effect relations. In the sections following, we examine the research designs that are used to examine each type of relation.

Correlational Designs

The primary goal of some studies, known as **correlational designs,** is to determine whether children who differ in one characteristic also differ in other characteristics. For example, a researcher might examine whether toddlers' aggressiveness is related to the number of hours they spend in day care or whether adolescents' popularity is related to their IQ.

The association between two variables is known as their **correlation.** When variables are strongly correlated, knowing a child's score on either one allows accurate prediction of the child's score on the other. For example, the fact that the number of hours per week that children spend reading correlates highly with their reading-test scores (Guthrie, Wigfield, Metsala, & Cox, 1999) means that a child's reading-test score can be accurately predicted if one knows how much time the child spends reading. It also means that the number of hours the child spends reading can be predicted if one knows the child's reading-test score.

Correlations can be either positive or negative in direction. The direction is positive when high values of one variable are associated with high values of the other; the direction is negative when high values of one are associated with low values of the other. Thus, the correlation between time spent reading and reading-test scores would be positive, because children who spend high amounts of time reading also have high reading-test scores. An obvious example of a negative correlation would be that between obesity and running speed; the more obese the child, the slower his or her running speed would tend to be.

Both the direction and strength of a correlation are indicated by a statistic called the **correlation coefficient.** The direction of the correlation is indicated by whether the sign in front of the number is positive or negative. Thus, in Figure 1.4a and 1.4b, variables 1 and 2 are positively related (that is, the higher the value of variable 1, the higher the value of variable 2). Conversely, in Figure 1.4c and 1.4d, variables 1 and 2 are negatively related (that is, the higher the value of variable 1, the lower the value of variable 2), so there is a minus sign in front of the number.

The strength of the relation between the two variables is indicated by the number within the correlation coefficient. Correlations range from 1.0 to –1.0. The

FIGURE 1.4 Five correlations (a) The strongest possible positive correlation; without exception, the higher the value of one variable, the higher the value of the other. (b) A strong but imperfect positive correlation; a higher value of one variable tends to go with a higher value of the other. (c) The strongest possible negative correlation; the higher the value of one variable, the lower the value of the other. (d) A strong but imperfect negative correlation. (e) A total lack of correlation; any value of one variable is equally likely to be accompanied by any value of the other.

higher the absolute value (the closer to 1.0 or –1.0), the stronger the relation between the variables; correspondingly, the lower the absolute value (the closer to 0), the weaker the relation. Thus, the correlations shown in Figure 1.4a and 1.4c, 1.00 and –1.00, are equally strong, the strongest possible, even though the directions of the relations are opposite. In both relations, knowing the value of variable 1 allows us to know the exact value of variable 2. The relations in Figure 1.4b and 1.4d are weaker, but they are still informative, in the sense that knowing the value of variable 1 allows a fairly accurate prediction of the value of variable 2. For example, in Figure 1.4d, if we know that the value of variable 1 is relatively high, we can predict that the value of variable 2 is relatively low. Finally, the value of the correlation coefficient in Figure 1.4e is 0. In this situation, knowing the value of variable 1 is useless for predicting the value of variable 2.

Correlation Does Not Equal Causation

When two variables are strongly correlated and there is a plausible cause–effect relation between them, it often is tempting to infer that one causes the other. However, this inference is not justified, for two reasons. The first is the **direction-of-causation problem:** a correlation does not indicate which variable is the cause and which the effect. In the above example of the correlation between time spent reading and reading achievement, greater time spent reading *might* cause increased reading achievement. On the other hand, the cause–effect relation could run in the opposite direction: greater reading skill might cause children to spend more time reading, because it makes reading more enjoyable. Or both could be true; there simply is no way to tell from the correlation.

The second reason that correlation does not imply causation is the **third-variable problem:** the correlation between two variables may actually be the result of some third, unspecified variable. Continuing with the reading example, growing up in an intellectual home environment may be the cause of both the greater time spent reading and the greater reading achievement. Again, we cannot infer causation from a correlation.

Experimental Designs

If correlations are insufficient to infer cause–effect relations, what is sufficient? The answer is **experimental designs,** a group of approaches that allow inferences about causes and effects to be drawn. The logic of experimental designs can be summarized quite simply. If (a) two or more groups of participants are comparable at the outset, and (b) the participants within each group are presented with experiences that differ in only one way from the experiences presented to participants in the other group, *and* (c) the participants in different groups behave differently after the experiences, *then* (d) the differing experiences must have caused the subsequent differences in behavior. In order to meet the first two requirements (a and b), experimental designs employ two basic procedures, *random assignment* and *experimental control.*

Random assignment Meeting the first requirement—that the people in each group be comparable at the outset—is crucial to being able to infer that it was the varying experiences that caused the later differences between the groups. Otherwise, those differences might have arisen from some preexisting difference between the people in the groups. Say, for example, that researchers wanted to determine whether Curriculum A is a more effective teaching tool than Curriculum B. If they gave Curriculum A to children at one school and Curriculum B to

variables attributes that vary across individuals and situations, such as age, gender, and expectations

correlational designs studies intended to indicate how variables are related to each other

correlation the association between two variables

correlation coefficient a statistic that indicates the direction and strength of a correlation

direction-of-causation problem the concept that a correlation between two variables does not indicate which, if either, variable is the cause of the other

third-variable problem the concept that a correlation between two variables may stem from both being influenced by some third variable

experimental designs a group of approaches that allow inferences about causes and effects to be drawn

random assignment a procedure in which each child has an equal chance of being assigned to each group within an experiment

experimental control the ability of the researcher to determine the specific experiences that children have during the course of an experiment

experimental group a group of children in an experimental design who are presented the experience of interest

control group the group of children in an experimental design who are not presented the experience of interest

independent variable the experience that children in the experimental group receive and that children in the control group do not receive

dependent variable a behavior that is measured to determine whether it is affected by exposure to the independent variable

naturalistic experiments a type of experimental design in which data are collected in everyday settings

children at another school, they would be unable to tell whether differences in knowledge following exposure to the curricula were caused by differences between the curricula or by other differences between the children at the two schools. It might be that the children at one school were smarter or more motivated and therefore learned more effectively.

The key to producing groups that are initially comparable is random assignment of participants to groups. **Random assignment** means that each child has an equal chance of being in each group, as would be the case if group membership were determined by flipping a coin for each child. When groups created through random assignment include a reasonably large number of children (typically fifteen to twenty children per group), initial differences between the groups tend to be minimal. For example, if forty children are divided randomly between two groups, each group is likely to have a few children who are unusually good readers, a few who are unusually bad readers, and many in between. Similarly, each group is likely to have a few children with very extroverted personalities, a few with very introverted personalities, and many in between. The logic implies that groups created through random assignment should be comparable on any variable.

Experimental control The second essential characteristic of an experimental design, **experimental control,** refers to the ability of the researcher to determine the specific experiences that children in each group encounter during the study. In the simplest experimental design, one with only two conditions, the groups are often referred to as the "experimental group" and the "control group." Children in the **experimental group** are presented with the experience of interest; children in the **control group** are treated identically except for not being presented that experience.

The experience that children in the experimental group receive and that children in the control group do not is referred to as the **independent variable.** The behavior that is hypothesized to be affected by exposure to the independent variable is referred to as the **dependent variable.** Thus, if a researcher hypothesized that showing children an anti-bullying film would reduce their rate of bullying, the researcher might randomly assign one group of children in a school or day camp to view the film and another group of children in the same school or camp not to view it. In this case, the anti-bullying film would be the independent variable and the amount of bullying that children engaged in after the procedure would be the dependent variable. If the independent variable, the anti-bullying film, had the desired effect, then it should promote a reduction in the dependent variable, the amount of bullying children engage in after watching the film.

One illustration of how experimental designs allow researchers to draw conclusions about causes and effects is an ingenious study of preschoolers' ability to use analogies to solve problems (Brown, Kane, & Echols, 1986). The study tested whether being asked questions about the similarities between two problems would allow 4- and 5-year-olds to extend to a new problem the lessons learned on a previous one. All the children in the study were first told a story about a genie who needed to transport jewels over a wall and into a bottle without crossing over the wall himself. The genie solved the problem by creating a tube from a piece of posterboard, placing the tube across the top of the wall so that one end led into the mouth of the bottle, and then rolling the jewels down the tube.

After hearing this story, half of the children were selected randomly to be in the experimental group. They were asked a set of questions that would focus their attention on the important parts of the genie's solution. What did the genie want to do? What made it hard to do? How did he solve the problem? The children in the control group were not asked such questions.

Then, children in both the experimental and the control groups were presented a second story, this one involving an Easter bunny who, while standing on one side of a narrow river, had to transfer eggs into a basket on the other side. All the children were asked how the bunny could use a piece of posterboard to make the transfer.

The researchers' hypothesis was that asking children questions that called attention to the key aspects of the genie story would help them draw the relevant analogy and solve the Easter bunny's problem. The results of the experiment supported this hypothesis. Almost 70% of children in the experimental group solved the problem, versus less than 20% of children in the control group. These results allowed the researchers to conclude that being asked the questions about the genie story caused the better problem solving, because the procedure presented to the experimental and control groups differed in only one way: whether questions about the genie's solution were asked. And since children were randomly assigned to the two groups, there was no reason to think that children in the experimental group were smarter, better motivated, or superior in any other way that would explain the results.

Although experimental designs such as this one have the unique advantage of allowing researchers to draw conclusions about the causes of events, they have limitations as well. Their greatest limitation is that the controlled circumstances of the laboratory are often quite different from the conditions of the everyday world. This fact raises questions concerning external validity, that is, whether findings obtained in the laboratory will generalize beyond it.

Naturalistic experiments One means of overcoming this problem is to conduct **naturalistic experiments.** As with naturalistic observation, the data gathered in naturalistic experiments are collected in everyday settings rather than in a laboratory, which increases the external validity of the findings. As with other experimental designs, naturalistic experiments involve random assignment of children to specific conditions, which allows causal conclusions to be drawn.

One classic naturalistic experiment focused on whether watching violent television programs made children more aggressive (Steuer, Applefield, & Smith, 1971). Preschoolers were randomly divided into an experimental group and a control group. Examination of children in the two groups during several play periods indicated that their initial levels of aggression were comparable. Then, over a period of several weeks, children in the experimental group were shown violent TV programs that had been broadcast on Saturday morning children's shows. Children in the control group were shown nonviolent Saturday morning programs during this period. After watching the TV programs, children in the experimental group, who had watched the violent shows, more often hit, kicked, choked, and squeezed their classmates during play periods than did children in the control group, who had watched the nonviolent programs. Thus, this naturalistic experiment demonstrated that watching violent programs was causally related to increased aggression in an everyday setting.

PETER BYRON

Both experimental studies and everyday observation suggest that watching violent TV programs can cause children to become more aggressive.

When the variables of interest are ones that allow children to be randomly assigned to groups, experimental designs are uniquely valuable for establishing cause–effect relations. However, for many variables of great interest, children cannot be randomly assigned to groups, which means that neither naturalistic nor laboratory experimental designs can be used. For example, researchers who want to study effects of temperament on the quality of friendships cannot randomly assign some children to have genial temperaments and others difficult ones. With these and many other important variables, correlational designs are the

TABLE 1.5

Advantages and Disadvantages of Correlational and Experimental Designs

Type of Design	Key Features	Advantages	Disadvantages
Correlational	Comparison of existing groups of children or examination of relations among each child's scores on different variables.	Only way to compare many groups of interest (boys–girls, rich–poor, etc.). Only way to establish relations among many variables of interest (IQ and achievement; popularity and happiness, etc.).	Third-variable problem Direction-of-causation problem.
Experimental	Random assignment of children to groups and experimental control of procedures presented to each group.	Allows causal inferences because design rules out direction-of-causation and third-variable problems. Naturalistic experiments can demonstrate cause–effect connections in natural settings.	Need for experimental control often leads to artificial experimental situations. Cannot be used to study many differences and variables of interest, such as age, sex, and temperament.

only option. The advantages and disadvantages of correlational and experimental designs are summarized in Table 1.5.

Designs for Examining Development

A great deal of research on child development focuses on the ways in which children change or remain the same as they grow older and gain experience. To study development over time, investigators utilize three research designs: cross-sectional, longitudinal, and microgenetic designs.

Cross-Sectional Designs

The most common and easiest way to study changes and continuities with age is to use the **cross-sectional** approach. This method compares children of different ages on a given behavior, ability, or characteristic. For example, in one cross-sectional study of children's friendships, sixth to twelfth graders at three schools were asked to name their best friend and up to ten other friends in their school (Urberg, Degirmencioglu, Tolson, & Halliday-Scher, 1995). The research indicated that some aspects of friendship changed with age: for example, the older children named fewer friends, but those they named were more likely to name them as friends as well. This finding is consistent with other research indicating that as children grow older, their friendship circles become smaller and their friendships more reciprocal. Other aspects of friendship did not change during the age span examined. For example, at all ages, children who were part of the ethnic majority at their school, regardless of whether that majority was white or black, were more likely to have their designation of friends reciprocated than were children who were part of the minority.

Cross-sectional designs are useful for revealing similarities and differences between older and younger children. However, they do not yield information about the stability of individual differences over time or about the patterns of change shown by individual children. This is where longitudinal approaches are valuable.

cross-sectional design a research method in which children of different ages are compared on a given behavior or characteristic over a short period of time

longitudinal design a method of study in which the same children are studied twice or more over a substantial period of time

microgenetic design a method of study in which the same children are studied repeatedly over a short period of time

Longitudinal Designs

The **longitudinal** approach involves following a group of children over a substantial period of time (usually two or more years) and observing changes and continuities in the children's development during that time. For example, in one longitudinal study, Brendgen and his colleagues (Brendgen et al., 2001) examined children's popularity with classmates each year from the time they were 7-year-olds to the time they were 12-year-olds. The individual children's popularity proved to be quite stable over this period: a substantial number of children were popular in the large majority of years; quite a few others were unpopular throughout. On the other hand, some individuals showed idiosyncratic patterns of change from year to year; the same child might be popular at age 8, unpopular at age 10, and of average popularity at age 12. Such findings about stability of individual differences over time and about individual patterns of change could only have been obtained in a longitudinal design.

If longitudinal designs are so useful for revealing stability and change over time, why are cross-sectional designs more common? The reasons are mainly practical. Studying the same children over long time periods involves the difficult and time-consuming task of locating the children for each reexamination. Inevitably, some of the children move away or they drop out of the study for other reasons. Such loss of participants may call into question the external validity of the findings, because the children who move or choose not to participate further may differ from those who participate throughout. When longitudinal research involves frequent repeated testing, the external validity of the findings may be threatened; for example, repeatedly encountering IQ tests could familiarize children with the type of items on the tests, thus improving their scores. For this reason, longitudinal designs are used primarily when the main issues are stability and change in individual children over time, issues that can only be studied longitudinally. When the central developmental issue involves age-related changes in typical performance, cross-sectional studies are more common.

TOM MCCARTHY / PHOTOEDIT

Being left out or unpopular is no fun for anyone. Longitudinal research has been used to determine whether the same children are left out year after year or whether popularity changes over time.

Microgenetic Designs

An important limitation of both cross-sectional and longitudinal designs is that they provide only a broad outline of the process of change. **Microgenetic designs,** in contrast, are specifically designed to provide an in-depth depiction of the processes that produce changes (Kuhn, 1995; Miller & Coyle, 1999; Siegler, 2000). The basic idea of this approach is to provide children who are thought to be on the verge of an important developmental change with heightened exposure to the type of experience that is believed to produce the change and to intensively study the children's behavior *while it is changing.*

One example of the microgenetic approach is Siegler and Jenkins's (1989) study of how kindergartners discover the counting-on strategy, the approach in which addition problems are solved by counting from the larger addend. Before children discover this strategy, they usually solve addition problems by counting from 1. Counting from the larger addend rather than from 1 reduces the amount of counting and thus produces faster and more accurate performance.

Siegler and Jenkins hypothesized that children discover counting-on for themselves as they solve addition problems, rather than being taught it by a teacher or parent. To test this hypothesis, and to observe the discovery process, they presented children who did not yet use counting-on, but who were close to the age when most children discover it, with more addition problems than they would normally encounter before entering school. By videotaping the child's behavior on each problem, the researchers were able to identify when in the study, if ever, each child first counted-on. Identifying when each child discovered the new approach, in turn, allowed examination of the experiences that preceded the discovery, the children's emotional reaction to it, and their generalization of the new approach following its initial use.

BOB DAEMMRICH / STOCK BOSTON

Discovering how to reach goals is an inherently rewarding experience. Microgenetic designs can provide insight into both the process of discovery and children's emotional response to it.

Although some children quite quickly discovered the counting-on strategy, others took more than 200 problems before discovering it, and one child never did so. Examination of the problems immediately before the discovery revealed a surprising fact: necessity is not always the mother of invention. Quite a few children discovered the counting-on strategy while working on easy problems that they previously had solved correctly by counting from 1. Apparently, children make discoveries without external pressure to do so.

The microgenetic method also revealed that children's very first use of the new strategy often was accompanied by impressive insight and excitement, like that shown by Lauren:

Experimenter: How much is 6 + 3?
Lauren: (long pause) 9.
E: OK, how did you know that?
L: I think I said . . . I think I said . . . oops, um . . . 7 was 1, 8 was 2, 9 was 3.
E: How did you know to do that? Why didn't you count 1, 2, 3, 4, 5, 6, 7, 8, 9?
L: (with excitement) 'Cause then you have to count all those numbers.

Despite her insightful explanation of counting-on and her excitement over discovering it, Lauren rarely used the new strategy on the problems that followed. Only after being presented problems such as 3 + 22, which are almost impossible for kindergartners to solve by counting from 1 but relatively easy for them to solve by counting from the larger addend, did Lauren (and other children who had discovered counting-on) frequently employ the new strategy. Other microgenetic studies have also shown that generalizing discoveries to new problems can be as challenging as making the discovery in the first place (Miller & Coyle, 1999).

As this example illustrates, microgenetic methods provide insight into the process of change and into individual differences in change processes over brief periods. However, these methods do not yield information about stability and change over long time periods. They therefore are typically used when the basic pattern of age-related change has already been established and the goal becomes to understand how the changes occur. Table 1.6 outlines the strengths and weaknesses of the three approaches to studying changes with age and experience: cross-sectional, longitudinal, and microgenetic designs.

TABLE 1.6

Advantages and Disadvantages of Designs for Studying Development

Design	Key Features	Advantages	Disadvantages
Cross-sectional	Children of different ages are studied at a single time.	Yields useful data about differences among ages groups. Quick and easy to administer.	Uninformative about stability of individual differences over time. Uninformative about similarities and differences in individual children's patterns of change.
Longitudinal	Children are examined repeatedly over a prolonged period of time.	Indicates the degree of stability of individual differences over long periods. Reveals individual children's patterns of change over long periods.	Difficult to keep all participants in study. Repeatedly testing children can threaten external validity of study.
Microgenetic	Children are observed intensively over a relatively short time period while a change is occurring.	Intensive observation of changes while they are occurring can reveal process of change. Reveals individual change patterns over short periods in considerable detail.	Does not provide information about typical patterns of change over long periods. Does not reveal individual change patterns over long periods.

Ethical Issues in Child-Development Research

All research with human beings raises ethical issues; this is especially true with studies of child development. Researchers have a vital responsibility to anticipate potential risks that the children in their studies may encounter, to minimize such risks, and to make sure that the benefits of the research outweigh the potential harm.

The Society for Research on Child Development, an organization devoted to research on children, has formulated a code of ethical conduct for investigators to follow (SRCD, 1999, pp. 283–284). Some of the most important ethical principles in the code are:

1. Be sure that the research does not harm children physically or psychologically.
2. Obtain informed consent for participating in the research, preferably in writing, from parents or other responsible adults and also from children if they are old enough that the research can be explained to them. The experimenter should inform children and relevant adults of all aspects of the research that might influence their willingness to participate and should explain that refusing to participate will not result in any adverse consequences to them.
3. Preserve individual participants' anonymity, and do not use information for purposes other than that for which permission was given.
4. Discuss with parents or guardians any information yielded by the investigation that is important for the child's welfare.
5. Try to counteract any unforeseen negative consequences that arise during the research. If such negative consequences arise, redesign procedures to avoid similar problems.
6. Correct any inaccurate impressions that the child may develop in the course of the study. When the research has been completed, explain the general findings to participants at a level they can understand.

Recognizing the importance of such ethical issues, universities and governmental agencies have established institutional review boards, in which independent scientists, and sometimes others from the community, evaluate the proposed research to ensure that it does not violate ethics guidelines. However, the individual investigator, who knows the most about the research and is in the best position to anticipate potential problems, bears the ultimate responsibility for seeing that his or her study meets high ethical standards.

review:

The scientific method, in which all hypotheses are treated as potentially incorrect, has allowed contemporary understanding of child development to progress well beyond the understanding of even the greatest thinkers of the past. This progress has been built on a base of four types of innovations:

1. measures that are reliable and valid;
2. data-gathering situations that yield useful information about children's behavior, such as interviews, naturalistic observations, and structured observations;
3. designs that allow identification of associations and cause–effect relations among variables, notably correlational and experimental designs;
4. designs that allow analysis of the continuities and changes that occur with age and experience, notably cross-sectional, longitudinal, and microgenetic designs.

Conducting scientific experiments also requires meeting high ethical standards, including not in any way harming the children who participate; obtaining informed consent for their participation in the research; preserving anonymity of all participants; and, after the study, explaining the findings to parents and, when possible, to children, at a level they can understand.

Chapter Summary

Why Study Child Development?

- Learning about child development is valuable for many reasons: it can help us become better parents, inform our views about social issues that affect children, and improve our understanding of human nature.

Historical Foundations of Child Development

- Great thinkers such as Plato, Aristotle, Locke, and Rousseau raised basic questions about child development and proposed interesting hypotheses about them, but lacked the scientific methods to answer them. Early scientific approaches, such as those of Freud and Watson, began the movement toward modern research-based theories of child development.

Enduring Themes in Child Development

- The field of child development is an attempt to answer a set of fundamental questions:
  1. How do nature and nurture together shape development?
  2. How do children contribute to their own development?
  3. In what ways is development continuous, and in what ways is it discontinuous?
  4. How does change occur?
  5. How does the sociocultural context influence development?
  6. How do children become so different from each other?
  7. How can research promote children's well-being?
- Every aspect of development, from the most specific behavior to the most general trait, reflects both people's biological endowment (their nature) and the experiences that they have had (their nurture).
- Even infants and young children actively contribute to their own development through their attentional patterns, use of language, and choices of play activities.
- Most developments can appear either continuous or discontinuous, depending on how often and how closely we look at them.
- Developmental change often occurs through a process of variation and selection, similar to biological evolution.
- The contexts that shape development include the people with whom children interact directly, such as family and friends; the institutions in which they participate, such as schools and religious organizations; and societal attitudes, such as those regarding race, ethnicity, and social class.
- Individual differences, even among siblings, reflect differences in children's genes, in their treatment by other people, in their interpretations of their own experiences, and in their choices of environments.
- Principles, findings, and methods from child-development research are being applied to improving the quality of children's lives.

Methods for Studying Child Development

- The scientific method has made possible great advances in understanding children. It involves choosing a question, formulating a hypothesis relevant to the question, developing a method to test the hypothesis, and using data to decide whether the hypothesis is correct.
- For a measure to be useful, it must be relevant to the hypothesis, reliable, and valid. Reliability means that independent observations of a given behavior are consistent. Validity means that a measure assesses what it is intended to measure.
- Among the main situations used to gather data about children are interviews, naturalistic observation, and structured observation. Interviews are especially useful for revealing children's subjective experience. Naturalistic observation is particularly useful when the primary goal is to describe how children behave in their everyday environments. Structured observation is most useful when the main goal is to describe how different children react to the identical situation.
- Correlation does not imply causation. The two differ in that correlations indicate the degree to which two variables are associated, whereas causation indicates that changing the value of one variable will change the value of the other.
- Experimental designs are especially valuable for revealing the causes of children's behavior.
- Data about development can be obtained through cross-sectional designs (examining different children of different ages), through longitudinal designs (examining the same children at different ages), or through microgenetic designs (presenting intensive experience over a relatively short period and analyzing the change process in detail).
- It is vital for researchers to adhere to high ethical standards. Among the most important ethical principles are striving to ensure that the research does not harm children physically or psychologically; obtaining informed consent from parents and, where possible, from children; preserving participants' anonymity; informing parents of anything needed to preserve the child's welfare; counteracting any negative outcomes that arise in the research; and correcting any inaccurate impressions that children form during the study.

Critical Thinking Questions

1. Why is it important to understand child development even if you do not have children of your own?
2. Why do you think that the children who spent less than six months in orphanages in Romania were able to catch up physically, intellectually, and socially, whereas those who spent more time there have not been able to catch up so far? Do you think that they will catch up in the future?
3. In what ways is it fortunate and in what ways unfortunate that children shape their own development to a substantial extent?
4. Did reading about sleeping arrangements in the United States and in other cultures influence what you would like to do if you have children? Explain why or why not.
5. Given what you learned in this chapter about child-development research, can you think of practical applications of the research that seem both feasible and important to you?

Key Terms

nature, p. 10
nurture, p. 10
continuous development, p. 14
discontinuous development, p. 14
stage theories, p. 15
variation, p. 18
selection, p. 18
sociocultural context, p. 19
socioeconomic status, p. 21
scientific method, p. 24
hypotheses, p. 24
reliability, p. 25
interrater reliability, p. 25
test–retest reliability, p. 26
validity, p. 26
internal validity, p. 26
external validity, p. 26
structured interview, p. 27
clinical interview, p. 27
naturalistic observation, p. 28
structured observation, p. 29
variables, p. 30
correlational designs, p. 30
correlation, p. 30
correlation coefficient, p. 30
direction-of-causation problem, p. 31
third-variable problem, p. 31
experimental designs, p. 31
random assignment, p. 32
experimental control, p. 32
experimental group, p. 32
control group, p. 32
independent variable, p. 32
dependent variable, p. 32
naturalistic experiments, p. 33
cross-sectional design, p. 34
longitudinal design, p. 34
microgenetic design, p. 35

CHAPTER 2

Prenatal Development, Birth, and the Newborn Period

MARC CHAGALL, *Pont Marie,* 1945–50

THEMES

- Nature and Nurture
- The Active Child
- Continuity/Discontinuity
- Mechanisms of Change
- The Sociocultural Context
- Individual Differences
- Research and Children's Welfare

Picture the following scenario. A developmental psychologist approaches her research subject, intent on investigating the subject's perceptual capacities and ability to learn from experience. First, she plays a loud sound through a speaker near the subject's ear and notes with satisfaction that the subject moves vigorously in response, concluding that the subject can hear the sound. Now she continues to play the same tone, over and over. As everyone else in the lab gets tired of hearing the same sound repeatedly, the subject seems to do the same, responding less and less to the repetitions of the sound and eventually not reacting to it at all. Has the subject learned to recognize the sound or just gone to sleep? To find out, the researcher now presents a different sound, and the subject returns to responding vigorously. The subject can apparently recognize the old sound and tell that the new sound is different from it, evidence that some simple learning has occurred. Wanting to see if the subject is capable of learning something more complex and in a more natural setting, the researcher sends the subject home, asking the subject's mother to read aloud from a Dr. Seuss book for several minutes a day for six weeks. Before the researcher sees the subject again, something quite dramatic happens: the subject is born!

This scenario is not at all fanciful: indeed, as you will discover later in this chapter, it is an accurate description of a fascinating and informative study that helped to revolutionize the understanding of prenatal development (DeCasper & Spence, 1986). As you will also discover in this chapter, researchers have been asking many questions about the sensory and learning capabilities of fetuses. And they have been finding that while in the womb, fetuses can detect a range of stimuli coming from the outside world and can learn from their experience and remain affected by it after birth.

In addition to discussing these aspects of prenatal development in this chapter, we will also consider some of the environmental hazards that can harm the developing fetus. We will then briefly review the process of being born, primarily from the infant's point of view. Finally, we will examine some aspects of neonatal behavior and discuss problems associated with premature birth.

In our discussion of the earliest periods of development, most of the developmental themes we described in Chapter 1 will play prominent roles. The most prominent will be *nature and nurture,* as we emphasize how every aspect of development before birth results from an intermingling of biological and environmental factors. Our genes contain a program for development, but that program does not dictate the final form to be achieved; rather, it provides a set of relatively simple instructions from which very complex forms ultimately emerge. Prenatal development consists of a cascade of minor events, with each event leading to another minor event and then another. In the end, something very complicated has happened, but not because that end point was specified at the beginning (see Figure 2.1).

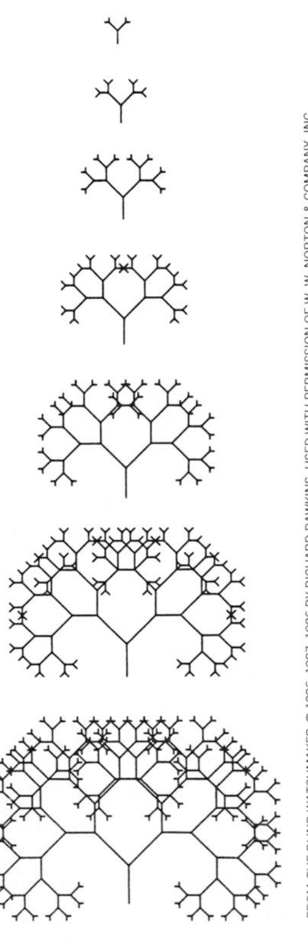

FIGURE 2.1 Emergent structure A structure of great complexity can emerge from a simple starting condition through the repeated application of a few very simple instructions. Can you figure out what rules were used to generate the figure?

The *active child* theme will also be featured, because the activity of the fetus contributes in numerous vital ways to its development. Normal prenatal development depends on fetal behavior, from squirming around in the womb to making breathing motions (both necessary for muscle development) to secreting hormones essential for the differentiation of the sex organs. Another theme we will highlight is the *sociocultural context* of prenatal development and birth, as we note large differences in how people in different societies think about the beginning of life and how the birth process is handled. *Individual differences* come into play at many points throughout the chapter, starting with gender differences in survival rates from conception on. The theme of *continuity/discontinuity* is also prominent: despite the dramatic transition between prenatal and postnatal life, the behavior of newborns shows clear relations to their behavior and experience inside the womb. Finally, the theme of *research and children's welfare* underlies our discussion of the role of poverty in prenatal development and birth outcomes, as well as our description of intervention programs designed to foster the development of preterm infants.

epigenesis the idea that there is an emergence of new structures and functions rather than there simply being growth of smaller structures into larger ones

embryology the study of prenatal development

Prenatal Development

Hidden from view, the process of prenatal development has always been mysterious and fascinating, and beliefs about the origins of human life and development before birth have been an important part of the lore and traditions of all societies (see DeLoache & Gottlieb, 2000). Enormous variability exists across as well as within cultures with respect to when life is believed to begin. (Box 2.1 describes what people in one society believe about this topic.) When we look back in history, we also see great differences in how people have thought about prenatal development. In the fourth century B.C., Aristotle posed the fundamental question about prenatal development that was to underlie Western thought for the next fifteen centuries: Does prenatal life start with the new individual already preformed, composed of a full set of tiny parts, or do the many parts of the human body develop in succession? Aristotle rejected the idea of preformation in favor of what he termed **epigenesis**—the emergence of new structures and functions during development (a view of development that is highly influential today; Wolpert, 1991). Seeking support for his idea, he took what was then the very unorthodox step of opening fertile chicken eggs to see for himself. He did indeed observe chick organs in various stages of development. Nevertheless, the idea of preformationism persisted long after Aristotle, evolving into a dispute about whether the miniature, preformed human was lodged inside the mother's egg or the father's sperm (see Figure 2.2).

The notion of preformation may strike you as a bit silly, even simpleminded. Remember, however, that our forebears had no way of knowing about the existence of cells and genes, to say nothing of the many discoveries that have led to a recent revolution in **embryology,** the study of prenatal development. Modern scientists have a variety of techniques for studying physical and behavioral development in the womb. Many of the mysteries that perplexed our ancestors have now been solved, but as is always true in science, new mysteries have replaced them.

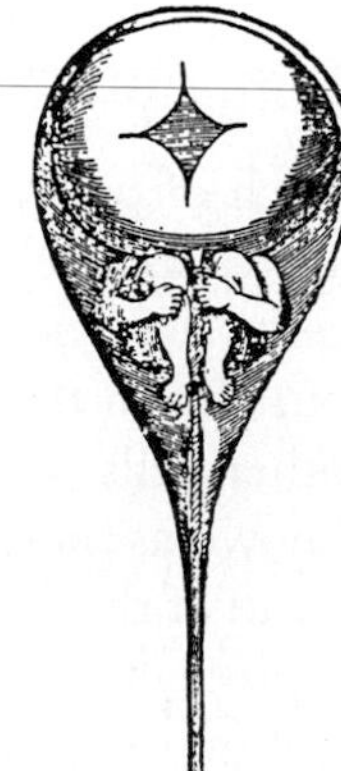

FIGURE 2.2 Preformationism
A seventeenth-century drawing of a preformed being inside a sperm. This drawing was based on the claim of committed preformationists that when they looked at samples of semen under the newly invented microscope they could actually see a tiny figure curled up inside the head of the sperm. They believed that the miniature person would enlarge after entering an egg. (From Moore & Persaud, 1993, p. 7). As this drawing illustrates, we must always take care not to let our cherished preconceptions so dominate our thinking that we see what we want to see—not what is really there.

a closer look 2.1

Beng Beginnings

Few topics have generated more intense debate and dispute in the United States in recent years than the issue of what point in development marks the beginning of life — the moment of conception or somewhere between conception and birth. The irony is that few who engage in this debate recognize how complex the issue is or the degree to which societies throughout the world have different views on this issue.

One example of this variety comes from the Beng, a people in the Ivory Coast of West Africa, who believe that every infant is a reincarnation of an ancestor (Gottlieb, 2000). According to the Beng, the ancestor's spirit, its *wru,* is not fully committed to an earthly life and it maintains a double existence, traveling back and forth between the everyday world and *wrugbe,* or "spirit village." (The term can be roughly translated as "afterlife," but "before-life" might be just as appropriate.) Until the umbilical stump drops off, the newborn is not considered to have emerged from *wrugbe* or to be a person. There is no funeral for a newborn who dies, for the infant's passing is simply conceived as a return in bodily form to the space that the infant was still psychically inhabiting.

These beliefs underlie many aspects of Beng infant-care practices. One is the application, many times a day, of an herbal mixture to the newborn's umbilical stump to hasten its drying out and dropping off — thereby initiating the infant's spiritual journey from *wrugbe* to earthly life and its emergence as a person. The journey from *wrugbe* is difficult and takes several years to complete; in the meantime, there is always the danger that the infant or young child will be homesick for its life in *wrugbe* and decide to leave its earthly existence. To prevent this, parents try to make their babies comfortable and happy so they will want to stay in this life. Among the many recommended procedures is elaborately decorating the infant's face and body so it will be attractive and elicit attention from others. Sometimes diviners are consulted, especially if the baby seems to be unhappy; a common diagnosis for prolonged crying is that the baby wants a different name, one from its previous life in *wrugbe.*

So when does life begin for the Beng? In one sense, a Beng individual's life begins well *before* birth, since he or she is a reincarnation of an ancestor. In another sense, however, life begins sometime *after* birth, when the individual is first considered to be a person.

COURTESY OF ALMA GOTTLIEB

The mother of this Beng baby has spent considerable time painting the baby's face in an elaborate pattern. She does this every day in an effort to make the baby attractive so other people will help keep the baby happy in this world.

Conception

Each of us originated as a single cell that resulted from the union of two highly specialized cells—a sperm from our father and an egg from our mother. These sex cells, also known as **gametes** or **germ cells,** are unique not only in their function but also in the fact that each one contains only half the genetic material found in other cells. Germ cells are produced through a special process of cell division known as **meiosis,** in which the eggs and sperm receive only 23 chromosomes, instead of the 46 present in all other cells of the body. This reduction is necessary for reproduction: if either the egg or sperm contained the full number of chromosomes, they could not merge, because no cell can survive with double the normal amount of genetic material. A major difference in the formation of these two types of gametes is the fact that all the eggs a woman will ever have are formed during her own prenatal development, whereas men produce new sperm continuously.

The process of reproduction starts with the launching of an egg (the largest cell in the human body) from one of the woman's ovaries into the fallopian tube (see Figure 2.3). As the egg moves through the tube toward the uterus, it emits a chemical substance that acts as a sort of beacon, a "come hither" signal that attracts sperm toward it.

gametes (germ cells) reproductive cells that contain only half the genetic material of all other normal cells in the body

meiosis specialized cell division necessary for reproduction that produces cells (gametes) that have only half of the normal complement of chromosomes

conception the union of an egg and sperm

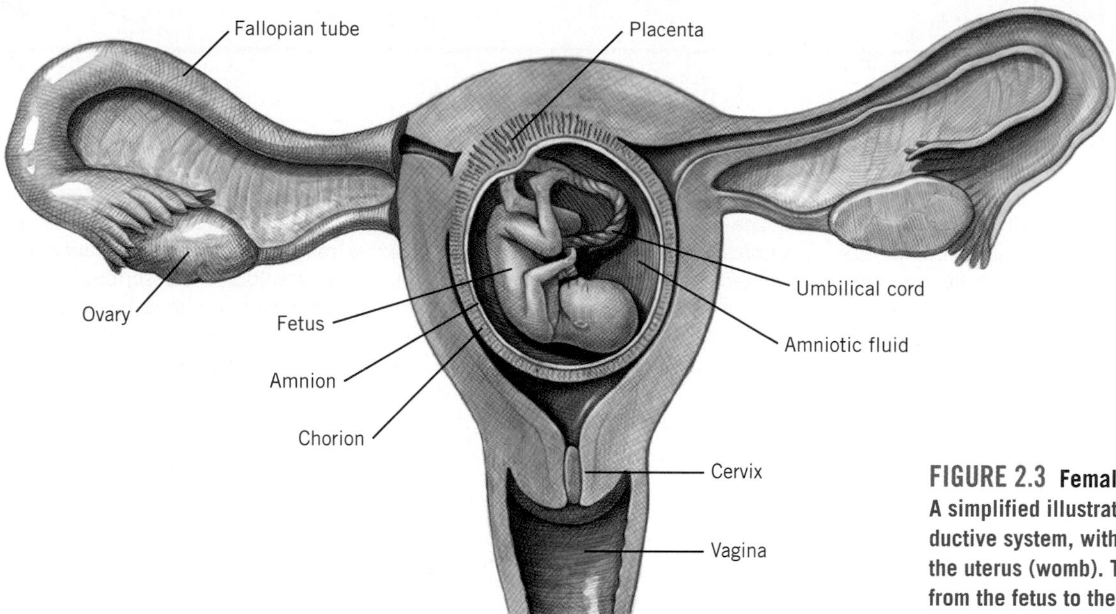

FIGURE 2.3 Female reproductive system A simplified illustration of the female reproductive system, with a fetus developing in the uterus (womb). The umbilical cord runs from the fetus to the placenta, which is burrowed deeply into the wall of the uterus. The fetus is floating in amniotic fluid inside the amniotic sac.

If an act of sexual intercourse takes place near the time the egg is released, **conception,** the union of sperm and egg, will be possible. In every ejaculation, as many as 500 million sperm are pumped into the woman's vagina. Each sperm, a streamlined vehicle for delivering the man's genes to the woman's egg, consists of little more than a pointed head packed full of genetic material (the 23 chromosomes) and a long tail. The sperm's tail whips around to propel it through the woman's reproductive system.

To be a candidate for initiating conception, a sperm must travel for about 6 hours, journeying 6 to 7 inches from the vagina through the uterus to the fallopian tube. The rate of attrition on this journey is enormous: of the millions of sperm that enter the vagina, only about 200 ever get near the egg (see Figure 2.4). There are many causes for this high failure rate. Some failures are due to chance: many of the sperm get tangled up with other sperm milling about in the vagina, and others simply happen to travel up the wrong fallopian tube (i.e., the

FIGURE 2.4 (a) Sperm nearing the egg Of the millions of sperm that started out together, only a few ever get near the egg. The egg is the largest human cell (the only one visible to the naked eye), but the sperm are among the smallest. **(b) Sperm penetrating the egg** This sperm is whipping its tail around furiously to drill itself through the outer covering of the egg.

(a)

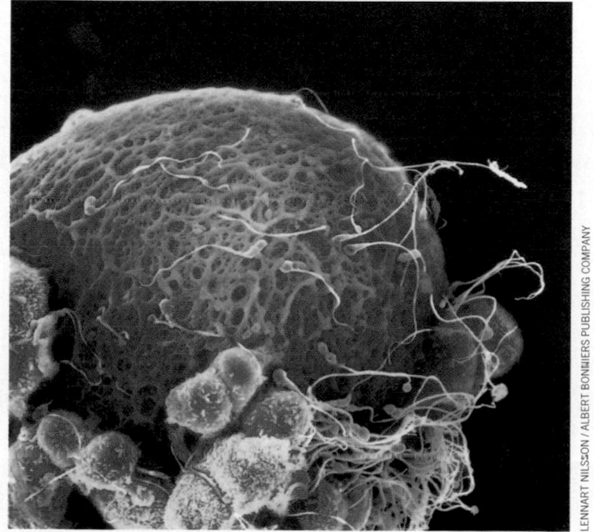

LENNART NILSSON / ALBERT BONNIERS PUBLISHING COMPANY

(b)

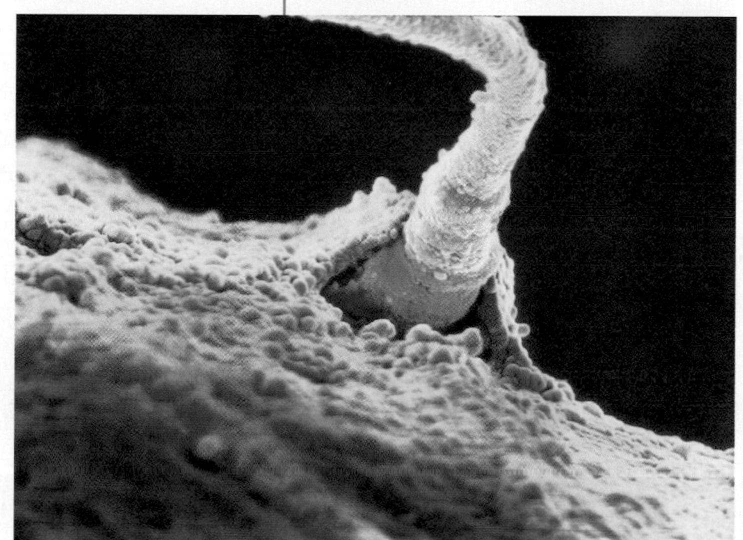

LENNART NILSSON / ALBERT BONNIERS PUBLISHING COMPANY

individual differences 2.2

The First Sex Differences

The proverbial competition between the sexes might be said to begin with the sperms' race to fertilize the egg, a race won much more often by the "boys." Those sperm that possess a Y chromosome (the genetic basis for maleness) are lighter and swim faster, so they get to the egg before those bearing an X chromosome. As a result, many more genetic males are conceived than females; experts estimate that there are approximately 120 to 150 male zygotes for each 100 female ones.

The girls win the next big competition—survival. The birth ratio is only 106 males to 100 females. Where are the missing males? Obviously, they are miscarried at a much greater rate than females, suggesting greater prenatal vulnerability for males. This heightened vulnerability is not limited to the prenatal period; boys suffer disproportionately from most developmental disorders, including language and learning disorders, dyslexia, attention-deficit disorder, mental retardation, and autism. The greater fragility of males continues throughout life, as reflected in the figure.

Differential survival is not always left in the hands of nature. In many societies, both historically and currently, male offspring are more highly valued than females, and parents resort to infanticide to avoid having daughters. For example, Inuit families in Alaska traditionally depended on male children to help in the hunt for food, and in former times Inuit girls were often killed at birth. Chinese parents, in both the past and present, count on their sons to take care of them in their old age. In modern China, the "one-child" policy, a measure designed to reduce population growth by forbidding couples to have more than one child, has resulted in many female babies being killed or abandoned to make room for a male child. A more technological approach is currently practiced in India and South Korea (and probably elsewhere): prenatal tests are used to determine the gender of the fetus, and female fetuses are selectively aborted. These cases dramatically illustrate the contextual model of development described in Chapter 1, showing how cultural values, government policy, and available technology all affect developmental outcomes.

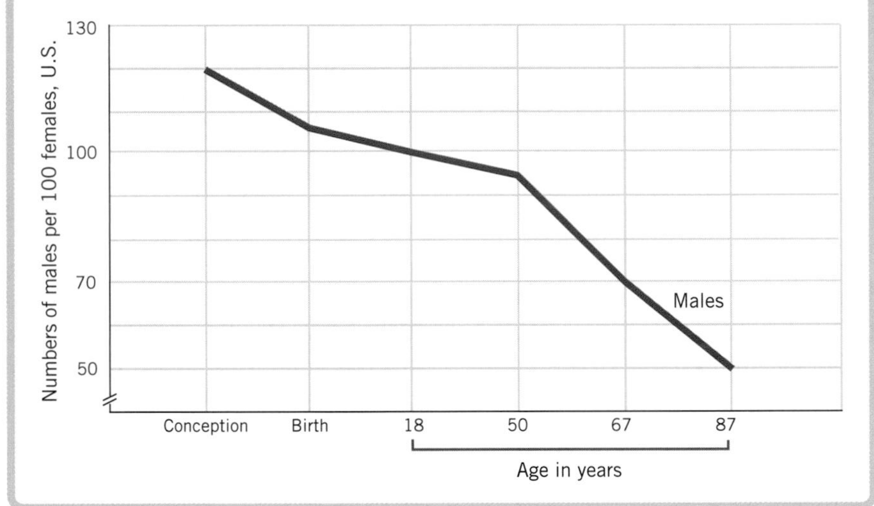

Source: Lerner & Libby (1976)

Males are more vulnerable than females across the life span. In the United States, at conception, there are more males than females, but that advantage quickly disappears. The two sexes become equal in number at around 18 years; from then on there are increasingly more females than males in the population, particularly in old age. As Herb Caen, the famous San Francisco columnist, commented: "As of the 1990 census, the number of people aged 80 and over in S.F. was 26,962, broken down to 8,766 broken down males and 18,196 females, all complaining 'Can't live with 'em, can't live without 'em'" (Caen, 1996).

one that does not currently harbor an egg). Other failures have to do with problems with the sperm themselves: a substantial portion have serious genetic or other defects that prevent them from propelling themselves vigorously enough to reach and fertilize the egg. Thus, any sperm that does get to the egg is reasonably likely to be healthy and structurally sound, revealing a Darwinian-type "survival of the fittest" process operating during fertilization. (Box 2.2 describes the consequences of this selection process for the conception of males and females.)

As soon as one sperm's head broaches the outer membrane of the egg, a chemical reaction seals the membrane, preventing other sperm from entering. The tail of the sperm falls off, the contents of its head gush into the egg, and the nuclei of the two cells merge. The fertilized egg, known as a **zygote,** now has a full complement of human genetic material, half from the mother and half from

zygote the fertilized egg formed from the union of an egg cell and a sperm cell

TABLE 2.1

Periods of Prenatal Development

Conception to two weeks	Zygote	Begins with conception and lasts until the zygote becomes implanted in the uterine wall. Rapid cell division takes place.
3rd to 8th week	Embryo	Following implantation, major development occurs in all the organs and systems of the body. Development takes place through the processes of cell division, cell migration, cell differentiation, and cell death, as well as hormonal influences.
9th week to birth	Fetus	Continued development of physical structures and rapid growth of the body. Increasing levels of behavior, sensory experience, and learning.

the father. The first of the three periods of prenatal development (see Table 2.1) has begun and will, if all goes well, continue for approximately 9 months (on average, 38 weeks, or 266 days).

Developmental Processes

Before describing the course of prenatal development, we need to briefly outline four major developmental processes that underlie the transformation of a zygote into an embryo and then a fetus. The first of these processes is *cell division.* Within 12 hours or so after fertilization, the zygote divides into two equal parts, each containing a full complement of genetic material. These two cells divide into four; those four into eight, and so on. Through continued cell division over the course of 38 weeks, the barely visible zygote becomes a newborn consisting of trillions of cells.

A second major process, which occurs during the embryonic period, is *cell migration,* the movement of newly formed cells from their point of origin to somewhere else in the embryo. Among the many cells that migrate are the neurons in the cortex, the outer layer of the brain. These cells originate deep inside the embryonic brain and then, like pioneers settling new territory, travel in waves "through the part of the cortex that has already been settled to establish a new community, a new layer of cells, beyond them" (Vaughn, 1996, p. 146).

The third process that is crucial to further prenatal development is *cell differentiation.* Initially, all embryonic cells, also known as stem cells, are equivalent and interchangeable: none have any fixed fate or function. Cells remain flexible for a short time after they have migrated to a new position. After several cell divisions, however, cells start to differentiate, or specialize, becoming different from one another in terms of both structure and function. In humans, stem cells develop into roughly 350 different types of cells, which from then on perform a particular function on behalf of the organism. (Because of this flexibility, very early embryonic stem cells offer the promise of treating a variety of illnesses, including Parkinson's disease and Alzheimer's disease. Injected into a person suffering from illness or injury, these cells have the capacity to develop into healthy cells to replace diseased or damaged ones.)

The process of differentiation is one of the major mysteries of prenatal development. Since all cells in the body have the identical genetic makeup, what determines what type of cell a given stem cell will become? The full answer is far from clear, but scientists believe that the *location* in which a cell ends up by chance

a closer look 2.3

Phylogenetic Continuity

At various times throughout this book, we will describe research done with nonhuman animals to make or support some point about human development. In doing so, we subscribe to the principle of **phylogenetic continuity** — the idea that because of our common evolutionary history, humans share some characteristics and developmental processes with other animals, especially mammals. Indeed, the child and the chimp in the photo have over 99% of their genes in common. In Chapter 3, we will consider how the 1% that they do not share contributes to making them so different.

The assumption that animal models of behavior and development can be useful and informative for human development underlies a great deal of research. For example, much of our knowledge of the effects of alcohol consumption by pregnant women comes from research with animals. Because scientists suspected that drinking alcohol while pregnant caused the constellation of defects now known as *fetal alcohol syndrome,* described later in this chapter (page 62), they experimentally exposed fetal mice to alcohol in their mothers' wombs. One of the results was the discovery that this intervention resulted in misformed facial features remarkably similar to the facial anomalies of children born to alcoholic mothers. This fact increased researchers' confidence that the problems commonly associated with fetal alcohol syndrome are, in fact, caused by alcohol rather than by some other factor that might also characterize alcoholic women.

One of the most fascinating discoveries in recent years, discussed later in this chapter, is the existence of fetal learning. Well before this phenomenon was demonstrated for human fetuses, it was documented in research on one of comparative psychologists' favorite creatures — the rat. Some natural preferences exhibited by newborn rat pups, including preferences important for survival, are based on learning that took place in the womb. To survive, newborns must find a milk-producing maternal nipple. How do they know where to go? In the process of giving birth, the nipples on the underside of the mother rat's belly get smeared with amniotic fluid. The familiar scent of the amniotic fluid lures her babies to where they need to be — with their noses, and hence their mouths, near a nipple (Blass, 1990).

How do we know that newborn rats' first nipple attachment is based on their recognition of amniotic fluid? For one thing, if the mother's belly is washed clean of amniotic fluid, her pups fail to find her nipples, and if half her nipples are washed, the pups will be attracted to the unwashed ones with amniotic fluid still on them (Blass & Teicher, 1980). Even more impressive, when researchers introduce odors or flavors into the amniotic fluid, either by directly injecting them or by adding them to the mother's diet, her pups prefer those odors and tastes after birth (Hepper, 1988; Pedersen & Blass, 1982; Smotherman & Robinson, 1987). These and other experimental demonstrations of fetal learning in rodents inspired researchers to look for similar processes in human fetuses. As you will see later, they found them.

KAREN HUNTT / NATIONAL GEOGRAPHIC IMAGE COLLECTION

Child and chimp have 99% of their genes in common.

determines its further development. Thus, nothing in the cell itself determines whether it will become part of the developing embryo or part of the various extraembryonic structures that support its development.

The initial flexibility and subsequent inflexibility of cells, as well as the importance of location, is vividly illustrated by classic research with frog embryos. If the region of a frog embryo that would normally become an eye is grafted onto its belly very early in development, the transplanted region will develop as a normal part of the belly. Thus, although the cells were initially in the right place to become an eye, they had not yet become specialized. Later on, the same operation

phylogenetic continuity the idea that because of our common evolutionary history, humans share some characteristics and developmental processes with other animals, especially mammals results in an eye—alone and unseeing—lodged in the belly of the frog embryo (Wolpert, 1991).

The fourth developmental process is something we do not normally think of as developmental at all—death. However, the selective death of certain cells is the "almost constant companion" to the other developmental processes we have described (Wolpert, 1991). Its role is readily apparent in hand development (see Figure 2.5), where the formation of fingers depends on the death of the cells in between the ridges in the hand plate. Some cell death is thought to be a form of programmed suicide, or **apoptosis;** in other words, dying is part of the developmental program for those cells that selectively disappear from the hand plates.

In addition to these four developmental processes, we need to call attention to the influence of *hormones* on prenatal development. For example, hormones play a crucial role in sexual differentiation. All human fetuses, regardless of the genes they carry, can develop either male or female genitalia. What causes development to proceed one way or the other is the presence or absence of *testosterone,* a male hormone. If testosterone is present, male sex organs develop; if it is absent, female genitalia develop. The source of this influential hormone is the male fetus itself. Around the eighth week after conception, the testes begin to produce testosterone, and this self-generated substance changes the fetus forever. This is just one of the many ways in which the fetus acts as an instigator of its own development.

We now turn our attention to the general course of prenatal development that results from all the above influences, as well as other developmental processes.

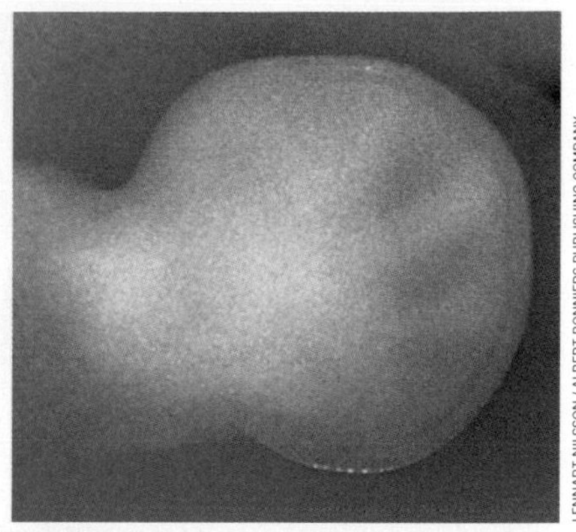

LENNART NILSSON / ALBERT BONNIERS PUBLISHING COMPANY

FIGURE 2.5 Embryonic hand plate
Fingers will emerge from the hand plate of this 7-week-old embryo. The fingers are formed as a result of the death of the cells between the ridges you can see in the plate. If these cells did not expire, the baby would be born with webbed rather than independent fingers.

Early Development

On its journey through the fallopian tube to the womb, the zygote doubles its number of cells roughly twice a day. By the 4th day after conception, the cells arrange themselves into a hollow sphere, the **blastocyst**, with a bulge of cells—called the **inner cell mass**—on one side.

This is the stage at which **identical twins** most often originate. They result from a splitting in half of the inner cell mass, and thus they both have exactly the same genetic makeup (Moore & Persaud, 1993). In contrast, **fraternal twins** result when two eggs happen to be released from the ovary into the fallopian tube and both are fertilized. Because they originate from two different eggs and two different sperm, fraternal twins are no more alike genetically than any pairs of siblings.

By the end of the 1st week following fertilization, if all goes well (as it does for fewer than half the zygotes that are conceived), a momentous event occurs—implantation, the process in which the zygote embeds itself in the uterine lining and becomes dependent on the mother for sustenance. Well before the end of the 2nd week, it will be completely embedded within the uterine wall.

After implantation, the encapsulated ball of cells starts to differentiate. In a process known as **gastrulation,** the inner cell mass becomes the **embryo,** and the rest of the cells develop into its support system. The inner cell mass is initially a single layer thick, but during the 2nd week, it folds itself into three layers, each with a different developmental destiny. The top layer becomes the nervous system, the nails, teeth, inner ear, lens of the eyes, and the outer surface of the skin. The middle layer eventually becomes muscles, bones, the circulatory system, the inner layers of the skin, and other internal organs. The bottom layer develops into the digestive system, lungs, urinary tract, and glands. A few days after the embryo has differentiated into these three layers, a U-shaped groove forms down the center of

apoptosis programmed cell death

blastocyst the hollow sphere of cells into which the zygote arranges itself at around the 4th day of development

inner cell mass the bulge of cells on the inside of the blastocyst that eventually forms into the embryo

identical twins twins that result from the splitting in half of the inner cell mass at the zygote stage, which gives each zygote exactly the same genetic makeup

fraternal twins twins that result when two eggs happen to be released into the fallopian tube at the same time and are fertilized by two different sperm. Fraternal twins share only half their genetic makeup.

gastrulation the process by which cells start to differentiate after the zygote implants into the uterine lining; the inner cell mass becomes the embryo, and the rest of the cells become its support system

embryo the name given to the developing organism from the 3rd to 8th week of prenatal development

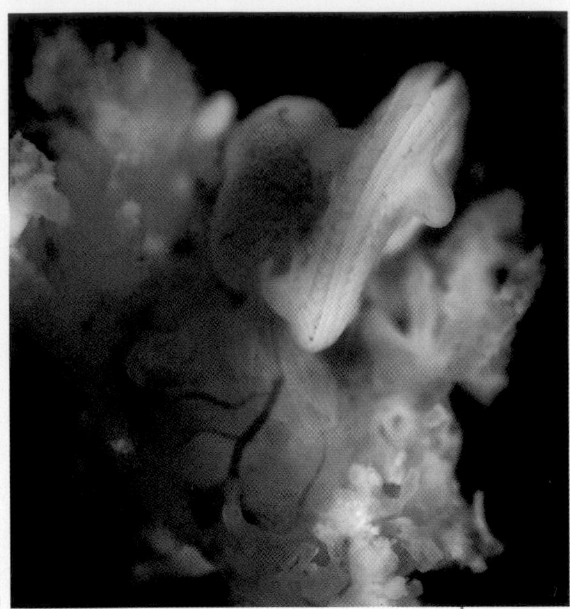

FIGURE 2.6 Neural tube In the 4th week, the neural tube begins to develop into the brain and spinal cord. In this photo, the neural groove, which fuses together first at the center and then outward in both directions as if two zippers were being closed, has been "zipped shut" except for one part still open at the top. Spina bifida, a congenital disorder in which the skin over the spinal cord is not fully closed, can originate at this point. After closing, the top of the neural tube will develop into the brain.

the top layer. The folds at the top of the groove move together and fuse, creating the **neural tube** (Figure 2.6). One end of the neural tube will swell and develop into the brain, and the rest will become the spinal cord.

The support system that is developing simultaneously with the embryo is elaborate and essential to its development. One key element of this support system is the **placenta,** a unique organ that permits the exchange of materials carried in the bloodstreams of the fetus and its mother. It is an extraordinarily rich network of blood vessels, including minute ones extending into the tissues of the mother's uterus, with a total surface area of about ten square yards—approximately the amount of driveway covered by the family car (Vaughn, 1996). Blood vessels running from the placenta to the embryo and back again are contained in the **umbilical cord.**

Although the placenta enables the blood systems of the mother and fetus to come extremely close to one another, it prevents their blood from actually mixing. However, the placental membrane is semipermeable, meaning that while some elements cannot pass through it, others can. Oxygen, nutrients, minerals, and some antibodies—all of which are just as vital to the fetus as they are to us—are transported to the placenta by the mother's circulating blood. They then cross the placenta and enter the fetal blood system. Waste products (e.g., carbon dioxide, urea) from the fetus cross the placenta in the opposite direction and are removed from the mother's bloodstream by her normal excretory processes.

The placental membrane also serves as a defensive barrier against a host of dangerous toxins and infectious agents that can inhabit the mother's body and could be harmful or even fatal to the fetus. Unfortunately, being semipermeable, the placenta is not a perfect barrier, and, as we will see later, a variety of harmful elements can cross it and attack the fetus. One other function of the placenta is the production of hormones, including estrogen, which increases the flow of maternal blood to the uterus, and progesterone, which suppresses uterine contractions that could expel the fetus prematurely (Nathanielsz, 1994).

A second vital part of the support system is the **amniotic sac,** a membrane filled with a clear, watery fluid in which the fetus floats. The amniotic fluid operates as a protective buffer for the developing fetus in several ways, such as providing it with a relatively even temperature and cushioning it against jolting. Also, because the fetus is floating, it can exercise its tiny, weak muscles relatively unhampered by the effects of gravity.

neural tube a U-shaped groove formed from the top layer of differentiated cells in the embryo that eventually becomes the brain and spinal cord

placenta an organ with an extraordinarily rich network of blood vessels that permits the exchange of materials between the bloodstreams of the fetus and its mother while keeping the two circulatory systems separate

umbilical cord a tube that contains the blood vessels that travel from the placenta to the developing organism and back again

amniotic sac a membrane that is filled with a clear, watery fluid in which the fetus floats and that acts as a protective buffer for the fetus in several ways

cephalocaudal development the pattern of growth in which areas near the head develop earlier than areas farther away from the head

An Illustrated Summary Of Prenatal Development

The course of prenatal development from the 4th week on is illustrated in Figures 2.7 through 2.14, and significant milestones are highlighted in the accompanying text. The fetal behaviors that are mentioned will be discussed in detail in a later section. Notice that earlier development takes place at a more rapid pace than later development and that the areas nearer the head develop earlier than those farther away (e.g., head before body, hands before feet)—a general tendency known as **cephalocaudal** (head-to-body) **development.**

Figure 2.7: At 4 weeks after conception, the embryo's tiny body is curved so tightly that the head and the tail-like structure at the other end are almost touching. Several facial features have their origin in the set of four folds in the front of the embryo's head; the face gradually emerges as a result of these tissues moving

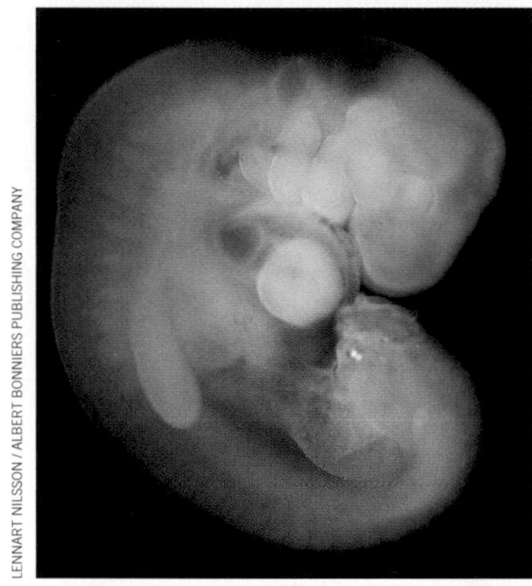
LENNART NILSSON / ALBERT BONNIERS PUBLISHING COMPANY

FIGURE 2.7 Embryo at 4 weeks

and stretching, as parts of them fuse and others separate. The round area near the top of the head is where the eye will form, and the round gray area near the back of the "neck" is the primordial inner ear. A primitive heart is visible; it is already beating and circulating blood. An arm bud can be seen in the side of the embryo; a leg bud is also present but less distinct.

Figure 2.8: This 5- to 6-week-old embryo floats freely in the amniotic fluid. In the 5th and 6th weeks, rapid brain development is occurring, as can be seen in the bulging forehead. The beginnings of an eye is apparent, and a nose is forming. Separate fingers are beginning to appear. The first spontaneous movements are occurring, as the embryo arches its back. However, because the embryo is so small and is surrounded by amniotic fluid, these movements cannot be felt by the mother.

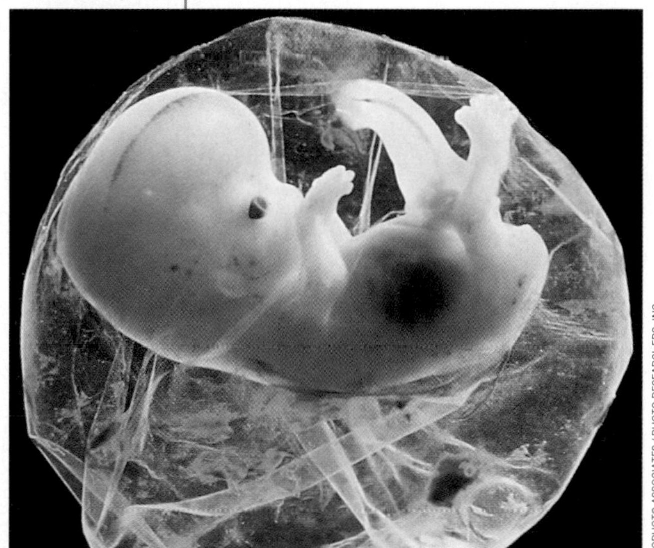
BIOPHOTO ASSOCIATES / PHOTO RESEARCH-ERS, INC.

FIGURE 2.8 Embryo at 5–6 weeks

Figure 2.9: The head constitutes roughly half the length of this 9-week-old fetus. The ears are forming. All the internal organs are present, although most must undergo further development. Sexual differentiation has started. Ribs are forming; elbows, fingers, and toes have emerged; and nails are growing. The umbilical cord connecting the fetus to the placenta is shown (the fetal membranes have been pulled to the side). The fetus has become responsive to external tactile stimulation: a touch to one side of the mouth area causes the head to turn away.

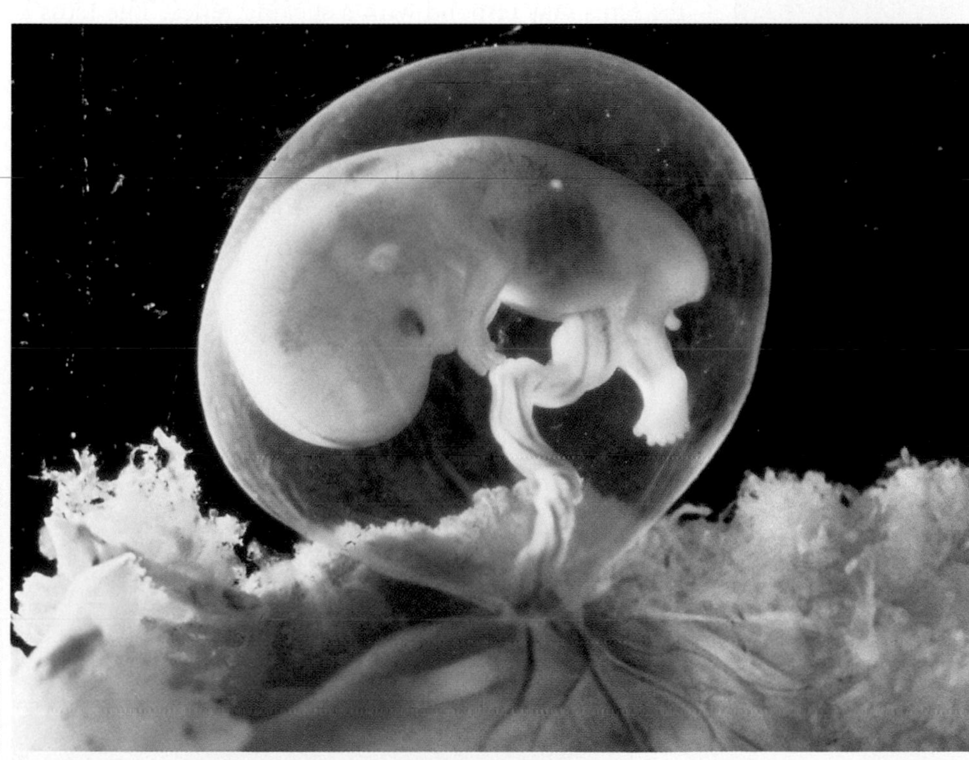
LENNART NILSSON / ALBERT BONNIERS PUBLISHING COMPANY

FIGURE 2.9 Fetus at 9 weeks

FIGURE 2.10
Fetus at 11–12 weeks

JOHN WATNEY / PHOTO RESEARCHERS, INC.

Figure 2.10: In weeks 11 and 12, the eyes are sealed shut. The fingers are clearly separated, and the external genitalia have developed. The fetus's movements have increased dramatically: the chest makes breathing movements, and some reflex behaviors—grasping, swallowing, sucking—are present. The arms and legs are in vigorous, almost constant motion, although these fetal movements are still not felt by the mother.

Figure 2.11: During the last 5 months of prenatal development, the growth of the lower part of the body accelerates. The intense kick by the 16-week-old fetus will be felt by its mother, although only as a mild "flutter."

Figure 2.12: This 18-week-old fetus is clearly sucking its thumb. If the hand happens to brush against its mouth, the fetus may respond with a sucking reflex. The fetus is covered with very fine hair, and a greasy coating will protect the fetal skin from its long immersion in liquid.

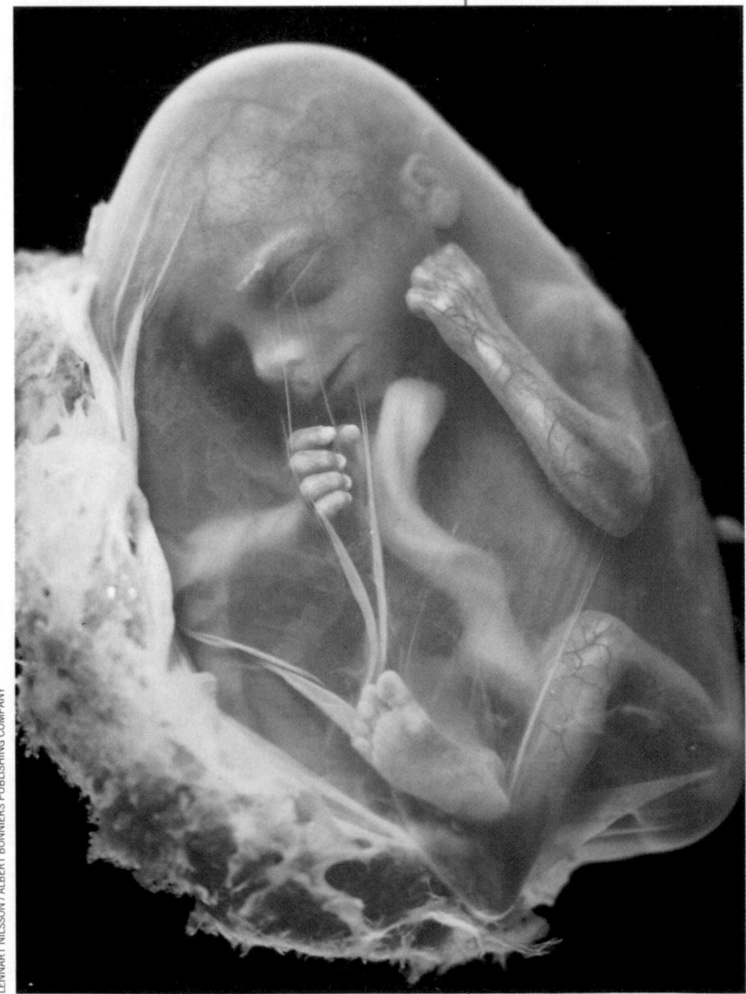
LENNART NILSSON / ALBERT BONNIERS PUBLISHING COMPANY

FIGURE 2.11 Fetus at 16 weeks

LENNART NILSSON / ALBERT BONNIERS PUBLISHING COMPANY

FIGURE 2.12
Fetus at 18 weeks

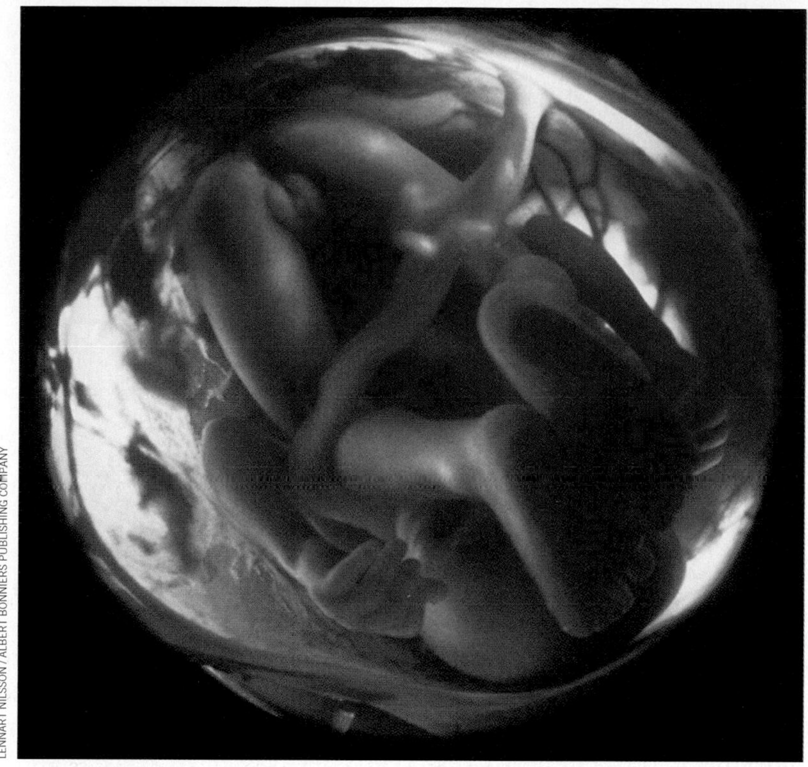

LENNART NILSSON / ALBERT BONNIERS PUBLISHING COMPANY

FIGURE 2.13 Fetus at 20 weeks

Figure 2.13: By the 20th week, the fetus is in a head-down position more of the time and is rapidly putting on weight. Free space in the amniotic sac is decreasing, and fetal movements will diminish. The components of facial expressions are present—the fetus is capable of raising its eyebrows, wrinkling its forehead, and moving its mouth.

Figure 2.14: The 28th week marks the point at which the brain and lungs are developed well enough that, if born early, the fetus has a chance of surviving on its own, without medical intervention. The eyes can open, and they move, especially during periods of REM (rapid eye movement) sleep. The auditory system is now functioning, and the fetus hears and reacts to a variety of sounds. The brain waves of this fetus are very similar to those of a newborn. During the last 3 months of prenatal development, the fetus grows dramatically in size, essentially tripling its weight. The mother becomes increasingly uncomfortable, and so, presumably, does the fetus in the cramped confines of the womb.

The typical result of this 9-month period of rapid and remarkable development is a healthy newborn.

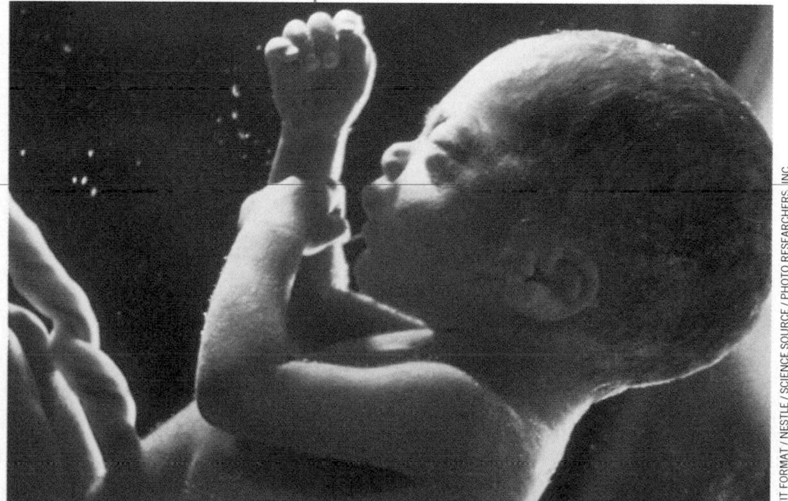

PETIT FORMAT / NESTLE / SCIENCE SOURCE / PHOTO RESEARCHERS, INC.

FIGURE 2.14 Fetus at 28 weeks

Fetal Behavior

As we have noted, the fetus is an active participant in, and contributor to, its own physical and behavioral development. Indeed, the normal formation of organs and muscles depends on fetal activity, and the fetus rehearses the behavioral repertoire it will need at birth.

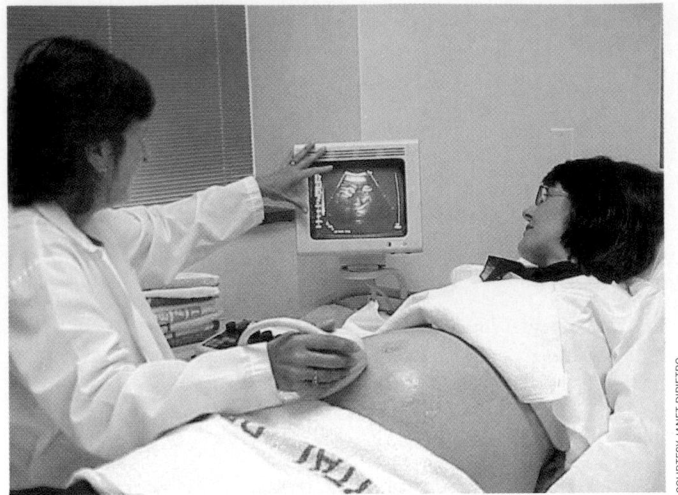

COURTESY JANET DIPIETRO

Developmental psychologist Janet DiPietro is using ultrasound to study the movement patterns of this woman's fetus.

Movement

Every mother knows that her baby was active in the womb, but few realize how early their child started moving. From 5 or 6 weeks after conception, the developing organism moves spontaneously, starting with a simple bending of the head and spine that is soon followed by the onset of numerous kinds of increasingly complex movements over the next weeks (De Vries, Visser, & Prechtl, 1982). One of the earliest distinct patterns of movement to emerge (at around 7 weeks) is, remarkably enough, hiccups. Why should a fetus hiccup? According to a scientific paper on the phenomenon of fetal hiccups, the "stimulus for hiccups and the mechanisms regulating their occurrence remain as poorly defined for the fetus as they are for the adult" (Stark & Myers, 1995, p. 61). In other words, no one knows.

Other fetal movements include moving arms and legs, wiggling fingers, grasping the umbilical cord, moving head and eyes, yawning, sucking, and others. The fetus can also completely change position in the womb by a kind of backward somersault. These various movements are initially jerky and uncoordinated but gradually become more integrated. By 12 weeks, most of the movements that will be present at birth have appeared (De Vries et al., 1982), although the mother is still unaware of them. Later on, when mothers can readily feel the movement of their fetuses, their reports indicate that how much a fetus moves—its activity level—is quite consistent over time: some fetuses are characteristically very active, whereas others are more sedentary (Eaton & Saudino, 1992). Thus, individual differences are apparent in fetal behavior. Further, there is continuity from prenatal to postnatal behavior. For example, more active fetuses are more active infants (DiPietro, Costigan, Shupe, Pressman, & Johnson, 1998).

A particularly important form of fetal movement is *swallowing*. The fetus drinks amniotic fluid, which passes through its gastrointestinal system. Most of the fluid is then excreted back out into the amniotic sac. One benefit of this activity is that the tongue movements associated with drinking and swallowing promote the normal development of the palate (Walker & Quarles, 1962). In addition, the passage of amniotic fluid through the stomach and intestines helps those organs mature properly, so that the digestive system is functional at birth. Thus, swallowing amniotic fluid prepares the fetus for survival outside the womb.

A second form of fetal movement anticipates the fact that at birth the newborn has only a few moments to start breathing. For that to happen, the lungs and the rest of the respiratory system, including the muscles that move the diaphragm in and out, must be mature and functional. The fetus gets ready by exercising: from as early as 10 weeks, it engages in "fetal *breathing,*" moving its chest wall in and out (Nathanielsz, 1994). The fetus does not take in air, of course; rather, small amounts of amniotic fluid are pulled into the lungs and then expelled. Unlike breathing after birth, which must be continuous, fetal breathing goes on only about 50% of the time (James, Pillai, & Smoleniec, 1995).

Behavioral Cycles

Once the fetus begins to move, it is in almost constant motion for the next month or so. Then periods of inactivity gradually begin to occur. Rest–activity cycles—bursts of high activity alternating with little or no activity for a few minutes at a time—emerge as early as 10 weeks and become very stable during the second half of pregnancy (Robertson, 1990). In the latter half of the prenatal period, the fetus moves only about 10% to 30% of the time (DiPietro et al., 1998). Fetuses that are anencephalic (a rare anomaly in which the cerebral cortex is missing) remain highly active throughout pregnancy, suggesting that the cortex is involved in the inhibition of fetal movement (James et al., 1995).

Longer-term patterns, including daily (circadian) rhythms, also become apparent, with the fetus less active in the early morning and more active in the late evening (Arduini, Rizzo, & Romanini, 1995). It always seems to pregnant women that their fetuses wake up and start doing acrobatics just as they themselves are trying to go to sleep. It seems they are right.

Near the end of pregnancy, the fetus spends over three-fourths of its time in quiet and active sleep states like those of the newborn (James et al., 1995) (see page 69). The active sleep state is characterized by REM, just as it is in infants and adults. Sleep states in the last weeks before birth are highly similar to those 2 weeks after birth (Groome, Swiber, Atterbury, Bentz, & Holland, 1997).

Fetal Experience

There is a popular idea—promoted by everyone from scholars to cartoonists—that we spend our lives longing for the peaceful days in our mother's womb. But is the womb a haven of peace and quiet? Although the uterus and the amniotic fluid buffer the fetus from much of the stimulation impinging on the mother, research has made it clear that the fetus experiences an abundance of stimulation. The sensory structures with which we experience the external world are present relatively early in prenatal development; they play a vital role in fetal development and, as we will see in the next section, fetal learning.

Touch

The fetus experiences tactile stimulation as a result of its own activity. In the process of moving, the fetus's hands come into contact with other parts of its body; fetuses have been observed grasping their umbilical cords, rubbing their faces, and, as you saw in Figure 2.12, sucking their thumbs. As the fetus grows larger, it increasingly often bumps against the walls of the uterus.

Taste

The amniotic fluid that the fetus swallows contains a variety of flavors (Maurer & Maurer, 1988). The fetus can detect these flavors and likes some better than others. Indeed, the fetus has a sweet tooth. The first evidence of fetal taste preferences came from a medical study performed over sixty years ago (described by

Gandelman, 1992). A physician named DeSnoo devised an ingenious treatment for women with excessive amounts of amniotic fluid. He injected a sweet flavor (saccharin) into their amniotic fluid, hoping that the fetus would help the mother out by ingesting increased amounts of fluid, thereby diminishing the excess. To find out if his procedure worked, DeSnoo also injected into the amniotic fluid a dye that shows up in urine. He reasoned that the more of the sweetened fluid the fetus drank, the more dye it would take in; the more dye it ingested, the more that would pass from the fetus across the placenta to the mother and be excreted in her urine. Thus, all he had to do was assess how much dye showed up in the mother's urine. DeSnoo found that the urine of mothers who had had the saccharin–dye combination injected into their amniotic fluid was more tinted than that of mothers who had received only the dye. Thus, the fetuses in this study drank more amniotic fluid when it had been sweetened, indicating that taste sensitivity and flavor preferences exist before birth.

Smell

Researchers have recently demonstrated that amniotic fluid can take on odors from what the mother has eaten (Mennella, Johnson, & Beauchamp, 1995), which confirmed what obstetricians have long reported—that during birth they can smell scents like curry and coffee in the amniotic fluid of women who had recently consumed them. Indeed, human amniotic fluid has been shown to be rich in odorants (although many do not sound very appealing—including those described as being pungently rancid, goaty, or having a "strong fecal note") (Schaal, Orgeur, & Rognon, 1995). Through fetal breathing, amniotic fluid comes into contact with the fetus's odor receptors. Hence, scientists have concluded that the fetus has olfactory experience (Schaal et al., 1995).

Hearing

Picture scientists hovering over a pregnant woman, ringing bells, striking a gong, clapping blocks of wood together, and even sounding an automobile horn. (It reminds you of the opening to this chapter, doesn't it?) In an effort to ascertain what auditory stimulation is available in the womb, scientists have presented these and other sounds to the protruding abdomen of a mother-to-be to see if her fetus reacts. We know that many sounds originating outside the woman's body are audible in the womb, because miniature recording devices have been inserted in the uterus immediately before birth (Lecanuet, Granier-Deferre, & Busnel, 1995; Querleu, Renard, Boutteville, & Crepin, 1989). External sounds that are audible include the voices of people talking to the woman. In addition, the prenatal environment includes many sounds generated internally by the mother—her heartbeat, her blood pumping through her vascular system, her breathing, her swallowing, and various rude noises made by her digestive system. A particularly prominent and frequent source of sound stimulation is the mother's voice as she talks, with the clearest aspects being the general cadence, intonation, and stress pattern of her speech.

The fetus responds to these various sounds from at least the 6th month of pregnancy on. During the last trimester, external noises elicit changes in fetal movements and heart rate (Kisilevsky, Fearon, & Muir, 1998; Lecanuet et al., 1995; Zimmer, Chao, Guy, Marks, & Fifer, 1993). The fetus's heart rate also changes (decelerates) briefly when the mother starts speaking (Fifer & Moon, 1995). As we will discuss in the next section on fetal learning, the fetus's extensive auditory experience with human voices has some lasting effects.

Sight

Although it is not totally black inside the womb, only a little light filters through. There is some evidence of fetal reaction to a bright light shone directly against the stretched skin of the mother's abdomen (Vaughn, 1996), but the visual experience of the fetus is presumably negligible.

habituation a simple form of learning that is shown by a decrease in response to repeated or continued stimulation

Fetal Learning

In the preceding sections, we have emphasized the impressive behavioral and sensory capabilities of the fetus in the early stages of development. Even more impressive is the extent to which the fetus learns from many of its experiences in the womb.

Direct evidence for human fetal learning comes from studies of habituation, one of the simplest forms of learning (Thompson & Spencer, 1966). **Habituation** involves a decrease in response to repeated or continued stimulation (see Figure 2.15). If you shake a rattle beside an infant's head, the baby will likely turn toward it. At the same time, the infant's heart rate may slow momentarily. (Transitory heart rate deceleration is a sign of interest.) If you repeatedly shake the rattle, however, the head-turning and heart rate changes will eventually stop. This decreased response is evidence of learning and memory; only if the infant remembers the stimulus from one presentation to the next can the stimulus lose its novelty. When a new stimulus occurs, the habituated response *recovers* (increases). Shaking a bell, for example, may reinstate the head-turning and heart rate responses. (Developmental psychologists have exploited habituation to study a great variety of topics, and in several later chapters you will read about a number of studies that have used it.)

In one habituation study of prenatal learning of speech sounds, a team of French investigators (Lecanuet et al., 1995) repeatedly presented fetuses in their 9th month of gestation with a syllable pair—"babi." (A speaker was placed over the mother's abdomen, and a recording of the syllable pair was played through it, loud enough to penetrate the womb.) The initial presentations elicited a brief but noticeable deceleration in the heart rate of the fetus. As the sound was repeated, the amount of change in heart rate grew smaller. Then the order of the two syllables was reversed, creating the new stimulus "biba." At this point, the heart rate response increased. Thus, the fetus had habituated to the familiar stimulus (i.e., had learned to recognize it) and could discriminate between one syllable pair and another. Fetuses pay attention to and habituate to a wide variety of sounds in addition to human voices (e.g., Kisilevsky & Muir, 1991; Lecanuet et al., 1995).

The earliest at which fetal habituation has been observed to date is 32 weeks' gestation, indicating that the central nervous system is sufficiently developed at this point for learning and memory to occur (Sandman, Wadhwa, Hetrick, Porto, & Peeke, 1997). Long-term learning and retention have also been demonstrated. A group of 37-week-old fetuses who had heard their mothers recite a short rhyme three times a day for four weeks recognized the familiar poem, as shown by greater heart-rate deceleration to the familiar poem than to a novel one (DeCasper, Lecanuet, Busnel, Granier-Deferre, & Maugeais, 1994).

FIGURE 2.15 Habituation Habituation occurs in response to the repeated presentation of a stimulus. As the first stimulus is repeated and becomes familiar, the response to it gradually decreases. When a novel stimulus occurs, the response recovers. The decreased response to the repeated stimulus indicates the formation of memory for it; the increased response to the novel stimulus indicates discrimination of it from the familiar one, as well as a general preference for novelty.

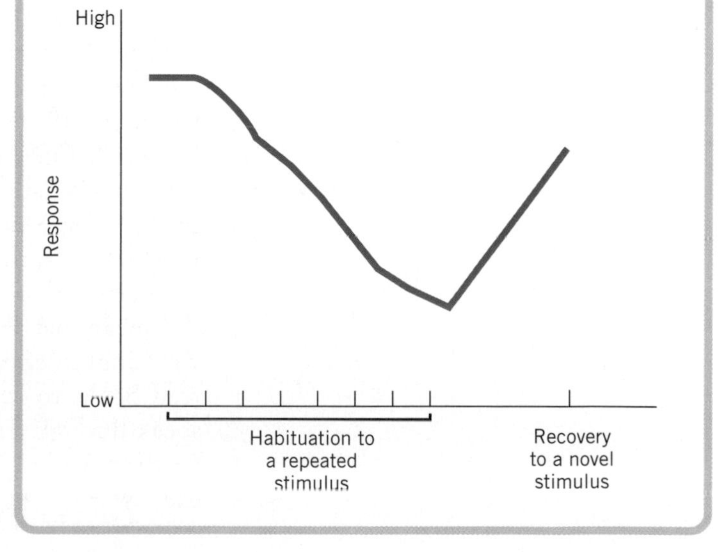

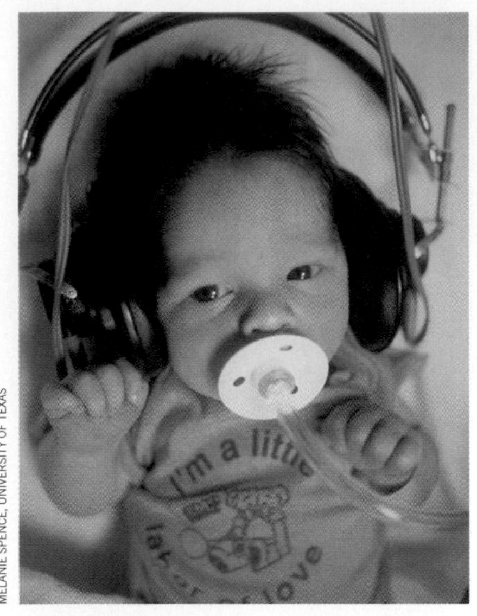

MELANIE SPENCE, UNIVERSITY OF TEXAS

This newborn can control what he gets to listen to. His pacifier is hooked up to a computer, which is in turn connected to a tape player. If the baby sucks in one pattern (predetermined by the researchers), he will hear one tape. If he sucks in a different pattern, he will hear a different tape. Researchers have used this technique to investigate many questions about infant abilities, including the influence of fetal experience on newborn preferences.

The effects of prenatal learning have also been observed *after* birth. In a classic study, Anthony DeCasper and Melanie Spence (1986) asked pregnant women to read aloud twice a day from *The Cat in the Hat* (or another Dr. Seuss book) during the last 6 weeks of their pregnancy. Thus, the women's fetuses were repeatedly exposed to the same highly rhythmical pattern of speech sounds. The question was whether they would recognize the familiar story after birth. To see, the researchers tested them as newborns. The infants were fitted with miniature headphones and given a special pacifier to suck on. The pacifier was wired to a computer that recorded the pattern of the baby's sucking. When the infant sucked in one particular pattern, he or she heard the familiar story through the headphones, but sucking in a different pattern produced a different story. The babies quickly modified their sucking to the pattern that enabled them to hear the familiar story. Thus, these newborns apparently recognized and preferred the story their mothers had read to them while they were still in the womb.

Newborns also have a natural preference for a familiar *smell*—the scent of the amniotic fluid in which they lived for 9 months. In one set of studies that shows this preference, newborns were presented with two pads, one saturated with their own amniotic fluid and the other saturated with the amniotic fluid of a different baby. With the two pads located on either side of their heads, the infants revealed a preference for the scent of their own amniotic fluid by keeping their heads oriented longer toward that scent (Marlier, Schaal, & Soussignon, 1998).

Long-lasting preferences based on prenatal experience have been demonstrated for *taste* (Mennella, Jagnow, & Beauchamp, 2001). Pregnant women were asked to drink carrot juice four days a week for three weeks near the end of their pregnancy. When their babies were tested at around 5½ months of age, they reacted more positively to cereal prepared with carrot juice than to the same cereal prepared with water. Thus, the flavor preferences of these 5½-month-old infants reflected the influence of their experience in the womb several months earlier. This finding has substantial theoretical and practical significance. On the theoretical side, it is a very powerful demonstration of the persistent effect of prenatal learning. On the practical side, it may shed light on the strength of cultural food preferences. A child whose mother ate a lot of chili peppers, ginger, and cumin, for example, may be more favorably disposed from the beginning to Indian food than a child whose mother's diet was much more bland.

Newborns also show numerous *auditory* preferences based on prenatal experience. To begin with, they prefer to listen to their own mother's voice over the voice of another woman; in other words, the fetus learns to recognize, and subsequently prefers, the particular voice it has heard the most (DeCasper & Fifer, 1980). Further, the newborn baby prefers a version of its mother's voice that sounds most familiar—one that has been filtered so as to mimic how it sounded in the womb (Moon & Fifer, 1990; Spence & Freeman, 1996). Finally, newborns would rather listen to the language they heard in the womb than to another language (Mehler et al., 1988; Moon, Cooper, & Fifer, 1993). French newborns prefer listening to French over Russian, for example.

There can be little question that the human fetus is listening and learning. Does this mean that parents-to-be should sign up for programs that promise to "educate your unborn child"? Such programs exhort the mother-to-be to talk to her fetus, read books to it, play music for it, and so on. The father-to-be is instructed to speak through a megaphone aimed at his wife's bulging belly in the hope that the newborn will recognize his voice as well as the mother's. Is there any point in such exercises?

Probably not. Although it seems possible that hearing Dad's voice more clearly and more frequently might lead the newborn to prefer it over unfamiliar voices, such a preference probably develops very shortly after birth anyway. And it is quite clear that some of the advertised advantages of prenatal training would not occur. Because of the level of development of the fetus's brain, it would be impossible for it to learn words or any kind of factual knowledge, no matter how much the mother-to-be might read aloud. The fetus will only learn about her voice and the general patterns of her language—not any specific content. We suspect that the craze for "prenatal education" will go the way of other ill-conceived attempts to shape early development to adult desires.

Hazards To Prenatal Development

Thus far, our focus has been on the normal course of development before birth. Unfortunately, prenatal development is not always free of error or misfortune. The most dire, and by far the most common, misfortune is spontaneous abortion (commonly referred to as miscarriage). The best estimate is that around 45% or more of pregnancies spontaneously abort before the woman has any idea she is pregnant (Moore & Persaud, 1993). The majority of embryos that miscarry very early have severe defects, such as missing an entire chromosome or possessing an extra one, that make further development impossible. Of pregnancies that women are aware of, 15% to 20% end in a miscarriage. Few couples realize how common this experience is, making it all the more painful if it happens to them.

Most infants who survive the danger of miscarriage are born fully normal. This is the case for well over 90% of all newborns in the United States today, and most of the rest have only minor defects. There are, however, numerous factors operating before birth that can cause less fortunate outcomes (Lamb & Lang, 1992). Genetic factors, which are the most common, will be discussed in the next chapter. Here, we consider the nature of environmental influences that can have deleterious effects on prenatal development.

Environmental Influences

A vast array of environmental agents have the potential to cause harm during prenatal development. They range from alcohol and drugs that the mother takes into her body to air pollution and radiation in the world around her. These agents, which are referred to as **teratogens,** can cause anything from relatively mild and easily corrected problems to death.

A crucial factor in the severity of the effects of potentially harmful agents is *timing.* Many agents cause damage only if exposure occurs during a **sensitive period** in prenatal development (see Figure 2.16). Each of the major organ systems has its own sensitive period, which is the time when its basic structures are being formed. There is no more dramatic or straightforward illustration of the importance of timing than the thalidomide tragedy that occurred in the 1960s. Many pregnant women who took this new, presumably safe sedative gave birth to babies with major limb deformities; some babies were born with no arms and with flipperlike hands growing out of their shoulders. However, these serious defects occurred only if the pregnant woman took the drug between the 4th and 6th week after conception, the time when her fetus's limbs were emerging and developing (look again at Figures 2.7 to 2.14). Taking thalidomide either before the arms or legs started to develop or after they were basically formed had no untoward effect.

teratogens environmental agents that have the potential to cause harm during prenatal development. The harm can range from easily correctible problems to death.

sensitive period the period of time during which a developing organism is most vulnerable to damage by outside agents

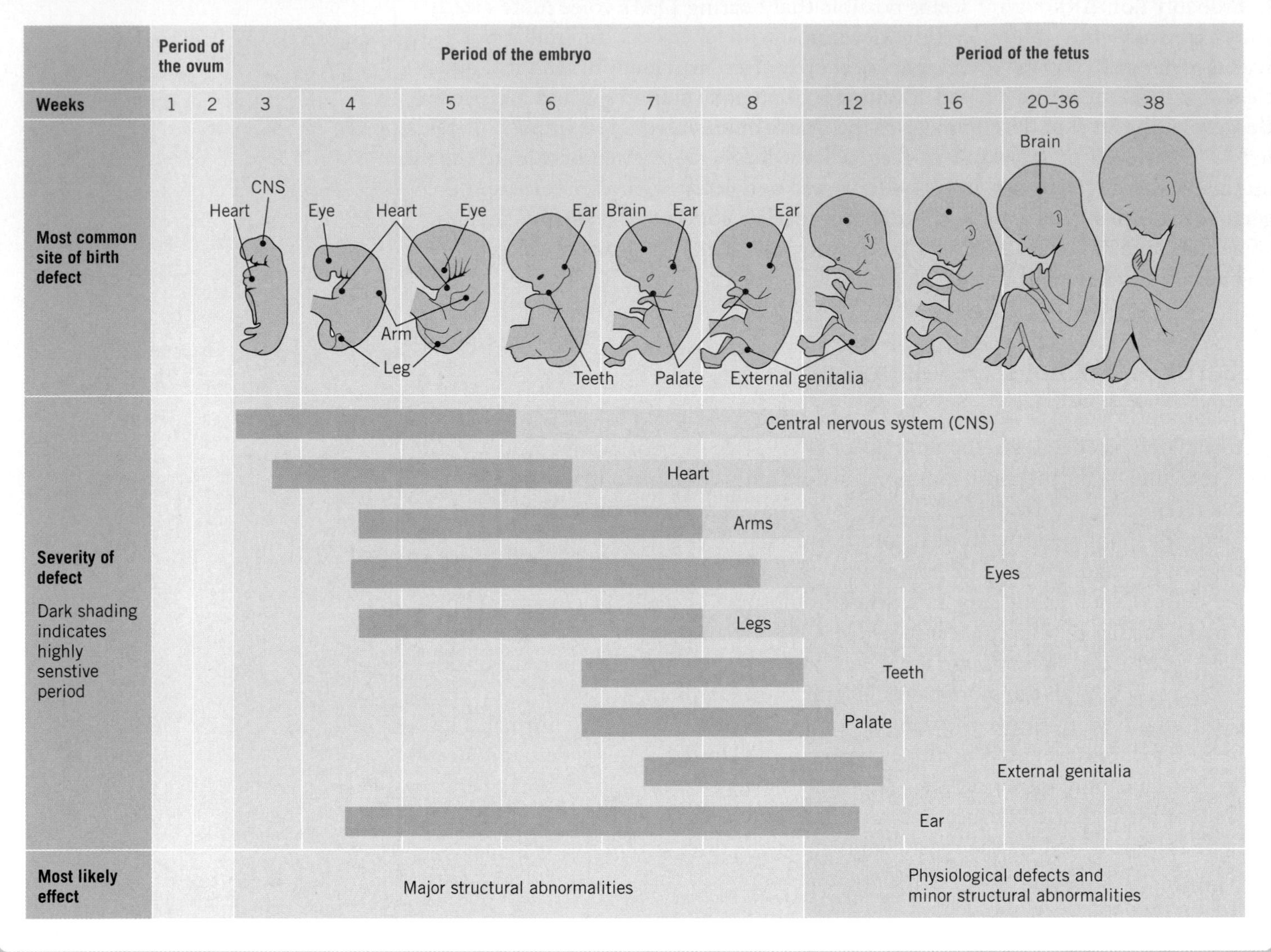

FIGURE 2.16 Stages of prenatal development **The most sensitive or critical period of prenatal development is the embryonic period. During the first two weeks, before implantation in the uterus, the zygote is generally not susceptible to environmental factors. Every major organ system of the body undergoes all or a major part of its development between the 3rd and the end of the 8th week. The dark green portions of the bars in the figure denote the times of most rapid development when major defects can form. The light green portions indicate periods of continued but less rapid development when minor defects may occur. (Adapted from Moore & Persaud, 1993.)**

dose–response relation the fact that the greater the exposure to a potential teratogen the fetus receives, the more likely it is that a defect will occur and the more severe the defect is likely to be

As you can see in Figure 2.16, the sensitive period for many organ systems—and hence the time when the most significant teratogenic damage can result from something the mother does or experiences—is before the woman might realize she is pregnant. This is especially problematic, because a substantial proportion of all births are unplanned. Hence, sexually active people of childbearing age need to be concerned with preventing birth defects.

Another crucial factor influencing the severity of teratogenic effects is the *amount and length of exposure.* Most teratogens show a **dose–response relation:** the greater the exposure to a potential teratogen the fetus receives, the more likely it is that a defect will occur and the more severe any defect is likely to be.

Given the importance of avoiding environmental agents that have teratogenic effects, it is often, unfortunately, very difficult to identify them and to determine exactly what effects they may have. One reason is that they so often occur in combination, making it difficult to separate out their effects. For families in urban poverty, for example, it is hard to tease apart the effects of poor maternal diet, exposure to air-borne lead, inadequate prenatal care, and psychological stress resulting from unemployment, single parenthood, and living in crime-ridden neighborhoods. Furthermore, the presence of multiple factors can have a *cumulative impact.* A given agent may have little discernible effect by itself but might have an impact in combination with other harmful agents. Alcohol, cigarettes, and addictive drugs all carry some risk, but the fetus of a woman who abuses all three is at particularly high risk. Moreover, a woman who drinks, smokes, and/or uses drugs while pregnant is likely to continue doing so after giving birth and hence is likely to provide poorer care for her child than she might otherwise do.

The effects of teratogens can also vary according to *individual differences* in susceptibility (probably in both the mother and the fetus). Thus, a substance that is harmless to most people may trigger problems in a minority who have a genetic susceptibility to it. The opposite can also occur. Although HIV infection is very harmful to a woman who contracts it, the majority of infants born to women with HIV or full-blown AIDS have not contracted the HIV virus themselves (Valleroy, Harris, & Way, 1990).

TABLE 2.2

Some Environmental Hazards to Fetus or Newborn

Drugs	Maternal Disease
Alcohol	AIDS
Birth control pills (sex hormones)	Chicken pox
Cocaine	Chlamydia
Heroin	Cytomegalovirus
Marijuana	Gonorrhea
Methadone	Herpes simplex (genital herpes)
Tobacco	Influenza
Environmental Pollutants	Mumps
Lead	Rubella (German measles)
Mercury	Syphilis
PCBs	Toxoplasmosis

Note: This list of dangerous elements is *not* comprehensive; there are many other agents in the environment that can have a negative impact on developing fetuses or on newborns during the birth process.

Finally, identifying teratogens is also made difficult by the existence of *sleeper effects,* in which the impact of a given agent may not be apparent for many years. For example, the hormone DES was commonly given in the 1940s to 1960s to discourage miscarriage, with no apparent ill effects on babies born to women who had received it. However, in adolescence and adulthood, these offspring turned out to have elevated rates of cervical and testicular cancer.

Having discussed some of the basic factors involved in environmental influences, we turn now to some of the specific teratogens that can adversely affect prenatal development. Because an enormous number of potential teratogens have been identified, we will focus only on some of the most common ones, emphasizing in particular those that are related to the pregnant woman's behavior. Table 2.2 includes the agents discussed in the text as well as some additional ones, but you should be aware that there are numerous others known or suspected to be hazardous to prenatal development.

Legal drugs Although many prescription and over-the-counter drugs are perfectly safe for pregnant women to take, some are not. Many (such as thalidomide and DES) that were initially believed to be harmless later turned out to be teratogens. Pregnant women (and women who have reason to think they might be or might soon become pregnant) should take drugs only under the supervision of a physician. The two legal "drugs" that cause by far the most havoc for fetal development are cigarettes (nicotine) and alcohol.

Cigarette Smoking We all know that smoking is unhealthy for the smoker, and there is an abundance of evidence that it is not good for the smoker's fetus either. When a pregnant woman smokes a cigarette, she gets less oxygen, and so does her fetus. A sign of this is that the fetus makes fewer breathing movements after Mom lights up. In addition, the fetuses of smokers metabolize some of the cancer-causing agents contained in tobacco. And because the mother-to-be inhales gases even when someone else, such as the father, is doing the smoking, passive smoking can have an indirect effect on fetal oxygen.

This woman is endangering the health of her fetus.

PHOTRI / JACK NOVAK / CORBIS STOCK MARKET

The main consequence that maternal smoking has for the fetus is retarded growth and low birth weight, both of which compromise the health of the newborn. Babies born to heavy smokers weigh on average 200 grams less than babies of nonsmokers (Moore & Persaud, 1993). In addition, evidence suggests that smoking may be linked to increased risk of SIDS (sudden infant death syndrome, discussed in Box 2.4) and a variety of problems, including lower IQ, hearing deficits, and cancer.

In spite of the well-established negative effects of maternal smoking on fetal development, almost 13% of women in the United States smoke during their pregnancies (National Center for Health Statistics, 2001). The rate is especially high (19%) for pregnant 18- and 19-year-olds. Most of these women also continue to smoke after giving birth; thus, their children are exposed to a known teratogen before birth, as well as to a known health hazard after birth.

Alcohol When a pregnant woman drinks, the alcohol in her blood crosses the placenta into both the fetus's bloodstream and the amniotic fluid. Thus, the fetus gets alcohol directly and also by drinking an amniotic-fluid cocktail. Concentrations of alcohol in the blood of mother and fetus quickly become equal, but the fetus has less ability to metabolize and remove alcohol from its blood, so it remains in the fetus's system longer.

The most dramatic teratogenic effect of maternal alcohol consumption occurs when the fetus is exposed to large amounts of alcohol over a long period of time. Babies born to alcoholic women often exhibit a condition known as **fetal alcohol syndrome (FAS)** (Jones & Smith, 1973; Streissguth, Bookstein, Sampson, & Barr, 1993). The most obvious symptoms of FAS are facial deformities like those shown in Figure 2.17. Less visible FAS effects can include varying degrees of mental retardation, attention problems, and hyperactivity, as well as defects of various organs. Maternal alcohol abuse is believed to be the most common nongenetic cause of mental retardation (Moore & Persaud, 1993). Furthermore, many children who were prenatally exposed to large amounts of alcohol do not have full-blown FAS but do exhibit a variety of neuropsychological impairments, including attention problems and hyperactivity (Mattson, Riley, Delis, & Jones, 1998).

FIGURE 2.17 Effects of FAS This child of an alcoholic mother, shown as an infant, a preschooler, and a school-age child, displays the symptoms of fetal alcohol syndrome (FAS). The characteristic features caused by extensive exposure to alcohol in the womb include facial abnormalities (a smooth upper lip, short nose, and narrow, widely-spaced eyes), as well as neuropsychological deficits (including attention, learning, and memory problems). Roughly 1 in every 1,000 infants born in the United States has FAS.

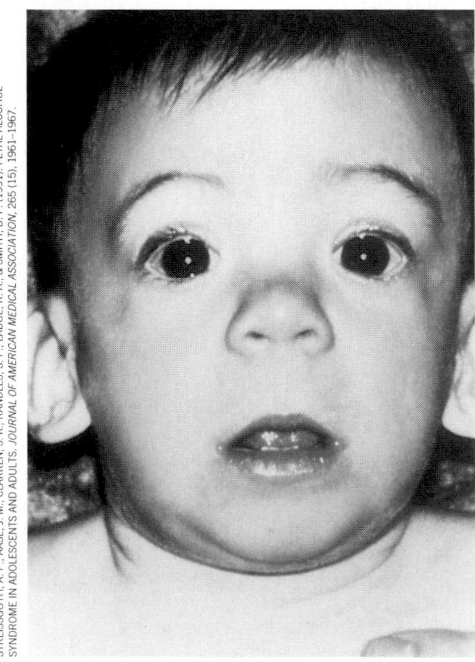

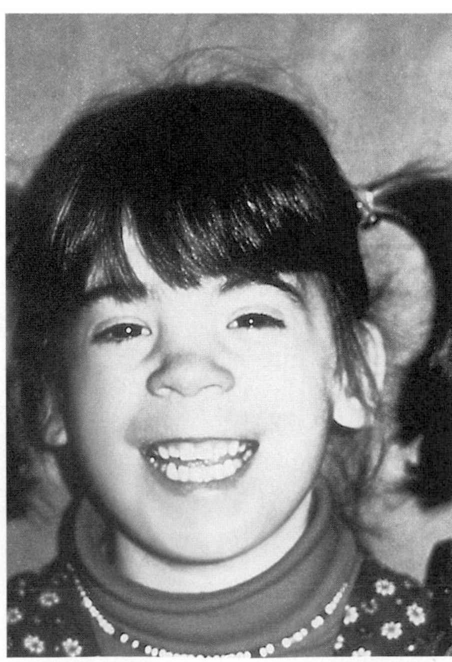

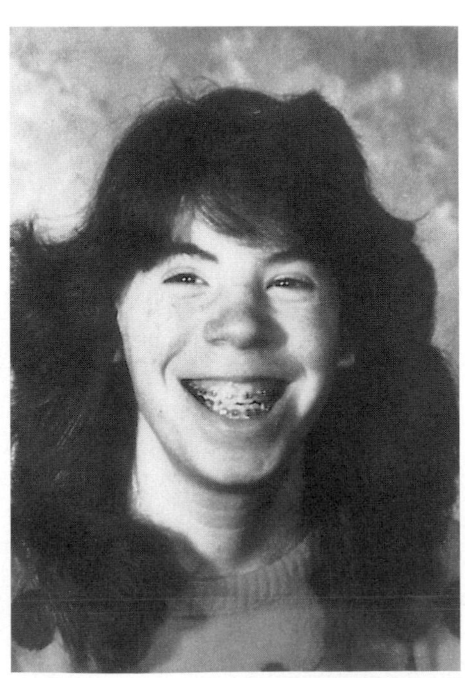

applications 2.4

Face Up to Wake Up

For parents, nothing is more terrifying to contemplate than the death of their child. New parents are especially frightened by the specter of **SIDS — sudden infant death syndrome.** SIDS refers to the unexpected death of an infant less than 1 year of age that has no identifiable cause. An apparently healthy baby is put to bed for the night, usually, and found dead in the morning. Although SIDS is rare, nearly 3,000 infants are victims in the United States each year, the majority between 2 and 4 months of age.

The causes of SIDS are still not fully understood, but researchers have identified some steps parents can take to decrease the risk to their baby.

The most important one is that *a baby should be put on his or her back to sleep.* Research has firmly established that sleeping on the stomach increases the risk of SIDS more than any other single factor (e.g., Willinger, 1995). The incidence of SIDS has been lowered in recent years through a worldwide health education program to convince parents to have their infants sleep on their backs, like the baby in the photo.

Second, to lower the risk of SIDS, *parents should not smoke.* If they do smoke, they should not smoke around the baby. Infants whose mothers smoke during pregnancy and/or after the baby's birth are more than 3½ times as likely to succumb to SIDS than babies not exposed to smokers in their home (Klonoff-Cohen et al., 1995).

Third, *babies should sleep on a firm mattress with no pillow.* Research has shown that soft bedding is associated with heightened risk, presumably because blankets and pillows can trap air around the infant's face, causing the baby to breathe in its own carbon dioxide instead of oxygen.

Fourth, *infants should not be wrapped in lots of blankets or clothes.* Being overly warm seems to be associated with SIDS.

COURTESY OF THE CJ FOUNDATION FOR SIDS

"Face Up to Wake Up." The motto of the foundation dedicated to lowering the incidence of SIDS is part of a worldwide campaign to educate parents about the risk of putting babies to sleep on their stomachs.

Even moderate drinking during pregnancy (i.e., less than one drink per day) can have both short- and long-term negative effects on development (e.g., Hunt, Streissguth, Kerr, & Olson, 1995; Streissguth, Barr, & Martin, 1983). In addition, binge drinking (occasionally having several drinks over a short period of time) is believed to be particularly harmful (Moore & Persaud, 1993); in other words, drinking a given amount of alcohol relatively quickly may be more dangerous than drinking the same amount over a longer period of time.

Evidence is accumulating that most of the deleterious effects of alcohol consumption occur because the presence of alcohol in the fetus's bloodstream triggers widespread cell death in the fetal brain (see Barinaga, 2000). It appears that alcohol-induced cell death may be particularly likely to occur in the last trimester of pregnancy.

Given the potential outcomes and the fact that "there is no known safe level of alcohol consumption for a pregnant woman" (National Clearinghouse for Alcohol and Drug Information, 1995), the best approach for expectant mothers is to avoid alcohol altogether.

fetal alcohol syndrome (FAS) the effects of maternal alcoholism on a fetus, including facial deformity, varying degrees of mental retardation, attention problems, hyperactivity, and organ defects

SIDS (sudden infant death syndrome) the unexpected death of an infant less than 1 year of age that has no identifiable cause

Illegal drugs Almost all commonly abused illegal drugs have been shown to be or are suspected to be dangerous for prenatal development. It has proved difficult to pin down exactly how dangerous various ones are, because, as we discussed earlier, pregnant women who use one illegal substance often use others and often smoke cigarettes and drink alcohol as well (Lester, 1998). Although marijuana (the most commonly used illegal substance in the United States) is suspected of having negative effects on fetal development, research has not provided conclusive evidence of such a link. Cocaine in its various forms is the second most common illegal drug abused by American women of childbearing age (Hawley & Disney, 1992). Although some early reports indicating a host of devastating effects of maternal use of cocaine turned out to be exaggerated, it is well established that cocaine use is associated with intrauterine growth retardation, premature birth, and small head size (Hawley & Disney, 1992). Newborn and older infants of coke addicts have impaired ability to regulate arousal and attention (e.g., DiPietro, Suess, Wheeler, Smouse, & Newlin, 1995; Karmel & Gardner, 1996; Lester & Tronick, 1994; Lewkowicz, Karmel, & Gardner, 1998). Some tend to be lethargic and underaroused; others are highly excitable and irritable, with a characteristic high-pitched cry that adults find very grating. Longitudinal studies of the development of cocaine-exposed children have reported persistent, although sometimes subtle, cognitive and social deficits (Lester, 1998). These deficits can be ameliorated to some degree, as may be shown by improved outcomes, in children adopted into supportive middle-class families (Koren, Nulman, Rovet, Greenbaum, Loebstein, & Einarson, 1998).

Environmental pollutants As we are all aware, we are surrounded by a variety of pollutants in our air, water, and food, some of which can have teratogenic effects. This fact was made apparent in the 1950s, when Minamata Bay in Japan was contaminated by high levels of mercury. Infants born to mothers who ate fish from the bay had serious neurological and behavioral disturbances. More recently, Midwestern mothers who consumed a diet high in Lake Michigan fish with high levels of PCBs (polychlorinated biphenyls) had newborns who were smaller than average and had small heads. The children with the highest prenatal exposure to PCBs had slightly lower IQ scores as long as 11 years later (Jacobson & Jacobson, 1996; J. L. Jacobson, et al., 1992). Another example of detrimental effects of environmental pollution is the link between lead pollution from automobile emissions and paint chips and a variety of neurobehavioral and other problems in newborns, an issue particularly important for expectant mothers who live in decaying urban neighborhoods near busy freeways (Tesman & Hills, 1994).

Occupational hazards Another category of worrisome environmental agents are those in the workplace. Many women have jobs that bring them into contact with a variety of potentially hazardous elements. Tollbooth collectors, for example, are exposed to high levels of automobile exhaust; farmers, to pesticides; and factory workers, to numerous chemicals. Employers and employees alike are grappling with how to protect pregnant women from potential teratogens without subjecting them to job discrimination.

Maternal Factors

Because she constitutes the most immediate environment for her fetus, certain characteristics of the mother-to-be herself can affect prenatal development. These characteristics include age, nutritional status, health, and stress level.

Age The age of the pregnant woman is related to the outcome of her pregnancy. Pregnancy is most likely to result in a healthy baby if the mother is older than 15 but younger than 35. Older mothers tend to have more health problems in general, making it more difficult to have a successful pregnancy. In addition, the older a woman is, the older her eggs are and the more likely they are to fail to divide properly. The result is a higher incidence of both fetal death and of infants born with certain genetic syndromes, such as Down syndrome (see Chapter 3, p. 91). Very young mothers are also at risk. They tend to be of lower socioeconomic status (SES) and are more likely to have inadequate diets and prenatal care. The high rate of pregnancies among teenagers in the United States remains a cause for concern, even though it has declined in recent years.

Nutrition The fetus depends on its mother for all its nutritional requirements. If a pregnant woman has an inadequate diet, her unborn child may also be nutritionally deprived (Pollitt et al., 1996). Growth of the brain is especially affected: malnourished newborns have smaller brains containing fewer brain cells than do well-nourished newborns. They tend to be unresponsive and irritable (Lozoff, 1989).

Because malnutrition is more common in impoverished families, it often coincides with the host of other risk factors associated with poverty, making it difficult to isolate its effects on prenatal development (Lozoff, 1989; Sigman, 1995). However, one study of development in very extreme circumstances was able to assess the effects of malnutrition independent of SES (Stein et al., 1975). In parts of Holland during World War II, people of all income and education levels suffered severe famine. Examination of health records of Dutch women who were pregnant at that time revealed that maternal malnutrition had a distinct negative impact on prenatal development, with the severity of the impact depending on when the malnutrition occurred. Women who became malnourished only in the last few months of pregnancy tended to have small, underweight babies with small heads. Babies born to mothers whose malnutrition started in the first few months of pregnancy often had serious physical defects.

Disease Although most maternal illnesses that occur during a pregnancy have no impact on the fetus, some do. For example, if contracted early in pregnancy, rubella (the three-day measles) can have devastating developmental effects, including major malformations, deafness, blindness, and mental retardation. As a result of immunization programs, this disease has become uncommon, but any woman of childbearing age who does not have immunities against it should be vaccinated before becoming pregnant.

The sexually transmitted diseases (STDs) that have become increasingly common throughout the world are quite hazardous to the fetus. Cytomegalovirus, currently the most frequent prenatal source of infection, can damage the fetus's central nervous system and cause other defects. Genital herpes can be very dangerous: if the infant comes into contact with active lesions in the birth canal, blindness or even death can result. HIV infection can sometimes be passed to the fetus in the womb or during birth, as well as through breast milk after birth.

Stress There has long been concern that severe emotional stress during pregnancy would negatively affect prenatal development, since stress leads to the release of hormones that divert oxygen to organs other than the uterus. However, because people tend to drink and smoke more than usual when they are highly stressed, it has been difficult to isolate the role of stress per se. An ingenious study succeeded by taking advantage of the fact that during World War II, alcohol and cigarettes were virtually nonexistent in parts of Europe. A pair of Finnish investigators (Huttunen & Niskanen, 1978) examined the health records of adults whose fathers had died, half of them while their mothers were pregnant with them, and the other half during the first few months after they were born. (The researchers took it for granted that a woman whose husband had recently died was undergoing severe stress.) Thus, the two groups were highly comparable in that none of them had grown up with their natural father and they had all spent their early lives with a mother who was under severe stress but who had no access to cigarettes or alcohol. The results of the study revealed that the adult children of mothers who experienced severe stress while pregnant had a higher rate of emotional problems and behavior disorders. Recently, a number of careful studies have established a link between maternal stress and measure of physiological functioning of the fetus (DiPietro, Hodgson, Costigan, Hilton, & Johnson, 1996), as well as preterm birth and low birthweight (Wadhwa, 1998).

review:

The most rapid period of development starts at conception, with the union of the egg and sperm, and continues for roughly 9 months, divided into three developmental periods—germinal, embryonic, and fetal. Every major organ system undergoes all or a substantial part of its development between the 3rd and 8th week following conception, making this a sensitive period for potential damage from environmental hazards. The processes through which prenatal development occurs include cell division, cell migration, cell differentiation, and cell death.

Scientists have recently learned an enormous amount about the behavior and experience of the developing organism, which begins to move at 5 to 6 weeks. Some behaviors of the fetus contribute to its development, including swallowing amniotic fluid and breathing motions. The fetus has relatively rich sensory experience from stimulation both within and outside the womb, and this experience is the basis for fetal learning. Researchers have recently established the persistent effects of fetal learning after birth.

Many environmental agents can have a negative impact on prenatal development, with cigarette smoking and alcohol consumption being the most common problems in the United States. Maternal factors (malnutrition, illness, etc.) can also cause problems for the developing fetus. Timing is crucial for some teratogens; the severity of effects is generally related to the amount and length of exposure, as well as to the number of different negative factors with which a fetus has to contend.

The Birth Experience

For 9 months, the expectant mother has been harboring a foreign object in her body. Approximately 38 weeks after conception, contractions of the muscles of the uterus begin, initiating the birth of the baby. Typically, the baby has already contributed to the process by, for one thing, rotating itself into the normal head-down position.

Uterine contractions, as well as the baby's progress through the birth canal, are painful for the mother, so women in labor are often given pain-relieving drugs. Although these drugs can help the mother get through childbirth more comfortably, they do not help her baby. Many obstetric medications slow labor, and anything that prolongs labor increases the chance of fetal *hypoxia* (oxygen deprivation) and thus increases the risk of brain damage. Also, delivery drugs given to the mother can result in a "drugged" baby—a baby with a decreased supply of oxygen who is less attentive, has poorer muscle tone, exhibits less vigorous reflexes, and so forth (Brackbill, McManus, & Woodward, 1985; Brazelton, Nugent, & Lester, 1987). The extent of these effects depends on which particular drugs are used and how high the dosage is. Fortunately, the effects are generally not long-lasting.

Is being born as painful as giving birth? Reasoning by analogy from the mother's pain, many people have asserted that the birth experience for the fetus is indeed painful, even traumatic. However, although we obviously cannot know for certain, there is good reason to doubt that birth is either traumatic or even particularly painful for the baby. A simple experiment is instructive in this regard. Compare how much pain you feel when you pinch a piece of skin on your forearm and pull on it versus when you wrap your hand around your forearm and squeeze as tightly as you can. The stretching is painful, but the squeezing is not. The mother's pain comes from her tissues being greatly stretched, but the baby experiences squeezing. Hence, the experiences of the two participants are unlikely to be comparable (Maurer & Maurer, 1988). Childbirth programs based on the assumption that birth is painful and traumatic for newborns are probably based on faulty premises.

In fact, the squeezing that the fetus experiences during birth serves several important functions. First, it temporarily reduces the overall size of the head, allowing the disproportionately large head of the fetus to pass safely through the mother's pelvic bones. This is possible because the skull is composed of separate plates that can overlap one another slightly during birth (see Figure 2.18). The "soft spot," or *fontanel,* in the top of the baby's head is simply a space between separate skull plates. Over the weeks following birth, the fontanel gradually disappears as the plates fuse together.

Another function of the squeezing of the baby's head during birth is to stimulate the production of hormones that will help the fetus withstand hypoxia during birth and regulate breathing after birth. It also serves to inhibit the fetus from breathing until the head has emerged from the birth canal. The squeezing of the infant's body forces amniotic fluid out of the lungs, in preparation for the newborn's first, crucial gasp of air (Lagercrantz & Slotkin, 1986; Nathanielsz, 1994). The birth cry is a very efficient mechanism for jump-starting respiration: a good, lusty cry not only obtains some essential oxygen but also forces open the small air sacs in the lungs, making subsequent breaths easier.

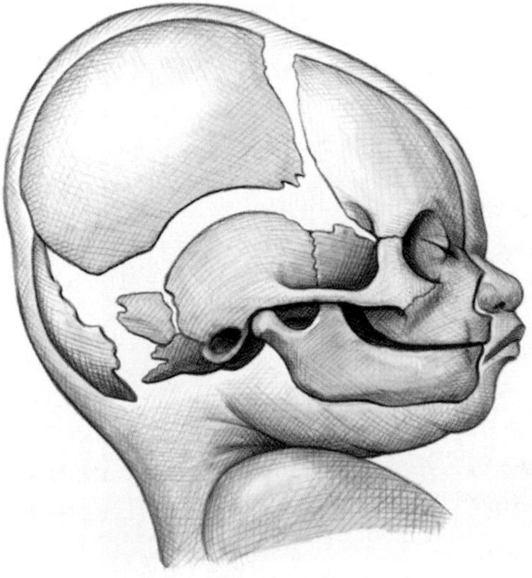

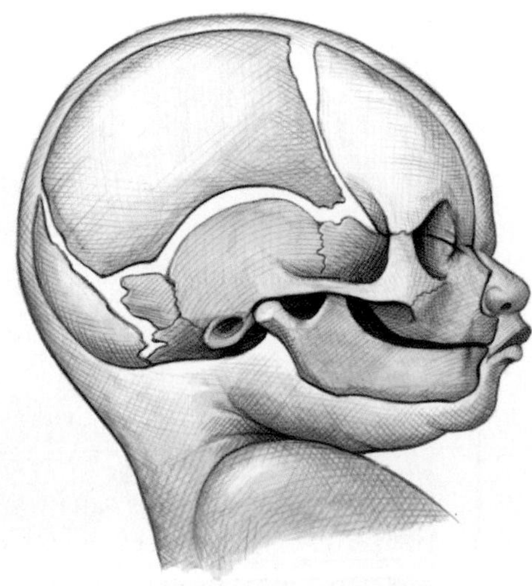

FIGURE 2.18 Head plates Pressure on the head during birth can cause the separate plates of the skull to overlap, resulting in a temporarily misshapen head. Fortunately, the condition rapidly corrects itself after birth.

Diversity Of Childbirth Practices

Although the biological aspects of birth are pretty much the same everywhere, childbirth practices vary enormously. As with many human behaviors, what is considered a normal and desirable birth custom in one society may seem strange or deviant—or even dangerous—in another.

All cultures pursue the dual goals of safeguarding the *survival and health* of both the mother and the baby and ensuring the *social integration* of the new person. Groups differ, however, regarding the relative importance they give to these different goals. We can see these differences by comparing the childbirth practices of two cultures—Bali and the United States.

An expectant mother on the South Pacific island of Bali assumes that her husband and other kin, along with any children she may already have, will all want to be present at the joyous occasion of the birth of a new child. Her female relatives, as well as a midwife, actively help her throughout the birth, which occurs in her home. Having already been present at many births, the Balinese woman knows what to expect from childbirth, even when it is her first child (Diener, 2000).

A very different scenario has been traditional in the United States, where the woman in labor withdraws almost totally from her everyday life. In most cases, she enters a hospital to give birth, attended by only one person emotionally close to her—usually her husband. The birth is supervised by a variety of medical personnel, most of whom are strangers. Having never witnessed a birth, the first-time mother may not have very realistic expecations about the birth process. Furthermore, she has a good chance—over 20%, in fact—of having her infant surgically removed from her uterus in a cesarean delivery.

Underlying the Balinese approach to childbirth is great emphasis on the social goal of immediately integrating the newborn into the family and community. The baby is considered a reincarnated soul of an ancestor, and thus is related to many more people than just its biological parents. Accordingly, many kin are present to support mother and baby. In contrast, modern Western groups have elevated the physical health of the mother and newborn above all other concerns. The belief that childbirth is safer in a hospital setting outweighs the resulting social isolation of mother and baby.

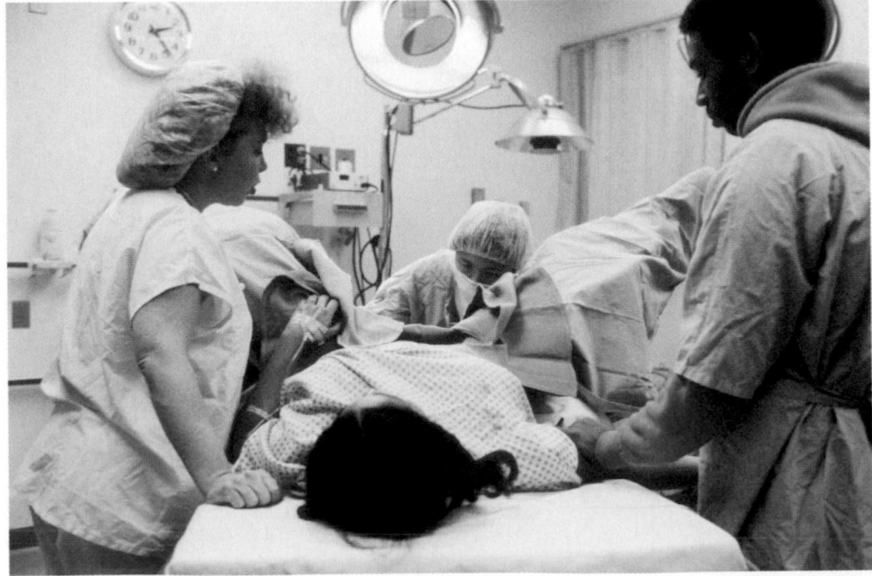
HARRIET GANS/THE IMAGE WORKS

The medical model of childbirth prevails in the United States.

The practices of both societies have changed to some degree. In the United States, the social dimensions of birth have come to be increasingly recognized by doctors and hospitals, who generally attempt to accommodate the birth process as a family event. As in Bali, various family members—sometimes even including the parents' other children—are encouraged to be present to support the laboring mother and to share a family experience. This shift has been accompanied by more moderate use of delivery drugs, thereby enhancing the woman's participation in childbirth and her ability to interact with her newborn. In addition, many expectant parents attend childbirth education classes, where they acquire some of the knowledge their Balinese counterparts have picked up through routine attendance at births. Pregnant women and their partners are taught general information about what to expect during childbirth, as well as specific breathing and relaxation techniques to control pain. In recognition of the social dimension of childbirth, social support is a key component of these programs; the pregnant woman's husband or some other supportive person is trained to assist her during the birth. Such childbirth programs are generally beneficial (Lindell, 1988), and obstetricians routinely advise expectant couples to enroll in them. At the same time that these changes are occurring in the United States, in traditional, nonindustrialized societies like Bali, Western medical practices are increasingly adopted in an effort to improve newborn survival rates. Such changes result both from shifts in the priority placed on different goals and from the evolution of new strategies to achieve goals.

review: Research on the birth process has revealed that many aspects of the experience of being born, including squeezing in the birth canal, have adaptive value and increase the likelihood of survival for the newborn. Great differences exist across cultures in beliefs and practices related to childbirth, with one clear difference having to do with the emphasis on immediately integrating the newborn into the community.

state refers to an infant's level of arousal and engagement in the environment, ranging from deep sleep to intense activity. State is an important mediator of young infants' experience of the world.

The Newborn Infant

A healthy newborn is ready and able to continue the developmental saga in a new environment. The baby begins interacting with that environment right away, exploring and learning about both the physical and social entities in it. Newborns' exploration of this uncharted territory is very much influenced by their state of arousal.

State of Arousal

State refers to a continuum of arousal, ranging from deep sleep to intense activity. As you well know, your state dramatically affects your interaction with the environment—with what you notice, do, learn, think about. It also affects the ability of others to interact with you. State is an even more important mediator of young infants' experience of the world around them.

Figure 2.19 depicts the average amount of time in a 24-hour period that Western newborns typically spend in each of six states, ranging from quiet sleep to crying. Within this general pattern, however, there is a great deal of variation. Some infants cry relatively rarely, whereas others

FIGURE 2.19 Newborn states The average proportion of time, in a 24-hour day, that Western newborns spend in each of six states. There are substantial individual and cultural differences in how much time babies spend in the different states.

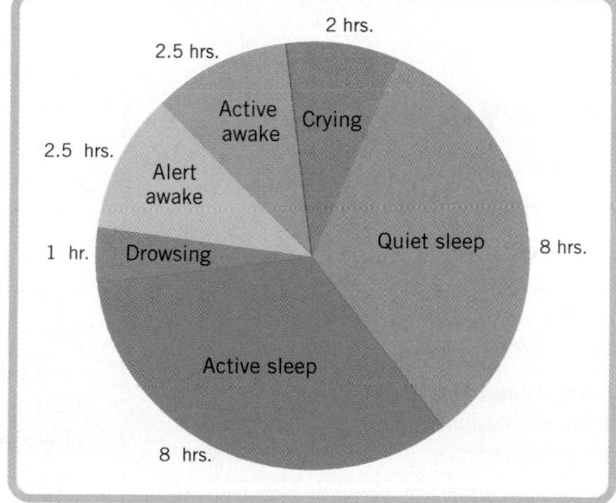

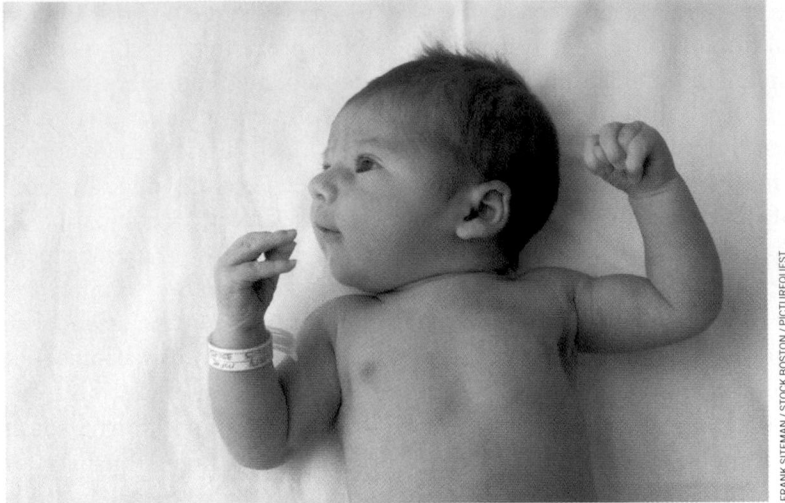

FRANK SITEMAN / STOCK BOSTON / PICTUREQUEST

FIGURE 2.20 Quiet alert state The parents of this quiet alert newborn have a good chance of having a pleasurable interaction with the baby.

cry for hours every day; some babies sleep much more, and others much less, than the 16-hour average shown in the figure. Some infants spend more than the average of 2½ hours in the awake-alert state, in which they are fairly inactive but attentive to the environment. To appreciate how these differences might affect parent–infant interaction, imagine yourself as the parent of a newborn who cries more than the average, sleeps little, and spends less time in the awake-alert state. Now imagine yourself with a baby who cries relatively little, sleeps well, and spends an above-average amount of time quietly attending to you and the rest of his or her environment (see Figure 2.20). Clearly, you would have many more opportunities for pleasurable interactions with the second newborn.

We will next consider in detail the two newborn states that are of particular concern to parents—sleeping and crying—both of which have been studied extensively.

Sleep

Figure 2.21 summarizes several important facts about sleep and its development, two of which are of particular importance. First, "sleeping like a baby" means, in part, sleeping a lot; on average, newborns sleep approximately twice as much as young adults do. Total sleep time declines regularly during childhood and continues to decrease, although more slowly, throughout life.

Second, the pattern of two different sleep states—*REM* and *non-REM* sleep—changes dramatically with age. **REM (rapid eye movement)** sleep is an active sleep state that is associated with dreaming in adults and is characterized by quick, jerky eye movements under closed lids; a distinctive pattern of brain activity; body movements; and irregular heart rate and breathing. **Non-REM sleep,** in contrast, is a quiet or deep sleep state characterized by the absence of motor activity or eye movements and regular, slow brain waves, breathing, and heart rate. As you can see in Figure 2.21, at birth, REM sleep constitutes fully 50% of a newborn's total sleep time. The proportion of REM sleep declines quite rapidly to only 20% by 3 or 4 years of age and remains low for the rest of life.

Why do infants spend so much time in REM sleep? Some researchers believe that it helps develop the infant's visual system. The human visual system, including the visual area of the brain, is relatively immature at birth, and its normal development depends on visual stimulation. However, relatively little visual stimulation is experienced by either the fetus residing in the womb or by the sleeping newborn

REM (rapid eye movement) an active sleep state that is associated with dreaming in adults and is characterized by quick, jerky eye movements under closed lids

non-REM sleep a quiet or deep sleep state characterized by the absence of motor activity or eye movements and regular, slow brain waves, breathing, and heart rate

autostimulation theory the idea that brain activity during REM sleep in the fetus and newborn makes up for natural deprivation of external stimuli and facilitates the early development of the visual system

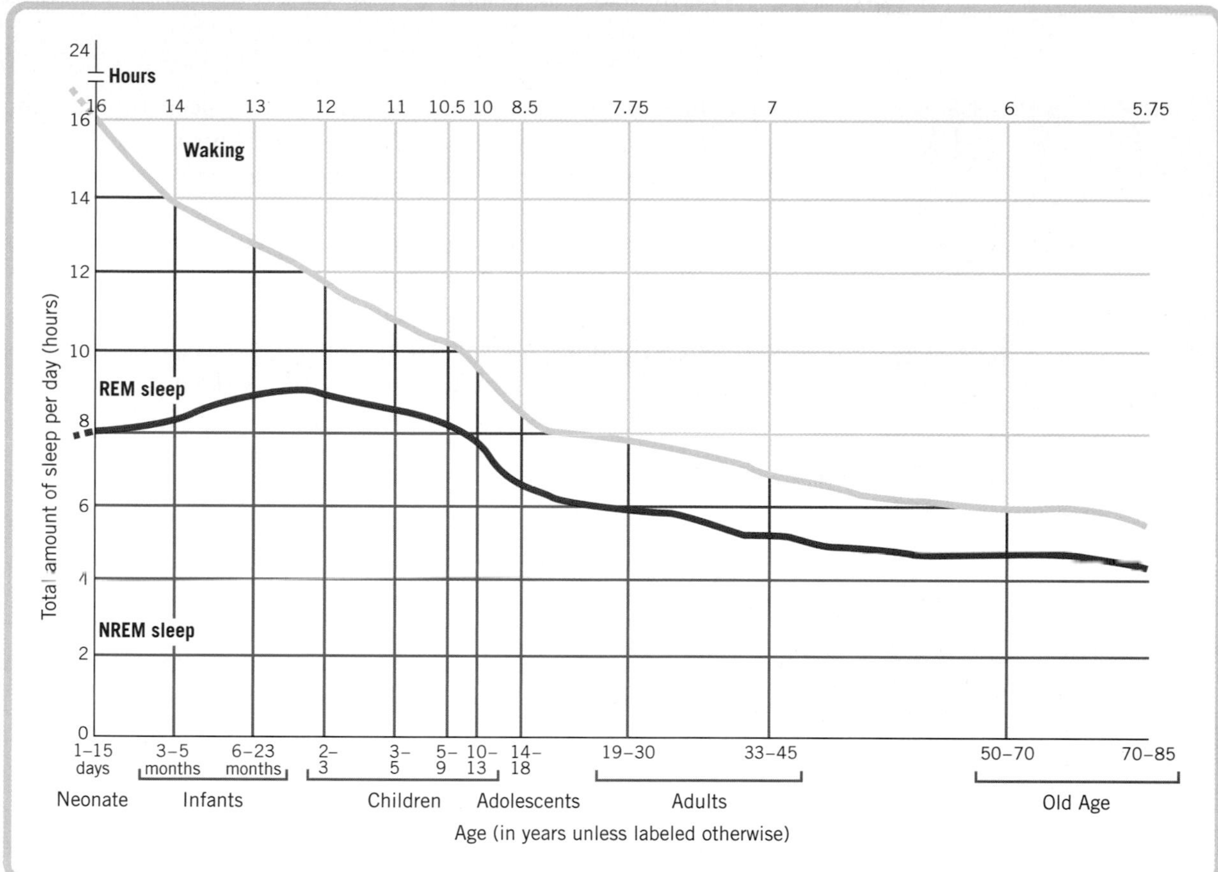

FIGURE 2.21 Total sleep and proportion of REM and non-REM sleep across the life span Newborns average a total of 16 hours of sleep, roughly half of it in REM sleep. The total amount of sleep declines sharply throughout early childhood and continues to decline much more slowly throughout life. From adolescence on, REM sleep constitutes only about 20% of total sleep time. (Adapted from Roffwarg, Muzio, & Dement, 1966, and from a later revision by these authors.)

whose eyes are closed roughly two-thirds of every day. During REM sleep, there is a high degree of electroencephalographic (EEG) activity in the brain, especially in the visual areas. According to the **autostimulation theory** (Roffwarg, Muzio, & Dement, 1966), this internally generated brain activity during REM sleep helps to make up for the natural deprivation of external stimulation and hence facilitates the early development of the visual system in the fetus and newborn.

If the autostimulation theory is correct, then infants who receive a higher level of stimulation when awake should engage in less REM activity when asleep. This prediction was confirmed by the finding of an inverse relation between waking visual experience and REM sleep (Boismeyer, 1977). Newborns were presented with complex patterns to look at while awake. The infants who had experienced a high level of extra visual stimulation spent less of their subsequent sleep time in REM sleep than did infants exposed to lower levels of visual stimulation.

Another difference between the sleep of young infants and older individuals (not reflected in Figure 2.21) is in sleep–wake cycles. Newborns generally cycle between sleep and waking states several times in a 24-hour period, sleeping slightly more at night than during the day (Whitney & Thoman, 1994). In other words, they are likely to be awake during part of their parents' normal sleep time. Gradually, infants develop the more mature pattern of sleeping through the night, although the age at which they do so depends very much on cultural practices and pressures. For example, most infants in the United States sleep through the night by around 4 months of age (Berg & Berg, 1987). This change is actively encouraged by most parents, who find the infant's initial sleep pattern disruptive, stressful, and exhausting (Halpern, Anders, Garcia-Coll, & Hua, 1994). Many different strategies are employed by tired parents, from the adoption of elaborate, often extended bedtime rituals to gritting their teeth and letting the baby cry himself or herself to sleep. In contrast, the parents of Kipsigis infants in rural

TERRY WILD STUDIO

Most American parents want to avoid the 2 A.M. fate of this young father. They regard their baby's sleeping through the night as a developmental triumph—the sooner, the better.

Kenya put little or no pressure on their infants to sleep through the night. Babies are almost always with their mothers: during the day they are often carried on her back as she goes about her daily activities, and at night they sleep with her and are allowed to nurse whenever they awaken. As a consequence, these babies distribute their sleeping throughout the night and day for several months (Harkness & Super, 1995; Super & Harkness, 1986). Thus, cultures vary not only in terms of where babies sleep, as you learned in Chapter 1, but also in terms of how hard parents attempt to influence their babies' sleep.

Crying

How do you feel when you hear a baby cry? We imagine that, like most people, you find the sound of a crying infant extremely unpleasant. Why is crying so aversive for us?

From an evolutionary point of view, infant crying and adult aversion to it could have adaptive significance. Infants cry for many reasons, including illness, pain, and hunger, that require the attention of caregivers. Adults' high level of motivation to stop an infant's crying leads them to take care of the infant's needs and hence would promote the infant's survival. Indeed, some have suggested that in times of hardship, such as famine, cranky babies are more likely to survive than more placid ones, possibly because they elicit adult attention and get more than their share of scarce food resources (DeVries, 1984).

Parents, especially novice parents, are often puzzled and anxious about why their baby is crying. Indeed, the majority of first calls to pediatricians have to do with parents' concerns about what they judge to be excessive crying (Harkness et al., 1996). With experience, parents become better at interpreting characteristics of the cry itself (a sharp, piercing cry usually signals pain, for example) and at using context (how long it has been since the last feeding) (Green, Jones, & Gustafson, 1987).

The peak period for crying is the first 3 months; it declines from an average of 2 hours a day in newborns to a total of 1 hour a day for the rest of the first year (St. James-Roberts & Halil, 1991). On a daily basis, the peak time for crying is late afternoon or evening. The phenomenon of "evening crying," which can be quite disappointing to parents looking forward to interacting with their offspring at the end of the workday, may be due to an accumulation of excess stimulation over the course of the day (Maurer & Maurer, 1988).

The nature of crying and the reasons for it change with development. Early on, crying reflects discomfort from pain, hunger, cold, or overstimulation, although from the beginning infants also cry from frustration (Lewis, Alessandri, & Sullivan, 1990; Stenberg, Campos, & Emde, 1983). Crying gradually becomes more of a communicative act; the crying of older babies often seems geared to "tell" caregivers something and to get them to respond (Gustafson & Green, 1988).

Soothing Given how much we dislike listening to crying babies, what works best to console them? Most of the traditional standbys—rocking, singing lullabies, holding the baby up to the shoulder (Korner & Thoman, 1970), giving a pacifier (R. Campos, 1989)—do work reasonably well. In general, many effective soothing techniques involve moderately intense and continuous or repetitive stimulation. One such technique used in many cultures is **swaddling,** which involves wrap-

swaddling a soothing technique, used in many cultures, which involves wrapping a baby tightly in cloths or a blanket, thereby restricting limb movement

colic excessive crying for no apparent reason

ping a baby tightly in cloths or a blanket, thereby restricting limb movement. The tight wrapping provides a constant high level of tactile stimulation and warmth. This technique is practiced in cultures as diverse and widespread as those of the Navajo and Hopi in the American Southwest (Chisolm, 1963), the Quechua in Peru (Tronick, Thomas, & Daltabuit, 1994), and rural villagers in Turkey (Delaney, 2000). Another traditional approach, distracting an upset infant with interesting objects or events, can also have a soothing effect, but the distress often resumes as soon as the interesting stimulus is removed (Harman, Rothbart, & Posner, 1997).

Touch can also have a soothing effect on infants, which may be one reason mothers so often touch their babies when interacting with them (Stack & Muir, 1990). In interactions with an adult, infants fuss and cry less, and they smile and vocalize more, if the adult pats, rubs, or strokes them (Field et al., 1996; Peláez-Nogueras, Field, Hossain, & Pickens, 1996; Stack & Arnold, 1998; Stack & Muir, 1992). Carrying young infants, as is routinely done in many societies around the world, reduces the amount of crying that young babies do (Hunziker & Barr, 1986).

In laboratory studies, a dramatic soothing effect has been achieved by giving a distressed newborn a small taste of something sweet. After receiving a tiny drop of a sweet solution, such as sucrose, on the tongue, newborns soon stop crying and thrashing about (Barr, Quek, Cousineau, Oberlander, Brian, & Young, 1994; Blass & Ciaramitaro, 1994; Smith & Blass, 1996). The taste of sucrose has an equally dramatic effect on pain sensitivity; newborn boys given a sweetened pacifier to suck during circumcision cry much less than babies who do not receive this simple intervention (Blass & Hoffmeyer, 1991).

PHOTODISC

Carrying infants close to the parent's body results in less crying. Many Western parents are now emulating the traditional carrying methods of other societies around the world.

Response to distress One question that often concerns parents is whether they should always respond as quickly and consistently as possible to a distressed infant. They wonder if that approach will reward the infant for crying and hence increase how much he or she cries, as some investigators have argued (Gewirtz & Boyd, 1977). Or, as others have claimed, would prompt reliable responding instill a sense of confidence and actually lead to less fussing and crying (Bell & Ainsworth, 1972)? It appears that, as is so often the case, the middle road may be best. In a longitudinal study, Hubbard and van IJzendoorn (1991) found that infants whose mothers delayed responding to their cries tended to have less frequent crying bouts than did infants whose mothers responded more rapidly. The key may be taking into account the severity of the infant's distress. If a parent responds quickly to severe distress but less promptly to minor upset, the infant may learn to regulate the latter type of distress on his or her own and hence end up crying less overall.

Colic No matter how hard their parents try to soothe them, some infants seem impervious to their efforts. Excessive crying for no apparent reason during the first few months of life is known as **colic** (Wessel, Cobb, Jackson, Harris, & Detwiler, 1954). Not only do "colicky" babies cry a lot, but they also tend to have high-pitched, grating cries that are very unpleasant to listen to and are often perceived as sounding "sick" (Barr, Rotman, Yaremko, Leduc, & Francoeur, 1992; Lester, Boukydis, Garcia-Coll, Hole, & Peucker, 1992; Zeskind & Barr, 1997). Unfortunately, colic is not a rare condition: more than one in ten young infants in the United States suffer from it (along with their parents) during their first 3 months. Fortunately, it typically lasts only those first few months and leaves no ill effects (Stifter & Braungart, 1992; St. James-Roberts, Conroy, & Wilsher, 1998). One of the best things parents with a colicky infant can do is to seek social support and relief from the frustration and feelings of inadequacy caused by being unable to soothe their baby.

Negative Outcomes at Birth

Although the most common outcome of a recognized pregnancy for a woman in an industrialized society is the full-term birth of a healthy baby, the outcome is sometimes less positive. The most dire result is the death of an infant. The most common less dire negative outcome is low birth weight, which, if extreme, can have long-term consequences.

Infant Mortality

Infant mortality—death during the first year after birth—has become a relatively rare event in the Western industrialized world, thanks to decades of improvements in public health and general economic levels. In the United States, the 1999 infant mortality rate was 7 deaths per 1,000 live births, the lowest in American history (Mathews, MacDorman & Menacker).

Although the infant mortality rate in the United States is low in absolute terms, it is high in comparison with that of many other industrialized nations. In 1996, the United States ranked 23rd in the world in terms of the number of infants who failed to survive their first year after birth (Table 2.3). The relative ranking of the United States has gotten steadily worse over the past several decades, because the infant mortality rates in many other countries have decreased faster and further.

The rates of infant mortality are starkly different for subsets of the U.S. population. African-American infants are more than twice as likely to die before their first birthday as Euro-American infants are. Indeed, the infant mortality rate for African-Americans is similar to that in many underdeveloped countries.

Why do more babies die in the United States—the richest country in the world—than in twenty-two other countries? Why are African-American infants' chances of survival so much poorer than those of Euro-American infants? There are many reasons, most having to do with poverty. For example, many low-income mothers-to-be, including a disproportionate number of African-Americans, have no health insurance and have limited access to good health and prenatal care (Kopp & Kaler, 1989; National Center for Health Statistics, 1998). In contrast, all the countries that rank above the United States with respect to infant mortality have some form of government-sponsored health care that guarantees pregnant women prenatal care at low or minimal cost.

In less developed countries, especially those suffering from a breakdown in social organization due to war, famine, major epidemics, or persistent extreme poverty, the infant mortality rates can be staggering. A particularly poignant example comes from the poorest areas of

TABLE 2.3

Infant Mortality Worldwide — 1996

Country	Deaths per 1,000 live births	Country	Deaths per 1,000 live births
Singapore	3.8	Belgium	5.6
Japan	3.8	Canada	5.6
Finland	4.0	Denmark	5.7
Sweden	4.0	Netherlands	5.7
Norway	4.0	Australia	5.8
Hong Kong	4.0	Italy	6.0
Switzerland	4.7	Czech Republic	6.0
Spain	4.7	United Kingdom	6.1
France	4.9	New Zealand	6.7
Germany	5.0	Portugal	6.9
Austria	5.1	**United States**	7.3
Ireland	5.5		

Source: Guyer et al. (1999)

a small city in northeast Brazil, where extreme poverty, chaotic social services, disrupted families, and an infant mortality rate as high as 90% set up conditions for a vicious cycle (Scheper-Hughes, 1992). Because any baby born in this area has a very high risk of dying and family resources are so slim, mothers look for some evidence that a new baby "wants to live" before they invest very much in the child, either economically or emotionally. They are likely to feed and care for the infant only minimally while engaging in "watchful waiting" for signs of "child sickness" (symptoms of which are the same as those of malnutrition and dehydration). Thus, underfeeding and neglect produce an infant who displays evidence that he or she "has no knack for life" or "wants to die," leading to further deprivation and neglect. When the almost inevitable occurs and the baby dies, the mother is not supposed to express grief, for it is believed that a mother's tears "will make the road from heaven to earth slippery and [the baby] will lose his footing and fall."

Low Birth Weight

The average newborn in the United States weighs 7½ pounds (most are between 5½ and 10 pounds), but approximately 7.5% of U.S. newborns weigh less than 5½ pounds (2,500 grams) and are considered to be of **low birth weight (LBW)** (National Center for Health Statistics, 2000). The rate is much higher for African-Americans (12%) and is strongly associated with poverty. Worldwide, it is estimated that over 18 million infants are born at less than 2,500 grams, 93% of them in developing countries (UNICEF, 2001). Some LBW infants are referred to as **premature** or preterm, because they are born at 35 weeks after conception or earlier, instead of the normal term of 38 weeks. Other LBW infants are referred to as **small for gestational age (SGA):** they may be either preterm or full-term, but they weigh substantially less than is normal for whatever their gestational age is. As a group, LBW newborns have a heightened level of medical complications, including brain damage incurred before or after birth (Beckwith & Rodning, 1991). Very LBW babies (those weighing less than 1,500 grams, or 3.3 pounds) are particularly vulnerable.

There are numerous causes of LBW and prematurity, including many of the risk factors discussed earlier. The mother's past health history is also relevant. For example, women who suffered from growth retardation during their own prenatal development are at greater risk for premature delivery (Nathanielsz, 1994), thus perpetuating the effects of poverty over generations. Simultaneous pregnancies—twins, triplets, and the multiple births that have become more common due to increased use of fertility drugs—are another cause of early births and LBW. (Box 2.5, p. 76, discusses some of the challenges faced by parents of LBW infants.)

Long-term outcomes What outcome can be expected for LBW newborns who survive? This question becomes increasingly important as newborns of ever lower birth weights—often as low as 1,000 grams (about 2¼ pounds)—are kept alive by modern medical technology. The answer includes both bad news and good news.

The bad news is that, *as a group*, LBW infants *on average* have more developmental problems than do babies of normal weight and term, especially if they experience medical complications (Goldson, 1996; Kopp & Kaler, 1989). They suffer from somewhat higher levels of hearing, language, and cognitive impairments. In preschool and elementary school, they are more likely to be distractible and hyperactive and to have learning disabilities. This group is also more likely to experience a variety of social problems, including poor peer and parent–child

low birth weight (LBW) a birth weight of less than 5½ pounds (2,500 grams)

premature any child born at 35 weeks after conception or earlier, as opposed to the normal term of 38 weeks

small for gestational age (SGA) babies that weigh substantially less than is normal for whatever their gestational age

applications 2.5

Parenting a Low-Birth-Weight Baby

Parenthood is challenging under the best of circumstances, but it is especially so for the parents of a preterm or LBW baby. First, they have to accept their disappointment over the fact that they do not have the perfect baby they imagined, and they may also have to cope with feelings of guilt ("What did I do wrong?"), inadequacy ("How can I take care of such a tiny, fragile baby?"), and fear ("Will my baby survive?"). Caring for a healthy baby takes a great deal of time, but caring for an LBW baby can be especially time-consuming and stressful and, if the infant requires extended intensive care treatment, very expensive.

Parents of an LBW baby have a great deal to learn. In the hospital, they need to learn how to interact successfully with a fragile baby confined to an isolette with its tiny body hooked up to life-support equipment. When their infant comes home, the parents have to cope with a baby that is relatively passive and unresponsive, without overstimulating the infant in an effort to get some response (Brazelton, 1990; Brazelton et al., 1987; Patteson & Barnard, 1990). LBW infants also tend to be more fussy than the average baby and difficult to soothe when they become upset (Brachfeld, Goldberg, & Sloman, 1980; Greene, Fox, & Lewis, 1983). To compound matters, they often have a high-pitched cry that is particularly unpleasant (Lester & Zeskind, 1978; Lester et al., 1989).

Another problem for parents is the fact that LBW infants have relatively disorganized behavioral states, their feeding schedules are irregular, and they have more trouble falling asleep, waking up, and staying alert than do infants of normal birth weight (DiVitto & Goldberg, 1979; Meisels & Plunkett, 1988). Thus, it takes longer for the baby to get on a regular, predictable schedule, making the parents' life more hectic.

Parents need to understand that their preterm baby's early development will not follow the same timetable as a full-term infant. Developmental milestones will be delayed. Instead of being delighted by their infant's beginning to smile at them at around 6 weeks, the parents of a preterm infant may have to wait several more weeks for their baby to look them in the eye and break into a heart-melting and deeply rewarding smile. Thus, preterm infants are not only more challenging to care for but in many ways they are also less rewarding to interact with. One consequence is that children who were born preterm are more often victims of parental child abuse (Frodi & Lamb, 1980; Parke & Collmer, 1975).

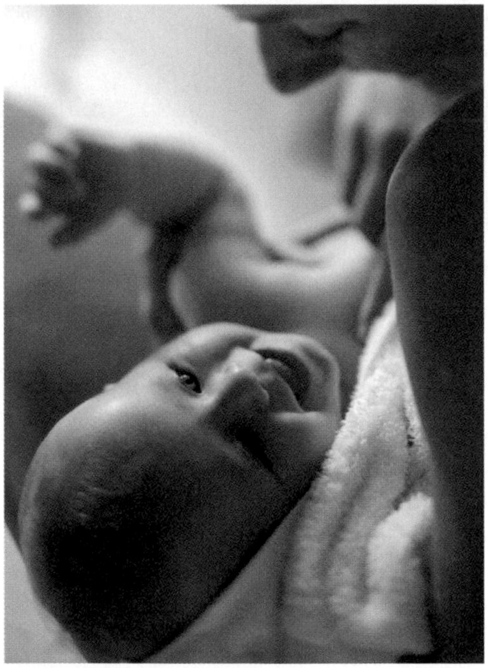

One step that can be helpful to parents of an LBW or preterm infant is learning more about infant development. An intervention program that trained mothers in how to interpret their preterm babies' signals resulted in gains in the children's mental-test performance (Achenbach, Phares, Howell, Rauh, & Nurcombe, 1990). More general knowledge can also be helpful. The preterm infants of mothers who had a relatively high level of knowledge about infancy performed better on a developmental test than did a group whose mothers were less knowledgeable about babies (but were otherwise comparable) (Dichtelmiller, Meisels, Plunkett, Bozynski, & Mangelsdorf, 1992).

In addition, any parent who is trying to deal with an LBW baby or an infant with other problems would do well to seek social support from someone — a spouse or partner, other family members, friends, or a formal support group for parents. In general, one of the best-documented phenomena in psychology is that we cope better with virtually any life problem when we have support from other people.

JAING JIN / SUPERSTOCK

Parents of an LBW baby usually have to wait longer for the joy of being the target of their child's first social smile.

relations (Landry et al., 1990). The lower their weight at birth, the more likely it is they will have any of these difficulties (Beckwith & Rodning, 1991).

The good news is that the *majority* of LBW children turn out quite well. The negative effects of their birth status gradually diminish so that children who were slightly to moderately underweight as newborns generally end up within the normal range on most developmental measures (Kopp & Kaler, 1989; Liaw & Brooks-Gunn, 1993; Meisels & Plunkett, 1988; Sameroff & Chandler, 1975; Vohr & Garcia-Coll, 1988).

Intervention programs What can be done to improve the chances that a given LBW infant will overcome his or her poor start in life? Developmental specialists have designed a variety of intervention programs to try to improve the current status and future outcome of LBW newborns. Parents are active participants in many of these programs, a marked change from past practice. Hospitals formerly did not allow parents to have any contact with their LBW infants, mainly because of fear of infection. Hospitals now actively encourage parents to have as much physical contact and social interaction as their hospitalized infant's physical condition allows.

One widely implemented intervention is based on the idea that touch is normally an important part of the life of newborns as they are picked up, cuddled, carried around, poked, and prodded. Many LBW infants experience little tactile stimulation because of the precautions that must be taken with them, including keeping them in special isolettes, hooked up to various life-support machines. To compensate, Tiffany Field and her colleagues (Field, 1990; Field, Scafidi, & Schanberg, 1987) developed a special therapy that involves massaging the babies and flexing their arms and legs (Figure 2.22). LBW babies who receive this therapy are more active and alert and gain weight faster than those who are not massaged. As a consequence, they get to go home earlier.

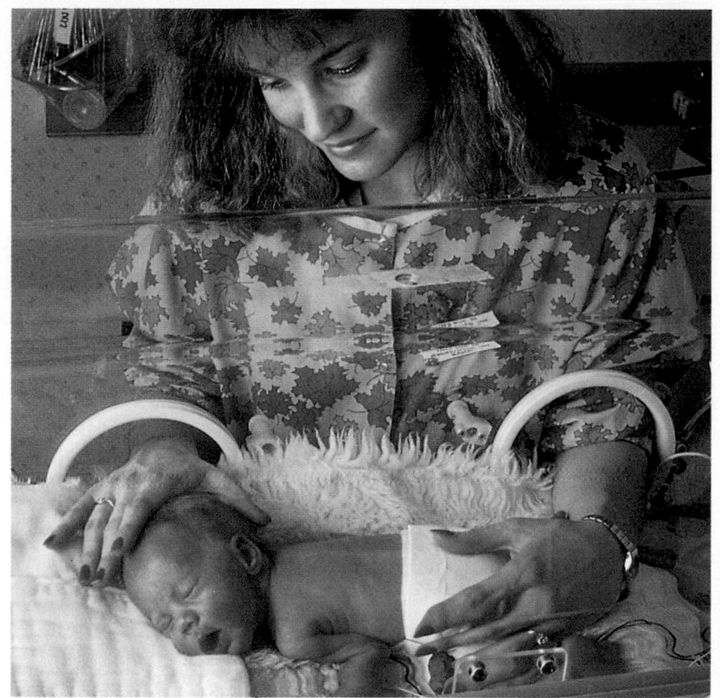

STEVIE GRAND / SCIENCE PHOTO LIBRARY / PHOTO RESEARCHERS, INC.

FIGURE 2.22 Infant massage Everybody enjoys a good massage, but hospitalized newborns particularly benefit from extra touching.

A large number of intervention programs with LBW newborns extend beyond their hospital stay, some for several years (e.g., Ramey & Campbell, 1992). One successful approach was demonstrated in the Infant Health and Development Project (Gross, Spiker, & Haynes, 1997; McCarton, Brooks-Gunn, Wallace, & Bauer, 1997). All the LBW infants received good health care, with half randomly assigned to the intervention group and half to a control group. The intervention included home visits and an intensive early childhood education program administered at a day-care center. The intervention lasted for three years, and the children were to be followed to the age of 8 years.

The degree to which this intervention program was successful differed for those LBW children who had weighed between 2,000 and 2,500 grams at birth and those who had weighed less than 2,000 grams. The IQ scores of the heavier LBW children in the intervention group were higher than those of the control-group children of comparable weight, with an advantage of 14 points at 3 years of age but a smaller difference (4 points) at age 8. The IQ scores of the lighter LBW children were higher in the intervention group at 3 years of age, but not at later ages. Similar results occurred for measures of behavioral problems. The intervention program was most beneficial for children with only a few risk factors and least beneficial for children from multirisk families.

This intervention project illustrates three important general points relevant to intervention efforts designed for high-risk infants. First, many intervention programs produce only modest gains, and the positive results often diminish over time. Second, the success of any intervention depends on the initial health status of the infant. Many programs for LBW babies have been of more benefit to those infants who are less tiny to begin with. This fact is cause for concern, as modern

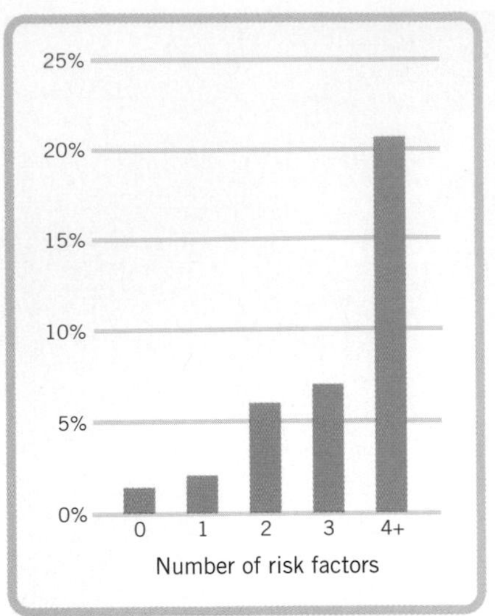

FIGURE 2.23 Multiple risk factors Children who grow up in families with multiple risk factors are more likely to develop psychiatric disorders than children from families with only one or two problematic characteristics (Rutter, 1979).

medical technology makes it possible to save the lives of infants who have a high risk of permanent, serious impairment. The third point is the importance of cumulative risk: the more risks the infant endures, the lower the chances of a good outcome. Because this principle applies to all aspects of development, we will examine it in greater detail in the next section.

Multiple-Risk Model

Risk factors tend to occur together in the world. For example, a woman who is so addicted to alcohol, cocaine, or heroin that she continues to abuse the substance even though she is pregnant is likely to be under a great deal of stress and unlikely to eat well, take vitamins, earn a good income, seek prenatal care, or take good care of herself in other ways. Further, whatever the cumulative effects of these prenatal risk factors, they will likely be compounded by the mother's continuation of her unhealthy lifestyle and by her resulting inability to provide good care for her child (Hawley & Disney, 1992; Kopp & Kaler, 1989; Myers, Olson, & Kaltenbach, 1992; Weston, Ivins, Zuckerman, Jones, & Lopez, 1989).

As you will see repeatedly throughout this book, a negative developmental outcome—whether in terms of prenatal or later development—is more likely when there are multiple risk factors. In a classic demonstration of this fact, Michael Rutter (1979) reported a heightened incidence of psychiatric disorders among English children growing up in families with four or more risk factors (including marital distress, low SES, paternal criminality, and maternal psychiatric disorder) (Figure 2.23). Thus, the risk of developing a disorder is slightly elevated for the child of parents who fight a lot, but if the child's family is poor, the father engages in criminal behavior, and the mother suffers from emotional problems, the child's risk is multiplied nearly tenfold. Similar patterns have been reported for intelligence test scores (Sameroff, Seifer, Baldwin, & Baldwin, 1993) and social-emotional competence (Sameroff, Seifer, Zax, & Barocas, 1987).

Poverty as a Developmental Hazard

Because it is such an important point, it cannot be emphasized enough: the existence of multiple risks is strongly related to socioeconomic status. Consider some of the factors we have discussed that are known to be dangerous for fetal development: inadequate prenatal care, poor nutrition, illness, emotional stress, cigarette smoking, drug abuse, and exposure to environmental and occupational hazards. All these factors are more likely to be experienced by a woman living below the poverty line than by a middle-class woman. It is no wonder then that the outcome of pregnancy on the whole is less positive for lower-SES infants than for babies born to middle-class parents (Kopp, 1990; Minde, 1993; Sameroff, 1986). Nor should it be surprising that among LBW infants, the eventual developmental outcome is poorer for those in lower-SES families (Drillien, 1964; Gross et al., 1997; Kalmar, 1996; Largo et al., 1989; Lee & Barratt, 1993; McCarton et al., 1997; Meisels & Plunkett, 1988; Siegel, 1985).

An equally sad fact is that in many countries, minority families are overrepresented in the lowest SES levels. One of the most striking examples is that of African-Americans. Although 17% of all children in the United States grow up in families whose income places them below the poverty line, 33% of African-American children live in poverty (National Center for Children in Poverty, 2001). Thus, their socioeconomic status places many African-American fetuses, newborns, and children at increased risk for developmental difficulties.

developmental resilience successful development in the face of multiple and seemingly overwhelming developmental hazards

Risk and Resilience

There are, of course, individuals who, faced with multiple and seemingly overwhelming developmental hazards, nevertheless do well. In studying such children, researchers employ the concept of **developmental resilience** (Garmezy, 1983; Masten, Best, & Garmezy, 1990). Resilient children often have two factors in their favor—(1) responsive care from someone and (2) certain personal characteristics, especially intelligence, responsiveness to others, and a sense of being capable of achieving their goals. Recall that in Werner's (1989) study of the children of Kauai (Chapter 1) a crucial factor in the outcome of children who had had a problematic start in life was whether some person took an active interest in their welfare.

In summary, development is highly complex, right from the moment of conception on. As you will see throughout this book, that complexity continues. Although early events and experiences can profoundly affect later development, developmental outcomes are never a foregone conclusion.

review:

The experience of newborn infants is mediated by internal states of arousal, ranging from deep sleep to intense crying, with large individual differences in the amount of time spent in the different states. Newborns spend roughly half their time asleep, and the amount of sleep declines steadily for many years. Researchers believe that the large proportion of their sleep that newborns spend in REM sleep is important for the development of the visual system and brain. Infants' crying is a particularly salient form of behavior for parents, and it generally elicits attention and caretaking. Some infants suffer from colic, but it does not leave lasting ill effects. Effective soothing techniques provide moderately intense, continuous, or repetitive stimulation. How parents respond to their young infant's distress is related to later crying.

Negative outcomes of pregnancy are higher for families living in poverty and for African-Americans. The United States ranks 23rd in the world in terms of infant mortality. Approximately 7.5% of all babies born in the United States are of low birth weight. Although most will suffer few lasting effects, the long-term outcome of severely LBW babies is often problematic. Several large-scale intervention programs have successfully improved the outcome of LBW infants.

According to the multiple-risk model, the more risks that a fetus or child faces, the more likely the child is to suffer from a variety of developmental problems. Low SES is associated with many developmental hazards. Despite multiple risks that many children experience, some show remarkable resiliency and thrive.

Chapter Summary

Prenatal Development

- Nature and nurture combine forces in prenatal development. Much of this development is generated by the fetus itself, making the fetus an active player in its own progress. Substantial continuity exists between what goes on before and after birth in that infants demonstrate the effects of what has happened to them in the womb.
- Prenatal development begins at the cellular level with conception, the union of an egg from the mother and a sperm from the father to form a zygote. The zygote multiplies and divides on its way through a fallopian tube.
- The zygote undergoes the processes of cell division, cell migration, cell differentiation, and cell death (apoptosis), all

to further the development of the organism. These processes continue throughout prenatal development.

- When the zygote becomes implanted on the uterine wall, it becomes an embryo. From that point, it is dependent on the mother to obtain nourishment and oxygen and to get rid of waste products through the placenta.
- Fetal behavior begins 5 or 6 weeks after conception with simple movements, undetected by the mother, that become increasingly complex and organized into patterns. The fetus practices behaviors vital to independent living, including swallowing and a form of intrauterine breathing.
- The fetus experiences a wealth of stimulation both from within the womb and from the external environment. The fetus learns from this experience, which has been demonstrated by studies that show persistent taste preferences and fine discriminations between familiar and novel sounds, especially language, by both fetuses and newborns.
- There are many hazards to prenatal development. The most common fate of a fertilized egg is spontaneous abortion (miscarriage). A wide range of environmental factors can be hazardous to prenatal development. These include teratogens from the external world and certain maternal characteristics and habits, such as maternal age, poor maternal nutrition, use of legal and illegal drugs, and exposure to environmental pollutants.

The Birth Experience

- Approximately 38 weeks after conception, the baby is ready to be born. Usually, the child has rotated into a head-down position that facilitates birth.
- The process of being squeezed through the birth canal has several beneficial effects on the newborn, including preparing the infant to take its first breath.
- How the process of childbirth is managed varies greatly from one society to another and is in part related to which goals and values are emphasized by the culture.

The Newborn Infant

- Newborns display six states of arousal, ranging from deep sleep to active crying.
- The amount of time infants spend in the different states varies greatly, both across individuals and across cultures.
- REM sleep seems to compensate for the lack of visual stimulation that results from the newborn's sleeping many hours a day.
- The sound of a baby crying is a very aversive stimulus for others, and adults employ many strategies to soothe distressed infants.
- Infants born weighing less than 5½ pounds (2,500 grams) are referred to as being of low birth weight. LBW infants are at risk for a variety of developmental problems, and the lower the birth weight, the greater the risk of enduring difficulties.
- A variety of intervention programs have been designed to improve the course of development of LBW babies, but the success of such programs depends very much on the number of risk factors that threaten the baby.
- The multiple-risk model refers to the fact that infants with a number of risk factors have a heightened likelihood of continued developmental problems. Poverty is a particularly insidious risk to development, in part because it is inextricably linked with numerous negative factors.
- Some children display resilience even in the face of substantial risk factors. Resilience seems to result from certain personal characteristics and from attention and emotional support from other people.

Critical Thinking Questions

1. A recent cartoon showed a pregnant woman walking down a street carrying a tape player with a set of very large headphones clamped around her protruding abdomen. Why? What research might provide the basis for her behavior, and what assumptions is she making about what the result might be? If you or your partner were pregnant, do you think you would do something like this?
2. We hear a great deal about the terrible and tragic effects of illegal drugs like cocaine and diseases like AIDS on fetal development. However, which two of the maternal behaviors associated with prenatal harm that were described in this chapter are actually the most common in the United States today?
3. Describe some of the cultural differences that exist in beliefs and practices with respect to conception, pregnancy, and childbirth. Is there any practice of another society that appeals to you more than practices with which you are familiar?
4. Explain the basic idea of the multiple-risk model and how it relates to poverty in terms of prenatal development and birth outcomes.

Key Terms

epigenesis, p. 43
embryology, p. 43
gametes (germ cells), p. 44
meiosis, p. 44
conception, p. 45
zygote, p. 46
phylogenetic continuity, p. 48
apoptosis, p. 49
blastocyst, p. 49
inner cell mass, p. 49
identical twins, p. 49
fraternal twins, p. 49
gastrulation, p. 49
embryo, p. 49
neural tube, p. 50
placenta, p. 50
umbilical cord, p. 50
amniotic sac, p. 50
cephalocaudal development, p. 50
habituation, p. 57
teratogens, p. 59
sensitive period, p. 59
dose–response relation, p. 60
fetal alcohol syndrome (FAS), p. 62
SIDS (sudden infant death syndrome), p. 63
state, p. 69
REM (rapid eye movement), p. 70
non-REM sleep, p. 70
autostimulation theory, p. 71
swaddling, p. 72
colic, p. 73
low birth weight (LBW), p. 75
premature, p. 75
small for gestational age (SGA), p. 75
developmental resilience, p. 78

CHAPTER 3

Biology and Behavior

PABLO PICASSO, *Woman Drawing Surrounded by Her Children*, 1950

Try the following thought experiment: A male and female astronaut aboard a distant space station fall in love and, eventually, the woman becomes pregnant. Unable to return to Earth, she gives birth on the station and the couple starts to raise little Lucy in the sky. Like all children, Lucy has inherited genetic material from her parents—in her case, healthy, high-achieving parents—but both before and after birth, her development will take place in an environment radically different from Earth. What will Lucy be like? How will her development proceed? In what ways would you expect her to be similar to children back on Earth, and in what ways do you think she would be different?

Start by thinking of all the aspects of Lucy's environment that will be very different from what she would have experienced on Earth. Here are a few examples:

Weightlessness. Lucy will not experience the effects of gravity on her body and movements. She will see many solid objects floating through the air.

Restricted space. Most of Lucy's visual experience will be within the space station, so she will rarely look at objects more than a few yards or thousands of miles away.

Restricted range of sounds. Lucy will hear only a few human voices, and her general auditory experience will be quite limited—no glasses shattering on the floor, no sirens, barking dogs, squealing tires, and so forth.

Limited social experience. Lucy will interact with a small number of adults and no children at all.

You can no doubt think of many more ways in which Lucy's experience will be unusual. How will her extraordinary environment affect her development? The underlying question here is to what extent the development of a genetically normal human being depends upon being reared in a normal human environment. Keep Lucy in mind as you read this chapter.

The focus of this chapter is the key physical underpinnings of human development—that is, the inheritance and influence of genes, the development and early functioning of the brain, and important aspects of physical development and maturation. Every cell in our bodies carries, and is affected by, the genetic material we inherited at our conception. Every behavior we engage in is directed by our brain, and how our brain functions depends, in part, on how it develops during the first few years of life. Everything we do at every age occurs with a physical body that changes very rapidly and dramatically in the first few years and in adolescence, and more slowly and subtly at other times.

Several of the themes that were set out in Chapter 1 figure prominently in this chapter. Issues of *nature and nurture,* as well as *individual differences* among children, are prominent throughout this whole chapter and especially the first section, which focuses on the interaction of genetic and environmental factors in development. *Continuity* in development is also highlighted throughout. We again emphasize the activity-dependent nature of developmental processes and the *active child's* part in charting the course of his or her own development.

Nature and Nurture

Everything about you—from your physical structure, intellectual capacity, and personality characteristics to your preferences in hobbies and food—is a joint consequence of the genetic material you inherited from your parents and the environment you have experienced from conception to this instant. These two factors—heredity and environment—work in concert to influence both the ways in which you are like other people and the ways in which you are unique.

People have long been aware that some traits and characteristics "run in families." For as long as there have been domesticated animals, farmers have practiced selective breeding to improve certain characteristics of their livestock—the size of their horses; the milk yield of their goats, cows, or yaks; the quality of their sheep's wool. Some ancient knowledge of heredity was quite sophisticated, even by modern standards. For example, a passage in the Talmud advised against circumcising an infant whose mother had a brother who was a "bleeder" (hemophiliac), for fear that the infant would bleed to death. (Later in this chapter, when you read about sex-linked inheritance patterns, you will see just how impressive this early understanding was.)

People have also long been aware that the environment plays a role in development as well—that a nutritious diet, for example, is necessary for livestock to produce a good milk supply or fine-quality wool. The Old Testament advice to "train up a child in the way he should go" (Proverbs 22:6) clearly reveals a concern with the role of nurture in development.

CHRISTINA SALVADOR / CORBIS SYGMA

The phenomenal athletic ability of golf great Tiger Woods is almost certainly due to the combination of nature—the genes he inherited from his parents—and nurture—the extensive coaching he received from his father.

When scientists first began to investigate the contributions of heredity and environment to development, they generally emphasized one factor or the other—heredity *versus* environment, nature *or* nurture—as the prime influence. In nineteenth-century England, for example, Francis Galton, a cousin of Charles Darwin, empirically investigated the role of heredity in a variety of human achievements. In one early effort (Galton, 1869), he identified men who had achieved "eminence" in a variety of fields, including science, law, religion, literature, music, and the military. From biographies and other documents (as well as general reputation), he concluded that talent runs in families: very close relatives of an eminent man (his father, brother, son) were more likely to be high achievers themselves than were less close relatives.

Among Galton's cases of closely related eminent men were John Stuart Mill and his father, both respected English philosophers. Ironically, Mill himself did not subscribe to Galton's view of the predominance of hereditary influences. He pointed out that most of Galton's eminent men were also members of well-to-do families, and he attributed the relation between their achievement and their kinship to the fact that they were similar in economic well-being, social status, education, and other advantages and opportunities. In short, according to Mill, Galton's subjects rose to eminence more because of environmental factors than hereditary ones.

Advancing beyond the nature versus nurture argument engaged in by Galton and Mill (and by many others) required advances in knowledge about both genetic and environmental factors. Our modern understanding of how characteristics are transmitted from parent to offspring originated with insights achieved by Gregor Mendel, a nineteenth-century Austrian monk who observed patterns of inheritance in the pea plants in his monastery garden. Some aspects of these inheritance patterns were later discovered to occur in all living things. Further advances were made throughout the twentieth century, with a signal achievement being Watson and Crick's 1953 insight into the structure of DNA, the basic component of hereditary transmission.

The subsequent understanding of genetic processes has increased enormously, and international teams of scientists are currently in the midst of rapid and exciting

"We think it has something to do with your genome."

progress in figuring out the function of the roughly 30,000 to 60,000 genes that make up the human **genome,** the entire set of human genes. One of the insights that resulted from mapping the human genome is how much we have in common with other species. The general structure of our genes is common to all living things on earth; we humans share a large proportion of our genes with bears, beans, barnacles, and bacteria. Most of our genes are devoted, in decreasing order, to making us animals, vertebrates, mammals, primates, and—finally—humans.

As researchers have achieved better understanding of the role of hereditary factors in development, they have also come to appreciate the limits of what these factors can account for on their own. Similarly, as knowledge has grown concerning the influence of experience on development, it has become clear that experience alone rarely provides a satisfactory account. Development results from the close and continual interplay of genes and experience, from nature and nurture, and this topic is the focus of the following section.

Genetic and Environmental Forces

genome the complete set of genes that an organism possesses

genotype the genetic material an individual inherits

phenotype the observable expression of the genotype, including both body characteristics and behavior

environment every aspect of the individual and his or her surroundings other than genes

The close and continual interplay of genes and experience is exceedingly complex. To simplify our discussion of interactions among genetic and environmental factors, we will organize it around the model of hereditary and environmental influences shown in Figure 3.1. Three key elements of the model are the **genotype**—the genetic material an individual inherits; the **phenotype**—the observable expression of the genotype, including both body characteristics and behavior; and the **environment**—every aspect of the individual and his or her surroundings other than the genes themselves.

These three elements are involved in four relations that are fundamental in the development of every child: (1) the parents' genetic contribution to the child's genotype, (2) the contribution of the child's genotype to his or her own phenotype, (3) the contribution of the child's environment to his or her phenotype, and (4) the influence of the child's phenotype on his or her environment. We will now consider each of these four relations in turn.

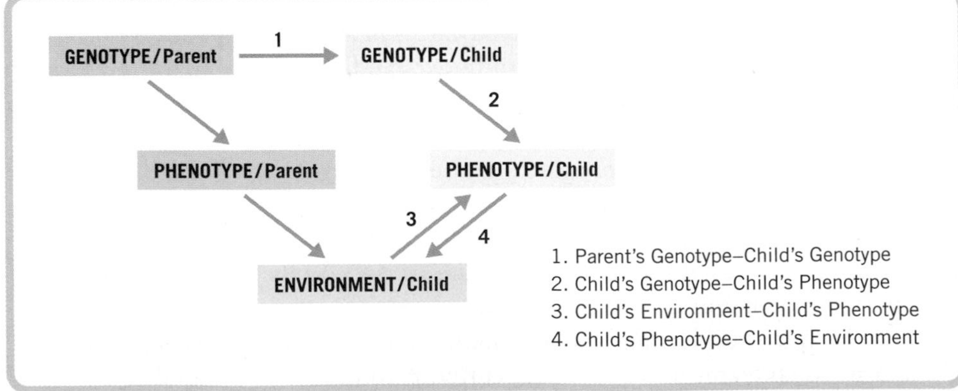

FIGURE 3.1 Development Development is a joint function of genetic and environmental factors. The four numbered relations are discussed in detail in the text.

1. Parent's Genotype—Child's Genotype

Relation 1, between the parent's genotype and the child's genotype, concerns the process of the transmission of genetic material—chromosomes and genes—from parent to offspring. The nucleus of every cell in the body contains **chromosomes,** long threadlike molecules made up of two twisted strands of **DNA (deoxyribonucleic acid).** DNA carries all the biochemical instructions involved in the formation and functioning of an organism. These instructions are "packaged" in **genes,** the basic unit of heredity in all living things. Genes are sections of chromosomes; more specifically, each gene is a segment of DNA that is the code for the production of one particular *protein.* Some proteins are the building blocks of the body's cells; others regulate the cells' functioning. Genes affect development and behavior only through the manufacture of proteins—"DNA's information translated into flesh and blood" (Levine & Suzuki, 1993, p. 19).

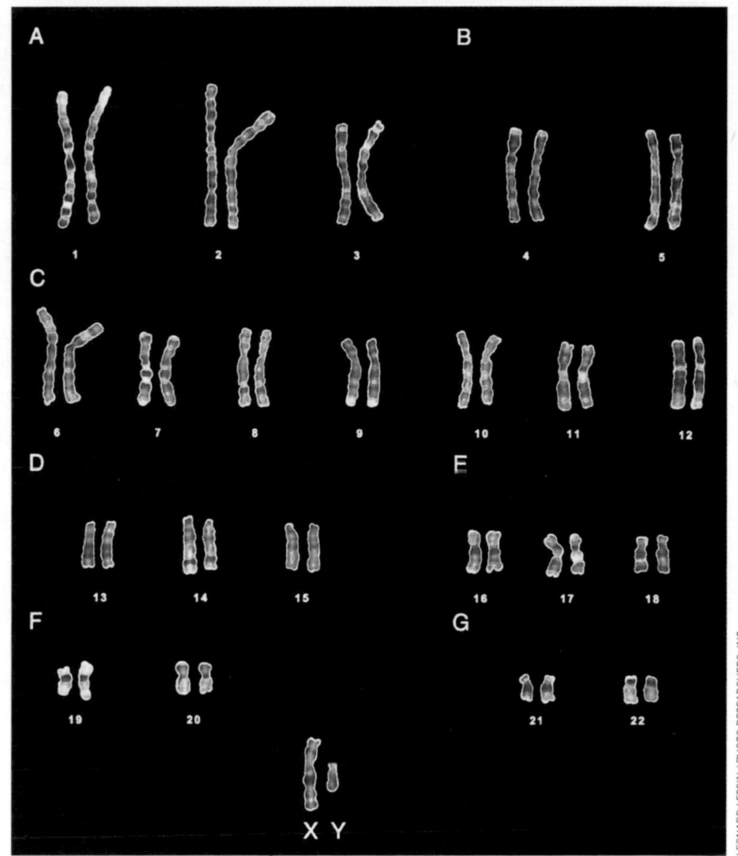

FIGURE 3.2 Karyotype This photograph, called a karyotype, shows the 23 pairs of chromosomes in a male human. The pairs of chromosomes have been arranged together in the photo, numbered according to size. The two members of the 23rd pair—the sex chromosomes—differ markedly in size; the Y chromosome that determines maleness is much smaller than the X chromosome.

Human heredity Humans normally have a total of 46 chromosomes in the nucleus of every cell, except eggs (ova) and sperm cells. (Recall from Chapter 2 that, as a result of meiosis, the cell division that produces germ cells, eggs and sperm each contain only 23 chromosomes.) The 46 chromosomes are actually 23 pairs (Figure 3.2). With one exception, the two members of each chromosome pair are of the same general size and shape and carry genes of the same type. That is, each pair carries, at corresponding locations, sequences of DNA that are relevant to the same traits. One member of each chromosome pair was inherited from each parent. Thus, every individual has two copies of each gene, one on the chromosome inherited from the father and one on the chromosome from the mother. Your children will each receive half of your genetic material, and your grandchildren will have one-quarter (just as you have half your genes in common with each of your parents and one-fourth with each grandparent).

Sex determination As noted above, there is one important exception to the statement that the two members of a chromosome pair are of the same size and shape (roughly the shape of the letter *x*) and contain the same genes. That exception involves the **sex chromosomes,** which determine an individual's sex. Females have two identical, largish sex chromosomes, called X chromosomes, but males have one X and one much smaller Y chromosome (so called because it has the shape of the letter *y*). Because a female has only X chromosomes, the meiotic division of her germ cells results in all her eggs having an X. However, because a male is XY, half his sperm contain an X chromosome and half a Y. For this reason, it is always the father who determines the sex of offspring: if an X-bearing sperm fertilizes an egg, a female (XX) zygote results; if the egg is fertilized by a Y-bearing sperm, the zygote is male (XY). It is the *presence* of a Y chromosome—not the fact of having only one X chromosome—that makes an individual male. A gene on the Y chromosome encodes the protein that triggers the formation of testes by activating genes on other chromosomes. Subsequently, the testosterone produced in the testes takes over the molding of maleness (Jegalian & Lahn, 2001).

chromosomes long, threadlike molecules that transmit genetic information. Chromosomes are made up of DNA.

DNA (deoxyribonucleic acid) molecules that carry all the biochemical instructions involved in the formation and functioning of an organism

genes sections of chromosomes that are the basic unit of heredity in all living things

sex chromosomes the chromosomes that determine an individual's gender

R. ELLIS / CORBIS SYGMA

These Elvis impersonators look like Elvis, sneer like Elvis, and even sing like Elvis (sort of). But they are not the King. The probability that any two humans have the same genotype is essentially zero.

Diversity and individuality As we have seen, genes guarantee that we will be similar in certain ways to other people both at the species level (we are all bipedal and have opposable thumbs, for example) and at the individual level (i.e., family resemblances). Genes also guarantee differences, both at the species and individual levels. Several mechanisms contribute to genetic diversity among people.

One such mechanism is **mutation,** a change in a section of DNA. Some mutations are random, spontaneous errors, while others are caused by environmental factors. Most are deleterious. Mutations that occur in germ cells can be passed on to offspring; many inherited diseases and disorders originated from a mutated gene. (Box 3.1 discusses the genetic transmission of diseases and disorders.)

Occasionally, however, a mutation that occurs in a germ cell or early in prenatal development makes individuals more viable, that is, more likely to survive, perhaps by increasing their resistance to some disease or by increasing their ability to adapt to some crucial aspect of their environment. Such favorable mutations provide the basis for evolution, because a person with the mutated gene is more likely to survive long enough to produce offspring, who, in turn, are likely to possess the mutated gene, thus heightening their chance of surviving and reproducing.

A second mechanism that promotes variability among individuals is the *random assortment* of chromosomes in the formation of egg and sperm. During meiosis, the 23 pairs of chromosomes are shuffled randomly, with chance determining which member of each pair goes into each new egg or sperm. This means that, for each germ cell, there are 2^{23}, or 8.4 million, possible combinations of chromosomes. Thus, when two germ cells—sperm and egg—unite, the odds are essentially zero that any two individuals—even members of the same family—would have the same genotype (except, of course, identical twins). Further variation is introduced by the fact that during meiosis the two members of a pair of chromosomes sometimes swap pieces; in a process known as **crossing over,** sections of DNA switch from one chromosome to the other. Consequently, the chromosomes that parents pass to their offspring are constituted differently from their own.

2. Child's Genotype—Child's Phenotype

We now turn to Relation 2 shown in Figure 3.1, the relation between one's genotype and one's phenotype. Notice that in the figure the child's phenotype has arrows pointing toward it from both the child's genotype and the environment, indicating that the characteristics of any child are a joint function of his or her unique genetic endowment and unique environment. In this section, we focus on genetic factors that affect the phenotype. In subsequent sections we will focus on how the phenotype is affected by environmental factors.

Our examination of the genetic contribution to the phenotype begins with a key fact: Although every cell in your body contains copies of all the genes you received from your parents, only some of those genes are expressed. At any time in any cell in the body, some genes are active, while others are not. Some genes that are hard at work in neurons are totally at rest in toenail cells. There are several reasons for this.

Gene expression: Developmental changes Human development proceeds normally, from conception to death, only if genes get turned on or off in the right place, at the right time, and for the right length of time. Some genes are turned on in only a few cells and for only a few hours and then are switched off permanently. Other genes are involved in the basic functioning of almost all cells almost all the time.

The switching on and off of genes is controlled in several ways, including by **regulator genes**—genes that control the activity of other genes—and by

mutation a change in a section of DNA. Mutations can contribute to genetic diversity among people, but most have a deleterious effect on the individual.

crossing over the process by which sections of DNA switch from one chromosome to the other. Crossing over promotes variability among individuals.

regulator genes genes that control the activity of other genes hormones. The activation or inactivation of one gene is always part of a chain of genetic events. When one gene switches on, it causes another gene to turn on or off, which has an impact on the status of yet other genes, and so on. The continuous switching on and off of genes underlies development throughout life, from the initial prenatal differentiation of cells to the gene-induced events of puberty to many of the changes related to aging, such as graying hair, reduced organ capacity, and menopause.

alleles two or more different forms of a gene for a particular trait

dominant allele the allele that, if present, gets expressed

recessive allele the allele that is not expressed if a dominant allele is present

homozygous a description of a person who inherits two of the same allele for a trait

heterozygous a description of a person who inherits two different alleles for a trait

Gene expression: Dominance patterns Many of an individual's genes are never expressed, and many others are only partially expressed. This is because about a third of human genes have two or more different forms, known as **alleles.** The alleles of a given gene influence the same trait or characteristic (e.g., eye color), but they contribute to different developmental outcomes (e.g., brown, blue, hazel, gray eyes).

Let's consider the simplest pattern of gene expression—the pattern of inheritance discovered by Mendel. Some genes have only two alleles, one of which is **dominant** and the other **recessive.** In this pattern, a person inherits either two of the same allele—and is said to be **homozygous** for the trait in question—or two different alleles—and is said to be **heterozygous** for the trait. When an individual is heterozygous for a trait, the instructions of the dominant allele will be expressed. When an individual is homozygous, with either two dominant or two recessive alleles, the corresponding trait will be expressed. (See Figure 3.3.)

To illustrate, let's consider two traits of no importance to human survival: the ability to roll one's tongue lengthwise and curly hair. If you can roll your tongue lengthwise into the shape of a tube, then at least one, but not necessarily both, of your parents must also possess this remarkable talent. From this statement (and Figure 3.3), you should be able to figure out that tongue rolling is governed by a dominant allele.

Turning to our second trait, if you have straight hair, then both of your parents must carry an allele for this trait. It is possible, however, that neither of them actually has straight hair. Because straight hair is governed by a recessive gene and curly hair by a dominant gene, Moe and Larry, with their radically different hairdos shown on page 10, could have had the same parents, both with hair like Larry's. They could not have had parents who looked like Moe.

The sex chromosomes present an interesting wrinkle in the story of dominance patterns. The Y chromosome, being smaller than the X chromosome, has only about a third as many genes on it. As a result, its alleles are less likely to be expressed. Suppose, for example, that a woman inherits a recessive allele on the X chromosome from her mother. Chances are, she will have a dominant allele on the chromosome from her father to suppress it. Now suppose that a man inherits the same recessive allele on the X chromosome from his mother. Chances are, because the Y chromosome from his father is so small, he will not have a dominant allele to override it, so he will develop the trait.

We now have a clue to the greater vulnerability of males described in the previous chapter (Box 2.2): they are more likely to suffer a variety of inherited disorders caused by recessive alleles on their X chromosome. Well-known examples of X-linked disorders (those transmitted on the X chromosome and hence more common in males) include *hemophilia* (a disorder in which blood

FIGURE 3.3 Mendelian inheritance patterns Below are the Mendelian inheritance patterns for two brown-haired parents who are both heterozygous for hair color. The allele for brown hair (B) is dominant, and that for blond hair (b) is recessive. Note that these parents have three chances out of four of producing children with brown hair. They have two chances in four of producing brown-haired children who carry the gene for blond hair.

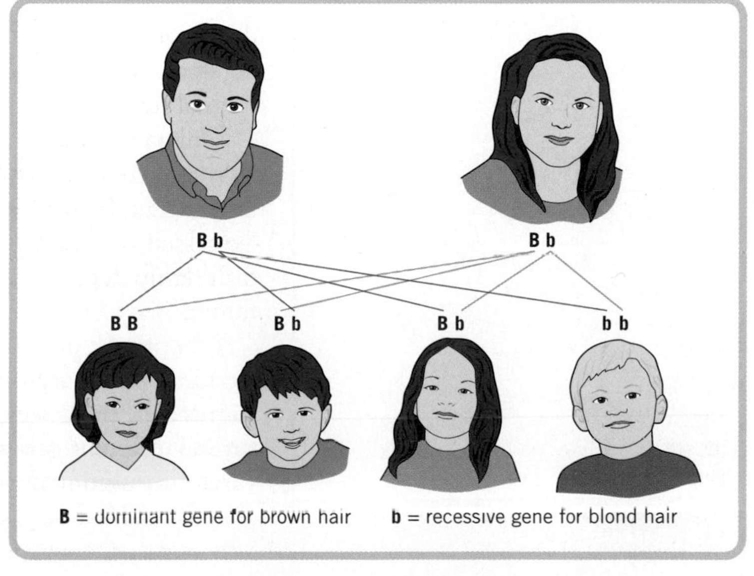

applications

Genetic Transmission of Diseases and Disorders

Some 5,000 human diseases and disorders are presently known to have genetic origins. Such conditions can be inherited in several different ways.

Dominant–Recessive Patterns

Many conditions show straightforward Mendelian (dominant–recessive) patterns of inheritance. For many serious genetic disorders, only an individual with two recessive alleles will have the condition. Recessive-gene diseases include PKU (discussed on p. 92) and sickle-cell anemia (discussed below), as well as Tay-Sachs disease, cystic fibrosis, and many others. Disorders that are caused by a dominant gene include Huntington's disease and neurofibromatosis.

In some cases, a single gene can have both deleterious and beneficial effects. Sickle-cell anemia is a debilitating and sometimes fatal blood disorder that affects about 1 out of every 50 West Africans and 1 in 400 African-Americans (Levine & Suzuki, 1993). A child who inherits a sickle-cell gene from both parents will suffer from from the disease. People with one normal and one sickle-cell gene have some abnormality in their blood cells but usually experience no negative effects. In fact, if they live in regions of the world—like Africa—where malaria is common, they benefit, because the sickle cells confer resistance against this deadly disease. In the nineteenth century, as Europeans (who lack the sickle-cell gene) began exploring Africa, malaria came to be known as the "white man's disease."

LEVINE & SUZUKI, 1993

Several cases of XY females have been detected through testing done to prevent males competing as females in the Olympics. Spanish athlete Maria Jose Martinez Patino (an XY female) was barred from Olympic competition for many years after her condition was discovered through genetic testing. She eventually won the right to compete in the 1992 Barcelona games.

Polygenic Inheritance

Many common human diseases and disorders are believed to result from the combined action of multiple genes, often in conjunction with environmental factors. Among the many diseases in this category are some forms of cancer and heart disease. Psychiatric disorders, such as schizophrenia, and behavior disorders, such as attention-deficit hyperactivity disorder (ADHD), also belong to this category.

Sex-Linked Inheritance

As mentioned in the text, some conditions are carried on the X chromosome and are much more common in males. (Females can inherit such conditions, but only in the very rare event that they inherit recessive alleles on both of their X chromosomes.) Sex-linked disorders range from relatively minor problems, like male-pattern baldness and red–green color blindness, to very serious disorders, including hemophilia and Duchenne's muscular dystrophy.

Chromosomal Anomalies

Another category of genetic disorder originates with errors in germ-cell division that

does not clot normally), red–green color blindness (inability to tell the difference between shades of red and green), and *fragile X syndrome* (a disorder involving mental retardation).

Only a few human traits follow the simple Mendelian pattern described above, in which there are two alleles, one dominant and one recessive, affecting one particular trait. Instead, a single gene can affect multiple traits, both alleles can be fully expressed or blended in heterozygous individuals, and some genes are expressed differently depending on whether they are inherited from the mother or from the father.

Inheritance patterns are even more complicated for most of the traits and behaviors of primary interest to behavioral scientists. These traits, such as shyness, aggression, thrill seeking, and empathy, involve **polygenic inheritance,** in which several different genes contribute to any given phenotypic outcome. There is great variability among people on such characteristics and few neat categories like being able or unable to roll your tongue or having curly or straight hair.

3.1

result in a zygote that has either more or less than the normal complement of chromosomes. Most such zygotes cannot survive, but some do. Down syndrome is caused by extra chromosomal material, most often an additional copy of chromosome 21. It most commonly originates when the mother's egg cells do not divide properly, and the egg that is fertilized contains an extra copy of chromosome 21. The probability of such errors in cell division increases with age, and the incidence of giving birth to a child with Down syndrome is markedly higher for women over 35 than for younger women. The child pictured here shows some of the facial features common to individuals with Down syndrome, which is also marked by mental retardation (ranging from mild to severe), a number of physical problems, and a sweet temperament.

Other disorders arise from extra or missing sex chromosomes. For example, Kleinfelter syndrome, which occurs in males, involves an extra X chromosome (XXY); Turner syndrome, which occurs in females, involves having only one (XO). Turner syndrome (which affects 1 in 2,500 females) is characterized by short stature and stunted sexual development at puberty. Girls whose X chromosome came from their mother have more social and academic difficulties than those who inherited their sole X chromosome from their father. This is an example of a gene that functions differently depending on the parent from whom it was inherited.

Regulator Gene Defect

A defect in the regulator gene that initiates the development of a male can interrupt the normal chain of events, occasionally resulting in a newborn that has female genitalia but is genetically male (an XY female). Such cases often come to light when a young woman fails to begin menstruating or when a fertility clinic discovers that the reason a couple has failed to conceive is that the person trying to get pregnant is genetically male.

RICHARD HUTCHINGS / SCIENCE SOURCE/PHOTO RESEARCHERS, INC.

The most common *identified* cause of mental retardation is Down syndrome, which occurs in about 1 of every 1,000 births in the United States. The risk increases dramatically with the age of the parents, especially the mother; by the age of 45, the mother has 1 chance in 32 of having a baby with Down syndrome. The degree of retardation varies greatly and depends in part on the kind of care and encouragement childen receive.

3. Child's Environment—Child's Phenotype

We now come to Relation 3 in our model—the impact of the environment on the child's phenotype. (Remember, the environment includes everything not in the genetic material itself.) As the model indicates, the child's observable characteristics result from environmental factors acting in concert with the child's genetic makeup. (Think about Lucy as you read this section.)

Because of the continuous interaction of genotype and environment, a given genotype will develop differently in different environments. This idea is expressed by the concept of the **norm of reaction** (Dobzhansky, 1955), which refers to all the phenotypes that could theoretically result from a given genotype in relation to all the environments in which it could survive and develop. According to this concept, for any given genotype in varying environments, one would expect a range of outcomes. A child with a given genotype whose environment is free of lead might be well above average in intelligence; the same child might suffer brain damage and mental retardation if he or she chews on lead paint chips littering the

polygenic inheritance inheritance in which traits are governed by more than one gene

norm of reaction the concept that encompasses all the phenotypes that can theoretically result from a given genotype in relation to all the environments in which it can survive and develop

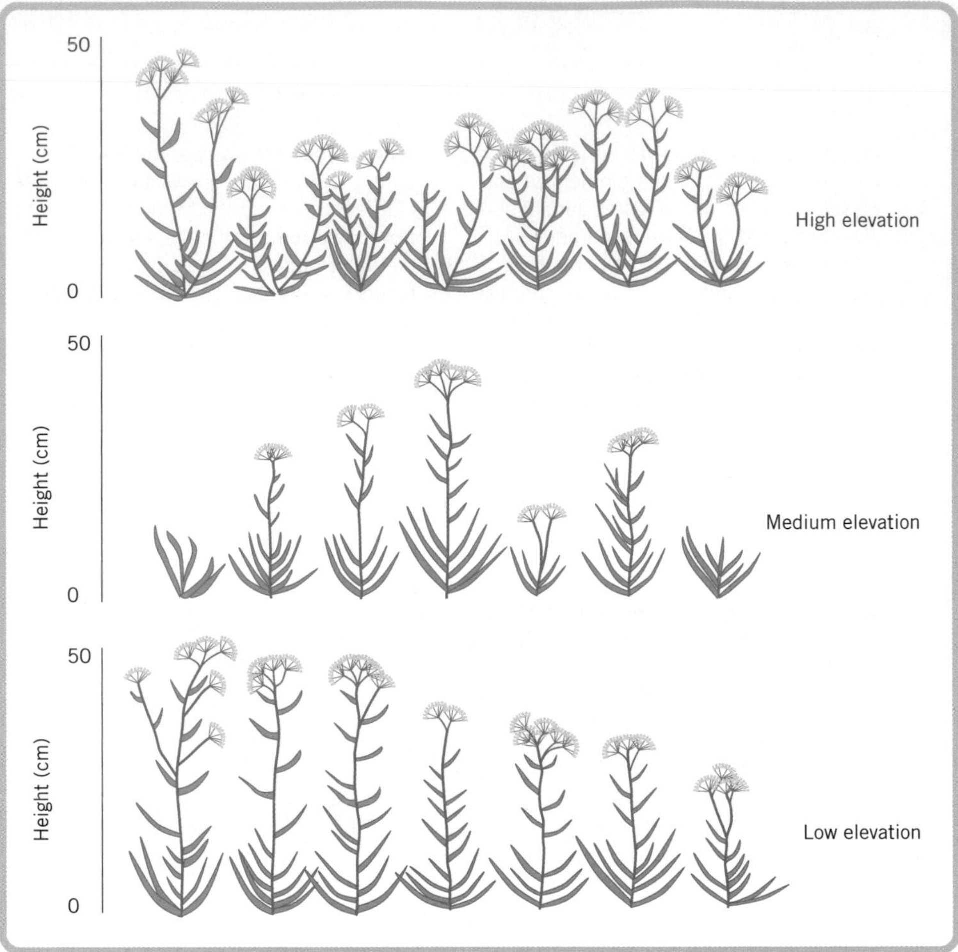

FIGURE 3.4 The norm of reaction concept Three cuttings were made from each of seven individual plants. One cutting from each plant was then planted at each of three different elevations, ranging from sea level to high mountains. As you can see, the order of the heights of the plants growing at the higher elevations is different from the ordering of the plants at sea level. No plant is consistently either the tallest or the shortest across the three environments. "The phenotype is the unique consequence of a particular genotype developing in a particular environment" (Lewontin, 1982, pp. 22–23).

home. Figure 3.4 offers a straightforward illustration of the norm of reaction in a genotype–environment interaction.

Classic example of genotype–environment interaction Genotype–environment interactions can be studied directly through research in which scientists randomly assign animals with known genotypes to be raised in a wide variety of environmental conditions. If genetically identical animals develop differently in different environments, researchers can infer that environmental effects must be responsible. Scientists cannot, of course, randomly assign humans to different rearing conditions, but we still have powerful examples of genotype–environment interactions for humans.

One such example is **phenylketonuria (PKU),** a disorder related to a defective recessive gene on chromosome 12. Individuals who inherit this gene from both parents cannot metabolize phenylalanine, an amino acid present in many foods and in artificial sweeteners. If they eat a normal diet, phenylalanine accumulates in the bloodstream and prevents normal brain development, resulting in severe mental retardation. However, if infants with the PKU gene are identified shortly after birth and placed on a stringent diet free of phenylalanine, retardation can be avoided. Thus, a given genotype results in quite different phenotypes—severe retardation or relatively normal intelligence—depending on environmental circumstances.

phenylketonuria (PKU) a disorder related to a defective recessive gene on chromosome 12 that prevents metabolism of phenylalanine. Without early diagnosis and a properly restricted diet, PKU can lead to severe mental retardation.

Parental contributions to child's environment Obviously, a highly salient and important part of a child's environment is his or her parents—the general home environment they provide, the manner in which they interact with the child, the experiences they arrange for the child, the encouragement they offer the child for particular behaviors and activities, and so on. Less obvious is the idea that the environment that parents provide for their children is due in part to their own genetic makeup. Parents' behavior toward their children (e.g., how warm or reserved they are, how patient or explosive) is genetically influenced, as are the kinds of activities and resources to which they expose their children (Plomin & Bergeman, 1991). Thus, the child of a parent with a high level of musical ability is likely to hear more music while growing up than is a child of less musically talented parents. To take another example, if we assume that interest in reading and reading skill are substantially influenced by genetic factors, it is easy to imagine the effect of parental genotype on children's environment. Parents who enjoy and value reading and who are skilled readers are likely to read often for pleasure and information, and they are also likely to read frequently to their children. In addition, committed readers are likely to buy lots of books and magazines and to have them around the house. They are also more likely to take their children to library story hours and to encourage them to have their own library card. In contrast, parents for whom reading is challenging and not a source of pleasure are less likely to provide a highly literate environment for their children (Scarr, 1992).

COURTESY OF JUDY DELOACHE

This parent enjoys reading novels for pleasure and reads extensively for her work. She is providing a rich literary environment for her young child.

4. Child's Phenotype—Child's Environment

Finally, Relation 4 in the model restates the *active child* theme—the child as a source of his or her own development. As noted in Chapter 1, children are not just the passive recipients of a preexisting environment. Rather, in two important ways they are active creators of the environment in which they live. First, by virtue of their nature and behavior, they actively evoke certain kinds of responses from others (Scarr, 1992; Scarr & McCartney, 1983). Babies who enjoy being cuddled are more likely to receive cuddling than are squirmy babies. Impulsive children no doubt hear "No," "Don't," "Stop," and "Be careful" more often than inhibited children do. Indeed, there is evidence that the degree to which parent–child relationships are mutually responsive is largely a function of the child's genetically influenced behavioral characteristics, that is, the behavior that children evoke from their parents (Deater-Deckard & O'Connor, 2000).

The second way in which children create their own environment is by actively selecting surroundings and experiences conducive to their interests, talents, and personality characteristics (Scarr, 1992). As soon as infants become capable of self-locomotion, for example, they start seeking out objects in the environment that they want to explore—and not necessarily objects their parents approve of their exploring! Beginning in the preschool years, children's friendship opportunities increasingly depend on their own characteristics, as they choose playmates and pals with whom they feel compatible—the "birds of a feather flock together" phenomenon. And, as we noted in Chapter 1, with age, children play an increasingly active role in selecting their own environment. As they gain more autonomy, they increasingly select aspects of the environment that fit their temperament and abilities. To go back to the example mentioned earlier, children who enjoy reading will read more books than children who find reading tedious. The more they read, the more skillful readers they become, leading them to choose increasingly more challenging books, leading them, in turn, to acquire advanced vocabulary and enhanced general knowledge.

Our discussion of the four kinds of gene–environment interactions has emphasized the vast complexity of the developmental process. Understanding how nature and nurture work together in this process is a daunting task but one in which a great deal of progress has been made, as you will see in the following section on how developmental scientists have been probing these interactions.

Behavioral Genetics

The rapidly expanding area of psychology known as **behavioral genetics** is concerned with how variation in behavior and development results from the combination of genetic and environmental factors. Behavioral geneticists ask the same sort of question Galton asked about eminence: "Why are people different from one another?" (Plomin, 1990). Why, in any group of human beings, do we vary in terms of how smart, sociable, depressed, aggressive, and religious we are? The behavioral geneticists' answer is that *all* behavioral traits are **heritable,** that is, influenced to some degree by hereditary factors, and that they all develop within an environment (Turkheimer, 2000). The traits that have been of primary interest to behavioral geneticists—intelligence, sociability, mood, aggression, and the like—are both *polygenic,* that is, affected by the combination of many genes, and **multifactorial,** that is, affected by many environmental factors as well. Thus, the sources of variation are vast. To fully answer Galton's question, behavioral geneticists try to tease apart genetic and environmental contributions to the differences observed among a population of people or other animals.

Two premises underlie this endeavor: (1) To the extent that genetic factors are important for a given trait or behavior, individuals who are genotypically similar should be phenotypically similar. In other words, behavior patterns should "run in families"; children should be more similar to their parents and siblings than to second- or third-degree relatives or unrelated individuals. (2) To the extent that shared environmental factors are important, individuals who have been reared together should be more similar than people who have not.

Behavioral Genetic Research Designs

As it was for Galton, the mainstay of modern behavioral genetics research is the *family study.* In order to examine genetic and environmental contributions to a given trait or characteristic, behavioral geneticists first measure that trait in people who vary in terms of genetic relatedness—parents and children, identical and fraternal twins, nontwin siblings, and so on. Next, they compare correlations between the measure of the trait in pairs of individuals who represent different categories of family relationships. (As you may recall from Chapter 1, a correlation coefficient expresses the extent to which two variables are related; the higher the correlation, the more precisely scores on one variable can be predicted from scores on the other.) Then they compare the resulting correlations to see if they are (1) higher for closely related individuals than for less closely related or unrelated people and (2) higher for individuals who share the same environment than for people who do not.

There are several specialized family-study designs that are particularly helpful in assessing genetic and environmental influences. One is the *twin-study* design, which compares the correlations for identical (monozygotic) twins with those for same-sex fraternal (dizygotic) twins. As you will recall, identical twins have 100% of their genes in common, whereas fraternal twins are only 50% genetically similar

behavioral genetics the science concerned with how variation in behavior and development results from the combination of genetic and environmental factors

heritable anything (characteristics, traits, etc.) influenced by heredity

multifactorial refers to the involvement of many factors in any outcome (just like nontwin siblings). The degree of similarity in the environment of the two types of twins is generally assumed to be equal or nearly so. Both types of twins shared the same womb, were born at the same time, are always the same age when tested. Furthermore, if they grow up together, they live in the same family and community. Thus, assuming different levels of genetic similarity and essentially equal environmental similarity, the difference between the correlations for the two types of twins is treated as an index of the importance of genetic factors in development. If the correlation between identical twins on a given trait or behavior is substantially higher than that between fraternal twins, it is assumed that genetic factors are substantially responsible for the difference.

Another family-study design used for assessing genetic and environmental influences is the *adoption study,* in which researchers examine whether adopted children's scores on a given measure are correlated more highly with those of their biological parents and siblings or with those of their adoptive parents and siblings. Genetic influences are inferred to the extent that children resemble their biological relatives more than their adoptive ones. The ideal behavioral genetics design—adoptive twin studies—combines the other two. It compares identical twins who grew up together versus identical twins who were separated shortly after birth and raised apart. If the correlations for twins reared apart are similar to those for twins reared together, it suggests that environmental factors have little effect. Conversely, if the correlations between identical twins who grew up in different environments are lower than the correlations for those who grew up together, a strong environmental influence is inferred. Box 3.2 describes some of the remarkable findings that have emerged from studies of twins reared apart, as well as some of the problems with such research.

Family studies of intelligence By far, the characteristic that has most often been the focus of behavioral genetics family studies is intelligence. As can be seen in Table 3.1, which summarizes the results of over 100 family studies of IQ through adolescence, the pattern of results reveals both genetic and environmental influences. Genetic influence is shown by generally higher correlations for higher degrees of genetic similarity. Most notable is the finding that identical twins resemble one another more than do same-sex fraternal twins.

At the same time, environmental influences are reflected in the fact that identical twins are not identical in terms of IQ. Further evidence for an environmental role is that twins who are reared together are more similar than those adopted into different families. In fact, in general—at least through adolescence—correlations are higher for people who share the same family environment (whether they are biologically related or not) than for individuals of the same degree of genetic relatedness who live apart. Note, however, that the correlations for adoptive families are probably inflated by selective placement, because adoption agencies generally try to place children with adoptive families of the same general background and race.

After adolescence, the picture is quite different from that presented in Table 3.1. In adulthood, the

TABLE 3.1

Summary of Family Studies of Intelligence

Average Familial IQ Correlations (*R*)

Relationship	Average *R*	Number of Pairs
	Reared-together biological relatives	
MZ twins	0.86	4,672
DZ twins	0.60	5,533
Siblings	0.47	26,473
Parent–offspring	0.42	8,433
Half-siblings	0.35	200
Cousins	0.15	1,176
	Reared-apart biological relatives	
MZ twins	0.72	65
Siblings	0.24	203
Parent–offspring	0.24	720
	Reared-together nonbiological relatives	
Siblings	0.32	714
Parent–offspring	0.24	720

Note: MZ = monozygotic; DZ = dizygotic.
Source: McGue, Bouchard, Iacono, & Lykken (1993)

individual differences 3.2

Identical Twins Reared Apart

Oskar Stohr and Jack Yufa are identical twins who were separated shortly after their birth in Trinidad. Oskar was raised by his grandmother in Germany as a Catholic and a Nazi. Jack was raised by his father, in the Caribbean, as a Jew. Despite their very different backgrounds, when the brothers first met as middle-aged men recruited for a research study in Minneapolis, they discovered a remarkable number of similarities between them:

> They share idiosyncrasies galore: they like spicy foods and sweet liqueurs, are absent-minded, have a habit of falling asleep in front of the television, think it's funny to sneeze in a crowd of strangers, flush the toilet before using it, store rubber bands on their wrists, read magazines back to front, dip buttered toast in their coffee. Oskar is domineering toward women and yells at his wife, which Jack did before he was separated. (Holden, 1980, p. 1324)

Jack and Oskar are participants in the Minnesota Study of Twins Reared Apart, an extensive study of identical twins separated early in life (Bouchard, Lykken, McGue, Segal, & Tellegen, 1990). Over 100 pairs of such twins have been located, recruited for the study, and brought to Minneapolis to undergo an extensive battery of physiological and psychological tests. In many cases, twin siblings were meeting for the first time since they were infants. (The reunited twins in the photo showed almost as many striking similarities as did Jack and Oskar, including their choice of occupation as firemen.) The motivation for this large-scale study is to examine genetic and environmental contributions to development and behavior by examining individuals who are genetically identical but who grew up in different environments.

The Minnesota team of investigators has been struck by the extent of similarity they have found in the separated twins they have studied; they have identified genetic contributions to "almost every behavioral trait so far investigated from reaction time to religiosity" (Bouchard et al., 1990). Particularly strong correlations have been found for traits as diverse as IQ, reaction to stress, aggression, and traditionalism.

As striking as the similarities between separated twins may be, there are several problems with automatically concluding that these similarities can be attributed to genetic factors. One is the issue of selective placement mentioned in the text: the environments of the separated siblings are often similar in many ways. It is extremely rare for separated twins to be raised like Jack and Oskar, with different languages, religions, and cultures. In fact, the majority of the twins in most behavioral genetics studies are from predominantly white, middle-class families in Western countries. As one behavioral geneticist commented:

> Take one of those kids and put him in a *really* different environment, like in a family of bushmen in Africa, or in a farming village in mainland China, and *then* come back twenty years later and see if you find two firemen who dress the same! (Levine & Suzuki, 1993, p. 241)

BOB SACHA

Identical twins Gerald Levey and Mark Newman were separated at birth and reared separately in middle-class Jewish homes in the New York area. When reunited at the age of 31, they discovered they were both firemen with droopy moustaches, wearing aviator-style sunglasses.

correlation for identical twins remains about the same as in the table (above .80), but the correlation for fraternal twins is lower (around .40, compared with .60 in the table) (Pedersen, Plomin, Nesselroade, & McClearn, 1992). The correlation for genetically unrelated individuals who were reared together is essentially zero (McGue, Bouchard, Iacono, & Lykken, 1993).

These patterns are consistent with the idea of phenotype–environment correlation discussed earlier—the fact that people actively construct their environment (McGue et al., 1993; Scarr & McCartney, 1983). As children get older, parental influence over their activities declines, and they increasingly control their own experiences. It may be that identical twins' IQs remain similar into adulthood because they select similar levels of intellectual stimulation, whereas fraternal twins become increasingly dissimilar because they choose divergent experiences for themselves (Scarr & McCartney, 1983).

Heritability

In their approach to the nature–nurture question, many behavioral geneticists attempt to quantify the degree to which genes contribute to various traits. To estimate how much of the variability in measures of a given trait is attributable to genetic and environmental factors, they derive heritability estimates from correlations of the type shown in Table 3.1. **Heritability** is a statistical estimate of the proportion of the measured variance on a given trait among individuals in a given population that is attributable to genetic differences among those individuals.

heritability a statistical estimate of the proportion of the measured variance on a given trait among individuals in a given population that is attributable to genetic differences among those individuals

An important point to understand about heritability estimates is that they tell us nothing about the relative contributions of genetic and environmental factors to the development of an individual. Instead, they estimate the amount of the variation among a given population of people that is due to differences in their genes. A simple analogy is provided in Figure 3.5. The heritability score for intelligence, for example, is generally considered to be approximately 50%, based on estimates that range from 30% to 70% (Plomin, 1990). This means that, for the population studied, roughly 50% of the variation in IQ scores is due to genetic differences among the members of the population. (It does *not* mean that 50% of your IQ score is due to your genetic makeup and 50% is due to your experience.) Note that this heritability score indicates that the environmental contribution to the variation in IQ is also approximately 50%.

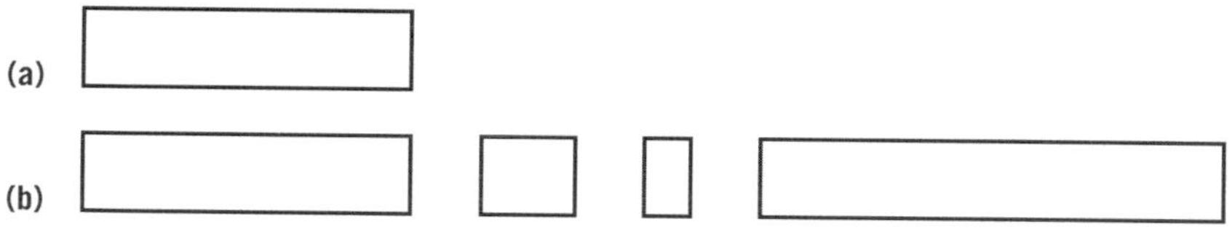

(a)

(b)

FIGURE 3.5 Genes *and* environment Which is more important for determining the area of rectangle (a)—its length or its width? Obviously, this is a meaningless question, because area is the product of both dimensions simultaneously. However, for the *group* of rectangles in (b) we *can* ask what contribution each dimension makes to variations in area among the members of the group. Here, most of the variation is due to differences in width. By analogy, asking whether some trait of an individual person is more due to genes or to environment is meaningless; but we can sensibly ask how much of the variation among a group of individuals can be attributed to each factor.

Behavioral genetic analyses have been applied to many diverse aspects of human behavior, several of which you will encounter in other chapters of this book. To cite just a few examples, substantial heritability has been reported for *infant activity level* (Saudino & Eaton, 1991), *temperament* (Goldsmith, Buss, & Lemery, 1997), *reading disability* (DeFries & Gillis, 1993), and *antisocial behavior* (Gottesman & Goldsmith, 1994). Substantial heritability has even been reported for *divorce* (McGue & Lykken, 1992) and *TV viewing* (Plomin, Corley, DeFries, & Fulker, 1990).

The implausibility of there being "broken home" or "couch potato" genes reminds us of an important point: in spite of the common use of the phrase, there are no genes "for" particular behavior patterns. As we stressed before, genes do nothing more than code for proteins, so they affect behavior only insofar as those proteins affect the sensory, neural, and other physiological processes involved in behavior. Thus, the heritability score for divorce may be related to a genetic predisposition to, for example, seek out novelty, and the score for TV viewing may be related to a genetically based low activity level or short attention span.

Heritability estimates have been criticized, both from within psychology (e.g., Gottlieb, 1992; Gottlieb, Wahlsten, & Lickliter, 1997; Lerner, 1995) and from outside it (e.g., Levine & Suzuki, 1993; Lewontin, 1982). Part of the criticism stems from the fact that heritability estimates are often misapplied and misinterpreted. For example, many people fail to realize the point we just emphasized: *Heritability scores apply only to populations, not to individuals.* This point is often misunderstood or ignored, especially in popular accounts of behavioral genetics research.

Further, *a heritability estimate applies only to a particular group living in a particular environment at a particular time.* The IQ correlations shown in Table 3.1, and the heritability estimates derived from them, may not be the same for impoverished families in the United States, upper-class Hindus in India, or Turkish farmers. We have already seen that they are not even the same for the same individuals in childhood and adulthood.

In addition, heritability estimates vary according to the level of genetic and environmental similarity of the population in question. For a dramatic (if not very realistic) example, suppose that in a futuristic world, a large number of clones (genetically identical individuals) were raised in a variety of different environments. The heritability score for any trait in this population would be zero, because, without any variation in genetic makeup, none of the variability in outcome could be attributed to genetic factors. Or suppose the opposite, that people of widely varying genetic backgrounds were all reared in virtually identical environmental circumstances in which everyone had superb nutrition and medical care, nice homes, loving families, and so forth. In this case, the heritability estimate would be extremely high, because almost none of the differences among these people could be attributed to differing environments.

Returning to the real world, consider the case of height. Research conducted almost exclusively with North Americans and Europeans, mostly white, mostly growing up with adequate nutrition, puts the heritability of height at around 90%. What if a large segment of this population were to experience a severe famine, while the rest remained well fed? Would heritability still be 90%? No—because the variability due to environmental factors would increase dramatically (and hence the variability that could be attributed to genetic factors would decrease equally dramatically).

A related, frequently misunderstood point is that *high heritability does not imply immutability.* The fact that a trait is highly heritable does *not* mean that there is little point in trying to improve the course of development related to that trait. Thus, for example, the fact that the heritability estimate for IQ is relatively high does not mean that the intellectual performance of young children cannot be improved by appropriate intervention efforts (as discussed in the preceding two chapters).

Finally, because they are relevant only within a given population, heritability estimates tell us nothing about differences *between* groups. The heritability score for IQ, for example, provides little insight into the meaning of differences in the IQ scores of different groups of Americans. European-Americans, on average, score 15 points higher on IQ tests than African-Americans do. Some people mistakenly assume that because IQ is estimated to be 50% heritable, the difference between the groups' IQ scores is genetically based. This assumption is totally unwarranted, given the large disparities between the groups in family income and education, quality of neighborhood schools, health care, and myriad other factors.

Environmental Effects

Every examination of genetic contributions to behavior and development is also, necessarily, a study of environmental influences: estimating heritability automatically estimates the proportion of variance *not* attributable to genetics. Because heritability estimates rarely exceed 50%, a large contribution from environmental factors is indicated. Researchers try to assess the extent to which aspects of our environment that we share with our relatives make us more alike and to what extent nonshared experiences make us different.

The most obvious source of shared environment is growing up together in the same family, and a standard estimate of *shared-environment* effects is based on the degree of similarity among adoptive siblings—biologically unrelated individuals who grew up together (Plomin, DeFries, McClearn, & Rutter, 1997). Shared-environment effects are also reflected in greater similarity between twins or other relatives than is accounted for by their genetic similarity. For example, substantial shared environmental influence has been inferred for positive affect in toddlers and young children because fraternal and identical twins reared together were equally similar in the degree to which they showed pleasure (Goldsmith et al., 1997). The source of this effect is unclear, but it could be due to some aspect of maternal behavior or personality, such as extraversion.

Behavioral geneticists have reported surprisingly little effect of shared environment on some aspects of development. For example, with respect to personality, the correlations for adoptive siblings are often near zero (Rowe, 1994). The same is true for some types of psychopathology, including schizophrenia (Gottesman, 1991). Growing up in an adoptive family with a schizophrenic sibling does not increase the risk that a child will be schizophrenic. In addition, the risk of schizophrenia is the same for the biological child of a schizophrenic parent regardless of whether that child is raised by the mentally disturbed parent or is adopted away at birth (Kety et al., 1994).

Nonshared-environment effects include effects of experiences that are unique to the individual. Even when children are growing up in the same family, they do not have all the same experiences—either inside or outside the family. Some behavioral geneticists have concluded that, for the most part, the primary effect of nonshared environmental factors is to increase the differences among family members rather than to make them more similar (Plomin & Daniels, 1987). Nonshared-environment effects are estimated from the remainder of the variance not attributable to genes or shared environment. With identical twins who were reared together, this would be the extent to which they are dissimilar on some trait. Because they are 100% alike genetically, any difference between them must be due to aspects of the environment that they did not experience in common. For many measures, this figure is around 50%.

Siblings may have quite different experiences *within the family* because of their different ages and birth order; for example, in a large family, the oldest child may have been reared by relatively young, energetic, but inexperienced, parents, whereas a much younger sibling may grow up with older, more sedentary, but more knowledgeable, parents. In addition, siblings may experience their parents' behavior toward them differently (what might be called the "Mom always loved you best" syndrome), as discussed in Chapter 1 (p. 22). Further, siblings can be affected quite differently by an event they experience in common, such as the divorce of their parents (Hetherington & Clingempeel, 1992). Finally, siblings may be highly motivated to differentiate themselves from one another (Sulloway, 1996). The younger sibling of a star student may strive to be a star athlete instead, and a child who observes a sibling disappearing into a self-destructive pattern of drug and alcohol abuse may become determined to follow a different path.

Siblings, especially those of different sex, have even more divergent experiences outside the home, such as belonging to different peer groups (Harris, 1995). Highly active brothers who both like physical challenges and thrills will have very different experiences if one joins the gymnastics team while the other hangs out with delinquents. Idiosyncratic life events—suffering a serious accident or illness, having an inspiring teacher, being bullied on the playground—can contribute further to making siblings develop differently.

review::

The four relations shown in Figure 3.1 depict the complex interplay of genetic and environmental forces in development. (1) The course of children's development is influenced by the genetic heritage they receive from their mother and father, with their sex determined solely by their father's contribution. (2) The relation between children's genotype and phenotype depends in part on dominance patterns in the expression of some genes, but most traits of primary interest to behavioral scientists are influenced by multiple genes (polygenic inheritance). (3) As the norm-of-reaction concept specifies, any given genotype will develop differently in different environments. A particularly salient part of children's environment is their parents, including their parents' own genetic makeup, which influences how parents behave toward their children. (4) Their own genetic makeup influences children to select and shape their own environment and the experiences they have in it.

The field of behavioral genetics is concerned with how development results from the interaction of genetic and environmental factors. Using the family-study methodology, behavioral geneticists compare the correlations among individuals who vary in the degree of genetic relatedness and in similarity of their rearing environments. Heritability scores are estimates of the proportion of the variance among individuals in a given population on a given trait that is attributable to genetic differences among them. Most behavioral traits that have been measured show substantial heritability; at the same time, heritability estimates reveal the close partnership of heredity and environment in development and the inappropriateness of thinking of nature and nurture as pitted against one another in a struggle for supremacy.

Brain Development

As you will see, the collaboration between nature and nurture is also central in the development of the brain and nervous system. Before discussing developmental processes in the formation of the brain, however, we need to consider the basic nature of this "most complex structure in the known universe" (Thompson, 2000, p. 1).

Fundamental to all aspects of behavioral development is the development of the central nervous system (CNS) and especially the brain. Without a functioning brain, there is no behavior. Indeed, the absence of brain activity is the legal definition of death. The brain is the font of all thought, memory, desire, disgust, imagination, personality—in short, the capacities and characteristics that make us who we are.

Over the evolutionary history of our species (that is, over the past 3 million years), the human brain expanded greatly in size. Although humans do not have the largest brains of all animals, we do have the greatest brain size relative to our body size (more than six times larger than one would expect based on other animals) (Kolb & Whishaw, 1996). Most of our brain size is achieved in the first years of development. A newborn's brain is only 25% as big as the average adult's brain, but a 3-year-old's brain is 80% as large.

The central role of the brain in human behavior was recognized as early as 3000 B.C. by the Egyptians. According to one ancient text, "If thou examinist a man having a smash in his temple. . . . If thou callest to him he is speechless and cannot speak" (quoted in Changeux, 1985, p. 4).

neurons cells that are specialized for sending and receiving electrical messages between the brain and all parts of the body, as well as within the brain itself

cell body a component of the neuron that contains the basic biological material that keeps the neuron functioning

dendrites neural fibers that receive input from other cells and conduct it toward the cell body in the form of electrical impulses

axons neural fibers that conduct electrical signals away from the cell body to connections with other neurons

Structures of the Brain

The brain is composed of a very large number of structures at a variety of different levels. We limit our discussion to two that are central to our discussion of the development of brain and behavior—the neuron and the cortex, as well as some of their various substructures.

The Neuron

The business of the brain is processing information. The basic units of the brain's remarkably powerful informational system are the more than 100 billion **neurons** (Figure 3.6), cells that are specialized for sending and receiving electrical messages between the brain and all parts of the body, as well as within the brain itself. *Sensory neurons* transmit information from sensory receptors that detect stimuli in the external environment or within the body itself; *motor neurons* transmit information from the brain to muscles and glands; and *interneurons* act as intermediaries between sensory and motor neurons.

Although they vary substantially in size, shape, and function, all neurons comprise three main components: (1) a **cell body,** which contains the basic biological material that keeps the neuron functioning; (2) **dendrites,** fibers that receive input from other cells and conduct it toward the cell body in the form of electrical impulses; and (3) an **axon,** a fiber (anywhere from a few micrometers to over a meter in length) that conducts electrical signals away from the cell body to connections with other neurons.

These connections, called **synapses,** are microscopic junctions between the axon terminal of one neuron and the dendritic branches or cell body of another. Neurons communicate with one another at synapses through a complex process in which their electrical impulses are translated into chemical messages that cross the synapses and are then translated back into electrical impulses in the receiving neuron. The total number of synapses is staggering—many trillions—with some neurons having as many as 15,000 synaptic connections with other neurons.

The brain contains other types of cells besides neurons, most notably **glial cells,** which outnumber neurons by ten to one. These cells perform a variety of critical supportive functions. One is the formation of a **myelin sheath** around certain axons, which insulates them and increases the speed and efficiency of information transmission.

synapses microscopic junctions between the axon terminal of one neuron and the dendritic branches or cell body of another. Synapses are where the communication between neurons happens.

glial cells cells in the brain that provide a variety of critical supportive functions.

myelin sheath a fatty sheath that forms around certain axons in the body and increases the speed and efficiency of information transmission in the nervous system

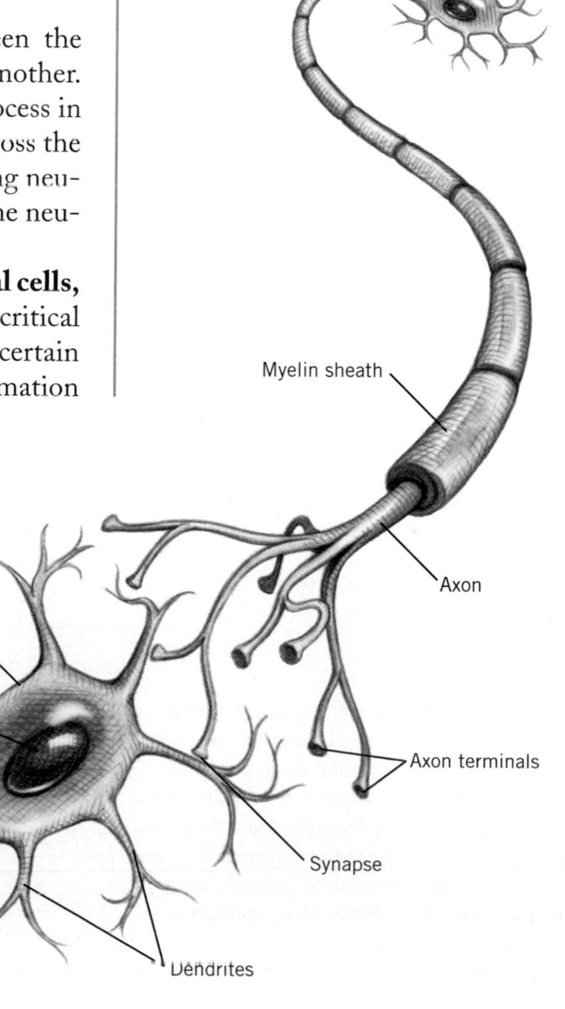

FIGURE 3.6 The neuron The *cell body* manufactures proteins and enzymes that support cell functioning, as well as *neurotransmitters,* the chemical substances that facilitate communication among neurons. The *axon* is the long shaft that conducts electrical impulses away from the cell body. Many neurons are covered with a *myelin sheath,* which enhances the speed and efficiency with which signals travel along the axon. Branches at the end of the axon have terminals that release neurotransmitters into the *synapses*—the small spaces between the axon terminals of one neuron and the dendrites or cell body of another. The *dendrites* conduct impulses toward the cell body. An axon can have synapses with thousands of other neurons. (Adapted from Banich, 1997.)

cerebral cortex the "gray matter" of the brain that plays a primary role in what is thought to be particularly human-like functioning, from seeing and hearing to writing to feeling emotion

lobes major areas of the cortex

occipital lobe the lobe of the brain that is primarily involved in processing visual information

temporal lobe the lobe of the brain that is associated with memory, visual recognition, and the processing of emotion and auditory information

parietal lobe the lobe of the brain that governs spatial processing as well as integrating sensory input with information stored in memory

frontal lobe the lobe of the brain associated with organizing behavior and the one that is thought responsible for the human ability to plan ahead

association areas parts of the brain which lie between the major sensory and motor areas that process and integrate input from those areas

The Cortex

The **cerebral cortex,** which is shown in Figure 3.7, is considered the "most human part of the human brain" (McEwen & Schmeck, 1994). There are, of course, numerous subcortical structures, but we will focus primarily on the cortex, which constitutes 80% of the brain, a much greater proportion than in other species (Kolb & Whishaw, 1996). Almost all of the evolutionary increase in overall human brain size was due to expansion of the cerebral cortex. The folds and fissures that are apparent in Figure 3.7 form during development as the brain grows within the confined space of the skull; all these convolutions make it possible to pack more cortex into the limited area.

The cortex plays a primary role in a wide variety of mental functions, from seeing and hearing to reading, writing, and doing arithmetic, to feeling compassion and communicating with others. As Figure 3.7 shows, the major areas of the cortex—the **lobes**—can be characterized in terms of the general behavioral categories with which they are associated. The **occipital lobe** is primarily involved in processing visual information. The **temporal lobe** is associated with memory, visual recognition, and the processing of emotion and auditory information. The **parietal lobe** is important for spatial processing. It is also involved in the integration of information from different sensory modalities, and it plays a role in integrating sensory input with information stored in memory and with information about internal states. The **frontal lobe,** the brain's "executive," is involved in many uniquely human abilities. It is particularly important for foresight—planning ahead and organizing behavior to achieve a goal. Information from multiple sensory systems is processed and integrated in the **association areas** that lie in between the major sensory and motor areas.

Although it is convenient to think of different cortical areas as if they were functionally specific, it is misleading to do so. Research is making it increasingly clear that complex mental functions are mediated by multiple areas of the brain. A given area may be critical for some ability, but that does not mean that control of that ability is located in that one area. (Box 3.3, pp. 104–106, examines some of the techniques that researchers use to learn about the functioning of specific brain areas.)

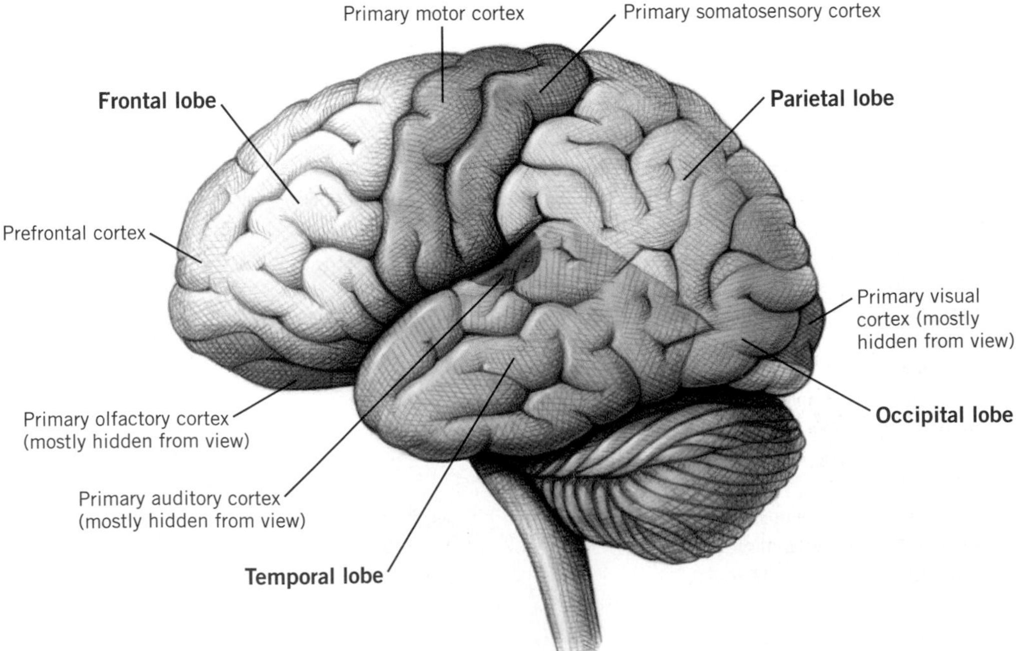

FIGURE 3.7 The human cerebral cortex This view of the left hemisphere of an adult brain shows the four major cortical regions—known as the lobes—which are divided from one another by deep fissures. Each of the primary sensory areas receives information from a particular sensory system, and the primary motor cortex controls the body's muscles. Information from multiple sensory areas is processed in association areas.

Cerebral lateralization The cortex is divided into two separate halves, or **cerebral hemispheres.** For the most part, sensory input from one side of the body goes to the opposite side of the brain, and the motor areas of the cortex control movements of the opposite side of the body. Thus, if you pick up a hot pot with your right hand, it is the left side of the brain that registers the pain and sends the message to let go immediately.

The left and right hemispheres are connected, primarily by a dense tract of nerve fibers known as the **corpus callosum,** which enables the two halves of the brain to communicate with one another. The two hemispheres are specialized for different modes of processing, a phenomenon referred to as **cerebral lateralization.** For example, in most people, the left hemisphere processes information in a piecemeal, linear manner as required for logical analysis, language, and sequential tasks; in contrast, the right hemisphere processes in a holistic manner that is better for dealing with spatial information. (This pattern is characteristic of right-handed, but not left-handed, individuals—lefties' brains are less clearly lateralized.)

cerebral hemispheres the two halves of the cortex. For the most part, sensory input from one side of the body goes to the opposite hemisphere of the brain.

corpus callosum a dense tract of nerve fibers that enable the two hemispheres of the brain to communicate

cerebral lateralization the phenomenon that each hemisphere of the brain is specialized for different modes of processing.

neurogenesis the proliferation of neurons through cell division

spines formations on the dendrites of neurons that increase the dendrites' capacity to form connections with other neurons

myelination the formation of myelin (a fatty sheath) around the axons of neurons that speeds and increases information-processing abilities

Developmental Processes

How does the incredibly complex structure of the human brain come into being? You will not be surprised to hear that, once again, a partnership of nature and nurture is involved. Some aspects of the construction of the brain are set in motion and tightly controlled by the genes, relatively independent of experience. But, as you will see, other aspects are profoundly influenced by experience.

Neurogenesis

In the 3rd or 4th week of prenatal life, cells in the newly formed neural tube begin dividing at an astonishing rate—at peak production, 250,000 new cells are born every minute (Cowan, 1979). **Neurogenesis,** the proliferation of neurons through cell division, is virtually complete by around 18 weeks after conception (Rakic, 1995).

After their "birth," neurons, which consist of little more than a cell body at this point, migrate to their ultimate destinations. Some neurons are pushed along passively by the newer cells formed after them, whereas others, such as those destined for the cortex, actively propel themselves toward their new home.

Once neurons reach their destination, they grow and differentiate. Neurons first grow an axon and then a "bush" of dendrites (refer back to Figure 3.6), and then they take on specific structural and functional characteristics as they form the different structures of the brain. Axons elongate as they grow toward specific targets, which, depending on the neuron in question, might be anything from another neuron in the brain to a bone in the big toe. The main change in dendrites is "arborization"—an enormous increase in the size and complexity of the dendritic "tree" as a result of growth, branching, and the formation of **spines** on the branches, all of which increase the dendrites' capacity to form connections with other neurons. In the cortex, the period of most intense growth and differentiation comes after birth.

The process of **myelination,** the formation of an insulating myelin sheath around some axons, begins in the brain before birth and continues into adolescence or even later. The various cortical areas become myelinated at very different rates, possibly contributing to the different rates of development for some kinds of behavior.

a closer look

Mapping the Mind

Developmental researchers employ a variety of techniques to determine what areas of the brain are associated with particular behaviors, thoughts, and feelings and how brain functions change with age. The existence of increasingly powerful techniques for investigating brain function has sparked a revolution in our understanding of the brain and its development. Here, we provide examples of research using various techniques to map the mind and its workings.

Neuropsychological Approach

Researchers have long drawn inferences about brain function from the effects of brain damage on behavior. If a particular function is lost or impaired following damage to a given area of the brain, it is evidence that that part of the brain must be involved in that function. An example of the neuropsychological approach comes from research by Adele Diamond (1991), who has demonstrated that healthy human infants and adult monkeys with lesions in the prefrontal cortex make similar kinds of errors in searching for hidden objects (see the photos). In various studies, infants and monkeys watched as a desirable object was hidden, and after a short delay, they successfully retrieved it. On the next trial, as the subject again watched, the object was hidden at a new location. This time, however, both the healthy infants and the brain-damaged monkeys usually erred, reaching to where they had previously found the toy instead of where they had just seen it being hidden. Older infants and intact monkeys do not make this error.

Based on this and other research, Diamond concluded that in both humans and monkeys the prefrontal cortex is involved in coordinating two skills essential to the searching task—remembering the location of an object and inhibiting the tendency to respond to its previous location. She inferred from the infants' failure on the task that this area of the brain is still relatively immature before 9 months of age.

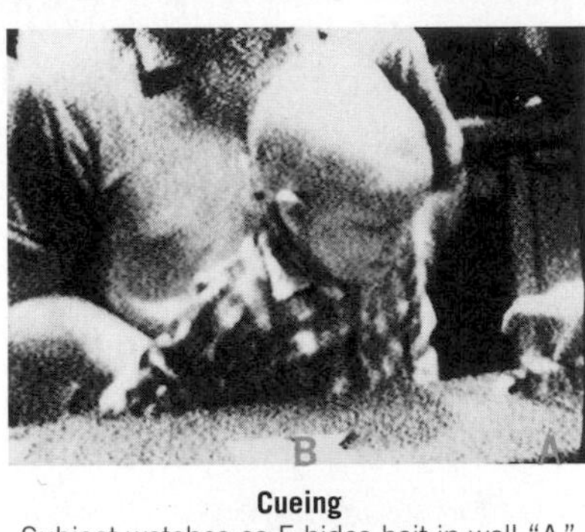

Cueing
Subject watches as E hides bait in well "A."

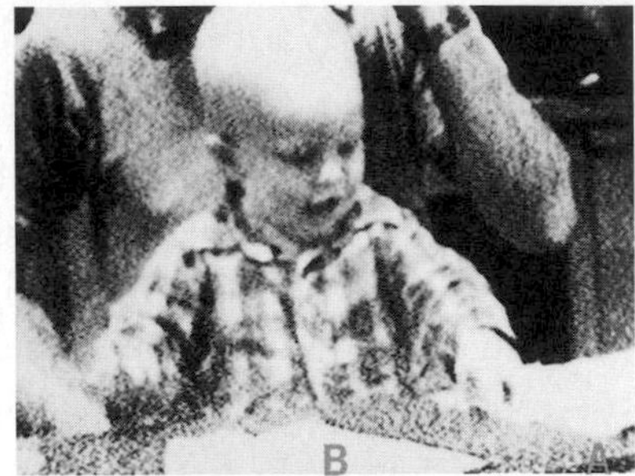

Response
Subject reaches correctly to well "A."

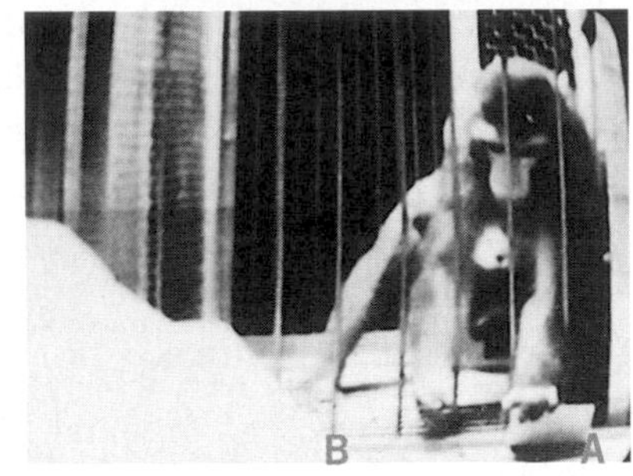

Cueing
Subject watches as E hides bait in well "B."

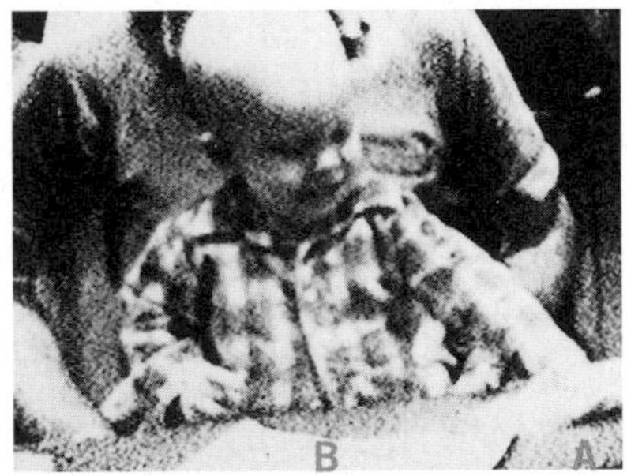

Response
Subject reaches incorrectly to well "A," which is now empty.

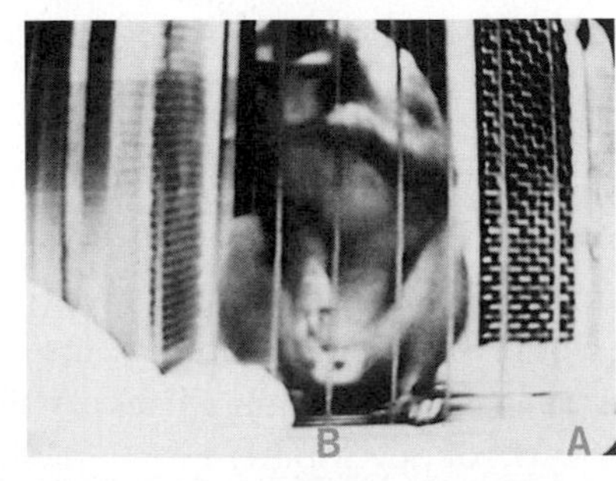

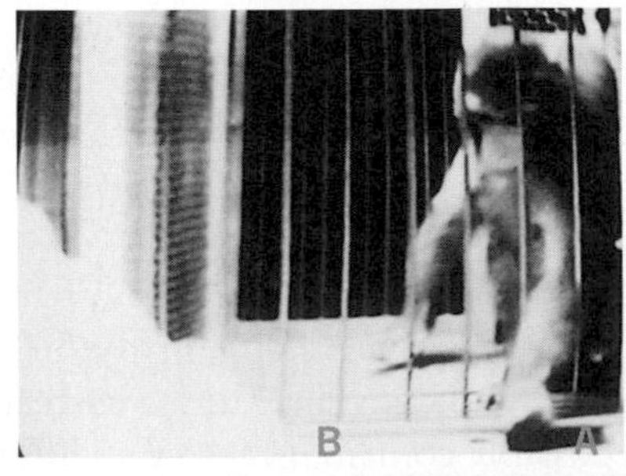

ADELE DIAMOND

Animal–human parallel **Similar search errors by a human infant and an adult monkey with brain damage. After observing an object being hidden in location A followed by a short delay, both baby and monkey successfully retrieve it. However, if they observe the same object being hidden in location B, both baby and monkey repeat their previous action and mistakenly search at location A, where they had found it before. (From Diamond, 1991.)**

3.3

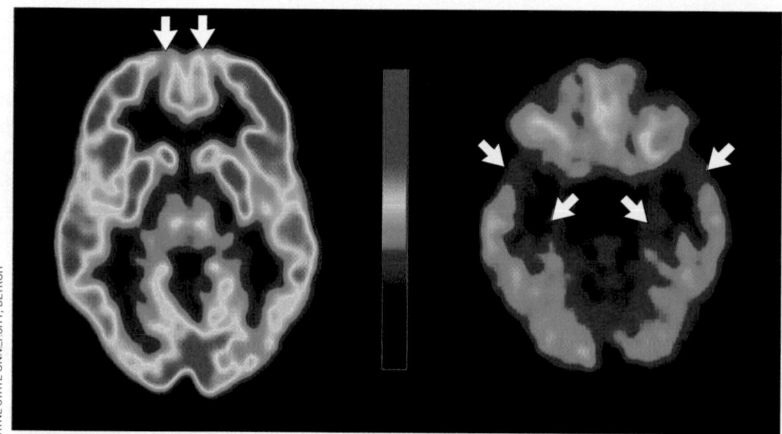

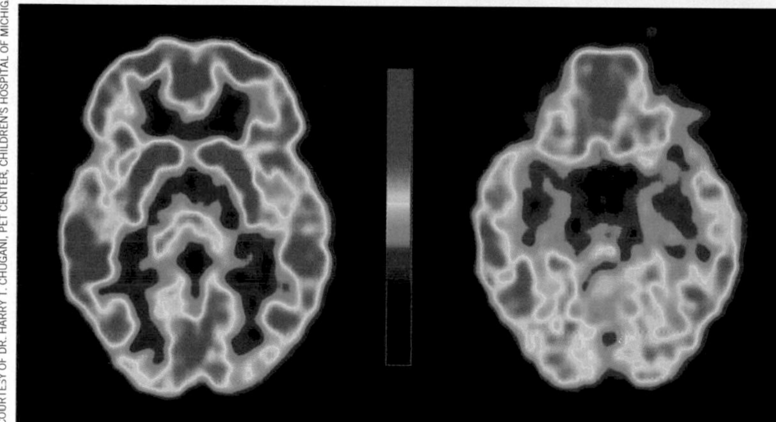

COURTESY OF DR. HARRY T. CHUGANI, PET CENTER, CHILDREN'S HOSPITAL OF MICHIGAN, WAYNE STATE UNIVERSITY, DETROIT

PET images ***Top:*** **Two sections of the brain of a 9½ year old girl who spent her first 32 months in a Romanian orphanage before being adopted.** ***Bottom:*** **Two sections of the brain of a 10½ year old girl who had a normal home environment. Areas of greater brain activity show up as bolder concentrations of red, whereas deep blue indicates low activity. The arrows point to the areas of unusually low metabolic activity in the brain of the Romanian child.**

Positron Emission Tomography (PET)

The neuroimaging technique known as a PET scan produces colorful pictures representing levels of brain activity. A radioactive substance is injected into a person's bloodstream, and the PET scanner records the extent of radiation given off in different areas of the brain. (See PET scans to left.) Because of the need to inject radioactive materials, most developmental data using this technique have come from children whose brains were being scanned for diagnostic purposes.

PET scans have revealed intriguing developmental changes in brain metabolism (Chugani, Phelps, & Mazziotta, 1987). As the graph shows, metabolic activity in the cortex is very low in the first years of life, increases rapidly to its peak between 4 and 8 years of age, and then slowly declines throughout adolescence to the low level characteristic of adulthood.

Functional Magnetic Resonance Imaging (fMRI)

Functional MRI also produces images reflecting cerebral blood flow related to brain activity, but the method is based on using a powerful magnet to pinpoint which areas of the brain are active during particular mental states. MRI images are similar to those that result from PET.

Because the person whose brain is being imaged must be able to tolerate the noise and close confinement of an MRI machine and must be able to remain very

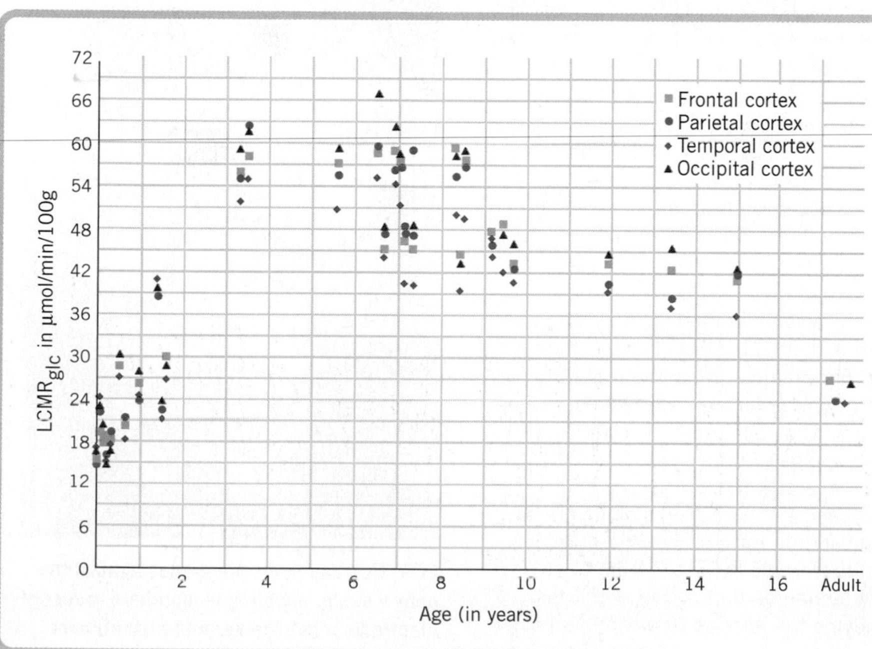

FROM CHUGANI, PHELPS, & MAZZIOTTA, 1987

Changes in cortical metabolism during development **The rate of glucose consumption by the brain, including the four lobes of the cortex, is highest between 4 and 8 years of age.**

*(**a closer look** is continued on the next page)*

(continued from the previous page)

3.3

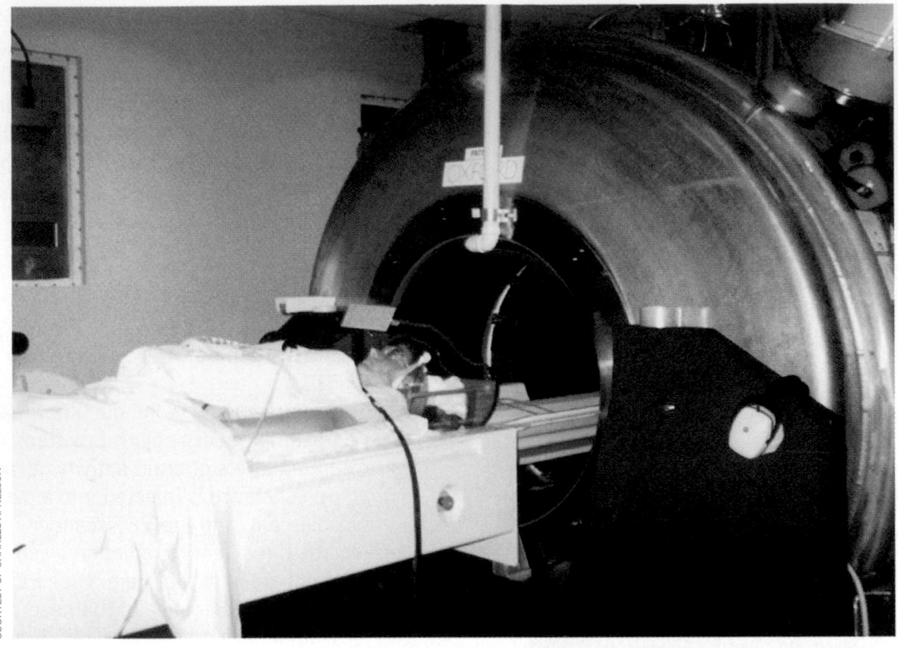

COURTESY OF CHARLES A. NELSON

Functional MRI **This 10-year-old boy is about to have an *fMRI* scan of his brain. The cot on which the child is lying will be pushed into the scanner, then the child will be shown visual stimuli projected onto a mirror directly above his eyes. He will press buttons on the box in his right hand to indicate when he perceives particular target stimuli. Changes in blood flow within the child's brain will be detected magnetically and transformed into a computerized image of brain activity.**

still, most fMRI studies with children have been done with 6-year-old and older participants (see photo above). In some of the first fMRI research done with children, patterns of brain activation in a memory task were similar to those of adults, suggesting that brain imaging techniques may be useful for studying normal cognitive functioning across a wide age range (Casey et al., 1995).

Electrophysiological Recording

Developmental researchers use EEG (electroencephalographic) recordings to trace connections between electrical activity in the brain and ongoing thoughts and emotions. Because EEG records are obtained through electrodes that simply rest on the scalp, this method is very often used with children and even infants (see photo at right). Through EEG recordings, researchers have discovered that in infants, just as in adults, greater electrical activity on the left side of the frontal area is associated with approach reactions (e.g., a positive emotion such as joy), whereas withdrawal responses (e.g., negative emotion such as anger or fear) involve greater activity on the right side (Sutton & Davidson, 1997). Similarly, in playful, pleasurable interactions with their mothers, infants generally show greater activation in the left frontal area of the brain. However, infants of depressed mothers show no difference in left and right activation in the frontal area, suggesting that interacting with their mothers may not be highly pleasurable (Dawson, Klinger, Panagiotides, Speiker, & Frey, 1992).

EEG activity in infants and young children is related to later cognitive functioning. For example, the pattern of EEG activity in newborns is correlated with attention and cognitive processing at 12 years of age (Parmelee et al., 1994). Also, in a task that involves comparing numbers, similar patterns of electrical activity are observed in 5-year-olds and adults (Temple & Posner, 1998).

A technique that is very useful for studying the relation between brain activity and specific kinds of stimulation is the recording of ERPs (event-related potentials), which are changes in the brain's electrical activity that occur in response to the presentation of a particular stimulus. For example, the ERP of 7-month-old infants differs when they are shown pictures of faces with happy versus fearful facial expressions (Nelson & de Haan, 1996). Maltreated children show a heightened ERP in response to angry (as opposed to happy) faces (Pollack, Cicchetti, Klorman, & Brumaghim, 1997). Studies of ERPs to auditory stimuli have shown that newborns' ability to discriminate among speech sounds is directly related to their language skills at 3 years of age (Molfese & Molfese, 1994).

Other Techniques

Although the above are the main techniques that have been used in developmental research to date, advances are being made at a rapid pace. "There is universal agreement that the twenty-first century will be a time of unprecedented discoveries linking the anatomical structures and physiological systems of the brain to the human mind" (Posner, Rothbart, Farah, & Bruer, 2001, p. 293).

COURTESY OF CHARLES A. NELSON

EEG **This cap holds electrodes against the baby's scalp, enabling researchers to record electrode activity generated from all over the baby's brain.**

Synaptogenesis

One result of the extraordinary growth of axonal and dendritic fibers is an exuberant explosion of neuronal connections. In the process of **synaptogenesis,** each neuron forms synapses with thousands of others, resulting in the formation of the trillions of connections referred to earlier. Figure 3.8 shows the process of synaptogenesis in the cortex. As you can see, synaptogenesis begins prenatally and proceeds very rapidly both before birth and for some time afterward. Note that the timing and rate of synapse production vary for different areas of the cortex; synapse generation is complete much earlier in the visual cortex, for example, than in the frontal area.

synaptogenesis the process by which neurons form synapses with other neurons, resulting in trillions of connections

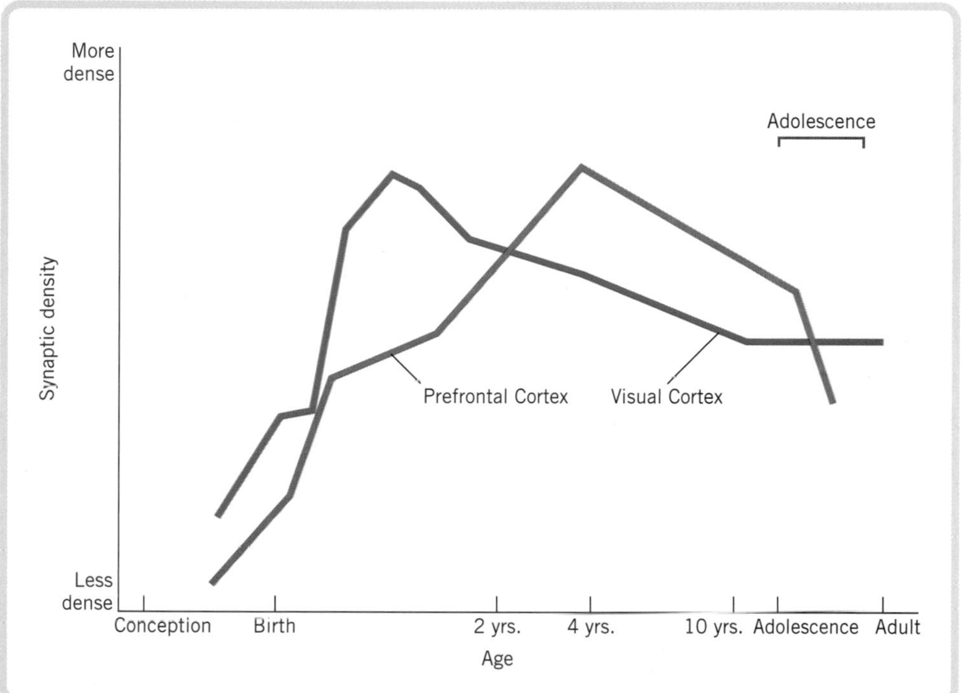

FIGURE 3.8 Synaptogenesis and the elimination of synapses Mean synaptic density (the number of synapses in a given space) first increases sharply as new synapses are overproduced and later declines gradually as excess synapses are eliminated. Note that the time scale is compressed at later stages. (From Huttenlocher & Dabholkar, 1997.)

Synapse Elimination

We now come to what is one of the most remarkable things about the development of the human brain. The wildly exuberant generation of neurons and synapses results in a huge surplus—many more neural connections than any one brain can use (Huttenlocher, 1994; Rakic, 1995). This overabundance of synapses includes a surplus of connections between different parts of the brain: too many neurons in what will become the auditory cortex, for example, are linked with those in the visual area, and both of these areas are overly connected to neurons involved in taste and smell. So, after creating this great synaptic superfluity, the brain starts eliminating it. As you learned in the previous chapter, death is a normal part of development, and nowhere is that more evident than in the systematic pruning of excess synapses that begins prenatally and continues for years after birth. The 6-month-old has almost twice as many synapses in the visual cortex as he or she will have as an adult.

Synaptic pruning occurs at different times in different areas of the brain, and the process of synapse elimination is not fully complete until adolescence (Huttenlocher & Dabholkar, 1997). You can see from Figure 3.8 that the elimination of synapses in the visual cortex begins near the end of the first year of life and continues until roughly 10 years of age, whereas synapse elimination in the frontal area shows a slower time course. During peak pruning periods, as many as 100,000 synapses may be eliminated per second (Kolb, 1995)!

Compare this pattern with the PET scan data shown in Box 3.3, and you will see that there are clear parallels between age changes in cerebral metabolic rate and synaptogenesis and synapse elimination. It is thought that the high level of metabolic activity throughout early childhood meets the high energy demands of synaptogenesis in the cortex and that the decline of metabolic activity in later childhood occurs as synaptic pruning reduces the energy needs of the brain (Chugani et al., 1987; Huttenlocher, 1994).

The Importance of Experience

What determines which of the brain's excess synapses will be pruned and which maintained? Experience plays a central role in a case of "use it or lose it." In a competitive process that has been dubbed "neural Darwinism" (Edelman, 1987), those synapses that are frequently activated are selectively preserved (Changeux & Danchin, 1976). The more often a synapse is activated, the stronger the connection between the neurons involved becomes. Conversely, when a synapse is rarely active, it is likely to disappear; the axon of one neuron withdraws and the dendritic spine of the other is pruned away.

The capacity of the brain to be affected by experience is known as **plasticity.** A good example of the power of plasticity in organizing the nervous system is a simple and not uncommon eye problem known as *strabismus* (Huttenlocher, 1994). Strabismus, commonly referred to as "lazy eye" or "crossed eyes," involves a lack of coordination in the movement of the eyes. As a result of the discordant sensory information the brain receives from the eyes, the child experiences blurred vision. In response, the child's brain starts suppressing messages from one eye, relying on the messages from the other (leaving the child with nonblurry, but monocular, vision). The eventual result is *amblyopia*—blindness in the suppressed eye, presumably because synapses linking that eye and the brain have disappeared due to inactivity. Strabismus can be corrected by putting a patch over the dominant eye, but this action must be taken before 6 years of age or the suppressed eye can become essentially disconnected from the brain.

The obvious question now is: Why does the human brain—the product of millions of years of evolution—take such a devious developmental path, producing a huge excess of synapses, only to destroy a substantial proportion of them? It is generally believed that this form of plasticity, in which the final wiring of the brain is left to experience, confers important advantages that outweigh the drawbacks. One advantage is *economy*—less information needs to be coded in the genes. This economizing may in fact be a necessity: although almost half of the entire set of human genes is thought to be involved in the formation and functioning of the nervous system, this number is enough to specify only a very small fraction of the normal complement of neurons and neural connections. Nurture joins forces with nature to complete the job.

The collaboration between nature and nurture in building the brain occurs differently for two kinds of experience. One kind is the general experiences that almost all normal infants have just by virtue of being human. The second kind is the specific, idiosyncratic experiences the child will have as a result of his or her own life circumstances—growing up in the United States or in the Amazon rain forest, experiencing frequent cuddling or abuse, being an only child or one of many siblings, and so on.

Experience-Expectant Processes

William Greenough refers to the role of the general human experience in brain development as **experience-expectant** plasticity. According to this view, the normal wiring of the brain is in part a result of the kinds of general experiences that have been present throughout human evolution, experiences that every human who inhabits any reasonably normal environment will have—patterned visual stimulation, voices and other sounds, movement and manipulation, and so forth (Greenough & Black, 1992). As a consequence, the brain can "expect" input from these reliable sources to selectively activate and stabilize some synapses, simultaneously causing the elimination of inactive ones. This is the source of the economizing noted earlier; it is due to experience-expectant plasticity that much less has to be coded into the genes to guarantee normal development. Thus, our experience of the external world plays a fundamental role in shaping the most basic aspects of our internal structure.

The downside of experience-expectant plasticity is that it is accompanied by vulnerability. If for some reason the experience that the developing brain is "expecting" to fine-tune its circuits is not present, whether because of stimulus deprivation or nonfunctional sensory receptors, development may be impaired. Consider, for example, the blindness in one eye that can result from strabismus (described previously), and the fact that total blindness can result from congenital cataracts. In both cases, the blindness occurs because the developing brain fails to receive the expected visual stimulation needed to mold the visual system, and the synapses that normally would be involved in seeing get pruned away.

When an expected form of sensory experience is absent, what happens to areas of the brain that normally would have become specialized as a result of that experience? A wealth of data from animals indicates that such areas can become at least partially reorganized to serve some other function. Evidence of such reorganization in humans comes from Helen Neville's (1990) studies of congenitally deaf adults who, as children, had learned American Sign Language (ASL), a full-fledged, but visually based, language. Deaf individuals rely heavily on peripheral vision for language processing; they typically look into the eyes of a person who is signing to them, while using their peripheral vision to monitor the hand and arm motions of the signer. ERP recordings of brain activity (see Box 3.3) showed that deaf individuals' responses to peripheral visual stimuli that are several times stronger than those of hearing people. In addition, their responses are distributed differently across brain regions. The evidence suggests that, due to deprivation of auditory experience, brain systems that would normally be involved in hearing and in spoken language processing become organized to process visual information instead.

plasticity the capacity of the brain to be affected by experience

experience-expectant plasticity the process through which the normal wiring of the brain occurs in part as a result of the kinds of general experiences that every human who inhabits any reasonably normal environment will have

Sensitive periods As suggested by the foregoing examples, a key element in experience-expectant plasticity is timing. There are a few *sensitive periods* when the human brain is especially sensitive to particular kinds of external stimuli. It is as though a time window were temporarily opened, inviting environmental input to help organize the brain. Gradually, the window closes. The neural organization that occurs (or does not occur) during sensitive periods is typically irreversible.

As we discussed in Chapter 1, the extreme deprivation that the Romanian orphans suffered early in life, when children normally experience a wealth of social and other environmental stimulation, is considered an example of a sensitive-period effect. Remembering our friend Lucy, do you think she will get enough "expected" experience for her brain to develop normally?

experience-dependent plasticity the process through which neural connections are created and reorganized throughout life as a function of an individual's experiences

Experience-Dependent Processes

The brain is also sculpted by idiosyncratic experience through what Greenough calls **experience-dependent** plasticity. In other words, neural connections are created and reorganized throughout life as a function of an individual's experiences. (If you remember anything of what you have been reading in this chapter, you have formed new neural connections.)

The role of experience-dependent plasticity is revealed in comparisons of animals who were reared either in complex environments full of objects to explore or in dull laboratory cages with no toys. The brains of rats (and cats and monkeys) that develop in one of these two environments differ. Those who have spent lots of their life exploring and manipulating novel objects have more dendritic spines on their cortical neurons, more synapses per neuron, and more synapses overall, as well as a generally thicker cortex and more of the supportive tissues (such as blood vessels and glial cells) that maximize neuronal and synaptic function. All this extra hardware seems to have a payoff, in that rats reared in the complex environment perform better in a variety of learning tasks (e.g., Juraska, Henderson, & Muller, 1984). Synapse formation in response to a stimulating environment is not limited to early development: even middle-aged rats show increased dendritic branching after spending time in a more complex environment (Greenough & Black, 1992).

In addition to such general effects of experience on brain structure, highly specific effects can also occur. For example, rats that are trained to use either just one or both forelimbs to get a food reward have increased dendritic material in the particular area of the motor cortex that controls the movement of the trained limb(s) (Greenough, Larson, & Withers, 1985; Tomie & Whishaw, 1990). Similar effects seem to occur in humans. For example, a study of violinists and cellists revealed that, compared with control subjects, the musicians had increased cortical representation of the fingers of the left hand (Elbert, Pantev, Wienbruch, Rockstroh, & Taub, 1995). In other words, after years of practice, more cortical cells were devoted to receiving input from and controlling the fingers that manipulate the strings of the instruments. Similarly, skilled Braille readers exhibit enlarged cortical representation of the left hand, which is the hand they use to read Braille text (Pascual-Leone, Cammarota, Wasserman, Brasil-Neto, Cohen, & Hallett, 1993).

How do the cortical representations of their hands differ for these professional musicians?

CALEB RAYNE / BANGOR DAILY NEWS / THE IMAGE WORKS

DAVE ZAJAC, THE HERALD/AP/WIDE WORLD PHOTOS

Brain Damage and Recovery

Plasticity and timing also play an important role in recovery from brain damage. Because of the plasticity of the brain early in life, it can become rewired—at least to some degree. Thus, in some respects, children who suffer from brain damage have a better chance of recovery of function than do adults who suffer similar damage.

The strongest evidence of less severe impairment from earlier injury is that young children who suffer damage to the language area of the cortex generally recover and rarely have *aphasia*—loss of language—later in life. After damage to the part of the left hemisphere where language is primarily represented in right-handed people, language functions shift elsewhere in the young brain, often into the intact right hemisphere. As a result, language is spared. In contrast, adults undergo no such reorganization of language functions after brain damage, so, depending on what particular area of the left hemisphere is damaged, they may have a permanent loss in the ability to comprehend or produce speech. Greater recovery from early brain injury has also been observed for functions other than language. For example, adults who had damage to the frontal area of the cortex during adulthood are worse at producing appropriate facial expressions than adults whose frontal lobe injury occurred in childhood (Kolb, 1995).

It is not always true, however, that the chance of recovery from early brain injury is greater than it is for later injury. It depends on how extensive the damage is and what aspect of brain development is occurring at the time of the damage. Consider, for example, the offspring of Japanese women who were exposed, while pregnant, to massive levels of radiation from the atomic bombs dropped in 1945. The rate of mental retardation was much higher for surviving children whose exposure had occurred very early, during the time of rapid neurogenesis and migration of neurons (Otake & Schull, 1984). Similarly, brain injury during the first year after birth generally results in more severe impairment in IQ than later injury (Kolb, 1995).

Furthermore, even when children appear to have made a full recovery from an early injury, deficits may emerge later. This was demonstrated in a study in which cognitive performance was compared for a group of children who had been born with cerebral damage and a control group of children with no brain damage (Banich, Levine, Kim, & Huttenlocher, 1990). As Figure 3.9 shows, the two groups of children did not differ in their performance on two subscales of an IQ

FIGURE 3.9 Emergent effects of early brain damage At six years of age, children with congenital brain damage scored the same as normal children on two subscales of an intelligence test. However, the children with brain damage failed to improve and fell progressively further behind the normal children, so that by adolescence there were large differences between the two groups.

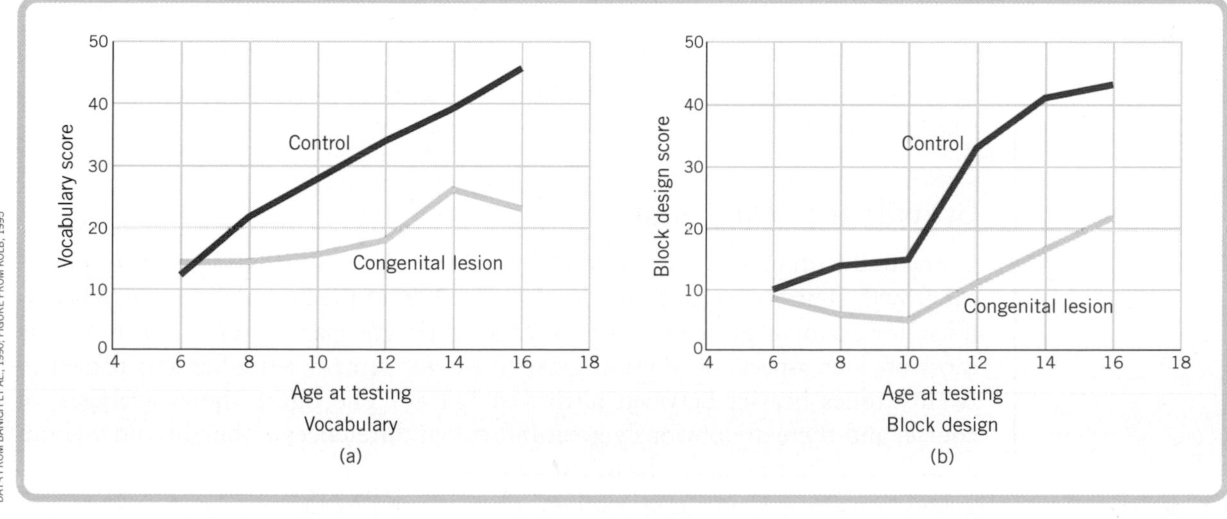

DATA FROM BANICH ET AL., 1990; FIGURE FROM KOLB, 1995

test at 6 years of age, but at later ages they showed notable differences. As the normal children's performance improved with age, that of the brain-damaged children did not, and they fell progressively behind. This result illustrates the difficulty of predicting the development of children with cerebral injuries; behavior that appears normal early on may become progressively less normal.

From the above discussion, we can generalize that the worst time to suffer brain damage is very early, during prenatal development and the first year after birth, when neurogenesis and neuron migration are occurring. Recovery can be impossible when basic brain structures are malformed. The "best" time appears to be in early childhood, when synapse generation and pruning are occurring—that is, when plasticity is highest—making rewiring of the brain and hence recovery of function possible. Later, when these developmental processes are mostly completed and plasticity is low, successful recovery from brain damage is less likely.

review:

Nature and nurture cooperate in the construction of the human brain. Some important brain structures include the neurons, which communicate with one another at synapses; the cortex, in which different functions are localized in different areas; and the cerebral hemispheres, which are specialized for different kinds of processing. The processes involved in the development of the brain include neurogenesis and synaptogenesis, followed by the systematic elimination of synapses as a function of experience. As a result of experience-expectant plasticity, the brain is shaped by experiences that are available in interaction with every normal environment. Because of experience-dependent plasticity, the brain is also structured by an individual's idiosyncratic experiences throughout life.

Because of the importance of experience in brain development, sensitive periods exist during which specific experience must be present for normal development. Timing is also a crucial factor in the ultimate impact of brain damage.

The Body: Physical Growth and Development

In Chapter 1, we emphasized the multiple contexts in which development occurs. Here we focus on the most immediate context for development—the body itself. Everything we think, feel, say, and do involves our physical selves; behavior is embodied, and changes in the body lead to changes in behavior. In this section, we present a broad overview of the normal pattern of physical growth and maturation from birth to adolescence. We will also examine some of the factors that can disrupt this pattern.

Growth and Maturation

Compared with most other species, humans undergo a prolonged period of physical growth. The body grows and develops for 20% of the human life span, whereas mice, for example, grow during only 2% of their life span. Figure 3.10 shows the most obvious aspects of physical growth: we get three times taller and fifteen to twenty times heavier between birth and age 20. The figure shows averages, of course, and there are obviously great individual differences in height and weight, as well as in the timing of physical development.

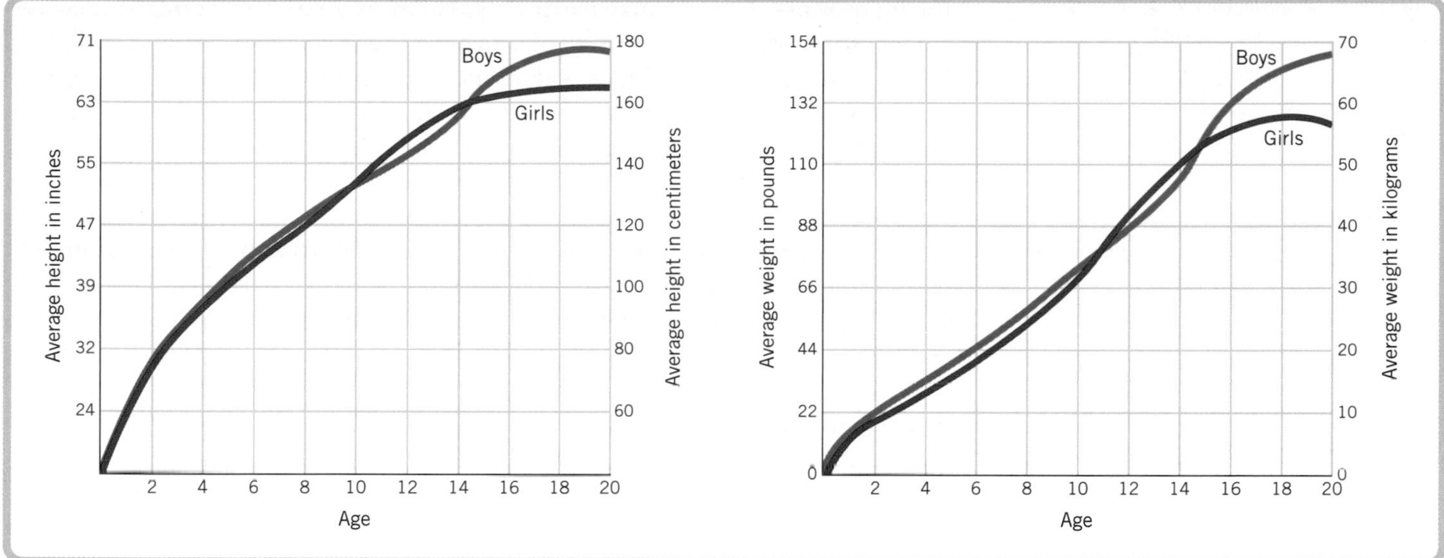

FIGURE 3.10 Growth curves Growth curves for height and weight from birth to twenty years of age. The steeper the slope, the more rapid the change in height or weight. These curves are based on the measurements of 175 well-nourished Americans; very different patterns would be observed for individuals developing in poorer areas of the world. (From R. M. Malina, 1975.)

Growth is uneven over time, as you can tell from the differences in the slopes in Figure 3.10. The slopes are steepest when the most rapid growth is occurring—in the first two years and in early adolescence. Early on, boys and girls grow at roughly the same rate, and they are essentially equal in height and weight until around 10 to 12 years of age. Then girls experience their adolescent growth spurt, at the end of which they are somewhat taller and heavier than boys. (Remember those awkward middle-school years when the girls tended to tower over the boys, much to the discomfort of both?) When adolescent boys experience their growth spurt, about two years after the girls, they permanently pass girls in both height and weight. Full height is achieved, on average, by around the age of 15½ for girls and 17½ for boys.

Growth is also uneven across the different parts of the body. Following the principle of cephalocaudal development described in Chapter 2, the head region is initially relatively large—fully 50% of body length at 2 months—but is only about 10% of body length in adulthood. The gawkiness of young adolescents stems in part from the fact that their growth spurt begins with dramatic increases in the size of the hands and feet; it's easy to trip over your own feet when they're disproportionately larger than the rest of you.

Body composition also changes with age. The proportion of body fat is highest in infancy, gradually declining thereafter until around 6 to 8 years of age. In adolescence, it decreases in boys but increases in girls, and that increase helps trigger the onset of menstruation. The proportion of muscle grows slowly until adolescence, when it increases dramatically, especially in boys.

At this point, the slight gap that has existed for years in the sports-related skills of boys and girls increases substantially; few adolescent girls can run as fast or throw a ball as far as most boys can (Malina & Bouchard, 1991). The widening gap is probably not due solely to differences in muscle development, as American boys have traditionally received more encouragement than girls have to develop

This star athlete goes against the trend in the United States for girls to be less active and to participate less in competitive sports than boys. Does she represent the wave of the future, or will boys continue to be more prominently represented in athletic activities?

RAOUL MINSART/CORBIS

puberty the developmental stage marked by the ability of the body to reproduce. This stage is accompanied by dramatic bodily changes.

menarche the onset of menstruation

body image how an individual perceives and feels about his or her physical appearance

secular trends marked changes in physical development that have occurred over generations

failure-to-thrive (nonorganic) — (FTT) a condition in which infants become malnourished and fail to grow or gain weight for no obvious medical reason

athletic prowess. The gap may narrow somewhat as a result of dramatic increases in the past few decades in girls' involvement in high school sports. However, boys still outnumber girls on athletic teams, and adolescent girls are much less physically active in general than are their male peers (Centers for Disease Control, 1999; National Federation of State High School Associations, 1997).

In adolescence, a series of dramatic bodily transformations are associated with **puberty,** which is defined as the development of the ability to reproduce. In girls, puberty typically begins with enlargement of the breasts and the general growth spurt in height and weight, followed by the appearance of pubic hair and then the onset of menstruation, known as **menarche.** For boys, puberty generally starts with the growth of the testes, followed by pubic hair, the general growth spurt, growth of the penis, and the capacity for ejaculation.

Substantially before puberty is complete, sexual attraction begins. According to surveys of American adults, sexual attraction is first experienced around 10 years of age, regardless of whether the attraction is for individuals of the other sex or the same sex (McClintock & Herdt, 1996). The onset of sexual attraction correlates with maturation of the adrenal glands, the major source of sex steroids other than the testes and ovaries.

These many developmental changes in the body are accompanied by psychological and behavioral changes. For example, the increase in body fat that girls experience in adolescence may be related to sex differences in **body image,** that is, how an individual perceives and feels about his or her physical appearance. Beginning in early adolescence, American girls tend to have more negative attitudes toward their bodies than boys do, and teenage girls typically want to lose several pounds regardless of how much they actually weigh (Tyrka, Graber, & Brooks-Gunn, 2000). The cultural stereotype that "any fat is bad" is shared by increasingly younger children (Cramer & Steinwert, 1998).

Variability

There is great variability across individuals and groups in all aspects of physical development, as reflected in the following examples. The average child growing up in North America or northern Europe is around 4 inches taller than the average child in Kenya, India, or New Guinea (Eveleth & Tanner, 1990). The rate of maturation is generally somewhat faster for African-American children than for their Euro-American peers, and the onset of puberty is slightly earlier for African-American girls. The onset of menstruation is often delayed in girls with a very low proportion of body fat, such as long-distance runners and dancers (Brooks-Gunn, 1987).

This variability in physical development is due to both genetic and environmental factors. Genes affect growth and sexual maturation in large part by influencing the production of hormones, especially growth hormone (secreted by the pituitary gland) and thyroxine (released by the thyroid gland). The influence of environmental factors is particularly evident in **secular trends,** marked changes in physical development that have occurred over generations. In contemporary industrialized nations, adults are several inches taller than their same-sex great-grandparents were. This change is assumed to result primarily from improvements in nutrition and general health. Another secular trend does not reflect an improvement in health status. In the United States today, girls begin menstruating a few years earlier than their ancestors did. Because menstruation requires a certain level of body fat, this change is believed to be related to higher levels of obesity among children today.

Environmental factors can also play a role in disturbances of normal growth. For example, severe chronic stress, such as that associated with a home environment involving serious marital discord, alcoholism, or child abuse, can impair growth by lowering the pituitary gland's production of growth hormone (Powell, Brasel, & Blizzard, 1967). A combination of genetic and environmental factors is apparently involved in nonorganic **failure-to-thrive (FTT),** a condition in which infants become malnourished and fail to grow or gain weight for no obvious medical reason. FTT is associated with disturbances in mother–infant interaction that are thought to stem from characteristics of both child and mother (Bithoney & Newberger, 1987; Drotar, 1992; Drotar, Eckerle, Satola, Pallotta, & Wyatt, 1990). Some mothers experience difficulty and frustration coping with infants who may not have much interest in food and who may have trouble staying awake to feed. The frustrated mother of a very poor eater may "run out of tricks" to get her baby to eat, eventuating in the child's becoming malnourished (Maldonado Duran, 2000). If the parents develop improved strategies for coping with their child's feeding problems and the chronically stressful situation is improved, the infant is likely to show quick catch-up growth.

Nutritional Behavior

The health of our bodies depends on what we put into them, including the amount and kind of food we eat. Thus, the development of eating or nutritional behavior is a crucial aspect of child development from infancy onward.

Infant Feeding

Like all mammals, human newborns obtain life-sustaining nourishment through suckling, although they require more assistance in this endeavor than do most other mammals. Until a few decades ago, breast feeding was, throughout the history of the human species, the only or primary source of nourishment for infants. Mother's milk has many virtues (Newman, 1995). It is naturally free of bacteria, strengthens the infant's immune system, and contains the mother's antibodies against the infectious agents the baby is likely to encounter after birth. However, in spite of the well-established nutritional superiority of breast milk, as well as the fact that it is free, the majority of infants in the United States are exclusively or predominantly formula-fed.

In the United States and other developed countries, infant formula can support normal growth and development, although with a somewhat higher rate of infections than with breast milk. In undeveloped countries, however, formula feeding can exact a costly toll. Much of the world does not have safe water, so infant formula is often mixed with polluted water in unsanitary containers. Further, poor, uneducated parents often dilute the formula in an effort to make the expensive powder last longer. In such circumstances, parents' attempts to promote the health of their babies end up having the opposite effect (Popkin & Doan, 1990).

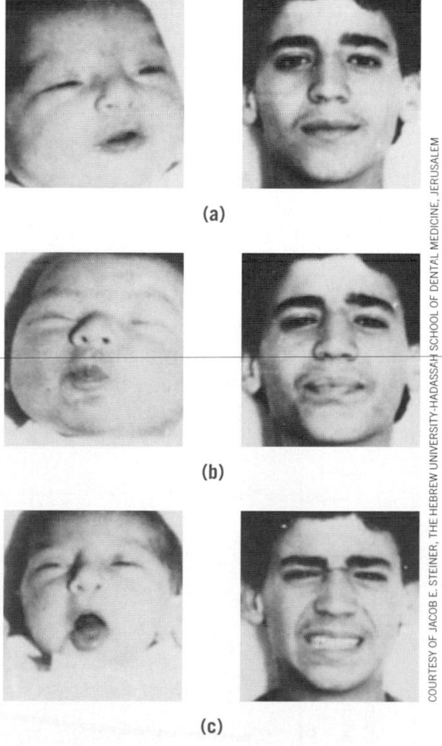

FIGURE 3.11 Taste preferences Taste preferences and reactions to different flavors are very similar in newborns and adults. (a) A sweet solution evokes a hint of a smile, (b) a sour solution causes a pucker, and (c) a bitter solution elicits a grimace.

Development of Food Preferences and the Regulation of Eating

Food preferences are a primary determinant of what we eat throughout life, and some are clearly innate. Figure 3.11 depicts some of the unlearned, reflexive facial expressions that newborns make in response to three basic tastes—sweet, sour, and bitter. Interestingly, these are the same facial expressions that adults make in response to these tastes (Rosenstein & Oster, 1988; Steiner, 1979). Newborns' strong preference for sweetness is reflected both in smiling in response to sweet flavors and in the fact that they will drink larger quantities of sweetened water than plain water (Lipsitt, 1977). These innate preferences may have an evolutionary origin, as poisonous substances are often bitter or sour but almost never sweet.

Infants' taste sensitivity is evident in their reactions to their mother's milk, which can take on the flavor of what she eats. Babies nurse longer and take more breast milk when their mother has ingested either garlic or vanilla flavors (Menella & Beauchamp, 1993b, 1996), but they drink less breast milk after their mother has downed a beer (Menella & Beauchamp, 1993a).

From infancy on, experience has a major influence on what foods children like and dislike and on what and how much they eat. For example, preschool children's liking for particular foods increases if they observe other children enjoying them (Birch & Fisher, 1996). Children's eating is also influenced by what their parents encourage and discourage. This influence does not always work in the way the parents intend, however. For example, standard parental strategies of cajoling and bribing young children to eat new or healthier foods—"If you eat your spinach, you can have some ice cream"—can be doubly counterproductive. The most probable result is that the child will dislike the healthy food even more and have an even stronger preference for the sweet, fatty food used as a reward (Birch & Fisher, 1996). (See Box 3.4 for recommendations on feeding young children.)

Parents might put less effort into trying to control their children's eating behavior if they realized that young children are actually quite good at regulating the amount of food they consume. Research has shown that preschool children adjust how much they eat at a given time based on how much they consumed earlier. In some studies, children ate less of a food if they had been served a snack earlier than they did if they had not had the snack (Birch & Fisher, 1996). (In contrast, a group of adults ate pretty much the same amount of the second course whether they had had the snack or not.) In general, children whose parents try to control their eating habits tend to be worse at regulating their food intake themselves than children of parents who let their children have more control over their eating (Johnson & Birch, 1994).

Eating Disorders

Appropriate regulation of eating is important for healthy physical and psychological development, and abnormal eating patterns can have serious negative consequences.

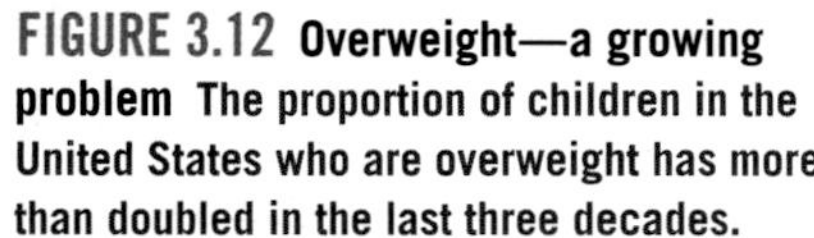

FIGURE 3.12 Overweight—a growing problem The proportion of children in the United States who are overweight has more than doubled in the last three decades.

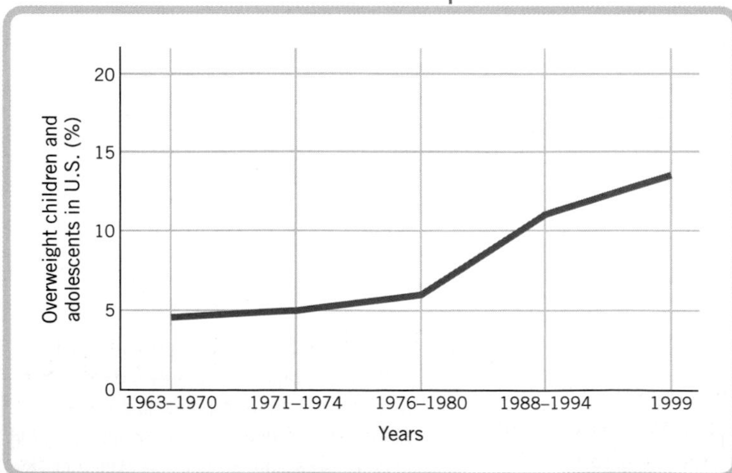

Source: National Center for Health Statistics (1999)

Obesity Many people have difficulty regulating their eating appropriately; the most common problem in the United States is overeating and its many consequences (Hill & Peters, 1998). In an epidemic of fatness, the proportion of overweight Americans has almost tripled in the past two decades. Currently, over half of American adults weigh more than is healthy, and nearly a quarter are obese. The proportion of American children and adolescents who are overweight has more than doubled in the past two decades (see Figure 3.12) with the increase being especially marked for Latinos and African-Americans. The outlook for these children is grim, because most fat children become fat adults and struggle with weight problems throughout their lives.

applications 3.4

Eat Your Peas, Please

Parents can have a powerful impact on what their young children eat, as well as on their children's ability to regulate their own diet in the long run. Research has established that some common parental practices have unintended negative consequences on children's self-regulation and that other approaches are beneficial. The accompanying lists of dos and don'ts are adapted from Birch and Fisher (1996).

Dos and Don'ts on Feeding Children

DO

Take responsibility for what foods are available to your child.

- Make sure the child has access primarily to healthful foods.
- Allow some junk foods, but only a limited amount. The probable result of prohibiting all junk food is increased liking for it.

Expect an initial negative reaction to any new food.

- Present new foods repeatedly, encouraging your child to take a small bite.
- Communicate an expectation that the child will try new foods.

Assume your child can appropriately regulate how much to eat from a variety of nutritious foods.

- Expect variability in the amount and kind of food eaten at a given meal; children vary widely in how much they eat from meal to meal, but they eat consistent amounts over 24-hour periods.

Encourage your child to learn to regulate his or her own eating behavior.

DON'T

Don't let your child select what to eat from an unlimited set of foods.

- Be aware that the probable result of giving children full control over their food choices is a diet heavy in sugar and fat.

Don't assume from an initial rejection of a new food that it will continue to be rejected.

Don't force or coerce your child to eat; any short-term success will be negated by the creation of counterproductive likes and dislikes.

Don't expect consistency in how much your child eats from one meal to the next.

Don't try to control your child's eating behavior.

- Don't force your child to eat a specific amount that you think he or she should consume; doing so undermines children's ability to regulate how much they eat.
- Don't reward your child for eating nonpreferred foods; this will decrease your child's liking for them even further.
- Don't use a preferred but nonnutritious food as a reward; doing so will probably make your child like it even more.

Why do some people but not others become overweight? Figure 3.13 offers two clues. First, fatness runs in families (Matheny, 1990; Plomin et al., 1997). Second, overweight individuals eat more than thin people do (although they tend to underreport how much they consume) (Allison & Pi-Sunyer, 1994). Thus, both genetic and environmental factors probably play a role in obesity.

With respect to genetic factors, there is a strong correlation between the weight of adopted children and that of their biological parents but not that of their adoptive parents. In addition, identical twins are more similar in weight than fraternal twins are, and even identical twins reared apart are similar in weight (Grilo & Pogue-Geile, 1991; Stunkard, Foch, & Hrubeck, 1986; Stunkard, Sorenson, et al., 1986).

NATIONAL GALLERY OF CANADA, OTTAWA: JACOB JORDAENS, *AS THE OLD SING, SO THE YOUNG PIPE*, 1638

FIGURE 3.13 "Fat runs in families" The overweight children and adults in this painting are all genetically related, and they are all overeating.

Environmental factors also play a role in the obesity epidemic. Indeed, becoming obese in the United States could be considered a normal response to the contemporary American environment (Hill & Peters, 1998). This environment offers a superfluity of rich food, with portion sizes that have increased dramatically. In addition, youngsters increasingly devote their leisure time to sedentary pursuits—playing video games, using computers, and especially watching television. One-third of children and adolescents watch television for more than 3 hours a day, and young couch potatoes who spend more than 5 hours a day in front of the tube are much more likely to be obese than are children who average 2 hours or less (Gortmaker, Must, Sobol, et al., 1996). (Interestingly, overweight people tend to own overweight dogs [Allison & Pi-Sunyer, 1994].)

Obesity puts people at risk for a wide variety of health problems, from heart disease to diabetes. In addition, obese people often suffer the consequences of negative stereotypes and discrimination. For example, adults who were overweight as adolescents are more often unmarried and have lower household incomes than people who were of normal weight in their teens (Gortmaker, Must, Perrin, Sobol, & Dietz, 1993). Social discrimination has been reported in areas ranging from housing to college admissions (Friedman & Brownell, 1995). A particularly striking example is the case of a Tennessee woman who was refused a seat in a movie theater on the grounds that she constituted a fire hazard (Allison & Pi-Sunyer, 1994).

There is, unfortunately, no easy cure for obesity in children. Some long-term success has been reported for a family-based weight-loss program in which both parents and children modified their eating and exercise patterns and reinforced each others' progress (Epstein, Valoski, Wing, & McCurley, 1994). Support from family and friends is important in children's successful maintenance of changes in their eating behavior and activity level.

Bulimia **Bulimia** is an eating disorder that is characterized by eating binges followed by self-induced vomiting, fasting, and other drastic efforts to avoid gaining weight. Between 1% and 5% of residents in Western countries are bulimic, and 9 out of 10 of them are women. Most developed the disorder in their teens or early adulthood. Bulimia sufferers tend to have very low self-esteem, beginning in childhood. Risk factors include being obese in childhood or having an obese parent, early menstruation (with accompanying changes in body shape), and various psychiatric problems (Fairburn et al., 1997). About half the women who are diagnosed with bulimia overcome the disorder within 5 to 10 years, while 20% continue to suffer with it. The remainder continue to have milder eating problems (Keel & Mitchell, 1997).

Anorexia **Anorexia nervosa** is a much rarer eating disorder than bulimia (it afflicts no more than 1% of the U.S. population), but it is an extremely severe one in which individuals starve themselves. Like bulimia, anorexia occurs predominantly in females, with its onset typically occurring in adolescence when girls begin to put on body fat and start dieting in response (Attie, Brooks-Gunn, & Peterson, 1990). Typically, anorexic individuals develop an extremely distorted body image, perceiving themselves as grotesquely obese: a girl so emaciated she can barely stand up may firmly believe she is too fat to get through a doorway.

The cause of anorexia is unknown, but those who suffer from it tend to be conscientious, well-behaved, good students from middle-class families and are often perfectionists with very high standards for themselves. They also tend to have controlling parents who hold high expectations for them. Many clinicians believe that the extreme, self-imposed dieting of anorexic individuals is an effort to establish autonomy and control over a part of their life (Graber, Brooks-Gunn, Paikoff, & Warren, 1994). Treatment of anorexia is especially difficult, because patients do not believe they have an eating problem; they think their only problem is being too fat. About 5% of anorexic individuals—who were perfectly healthy before they started dieting—actually die of starvation (Harris, 1991).

bulimia an eating disorder that is characterized by eating binges followed by self-induced vomiting, fasting, and other drastic efforts to avoid gaining weight

anorexia nervosa an eating disorder in which individuals starve themselves because of an extremely distorted body image

marasmus malnutrition brought about by the ingestion of too few calories

kwashiorkor malnutrition brought about by inadequate protein

Undernutrition

Forty percent of all the world's children under the age of 5—approximately 190 million youngsters—are undernourished or malnourished (Pollitt et al., 1996). The nutritional deficits they experience can involve an inadequate supply of total calories, of protein, of vitamins and minerals, or any combination of these deficiencies (Sigman, 1995). This problem is most obvious in the severe cases of malnutrition of infants and young children with **marasmus** (too few calories) or **kwashiorkor** (inadequate protein) in developing nations. The less extreme condition of undernutrition is much more common, especially in developed countries. In the United States in 1992, 12 million children were estimated to be undernourished (Brown & Pollitt, 1996).

Undernutrition and malnutrition are almost always associated with poverty and myriad related factors, including limited access to health care and parents' limited education. Furthermore, the stress of poverty may constrict some mothers' ability or inclination to provide attentive care for their children, putting them at risk for undernutrition (Valenzuela, 1997).

The interaction of malnutrition with poverty and other forms of deprivation adversely affects all aspects of development. Figure 3.14 presents a model of how the complex interaction of these multiple factors impairs cognitive development (Brown & Pollitt, 1996). As you can see, malnutrition can have *direct* effects on the

FIGURE 3.14 Malnutrition and cognitive development Malnutrition, combined with poverty, affects many aspects of development and can lead to impaired cognitive abilities. (From Brown & Pollitt, 1996.)

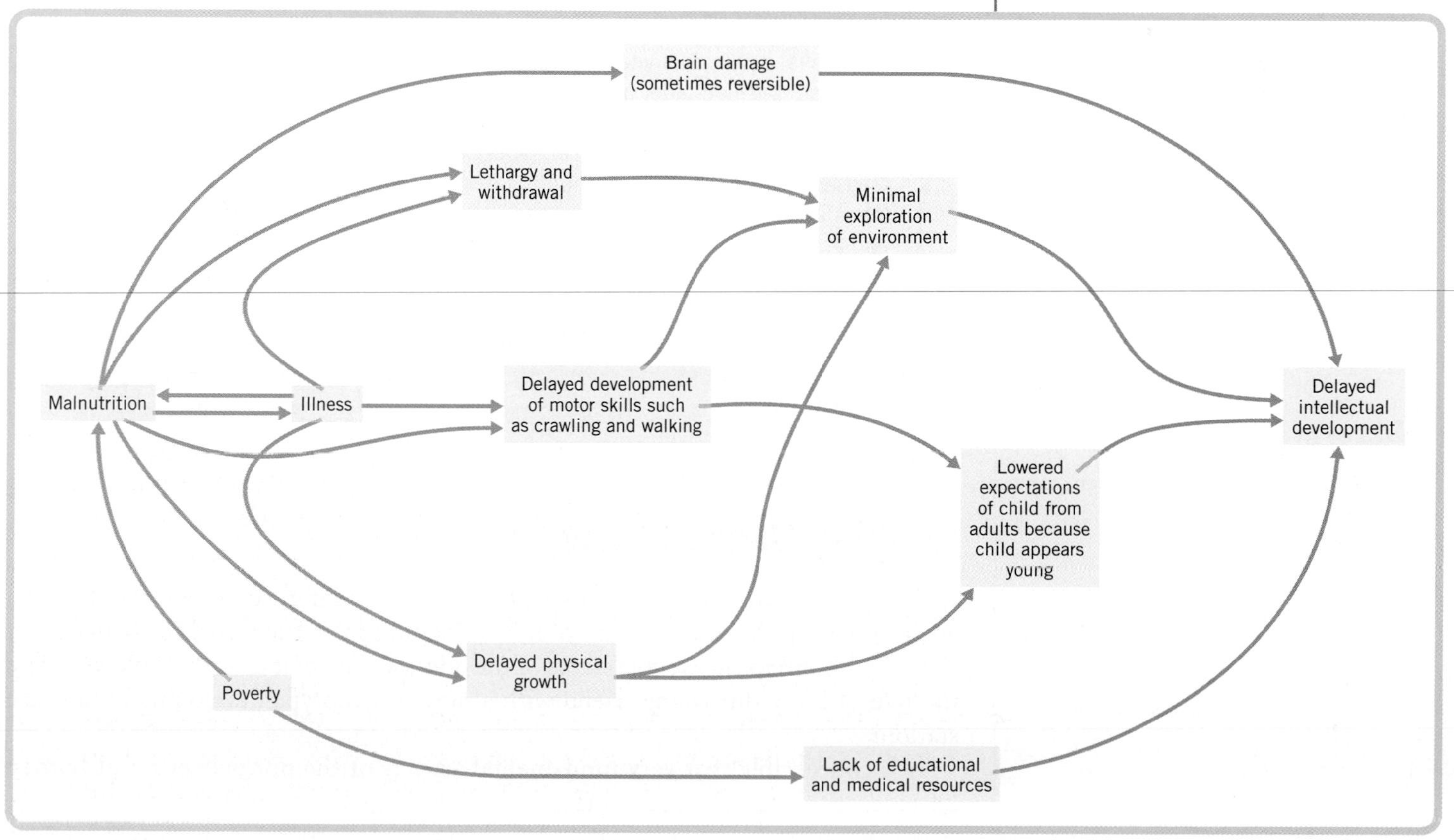

structural development of the brain, general energy level, susceptibility to infection, and physical growth. With inadequate energy, malnourished children tend to reduce their energy expenditure and withdraw from stimulation, making them quiet and passive in general, less responsive in social interactions, less attentive in school, and so on. Apathy, slowed growth, and delayed development of motor skills also retard the children's exploration of the environment, further limiting their opportunities to learn. Because of their small size and delayed development, malnourished children may be perceived as younger and less competent than they actually are, leading adults to expect and demand less of them. When relatively little is expected from them by their parents and teachers, they are unlikely to derive the same benefits from attending school that a healthy child gets, thereby losing out further on one of the most important sources of intellectual growth. All these factors, exacerbated by a generally impoverished environment and inadequate resources, converge to lead to delayed intellectual development.

Can anything be done to help malnourished and undernourished youngsters? Because so many interacting factors are involved, it is not easy to do so; but neither is it impossible, as shown by several large-scale intervention efforts throughout the world (Sigman, 1995). In one successful long-term project in Guatemala led by Ernesto Pollitt, for example, a high-protein dietary supplement started in infancy correlated with an increase in performance on several tests of cognitive functioning in adolescence (Pollitt, Gorman, Engle, Martorell, & Rivera, 1993). Although it is possible to improve the developmental status of malnourished children, it would be better, both for the children themselves and for society in general, to prevent the occurrence of malnutrition in the first place. As Brown and Pollitt (1996) note: "On balance, it seems clear that prevention of malnutrition among young children remains the best policy—not only on moral grounds but on economic ones as well" (p. 702).

review:

Nutritional behavior is vital to general health. Preferences for certain foods are evident from birth on, and, as children develop, what they choose to eat is influenced by many factors, including the preferences of their friends and their parents' attempts to influence their eating behavior. Obesity among both adults and children has increased dramatically in the United States in recent decades, as exposure to rich foods in large portions has increased and physical activity has decreased. Bulimia and anorexia are relatively rare eating disorders, but they can have quite severe consequences. Throughout the world, the most common nutritional problem is undernutrition. Malnutrition is very closely associated with poverty, and the combined effects of malnutrition and poverty have a wide variety of deleterious effects on development.

Looking Back at Lucy

Knowing what you now know about the intimate relation between heredity and environment in the development of human beings, from the initial construction of the baby's brain to the weight status of the adolescent, what do you think would be the fate of Lucy, our young friend with a normal genotype developing on a space station?

It is conceivable that very fundamental aspects of the normal course of human development would be quite different for her. Clearly, her environment would be restricted compared with that of a child on Earth. To what extent would it matter? Would her brain be organized differently as a result of her extremely limited range of visual and auditory stimulation? With no peers and only a few adults for company, would she be more like her parents than the average earthbound child, or less like them? Is it possible that in her very low-gravity environment, her muscles (as well as her bones) might not develop sufficiently to support normal physical growth? If so, she might be incapable of the behaviors through which infants explore and learn about the world. We cannot, of course, know the answers to these or the hundreds of other questions we could easily ask, but thinking about Lucy emphasizes the intimate bond between nature and nurture in human development.

Chapter Summary

Nature and Nurture

- The complex interplay of nature and nurture was the constant theme of this chapter. In the drama of development, genotype, phenotype, and environment all play starring roles, and the plot moves forward as they interact in many obvious and many not-so-obvious ways.
- The starting point for development is the genotype—the genes inherited at conception from one's parents. Only some of those genes are expressed in the phenotype, one's observable characteristics. Whether or not *some* genes are expressed at all is a function of dominance patterns. Gene expression, the switching on and off of genes over time, underlies many aspects of development.
- The eventual outcome of a given genotype is always contingent on the environment in which it develops. Parents and their behavior toward their children are a salient part of the children's environment. Parents' behavior toward their children is influenced by their own genotypes. Similarly, the child's development is influenced by the aspects of the environment he or she seeks out and the different responses the child's characteristics and behavior evoke from other people.
- The field of behavioral genetics is concerned with the joint influence of genetic and environmental factors on behavior. Through the use of a variety of family-study designs, behavioral geneticists have discovered a wide range of behavior patterns that "run in families." Many behavioral geneticists use heritability estimates to statistically evaluate the relative contributions of heredity and environment to behavior.

Brain Development

- A burgeoning area of developmental research focuses on the development of the brain—the most complex structure in the known universe. Neurons are the basic units of the brain's informational system. These cells transmit information via electrical signals. Impulses are transmitted from one neuron to another at synapses.
- The cortex is referred to as the most human part of the human brain, because it is involved in a wide variety of higher mental functions. Different areas of the cortex are specialized for general behavioral categories. The cortex is divided into two cerebral hemispheres, each of which is specialized for certain modes of processing, a phenomenon known as cerebral lateralization.
- Brain development involves several processes, beginning with neurogenesis and differentiation of neurons. In synaptogenesis, an enormous profusion of connections between neurons is generated, starting prenatally and continuing for the first few years after birth. Through synaptic pruning, excess connections among neurons are eliminated.
- Experience plays a crucial role in the strengthening or elimination of synapses and hence in the normal wiring of the brain. The fine-tuning of the brain involves experience-expectant processes, in which existing synapses are preserved as a function of stimulation that virtually every human encounters, and experience-dependent processes, in which new connections are formed as a function of learning.
- Plasticity refers to the fact that nurture is the partner of nature in the normal development of the brain. This fact makes it possible in certain circumstances for the brain to rewire itself in response to damage. It also makes the developing brain vulnerable to the absence of stimulation at sensitive periods in development.
- The ability of the brain to recover from injury depends on the age of the child. Very early damage, when neurogenesis and synaptogenesis are occurring, can have especially devastating effects. Damage during the preschool years, when synapse elimination is occurring, is less likely to have permanent deleterious effects.

The Body: Physical Growth and Development

- Humans undergo a particularly prolonged period of physical growth, during which growth is uneven, proceeding more rapidly early in life and in adolescence. Puberty ushers in many physical and behavioral changes, including sex differences in body proportions and in muscle-to-fat ratios, with accompanying changes in body image and activity. Secular trends have been observed in increases in average height and age of onset of menarche.
- Food preferences begin with innate responses by newborns to basic tastes, but additional preferences develop as a result of experience. Parents have a large impact on their children's ability to successfully regulate their own eating. Problems with the regulation of eating are evident in the United States, where an epidemic of obesity is clearly related to both environmental and genetic factors. Bizarre eating patterns and aversions threaten the health of sufferers of serious eating disorders such as bulimia and anorexia, both of which are more common in young females.
- In most of the rest of the world, the dominant problem is getting enough food, and nearly half of all the children in the world suffer from undernutrition. Inadequate nutrition is closely associated with poverty, and it leads to a variety of behavioral and physical problems in virtually every aspect of the child's life. Prevention of undernutrition is needed to allow millions of children to develop normal brains and bodies.

Critical Thinking Questions

1. A major focus of this chapter was the interaction of nature and nurture. Consider yourself and your family (regardless of whether you were raised by your biological parents). Identify some aspect of who you are that illustrates each of the four relations described in the text. (1) How and when was your sex determined? (2) What are some alleles you are certain or relatively confident you share with other members of your family? (3) What might be an example of a gene-environment interaction in your parents' behavior toward you? (4) Give an example of your active selection of your own environment that might have influenced your subsequent development.
2. "According to behavioral geneticists, 50% of a person's IQ is due to heredity and 50% to environment." Discuss what is wrong with this statement, describing both what heritability estimates mean and what they do not mean.
3. Relate the developmental processes of synaptogenesis and synapse elimination to the concepts of experience-expectant and experience-dependent plasticity.
4. Consider Figure 3.14 on malnutrition and cognitive development. Imagine an undernourished 6-year-old child living in the United States. Go through the figure and generate a specific example of something that might happen to this child at each point in the diagram.

Key Terms

genome, p. 86
genotype, p. 86
phenotype, p. 86
environment, p. 86
chromosomes, p. 87
DNA (deoxyribonucleic acid), p. 87
genes, p. 87
sex chromosomes, p. 87
mutation, p. 88
crossing over, p. 88
regulator genes, p. 88
alleles, p. 89
dominant allele, p. 89
recessive allele, p. 89
homozygous, p. 89
heterozygous, p. 89
polygenic inheritance, p. 90
norm of reaction, p. 91
phenylketonuria (PKU), p. 92
behavioral genetics, p. 94
heritable, p. 94
multifactorial, p. 94
heritability, p. 97
neurons, p. 101
cell body, p. 100
dendrites, p. 100
axons, p. 100

synapses, p. 101
glial cells, p. 101
myelin sheath, p. 101
cerebral cortex, p. 102
lobes, p. 102
occipital lobe, p. 102
temporal lobe, p. 102
parietal lobe, p. 102
frontal lobe, p. 102
association areas, p. 102
cerebral hemispheres, p. 103
corpus callosum, p. 103
cerebral lateralization, p. 103
neurogenesis, p. 103
spines, p. 103
myelination, p. 103
synaptogenesis, p. 107
plasticity, p. 108
experience-expectant plasticity, p. 109
experience-dependent plasticity, p. 110
puberty, p. 114
menarche, p. 114
body image, p. 114
secular trends, p. 114
failure-to-thrive (nonorganic)—(FTT), p. 115
bulimia, p. 118
anorexia nervosa, p. 118
marasmus, p. 119
kwashiorkor, p. 119

CHAPTER 4

Theories of Cognitive Development

DIEGO RIVERA, *Fin del Corrido,* c. 1922–1928

THEMES

- Nature and Nurture
- The Active Child
- Continuity/Discontinuity
- Mechanisms of Change
- The Sociocultural Context
- Individual Differences
- Research and Children's Welfare

A 7-month-old infant, sitting on his father's lap, becomes intrigued with the father's glasses, grabs one side of the frame, and yanks it. The father says, "Ow!" and the boy lets go, but he then reaches up and yanks it again. This leads the father to wonder how he can safeguard the glasses without causing the child to start screaming. Fortunately, the father, a developmental psychologist, soon realizes that Jean Piaget's theory of cognitive development suggests a simple solution: put the glasses behind his back. According to Piaget's theory, removing the glasses from sight should lead a baby of this age to act as if they never existed. The strategy works exactly as planned; after the father puts the glasses out of sight, the boy shows no further interest in them and turns his attention elsewhere. The father silently thanks Piaget.

This experience, which one of us actually had, illustrates in a small way how understanding theories of child development can yield practical benefits. It also illustrates three broader advantages of knowing about such theories:

1. Developmental theories provide a framework for understanding important phenomena. Theories make clear the significance of observations, both from research studies and from everyday life. A guest who observed the glasses incident but who did not know about Piaget's theory might have found the experience mildly amusing but not of any particular significance. Within Piaget's theory, however, this passing event exemplifies a very general and profoundly important developmental phenomenon: infants below 8 months of age react to the disappearance of an object as though they do not understand that the object still exists. Thus, theories of child development place particular experiences and observations in a larger context and deepen our understanding of their significance.

2. Developmental theories raise crucial questions about human nature. After observing in an informal experiment that infants below 8 months of age rarely reached for a favorite object after he covered it with a cloth or otherwise put it out of sight, Piaget concluded that before that age, infants do not realize that hidden objects still exist. Others have challenged this explanation, arguing that infants younger than 8 months do in fact understand that hidden objects continue to exist, but that deficiencies of memory or problem-solving skills prevent them from acting on that understanding to retrieve hidden objects (Baillargeon, 1993; Munakata, McClelland, Johnson, & Siegler, 1997). Despite these disagreements about how best to interpret infants' behavior, all of the researchers agree that Piaget's theory raises a crucial question about human nature: Do infants realize from the first days of life that hidden objects continue to exist, or is this something that they learn only later?

3. Developmental theories motivate new research. Theories also stimulate new studies, whose findings can support, fail to support, or require refinements of the original claims. For example, Piaget's ideas led Bower and Wishart (1972) to test whether 7-month-olds' failure to reach for hidden objects was due to their being insufficiently motivated or insufficiently skillful at reaching to obtain them. To test this hypothesis, the researchers created a situation similar to Piaget's object-permanence experiment except that they placed the object, an attractive toy, under a transparent cover rather than under an opaque one. In this situation, infants quickly removed the cover and regained the toy, thus demonstrating that they were both motivated to obtain it and sufficiently skilled to do so. This finding supported Piaget's original interpretation. In contrast, an experiment conducted by Diamond (1985) indicated a need to refine Piaget's theory. Diamond varied the amount of time between when the toy was hidden and when the infant was allowed to reach for it. She found that even 6-month-olds could succeed if allowed to reach immediately, that 7-month-olds could wait as long as 2 seconds and still succeed, that 8-month-olds could wait as long as 4 seconds and still succeed, and so on. Diamond's finding indicated that memory for the location of hidden objects, as well as the understanding that they continue to exist, is crucial to success on the task. Thus, theories of child development are useful because they provide frameworks for understanding important phenomena, raise fundamental questions about human nature, and motivate new research.

Because child development is such a complex and varied process, no single theory accounts for all of it. The most informative current theories focus primarily either on cognitive development or on social development. Providing a good account of development in either of these areas is an immense challenge, because each of them spans a huge range of topics. Cognitive development spans the growth of such diverse capabilities as perception, attention, language, problem solving, reasoning, memory, and conceptual understanding. Social development spans the growth of equally diverse areas: emotions, personality, relationships with peers and family members, self-understanding, aggression, and moral understanding and behavior. Taking into account both sets of capabilities, we can easily understand why no one theory has captured the entirety of child development. Therefore, we consider theories of cognitive development in this chapter and theories of social development in Chapter 9.

The present chapter examines four particularly influential theories of cognitive development: Piagetian, information-processing, core-knowledge, and sociocultural. For each of the four theories, we consider the assumptions about children's nature on which the theory is based, the issues on which the theory focuses, and practical examples of its educational usefulness.

These four theories are influential in large part because they convey important insights into the basic questions about development described in Chapter 1. Each theory addresses all the issues to some extent, but each one emphasizes different issues. For example, Piaget's theory focuses on *continuity/discontinuity* and the *active child*, whereas information-processing theories focus on *change mechanisms* (Table 4.1). Together, the four theories allow a broader appreciation of cognitive development than any one of them does by itself.

TABLE 4.1

Main Questions Addressed by Theories of Cognitive Development

Theory	Main Question Addressed
Piagetian	Nature–nurture, continuity/discontinuity, the active child
Information-processing	Nature–nurture, how change occurs
Core-knowledge	Nature–nurture, continuity/discontinuity
Sociocultural	Nature–nurture, influence of the sociocultural context, how change occurs

Piaget's Theory

Jean Piaget's studies of cognitive development are a testimony to how much one person can contribute to a scientific field. Before he began his work, around 1920, there was no recognizable field of cognitive development. Yet even today, Piaget's theory remains the standard against which all other developmental theories are measured. What accounts for its longevity?

One reason is that Piaget's observations and descriptions of children vividly convey the flavor of their thinking at different ages. Another reason is the exceptional breadth of the theory. It extends from the first days of infancy through adolescence and examines content areas as diverse as conceptualization of time, space, and distance; language use; memory; understanding of other people's perspectives; scientific reasoning; and moral judgment. Even today, it remains the broadest theory of cognitive development. A third reason for its longevity is the surprising and thought-provoking observations that Piaget used to support the theory. Yet a fourth reason is the theory's intuitively plausible depiction of the interaction of nature and nurture and the recognition of both continuities and discontinuities in development.

YVES DEBRAINE / BLACK STAR

Jean Piaget, whose work has had a profound influence on developmental psychology, observing children at play.

View of Children's Nature

Piaget's fundamental assumption about children was that from birth onward they are active mentally as well as physically, with their activity greatly contributing to their own development. His approach is often labeled *constructivist,* because it depicts children as constructing knowledge for themselves in response to their experiences. Three of the most important of children's constructive processes, according to Piaget, are generating hypotheses, performing experiments, and drawing conclusions. If this description reminds you of scientific problem solving, you are not alone: the "child as scientist" is the dominant metaphor within Piaget's theory. Consider this description of his infant son:

> Laurent is lying on his back. . . . He grasps in succession a celluloid swan, a box, etc., stretches out his arm and lets them fall. He distinctly varies the position of the fall. When the object falls in a new position (for example, on his pillow), he lets it fall two or three more times on the same place, as though to study the spatial relation.
>
> (Piaget, 1952b, pp. 268–269)

In simple activities, such as Laurent's game of "drop the toy from different places and see what happens," Piaget perceived the beginning of scientific experimentation.

This example also illustrates a second basic Piagetian assumption: Children learn many important lessons on their own, rather than depending on instruction from adults or older children. To further illustrate this point, Piaget cited a friend's recollection from childhood:

> He was seated on the ground in his garden and he was counting pebbles. Now to count these pebbles he put them in a row and he counted them one, two, three up to 10. Then he finished counting them and started to count them in the other direction. He began by the end and once again he found that he had 10. He found this marvelous. . . . So he put them in a circle and counted them that way and found 10 once again.
>
> (Piaget, 1964, p. 12)

This incident also exemplifies a third of Piaget's basic assumptions: Children are intrinsically motivated to learn and do not need rewards from adults to do so. When they acquire a new capability, they apply it as often as possible. They also reflect on the lessons of their experience, because they want to understand themselves and everything around them.

Central Developmental Issues

In addition to his view that children actively shape their own development, Piaget offered important insights regarding the roles of nature and nurture and of continuities and discontinuities in development.

Nature and Nurture

Piaget believed that nature and nurture interact to produce cognitive development. In his view, nurture includes every kind of experience the child encounters. Nature includes the child's maturing brain and body; ability to perceive, act, and learn from experience; and motivation to meet two basic functions that are central to cognitive growth: adaptation and organization. **Adaptation** is the tendency to respond to the demands of the environment in ways that meet one's goals. **Organization** is the tendency to integrate particular observations into coherent knowledge. Because both adaptation and organization involve children's response to experience, it can be said that it is part of children's nature to respond to their nurture.

Sources of Continuity

Piaget depicted development as involving both continuities and discontinuities. The main sources of continuity are three processes—assimilation, accommodation, and equilibration—that work together from birth to propel development forward.

Assimilation is the process by which people translate incoming information into a form that they can understand. To illustrate, when one of our children was 2 years old, he saw a man who was bald on top of his head and had long frizzy hair on the sides. To his father's horror, the toddler gleefully shouted, "Clown, clown." (Actually, it sounded more like "Kown, kown.") The man apparently looked enough like a "kown" that the boy could assimilate him to his clown concept.

Accommodation is the process by which people adapt current knowledge structures in response to new experiences. In the "kown" incident, the boy's father explained to his son that the man was not a clown and that even though his hair was like a clown's, he wasn't wearing a funny costume and wasn't doing silly things to make people laugh. With this new information, the boy was able to accommodate his idea to the standard concept of "clown," allowing other men with bald pates and long side hair to pass by in peace.

Finally, **equilibration** is the process by which children (or other people) balance assimilation and accommodation to create stable understanding. Equilibration includes three phases. First, children are satisfied with their understanding of a phenomenon; Piaget labeled this a state of *equilibrium,* because children do not see any discrepancies between their experiences and their understanding. Then, children perceive that their understanding is inadequate; Piaget said that children at this point are in a state of *disequilibrium,* because they recognize shortcomings in their understanding but cannot generate a superior alternative. Finally, children develop a more sophisticated understanding that eliminates the shortcomings of the old one. This new understanding provides a more stable equilibrium, in the sense that a wide range of new experiences can be understood within it.

To illustrate how equilibration works, suppose that a girl in preschool believes that only animals are living things, because only they can move in ways that help them live. (In fact, this is what most 4- to 7-year-olds in a wide range of cultures

adaptation the tendency to respond to the demands of the environment in ways that meet one's goals

organization the tendency to integrate particular observations into coherent knowledge

assimilation the process by which people translate incoming information into a form that they can understand

accommodation the process by which people adapt current knowledge structures in response to new experiences

equilibration the process by which children (or other people) balance assimilation and accommodation to create stable understanding do believe [Hatano et al., 1993].) Sooner or later, the girl will realize that plants also move in ways that promote their survival (e.g., toward sunlight). This new information would be difficult to assimilate into her previous thinking. The disparity between the girl's previous understanding of living things and her new knowledge about plants would create a state of disequilibrium, in which she was unsure what it means to be alive. Later, her thinking would accommodate to the new information about plants. That is, she would realize that animals and plants both move in adaptive ways and that because adaptive movement is a key characteristic of living things, plants as well as animals must be alive (Opfer & Gelman, 2001). This constitutes a more advanced equilibrium, because subsequent information about plants and animals will not contradict it. Through innumerable such equilibrations, children gradually extend their understanding of the world around them.

Sources of Discontinuity

Although Piaget placed some emphasis on continuous aspects of cognitive development, the most famous part of his theory concerns discontinuous aspects, that is, distinct stages of cognitive development. Piaget viewed these stages as products of the basic human tendency to organize knowledge into structures. Each stage represents a coherent way of understanding one's experience, and each transition between stages represents a discontinuous intellectual leap from one coherent way of understanding to the next, higher one. The following are the central properties of Piaget's stage theory:

1. *Qualitative change.* Piaget believed that children of different ages think in qualitatively different ways. For example, he proposed that children in early stages of cognitive development conceive of morality in terms of the outcomes of a person's behavior, whereas children in later stages conceive of it in terms of the person's intent. A 5-year-old would judge someone who accidentally broke a whole jar of cookies as having been more naughty than someone who deliberately stole a single cookie; an 8-year-old would reach the opposite conclusion. This difference represents a *qualitative change,* because the two children are basing their moral judgments on entirely different criteria.

2. *Broad applicability.* The type of thinking characteristic of each stage pervades children's thinking across diverse topics and contexts.

3. *Brief transitions.* Children do not move from one stage to the next overnight. Before entering a new stage, they pass through a brief transitional period in which they fluctuate between the type of thinking characteristic of the new, more advanced stage and the type of thinking characteristic of the old, less advanced one.

4. *Invariant sequence.* People in all places and in all historical periods progress through the stages in the same order. No stages are ever skipped.

Piaget's stage theory provides a simple and elegant way of thinking about cognitive development. In reality, the developmental process is considerably more complicated than the theory implies. However, the theory does provide a helpful overview of age-related patterns of cognitive development, as well as many useful insights into those patterns.

We now turn to the specifics of Piaget's stage theory. Piaget hypothesized that children progress through four stages of cognitive development: the *sensorimotor* stage, the *preoperational* stage, the *concrete operational* stage, and the *formal operational* stage. With each stage, children add new ways of knowing their world to those that they already possess:

1. In the **sensorimotor stage** (birth to 2 years), infants' intelligence develops, and is expressed, through their sensory and motor abilities. Infants begin life with reflexes; with perceptual abilities such as seeing and hearing; and with the basic learning mechanisms of assimilation, accommodation, and equilibration. Through the maturation of their sensorimotor abilities and the application of these learning mechanisms to their experiences, infants learn about people and objects and construct rudimentary forms of fundamental concepts such as time, space, and causality. Throughout the period, they live largely in the here and now: their intelligence is bound to their immediate perceptions and actions.
2. In the **preoperational stage** (2 to 7 years), toddlers and preschoolers become able to represent their experiences in language, mental imagery, and symbolic thought. This allows them to remember their experiences for longer periods of time and to form more sophisticated concepts. However, as suggested by the term *preoperational,* children at this stage are viewed by Piaget as unable to perform *operations* (reversible mental activities)—such as reasoning that pouring water into a differently shaped glass must leave the amount of water unchanged, because the water could be returned to the original glass and the amount would be identical. The inability to perform such operations results in young children having difficulty thinking in consistent, logical ways. Instead, they focus on single, perceptually striking aspects of an event or problem, even when multiple aspects are important.
3. In the **concrete operational stage** (7 to 12 years), children can reason logically about concrete objects and events. However, they have difficulty thinking in purely abstract terms and in combining information systematically.
4. In the final stage of cognitive development, the **formal operational stage** (12 years and beyond), children can think deeply not only about concrete events but also about abstractions and purely hypothetical situations. They also can perform systematic scientific experiments and draw appropriate conclusions from them.

With this overview of Piaget's theory, we can consider in greater depth some of the major changes that take place in each stage.

sensorimotor stage the period (birth to 2 years) within Piaget's theory in which intelligence is expressed through sensory and motor abilities

preoperational stage the period (2 to 7 years) within Piaget's theory in which children become able to represent their experiences in language, mental imagery, and symbolic thought

concrete operational stage the period (7 to 12 years) within Piaget's theory in which children become able to reason logically about concrete objects and events

formal operational stage the period (12 years and beyond) within Piaget's theory in which people become able to think about abstractions and hypothetical situations

The Sensorimotor Stage (Birth to 2 Years)

On the first day of a child-development class several years ago, one of us asked the students, "What do you think are the most important characteristics of infants' intelligence?" Quite a few students offered no characteristics, saying that they did not think infants had intelligence. Others chose physical coordination, alertness, and recognition of people and objects as the most important properties—quite different qualities from the ones they thought characterize intelligence later in childhood. These impressions were reasonable, given the narrow range of infants' behavior and their general helplessness.

Part of Piaget's genius, however, was that he perceived infants' intelligence to include much more than their limited behaviors would suggest. He realized that in infants' awkward flailings and graspings lay the seeds of some of humankind's most advanced thought processes. Many of the clearest examples of the *active child* theme come from Piaget's descriptions of this stage.

Over the course of the first two years, according to Piaget, infants' sensorimotor intelligence develops through six increasingly complex substages, each one built upon the achievements of the preceding one. At first, this may seem like a lot of substages to go through in such a short time. However, considering that between birth and the age of 3, the brain triples in weight (with weight being an index of brain maturation during this period), the number of substages does not seem excessive. The profound developments that Piaget describes as occurring during infancy call attention to a general principle: Children's thinking grows especially rapidly in the first few years.

In the description of Piaget's six sensorimotor substages that follows, the age range that accompanies each substage is approximate. Different infants develop at different rates, but the age ranges do indicate when these developments typically occur.

Substage 1 (Birth to 1 Month)

Infants are born with many reflexes. When objects move in front of their eyes, they visually track them; when objects are placed in their mouths, they suck them; when objects come into contact with their hands, they grasp them; when they hear noises, they turn their heads toward them; and so on. Piaget believed that these simple reflexes and perceptual abilities are essential tools for building intelligence.

During their first month, infants begin to modify their reflexes to make them more adaptive. In the first days after birth, for example, they suck in a similar way regardless of the type of object they are sucking. Within a few weeks, however, they adjust their sucking according to the object in their mouth. Thus, they suck differently on a milk-bearing nipple than on their finger. As this example illustrates, even in their first month, infants accommodate their actions to the parts of the environment with which they interact.

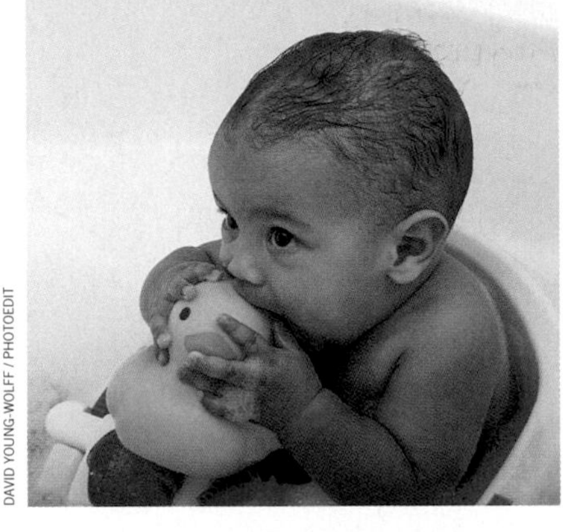

DAVID YOUNG-WOLFF / PHOTOEDIT

Piaget proposed that when infants suck on objects, they not only gain pleasure but also knowledge about the world beyond their bodies.

Substage 2 (1 to 4 Months)

In this period, infants begin to organize separate reflexes into larger behaviors, most of which are centered on their own bodies. Instead of just grasping objects that touch their palms and sucking on objects that come into their mouths, as they did in substage 1, during substage 2, infants integrate these actions. When holding objects with their hands, for example, they often bring them to their mouths. Thus, their reflexes begin to serve as building blocks for more complex behaviors.

Substage 3 (4 to 8 Months)

Whereas in the first two substages, infants' actions are reflex-bound and are centered on their own bodies, in substage 3, infants become increasingly interested in the world around them—people, animals, toys, and other objects and events beyond their own bodies. A hallmark of this substage is the repetition of actions on the environment that bring pleasurable or interesting results. Banging rattles, for example, is often a favorite activity for infants in substage 3.

Piaget (1954) made a striking and controversial claim about a deficiency in infants' thinking during this period, the one referred to in the anecdote at the beginning of the chapter about the father hiding his glasses. The claim was that through the age of 8 months, infants lack the concept of **object permanence,** that is, the knowledge that objects continue to exist even when they are out of view. This claim, like most of Piaget's ideas about infants, was based largely on his observations of his own children, Laurent, Lucienne, and Jacqueline. The following account of an experiment with Laurent reflects the type of observation that inspired Piaget's belief about object permanence:

At age 7 months, 28 days, I offer him a little bell behind a cushion. So long as he sees the little bell, however small it may be, he tries to grasp it. But if the little bell disappears completely he stops all searching.

I then resume the experiment using my hand as a screen. Laurent's arm is outstretched and about to grasp the little bell at the moment I make it disappear behind my hand which is open and at a distance of about 15 cm. from him. He immediately withdraws his arm, as though the little bell no longer existed.

(Piaget, 1954, p. 39)

Thus, in Piaget's view, for infants younger than 8 months, the adage "Out of sight, out of mind" is literally true. They are able to mentally represent only objects that they can perceive at the moment.

object permanence the knowledge that objects continue to exist even when they are out of view

A-Not-B error the tendency to reach where objects have been found before, rather than where they were last hidden

Substage 4 (8 to 12 Months)

By the end of the first year, infants search for hidden objects rather than acting as if they had vanished, thus indicating that they mentally represent the objects' continuing existence even when they no longer see them. These initial representations, however, are fragile; infants form them only under favorable circumstances. The fragility of 8- to 12-month-olds' representations of objects is reflected in the **A-Not-B error.** Once infants of that age have reached for and found a hidden object several times in one place (location A), when they see the object hidden at a different place (location B), and cannot immediately search for it, they tend to reach where they have found the object before (Figure 4.1). Not until around their first birthday do infants consistently search first at the object's current location.

(a)

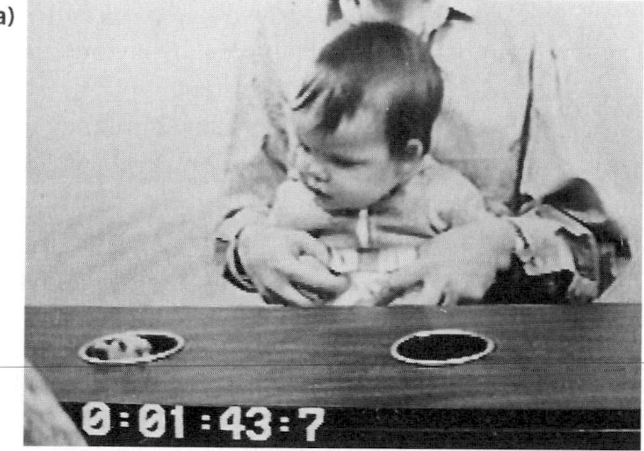

(b)

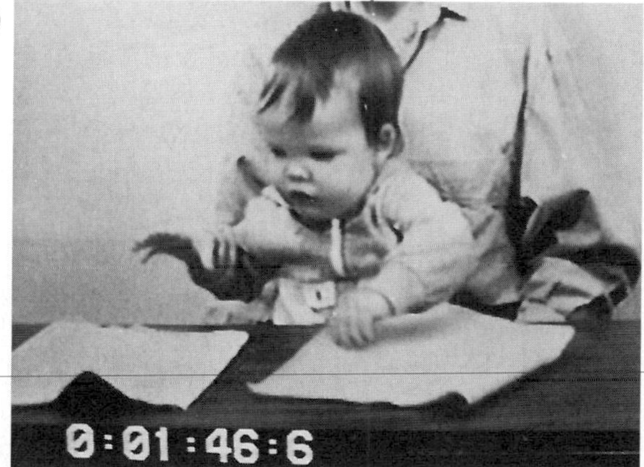

(c)

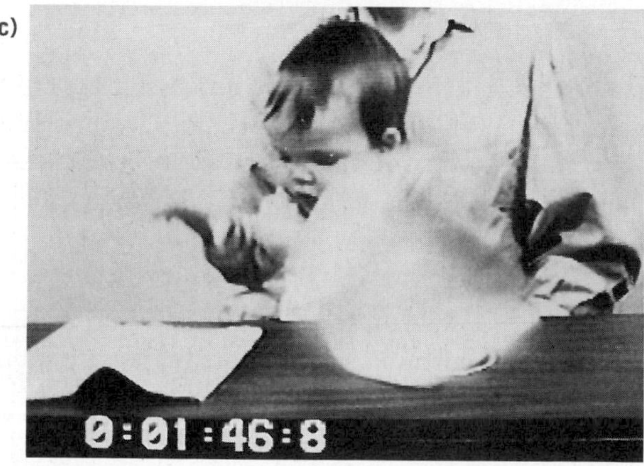

(d)

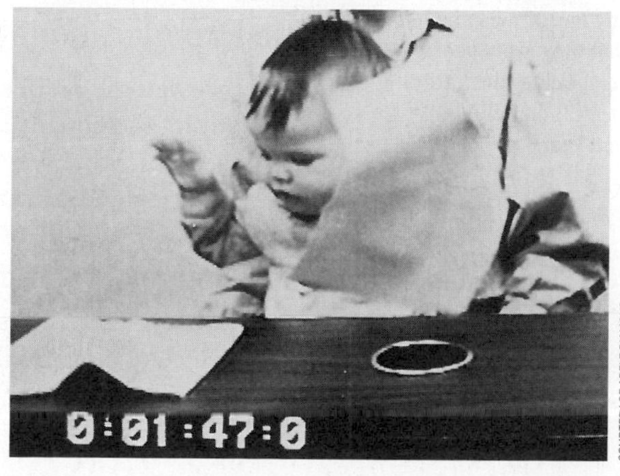

FIGURE 4.1 Piaget's A-Not-B task Just prior to this videotaped sequence, the infant saw a toy hidden in the circular hiding place to her left, saw it covered with a cloth, and retrieved it from under the cloth. (a) Now she sees the toy placed in the circular hiding place to her right. Rather than picking up the cloth on the right, which covers the toy now, she (b) reaches for the cloth on the left, which covers the place where she found the toy before, and (c, d) picks up that cloth.

deferred imitation the repetition of other people's behavior a substantial time after it originally occurred

symbolic representation the use of one object to stand for another

egocentrism the tendency to perceive the world solely from one's own point of view

Substage 5 (12 to 18 Months)

At around 1 year of age, infants begin to actively and avidly explore the potential uses to which objects can be put. The "child as scientist" example presented earlier, in which Laurent varied the positions from which he dropped different objects to see what would happen, provides one instance of this emerging competency. Similar examples occur in every family. Few parents forget their 12- to 18-month-olds' sitting in their high chairs, banging various objects against the high chair's tray—first a spoon, then a plate, then a cup—seemingly fascinated by the distinctive sounds made by the different objects. Much less do they forget their infants' dropping various bathroom articles into the toilet, or showering a bag of flour over the kitchen floor, just to see what happens. In such memorable incidents, Piaget perceived not bad intentions but the beginnings of scientific experiments.

Substage 6 (18 to 24 Months)

In this final period of the sensorimotor stage, according to Piaget, infants become able to form enduring mental representations. The first sign of this new capability is **deferred imitation,** that is, the repetition of other people's behavior minutes, hours, or days after it occurred. Consider Piaget's observation of 1-year-old Jacqueline:

> Jacqueline had a visit from a little boy . . . who, in the course of the afternoon, got into a terrible temper. He screamed as he tried to get out of a playpen and pushed it backward, stamping his feet. . . . The next day, she herself screamed in her playpen and tried to move it, stamping her foot lightly several times in succession.
> (Piaget, 1951, p. 63)

Piaget indicated that Jacqueline had never before thrown such a tantrum. Presumably she had watched and remembered her playmate's behavior, maintained a representation of it overnight, and imitated it the next day.

When we consider Piaget's whole account of development during infancy, several notable trends are evident. At first, infants' activities center on their own bodies; later, their activities include the world around them. Early goals are concrete (shaking a rattle and listening to the sound it makes); later goals often are more abstract (varying the heights from which objects are dropped and observing how the effects vary). Infants also become increasingly able to form mental representations, moving from "out of sight, out of mind" to remembering a playmate's actions from a full day earlier. Such enduring mental representations make possible the next stage, preoperational thinking.

COURTESY OF JUDY DELOACHE

This toddler's techniques for applying eye makeup may not exactly mirror those he has seen his mother use, but they are close enough to provide a compelling illustration of deferred imitation, a skill that children gain during their second year.

The Preoperational Stage (Ages 2 to 7)

Piaget viewed the preoperational period as including a mix of impressive cognitive acquisitions and equally impressive limitations. Perhaps the foremost acquisition is the development of *symbolic representations;* among the most striking weaknesses are *egocentrism* and *centration.*

Development of Symbolic Representations

Have you ever seen preschoolers use a popsicle stick to represent a gun or play with a piece of cloth as if it were a pillow? Forming such personal representations is common among 3- to 5-year-olds. It is one of the ways in which they exercise their emerging capacity for **symbolic representation**—the use of one object to stand for another. Typically, these personal symbols physically resemble the objects they represent. The popsicle stick's shape somewhat resembles that of a gun barrel; the cloth's texture is similar to that of the pillow, and both are comforting.

As children develop, they rely less on these self-generated symbols and more on conventional ones. For example, when 5-year-olds play games involving pirates, they might wear a patch over one eye and a kerchief over their head because that is the way pirates are commonly depicted. Heightened symbolic capabilities during the preoperational period are also evident in the growth of drawing. Children's drawings during this age range make increasing use of conventions, such as representing the leaves of flowers as V's (Figure 4.2).

FIGURE 4.2 A 4-year-old's drawing of a summer day Note the use of simple artistic conventions, such as the V-shaped leaves on the flowers (Dennis, 1992, p. 234).

Egocentrism

Although Piaget noted important positive developments in children's thinking during the preoperational stage, he placed greater emphasis on the limitations that remained. Among the most important is **egocentrism,** that is, perceiving the world solely from one's own point of view. One example of this limitation involves preschoolers' difficulty in taking other people's spatial perspectives. Piaget and Inhelder (1956) demonstrated this difficulty by having 4-year-olds sit at a table in front of a model of three mountains of different sizes (Figure 4.3). The children were asked to identify which of several photographs depicted what a doll would see if it were sitting on chairs at various points around the table. Solving this problem required children to recognize that their own perspective was not the only one possible and to imagine what the view would be from another location. Most 4-year-olds, according to Piaget, cannot do this.

FIGURE 4.3 Piaget's three-mountains task When asked to choose the picture that shows what the doll sitting in the seat across the table would see, most children below age 6 choose the picture showing how the scene looks to them, illustrating their difficulty in separating their own perspective from that of others.

The same difficulty in taking other people's perspectives is seen in quite different contexts, for example, in communication. As illustrated in Figure 4.4, preschoolers often talk right past each other; they seem blithely unaware that their listener is paying no attention whatsoever to what they are saying. Preschoolers' egocentric communication also is evident when they make statements that assume knowledge that they themselves possess but that their listeners are unlikely to share. For example, 2- and 3-year-olds frequently tell preschool teachers things like, "He took it from me," in situations where the teacher has no idea what person or object the child is referring to. Egocentric thinking is also evident in preschoolers' explanations of events and behavior. Consider the following interviews with preschoolers that occurred on a popular television show of the 1950s:

> *Interviewer:* Any brothers or sisters?
> *Child:* I have a brother a week old.
> *I:* What can he do?
> *C:* He can say "Mamma" and "Daddy."
> *I:* Can he walk?
> *C:* No, he's too lazy.
>
> *Interviewer:* Any brothers or sisters?
> *Child:* A 2-months-old brother.
> *I:* How does he behave?
> *C:* He cries all night.
> *I:* Why is that, do you think?
> *C:* He probably thinks he's missing something on television.
>
> (Linkletter, 1957, p. 6)

FIGURE 4.4 Egocentrism An example of young children's egocentric conversations.

Over the course of the preoperational period, egocentric speech becomes less common. An early sign of progress is children's verbal quarrels, which become increasingly frequent during this period. The fact that a child's statements elicit a playmate's disagreement indicates that the playmate is at least paying attention to what the other child is saying and the differing perspective that it implies. Children also become better able to envision spatial perspectives other than their own. Of course, we all remain somewhat egocentric throughout our lives, but we do improve.

Centration

A related limitation of preschoolers' thinking is **centration,** that is, focusing on a single, perceptually striking feature of an object or event to the exclusion of other, less striking features. Children's approaches to balance scales provide a good example of centration. If presented with a balance scale like that in Figure 4.5 and asked "Which side will go down?" 5- and 6-year-olds center on the amount of weight on each side, ignore the distance of the weight from the fulcrum, and say that whichever side has more weight will go down (Inhelder & Piaget, 1958).

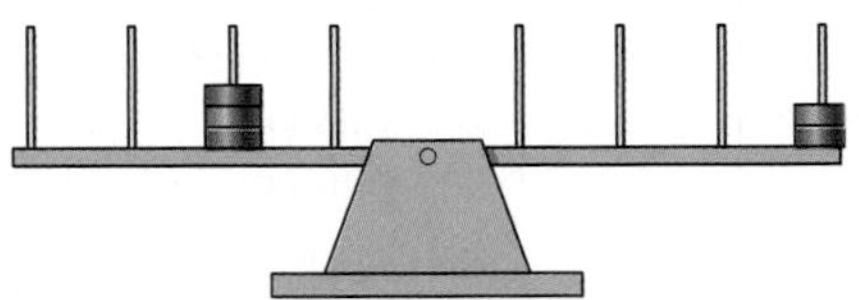

FIGURE 4.5 Balance scale study by Case (1992) When asked to predict which side of a balance scale, like the one shown above, would go down if the arm were allowed to move, 5- and 6-year-olds almost always center their attention on the amount of weight and ignore the distances of the weights from the fulcrum. Thus, they would predict that the left side would go down, although the right side actually would.

Another good example of centration comes from Piaget's research on children's understanding of the concepts of time, speed, and distance. This research arose from an encounter between Piaget and the great physicist Albert Einstein. In 1928, Einstein attended a lecture by Piaget and afterward asked about the order in which children acquire the concepts of time and velocity (speed), concepts of fundamental importance within Einstein's own theory. To find the answer to this question, Piaget (1946) presented 4- to 10-year-olds with two toy trains running along parallel tracks in the same direction (Figure 4.6). After the cars stopped moving, Piaget asked the children, "Which train traveled for the longer time (or for the longer distance, or at the faster speed)?"

Most 4- and 5-year-olds focused entirely on one dimension of the events—the trains' stopping points. They claimed that the train that stopped farther down the track also had traveled for the longer time (or farther, or faster). They ignored where and when the trains started, when they stopped, and the total time for which they traveled. Not until roughly age 9 did they consider more than one dimension of the problem.

The example illustrates another quality often seen in preoperational thinking—a focus on static states rather than transformations. The trains' stopping points are static positions; they remain constant after the trains have completed their travel. The time, speed, and distance for which the trains traveled all involve transformations, which are not available for inspection after the trains stop moving. Children in the preoperational stage frequently ignore transformations and focus instead on static states, even when doing so leads to incorrect judgments.

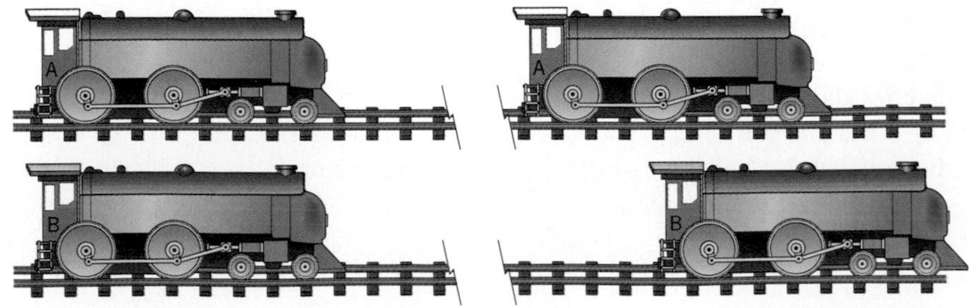

FIGURE 4.6 Piaget's train problem If two trains start and stop at the same time, but one stops farther up the track, children below age 8 usually say that the train that stopped farther up the track traveled for more time.

To summarize, Piaget proposed that 2- to- 7-year-olds have difficulty taking perspectives other than their own, that they center on perceptually salient dimensions at the expense of dimensions that are less salient but equally or more important, and that they focus on static states over transformations. In the next period of cognitive development, the concrete operations stage, children largely overcome these limitations.

centration the tendency to focus on a single, perceptually striking feature of an object or event

conservation concept the idea that merely changing the appearance of objects does not change their key properties

The Concrete Operations Stage (Ages 7 to 12)

At around age 7, according to Piaget, children begin to reason logically about concrete features of the world. Development of the conservation concept, one of Piaget's most famous discoveries, exemplifies this progress.

The idea of the **conservation concept** is that merely changing the appearance or arrangement of objects does not change their key properties, such as quantity of material. Three variants of the concept that are commonly studied in children are conservation of liquid quantity, conservation of solid quantity, and conservation of number (Piaget, 1952a). In all three cases, the tasks used to measure children's understanding share a three-phase procedure (Figure 4.7). First, children see two objects or sets of objects—such as two glasses of orangeade, two clay balls, or two rows of pennies—that are identical in number or quantity. Once children agree that the dimension of interest (e.g., the amount of orangeade) is equal, the second phase follows. Here, one object or set of objects is transformed in a way that makes it look different but does not change the dimension in question. A glass of orangeade might be poured into a taller, narrower, glass; a short, thick clay sausage

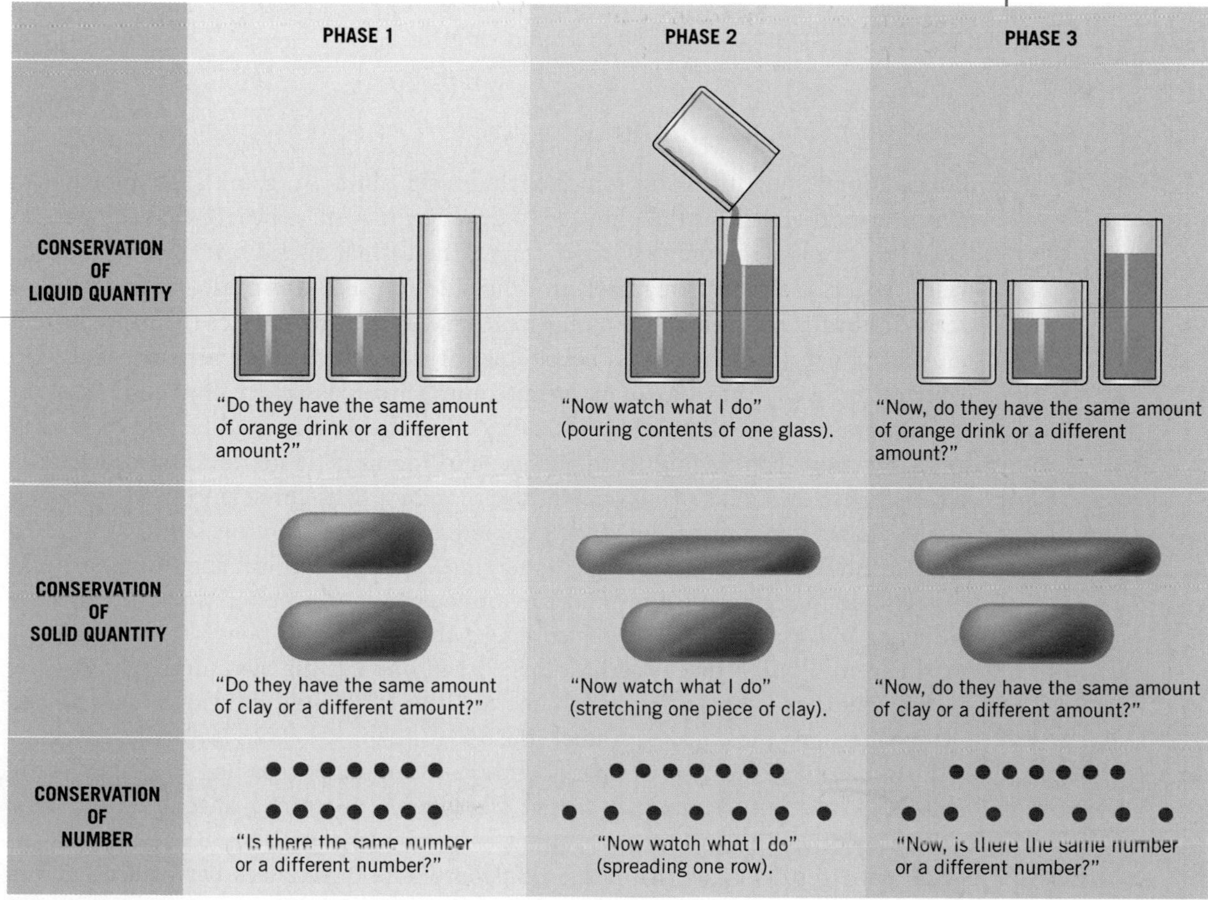

FIGURE 4.7 Procedures used to test conservation of liquid quantity, solid quantity, and number Most children below age 7 say that the taller liquid column has more liquid, the longer sausage has more clay, and the longer row has more objects.

might be molded into a long, thin sausage; or a row of pennies might be lengthened. Finally, in the third phase, children are asked whether the dimension of interest, which they earlier had said was equal for the two objects or sets of objects, is still equal. Children age 7 and older generally say yes, which of course is correct.

However, 4- and 5-year-olds generally answer no. On conservation-of-liquid-quantity problems, they claim that the taller, narrower glass has more orangeade; on conservation-of-solid-quantity problems, they claim that the long, thin sausage has more clay than the short, thick one; and so on.

All the weaknesses that Piaget perceived in preoperational children's thinking seem to contribute to their difficulty with conservation problems. They center their attention on the single, perceptually salient dimension of height or length, ignoring other relevant dimensions. They respond to appearances rather than to the underlying reality and fail to understand that their own perspective can be misleading. They focus on the static state (height of the liquid column or length of the clay sausage) and ignore the transformation that was performed (pouring the orangeade or reshaping the clay).

The same progress in thinking that allows children in the concrete operations stage to solve conservation problems also allows them to solve many other problems that require attention to multiple dimensions and consideration of transformations. For example, they master the train problem that was used to measure understanding of time, speed, and distance, and they consider distance from the fulcrum as well as weight on the balance-scale problem.

This successful reasoning, however, is largely limited to concrete situations. Highly abstract thinking remains very difficult, as does reasoning about hypothetical situations. Only during the formal operations stage, according to Piaget, do children become able to think well about hypothetical situations and abstractions, as well as concrete situations.

The Formal Operations Stage (Age 12 and Beyond)

Formal operational thinking, which includes the ability to think abstractly and to reason hypothetically, is the pinnacle of the Piagetian stage progression. Piaget believed that unlike the previous three stages, the formal operations stage is not universal; some adolescents reach it but others do not. For those adolescents who do reach it, formal operational thinking greatly expands and enriches their intellectual universe. Such thinking makes it possible for them to see the particular reality in which they live as only one of an infinite number of possible realities. This insight leads them to think about alternative ways that the world could be and to ponder deep questions concerning truth, justice, and morality. It no doubt also helps account for the fact that many people first acquire a taste for science fiction during adolescence. The alternative worlds depicted in science-fiction stories appeal to adolescents' desire to exercise their emerging capacity to think about our world as just one of many possibilities and to wonder whether a better world is possible. Inhelder and Piaget (1958) aptly expressed the intellectual power that formal operational thinking provides adolescents: "Each one has his own ideas (and usually he believes they are his own) which liberate him from childhood and allow him to place himself as the equal of adults" (pp. 340–341).

Another vital feature of formal operational thinking, according to Piaget, is the ability to reason systematically about all possible outcomes of a situation. This ability is crucial for scientific reasoning, in particular the ability to design and interpret the results of experiments. Consider some differences between children's and adolescents' ability to generate systematic scientific experiments to solve a pendulum problem (Inhelder & Piaget, 1958). In this problem, children are presented a pendulum frame, a set of strings of varying length with a loop at each end, and a set of metal weights of varying weight, any of which can be attached to any string. When the loop at one end of the string is attached to a weight, and the loop at the other end is attached to the frame of the pendulum, the string can be swung (Figure 4.8). The task is to determine which factor or factors influence the amount of time it takes the pendulum to swing through a complete arc: the length of the string, the heaviness of the weight, the height from which the weight is dropped, or some combination of these factors. Think for a minute: How would you go about solving this problem?

Most concrete operational children, like most adolescents, begin their experiments believing that the heaviness of the weight is the most important factor, and quite likely the only important one. Where children and adolescents differ is in how they test their beliefs. Concrete operational children typically design unsystematic experiments from which no clear conclusion can be drawn. For example, they might compare the travel time of a heavy weight on a short string released from a high point to the travel time of a light weight on a long string released from a low point. When the first pendulum goes faster, they would conclude that, just as they thought, heavy weights go faster.

In contrast, adolescents in the formal operational stage would frame the problem more abstractly. They would realize that any of the variables—weight, string length, and dropping point—might influence the time it took for the pendulum to swing through an arc and that they therefore should test how each variable influenced the travel time. To test the role of weight, they would compare times to complete an arc for a heavier weight and a lighter weight, attached to strings of equal length and dropped from the same height. To test the effect of string length, they would compare the travel times of a long and a short string, with equal weight dropped from an identical position. To test the influence of dropping point, they would vary the dropping point of a given weight attached to a given string. Such a systematic set of experiments would allow the formal operational reasoner to learn that only string length influences the pendulum's travel time; neither weight nor dropping point matters.

The attainment of such systematic formal operational reasoning does not mean that adolescents will always reason in advanced ways, but it does, according to Piaget, mark the point at which adolescents have the reasoning powers of intelligent adults. Some ways in which Piaget's theory can be applied to improving education are discussed in Box 4.1.

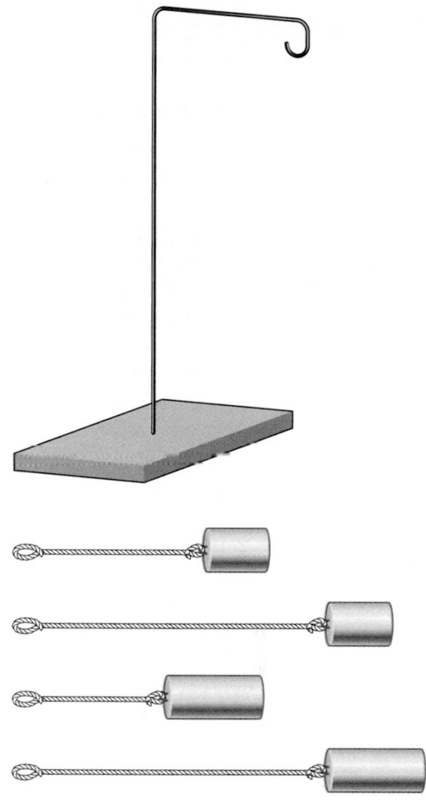

FIGURE 4.8 Inhelder and Piaget's pendulum problem The task is to compare the motions of longer and shorter strings, with lighter and heavier weights attached, in order to determine the influence of weight, string length, and dropping point on the time it takes for the pendulum to swing back and forth. Children below age 12 usually perform unsystematic experiments and draw incorrect conclusions.

TABLE 4.2

Piaget's Stages of Cognitive Development

Stage	Approximate Age	New Ways of Knowing
Sensorimotor	Birth to 2 years	Infants know the world through their senses and through their actions. For example, they learn what dogs look like and what petting them feels like.
Preoperational	2–7 years	Toddlers and young children acquire the ability to internally represent the world through language and mental imagery. They also begin to be able to see the world from other people's perspectives, not just from their own.
Concrete operational	7–12 years	Children become able to think logically, not just intuitively. They now can classify objects into coherent categories and understand that events are often influenced by multiple factors, not just one.
Formal operational	12 years onward	Adolescents can think systematically and reason about what might be as well as what is. This allows them to understand politics, ethics, and science fiction, as well as to engage in scientific reasoning.

applications 4.1

Educational Applications of Piaget's Theory

Piaget's view of children's cognitive development holds a number of general implications for how children should be educated (Ginsburg & Opper, 1988; Piaget, 1970). Most generally, it suggests that children's distinctive ways of thinking at different ages need to be considered in deciding how to teach them. For example, children in the preoperational and concrete operational stages would not be expected to be ready to learn purely abstract concepts such as inertia and equilibrium state, whereas adolescents in the formal operational stage would be expected to be ready to learn such concepts. Taking into account such general age-related differences in cognitive level before deciding when to teach particular concepts is often labeled a "child-centered approach."

A second implication of Piaget's approach is that children learn by interacting with the environment, both mentally and physically. One application of this emphasis on activity concerned understanding of the concept of speed (Levin, Siegler, & Druyan, 1990). The investigation focused on problems of a type beloved by physics teachers: "When a race horse travels around a circular track, do its right and left sides move at the same speed?" It appears obvious that they do, but in fact they do not. The part of the horse toward the outside of the track is covering a slightly greater distance in the same amount of time as the part toward the inside and therefore is moving slightly faster.

Levin and her colleagues devised a procedure that allowed children to actively experience how different parts of a single object can move at different speeds. One of the researchers purchased a metal bar almost 7 feet long, brought it to a room in her basement, and attached one end of it to a pivot that was mounted on the floor. Later, sixth graders were brought individually to the researcher's house and taken to the room that contained the metal bar and pivot. The researcher and the child took four walks around the pivot while holding onto the bar. On two of the walks, the child held the bar near the pivot and the experimenter held it at the far end; on the other two walks, they switched positions (see the figure). After each walk, children were asked whether they or the experimenter had walked faster.

The differences in the speeds required for walking while holding the inner and the outer parts of the metal bar were so dramatic that the children generalized their new understanding to other problems involving circular motion, such as cars moving around circular tracks on a computer screen. In other words, physically experiencing the concept accomplished what years of formal science instruction usually fail to do. As one boy said, "Before, I hadn't experienced it. I didn't think about it. Now that I have had that experience, I know that when I was on the outer circle, I had to walk faster to be at the same place as you" (Levin et al., 1990). Clearly, relevant physical activities, accompanied by questions that call attention to the lessons of the activities, can foster children's learning.

A child and an adult holding onto a bar as they walk around a circle. Twice, the child held the bar near the pivot; twice, the child held it at its end. The much faster pace needed to keep up with the bar when holding onto its end led children to realize that the end was moving faster than the middle (Levin, Siegler, & Druyan, 1990).

Piaget's Legacy

Although much of Piaget's theory was formulated many years ago, it remains a very influential approach to cognitive development. Some of its strengths were mentioned earlier. It provides a good overview of what children's thinking is like at different points in development. It offers a plausible and appealing perspective on children's nature. It surveys a remarkably broad spectrum of developments and covers the entire age span from infancy through adolescence. It includes countless fascinating observations of how children think.

However, subsequent analyses (Flavell, 1971, 1982; Miller, 2002) have also noted some crucial weaknesses in Piaget's theory. The following four weaknesses are among the most important:

1. The stage model depicts children's thinking as being more consistent than it is. According to Piaget, once children enter a given stage, their thinking shows the characteristics of that stage consistently across diverse concepts. Subsequent research, however, has shown that children's thinking is far more variable than this depiction suggests. Even with regard to a single concept such as conservation, performance on different tasks is quite variable. For example, most children succeed on conservation-of-number problems by age 5 or 6, whereas most do not succeed on conservation-of-solid-quantity problems until age 8 or 9 (Field, 1987; Siegler, 1981). Piaget recognized that such variability exists but was unable to explain it successfully.

2. Infants and young children are more cognitively competent than Piaget recognized. Piaget presented children with relatively difficult tests of understanding. This had the advantage of guaranteeing that a child who succeeded on one of his tasks had a good understanding of the concept being tested. However, the challenging tasks also led Piaget to miss infants' and young children's earliest knowledge of these concepts. For example, Piaget's test of object permanence required children to reach for the hidden object; as Piaget claimed, children do not do this until 8 or 9 months of age. However, alternative tests of object permanence, which analyze infants' eye fixations after the object has disappeared from view, indicate that infants have some grasp of the continuing existence of objects by 3 months of age (Baillargeon, 1987, 1993).

3. Piaget's theory understates the contribution of the social world to cognitive development. Piaget's theory focuses primarily on how children come to understand the world through their own efforts. From the day that children emerge from the womb, however, they live in a profoundly social environment that shapes their development in countless ways. A child's cognitive development reflects the contributions of other people and of the broader culture to a far greater degree than Piaget's theory acknowledges.

4. Piaget's theory is vague about the cognitive processes that give rise to children's thinking and about the mechanisms that produce cognitive growth. Piaget's theory provides any number of excellent descriptions of children's thinking. The theory is far less clear, however, about the processes that lead them to think in a particular way and that produce changes in their thinking. Assimilation, accommodation, and equilibration have a general air of plausibility, but how they operate is far from clear.

These weaknesses of Piaget's theory do not negate the magnitude of his achievement. His innumerable revealing tasks for testing children's abilities at different ages, his fascinating observations of age-related changes in children's behavior, and his integrated depiction of cognitive development from birth through adolescence combine to make his theory one of the major intellectual achievements of the twentieth century. However, appreciating the weaknesses as well as the strengths of his theory is necessary for understanding why alternative theories of cognitive development have become increasingly prominent.

In the sections that follow, we consider the three most prominent alternative theories: *information-processing, core-knowledge,* and *sociocultural.* Each type of theory can be seen as an attempt to overcome a major weakness of Piaget's approach. Information-processing theories emphasize precise characterizations of the processes that give rise to children's thinking and the mechanisms that produce cognitive growth. Core-knowledge theories emphasize early understandings of infants and young children that may have an innate evolutionary basis. Sociocultural theories emphasize the ways in which children's interactions with the social world, both with other people and with the products of their culture, guide cognitive development. In addition, theorists of all three persuasions agree that children's thinking is more variable than is recognized within Piaget's stage theory. The remainder of this chapter focuses on these three alternative theories.

review:

Piaget's theory of cognitive development emphasizes the interaction of nature and nurture, continuities and discontinuities, and children's active contribution to their own development. Piaget believed that a maturing brain, maturing abilities to perceive and act, and increasingly rich and varied experiences interacting with the environment allow children to adapt to an increasing range of circumstances.

According to Piaget, the continuities of development are produced by assimilation, accommodation, and equilibration. Assimilation involves simplifying incoming information so that it can be understood. Accommodation involves adapting one's thinking toward being more consistent with new experiences. Equilibration involves balancing assimilation and accommodation in a way that creates stable understandings.

The discontinuities of development involve four discrete stages—the sensorimotor stage (birth to age 2), in which infants begin to know the world through the perceptions of their senses and through their motor activities; the preoperational stage (ages 2 to 7), in which children become capable of mental representations but tend to be egocentric and to focus on a single dimension of an event or problem; the concrete operational stage (ages 7 to 12), in which children reason logically about concrete aspects of the environment but have difficulty thinking abstractly; and the formal operational stage (age 12 and beyond), in which preadolescents and adolescents become capable of abstract as well as concrete thought.

Among the most important strengths of Piaget's theory are its broad overview of development, attractive perspective on children's nature, inclusion of varied tasks and age groups, and endlessly fascinating observations. Among the theory's most important weaknesses are its vagueness regarding cognitive mechanisms, its underestimation of infants' and young children's cognitive competence, its lack of attention to the contribution of the social world, and its overstatement of the consistency of children's thinking.

Information-Processing Theories

SCENE: DAUGHTER AND FATHER IN THEIR YARD. A PLAYMATE RIDES IN ON A BIKE

Child: Daddy, would you unlock the basement door?
Father: Why?
C: 'Cause I want to ride my bike.
F: Your bike is in the garage.
C: But my socks are in the dryer.

(Klahr, 1978, pp. 181–182)

What reasoning could have produced this girl's enigmatic comment, "But my socks are in the dryer"? David Klahr, an eminent information-processing theorist, formulated the following model of the thought process that led to it:

Top goal: I want to ride my bike.
  Bias: I need shoes to ride comfortably.
  Fact: I'm barefoot.
    Subgoal 1: Get my sneakers.
    Fact: The sneakers are in the yard.
    Fact: They're uncomfortable on bare feet.
      Subgoal 2: Get my socks.
      Fact: The sock drawer was empty this morning.
      Inference: The socks probably are in the dryer.
        Subgoal 3: Get them from the dryer.

Fact: The dryer is in the basement.
Subgoal 4: Go to the basement.
Fact: It's quicker to go through the yard entrance.
Fact: The yard entrance is always locked.
Subgoal 5: Unlock the door to the basement.
Fact: Daddies have the keys to everything.
Subgoal 6: Ask daddy to unlock the door.

Klahr's analysis of his daughter's thinking illustrates several notable characteristics that are common to information-processing theories.[1] As noted previously, one distinctive feature is precise specification of the processes involved in children's thinking. Thus, Klahr attempted to identify what his daughter's exact goals were, what environmental obstacles she anticipated, and what reasoning led her to the strategy of asking him to unlock the basement door. Such **task analysis**—that is, identification of goals, relevant information in the environment, and potential processing strategies—helps information-processing researchers understand and predict children's behavior.

task analysis the research technique of identifying goals, relevant information in the environment, and potential processing strategies for a problem

A second distinctive characteristic that is evident in Klahr's information-processing analysis is an emphasis on thinking as a *process* that occurs over time. In his analysis, Klahr depicts his daughter as generating a sequence of subgoals and relevant facts, one after another, in planning how to reach the overall goal of riding her bike in comfort.

A third distinctive characteristic of information-processing theories is their underlying metaphor of the child as computational system. A computer's information processing is limited by its hardware and its software. The hardware limitations include the computer's memory capacity and the efficiency with which it executes basic operations. The software limitations include the strategies and knowledge available for particular tasks. People's information processing is limited by the same factors: memory capacity, efficiency of thought processes, and availability of relevant strategies and knowledge. The computational analogy is also evident in the resemblance between the step-by-step processes of computer programs and the step-by-step analyses in Klahr's and many other information-processing models of children's thinking (e.g., Gentner, Ratterman, Markman, & Kotovsky, 1995; Halford et al., 1995; Klahr & MacWhinney, 1998; Shrager & Siegler, 1998; Shultz, Schmidt, Buckingham, & Mareschal, 1995). In the information-processing view, cognitive development arises from children's gradually surmounting their processing limitations through increasingly effective execution of basic processes, expanding memory capacities, and acquisition of new strategies and knowledge.

View of Children's Nature

Information-processing theorists view children as undergoing continuous cognitive change. The term "continuous" applies in two senses. First, important changes are viewed as occurring constantly, rather than being restricted to special transition

[1] Here and throughout this section, we use the plural term "information-processing *theories*" rather than the singular term "information-processing *theory*" because information theories consist of a variety of related approaches, rather than reflecting the unified ideas of a single theorist such as Piaget. For the same reason, in subsequent sections we refer to "core-knowledge theories" and "sociocultural theories."

problem solving the process of attaining a goal by using a strategy to overcome an obstacle

periods between stages. Second, cognitive growth is viewed as typically occurring in small increments rather than abruptly. This depiction differs from Piaget's belief that children progress through qualitatively distinct stages separated only by relatively brief transition periods.

The Child as Problem Solver

Also basic to information-processing theories is the assumption that children are active problem solvers. As suggested by Klahr's analysis of his daughter's behavior, **problem solving** involves a goal, a perceived obstacle, and a strategy or rule for overcoming the obstacle and attaining the goal. Another description of a young child's problem solving reveals the same combination of goal, obstacle, and strategy:

> Georgie (a 2-year-old) wants to throw rocks out the kitchen window. The lawnmower is outside. Dad says that Georgie can't throw rocks out the window, because he'll break the lawnmower with the rocks. Georgie says, "I got an idea." He goes outside, brings in some green peaches that he had been playing with, and says: "They won't break the lawnmower."
>
> (Waters, 1989, p. 7).

In addition to illustrating the goal–obstacle–strategy sequence, this example points to two key cognitive processes that are emphasized in information-processing analyses of children's problem solving: planning and analogical reasoning.

Planning Problem solving is often more successful if people first plan what to do. Georgie did not just happen to gather the green peaches; they were part of his plan to continue throwing things out the window while obeying his father's instruction to stop throwing rocks.

Children begin to form simple plans by their first birthday. In one demonstration of this capability, Willatts (1990) presented 12-month-olds with a solid barrier, behind which lay a cloth with a string attached and a toy that was too far away for the baby to reach (Figure 4.9). Sometimes the toy was attached to the string; other times it was not. The babies were quicker to knock the barrier out of the way, grab the cloth, and pull the string when the toy was attached to the string than when it was not. Willatts's analysis of the children's information processing indicated that they had formulated a three-step plan for reaching the goal: remove the obstacle, pull in the cloth, and grab the string to get the toy.

COURTESY OF PETER WILLATTS, UNIVERSITY OF DUNDEE, SCOTLAND

FIGURE 4.9 Planning Procedure used by Willats (1990) to examine 12-month-olds' planning. To get the attractive toy, the baby needed to knock the barrier out of the way (left frame) and then pull in the towel connected by the string to the toy (right frame).

As children grow older, they make a greater variety of plans, including ones concerning how to get to friends' houses, what books to read for reports, and when to study for tests. This planning helps them solve a broader range of problems than they would be able to solve without planning (Hudson, Sosa, & Schapiro, 1997; Scholnick, Friedman, & Wallner-Allen, 1997). For example, when middle-school children were required to plan a strategy before playing a game of "20 Questions," they identified the answer after fewer questions than did their peers who were not required to plan (Ellis & Siegler, 1997). Despite the advantages of planning, however, many children fail to plan in situations in which it would help their problem solving (Berg, Strough, Calderone, Meegan, & Sansone, 1997). The question is why.

Analysis of the information-processing requirements of planning indicates that it requires a kind of strategy choice, in which the person decides to forgo immediate attempts to solve the problem in favor of analyzing which strategy is likely to be most effective. Within this perspective, several factors seem likely to lead children, especially young ones, to choose not to plan even when doing so would help them solve problems:

1. *Inhibiting action is difficult.* Planning requires children to inhibit their desire to move directly toward the goal. Ability to inhibit action is quite limited during early childhood; children below age 5 or 6 years have special difficulty resisting the desire to act (Dempster, 1993, 1995). A large part of the reason is that the frontal lobe, a part of the brain that plays an important part in inhibition, is one of the last parts of the brain to mature, with substantial maturation occurring between age 5 and adolescence (Ridderinkhof & Molen, 1997).

2. *Young children tend to be overoptimistic.* Optimism is an attractive quality, but young children have it in excess. They think that they can remember more, communicate more effectively, and imitate a model more accurately than they actually can (Bjorklund, 1997; Schneider, 1998). This overoptimism can lead them not to plan, because they think they will succeed without planning. The overoptimisim also can lead them to act rashly. For example, 6-year-olds who overestimate their physical abilities have more accidents than less optimistic children (Plumert, 1995). Older children are more realistic in assessing their capabilities, which contributes to their planning more often.

3. *Plans can fail.* As the Scottish poet Robert Burns (1786) wrote, "The best-laid schemes o' Mice an' Men / gang aft agley. . . ." Plans can fail either because they were inherently flawed or because they were badly executed. Children's and adolescents' plans often fail for both reasons (Schauble, 1996). This high failure rate makes planning a less attractive option than if planning were consistently successful.

As these examples imply, brain maturation, in combination with experiences that reduce overoptimism and demonstrate the value of planning, leads to an increase in the frequency and quality of planning well into adolescence (Chalmers & Lawrence, 1993). Even adolescents and adults, however, fail to plan in many situations in which doing so would help them solve problems (Friedman & Scholnick, 1997).

PHOTOS COURTESY OF JODIE PLUMERT

Young children's overoptimism sometimes leads them to engage in dangerous activities. This particular plan worked out fine, but not all do.

Analogical reasoning People often understand new problems in terms of familiar ones. For example, Goswami (1995) found that reminding 3- and 4-year-olds of the story "Goldilocks and the Three Bears" helped them solve problems in which they needed to order objects on dimensions such as temperature (boiling hot, hot, and warm food). Information-processing analyses indicate that, as in this example, successful analogical reasoning requires ignoring superficial dissimilarities (whether the objects are bears or food) and focusing on underlying parallel relationships (the ordering from greatest to least on size and temperature). Georgie's substitution of green peaches for rocks was another example of drawing on analogy to solve a problem.

As with planning, a rudimentary form of analogical reasoning emerges around children's first birthday. This early competence, however, is initially limited to situations in which the new problem closely resembles the old. Thus, when 10-month-olds saw their mothers demonstrate how to solve the barrier-and-toy problem shown in Figure 4.9, they applied the lesson to new parallel problems only when the new problems included several superficial features—colors, sizes, shapes, and locations of objects—similar to those in the original (Chen, Sanchez, & Campbell, 1997). In contrast, 13-month-olds also drew the analogy when the new and old problems shared fewer superficial features.

Superficial similarity between the original and new problems continues to influence analogical reasoning well beyond infancy. Even in middle childhood, younger children often require more surface similarity to draw an analogy than do older ones (Gentner, 1989). When asked to explain the statement "A camera is like a tape recorder," for example, 6-year-olds tend to cite superficial similarities, such as that both are often black; in contrast, 9-year-olds tend to cite deeper similarities, such as that both devices are used to record information (Gentner et al., 1995). The 9-year-olds' deeper understanding of the nature of tape recorders and cameras enables them to see analogies between the two devices that the less knowledgeable 6-year-olds miss.

Central Developmental Issues

Like all the theories described in this chapter, information-processing theories examine how *nature and nurture* work together to produce development. What makes information-processing theories unique is their emphasis on precise descriptions of *how change occurs.* The way in which information-processing theories address the issues of nature and nurture and how change occurs can be seen particularly clearly in their account of the development of memory and learning.

An Overview of the Development of Memory and Learning

Infants enter the world with the ability to execute a variety of basic processes that help them remember and learn from their experiences. Over the course of development, they become more efficient in executing these basic processes, and they acquire strategies and content knowledge that further enhance their memory and learning ability.

Basic Processes

The simplest and most frequently used mental activities are known as **basic processes.** They include associating events with each other, recognizing objects as familiar, generalizing from one instance to another, and **encoding** (representing in memory) specific features of objects and events.

These basic processes contribute to memory development and learning in two main ways. First, they help development get off the ground by allowing infants to learn and remember even in their earliest days. Second, with development, children execute basic processes more efficiently, which further enhances their memory and learning.

basic processes the simplest and most frequently used mental activities

encoding the process of representing in memory information that draws attention or is considered important

Encoding Although people often think of memory as a verbatim record of events, akin to a movie of their life, remembering is actually a far more selective activity. People *encode* information that draws their attention or that they consider important; however, they fail to encode a great deal of other information. This failure can probably be seen in your own memory of the American flag; although you have seen it many times, you most likely have not encoded exactly how the stars in the blue field are arranged.

"Mirror, mirror, on the wall, who's the fairest of the mall?"

FIGURE 4.10 Misencoding Misencoding common sayings can lead to memorable confusions.

Some crucial information, such as data on the relative frequency of events, is encoded automatically. For example, almost everyone can answer the following question, "Which letter occurs more often: *i* or *e*?" Yet no one tries to remember the relative frequency of letters of the alphabet. We just acquire a sense that *e* occurs more often through seeing it more often. People of all ages seem to automatically remember such frequency information, which is fortunate, because such automatic encoding of frequencies is crucial for learning (Hasher & Zacks, 1984). When children form concepts, they must encode features of objects and events and remember which features tend to go together. Learning the concept "bird," for example, requires the observation that animals that fly also tend to have feathers, to have beaks, and to live in trees. Such encoding of frequency information is present from early in infancy (Saffran, Aslin, & Newport, 1996).

Children do not encode all of the important information in the environment, however (Figure 4.10). Their limited encoding is evident on the balance-scale task, in which, as you may recall, the large majority of 5- and 6-year olds predict that the side with more weight will go down, regardless of the distance of the weights from the fulcrum. The reason for this exclusive reliance on weight seems to be that when shown a balance scale, children at this age do not encode information about distance from the fulcrum. This failure was demonstrated in an experiment in which 5- and 6-year olds were shown a balance scale with weights on pegs, and then, with that scale hidden from view, were asked to reproduce the arrangement of its weights on pegs with another balance scale that was without weights but otherwise identical. Most put the right number of weights on both sides (showing that they encoded weight), but they put them on the wrong pegs (showing that they did not encode distance from the fulcrum). In addition, teaching 5-year-olds to encode the distance of weights from the fulcrum, as well as the amount of weight, increased their ability to learn from subsequent experience with balance scales, relative to a control group of peers who had not been taught earlier to encode distance (Siegler, 1976). Thus, improved encoding leads to improved ability to learn.

Speed of processing The speed with which children execute basic processes increases greatly over the course of childhood. As shown in Figure 4.11, processing speed increases most rapidly at young ages but continues to increase well into adolescence (Hale, Frye, & Jessie, 1993; Kail, 1991, 1997; Miller & Vernon, 1997; Zelazo, Kearsley, & Stack, 1995). Everyone agrees on these facts.

Considerable controversy exists, however, about whether the increasing processing speed reflects biological maturation as well as experience. The role of experience is self-evident: everyone processes familiar information faster than unfamiliar information (think how much faster you are at understanding an English sentence than at understanding the equivalent sentence in whatever foreign language you studied in high school). Some researchers believe that all age-related improvements in processing speed are due to the increasing experience that comes with age (e.g., Chi, 1978); others believe that biological maturation also contributes (e.g., Case, 1992).

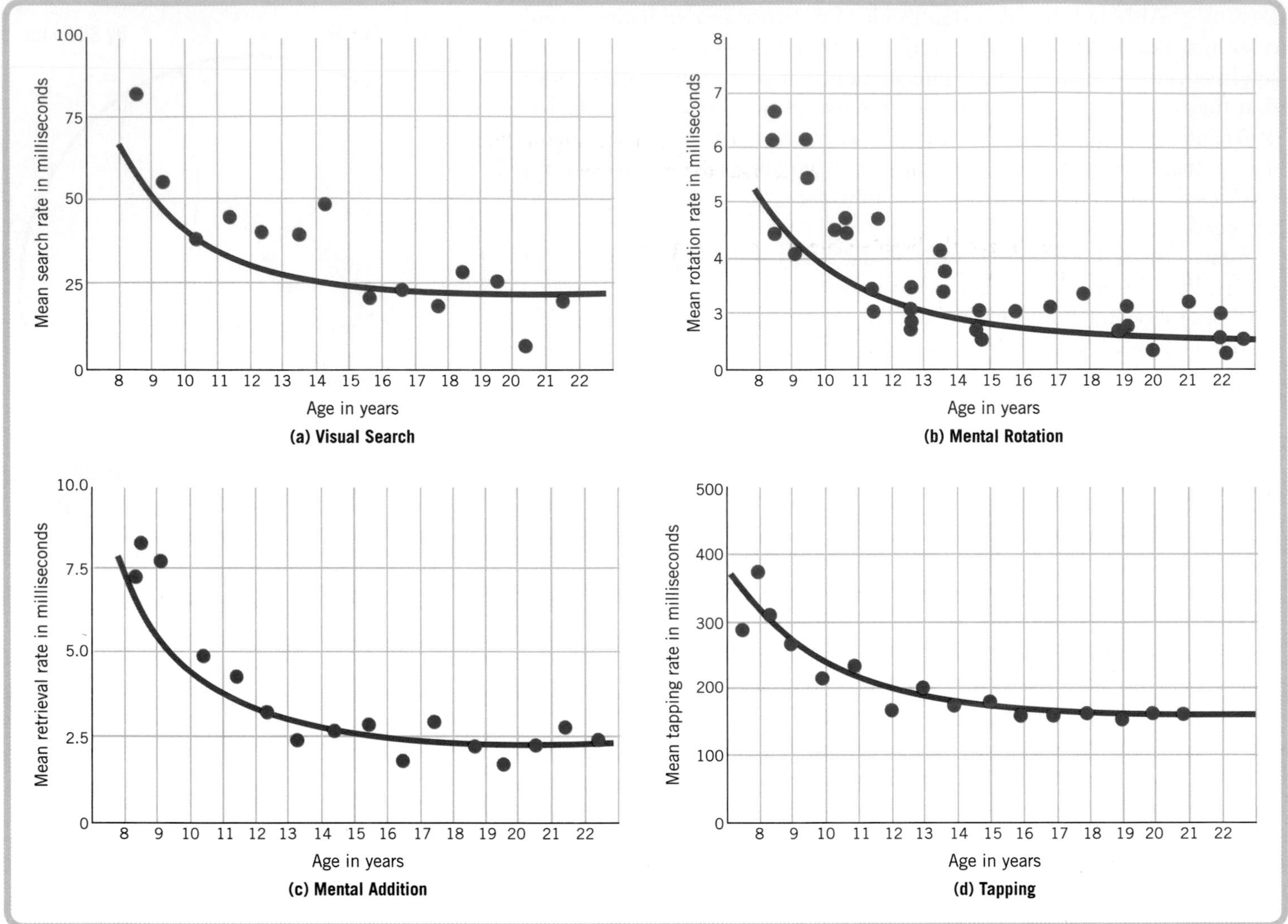

FIGURE 4.11 Increase with age in processing on four tasks **Note that on all four tasks, the increase is rapid in the early years and more gradual later.**

Recent evidence supports the view that biological maturation, as well as experience, contributes to increased processing speed. Eaton and Ritchot (1995) presented fourth graders with simple information-processing tasks with which everyone of the same age would have had roughly equal experience (for example, the task of indicating as quickly as possible whether an arrow was pointing left or right). They found that those fourth graders who were more physically mature than most of their classmates (i.e., who were a greater percentage of their parents' heights, and therefore of their own expected height) processed such information more quickly. Thus, biological maturation, as well as experience, seems to contribute to increasing processing speed.

One biological process that contributes to faster processing is *myelination.* As discussed in Chapter 3, many axons of neurons become covered with myelin, a fatty substance that insulates the axon and thus promotes faster and more reliable transmission of electrical impulses in the brain. Myelination begins during the prenatal period, but it continues throughout childhood and adolescence (Korner, 1991; Lecours, 1975). It seems to contribute to greater speed of processing not only by enhancing neural communication but also by increasing the child's ability to resist distractions (Dempster, 1993; Harnishfeger & Bjorklund, 1993).

Strategies

Information-processing theories point to the acquisition and growth of strategies as another major source of the development of learning and memory. A number of these strategies emerge between ages 5 and 8 years, among them the strategy of **rehearsal,** the process of repeating information over and over. The following newspaper item illustrates the usefulness of rehearsal for remembering information verbatim:

> A 9-year-old boy memorized the license plate number of a getaway car following an armed robbery, a court was told Monday. . . . The boy and his friend . . . looked in the drug store window and saw a man grab a 14-year-old cashier's neck. . . . After the robbery, the boys mentally repeated the license number until they gave it to police.
>
> (*Edmonton Journal,* January 13, 1981, cited in Kail, 1984)

Had the boys witnessed the same event when they were 5-year-olds, they probably would not have rehearsed the numbers and would have forgotten the license number before the police came.

Another widely used memory strategy that becomes increasingly prevalent at roughly the same age is **selective attention,** the process of intentionally focusing on the information that is most relevant to the current goal. If 7- and 8-year-olds are shown several toy animals and several household items, and are told that they later will need to remember the objects in only one category, they focus their attention on the objects in the indicated category. In contrast, given the same instructions, 3- and 4-year-olds pay roughly equal attention to the objects in both categories, which reduces their memory for the objects they need to remember (DeMarie-Dreblow & Miller, 1988).

When children first acquire memory strategies such as rehearsal and selective attention, their use of the strategies tends to be quite limited. The reason seems to lie in the same types of cost-benefit considerations that limit their use of planning. Initial uses of memory strategies do not improve recall as much as later uses, a phenomenon known as **utilization deficiency** (Bjorklund, Miller, Coyle, & Slawinsky, 1997; Miller & Seier, 1994). At the same time, the cost in mental effort required to use novel strategies is greater than the cost to use well-learned ones (Guttentag, 1984, 1985; Kee & Howell, 1988). Consistent with this cost-benefit analysis, researchers have found that either increasing the benefit of using a strategy (by paying children for successful recall) or decreasing the cost (by presenting material to which the strategy can be easily applied) increases the frequency of young children's use of memory strategies (Kunzinger & Wittryol, 1984; Ornstein & Naus, 1985).

Content Knowledge

Information-processing theories also point to a third source of development of memory and learning: improved knowledge. With age, children's knowledge about almost everything increases. Their greater knowledge improves recall of new material by making it easier to relate the new material to existing information (Schneider & Pressley, 1997). Content knowledge exerts such a large impact that when children know more about a topic than adults, their memory for new information about the topic often is better than that of the adults. For example, when children and adults are provided new information about children's TV programs and books, the children generally remember more of the information than do the

rehearsal the process of repeating information over and over to aid memory

selective attention the process of intentionally focusing on the information that is most relevant to the current goal

utilization deficiency the phenomenon that initial uses of strategies do not improve memory as much as later uses

CHARLES GUPTON / CORBIS STOCK MARKET

Through repeated visits to doctors' offices and through other experiences that occur in more or less fixed sequences, children form scripts that let them know what to expect in the future.

adults (Lindberg, 1980, 1991). Similarly, children who know a lot about soccer learn more from reading new soccer stories than do other children who are both older and have higher IQs but who know less about soccer (Schneider, Korkel, & Weinert, 1989).

One type of knowledge that is especially helpful for learning and remembering is **scripts,** that is, knowledge about how some type of everyday event usually goes. Many types of everyday events occur in a fixed sequence. For example, eating at a fast-food restaurant entails first lining up to order food, then paying for it, then receiving the food, and then bringing it to a table. By age 3 or 4 years, children form scripts that enable them to anticipate and remember eating at fast-food restaurants, as well as other scripts that enhance their ability to anticipate and remember birthday parties, bedtime routines, and other recurring situations (Fivush & Hammond, 1990; Nelson & Hudson, 1988).

With age and experience, children's scripts become increasingly detailed and firm. This helps the children remember what did not happen as well as what did, that is, to separate fact from fiction. For example, when 7-year-olds were asked about visits to the doctor's office three months after the visit, they almost always replied "no" to outlandish questions such as, "Did the nurse lick your knee?" (Ornstein, Shapiro, Clubb, Folmer, & Baker-Ward, 1997). In contrast, 3-year-olds often answered "yes" to such questions. The older children's better-developed scripts helped them know not only what was likely to happen but also what was not, and thus aided their memory.

Cognitive Processes Work Together

Although information-processing theories distinguish among basic processes, strategies, and content knowledge, such theories also emphasize that these processes work together, rather than in isolation, to produce cognitive growth. Efficient execution of basic processes enhances acquisition of new content knowledge; for example, children whose speed of processing is high tend to learn and remember more than those whose processing speed is slower (Kail, 1991). Similarly, possessing extensive content knowledge in an area enhances acquisition of new strategies; for example, strategies are better learned when the person teaching them illustrates their use with familiar content (Chi, 1981). Moreover, skillful strategy use increases the efficiency of basic processes; children who are skilled at rehearsal more effectively form associations involving the rehearsed material than do children who are less skilled at rehearsal (Miller & Seier, 1994). Thus, improvements in each type of memory process produce improvements in the others as well.

Alternative Information-Processing Theories

Students often have the impression that theories are like manufactured objects, complete and unchanging from the time they are made. Actually, however, theories are more like living things, continuously evolving. One form that this evolution takes is the generation of specific new theories within an existing class of theories. These new theories typically maintain the core assumptions of the general class, but they extend it and bolster its ability to deal with specific problems. In this section, we consider three relatively recent information-processing theories of this type—connectionist, dynamic-systems, and overlapping-waves theories. Each new alternative is designed to remedy a shortcoming of traditional information-processing approaches.

script the way in which some type of everyday event usually goes

sequential processing thinking that occurs one thought after another

connectionist theories a type of information-processing approach that emphasizes the simultaneous activity of numerous, interconnected processing units

parallel processing thinking that occurs simultaneously

neural-network approach a synonym for connectionist theories

Connectionist Theories

As exemplified by Klahr's analysis of his daughter's "socks in the dryer" comment, traditional information-processing approaches emphasize **sequential processing**—that is, thinking that occurs one thought after another. However, as **connectionist theories** emphasize, information processing also involves a great deal of **parallel processing,** in which various types of cognitive activity occur simultaneously. Researchers who take this approach have developed *connectionist models,* computer simulations that, like the brain, include large numbers of simple processing units, densely interconnected to each other in ways that produce parallel processing. The abstract resemblance to neural activity makes the connectionist approach—or **neural-network approach,** as it is also known—a promising candidate for modeling how thinking is achieved in the brain.

As illustrated in Figure 4.12, the processing units within connectionist models are organized into two or more layers. Most models include an input layer, whose processing units encode the initial representation of the situation; one or more hidden layers, whose units combine information from the input units; and an output layer, whose units generate the system's response to the situation. Connectionist models also include a learning rule, corresponding to the way in which children are thought to use feedback from other people and the physical environment to improve their performance on the task. Each time the system generates a wrong answer, the learning rule adjusts the strength of the connections in ways that will lead to a better answer if the same item or a related one is again presented. Thus, such models gradually learn which responses are appropriate for different input patterns.

Connectionist systems have proved able to learn a wide variety of concepts and skills, including object permanence, face recognition, and acquisition of word meanings and grammar (Johnson, 1998; MacWhinney & Chang, 1995; Marchman, 1992; Munakata, McClelland, Johnson, & Siegler, 1997). The models have demonstrated that developments that previously were thought to involve sudden, discontinuous changes may in fact reflect gradual, incremental processes. For example, McClelland and Rumelhart's (1986) model of how children learn to generate regular past-tense verb forms indicates that children may not learn the "*verb* + ed" rule all at once. Rather, they may slowly extend the form to more and more verbs, more and more consistently. In this case and in others where children have substantial experience with the particular task, connectionist models have generated patterns of learning that closely resemble those of children.

FIGURE 4.12 Information processing A connectionist model of children's representation of the object permanence task. Here, the input layer (bottom row) corresponds to children's representation of the object permanence situation in which one of two toys, hidden beneath one of two covers, is located at one of three locations. The output layer (top row) corresponds to children's responses to the situation with their eyes (left) and hands (right). The hidden layer includes processing units where the several types of information from the input layer are integrated. Within this model, children's looking patterns develop more rapidly than their reaching because the gaze/expectation system learns from every visual experience, whereas the reaching system only learns from experiences that occur within reaching distance.

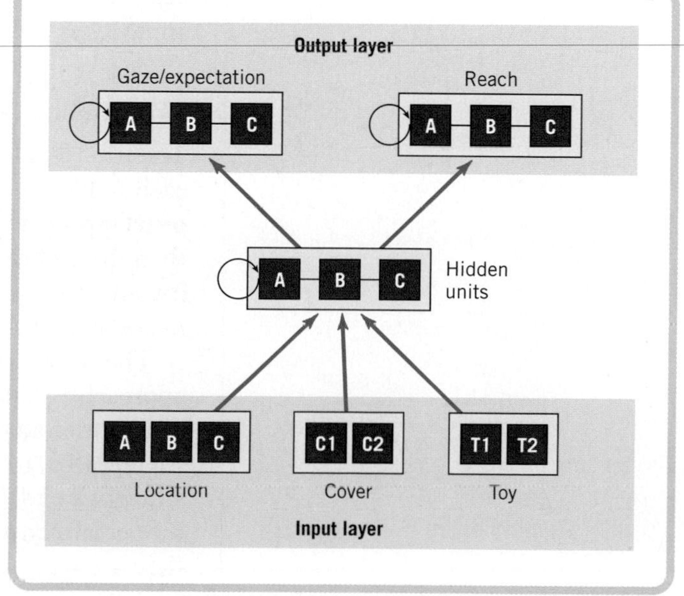

Dynamic-Systems Theories

The specificity that is among the greatest attractions of traditional information-processing approaches also has a downside: it can create the impression that different aspects of children's

dynamic-systems theories an information-processing approach that emphasizes how varied aspects of the child function as a single, integrated whole

overlapping-waves theories an information-processing approach that emphasizes the variability of children's thinking

thinking have nothing to do with each other. **Dynamic-systems theories** are intended to counter this impression by illustrating how varied aspects of the child—perception, motor activity, attention, language, memory, and emotions—function as a single, integrated whole to produce behavior (Thelen & Smith, 1998; van Geert, 1997).

A good example of how dynamic-systems theories lead to novel perspectives on development comes from Smith, Thelen, Titzer, and McLin's (1999) study of the A-Not-B error, a classic measure of conceptual understanding. As noted previously, this error, characteristic of 8- to 12-month-olds, involves children's searching for a toy where they found it earlier (location A), rather than where it was hidden most recently (location B). Piaget (1954) explained the A-Not-B error by hypothesizing that before their first birthday, infants lack a clear concept of the permanent existence of objects.

Viewing the A-Not-B error from a dynamic-systems perspective, Smith and her colleagues arrived at a different interpretation. They argued that the babies' previous attending and reaching to location A influenced their attending and reaching when the object was subsequently hidden at location B. On the basis of this premise, the researchers made several predictions that were later borne out. One was that the more often babies had found an object by reaching to one location, the more likely they would be to reach there again when the object was hidden at a different location. Another accurate prediction was that infants would reach wherever they were looking at the time when they began to reach. Thus, if an infant saw an object hidden, and the experimenter tapped another location just as the infant was about to reach, so that the infant would look at the tapped location, the infant usually reached to the tapped location where he or she was looking. A third accurate prediction was that the searching of older children (2-year-olds) for hidden objects also would be influenced by their history of looking, reaching, and finding a hidden object at a location other than the one where the object was most recently hidden (Spencer, Smith, & Thelen, 2001). Consistent with the view that multiple aspects of development influence each other, these experiments demonstrate that motor activities and attention influence success on the A-Not-B task, which is usually viewed as a measure of conceptual understanding of object permanence. More generally, by emphasizing the relations among motor activities, attention, and other aspects of children's behavior, dynamic-systems approaches are improving understanding of how development occurs.

Overlapping-Waves Theories

Traditional information-processing theories, and Piaget's theory as well, depict each child as thinking about a given task in a single way. According to **overlapping-waves theories,** however, children's thinking is far more variable than these portrayals suggest. Understanding the sources of this cognitive variability, and the ways in which it improves children's thinking and learning, is the major goal of the overlapping-waves approach.

The basic depiction of development suggested by the overlapping-waves approach is illustrated in Figure 4.13. At any given time, children possess several different strategies for solving a given problem. At the youngest age depicted in Figure 4.13, for example, children usually use strategy 1, but they sometimes use strategy 2 or 4. With age and experience, the strategies that produce more successful performance become more prevalent; new strategies also are generated and, if they are more effective than previous approaches, are used increasingly. Thus, by

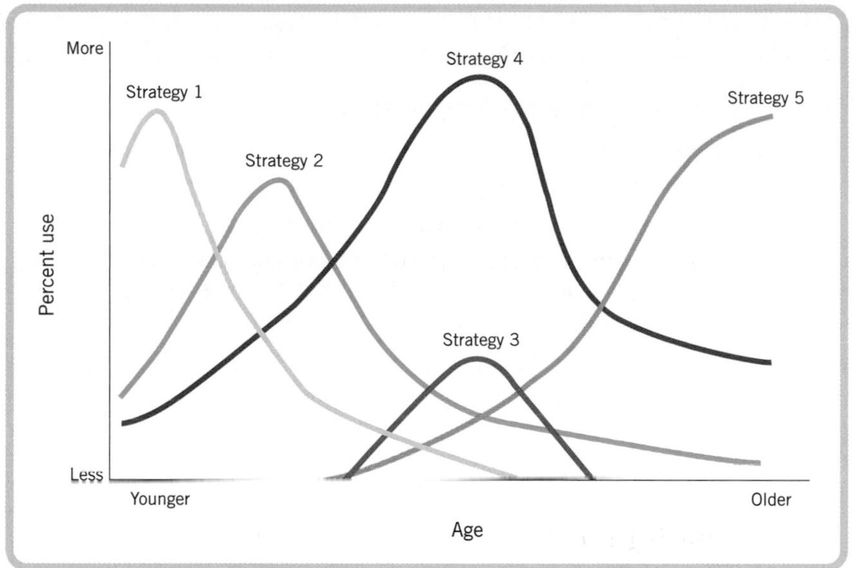

FIGURE 4.13 The overlapping-waves model The overlapping waves model proposes that at any one age, children use multiple strategies; that with age and experience, they rely increasingly on more advanced strategies (the ones with the higher numbers); and that development involves changes in use of existing strategies as well as discovery of new approaches.

the middle of the age range in Figure 4.13, children have added strategies 3 and 5 to the original group and have almost stopped using strategy 1.

Variable strategy use has been found in many recent studies of tasks on which children of a given age previously had been portrayed as using only a single strategy. These tasks include arithmetic, time telling, reading, spelling, number conservation, scientific experimentation, and recall from memory (Alibali, 1999; Chen & Siegler, 2000; Kuhn, Garcia-Mila, Zohar, & Anderson, 1995; Lemaire & Siegler, 1995; Miller & Coyle, 1999; Schauble, 1996). On tests of number conservation, for example, 5-year-olds often use the strategy that Piaget described: choosing the longer row as having more objects. However, the same child who on one trial uses that approach will on other trials correctly reason that just spreading a row does not change the number of objects, and on yet other trials will count the number of objects in the rows (Siegler, 1995).

Overlapping-waves theories also hypothesize that children benefit from this strategic variability. One reason is that it allows them to adapt to differences among problems and situations. For example, when asked to remember short lists of numbers or lists that are easy to encode (e.g., 7, 8, 9, 10, 11), 5-year-olds are less likely to use rehearsal than when presented with longer and less orderly lists (McGilly & Siegler, 1990). Another advantage of strategic variability is that it provides opportunities for children to adjust to their own growing competence. To illustrate, for 1-year-olds, walking down sloped ramps is fairly dangerous, so they often choose to slide down on their bellies, backs, or behinds (Adolph, 1997). However, as their balance and coordination develop, they become increasingly able to walk down the same ramps and choose to do so increasingly often. For these reasons and others, the more strategies children know, the better their learning tends to be (Perry, Church, & Goldin-Meadow, 1988; Siegler, 1995). Thus, just as connectionism is improving understanding of development on frequently encountered tasks, and dynamic-systems theories are improving understanding of relations among motor activities, attention, and conceptual understanding, overlapping-waves theories are improving understanding of strategic development. Box 4.2 illustrates how this focus on strategic development can improve education.

applications 4.2

Educational Applications of Information-Processing Theories

As noted earlier, one of the features shared by all information-processing approaches is an emphasis on task analysis. In addition to their usefulness as a research tool, such analyses allow teachers to assess the source of individual children's learning problems and to target instruction to the child's specific difficulty.

The instructional usefulness of task analysis was illustrated in Brown and Burton's (1978) study of the conventional long subtraction algorithm—e.g., the formula for solving problems such as

$$\begin{array}{r} 276 \\ -\,182 \\ \hline \end{array}$$

The analysis indicated that successful execution of this procedure requires several levels of skills and knowledge. At the highest level, executing the procedure requires that students first do the subtraction in the rightmost column, then the subtraction in the second column from the right, and so on. At a more specific level, it requires meeting the subgoal of reducing the value of the top number by the value of the bottom number. This, in turn, requires knowing the single-digit subtraction facts, knowing how to borrow from numbers other than 0, knowing how to borrow from 0, and knowing how to borrow across 0s.

Many elementary school children have trouble learning the long subtraction algorithm, especially the part concerning borrowing across 0s. Not knowing the correct approach, they generate "bugs," or systematic erroneous strategies. Consider one boy's pattern of correct answers and errors in the problems presented in the table. A superficial look reveals merely that the boy who generated this pattern erred on three of the five problems. When grading such a paper, many teachers would write something like "You can do better" and leave it at that. However, task analysis yields a more precise interpretation of the difficulty. The boy knows the single-digit subtraction facts and the basic borrowing procedure, but he does not know how to borrow from 0, as indicated by the fact that all three of his errors arose on problems where the top number included a 0.

Further analysis of the boy's errors and the problems that elicited them reveals two bugs that would generate these particular answers. First, whenever a problem required subtraction from 0, the boy adopted the strategy of flipping the two numbers in the column with the 0. For example, on 605 – 379 he treated 0 – 7 as 7 – 0, and wrote "7" as the answer. Second, whenever the problem required borrowing from the number to the left of the 0, the boy did not reduce the number (e.g., he did not reduce the 6 to 5 in 605 – 379). This failure makes sense in the context of the first bug; after all, when the boy flipped the 0 and the 7, he did not borrow anything from the 6. Thus, the task analysis indicates that the boy has two interwoven difficulties in borrowing from 0. More generally, diagnosing the specific bugs that give rise to incorrect performance is a requisite first step in clearly explaining to children who are having difficulty why they are wrong and what they should do instead (Baffes & Mooney, 1996; Mark & Greer, 1995).

Example of a Subtraction "Bug"

307	856	606	308	835
– 182	– 699	– 568	– 287	– 217
285	157	168	181	618

review: Information-processing theories envision children as active learners and problem solvers who continuously devise means for overcoming their processing limits and reaching their goals. Planning, analogical reasoning, and rule formation are among the processes that information-processing theories envision as contributing most to the development of problem solving. Cognitive growth in general, and development of memory and learning in particular, are seen as involving increasingly efficient execution of basic operations, construction of more effective strategies, and acquisition of new content knowledge. In recent years, connectionist, dynamic-systems, and overlapping-waves theories have joined traditional information-processing analyses as means of understanding how change occurs.

Core-Knowledge Theories

I didn't break the lamp, and I won't do it again.

—3-year-old, speaking to her mother (cited in Vasek, 1986)

core-knowledge theories approaches that emphasize the sophistication of infants' and young children's thinking in areas that have been important throughout human evolutionary history

Although transparent from an adult's perspective, this 3-year-old girl's attempted cover-up reflects surprisingly sophisticated thinking. She realizes that her mother does not know all that she herself knows about how the lamp was broken, so she attempts to deny responsibility. At the same time, she knows that her mother may not believe her, so she hedges her bets. The girl's skill at deception is typical for her age. When more than fifty 3-year-olds were encouraged by an experimenter to deceive another adult as to the whereabouts of a "treasure" they had seen a doll hide, the majority destroyed clues that the doll had "accidentally" left on the scene and lied when asked about the treasure's location (Chandler, Fritz, & Hala, 1989).

Such studies of deception illustrate two characteristic features of research inspired by **core-knowledge theories.** One is that the research focuses on areas—such as understanding of other people—that have been important throughout human evolutionary history. Other key areas that are viewed as core knowledge include recognizing the difference between living and nonliving things, identifying human faces, finding one's way around the environment, and learning language.

A second feature of the core-knowledge approach that is reflected in deception studies is the assumption that in certain areas of probable importance in human evolution, young children reason in ways that are considerably more advanced than Piaget's theory suggested were possible. If children under the age of 6 or 7 were completely egocentric, they would assume that other people's knowledge is the same as their own; from this perspective, there would be no point to making a false statement, because the other person would know it was false. Yet the findings of studies of young children's deceptions indicate that 3-year-olds understand that other people can be fooled. The question is how children come to have such sophisticated knowledge so early in life.

Indirect ways of breaking bad news are a specialty of young children.

View of Children's Nature

Core-knowledge theories depict children as active learners, constantly striving to solve problems and to organize their understanding into coherent wholes. In this respect, these theories' perspective on children's nature resembles those of Piagetian and information-processing theories.

The way in which core-knowledge theories differ most strongly from Piagetian and information-processing theories is in their view of children's innate capabilities. Piaget and information-processing theorists believe that children enter the world equipped only with general learning abilities and that they must actively apply these abilities to gradually increase their understanding of all types of content. In contrast, core-knowledge theorists view children as entering the world not only with general learning abilities but also with specialized learning abilities that allow them to quickly and effortlessly acquire information of evolutionary importance. Where the central metaphors within Piagetian and information-processing theories are the child as scientist and the child as computational system, the central metaphor in the core-knowledge approach is the child as well-equipped product of evolution. This metaphor is strikingly apparent in the following statement by Rochel Gelman and Earl Williams, major proponents of the core-knowledge approach:

> The brain is no less a product of natural selection than the rest of the body's structures and functions. . . . Hearts evolved to support the process of blood circulation, livers evolved to carry out the process of toxin extraction, and mental structures evolved to enable the learning of certain types of information necessary for adaptive behavior.
>
> (Gelman & Williams, 1998, p. 600)

Studies of animals other than humans provide many striking examples of specialized learning mechanisms (Gallistel, Brown, Carey, Gelman, & Keil, 1991; Keil, 1998). Most songbirds, for example, are not born knowing the songs characteristic of their species, but they are born with learning mechanisms that allow them to master the melodies rapidly once they hear them (Marler, 1991). Similarly, rats and ants are not born knowing the spatial layout of their home territory, but they are biologically prepared to learn it quickly (Gallistel, 1990).

Core-knowledge theorists maintain that humans possess similar specialized learning mechanisms, some of which are unique to our species. Language acquisition provides a good example. The noted linguist Noam Chomsky proposed that humans, but not other animals, are born with specific language-acquisition mechanisms that allow them to rapidly master the complicated systems of grammatical rules that are present in every human language. One type of evidence for such mechanisms is the universality of language acquisition. Virtually all children in all societies master the basic grammar of their native language quickly and effortlessly, even though adults almost never tell them these complex rules. In contrast, acquisition of other complex rule systems—such as those in spelling, geometry, and algebra—is not universal and requires extensive instruction from adults and considerable effort from children.

Another reason for believing that children possess mechanisms that are specialized for learning language is that certain areas in the middle of the left hemisphere of the brain are consistently active in processing grammar. Any damage to those left hemisphere areas harms grammatical competence to a much greater extent than does similar damage to the corresponding areas of the brain's right hemisphere. The behavioral and physiological data together provide good reason to believe that people possess specialized mechanisms for learning language. Similar combinations of behavioral and physiological data suggest that people also possess specialized mechanisms for learning about other areas of evolutionary importance, such as spatial layouts and human faces (Johnson, 1998). Thus, whereas Piaget and information-processing theorists depict intelligence as a unified whole that generates understanding of all domains, core-knowledge theorists depict intelligence as a mixture of general learning abilities and powerful specialized abilities for learning to solve evolutionarily important problems, that is, problems that have been important for survival throughout human existence.

Central Developmental Issues

Like Piaget and information-processing theorists, core-knowledge theorists believe that development is produced by the interaction of nature and nurture. Unlike most theorists who take the other two approaches, however, these theorists believe that children's nature also includes innate understanding of crucial concepts.

Domain Specificity

The innate understandings proposed by core-knowledge theorists are assumed to be **domain specific,** that is, limited to a particular area, such as living things or the properties of inanimate objects. Such domain-specific understandings allow infants to distinguish between living and nonliving things; to anticipate that nonliving physical objects they encounter for the first time will remain stationary unless an external force is applied to them; to anticipate that animals they encounter for the first time might well move on their own; and to learn quickly in these and

domain specific limited to a particular area, such as living things or people other areas of probable evolutionary importance. Two prominent advocates of core-knowledge approaches, Susan Carey and Elizabeth Spelke, summarized their view of domain specificity as follows:

> We argue that human reasoning is guided by a collection of innate domain-specific systems of knowledge. Each system is characterized by a set of core principles that define the entities covered by the domain and support reasoning about these entities. Learning, in this view, consists of the enrichment of the core principles.
>
> (Carey & Spelke, 1994, p. 169)

Consistent with this emphasis on innate domain-specific understanding, core-knowledge theorists have devoted a great deal of attention to early understanding of major domains—language, space, number, physical objects, plants and animals, and people. This research will play an important role in the next three chapters.

Children's Informal Theories

A number of core-knowledge theorists have proposed that young children actively organize their understanding of the most important domains into informal theories (Carey, 1985; Gopnik & Meltzoff, 1997; Wellman & S. Gelman, 1998). In particular, children are thought to form naive theories of *physics* (knowledge of objects), *psychology* (knowledge of people), and *biology* (knowledge of plants and animals). These informal theories, of course, are not precisely specified deductive systems, but they do share three important characteristics with formal scientific theories:

1. They identify fundamental units for dividing up the vast number of objects and events in the world into a few basic categories.
2. They explain many particular phenomena in terms of a few basic principles.
3. They explain events in terms of unobservable causes.

Each of these characteristics is evident in preschoolers' understanding of biology (Hatano & Inagaki, 1996; Keil, 1998). Consistent with the first characteristic, preschoolers divide all objects into people, other animals, plants, and nonliving things (S. Gelman, in press). Consistent with the second characteristic, preschoolers understand broadly applicable principles, such as that a desire for food and water underlies a wide range of behaviors of animals. Consistent with the third characteristic, preschoolers know that vital activities of animals and plants, such as reproduction and movement (in the case of animals), are caused by something inside them, as opposed to the external forces that determine the behavior of inanimate objects.

Why would children form intuitive theories of physics, biology, and psychology? According to core-knowledge theorists Henry Wellman and Susan Gelman (1998), the reason probably lies in our evolutionary past. Children have always needed to know about physical objects in order to perceive the environment accurately and to move around it without hurting themselves. They have needed to know about animals and plants to avoid predators and poisons. They have needed to understand other people in order to communicate their wants and needs. Again, the core-knowledge metaphor of the child as a well-equipped product of evolution is clear.

When do children first possess such core theories? Spelke (1988, 1994) speculates that infants begin life with a primitive theory of physics, that is, of inanimate objects. This theory includes the knowledge that the world is composed of physical objects that occupy space, move only in response to external forces, and move

applications 4.3

Educational Applications of Core-Knowledge Theories

Operating from the principle that people's existing knowledge greatly influences their learning, Hatano and Inagaki (1996) noted several implications of findings regarding children's naive theories of biology that could be used to help children gain a more advanced understanding of the subject. One such implication is that by the time children enter kindergarten, their theory of unobservable causes—such as those related to animals' vital activities—can be built upon to teach them concepts that are usually thought to be beyond their grasp. For example, they can understand that invisible germs cause diseases and that invisible genes cause resemblances between parents and children (Kalish, 1996; Springer, 1996).

A second instructional implication derives from a more specific finding: Children's early theories of biology are influenced by their knowledge about human beings. Young children extrapolate from what they know about people to predict the qualities of other animals, a process known as **personification** (Carey, 1985; Inagaki & Hatano, 1991). Although personification leads to many valid conclusions, it also interferes with understanding some biological concepts. For example, it makes it difficult for children to understand that plants are alive, because plants clearly do not form intentions and pursue goals in the same sense as people do. Instructional programs that emphasize that plants actually do move in ways that help them function—for example, in moving toward sunlight—can help young children overcome such misconceptions (Opfer, 2001).

in continuous ways through space rather than jumping from one position to another. As one source of evidence, Spelke cited Baillargeon's (1987, 1994) finding that 3-month-olds show surprise when, thanks to a clever arrangement of mirrors, a solid object appears to move through the space occupied by another solid object. She also noted that 2-month-olds show surprise when, again due to trickery, moving objects seem to suddenly jump from one point to another without passing through intermediate positions or when unattached objects start and stop moving simultaneously (Spelke, Breinlinger, Macomber & Jacobson, 1992).

Wellman and Gelman (1998) suggested that the first theory of psychology may emerge at around 18 months of age and the first theory of biology at around 3 years. The first theory of psychology is organized around the insight that people's actions, not just one's own but other people's, too, reflect their goals and desires. For example, the 2-year-old realizes that other people will want to eat if they are hungry regardless of whether he or she is (Wellman & Gelman, 1998). The first theory of biology is organized around the realization that people and other animals are living things, different from nonliving things and plants. For example, 3- and 4-year-olds realize that animals, but not manufactured objects, move on the basis of their own power (Gelman & Gottfried, 1996).

Of course, a huge amount of development occurs beyond these initial theories. Some of the development involves building on the original organization and filling in details. For example, even 3-month-olds understand that an object (e.g., a glass) will fall unless at least some of it is supported by another object (e.g., a table), but not until about 7 months do infants understand that when only a small percentage of an object is supported, the object will fall (Baillargeon, 1994). In other cases, children may replace rudimentary theories with more advanced ones. For example, Hatano and Inagaki (1996) noted that not until the age of 7 years are children convinced that the category of living things includes plants as well as animals, because plants share with animals the properties of growth, reproduction, and adaptive movement—the key attributes of living things.

As with the research on infants' initial conceptual understanding, research on children's informal theories is examined in more depth in later chapters. Box 4.3 focuses on implications of core-knowledge theories for instruction.

personification generalizing knowledge about people to infer properties of other animals

sociocultural theories approaches that emphasize the contribution to children's development of other people and the surrounding culture

guided participation a process in which more knowledgeable individuals organize situations in ways that allow less knowledgeable people to learn

review:

Core-knowledge theorists envision children as the well-equipped products of evolution. They focus on development of understanding in domains of likely evolutionary importance: space, time, language, biology, and so on. Researchers who take this approach have demonstrated that infants and young children possess surprising understanding of these domains. Core-knowledge theorists believe that this early competence is made possible by innate, domain-specific understanding and specialized learning mechanisms. Children are viewed as active thinkers who form theories that divide objects and events into a few basic categories, include powerful principles, and explain events in terms of unobservable causes.

Sociocultural Theories

A mother and her 4-year-old daughter, Sadie, assemble a toy, using a diagram to guide them:

> *Mother:* Now you need another one like this on the other side. Mmmmm . . . there you go, just like that.
> *Sadie:* Then I need this one to go like this? Hold on, hold on. Let it go. There. Get that out. Oops.
> *M:* I'll hold it while you turn it. *(Watches Sadie work on toy)* Now you make the end.
> *S:* This one?
> *M:* No, look at the picture. Right here *(points to diagram)*. That piece.
> *S:* Like this?
> *M:* Yeah.
>
> (Gauvain, 2001, p. 32)

This interaction probably strikes you as completely unexceptional—and it is. From the perspective of **sociocultural theories,** however, it and thousands of other unexceptional interactions like it are of the utmost importance, because they are the motors that move development forward.

One noteworthy characteristic of the event, from the sociocultural perspective, is that Sadie is learning to assemble the toy in an interpersonal context. Sociocultural approaches emphasize that much of development takes place through direct interactions between children and other people—parents, siblings, teachers, playmates, and so on. Rather than viewing children as individuals trying to make sense of the world through their own efforts, sociocultural theories view children as social beings, enmeshed in the lives of other people who want to help them acquire the skills and knowledge valued by their culture. Thus, whereas Piagetian, core-knowledge, and information-processing theories emphasize children's active roles in their own development, sociocultural theories emphasize the developmental importance of children's interactions with other people.

This interaction between Sadie and her mother is also noteworthy because it exemplifies **guided participation,** a process in which more knowledgeable individuals organize activities in ways that allow less knowledgeable people to engage in them at a higher level than they could manage on their own (Rogoff, 1990). Sadie's mother, for

Through guided participation, parents can help children not only accomplish immediate goals but also learn skills, such as how to use written instructions and diagrams to assemble objects.

ELLEN B. SENISI

cultural tools the innumerable products of human ingenuity that enhance thinking

example, holds one part of the toy so that Sadie can screw in another part; without her mother's help, Sadie would be unable to screw the two parts together and thus could not improve her skill at the task. Similarly, Sadie's mother points to the relevant part of the diagram, enabling Sadie to decide what to do next and also to learn how diagrams convey information. As this episode illustrates, guided participation often occurs in situations in which the explicit purpose is to achieve a practical goal, such as assembling a toy, but in which learning also occurs as a by-product of the activity.

A third noteworthy characteristic of the interaction between Sadie and her mother is that it occurs in a broader cultural context. This context includes not only other people but also the innumerable products of human ingenuity that sociocultural theorists refer to as **cultural tools:** symbol systems, artifacts, skills, values, and so on. In the example of Sadie and her mother, the relevant symbol systems include the language they use to convey their thoughts and the diagram they use to guide their assembly efforts; the relevant artifacts include the toy and the printed sheet on which the diagram appears; the relevant skills include the proficiency in language that allows them to communicate with each other and the procedures they use to interpret the diagram; and the values include the culture's approval of parents' interacting with their children in the way that Sadie's mother does and of young girls' learning mechanical skills. In the background are broader technological, economic, and historical factors. The interaction would not be occurring in the absence of the technology needed to manufacture toys and print diagrams, an economy that allows parents the leisure for such interactions, and a history leading up to the symbol systems, artifacts, skills, values, technologies, and economy reflected in the interaction. Thus, sociocultural theories can help us appreciate the many aspects of culture embodied in even the smallest everyday interactions.

View of Children's Nature

The giant of the sociocultural approach to cognitive development, and in many ways its originator, was the Russian psychologist Lev Semyonovich Vygotsky. Although Vygotsky and Piaget were contemporaries, much of Vygotsky's most important work was largely unknown outside the Soviet Union until the 1970s. Its appearance created a stir, in part because Vygotsky's view of children's nature was so different from Piaget's.

The Russian psychologist Lev Vygotsky, the father of the sociocultural approach to child development.

DAVIDSON FILMS, INC.

Vygotsky's Theory

As noted earlier, Piaget depicted children as little scientists, trying to understand the world on their own. Vygotsky, in contrast, portrayed them as social beings, intertwined with other people who are eager to help them gain skills and understanding. Where Piaget viewed children as intent on mastering physical, mathematical, and logical concepts that are the same in all times and places, Vygotsky viewed them as intent on participating in activities that happen to be prevalent in their local setting. Where Piaget emphasized qualitative changes in thinking, Vygotsky emphasized continuous, quantitative changes.

These Vygotskyian views gave rise to the central metaphor within sociocultural theories: children as social beings, shaped by and shaping their cultural contexts. This perspective on children's nature has been incorporated into all contemporary sociocultural theories, including those of Barbara Rogoff (1990), Michael Cole (1996), and Michael Tomasello (1999).

Children as Teachers and Learners

According to Michael Tomasello, human beings are unique in two interlocking ways that are crucial to our ability to create complex, rapidly changing cultures. One of these uniquely human characteristics is the inclination to teach others of the species; the other is the inclination to attend to and learn from such teaching (Tomasello, 1999; Tomasello, Kruger, & Ratner, 1993). In every human society, adults communicate facts, skills, values, and traditions to their young. This is what makes culture possible; as Sir Isaac Newton noted, it enables the new generation to stand on the shoulders of the old and thus to see farther. The inclination to teach is not limited to adults. All normal 2-year-olds spontaneously point to objects to call other people's attention to features that they themselves find interesting; such rudimentary teaching behaviors that are not directly tied to survival are not seen in other species. This inclination to learn from teaching and to teach is what enables children to be socialized into their culture and to pass it on to others.

BOB DAEMMRICH / STOCK BOSTON

A Mayan mother teaches her daughter weaving skills by involving her in the process. The inclination to teach and the ability to learn from teaching are among the most distinctive human characteristics.

Children as Products of Their Culture

Sociocultural theorists believe that many of the *processes* that produce development, such as guided participation, are the same in all societies. However, the *content* that children learn—the particular symbol systems, artifacts, skills, and values—vary greatly from culture to culture and shape children's thinking accordingly.

One approach that sociocultural researchers have used to study the impact of culturally specific activities on children's thinking is to intensively examine particular kinds of learning in their cultural context. The value of such research is illustrated by experiments designed to examine the effects of abacus expertise on East Asian children's mental arithmetic (Hatano & Osawa, 1983; Stigler, 1984). Child abacus experts were found to excel at mental arithmetic even when no abacus was present. Their superiority came from their solving complex mental arithmetic problems by imagining an abacus, visualizing how they would solve the problem on it, and then reading the answer from the imagined final placement of beads (Figure 4.14). Needless to say, this strategy only appears in societies where abacuses are used. However, the finding also illustrates a general principle: The artifacts and skills of a culture shape the thinking of people in that culture.

ARIEL SKELLEY / CORBIS STOCK MARKET

FIGURE 4.14 Cultural tools shape learning As illustrated by this photo of an East Asian father teaching his children to use an abacus, the tools available in a culture shape the learning of children within that culture.

Central Developmental Issues

Among the most important aspects of Vygotsky's legacy is the idea that cognitive change originates in social interaction. Vygotsky and contemporary sociocultural theorists also have proposed a number of more specific ideas about *how change occurs*. One of these ideas—guided participation—was discussed earlier. In this section, we examine three related concepts that play prominent roles in sociocultural analyses of change: intersubjectivity, social scaffolding, and the zone of proximal development.

Intersubjectivity

Sociocultural theorists believe that the foundation of human cognitive development is our ability to establish **intersubjectivity,** the mutual understanding that people share during communication (Gauvain, 2001; Rogoff, 1990; Rommetveit, 1985). The idea behind this imposing term is both simple and profound: effective communication requires participants to focus on the same topic and also on each other's reaction to whatever is being communicated. Such a "meeting of the minds" is indispensable for effective teaching and learning.

The roots of intersubjectivity are evident early in infancy. By age 2 to 3 months, infants show greater animation and interest when their mothers respond to their actions than when the mothers act in ways that are independent of them (Murray & Trevarthen, 1985). By age 6 months, infants can learn novel behaviors by observing other people's behavior (Collie & Hayne, 1999).

These developments set the stage for the emergence of a capability that is at the heart of intersubjectivity—**joint attention,** a process in which infants and their social partners intentionally focus on a common referent in the external environment. The emergence of joint attention is evident in numerous ways. Between the ages of 9 and 15 months, infants increasingly look toward the same objects as their social partners, monitor changes in their partners' looking, adjust where they are looking if the partner focuses on a new object, and actively direct adults' attention toward objects that interest them (Adamson & Bakeman, 1991; Gauvain, 2001; Scaife & Bruner, 1975; Tomasello & Farrar, 1986). At about the same age, children also begin to show the related behavior of **social referencing,** the tendency to look to social partners for guidance about how to respond to unfamiliar or threatening events (Campos & Stenberg, 1981).

LAURA DWIGHT

Joint attention, the process through which social partners focus on the same external object, underlies the human capacity to teach and to learn from teaching.

Joint attention greatly increases children's ability to learn from other people. One important example involves language learning. When an adult tells a toddler the name of an object, the adult usually looks or points directly at it; children who are looking at the same object are in a better position to learn what the word means than ones who are not (Baldwin, 1991). The effectiveness of such joint attention is reflected in the fact that the younger the age at which infants begin to show joint attention, the faster their subsequent language acquisition (Carpenter, Nagell, & Tomasello, 1998).

Intersubjectivity continues to develop well beyond infancy, as children become increasingly able to take the perspectives of other people. For example, 4½-year-olds are more likely than 3-year-olds to reach agreement with peers on the rules of games they are about to play and the roles that each child will assume (Goncu, 1993). The continuing development of such perspective-taking abilities also leads to school-age children becoming increasingly able to teach and learn from each other (Gauvain, 2001).

Social Scaffolding

When putting up tall buildings, construction workers are aided by the use of metal frameworks called scaffolds, which allow them to work high above the ground. Once a building's main structure is in place, it can support further work, thus allowing the scaffolding to be removed. In an analogous fashion, children's learning is aided by **social scaffolding,** in which more competent people provide a temporary framework that supports children's thinking at a higher level than children

applications 4.4

Educational Applications of Sociocultural Theories

In recent years, the educational system of the United States has been criticized for promoting rote memorization of facts rather than deep understanding; for promoting competition rather than cooperation among students; and for generally failing to create enthusiasm for learning (Bruner, 1996). The emphasis of sociocultural theories on the centrality of culture implies that one way to improve schooling is to change the culture of schools. The culture should be one in which instruction is aimed at deep understanding, in which learning is a cooperative activity, and in which learning a little makes children want to learn more.

One impressive effort to meet these goals is Ann Brown's (1997) *community-of-learners* program. Efforts to build communities of learners have focused on 6- to 12-year-olds, most of them African-American children attending inner-city schools. Courses center around projects that require research on some large topic, such as interdependence between animals and their habitats. The class divides into small groups, each of which focuses on a particular aspect of the topic. With the topic of the interdependence between animals and habitats, for example, one group might study predator–prey relations; another, reproductive strategies; another, protection from the elements; and so on. At the end of roughly ten weeks, new groups are formed, each including one child from every original group. Children in the new groups are asked to solve a problem that encompasses all the aspects studied by the previous groups, such as designing an "animal of the future" that would be particularly well adapted to its habitat. Because each child's participation in the previous group has resulted in the child's gaining expertise on the aspect of the problem studied by that group, and because no other child in the new group has that expertise, all of the children's contributions are essential for the new group to succeed. This has been labeled the *jigsaw approach,* because, as in a jigsaw puzzle, each piece is necessary for the solution.

A variety of people help foster such communities of learners. Classroom teachers introduce the big ideas of the unit, encourage the class to pool its knowledge to achieve deeper understanding, push children to provide evidence for their opinions, and ask them to summarize what they know and identify new learning goals. Outside experts are brought to classrooms to lecture and answer questions about the topic. Children and teachers exchange e-mails with groups at other schools who are working on the same problem to see how they are approaching issues that arise.

Creating such communities of learners has both cognitive and motivational benefits. Participation in such groups leads to children's becoming increasingly adept at constructing high-quality solutions to the problems they try to solve. It also leads to their learning such general skills as identifying key questions and comparing alternative solutions to a problem. Finally, because the children all depend on each other's contributions, the community-of-learners approach encourages mutual respect and individual responsibility for the success of the entire group. In short, the approach creates a culture of learning.

could manage on their own (Wood, Bruner, & Ross, 1976). Ideally, this framework includes explaining the goal of the task, demonstrating how the task should be done, and helping the child execute the most difficult parts. This, in fact, is the way parents tend to teach their children (Pratt, Kerig, Cowan, & Cowan, 1988; Saxe, Guberman, & Gearhart, 1987; Wood, 1986). Through the process of social scaffolding, children become capable of working at a higher level than if they had not received such help. At first, this higher-level functioning requires extensive support, then it requires less support, and eventually it becomes possible without any support. The higher the quality of the scaffolding, the greater the child's learning (Pacifici & Bearison, 1991).

The quality of scaffolding that people provide tends to increase with increases in their age and experience. Adults' scaffolding tends to be of higher quality than children's, and older children's of higher quality than younger ones'. In part, this is because adults usually encourage learners to participate actively in the task and help them learn strategies for proceeding independently in the future (Ellis & Rogoff, 1986; Gauvain, 2001). Children, in contrast—even ones who are as knowledgeable about a task as adults are—often just tell less knowledgeable peers what to do or do the task themselves. Not surprisingly, 5- to 9-year-olds who have previously solved problems with their parents do better on similar new problems than peers who have previously solved the same kinds of problems with other children (Radiszewska & Rogoff, 1988).

intersubjectivity the mutual understanding that people share during communication

joint attention a process in which social partners intentionally focus on a common referent in the external environment

social referencing the tendency to look to social partners for guidance about how to respond to unfamiliar or threatening events

social scaffolding a process in which more competent people provide a temporary framework that supports children's thinking at a higher level than children could manage on their own

zone of proximal development (ZPD) the range of performance between what children can do unsupported and what they can do with optimal support

Zone of Proximal Development

In analyzing the process of social scaffolding, Vygotsky (1978) used the term **zone of proximal development (ZPD)** to refer to the range of performance between what children can do unsupported and what they can do with optimal support. Implicit in this label is the idea that development is most likely when children's thinking is supported by more knowledgeable people at a somewhat higher level than the children could manage unaided—but not so far beyond their unaided level that they would be lost.

Both mothers and fathers adjust their contribution to children's problem solving in a way that suggests that they implicitly understand the ZPD concept (Conner, Knight, & Cross, 1997; Gauvain, 2001; Pratt et al., 1988). They direct their instructional efforts at the upper end of the child's capabilities, and as children become competent with simple aspects of the task, parents encourage them to think about the problem at higher levels. For example, on a task requiring children to place miniature furniture in the appropriate rooms of doll houses (Freund, 1990), parents initially focused on low-level, concrete goals with 3-year-olds ("Put the stove in the kitchen") but focused on higher-level, more abstract goals with 5-year-olds ("First do the kitchen, then the dining room"). The degree to which parents emphasized higher-level capabilities as children gained competence with lower-level ones was associated with superior problem solving when children were later asked to solve problems on their own. As discussed in Box 4.4, concepts from sociocultural theories have also proved useful for improving education in classrooms.

review:

Sociocultural approaches view children as social beings, shaped by, and shaping, their cultural contexts. These approaches emphasize that children develop in a cultural context of other people and human inventions, such as symbol systems, artifacts, skills, and values. Through guided participation, more knowledgeable people help children gain skill in using these cultural tools; using the tools, in turn, further transforms children's thinking. Culture is made possible by the human propensity to think and learn and by our ability to establish intersubjectivity with other people. Through processes such as social scaffolding, sensitivity to children's zone of proximal development, and creation of communities of learners, older and more skilled individuals help children acquire the skills, knowledge, and values of their culture.

A Grand Unified Theory?

While reading this chapter, you may have wondered, "Why not construct a theory that combines the strengths of all four theories?" Such a theory would convey the panoramic overview of Piaget's theory, the precise description of cognitive processes and change mechanisms of information-processing theories, and the insights about early competence and the contributions of the social world of core-knowledge and sociocultural theories.

This question can be answered in two ways. One is that the theories have many contradictory features that would be difficult if not impossible to reconcile within a single coherent theory. They differ greatly in their views of children's nature, of whether development includes discontinuities, of whether children possess domain-specific learning mechanisms, and of the role of the social world. Creating a formal unified theory from among them is probably impossible.

On the other hand, creating informal theories that incorporate insights from all four theories is not only possible—it is what most researchers do. They borrow wisdom from wherever they can find it. Just as children have multiple ways of thinking about most subjects, so do researchers. When researchers consider how the social world shapes development, for example, they utilize insights from sociocultural theorists, even if that is not their primary orientation. Likewise, they draw on insights from the other three theories when concerned with the questions on which they focus. In reading further chapters, we hope you also will be able to keep in mind the four theories and use them where they make sense to you.

Chapter Summary

Theories of development are important because they provide a framework for understanding important phenomena, raise major issues regarding human nature, and motivate new research. Four major theories of cognitive development are Piagetian, information-processing, core-knowledge, and sociocultural.

Piaget's Theory

- Among the reasons for the longevity of Piaget's theory are that it vividly conveys the flavor of children's thinking at different ages, extends across a broad range of ages and content areas, and provides many fascinating and surprising observations of children's thinking.
- Piaget's theory is often labeled "constructivist," because it depicts children as actively constructing knowledge for themselves in response to their experience. Piaget's theory posits that children learn through two processes that are present from birth—assimilation and accommodation—and that they balance their contributions through a third process, equilibration. These processes produce continuities across development.
- Piaget's theory divides cognitive development into four broad stages: the sensorimotor stage (birth to age 2), the preoperational stage (ages 2 to 7), the concrete operations stage (ages 7 to 12), and the formal operations stage (age 12 years and beyond). These stages reflect discontinuities in development.
- In the sensorimotor stage, infants' intelligence is expressed primarily through motor interactions with the environment. They gain concepts such as object permanence and become capable of deferred imitation.
- In the preoperational stage, children become able to represent their experiences in language, mental imagery, and thought, but because of cognitive limitations such as egocentrism and centration, they have difficulty solving many problems, including conservation, balance-scale, and speed, time, and distance problems.
- In the concrete operations stage, children become able to reason logically about concrete objects and events but have difficulty reasoning in purely abstract terms and in succeeding on tasks requiring hypothetical thinking, such as the pendulum problem.
- In the formal operations stage, children gain the full cognitive capabilities of adults.
- The primary weaknesses of Piaget's theory are that it depicts children's thinking as being more consistent than it is, underestimates infants' and young children's cognitive competence, understates the contribution of the social world to cognitive development, and only vaguely describes the mechanisms that give rise to thinking and cognitive growth.

Information-Processing Theories

- Information-processing theories focus on the specific mental processes that underlie children's thinking. Even in infancy, children are seen as actively pursuing goals, encountering processing limits, and devising strategies that allow them to surmount the processing limits and attain the goals.
- Among the leading contributors to the growth of problem solving are the development of planning and analogical reasoning.
- The development of memory and learning in large part reflects improvements in basic processes, strategies, and content knowledge.
- Basic cognitive processes allow infants to learn and remember from birth onward. Among the most important basic processes are association, recognition, generalization, and encoding.

- The use of strategies enhances learning and memory beyond the level that basic processes alone could provide. Rehearsal and selective attention are two important strategies.
- Increasing content knowledge enhances memory and learning of all types of information.
- Alternative information-processing approaches, including connectionist, dynamic-systems, and overlapping-waves approaches, have arisen to address weaknesses in traditional approaches.

Core-Knowledge Theories

- Core-knowledge theories are based on the view that children begin life with a wide range of specific cognitive competencies.
- Core-knowledge approaches also hypothesize that children are especially adept at acquiring evolutionarily important information, such as language, spatial layouts, and face recognition.
- These approaches also posit that from early ages, children organize information about the most important domains into informal theories, such as theories of physics, biology, and psychology.

Sociocultural Theories

- Starting with Vygotsky's theory, sociocultural theories have focused on the way that the social world molds development. Development is shaped not only by interactions with other people and the skills learned from them but also by the artifacts with which children interact and the values and traditions of the larger society.
- Sociocultural theories view people as differing from other animals in their propensity to teach and their ability to learn from teaching.
- Establishing intersubjectivity between people through such processes as joint attention and social referencing is essential to learning.
- Sociocultural theories describe people as learning through guided participation, social scaffolding, and teaching that is aimed at the child's zone of proximal development.

Critical Thinking Questions

1. Piaget's theory has been prominent for more than seventy years. Do you think it will continue to be prominent for the next thirty years as well? Why or why not?
2. Do you think that the term *egocentric* is a good description of preschoolers' overall way of seeing the world? On the basis of what you learned in this chapter and your own experience, explain your answer and indicate in what ways preschoolers are egocentric and in what ways they are not.
3. Does the evolutionary perspective of core-knowledge theories seem sound to you? Explain and give examples of how learning in core-knowledge domains may or may not have contributed to human evolution.
4. Information-processing analyses tend to be more specific than analyses generated by other theories. Do you see this specificity as an advantage or a disadvantage? Why?
5. Imagine you are trying to help a 6-year-old learn a skill that you possess. Using the ideas of guided participation, social scaffolding, and the zone of proximal development, describe how you might go about this task.

Key Terms

adaptation, p. 129
organization, p. 129
assimilation, p. 129
accommodation, p. 129
equilibration, p. 129
sensorimotor stage, p. 131
preoperational stage, p. 131
concrete operational stage, p. 131
formal operational stage, p. 131
object permanence, p. 132
A-Not-B error, p. 133
deferred imitation, p. 134
symbolic representation, p. 135
egocentrism, p. 135
centration, p. 136

conservation concept, p. 137
task analysis, p. 143
problem solving, p. 144
basic processes, p. 146
encoding, p. 146
rehearsal, p. 149
selective attention, p. 149
utilization deficiency, p. 149
script, p. 150
sequential processing, p. 151
connectionist theories, p. 151
parallel processing, p. 151
neural-network approach, p. 151
dynamic-systems theories, p. 152
overlapping-waves theories, p. 152
core-knowledge theories, p. 155
domain specific, p. 156
personification, p. 158
sociocultural theories, p. 159
guided participation, p. 159
cultural tools, p. 160
intersubjectivity, p. 162
joint attention, p. 162
social referencing, p. 162
social scaffolding, p. 162
zone of proximal development (ZPD), p. 164

CHAPTER 5

Infancy

PABLO PICASSO, *Maternité*, 1921

THEMES

- Nature and Nurture
- The Active Child
- Continuity/Discontinuity
- Mechanisms of Change
- The Sociocultural Context
- Individual Differences
- Research and Children's Welfare

Four-month-old Benjamin, perched on the kitchen counter in his infant seat, is watching his parents wash the dinner dishes (see photo opposite). What he observes includes two people who move on their own, as well as a variety of glass, ceramic, and metal objects of differing sizes and shapes that move only when picked up and manipulated by the people. Other elements of the scene never move. As the people go about their task, distinctive sounds emanate from their moving lips, while different sounds occur as they deposit silverware, skillets, glasses, and sponges on the kitchen counter. At one point, Benjamin sees a cup completely disappear from view as his father places it on the counter behind a cooking pot; it reappears a moment later when the pot is moved. He also sees objects disappear as they pass through the suds and into the water, but he never sees one object pass through another. The objects that are placed on the counter stay put, until Benjamin's father deposits a crystal goblet with more than half of its base hanging over the counter's edge. The resulting loud crashing sound startles all three people in the room, and Benjamin is further startled when the two adults start emitting sharp, loud sounds toward one another, quite unlike the soft, pleasant sounds they had been producing before. When Benjamin begins crying in response, the adults rush to him, patting him and making soft, especially pleasant sounds to him.

This example, to which we will return throughout the chapter, illustrates the enormous amount of information that is available for an infant to observe and learn from in even the most everyday situations. In learning about the world through such situations, Benjamin, like most infants, avidly explores everything and everyone around him, using every tool he has: he gathers information by looking and listening, as well as by tasting, smelling, and feeling. His area of exploration will gradually expand as he becomes capable first of reaching for objects and then of manipulating them, making it possible for him to discover more about them. When he starts to move around under his own power, even more of the world will become available to him, including things his parents would prefer that he not investigate, such as electrical outlets and cat litter. Never will Benjamin explore so voraciously or learn so rapidly as in the first few years of his young life.

In this chapter, we discuss development in four closely related areas: perception, action, learning, and cognition. Our discussion focuses primarily on infants and toddlers. One reason for concentrating on this period is that extremely rapid developmental change occurs in all four areas during the first two years of a child's life. A second reason is the fact that development in these four domains is particularly intertwined in this period: the minirevolutions that transform infants' behavior and experience in one domain lead to minirevolutions in others. For example, the large improvements in visual abilities that occur in their first few months enable infants to see more of the people and objects around them, thereby dramatically enlarging the opportunities they have to learn new information.

A third reason for concentrating on infancy in this chapter is the fact that the majority of recent research on perceptual and motor development has been done with infants and young children. There is also a large body of fascinating research on learning and cognition in the first few years. We will review some of this research here and cover subsequent development in these areas in later chapters. A final, research-related reason for focusing on infants in this chapter is that the methods used to investigate infants' development in these four domains are, of necessity, quite different from those that researchers are able to use to study older children.

Our examination of key developments in infancy will feature several enduring themes. The *active child* theme is vividly embodied by infants' eager explorations of their environment. *Continuity/discontinuity* comes up repeatedly in research that addresses the relation between behavior and development in infancy and development later in life. In some sections, the *mechanisms of change* theme is also prominent, as we explore the role that variability and selection play in infants' development. In our discussion of early motor development, we will examine contributions made by the *sociocultural context.*

The theme that most pervades this chapter, however, is the interaction of *nature and nurture* in development. For at least 2,000 years, a not always amicable debate has existed between those philosophers and scientists who emphasize innate knowledge and those who emphasize learning in the development of human beings (Spelke & Newport, 1998). These different emphases are quite evident in the core-knowledge and connectionist accounts reviewed in Chapter 4. The desire to shed light on this age-old debate is one reason that an enormous amount of research has been conducted in the past few decades on perception, action, learning, and cognition in infancy. As you will see, what developmental scientists have recently learned about babies has revealed that their development is even more complicated and remarkable than previously suspected.

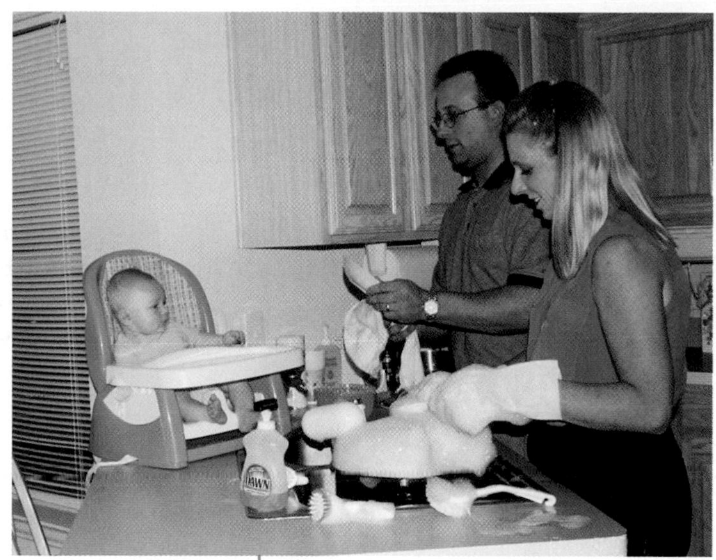

Baby Benjamin looking and listening as his parents do the dishes.

Perception

Parents of new babies cannot help wondering what their children experience—how much they can see, how well they can hear, and so on. William James, one of the earliest psychologists, believed that the world of the newborn is a "big blooming, buzzing confusion." Modern researchers do not share his view. Indeed, remarkable advances in knowledge about early sensation and perception indicate that infants come into the world with all their sensory systems functioning to some degree and that subsequent development occurs at a very rapid pace. **Sensation** refers to the processing of basic information from the external world by the sensory receptors in the sense organs (eyes, ears, skin, etc.) and brain. **Perception** is the process of organizing and interpreting sensory information. In our opening example, sensation involved light and sound waves activating receptors in Benjamin's eyes, ears, and brain; perception involved, for example, his experiencing the visual and auditory stimulation provided by the crashing goblet as a single coherent event.

In this section, we devote the most attention to vision, both because of its fundamental importance to humans and because so much more research has been conducted on vision than on the other senses. We will also discuss hearing and, to a lesser degree, taste, smell, and touch, as well as the coordination between multiple sensory modalities.

sensation the processing of basic information from the external world by the sensory receptors in the sense organs (eyes, ears, skin, etc.) and brain

perception the process of organizing and interpreting sensory information

Vision

With roughly 40% to 50% of our cerebral cortex involved in visual processing (Kellman & Arterberry, 1998), humans rely more heavily on vision than most

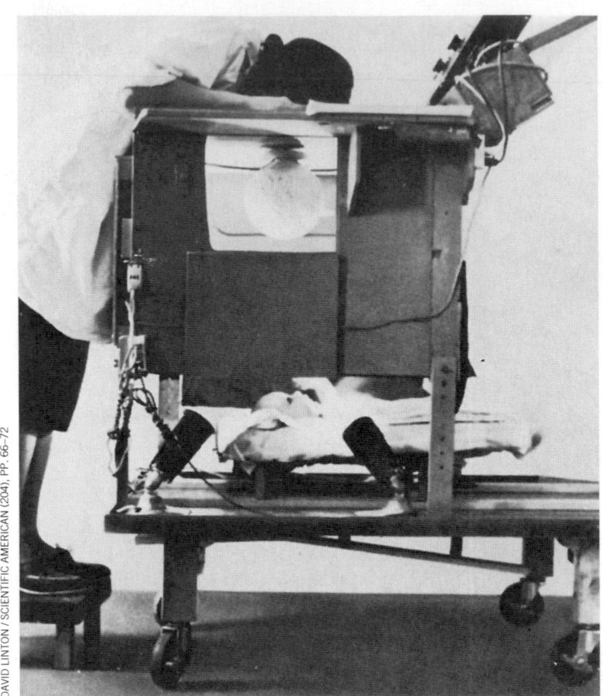

DAVID LINTON / SCIENTIFIC AMERICAN (204), PP. 66–72

This simple apparatus was designed by Robert Fantz to present visual stimuli to infants. The observer looked through a peephole at the infant's eyes and recorded how long the baby looked at the stimuli. The "Fantz box" was replaced by much more elaborate and precise equipment, but it ushered in the modern era of infancy research.

species do. As recently as a few decades ago, it was generally assumed that newborns' vision was so poor as to be barely functional. However, once researchers started carefully studying the looking behavior of newborns and young infants, they discovered that the old assumption was far too pessimistic. In fact, newborns begin visually exploring the world minutes after leaving the womb. They scan the environment, and when their gaze encounters a person or object, they pause to look at it (Haith, 1980). Although newborns do not see what they look at as clearly as adults do, their vision improves extremely rapidly in their first months.

The evidence that enables us to say this so confidently was made possible by researchers' invention of a variety of ingenious methods to study infants. The first research breakthrough was achieved with the **preferential-looking technique,** a method for studying visual attention in infants. In this technique, pioneered by Robert Fantz (1961), different visual stimuli are typically displayed on two side-by-side screens. If an infant looks longer at one of the two stimuli, the researcher can infer that the baby can tell the difference between them and has a preference for one over the other. Fantz established that newborns, just like everyone else, would rather look at something than at nothing. When a pattern of any sort—black and white stripes, newsprint, a bull's-eye, a schematic face—was paired with a plain surface, the infants preferred (i.e., looked longer at) the pattern. Another method that was adapted to study sensory and perceptual development in infants is habituation, which you encountered in Chapter 2 as a research tool for studying fetal development. As you may recall, this procedure involves repeatedly presenting a given stimulus until the infant's response to it declines, or habituates. Then a novel stimulus is presented. If the infant's response increases, the researcher infers that the baby can discriminate between the old and new stimuli. Although extremely simple, these procedures have turned out to be enormously powerful for studying infants' perception and understanding of the world.

Visual Acuity

The new methods enabled researchers to assess infants' **visual acuity,** that is, to estimate how clearly they can see. Infants' visual acuity can be estimated by showing them, for example, a plain gray square paired with black and white stripes of varying widths (Figure 5.1). Because infants prefer looking at a pattern to looking at a homogeneous surface, the narrowest stripes an infant prefers relative to the gray square can be assumed to be the smallest pattern he or she can distinguish (Fantz, Fagan, & Miranda, 1975; Gwiazda, Brill, Mohindra, & Held, 1980). (If you prop your textbook up with Figure 5.1 visible, and then walk backward away from it, the stripes in the figure gradually will blur together into a gray field and you will no longer be able to tell the difference between the two stimuli. An optometrist could use the distance at which you can no longer make out the stripes to estimate your visual acuity.) Research using this and similar techniques has established that visual acuity develops so rapidly that by 8 months of age, an infant's vision approaches that of an adult, although it continues to improve for several years thereafter (Kellman & Arterberry, 1998).

Infants display a variety of other visual preferences that are related to their basic sensory abilities. For example, they generally prefer to look at patterns of high

preferential-looking technique a method for studying visual attention in infants that involves showing infants two patterns or two objects at a time to see if the infants have a preference for one over the other

visual acuity the sharpness of visual discrimination

contrast sensitivity the ability to detect differences in light and dark areas in a visual pattern

retina the back surface of the eye containing the light-sensitive neurons, the rods and cones, that translate light into messages that are sent to the brain

fovea the central region of the retina

visual contrast—such as a black-and-white checkerboard (Banks & Dannemiller, 1987). This is because young infants have poor **contrast sensitivity;** they can detect a pattern only when it is composed of highly contrasting elements. One reason for poor contrast sensitivity has to do with the anatomy of the newborn's eye, particularly the **retina,** the back surface of the eye. The retina contains the light-sensitive neurons—the rods and cones—that translate light into messages that are sent to the brain. The cones, which are involved in seeing fine detail and color, are highly concentrated in the **fovea,** the central region of the retina (Kellman & Banks, 1997). Newborns' cones have a different size and shape from those of adults, and they are also spaced farther apart than cones in the adult eye. As a consequence, newborns' cones catch only 2% of the light striking the fovea, whereas adults' cones catch 65% of the light (Banks & Shannon, 1993).

FIGURE 5.1 Visual acuity An infant's visual acuity can be estimated by comparing how long the baby looks at a striped pattern such as this one versus a plain gray square of the same size and overall brightness. This simple test, first developed by researchers interested in visual development, is frequently used to diagnose early visual problems (From Maurer & Maurer, 1988)

Another restriction on young infants' visual experience is that, for the first month or so, they do not share adults' experience of a richly colorful world. At best, they can, under certain conditions, distinguish some shades from white (Adams, 1995). By 2 or 3 months of age, infants' color vision is similar to that of adults (Kellman & Arterberry, 1998). Indeed, it is similar to the extent that 4- and 5-month-olds prefer (look longest at) the same colors that adults rate as most pleasant—red and blue (Bornstein, 1975). They also perceive the boundaries between colors in more or less the same way as adults do: they respond equivalently to two shades that adults label as the same color (e.g., "blue"), but they discriminate between two shades that adults refer to with different color names (e.g., "blue" and "green") (Bornstein, Kessen, & Weiskopf, 1976).

Visual Scanning

As we mentioned earlier, newborns start visually scanning the environment right away. From the beginning, they are attracted to moving stimuli, which they have trouble tracking because their eye movements are jerky and often do not stay with the object they are trying to follow. Not until 2 or 3 months of age are infants able to track moving objects smoothly, and then only if an object is moving slowly (Aslin, 1981).

Another limitation on young infants' visual experience of the world (and hence on what they can learn) is that their visual scanning is restricted. With a simple figure like a triangle, infants younger than 2 months old look almost exclusively at one corner. With more complex shapes, they tend to limit their scanning to the outer edges (Haith, Bergman, & Moore, 1977; Milewski, 1976; Salapatek & Kessen, 1966). Thus, as Figure 5.2 shows, when 1-month-olds look at a line drawing of a face, their fixations tend to concentrate on the perimeter—on the chin or hairline, where there is relatively high contrast with the background. By 2 months of age, infants scan much more broadly, which enables them to pay attention to both overall shape and inner details.

Based on what you just read, can you predict how a 1-month-old and a 2-month-old would respond to a picture of a face with its features properly arranged versus one with its features scrambled? Because 1-month-olds look primarily at the perimeter of the face patterns, they would not notice the difference between the two pictures and hence would not prefer the normal over the freakish one. In

(a)

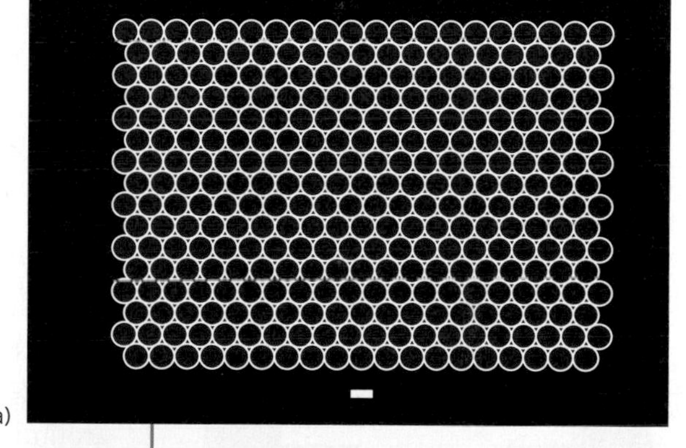

(b)

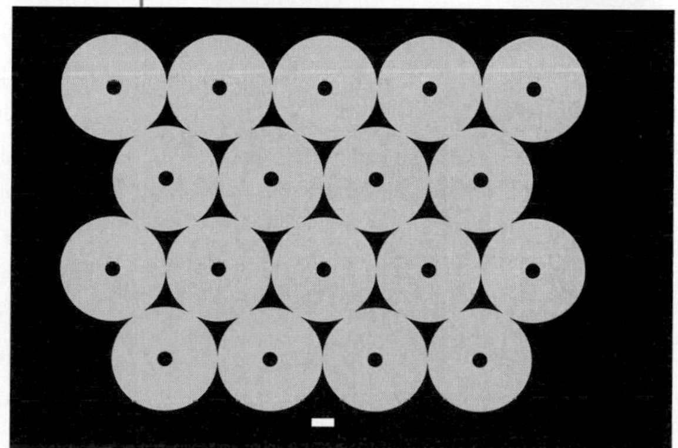

These schematic drawings represent the effective light-collecting areas for the foveal cones of (a) a newborn and (b) an adult. Because of differences in the size, shape, and spacing of their cones, the newborn's cones are much less sensitive than those of the adult. (From Banks & Shannon, 1993)

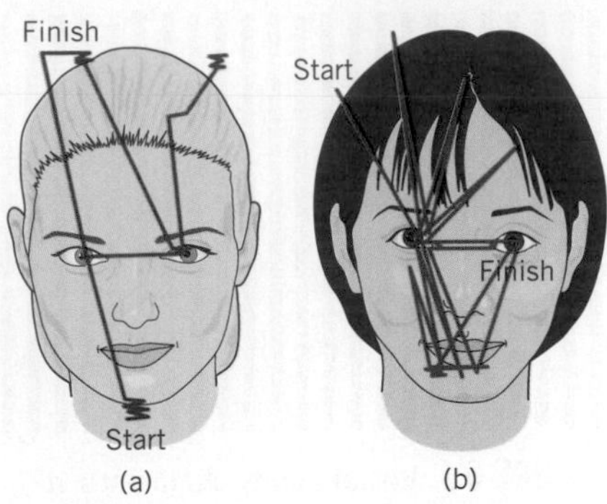

FIGURE 5.2 Visual scanning The lines superimposed on these face pictures show where two babies fixated on the images. (a) A 1-month-old looked primarily at the outer contour of the face and head, with a few fixations of the eyes. (b) A 2-month-old fixated primarily on the internal features of the face, especially the eyes and mouth. (From Maurer & Salapatek, 1976)

FIGURE 5.3 Subjective contour When you look at this figure, you no doubt see a square—what is called a *subjective contour,* because it does not actually exist on the page. Seven-month-olds also see the overall pattern here and detect the illusory square. (From Bertenthal, Campos, & Haith, 1980)

perceptual constancy the perception of objects as being of constant size, shape, color, etc., in spite of physical differences in the retinal image of the object

contrast, because 2-month-olds also look at the inner features, as well as the outer ones, they would reliably prefer the normal face (Maurer, 1985). Box 5.1 describes more about infants' reaction to human faces.

Pattern Perception

Accurate perception of the world requires more than acuity and systematic scanning; it also requires an active process of analyzing and integrating the separate elements of a visual display into a coherent pattern. To perceive the face in Figure 5.2, as 2-month-olds apparently do, they must not only see the separate elements but also integrate them.

A striking demonstration of active pattern perception in infancy comes from research using the stimulus shown in Figure 5.3. When you look at it, you no doubt perceive a square, even though no square actually exists. This perception of subjective contour results from your active integration of the separate elements in the stimulus into a single pattern. If you simply looked at the individual depicted shapes in turn, no square would pop out. There is strong evidence that 7-month-olds also perceive the subjective square in Figure 5.3 (Bertenthal, Campos, & Haith, 1980), and even younger infants may also be able to perceive subjective contour in similar stimuli (Ghim, 1990).

Infants are also able to perceive coherence among moving elements. In research by Bennett Bertenthal and his colleagues (Bertenthal, 1993; Bertenthal, Proffitt, & Kramer, 1987), infants watched a film of moving points of light. Adults who watch this film immediately and confidently identify what they see as a person walking; the moving lights appear to be attached to the major joints and head of an adult human being. Five-month-olds apparently see the same thing; they look longer at the humanlike light-point displays than at ones that involve an equal amount of movement but not a pattern of human movement.

Object Perception

One of the most remarkable things about our perception of objects in the world around us is how stable that perception is. When another person approaches or moves away from us, or slowly turns in a circle, our retinal image of the person changes in size and shape, but we do not have the impression that the person gets larger or smaller or changes shape. Instead, we perceive a constant shape and size, a phenomenon known as **perceptual constancy.** For a good demonstration of size constancy, look in the mirror and notice that the image of your face seems to be the normal size of a face. Then steam up the mirror and trace the outline of your face on the mirror. You will find that the outline is actually a great deal smaller than your real face. The origin of perceptual constancy was a traditional component in the debates between empiricists and nativists, with the former arguing that our perception of the constant size and shape of objects develops as a function of experience, whereas the latter argued that this perceptual regularity stems from inherent properties of the nervous system.

The nativist view gets a nod from research showing good evidence of perceptual constancy in newborns. In a study of *size* constancy (Slater, Mattock, & Brown, 1990), newborns were repeatedly shown a cube at varying distances, so the size of the retinal image differed from one trial to the next. The question was whether the newborns would perceive these events as multiple presentations of a single object or as similar objects of different sizes. To answer this question, the researchers subsequently presented the newborns with the original cube along with a second one that was identical except that it was twice as large. The crucial element of the study was

a closer look 5.1

Beauty and the Baby

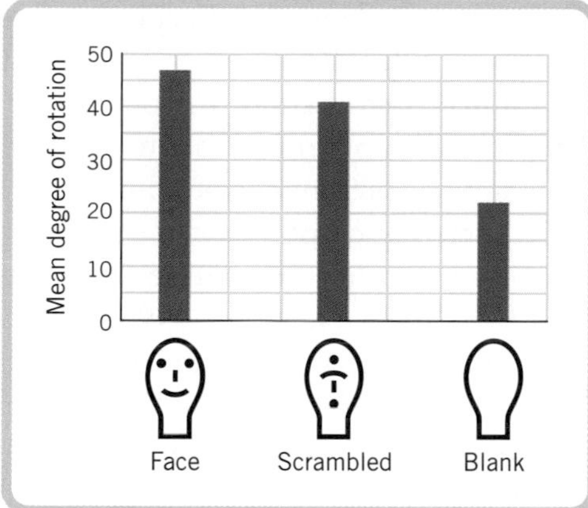

Newborns visually track a regular schematic face for longer than they do a scrambled or blank face. (From Johnson et. al., 1991)

A particularly fascinating aspect of infant perception has to do with the reaction of human infants to that most social of all stimuli—the human face. Newborns show special sensitivity to face stimuli in one situation: when a schematic drawing of a face (see the figure) is slowly moved in front of them, newborns visually track a pattern with the facial features in their regular positions longer than they track one with the features scrambled (Johnson, Dziurawiec, Ellis, & Morton, 1991). The key factor responsible for this preference seems to be the presence of two salient blobs, horizontally aligned, with a single blob centered below them, all contained inside an oval or square shape. In other words, newborns' tracking response is elicited by facelike structures with eyelike and mouthlike elements, but not necessarily by faces per se (Johnson & Morton, 1991; Simion, Valenza, Umiltà, & Barba, 1998).

Infants quickly develop preferences for particular real faces. After about 12 hours' cumulative exposure to their mother over the first few days after birth, infants look longer at her face than at the face of an unfamiliar woman, whether they are tested with video presentations (Walton, Bower, & Bower, 1992) or with live people (Bushnell, 1998; Bushnell, Sai, & Mullin, 1989).

With age, meaning plays an increasing role in infants' response to faces. Although infants come to discriminate among a variety of facial expressions between the ages of 4 and 10 months, they do not reliably prefer one over the other: they look equally long at a face displaying an angry frown as at one with a beaming smile (Nelson, 1987; Walker-Andrews, 1997). Between 5 and 7 months of age, infants notice common emotional expressions in faces and voices (Soken & Pick, 1992; Walker-Andrews, 1997). When they hear a voice expressing positive affect, they look preferentially at a smiling face, but they look longer at an angry face when they hear an angry voice. By the end of the year, they generally prefer smiling faces to fearful or angry ones. Thus, infants eventually come to understand the significance of different facial expressions.

One of the most intriguing aspects of infants' facial preferences is the fact that, along with all the rest of us, babies like a pretty face. Infants look longer at faces that are judged by adults to be highly attractive than at faces judged to be less appealing. This preference has been shown for infants between 2 and 6 months of age (Langlois, Ritter, Roggman, & Vaughn, 1991; Langlois et al., 1987; Rubenstein, Kalakanis, & Langlois, 1999) and even for newborns (Slater et al., 1998, 2000).

Older infants' preference for prettiness, like adults, also affects their behavior toward real people. This was demonstrated in an extraordinarily clever and well-designed study in which 12-month-olds interacted with a woman whose face was either very attractive or very unattractive (Langlois, Roggman, & Rieser-Danner, 1990). The first key feature of this study was that the attractive woman and the unattractive woman were one and the same!

This duality of appearance was achieved through the use of extremely natural-looking professional masks that were painstakingly applied before the woman interacted with the infants. On a given day, the young woman who would test the babies emerged from her makeup session looking either fabulous or not so fabulous, depending on which mask she was wearing. The masks were carefully designed to conform to what adults judge to be a very attractive face and a relatively unattractive one (without being abnormal or deformed). When interacting with the woman, the infants behaved differently as a function of which mask she was wearing. They exhibited more pleasure, became more involved in play, and were less likely to withdraw when she was wearing the attractive mask than when she had on the unattractive one.

A second key feature of this study—the control that makes the results so strong—is that the young woman never knew on any given day which mask she had on. Thus, the children's behavior could not have been cued by her behavior; it could only have been due to her appearance—to whether she looked more like Marilyn Monroe or Marilyn Manson.

This toddler reacts more positively to this very attractive young woman than she would to a less attractive individual.

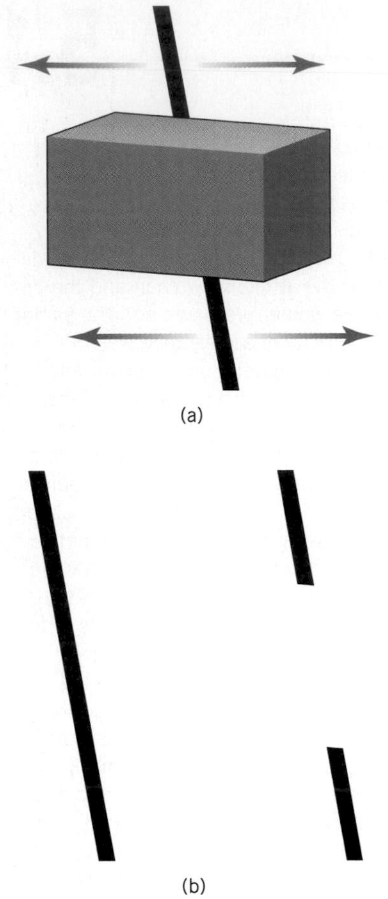

FIGURE 5.4 Object segregation Infants who see the display at the top of this figure (a) perceive it as two separate objects, a rod moving behind a block. After habituating to the display, they look longer at two rod segments than at a single rod (b), indicating that they find the single rod familiar but the two segments novel. If they first see a display with no movement, they look equally long at the two test displays. This result reveals the importance of movement for *object segregation.* (From Kellman & Spelke, 1983)

that the second cube was twice as far away, so it produced the same-size retinal image as the first one. The infants looked longer at the new cube, indicating that they saw it as different in size from the original one. This in turn revealed that they had perceived the multiple presentations of the original cube as a single object of a constant size even though its retinal size varied. Thus, visual experience does not seem to be necessary for size constancy (Granrud, 1987; Slater & Morison, 1985).

Another crucial perceptual ability is **object segregation,** the perception of the boundaries between objects. To appreciate the importance of this ability, try to imagine that you are seeing the objects in your present surroundings for the first time. How can you tell where one object starts and another one ends? A gap between two objects provides clear evidence of two separate entities, and young infants are sensitive to this information (Spelke & Newport, 1998). But what if there are no visible gaps? Suppose, for example, that as baby Benjamin watches his parents washing dishes, he sees a cup sitting on a saucer. Will he perceive this arrangement as one or two objects? Lacking experience with china, Benjamin may be unsure: the difference in shape suggests two objects, but the common texture suggests only one. Now suppose Ben's mother picks up the cup to dip it in the suds. Will he still be uncertain? No, because even for an infant, independent motion of cup and saucer signals that they are separate things.

The importance of motion for object segregation in infants was initially demonstrated in a classic experiment by Kellman and Spelke (1983). First, 4-month-olds were presented with a display, shown in Figure 5.4a, which adults perceive as a single rod moving back and forth behind a block of wood. After habituating to the display, the infants were shown the two test displays in Figure 5.4b. The investigators reasoned that if the infants, like adults, assumed that there was a single rod behind the block during habituation, they would look longer at the two rod segments because that display would be novel. This is exactly what the babies did.

What caused the infants to assume that the two rod segments they could see were a single, unitary object? The answer is common movement, the fact that the two segments always moved together in the same direction and at the same speed. Four-month-olds who saw a display that was the same as the one in Figure 5.4a, except that the rod was stationary, looked equally long at the two test displays. In the absence of common movement, the display was ambiguous. Subsequent research established that even 2-month-olds (although not newborns) perceive a single rod if the block is quite narrow so that more of the rod is visible as it moves back and forth (Johnson & Aslin, 1995; Slater, Johnson, Brown, & Badenoch, 1996).

Common movement is such a powerful cue that it makes even perceptually distinct elements look like a unitary object. It does not matter if the two parts of the object moving behind the block differ in color, texture, and shape (Kellman & Spelke, 1983), nor does it make much difference how they move (side to side, up and down, etc.) (Kellman, Spelke, & Short, 1986).

As they get older, infants use additional sources of information for object segregation, including their general knowledge about the world (Needham, 1997; Needham & Baillargeon, 1997; Needham, Baillargeon, & Kaufman, 1997). Consider the rather peculiar-looking displays shown in Figure 5.5. The differences in color, shape, and texture between the box and the tube in Figure 5.5a suggest that there are two separate objects, although you cannot really be sure. However, your knowledge that objects cannot float in midair tells you that Figure 5.5b has to be a single object; that is, the tube *must* be attached to the box.

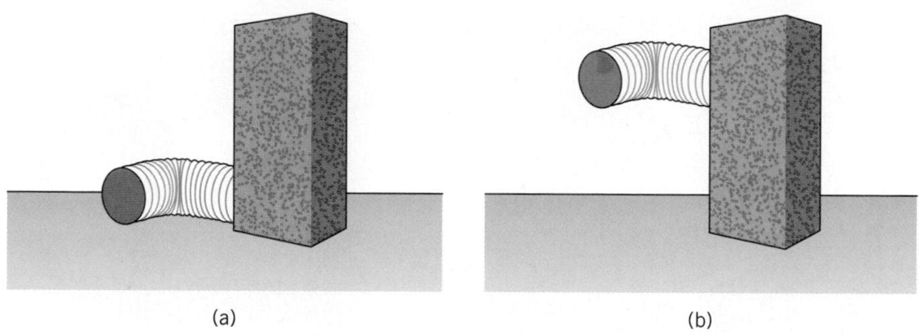

FIGURE 5.5 Knowledge and object segregation (a) It is impossible to know for sure whether this figure is one object or two. (b) Because of your knowledge about gravity and support, you can be sure that *this* figure is a single (albeit very odd) object. (From Needham, 1997)

Like you, 8-month-olds interpret these two displays differently. When they see a hand reach in and pull on the tube in Figure 5.5a they look longer (presumably they are more surprised) if the box and tube move together than if the tube comes apart from the box, indicating that they perceive the display as two separate objects. However, the opposite pattern occurs in Figure 5.5b: now the infants look longer if the tube alone moves, indicating that they perceive a single object.

Depth Perception

To navigate about the environment, we need to know where we are with respect to the objects and landmarks around us. We use many sorts of depth and distance cues to tell us whether we can reach the coffee cup on our desk or whether the approaching car is far enough away that we can safely cross in front of it. From the beginning, infants are sensitive to some of these cues, and they rapidly become sensitive to the rest.

One such cue that infants are sensitive to very early is **optical expansion:** As an object comes toward us, its visual image increases in size, causing more and more of the background to be occluded. When an image of an approaching object expands symmetrically, we know the object is headed right for us, and a sensible response is to duck. Babies cannot duck, but infants as young as 1 month old blink defensively at an expanding image that appears to be an object coming straight toward them (Ball & Tronick, 1971, Nanez & Yonas, 1994; Yonas, 1981).

Another depth cue that emerges early is due to the simple fact that we have two eyes. The retinal image of an object is never quite the same in the two eyes, so the eyes never send quite the same signal to the brain—a phenomenon known as **binocular disparity.** The closer the object we are looking at, the greater the disparity between the two images; the farther away the object, the less disparity there is. In a process known as **stereopsis,** the visual cortex combines the differing neural signals, resulting in the perception of depth. This form of depth perception emerges quite suddenly at around 4 months of age and is generally complete within a few weeks (Held, Birch, & Gwiazda, 1980), presumably due to the maturation of the visual cortex.

At around 6 or 7 months of age, infants begin to become sensitive to a variety of **monocular** depth cues (so called because they denote depth even if one has one eye closed) (Yonas, Arterberry, & Granrud, 1987). These cues are also known as **pictorial** cues, because they can be used to portray depth in pictures. One example is relative size: objects that are larger appear to be closer than smaller objects. Another is interposition: near objects partially occlude ones that are farther away.

In one of the earliest—and cleverest—studies of infants' sensitivity to monocular depth cues, Albert Yonas and his colleagues (Yonas, Cleaves, & Pettersen, 1978)

object segregation the identification of separate objects in a visual array

optical expansion a depth cue in which an object occludes increasingly more of the background, indicating that the object is approaching

binocular disparity the difference between the retinal image of an object in each eye that results in two slightly different signals being sent to the brain.

stereopsis the process by which the visual cortex combines the differing neural signals, caused by binocular disparity, resulting in the perception of depth

monocular or **pictorial cues** the perceptual cues of depth that can be perceived by one eye alone. Examples are relative size and interposition.

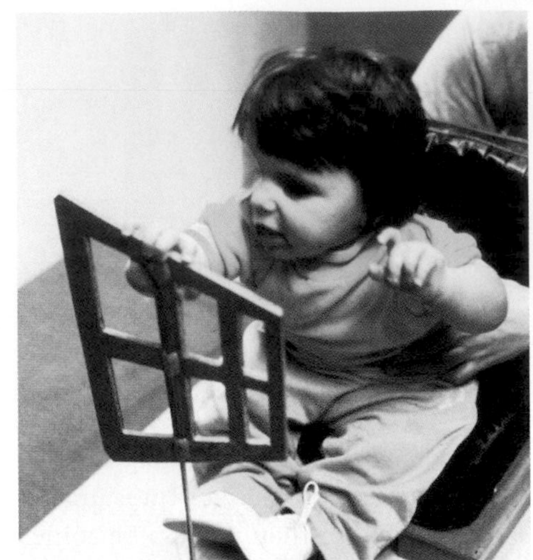

BOTH: ALBERT YONAS

FIGURE 5.6 Monocular depth cues This 7-month-old infant is using the monocular depth cue of *relative size.* Wearing an eye patch to take away binocular depth information, he is reaching to the longer side of a trapezoidal window. This behavior indicates that the baby sees it as the nearer, and hence more readily reachable, side of a regular window. (Yonas et al., 1978)

capitalized on the fact that infants will reach toward whichever of two objects is nearer. The investigators put a patch over one eye of 5- and 7-month-olds and presented them with a trapezoidal window with one side considerably longer than the other (Figure 5.6). When viewed by an adult with one eye closed (so binocular depth information is not available), the window appears to be a standard rectangular window sitting at an angle with one side closer to the viewer. The 7-month-olds (but not the younger babies) reached toward the longer side. The only reason they would have to prefer that side is if they perceived it as being nearer. Hence, this result reveals sensitivity to monocular depth cues. (Box 5.2 reviews research on infants' perception of pictures and photographs.)

EMPEROR AUGUSTUS AND THE SIBYL, 1535 BY PARIS BARDONE (1500–1571). PUSHKIN MUSEUM, MOSCOW, RUSSIA / BRIDGEMAN ART LIBRARY

This Renaissance painting contains multiple examples of the two pictorial cues of relative size and interposition, as well as other cues, such as the convergence of parallel lines in the distance.

a closer look 5.2

Picture Perception

A special case of perceptual development concerns pictures. Pictures are ubiquitous in modern societies, and we acquire an enormous amount of information through them. When can infants perceive and understand these important cultural artifacts?

Even young infants perceive pictures in much the same way that you do. In a classic study, Hochberg and Brooks (1962) raised their own infant son with no exposure to pictures at all: no pictures on the walls of their home; no family photos; no picture books; no patterns on sheets, clothing, or toys. They even removed the labels from canned foods. Nevertheless, when tested at 18 months, the child readily identified people and objects in photographs and line drawings. Later research established that infants as young as 5 months old can recognize people and objects in photographs and drawings of them (e.g., DeLoache, Strauss, & Maynard, 1979; Dirks & Gibson, 1977), and even newborns can recognize two-dimensional versions of three-dimensional objects (Slater, Rose, & Morison, 1984).

Despite their precocious perception of pictures, infants do not understand their nature. The four babies shown here—two from the United States and two from a rural village in West Africa—are all trying to grasp depicted objects. Although these babies can perceive the difference between pictures and objects, they do not yet understand what two-dimensionality means; hence, they attempt to treat pictured objects as if they were real objects—with an inevitable lack of success. By 19 months of age and after substantial experience with pictures, American infants no longer manually investigate pictures, apparently having learned the appropriate cultural use of pictures—to look at and talk about, but not to feel, pick up, or eat (DeLoache, Pierroutsakos, Uttal, Rosengren, & Gottlieb, 1998; Pierroutsakos & DeLoache, 2002).

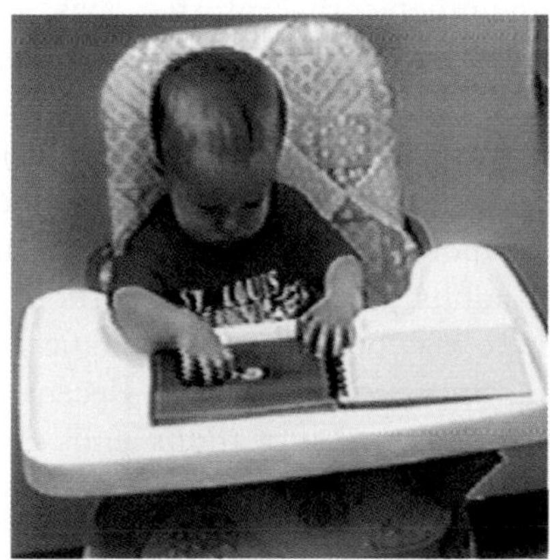

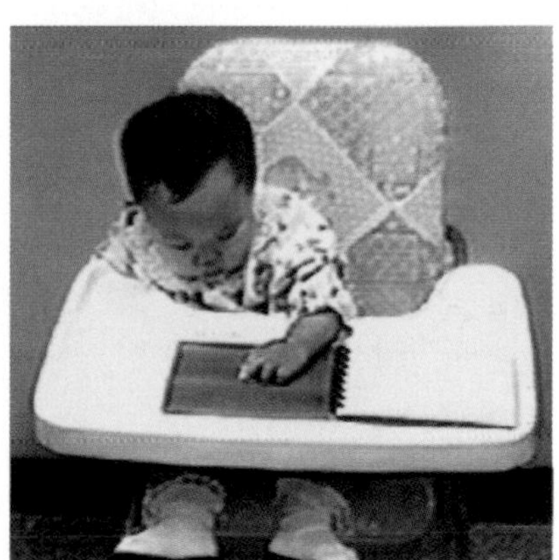

These 9-month-old infants—two from the United States and two from West Africa—are responding to pictures of objects as if they were real objects. They do not yet know the true nature of pictures. (From DeLoache, Pierroutsakos, Uttal, Rosengren, & Gottlieb, 1998)

Auditory Perception

Another rich source of infants' information about the world is sound. The human auditory system is relatively well developed at birth, although newborns can still be characterized as a bit hard of hearing (Trehub & Schellenberg, 1995). The faintest sound a newborn responds to is roughly four times louder than the quietest sound an adult can detect (Maurer & Maurer, 1988). Not until 5 to 8 years of age does hearing approach adult levels.

When they hear a sound, newborns tend to turn toward it, a phenomenon referred to as **auditory localization** (Morrongiello, Fenwick, Hillier, & Chance,

auditory localization perception of the location in space of a sound source

1994). One dedicated scientist tested his 10-minute-old daughter while still in the delivery room and found that she turned her head toward a clicking sound he made to the side of her head (Wertheimer, 1961). Because they turn their heads very slowly, newborns are most likely to localize the source of a sound that continues for several seconds (Clarkson & Clifton, 1991).

Infants are remarkably adept at perceiving pattern in the stream of sound they hear, and they are especially proficient at detecting subtle differences in the sounds of human speech. Because infants' speech perception is so important to language development, we will review it in detail in Chapter 6. Here we will focus on another realm in which infants display a surprising degree of perceptual sensitivity—music.

Music Perception

The nineteenth-century essayist Thomas Carlyle referred to music as "the speech of angels," suggesting a similar basis for these two auditory modes. In support of this idea, modern researchers have demonstrated that 7-month-old infants learn sequences of musical tones in much the same way they learn sequences of linguistic sounds, suggesting a common learning mechanism (Saffran, Johnson, Aslin, & Newport, 1999). Further, scientists have discovered similarities in how the brains of adults process some aspects of speech and music, leading to speculation that there may be an innate, biological foundation for music perception just as there is known to be for language. Recent research showing that infants' response to music is similar to that of adults lends support to this idea.

For one thing, infants share the strong preferences that adults have for some musical sounds over others. From Pythagoras to Galileo to the current day, many scholars have argued that consonant tones are inherently pleasing to human ears, whereas dissonance is unpleasant (Schellenberg & Trehub, 1996; Trehub & Schellenberg, 1995). To see if infants agree, researchers employ a procedure in which a visual stimulus is attached to the front of a speaker that plays a tape. When music starts emanating from the speaker, infants tend to look toward it. The length of time infants look at the display is taken as a measure of their interest in or preference for the music emanating from the speaker. Studies have shown that 4-month-olds pay more attention to a consonant version of a folk song than to a dissonant one (Zentner & Kagan, 1996, 1998) and that 6-month-olds prefer a consonant version of a minuet over a predominantly dissonant one (Trainor & Heinmiller, 1998).

Infants also respond to rhythm in music. Although they do not exactly tap their toes in time to the beat, infants do move to it, bouncing perceptibly while listening to lively, rhythmic band music (Trehub, 1993). Infants are likewise sensitive to temporal organization in music. In one study, for example, infants as young as 4½ months listened longer to Mozart minuets with 1-second pauses between natural phrase boundaries in the music than to the same music with the pauses inserted in the middle of the phrases (Krumhansl & Jusczyk, 1990).

Equally impressive is infants' sensitivity to melody, as demonstrated by a study in which Chang and Trehub (1977) habituated 5-month-olds to a simple melody. When the same melody was then played at a higher or lower pitch, the infants remained habituated. It was the same song to them. However, when the identical notes were played in a different order (thereby destroying the melodic pattern), the babies showed renewed interest. Thus, the infants responded like adults, who perceive a melody to be the same regardless of whether it is played on a piccolo or a tuba, but perceive it to be a different tune if the notes are rearranged.

Given that infants and adults show many similarities in musical perception and preferences, it is not surprising that there is some evidence of similar brain activity in their processing of music as well. For example, infants' detection of melody relies primarily on right-hemisphere processing, just as it does in most adults (Balaban, Anderson, & Wisniewski, 1998). Their shared sensitivity to musical stimuli may be part of the reason that caregivers the world over sing to their babies (Trehub & Schellenberg, 1995).

Taste and Smell

As you learned in Chapter 2, sensitivity to taste and smell develops before birth, and newborns show an innate preference for sweet flavors. Preferences for smells are also present very early in life, including a general attraction to the odor of breast milk, the natural food source for human infants (Porter, Makin, Davis, & Christensen, 1991, 1992). Smell plays a powerful role in how a variety of infant mammals learn to recognize their mothers, and the same is probably true for human infants. This was shown by studies in which infants were given a choice between the scent of their own mother and that of another woman. A pad that an infant's own mother had worn next to her breast was placed on one side of the infant's head and a pad worn by a different woman was placed on the other side. Two-week-old infants turned more often and spent more time oriented to the pad that contained their mother's unique scent (MacFarlane, 1975; Porter et al., 1992).

Touch

Another important way that infants learn about the environment is through active touch, whether with their hands and fingers or mouth and tongue. Oral exploration dominates for the first few months, as infants mouth and suck on their own fingers and toes, as well as virtually any object they come into contact with. (This is why it is so important to keep small, swallowable objects away from babies.) Through their ardent oral exploration, babies presumably learn about their own bodies (or at least the parts they can get their mouths on), as well as about the texture, taste, and other properties of the objects they encounter.

From around the age of 4 months, as infants gain greater control over their hand and arm movements, manual exploration increases and gradually takes precedence over oral exploration. Infants actively rub, finger, probe, and bang objects, and their actions become increasingly specific to the properties of the objects. For example, they tend to rub textured objects and bang rigid ones. The increase in manual control also facilitates visual exploration in that infants can hold interesting objects in order to examine them more closely, rotating the objects to view them from different angles and transferring them from hand to hand to get a better look at them (Bushnell & Boudreau, 1991; Lockman & McHale, 1989; Palmer, 1989; Rochat, 1989; Ruff, 1986).

Intermodal Perception

Most events that we or infants experience involve simultaneous stimulation through multiple sensory modalities. In the crystal-goblet-falling-on-tile-floor event witnessed by Benjamin, both visual and auditory stimulation were provided by the shattering glass. Through the phenomenon of **intermodal perception,** the combining of information from two or more sensory systems, Ben's parents perceived the auditory and visual stimulation as a unitary, coherent event involving sight and sound. It is likely that Ben did, too, although how and when intermodal perception develops has been a topic of considerable debate.

According to Piaget (1954) and others (e.g., Bryant, 1974), information from different sensory modalities is initially separate, and only after some months do infants become capable of forming associations between how things look and how they sound, taste, feel, and so on. In contrast, Eleanor Gibson (1988) and her colleagues (e.g., Bahrick, 1994; Spelke, 1979) argue that from very early on infants integrate information from different senses. A very simple example is newborns' turning toward a sound they hear (the phenomenon of auditory localization discussed on pp. 178–179), indicating that the babies expect a sound to be associated with an object.

Very young infants also link their oral and visual experience. In studies with 1-month-olds (Meltzoff & Borton, 1979) and newborns (Kaye & Bower, 1994), the infants sucked on pacifiers that they were prevented from seeing. They were then shown a picture of the pacifier they had sucked on and a picture of a novel pacifier of a different shape or texture. The infants looked longer at the picture of the pacifier they had sucked on. Thus, these infants could visually recognize an object they had experienced only through oral exploration.

When infants become able to explore objects manually, they readily integrate their visual and tactile experience. In one study, for example, 4-month-olds were allowed to hold and feel, but not see, a pair of rings that were connected by either a rigid bar or a string. When the babies were shown both types of rings, they recognized the ones they had previously explored with their hands (Streri & Spelke, 1988). A different version of visual–tactile integration is shown by the fact that 5-month-old infants can detect a relation between their own limb movements and a video display of those movements, as shown by the fact that they look longer at a video that is not synchronized with their movements than at one that is (Bahrick & Watson, 1985; Rochat & Morgan, 1995; Schmuckler, 1996).

Using a very clever technique, researchers have discovered that infants also possess a variety of forms of auditory–visual intermodal perception. This technique involves simultaneously presenting two films, side by side, while playing a soundtrack that is synchronized with one of the films but not the other. If an infant shows greater response to the film that is consistent with the soundtrack, it is taken as evidence that the infant detects the common structure in the auditory and visual information.

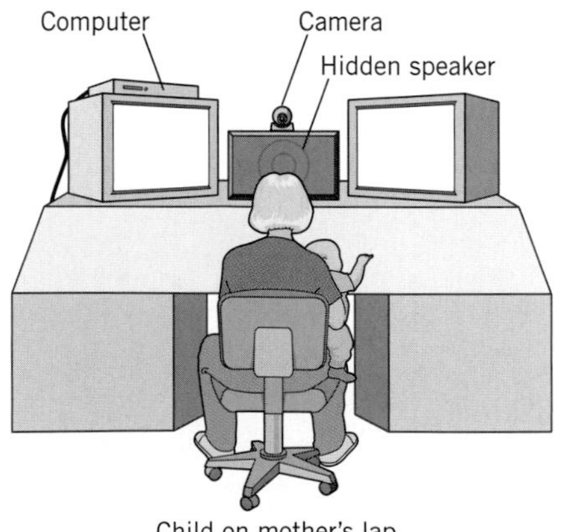

A set-up like this one enables researchers to study auditory–visual intermodal perception. The two computer screens display different films, one of which is coordinated with a soundtrack. The video camera records the infant's looking toward the two screens.

In an early study using this procedure, Elizabeth Spelke (1976) showed 4-month-olds two videos, one of a person playing peekaboo and the other of a hand beating a drumstick against a block. The infants responded more to the film that matched the sounds they were hearing. When they heard a voice saying "Peekaboo," they looked more at the person, but when they heard a beating sound, they looked longer at the hand. In subsequent studies, infants showed finer discriminations. For example, 4-month-olds responded more to a film of a "hopping" toy animal that contacted the surface in synchrony with sounds of impact than to a film in which the impact sounds occurred while the animal was in midair (Spelke, 1979).

Similar studies have found that infants seem especially well tuned to the relation between human faces and voices. Four-month-olds who are shown side-by-side films of a person talking and hear a talking voice look longer at the face whose lip movements are synchronized with the speech (Spelke & Cortelyou, 1980;

Walker, 1982). Four-month-olds even detect the relation between specific speech sounds, such as "a" and "i," and the specific lip movements associated with them (Kuhl & Meltzoff, 1982, 1984).

review:

Using a variety of special techniques, developmental psychologists have discovered an enormous amount about perceptual development in infancy. They have documented rapid development of basic visual abilities from birth over the next few months, discovering that by approximately 8 months of age infants' visual acuity, scanning patterns, and color perception are similar to those of adults. Some forms of depth perception are present at birth, whereas others develop in the ensuing months. By 5 to 7 months of age, infants actively integrate separate elements of visual displays to perceive coherent patterns. They use many sources of information, including movement and their knowledge of their surroundings, for object segregation.

Research on auditory perception has shown that right from birth, babies turn toward sounds they hear. They are quite sensitive to musical stimuli and display many of the same preferences adults do, such as a preference for consonance over dissonance. Smell and touch both play an important role in infants' interaction with the world around them. The crucial ability to link what they perceive in separate modalities to experience unitary, coherent events is present in a simple form at birth, but more complex associations develop gradually. Thus there is much in recent research to encourage anyone of a nativist persuasion. At the same time, most perceptual skills also show development over time, much of which clearly involves learning.

intermodal perception the combining of information from two or more sensory systems

reflexes innate, fixed patterns of action that occur in response to particular stimulation

Motor Development

As you learned in Chapter 2, human movement starts well before birth while the fetus floats weightlessly in amniotic fluid. After birth, the newborn's movements are jerky and relatively uncoordinated, in part because of physical and neurological immaturity and in part because the baby is experiencing the full effects of gravity for the first time. As you will see in this section, the story of how the uncoordinated newborn, trapped by gravity, becomes the toddler confidently and competently moving about and exploring the environment is much more complicated, and more interesting, than was previously believed.

Reflexes

Newborns do start off with some tightly organized behaviors. These behaviors are neonatal **reflexes**—innate, fixed patterns of action that occur in response to particular stimulation. Some reflexes, such as withdrawal from a painful stimulus, have clear adaptive value; others have no known adaptive significance. In the *grasping* reflex, newborns close their fingers around anything that contacts the palm of their hand. A touch on the cheek near the mouth sets off the *rooting* reflex, in which babies turn their head in the direction of the touch and open their mouth. Thus, when their cheek comes into contact with their mother's breast, they turn toward the breast, opening their mouth as they do. Oral contact with the nipple then sets off a *sucking* reflex, which occurs with any stimulus inside the mouth. Obviously, these two reflexes increase the baby's chance of getting nourishment and ultimately of surviving. No benefit is known to be associated with other reflexes, such as the *tonic neck reflex;* when the infant's head is turned to the right, the right arm extends and the left arm flexes, and at the same time the right knee flexes.

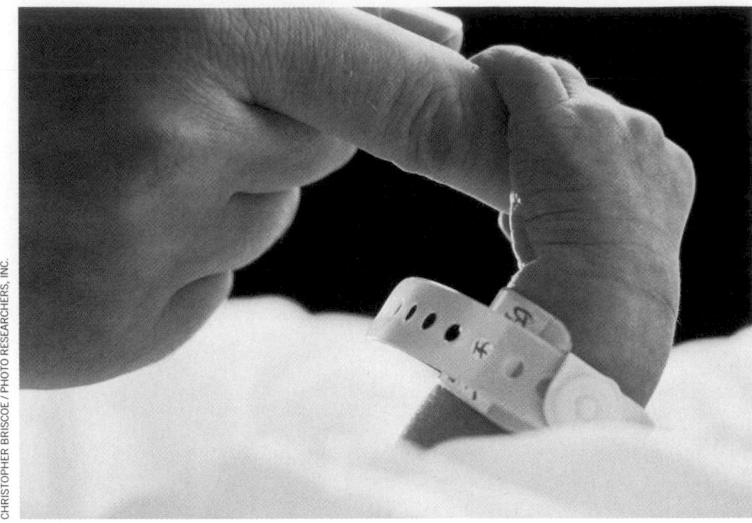

CHRISTOPHER BRISCOE / PHOTO RESEARCHERS, INC.

Neonatal reflexes: (a) Grasping

ELIZABETH CREWS / THE IMAGE WORKS

(b) Rooting

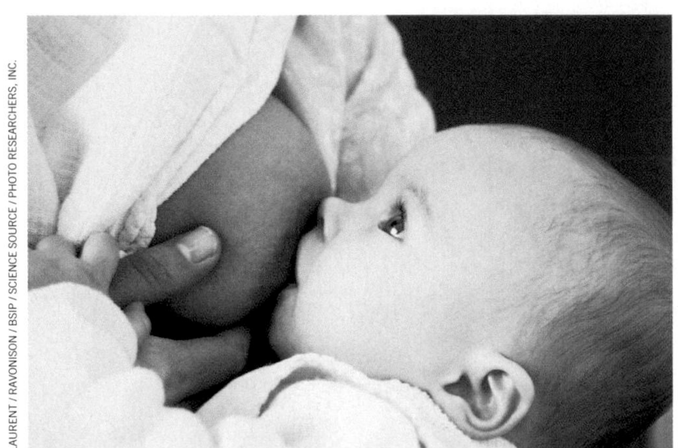

LAURENT / RAVONISON / BSIP / SCIENCE SOURCE / PHOTO RESEARCHERS, INC.

(c) Sucking

LAURA DWIGHT / PETER ARNOLD, INC.

(d) Tonic neck reflex

The presence of strong reflexes at birth is a sign that the newborn's central nervous system is in good shape. Brain damage can be signaled by reflexes that are either abnormally weak or vigorous. Most of the neonatal reflexes disappear on a regular schedule, although some—including coughing, sneezing, blinking, and withdrawing from pain—remain throughout life. Persistence of a neonatal reflex beyond the point at which it is expected to disappear warns of a possible neurological problem.

Motor Milestones

Infants progress quickly in acquiring the basic movement patterns of our species, shown in Figure 5.7. As you will see, the achievement of each of the major "motor milestones" of infancy, especially walking, constitutes a major advance in the infant's experience of the world.

The average ages that Figure 5.7 gives for the development of each of these important motor skills are based on research with Western, primarily North American, infants. Keep in mind, however, that cultural factors can affect the

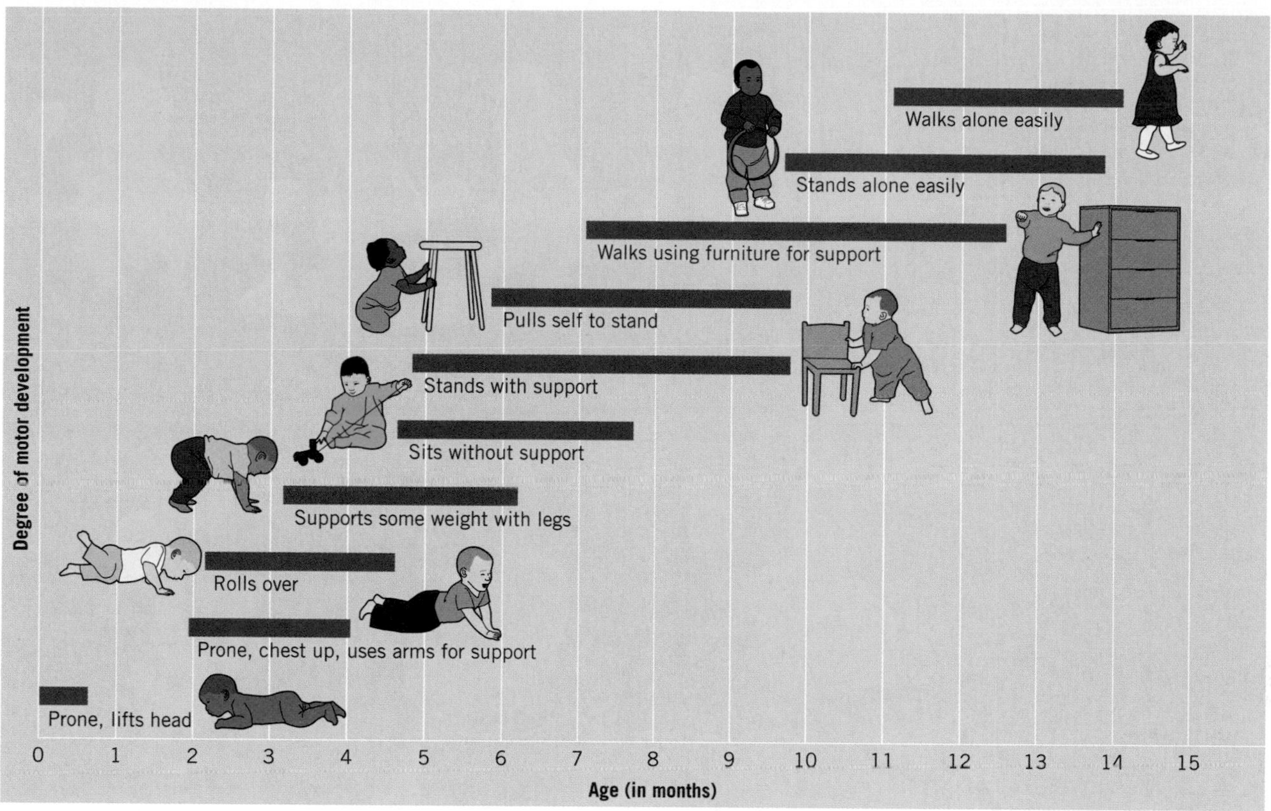

FIGURE 5.7 The major milestones of motor development in infancy The average age and range of ages for achievement of each milestone are shown. Note that these age norms are based on research with healthy, well-nourished North American infants. (Adapted from Santrock, 1988)

course of motor development and that the degree to which motor skills are encouraged and facilitated varies from one culture to another. Some cultures actively discourage early locomotion. In modern urban China, for example, infants are typically placed on soft beds, surrounded by thick pillows to prevent falling. This arrangement does not enable the infants to develop the muscle strength required to support the upper trunk, which is necessary for crawling. Parents also try to prevent infants from crawling because of their concern about the cleanliness of children's hands (Campos, Anderson, Barbu-Roth, Hubbard, Hertenstein, & Witherington, 2000). Among the Ache, a nomadic people who live in the rain forest of Paraguay, infants spend almost all of their first three years of life being carried by, or kept very near, their mothers. Because the Ache typically clear only very small areas of the forest for their temporary camps, any babies who venture more than a few feet away from their mothers are quickly retrieved (Kaplan & Dove, 1987). In direct contrast, the Kipsigis in rural Kenya actively encourage the motor development of their infants; for example, they help their babies practice sitting by propping them up in shallow holes dug in the ground to support their backs (Super, 1976). Other groups, in West Africa and the West

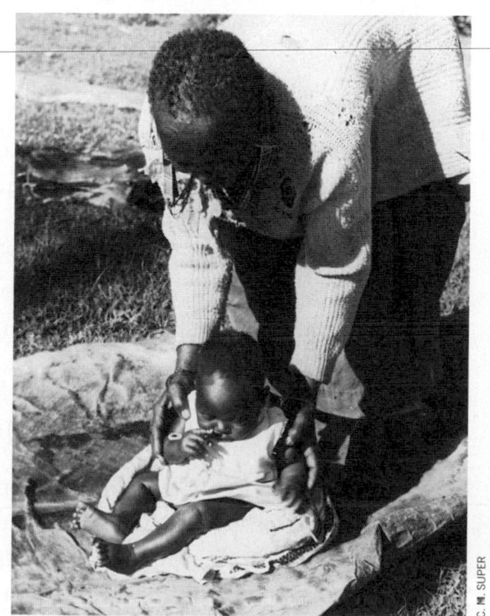

To encourage her infant to sit independently, this Kipsigis mother in rural Kenya has dug a small hole in the sand to prop up the baby. This mother believes it is important to help infants develop motor skills. (Super, 1976)

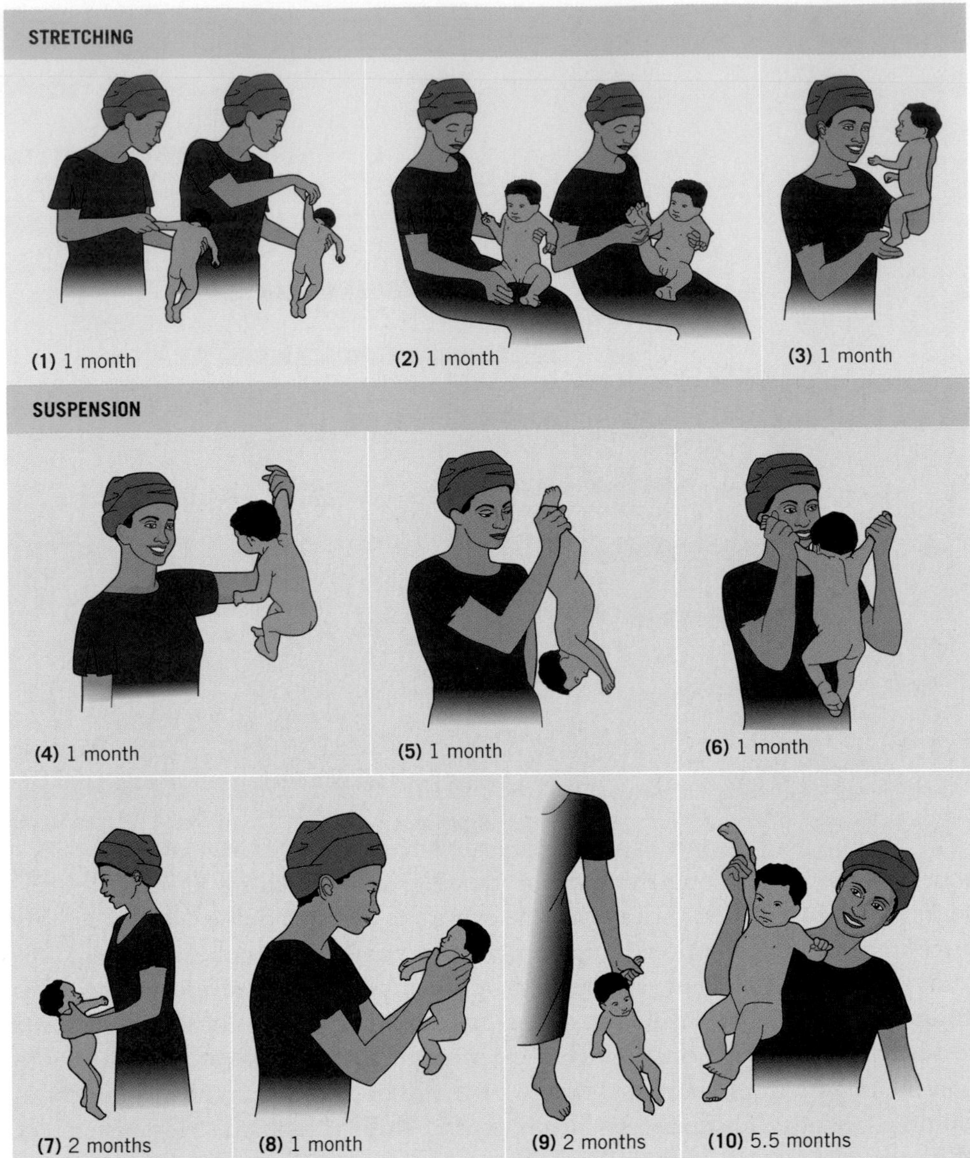

Mothers in Mali believe it is important to exercise their infants to promote their physical and motor development. The maneuvers shown here do not harm the babies and do hasten their early motor skills. (Adapted from Bril & Sabatier, 1986)

Indies, institute an aggressive program of massage, manipulation, and stimulation designed to facilitate their infants' motor development (Hopkins & Westra, 1988).

These widely varying cultural practices can have an impact on infants' development. Researchers have documented somewhat slower motor development in Ache and Chinese infants compared with the norms shown in Figure 5.7; Kipsigis babies and the infants who undergo exercise regimes, on the other hand, are advanced in their motor-skill development.

Current Views of Motor Development

Two early pioneers in the study of motor development, Arnold Gesell and Myrtle McGraw, were impressed by infants' orderly acquisition of the skills shown in Figure 5.7. They concluded that infants' motor development is governed by neurological maturation of the brain, especially the increasing control of behavior by the cortex (Gesell & Thompson, 1938; McGraw, 1943).

a closer look 5.3

"The Case of the Disappearing Reflex"

One of the primary proponents of the dynamic-systems point of view we discussed in Chapter 4 is Esther Thelen. Early research by Thelen and her colleagues provides an excellent example of this approach to investigating motor development, as well as a good example of how to formulate hypotheses and test them in general. In one study, they held infants under the arms and submerged them waist-deep in water. As you read the following paragraphs, see how soon you can figure out the rationale for this somewhat strange-sounding, but in fact extremely clever and informative, experiment.

This particular study was one in a series of investigations of what Thelen (1995) refers to as "the case of the disappearing reflex." The reflex in question, the **stepping reflex,** can be elicited by holding a newborn under the arms so that his or her feet touch a surface; the baby will reflexively perform stepping motions, lifting first one leg and then the other in a coordinated pattern as in walking. The reflex typically disappears at around 2 months of age. It was long assumed that the stepping reflex disappears from the infant's motor repertoire as a result of cortical maturation.

However, the results of a classic study by Zelazo, Zelazo, and Kolb (1972) were inconsistent with this view. In this research, 2-month-old infants were given extra practice exercising their stepping reflex, and as a result, the infants continued to show the reflex long after it would otherwise have disappeared. Other research also showed persistence of the stepping pattern long beyond 2 months of age. For one thing, the rhythmical kicking that babies engage in when they are lying down involves the same pattern of alternating leg movement as stepping does. However, unlike stepping, kicking continues throughout infancy (Thelen & Fisher, 1982). For another, when 7-month-olds in whom the stepping reflex has disappeared are supported on a moving treadmill, they step smartly (Thelen, 1986). If the stepping reflex can be prolonged or elicited long after it is scheduled to disappear, cortical maturation cannot account for its vanishing. Why then does it normally disappear?

COURTESY OF ESTHER THELEN

This infant, who no longer shows a stepping reflex on dry land, does show it when suspended in water.

A clue was provided by the observation that chubbier babies generally begin walking (and crawling) somewhat later than slimmer ones. Thelen reasoned that infants' very rapid weight gain in the first few weeks after birth may cause their legs to get heavier faster than they get stronger. More strength is needed to step while upright than to kick while lying down, and more is needed to lift a fat leg than a thin one. Thus, Thelen hypothesized that the solution to the mystery might have more to do with brawn than brains.

To test this hypothesis, two elegant experiments were conducted (Thelen, Fisher, & Ridley-Johnson, 1984). In one, the researchers put weights, roughly equivalent to the amount of fat typically gained in the first few months, on the ankles of infants who still had a stepping reflex. The babies suddenly stopped stepping. In the second study, infants who no longer showed a stepping reflex were suspended waist-deep in a tank of water (see the photo). As predicted, with the buoyancy of the water supporting their weight, the babies resumed stepping. Thus, the scientific detective work of these investigators established that the normal disappearance of the stepping reflex is not, as was previously assumed, caused by cortical maturation; rather, the movement pattern (and its neural basis) remains but is masked by the changing ratio of leg weight to strength. Only by considering multiple variables simultaneously was it possible to solve the mystery of the disappearing reflex.

Current theorists, many of whom take a dynamic-systems approach (see Chapter 4), emphasize that motor development results from a confluence of numerous factors, including neural mechanisms but also including increases in infants' strength, posture control, balance, and perceptual skills, and changes in their body proportions and motivation (Bertenthal & Clifton, 1998; Lockman & Thelen, 1993; Thelen, 1995). (Box 5.3 offers a detailed account of a program of research exemplifying this approach.) To get a sense of the role these factors play, think for a moment about how each might influence the attainment of the motor milestones. They all play a part in the gradual transition from newborns unable even to lift their head to toddlers who walk independently by holding their upper body erect while coordinating the movement of their legs that have grown strong enough to support their weight. Every advance in this transition is fueled by what infants can perceive of the external world and their motivation to experience more of it.

stepping reflex a neonatal reflex in which an infant lifts first one leg and then the other in a coordinated pattern like walking

The Expanding World of the Infant

Infants' mastery of each of the milestones shown in Figure 5.7 greatly expands their world: there is more to see when they can sit up, more to explore when they can reach for things themselves, and even more to discover when they can move about on their own. In this section, we consider some of the ways that motor development affects infants' experience of the world.

Reaching

The development of reaching sets off a minirevolution in the infant's life: "once infants can reach for and grasp objects, they no longer have to wait for the world to come to them" (Bertenthal & Clifton, 1998). However, as Figure 5.7 indicates, reaching takes time to develop. That is because this seemingly simple behavior actually involves a complex interaction of multiple, independent components, including muscle development, postural control, development of various perceptual and motor skills, and so on (Spencer, Vereijken, Diedrich, & Thelen, 2000; Thelen, Corbetta, Kamm, Spencer, Schneider, & Zernicke, 1993). For reaching to occur at all, infants must first be motivated to get their hands on an object. This component seems to be automatic: infants are intrinsically interested in interacting with the world around them. For the first few months, however, they are limited to **prereaching movements**—clumsy swiping toward the general vicinity of objects they see (von Hofsten, 1982).

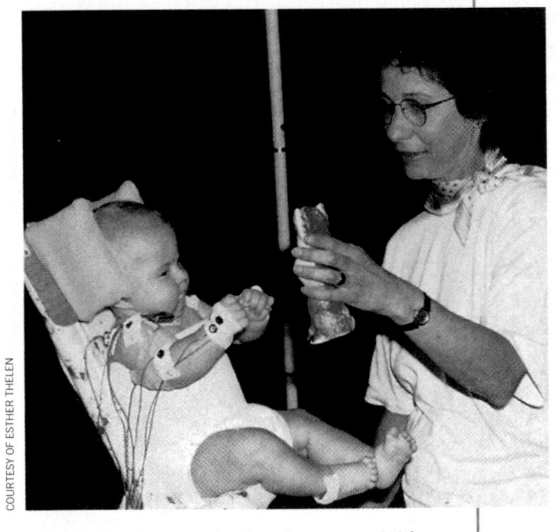

COURTESY OF ESTHER THELEN

The electrodes attached to the arms of this baby in Esther Thelen's lab are connected to a computer, so the infant's reaching movements can be analyzed in great detail.

At around 3 to 4 months of age, infants begin successfully reaching for objects, although their movements are still somewhat jerky and poorly controlled. Improved control of the head and upper torso are key to making reaching possible. Underlying this increase in postural control are other advances, including increased strength of the muscles in the neck, shoulders, and arm, as well as increased ability to modulate the force used to move the arm to a target (Spencer & Thelen, 2000).

At around 7 months, as infants gain the ability to sit independently, their reaching becomes quite stable, and the trajectory of their reaches is consistently smooth and straight to the target (Rochat, 1992; Spencer et al., 2000; Thelen et al., 1993; von Hofsten, 1979, 1991). Infants' sphere of influence is enlarged by the achievement of stable sitting and reaching, because they can now lean forward to capture objects that would previously have been out of reach (Rochat & Goubet, 1995).

Some aspects of infants' reaching behavior indicates that they rely on the "feel" of their hand and arm moving in relation to their body and to external objects. One form of evidence for this is the fact that vision is not necessary for accurate reaching: 4- to 8-month-old infants in a completely dark room will reach for an invisible object that is making a sound (Clifton, Rochat, Litovsky, & Perris, 1991). They coordinate their perception of the sound's location with the feedback from their arm and hand movement. A second form of evidence is that when reaching for objects they can see, infants rarely reach for ones that are too distant, suggesting that they have some sense of how long their arms are (Bertenthal & Clifton, 1998). Infants' reaching shows other signs of anticipation; for example, they adjust their reaching hand to the size, shape, or orientation of a desired object, opening their fingers wider when approaching a larger object (Lockman, Ashmead, & Bushnell, 1984; Newell, Scully, McDonald, & Baillargeon, 1989). Most impressive, infants can make contact with a moving object by anticipating its trajectory and aiming their reach slightly ahead of it (Robin, Berthier, & Clifton, 1996; von Hofsten, 1980; von Hofsten, Vishton, Spelke, Feng, & Rosander, 1998).

applications 5.4

A Recent Secular Change in Motor Development

In the late 1990s, pediatricians noticed a surprising increase in the number of visits they received from parents worried because their infants either began crawling quite late or never crawled at all. Many babies had simply gone from sitting to walking.

The cause for this genuine secular change in motor development seems to be traceable to the campaign, described in Box 2.4 (p. 63), urging parents to put their babies to sleep on their backs (Davis, Moon, Sachs, & Ottolini, 1998). As we discussed in Chapter 2, this public health effort was very successful in changing parents' behavior and has resulted in a remarkable reduction in the incidence of SIDS (sudden infant death syndrome).

It appears that lying on their backs makes infants less likely to roll over on schedule. One source of this effect may be motivational: the better view of the environment that they have on their backs may lessen infants' motivation to roll over onto their stomachs, where the view is quite restricted. But, spending less time on their tummies, the babies have less opportunity to discover that they can propel themselves forward by squirming. With less practice pushing themselves up from lying on their stomachs, the infants' arm strength may develop somewhat more slowly.

In any event, the research is reassuring: when observed at 18 months, there was no difference in the development of infants who had or who had not crawled on schedule.

Self-Locomotion

At around 8 months of age, infants become capable for the first time in their lives of **self-locomotion,** that is, of moving themselves around in the environment. No longer limited to being only where someone else carries or puts them, they find that the world available to them becomes vastly greater.

"FIRST STEPS, AFTER MILLET," BY VINCENT VAN GOGH. THE METROPOLITAN MUSEUM OF ART

Infants' first success at moving forward under their own power typically takes the form of crawling. (Box 5.4 describes an interesting example of a recent increase in variability in the onset of crawling.) Many (perhaps most) infants begin by belly crawling or using other idiosyncratic patterns of self-propulsion, one of which researchers refer to as the "inchworm belly-flop" style (Adolph, Vereijken, & Denny, 1998). Most belly crawlers then shift to hands-and-knees (or in some cases, hands-and-feet) crawling, which is less effortful.

When infants first begin walking independently, at around 13 to 14 months, they adopt various conservative strategies to keep themselves upright and moving forward. They place their feet relatively wide apart, which increases their base of support; they slightly flex at the hip and knee, thereby lowering their center of gravity; they keep their hands in the air to facilitate balance; and they have both feet on the ground 60% of the time (as opposed to only 20% for adults) (Bertenthal & Clifton, 1998; Clark & Phillips, 1993). The result is a toddling gait that inspired the name commonly applied to infants in their second year.

The everyday life of the newly mobile crawler or walker is replete with challenges to locomotion—slippery floors, spongy carpets, paths cluttered with objects and obstacles, stairs, sloping lawns, and so on. Infants must constantly evaluate whether their developing skills are adequate to enable them to travel from one point to another. Eleanor Gibson and her colleagues (Gibson, Riccio, Schmuckler, Stoffgren, Rosenberg, & Taormina, 1987; Gibson & Schmuckler, 1989) have studied the relation between perception and locomotion and have found that infants adjust their mode of locomotion according to the properties they perceive in

prereaching movements clumsy swiping movements by young infants toward the general vicinity of objects they see

self-locomotion the ability to move oneself around in the environment

a closer look

"Travel Broadens the Mind"[1]

The interdependence of different developmental domains is beautifully illustrated by a rich and fascinating series of experiments conducted over three decades. This work started with a landmark study by Eleanor Gibson and Richard Walk (1960) addressing the question of whether infants can perceive depth, and it has culminated in research linking depth perception, locomotion, cognitive abilities, emotion, and the social context of development.

To answer the depth-perception question, Gibson and Walk used an apparatus known as the "visual cliff." As the photo shows, the visual cliff consists of a thick sheet of plexiglass that can support the weight of an infant or toddler. A platform across the middle divides the apparatus into two sides. A checked pattern right under the glass on one side makes it look like a solid, safe surface. On the other side, the same pattern is far beneath the glass, and the contrast in the apparent size of the checks makes it look as though there is a dangerous drop-off—a cliff—between the two sides.

Gibson and Walk reported that 6- to 14-month-old infants would readily cross the shallow side of the visual cliff. They would not, however, cross the deep side, even when a parent was beckoning to them to come across it. The infants were apparently unwilling to venture over what looked like a precipice—strong evidence that they perceived and understood the significance of the depth cue of relative size.

As is always the case in science, new questions immediately arose, starting with how early infants can perceive depth information. This question was addressed by the simple expedient of slowly lowering 1½-month-old infants over the visual cliff while monitoring their heart rate (Campos, Langer, & Krowitz, 1970). A very interesting result emerged: the infants' heart rate decelerated over the deep side, indicating that they could perceive the difference in depth and found the deep side more interesting than the shallow one. However, the infants showed no fear of the deep side. So when and how does fear of heights emerge?

In a series of studies, Joseph Campos and his colleagues established that self-produced locomotion plays a vital role in the development of fear or wariness of heights (summarized in Campos, Anderson, Barbu-Roth, Hubbard, Hertenstein, & Witherington, 2000; and Campos, Bertenthal, & Kermoian, 1992). First, they compared infants of the same age but with different amounts of locomotor experience. Seven-month-olds who had been crawling on their own for a while showed a fear response (heart rate acceleration) when lowered over the deep side of the visual cliff; noncrawlers of the same age noticed the deep side (as shown by heart rate deceleration) but showed no sign of fear or wariness.

Next, the researchers did an experimental study with 7-month-old noncrawlers. Half the infants were given at least 32 hours' experience navigating around their homes in wheeled walkers. When tested on the visual cliff, these babies displayed more wariness of the deep side than did the infants of the same age with no walker experience.

An additional piece of evidence came from what is sometimes called an "experiment in nature"—a naturally occurring situation that provides scientists with answers to important questions that they could never, for ethical reasons, design experiments to ask. In this case, the researchers studied an infant who, due to a congenital hip problem, had been in a body cast for his first 8½ months and therefore had been deprived of locomotor experience. When the cast was removed, the boy showed no fear when lowered over the deep side of the visual cliff, even though he was well past the age at which infants typically show this reaction. After a few weeks of crawling experience, however, he showed the classic pattern of wariness.

It thus appears that experience moving themselves around in the environment plays a very important role in babies' de-

COURTESY OF PROFESSOR JOSEPH J. CAMPOS, UNIVERSITY OF CALIFORNIA, BERKELEY

An infant refusing to cross the deep side of the *visual cliff,* even though his mother is calling and beckoning to him from the other side.

veloping understanding of the significance of differences in the height of surfaces. Fortunately, the experience does not necessarily require hard knocks: infants do not have to do a nosedive off the bed or take a tumble down the stairs to associate drop-offs with danger. Often, relevant information comes from their parents via what is termed **social referencing,** the use of another person's emotional reaction to interpret an ambiguous situation (Campos & Stenberg, 1981; Rosen, Adamson, & Bakeman, 1992; Walden & Baxter, 1989). Imagine seeing your 7-month-old at the top edge of a flight of stairs. You would almost certainly look and sound frightened as you yell, "STOP!" and rush to snatch the baby from harm's way. Your baby would use your emotional reaction to infer that stairs are dangerous, without having to actually plunge down them.

Infants' use of the emotional reactions of others has been demonstrated using a visual cliff with a relatively shallow apparent drop-off that looks less threatening than the standard, deep one (Sorce, Emde, Campos, & Klinnert, 1985). Again, a parent stood at the other end of the apparatus, so the infant had a reason to want to cross the deep side. The key feature of this study was that the parent made either a happy or a fearful face: if the parent was smiling happily, the infant scampered across; if the parent looked fearful, the infant was likely to remain on the safe haven of the shallow side.

The advent of self-produced locomotion is related to a variety of emotional experiences other than wariness and fear. Infants who have become capable of a new form of self-locomotion, whether by using a walker, crawling, or walking, are happy to be moving about on their own. Newly walking infants have been described as "euphoric" and as experiencing a "love affair with the world" (Mahler, Pine, & Bergman, 1975).

Moreover, the advent of self-locomotion causes the general affective climate of the family to change, both positively and negatively. Infants tend to smile more and engage in more frequent positive interactions with their mothers (Bertenthal & Campos, 1990; Biringen, Emde, Campos, & Appelbaum, 1995; Campos, Kermoian, & Zumbahlen, 1992; Gustafson, 1984). At the same time, however, newly mobile youngsters create new challenges for their parents, and anger becomes more common, both for infants and parents. For the infants, dirt in a potted plant, volume controls on the stereo, electrical outlets, and anything breakable seem to all call out to them to be investigated. As a result, their parents start issuing prohibitions—"No!" "Don't!" "Put that down!" This frustrates the infants and provokes anger, just as the infants' persistent efforts to explore prohibited items elicits anger in their parents (Campos et al., 1992). Thus, the milestones that can be a source of joy for babies and pride for parents also constitute a source of frustration and family conflict.

This example is a vivid illustration of the fact that development in a given domain—whether perceptual, motor, emotional, social, or any other—interacts intimately with development in other domains. It points clearly to the powerful role of self-produced locomotion in stimulating widespread developmental changes. Perhaps we should not be surprised at how powerful it is. After all, no animal takes so long to begin moving about on its own, and probably no animal experiences such joy when it finally does.

[1]The apt title of an article by Joseph Campos and his colleagues. (2000)

social referencing the use of another person's emotional reaction to interpret an ambiguous situation

BILL LOSH / FPG / GETTY IMAGES

Social referencing: **This toddler is relying on her mother's encouraging behavior to conclude that it is perfectly safe for her to hurl her body into the swimming pool.**

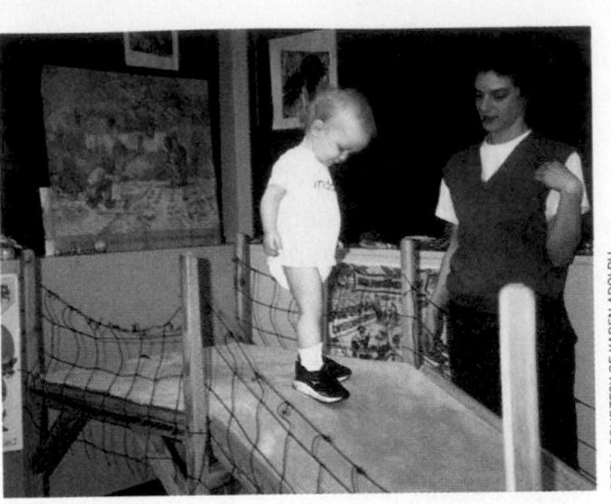

BOTH: COURTESY OF KAREN ADOLPH

FIGURE 5.8 Integrating perceptual information with new motor skills Researcher Karen Adolph will need to rescue the newly-crawling young infant on the left, who does not realize that this slope is too steep for her current level of crawling expertise. In contrast, the experienced walker on the right is judiciously deciding that the slope is too steep for him to walk down.

the surface they want to traverse. For example, infants who had promptly walked across a rigid plywood walkway prudently reverted to crawling in order to cross a water bed. (Box 5.5 focuses further on the close relation between perception and locomotion.)

In related research, Karen Adolph and her colleagues have discovered a surprising degree of specificity in infants' learning to judge what they can accomplish with new locomotor and postural skills (Adolph, 1997, 2000; Adolph, Eppler, & Gibson, 1993; Eppler, Adolph & Weiner, 1996). This research exemplifies the type of *mechanism of change,* described in Chapter 1, in which variation and selection produce developmental change. The investigators asked parents to entice their infants to travel down sloping laboratory walkways that were inclined to varying degrees, while an experimenter hovered nearby in case it was necessary to catch an overly adventurous infant (Figure 5.8). In their first weeks of crawling, infants (averaging around 8½ months in age) unhesitatingly and competently went down shallow slopes. Confronted with slopes that were too steep to crawl down, the babies typically studied them for some time, but then launched themselves headfirst anyway (requiring the experimenter to catch hold of them). With more weeks of practice at crawling, the babies got better both at judging whether they could get down a given slope and at devising descent strategies: they began to inch cautiously down somewhat steep slopes but avoided very steep slopes altogether. However, when the infants started walking, they again misjudged which slopes they could get down using their new mode of locomotion. Thus, infants apparently have to learn through experience how to integrate perceptual information with each new motor behavior they develop (Bertenthal & Clifton, 1998; Lockman, 1984).

review: All normally developing infants display a similar sequence of milestones in the development of motor behavior, starting with a common set of neonatal reflexes. Researchers have increasingly emphasized the pervasive interconnectedness between infants' motor behavior, perception, and motivation, as well as the many ways that infants' experience of the world changes with each advance. In the development of self-locomotion (crawling, walking), infants adopt a variety of different movement patterns to get around and to cope with different environmental challenges.

Learning

Who do you think learned more today—you or a 10-month-old infant? We'd bet on the baby, just because there is so much that is new to the infant. Think back to baby Benjamin in the kitchen with his parents. A wealth of learning opportunities was embedded in that everyday scene. Benjamin was, for example, gaining experience with some of the differences between animate and inanimate entities; with the particular sights and sounds that go together in events; with the consequences of objects losing support (including the effect of this event on his parents' emotional state); and so on. He also experienced consequences of his own behavior, such as his parents' response to his crying.

In this section, we review six different types of learning by which infants profit from their experience and acquire knowledge of the world. These types of learning include habituation, basic perceptual learning, the formation of simple visual expectancies, classical conditioning, instrumental (operant) conditioning, and observational learning. Some of the questions that developmental psychologists have addressed with respect to infants' learning include at what age the different forms of learning appear, how long-lasting the learning that takes place in infancy is, and in what ways learning in infancy is related to later cognitive abilities. Another important question concerns the extent to which infants find some things easier or more difficult to learn.

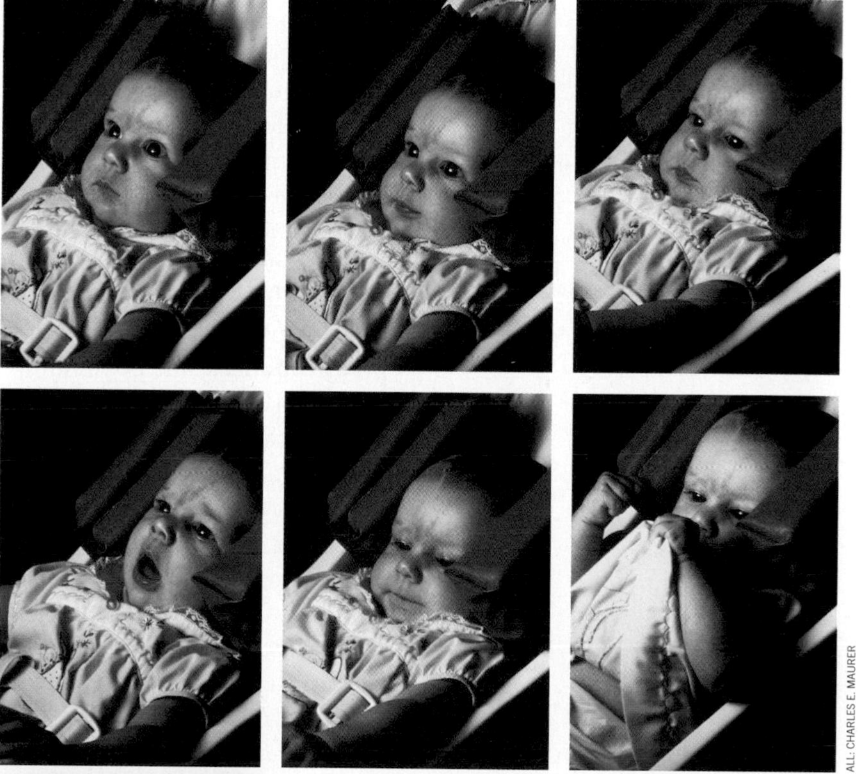

ALL: CHARLES E. MAURER

FIGURE 5.9 Habituation This 3-month-old provides a vivid demonstration of *habituation.* She is seated in front of a screen on which photographs are displayed. At the first appearance of a photo of a face, her eyes widen and she stares intently at it. With three more presentations of the same picture, her interest wanes and a yawn appears. By its fifth appearance, other things are attracting the baby's attention, and by the sixth even her dress is more interesting. When a new face finally appears, her interest in something novel is evident. (From Maurer & Maurer, 1988)

Habituation

Probably the simplest and earliest form of learning is recognizing something that has been experienced before. As we discussed in Chapter 2 and again earlier in this chapter, babies—like everybody else—tend to respond relatively less to stimuli they have previously experienced and relatively more to novel ones (see Figure 5.9). *Habituation*—a decrease in response to repeated stimulation—reveals that learning has occurred; the infant has a memory representation of the repeated, and now familiar, stimulus. When a new stimulus is perceived as novel, dishabituation—an increase in response—occurs. Habituation is highly adaptive: diminished attention to what is old and known enables infants to pay attention to, and learn about, what is new.

The speed with which an infant habituates is believed to reflect the general efficiency of the infant's processing of information. Related attentional measures, including duration of looking and degree of novelty preference, are also taken as measures of speed and efficiency of processing. A substantial and surprising degree of continuity has been found between these measures in infancy and general cognitive ability later in life. Infants who habituate relatively rapidly, who take relatively short looks at visual stimuli, and/or who show a greater preference for novelty tend to have higher IQs when tested as much as eighteen years later (Bornstein & Sigman, 1986; Colombo, 1995; McCall & Carriger, 1993; Rose & Feldman, 1995, 1997; Sigman, Cohen, & Beckwith, 1997). Thus, one of the earliest and simplest forms of human learning is fundamental to basic cognitive development.

Perceptual Learning

From the beginning, infants actively search for order and regularity in the world around them, and they learn a great deal from simply paying close attention to the objects and events they perceive. According to Eleanor Gibson (1988), the key process in perceptual learning is **differentiation**—extracting from the constantly changing stimulation in the environment those elements that are invariant, that remain stable. For example, infants learn the association between tone of voice and facial expression because, in their experience, for example, a pleasant, happy, or excited tone of voice usually occurs with a smiling face, and a harsh, angry tone of voice invariably occurs with a frowning face, never with a smiling one. With age and experience, infants become increasingly efficient at extracting relevant information, and they are able to make finer and finer discriminations among stimuli.

A particularly important part of perceptual learning is the infant's discovery of **affordances,** the possibilities for action offered, or afforded, by objects and situations (Gibson, 1988). They discover, for example, that small—but not large—objects can be picked up, that liquid can be spilled, that chairs of a certain size can be sat in, and so forth. Infants discover affordances by figuring out the relations between their own bodies and abilities and the things around them. As we discussed earlier, for example, infants come to appreciate that solid, flat surfaces afford stable walking, but squishy or steeply sloping ones do not (Adolph, 1997; Gibson et al., 1987; Gibson & Schmuckler, 1989).

Perceptual learning is involved in many, but not all, examples of intermodal coordination. As we noted previously, learning is not required to detect a unitary event involving sight and sound, so baby Benjamin naturally perceives a single, coherent event the first time he sees and hears a crystal goblet crashing on the floor. However, one does have to learn what particular sights and sounds go together, so only through experience does Ben know that tinkling sounds are associated with breaking glass. As you have seen, infants are sensitive early on to the synchrony of lip movements and vocal sounds, but they must learn to relate the unique sight of their mother's face with the unique sound of her voice (which they accomplish by 3½ months of age; Spelke & Owsley, 1979). The necessity for perceptual learning is especially clear for events that involve arbitrary relations, such as an association between the color of a cup and the taste of the food inside. The fact that 7-month-olds can be taught color–taste associations in the lab (Reardon & Bushnell, 1988) would come as no surprise to those parents whose infants clamp their mouths shut at the sight of a spoon conveying anything green.

differentiation the extraction from the constantly changing stimulation in the environment of those elements that are invariant, or stable

affordances the possibilities for action offered by objects and situations

Visual Expectancy

Another very simple form of learning that is evident early in life is the formation of expectancies for future events based on past experience. This type of learning has been studied by presenting infants with a series of simple stimuli (lights or pictures) that appear in a set of different locations on a screen in front of them (Haith, Hazen, & Goodman, 1988; Haith, Wentworth, & Canfield, 1993). The stimuli appear in either a random or a regular, predictable sequence, such as an alternating left–right sequence. When presented with a simple, regular sequence, 3-month-olds begin within minutes to anticipate where the next stimulus will be, looking to that side in advance of its appearance. Many infants are also capable of detecting the regularity of more complex sequences of events (such as left–left–left–right; Canfield & Haith, 1991). Infants' ability to form these simple expectations is related to later intellectual functioning: performance in the visual expectancy task at 3½ months of age is positively correlated with IQ at 4 years of age (Dougherty & Haith, 1997).

Classical Conditioning

Another important form of learning is **classical conditioning,** which was first discovered by Pavlov in his famous research with dogs (who learned an association between the sounding of a bell and the arrival of food and gradually came to salivate at the sound of the bell alone). Classical conditioning plays a role in infants' everyday learning about the relations between environmental events that have relevance for them. Consider the role of classical conditioning in infants' sucking. Babies' mealtimes occur frequently and have a predictable structure. First, the hungry infant is picked up by the mother (with her unique constellation of perceptual features) and held in a particular way. Then a breast or bottle contacts the infant's mouth, eliciting the sucking reflex. This causes milk to flow into the infant's mouth, and the infant experiences the pleasurable sensations of a delicious taste and the satisfaction of hunger. Learning, in the form of classical conditioning, is revealed when an infant's sucking motions, which initially occurred reflexively after stimulation of the infant's mouth, start to be made earlier in the sequence of events, for example, to the mere sight of the bottle or breast.

Classical conditioning involves an **unconditioned stimulus (UCS)** (the insertion of the nipple into the infant's mouth) that reliably elicits a reflexive, unlearned response—an **unconditioned response (UCR)** (the sucking reflex). Learning, or conditioning, can occur if an initially neutral stimulus—the **conditioned stimulus (CS)**—repeatedly occurs just before the unconditioned stimulus (the baby sees the breast or bottle before receiving the nipple). Gradually the originally reflexive response—now the learned or **conditioned response (CR)**—comes to occur to the initially neutral stimulus (anticipatory sucking movements now begin as soon as the baby sees the breast or bottle). In other words, the sight of the bottle or breast has become a signal of what will follow. Gradually, the infant may also come to associate the mother herself with the whole sequence, including the pleasurable feelings that result from feeding. If so, these feelings could eventually be evoked simply by the presence of the mother.

A laboratory example of conditioned sucking comes from a study by Elliott Blass and his colleagues (Blass, Ganchrow, & Steiner, 1984). The researchers

classical conditioning a form of learning that consists of associating an initially neutral stimulus with a stimulus that always evokes a particular reflexive response

unconditioned stimulus (UCS) in classical conditioning, a stimulus that evokes a reflexive response

unconditioned response (UCR) in classical conditioning, a reflexive response that is elicited by the unconditioned stimulus

conditioned stimulus (CS) in classical conditioning, the neutral stimulus that is repeatedly paired with the unconditioned stimulus

conditioned response (CR) in classical conditioning, the originally reflexive response that comes to be elicited by the conditioned stimulus stroked the foreheads of newborns just before putting a small dose of sugar water into their mouths, and soon the infants began puckering their lips and sucking (CR) just to the touch on their forehead (CS)—in advance of anything actually being in their mouths.

It is thought that many emotional responses are initially learned through classical conditioning. One of the first demonstrations of emotional conditioning was the case of Little Albert (Watson & Rayner, 1920), whom John B. Watson, the founder of behaviorism (mentioned in Chapter 1), had conditioned to fear a white rat. When Watson first exposed 9-month-old Albert to a perfectly nice white rat in the laboratory, the boy initially had a positive reaction. On subsequent exposures, however, a loud, frightening noise was repeatedly paired with the rat. After a number of such pairings, Albert became afraid of the rat itself. (In this example, the fear-eliciting noise was the UCS, the rat was the CS, and Albert's fear response was the UCR [to the noise] and the CR [to the rat].) In an everyday example of classically conditioned fear, infants and young children often show fear at the white coat of a doctor or nurse, based on their previous association between people wearing white coats and painful injections. (To counteract this problem, modern pediatricians often sport lab coats with pictures of cartoon characters, to which children have a positive response.)

Just as some stimulus–stimulus relations are easier to learn than others, as noted in the perceptual learning section, studies have shown that some stimulus–response relations can be classically conditioned more readily than others. For example, newborns learned to turn their heads to a touch on the forehead when they heard a clicking sound but not when they heard "psst" or "shhh" (Blass, 1990). One probable reason was that the click was more successful in eliciting their attention. Similarly, 4-month-olds learned to associate a face and voice when the facial expression and voice quality were congruent (e.g., a consoling voice and a sad face) but not when they were incongruent (the same voice and a smiling face) (Kaplan, Zarlengo-Strouse, Kirk, & Angel, 1997).

Instrumental Conditioning

A key form of learning for infants (and everyone else) is learning about the consequences of one's own behavior. In everyday life, infants learn that shaking a rattle produces an interesting sound, that cooing at Dad gets him to coo back, and that exploring the dirt in a potted plant leads to a parental reprimand. This kind of learning, referred to as **instrumental conditioning,** or *operant conditioning,* involves learning the relation between one's own behavior and the reward or punishment it results in. Most instrumental conditioning research with infants involves **positive reinforcement,** that is, a reward that reliably follows a behavior and increases the likelihood that the behavior will be repeated. Thus, there is a *contingency* relation between the infant's behavior and the reward: *if* the infant makes the response, *then* he or she receives the reinforcement. Table 5.1 shows a few examples of the great variety of ingenious situations researchers have engineered in order to examine instrumental learning in infants.

TABLE 5.1

Studying Instrumental Conditioning in Infants

Age Group	Learned Response	Reinforcement
Newborns	Head turn to side	Drink of sucrose water
3 weeks	Sucking pattern	Interesting visual display
5–12 weeks	Sucking pattern	Keep a movie in focus
6 months	Push a lever	Cause a toy train to move along a track

Source: Bruner (1973); Hartshorn & Rovee-Collier (1997); Siqueland & DeLucia (1969); Siqueland & Lipsitt (1966)

Carolyn Rovee-Collier (1997) and her colleagues designed a very simple but clever procedure to study instrumental learning and memory in young infants:

they tie a ribbon around an infant's ankle and connect it to a mobile hanging above the infant's crib (Figure 5.10). In the course of naturally kicking their legs, infants as young as 2 months old learn within minutes the relation between their leg movements and the enjoyable sight of the jiggling mobile. They then quite deliberately and often joyfully increase their rate of foot kicking. The interesting mobile movement thus serves as reinforcement for the kicking behavior. An additional feature of this procedure is that the intensity of the reward—the amount of movement of the mobile—depends on the intensity of the baby's behavior.

Although infants can learn a great variety of contingency relations, there are a number of limitations on the learning process. For example, the younger the infant, the closer together the response and reinforcement have to be both in time and space: young babies learn only if there is a minimal delay between their response and the subsequent reinforcement and only if the reinforcement occurs very near to where the response was made. Thus, they might learn the relation between pressing a button and a light coming on, but only if the light is located quite near the button and comes on shortly after the button is pressed (Millar, 1990).

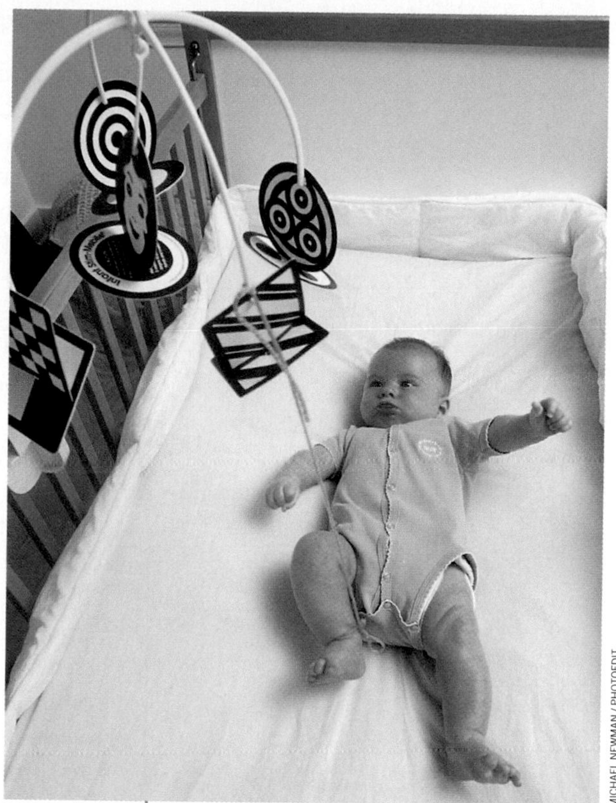

MICHAEL NEWMAN / PHOTOEDIT

FIGURE 5.10 Contingency This young infant learned within minutes that kicking her leg would cause the mobile to move in an interesting way; she learned the *contingency* between her own behavior and an external event.

Infants' intense motivation to explore and master their environment, which we have emphasized in our *active child* theme, shows up in instrumental learning situations: infants work hard at learning to predict and control their experience, and they dislike losing control once it has been established. Researchers have described facial expressions of joy and interest while infants as young as 2 months old were learning a contingency relation, and expressions of anger when a learned response no longer produced the expected results (Lewis, Alessandri, & Sullivan, 1990; Sullivan, Lewis, & Alessandri, 1992). When newborns failed to receive the sucrose they had learned would follow a head-turn response, seven out of eight cried (Blass, 1990).

Infants may also learn that there are situations over which they have no control. For example, infants of depressed mothers tend to smile less and show lower levels of positive affect than do infants whose mothers are not depressed. In part, this may be because infants of depressed mothers learn that such friendly displays are seldom rewarded by their preoccupied parent (Campbell, Cohn, & Meyers, 1995).

It is also possible for infants to conclude erroneously that they have no effect in a given situation. In research by Watson and Ramey (1972), one group of 2-month-old infants learned a contingency relation between head turning and the movement of a mobile. Whenever the babies turned their head to the right (or left), a mobile above their crib rotated, a sight the babies found very pleasurable. As a result, the rate of head turning in the appropriate direction increased. A second group of infants had experience with the same mobile, but its movement was unrelated to their behavior. The important part of this study came when the babies in the second group were presented with a new mobile that they could in fact control with a head-turn response: they failed to learn the contingency; that is, they did not figure out the relation between their own behavior and the movement of the mobile. Thus, their experience with a noncontingent relation prevented them from learning a contingent one. This research suggests that infants are learning more than just the particular contingency relations to which they are exposed; they are also learning about the relation between themselves and the world and the extent to which they can have an impact on it.

instrumental conditioning *(operant conditioning)* learning the relation between one's own behavior and the consequences that result

positive reinforcement a reward that reliably follows a behavior and increases the likelihood that the behavior will be repeated

Observational Learning

A particularly potent source of infants' learning is their observation of other people's behaviors. Parents, who are often amused and sometimes embarrassed by their toddler's reproduction of their own behavior, are well aware that their offspring learn a great deal through simple observation.

The ability to imitate the behavior of other people appears to be present very early in life, albeit in an extremely limited form. Andrew Meltzoff and Keith Moore (1977, 1983) found that after newborns watch an adult model slowly and repeatedly stick out his or her tongue, they often stick out their own tongue (Meltzoff & Moore, 1977). Ever since this finding was first reported, investigators have disputed whether this behavior is really evidence of imitation and whether, as Meltzoff and Moore claimed, newborns are sensitive to some aspects of the correspondence between an adult's body and their own (Anisfeld et al., 2001).

By the age of 6 months, however, infant imitation is indisputable. Six-month-old infants not only imitate tongue protrusion but they also attempt to poke their tongue out to the side when that is what they have seen an adult do (Meltzoff & Moore, 1994). From this age on, the scope of infant imitation expands. Infants begin to imitate novel actions they have seen performed on objects (such as an experimenter leaning over from the waist to touch his or her forehead to a box). Some time after observing such a display, the infants are presented with the same objects the experimenter had acted on. Infants as young as 6 to 9 months old imitate some of the novel actions they have witnessed, even after a delay of 24 hours (Barr, Dowden, & Hayne, 1996; Meltzoff, 1988b), and 14-month-olds do so after a full week (Meltzoff, 1988a).

Older infants' imitations reflect some understanding not only of human action but of intention as well. Evidence for this claim comes from research in which 18-month-olds observed an adult attempting, but failing, to pull apart a small dumbbell toy (Meltzoff, 1995). The adult pulled on the two ends, but his hand "slipped off," and the dumbbell remained in one piece (Figure 5.11a). When the infants were subsequently given the toy, they pulled the two ends apart, imitating what the adult had *intended* to do, not what he had actually done. Infants' imitative actions are limited to human acts, as shown by a different group of 18-month-olds who watched a mechanical device with pincers that grasped the two ends of the dumbbell. Some infants saw the pincers pull apart the dumbbell, and others saw the pincers slip off the end, just as the human hand had done (Figure 5.11b). Regardless of what the infants had seen the mechanical device do, they rarely attempted to pull apart the dumbbell themselves. Thus, infants attempt to reproduce the behavior and intentions of other people, but not of inanimate objects.

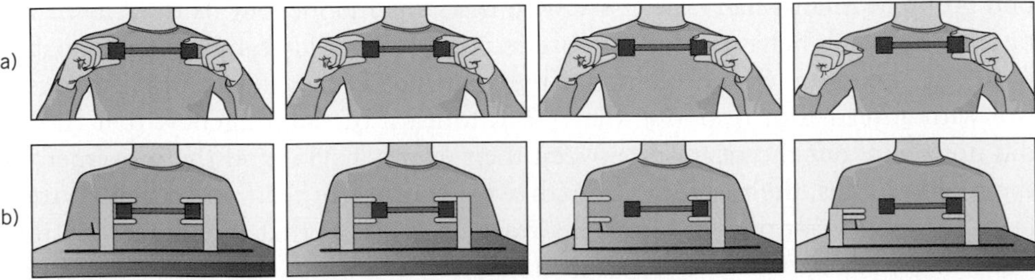

FIGURE 5.11 Imitating intentions **(a) When 18-month-olds see a person apparently try, but fail, to pull the ends off a dumbbell, they imitate pulling the ends off—the action the person *intended* to do, not what the person actually did. (b) They do not imitate a mechanical device at all. (From Meltzoff, 1995)**

Babies are by no means restricted to learning from the behavior of live adult models. Infants as young as 15 months of age imitate actions they have seen an adult perform on television (Barr & Hayne, 1999; Meltzoff, 1988a). Peers can also serve as models for young toddlers: well-trained 14-month-old "expert peers" demonstrated novel actions for their age-mates, either at their preschool or in a laboratory (Hanna & Meltzoff, 1993). For example, they pushed a button hidden inside a box to sound a buzzer. Children who were tested in their own homes 48 hours later imitated what they had seen the child model do earlier.

review: Infants begin learning about the world immediately. They habituate to repeatedly encountered stimuli, form expectancies for repeated event sequences, and learn associations between particular sights and sounds that regularly occur together. Classical conditioning, which has been demonstrated in newborn and older infants, is believed to be especially important in the learning of emotional reactions. Infants are highly sensitive to a wide range of contingency relations between their own behavior and what follows it. A particularly powerful form of learning for older infants is observational learning: from 6 months of age on, infants learn many new behaviors simply by watching what other people do. Although an enormous amount of learning goes on during the infancy period, some associations or relations are easier for babies to learn than others are. In observational learning, for example, intentionality is a key factor.

Cognition

Clearly, infants are capable of learning in a variety of ways. But do they actually think? This is a question that has intrigued parents and developmental psychologists alike (Kagan, 1972). Baby Benjamin's parents have no doubt looked with wonderment at their child, asking themselves, "What is he thinking? *Is* he thinking?" Developmental scientists have been hard at work over the past twenty years or so trying to find out to what extent infants engage in cognition (knowledge, thought, reasoning), asking how infants interpret events that they experience, what inferences they are capable of drawing, what predictions they can make, and so on. The resulting explosion of fascinating research has established that infants' cognitive abilities are much more impressive than previously believed. The origin of these impressive skills is, however, a matter of considerable debate, and there is currently a range of theoretical positions differing in the extent to which nature or nurture is emphasized.

According to the core-knowledge position, which we described in Chapter 4, it is necessary to credit infants with innate knowledge in a few domains of particular importance (Carey & Spelke, 1994; Gelman & Williams, 1998; Scholl & Leslie, 1999; Spelke, 2000). Core-knowledge theorists maintain that infants are born with some knowledge about the physical world, such as that two objects cannot occupy the same space, that physical objects move only if something sets them in motion, and so on. Other theorists emphasize that infants possess specialized learning mechanisms that enable them to acquire knowledge rapidly and efficiently in these domains (Baillargeon, 1994, 1995; Baillargeon, Kotovsky, & Needham, 1995). Still other theorists emphasize general learning mechanisms through which infants' mental representations of the physical world are gradually strengthened (Munakata, McClelland, Johnson, & Siegler, 1997). Finally, at the other end of the spectrum from the core-knowledge theories is the view that infants may not have knowledge representations at all and that perceptual-motor processes may be responsible for much of what has been described as cognition in infancy (Haith & Benson, 1998; Smith, 1999).

Thinking About Things

A large part of what we know about infant cognition has come from research on the development of knowledge about objects, research originally inspired by Jean Piaget's theory of sensorimotor intelligence. As you learned in Chapter 4, Piaget believed that young infants' understanding of the world is severely limited by an inability to mentally represent and think about anything that is not perceptually available at the moment. In other words, he thought that infants' knowledge is limited to the "here and now"—that they are aware of the existence of only those things they can currently see, hear, touch, and so on. Thus, if an infant loses sight of an object for some reason (e.g., the baby drops it and can no longer see it or someone hides it under a cloth), it disappears not only from the infant's sight but also from the infant's mind. In Piaget's words, the object is "a mere image which re-enters the void as soon as it vanishes" (Piaget, 1954, p. 11). Piaget's observation that infants younger than 8 months of age do not search for objects they cannot see led him to formulate his concept of *object permanence,* which refers to the understanding that objects exist independently of one's perception of them and action on them.

A substantial body of research has supported Piaget's claim that young infants do not manually search for hidden objects. However, as noted in Chapter 4, skepticism gradually arose about his explanation of this fascinating phenomenon. A great deal of evidence indicates that young infants are in fact able to mentally represent and think about the existence of invisible objects and events.

The simplest evidence for young infants' ability to represent an object that has vanished from sight is the fact that they will reach for objects in the dark. When young infants are shown an attractive object and the room is then plunged into darkness, causing the object (and everything else) to disappear from view, most babies reach to where they last saw the object, indicating they expect it to still be there (Hood & Willatts, 1986; Perris & Clifton, 1988; Stack, Muir, Sherriff, & Roman, 1989).

Young infants even seem to be able to think about some characteristics of invisible objects, as evidenced by their reaching differently depending on what they know about an object they cannot see. When 6-month-olds sitting in the dark heard the sound of a familiar large object, they reached toward it with both hands (just as they had in the light); but they reached with only one hand when the sound they heard was that of a familiar small object (Clifton, Rochat, Litovsky, & Perris, 1991). Similarly, 6½-month-olds watched as a ball fell noisily through a tube and came to rest at one location or another. With the lights out, the infants, relying on the noise of the ball's movement as a guide, reached toward the ball's current location (Goubet & Clifton, 1998).

The majority of the evidence that young infants can represent and think about invisible objects comes from research using the **violation-of-expectancy** procedure. Its logic is similar to that of the visual-preference method we discussed earlier (p. 172). The basic assumption is that if infants observe an event that violates something they know about how the world works, they will be surprised or at least

violation-of-expectancy a procedure used to study infant cognition in which infants are shown an event that should evoke surprise or interest if it violates something the infant knows or assumes to be true show interest. Thus, an event that is impossible or inconsistent with respect to the infant's knowledge should evoke a greater response (such as longer looking or a change in heart rate) than does a possible or consistent event.

The violation-of-expectancy technique was used in a classic series of studies designed by Renée Baillargeon and her colleagues (Baillargeon, 1987b; Baillargeon, Spelke, & Wasserman, 1985) to see if infants too young to search for an invisible object might nevertheless have a mental representation of its existence. In some of these studies, infants were first habituated to the sight of a screen rotating back and forth through a 180° arc (Figure 5.12). Then a box was placed in the screen's path, and the infants saw two test events. In one, the *possible event,* the screen rotated upward, occluding the box as it did so, and stopped when it contacted the box. In the *impossible event,* the screen continued to rotate a full 180°, appearing to pass through the space occupied by the box (which the experimenter had surreptitiously removed).

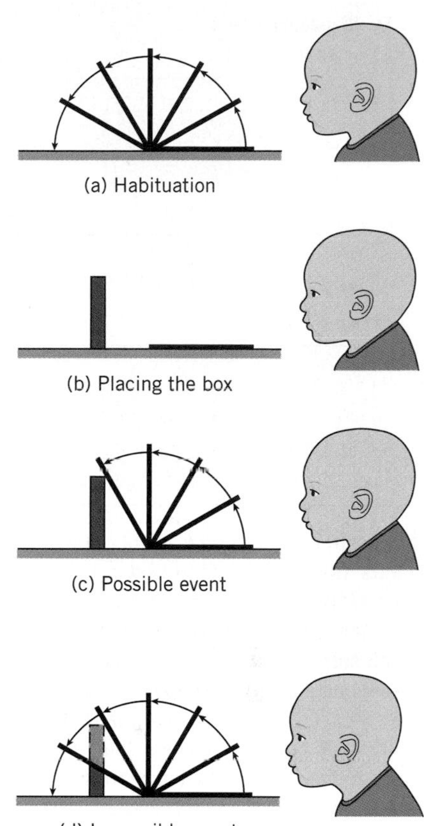

FIGURE 5.12 Possible versus impossible events In a classic series of tests of object permanence, Renée Baillargeon and her colleagues first habituated young infants to the sight of a screen rotating through 180 degrees. Then a box was placed in the path of the screen. In the *possible event,* the screen rotated up, occluding the box, and stopped when it reached the top of the box. In the *impossible event,* the screen rotated up, occluding the box, but then continued on through 180 degrees, appearing to pass through the space where the box was. Infants looked longer at the impossible event, showing they mentally represented the presence of the invisible box. (From Baillargeon, 1987a)

Infants as young as 4½ months of age, and even some 3½-month-olds, looked longer at the impossible event than at the possible one. The researchers reasoned that the full rotation of the screen (to which the infants had previously been habituated) would have been more interesting or surprising than the partial rotation only if the infants had expected the screen to stop when it reached the box. And the only reason for them to have had that expectation was if they thought the box was still present—that is, if they mentally represented an object they could no longer see. Further, the infants apparently expected the box to remain in place and did not expect the screen to be able to pass through it. Thus, research using two very different assessments—reaching in the dark and visual attention—provides converging evidence that infants who do not yet search for hidden objects nevertheless can represent the objects' continued existence.

Other studies have provided further evidence regarding young infants' ability to reason about some of the characteristics of invisible objects. For example, some studies showed that the *height* of the box behind the rotating screen affected 6½-month-olds' expectations about where the screen should stop. They expected the screen to rotate farther when there was a short box in its path than when there was a taller one (Baillargeon, 1991). Infants' expectations have also been shown to be influenced by *texture:* after handling a hard, rigid object and a soft, compressible one, 7½-month-olds looked longer when the screen appeared to rotate through the hard object than when it appeared to squash the soft one (Baillargeon, 1987a).

This research shows that young infants share more of adults' expectations about objects than Piaget believed was possible. Additional studies have examined infants' ability to generate an interpretation of a puzzling event—something adults do frequently. Young infants (3½- and 5½-month-olds) were shown the display in Figure 5.13a (Baillargeon & DeVos, 1991; Baillargeon & Graber, 1987). On alternate trials, they saw either a tall or a short toy rabbit travel behind a screen and then, after an appropriate interval, reappear on the other side. Before the test events, the rectangular screen was replaced by one with a window cut out of its top half (Figure 5.13b). For the possible test event, the infants saw the short rabbit (which was shorter than the bottom edge of the window) move behind the screen and emerge at the other side. For the impossible event, they saw the tall rabbit disappear behind the screen and a few seconds later emerge on the other side—but without ever having appeared in the window. (As you have no doubt surmised, the experimenters secretly used two tall rabbits—one on each side of the screen.)

Familiarization Events

(a)

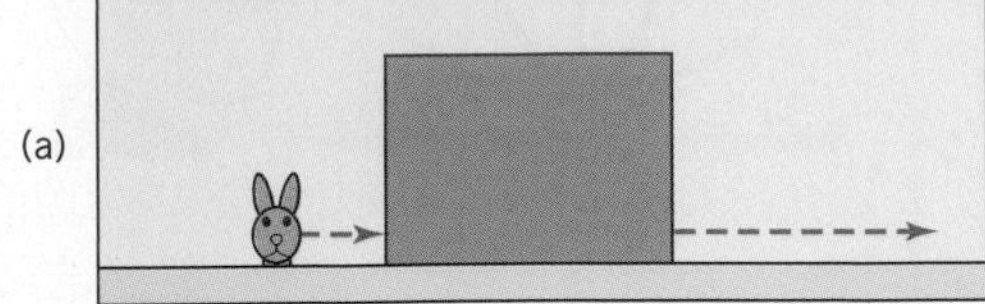

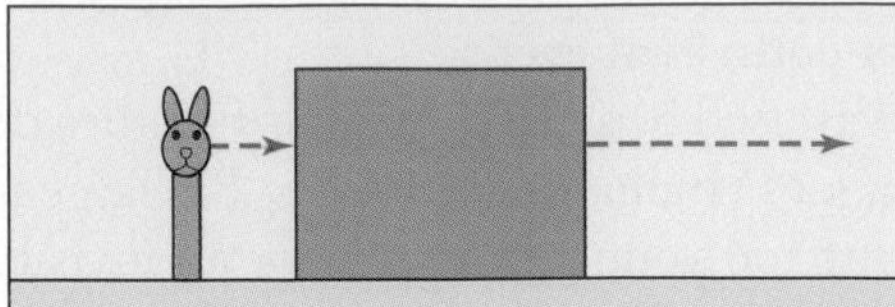

Test Events

(b)

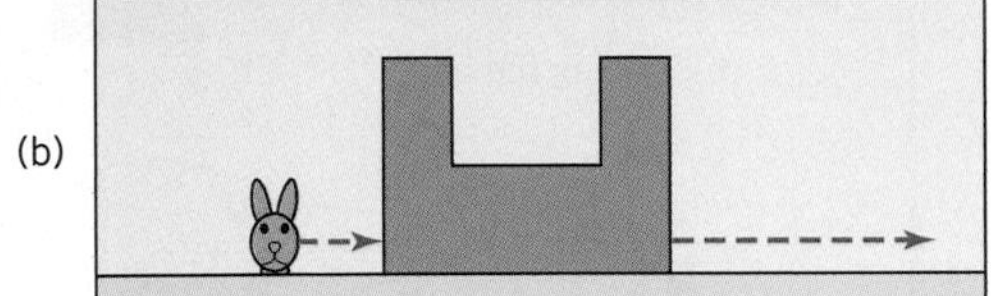

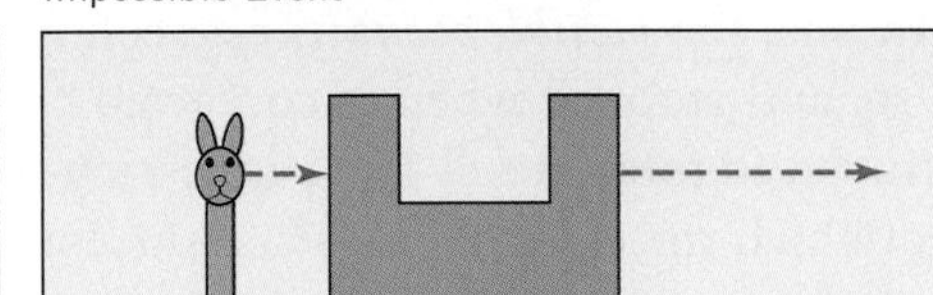

FIGURE 5.13 Knowledge about invisible objects (a) *Familiarization events:* Infants watch as, on successive trials, a short and then a tall toy rabbit moves out from behind the left side of a screen, passes behind the screen, and emerges on the other side. (b) *Test events:* In the possible event, the small rabbit passes from one side of the screen to the other without appearing in the window. In the impossible event, the tall rabbit does the same. Infants look longer at the impossible event. (From Baillargeon & Graber, 1987; Baillargeon & DeVos, 1991)

The infants looked longer when the tall rabbit failed to appear in the window than when the short rabbit did not appear. This result indicates that they mentally represented both the existence and the height of the objects and expected the tall rabbit to be visible in the window. This conclusion was supported by what happened when another group of infants was first shown that there were two tall rabbits behind the screen, one on either side of the window. Infants who received this hint did not look longer in the test trial in which the tall rabbit failed to appear in the window. Knowledge that there were two rabbits involved removed the mystery from the event.

We thus see that when researchers study infants' looking behavior rather than their searching behavior, they find evidence that infants have a substantially greater understanding of the permanence of objects than Piaget realized. However, as noted in Chapter 4, once infants begin searching for hidden objects, at around the age of 8 months, they make a rather surprising kind of error that Piaget (1954) discovered—the *A-Not-B error*. If a toy is hidden twice, at location A in the first trial and at location B in the second trial, infants between 8 and 12 months of age will search correctly at A on the first trial, but on the second, they will often search again at A. Piaget interpreted this behavior as evidence that, before the age of 12 months, infants do not understand that an object exists independently of their actions on it, and hence they expect to find an object where they previously found it.

A great deal of subsequent research has produced a wealth of observations about what makes the A-Not-B error more or less likely to occur (Marcovitch & Zelazo, 1999; Wellman, Cross, & Bartsch, 1987). Among the findings are that infants make the error less often as they get older, and are less likely to go back to A if the A and B locations are distinctly different in appearance (Bremner, 1978). Infants commit the A-Not-B error more often as the delay between the A and B trials increases (Diamond, 1985) and as the number of times the object has been hidden at A increases (Marcovitch & Zelazo, 1999).

One of the most remarkable things about the A-Not-B error is that it occurs, albeit less frequently, even when the toy is not actually hidden: after retrieving a toy at location A, infants often return to A even if the toy at B is fully visible under a transparent cover (Bremner & Knowles, 1984; Harris, 1974; Sophian & Yengo, 1985). Infants respond in the same way even if there are simply two objects fully visible at two locations; after reaching for an object that the experimenter has picked up and waved around and then put down in location A, infants tend to go back to A after seeing a similar object waved around and then put down at location B (Figure 5.14) (Smith, Thelen, Titzer, & McLin, 1999).

Visual-attention tests of the A-Not-B error reveal the same discrepancy between looking and searching that we discussed previously for basic object permanence. When 7- to 11-month-old infants simply observe hiding events, first at A and then at B, they tend to look at the correct location, B; that is, they do not make the A-Not-B error (Hofstadter & Reznick, 1996). Furthermore, in violation-of-expectancy tests, 8- to 12-month-old infants, who would commit the A-Not-B search error, look longer when a toy they observed being hidden at A is revealed at B than when it reappears at A (Ahmed & Ruffman, 1998; Baillargeon, DeVos, & Graber, 1989). It is not fully clear why infants appear more competent when tested via visual-attention measures versus tests that require them to take action, and this is a topic of intense investigation.

Many explanations have been offered for the A-Not-B error. Diamond (1985) attributes it to the combination of memory limitations and poor inhibitory control associated with immaturity of the prefrontal cortex (a brain region that, as discussed in Chapter 3, is involved in many higher-level cognitive functions). According to other accounts, a representational system, which favors responding on the basis of a mental representation of the object's current location, competes with and gradually comes to dominate a response system, which favors the repetition of a previously successful motor response (Marcovitch & Zelazo, 1999). For some theorists, response perseveration wins out in the A-Not-B task because of deficiencies on the representational side. For example, Aguiar and Baillargeon (2000) propose that young infants do not adequately analyze the difference between the A and B trials, and hence simply do again what worked before. In contrast, following from the dynamic-systems emphasis on lower-level factors described in Chapter 4, Linda Smith and her colleagues (Smith et al., 1999) emphasize the response side (see p. 152), arguing that a strong tendency to repeat a previous motor behavior is the primary factor responsible for repeatedly searching at A. Each of these accounts explains some of the research results, but none are consistent with all the data.

Developmentalists have thus learned a great deal about infants' thinking about things, especially about their ability to keep absent objects in mind. However, the full integration of their findings has yet to be achieved.

Physical Knowledge

Infants' knowledge about the physical world is not limited to what they know and are learning about objects. One domain that has been extensively studied is the understanding of *gravity*, a phenomenon about which infants who have never heard the word "gravity" soon know a great deal: they know that objects do not float in midair, that an object that is inadequately supported will fall, that balls roll

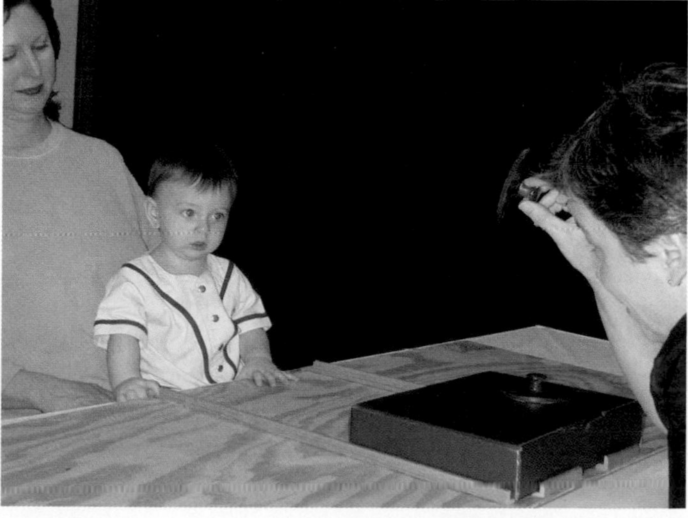

BOTH: COURTESY OF DR. LINDA B. SMITH

FIGURE 5.14 The A-Not-B error Babies show the A-Not-B pattern even if the object is not hidden but just waved around at first one and then another position. On the next trial, when developmental psychologist Linda Smith waves the other object in the air, the baby will reach for the one he picked up before.

means–end problem solving the process of using an action (the means) to achieve a goal (the end)

down but not up slopes, that a nonround object placed on a stable surface will stay put, and so forth.

This knowledge starts to develop in the first year. By 7 months of age (but not 5), infants look longer when they see a ball that is released on a slope move upward than when it moves down; this indicates that they had expected it to go down. Similarly, they look longer at an object that slows down as it travels down a slope than at one that picks up speed on a downward trip (Kim & Spelke, 1992).

Infants also gradually come to understand under what conditions one object can support another. Figure 5.15 summarizes infants' reactions to simple support problems involving boxes and a platform (Baillargeon, Needham, & DeVos, 1992; Needham & Baillargeon, 1993). At 3 months of age, infants are surprised (they look longer) if a box that is released in midair remains suspended (as in Figure 5.15a), rather than falling. However, as long as there is any contact at all between the box and the platform (as in Figure 5.15b and 5.15c), these young infants do not appear to be surprised when the box remains stationary. By approximately 5 months of age, they appreciate the relevance of the *type* of contact involved in support. They now know that the box will be stable only if it is released on top of the platform, so they would be surprised by the display in Figure 5.15b. Roughly a month later, they recognize the importance of the *amount* of contact, and hence they look longer when the box in Figure 5.15c stays put with only a small portion of its bottom surface on the platform. Shortly after their first birthday, infants also take into account the *shape* of the object and hence are surprised if an asymmetrical object like that shown in Figure 5.15d remains stable.

FIGURE 5.15 Infants' developing understanding of support relations (Adapted from Baillargeon, 1998)

Violation detected at each stage

Initial concept: Contact/No contact

(a) 3 months

Variable: Type of contact

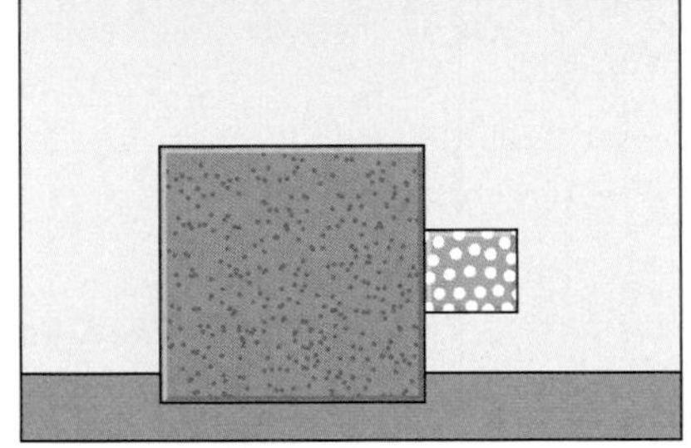

(b) 5 months

Variable: Amount of contact

(c) 6.5 months

Variable: Shape of the box

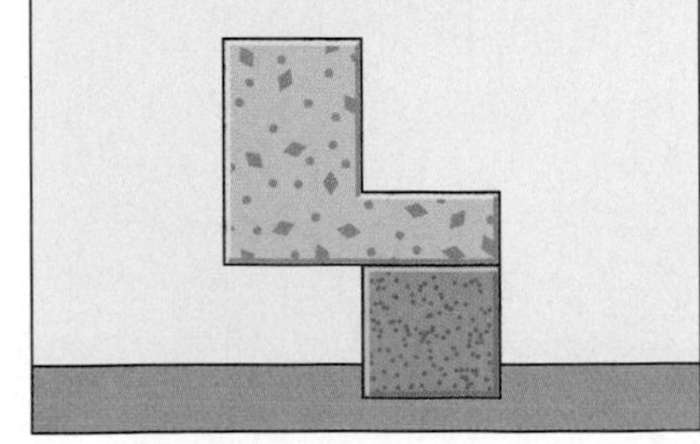

(d) 12.5 months

Infants presumably develop this progressively refined understanding of support relations between objects as a result of experience. They observe innumerable occasions of adults placing objects on surfaces, and once in a while, as in the crashing crystal observed by baby Benjamin, they see the consequences of inadequate support. And, of course, they collect additional data through their own manipulation of objects, including lots more evidence than their parents would like about what happens when a milk cup is deposited on the very edge of a high chair tray.

Problem Solving

A major landmark in infants' cognitive development is their gaining the ability to use their knowledge about objects and various physical phenomena to solve problems—from how to get desirable objects that are out of reach, to how to activate a jack-in-the-box. Such **means–end problem solving** by infants was first studied by Piaget (1952). In one of the simple tasks he devised, a desirable toy is placed out of reach of the infant on the far end of a cloth, the near end of which is well within the infant's grasp. Not until around 8 months (the same age they start searching for hidden objects) will infants immediately pull on the near end of the cloth as a means of getting the toy (Willatts, 1985, 1999). Before that age, they will strain toward the desired object, trying in vain to reach it directly while ignoring the cloth that would enable them to succeed.

BOTH: COURTESY OF PETER WILLATTS, UNIVERSITY OF DUNDEE, SCOTLAND

An 8-month-old pulls on a cloth as the means to solving the problem she faces here—getting the out-of-reach toy she wants.

One source of difficulty in this kind of problem is that infants must *inhibit* responding to the fascinating toy they want and instead direct their attention and action to something else—the boring cloth covering it or lying underneath it. The difficulty of response inhibition was made especially apparent by a study in which infants were presented with a transparent box with a desirable toy inside it. The experimenter showed the infants that the side walls of the box were open, held the box firmly on the table, and invited the babies to get the toy. Thus, the infants could see the toy through the front wall of the box, but to get it, they first had to reach away from it—around and through one of the open sides of the box. Infants failed to solve this seemingly simple problem until around 11 months of age (Diamond & Gilbert, 1989), partly because they persisted in trying to reach directly through the transparent front wall of the box.

Looking Ahead

The intense activity focused on cognition in infancy has produced a wealth of fascinating findings. This new information has not, however, resolved the basic issues about how cognition develops in infancy. The evidence we have reviewed reveals a remarkable constellation of abilities and deficits. Infants can be both surprisingly smart and surprisingly clueless. They can infer the existence of an unseen object but cannot retrieve it. They appreciate that objects cannot float in midair but think that any kind and amount of contact at all provides sufficient support. The challenge for theorists is to account for both the competence and the incompetence of infants' thinking. For the moment, the field's state of knowledge has been characterized as a strange state of empirical richness combined with theoretical disarray (Spelke & Newport, 1998).

review:: Building on the brilliant insights and observations of Jean Piaget, and using an array of extremely clever methods, modern researchers have made a host of fascinating discoveries about the cognitive processes of infants. We know that infants mentally represent not only the existence of hidden objects but also characteristics such as the object's size, height, or noise-making properties. Nevertheless, they are easily confused by multiple hiding events. Infants' understanding of the physical world grows steadily, as shown by their appreciation of support relations and their increasing ability to solve everyday problems.

Chapter Summary

Perception

- The human visual system is relatively immature at birth; young infants have poor acuity, low contrast sensitivity, minimal color vision, and limited visual scanning ability. Modern research has demonstrated, however, that newborns begin visually scanning the world minutes after birth and that very young infants show preferences for strongly contrasted patterns, for the same colors adults prefer, and, especially, for certain human faces.
- Some visual abilities, including perception of constant size and shape, are present at birth; others develop rapidly over the first year. Binocular vision develops quite suddenly at around 4 months of age, and the ability to identify object boundaries—object segregation—is also present at that age. By 7 months, infants are sensitive to a variety of monocular, or pictorial, depth cues; and pattern perception has developed to the point that infants can perceive illusory (subjective) contours, as adults do.
- The auditory system is comparatively well developed at birth, and newborns will turn their heads to localize a sound. Young infants' remarkable proficiency at perceiving pattern in auditory stimulation underlies their sensitivity to musical structure.
- Infants are sensitive to smell from birth. They learn to identify their mother in part by her unique scent.
- Through active touching, using both mouth and hands, infants explore and learn about themselves and their environment.
- Research on the phenomenon of intermodal perception has revealed that from very early on, infants integrate information from different senses, linking their visual with their aural, olfactory, and tactile experiences.

Motor Development

- Motor development, or the development of action, proceeds rapidly in infancy through a series of "motor milestones," starting with the strong reflexes displayed by newborn babies. Recent research has demonstrated that the regular pattern of development results from the confluence of many factors, including the development of strength, posture control, balance, and perceptual skills. This pattern of motor development varies in different cultures, however, as a result of their unique cultural practices.
- Each new motor achievement, from reaching to self-locomotion, expands the infant's experience of the world but also presents new challenges. Infants adopt a variety of strategies to move around in the world successfully and safely.

Learning

- Various kinds of learning are present in infancy. Infants habituate to, and form expectancies about, stimuli that are repeated. Through active exploration, they engage in perceptual learning. They also learn through classical conditioning, which involves forming associations between natural and neutral stimuli, and through instrumental conditioning, which involves learning about the contingency between one's own behavior and some outcome. Babies clearly enjoy learning to control their experience.
- From the second half of the first year on, observational learning—watching and imitating the behavior of other people—is an increasingly important source of information.

Cognition

- Powerful new research techniques—most notably the violation-of-expectancy procedure—have established that infants display impressive cognitive abilities. Much of this work on mental representation and thinking was originally inspired by Jean Piaget's concept of object permanence. But it has been revealed that, contrary to Piaget's belief, young infants can mentally represent invisible objects and even draw simple inferences from observed events.
- When infants begin searching for invisible objects, they commit the A-Not-B error, searching for the object where they last found it rather than where they just saw it being hidden. Several different explanations have been proposed for this error; some emphasize problems in the response side, whereas others emphasize representational factors.
- Other research, focused on infants' developing knowledge of the physical world, has demonstrated their understanding of some of the effects of gravity. It takes babies several months to work out the conditions under which one object can provide stable support for another.
- A major landmark in infants' cognitive development is their gaining the ability to use knowledge about objects to solve physical problems—such as pulling on the edge of a cloth to bring a desired toy within reach. Such means–end problem solving (first studied by Piaget) develops at about 8 months of age.
- Although many fascinating phenomena have been discovered in the area of infant cognition, basic issues about cognitive development remain unresolved. Theorists are sharply divided on how to account for the abilities, on the one hand, and the deficiencies, on the other hand, in infants' thinking.

Critical Thinking Questions

1. The major theme throughout this chapter was nature and nurture. Consider the following research findings discussed in the chapter: infants' preference for consonance (versus dissonance) in music, their preference for faces that adults consider attractive, and their ability to represent the existence and even the height of an occluded object. To what extent do you think these preferences and abilities rest on innate factors, and to what extent are they the result of experience?
2. As you have seen from this chapter, researchers have learned a substantial amount about infants in the recent past. Were you surprised at some of what has been learned? Describe to a friend something from each of the main sections of the chapter that you would never have suspected an infant could do or would know. Similarly, tell your friend a few things that you were surprised to learn infants do not know or that they fail to do.
3. Suppose you were the parent of a young infant, and you were concerned that your baby might not be able to see very well. How could a developmental psychologist test your baby's vision?
4. Explain why infancy researchers did the following things (each of which seems somewhat odd if one does not know the rationale behind it). What hypotheses were they trying to test?
   a. Suspended infants in water up to their waists
   b. Showed infants with one eye patched a misshapen window
   c. "Hid" a toy under a transparent container
   d. Pretended to be unable to pull the end off a dumbbell

Key Terms

sensation, p. 171
perception, p. 171
preferential-looking technique, p. 172
visual acuity, p. 172
contrast sensitivity, p. 173
retina, p. 173
fovea, p. 173
perceptual constancy, p. 174
object segregation, p. 176
optical expansion, p. 177
binocular disparity, p. 177
stereopsis, p. 177
monocular or pictorial cues, p. 177
auditory localization, p. 179
intermodal perception, p. 182
reflexes, p. 183
stepping reflex, p. 187
prereaching movements, p. 188
self-locomotion, p. 189
social referencing, p. 191
differentiation, p. 194
affordances, p. 194
classical conditioning, p. 195
unconditioned stimulus (UCS), p. 195
unconditioned response (UCR), p. 195
conditioned stimulus (CS), p. 195
conditioned response (CR), p. 195
instrumental conditioning, p. 196
positive reinforcement, p. 196
violation-of-expectancy, p. 200
means–end problem solving, p. 204

CHAPTER 6

Development of Language and Symbol Use

ROMARE BEARDEN, *Early Carolina Morning*, 1978

THEMES

- Nature and Nurture
- The Active Child
- Continuity/Discontinuity
- Mechanisms of Change
- The Sociocultural Context
- Individual Differences
- Research and Children's Welfare

"Woof." (used at the age of 11 months to refer to neighbor's dog)
"Hot." (used at the age of 14 months to refer to stove, matches, candles, light reflecting off shiny surfaces, etc.)
"Read me." (used at the age of 21 months to ask mother to read a story)
"Why I don't have a dog?" (27 months of age)
"If you give me some candy, I'll be your best friend. I'll be your two best friends." (48 months of age)
"Granna, we went to Cagoshin [Chicago]." (65 months of age)
"It was, like, ya' know, totally awesome, dude." (192 months of age)

These utterances, which we will return to throughout the chapter, were all produced by one boy in the process of becoming a native speaker of the English language (Clore, 1981). In beginning to learn his native language, this boy displayed the capacity that most sets humans apart from other species: the creative and flexible use of symbols, including language and many kinds of nonlinguistic symbols (print, numbers, pictures, models, maps, etc.). **Symbols** are systems for (1) representing our thoughts, feelings, and knowledge, and (2) communicating them to other people. Our ability to use symbols vastly expands our cognitive and communicative power. It frees us from the present, enabling us to learn from the generations of people who preceded us and to contemplate the future. Because symbols are such an important source of learning and knowledge, becoming symbol-minded is a crucial developmental task for all children everywhere in the world (DeLoache, 2002).

In this chapter, we will focus first and primarily on the acquisition of language, the preeminent symbol system, the "jewel in the crown of cognition" (Pinker, quoted in Kolata, 1987). We will then discuss children's mastery and creation of nonlinguistic symbols, such as pictures and models, as well as the development of symbolic, or pretend, play.

The dominant theme in this chapter will once again be *nature and nurture*. Considerable debate has focused on the relative contributions of nature and nurture in children's language development. A related disagreement concerns the extent to which language acquisition is made possible by abilities that are specialized for learning language versus by general-purpose cognitive mechanisms that support all sorts of learning.

MYRLEEN FERGUSON CATE / PHOTOEDIT

These children are intent on mastering one of the many important symbol systems in the modern world.

The *sociocultural context* is another theme that is prominent in this chapter. We will frequently discuss research conducted with children from different language communities, citing both similarities and differences in language acquisition across cultures. This comparative work often provides crucial evidence for or against theoretical claims about language development. A third theme that recurs throughout the chapter is *individual differences;* as you will see, there is great variability in the timing of most aspects of language development. For any given milestone, some children will achieve it much earlier, and some much later, than others. The *active child* theme also puts in repeated appearances here. Infants and young children pay close attention to language and a wide variety of symbolic artifacts, and they work hard at figuring out how to communicate with other people.

symbols systems for representing our thoughts, feelings, and knowledge and for communicating them to other people

language comprehension understanding what others say (or sign or write)

language production actually speaking (or signing or writing) to others

generativity the idea that by using the finite set of words in our vocabulary, we can put together an infinite number of sentences and express an infinite number of ideas

Language Development

What can the average 5- to 10-year-old do almost as well as you can? Not much, but one very important thing is using language, whether spoken or manually signed. By 5 years of age, children have mastered the basic structure of their native language. The sentences uttered by the average first-grade student are just as correct grammatically as those produced by the average college freshman. Although their powers of expression may be less sophisticated than yours and their vocabularies smaller, first graders' basic linguistic competence is not.

Using language involves both **language comprehension,** which refers to understanding what others say (or sign or write), and **language production,** which refers to actually speaking (or signing or writing) to others. As you will see repeatedly in this chapter, *language comprehension precedes language production:* children understand words and linguistic structures that other people use before they include them in their own utterances (Goldin-Meadow, Seligman, & Gelman, 1976). This is, of course, not unique to young children; you no doubt understand many words that you never actually use. In our discussion, we will be concerned with developmental processes involved in both comprehension and production, as well as the relation between them.

The Components of Language

Each of the thousands of languages in the world is based on a complex system of rules for combining different kinds of elements at different levels of a hierarchy: sounds are combined to form words, words are combined to form sentences, and sentences are combined to form narratives. Thus, acquiring a language involves learning the language's sounds and sound patterns, its specific words, and the ways in which the language allows words to be combined. It also involves learning how language is employed for communication with other people. The enormous benefit that emerges from this combinatorial process is **generativity;** using the finite set of words in our vocabulary, we can generate an infinite number of sentences, expressing an infinite number of ideas.

The generative power of language comes at a cost, however, and the cost is complexity. To appreciate the challenge that this complexity presents to children who must master their native language, imagine yourself as a stranger in a strange land. Someone walks up to you and says, "Jusczyk blickets Nthlakapmx." You would have absolutely no idea what this person had just said. Why?

phonemes the elementary units of meaningful sound used to produce languages

phonological development the acquisition of knowledge about the sound system of a language

morphemes the smallest units of meaning in a language, composed of one or more phonemes

semantic development the learning of the system for expressing meaning in a language, including word learning

syntax rules in a language that specify how words from different categories (nouns, verbs, adjectives, etc.) can be combined

syntactic development the learning of the syntax of a language

pragmatic development the acquisition of knowledge about how language is used

metalinguistic knowledge an understanding of the properties and function of language—that is, an understanding of language as language

First, you may have difficulty even perceiving some of the sounds that the speaker is uttering. **Phonemes** are the elementary units of sound used to produce languages, and they distinguish meaning. For example, "rake" differs by only one phoneme from "lake" (/r/ versus /l/), but the two words have quite different meanings to English speakers. Languages employ different sets of phonemes; English, for example, uses 45 of the roughly 200 sounds used in the world's languages. The phonemes that distinguish meaning in any one language overlap with, but also differ from, those in other languages. For example, the sounds /r/ and /l/ do not carry different meaning in Japanese. Further, combinations of sounds that are common in one language may never occur in others. When you read the stranger's utterance in the preceding paragraph, you probably had no idea how to pronounce "Nthlakapmx," because the sound combinations that the letters of this word represent do not occur in English. Thus, the first step in children's language learning is **phonological development,** the acquisition of knowledge about the sound system of their language.

Another reason you would not know what the stranger had said to you, even if you could have perceived the sounds being uttered, is that you would have had no idea what the sounds mean. The smallest units of meaning are **morphemes,** which are composed of one or more phonemes. Morphemes, alone or in combination, constitute words. The words *I* and *dog,* for example, are both single morphemes, because each of them refers to a single entity. The word *dogs* contains two morphemes, one designating a familiar furry entity and the second indicating more than one of them. Thus, the second step in language acquisition is **semantic development,** that is, learning the system for expressing meaning in a language, including word learning.

However, even if you were told the meaning of each individual word the stranger had used, you would still not understand the utterance, because in all languages meaning depends on how words are put together. To express an idea of any complexity, we combine words into sentences, but only some combinations are permissible. For every language, a large set of rules—the **syntax** of the language—specifies how words from different categories (nouns, verbs, adjectives, etc.) can be combined. In English, many grammatical rules pertain to the *order* in which words can appear in a sentence, and word order affects meaning. "John loves Mary" does not mean the same thing as "Mary loves John." In some other languages, which person is the lover and which the beloved would be conveyed by word endings or subtle differences in sound rather than by word order. **Syntactic development** involves learning the syntax, the rules for combining words, of a language.

Finally, a full understanding of the interaction with the stranger would necessitate some knowledge of the cultural rules for using language. In some societies, it would be quite bizarre to address a stranger in the first place, whereas in others it is commonplace. **Pragmatic development** refers to acquiring knowledge about how language is used.

Our example of the bewilderment one experiences when listening to someone speak a language one does not know is useful for delineating the components of language use. However, as an analogy to what infants and young children face in learning language, it is limited. An adult who hears someone speaking an unfamiliar language already knows what language is, knows that the sounds the person is uttering constitute words, knows that words are combined to form sentences, and so on. In other words, adults have considerable **metalinguistic knowledge** about the properties of language and language use that young language learners do not.

Thus, learning to comprehend and produce language involves phonological, semantic, syntactic, and pragmatic development, as well as metalinguistic knowledge about language. The same factors are involved in learning languages that are signed (although the basic elements are gestures rather than sounds). There are over 200 sign languages, including American Sign Language (ASL), which are based on gestures, both manual and facial. They are true languages, and the course of acquisition of a sign language is remarkably similar to that of a spoken language. As you will see, research on the development of sign language has provided a great deal of insight into the nature of language acquisition in general.

What Is Required for Language?

What does it take to be able to learn a language in the first place? Full-fledged language is achieved only by humans, but only if they have experience with other humans using language for communication.

A Human Brain

A probable prerequisite for full-fledged language development is a human brain. Language is a *species-specific* behavior, in that only humans acquire language in the normal course of development in their normal environment. Furthermore, it is *species-universal* in that virtually all young humans learn language. It takes highly abnormal environmental conditions or relatively severe cognitive impairment to disrupt children's language development.

In contrast, no other animals naturally develop anything approaching the complexity or generativity of human language, even though they can communicate with one another. For example, birds claim territorial rights via birdsong (Marler, 1970), and vervet monkey calls reveal the presence of a predator and indicate whether the predator is a hawk or a snake (Seyfarth & Cheney, 1993).

Researchers have had some success in training nonhuman primates to use complex communicative systems. One of the early efforts was a very ambitious project in which a dedicated couple raised a chimpanzee in their own home, with their own children, to see if the chimp, named Vicki, would learn to speak (Hayes & Hayes, 1951). Although Vicki clearly learned to comprehend some words and phrases, she produced virtually no recognizable words. Concluding that nonhuman primates lack the vocal apparatus for producing speech, later researchers attempted to teach them sign language. Washoe, a chimpanzee, and Koko, a gorilla, became famous for their ability to communicate with their human trainers and caretakers by signing (Gardner & Gardner, 1969; Patterson & Linden, 1981). Washoe was able to label a variety of objects and could make requests ("more fruit," "please tickle") and comments ("Washoe sorry"). However, the general consensus is that, impressive though Washoe's and Koko's performances were, they did not qualify as language, because there was little evidence of syntactic structure in their "utterances" (Terrace, Petitto, Sanders, & Bever, 1979; Wallman, 1992).

The most successful sign-learning nonhumans are Kanzi and Panbisha, bonobos, or pygmy chimpanzees. Kanzi learned to communicate with humans by using a specially designed keyboard composed of numerous symbols that denote specific objects and actions ("give," "eat," "banana," "hug," etc.) (Savage-Rumbaugh, Murphy, Sevcik, Brakke, Williams, & Rumbaugh, 1993). Kanzi became very adept at using the keyboard to answer questions, to make requests, and even to offer comments. He often combines signs, but whether they can be considered rule-governed sentences is not clear. Kanzi also understands many words and phrases spoken to him by his human caretakers, and he is even sensitive to word order. For example, when asked to "give the shot [a syringe] to Liz" (a caretaker),

COURTESY OF THE LANGUAGE RESEARCH CENTER, GEORGIA STATE UNIVERSITY, PHOTO BY LIZ PUGH

Panbisha, a bonobo chimpanzee, communicates with her caretakers by using a specially designed set of symbols that stand for a wide variety of objects, people, and actions.

he handed the syringe to her; however, when instructed to "give Liz a shot," he touched the syringe to her arm.

Whatever the ultimate decision regarding the extent to which Kanzi or other nonhuman primates should be credited with language, several things are clear. Even the most basic language achievements of nonhuman primates come only after a great deal of concentrated effort by humans to teach the animals, whereas human children master the rudiments of their language by the age of 5 with little explicit teaching. At age 5, human children understand thousands of words, whereas nonhuman primates have relatively small vocabularies. Furthermore, although the most advanced nonhuman communicators combine symbols in utterances, there is little evidence for syntactic structure, which is a defining feature of language (Tomasello, 1994). In short, only the human brain acquires a communicative system with the complexity, structure, and generativity of language.

Brain–language relations A vast amount of research has examined brain–language relations. One thing that is clear is that language processing involves a substantial degree of functional localization. At the broadest level, there are hemispheric differences in language functioning that we discussed to some extent in Chapter 3. For the 90% of people who are right-handed, language is primarily represented and controlled by the left hemisphere of the cerebral cortex. This association was first formally reported in 1861 by Paul Broca, a French physician, whose observations of language deficits in patients with various forms of brain injuries led him to conclude that "we speak with the left hemisphere."

Developmental evidence for left-hemisphere specialization for language also comes from EEG studies showing that for both adults and children, listening to speech is associated with greater electrical activity in the left hemisphere than in the right. The same is true for young infants, who show greater left-hemisphere activity when listening to speech but greater right-hemisphere response to nonspeech sounds (Molfese & Betz, 1988; Molfese, Freeman, & Palermo, 1975). Thus, the left hemisphere shows some specialization for language (or language-like stimuli) at a very early age, although the degree of hemispheric specialization for language increases with age (Mills, Coffey-Corina, & Neville, 1997; Witelson, 1987).

Specialization for language is also evident *within* the left hemisphere (Figure 6.1). Aphasia, the condition in which language functions are severely impaired, can result from damage to some, but not other, parts of the left hemisphere. One form of aphasia, Broca's aphasia, is typically associated with injury in the front part of the left hemisphere, near the motor cortex—an area known as Broca's area.

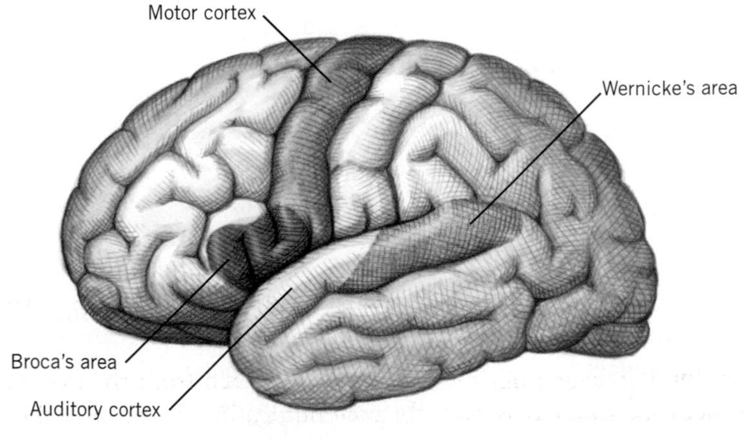

FIGURE 6.1 Lateralization of language In most people, the left hemisphere of the cerebral cortex is specialized for language. Damage to Broca's and Wernicke's areas can produce severe impairments in language functions, known as aphasia.

Patients with Broca's aphasia have difficulty producing speech; they may say a single word over and over or haltingly produce short strings of words with little or no grammatical structure, as in this example:

> Yes . . . ah . . . Monday . . . and Dad . . . er . . . hospital . . . and ah . . . Wednesday . . . Wednesday, nine o'clock . . . and oh . . . Thursday . . . ten o'clock, ah doctors . . . two . . . an' doctors . . . and er . . . teeth . . . yah.
>
> (Goodglass, 1979, p. 256)

A different aphasia, Wernicke's aphasia (named for the nineteenth-century neurologist who first described it), is typically associated with damage in an area next to the auditory cortex (Wernicke's area). Patients with this type of aphasia have no trouble producing speech, but what they say makes no sense, and their language comprehension is also impaired.

> I feel very well. My hearing, writing has been doing well. Things that I couldn't hear from. In other words, I used to be able to work cigarettes I didn't know how . . . Chesterfeela, for 20 years I can write it.
>
> (From Goodglass, 1993, p. 86)

Left-hemisphere damage produces aphasia in deaf signers just as it does for users of spoken language. This suggests that the left hemisphere is actually specialized for the kind of analytic, serial processing required for language, not for the specific modality (spoken words or signs) in which it is expressed (Bellugi, Poizner, & Klima, 1989).

Critical period for language development A considerable body of evidence has given rise to the hypothesis that the early years constitute a **critical period** during which language develops readily and that after this period (sometime between age 5 and puberty), language acquisition is much more difficult and ultimately less successful. Relevant to this hypothesis, there are several reports of children who failed to develop language after being deprived of early linguistic input.

The most famous case is that of Victor, the "Wild Child," who had apparently been abandoned by his parents and had lived on his own for many years in the woods near Aveyron, France. When discovered in 1800, the boy, who appeared to be around 12 years of age, was naked, sometimes walked on all fours, and was frightened of people. Although he could make various sounds, he had no language. After a number of years of intense socialization and language training, Victor learned to behave appropriately in social situations most of the time, but he never learned more than a few words (Lane, 1976).

A modern-day "wild child," Genie, came to light in the United States in 1970. From the age of approximately 18 months until she was rescued at age 13, Genie's parents had kept her locked up alone in a room, tied up day and night. During her imprisonment, no one spoke to her; when her father brought her food, he growled at her like an animal. At the time of her rescue, Genie's development was stunted—physically, motorically, and emotionally—and she could barely speak. With intensive training, she made some progress, but her language ability never developed much beyond the level of a toddler's: "Father take piece wood. Hit. Cry" (Curtiss, 1977, 1989; Rymer, 1993).

Do the extraordinary cases of these two children support the critical-period hypothesis? Possibly, but it is difficult to know for sure. It could be that Victor was retarded from infancy and even that he was abandoned for that reason. Genie's failure to develop language might have resulted as much from the bizarre and inhuman treatment she suffered as from the communication deprivation she endured.

critical period the time during which language develops readily and after which (sometime between age 5 and puberty) language acquisition is much more difficult and ultimately less successful

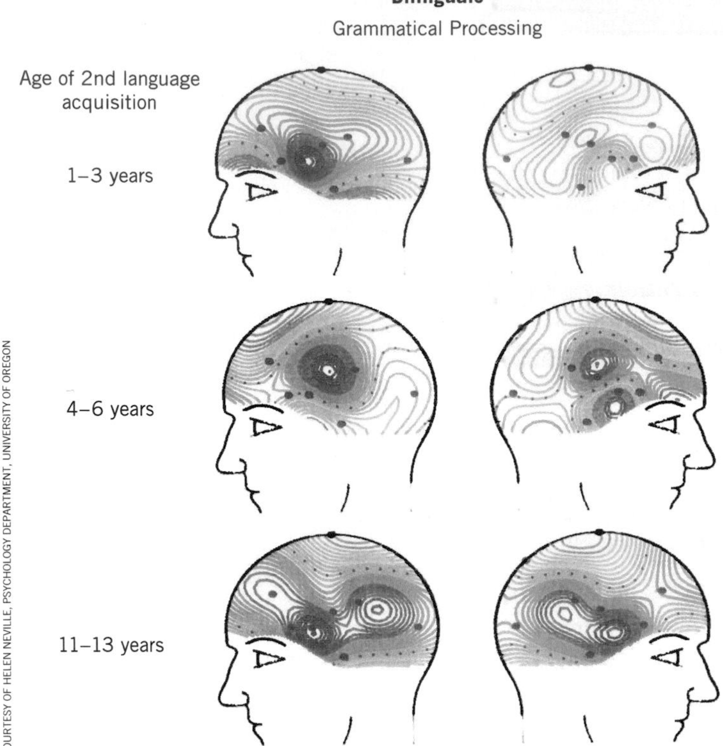

FIGURE 6.2 Hemispheric differences in language processing Adults who learned a second language at 1 to 3 years of age show the normal pattern of greater left-hemisphere activity in a test of grammatical knowledge. (Darker colors indicate greater activation.) Those who learned the language later show increased right-hemisphere activity. (Adapted from Neville & Bavelier, 1999)

Other areas of research provide much stronger evidence for the critical-period hypothesis. As noted in Chapter 3, brain damage is generally more likely to lead to permanent language impairment if it occurs in adulthood than if it occurs in childhood, presumably because other areas of the young brain are able to take over language functions (see Johnson, 1998). (See Chapter 3, pp.111–112 to review the role of timing in the long-term effects of brain damage.)

Additional strong support for the critical-period hypothesis comes from studies of adults who learned a second language at different ages. Research by Helen Neville and her colleagues (Neville & Bavelier, 1999; Weber-Fox & Neville, 1996) has shown different patterns of cerebral organization in late learners of a second language and in those who learned it early. As Figure 6.2 shows, people who learned English at 4 years of age or later showed less left-hemisphere localization of those aspects of brain organization related to grammatical processing in English than did people who learned the language at a younger age.

In a very important behavioral study, researchers tested the English proficiency of Japanese and Korean immigrants who had come to the United States and had begun learning English either as children or as adults (Johnson & Newport, 1989). The results, shown in Figure 6.3, reveal that knowledge of English grammar was related to the age at which these individuals began learning English, but not to the length of their exposure to the language (i.e., how long they had been in America). The most proficient were those who had begun learning English before the age of 7. The same pattern of results has been described for the learning of one's first language. Similarly, the ASL proficiency of deaf adults depends on the age at which they first started learning it—the earlier they began, the more skilled they were as adults (Newport, 1990).

Elissa Newport (1991) has proposed an intriguing hypothesis for these results and for why children are generally better language learners than adults. According to her "less is more" account, because of perceptual and memory limitations, young children extract and store smaller chunks of the language they hear than adults do. Because it is far easier to figure out the underlying structure of shorter samples of speech than longer ones, young learners' limited cognitive abilities may actually make the task of analyzing and learning language easier.

The evidence for a critical period in language acquisition has some very clear practical implications. For one thing, deaf children should be exposed to sign language as early as possible. For another, foreign-language training in the schools, discussed in Box 6.1, should begin in the early grades; by the time students reach high school, their language-learning capability has already declined.

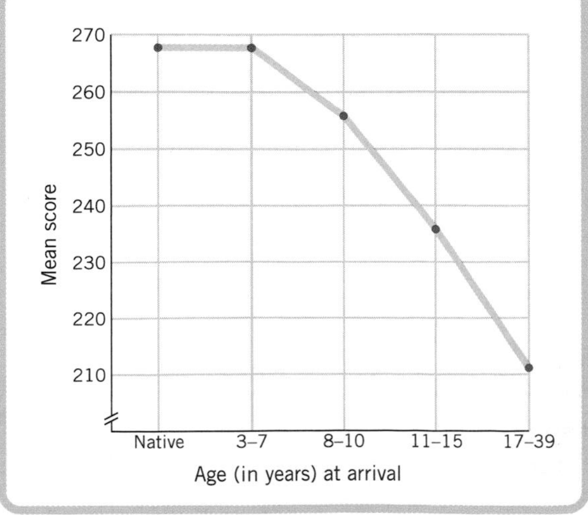

FIGURE 6.3 Test of critical-period hypothesis Performance on a test of English grammar of adults originally from Korea and China is directly related to the age at which they came to the United States and were exposed to English. The scores of adults who emigrated before the age of 7 are indistinguishable from those of native speakers of English. (Adapted from Johnson & Newport, 1989)

applications 6.1

Two Languages Are Better Than One

The topic of **bilingualism,** the ability to use two languages, has attracted substantial attention in recent years as increasing numbers of children are developing bilingually. Indeed, almost half of the children in the world are regularly exposed to more than one language.

Some children begin learning two languages very early in life, often because their parents or other family members speak different languages. Does early exposure to two languages cause confusion and make the task of language learning more difficult? Research on bilingual acquisition gives little cause for concern.

For the most part, children who are acquiring two languages do not seem to confuse them; indeed, they appear to build two separate linguistic systems (deHouwer, 1995). They do not mistakenly use the phonological system of one language to pronounce words in the other. Although a word from one language may occasionally get mixed into a sentence in the other, children keep the grammatical rules of the two languages separate.

Learning two languages is, of course, more work than learning just one, and children developing bilingually may initially lag behind slightly on some language measures (Oller & Pearson, in press; Pearson & Fernandez, 1994). However, both the course and the rate of development are generally very similar for bilingual and monolingual children (deHouwer, 1995). In addition, there are cognitive benefits to bilingualism: children who are competent in two languages perform better on a variety of cognitive tests than do children who are monolingual (Bialystok, Shenfield, & Codd, 2000; Hakuta, Ferdman, & Diaz, 1987; Peal & Lambert, 1962). Thus, the advantages of acquiring two languages outweigh the minor disadvantages.

More difficult issues arise with respect to formal acquisition of a second language later on in school. A major debate in the United States has centered around bilingualism in the classroom and what approach to take in educating school-age children who are not fluent in English. The debate over bilingual education is extremely complicated and tied up with a host of political, ethnic, and racial issues. One side of this debate advocates *total immersion,* in which children are communicated with and taught exclusively in English, with the goal of helping them become proficient in English as quickly as possible. The other side recommends an approach that initially provides children with instruction in basic subjects in their native language and gradually increases the amount of instruction provided in English. In support of this view, there is evidence (1) that children often fail to master basic subject matter when it is taught in a language they do not fully understand; and (2) that when both languages are integrated in the classroom, children learn the second language more readily, participate more actively, and are less frustrated and bored (Augusta & Hakuta, 1998; Crawford, 1997; Hakuta, 1999). This approach also helps prevent *semilingualism*—inadequate proficiency in both languages—which can occur if children become less proficient in their original language as a result of being taught a second one in school.

ELIZABETH CREWS / THE IMAGE WORKS

Although the issue of bilingualism in the classroom has been a topic of intense debate in the United States, research on bilingual language acquisition reveals a variety of benefits.

A Human Environment

Possession of a human brain is not enough for language to develop. Children must also be exposed to other people using language—any language, signed or spoken. Adequate experience hearing others talk is readily available in the environment of almost all children anywhere in the world (Jaswal & Fernald, 2002). Like Benjamin watching his parents do the dinner dishes (Chapter 5), infants and

bilingualism the ability to use two languages

young children overhear countless conversations, and in most societies, some speech is specifically directed to them. Much of the speech directed to infants occurs in the context of daily routines—during thousands of mealtimes, diaper changes, baths, and bedtimes, as well as in countless games like peekaboo and "eentsie-weentsie spider." As children get older, they are increasingly involved in interactive conversations with older siblings and adults.

Infant-directed speech Imagine yourself on a bus; behind you, someone is talking to another person. Could you guess whether that person was addressing an infant or an adult? We have no doubt that you—or anyone else—could, even if you were in another country where you didn't speak the local language. The reason is that in virtually all societies, adults adopt some distinctive mode of speech when talking to babies and very young children. This special way of speaking was originally dubbed "motherese" (Newport, Gleitman, & Gleitman, 1977), but the current term **infant-directed speech (IDS)** recognizes the fact that this special style of speech is not used just by mothers. Indeed, even young children adopt it when talking to babies (Sachs & Devin, 1976; Shatz & Gelman, 1973). As we describe the characteristics of IDS, keep in mind that it is not used in all cultures and that the IDS of American mothers tends to be more extreme than that of virtually any other group (Fernald, 1989).

Characteristics of Infant-Directed Speech Possibly the most obvious quality of speech directed toward infants is its emotional tone. As Darwin (1877) put it, it is "the sweet music of the species," speech suffused with affection. Another obvious characteristic of IDS is exaggeration (see Boysson-Bardies, 1999). People talking to babies do so in a much higher voice than they would ever use with an adult (except possibly a lover), and they make extreme changes in intonation patterns, swooping abruptly from very high-pitched sounds to very low ones. They also talk more slowly and clearly and elongate the pauses between their utterances. All this exaggerated speech is accompanied by exaggerated facial expressions. Many of these characteristics have been noted in adults speaking other languages, including Arabic, French, Italian, Japanese, Mandarin Chinese, and Spanish (see Boysson-Bardies, 1999), as well as in deaf mothers signing to their infants (Masataka, 1992).

Although the prevalent emotional tone of IDS is warm and affectionate, parents of older infants vary their emotional tone to impart important information. For example, a mother's "No" uttered with sharply falling intonation tells the baby that the mother disapproves of something, whereas a cooed "Yeesss" indicates approval. The same intonational qualities are used by mothers to signal approval and disapproval across languages, from English to Italian to Japanese (Fernald, Taeschner, Dunn, Papousek, Boysson-Bardies, & Fukui, 1989). That infants use the intonation of their mothers' messages to interpret meaning was clearly established by Anne Fernald (1989) in a series of clever experiments. In one, 8-month-old infants were presented with an attractive toy, and their mothers made either an approving statement ("Yes, good boy") or a disapproving one ("No, don't touch"). Half the statements of each type were said in a cooing, encouraging tone of voice and half in a sharp, prohibitive tone. The infants played with the toy more when their mother's tone of voice was encouraging, regardless of what she actually said.

Do infants care how they are spoken to? They seem to. In fact, they prefer IDS to speech directed at an adult—even

The infant-directed speech (IDS) used by this father grabs and holds his baby's attention.

MICHAEL NEWMAN / PHOTOEDIT

when IDS is spoken to an infant other than themselves (Cooper & Aslin, 1994; Fernald, 1985; Pegg, Werker, & McLeod, 1992) and even when it is in a language other than their own. For example, in one study, both Chinese and American infants listened longer to a Cantonese-speaking Chinese woman talking to a baby than to the same woman talking to an adult friend (Werker, Pegg, & McLeod, 1994). Furthermore, infants (and even adults) learn more new words in a foreign language if the words are presented in IDS than if they are presented in adult-directed speech (Golinkoff & Alioto, 1995; Golinkoff, Alioto, & Hirsch-Pasek, 1996).

Although IDS is very common throughout the world, it is not universal. Among the Kwara'ae of the Solomon Islands in the South Pacific (Watson-Gegeo & Gegeo, 1986), the Kaluli of New Guinea (Schieffelin & Ochs, 1987), and the Ifaluk of Micronesia (see Le, 2000), adults believe that infants lack any capacity for understanding speech, so there is no point in speaking to them. When Kaluli infants begin to speak, showing some understanding, their parents initiate very direct language training, saying words or sentences and instructing their child to repeat what they just said. Whether parents speak directly to their infants or not may affect the speed of their early language learning, but not the level of mastery they eventually achieve (Lieven, 1994).

BOB AND IRA SPRING / STOCK CONNECTION / PICTUREQUEST

Around the world, parents in some cultures talk directly to their babies, whereas parents in other cultures do not.

We thus see that infants begin life equipped with the two basic necessities for acquiring language: a human brain and a human environment. So long as they do not suffer severe brain damage or grow up in conditions of extreme social deprivation, they will acquire their native language. We turn now to the many steps through which that remarkable accomplishment proceeds.

The Process of Language Acquisition

Acquiring a language involves both listening and talking (or looking and signing); it requires both comprehending what other people communicate to you and producing intelligible language of your own. Infants start out paying attention to what people say or sign, and they know a great deal about language long before their first linguistic productions.

Speech Perception

As you saw in Chapter 2, the task of language learning begins in the womb, as fetuses develop a preference for listening to their mother's voice and the language they hear her speak. The basis for this very early learning is **prosody,** the characteristic rhythm, tempo, cadence, melody, intonational patterns, and so forth with which a language is spoken. Differences in prosody are in large part responsible for why languages sound so different from one another, and they also contribute to why speakers of the same language can sound so different. Consider, for example, the different sounds of Japanese, French, and German, and contrast the melodic speech of British speakers with the relatively flat speech of Americans.

Sensitivity to prosody is not enough to learn language, however. One must be able to distinguish among the speech sounds that make a difference in a given language. To learn English, for example, one must distinguish between *bat* and *pat, dill* and *kill, Ben* and *bed.* Remarkably, infants do not have to learn to hear these differences; young infants perceive speech sounds in very much the same way that adults do.

infant-directed speech (IDS) the distinctive mode of speech that adults adopt when talking to babies and very young children

prosody the characteristic rhythm, tempo, cadence, melody, intonational patterns, and so forth with which a language is spoken

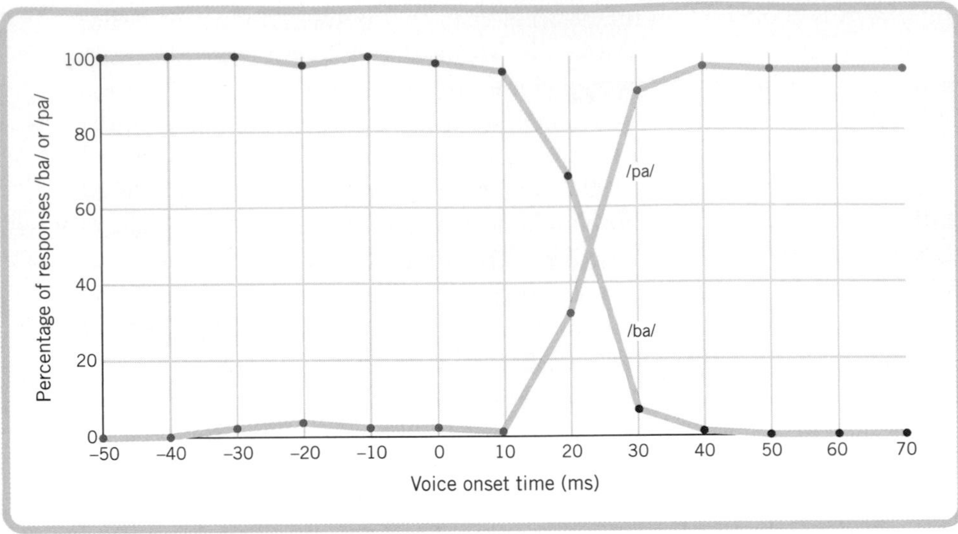

FIGURE 6.4 Categorical perception of speech sounds by adults When adults listen to a tape of artificial speech sounds that gradually change from one sound to another, such as /ba/ to /pa/ or vice versa, they suddenly switch from perceiving one sound to perceiving the other. (Adapted from Wood, 1976)

Categorical perception of speech sounds Both adults and infants perceive speech sounds as belonging to discrete categories. This phenomenon, referred to as **categorical perception,** has been established by studying people's response to artificial speech sounds. In this research, a speech synthesizer is used to gradually and continuously change one speech sound, such as /b/, into a related one, such as /p/. These two phonemes are on an acoustic continuum; they are produced in exactly the same way, except for one crucial difference—the length of time between when air passes through the lips and when the vocal cords start vibrating. This lag, referred to as **voice onset time (VOT),** is much shorter for /b/ (15 milliseconds) than for /p/ (100 ms). Researchers create tape recordings of artificial speech sounds that vary along this VOT continuum, so that each successive sound is slightly different from the one before, with /b/ gradually changing into /p/. However, adult listeners do not perceive this continuously changing series of sounds (Figure 6.4). Instead, they hear /b/ repeated several times and then hear an abrupt switch to /p/; all the sounds with a VOT of less than 25 ms are perceived as /b/, and all those of greater than 25 ms are perceived as /p/. Thus, adults automatically divide the continuous signal into two discontinuous categories—/b/ and /p/.

Young babies make the same kind of sharp distinctions between speech sounds. This remarkable fact was established using the habituation technique familiar to you from previous chapters. In the original, classic study (one of the 100 most frequently cited studies in psychology), 1- and 4-month-olds sucked on a pacifier hooked up to a computer (Eimas, Siqueland, Jusczyk, & Vigorito, 1971). Their sucking resulted in speech sounds being broadcast for them to listen to. After hearing the same sound repeatedly, the babies gradually sucked less enthusiastically. Then a new sound was played. If the infants' sucking response to the new sound increased, it could be inferred that the infants discriminated the new sound from the old one.

The crucial factor in this study was the relation between the new and old sounds—specifically, whether they were from the same or different adult categories. For one group of the babies, the new sound was from a different adult category; thus, after habituation to a series of sounds that adults perceive as /b/, sucking now produced a sound that adults identify as /p/. For the second group, the old and new sounds were within the same category (i.e., adults would perceive them both as /b/). A critical feature of the study is that for both groups, the new and old

categorical perception the perception of speech sounds as belonging to discrete categories

voice onset time (VOT) the length of time between when air passes through the lips and when the vocal cords start vibrating

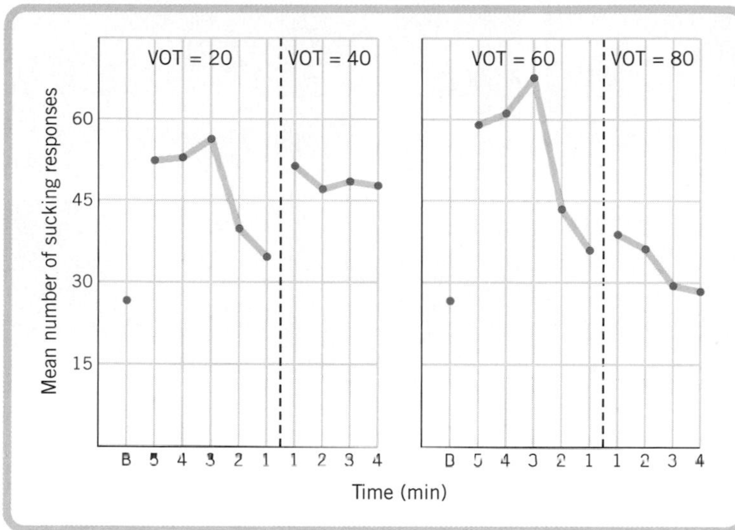

FIGURE 6.5 Categorical perception of speech sounds by infants One- and four-month-old infants were habituated to a tape of artificial speech sounds. One group repeatedly heard a /ba/ sound with a VOT of 20, and they gradually habituated to it. When the sound changed to /pa/, with a VOT of 40, they dishabituated, indicating that they perceived the difference between the two sounds, just as adults do. Another group was habituated to a /pa/ sound with a VOT of 60. When the sound changed to another /pa/ with a VOT of 80, the infants did not dishabituate, suggesting that, like adults, they did not discriminate between these two sounds. (Adapted from Eimas et al., 1971)

sounds differed equally in terms of VOT. As Figure 6.5 shows, the infants increased their rate of sucking when the new sound came from a different phonemic category (from /p/ instead of /b/). Habituation continued, however, when the new sound was within the same category as the original one. Since this classic study, a substantial body of research has established that infants, just like adults, show categorical perception of numerous speech sounds (Aslin, Jusczyk, & Pisoni, 1998).

One difference between infants and adults, however, is that young infants actually make *more* distinctions than adults do. This rather surprising phenomenon occurs because all languages use only a subset of the large variety of phonemic categories that exist. As noted earlier, the sounds /r/ and /l/ make a difference in English, but not in Japanese. Similarly, speakers of Arabic, but not English, perceive a difference between the /k/ sound in "keep" and "cool." Adults simply do not perceive most differences in speech sounds that are not important in their native languages, which partly accounts for why it is so difficult for adults to learn a second language.

In contrast, infants do distinguish between phonemic contrasts that are not made in their own language. For example, Kikuyu infants in Africa are just as good as American infants at discriminating English contrasts not found in Kikuyu (Streeter, 1976). Studies done with infants from English-speaking homes have shown that they can discriminate non-English distinctions made in languages ranging from German and Spanish to Thai, Hindi, and Zulu (see Jusczyk, 1997, for a review of this work).

This research reveals an ability that is both innate, in the sense that it is present at birth, and independent of experience, because infants can discriminate between speech sounds they have never heard before. Presumably, this capacity for categorical perception of speech sounds is enormously helpful to infants, as it essentially primes them to start learning any language in the world. Note, however, that categorical perception also occurs for some nonspeech sounds (see Aslin et al., 1998) and that the ability to distinguish speech sounds is not a uniquely human skill: nonhumans, including monkeys, chinchillas, and Japanese quail, also respond categorically to speech sounds (Kluender, Diehl, & Killeen, 1987; Kuhl & Miller, 1978; Kuhl & Padden, 1983). These facts suggest that, helpful though categorical perception of phonemes may be to human infants, it does not reflect a mode of processing specialized for language.

FIGURE 6.6 Speech perception This infant is participating in a study of speech perception in the laboratory of Janet Werker. The baby has learned to turn his head to the sound source whenever he hears a change from one sound to another. A correct head turn is rewarded by an exciting visual display, as well as by the applause and praise of the experimenter. To make sure that the mother does not influence her child's behavior, she is wearing headphones so she cannot hear what the baby hears. (From Werker, 1989)

Developmental changes in speech perception The ability of young infants to discriminate among speech sounds they have never heard before does not last long. By the end of their first year, their speech perception is similar to that of their parents. The initial demonstration of this shift was carried out by Janet Werker and her colleagues, who tested the ability of infants of different ages to discriminate speech sounds (Werker, 1989; Werker & Lalonde, 1988; Werker & Tees, 1984). The infants were all from English-speaking homes, and they were tested with speech contrasts that are not used in English but that are important in two other languages—Hindi and Nthlakapmx (a language spoken by North American Indians in the Pacific Northwest). To test the discriminatory capabilities of 6- to 12-month-old infants, the researchers used a simple conditioning procedure, shown in Figure 6.6. The infants learned that whenever they heard a change in the series of sounds they were listening to, they could see an interesting sight by turning their head to one side. Thus, discrimination among speech sounds was inferred if the infants quickly turned their heads in the correct direction following a sound change.

Figure 6.7 shows that at 6 to 8 months of age, the infants readily discriminated among the sounds they heard; they could tell one Hindi syllable from another, and they could also distinguish between two sounds in Nthlakapmx. At 12 months, however, infants no longer heard the differences they had detected a few months before. A similar change occurs for vowels, although at a slightly earlier age (Kuhl, 1991; Kuhl, Williams, Lacerda, Stevens, & Lindbloom, 1992; Polka & Werker, 1994).

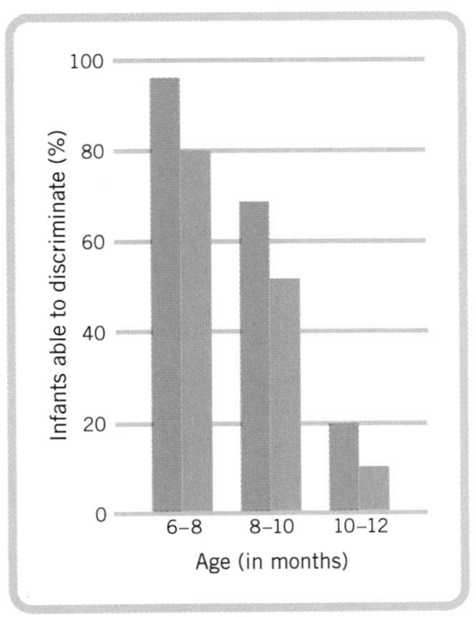

FIGURE 6.7 Age changes in infants' speech perception Infants' ability to discriminate between speech sounds *not* in their native language declines between 6 and 12 months of age. Six-month-olds from English-speaking families readily discriminate between syllables in Hindi (blue bars) and Nthlakapmx (green bars), but 10- to 12-month-olds do not. (Adapted from Werker, 1989)

Sensitivity to regularities in speech In addition to focusing on the speech sounds that are used in their native language, infants become increasingly sensitive to many of the numerous regularities in that language. One example is stress pattern, an element of prosody. In English, the first syllable in two-syllable words is much more often stressed than the second syllable is (as in "English," "often," and "second"). Nine-month-old American infants pay attention longer to lists of words that follow this pattern than to words in which the second syllable is stressed (Jusczyk, Cutler, & Redanz, 1993).

The discovery that infants are sensitive to this regular feature of the language they hear was made possible through a very simple procedure designed to assess infants' auditory preferences. Lights mounted near two loudspeakers located in panels on either side of the infants are used to draw the infant's attention to one side or the other. As soon as the infant turns to look at the light, an auditory stimulus is played through the speaker, and it continues as long as the baby is looking in that direction. The length of time the infant spends looking at the light—and hence listening to the sound—is taken as a measure of the degree to which the infant is attracted to that sound. As you will see, this head-turn preference procedure has been used extensively to address questions about language development in infancy.

Another regularity to which infants are surprisingly sensitive concerns the **distributional properties** of the speech they hear. In any language, certain sounds are more likely to appear together than are others. Sensitivity to such regularity in the speech stream was demonstrated in an elegant series of experiments in which babies learned new words based purely on statistical regularities (Aslin, Saffran, & Newport, 1998; Saffran, Aslin, & Newport, 1996). The infants in this study listened to a 2-minute tape of four different three-syllable "words" (e.g., *tupiro, golabu, bidaku, padoti*) repeated in random order with no pauses between the "words." Then, on a series of test trials, the babies were sometimes presented with the same "words" and sometimes with "nonwords"—the same syllables combined in different combinations. They listened longer to the novel "nonwords." To have exhibited this preference, the babies must have noticed and remembered how often certain syllables occurred together in the sample of speech they heard; they learned, for example, that "bi" was always followed by "da" and that "da" was always followed by "ku," but that "ku" was followed by any of three other syllables ("tu," "go," or "pa"). Thus, the infants used the recurrent patterns to fish words out of the passing stream of speech.

How quickly could you pick out a word from a stream of speech like the one shown here? It takes 8-month-old infants only 2 minutes.

Another feature of how people speak—the minute pauses that occur between words—provides useful information for older infants. Eleven-month-olds listened longer to speech in which 1-second pauses had been inserted between successive words than to passages in which the pauses occurred between syllables within words (Myers et al., 1996). (Notice the similarity between this result and younger infants' preference for Mozart minuets with pauses between musical phrases that we described in Chapter 5.)

As demonstrated in the research on speech perception we have reviewed, infants work very hard right from the beginning to identify patterns in the sounds they hear other people producing. They start out with the ability to make crucial distinctions among speech sounds but then narrow their focus to the sounds that they hear with regularity, the ones that make a difference in the language they are to acquire. With increasing exposure to language, infants identify remarkably subtle regularities in what they hear.

Preparation for Speech Production

In their first months, babies are getting ready to talk. The repertoire of sounds they can produce is extremely limited for the first two months. They cry, sneeze, sigh, burp, and smack their lips, but their vocal tract is not sufficiently developed to allow them to produce anything like real speech sounds. Then, at around 6 to 8 weeks of age, infants suddenly begin producing simple speech sounds—long, drawn-out vowel sounds, such as "ooohh" or "aaahh," or consonant–vowel combinations such as "goo." Lying in their cribs, young infants entertain themselves with vocal gymnastics, switching from low grunts to high-pitched cries, from soft murmurs to loud shouts. They click, smack, blow raspberries, squeal, all with apparent fascination and delight. Through this practice, infants' motor control over their vocalization steadily improves.

distributional properties the phenomenon that in any language, certain sounds are more likely to appear together than are others

At the same time that their sound repertoire is expanding, infants become increasingly aware that their vocalizations elicit responses from others, and they begin to engage in dialogues of reciprocal ooohing and aaahing, cooing and gooing, with their parents. With improvement in their motor control of vocalization, they increasingly imitate the sounds of their "conversational" partners, even producing higher-pitched sounds when interacting with their mothers and lower-pitched sounds when interacting with their fathers (Boysson-Bardies, 1999). The tendency of infants to imitate the speech sounds they hear has been demonstrated in the laboratory: 5-month-olds who listened to a tape of a simple vowel sound produced a similar sound in response (Kuhl & Meltzoff, 1984).

Babbling Sometime between 6 and 10 months of age, but on average at around 7 months, a major milestone occurs: babies begin to babble. Standard babbling involves producing syllables made up of a consonant followed by a vowel ("pa," "ba," "ma") that are repeated in strings ("papapa"). Although it was formerly believed that infants babble a wide range of sounds from their own and other languages (Jakobson, 1941), more recent research has revealed that babies actually babble a fairly limited set of sounds, including some not in their native language (Boysson-Bardies, 1999; Locke, 1983).

A key component in the development of babbling is receiving feedback from the sounds one is producing. Although congenitally deaf infants produce vocalizations similar to those of hearing babies until around 5 or 6 months of age, their vocal babbling occurs very late and is very limited (Oller & Eilers, 1988). This finding is contrary to earlier claims that deaf infants begin to babble vocally at the same time as hearing babies do (e.g., Lenneberg, 1967). However, some congenitally deaf babies do babble right on schedule—those who are regularly exposed to sign language. According to Petitto and Marentette (1991), at around 8 months of age, deaf infants exposed to ASL begin to babble *manually,* producing repetitive hand movements that are components of full ASL signs, just as vocally babbled sounds are components of words. Thus, like infants learning a spoken language, deaf infants seem to experiment with the elements that are combined to make meaningful words in their native language (Figure 6.8).

FIGURE 6.8 Silent babbling Babies who are exposed to the sign language of their deaf parents engage in "silent babbling." A subset of their hand movements differ from those of infants exposed to spoken language in that their slower rhythm corresponds to the rhythmic patterning of adult sign. (Adapted from Petitto, Holowka, Sergio, & Osstry, 2001)

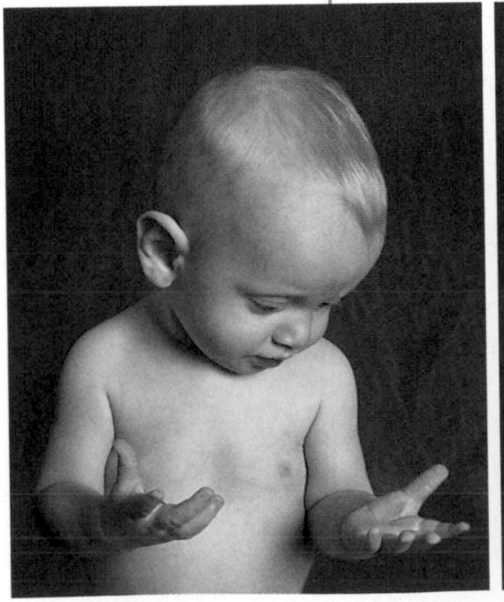

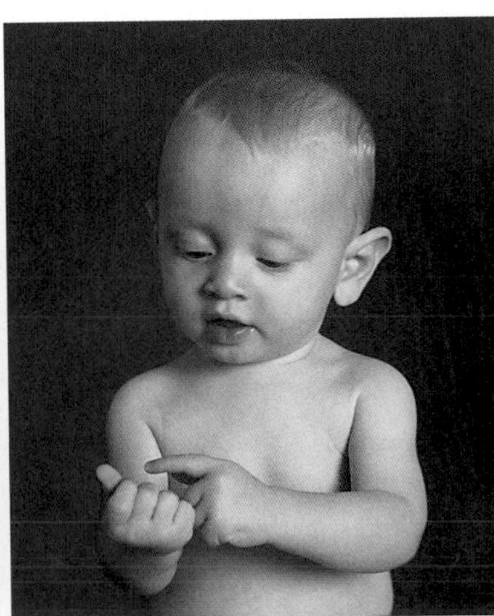

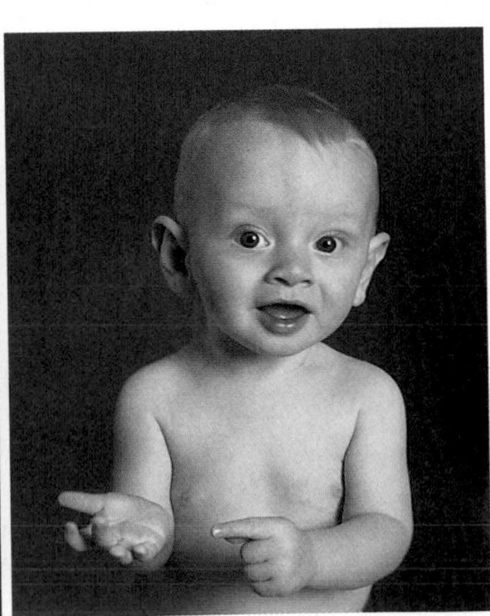

PHOTOS BY JEFFREY DEBELLE / © DR. LAURA ANN PETITTO

As infants' babbling becomes more varied, it gradually takes on the sounds, rhythm, and intonational patterns of the language the infants hear daily. In a simple but clever experiment, French adults listened to the babbling of a French 8-month-old and an 8-month-old from either an Arabic- or Cantonese-speaking family. When asked to identify which baby was the French one in each pair, the adults chose correctly 70% of the time (Boysson-Bardies, Sagart, & Durant, 1984). Thus, before they utter their first meaningful words, infants are, in a sense, native speakers of a language.

intersubjectivity the sharing of a common focus of attention by two or more people

joint attention when the baby and the parent are looking at and reacting to the same thing in the world around them; often established by the parent's following the baby's lead, looking at and commenting on whatever the infant is studying

Early interactions Before we turn to the next big step in language production—recognizable words—it is important to consider the social context that promotes language development in most societies. Even before infants start speaking, they display the beginnings of communicative competence, the ability to communicate intentionally with another person.

The first indication of this communicative competence is turn taking. In a conversation, mature participants alternate between speaking and listening. Jerome Bruner and his colleagues (Bruner, 1977; Ratner & Bruner, 1978) have proposed that learning to take turns in social interactions is facilitated by parent–infant games, such as peekaboo and "Give-and-Take," in which caregiver and baby take turns giving and receiving objects. (Infants are initially much better at offering an object than they are at relinquishing it.) In these "action dialogues" (Bruner, 1977), the child alternates between active and passive roles, just as one alternates between speaking and listening in conversations.

Successful communication also requires **intersubjectivity:** two interacting partners must share a common focus of attention. Early on, **joint attention** is established by the parent's following the baby's lead, looking at and commenting on whatever the infant is looking at. Around 6 months of age, infants become capable of following the direction of another's gaze, as long as the person is looking at something in plain view. By 18 months of age, infants can use the direction of an adult's gaze to determine the location of an object they cannot currently see (Butterworth & Grover, 1988).

A sure method of establishing joint attention with another adult is to point toward whatever you want to talk about. If you try this with a young infant, however, the baby is likely to stare intently at your outstretched finger rather than look toward the object at which you are pointing. But by around 9 months of age, most babies look in the direction in which the finger is pointing. A few months later, they begin to point themselves (Butterworth, 1998), and by 2 years of age, pointing is deliberately employed to direct the attention of another person (Moore & D'Entremont, 2001). These early interactions thus provide infants with a framework for incorporating words to communicate with others.

We have thus seen that infants take their time getting ready to talk. Through babbling, they gain some initial level of control over the production of sounds that are necessary to produce recognizable words. As they do so, they already begin to sound like their parents. Through early interactions with their parents, they develop interactive routines similar to those required in the use of language for communication.

First Words

Infants first learn words simply as familiar patterns of sounds without attaching any meaning to them; but then, in a major revolution, words become vehicles of meaning. Thus, infants first *recognize* words, and then they begin to *comprehend* them. Next, they begin producing some of the words they have learned.

Early word recognition The first task in learning words is picking them out of the speech stream. The first familiar sound to perceptually pop out of the language a child hears is his or her own name. Infants as young as 4½ months of age will listen longer to a tape repeating their own name than to a tape of a different but similar name (Mandel, Jusczyk, & Pisoni, 1995). At 7 to 8 months of age, infants readily learn to recognize *new* words and remember them for weeks (Jusczyk & Aslin, 1995; Jusczyk & Hohne, 1997).

The problem of reference Once infants can recognize recurrent units from the speech they hear, the stage is set for a truly major advance. They are ready to address the problem of **reference,** to start associating words and meaning. Figuring out which of the multitude of possible referents is the right one for a particular word is, as the philosopher Willard Quine (1960) pointed out, a very complex problem. If a child hears someone say "bunny" in the presence of a rabbit, how does the child know whether this new word refers to the rabbit itself, to its fuzzy tail, to the whiskers on the right side of its nose, or to the twitching of its nose? That the problem of reference is a real problem is illustrated by the case of a toddler who thought "Phew!" was a greeting, because it was the first thing her mother said on entering the child's room every morning (Ferrier, 1978).

There is evidence that infants begin associating highly familiar words with their referents at around 6 months of age; when 6-month-olds hear either "Mommy" or "Daddy," they look toward the appropriate person (Tincoff & Jusczyk, 1999). Infants gradually come to understand the meaning of less frequently heard words, and the pace of their vocabulary building varies greatly from one child to another. According to parents' reports on 1,000 children in the United States, 10-month-olds' *comprehension vocabulary*—the words a child understands (but may not be able to say)—ranges from 11 to 154 words (Fenson et al., 1994).

Early word production Gradually, infants begin to say some of the words they understand. Most produce their first words between 10 and 15 months of age. The term *productive vocabulary* refers to the words a child is able to say.

What qualifies as a "first word"? It can be any specific utterance that the child makes consistently to refer to or to express something. Even with this loose criterion, identification of a child's earliest few words can be problematic. For one thing, doting parents often overinterpret their child's babbling. For another, very early words may differ from the corresponding adult form. For example, *Woof* was one of the first words of the boy whose linguistic progress was illustrated at the beginning of this chapter. It was used to refer to the dog next door—both to excitedly name the animal when it appeared in the neighbors' yard and to wistfully request the dog's presence when it was absent.

Initially, infants' early word production is limited by their ability to pronounce the words they already know well enough that an attentive parent can discern their meaning. To make life easier for themselves, infants adopt a variety of simplification strategies (Gerken, 1994). For example, they leave out the difficult bits of words, turning *banana* into "nana," or they substitute easier sounds for hard-to-say ones—"bubba" for *brother,* "wabbit" for *rabbit.* Sometimes they reorder parts of words to put an easier sound at the beginning of the word, as in the common "pasketti" (for *spaghetti*) or the more idiosyncratic "Cagoshin" (shown at the beginning

reference in language and speech, the associating of words and meaning

holophrastic period the period when children begin using the words in their small productive vocabulary one word at a time

of the chapter as the way one child continued for several years to say *Chicago*). Children's early language is subject to a number of other factors that sometimes cause their parents concern. Some of these factors are discussed in Box 6.2.

Once children start talking, around the end of the first year, what do they talk about? The early productive vocabularies of children in the United States include names for people, objects, and events from the child's everyday life (Clark, 1979; Nelson, 1973). Children name their parents, siblings, and pets, as well as ecologically important objects such as cookies, juice, and balls. Frequent events and routines are also labeled—"up," "bye-bye," "night-night." Important modifiers are also used—"mine," "hot," "all gone."

Nouns predominate in the early productive vocabularies of children learning English, possibly in part because the meanings they represent are easier to pick up from observation than are the meanings of verbs; nouns can label entities, whereas verbs represent relations among entities (Gentner, 1982). In addition, the proportion of nouns in very young children's vocabularies is related to the proportion of nouns in their mother's speech to them (Pine, 1994), and middle-class American mothers (the group most frequently studied) do a great deal of object labeling for their infants, much more than do mothers in some other cultures, such as Japan (Fernald & Morikawa, 1993).

Infants begin using the words in their small productive vocabulary only one word at a time. This period of one-word utterances is referred to as the **holophrastic period,** because the child typically expresses a "whole phrase" with a single word. "Drink" can refer to the child's desire to have his mother pour him a

individual differences 6.2

Variability in Language Development

Parents often become concerned if their child seems to lag behind his or her peers in reaching any of the major milestones in language development. When should they worry? The most important thing parents need to recognize is that there are huge individual differences in many aspects of language acquisition, and most of them do not predict later problems.

One form of variation that language researchers have identified is **style,** that is, the strategies young children enlist in beginning to speak. Some children display a **referential** or **analytic style,** whereas others are characterized as having an **expressive** or **holistic style** (Bates, Dale, & Thal, 1995; Bloom, 1975; Nelson, 1973). A third style is **wait-and-see** (Boysson-Bardies, 1999).

Boysson-Bardies (1999) has described these three styles using French infants as examples. Children characterized as referential tend to analyze the speech stream into individual phonetic elements and words, and their first utterances tend to be isolated, often monosyllabic words. This style is exemplified by Emilie, whose first twenty words were almost all monosyllables starting with the same three consonants that had dominated her earlier babbling. Thus, from the adult words she heard, she seemed to systematically select those beginning with the sounds she had already mastered. Her simple and efficient strategy enabled Emilie to rapidly increase her vocabulary.

Children characterized as expressive give more attention to the overall sound of language—its rhythmic and intonational patterns—than to the phonetic elements of which it is composed. This style was adopted by Simon, whose strategy might be characterized as "conversation first." Rather than beginning with small units of speech as Emilie did, sociable Simon joined in the conversations of adults with long "sentences" or even "questions," all uttered with perfect French intonational patterns. However, these utterances included hardly any recognizable words.

Children described as "wait-and-see" begin to talk late—some of them very late. Henri babbled very little, and even after he began to understand many words, he remained silent. Until the age of 20 months, he rarely said anything beyond "papa," "maman," and "non." Henri had, however, been listening carefully for a long time, because at the age of 20 months he suddenly began saying a large number of clearly articulated words and then rapidly acquired more.

Although these different styles reflect substantial differences in *how* children go about beginning to talk, they have little if any effect on the ultimate outcome of the process. "All children reach their destination—the acquisition of their native language—no matter which strategy they adopt at the outset" (Boysson-Bardies, 1999, p. 176).

As noted earlier in the chapter, children also differ dramatically in the age at which they speak their first recognizable word and produce their first sentence, and the size of their early vocabularies varies widely as well. However, most young children who lag behind others or who are below average in productive vocabulary—even those who are far below the norm—catch up within a few years. Parents worried about their slow-to-talk child can take heart from the fact that Albert Einstein is reported not to have talked before 4 or 5 years of age.

Thus, as long as there are no other signs of developmental problems, parents should not worry overly much if their child is a late talker. There is, however, cause for concern about a young child whose *comprehension* of language is lagging, because this kind of delay may signal a hearing problem or cognitive difficulties predictive of later problems (Bates et al., 1995).

style the strategies that young children enlist in beginning to speak

referential (analytic) style speech strategy that analyzes the speech stream into individual phonetic elements and words; the first utterances of children who adopt this style tend to use isolated, often monosyllabic words

expressive (holistic) style children who use this speech strategy give more attention to the overall sound of language—its rhythmic and intonational patterns—than to the phonetic elements of which it is composed

wait-and-see style the children who use this speech strategy often begin to speak very late but then have a large vocabulary and quickly acquire more words

overextension the use of a given word in a broader context than is appropriate

glass of juice. "Juice" could, of course, refer to the very same desire. Children who produce only one-word utterances are not limited to single ideas; they manage to express themselves by stringing together successive one-word utterances. An example is a little girl with an eye infection who pointed to her eye, saying, "Ow," and then after a pause, "Eye" (Hoff, 2001).

The rate of children's vocabulary development is influenced by the sheer *amount* of talk that they hear: the more speech mothers address to their toddlers, the more rapidly the children learn new words (Huttenlocher, Haight, Bryk, Seltzer, & Lyons, 1991). Correspondingly, more highly educated mothers talk to their children more than do less-educated mothers, and their children have increasingly larger vocabularies than do the children of less-educated parents (Fenson et al., 1994; Hart & Risley, 1994; Hoff-Ginsberg, 1993, 1994; Huttenlocher et al., 1991).

What young children want to talk about quickly outstrips the number of words in their limited vocabularies, so they make the words they do possess perform double duty. One way they do this is through **overextension**—using a given word in a broader context than is appropriate, as when children use *dog* for any four-legged

TABLE 6.1

Examples of Young Children's Overextensions of Word Meaning

Word	Referents
ball	ball, balloon, marble, apple, egg, spherical water tank (Rescorla, 1980)
cat	cat, cat's usual location on top of TV when absent (Rescorla, 1980)
moon	moon, half-moon-shaped lemon slice, circular chrome dial on dishwasher, half a Cheerio, hangnail (Bowerman, 1978)
snow	snow, white flannel bed pad, white puddle of milk on floor (Bowerman, 1978)
baby	own reflection in mirror, framed photograph of self, framed photographs of others (Hoff, 2001)

animal, *daddy* for any man, *moon* for a dishwasher dial, or *hot* for any reflective metal (Table 6.1). Most overextensions represent an effort to communicate rather than a lack of knowledge, as demonstrated by research in which children who overextended some words were given comprehension tests (Naigles & Gelman, 1995; Thompson & Chapman, 1977). In one study, for example, children were shown pairs of pictures of entities for which they generally used the same label—for instance, a dog and a sheep, both of which they normally referred to as "dog." However, when asked to point to the sheep, they chose the correct animal. Thus, these children understood the meaning of the word *sheep,* but because it was not in their productive vocabulary, they used a related word that they could say to talk about the animal.

Word learning After the appearance of their first words, children typically plod ahead slowly, reaching a productive vocabulary of fifty or so words by around 18 months of age. Suddenly, the plodding is over, as most children begin the "vocabulary explosion," or "word spurt" (Figure 6.9) (Benedict, 1979; Goldfield & Reznick, 1990). Word learning shifts from first gear to overdrive, with new words being said for the first time every day. Children's comprehension vocabulary shows similar rapid growth; from 18 months of age to the time they are in first grade, children are estimated to learn an average of five to ten new words every day (Anglin, 1993; Carey, 1978).

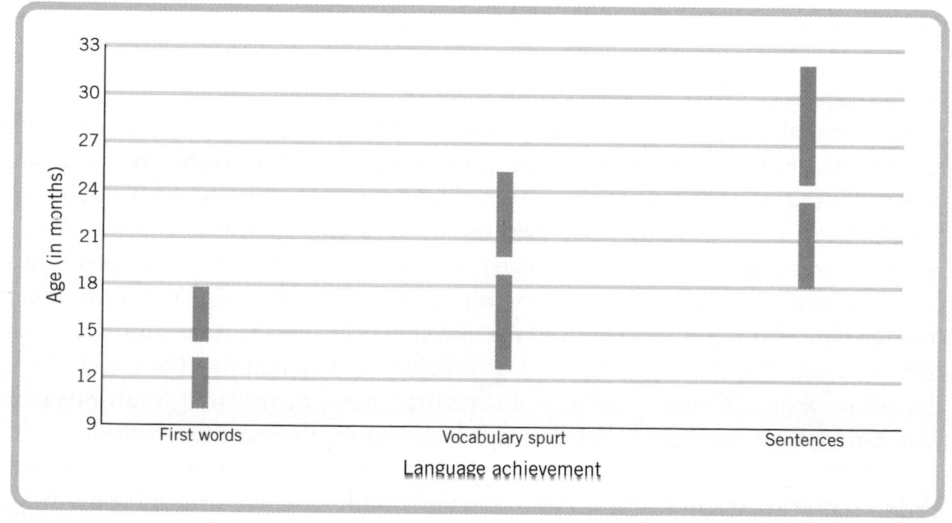

FIGURE 6.9 Language achievement On average, American children say their first word at around 13 months, experience a vocabulary spurt at around 19 months, and begin to produce simple sentences at around 24 months. However, the bars around the means show that there is great variability in when different children achieve each of these milestones. (Adapted from Bloom, 1998)

COURTESY OF JEAN BRIGGS

This young Inuit child is playing a naming game; her mother has just asked her to point to her nose.

What accounts for the speed of young children's word learning? When we look closely, we see that there are multiple sources of support for learning new words: young learners receive assistance from the people around them, and they also help themselves.

Adult Influences on Word Learning In addition to using IDS, which makes word learning easier, caregivers do other helpful things, including putting vocal stress on new words and saying them in the final position in a sentence. Also helpful is adults' tendency to label objects that are already the focus of the child's attention, thereby reducing uncertainty about the referent (Masur, 1982; Tomasello, 1988; Tomasello & Farrar, 1986). Another stimulus to word learning comes from the naming games many families play with young children, asking the child to point to a series of named items—"Where's Daddy?" "Where's Mommy?" "Where's your tummy?" Repetition also helps; young children are more likely to acquire words their parents use frequently (Huttenlocher et al., 1991).

Children's Contributions to Word Learning When confronted with novel words whose meaning they do not know, children actively exploit the context in which the new word was used in order to infer its meaning. A classic study by Susan Carey and Elsa Bartlett (1978) demonstrated **fast mapping**—the process of rapidly learning a new word simply from the contrastive use of a familiar and an unfamiliar word. In the course of everyday activities in a preschool classroom, an experimenter drew a child's attention to two trays, asking the child to get "the *chromium* tray, not the red one." The child was thus provided with a contrast between a familiar term (*red*) and an unfamiliar one (*chromium*). From this simple contrast, the children in the class inferred that the name of the color of the requested object was "chromium." After this single exposure to a novel word, about half the children showed some knowledge of it a week later by correctly picking the *chromium* one from an array of paint chips.

Some theorists have proposed that the many inferences children make in the process of learning words are guided by a number of assumptions (sometimes referred to as principles, constraints, or biases) that limit the possible meanings children entertain for a new word. For example, Ellen Markman and her colleagues (Markman, 1989; Woodward & Markman, 1998) propose that the *whole-object* assumption leads children to expect a novel word to refer to a whole object, rather than a part, property, action, or other aspect of the object. Thus, in the case of Quine's rabbit problem, the whole-object assumption results in children's taking *bunny* to apply to the whole animal, not just to its tail or whiskers or the twitching of its nose.

Children also expect that a given entity will have only one name (an expectancy referred to as the *mutual exclusivity* assumption by Woodward and Markman [1998] and as the *novel name–nameless category* principle by Golinkoff, Mervis, and Hirsh-Pasek [1994]). Early evidence for this assumption came from a study in which 3-year-olds saw pairs of objects—a familiar object for which the children had a name and an unfamiliar one for which they had no name. When the experimenter said, "Show me the blicket," the children selected the object for which they had no name (Markman & Wachtel, 1988). Thus, they mapped the novel label to the novel object. Even 13-month-old infants map a novel label to an object for which they have no name (Woodward, Markman, & Fitzsimmons, 1994).

In addition to their general tendency to map novel words onto novel objects, children pay attention to the *social context* in which language is used, exploiting a

fast mapping the process of rapidly learning a new word simply from the contrastive use of a familiar and an unfamiliar word

pragmatic cues aspects of the social context used for word learning variety of **pragmatic cues** for word learning. For example, children use an adult's focus of attention as a cue to word meaning. In one study by Dare Baldwin (1993), an experimenter showed 18-month-olds two novel objects and then concealed them in separate containers. Next, the experimenter peeked into one of the containers and commented, "There's a modi in here." The adult then removed and gave both objects to the child. When asked for the "modi," the children picked the object that the experimenter had been looking at when saying the label. Thus, the infants used the relation between eye gaze and labeling to learn a novel name for an object before they had ever seen it (see Figure 6.10).

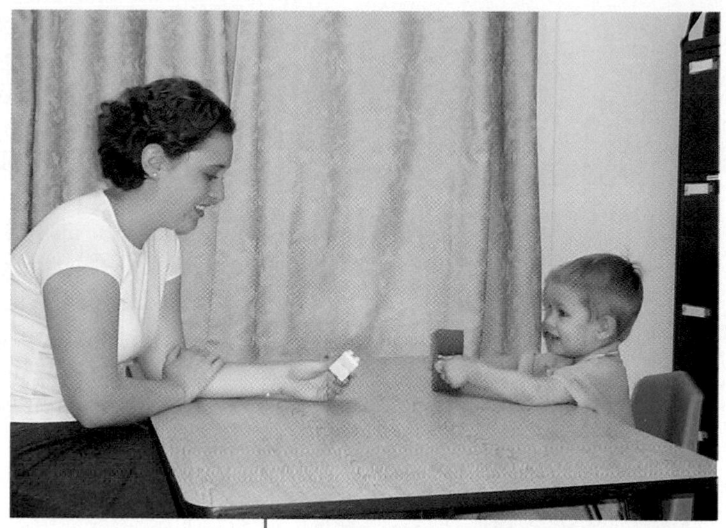
COURTESY OF JUDY DELOACHE

FIGURE 6.10 Pragmatic cues for word learning This child will assume that the novel word the experimenter is saying is the name of the object she is looking at, even if the child is looking at a different object when he hears the word.

Another pragmatic cue that children use to draw inferences about a word's meaning is *intentionality.* For example, in one study, 2-year-olds heard an experimenter announce, "Let's dax Mickey Mouse." The experimenter then performed two actions on a Mickey Mouse doll, one carried out in a coordinated and apparently intentional way, followed by a pleased comment ("There!"), and the other carried out in a clumsy and apparently accidental way, followed by an exclamation of surprise ("Whoops!"). The children interpreted the novel verb *dax* as referring to the action the adult seemed to have intended to do (Tomasello & Barton, 1994). Similarly, 18-month-olds used an adult's emotional response to learn a novel object label (Tomasello, Strosberg, & Akhtar, 1996). After announcing her intention to "find the gazzer," an adult picked up and rejected one object with obvious disappointment and then gleefully seized a second object. The children inferred that the second object was a "gazzer."

In learning new words, young children also use the *linguistic context* in which novel words appear to help infer their meaning. In one of the earliest experiments on language acquisition, Roger Brown (1957) established that the grammatical form of a novel word influences children's interpretation of it. He showed preschool children a picture of a pair of hands kneading a mass of material in a container (Figure 6.11). The picture was described to one group of children as "sibbing," to another as "a sib," and to a third as "some sib." The children subsequently interpreted the new word *sib* as referring to the action, the container, or the material, depending on which grammatical form (verb, count noun, or mass noun) of the word they had heard.

FIGURE 6.11 Linguistic context When Roger Brown, a pioneer in the study of language development, described this picture as "sibbing," "a sib," or "some sib," preschool children made different assumptions about the meaning of "sib." (Brian Kovaleski)

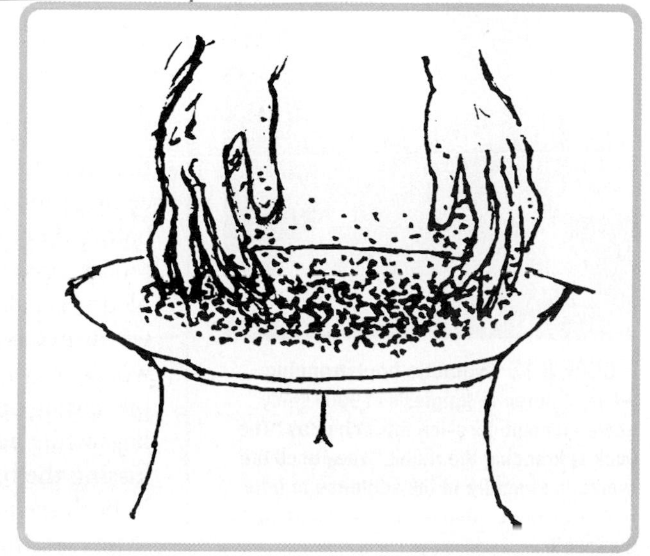

More recent evidence has shown that 2- and 3-year-old children use the grammatical category of novel words to help interpret their meaning (e.g., Hall, Waxman, & Hurwitz, 1993; Markman & Hutchinson, 1984; Waxman, 1990). Hearing "This is a dax" applied to an object, they assume that *dax* refers to that object, as well as to other members of the same category. In contrast, hearing "This is a dax one," they assume that *dax* refers to a property of the object (e.g., its color or texture). These noun-category and adjective-property linkages are made by infants and toddlers (e.g., Waxman & Hall, 1993; Waxman & Markow, 1995, 1998). Thus, children expect words from different grammatical categories to have different types of meanings.

Novel nouns particularly heighten children's attention to shape, possibly because shape is a good cue to category membership.

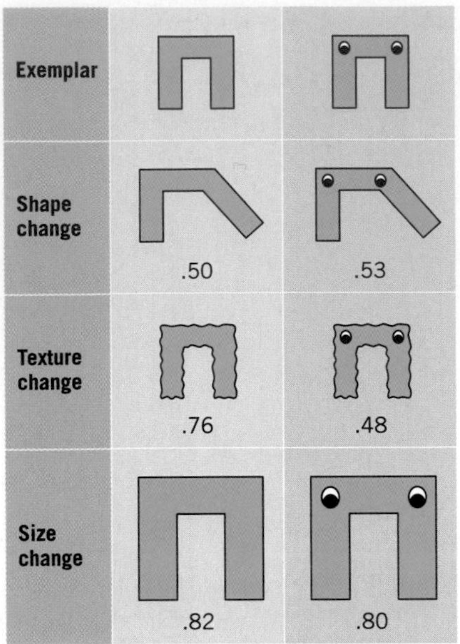

FIGURE 6.12 Shape bias Children are shown the examplar at the top of this figure, and then they are tested to see which of the stimuli below they assume shares the same label as the examplar. The numbers show that the children most often extend a label to objects of the same shape, even if the surface texture or size changes. (Adapted from Landau, Smith, & Jones, 1988)

Children readily extend a novel noun to novel objects of the same shape, even when those objects differ dramatically in size, color, and texture (Landau, Smith, & Jones, 1988; Smith, Jones, & Landau, 1992). Thus, a child who hears a U-shaped wooden block called "a dax" will assume that *dax* also refers to a U-shaped object covered in blue fur or to a U-shaped piece of red wire but not to a wooden block of a different shape (Figure 6.12).

Children also use the grammatical structure of whole sentences to figure out meaning—a strategy referred to as **syntactic bootstrapping** (Fisher, 2000; Fisher, Gleitman, & Gleitman, 1991; Landau & Gleitman, 1985). One demonstration of this phenomenon involved showing 2-year-olds a videotape of a duck using his left hand to push a rabbit down into a squatting position while both animals waved their right arms in circles (Figure 6.13) (Naigles, 1990). (The roles of the rabbit and duck were played by adults in costumes.) As they watched, some children were told, "The duck is kradding the rabbit"; the others were told, "The rabbit and the duck are kradding." All the children then saw two videos side by side, one showing the duck pushing on the rabbit and the other showing both animals waving their arms in the air. Instructed to "Find kradding," the two groups looked at the event that matched the syntax they had heard while watching the initial video. Those who had heard the first sentence had apparently taken "kradding" to mean what the duck had been doing to the rabbit, whereas those who had heard the second sentence thought it meant what both animals had been doing. Thus, the children had arrived at different interpretations for a novel verb depending on the *structure* of the sentence in which it was embedded.

We thus see that infants and young children have a remarkable ability to learn new words as object names. Interestingly, they are equally able to learn nonlinguistic "labels" for objects. Infants between 13 and 18 months of age map gestures or nonverbal sounds (e.g., squeaks and whistles) onto novel objects just as readily as they map words (Namy, 2001; Namy & Waxman, 1998; Woodward & Hoyne, 1999). Later, by 20 to 26 months of age, they accept only words as names.

LETITIA R. NAIGLES, UNIVERSITY OF CONNECTICUT

FIGURE 6.13 Syntactic bootstrapping When children in Naigles's (1990) study heard an adult describe this scene as "The duck is kradding the rabbit," they used the syntactic structure of the sentence to infer that *kradding* is what the duck was doing to the rabbit.

Putting Words Together

A major landmark in early language development is achieved when children start combining some words into sentences, an advance that enables them to express increasingly complex ideas. The degree to which children develop syntax, and the speed with which they do it, is what most distinguishes their language abilities from those of nonhuman primates.

First sentences Most children begin to combine words into simple sentences by the end of their second year. However, in another example of comprehension preceding production, young children know something about word combinations well before they produce any. For example, 12- to 14-month-olds listen longer to sentences whose word order is normal than to sentences whose word order is scrambled (Fernald & McRoberts, 1995). Also, 13- to 15-month-olds appreciate that words in combination carry a meaning distinct from the meaning of the individual words. Kathy Hirsch-Pasek and Roberta Golinkoff (1991) demonstrated this by presenting infants with two videotaped scenes—one of a woman kissing some keys while holding up a ball and the other of the woman holding up the keys while kissing the ball. Thus, the same elements—kissing, keys, and a ball—were present in both scenes. Yet when the infants heard the sentence "She's kissing the keys" or "She's kissing the ball," they looked preferentially at the appropriate scene.

Children's first sentences are two-word combinations; their separate utterances of "More," "Juice," and "Drink" become "More juice" and "Drink juice." These two-word utterances have been described as **telegraphic speech,** because, just as in telegrams, nonessential elements are missing (Brown & Fraser, 1963). Consider the following examples of standard two-word utterances: "Read me," "Mommy tea," "Ride Daddy," "Big pants," "Hurt knee," "All wet," "More boy," "Key door," "Andrew sleep" (Braine, 1976). These primitive sentences do not include a number of elements that would appear in adult utterances, including function words (such as *a, the, in*), auxiliary verbs (*is, was, will, be*), and word endings (indicating plurals, possessives, or verb tenses). Children's early sentences possess this telegraphic quality in languages as diverse as English, Finnish, Luo (Kenya), and Kaluli (New Guinea) (Boysson-Bardies, 1999).

syntactic bootstrapping the strategy of using the grammatical structure of whole sentences to figure out meaning

telegraphic speech the term describing children's first sentences that are generally two-word utterances

For young children learning languages like English, in which word order is crucial for meaning, their early, simple sentences follow a consistent word order: a child might say "Eat cookie" but would be unlikely ever to say "Cookie eat." Many theorists have cited this preservation of correct word order in young children's early utterances as evidence that young children possess grammatical rules similar to those that govern adult speech (e.g., Gleitman, Gleitman, Landau, & Wanner, 1988). Others interpret two-word utterances as governed by grammatical rules, but rules that are unique to the language of children (Bloom, 1970; Braine, 1963). Still others argue that the regularity of early word combinations is simply a matter of children's imitating the order of words they hear in adult speech (Tomasello, 1992).

Many children continue to produce one- and two-word utterances for some time, whereas others quickly move on to three-word and longer sentences. Figure 6.14 shows the rapid increase in the mean length of utterances of three children in Roger Brown's (1973) classic study of language development. As you can see from the figure, Eve started her explosive increase in sentence length much earlier than the other two children did. The length of children's utterances increases in part because they begin to systematically incorporate some of the elements that were missing from their telegraphic speech (deVilliers & deVilliers, 1973). Consider, for example, the sentence "I eating cookies," said by a 2-year-old. A short time before, this child might only have said "Eat cookie" to communicate exactly the same idea. Now, however, three additional elements are present—the first-person pronoun, the *-ing* ending on the verb, and the plural *-s* added to *cookie.* (Sometime soon the child will add the auxiliary verb *am.*)

Once children are capable of producing four-word sentences, typically at around 2½ years of age, they begin to produce complex sentences, that is, sentences that contain more than one clause (Bowerman, 1979): "Can I do it when we get home?" "I want this doll because she's big" (Limber, 1973).

Practice Makes Perfect An important source of children's increasing proficiency at using language is their own hard work. Toddlers actively practice their developing language skills, often in solitary practice

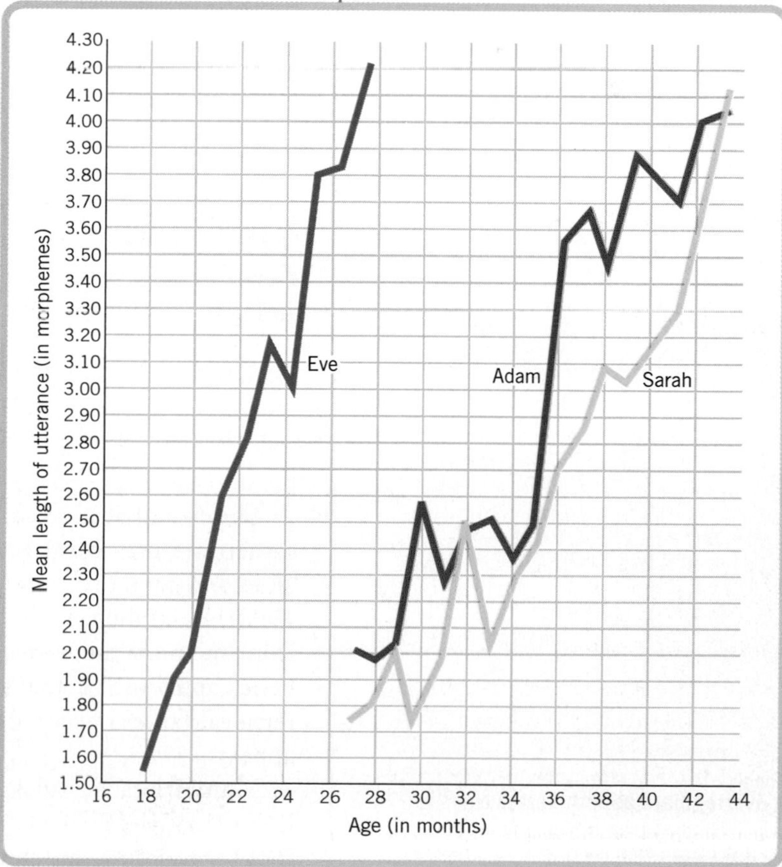

FIGURE 6.14 Length of utterance The relation between age and the mean length of utterance for the three children—Adam, Eve, and Sarah—studied by Roger Brown. (From Brown, 1973)

sessions conducted in their beds before falling asleep. Ruth Weir (1962) recorded the crib talk of her 2½-year-old son in which he explored and practiced a variety of grammatical forms, as in this example:

> Block.
> Yellow block.
> Look at the yellow block.
>
> There is the light.
> Where is the light?
> Here is the light.

Grammatical rules As noted above, there is some debate regarding whether the regularity of toddlers' word order reflects an internalization of grammatical rules. The strongest evidence in support of the idea that young children are learning the grammatical rules of their language comes from their production of word endings. In English, the rules for pluralizing nouns and putting verbs into the past tense are, with some exceptions, highly regular: add *-s* to nouns and *-ed* to verbs. These simple rules suffice for the vast majority of English words.

Young children follow these rules, as was established by a classic experiment by Jean Berko (1958) in which young children were shown a picture of a nonsense animal, which the experimenter referred to as "a wug." Then a picture of two of the creatures was produced, and the experimenter said, "Here are two of them; what are they?" Children as young as 4 readily answered correctly: "Wugs." Thus, these children created the correct plural form for a totally novel word.

Other evidence that is consistent with the idea that children learn rules comes from what they do with words that violate the standard rules. Take the plural of *man* and the past tense of *go,* for example. Children use the correct irregular forms of these words, saying "men" for the plural of *man* and "went" for the past tense of *go.* However, some time after they learn the appropriate regular endings, they start making occasional **overregularization** errors, in which they treat irregular forms as if they were regular. Thus, a child who previously said "men" and "went" now sometimes produces novel forms such as "mans" and "goed," as well as "foots," "feets," "breaked," "broked," and even "branged," and "walkeded" (Berko, 1958; Kuczaj, 1977; Xu & Pinker, 1995). The following dialogue between a 2½-year-old and his father illustrates this kind of error, as well as the difficulty of correcting it:

> *Child:* I used to wear diapers. When I growed up (pause)
> *Father:* When you grew up?
> *Child:* When I grewed up, I wore underpants.
>
> (Clark, 1993)

The fact that a given child sometimes commits overregularization errors and sometimes uses correct irregular word endings led Gary Marcus to propose the "rule and memory" model of children's grammar (Marcus, 1996; Marcus et al., 1992). According to this model, these errors occur when children fail to retrieve from memory the correct form they have learned for a given irregular verb and hence apply the general rule by default. With experience using the language, such retrieval failures occur less frequently, and overregularization errors gradually disappear.

Many syntactic rules have multiple components, and young children master them step by step. One example involves negation. The word *no* is a very useful tool for toddlers, and it accounts for many one-word utterances in children's ear-

overregularization speech errors in which children treat irregular forms of words as if they were regular liest speech. A little later, *no* is frequently combined with one or two other words to express a variety of meanings, including refusal to do something ("No bath"), the nonexistence of something ("No more cookie"), or denial ("No the sun shining") (Klima & Bellugi, 1967). In young children's early negative sentences, the negative term most often occurs at the beginning of the sentence, and the subject is omitted ("No want juice," "No fit") (Klima & Bellugi, 1966). At around the age of 3, children start to incorporate the negative element into the sentence and add appropriate auxiliary verbs, at which point "No want bath" becomes "I don't want a bath."

Another syntactic rule that children begin to acquire quite early in the preschool period and then master step by step involves the interrogative, which is key to their ability to ask questions and hence to get desired information from others. Initially, children simply use rising intonation to convert a statement into a query, as in "I ride train?" At around age 2, children who are learning English start asking "wh" questions, that is, questions that focus on who, what, where, when, and why, as well as how. In their earliest "wh" questions, children simply put the "wh" word at the beginning of an affirmative statement (Klima & Bellugi, 1967), as in the plaintive query listed at the beginning of the chapter—"Why I don't have a dog?" Eventually, children work out the correct question form in English, which requires inverting the subject and verb of the sentence to ask, for example, "Why don't I have a dog?"

Parents play a role in their children's grammatical development, although a more limited one than you might expect. Clearly, they provide a model of grammatically correct speech. In addition, children's grammatical development is facilitated to some extent if their parents frequently fill in missing parts of their children's incomplete utterances (Nelson, Denninger, Bonvillian, Kaplan, & Baker, 1984; Newport et al., 1977), as when a parent responds to a child's "No bed" by saying, "You really don't want to go to bed right now, do you."

One might think that parents also contribute to children's language development by expressly correcting the frequent speech errors their children make. In fact, parents generally ignore even wildly ungrammatical mistakes, accepting sentences such as "I magicked it," "Me no want go," or "I want dessert in front of dinner" (Becker-Bryant & Polkosky, 2001; Brown & Hanlon, 1970). It would be hard to do otherwise, since so much of children's speech is like this. And, as the parent who tried to correct his son's use of "growed" discovered, such efforts are largely futile anyway. Parents do, however, tend to correct some of their children's utterances—their statements that are factually incorrect. Thus, parents are more concerned with the truth of what their children say than with its grammatical correctness.

Learning how to combine words to create interpretable sentences is the crowning achievement in language acquisition. Possibly no linguistic development is more stunning than the progress children make in a few years from simple two-word utterances to complex sentences that conform to the grammatical rules of the child's language. Even their errors reveal an increasingly sophisticated representation of the grammatical structure of their native language. This accomplishment is made all the more impressive by evidence that parental feedback plays a relatively minor role in it.

The child in this cartoon has mastered one of the more difficult aspects of English grammar—the passive voice.

collective monologues young children's talk with one another that often tends to be a series of non sequiturs, with the content of each child's turn having little or nothing to do with what the other child has just said

narratives descriptions of past events that have the basic structure of a story

Conversational Skills

Young children are eager to participate in conversations with others, but their conversational skills initially lag well behind their burgeoning language skills. For one thing, much of very young children's speech is directed to themselves, rather than to another person. Vygotsky (1962) believed that this *private speech* of young children serves an important regulatory function: children talk to themselves as a strategy to organize their actions (Behrend, Rosengren, & Perlmutter, 1992). Private speech often accompanies solitary play, but as much as half of young children's speech in the company of other children or adults is addressed to themselves (Schoeber-Peterson & Johnson, 1991). Gradually, private speech is internalized as thought, and children become capable of mentally organizing their behavior, so they no longer need to talk out loud to themselves.

As noted in Chapter 4, when young children converse with other children, their conversations tend to be egocentric. Piaget (1926) labeled young children's talk with their peers as **collective monologues.** Even when they take turns speaking, their conversations tend to be a series of non sequiturs, with the content of each child's turn having little or nothing to do with what the other child has just said. The following conversation between two American preschoolers gives a good idea of what Piaget observed:

> *Jenny:* My bunny slippers . . . are brown and red and sort of yellow and white. And they have eyes and ears and these noses that wiggle sideways when they kiss.
>
> *Chris:* I have a piece of sugar in a red piece of paper. I'm gonna eat it but maybe it's for a horse.
>
> *Jenny:* We bought them. My mommy did. We couldn't find the old ones. These are like the old ones. They were not in the trunk.
>
> *Chris:* Can't eat the piece of sugar, not unless you take the paper off.
>
> (Stone & Church, 1957, pp. 146–147)

Gradually, children's capacity for sustained conversation increases. In a longitudinal study of parent–child conversations of four children from the age of 21 months to 36 months, Bloom, Rocissano, and Hood (1976) found that the proportion of children's utterances that were on the same topic and added new information to what an adult had just said more than doubled (from around 20% to over 40%). In contrast, the proportion of utterances following an adult's statement that were on unrelated topics fell dramatically (from around 20% to almost 0). With peers, children of this age still have considerable difficulty sustaining a dialogue. The conversations of preschool peers are much longer and more complex when they occur in the context of pretend play, in part because pretense is often based on highly familiar routines, such as cooking or caring for a baby (French, Lucariello, Seidman, & Nelson, 1985; Nelson & Gruendel, 1979).

Parents typically help young children talk about past events.

MYRLEEN FERGUSON CATE / PHOTOEDIT

A particular aspect of young children's conversations that changes dramatically in the preschool period is the extent to which they talk about the past. At most, 3-year-olds' conversations include occasional brief references to past events. In contrast, 5-year-olds produce **narratives**—descriptions of past events that have the basic structure of a story (Miller & Sperry, 1988; Nelson, 1993). One thing that makes longer, more coherent narratives possible is better understanding of the basic structure of stories (Peterson & McCabe, 1988; Shapiro & Hudson, 1991; Stein, 1988).

Parents actively assist their children to develop the ability to produce coherent accounts of past events by providing what has been referred to as *scaffolding* (discussed in Chapter 4) for their children's narratives (Bruner, 1975). An effective way to structure children's conversations about the past is to ask them elaborative questions, that is, questions that enable them to say something—anything—that advances the story:

> *Mother:* And what else happened at the celebrations?
> *Child:* I don't know.
> *Mother:* We did something special with all the other children.
> *Child:* What was it?
> *Mother:* There were a whole lot of people over at the beach, and everyone was doing something in the sand.
> *Child:* What was it?
> *Mother:* Can't you remember what we did in the sand? We were looking for something.
> *Child:* Umm, I don't know.
> *Mother:* We went digging in the sand.
> *Child:* Umm, and that was when um the yellow spade broke.
> *Mother:* Good girl, I'd forgotten that. Yes, the yellow spade broke, and what happened?
> *Child:* Um, we had to um dig with the other end of the yellow bit one.
> *Mother:* That's right. We used the broken bit, didn't we?
> *Child:* Yeah.
>
> (Farrant & Reese, 2002)

The child in this conversation does not actually say much, but the parent's questions help the child think about the event, and the parent also provides a conversational model. Toddlers whose parents scaffold their early conversations by asking useful, elaborative questions produce better narratives on their own a few years later (Fivush, 1991; McCabe & Peterson, 1991; Reese & Fivush, 1993).

We thus see that young children put their burgeoning linguistic skills to good use, becoming more effective communicative partners in conversations with other people. Initially, they still need substantial support from a more competent partner, but their conversational skills increase quite regularly.

Later Development

From 5 or 6 years of age on, children continue to develop language skills, although with less dramatic accomplishments. For example, the ability to sustain a conversation that improved so dramatically in the preschool years continues to improve for many years thereafter. Figure 6.15 shows that, as children get older, their conversational contributions are increasingly often related to the topic under discussion. In addition, the length of their dialogues on a single topic increases substantially (Dorval & Eckerman, 1984). School-age children become increasingly capable of reflecting upon and analyzing language, and they master more complex grammatical rules, such as the use of passive constructions.

One consequence of schoolchildren's more reflective and analytic language skills is their increasing appreciation of the multiple meanings of words, which is responsible for the emergence of the endless series of puns, riddles, and "knock-knock" jokes with which primary school children delight themselves and torture their parents (Ely & McCabe, 1994). They also are able to learn the meaning of new words simply from hearing them defined (Pressley, Levin, & McDaniel, 1987), a factor that

FIGURE 6.15 Conversations become more relevant with age As children get older, their conversational turns become increasingly more related to what the other person has just said.

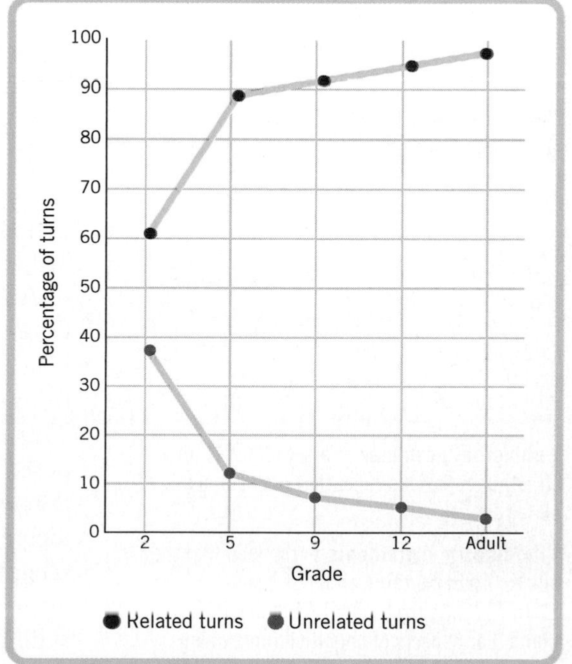

helps their comprehension vocabulary expand—from the 10,000 words that the average 6-year-old knows to the 40,000 words estimated for fifth graders (Anglin, 1993) to the average college-student vocabulary that has been estimated to be as high as 150,000 words (Miller, 1977).

We thus see that by 5 or 6 years of age, children have accomplished a prodigious feat. This accomplishment includes producing the sounds that make up words in their language (phonological development), learning the meaning of thousands of words (semantic development), and mastering the grammatical structure of the language (syntactic development). They have also learned a great deal about the appropriate uses of their language and have become relatively skilled conversationalists (pragmatic development). Theorists of language development have proposed widely varying accounts of this remarkable accomplishment.

Current Theoretical Issues in Language Development

There is virtually universal agreement among language development researchers that children develop language as a result of the interaction between characteristics of the human brain and the language to which they are exposed. Researchers disagree, however, with respect to the relative roles of nature and nurture in language development, the degree to which language acquisition is supported by language-specific versus general-purpose cognitive abilities, and the role of social interaction and communication in language development.

Nativist Views

From Plato and Kant to their modern intellectual descendants, nativists have argued that language is too complex to come from experience alone, so there must be some preexisting, innate structures that enable young humans to acquire it. The most influential modern version of this point of view was advanced by Noam Chomsky (1957, 1959, 1988), a linguist who argues that using a language requires knowledge of a set of highly abstract, unconscious rules. These rules, which Chomsky referred to as **universal grammar,** are common to all languages, and they are what makes it possible for people to learn particular languages. Thus, every language has a set of syntactic rules that people must master in order to learn the language, and people are assisted in learning those rules by their inborn knowledge of the general form that languages can take. Because of this inborn knowledge, children require only minimal input to trigger language development; simply hearing other people use language is enough. Although Chomsky acknowledges that language fulfills a communicative function, he contends that this function has little to do with the nature of language or how it is acquired.

According to the nativist view, the cognitive abilities that support language development are highly specific to language. As Steven Pinker (1994) describes it, language is "a distinct piece of the biological makeup of our brains . . . distinct from more general abilities to process information or behave intelligently" (p. 18). This claim is taken one step further by the **modularity hypothesis,** which proposes that the human brain contains an innate, self-contained language module that is separate from other aspects of cognitive functioning (Fodor, 1983). The idea of specialized mental modules is not limited to language. As you learned in Chapter 4 and will see again in Chapter 7, innate, special-purpose modules have been proposed to underlie a variety of functions, including perception, spatial skills, and social understanding.

universal grammar a set of highly abstract, unconscious rules that are common to all languages

modularity hypothesis the idea that the human brain contains an innate, self-contained language module that is separate from other aspects of cognitive functioning

Nativist views of language development are supported by the fact that virtually all children exposed to full-fledged language acquire it, and no other animals do. Demonstrations of critical periods for language development, as well as specific links between brain structures and language abilities, are generally taken as supportive of the nativist position. Probably the strongest support for the idea that children come equipped with some fundamental knowledge of linguistic rules is the research reviewed in Box 6.3 on the invention of sign languages by groups of deaf children with no linguistic input from adults. The fact that these children spontaneously imposed grammatical structure onto their simple sign systems suggests preexisting structural knowledge, especially because aspects of the grammatical system that some of these children invented match that of some existing spoken languages.

The views of Chomsky and other nativists have been criticized for many things, especially for the idea of a universal grammar common to all languages (Maratsos, 1998; Slobin, 1985). They have also been criticized for focusing almost exclusively on syntactic development while ignoring the importance of the communicative role of language, and for proposing that language acquisition is supported by special language-specific mechanisms.

Interactionist Views

According to interactionist views, virtually everything about language development is influenced by its communicative function. To begin with, children are motivated to interact with others, to communicate their own thoughts and feelings, and to understand what other people are trying to communicate to them (Bloom, 1991; Bloom & Tinker, 2001; Snow, 1999). By paying close attention to the multitude of clues available in the language they hear and the social context in which language is used, children gradually discover the underlying regularities in language and its use.

In a strong version of this general view, Michael Tomasello and his colleagues argue that language is basically a social skill (Carpenter, Nagell, & Tomasello, 1998; Tomasello, 1995). The formal structural properties of language that Chomsky believed to be innate are instead mastered in the process of learning to communicate with other people; and language itself is properly thought of as a set of social conventions that enable people to communicate.

Interactionist theories are supported by the basic fact that the main (although not the only) purpose to which infants and young children apply their steadily increasing language skills is communicating with other people. The rapidly accumulating evidence of the remarkable sensitivity of infants and young children to a host of pragmatic cues and their ability to use even quite subtle aspects of the social context to interpret utterances are also consistent with this view. Evidence that undermines the claim for language-specific learning mechanisms supports this position. This includes the non-language-specific nature of categorical perception of speech sounds discussed earlier, as well as the fact that infants and young children accept nonverbal sounds or gestures as labels for objects just as readily as they accept speech sounds.

Critics of the interactionist position contend that even the most diligent attention to language and its accompanying behavior could never reveal the complex, abstract grammatical principles emphasized by Chomsky and other nativists. In this regard, they note that the very impressive demonstrations of infants' and young children's sensitivity to pragmatic cues cited by interactionists have involved semantic (word-learning) development rather than what they see as the more challenging problem of syntactic development.

a closer look

"I Just Can't Talk Without My Hands": What Gestures Tell Us About Language

Most people around the world spontaneously accompany their speech with gestures (Goldin-Meadow, 1999). The naturalness of gesturing is revealed by the fact that blind people gesture as they speak just as much as sighted individuals do, even when they know their listener is also blind (Iverson & Goldin-Meadow, 1998).

The intricate connection between gesture and speech has led some theorists to argue that human speech actually evolved from gesture (Corballis, 1999). Bipedalism, which emerged at least 4 million years ago, left the hands and arms free for purposes other than locomotion. The suggestion is that this freedom allowed a communication system based on gesture to develop and that this gesture system, capitalizing on changes in the structure of the vocal tract and the brain, later evolved into spoken language.

Turning from the development of the species to the development of individual children, we find that recognizable gestures often appear before recognizable spoken words. According to Linda Acredolo and Susan Goodwyn (1990), many "baby signs" are invented by children themselves. One participant in their research signed "alligator" by putting her hands together and opening and closing them to imitate snapping jaws; another indicated "dog" by sticking her tongue out as if panting; another signaled "flower" by sniffing. Some infants apparently have the cognitive capacity for referring to objects and events but have better motor control of their hands and bodies than of their vocal apparatus. Encouraging the use of referential gestures can have a positive impact on early language learning. Children whose parents taught them a set of baby signs when they were 11 months old had larger verbal vocabularies, both in comprehension and production, at 3 years of age (Goodwyn, Acredolo, & Brown, 2000).

SUSAN GOODWYN

This young participant in the research of Acredolo and Goodwyn is producing her idiosyncratic "baby sign" for pig.

Even more dramatic evidence of intimate connections between gesture and language comes from research on children who have *created* their own gesture-based languages. Susan Goldin-Meadow and her colleagues (Feldman, Goldin-Meadow, & Gleitman, 1978; Goldin-Meadow & Mylander, 1998) studied congenitally deaf American and Chinese children whose hearing parents had little or no proficiency in any formal sign language. These children and their parents made up "home signs" in order to communicate with one another. However, the children's gesture vocabulary quickly outstripped that of their parents. More important, the children, but not the parents, spontaneously imposed a structure—a rudimentary grammar—on their gestures. Both groups of children used a grammatical structure that occurs in some languages but not in either the English or Mandarin languages of their parents. As a

Connectionist Views

At the opposite end of the theoretical continuum from the nativist view are connectionist, or neural-network, accounts of language development (e.g., Bates & Elman, 1993). According to these accounts, the information needed to acquire language is contained in the language itself. Children do not need innate linguistic knowledge or special language-specific mechanisms to notice and learn the many statistical regularities in the speech they hear. Instead, language development is assumed to be based primarily on general-purpose learning mechanisms: it occurs as the result of the gradual strengthening of connections in the neural network.

This view is consistent with the speech-perception research described earlier, documenting young infants' impressive ability to analyze and identify structural features of the language they hear. In addition, connectionists have offered an influential alternative account of overregularization errors. Like connectionist analy-

6.3

result, the sign systems of the children were more similar to each other than to those of their own parents. The children's signs were also more complex than those of their parents.

The tendency of deaf children to spontaneously systematize inconsistent input from others has been reported by other researchers as well (Singleton & Newport, in press). A particularly extensive look at this phenomenon has been provided by a large-scale education program for the deaf begun in the Central American nation of Nicaragua in 1979 (Senghas & Coppola, 2001). When the program was initiated, hundreds of deaf children were brought together in two schools in the city of Managua. For most of the children, it was their first exposure to other deaf youngsters. The teachers in the school knew no formal sign language, nor did the children, who had only the simple home signs they had used to communicate with their families. The children quickly began to build on one another's existing informal signs, constructing a "pidgin" sign language—a relatively crude, limited communication system.

What happened next was even more intriguing. As younger students entered the schools, they rapidly transformed the rudimentary system used by the older students into a complex, fully consistent grammar, which came to be known as the Idioma de Signos Nicaraguense (ISN). The most fluent signers today are those who entered the schools at a young age after ISN had become highly sophisticated. Anselmo, a young man who was 7 years old when he first began attending one of the schools, summed up the life-transforming effect that acquiring a functional language had on his life: "I can remember my childhood, but I can also remember not having any way to communicate. Then my mind was just a blank." (quoted in Osborne, 1999, p. 89)

In addition to being an inherently fascinating story, these reports of language-inventing deaf children are of great theoretical significance. The fact that children go beyond the linguistic input they receive, spontaneously refining and systematizing their language, offers support for nativist claims of innate grammatical knowledge.

SUSAN MEISELAS / MAGNUM PHOTOS, INC.

Nicaraguan deaf children signing together in the language invented in their school.

ses of other phenomena (see Chapter 4, p. 151), this account is based on computer models of neural networks that have the capacity to modify themselves as a result of input. The model network is provided with a large body of language input similar to what children are exposed to in order to see if the network eventually produces output that simulates the speech of real children. One of the most successful models to date focuses on the acquisition of the past tense. From input of large numbers of English sentences with regular and irregular verbs, neural-network models can learn to form the past tense correctly. In the process, the models make the same kinds of overregularization errors that children make (Rumelhart & McClelland, 1986). Thus, with little built-in (innate) grammatical knowledge and no language-specific learning mechanisms, these models can learn from experience, and the course of their learning can look surprisingly similar to that of young children.

Although connectionist accounts have achieved impressive success with respect to modeling a few specific aspects of language development, such as the past tense in English, most aspects of language acquisition have yet to be modeled. In addition, connectionist models are always open to criticism regarding the features that were built into the models in the first place and how well the input provided to them matches the input from which children induce the structure of their language.

review:

The process of acquiring language is very complex, involving development of many different kinds of knowledge and skills that underlie the comprehension and production of language, whether spoken or signed. In the space of a few years, children take giant steps in mastering the phonology, semantics, syntax, and pragmatics of their native language. This remarkable achievement is made possible by the joint prerequisites of a human brain and exposure to human communication. The current theoretical accounts of language development differ with respect to how much emphasis they put on nature and nurture. Nativists like Chomsky and Pinker clearly emphasize innate linguistic knowledge and language-specific learning mechanisms, whereas connectionists argue that language learning can emerge from general-purpose learning mechanisms. Interactionists place particular emphasis on the communicative function of language and children's motivation to understand and interact with other people. The vast literature on language development provides some support for all of these views, but none of them provide the full story of children's acquisition of the "jewel in the crown of cognition."

Nonlinguistic Symbols and Development

Although language is our preeminent symbol system, humans have invented a wealth of other kinds of symbols to communicate with one another. Virtually anything can serve as a nonlinguistic symbol so long as someone intends it to stand for something other than itself (DeLoache, 1995). The list of symbols you regularly encounter is long and varied, ranging from the printed words, numbers, graphs, photographs, and drawings in your textbooks to thousands of everyday items such as TV, movies, computer icons, maps, clocks, and so on. Because symbols are so central to our everyday lives, as discussed in Box 6.4, mastering the various symbol systems important in their culture is a crucial developmental task for all children.

Symbolic proficiency involves both the mastery of the symbolic creations of others and the creation of new symbolic representations. We will first discuss early symbolic functioning, starting with research on very young children's ability to exploit the informational content of symbolic artifacts. Then we will focus on children's creation of symbols through pretend play and drawing. In Chapter 8, we will examine development in older children of two of the most important of all symbolic activities—reading and mathematics.

Using Symbols as Information

One of the vital functions of many symbols is that they provide useful information. For example, a map—whether a crude pencil sketch on the back of an envelope or a multicolor map in an expensive world atlas—can be crucial for locating a

applications 6.4

Digital Development

> Across the world there is a passionate love affair between children and computers.... They seem to know that in a deep way [computer technology] already belongs to them. They know they can master it more easily and more naturally than their parents. They know they are the computer generation.
>
> (Papert, 1996, p. 000)

Children in many contemporary societies are spending increasing amounts of time in front of flickering screens. Although television has long taken up many hours of youngsters' time, computers and video games rival the "boob tube" as daily preoccupations. National surveys in the United States, for example, indicate that children between 2 and 17 years of age who have access to computers and video games spend 4 to 5 hours a day in front of some kind of screen. A peak of nearly 6 hours a day comes between the ages of 8 and 13 (Roberts, Foehr, Rideout & Brodie, 1999; Stanger & Gridina, 1999).

What is the impact of the time children spend with these new technologies? As with every new technology, a great deal of public attention has focused on both the potential benefits and perils associated with children's deep immersion in the digital age. With respect to computers, many believe that they are an important educational resource for children, especially for doing their homework. Although there has been relatively little research on whether home computer use improves school achievement, the results of several studies are encouraging, suggesting that it may very well be helpful (Subrahmanyam, Kraut, Greenfield, & Gross, 2000). (At the same time, however, research has revealed that the predominant computer activity for children is playing games [Subrahmanyam et al., 2000].)

There is also evidence that some kinds of video games may have specific cognitive benefits. In one study, 10- and 11-year-olds practiced a video game in which they used a joystick to guide a marble along a grid, preventing the marble from falling and protecting it from attacks by intruders. Afterward, they showed enhanced performance on a test of spatial skills that involved visualizing and mentally manipulating images (Subrahmanyam & Greenfield, 1994).

Whatever its possible benefits, children's extensive involvement with computers and video games has raised a number of concerns. The child who is glued to a computer screen or video game is not out playing in the park or otherwise engaging in robust physical activity. The sedentary nature of computer use, like television watching, is believed to contribute to the current epidemic of obesity in the United States. (Ironically, the single form of exercise provided by extensive video game playing has produced a unique physical syndrome dubbed "nintendinitis"—a form of painful tendonitis in the thumb resulting from repeated button pressing [Brasington, 1990].)

Particular concerns have been expressed about the solitary nature of children's home computer and video game use and the possibility that it may rob them of time with friends. Consistent with these concerns, around 20% of children in the United States between ages 8 and 18 have a computer in their bedroom, and more than 60% of the time they spend logged onto the computer is spent alone (Roberts et al., 1999). However, some recent evidence may help allay some of these concerns about social deprivation. For one thing, much of the time that children spend on the computer is devoted to interpersonal communication via the Internet. Second, research indicates that moderate video game playing seems to have no significant impact on children's social skills and interactions. In fact, computer games can actually bring together peers and family members who enjoy playing the same games (Colwell, Grady, & Rhiati, 1995; Mitchell, 1985).

Another serious area of concern centers on the possibility that computers will further exacerbate important social problems. In Chapters 9 and 14, we will review issues having to do with the effects of media violence on aggression in children and with the possibility of a gender gap in computer skills.

An equally important issue is the fear that unequal access to computers may deepen existing socioeconomic inequalities (see Becker, 2000). As of a U.S. census survey published in 1998, only 22% of children in families with annual incomes under $20,000 had access to a computer at home. In contrast, over 91% of children in families with incomes of more than $75,000 had at least one home computer. However, having a computer is only part of the story. Higher-SES families are more likely to have newer, more powerful computers and to have more than one of them. Thus, children from lower-SES families are far less likely to be able to use computers to do homework, to use the Internet, or to play sophisticated games. The disparity in access to computers is less extreme at school, where computers are used extensively in classrooms in low-SES neighborhoods. However, teachers in high-SES schools tend to make more creative and innovative use of classroom computers. In sum, the picture on this issue is rather dismal: the digital divide between children from wealthier and poorer families is very wide, and may be growing even wider.

FELICIA MARTINEZ / PHOTOEDIT

An ardent member of the computer generation.

ALL: COURTESY OF JUDY DELOACHE

FIGURE 6.16 Scale model task In a test of young children's ability to use a symbol as a source of information, a 3-year-old child watches as the experimenter (Judy DeLoache) hides a miniature troll doll under a pillow in a scale model of an adjacent room. The child searches successfully for a larger troll doll hidden in the corresponding place in the actual room, indicating that she appreciates the relation between the model and room. The child also successfully retrieves the small toy she originally observed being hidden in the model.

particular place. To use a symbolic artifact such as a map requires **dual representation;** that is, the artifact must be represented mentally in two ways at the same time, as a real object and as a symbol for something other than itself (DeLoache, 1995, 2000). Thus, to exploit the wealth of symbolic artifacts important in the daily lives of residents of modern Western societies, children must become adept at achieving dual representation.

Very young children can have substantial difficulty with dual representation, limiting their ability to use information from symbolic artifacts (DeLoache, 1987, 2001). This has been demonstrated by research in which a young child watches as an experimenter hides a miniature toy in a scale model of a regular-size room next door (Figure 6.16). The child is then asked to find a larger version of the toy that the child is told "is hiding in the same place in the big room." Three-year-olds readily use their knowledge of the location of the miniature toy in the model to figure out where the large toy is in the room. In contrast, most 2½-year-old children fail to find the large toy; they seem to have no idea that the model tells them anything about the room. Perhaps because the model is so salient and interesting as a three-dimensional object, very young children have trouble managing dual representation and fail to notice the symbolic relation between the model and the room it stands for.

This interpretation received strong support in a study in which dual representation was not necessary to reason between a model and a larger space (DeLoache, Miller, & Rosengren, 1997). An experimenter showed 2½-year-old children a "shrinking machine" (really an oscilloscope with lots of dials and lights) and told them that the machine could "make things get little." They watched as a troll doll was hidden in a movable tentlike room (approximately 8 feet by 6 feet) and the shrinking machine was "turned on." Then the children and experimenter waited in another room while the shrinking machine worked. When they returned, a scale model of the tentlike room stood in place of the original. (Assistants had, of course, removed the original tent and replaced it with the scale model.) When asked to find the troll, the children succeeded.

Why should the idea of a shrinking machine enable these 2½-year-olds to do better? The answer is that if the child believes the experimenter's claims about the shrinking machine, then in the child's mind the model simply *is* the room. Hence, there is no symbolic relation between the two spaces and no need for dual representation.

The difficulty that young children have with dual representation and symbols is evident in other contexts as well. For example, investigators often use anatomically detailed dolls to interview young children in cases of suspected sexual abuse, assuming that the relation between the doll and themselves would be obvious. However, children younger than 5 years of age often fail to make any self–doll connection, so the use of a doll does not improve their memory reports and may even make them less reliable (Bruck, Ceci, Francoeur, & Renick, 1995; DeLoache & Marzolf, 1995; DeLoache & Smith, 1999; Goodman & Aman, 1990).

Increasing ability to achieve dual representation—to immediately interpret a symbol in terms of what it stands for—enables children to discover the abstract nature of various symbolic artifacts. For example, unlike younger children, school-age children realize that the red line on a road map does not mean that the real road will also be red (Liben, 1999). Older children are also able, when properly instructed, to use objects such as rods and blocks of different sizes that represent different numerical quantities to help them learn to do mathematical operations (Uttal, Liu, & DeLoache, 1999).

dual representation the idea that the use of a symbolic artifact can only be achieved if it is represented mentally in two ways at the same time: both as a real object and as a symbol for something other than itself

pretend play make-believe activities in which children often create new symbolic relations—for example, using a broom to represent a horse

object substitution a form of pretense in which an object is used as something other than itself

Pretend Play

In **pretend play,** children often create new symbolic relations. Initially, children simply pretend to engage in familiar activities, sometimes using realistic toys or real objects. For example, a child might lay her head down and close her eyes, making-believe she is asleep, or she might talk animatedly into a toy telephone. Most researchers place the emergence of true *symbolic play* at around 18 months of age, when children become capable of creating temporary symbols by using one object "as if" it were something other than itself: a banana serves as a telephone receiver, a broom becomes a horse (Huttenlocher & Higgins, 1978; McCune, 1995; Ungerer, Zelazo, Kearsley, & O'Leary, 1981). In performing such **object substitutions,** children mentally "decouple" the object's real attributes so that they can pretend it is something else. Most of the real features of the banana are ignored in order to pretend to talk into it (Leslie, 1987).

Toddlers' pretend play becomes increasingly complex as they begin to combine a series of different pretend actions into a reasonably coherent scenario and begin to coordinate their own symbolic play with that of others. Consider, for example, "tea party" rituals in which a child and parent "pour tea" for each other from an imaginary teapot, daintily "sip" it, "eat" imaginary cookies and comment on how very delicious they are, and so on. Young children's pretend play is typically more sophisticated when they are playing with a parent or older sibling who can scaffold the play sequence than when they are pretending with a peer (Farver & Wimbarti, 1995; Tamis-LeMonda & Bornstein, 1994; Zukow-Goldring, 1995).

Even as their pretense becomes highly skilled and sophisticated, children only gradually come to appreciate the role of the mind in pretending. In research related to the theory-of-mind perspective, discussed in Chapter 4, Angeline Lillard (1998) has investigated children's understanding of pretense by showing children age 4 and older a puppet named Moe who is made to hop around as the experimenter comments, "Look, Moe is hopping just like a kangaroo." Then children are also told other things about Moe, such as, "Moe doesn't know anything about kangaroos" or "Moe isn't thinking about kangaroos right now." The children are then asked, "Is Moe *pretending* to be a kangaroo?" Most 4- and 5-year-olds respond that Moe is indeed pretending, basing their judgment on his actions rather than his mental state and revealing an incomplete understanding of the mental basis of pretense. Understanding that pretending is primarily a mental activity develops gradually and is not fully in place until around age 9.

LAURA DWIGHT

Parents often engage in pretend play with their young children. In a favorite play ritual—the "tea party"—mother and child eat imaginary cookies and sip nonexistent tea.

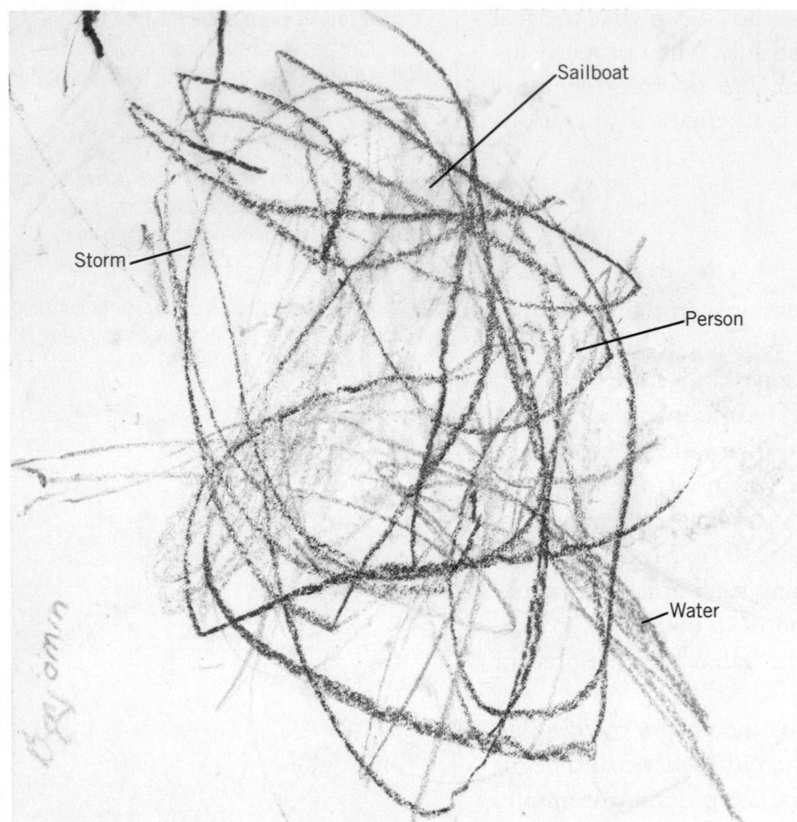

FIGURE 6.17 Early drawing Appearances to the contrary, this is not random scribbling, as shown by what the 2-year-old who produced it said about his work. As he drew the triangular shape, he said it was a "sailboat." A set of wavy lines was labeled "water." Some scribbled lines under the "sailboat" were denoted as the "person driving the boat." Finally, the wild scribbles drawn over the rest were "a storm." Thus, each element was representational to some degree, even though the picture as a whole was not.

Drawing

Drawing pictures is a common symbolic activity that parents in many societies encourage their children to undertake. When young children first start making marks on paper, their focus is almost exclusively on the activity per se, with no attempt to produce recognizable images. At around 3 or 4 years or age, most children begin trying to draw pictures *of* something; they try to produce representational art.

Children's artistic ideas often outstrip their motor and planning capabilities (Yamagata, 1997). Figure 6.17 shows what at first appears simply to be a classic scribble. However, thc 2½-year-old artist was narrating his efforts as he drew, and a recording of what he said makes it clear that he represented each of the individual elements of his picture reasonably well but was unable to coordinate them spatially on the paper.

The most common subject for young children is the human figure. Just as infants who are first beginning to speak simplify the words they produce, young children simplify their drawings of the human figure, as shown in Figure 6.18. Note that to produce these very crude, simple shapes, the child must plan the drawing and must spatially coordinate the individual elements. Even children's early "tadpole" people have the legs on the bottom and the arms on the side. Gradually, additional elements are incorporated, typically starting with a body drawn beneath the circle that now represents only a head.

Figure 6.19 reveals some of the strategies children use to produce more complex pictures. The child in this case has drawn quite a complex picture, including his home, his school, the road in between them, and four other homes along the road. One strategy he used was to rely on a well-practiced formula for representing houses: a pentagon with a door and roof line. Another was to coordinate the placement of each house with respect to the road, although at the cost of the overall coordination among the houses. Eventually, some children become highly skilled at representing the relations among the multiple elements in their pictures.

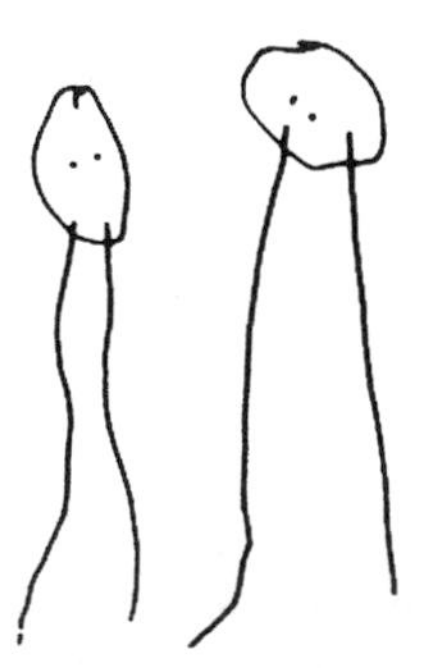

FIGURE 6.18 Tadpole drawings Young children's early drawings of people typically take this "tadpole" form. (From Goodnow, 1977)

FIGURE 6.19 More complex drawings This child's drawing relies on some well-practiced strategies, but the child has not yet worked out how to represent complex spatial relationships. (From Goodnow, 1977)

A particularly interesting case of early talent is Nadia, an autistic child who drew the first horse in Figure 6.20 at the age of 4. Her extraordinary drawing ability coexisted with very poor language and motor skills, and declined with age (see the second horse). Researchers have been particularly interested in autistic individuals who, like Nadia, have exceptional artistic abilities (Selfe, 1995), in part because of the relevance of these rare cases to the modularity hypothesis introduced earlier. Such extraordinary drawing talent amid general mental retardation is suggestive of an encapsulated ability that is unaffected by general intellectual and other deficits. These cases provide only modest support for the modularity hypothesis, however, because autistics' drawing skill may also arise from the obsessive attention to detail observed in many autistic individuals.

(a)

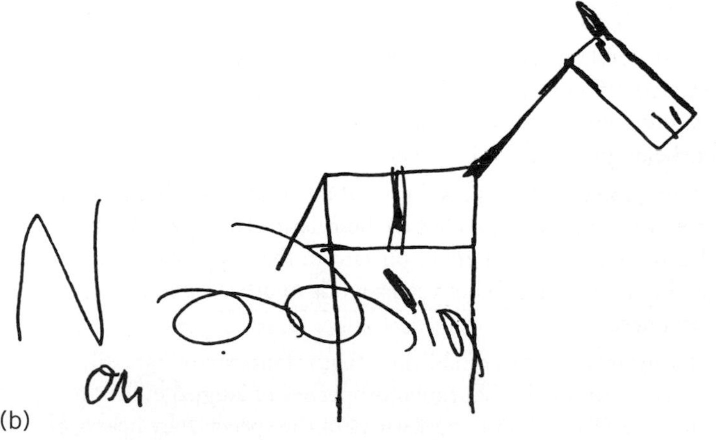

(b)

FIGURE 6.20 Autistics' artistry (a) Nadia, an autistic child with extraordinary artistic ability, became famous for drawings such as this one, made when she was 4 years of age. (b) By the age of 25, Nadia's former talent was no longer evident. (From Selfe, 1995)

review:

Nonlinguistic symbols play an important role in the lives of young children. Young children become increasingly sensitive to the informational potential of symbolic objects created by others, an important step toward skillful use of the many symbol systems that are critical to modern life. In most, but not all, societies, children create novel symbol–referent relations in the course of symbolic play. Symbolic creativity is also evident in the products of young artists.

Chapter Summary

A critical feature of what it means to be human is the creative and flexible use of a variety of language and other symbols. The enormous power of language comes from generativity—the fact that a finite set of words can be used to generate an infinite number of sentences.

Language Development

- Acquiring a language involves learning the complex system of phonological, semantic, syntactic, and pragmatic rules that govern the sounds, meaning, grammatical structure, and use of the language. The only exception is that sign languages employ gestures rather than sounds as elementary units.
- Language ability is species-specific; the first prerequisite for its full-fledged development is a human brain, areas of which are specialized for the comprehension and production of language. Researchers have succeeded in teaching nonhuman primates remarkable symbolic skills but not full-fledged language.
- The first few years of human life constitute a critical period for language acquisition; people who learn a language after childhood are never as skilled as those who learn it earlier.
- A second prerequisite for language development is a human environment. All hearing children receive an enormous amount of language input. Much of it comes in the special way in which adults and older children in most societies talk to babies. Infant-directed speech (IDS) differs in many ways from speech addressed to older individuals, being marked by higher pitch; extremes in intonation; warm, affectionate tone; and exaggerated facial expressions.
- Remarkable speech-perception abilities have been demonstrated in infants. Like adults, infants exhibit categorical perception of speech sounds, perceiving physically similar sounds as belonging to discrete categories.
- Young infants are actually better than adults at discriminating between speech sounds not in their native language. As they learn the sounds that are important in that language, their ability to distinguish between sounds in other languages declines.
- Recent research has established that infants are remarkably sensitive to the distributional properties of language; they notice a variety of subtle regularities in the speech they hear and use these regularities to pick out words from the passing stream of speech.
- From their first months, babies are preparing for speech production by making a variety of sounds, steadily gaining motor control over these vocalizations. Infants begin to babble at around 7 months of age. Hearing infants produce sounds like "bababa"; and some deaf infants who are exposed to sign language produce hand movements with the same sort of repetitive pattern. Gradually, vocal babbling begins to sound more like the baby's native language.
- The second half of an infant's first year is also characterized by learning how to interact and communicate with other people, including the ability to establish joint attention with another person by following the direction of that person's gaze or pointing to direct someone else's attention so a topic can be shared.
- Word recognition (associating highly familiar words with their referents) begins to emerge at about 6 months of age.
- The production of recognizable words begins at around 1 year of age. In the holophrastic period, young children say only one word at a time. With their severely limited vocabularies, they often make overextension errors, using a particular word in a broader context than is appropriate.
- At around 18 months of age, a "vocabulary explosion" occurs, as children start learning new words at a very rapid pace. Aided by adults or by their own efforts, they rely on a variety of assumptions and strategies to figure out what the new words mean.
- By the end of their second year, most infants produce short sentences, often described as telegraphic speech because only the most important words are included. The length and complexity of their utterances gradually increase, and they spontaneously practice their emerging linguistic skills.
- There is ongoing debate about whether toddlers' ability to follow regular word order (in languages like English where word order is crucial to meaning) reflects an innate knowledge of grammatical rules.
- At around 4 years of age, English-speaking children make overregularization errors, in which they treat irregular forms as if they were regular. These errors have often been taken as evidence of rule learning. Further grammatical development involves learning negative and interrogative forms.
- Children develop their burgeoning language skills as they go from collective monologues to sustained conversation—the ability to tell coherent narratives about their experiences.
- Virtually all current theories of language development acknowledge that it involves an interaction between innate factors and experience. Among these theories are nativist, interactionist, and connectionist views.
- Nativists, such as the influential linguist Noam Chomsky, posit innate knowledge of universal grammar, the set of highly abstract rules common to all languages. They believe that language learning is supported by language-specific skills.
- Interactionist theorists emphasize the communicative context of language development and use. They emphasize the impressive degree to which infants and young children use a host of pragmatic cues to figure out what others are saying.

- Connectionists fall at the other end of the theoretical continuum from nativists, arguing that language can develop in the absence of innate knowledge and that language learning requires only powerful general-purpose cognitive mechanisms—that is, that such learning occurs as a result of gradual strengthening of connections in the neural network.

Nonlinguistic Symbols and Development

- Symbolic artifacts like maps or models require dual representation. To use them, children must represent mentally both the object itself as well as its symbolic relation to what it stands for. Toddlers become increasingly skillful at achieving dual representation and using symbolic artifacts as a source of information.
- Young children create symbolic relations through their pretend play. The complexity of this play increases during the preschool years. Only gradually, however, do children come to understand the role of the mind in pretense.
- Drawing is a symbolic activity commonly engaged in by children and encouraged by adults. Young children's early scribbling quickly gives way to the intention to draw pictures *of* something, with a favorite theme being representations of the human figure.
- Developmentalists are interested in the rare cases of autistic children with remarkable artistic skill, in part because of the relevance of these children's isolated skills to the modularity hypothesis. Such skill, however, may also arise from the obsession with detail observed in many autistic individuals.

Critical Thinking Questions

1. Drawing on the many references to parental behaviors relevant to language development that were discussed in this chapter, give some examples of ways parents are known to influence their children's language development.
2. Language development is a particularly complex aspect of child development, and no single theory accounts successfully for all that is known about how children acquire language. Which of the three theoretical views that were presented seem to you to do the best job of explaining what you learned about language development in this chapter?
3. Imagine that you are the director of a day-care center for infants and toddlers. A couple comes to your center seeking to enroll their 1-year-old, who has been deaf since birth. What would you want to know about how these parents interact with their child at home? If you decided to accept the child into your center, what practices would be important to introduce into the center to provide for this child?
4. Many parallels were drawn between the process of language acquisition in children learning spoken and in those learning signed languages. What do these similarities tell us about the basis for human language?

Key Terms

symbols, p. 210
language comprehension, p. 211
language production, p. 211
generativity, p. 211
phonemes, p. 212
phonological development, p. 212
morphemes, p. 212
semantic development, p. 212
syntax, p. 212
syntactic development, p. 212
pragmatic development, p. 212
metalinguistic knowledge, p. 212
critical period, p. 215
bilingualism, p. 217
infant-directed speech (IDS), p. 218
prosody, p. 219
categorical perception, p. 220
voice onset time (VOT), p. 220
distributional properties, p. 223
intersubjectivity, p. 225
joint attention, p. 225
reference, p. 226
holophrastic period, p. 227
style, p. 228
referential (analytic) style, p. 228
expressive (holistic) style, p. 228
wait-and-see style, p. 228
overextension, p. 228
fast mapping, p. 230
pragmatic cues, p. 231
syntactic bootstrapping, p. 232
telegraphic speech, p. 233
overregularization, p. 234
collective monologues, p. 236
narratives, p. 236
universal grammar, p. 238
modularity hypothesis, p. 238
dual representation, p. 244
pretend play, p. 245
object substitution, p. 245

CHAPTER 7

Conceptual Development

CHRISTIAN PIERRE / SUPERSTOCK

CHRISTIAN PIERRE, *Miracle of Life,* 1996

Imagine the following scene. Shawna, a 10-month-old, crawls into her 7-year-old brother's bedroom. The room contains many objects: a bed, a dresser, a chair, a dog walking around, a fish tank, a CD player, a receiver, speakers, a baseball, a baseball mitt, books, magazines, shoes, dirty socks, and other things. Shawna's brother possesses such concepts as furniture, clothing, reading material, sports equipment, and animals that help him understand what he sees in his room. But what does the room look like to Shawna? Babies don't have concepts of furniture, reading material, sports equipment, and the like, so the room would seem very different to her than it would to an older child. What concepts would Shawna have? Would she have concepts of living and nonliving things that would help her understand why the dog runs around on its own but the books never do, or would this difference seem strange? Would she have concepts of heavier and lighter that would allow her to understand why she could pick up a sock but not a chair, or would that be a mystery? And how would Shawna's concepts differ from those she had earlier in infancy and those she will acquire in the next few years?

As this hypothetical scene indicates, concepts are crucial for enabling people to make sense of the world. But what exactly are concepts, and how do they help us understand?

Concepts are general ideas or understandings that can be used to group together objects, events, qualities, or abstractions that are similar in some way. There are an infinite number of possible concepts, because there are infinite ways in which objects or events can be similar. For example, objects can have similar functions (e.g., all cups are for drinking), shapes (e.g., all football fields are rectangular), materials (e.g., all diamonds are made of compressed carbon), sizes (e.g., all giants are large), tastes (e.g., all Cokes taste sweet), and so on.

Concepts help us simplify the world and act effectively in it by allowing us to use our prior experience to interpret new situations. If we like the taste of one carrot, we probably will like the taste of others. Concepts also tell us how to react emotionally to new experiences, as when we exercise caution with all unfamiliar dogs after being bitten by one. Life without concepts would be unthinkable; every situation would be new, and we would have no idea what past experience was relevant in the new situation.

As surprising as it may seem, infants form concepts from the first months of life. But how are they able to do so? Having read Chapters 4, 5, and 6, you already know part of the answer. Each of the four theories of cognitive development that you read about in Chapter 4 identified key contributors to conceptual development. Core-knowledge theories, which emphasize *biological predispositions,* maintain that infants enter the world prepared by evolution to form certain kinds of concepts, such as the concept of a human face or the concept of a solid object. If infants are given even minimal relevant experience, they rapidly form these concepts. Jean Piaget's theory points to a second basis for infants' rapid conceptual development: their *physical interactions with objects.* These interactions help them learn about the properties of objects, for example, that rubber objects bounce and glass ones do not. Information-processing theories emphasize a third vital factor, *basic processing skills.* The process of association, for example, allows infants to connect the appearance of a cat with the sound of mewing and the feel of fur, and thus to form the concept "cat." Finally, sociocultural theories point to the ways in which *the social world* contributes to conceptual development. Parents, relatives, neighbors, and peers shape the concepts that infants form. They steer infants' attention toward information that they can grasp and help them interpret their experiences.

In Chapter 5, you encountered another basis of infants' rapid conceptual development: their sophisticated perceptual abilities. Infants can learn about the world by seeing, hearing, touching, tasting, and smelling. These perceptual abilities provide the data they need to form concepts.

concepts general ideas or understandings that can be used to group together objects, events, qualities, or abstractions that are similar in some way

Another major influence on conceptual development, discussed in Chapter 6, is language. Language and conceptual development build on each other. Learning a word is much easier if you already have some understanding of the concept to which it refers. Learning the term "lynx," for example, is much easier if you have seen a lynx. At the same time, language greatly enriches conceptual understanding and sometimes creates new concepts. If you say to a child, "A lynx is a kind of wildcat with short, soft fur," the child will form a concept of "lynx" despite never having seen one.

This background discussion of conceptual development suggests several of the themes that will be prominent in this chapter. One is *nature and nurture;* children's concepts reflect the interaction of their biological predispositions to attend to certain types of events and to process information in particular ways with the specific experiences that they have. Another recurring theme is the *active child;* from infancy onward, children's concepts reflect their active attempts to make sense of the world. A third major theme is *mechanisms of change;* researchers study conceptual development not only to understand what concepts children form but the processes by which they form them. And, of course, the theme of the *sociocultural context* pervades the chapter, since, as noted, the social world influences the very concepts that children form. We will examine several specific instances of this influence in terms of cross-cultural variations in certain areas of children's conceptual understanding.

KENNETH GARRETT / WOODFIN CAMP & ASSOCIATES

What does this infant see when he looks at this room?

The focus of this chapter is on the development of the most fundamental concepts, the ones that are useful in the greatest number of situations. These concepts fall into two groups. One group of fundamental concepts is used to categorize the kinds of things that exist in the world: people, plants and animals, and inanimate objects. The other group of fundamental concepts is used, along with the first group, to represent our experiences: space (where the experience occurred), time (when it occurred relative to other events and how long it lasted), causality (why it occurred), and number (how many things it involved or how often it occurred).

If you have ever worked on a newspaper, or taken a course that covered the basics of journalism, you may have noticed that these fundamental concepts correspond closely to the questions that every news story must answer: Who or What? Where? When? Why? and How many? The similarity between the concepts that are most fundamental for children and those that are most important in newspaper stories is no accident. Knowing who or what, where, when, why, and how many is essential for understanding almost any event.

Because early conceptual development is so crucial, this chapter focuses on development in the first five years. This obviously does not mean that conceptual growth ends at age 5. Children's understanding of the basic concepts deepens for many years thereafter, and older children acquire vast numbers of additional, more specialized concepts. Rather, the focus on conceptual development in the first five years reflects the fact that this is the period in which children acquire a basic understanding of the most fundamental concepts, the ones that are universal across societies, that allow children to understand their own and other people's experiences, and that provide the foundation for subsequent conceptual growth.

Understanding Who or What

From the moment they are born, children face the task of understanding their world in terms of who or what, that is, in terms of the objects they encounter. This task involves not only recognizing and distinguishing among these objects but also understanding their functions and relations to each other.

Dividing Objects into Categories

From early in development, children divide the things in the world into a few broad categories of the type shown at the top of the columns in Table 7.1: inanimate objects, people, and other living things (Wellman & Gelman, 1998). Forming these broad divisions is a crucial development, because different types of concepts apply to different types of objects (Keil, 1979). Some concepts apply to anything—all things have heights, weights, colors, and so on. Other concepts apply only to people and other animals—only people and other animals can run and learn, for example. Yet other concepts apply only to people; reading and shopping are two such cases. These distinctions among categories are important because they help children make accurate inferences about unfamiliar objects. When they are told "a platypus is a kind of animal," they know instantaneously that it can move, eat, grow, reproduce, and so on.

Proceeding down any of the columns in Table 7.1 illustrates a major way in which forming categories helps children figure out how the things in the world are related to each other. Children divide objects into **category hierarchies,** that is, categories related by set–subset relations. The furniture/chair/La-Z-Boy relation shown in Table 7.1 is one example. The category "furniture" includes all chairs; the category "chair" includes all La-Z-Boys. Forming such category hierarchies again greatly simplifies the world for children by allowing them to draw accurate inferences. If children are told that a La-Z-Boy is a kind of chair, they can use their general knowledge of chairs to infer that people sit on La-Z-Boys and that La-Z-Boys are neither lazy nor boys.

TABLE 7.1

Object Hierarchies

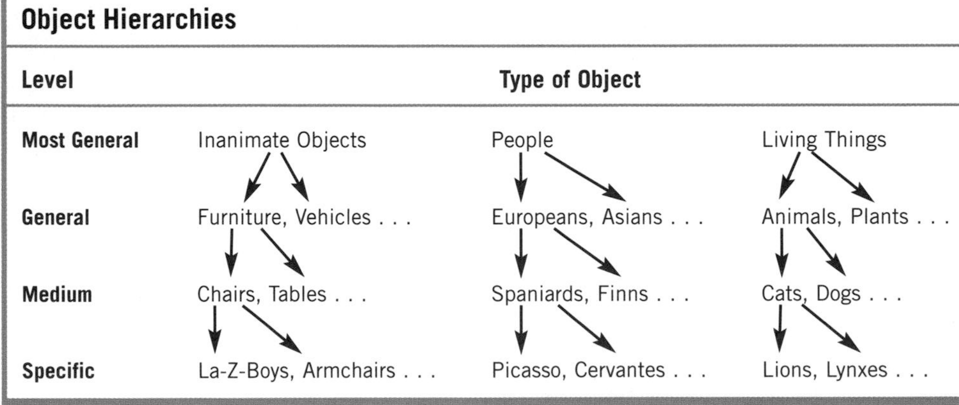

Level	Type of Object		
Most General	Inanimate Objects	People	Living Things
General	Furniture, Vehicles . . .	Europeans, Asians . . .	Animals, Plants . . .
Medium	Chairs, Tables . . .	Spaniards, Finns . . .	Cats, Dogs . . .
Specific	La-Z-Boys, Armchairs . . .	Picasso, Cervantes . . .	Lions, Lynxes . . .

Of course, infants are not born knowing about La-Z-Boys and chairs, nor are they born knowledgeable about the other categories shown in Table 7.1. In the next section, we examine some of the ways in which children form categories. The focus of the section will be on aspects of categorization that apply to all kinds of objects, living and nonliving.

Categorization in Infancy

Even in the first months of life, infants form categories of objects (Haith & Benson, 1998; Wellman & Gelman, 1998). This has been demonstrated in habituation experiments like those described in Chapter 5 (p. 193). For example, Quinn and Eimas (1996) found that as 3- and 4-month-olds were shown photographs of pairs of animals of a given type, such as two cats, they habituated; that is, they looked at the cat photographs for less and less time. However, when the infants were then shown a photo of the same type of animal and a photo of a related but different type of animal, such as a dog (Figure 7.1), they looked more at the new type of animal. Their habituation to the photos of the original type of animal suggests that despite fairly sizable differences in the appearances of the individual animals, the infants perceived them as members of a single category. The infants' subsequent preference for the photo of the other type of animal suggests that they saw it as a member of a different category.

category hierarchy categories that are related by set–subset relations, such as animal/dog/poodle

perceptual categorization the grouping together of objects with similar appearances

Infants can also form categories more general than "cats." Behl-Chadha (1996) found that 6-month-olds habituated after repeatedly being shown pairs of pictures of different types of mammals (cats, zebras, elephants, etc.) and then dishabituated when they were shown a picture of a bird or a fish. The infants apparently perceived similarities among the different mammals that led to their eventually losing interest in them. The infants also apparently perceived differences between the mammals and the bird or fish that led them to show renewed interest.

As suggested by this example, a key element in infants' thinking is **perceptual categorization,** the grouping together of objects that have similar appearances (Eimas & Quinn, 1994; Madole & Cohen, 1995). Prior to being tested in the Behl-Chadha (1996) study, few of the infants would have had any experience with zebras or elephants. Thus, the infants' differentiation between the large four-legged mammals and the birds and fish could be based only on the animals' differing appearances.

Infants categorize objects along many perceptual dimensions, including color, size, and movement. Often their categorization is based to a large extent on specific parts of objects rather than on the object as a whole; for example, infants younger than 18 months old rely heavily on the presence of legs to categorize objects as animals, and they rely on the presence of wheels to categorize objects as vehicles (Rakison & Butterworth, 1998; Rakison & Poulin-Dubois, 2001).

Trial 1

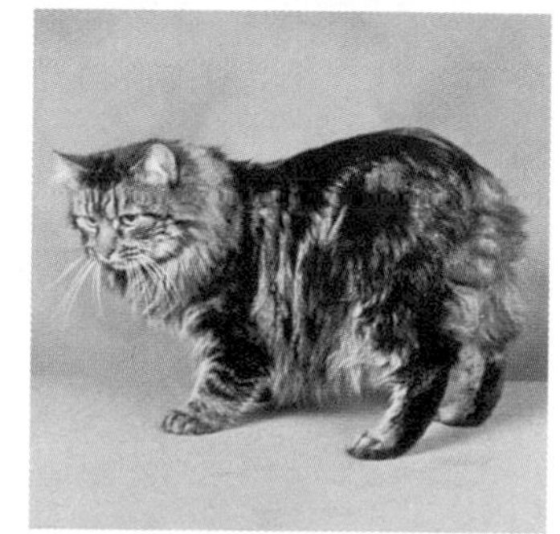

Trial 2

Trial 3

Test trial

FIGURE 7.1 Stimuli presented by Quinn and Eimas (1996). After habituating to repeated presentations of pairs of photos of cats that look quite different from each other (trials 1–3 above), 3- and 4-month-olds look longer at a different type of animal on the test trial (the dog in this example) than at another photo of a cat. Thus, despite lacking knowledge about cats and other animals, infants form categories that allow them to discriminate between members of the category and members of related but different categories.

As children approach their second birthday, they increasingly categorize objects on the basis of overall shape. When toddlers are shown an unfamiliar object and told that it is a "dax," they assume that other objects of the same shape are also "daxes," even when the objects differ from each other in size, texture, and color (Landau, Smith, & Jones, 1998). This is a useful assumption, because with many objects, shape indeed is similar for different members of a category. If we see a silhouette of a cat, hammer, or chair, we can tell from the shape what it is. However, we cannot do the same if we know only the object's color or size or texture.

By the end of their first year, infants also form categories on the basis of the objects' function (that is, the purpose for which the object is used). This capability was evident in a study in which 9- and 10-month-olds were shown castanets that produced clacking sounds when they were shaken (Baldwin, Markman, & Mellartin, 1993). When the babies were later given a similar-looking toy, they actively tried to reproduce the sound. If the similar-looking toy did not produce the expected sound, the infants tried repeatedly to reproduce it. They apparently expected that a toy that looked like the original would serve the same function—in this case, making the same interesting noise.

By the beginning of their second year, infants also can use their knowledge of categories to determine which actions go with which type of objects. In one demonstration of this phenomenon with 14-month-olds, each infant saw an experimenter tilt a small cup to a toy dog's mouth and say "Sip, sip, umm, good" (Mandler & McDonough, 1998). Next, the experimenter presented the infant with a toy from the same general category (for example, a rabbit), and a toy from a different category (for example, a motorcycle). Then the experimenter handed the infant the cup, again said "Sip, sip, umm, good," and watched what the child did. If the 14-month-olds had formed the category "animal," and could use it to guide their playing, they presumably would be more likely to pour the pretend water into the rabbit's mouth than onto the motorcycle. This is exactly what they did.

Categorization of Objects Beyond Infancy

As children move beyond infancy, their ability to categorize expands greatly. In this section, we first describe two of the most important trends in this growth—increasing understanding of category hierarchies and causal connections—both of which involve knowledge of relations among categories. Then we examine two major contributors to these and other improvements in categorization.

Category hierarchies As discussed previously, many categories are hierarchically related. The category of "tools" includes the subset "hammers"; the subset "hammers" includes the smaller subset "tack hammers"; and so on. As in this example, category hierarchies often include three main levels: a general one, the **superordinate level;** a very specific one, the **subordinate level;** and one in-between, the **basic level** (Rosch, Mervis, Gray, Johnson, & Boyes-Braem, 1976). Examples of such hierarchies include plants/trees/oaks; clothing/pants/Levis; toys/balls/golf balls; and so on.

superordinate level the most general level within a category hierarchy; for example, animal in the animal/dog/poodle example

subordinate level the most specific level within a category hierarchy; for example, poodle in the animal/dog/poodle example

basic level the middle level, and often the first level learned, within a category hierarchy; for example, dog in the animal/dog/poodle example

As its name suggests, the basic level is the one that children usually learn first. Thus, they typically form categories of medium generality, such as "tree," before they form more general categories, such as "plant," or more specific ones, such as "oak." The reasons are not hard to understand. A basic-level category such as "tree" has a number of consistent characteristics: bark, branches, hardness, large size, and so on. In contrast, the more general category "plant" has fewer consistent characteristics: plants come in a wide range of shapes, sizes, and colors. (Consider an oak, a rose, and grass.) Subordinate-level categories have the same consistent characteristics as the basic-level category, and some additional ones—all oaks have rough bark and pointed leaves, for example. However, it is relatively difficult to discriminate members of the subordinate-level category from others in the basic-level category (oaks versus maples or elms, for example). Thus, it is not surprising that children tend to form basic-level categories at the youngest ages.

Children's early categories often correspond closely to the categories that adults consider basic, but sometimes children form "child-basic" categories (Dromi, 1987; Mervis 1987). These are categories whose generality is somewhere between basic and superordinate categories. For example, the objects that 1- and 2-year-olds label "balls" include not only balls but also walnuts, round coin banks, large beads, round candles, and so on. Thus, their idea seems closer to the category "things that can roll" than to the adult concept of "ball." Similarly, toddlers' concept of "doggie" seems to correspond more closely to "medium-sized, four-legged mammal" than to the adult category "dog," since toddlers often apply the label "doggie" to cats and foxes as well as dogs.

How might children progress from child-basic to standard-basic categories? One key process involves understanding the role of object characteristics that are relatively subtle but that have important functions (Tversky & Hemenway, 1984). The wicks on round candles and the slots in round coin banks provide two examples. Both are unremarkable visually, and it is not surprising that toddlers frequently ignore them. However, these features are critical to the functions of the candles and coin banks. As children grasp the importance of the functions of these and similarly subtle features of other objects, their categories become more like those of adults. Consistent with this conclusion, 24-month-olds move from child-basic to standard-basic categories when an experimenter points out and explains the function of perceptually subtle but important features, such as the candle wicks (Banigan & Mervis, 1988).

Having formed basic-level categories, how do children go on to form superordinate and subordinate categories? Part of the answer is that parents and others use the child's basic-level categories as a foundation for explaining the more specific and more general categories. When parents teach children superordinate concepts, such as mammals, they typically illustrate the terms with basic-level examples that the child already knows (Callanan, 1985). They might say: "Mammals are animals such as foxes, bears, and cows." Parents also refer to basic-level categories to teach children subordinate level terms (Taylor & Gelman, 1989; Waxman & Senghas, 1992). For example, they might say: "Canaries are a kind of bird; they're small, yellow, and sing a lot." Such descriptions allow children to use what they already know about basic-level categories to form superordinate- and subordinate-level categories. The example also illustrates the importance of the social world in explaining how change occurs in conceptual development.

Causal understanding and categorization Preschoolers are notorious for their endless questions about causes and reasons: "Why do dogs bark?" "How does the telephone know where to call?" "Where does rain come from?" Although parents are often exasperated by such questions, the questions and the answers they elicit do serve an important function: they help children learn.

Understanding causal relations is crucial in forming many categories. How could children form the category of "light switches," for example, if they did not understand that light switches cause lights to go on? To study how understanding of causes influences category formation, Krascum and Andrews (1998) told two

FIGURE 7.2 Cause–effect relations Hearing that wugs are well prepared to fight and gillies to flee helped preschoolers categorize novel pictures like these as wugs or gillies (Krascum & Andrews, 1998). In general, understanding cause–effect relations helps people of all ages learn and remember.

groups of 4- and 5-year-olds about two categories of imaginary animals, "wugs" and "gillies." One group was told that wugs usually have claws, spikes on the end of their tail, horns on their head, and armor on their back, and that gillies usually have big ears, wings, a long tail, and long toes. Another group was provided the same information, plus a simple theory that explained why wugs and gillies are the way they are. They were told that wugs have claws, spikes, horns, and armor because they like to fight. In contrast, they were told, gillies do not like to fight; instead, they like to hide in trees. Their big ears let them hear approaching wugs, their wings let them fly away to treetops, and so on.

Then the children in both groups were shown pictures of fanciful animals and asked if each one was a wug or a gillie (Figure 7.2). Those children who were told why wugs and gillies have the features they do were better at classifying the pictures into the appropriate categories. When tested the next day, those children also remembered the categories better than children who were not given the explanation. Thus, understanding why objects are the way they are helps children learn and remember new categories.

Knowledge of Other People and Oneself

Although none of us fully understands either ourself or others, there is a commonsense level of understanding of people that just about everybody has. As discussed in Chapter 4 (pp. 135–136), this **naive psychology** is evident among children as young as 3 years old (Wellman & Gelman, 1998). At the center of naive psychology are three **psychological constructs,** that is, ideas that people commonly use to understand human behavior: desires, beliefs, and actions. We apply these three constructs almost every time we think about why someone did something. For example, why did Jimmy go to Billy's house? He *wanted* to play with Billy (a desire); he *thought* Billy was at home (a belief); so he *went* to Billy's house (an action). Why did Jenny turn on the TV? She *wanted* to watch *X-Files;* she *thought* that it was on at that time; so she *clicked* the remote.

Three properties of naive psychological constructs are noteworthy. First, most of them are invisible. No one can see a desire, a belief, a perception, a physiological state, and so on. We can see behaviors related to the construct, such as Jimmy's ringing Billy's doorbell, but we cannot see the desire that underlies the behavior. Second, the invisible constructs are all linked to each other in cause–effect relations. As an illustration, Jimmy might feel frustrated if Billy is not home, which could cause him to go back to his house and be mean to his younger brother. The third noteworthy property of these naive psychological constructs is that they develop extremely early.

Infants' Naive Psychology

Definitely by the age of 1 year, and quite likely earlier, infants think about other people in terms of several invisible constructs. One reason why such constructs regarding other people emerge so quickly is that infants find people interesting and appealing and pay careful attention to them. As you learned in Chapter 5, even very young infants prefer looking at people's faces rather than other objects. Infants also imitate people's facial movements, such as sticking out one's tongue, but they do not imitate the motions of inanimate objects.

This early interest in other people helps infants learn about them. Focusing on faces helps infants learn about the people whose bodies are attached to the faces.

Imitating other people and forming emotional bonds with them encourages the other people to interact more with the infants, thus creating additional opportunities for the infants to develop psychological understanding. Infants' learning about people is also furthered by the fact that infants, like older children and adults, want certain things to happen, intend certain actions to produce certain outcomes, feel certain emotions, and so on. Thus, infants can use their own experience to understand others (Harris, 1992).

In the first half of their second year, toddlers begin to show a grasp of two ideas that are crucial for psychological understanding: intentions and the self. First consider **intentions,** the desire to act in a certain way. To comprehend the relation between desires and actions or between beliefs and actions, infants must first realize that people's actions are usually intended to accomplish a goal (Baldwin & Moses, 1994). This goal-directed behavior distinguishes people's motions from those of inanimate objects, such as feathers and balls, and even from the motions of self-propelled objects, such as windup toys.

By the age of 18 months, infants can infer simple intentions of other people. One demonstration of this ability came from the procedure, described in Chapter 5, in which 18-month-olds saw an experimenter try unsuccessfully to pull the ends off a miniature dumbbell. The children subsequently imitated what the experimenter seemed to intend to do, rather than what she actually did (Meltzoff, 1995). A similar phenomenon is evident in language development. When an experimenter and a 19- or 20-month-old are looking at different objects, and the experimenter says "Look, a 'toma,'" most babies infer that the experimenter intended to label whatever object the experimenter was looking at; this inference leads the babies to choose that object when subsequently asked to "point to the 'toma'" (Baldwin, 1991, 1993).

Another crucial development in psychological understanding that occurs during this period involves the emergence of a basic understanding of the self. By 24 months of age, most children, upon looking in a mirror, recognize what they see as a self-image (Lewis & Brooks-Gunn, 1979). Also by the age of 24 months, more children smile at photos of themselves in photo albums than at photos of other children, again suggesting that they know who is in the photo (Lewis & Brooks-Gunn, 1979). Thus, basic understanding of both intentionality and the self develops by the age of 2.

Toward the end of their second year, children begin to recognize who is staring back at them in the mirror.

Development Beyond Infancy

Between the ages of 2 and 5 years, children build on their early-emerging psychological understanding to develop an increasingly sophisticated comprehension of themselves and other people. Two areas in which this development is especially impressive are play activities and understanding of people's minds.

The growth of play Play refers to activities that are pursued for their own sake, without any motivation other than the intrinsic enjoyment of engaging in them. The earliest play activities, such as banging spoons on high chair trays, tend to be solitary. However, over the next few years, children's increasing understanding of other people contributes to play also becoming much more social, as well as more complex.

As discussed in Chapter 6, one early milestone in the development of play is the emergence at around 18 months of *pretend play,* a type of activity in which children act as if they were in a different situation than their actual one. When children slide a block along the floor and say "vroom, vroom" as if the block were a car, or cradle their pillow in their arms and talk to it as if it were a baby, they are engaging

naive psychology a commonsense level of understanding of other people and oneself

psychological constructs ideas used to understand human behavior, such as desires, beliefs, and actions

intention the goal of acting in a certain way

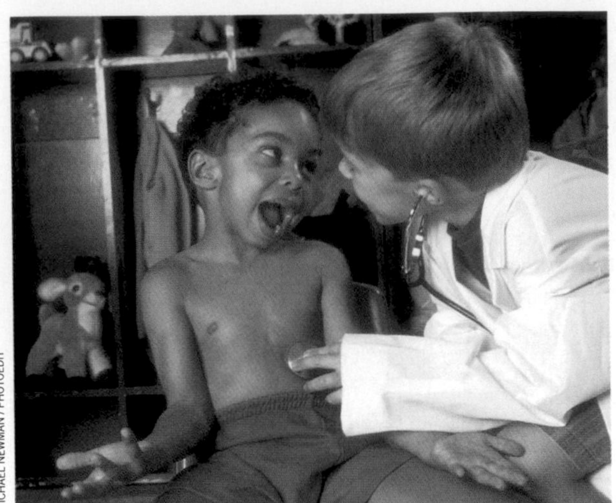

MICHAEL NEWMAN / PHOTOEDIT

Sociodramatic play, in which children create minidramas based on their experiences, both reflects children's understanding of the situation and helps them increase that understanding.

in pretend play. About a year later, they begin to participate in *sociodramatic play,* in which they engage in miniature dramas with other children, such as mother-comforting-baby or doctor-helping-sick-child (O'Reilly & Bornstein, 1993). By the elementary school years, play also includes activities, such as sports and board games, that have conventional rules that apply to all the participants.

Because play is such a universal and pervasive part of childhood, and because the form of play changes so much during development, major theorists such as Piaget and Vygotsky have speculated about its broader significance. In particular, they have wondered whether pretend and sociodramatic play simply reflect children's level of development or whether such play also advances that developmental level. Piaget (1928) believed that preschoolers' play reflects their general egocentrism and that it is only during the elementary school years, when fantasy play is increasingly subordinated to games with conventional rules, that play contributes to development. In contrast, Vygotsky (1978) argued that toddlers' and preschoolers' pretend and sociodramatic play can create zones of proximal development (Chapter 4, p. 164), which enable young children to think and act in more mature ways than they ordinarily would. Subsequent research indicates that Vygotsky was right: very young children's pretend play not only reflects their understanding of other people's psychological functioning; it also helps that understanding increase.

One source of evidence for this conclusion is that the amount of time that toddlers spend in pretend play with others at age 33 months is positively correlated with their comprehension of emotions at age 40 months (Youngblade & Dunn, 1995). The pretend play may lead young children to focus on how various situations would make them, or their play partner, feel and thus increase their understanding of other people. Consistent with this conclusion, children who participate in greater amounts of pretend play with other children also tend to be more socially mature and popular with other children, perhaps because they understand the other children's feelings better (Howes & Matheson, 1992). Language development and creativity in the preschool period also seem to be enhanced by pretend play (Fisher, 1992). Thus, although adults sometimes view fantasy play as unimportant or even as a waste of time, it actually seems to enhance children's social and intellectual development. (For a discussion of a particularly interesting kind of fantasy play—play involving imaginary companions—see Box 7.1.)

The growth of a theory of mind Between the ages of 2 and 5 years, children build on their initial naive psychology to form a **theory of mind,** a basic understanding of how the mind works and how it influences behavior. This theory of mind explains human mental functioning in terms of psychological constructs such as desires, beliefs, perceptions, and emotions. As children's theory of mind develops, their knowledge about these psychological constructs becomes organized into a network that describes the interrelations among the constructs at a general level (Wellman, 1990; Wellman & Gelman, 1998). As illustrated in Figure 7.3, preschoolers' theory of mind includes the knowledge that beliefs often originate in perceptions, such as seeing an event or hearing someone describe it. It also includes the knowledge that desires can originate from physiological states, such as hunger or pain, or from psychological states, as when we want to see a friend because we like her. Beyond this, preschoolers realize that desires and beliefs produce actions, and also that actions can change those same desires and beliefs.

theory of mind a basic understanding of how the mind works and how it influences behavior

individual differences 7.1

Imaginary Companions

Interest in, and understanding of, other people underlies one of the most fascinating aspects of many children's development: the creation of imaginary companions. Although children's talking about their invisible friends causes some parents to worry about the children's mental health, imagining such companions is actually entirely normal. In an intriguing series of studies, Marjorie Taylor (1999) found that 63% of children whom she interviewed at age 3 or 4 years and again at age 7 or 8 years reported having imaginary companions at one or both ages. Although most of the imaginary playmates were ordinary boys and girls who happened to be invisible, others were more colorful. They included Derek, a 91-year-old man who was said to be only 2 feet tall but able to hit bears; "The Girl," a 4-year-old who always wore pink and was "a beautiful person"; and Joshua, a possum who lived in San Francisco. Other imaginary companions were modeled after specific people; two examples were MacKenzie, an imaginary playmate who resembled the child's cousin MacKenzie, and "Fake Rachel," who resembled the child's friend Rachel.

Contrary to common speculation that children who invent imaginary playmates differ from their peers in broad characteristics such as personality, intelligence, and creativity, Taylor (1999) found no such broad differences between the two groups. However, she and other investigators did identify a few, relatively specific differences. Children who create imaginary playmates are more likely (1) to be firstborn or only children; (2) to watch relatively little television; (3) to be verbally skillful; and (4) to have advanced theories of mind (Singer & Singer, 1981; Taylor & Carlson, 1997). These relations make sense. Being without siblings may motivate some firstborn and only children to invent friends to keep them company; not watching much television frees time for imaginative play; and being verbally skilled and having an advanced theory of mind may enable children to imagine especially interesting companions and especially interesting adventures with them.

Companionship and enjoyment of fantasy are not the only reasons why children invent imaginary companions. Children also use them to deflect blame ("I didn't do it; Blebbi Ussi did"), to vent anger ("I hate you, Blebbi Ussi"), and to convey information that the child is reluctant to state directly ("Blebbi Ussi is scared of falling into the potty"). As Taylor (1999, p. 63) noted, "Imaginary companions love you when you feel rejected by others, listen when you need to talk to someone, and can be trusted not to repeat what you say." It thus is no wonder that so many children invent them.

Although the sight of their child feeding someone who isn't there might worry some parents, the majority of children enjoy the company of imaginary friends at some time in early childhood.

SHERRY WHITMORE

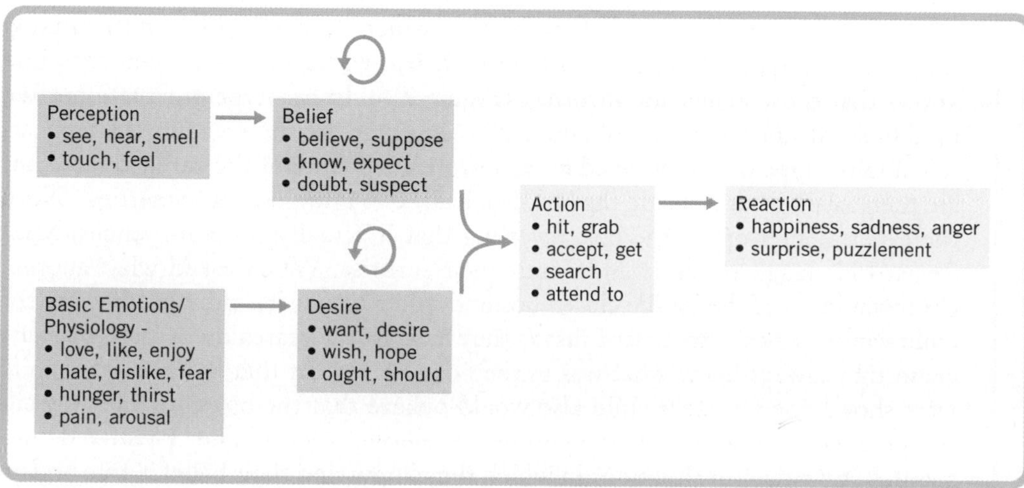

FIGURE 7.3 Developing a theory of mind Wellman's (1990) model of the basic categories in preschoolers' theory of mind and the relations among them. The heading of each box refers to the general category; the words below the heading are those that preschoolers commonly use when discussing the specific functions, feelings, actions, and states that fall within that category.

FIGURE 7.4 The Smarties task The Smarties task is frequently used to study preschoolers' theory of mind. Most 3-year-olds answer like the child in the cartoon, which suggests that they fail to realize that other people may have false beliefs that deviate from what the child knows to be true.

One of the first steps toward developing such a theory of mind is understanding the connection between others' desires and their actions. Henry Wellman, a leading student of children's understanding of psychology, has found that most 2-year-olds show such understanding. For example, 2-year-olds predict that characters in stories will act in accord with the characters' own desires, even when those desires differ from the children's own (Astington, 1993; Gopnik & Slaughter, 1991; Lillard & Flavell, 1992; Wellman & Woolley, 1990). Thus, if 2-year-olds themselves would rather play with trucks than dolls, but are told that a character in a story would rather play with dolls than trucks, they predict that, given a choice between playing with dolls or trucks, the character in the story will choose the dolls.

Although most 2-year-olds understand that *desires* can influence behavior, they show little understanding that *beliefs* also are influential. Thus, if 2-year-olds are told that a story character named Sam believes that a puppy is under the porch, but the 2-year-olds themselves know that the puppy is in the garage, they predict that Sam will look for the puppy where they know it is, rather than where Sam believes it to be (Wellman & Woolley, 1990). In contrast, most 3-year-olds predict that Sam will look where Sam believes the puppy is, regardless of their own knowledge. Three-year-olds' conversations also reflect their understanding of the relation between beliefs and actions. For example, they answer questions such as "Why is Billy looking for his dog?" by referring to beliefs ("He thinks the dog ran away") as well as desires ("He wants it") (Bartsch & Wellman, 1995). Thus, 3-year-olds possess the core of the desire–belief–action model depicted in Figure 7.3.

In addition to having a basic understanding that desires and beliefs affect behavior, 3-year-olds also have a more general understanding of mental entities. They realize that all types of mental processes—not just desires and beliefs but also thoughts, dreams, and memories—differ both from tangible objects, such as chairs, and from intangible physical entities, such as shadows and sounds. When asked why they cannot touch shadows, for example, they typically offer explanations such as "'Cause it is just something you couldn't feel." When asked why they cannot touch a dream, they typically explain that the dream is in their mind (Wellman, 1990). Most 3-year-olds also have some knowledge of how beliefs and desires originate. They know, for example, that seeing an event produces beliefs about it, whereas simply being next to someone who can see the event does not (Pillow, 1988).

At the same time, 3-year-olds' understanding of the relation between other people's beliefs and their own beliefs—a key part of their theory of mind—is limited in important and surprising ways. These limitations are evident when children are presented with **false-belief problems,** which test a child's understanding that other people will act in accord with their own beliefs even when the child knows that those beliefs are incorrect (Figure 7.4). In one type of situation often used to study understanding of false beliefs, children are shown a box that appears to contain a type of candy called Smarties, with a picture of the candy on it. They are then asked what is inside the box. Logically enough, they say "Smarties." Next, the experimenter opens the box, revealing that it actually contains pencils. Most 5-year-olds laugh or smile and admit their surprise. When asked what another child would say if shown the closed box and told to guess its contents, they say the child would answer "Smarties," just as they had. Not 3-year-olds! A large majority claim they always knew what was in the box and predict that if some other child were shown the box, that child also would believe that the box contained pencils (Gopnik & Astington, 1988; Wimmer & Perner, 1983). The 3-year-olds' responses show that, in situations in which they know that their belief is true and an alternative belief is false, they have difficulty understanding that other people could have the alternative belief.

Children in non-Western societies show similar developmental trends. For example, 3- to 5-year-old Pygmy children growing up in the African rain forest respond to false-belief problems similarly to 3- to 5-year-olds in North America and Europe (Avis & Harris, 1991). Such results indicate that 3-year-olds around the world find it difficult to separate what they know about the true state of affairs from their beliefs about what other people, lacking their experience, would know.

In this case, as in many others, however, difficult is not the same as impossible. Many 3-year-olds *are* able to succeed on false-belief tasks if the task is presented in a way that facilitates understanding. For example, on false-belief problems like the one involving Smarties, many 3-year-olds succeed if they collaborate with the experimenter to deceive another child in the same way that they themselves were deceived earlier. In one study, the experimenter told the child that the two of them were going to play a trick and asked the child to hide pencils in the candy box before it was shown to another child (Sullivan & Winner, 1993). Under these circumstances, most 3-year-olds predicted that the other child would say the box contained Smarties. Presumably, assuming the role of deceiver and hiding the pencils in the candy box helped 3-year-olds see the situation from the other child's perspective. Nonetheless, it is striking just how much difficulty 3-year-olds have with standard false-belief problems.

SUPERSTOCK

Despite leading very different lives, pygmy children in Africa and age peers in industrialized societies in North America and Europe respond to the false-belief task in the same way.

Similar limits on 3-year-olds' theory of theory of mind is revealed by **appearance–reality problems**—problems in which appearances and reality diverge. In one demonstration of this, John Flavell and his colleagues showed 3- to 5-year-olds sponges that looked just like rocks and gave them a chance to play with them so that the children could experience the objects' light weight and spongy texture (Flavell, Flavell, & Green, 1983). When asked what the objects actually were, children of all ages correctly answered "Sponges." When asked what the objects looked like, most 3-year-olds, but few 5-year-olds, also said "Sponges." The 3-year-olds also predicted that another child who saw the objects for the first time would know they were sponges. Thus, as with the Smarties task, the 3-year-olds thought that another child's behavior would reflect what they themselves knew to be the case rather than reflecting the other child's own beliefs. Also, as in the case of false-belief problems, the same age-trend appears across dissimilar cultures (Flavell, Zhang, Zou, Dong, & Qi, 1983).

Although the large majority of 5-year-olds find appearance–reality and false-belief problems laughably easy, one group finds them very difficult even when they are teenagers: children with **autism.** This syndrome, which involves a variety of intellectual and emotional difficulties, strikes roughly 4 in 10,000 children. Even compared with retarded children of the same age and IQ, autistic children are particularly befuddled by false-belief tasks and by other tasks that examine an individual's knowledge of other people's minds (Baron-Cohen, 1991).

The difficulties that most children with autism exhibit on false-belief tasks make sense given the many other interpersonal problems they experience. Children with autism rarely form close relationships with others; they tend to take a greater interest in objects than in people. Many engage in solitary repetitive behaviors, such as continually rocking back and forth or endlessly skipping around a room. Most of them also lack normal language skills. Even those who learn to talk reasonably well rarely use verbs referring to the mind, such as "think" and "know,"

false-belief problems tasks that test a child's understanding that other people will act in accord with their own beliefs even when the child knows that those beliefs are incorrect

appearance–reality problems problems in which appearances and reality diverge

autism a syndrome that tends to produce a number of intellectual and emotional limitations, particularly in understanding and relating to other people

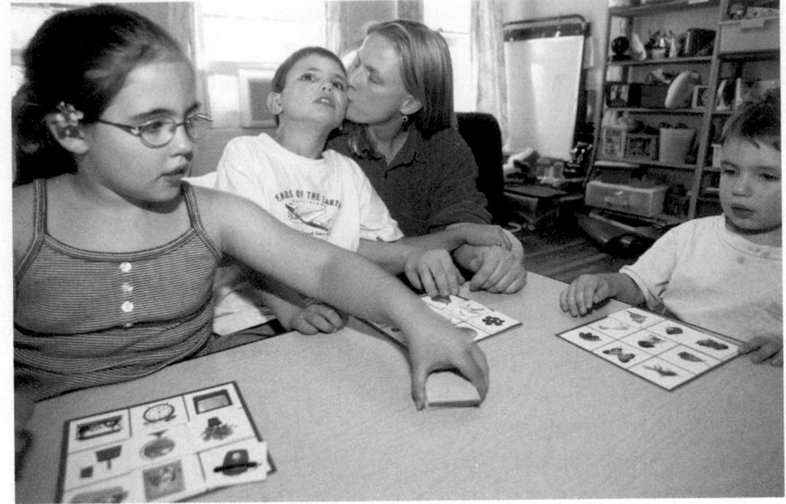

An autistic child, sitting in his mother's lap, shows a distinct lack of interest in her affection. Such lack of interest in other people is common among autistic children and seems related to their very poor performance on tasks that require understanding of other people's minds.

terms that most normal 2-year-olds use (Tager-Flusberg, 1992). In addition, most children with autism do not engage in pretend play (Baron-Cohen, 1993). Taken together, these symptoms suggest that children with autism have a special impairment in their "mind-reading mechanisms" (Baron-Cohen, 1993; Frith, 1989; Leslie, 1991).

Explaining the development of theory of mind The data from children with autism and from typical 2- and 3-year-olds indicate that life would be very different without "mind-reading mechanisms." However, the findings do not say what exactly causes the problems in understanding other people's thinking. Nor do the findings indicate what causes typical children's improvement on a broad range of theory-of-mind tasks between the ages of 3 and 5 years or what causes the lack of comparable improvement during this period among children with autism. These uncertainties have generated enormous controversy, and at this point there is great disagreement about how to answer them.

Investigators in one camp propose the existence of a **theory-of-mind module (TOMM),** a hypothesized brain mechanism devoted to understanding other human beings. Adherents of this position argue that among typical children exposed to a typical environment, the TOMM matures over the first 5 years, producing an increasingly sophisticated understanding of people's minds (Fodor, 1992; Leslie, 1994). Autistic children's difficulties in understanding other people are ascribed to a biologically impaired TOMM.

Investigators in a second group emphasize interactions with other people as crucial to the development of theory of mind (Perner, Ruffman, & Leekham, 1994; Siegal, 1991). They cite evidence that preschoolers with older siblings do better on false-belief tasks than do those without older siblings, presumably because the former have greater opportunity to learn about other people's minds (Jenkins & Astington, 1996; Ruffman, Perner, Naito, Parkin, & Clements, 1998). From this perspective, the tendency of children with autism not to interact with other people is a

Sharing experiences with older siblings helps younger siblings understand other people

major contributor to the children's difficulty in understanding other people's minds.

A third group of investigators emphasize the growth of general information-processing skills as essential to children's understanding other people's minds, especially in situations that require them to keep track both of what they themselves know to be true and what another person, lacking the child's knowledge, might understand (Frye, Zelazo, Brooks, & Samuels, 1996; Harris, 1991). In this view, typical 3-year-olds and children with autism do not possess the processing skills necessary to keep track of all of the conflicting information, whereas many typical 4-year-olds and almost all typical 5-year-olds do.

All three explanations relating to the development of a theory of mind seem to have merit. Maturation of regions of the brain that are especially important for understanding other people, increasing experience with other people, and improved information-processing capacity all seem to contribute to the growth of psychological understanding during the preschool years. And even more certain, by the age of 5 or 6, almost all children have a solid core understanding of other people that equips them to venture forward into the more complex social environment that they encounter when they start school.

theory-of-mind module (TOMM) a hypothesized brain mechanism devoted to understanding other human beings

personify to attribute qualities of human beings to other entities

Knowledge of Living Things

Children find living things fascinating. One sign of their fascination is how often they refer to them when they begin to talk. In a study of the first fifty words used by children, the two terms that were used by the greatest number of children were "dog" and "cat" (and variants such as "doggie" and "kitty") (Nelson, 1973). "Duck," "horse," "bear," "bird," and "cow" also were among the most common early terms. By the time they are 4 or 5 years old, children's fascination with living things translates into a surprising amount of knowledge about them, including knowledge of unobservable biological processes such as inheritance, illness, and healing.

Alongside this knowledge, however, are some very idiosyncratic beliefs. Consider the statement of a 6-year-old who claimed that he was a great fisherman. When asked the secret of his success, he said:

> When you throw in your line, the main thing is don't look hungry because if the fish sees you up there making faces and licking your lips, they'll know you want to eat them. But if you just pretend that you're not even interested in what's going on, they think that you just like them and want them to eat what you've thrown in, and they bite it.
>
> (Linkletter, 1957, p. 22).

This 6-year-old seems to have generalized his understanding of people's minds to those of fish. Such a tendency to **personify**—to attribute properties of human beings to other animals—is quite common among 4- to 6-year-olds. Many children of these ages also confuse essential properties of living and nonliving things. For example, about 40% of 5- and 6-year-olds in Israel and Japan say that plants are not alive (Hatano et al., 1993), and about 20% of Japanese children say that stones and chairs are alive. Erroneous notions such as these have led some experts to conclude that children have only a shallow and fragmented understanding

Children are interested in living things, plants as well as animals—especially when the plants taste good.

COURTESY OF SUWANNA AND DAVID SIEGLER

of living things until they are 7 to 10 years old (Carey, 1999; Slaughter, Jaakkola, & Carey, 1999). Others disagree, believing that by age 5 or 6, children understand the essential characteristics of living things and what separates them from nonliving objects (Keil, 1995; Springer, 1999). With this dispute in mind, we will now consider what young children do and do not know about living things and how this knowledge is acquired.

Distinguishing Living from Nonliving Things

As noted previously, infants are interested in people and, in their first year, distinguish between humans and nonliving things (Figure 7.5). Nonhuman animals also attract infants' interest, though infants act differently toward them than they do toward people. Nine-month-olds, for example, pay more attention to rabbits than they do to inanimate objects, but they smile less at rabbits than they do at people (Poulin-Dubois, 1999; Ricard & Allard, 1993).

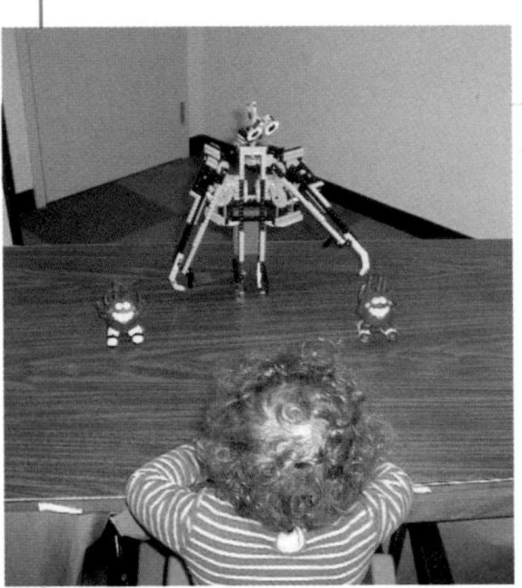

BOTH: COURTESY OF DIANE POULIN-DUBOIS

FIGURE 7.5 Distinguishing humans from nonliving things Task used by Poulin-Dubois (1999) to study infants' reactions when they see people and inanimate objects (in this case a robot) engaging in the same action. Both 9- and 12-month-olds show surprise when they see inanimate objects move on their own, suggesting that they understand that self-produced motion is a distinctive characteristic of people and other animals.

These behavioral reactions indicate that distinctions among people, other animals, and inanimate objects arise in the first year. However, the reactions do not show when children construct a general category of living things that includes plants as well as animals or when they recognize humans as a type of animal. It is difficult to assess this knowledge until children are 3- or 4-year-olds and their language development is sufficiently advanced that they can comprehend and answer questions about their knowledge. By this age, they clearly know quite a bit about similarities among living creatures and the differences between them and inanimate objects. These understandings do not involve just visible properties such as having legs, moving, and making distinctive noises. They also extend to invisible processes such as digestion and heredity (Wellman & Inagaki, 1997).

However, despite these understandings, even through age 5, children have difficulty thinking about human beings as animals, similar in many ways to other animals. They frequently deny that people are animals at all. One demonstration of the strength of young children's distinction between people and other animals came from asking 5-year-olds which two out of the following three things were most alike: people, chimpanzees, and caterpillars. In two different studies, most children said that the chimpanzees and caterpillars were more similar to each other than either of them were to people (Coley, 1993; Johnson, Mervis, & Boster, 1992).

Knowing how to think about the life status of plants also presents a challenge. On the one hand, most preschoolers know that plants, like animals but unlike inanimate objects, grow (Hickling & Gelman, 1995; Inagaki & Hatano, 1996), heal themselves (Backscheider, Shatz, & Gelman, 1993), and die (Springer, Nguyen, & Samaniego, 1996). On the other hand, most preschoolers believe that plants are not alive; not until they are 7 to 9 years old do clear majorities of children judge plants to be alive (Richards & Siegler, 1984). Part of the reason that this realization about plants takes so long to develop is that children seem to equate being alive with being able to move in adaptive ways, and the movement of plants toward goals that promote their survival, such as water and sunlight, is difficult to observe (Opfer & Gelman, 2001).

Understanding Biological Processes

Preschoolers understand that biological properties, such as growth, digestion, and healing, differ from psychological and physical ones (Wellman & Gelman, 1998). Thus, while they recognize that psychological processes, such as desires, influence what people do, they also recognize that there are strictly biological processes that are independent of one's desires. This distinction between psychological and biological processes leads preschoolers to predict that people who wish to lose weight, but who also eat a lot, will not get their wish (Inagaki & Hatano, 1993; Schult & Wellman, 1997). They also recognize that properties of living things often serve important functions for the organism, whereas properties of inanimate objects do not. Thus, 5-year-olds recognize that the green color of plants is crucial for them to make food, whereas the green color of emeralds has no function for the emerald (Keil, 1992). The extent of preschoolers' understanding of biological processes can be seen more fully by examining their specific ideas about inheritance, growth, and illness.

Inheritance Preschoolers obviously do not know about DNA or the mechanisms of heredity, but they do know that physical characteristics tend to be passed on from parent to offspring. If told, for example, that Mr. and Mrs. Bull have hearts of an unusual color, they predict that Baby Bull also will have one (Springer & Keil, 1991). Similarly, they believe that a baby mouse will eventually have hair of the same color as its parents, even if it is presently hairless.

Preschoolers also know that certain aspects of development are determined by heredity rather than environment. For example, 5-year-olds realize that an animal of one species raised by parents of another species will become an adult of its own species (Johnson & Solomon, 1996). At times, preschoolers' belief in heredity is too strong, leading them to deny the influence of the environment in situations where older children recognize its importance. Thus, preschoolers tend to believe that differences between boys and girls in play preferences and aptitudes are due totally to heredity. Not until age 9 or 10 do children recognize any environmental influence on gender differences (Taylor, 1993).

Related to this general belief in the importance of heredity is one of the most basic aspects of children's biological beliefs: **essentialism,** the view that living things have an essence inside them that makes them what they are (Atran, 1990; Gelman, Coley, & Gottfried, 1994). Thus, puppies have a certain "dogness" inside them, kittens have a certain "catness," roses have a certain "roseness," and so on. Preschoolers believe that animals inherit this essence from their parents and maintain it throughout their lives.

Growth, illness, and healing Preschoolers realize that growth, like inheritance, is a product of internal processes. Due to something going on inside living things (again, preschoolers are not sure what), plants and animals change from smaller and less complex to bigger and more complex (Rosengren, Gelman, Kalish, & McCormick, 1991). Three- and 4-year-olds also recognize that the growth of living things proceeds in only one direction (smaller to larger), whereas inanimate objects such as balloons can grow either smaller or larger.

Preschoolers also show a basic understanding of illness. Three-year-olds have heard of germs and have a general sense of how they operate. They know that eating food that is contaminated with germs can make you sick, even if you are unaware of the germs being there (Kalish, 1997). Conversely, they realize that psychological processes, such as being aware of germs in one's food, do not cause illness.

essentialism the view that living things have an essence inside them that makes them what they are

Finally, preschoolers know that plants and animals, unlike inanimate objects, have internal processes that allow them to heal. For example, 4-year-olds realize that a cat or a tomato plant that is scratched can repair itself but that a scratched car or chair cannot (Backscheider et al., 1993). They also know that when an animal's hair is cut, it will grow back, but if a doll's hair is cut, it never will. Thus, preschoolers possess considerable knowledge of biology.

How Do Children Acquire Biological Knowledge?

A variety of proposals have been advanced concerning how children learn about living things. One idea is much like that of the theory-of-mind module described previously in this chapter. It posits that humans are born with a "biology module"—a brain structure or mechanism that helps them to learn quickly about living things (Atran, 1990, 1994). Those who postulate a biology module make three main arguments:

- During earlier periods of our evolution, it was crucial for human survival that children learn quickly about animals and plants.
- Children throughout the world are fascinated by plants and animals and learn about them quickly and easily.
- Children throughout the world organize information about plants and animals in very similar ways (in terms of growth, reproduction, inheritance, sickness, and healing).

An alternative position is that the input about living things that children receive from the general culture and from their parents and teachers is a major contributor to the children's early understanding of growth, inheritance, and other biological processes (Callanan, 1990; Chi, Hutchinson, & Robin, 1989). Those who take this position find support in research on cross-cultural differences in children's biological knowledge. For example, 5-year-olds in Japan are more likely than age peers in the United States and Israel to attribute physical sensations—such as being able to feel pain and be cold—to inanimate objects (Hatano et al., 1993). The tendency of Japanese children to believe that inanimate objects possess such qualities echoes the Buddhist tradition, still influential in Japanese society, which views all objects as having certain psychological properties.

To examine the input that young children receive from their parents, Susan Gelman and her colleagues observed mothers as they read and commented on books about animals to their 1- and 2-year-olds (Gelman, Coley, Rosengren, Hartman, & Pappas, 1998). Many of the mothers' statements suggested that animals have intentions and goals; that different members of a particular category, such as dogs, have a lot in common; and that animals differ greatly from inanimate objects. Such parental teaching clearly contributes to children's acquisition of biological knowledge.

As with the parallel arguments regarding the sources of psychological understanding, both nature and nurture clearly play important roles in children's acquisition of biological understanding. Young children seem innately interested in learning about animals. If they were not so interested in learning about them, fewer books and television shows would be aimed at satisfying this curiosity. At the same time, the particulars of

The feelings of awe experienced by many children (and adults) upon seeing remains of great animals of the past were a major reason for the founding of natural history museums. Despite all the depictions of monsters and superheroes on television, in movies, and in video games, these fossils inspire the same sense of wonder in children growing up today.

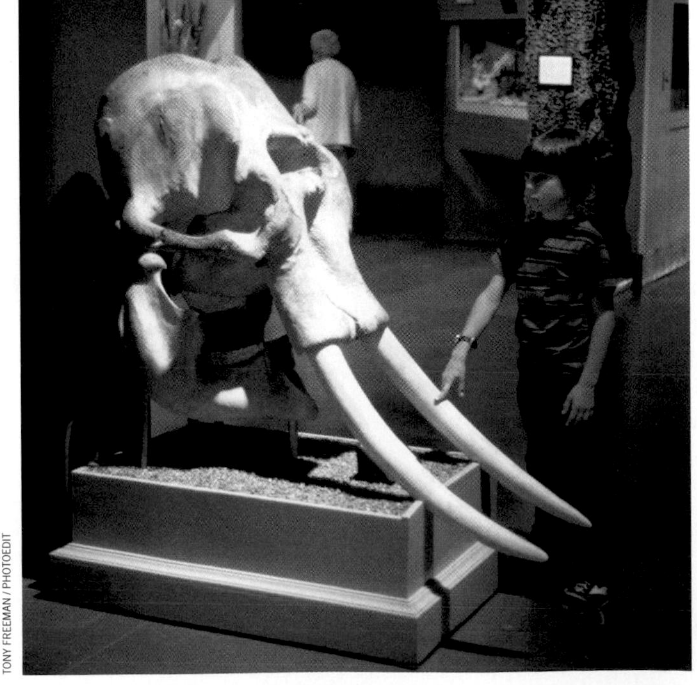

TONY FREEMAN / PHOTOEDIT

what children learn obviously are influenced by the information that is made available to them. The existence of books, television programs, and videocassettes about animals increases the knowledge of animals that children acquire. As we have seen again and again, nature and nurture work together to determine what children learn.

review:

From early in infancy, children form categories of similar objects. Such categorization helps them infer the properties of unfamiliar objects within a category. For example, if children learn that a new object is an animal, they know that it will grow, move, and eat. Children form new categories, and include new objects within an existing category, on the basis of similarities between the appearance and function of the new object and other objects already known to be category members.

One particularly important category is people. From the first days of life, infants are interested in other people and spend a great deal of time looking at them. By the age of 3, they form a simple theory of mind, which includes some understanding of the causal relations among intentions, desires, beliefs, and actions. Not until around the age of 5, however, do most children grasp the distinction between appearance and reality and become able to solve false-belief problems. The development of understanding of other people's minds during the preschool period has been attributed to biological maturation of a theory-of-mind module, to experience in interacting with other people, and to the growth of information-processing capabilities that allow children to understand increasingly complex social situations.

Another vital category is living things. During the preschool years, children gain a basic understanding of the properties of biological entities such as growth, heredity, illness, and healing. Not until children go to school, however, do most of them include plants in the category of living things. Explanations for children's relatively rapid acquisition of biological knowledge include maturation of brain mechanisms that lead them to be interested in living things and to learn about them quickly and easily, and the extensive exposure to biological information provided by most families and the broader culture.

Understanding Where, When, Why, and How Many

Making sense out of life requires accurately representing not only who or what was involved in an event, but also where, when, why, and how often the event occurred. To grasp the importance of these latter concepts, imagine what life would be like if you lost your understanding of any one of them, for example, your sense of time. Without a sense of time, you would not even know the order in which events occurred. Did you first get dressed and then go to class or did you first go to class and then get dressed? Your whole impression of your life as a continuous stream of events would be shattered. To put it mildly, this would create some problems. Similar problems would arise if you lost your sense of space or causality or number. Reality would resemble a dream, in which order and predictability are suspended and chaos rules.

As described in the previous section, the categories that children need to answer the questions Who? and What? are formed early in development, though understanding of people, other living things, and objects continues to develop throughout life. Development of understanding of space, time, causality, and number follows a similar path. In each case, development begins early in infancy, but major improvements continue for many years thereafter.

Space

People often equate spatial thinking with vision; in this view, we can think spatially only about layouts that we are presently seeing or have seen. Even in infancy, however, spatial thought can be based on senses other than vision, and such thought is possible when vision is not. Thus, when 3-month-olds are brought into a totally dark room in which they cannot see anything, they can use the noise that nearby objects make to identify their spatial location and to reach for and touch them (Clifton, Muir, Ashmead, & Clarkson, 1993).

Underlying both early and later spatial thinking is the specialization of certain parts of the brain for coding particular types of spatial information. Contrary to the popular notion that spatial thinking occurs solely in the right hemisphere, spatial thinking actually occurs in both hemispheres. However, the two sides differ in the degree to which they process different types of spatial information (Newcombe & Huttenlocher, 2000). Areas in the right hemisphere are especially active from early infancy onward in processing fine-grain, continuous, spatial information, such as the information used to recognize faces or to identify objects through exploring them with one's hands (Wittelson & Swallow, 1988). In contrast, certain areas in the left hemisphere are especially active in processing categorical spatial information, such as the information that a particular object is in the bathroom or next to the television (Chabris & Kosslyn, 1998; Newcombe & Huttenlocher, 2000).

People, like other animals, code space both relative to themselves and relative to the external environment (Gallistel, 1990). In the following sections we consider each of these types of coding.

Representing Space Relative to Oneself

From early in infancy, children code the locations of objects in relation to their own bodies. As noted in Chapter 5, when young infants are shown two objects, they tend to reach for the closer one (von Hofsten & Spelke, 1985). This shows that they can tell which object is closer, as well as the general direction of that object relative to themselves.

Over the ensuing months, infants' representations of space become increasingly durable, enabling them to locate objects they observed being hidden some seconds earlier. Most 7-month-olds accurately reach for objects that were hidden under one of two identical covers two seconds earlier but not for objects hidden four seconds earlier; most 12-month-olds, in contrast, accurately reach for objects hidden under one of the covers ten seconds earlier (Diamond, 1985).

These examples of infants' ability to code space involve the infants' remaining in a single location. Piaget (1971) proposed that this is the only kind of spatial coding that infants can do. The reason, according to his theory, is that the only spatial representations possible during the sensorimotor period are **egocentric representations,** in which the locations of objects are coded relative to the infants' position when they learned the locations. As evidence, Piaget reported experiments showing that if infants repeatedly found a toy to their right, they would continue to turn to their right to find it, even after they had been turned around so that the object was now on their left.

Subsequent studies have obtained similar findings for children in their first year. When 6- and 11-month-olds repeatedly see an interesting sight appear on their right, they initially continue to turn right even after they have been rotated so that the interesting sight is now on their left (Acredolo, 1978). This egocentrism is

egocentric representations coding of spatial locations relative to one's own body, without regard to the surroundings not absolute; if toys are hidden right next to a distinctive landmark, such as a large tower of blocks, infants usually find the toys despite the change in their own position. Still, the question remains: How do children become able to find objects when their own position has changed and when landmarks are not available to guide their search?

Self-locomotion, the ability to move on one's own, seems to play a large part in helping infants acquire a sense of space independent of their own location. Thus, infants who crawl, or who have had experience propelling themselves in walkers, more often remember the locations of objects on the object-permanence task (pp. 132–133) than do infants of the same age who do not crawl on their own, or do not have experience with walkers (Bai & Bertenthal, 1992; Bertenthal, Campos, & Kermoian, 1994). Infants with experience in self-locomotion also do better in representing depth, as evidenced by changes in their heart rate as they approach the visual cliff (Chapter 5, pp. 190–191).

The reasons why self-produced locomotion enhances infants' coding of space should be familiar to anyone who has both driven a car and been a passenger in one. As noted by Bertenthal, Campos, and Kermoian (1994), just as driving requires continuous updating of information about the surroundings, so does crawling or walking. In contrast, just as being a passenger in a car does not require such continuous updating of one's location, neither does being carried.

The impact of self-produced locomotion on infants' coding of space was evident in a study in which 10- and 11-month-olds were placed next to a large box with three transparent plexiglass sides and one open side (see Figure 7.6). The open side was the one farthest from the infants but closest to the experimenter (Benson & Uzgiris, 1985). The experimenter began by putting an attractive toy in

(a)
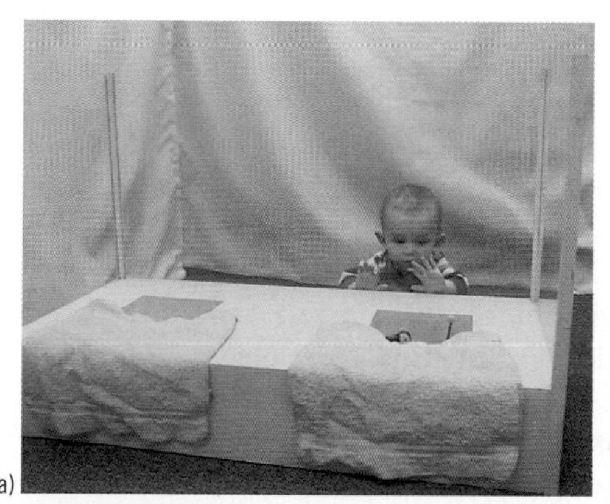

(b)
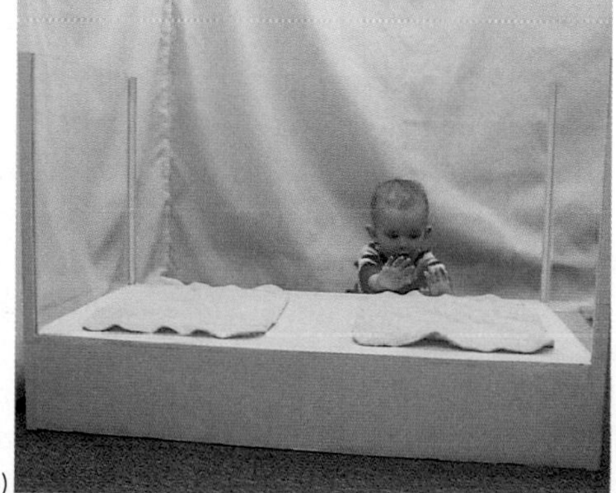

FIGURE 7.6 Self-locomotion and spatial representations A 10-month-old (a) sees a toy hidden in the well to his left behind a plexiglass window; (b) finds that he cannot reach through the plexiglass to get the toy, which now has a cloth over it; (c) having crawled to the open side of the apparatus, removes the cloth covering the toy, which is now on his right; (d) reaches for the toy; and (e) savors his success. Toddlers who locomoted on their own to the open side of the apparatus were more likely to reach to the correct location than were peers who were carried to the open side.

(c)
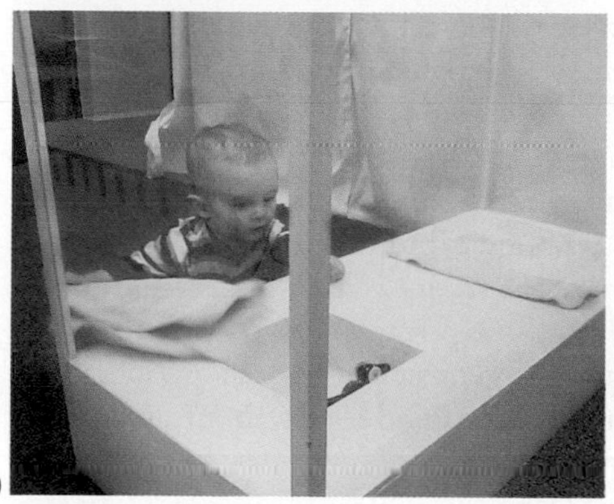

(d)

(e)

ALL: J. B. BENSON

one of two wells in the box and then placing identical pieces of cloth over both wells. Next, the infants were either induced to crawl on their own to the open side of the box or were carried there. Once on the open side, those who had crawled on their own were more likely to reach for the correct well to retrieve the toy. A related study that used a similar procedure and age group indicated that infants who crawled or walked also looked more at the location of the hidden object as they were moving than did infants who were carried (Acredolo, Adams, & Goodwin, 1984). Thus, the continuous updating of spatial representations that occurs during self-produced locomotion seems to be critical to infants' remembering the locations of hidden objects.

The power of self-locomotion to enhance older children's spatial coding was vividly illustrated by a study of kindergartners, all from the same class, who were asked to imagine being in their classroom while they were actually in their homes. Some were asked to mentally picture themselves walking from their seat in the classroom to the teacher's chair, then turning around to face the class. They then were asked to point to various locations in the classroom: the fishbowl, the alphabet chart, the coatroom door, and so on. Under these conditions, the 5-year-olds' pointing was very inaccurate. Other kindergartners were instructed to actually walk through their kitchen as they imagined walking from their seat to the teacher's chair and to turn around when they reached it. Under these conditions, the children's pointing to the imagined objects in their classroom was far more accurate. This result, like those with the infants, highlights the fundamental interconnection between the systems that produce self-generated motion through space and those that produce mental representations of space.

Development of Spatial Concepts in Blind and Visually Impaired People

The ever changing flow of visual information that accompanies self-locomotion is important not only for activating our sense of space while we are moving but also for enhancing long-term spatial development. Early visual experience may play an especially important role in spatial development. Evidence for this conclusion comes from cases in which surgery has restored vision to adults who were born blind (Carlson, Hyvarinen, & Raninen, 1986; von Senden, 1960). In most such cases, the corrective surgery in adulthood has not allowed people who were born blind to use visual information to effectively represent space.

Blind adults, even those blind from birth, tend to have a quite accurate sense of space, which helps them move around the environment skillfully.

ROBIN SACHS / PHOTOEDIT

These findings do not mean that children who are born blind cannot represent space. They actually tend to have a better sense of space than most people would guess. On tasks involving the representation of very small spaces, such as being guided in drawing two edges of a triangle on a piece of paper and then being asked to complete the triangle by drawing the third leg themselves, children who are born blind perform as well as sighted children who are blindfolded (Thinus-Blanc & Gaunet, 1997). On tasks involving representation of large spaces, such as those formed by exploring unfamiliar rooms, the spatial representations of people born blind also are surprisingly good—just about as good as those formed by sighted people who were blindfolded during the exploration period. Thus, although our representation of large spaces seems to benefit from early visual experience, many blind people develop impressive senses of space without ever seeing the world.

Representing Space Relative to the External Environment

As noted earlier, infants as young as 6 months old can code hidden objects' locations in terms of landmarks. However, for such young infants to use a landmark successfully, it needs to be the only obvious landmark in the environment and must be located right next to the hidden object.

With development, infants become increasingly able to choose among alternative landmarks. In research in which 12-month-olds are presented with a single yellow cushion, a single green cushion, and a large number of blue cushions, they have little trouble finding an object hidden under either the yellow or the green cushion (Bushnell, McKenzie, Lawrence, & Connell, 1995). By age 5 years, children can also represent an object's position in relation to multiple landmarks, such as when it is midway between a tree and a street lamp (Newcombe & Huttenlocher, 2000).

More difficult for forming spatial representations are situations in which children are moving around in an environment without landmarks or where the only landmarks are far from the target location. To understand the challenge of such tasks, suppose that you walked through a forest and didn't remember the exact turns you had taken. How would you find your way back? Some animals, such as ants, rodents, and geese, have a skill known as **dead reckoning,** the ability to keep track continuously of their locations relative to the starting point and thus to go directly back to it (Gallistel, 1990). This skill is very important for such creatures, who forage for food and then return to a fixed nest. Children (and adults) show dead reckoning to some degree—good enough to lead them in the right general direction (Loomis et al., 1993). Even blindfolded 2-year-olds who have been led on circuitous routes show better than chance ability to return toward the starting point (Muller & Wehner, 1988).

On the other hand, forming relatively precise coding of locations in the absence of straightforward landmarks continues to be difficult for people well beyond 2 years of age (Bremner, Knowles, & Andreasen, 1994). Six- and 7-year-olds are not very good at it (Overman, Pate, Moore, & Peleuster, 1996), nor are many adults (Gallistel, 1990). For example, when adults are asked to walk around the perimeter of an unfamiliar college campus and then to walk straight back to the starting point, many choose routes that take them nowhere near the original location (Cornell, Heth, Kneubuhler, & Sehgal, 1996).

The degree to which people develop spatial skills is strongly influenced by the importance of these skills in their culture. To demonstrate this point, Kearins (1981) compared the spatial abilities of Aboriginal children growing up in the Australian desert with those of their Euro-Australian peers growing up in Australian cities. Spatial ability is essential in Aboriginal culture, because much of life in this culture consists of long treks between distant oases and water holes. Needless to say, the Aborigines cannot rely on road signs; they must rely on their sense of space to find the water. Consistent with the importance of spatial skills in their everyday lives, Aboriginal children are superior to city dwellers in memory for spatial location, even in playing board games, a context that is more familiar to urban children (Kearins, 1981). Thus, consistent with the general importance of the sociocultural context, the uses that people make of spatial thinking in their everyday activities greatly influence the quality of spatial thinking that they achieve.

dead reckoning the ability to keep track continuously of one's location relative to the starting point and thus to go directly back to it

Time

As noted earlier, a basic sense of the flow of events through time seems to be innate; without such a sense of time, the world would seem utterly chaotic. However, a great deal of development beyond this base occurs in how children experience time and how they reason about it.

Experiencing Time

The most basic sense of time, and the one that emerges at the youngest age, involves the experience of time—that is, knowing what happened first, what happened next, and so on. Not surprisingly, given how mystifying life would be without such a sense of time, children represent the order in which events occur over time from early in infancy. In one study, in which 3-month-olds saw interesting photos first on their left, then on their right, then on their left, and so on, they began to look to the side where each new photo was to appear even before it was presented (Haith, Wentworth, & Canfield, 1993). This looking pattern indicated that the 3-month-olds detected the repetitive sequence of events over time and expected the sequence to continue. By 12 months of age, if not earlier, infants can detect the order of events they have seen only once; after seeing a pair of actions, they imitate the behaviors in the order in which they occurred (Bauer, 1995). By the age of 20 months, toddlers show similar proficiency with sequences of three events (Bauer, 1995) (see Figure 7.7). The fact that the toddlers maintain the original order when they imitate the three actions indicates that they mentally represented what came first, what next, and so on.

Estimating the duration of events (how long they took) is more difficult than remembering the order in which they occurred. Not surprisingly, this capability develops somewhat later. By the age of 5, however, children can learn to estimate quite accurately periods of three to thirty seconds if they are given feedback about the length of the time period (Fraisse, 1982). For example, if they are told that two tones will occur thirty seconds apart, are presented with the tones, and then are asked to generate the same time interval for themselves, most are able to do so fairly accurately. To estimate such brief durations, young children often count the number of seconds that are passing. This strategy sometimes is useful but not always. The problem is that preschoolers often fail to realize the importance of counting at an even rate (Levin, 1989). This difficulty is not unique to the concept of time. In general, maintaining consistent units of measurement poses a serious difficulty for children, regardless of whether they are dividing up food, measuring the length of a line, or estimating the passage of time (Miller, 1989).

What about longer time periods—periods of weeks, months, or years? William Friedman, a psychologist who has focused on children's understanding of time, has found that preschoolers possess some knowledge regarding such long periods. For example, when asked which of two past events occurred more recently, most 4-year-olds knew that a specific event, such as Valentine's Day, that happened a week ago was more recent than an event that happened seven weeks ago, such as Christmas (Friedman, 1991). Not until age 9, however, are children able to estimate whether their birthday or Christmas occurred more recently, if both occurred more than sixty days earlier (Friedman, Gardner, & Zubin, 1995). A similar developmental sequence is evident with regard to the timing of future events, though it occurs at slightly older ages. For example, 6- and 7-year-olds know which of two future events is farther away if the events are no more than two months in the

(a) 
(b) 
(c) 
(d) 

ALL: COURTESY OF PATRICIA BAUER

FIGURE 7.7 Imitating sequences of events Understanding the actions they are imitating helps toddlers perform the actions in the correct order. In this illustration of the procedure used by Bauer (1995) to demonstrate this point, a toddler imitates a previously observed three-step sequence to build a rattle. The child (a) picks up a block; (b) puts it into the bottom half of the container; (c) screws the top half of the container onto the bottom, thus completing the rattle; and (d) shakes it.

future, but it is not until age 10 that children know which of two events farther into the future is more distant (Friedman, 2000). Thus, with development, children expand their time horizons into both the past and the future.

Reasoning About Time

In addition to becoming increasingly proficient at estimating the passage of time, children in middle childhood also become increasingly proficient at reasoning about it. In particular, they become able to infer that if two events started at the same time, but one event ended later than the other, then the event that ended later lasted for a greater amount of time.

Children as young as 5 years old can make such logical inferences about time, but they do so only when the situation does not involve potentially distracting features. For example, when told that two dolls fell asleep at the same time and that one doll awoke before the other, 5-year-olds reason correctly that the doll that slept later also slept longer (Levin, 1982). As discussed in Chapter 4, however, when they see two toy trains travel in the same direction on parallel tracks, and one train stops farther down the track, 5-year-olds usually say that the train that stopped farther down the track traveled for a longer time regardless of when the trains started and stopped (Acredolo & Schmidt, 1981). The problem is that the 5-year-olds' attention is captured by the one train's being farther up the track, which leads them to focus on the spatial positions of the trains rather than on their own fragile concept of time. Piaget's (1969) observations of children's performance on this task, you will recall, were part of what led him to his concept of centration, the idea that preoperational-stage children often focus on a single dimension and ignore other, more relevant ones.

Causality

The famed eighteenth-century Scottish philosopher David Hume described causality as "the cement of the universe." His point was that causal connections unite discrete events into coherent wholes. Subsequent evidence has indicated that from early in development, children rely heavily on their understanding of causal mechanisms to infer why events occur. When children disassemble toys to find out how they work, or ask how flipping a switch makes a light go on, or wonder why their mother is yelling at them for minor transgressions, they are trying to understand causal mechanisms.

Causal mechanisms influence both physical and psychological events, but they operate somewhat differently in the two contexts (Corrigan & Denton, 1996). With physical events, causal mechanisms involve a transfer of energy from one object to another (think of a moving pool ball colliding with a stationary one). With psychological events, causal mechanisms produce motivations and reasons for feelings and actions (think of a mother's disappointed expression causing her son to feel sad). We have already discussed the development of children's understanding of psychological and biological causes in the sections of this chapter devoted to the understanding of people and other living things; in this section we focus on children's understanding of physical causation, involving the ways in which forces and energy produce their effects.

Causal Reasoning in Infancy

By 6 to 10 months of age, infants perceive causal connections among some physical events (Leslie, 1987; Oakes & Cohen, 1995). In a typical experiment showing infants' ability to perceive such links, Les Cohen and Lisa Oakes presented infants with a series of video clips in which a moving object collided with a stationary object, and the stationary object immediately started moving in the way one would expect (Cohen & Oakes, 1993). Different moving and stationary objects were used in each clip, but the basic "plot" remained the same. After seeing a few of these video clips, infants habituated to the collisions. Then they were shown a slightly different clip, in which the stationary object started moving before contact was made. Infants looked at the unusual event for a longer time than they had looked at the preceding trials. Presumably, the longer looking indicated that the new video clip violated their sense that inanimate objects do not move on their own.

Infants nearing the end of their first year also seem to expect larger objects to exert greater forces than smaller ones. Kotovsky and Baillargeon (1994) repeatedly showed 11-month-olds a video of a medium-sized moving object colliding with a stationary object and causing the stationary object to move a certain distance. After the infants habituated to this event, some were shown a video of a larger object, moving at the same speed as the medium-sized object had, hitting the stationary object and causing it to move farther than it had after it was hit by the medium-sized object. Other infants were shown a video of a smaller moving object, again moving at the same speed, hitting the stationary object and causing it to move farther than the medium-sized object had. Infants who witnessed the latter condition looked longer than infants who witnessed the former condition, apparently because they were surprised that the smaller object had greater impact.

Infants' and toddlers' understanding of causality influences not only their expectations about physical events but also their ability to remember and imitate sequences of actions. When 1-year-olds are shown a sequence of events whose order is arbitrary (for example, a Big Bird doll being put in a toy truck and then blocks being put in the truck) and then are asked to recall and imitate the actions in the order they saw them, they sometimes succeed (Bauer, 1995; Hertsgaard & Bauer, 1990). However, when they are asked to recall and imitate sequences of actions whose order is dictated by causality (for example, setting up a toy ramp at the back of a truck before having a toy car drive up the ramp into the truck), toddlers recall and imitate the sequence much more successfully. Especially striking, when they are shown a sequence of three actions, of which two are causally connected and one is not, they often imitate the two causally connected actions but leave out the irrelevant one (Bauer & Fivush, 1992). Thus understanding causal connections facilitates memory and imitation from at least the age of 1.

Development of Causality Beyond Infancy

Although infants in their first year possess the general idea of cause and effect, they apply the idea only in situations in which the cause–effect connections are obvious. A common theme that characterizes many particular developments in the understanding of causality beyond infancy is the continuous expansion of children's ability to identify causal relations even when the causes are not immediately apparent.

One illustration of this expansion comes from Zhe Chen and Robert Siegler's (2000) study of 1½- and 2½-year-olds' use of tools. The toddlers were presented with an attractive toy that was sitting on a table a foot beyond their reach. Between the child and the toy were six potential tools that varied in length and in the type of head at the end of the shaft (Figure 7.8). To succeed on the task, the toddlers needed to understand the causal relations that would make one tool more effective than the others for pulling in the toy. In particular, they needed to understand that a sufficiently long shaft and a head at right angles to the shaft were essential.

The 2½-year-olds succeeded considerably more often than the 1½-year-olds in obtaining the toy, both in their initial efforts to get it on their own and after being shown by the experimenter how they could use the optimal tool to get it. One reason for the older toddlers' greater success was that they used tools more often, as opposed to reaching with their hands across the table or asking their mothers for help. Another reason was that they more often chose the optimal tool when they did use a tool. The older toddlers also more often generalized what they had learned on the first problem to new, superficially different problems involving tools and toys with different shapes, colors, and decorations. The results indicated that the older toddlers had a deeper understanding of the causal relations between the tools' features and their likely success for

FIGURE 7.8 Problem solving Task used by Chen and Siegler (2000) to examine toddlers' problem solving. Choosing the right tool for getting the toy required children to understand the importance of both the length of the shaft and the angle of the head relative to the shaft. Older toddlers' greater understanding of these causal relations led them to more often use tools, rather than just reaching for the toy, and more often choose the right tool for the task.

raking in the toy. This deeper understanding allowed them to succeed more often in solving the problems.

In the next few years, children begin to search actively for causes when no cause is apparent. In one study, 3- to 5-year-olds were shown two objects that always moved together. The children were led to believe that the coordinated movement was caused by the two objects being connected by a hidden string, but when the children inspected the part of the apparatus where the string supposedly was housed, they found it empty. Many 4-year-olds and most 5-year-olds laughed, accused the experimenter of tricking them, and searched for the connection elsewhere. In contrast, almost no 3-year-olds did any of these things. The older preschoolers' searching indicated that they knew that some cause must have produced the effect, even if they could not identify what it was.

This emerging understanding that events must have causes seems to influence children's reactions to magic tricks. Most 3- and 4-year-olds fail to see the point of magic tricks; they grasp that something strange has happened but do not find the tricks humorous or actively try to figure out what caused the strange outcome (Rosengren & Hickling, 1994). By age 5, however, children become fascinated with magic tricks precisely because no obvious causal mechanism has produced the effect, and many want to search the magician's hat or other apparatus to see how such a stunt was possible. This increasing appreciation that even strange events must have causes, along with an increasing understanding of the mechanisms that connect causes and their effects, is crucial to the growth of causal reasoning. As discussed in Box 7.2, however, this increasing appreciation of causation does not immediately lead to the end of magical thinking.

Number

Like space, time, and causality, number is a central dimension of human experience. It is hard to imagine how the world would appear if we did not have at least a crude sense of number; we would not know how many fingers we have, how many people are in our family, and so on. All cultures have developed numerical systems, though in a few hunting-and-gathering societies, the systems are as simple as "1, 2, 3, many" (Dantzig, 1967). The fact that the simplest numerical systems stop at 3 may not be coincidental; infants also deal with sets of one, two, and three objects in much more sophisticated ways than they deal with larger sets. Below, we examine several basic aspects of the development of understanding of numbers.

Numerical Equality

Perhaps the most basic numerical understanding is that of **numerical equality,** the realization that all sets of *N* objects have something in common. When children recognize, for example, that two dogs, two cups, two balls, and two shoes all share the property of "twoness," they have a rudimentary understanding of numerical equality.

Infants as young as 5 months old appear to have such a sense of numerical equality, at least as it applies to sets of one, two, or three objects. We know this from studies using the familiar habituation paradigm. In these studies, young infants are shown a sequence of pictures, with each picture having the same number of objects but differing in other ways (Starkey, Spelke, & Gelman, 1990; van Loosbroek & Smitsman, 1990). For example, infants might be shown three stars arranged vertically, then three circles arranged horizontally, then three diamonds

numerical equality the realization that all sets of *N* objects have something in common

a closer look 7.2

Magical Thinking and Fantasy

Lest you conclude that by the age of 5, children's causal reasoning is pretty much like that of adults, consider the following conversation between two kindergartners and their teacher:

> *Lisa:* Do plants wish for baby plants?
> *Deana:* I think only people can make wishes. But God could put a wish inside a plant. . .
> *Teacher:* I always think of people as having ideas.
> *Deana:* It's just the same. God puts a little idea in the plant to tell it what to be.
> *Lisa:* My mother wished for me and I came when it was my birthday.
> (Paley, 1981, pp. 79–80)

This is not a conversation that would have occurred between two 10-year-olds and their teacher. Rather, as noted by Jacqui Woolley, a psychologist who has studied preschoolers' fantasies, it reflects one of the most charming aspects of early childhood: preschoolers and young elementary school children "live in a world in which fantasy and reality are more intertwined than they are for adults" (Woolley, 1997).

Young children's belief in fantasy and magic, as well as in normal causes, is evident in many ways. Most 4- to 6-year-olds believe that they can influence other people by wishing them into doing something, such as buying a particular present for the child's birthday (Vikan & Clausen, 1993). They believe that effective wishing takes a great deal of skill, and perhaps magic, but that it can be done. Many fear that monsters will cause them harm (Woolley, 1997). On the brighter side, many believe that getting in good with Santa Claus can make their hopes come true (Rosengren, Kalish, Hickling, & Gelman, 1994). As noted earlier in this chapter, preschoolers and young elementary school students often play with imaginary companions (Taylor, Cartwright, & Carlson, 1993). This world of the imagination is most prominent between the ages of 3 and 6, though aspects of it remain evident for years thereafter.

Research has shown that young children not only believe in magic; they also act on their belief. In one experiment, preschoolers were told that a certain box was magical and that if they placed a drawing in it and said magical words, the object depicted in the drawing would appear. Then the experimenter left the child alone with the box and a number of drawings. Children put drawings of the most attractive items into the box, said the "magical words," and were clearly disappointed when they opened the box and found only the drawings (Subbotsky, 1993, 1994).

How can we reconcile preschoolers' competence in causal reasoning with their belief in magic and Santa Claus? The key is to recognize that here, as in many other situations, children believe a variety of ideas at the same time. They think that magic may cause things to happen but do not depend on it when doing so could be embarrassing. In one demonstration of this limited belief in magic (Woolley & Phelps, 1994), an experimenter showed preschoolers an empty box, closed it, and then asked them to imagine a pencil inside it. The experimenter next asked the children whether there was now a pencil in the box; many said "yes." Then an adult came into the room and said that she needed a pencil to do her work. Very few of the preschoolers opened the box or handed it to her. Thus, when no further consequences would follow, many children said that the box contained a pencil, but they didn't believe strongly enough to act in a way that might look foolish to an adult.

How do children move beyond their belief in magic? One means is learning more about real causes; the more children know about the true causes of events, the less likely they are to explain them in magical terms (Woolley, 1997). Another means involves experiences that undermine the original beliefs, such as hearing a classmate say that there's no such thing as Santa Claus, or personal observations of two Santa Clauses passing each other on the street. Sometimes, however, children manage, at least temporarily, to avoid the disillusionment that such experiences can bring by distinguishing between flawed realizations of the ideal and the ideal itself—for example, between the real Santa Claus and imposters who dress up to look like him.

Belief in magic and fantastic creatures sometimes does not end in childhood. In Gallup polls, more than 20% of American adults have reported believing in ghosts and haunted houses (Gallup & Newport, 1991). Innumerable other adults indulge in superstitions such as not walking under ladders, avoiding cracks in sidewalks, and knocking on wood. Thus, many of us never entirely outgrow magical thinking.

arranged diagonally, and so on. After the infants habituate to the pictures of three objects, they are shown a picture with a different number of objects, (such as two squares). These studies indicate that 5-month-olds tend to discriminate one object from two and two objects from three. The tendency is weak—infants' discriminations are often based on the objects' total area or the length of their contours rather than on their number when both vary (Clearfield & Mix, 1999; Feigenson, Carey,

& Spelke, 2002). However, the fact that infants also discriminate among small numbers of events indicates that they do have a sense of number independent of area and contour. In one of the clearer demonstrations of this rudimentary numerical understanding, Wynn (1995) showed 6-month-olds a puppet that repeatedly jumped twice. After the infants habituated, they were shown the puppet jumping either once or three times. The infants' looking time increased, suggesting that the infants discriminated between two jumps and one or three.

Despite this early ability to deal with very small sets, it is not until children are 3 or 4 *years* old that they show comparable understanding of slightly larger sets. Even 36-month-olds have difficulty discriminating between four objects or events and five (Starkey, 1992; Strauss & Curtis, 1984). This surprising difference between infants' and toddlers' competence with very small sets and their incompetence with slightly larger ones is also crucial for evaluating claims that infants possess a rudimentary understanding of arithmetic.

Infants' Arithmetic

Some experts on infants' understanding of number have concluded that infants have a basic understanding of arithmetic (R. Gelman & Williams, 1998; Wynn, 1992). Here is the type of evidence on which they base their conclusion (Figure 7.9). A 5-month-old sees a doll on a stage. A screen comes up, hiding the doll from the infant's sight. Then the infant sees a hand place a second doll behind the screen and then sees the hand emerge from behind the screen without the doll, thus seeming to have left the second doll with the first one. Finally, the screen drops, revealing either one or two dolls. Most 5-month-olds look longer if only

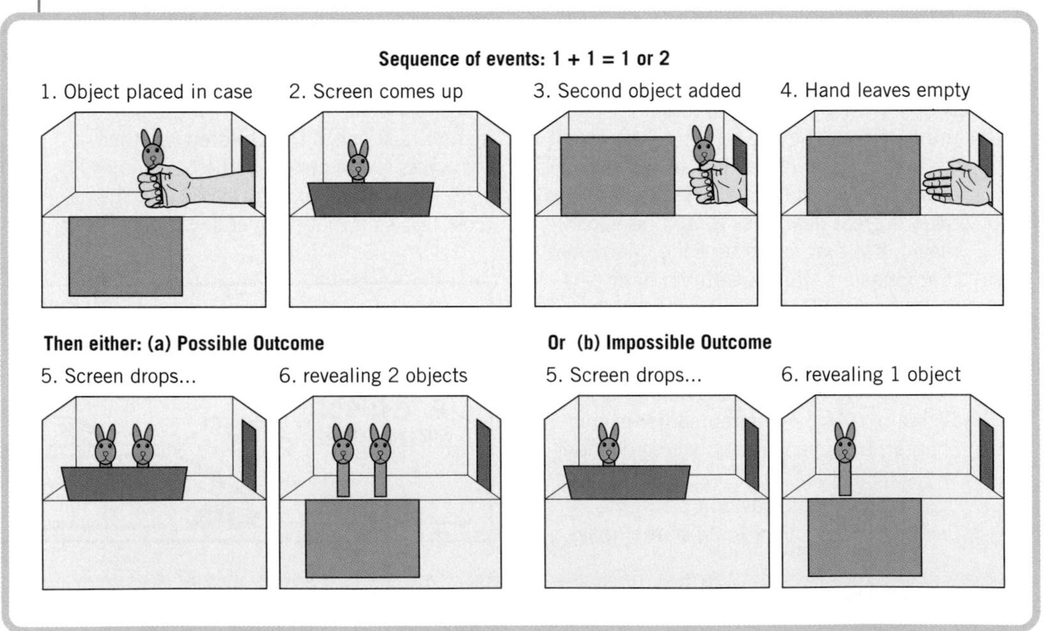

FIGURE 7.9 Task used by Wynn (1992) to examine infants' rudimentary understanding of addition The child saw (1) a single doll placed on a stage, (2) a screen raised to hide the doll, (3) a hand with a doll in it move toward and then behind the screen, and (4) the hand return empty after having been behind the screen. Then the screen dropped, revealing either (5 and 6) the possible event of two dolls on the stage or (7 and 8) the impossible event of one doll on the stage. Infants below 6 months of age looked for a longer time at the impossible event, suggesting their surprise at seeing one doll rather than two.

one object appears than if two do, suggesting that they expected that 1 + 1 should equal 2, and that they were surprised when they saw only one doll. Similar results are seen with subtraction: 5-month-olds look longer when the removal of one of two objects seems to result in two objects being present than when the removal results in only one being there (Wynn, 1992).

But do these findings show that infants understand arithmetic? The claim that they do has excited a great deal of argument. One reason for the controversy is that efforts to replicate the original result have had mixed success. Some studies have replicated it (Simon, Hespos, & Rochat, 1995); others have not (Wakeley, Rivera, & Langer, 2000). A more general reason for the controversy is that, as with the tasks described in the previous section, infants show competence only in situations where the total number of objects is limited to three or less. They do not show similar understanding of the effects of adding two objects to two other objects until they are much older—4 or 5 years old (Huttenlocher, Jordan, & Levine, 1994; Starkey, 1992).

The fact that infants' competence is limited to sets of three or fewer objects has led a second group of experts (Clearfield & Mix, 1999; Haith & Benson, 1998; Simon, 1997) to conclude that infants' responses on these tests of arithmetic are based not on understanding of arithmetic but instead on perceptual processes. For example, Haith and Benson (1998) proposed that infants rely on **subitizing,** a perceptual process by which adults and children can look at one, two, or three objects and almost immediately know how many objects are present. According to this interpretation, infants form a mental image of the object or objects that are initially present and of the objects that seem to be added to, or subtracted from, them, and they look for a longer time when the objects they see at the end of the problem appear different from that mental image. Consistent with this interpretation, when 5-month-olds are tested under conditions that increase the difficulty of forming a mental image, they do not show surprise when 1 + 1 = 1 (Uller & Huntley-Fenner, 1995). Thus, under some circumstances, infants show numerical competence with small sets of objects, but it remains uncertain whether this early competence means that they have a basic understanding of arithmetic.

Counting

By age 3, most children acquire a means—counting—for precisely establishing the number of objects in sets larger than three. Most 3-year-olds can count up to ten objects correctly. Preschoolers also seem to understand the basic principles underlying counting. Rochel Gelman and Randy Gallistel (1978) hypothesized that preschoolers understand the following five counting principles:

One-to-one correspondence: Each object should be labeled by a single number word.

Stable order: The numbers should always be recited in the same order.

Cardinality: The number of objects in the set corresponds to the last number stated.

Order irrelevance: Objects can be counted left to right, right to left, or in any other order.

Abstraction: Any set of discrete objects or events can be counted.

Much of the evidence that preschoolers understand these principles comes from their judgments of two types of counting procedures: incorrect counts and unusual but correct counts. When 4- or 5-year-olds see a puppet counting in a

subitizing a process by which adults and children can look at a few objects and almost immediately know how many objects are present

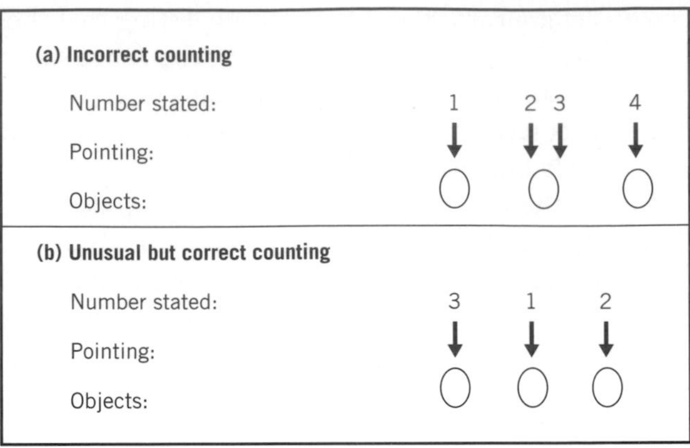

FIGURE 7.10 Counting procedures Counting procedures similar to those used by Frye et al. (1989) and Gelman et al. (1986). (a) An incorrect counting procedure. (b) An unusual but correct procedure.

way that violates the one-one correspondence principle—for example, by labeling a single object with two number words (Figure 7.10a)—they consistently say that the counting is incorrect (Frye, Braisby, Lowe, Maroudas, & Nicholls, 1989; Gelman, Meck, & Merkin, 1986). In contrast, when they see the puppet count in ways that are unusual but that do not violate any principle—for example, by starting counting in the middle of a row but counting all the objects (Figure 7.10b)—they judge the counting to be correct. Preschoolers readily say that they would not count that way themselves, but they also say that it is OK for the puppet to do so. Their ability to realize that procedures that they themselves would not use are nonetheless correct shows that they understand the principles that distinguish correct from incorrect counting.

Although children all over the world learn number words, the rate at which they do so is affected by the system of number words in their culture. For example, as noted by Kevin Miller and a group of collaborators, most 5-year-olds in China can count to 100 or more, whereas most of their counterparts in the United States cannot count nearly as high (Miller, Smith, Zhu, & Zhang, 1995). Part of the reason for the Chinese children's greater counting proficiency seems to be the greater regularity of their system of numbers, particularly in the teens. In both Chinese and English, the words for numbers above 20 follow a regular rule: "Decade name first, digit name second" (e.g., "twenty-one," "twenty-two," etc.). In Chinese, numbers between 10 and 19 follow the same rule (equivalent to "ten-one," "ten-two," etc.) In English, however, no simple rule generates the numbers between 10 and 19; each number has to be learned separately.

FIGURE 7.11 Counting level Although 3-year-olds in China and the United States can count to about the same point, 4- and 5-year-olds in China can count much higher than their U.S. peers. One reason for the faster development of Chinese children's counting ability appears to be that the Chinese words for numbers in the teens follow a consistent, easily learned pattern, whereas the English words for numbers in the teens must be memorized one by one. (Data from Miller et al., 1995)

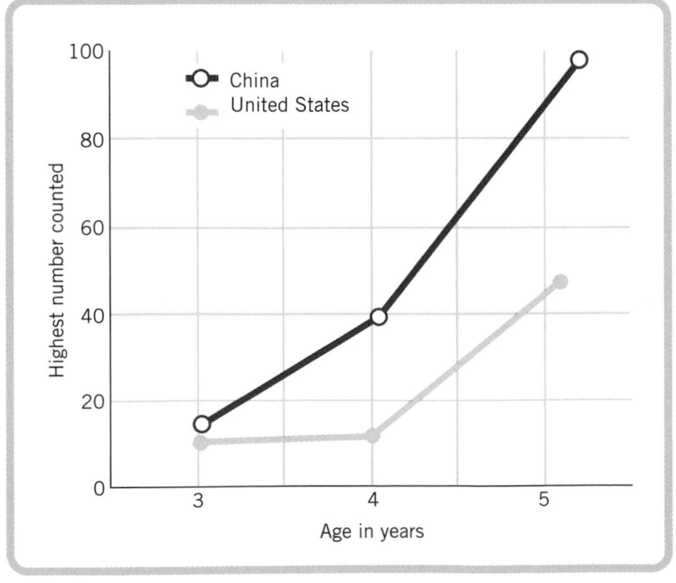

Figure 7.11 illustrates the apparent impact of this difference between the languages. Three-year-olds in the United States and China count comparably—both can recite the numbers 1 through 10. However, 4-year-olds in China quickly learn the teens and succeeding decades, whereas their peers in the United States experience prolonged difficulty with the teens. The difference in languages is not the only reason why the counting skill of U.S. children lags behind that of children in China; East Asian culture also places a much greater emphasis on mathematical skill. However, the greater simplicity of the Chinese system and those of other East Asian languages for naming teens seems to contribute to Chinese children's earlier mastery of counting.

Numerical Ordering

Although 5-month-olds recognize that sets of two or three have something in common with other sets that have the same number of entities, it is not until about a year later that infants form the general concept of larger number and smaller number. In one experiment (Strauss & Curtis, 1984), 16-month-olds were repeatedly shown two squares on a screen, one containing a single dot and the other, two dots. The children were rewarded each time they touched the square with two dots. Once they had learned to consistently touch the square with two dots, they were presented with two new squares, one containing three dots and one containing four. In this new situation, they usually touched the square with four dots, suggesting that they had formed the concept of larger and smaller numbers and had learned to choose the square with the greater number.

To confirm this conclusion, the experimenters ran a second experiment in which infants were rewarded for touching the square with one dot rather than two. When these infants subsequently were presented the larger sets, they chose the square with three dots rather than four. Thus, the conclusion that the 16-month-olds exhibited a basic understanding of larger and smaller number was supported.

As with other aspects of numerical understanding, it takes a long time for children to extend this competence to slightly larger numbers. For example, very few 3-year-olds consistently answer correctly such questions as "Which is more: *N* oranges or *M*?" when *N* and *M* are numbers between 5 and 9 (Siegler & Robinson, 1982). Some 4-year-olds solve such problems correctly, but even they often encounter difficulty when the numbers are close, as in "Which is more: 6 oranges or 7?" Not until the age of 5 do most children know the relative sizes of all, or almost all, numbers between 1 and 10. This knowledge, together with the other numerical understandings that children have developed during the preschool years, sets the stage for the very rapid growth of mathematical skills that occurs in the elementary school years.

review:

People, like other animals, are biologically prepared to code specific types of spatial information in specific parts of the brain. From their first year, children represent spatial locations both relative to their own bodies and relative to other features of the environment, such as landmarks. Self-produced movement seems to be crucial in the development of spatial representations.

A rudimentary sense of time also is present extremely early; by age 3 months if not earlier, infants possess a sense of experiential time, the order in which events happened. However, acquiring an accurate sense of duration takes until the age of 3 to 5 years, and learning to reason logically about time takes even longer.

A basic understanding of causality also emerges extremely early in development. Infants in their first year distinguish between physical causes and psychological causes. During the preschool and elementary school periods, children become increasingly adept at inferring causal relations, although a belief in magic and the supernatural coexists with this growing understanding of causal mechanisms, especially in the preschool years.

With small numbers, as with space, time, and causality, infants show a basic understanding within the first year. By age 3 or 4 years, they learn the principles underlying counting, such as that each object must be counted once and only once. By age 5 years, most learn the relative sizes of different numbers and how to count beyond 20. The rate of learning is influenced by the regularity of the number system in the child's language, as well as by the culture's emphasis on mathematics.

Chapter Summary

To understand their experiences, children must learn that the world includes several types of objects that are quite different from each other: people, other living things, and inanimate objects. Children also need a basic understanding of space, time, causality, and number, so that they will be able to code their experiences in terms of where, when, why, and how often events occurred.

Understanding Who or What

- Infants' early categories of objects are based in large part on perceptual similarity, especially similarity in the shapes of the objects. By the end of their first year, they also form categories of objects that serve the same function.
- By the age of 2 or 3 years, infants form category hierarchies of the type animal/dog/poodle, furniture/chair/La-Z-Boy, and so on.
- From infancy onward, children act differently toward people than toward other animals or inanimate objects. For example, infants smile more at people than at either rabbits or robots.
- By 18 months of age, toddlers understand that people have intentions, as demonstrated when the toddlers imitate what they believe an adult intended to do rather than what the adult actually did.
- Between the ages of 2 and 5 years, preschoolers develop a rudimentary theory of mind, according to which they organize their understanding of people's behavior. A key assumption of this theory of mind is that desires and beliefs lead to actions.
- Animals and plants, especially animals, are of great interest to young children. When animals are present, infants and toddlers pay careful attention to them.
- By the age of 4 years, children develop a quite elaborate understanding of living things, including coherent ideas about invisible processes such as growth, inheritance, illness, and healing. Both children's natural fascination with living things and the input they receive from the environment contribute to their knowledge about plants and animals.

Understanding Where, When, Why, and How Many

- Humans, like other animals, are biologically prepared to code space. Early in infancy, they code locations of other objects primarily in relation to their own location. As they gain the ability to move around on their own, they gain a sense of locations relative to the overall environment as well as to their own current location. From infancy onward, children also use landmarks to remember locations.
- Children who are born blind have surprisingly good mental representations of space.
- Just as infants are born with an ability to represent some aspects of space, so they are born with an ability to represent some aspects of time. Even 3-month-olds represent the order in which events occur. Infants of that age represent not only the past and present but also the future, as indicated by their using consistent sequences of past events to anticipate future events.
- By the age of 5 years, children also can reason about time, in the sense of inferring that if two events started at the same time, and one stopped later than the other, that event took longer. However, children can do this only when there are no interfering perceptual cues.
- The development of causal reasoning also begins in infancy. By 6 to 12 months, for example, infants understand the likely consequences of objects colliding. Understanding causal relations among actions helps 1-year-olds remember and imitate them.
- By age 4 or 5, children seem to realize that causes are necessary for events to occur. When no cause is obvious, they search for one. During the preschool period, though, children believe in magic as well as understanding many cause–effect relations.
- As with understanding of space, time, and causality, rudimentary understanding of number is present from early in infancy. Infants notice differences among sets of events that are repeated different numbers of time.
- By 3 years of age, most children learn to count as many as ten objects. Their counting seems to reflect an understanding of the principles that underlie counting, such as that each object should be labeled by a single number word.
- During the preschool period, children also become increasingly knowledgeable about the relative sizes of numbers, a type of knowledge that becomes vital when they learn arithmetic.

Critical Thinking Questions

1. Why is it useful for people to organize categories in hierarchies, such as animal/dog/poodle or vehicle/car/Honda?
2. How does paying close attention to objects' shapes help toddlers form categories and learn words?
3. What is naive psychology and why is it useful for young children?
4. Why do you think that 5-year-olds are so much better than 3-year-olds at false-belief problems?
5. Self-produced movement enhances children's representation of space. What evolutionary purpose might this serve?
6. Why do you think preschoolers believe in magic and fantasy when they are also capable of more sophisticated reasoning about causes and effects?

Key Terms

concepts, p. 252
category hierarchy, p. 254
perceptual categorization, p. 255
superordinate level, p. 256
subordinate level, p. 256
basic level, p. 256
naive psychology, p. 258
psychological constructs, p. 258
intention, p. 259
theory of mind, p. 260
false-belief problems, p. 262
appearance–reality problems, p. 263
autism, p. 263
theory-of-mind module (TOMM), p. 264
personify, p. 265
essentialism, p. 267
egocentric representation, p. 270
dead reckoning, p. 273
numerical equality, p. 278
subitizing, p. 281

CHAPTER 8

Intelligence and Academic Achievement

ZINADIA SEREBRIAKOVA, *The House of Cards,* c.1919

In 1904, the minister of education of France faced a problem. France, like other Western European and North American countries, had introduced universal public education around 1900. It soon became apparent, however, that some children were not learning well. Therefore, the minister wanted a means of identifying children who would have difficulty succeeding in standard classrooms, so that they could be given special education. His problem was: How could such children be identified?

One obvious way was to ask teachers to indicate which students in their classrooms were encountering difficulty. However, the minister worried that teachers might be biased in their assessments. In particular, he was concerned that some of them would be prejudiced against poor children and would say that they were not able to learn, even if they were. He therefore decided that what was needed was an objective test that would identify children who had difficulty learning. With this goal in mind, the minister asked Alfred Binet, a French psychologist who had been studying intelligence for fifteen years, to develop an easy-to-administer, objective test of intelligence.

Other psychologists of the time had tried to develop such a test and had failed. In retrospect, their failures were due to deficiencies in their theories of intelligence. The prevailing view at the time was that intelligence is based on simple skills, such as forming associations and detecting whether two objects are the same or different. According to this view, children who are more adept than their peers at such simple skills learn more quickly and thus become more intelligent. The theory was plausible—but wrong. It is now clear that simple skills are only weakly related to broader, everyday indicators of intelligence, such as school performance.

Binet had a different theory. He believed that the key components of intelligence were high-level abilities, such as problem solving, reasoning, and judgment, and he maintained that intelligence tests should assess such abilities directly. Therefore, on the test that he and his colleague, Théophile Simon, devised—the *Binet-Simon Intelligence Test*—children were asked (among other things) to interpret proverbs, solve puzzles, name objects, and sequence the frames of cartoons so that the joke made sense.

Binet's approach was successful in identifying children who would have difficulty learning from classroom instruction. More generally, children's performance on the Binet-Simon test correlated highly not only with their school grades at the time of testing but also with their grades years later. The success of this test bears out the adage "There is nothing so practical as a good theory."

In addition to the practical impact of his test, Binet's approach to intelligence has exercised a lasting influence on research on the topic. In most areas of cognitive development—perception, language, conceptual understanding, and so on—the emphasis is on age-related changes: how younger children differ from older ones. Following Binet's lead, however, research on intelligence has focused on *individual differences*—on how and why children of the same age differ from each other, and on the *continuity* of such individual differences over time. The nature of individual differences is one of the enduring themes throughout the field of child development, but nowhere is the focus on it more intense than in the study of intelligence.

Questions regarding the development of intelligence excite strong passions, and no wonder. Research in this area raises many of the most basic issues about human nature: the roles of heredity and environment, the influence of ethnic and racial differences, the effects of wealth and poverty, and the possibility of improvement. Almost everyone has opinions, often heartfelt ones, about why some people are more intelligent than others. Intelligence research also has added greatly to the understanding of many of the major themes of this book, especially the nature and origins of *individual differences,* the contributions of the *active child* and of the *sociocultural context,* the way in which *nature and nurture* together shape development, the degree of *continuity* in a key human trait, and the role of *research and children's welfare.* Before examining research on the development of intelligence, however, we pose a question that sounds innocuous but that actually is at the heart of many of the controversies: What *is* intelligence?

What Is Intelligence?

Intelligence is notoriously difficult to define, but this has not kept people from trying. Part of the difficulty is that intelligence can legitimately be described at three levels of analysis: viewed as one thing, a few things, or many things.

Intelligence as a Single Trait

Some researchers view intelligence as a single entity that influences all aspects of cognitive functioning. Supporting this idea is the fact that performance on almost all intellectual tasks is positively correlated. Children who do well on one intellectual task tend to do well also on others (Anderson, 1992). These positive correlations occur even among quite dissimilar intellectual tasks, for example, remembering lists of numbers and folding pieces of paper to reproduce printed designs. The omnipresent positive correlations have led to the hypothesis that each of us possesses a certain amount of ***g*,** or **general intelligence,** and that *g* influences our ability to think and learn on all intellectual tasks (Jensen, 1973; Spearman, 1927).

Numerous sources of evidence attest to the usefulness of viewing intelligence as a single entity. Measures of *g,* such as overall scores on intelligence tests, correlate positively with school grades and achievement test performance (Brody, 1992). At the level of cognitive processes, *g* correlates with information-processing speed (Deary, 1995) and with speed of neural transmission in the brain (Vernon, 1993). Measures of *g* also correlate strongly with people's knowledge of subjects they have not studied in school, such as medicine, law, art history, the Bible, and so on (Lubinski & Humphreys, 1997). Thus, there is good reason to view intelligence as a single entity that involves the ability to think and learn.

Intelligence as a Few Basic Abilities

There also are good arguments for viewing intelligence as more than a single general entity. The simplest such view holds that there are two types of intelligence: *crystallized intelligence* and *fluid intelligence* (Cattell, 1987). **Crystallized intelligence** is factual knowledge about the world: knowledge of word meanings, arithmetic facts, capitals of countries, and so on. **Fluid intelligence,** on the other hand, involves the ability to think on the spot, for example, by drawing inferences and understanding relations between concepts that have not been encountered previously. On intelligence tests, fluid intelligence is reflected in the ability to assemble novel puzzles, determine the next entry in a series of numbers, identify which one of four objects is related to the others, and so on.

_g_ (general intelligence) the part of intelligence that is common to all intellectual tasks

crystallized intelligence factual knowledge about the world

fluid intelligence ability to think on the spot to solve novel problems

The distinction between fluid and crystallized intelligence is supported by the fact that tests of each type of intelligence correlate more highly with each other than they do with tests of the other type. Thus, children who do well on one test of fluid intelligence tend to do well on other tests of fluid intelligence but not necessarily on tests of crystallized intelligence. In addition, the two types of intelligence have different developmental courses. Crystallized intelligence increases steadily from early in life to old age, whereas fluid intelligence peaks in early adulthood and slowly declines thereafter (Horn, Donaldson, & Engstrom, 1981).

A somewhat more complex view of intelligence proposes that the human intellect is composed of several abilities. One prominent proposal of this type, that of Thurstone (1938), portrayed intelligence as involving seven **primary mental abilities:** word fluency, verbal meaning, reasoning, spatial visualization, numbering, rote memory, and perceptual speed. The key evidence for the usefulness of dividing intelligence into these seven abilities is similar to that for the distinction between fluid and crystallized intelligence. Performance on various tests of a single ability tends to be more similar than performance on tests of any of the other abilities. For example, although both spatial visualization and perceptual speed are measures of fluid intelligence, children tend to perform more similarly on two tests of spatial visualization than they do on a test of spatial visualization and a test of perceptual speed. The trade-off between the two views is between the simplicity of the crystallized/fluid distinction and the greater precision of the seven primary mental abilities.

Intelligence as Multiple Processes

Yet other views see intelligence as comprising numerous, distinct processes. Information-processing analyses of how people solve intelligence test items (Carpenter, Just, & Shell, 1990; Hunt, 1978) and how they perform everyday intellectual tasks such as reading, writing, and arithmetic (Geary, 1994; Stanovich, 1992) reveal that a great many processes are involved. These include attending, perceiving, encoding, associating, generalizing, planning, reasoning, forming concepts, solving problems, generating and applying strategies, comprehending and producing language, and so on. Viewing intelligence as "many things" allows more precise specification of the processes involved in intelligent behavior than do approaches that view it as "one thing" or "a few things."

A Proposed Resolution

How can these competing perspectives on intelligence be reconciled? After studying intelligence for more than half a century, John Carroll (1993) proposed a grand, hierarchical integration: the **three-stratum theory of intelligence** (Figure 8.1). At the top of the hierarchy is *g;* in the middle are eight moderately general abilities (which include both fluid and crystallized intelligence and more specific skills, similar to the seven primary mental abilities); at the bottom are many specific processes. General intelligence influences all of the moderately general abilities, and both general intelligence and the moderately general abilities influence the specific processes. For example, knowing someone's general intelligence allows fairly reliable prediction of the person's general memory skills; knowing both of them allows quite reliable prediction of the person's memory span; and knowing all three allows very accurate prediction of the person's memory span for a particular type of material, such as words, letters, or numbers.

primary mental abilities seven abilities said by Thurstone to be crucial to intelligence

three-stratum theory of intelligence Carroll's model of intelligence, including *g* at the top of the hierarchy, eight moderately general abilities in the middle, and many specific processes at the bottom

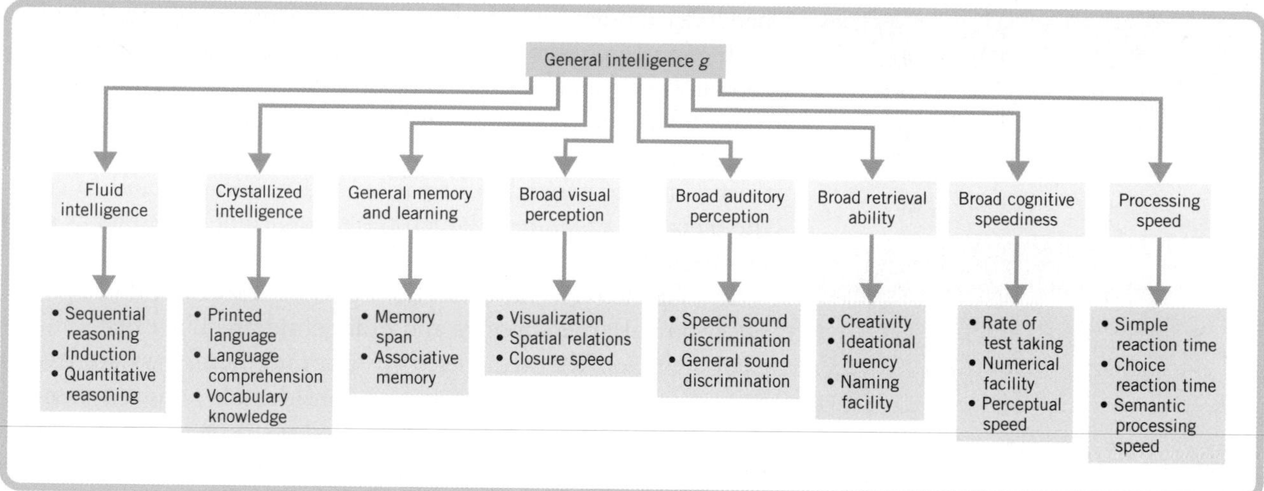

FIGURE 8.1 Carroll's three-stratum model of intelligence In Carroll's three-stratum model of intelligence, general intelligence (*g*) influences several intermediate-level abilities, and each intermediate-level ability influences a variety of specific processes. As this model suggests, intelligence can be usefully viewed as a single entity, as a small set of abilities, or as a very large number of particular processes.

Carroll's comprehensive analysis of the research literature indicated that all three levels of analysis outlined in this section are necessary to account for the totality of facts about intelligence. Thus, for the question, "Is intelligence one thing, a few things, or many things?" the correct answer seems to be "all of the above."

review:: Intelligence can be described at three levels of analysis. It can be viewed as a single general ability to learn, think abstractly, and adapt to novelty; as several moderately general abilities, such as spatial, verbal, and mathematical capacities; or as a vast collection of specific skills, processes, and content knowledge. All three levels are useful for understanding intelligence.

Measuring Intelligence

Although intelligence is usually viewed as an invisible *capacity* to think and learn, any measure of it must be based on *observable behavior.* Thus, when we say that a person is intelligent, we mean that the person acts in intelligent ways. One of Binet's profound insights was that the best way to measure intelligence is by observing people's actions on tasks that require a variety of types of intelligence: problem solving, memory, language comprehension, spatial reasoning, and so on. Modern intelligence tests continue to sample these and other aspects of intelligence.

The Contents of Intelligence Tests

Intelligence means somewhat different things at different ages (McCall, Eichorn, & Hogarty, 1977). For example, language ability is not a part of intelligence at 6 months of age, because infants this young neither produce nor understand words, but it is a vital part of intelligence at 6 years of age. The items on tests developed to measure intelligence at different ages reflect these changing meanings of intelligence. For example, on the Stanford-Binet intelligence test (a descendant of the original Binet-Simon test), 2-year-olds are asked to identify the objects depicted in line drawings (a test of recognition of objects), to find an object that they earlier

SPENCER GRANT / PHOTOEDIT

Many IQ tests measure spatial thinking through tasks like this one. Children are first shown a target pattern, like the one in the notebook on the desk; then they are asked to re-create the target pattern by assembling a set of small blocks, each with different smaller patterns on its six sides. Many children find such tasks interesting; others find them just frustrating.

had seen hidden (a test of learning and memory), and to place each of three objects in a hole of the proper shape (a test of perceptual skill and motor coordination). The version of the Stanford-Binet presented to 10-year-olds asks them to define words (a test of verbal ability), to explain why certain institutions exist (a test of general information and reasoning), and to count the blocks in a picture in which the existence of some blocks must be inferred (a test of problem solving and reasoning).

Intelligence tests have had their greatest success and widest application with preschoolers and older children. The exact abilities examined, and the items used to examine them, vary somewhat from test to test, but there is also considerable similarity among the leading tests. The most widely used instrument for children 6 years and older is the **Wechsler Intelligence Test for Children (WISC).**

The WISC is divided into two main sections: verbal and performance. The verbal section focuses on general knowledge of the world and skill in using language; it mainly measures crystallized intelligence. The performance section focuses on spatial and perceptual abilities; it mainly measures fluid intelligence. Each section includes six subtests, the last of which is optional, depending on whether the tester thinks all of the other tests are valid reflections of the child's capabilities. (If a child's attention wandered during a particular subtest or the child did not understand some of the questions, the tester discards the results of that subtest and substitutes those from the optional subtest.) The examples listed below reflect the types of items that appear on the test (the actual items are protected by copyrights and thus cannot be shown):

WISC Verbal Section

Information "How many nickels are in a quarter?" "What is the capital of France?"

Vocabulary "What is a helicopter?" "What is a treaty?"

Similarities "How are a hammer and a chisel alike?" "How are a mountain and a river alike?"

Arithmetic "Billy had 8 oranges and gave 3 to his friends; how many oranges did he have left?" "If 4 friends divided 48 cookies equally, how many did each one get?"

Comprehension "Why does each country have an army?" "Why do we have jails?"

Digit span "Repeat the following numbers in order when I'm finished: 5, 3, 7, 4, 9."

WISC Performance Section

Picture completion Children are shown a picture, such as a car with no wheels, and are asked: "What part of this picture is missing?"

Picture arrangement Children are asked to arrange several cartoon frames so that they tell a coherent story.

Block design Children are presented with nine cubes, each of which has two red sides, two white sides, and two sides that contain a red triangle and a white triangle. They then are shown a picture of a red and white square and are asked to arrange the cubes so that they match the picture.

Object assembly Children are presented puzzle pieces depicting parts of common objects and are asked to put them together to make the object. For example, if the pieces depicted the arms, legs, head, and other parts of the human body, the task would be to put the pieces together in a way that resembled a person.

Coding Children are presented a piece of paper on which are printed roughly 100 small geometric shapes: 25 squares, 25 circles, 25 triangles, and 25 diamonds. The shapes are presented in random order on the sheet. Whenever children see a given shape, they are supposed to write a certain symbol underneath it. For example, they might be asked to write a cross under every triangle they see and to write a dash under every circle. The goal is to write the symbols for as many of the shapes as possible within the allotted time.

Mazes Children are presented printed mazes and are asked to draw a line showing a path to a goal.

Wechsler Intelligence Scale for Children (WISC) a widely used test designed to measure the intelligence of children 6 years and older

IQ (intelligence quotient) a summary measure used to indicate a child's intelligence relative to others of the same age

normal distribution a pattern of data in which scores fall symmetrically around a mean value, with most scores falling close to the mean and fewer and fewer scores farther from it

standard deviation a measure of the variability of scores in a distribution; in a normal distribution, 68% of scores fall within 1 standard deviation of the mean and 95% of scores fall within 2 standard deviations

The Intelligence Quotient (IQ)

Intelligence tests such as the WISC and the Stanford-Binet provide an overall quantitative measure of a child's intelligence relative to that of other children of the same age. This summary measure is referred to as the child's **IQ (intelligence quotient).**

Understanding how IQ scores are computed, and why they are computed in this way, requires a little background. Early developers of intelligence tests observed that many easy-to-measure human characteristics, such as men's heights, women's heights, men's weights, and women's weights, fall into a **normal distribution.** As shown in Figure 8.2, normal distributions are symmetrical around a mean value, with most scores falling relatively near the mean. The farther a score is from the mean, the smaller the percentage of people who obtain it. For example, the mean height of adult males in the United States is around 5' 10". Many men are 5' 9" or 5' 11", but few men are 5' 2" or 6' 6". The farther a height from the mean, the smaller the number of men that height.

A similar distribution is found in the intelligence test scores of large, representative groups of children of a given age. This normal distribution means that most IQ scores are fairly close to the mean, with few children obtaining very high or very low scores. Early designers of IQ tests made an arbitrary decision that has been maintained ever since: a score of 100 is given to children who score exactly at the mean for their age at the time the test is developed. (The mean score can rise or fall in the years after the test is developed and, indeed, as discussed later in this chapter, such a change in mean IQ has occurred throughout the industrialized world in recent years.)

IQ scores reflect not only the mean for the test but also its **standard deviation.** As discussed on page 296, the standard deviation is a measure of the variability of scores within a distribution. By the definition of a normal distribution, 68% of scores in such a distribution must be between 1 standard deviation below the mean and 1 standard deviation above it, and 95% of scores must be between 2 standard deviations below the mean and 2 standard deviations above it.

On most IQ tests, the standard deviation is 15 points. Thus, as shown in Figure 8.2, a child scoring 1 standard deviation above the mean for his or her age (a score higher than 84% of children) receives a score of 115 (the mean of 100 plus the 15-point standard deviation). Similarly, a child scoring 1 standard deviation below the mean (a score higher than only 16% of children) receives a score of 85 (the mean of 100 minus the standard deviation of 15). As is also evident

FIGURE 8.2 A normal distribution, shown in both standard deviation units and in the IQ score assigned to that level of performance IQ scores fall into a normal distribution like the one shown here. The numbers along the base of the figure correspond to IQ scores. The number just below each IQ score indicates how many standard deviation units that score is below or above the mean; thus, an IQ of 55 is 3 standard deviations below the mean. The percentages in each interval indicate the percent of children whose scores fall within that interval; for example, less than 1% of children have IQ scores below 55 and slightly more than 2% score between 55 and 70.

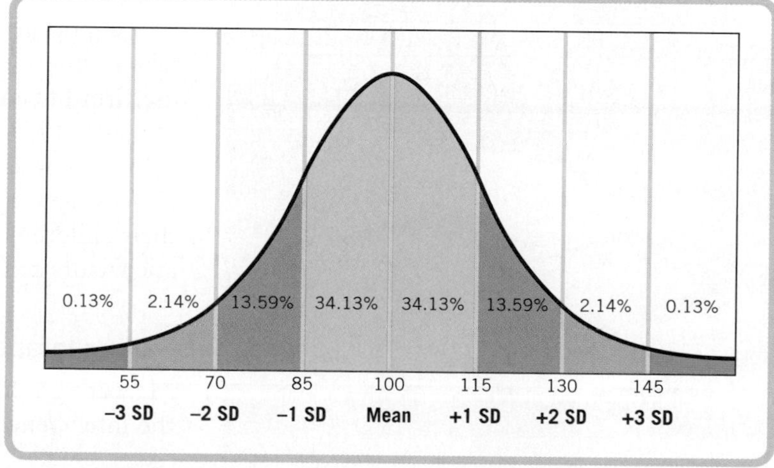

in Figure 8.2, about 95% of children obtain IQ scores within 2 standard deviations of the mean (between 70 and 130).

An advantage of this scoring system is that IQs at different ages are easy to compare, despite the great increases in knowledge that accompany development in all children. A score of 130 at age 5 means that a child's performance exceeded that of 98% of age peers; a score of 130 at age 10 means exactly the same thing. This property has facilitated analysis of the stability of IQ scores over time, a topic we turn to next.

Continuity of IQ Scores

If IQ is a consistent property of a person, then the IQ scores that people obtain at different ages should be highly correlated. Longitudinal studies that have measured the same children's IQ scores at different ages have, in fact, shown impressive continuity from age 5 years onward. For example, one study indicated that children's IQs at age 5 correlated .67 with their IQs at age 15 (Humphreys, 1989). This is a quite remarkable degree of continuity over a ten-year period. (Recall from Chapter 1 that a correlation of 1.00 indicates that two variables are perfectly correlated.) Indeed, IQ may be the most stable of all psychological traits (Brody, 1992).

Several variables influence the degree of stability of IQ scores over time. As might be expected, the closer in time that IQ tests are given, the more stability is found. Thus, the same study that found that IQ at ages 5 and 15 correlated .67 also found that IQ at ages 5 and 9 correlated .79 and that IQ at ages 5 and 6 correlated .87. For any given length of time between tests, scores are more stable at older ages. For example, in one study, IQ scores of 4- and 5-year-olds correlated .80, those of 6- and 7-year-olds correlated .87, and those of 8- and 9-year-olds correlated .90 (Brody, 1992).

The IQ scores of children whose parents take an interest in their academic success tend to increase over time.

LAURA DWIGHT

The fact that a person's IQ scores at different ages tend to be similar does not mean that the scores are likely to be identical. Children who take an IQ test at age 4 and again at age 17 show an average change, up or down, of 13 points; those who take the test at ages 8 and 17 show an average change of 9 points; and those who take it at ages 12 and 17 show an average change of 7 points (Brody, 1992). These changes are due in part to random variation, for example, in the child's alertness on the particular test days and in his or her knowledge of the items on the particular tests.

Changes in IQ scores over time may also be influenced by characteristics of children and of their parents other than intelligence. Scores tend to increase among children who believe that academic performance is very important. They also tend to increase among children whose parents take an interest in their children's learning and academic success and who use firm but moderate disciplinary procedures (McCall, Applebaum, & Hogarty, 1973). In contrast, IQ scores tend to decrease among children who view academic performance as unimportant and whose parents use either very stern or lax disciplinary procedures and show little interest in their children's performance in school. Thus, both random and systematic factors contribute to changes in children's IQs over time.

Testing Infants' Intelligence

Measuring infants' intelligence has proved more difficult than measuring the intelligence of older children. The main reason is that many abilities

individual differences 8.1

Gifted Children

By the time KyLee was 18 months old, he was fascinated with numbers: his favorite toys were plastic numbers and blocks with numbers on them. As he played with these toys, he said the number names over and over. When he was 2 years old, he saw a license plate with two 8s on it and said "8 + 8 = 16"; neither he nor his parents could explain how he knew this. By age 3 years, KyLee was playing math games on a computer every day. During one such game, he discovered the idea of prime numbers and thereafter was able to identify new prime numbers. Again, neither he nor his parents knew how he did this. Before he entered kindergarten, he could add, subtract, multiply, divide, estimate, and solve complex word problems. When asked if he ever got tired of numbers, he said, "No, never" and said that he was a "number boy" (Winner, 1996, pp. 38–39).

As noted by Ellen Winner, a psychologist who studies intellectually and artistically gifted children, some, like KyLee, show astonishing early facility in a particular area: numbers, drawing, reading, music, or some other realm. A smaller number of children are exceptional in a wide range of intellectual areas. These globally gifted children usually display several of the following signs of giftedness from very early in development (Robinson & Robinson, 1992):

- unusual alertness and long attention span in infancy
- rapid language development
- learning with minimal help from adults
- curiosity—asking deep questions and being dissatisfied with superficial answers
- high energy levels, often bordering on hyperactivity
- intense reactions to frustration
- precocious reading and interest in numbers
- exceptional logical and abstract reasoning
- unusually good memory
- enjoyment of solitary play

Exceptional early ability does not imply intellectual ability across the board, however. Children who are exceptional in several intellectual areas often are quite average in others. Some such children even show learning disabilities in certain areas (Benbow & Minor, 1990; Detterman, 1993). Similarly, exceptional early ability in an area is no guarantee of outstanding achievement in that area during adulthood (Benbow, 1992; Simonton, 1991). Factors such as motivation to excel, creativity, and perseverance in the face of difficulty also are essential for exceptional adult contributions.

Exceptionally early readers, such as this 3½-year-old, generally continue to be excellent readers throughout life.

ELIZABETH CREWS / THE IMAGE WORKS

that play large roles in later intelligence—language, mathematics, and logical reasoning, for example—are only minimally developed in infancy and therefore cannot be reliably measured at that time. Despite these difficulties, some tests of infants' intelligence have been formulated. Such tests, which measure perception, attention, early vocabulary, and basic motor abilities, have had some success in identifying babies with retardation and other developmental problems (e.g., Bayley, 1993; Colombo, 1993). However, they are not very useful for assessing the intelligence of more typical children.

review: Intelligence tests examine a range of abilities and types of knowledge, including vocabulary, verbal comprehension, arithmetic, memory, and spatial reasoning. The tests are used to obtain a general measure of intelligence, the IQ score. IQ tests are designed to produce average scores of 100, with higher scores indicating above-average intelligence and lower scores below-average intelligence. IQ scores of individual children tend to be quite stable over long periods of time, but they vary somewhat from one testing to the next.

IQ Scores as Predictors of Important Outcomes

IQ is a strong predictor of academic, economic, and occupational success. As noted earlier, IQ scores correlate positively and fairly strongly with school grades and achievement test performance, at the time of the test and years later (Brody, 1992). IQ scores also correlate positively with long-term educational achievement. In the United States, IQ in sixth grade correlates about .60 with the years of education that a person eventually obtains (Duncan, Featherman, & Duncan, 1972; Jencks, 1979).

In part, the positive relation between IQ and income and occupational success is due to the fact that standardized test scores serve as a gatekeeper, determining which students will be allowed to gain access to training and credentials required in lucrative professions. Even among people who initially have the same job, however, those with higher IQs tend to perform better (Hunter, 1986), earn more money (Jencks, 1979), and receive better promotions (Wilk, Desmarais, & Sackett, 1995). After a comprehensive review of research on intelligence, Brody (1992) concluded "IQ is the most important predictor of an individual's ultimate position within American society." A child's IQ is more closely related to the child's later occupational success than is the socioeconomic status of the family within which the child grows up, family income, the school the child attends, or any other variable that has been studied (Ceci, 1993; Duncan et al., 1972).

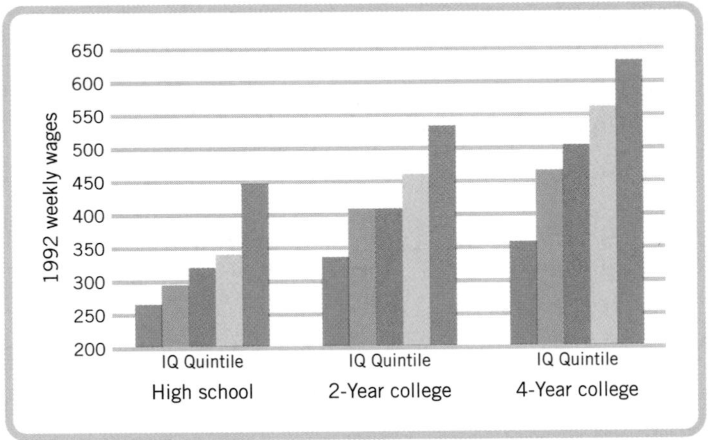

FIGURE 8.3 Effects of IQ and education on income IQ influences income, but so do other factors such as education. The relations are evident in these data, collected in the late 1980s, which indicate the average income of people who received different levels of education and who scored in different quintiles (fifths) of the IQ distribution. Within any given level of education, people of higher IQ earned more. Thus, among people with only a high school education, those who scored in the bottom 20% on an IQ test (the blue bar) averaged only a little more than $250/week, whereas those who scored in the top 20% (the purple bar) averaged almost $450/week. On the other hand, as shown by the purple bars, people in the top 20% in IQ score who had only a high school education earned an average of roughly $450/week, whereas those of comparable IQ but with a four-year college education earned almost $650/week. (Data from Ceci, 1996)

As strong a predictor as IQ is, it is far from the whole story in academic, economic, and occupational success. Motivation to succeed, creativity, physical and mental health, social skills, and a host of other qualities also exert important influences (Feldman, 1986; Sternberg, 2000; Tannenbaum, 1986). Figure 8.3 illustrates how the same set of data can provide evidence for the importance of both IQ and other factors. Consistent with the emphasis on the importance of IQ, the figure shows that for people with the same level of education, those with higher IQs earn more money. Consistent with the emphasis on the importance of other factors, the figure shows that among people of comparable IQs, those who complete more years of education earn more money. Thus, while IQ is a key contributor to educational, occupational, and economic success, other factors are also influential.

review: IQ scores are positively related to g\rades in school and achievement test performance, both at the time of the test and in the future. They are also positively related to occupational success in adulthood. However, they are not the only influence on these outcomes. Motivation, creativity, health, social skills and a variety of other factors contribute, too.

Genes, Environment, and the Development of Intelligence

No issue in psychology has produced longer or more acrimonious debate than the issue of how heredity and environment influence intelligence. Even people who recognize that intelligence, like all human qualities, is constructed through the continuous interaction of genes and environment often forget this fact and take extreme positions that are based more on emotions and ideology than on evidence. The purpose of the present discussion is to provide a coherent framework for thinking about the complex issues in this area and to summarize what is known.

A useful starting point for thinking about genetic and environmental influences on intelligence is provided by Bronfenbrenner's (1993) ecological model of development (discussed in detail in Chapter 9, pp. 346–348). This model envisions children's lives as embedded within a series of increasingly encompassing environments. The child, with a unique set of qualities, including his or her genetic endowment and personal experiences, is at the center. Surrounding the child is the immediate environment, especially the people and institutions the child interacts with directly: family, school, classmates, teachers, neighbors, and so on. Surrounding the immediate environment are more distant, and less tangible, environments that also influence development: cultural attitudes, the social and economic system, mass media, the government, and so on. We will now examine how qualities of the child, the immediate environment, and the broader environment contribute to the development of intelligence.

Qualities of the Child

Children contribute greatly to their own intellectual development. The contribution comes about through their genetic endowment, through the reactions they elicit from other people, and through their choice of environments in which to spend their time.

Genetic Contributions to Intelligence

As noted in Chapter 3 (pp. 95–97), genes have a substantial influence on intelligence. About 50% of the variation in IQs among Euro-Americans is attributable to genetic variation. (Recall from Chapter 3 that such an estimate—based on differing correlations between the IQs of identical twins, of fraternal twins, of cousins, and so on—means that about half of the differences in people's IQs can be attributed to genetic differences.)

A common stereotype is that the relative influence of heredity on intelligence is greatest early in life, when children's experience is limited, and that as children gain experience, the relative influence of the environment on intelligence grows. This stereotype has it exactly backward. The genetic contribution to intelligence is greater in older children than in younger ones. The IQs of adopted children and those of their biological parents (with whom they are not living) become increasingly correlated as the children grow up (Honzik, MacFarlane, & Allen, 1948). In contrast, the IQs of adopted children and their adoptive parents become less correlated as the children become older (Brody, 1992; DeFries, Plomin, & LaBuda, 1987; McGue, Bouchard, Iacono, & Lykken, 1993). One reason for this increasing genetic influence is that some genetic processes do not have their effects on IQ until later childhood and adolescence (Loehlin, 1989). For example, some

PATRICK BENNETT / CORBIS

Children influence their own development; these children's joyous reactions to their father's reading ensure that he will want to read to them in the future.

connections linking certain areas in the brain that are distant from each other are not formed until adolescence, and the extent of such connections reflects genetic influences (Thatcher, 1992). Another reason is that children's increasing independence with age allows them greater freedom to choose environments that are compatible with their own genetically based preferences, but not necessarily with those of the parents who are raising them (Scarr, 1992).

Genotype–Environment Interactions

As discussed in Chapter 3, the types of environments children encounter are partially influenced by their genotype. Sandra Scarr proposed that these gene–environment relations involve three types of effects: passive, evocative, and active (Scarr, 1992). *Passive effects* of the genotype arise when children are raised by their biological parents. These effects occur not because of anything the children do but because of the overlap between their parents' genes and their own. Thus, children whose genotypes predispose them to enjoy reading are likely to be raised in homes with books, magazines, and newspapers, because their parents also like to read. *Evocative effects* of the genotype emerge through children's eliciting or influencing other people's behavior. For example, even if a little girl's parents are not avid readers, they will read more bedtime stories to her if she seems interested in the stories than if she seems bored. *Active effects* of the genotype involve children's choosing environments that they enjoy. A high school student who likes reading will borrow books from the library and obtain books in other ways, regardless of whether her parents read to her when she was young. The evocative and active effects of the genotype help explain how children's IQs become more closely related to those of their biological parents, even if they are adopted and never see them (Matheny, Wilson, Dolan, & Krantz, 1981).

Gender and Intelligence

Despite widespread belief to the contrary, boys and girls are equivalent or almost equivalent in most aspects of intelligence. Boys tend to be overrepresented at both the upper and lower extremes; for example, four times as many boys as girls are highly precocious in math, and five times as many boys as girls are diagnosed with dyslexia, a reading disability (Benbow, 1988; Halpern, 1992). However, the average IQ scores of boys and girls are virtually identical (Hyde & McKinley, 1997).

Some small differences in average performance between boys and girls have been found in specific intellectual areas. Girls, as a group, tend to be stronger in verbal fluency, in writing, and in perceptual speed, with the differences in verbal fluency and perceptual speed appearing as early as the toddler years (Hedges & Nowell, 1995; Kimura & Hampson, 1994; Reinisch & Sanders, 1992). Boys, as a group, tend to be stronger in visual-spatial processing, in science, and in mathematical problem solving, with the differences in visual-spatial processing appearing as early as the age of 3 years and growing larger during adolescence (Halpern, 1997; Masters & Sanders, 1993). This pattern of differences is similar in different countries. For example, a study of eighth graders' science knowledge in forty-one countries showed differences favoring boys in 75% of the countries and no differences in the remaining 25% (Vogel, 1996). Although some research has suggested that these gender differences in intellectual abilities have decreased over the past few decades (e.g., Feingold, 1988), more systematic analyses indicate that the differences have actually been quite stable (Halpern, 1997; Hedges & Nowell, 1995; Voyer, Voyer, & Bryden, 1995).

What accounts for these differences is a matter of hot debate. Some argue that gender differences in intellectual abilities are primarily the result of biological differences (Collaer & Hines, 1995; Shaywitz et al., 1995). Others attribute the differences mainly to societal messages regarding the gender-appropriateness of different intellectual pursuits (e.g., "Math is for males") (Baenninger & Newcombe, 1989; Beal, 1994) or to peer pressure (Harris, 1995; Lytton, 1999; Lytton & Romney, 1991). Given the heated quality of the question, it is important to keep in mind the small magnitude of those differences that do exist. Although intellectual differences between boys and girls are more interesting than similarities are, they are also less prevalent.

Influence of the Immediate Environment

The influence that nurture has on the development of intelligence begins with the immediate environment of families and schools.

Family Influences

If asked to identify the most important environmental influence on their intelligence, most people probably would say "my family." Testing the influence of the family environment on children's intelligence, however, requires some means of assessing what the family environment is. How can we measure something as complex and multifaceted as a family environment, especially when that environment may be different for different children in the same family?

Bettye Caldwell and Robert Bradley (1979) tackled this complex problem by devising a measure known as the HOME (Home Observation for Measurement of the Environment). This measure samples various aspects of children's home life, including the organization and safety of living space; the intellectual stimulation offered by parents; whether children have books of their own; the amount of parent–child interaction; the parents' emotional support of the child; and so on. Table 8.1 shows the items and subscales used in the original HOME, which was designed to assess the family environments of children between birth and age 3. Subsequent versions of the HOME have been developed for application with preschoolers, school-age children, and adolescents (Bradley, 1994).

Throughout childhood, children's IQ scores are positively correlated with the quality of their family environment as measured by the HOME (Barnard, Bee, & Hammond, 1984; Luster & Dubow, 1992; Siegel, 1984). The HOME also predicts future IQ scores. HOME scores of families of 6-month-olds correlate positively with the IQ of the children at age 4½ (Bradley & Caldwell, 1984); and HOME scores of 2-year-olds correlate positively with IQ scores and school achievement of 11-year-olds (Bradley, 1989; Olson, Bates, & Kaskie, 1992). When HOME scores are relatively stable over time, IQ scores also tend to be stable; when HOME scores change, IQ scores also tend to change in the same direction (Bradley, 1989). Thus, assessing varied aspects of a child's family environment allows good prediction of the child's IQ.

Given this evidence, it is tempting to conclude that better-quality home environments cause children to have higher IQs. Whether that is actually the case is

TABLE 8.1

Items and Subscales on the HOME (Infant Version)

I. Emotional and Verbal Responsivity of Mother
1. Mother spontaneously vocalizes to child at least twice during visit (excluding scolding).
2. Mother responds to child's vocalizations with a verbal response.
3. Mother tells child the name of some object during visit or says name of person or object in a "teaching" style.
4. Mother's speech is distinct, clear, and audible.
5. Mother initiates verbal interchanges with observer—ask questions, makes spontaneous comments.
6. Mother expresses ideas freely and easily and uses statements of appropriate length for conversation (e.g., gives more than brief answers).
7. Mother permits child occasionally to engage in "messy" types of play.
8. Mother spontaneously praises child's qualities or behavior twice during visit.
9. When speaking of or to child, mother's voice conveys positive feelings.
10. Mother caresses or kisses child, mother's voice conveys positive feelings.
11. Mother shows some positive emotional responses to praise of child offered by visitor.

II. Avoidance of Restriction and Punishment
12. Mother does not shout at child during visit.
13. Mother does not express overt annoyance with or hostility toward child.
14. Mother neither slaps nor spanks child during visit.
15. Mother reports no more than one instance of physical punishment occurred during the past week.
16. Mother does not scold or derogate child during visit.
17. Mother does not interfere with child's actions or restrict child's movements more than three times during visit.
18. At least ten books are present and visible.
19. Family has a pet.

III. Organization of Physical and Temporal Environment
20. When mother is away, care is provided by one of three regular substitutes.
21. Someone takes child into grocery store at least once a week.
22. Child gets out of house at least four times a week.
23. Child is taken regularly to doctor's office or clinic.
24. Child has a special place in which to keep his or her toys and "treasures."
25. Child's play environment appears safe and free of hazards.

IV. Provision of Appropriate Play Materials
26. Child has some muscle-activity toys or equipment.
27. Child has push or pull toy.
28. Child has stroller or walker, kiddie car, scooter, or tricycle.
29. Mother provides toys or interesting activities for child during interview.
30. Provides learning equipment appropriate to age—cuddly toy or role-playing toys.
31. Provides learning equipment appropriate to age—mobile, table and chairs, high chair, play pen.
32. Provides eye–hand coordination toys—items to go in and out of receptacle, fit-together toys, beads.
33. Provides eye–hand coordination toys that permit combinations—stacking or nesting toys, blocks or building toys.
34. Provides toys that incorporate literature or music.

V. Maternal Involvement with Child
35. Mother tends to keep child within visual range and to look at him or her often.
36. Mother "talks" to child while doing her work.
37. Mother consciously encourages developmental advances.
38. Mother invests "maturing" toys with value via her attention.
39. Mother structures child's play periods.
40. Mother provides toys that challenge child to develop new skills.

VI. Opportunities for Variety of Daily Stimulation
41. Father provides some caretaking every day.
42. Mother reads stories at least three times weekly.
43. Child eats at least one meal per day with mother and father.
44. Family visits or receives visits from relatives.
45. Child has three or more books of his or her own.

Source: From "174 Children: A Study of the Relationship Between Home Environment and Cognitive Development During the First 5 Years" by R. H. Bradley and B. M. Caldwell, 1984. In A. W. Gottfried (Ed.) *Home Environment and Early Cognitive Development* (pp. 7–8), New York: Academic Press. Copyright © 1984 by Academic Press. Reprinted by permission.

not yet known, however. The uncertainty reflects two factors. First, the type of home intellectual environment that parents establish is almost certainly influenced by their genetic makeup. Second, almost all studies using the HOME have focused on families in which children live with their biological parents. These two circumstances may mean that parents' genes influence both the intellectual quality of the home environment and children's IQs; thus the home intellectual environment as such may not cause children to have higher or lower IQs. Consistent with this possibility, in the few studies in which the HOME has been used to study adoptive families, the correlations between it and children's IQs are lower than in studies of children living with their biological parents (Plomin, DeFries, McClearn, & Rutter, 1997). Thus, although scores on the HOME clearly correlate with children's IQs, causal relations between the two have not yet been established.

Shared and nonshared family environments When we think of a family's intellectual environment, we usually think of characteristics that are the same for all children within the family: the parents' emphasis on education, the number of books in the house, the frequency of intellectual discussions around the dinner table, and so on. As discussed in Chapter 3, however, each child within a given family also encounters unique, nonshared environments. In any family, only one child can be the firstborn and receive the intense, undivided attention early in life that this status often entails. Similarly, a child who has interests or personality characteristics like those of one or both parents may receive more positive attention than other children in the family. Children also occupy niches within their family, and the fact that one child is "the smart one" may lead siblings to withdraw from intellectual activity and instead become "the popular one," "the athletic one," or even "the bad one" (Scarr, 1992). If very deficient homes are excluded from consideration, such within-family variations in children's environment seem to have a greater impact on the development of intelligence than do between-family variations (Plomin & Daniels, 1987; Scarr & Weinberg, 1983; Teasdale & Owen, 1984). Consistent with this finding, most of the items on the HOME instrument (see Table 8.1) assess not the shared family environment but rather the environment of the individual child being considered: whether the mother speaks to that child during the visit, whether she praises the child, whether she responds to the child's verbal statements, and so on.

Influences of Schooling

Attending school makes children smarter. One type of evidence for this conclusion came from a study that examined IQ scores of older and younger Israeli children in the fourth, fifth, and sixth grades (Cahan & Cahan, 1989). As indicated by the gradual upward trends in the graphs in Figure 8.4, older children within each grade did somewhat better than younger children within that grade on each part of the test. However, the jumps in the graphs between grades indicate that children who were only slightly older, but who had a year more schooling, did much better than the slightly younger children in the grade below them. For example, on the Verbal Oddities subtest (which involves indicating which word in a series doesn't belong with the others), the results show a small gap between 126- and 127-month-old fourth graders but a large gap between both of them and 128-month-old fifth graders.

Another type of evidence indicating that going to school makes children smarter is that average IQ and achievement test scores rise during the school year and drop during summer vacation (Ceci, 1991; Huttenlocher, Levine, & Vevea, 1998). The way in which these changes vary with children's family backgrounds adds further support to the view that schooling makes children smarter (Alexander & Entwistle, 1996; Entwistle & Alexander, 1992; Heyns, 1978). Children from families of low socioeconomic status and those from families of high socioeconomic status make comparable gains in school achievement during the school year. However, over the summer, low-SES children's achievement test scores drop, whereas the scores of high-SES children stay constant or rise slightly. The likely explanation is that during the academic year, schools provide children of all backgrounds with relatively stimulating intellectual environments, but when school is not in session, children from

FIGURE 8.4 Relations of age and grade to performance on two parts of an IQ test The jumps between grade levels indicate that schooling exerts an effect on intelligence test performance beyond that of the child's age. (Data from Cahan & Cahan, 1989)

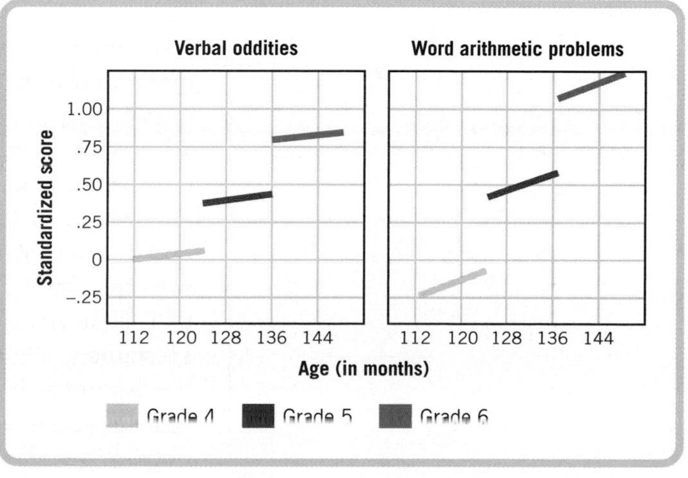

low-SES families are less likely to have the kinds of experiences that would maintain or increase their academic achievement.

One inference that you might draw from these findings is that most children would have higher levels of intellectual achievement if they went to school for more days each year. Several types of evidence suggest that this inference is probably correct. For example, children in European and Asian countries that have longer school years than the United States also have consistently higher school achievement (Geary, 1996; Stevenson & Stigler, 1992). Further, in an experiment with American kindergartners, lengthening the school year from the usual 180 days to 210 days (comparable to the school year in Europe and East Asia) increased mastery of math and reading (Frazier, & Morrison, 1998.) Attending summer school has a similarly positive effect, especially on understanding of mathematics, a subject that most children ignore when school is not in session (Cooper, Charlton, Valentile, & Muhlenbruck, 2000). Thus, attending school increases both IQ scores and specific academic skills.

Influence of Society

Intellectual development is influenced not only by characteristics of children, their families, and their schools but also by broader characteristics of the economic and social systems within which they develop. Developmental researchers are especially interested in understanding the economic and social characteristics that can interfere with children's development. Poverty is one particularly influential characteristic of this type. In this section, we first consider how poverty affects children's development in different societies and then examine how it contributes to differences in IQ and school achievement among racial and ethnic groups. Next we consider other factors that place intellectual development at risk. Finally we consider programs aimed at enhancing poor children's intellectual development.

Effects of Poverty

Growing up in impoverished circumstances can have large negative effects on children's IQ scores. Even after taking into account such factors as the mother's education, whether the home is headed by a single mother, and race, the adequacy of family income for meeting family needs is related to children's IQs (Duncan et al., 1994). Further, the more years children spend in poverty, the lower their IQs tend to be.

Poverty can exert negative effects on intellectual development in numerous ways. For example, chronic inadequate diet early in life can disrupt brain development, and either chronic or short-term inadequate diet at any point in life can impair immediate intellectual functioning. Reduced access to health services, inadequate parenting, and insufficient intellectual stimulation and emotional support in the home are other factors associated with poverty that can impair intellectual growth.

The relation between poverty and IQ is highlighted by the fact that in all countries that have been studied, children from wealthier homes score higher on IQ and achievement tests than do children from poorer homes (Keating & Hertzman, 1999; Case, Griffin, & Kelley, 1999). More telling still, in the developed countries where the income gap between rich and poor is widest, such as the United States, the difference between the intellectual achievement of children from rich and poor homes is much larger than in countries in which the gap is smaller—such as the Scandinavian countries and, to a lesser degree, Germany, Canada, and Great Britain. As shown in Figure 8.5, children from affluent families in the United States score about the same on tests of intellectual achievement as do children from affluent families in other countries. In contrast, children from poor families in the United States score far below children from poor families in countries with greater income equality. The key difference is that poor families in the United States are much poorer than their counterparts in other developed countries. Thus, in 1998, 19% percent of children in the United States lived in families with incomes below the poverty line (United States Census Bureau, 1999), more than double the percentage in Germany and triple the percentage in Switzerland and Sweden a decade earlier (Duncan, Bound, Laren, & Oleinick, 1991).

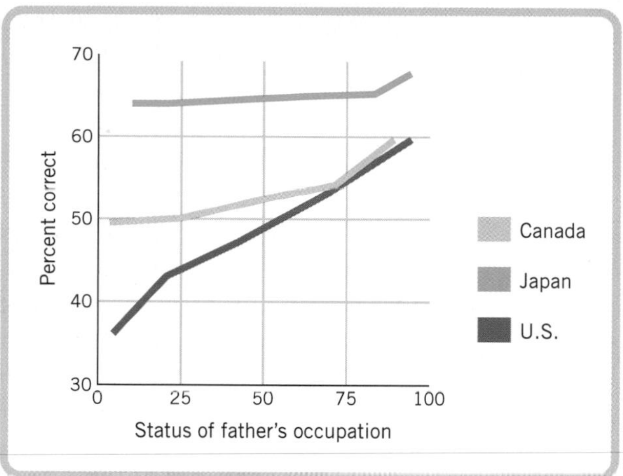

FIGURE 8.5 Relation in three countries between fathers' occupational status and children's math achievement U.S. children whose fathers hold low-status jobs perform far more poorly on math-achievement tests than do children whose fathers hold comparable jobs in Canada or Japan. In contrast, U.S. children whose fathers have high-status jobs perform as well as children whose fathers have comparable jobs in Canada and almost as well as children from similar backgrounds in Japan. (Data from Case et al.,1999)

Within the United States, the percentage of children living in poor families is much higher among African-Americans and Latinos than among Euro- and Asian-Americans. In 1998, 26% of African-Americans and Latinos lived in families with incomes below the poverty line, versus 8% of Euro-American children (U.S. Census Bureau, 2000). A study that examined families over a six-year period (Duncan et al., 1994) indicated that five times as many African-American families were poor during the entire period as were Euro-American families. Even among children whose families were not poor, nearly 50% of African-American children lived in neighborhoods with a high percentage of poor families, whereas fewer than 10% of Euro-American children did. These economic differences help explain the group differences in IQ that we will examine in the next section.

Some children who live in poverty overcome the odds and do well in school and in life. What distinguishes these *resilient children* (Werner, 1993) from others in similar circumstances? Bradley and his colleagues (1994) identified a group of children who, despite being born into poor families and also being born prematurely, functioned in the normal or superior range on cognitive, social, health, and growth measures at the age of 3 years. The researchers found that the parents of these children protected them in a number of ways from the usual deleterious effects of poverty. They were more likely than other impoverished parents to be responsive to their children and to provide them with safe play areas and varied learning materials. Thus, high-quality parenting can help children meet the challenges imposed by poverty.

Race, Ethnicity, and Intelligence

Few claims stir stronger passions than assertions that racial and ethnic groups differ in intelligence. It is therefore especially important both to know the facts and to know what can and cannot be concluded from them.

One fact is that *average* IQ scores of children of different racial and ethnic groups do differ. For example, the average IQ of Euro-American children is 10 to 15 points higher than that of African-American children. Average scores of children of Latinos and American Indians fall in between, and Asian-American children's average scores are higher than those of any other group in the United States (Suzuki & Valencia, 1997). These differences are explained in part by differences in social-class backgrounds. Within each social class, however, differences in mean IQs of African-American and Euro-American children also are present, though they are smaller than the ones that are present when social class is not held constant (Suzuki & Valencia, 1997).

A second fact is that statements about group differences in IQ scores refer to statistical averages rather than to any individual's score. Understanding this second fact is essential for interpreting the first one. Millions of African-American children have IQs higher than the average Euro-American child, and millions of Euro-American children have IQs lower than the average African-American child. There is far more variability *within* each racial group than *between* them. Thus, data on the average IQ of members of an ethnic or racial group tell us nothing about a given individual.

A third fact is that racial/ethnic groups differ in their profile of intellectual abilities as well as in overall scores. A study of 93 American Indian groups and subgroups indicated that their average score on the performance part of IQ tests was 100 but that their average score on the verbal part was 83 (Vraniak, 1994). Latino children likewise tend to have higher performance scores than verbal scores (Suzuki & Valencia, 1997), as do Asian-American children (Lynn & Hampson, 1986) and Japanese children who live in Japan (Kodama, Shinagawa, & Motegi, 1978; Suzuki & Valencia, 1997). In contrast, some studies of African-American children indicate that their scores on the verbal portion of the IQ tests tend to be higher than their scores on the performance portion (Taylor & Richards, 1991; Vance, Hankins, & McGee, 1979). There are many possible reasons for these differences in profiles of abilities. For example, the superior visual and spatial abilities of Asian-American children have been ascribed to neurological factors, nonverbal communication style, cultural values, and a host of other factors (Sue & Okazaki, 1990).

A fourth crucial fact is that differences in IQ scores of children from different racial and ethnic groups describe children's performance only in the environments in which the children live. The findings do not indicate their intellectual potential, nor do they indicate what would happen if the children lived in different environments. In one dramatic illustration of this fact, Scarr and Weinberg (1976, 1983) examined IQ scores of more than 100 African-American children who had been adopted by Euro-American parents. The adoptive parents were above average in income, education, and intelligence (mean IQ = 119), whereas the biological parents were roughly average on these dimensions. When African-American children who were adopted in their first year were tested at around age 7, their mean IQ was 110, higher than that of the average Euro-American child in the United States. Similar effects have been observed at later ages. In a study of African-American 16- to 22-year-olds who as infants had been adopted into relatively affluent and well-educated Euro-American families, the mean IQ was 106 (Scarr & Weinberg, 1983).

Thus, the current group differences in IQ in the general population are not inevitable. Indeed, with decreases in discrimination and inequality over the last half of the twentieth century, IQ differences between Euro-American and African-American children decreased (Brody, 1992).

Risk Factors and Intellectual Development

Articles in popular magazines on how to help all children reach their intellectual potential often focus on a single factor. Some articles emphasize the need to eliminate poverty; others emphasize the need to eliminate racism; still others emphasize the need to preserve two-parent families; and so on. However, no single factor, or even a small group of factors, is *the* key. Instead, a variety of factors in combination contribute to the problem of substantial numbers of children failing to reach their intellectual potential.

To capture the impact of these multiple influences, Arnold Sameroff and his colleagues developed an *environmental risk scale* (Sameroff, Seifer, Baldwin, & Baldwin, 1993). The scale was based on a number of features of the environment that put children at risk for low IQs (Table 8.2). Each child's risk score is a simple count of the number of major risks facing the child. Thus, a child growing up with a mother who is unemployed, high in anxiety, a high school dropout, and unmarried would have a risk score of 4 (assuming that none of the other risk factors applied).

TABLE 8.2

Risk Factors Related to IQ Scores

1. Head of household unemployed or working in low-status occupation.
2. Mother did not complete high school.
3. At least four children in family.
4. No father or stepfather in home.
5. African-American family.
6. Large number of stressful life events in past few years.
7. Rigidity of parents' beliefs about child development.
8. Maternal anxiety.
9. Maternal mental health.
10. Negative mother-child interactions.

Source: Sameroff et al. (1993)

Sameroff and his colleagues measured the IQs and environmental risks of more than 100 children when they were 4-year-olds and again when they were 13-year-olds. They found that the more risks in a child's environment, the lower the child's IQ tended to be. As shown in Figure 8.6, the effect was large. The average IQ of children whose environments did not include any of the risk factors was around 115; the average IQ of children whose environments included six or more risks was around 85. The sheer number of risks in the child's environment was a better predictor of the child's IQ than was any particular risk being present.

This study also provided an interesting perspective on why there is so much stability in children's IQ scores. It is not just that children maintain the same genotype; most also continue to live in a similar environment. The study revealed that there was just as much stability in the riskiness of children's environments at ages 4 and 13 years as there was in their IQ scores.

The number of risk factors in a 4-year-old's environment not only correlates highly with the child's IQ at age 4, it also predicts the likelihood of changes in the child's IQ between ages 4 and 13. That is, if two children have the same IQ at age 4, but one child lives in an environment with more risk factors, the child facing more risks probably will have a lower IQ at age 13 than the other child. Thus, environmental risks have both immediate and long-term effects on children's intellectual development.

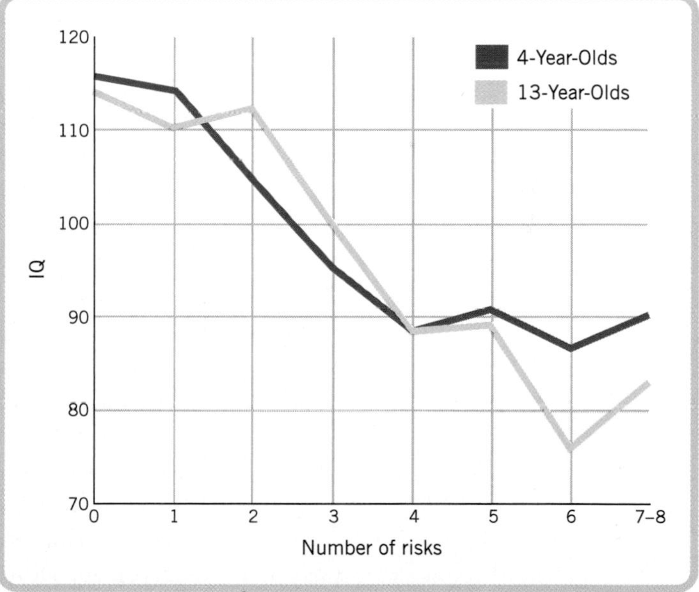

FIGURE 8.6 Risk factors and IQ For both younger and older children, the more risk factors there are in the environment, the lower the average IQ. (Data from Sameroff et al., 1993)

Although Sameroff and his colleagues described their measure as a "risk index," it is as much a measure of the goodness of children's environments as of the potential for harm. As previously noted, children whose environments include few or none of the risk factors generally have IQs that are well above average. Their high IQs reflect the benefits of their environments as much as the low IQs of other children reflect the adversity of theirs. Simply put, no one makes it alone: our successes, and our failures, result not only from our own abilities but also from the quality of support provided by our families, other people who influence us, and the broader society.

Programs for Helping Poor Children

During the early 1960s, a political consensus developed in the United States proposing that helping children from poor families should become a national priority. Psychological research contributed to this consensus by demonstrating that children's environments had significant effects on their cognitive growth (Dennis &

Najarian, 1957; Hunt, 1961). As a consequence, over the next few years, many intervention programs were initiated to enhance the intellectual development of poor children.

Most of these interventions were small-scale experimental programs, intended to test ideas about the types of intervention that would be most beneficial. Some were *home-based programs* that focused their educational efforts primarily on parents, especially mothers. The two main premises of these programs were that parents are the largest influence on children's early development and that improving parenting would help all children in the family. Other interventions were *center-based programs*, which operated much like traditional nursery schools, with teachers who interacted directly with children. Some programs were based on behaviorist theories and emphasized direct instruction in the skills and concepts needed to learn reading and arithmetic and reinforcement of children for learning them. Other programs were based on Piagetian theory and emphasized provision of stimulating environments that would encourage children to construct new skills and concepts without direct instruction or external reinforcement. Yet other programs were an eclectic mix of ideas from behaviorist and Piagetian theories and traditional preschool practices, such as singing songs and telling stories.

In a comprehensive analysis of eleven of the most prominent initial early-intervention programs—all of which focused on 2- to 5-year-old African-American children from low-income families—Irving Lazar and his colleagues found a consistent pattern (Lazar, Darlington, Murry, Roye, & Snipper, 1982). Participation in the programs, most of which lasted a year or two, initially increased children's IQ scores substantially—by 10 to 15 points. However, over the next two or three years, the gains decreased, and by the fourth year after the end of the programs, no differences were apparent between the IQ scores of participants and those of nonparticipants from the same neighborhoods and backgrounds. Similar patterns emerged in an analysis of programs that emphasized mathematics and reading achievement (McKey et al., 1985).

Fortunately, other effects of these experimental programs were more enduring. Only half as many program participants as nonparticipants were later assigned to special-education classes—14% versus 29%. Similarly, fewer participants were held back in school, and more participants subsequently graduated from high school.

This combination of findings may seem puzzling. If the intervention programs did not result in lasting increases in IQ or achievement test scores, why would they have led to fewer children being assigned to special-education classes or being held back in school? The likely reason is that the interventions had long-term effects on children's self-esteem, motivation, and classroom behavior. Some of the interventions also may have aided mothers' parenting skills and ability to communicate with teachers (Lazar et al., 1982). These effects would help children and their parents make favorable impressions on teachers, principals, and school psychologists and thus convince them in borderline cases that the children should be promoted along with their classmates.

Participation also led to benefits after children finished school. Participants in some of the programs later used the welfare system less and earned larger salaries (Haskins, 1989; McLoyd, 1998). Positive effects such as these suggest that early-intervention programs not only can help participants lead more successful lives; they also may more than repay their costs by reducing the need for social services. (As discussed in Box 8.2, one type of specialized, intensive program has shown the possibility of producing enduring gains in IQ and school achievement as well.)

applications 8.2

A Highly Successful Early Intervention: The Carolina Abecedarian Project

The difficulty of producing enduring gains in poor children's IQs and achievement test scores led some evaluators to conclude that intelligence is unalterable (Jensen, 1973; Westinghouse Learning Center, 1969). However, the same findings motivated other researchers to find out if interventions that started in infancy and that attempted to improve many aspects of children's lives might produce enduring increases in IQs, even though less intensive, later-starting efforts had not. One effort that has yielded a positive answer to these questions is the **Carolina Abecedarian Project,** a program that clearly illustrates the theme of how research can improve children's welfare (Campbell & Ramey, 1994, 1995; Ramey, Yates, & Short, 1984).

Children were selected to participate in the Abecedarian (pronounced "A-Bee-Cee-Darian") program on the basis of low family income, the absence of a father in the home, low maternal IQ and education, and other factors that put them at risk for developmental problems. More than 95% of the children who participated were African-American.

Children in the program began attending a special day-care center by the time they were 6-month-olds and continued to do so through the age of 5 years. The center operated for the entire working day (7:45 A.M.–5:30 P.M.), and the teacher–child ratio was optimal: 1:3 for children 3 years old and younger and 1:6 for 4-year-olds. The day-care center's program for children 3 years old and younger emphasized general social, cognitive, and motor development; for children over age 3, it also provided systematic instruction in math, science, reading, and music. At all ages, the program emphasized language development and ensured extensive verbal communication between teachers and children. Program personnel also worked with the children's mothers outside the day-care center to improve their understanding of child development. Families of children in the experimental program were provided nutritional supplements and access to high-quality health care. Families of children in a control group received similar health and nutritional benefits, but the children did not attend the day-care center.

This well-planned, multifaceted program proved to have lasting positive effects on the IQs and achievement levels of children in the experimental group. At the age of 15 years, ten years after the program had ended, these children had higher mean IQ scores than the children in the control group: 98 versus 93 (Ramey et al., 2000). Participants' achievement test scores in reading, social studies, and science also were higher. As with less encompassing intervention programs, fewer participants were ever held back in school or placed in special-education classes.

The five years of free, all-day educational child care also had positive effects on the lives of the children's mothers. Fifteen years after the end of the program, they were more likely to be employed than mothers of children in the control group and more likely to have obtained education beyond high school (Ramey et al., 2000). Teenage mothers showed the largest benefits.

What lessons can be drawn from the Abecedarian Project? One important lesson is the benefit of starting interventions early and continuing them for substantial periods of time. A version of the Abecedarian program that ended at age 3 did not produce long-term effects on intelligence, nor did a program that provided educational support from kindergarten through second grade (Burchinal et al., 1997; Ramey et al., 2000). A second crucial lesson is the need for caregivers of infants to interact with them in positive, responsive ways. High ratios of adults to infants in day-care centers make such interactions more likely, as does educating staff members in the need for such interactions. Probably the most important lesson is the most basic: *it is possible* to design interventions that have substantial, lasting, positive effects on poor children's intellectual development. This knowledge may inspire even more successful efforts to improve the lives of poor children.

Project Head Start In response to the same political consensus of the 1960s that led to small-scale early-intervention programs, the U.S. government initiated a large-scale intervention program: Project Head Start. In the past thirty-five years, this program has provided a wide range of services to more than 13 million children (McLoyd, 1998).

At present, Head Start serves roughly 1 million 3- to 5-year-olds per year in approximately 2,000 centers around the United States. Most participants are 4-year-olds. The population served is racially and ethnically diverse: a survey from the mid-1990s indicated that 36% of Head Start children were African-American, 33% were Euro-American, 24% Latino, 4% American Indian, and 3% Asian-American (National Center for Educational Statistics, 1995). Almost all the children are from families with incomes below the poverty line, mostly single-parent families. In the program, children receive medical and dental care and nutritious meals, and are provided with a safe and stimulating environment in a day-care center. Many parents of participating children work as caregivers at the

Carolina Abecedarian Project a comprehensive and successful enrichment program for children from low-income families

MARK RICHARDS / PHOTOEDIT

Among the benefits of Head Start is the provision of nutritious meals for children who otherwise might be at risk for malnutrition.

centers, serve on policy councils that help plan each center's directions, and receive help with their own vocational and emotional needs. Although centers vary, all are governed by a philosophy that emphasizes involving the family and community; building on children's strengths, rather than just trying to shore up weaknesses; and attending to children's social, emotional, and physical development as well as their intellectual growth.

Consistent with the findings of the smaller experimental intervention programs that have been aimed at 3- and 4-year-olds, participation in Head Start produces higher IQs and achievement test scores by the end of the program and for a few years thereafter. Beyond that, however, children's performance becomes indistinguishable from that of nonparticipants with similar backgrounds (McKey et al., 1985; McLoyd, 1998). On the other hand, participation in Project Head Start produces a number of other positive effects that do endure: improved social skills and health, lower frequency of being held back in school, greater likelihood of graduating from high school, and greater involvement of families in the educational process (Lee, Brooks-Gunn, Schnor, & Liaw, 1990; Zigler & Styfco, 1993). These are important gains and have contributed to the enduring political popularity of Head Start.

review:

The development of intelligence is influenced by qualities of the child, qualities of the immediate environment, and qualities of the broader society. The child's genetic inheritance is one important influence, an influence that steadily increases over the course of development. The intellectual environment provided by the child's family, and the schooling the child encounters, are also influential. More general factors, such as the family's economic status and educational level, and whether one or two parents are present, are also important.

Programs for helping preschoolers who are at risk for low IQs are often beneficial in a variety of ways, though their effect on IQ and achievement test scores usually fades over time. However, at least one early intervention program, the Abecedarian Project, reports positive effects on IQs and achievement into adolescence and adulthood.

Alternative Perspectives on Intelligence

The discussions of intellectual development in this chapter have relied on IQ tests as the main measure of intellectual development. Research using these tests has revealed a great deal about the development of intelligence. However, a number of contemporary theorists have argued that many important aspects of intelligence are not measured by IQ tests. The tests assess verbal, mathematical, and spatial capabilities, but they do not directly examine other abilities that seem to be inherent parts of intelligence: creativity, social understanding, knowledge of one's own strengths and weaknesses, and so on. This perspective has led Howard Gardner and Robert Sternberg to formulate theories of intelligence that encompass a wider range of human abilities than do traditional theories.

multiple intelligence theory Gardner's theory of intellect, based on the view that people possess at least eight types of intelligence

Gardner (1993) labeled his approach **multiple intelligence theory.** Its basic claim is that people possess eight intelligences: the linguistic, logical-mathematical, and spatial abilities emphasized in previous theories and measured on IQ tests, and also musical, naturalistic, bodily-kinesthetic, intrapersonal, and interpersonal abilities (see Table 8.3).

Gardner used several types of evidence to arrive at this set of intelligences. One involved deficits shown by people with brain damage. For example, some brain-damaged patients function well in most respects but have no understanding of other people (Damasio, 1999). This phenomenon suggested to Gardner that interpersonal intelligence was distinct from other types of intelligence. A second type of evidence that Gardner used to identify this set of intelligences was the existence of prodigies, people who from early in life show exceptional ability in one area but not in others. One such example is Mozart, who displayed musical genius while still a child but was otherwise unexceptional most ways. Consider this description of the 8-year-old Mozart by an adult for whom Mozart was demonstrating his virtuosity at the keyboard:

> He had not only a most childish appearance but likewise had all the actions of that stage of life. For example, whilst he was playing to me, a favorite cat came in, upon which he immediately left his harpsichord, nor could we bring him back for a considerable time. He would also sometimes run about the room with a stick between his legs by way of a horse.
>
> (Barrington, 1764; cited in Gould, 1992, p. 10)

TABLE 8.3

Gardner's Theory of Multiple Intelligences

Type of Intelligence	Description	Examples
Linguistic intelligence	Sensitivity to the meanings and sounds of words; mastery of syntax; appreciation of the ways language can be used	Poet Political speaker Teacher
Logical-mathematical intelligence	Understanding of objects and symbols, of the actions that can be performed on them and of the relations between these actions; ability for abstraction; ability to identify problems and seek explanations	Mathematician Scientist
Spatial intelligence	Capacity to perceive the visual world accurately, to perform transformations upon perceptions and to re-create aspects of visual experience in the absence of physical stimuli; sensitivity to tension, balance, and composition; ability to detect similar patterns	Artist Engineer Chess master
Musical intelligence	Sensitivity to individual tones and phrases of music; an understanding of ways to combine tones and phrases into larger musical rhythms and structures; awareness of emotional aspects of music	Musician Composer
Naturalistic intelligence	Sensitivity and understanding of plants, animals, and other aspects of nature	Biologist
Bodily-kinesthetic intelligence	Use of one's body in highly skilled ways for expressive or goal-directed purposes; capacity to handle objects skillfully	Dancer Athlete Actor
Intrapersonal intelligence	Access to one's own feeling life; ability to draw on one's emotions to guide and understand one's behavior	Novelist Therapist Patient
Interpersonal intelligence	Ability to notice and make distinctions among the moods, temperaments, motivations, and intentions of other people and potentially to act on this knowledge	Political leader Religious leader Parent Teacher Therapist

Source: Gardner (1993)

Mozart's musical genius was evident from early in childhood, leading some of the greatest musicians of his day to play music with him when he was still a child.

The existence of highly specialized musical talents such as Mozart's provides evidence for viewing musical ability as a separate intelligence.

Gardner proposed that individual children learn best through instruction that allows them to build on their intellectual strengths. Thus, a child who is high in spatial intelligence might learn history best through the extensive use of charts and graphs, whereas a child who is high in social intelligence might learn history best through group discussions and projects. Although Gardner's theory of intelligence is backed by less supporting evidence than traditional theories of intelligence, its emphasis on how instruction can build on individual children's strengths and its optimistic message have caused it to have a large influence on teaching.

Sternberg (2000) also argues that the emphasis of IQ tests on the type of intelligence needed to succeed in school is too narrow. However, the alternative view of intelligence that he proposes differs from that proposed by Gardner. Sternberg's **theory of successful intelligence** envisions intelligence as "the ability to achieve success in life, given one's personal standards, within one's sociocultural context" (p. 4). In his view, success in life reflects people's ability to build on their strengths, to compensate for their weaknesses, and to select environments in which they can succeed. When people choose a job, for instance, their understanding of the conditions that will motivate them to do their best may be as important to their success as their linguistic, spatial, and mathematical abilities.

Sternberg proposed that the degree to which people can succeed in life depends on three types of abilities: analytic, practical, and creative. *Analytic abilities* involve the types of linguistic, mathematical, and spatial skills that are measured by traditional intelligence tests. *Practical abilities* involve reasoning about everyday problems, such as how to resolve conflicts with other people. *Creative abilities* involve reasoning effectively in novel circumstances (for example, inventing games to divert one's children on a long car drive when they do not want to play the usual ones).

Considering all three types of abilities may enhance prediction of intellectual outcomes beyond that possible with traditional IQ tests. In one study, conducted with a predominantly lower-income African-American sample at a college with open admissions, the test of practical intelligence was a better predictor of grades than the test of analytic ability (Sternberg, 2000). Another study, conducted at an elite Ivy League school, showed that grades could be better predicted by measuring all three types of abilities than any one of them. An interesting feature of Sternberg's tests of practical and creative intelligence is that the students who excel on them are more diverse racially and economically than are those who excel on the more traditional analytic test. Thus, considering all three types of intelligence may allow identification of a wider range of talented people than considering only the type of analytic ability measured in traditional tests of intelligence.

The recent theories of intelligence proposed by Gardner, Sternberg, and others (e.g., Ceci, 1996) have inspired a rethinking of long-held assumptions about intelligence. Traditional views of intelligence and how it should be measured reflect historical factors (that intelligence tests were developed to predict performance in school, rather than success in life); value judgments (that access to honors classes and elite colleges should depend in large part on success on tests); and pragmatic considerations (skills that can be measured quickly and easily are more likely to be included on such tests). Yet intelligence and success in life clearly involve a broader range of capabilities than those measured by the traditional tests, and it may prove possible to improve testing by measuring this broader range of capabilities. There is not now, nor will there ever be, a single correct theory of intelligence. What is possible is a variety of theories, and tests based on them, that together reveal the varied ways in which people can be intelligent.

theory of successful intelligence Sternberg's theory of intellect, based on the view that intelligence is the ability to achieve success in life

phonemic awareness ability to identify component sounds within words

review: Howard Gardner and Robert Sternberg have formulated new theories of intelligence. Gardner's multiple intelligence theory proposes that there are eight intelligences: linguistic, logical-mathematical, spatial, musical, naturalistic, bodily-kinesthetic, intrapersonal, and interpersonal. Sternberg's theory of successful intelligence proposes that success in life depends on three types of abilities: analytic, practical, and creative. Both conceive of intelligence as a broader set of abilities than have traditional theories.

Acquisition of Academic Skills: Reading, Writing, and Mathematics

Among the most important uses to which children apply their intelligence is learning the skills and concepts taught at school. Because these skills and concepts are central to succeeding in modern society, and because they are difficult to master, children spend roughly 15,000 hours in school from the first through the twelfth grade. Much of this time is devoted to learning to read, write, and do math. In this section, we focus on how children acquire these skills and why some children have such difficulty mastering them.

Reading

Many children learn to read effortlessly, either before they go to school or after a small amount of instruction. Others, however, find the learning process difficult and frustrating. You can no doubt remember the painful experience of listening to classmates—and perhaps yourself—read aloud, haltingly and incorrectly, seeming to take forever to get through simple sentences, even in second and third grade. Why is it that some children learn to read so effortlessly, whereas others experience such difficulty? To answer this question, we must examine the typical path of reading development, as well as how and why children deviate from it.

The appeal of nursery rhymes to young children has always been obvious, but only recently have the benefits of such rhymes for phonemic awareness and reading acquisition become known.

DON SMETZER / PHOTOEDIT

Chall (1979) described five stages of reading development. These stages provide a good overview of the typical path to mastery:

Stage 0 (birth until the beginning of first grade): During this time, many children acquire key prerequisites for reading. These include knowing the letters of the alphabet and gaining **phonemic awareness,** that is, the ability to identify component sounds within spoken words.

Stage 1 (first and second grades): Children acquire **phonological recoding skills,** the ability to translate letters into sounds and to blend the sounds into words. (This ability is informally referred to as sounding out.)

Stage 2 (second and third grades): Children gain fluency in reading simple material.

Stage 3 (fourth through eighth grades): Children become able to acquire new information from print. To quote Chall, "In the primary grades, children learn to read; in the higher grades, they read to learn" (1979, p. 24).

Stage 4 (eighth through twelfth grades): Adolescents acquire skill not only in understanding information presented from a single perspective but also at coordinating multiple perspectives. This makes it possible for them to appreciate the subtleties in great novels, which almost always include multiple viewpoints.

This description of developmental stages provides a general sense of the reading acquisition process and a framework for understanding how particular developments fit into the broader picture.

Prereading Skills

Preschoolers acquire certain basic information about reading just from looking at books and having their parents read to them. They learn that (in English and other European languages) text is read from left to right; that after reaching the right end of a line, reading continues at the extreme left of the line below; and that words are separated by small spaces.

Many children, especially middle-class ones, also learn the names of most or all of the letters of the alphabet before they enter first grade. This tends not to be true of low-income, minority-group members, however. In one California sample, 71% of English-speaking 5-year-olds but only 4% of Spanish-speaking peers could name most of the uppercase letters correctly (Masonheimer, 1980, cited in Ehri, 1986). Kindergartners' mastery of letter names is positively correlated with their later reading achievement through at least seventh grade (Vellutino & Scanlon, 1987). However, there is no causal relation between the two; teaching the names of the letters to randomly chosen preschoolers does not increase their subsequent reading achievement (Adams, 1990). Instead, it appears that other variables, such as children's interest in books and parents' interest in their children's reading, stimulate both early knowledge of the alphabet and later high reading achievement.

Phonemic awareness, on the other hand, is both correlated with later reading achievement and a cause of it. To measure awareness of the component sounds within words, Juel (1988) and others have presented beginning first graders with questions such as "What are the two sounds in 'no'?" and "Say 'top.' Now, what would you have if you didn't say the 't'?" Performance on these simple phonemic-awareness tasks at the beginning of first grade is highly predictive of children's ability to sound out words at the end of first grade, above and beyond the influence of IQ and listening comprehension. Phonemic awareness in kindergarten also is predictive of ability to sound out words through the end of fourth grade (Bruck, 1992; Juel, 1988; Olson, Forsberg, & Wise, 1994; Wagner et al., 1997). Even more impressive, teaching phonemic-awareness skills to 4- and 5-year-olds causes them to become better readers (and spellers) for at least four years after the training (Bradley & Bryant, 1983; Byrne & Fielding-Barnsley, 1995).

Although explicit training in phonemic awareness can help foster the skill, children do not ordinarily receive such explicit training outside the laboratory. Where,

phonological recoding skills ability to translate letters into sounds and to blend sounds into words

visually based retrieval proceeding directly from the visual form of a word to its meaning

strategy-choice process procedure for selecting among alternative ways of solving problems then, does phonemic awareness come from in the natural environment? One relevant experience is hearing nursery rhymes. Many nursery rhymes highlight the contribution of individual sounds to differences among words (e.g., "I do not like green eggs and *ham;* I do not like them *Sam* I *am.*") Consistent with this analysis, 3-year-olds' knowledge of nursery rhymes correlates positively with their later phonemic awareness, above and beyond their IQs and their mother's educational level (Maclean, Bryant, & Bradley, 1987). Beyond this initial source, once children begin to read, the more they read, the more their phonemic awareness grows (Cardoso-Martins, 1991; Tunmer & Nesdale, 1985).

Word Identification

Rapid, effortless identification of words is crucial not only to reading comprehension but also to the enjoyment of reading. One remarkable finding makes the point: 40% of fourth graders who were poor at identifying words said they would rather clean their rooms than read (Juel, 1988). One went as far as to say, "I'd rather clean the mold around the bathtub than read." Thus, not only does being poor at word identification make the reading process slow and laborious; it also leads children to read no more than is absolutely necessary, which, in turn, slows subsequent learning.

Words can be identified in two main ways: *phonological recoding* and *visually based retrieval.* As previously indicated, phonological recoding involves converting the visual form of a word into a verbal, speechlike form and using the speechlike form to determine the word's meaning. **Visually based retrieval** involves proceeding directly from the visual form of the word to its meaning.

From early in first grade, children choose adaptively between these two approaches. They do so through a **strategy-choice process**, in which they choose the fastest approach that is likely to be correct (Siegler, 1988b). In the context of reading, this means that on easy words, children rely heavily on the fast but not always accurate approach of retrieval, and on hard words, they resort to the slower but surer strategy of phonological recoding. As shown in Figure 8.7, first graders are very skillful in adjusting their frequency of backup strategies to the difficulty of the particular word.

In addition to indicating how children choose between strategies at any one time, the strategy-choice model also helps clarify how children's choices change over time. Between the beginning of first grade and the end of second grade, most children progress from relying primarily on phonological recoding to relying primarily on retrieval. This change in word-identification strategies seems to be shaped by their own reading activities. Correctly identifying a word, either through retrieval or through phonological recoding, allows children to associate the visual appearance of the word with its meaning. The stronger the association between appearance and meaning becomes, the more likely that children will be able to retrieve the word's identity. Thus, on relatively easy words (i.e., ones that are short, occur frequently, and have regular letter–sound relations), retrieval quickly comes to predominate. On words that are longer, less common, and less regular in their letter–sound correspondences, phonological recoding remains predominant for a longer time, because associations between the words' letters and their meaning grow more slowly.

As is often the case in development, children's degree of mastery of the earlier-developing strategy contributes directly to their mastery of the later-developing capability. Children who are better at sounding out words have more opportunities

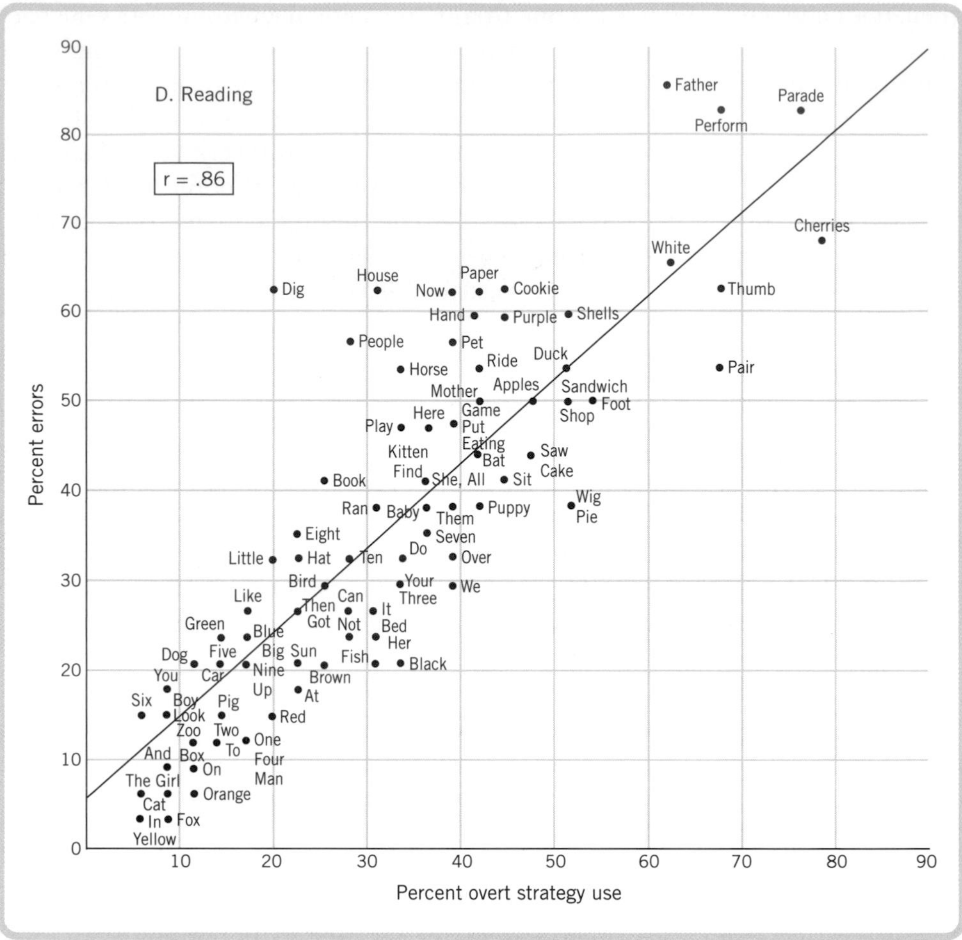

FIGURE 8.7 Young children's strategy choices in reading There is a strong positive correlation between the difficulty of a word, as defined by the percentage of errors children make on it, and the frequency of young children's using an overt strategy, such as audible phonological recoding, to read it. Thus, on easy words that children almost always read correctly, such as *in*, they generally used retrieval to identify the word, but on difficult words that elicited many errors, such as *parade*, children often fell back on overt strategies such as sounding out. (Siegler, 1986)

to associate the printed form of the word with its meaning. Thus, ironically, strong phonological recoding skills enable children to stop using phonological recoding earlier and to shift more completely to visually based retrieval. It is not surprising, therefore, that reading instruction that emphasizes phonics, and the strategy of phonological recoding, helps to produce fast and accurate word identification (Adams, Treiman, & Pressley, 1998). (Box 8.3 discusses the relation between poor phonological recoding skills and the reading disability known as dyslexia.)

Comprehension

The point of learning to read individual words is to be able to comprehend the longer text in which the individual words appear. Reading comprehension involves forming a **mental model** of the situation or idea being depicted in the text and continuously updating it as new information appears (Johnson-Laird, 1983; Oakhill & Cain, 2000). All of the factors that influence the development of cognition in general—basic processes, strategies, metacognition (knowledge about people's thinking), and content knowledge—also influence the development of reading comprehension.

Basic processes and capacities such as encoding (identification of key features of an object or event) and automatization (executing a process with minimal demands on cognitive resources) are crucial to reading comprehension. The reason is simple: children who are able to identify the key features of words without using cognitive resources have more resources left to devote to comprehension. Fast and

mental model processes used to represent a situation or sequence of events

dyslexia inability to read well despite normal intelligence

phonological processing ability to discriminate and remember sounds within words

individual differences 8.3

Dyslexia

Some children who are of normal intelligence and who grow up with parents who encourage them to read nevertheless read very poorly. This inability to read well despite normal intelligence, referred to as **dyslexia,** affects roughly 3% to 5% of children in the United States (Rayner & Pollatsek, 1989).

Most children with dyslexia are poor at reading primarily because of a general weakness at **phonological processing.** This weakness is evident in the children's poor ability to discriminate between phonemes, their poor short-term memory for verbal material (as indicated, for example, by poor ability to recall an arbitrary list of words), and their slow recall of the names of objects (Vellutino, Scanlon, & Spearing, 1995). Determining the sounds that go with vowels is especially difficult for children with dyslexia, at least in English, where a single vowel can be pronounced in many ways (consider the sounds that accompany *a* in "hate," "hat," "hall," and "hard"). Because of this poor phonological processing, dyslexic children have great difficulty mastering the letter–sound correspondences used in phonological recoding (Shankweiler et al., 1995; Stanovich & Siegel, 1994). For example, as shown in the figure, when asked to read pseudowords such as *parding,* dyslexic 13- and 14-year-olds perform at the same level as typical 7- and 8-year-olds (Siegel, 1993). As would be expected from the strategy-choice model described earlier, this difficulty with phonological processing causes most dyslexic children to be poor at visually based retrieval as well as at sounding out words (Manis, Seidenberg, Doi, McBride-Chang, & Peterson, 1996). The problem can be a lasting one: individuals who have poor phonological processing skills in early elementary school usually are poor readers as adults as well (Wagner et al., 1997).

Studies of brain functioning support the view that poor phonological processing is at the heart of dyslexia. When dyslexic adults read, two areas of their brains are less active than the corresponding areas in typical adults reading the same words (Shaywitz et al., 1998). One such area, located toward the back of the brain, is directly involved in phonological processing; the other area, more toward the middle of the brain, is involved in integrating visual and auditory data (in this case, integrating the letters on the page with accompanying sounds).

How can dyslexic children be helped? One tempting inference is to conclude that because these children have difficulty learning phonics, they would learn better through an approach that de-emphasizes letter–sound relations and instead emphasizes either visually based retrieval or reliance on context. These alternative methods work poorly, however (Lyon, 1995). There is simply no substitute for being able to sound out unfamiliar words. Instead, what seems to work best is to teach children with dyslexia to use strategies that enhance their phonological recoding (Lovett et al., 1994). Effective strategies include drawing analogies to known words with similar spellings; generating alternative pronunciations of vowels when the first attempt at sounding out does not yield a plausible word; and, with long words, "peeling off" prefixes and suffixes and then trying to identify the rest of the word. Using such strategies helps children with dyslexia to improve their reading-achievement scores and spelling (Lovett et al., 1994).

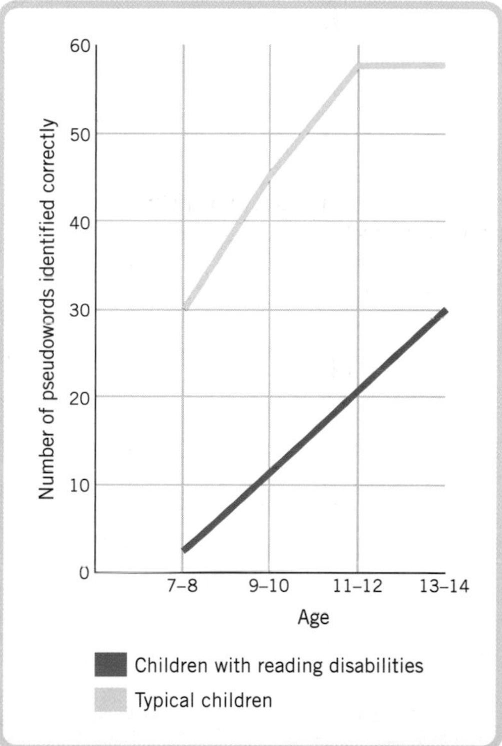

Number of pseudowords identified correctly by 7- to 14-year-olds with and without reading disabilities. Note that 13- and 14-year-olds with reading disabilities correctly identified no more words than typical 7- and 8-year-olds. The poor phonological recoding skills of children with learning disabilities leads them to have special difficulty with pseudowords that, because they are totally unfamiliar, can be pronounced only by using phonological recoding. (Data from Siegel, 1993)

accurate word identification correlates positively with reading comprehension at all points from the first grade through adulthood (Saarnio, Oka, & Paris, 1990; Vellutino, 1991).

Development of reading comprehension also is aided by acquisition of strategies. For example, good readers proceed slowly when they need to master written material thoroughly and speed up when they need only a rough sense of it (Pressley, El-Dinary, Stein, Marks, & Brown, 1992). Proficiency in making such adjustments develops surprisingly late, however. Even when 10-year-olds are told that some

comprehension monitoring the process of keeping track of one's understanding of a verbal description or text

material is crucial and other material is not, they tend to read all of the material at the same speed. In contrast, 14-year-olds skim the nonessential parts and spend more time on the important ones (Kobasigawa, Ransom, & Holland, 1980).

Increasing metacognitive knowledge also contributes to improvements in reading comprehension. With age and experience, readers increasingly monitor their understanding of what they are reading and reread passages they do not understand (Baker, 1994). Such **comprehension monitoring** differentiates good readers from poor ones at all ages from the first grade through adulthood. Instructional approaches that focus on comprehension monitoring and other metacognitive skills, such as anticipating questions that a teacher might ask about the material, have been found to improve reading comprehension (Palincsar & Magnusson, 2001; Rosenshine & Meister, 1994).

Perhaps the greatest influence on the development of reading comprehension is content knowledge. The growth of content knowledge frees cognitive resources for focusing on what is new or complex in the text. It also allows readers to draw reasonable inferences about information left unstated in the text. Thus, when reading the headline "Yankees Beat Braves," knowledgeable readers realize that the headline concerns baseball; it is unclear how less knowledgeable readers would interpret such a headline.

Children's reading comprehension is also influenced by the amount of reading they do, which varies greatly. For example, U.S. fifth graders whose reading-achievement test scores are in the 90th percentile for their grade report reading roughly 200 times as much as peers who score in the 10th percentile (Anderson, Wilson, & Fielding, 1988). High reading ability leads children to read more; children who read more, in turn, show greater gains over time in reading comprehension than do children of equal ability who read less (Guthrie, Wigfield, Metsala, & Cox, 1999).

Children's reading comprehension is influenced not only by their own activities but also by those of their parents. Preschoolers whose parents tell and read them stories learn how such stories tend to go, and this helps them understand new stories once they start reading (Bus, van Ijzendoorn, & Pellegrini, 1995; Scarborough & Dobrich, 1994). Differences between the reading comprehension skills of children from middle- and low-income families in part reflect differences in how much parents read to them during the preschool years. For example, a study conducted in Israel showed that in an affluent school district with high reading-achievement scores, 96% of parents of preschoolers read to them daily. The same was true of only 15% of parents of preschoolers in a poor district with low scores (Feitelson & Goldstein, 1986).

The straightforward implication of these findings is that if preschoolers from poor families were read to daily, they too would become better readers. The evidence is consistent with this inference. A study in Mexico showed that having a graduate student read storybooks to 2-year-olds daily over a six-week period improved the children's vocabulary and ability to use language relative to those of a control group of peers who were not read to (Valdez-Menchaca & Whitehurst, 1992). Similar effects have been observed among Head Start children whose parents and teachers were encouraged to read stories to them and to use facilitating techniques, such as encouraging the children to explain the characters' goals and motivations (Whitehurst et al., 1994). Persuading low-income parents to enroll in such programs and to read to their children on a continuing basis is not easy (Adams et al., 1998; Whitehurst et al., 1994), but when parents do so, their children benefit.

Writing

Much less is known about the development of children's writing than about the development of their reading, but what is known shows interesting parallels between the two.

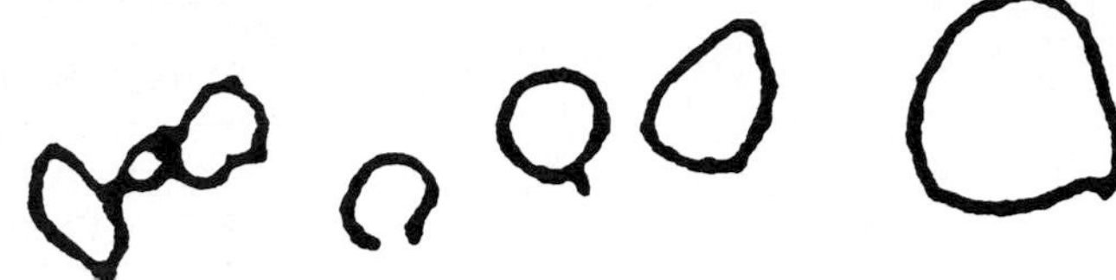

FIGURE 8.8 A 3½-year-old's effort to write a shopping list for a teddy bear The child's symbols, although unconventional, indicate an understanding that each word requires a separate symbol. (Jones, 1990)

Prewriting Skills

The development of writing, like the development of reading, begins before children receive formal schooling. Figure 8.8 displays a typical 3-year-old's "shopping list." The marks are not conventional letters of the alphabet, but they look vaguely like them and are arranged in a linear horizontal sequence. By age 4, children's "writing" is sufficiently advanced that adults have no trouble distinguishing it from the figures 4-year-olds produce when asked to draw a flower or a house (Tolchinsky-Landsmann & Levin, 1985).

Preschoolers' "writing" indicates that they expect meaning to be reflected in print. They use more marks to represent words that signify many objects, such as "forest," than to represent words that signify a single object, such as "tree" (Levin & Korat, 1993). Similarly, when asked to guess which of several words names an object, they generally choose longer words for larger objects. Although written language obviously does not follow this "rule," the children's guess seems reasonable.

Generating Written Text

Learning to write (in the sense of writing a story) is a good deal more difficult than learning to read. This is not surprising, because writing requires focusing simultaneously on multiple goals, both low level and high level. The low-level goals include forming letters, spelling words, and using correct capitalization and punctuation. The high-level goals include making arguments comprehensible without the intonations and gestures that help us express ourselves when we speak, organizing individual points in a coherent framework, and providing the background information that readers need to understand the writing (Boscolo, 1995). The difficulties of meeting both the low-level and high-level goals result in children's writing the type of story illustrated in Figure 8.9.

FIGURE 8.9 A fourth grader's story The intended title of this story, which was written by a fourth grader, was "The Kid Who Lost Things." See if you can figure out the rest.

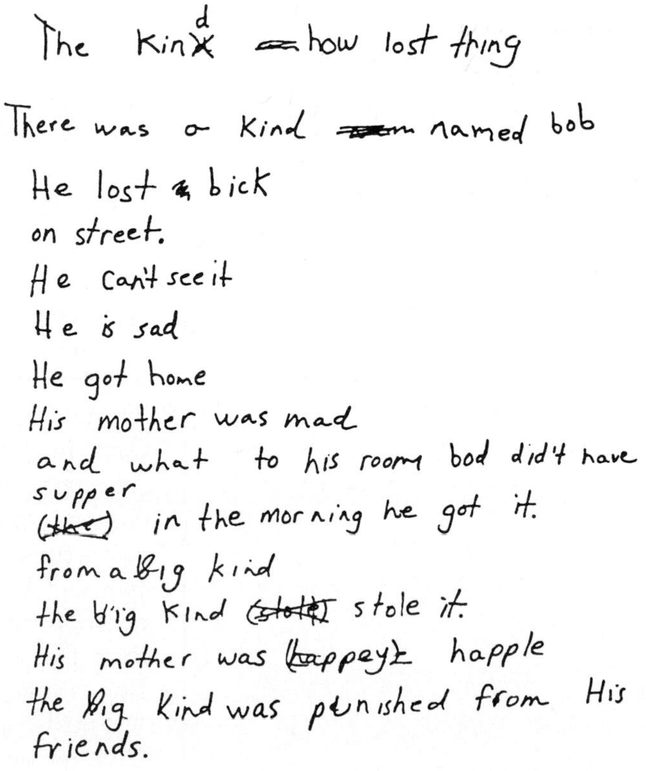

The Kind how lost thing

There was a Kind named bob
He lost a bick
on street.
He can't see it
He is sad
He got home
His mother was mad
and what to his room bod did't have supper
(the) in the morning he got it.
from a big kind
the big Kind (stole) stole it.
His mother was (happey) happle
the big Kind was punished from His friends.

As with development of reading comprehension, growth of writing proficiency reflects improvements in basic capacities, strategies, metacognition, and content knowledge. Automatizing low-level skills, such as spelling and punctuation, aids writing not only because correct spelling and punctuation make writing easier to understand but also because automatizing the low-level skills frees cognitive resources for pursuing the higher-level goals of writing. Consistent with this conclusion, children's proficiency at low-level skills such as spelling correlates positively with the quality of their essays (Juel, 1994).

Acquisition of writing strategies also helps children reduce the cognitive demands of writing. One common strategy is to sequence high-level goals in a standard organization that can be used repeatedly. Harriet Waters, a psychologist whose proud

TABLE 8.4

Stories Written at Beginning, Middle, and End of Year for Class News Assignment

SEPTEMBER 24, 1956
Today is Monday, September, 24, 1956. It is a rainy day. We hope the sun will shine.
We got new spelling books. We had our pictures taken. We sang Happy Birthday to Barbara.

JANUARY 22, 1957
Today is Tuesday, January 22, 1957. It is a foggy day. We must be careful crossing the road.
This morning, we had music. We learned a new song.
Linda is absent. We hope she comes back soon.
We had arithmetic. We made believe that we were buying candy. We had fun.
We work in our English books. We learned when to use is and are.

MAY 27, 1957
Today is Monday, May 27, 1957. It is a warm, cloudy day. We hope the sun comes out.
This afternoon, we had music. We enjoyed it. We went out to play.
Carole is absent. We hope she comes back soon.
We had a spelling lesson, we learned about a dozen.
Tomorrow we shall have show and tell.
Some of us have spelling sentences to do for homework.
Danny brought in a cocoon. It will turn into a butterfly.

Source: Waters (1980)

mother saved all of her daughter's "class news" assignments from second grade, was one child who employed such an approach (Waters, 1980). As shown in Table 8.4, in each class news essay, Waters first stated the date, then discussed the weather, and then discussed events of the school day, a strategy that greatly simplified her writing task. For older children, formulating outlines serves a similar purpose of dividing the task of writing into manageable parts: first figure out what you want to say; then figure out how to say it.

Metacognitive understanding plays several crucial roles in writing. Perhaps the most basic type of metacognitive understanding is recognizing that readers may not have the same knowledge as the writer and that one therefore should include all the information that readers need to allow them to grasp what is being said. Good writers consistently exhibit such understanding by high school; poor writers often do not (Scardamalia & Bereiter, 1984). A second crucial type of metacognitive knowledge involves understanding the need to plan one's writing, rather than just jumping in and starting to write. Good writers spend much more time than poor writers planning what they will say before they begin writing (Kellogg, 1994). Understanding the need for revision is a third key type of metacognitive knowledge. Although good writers produce better first drafts than poor writers, they also spend more time revising what they have written (Fitzgerald, 1992).

Fortunately, as with reading, instruction aimed at inculcating metacognitive understanding can enhance writing skills (Graham & Harris, 1992; Harris & Graham, 1992). In particular, third to sixth graders' writing improves when they are taught to routinely ask themselves basic questions such as: Who is the main character in this story? What does the main character do? How do the other characters respond? How does the main character respond to the other characters' responses? What happens in the end? Encouraging children to focus on such questions leads to better first drafts; further encouraging them to assess how well their first draft addresses such questions improves revisions (Beal, Garrod, & Bonitatibus, 1990).

Finally, as in reading, content knowledge plays a crucial role in writing. Children generally write better when they are familiar with the topic than when they are not (Bereiter & Scardamalia, 1982). Thus, the standard advice "Write what you know" applies to children as well as to aspiring authors.

ADHD (attention-deficit hyperactivity disorder) a syndrome that involves difficulty in sustaining attention

individual differences 8.4

Attention-Deficit Disorder

Acquiring academic skills such as reading and writing requires children to focus their attention for prolonged periods of time. Without sustained attention, how can children write a story or book report, especially if they are surrounded by potential distractions? Everyone finds such situations challenging, but some children (and adults) encounter special difficulty with them. These are people with **ADHD (attention-deficit hyperactivity disorder).**

Although the term ADHD is relatively new, the syndrome—variously labeled *hyperactivity, minimal brain dysfunction,* and *attention-deficit disorder*—has long been recognized. Children with ADHD tend to be of normal intelligence and do not typically show serious emotional disturbances. However, they have difficulty sticking to plans, following rules and regulations, and persevering on tasks that require sustained attention (especially ones they find uninteresting). Many are hyperactive, constantly fidgeting, drumming on their desks, and moving around, even when they are supposed to be sitting quietly in their seats in the classroom. Many also encounter problems in suppressing aggressive reactions when they are frustrated. All these symptoms seem to reflect an underlying difficulty in inhibiting impulses to act (Barkley, 1997). The difficulty is greatest when interesting distractors are available. In one study, 6- to 12-year-old boys diagnosed with ADHD paid attention to an educational television program *(3-2-1 Contact)* for only half as much time as boys without ADHD when distracting toys were in the room but were equally attentive when no distracting toys were present (Landau, Lorch, & Milich, 1992).

By current definitions, ADHD affects 3% to 5% of children in the United States (American Psychiatric Association, 1994). The large majority of children diagnosed with ADHD are boys. However, this sex difference may be due not to a difference in frequency of the syndrome but to the fact that boys with ADHD are more likely to engage in disruptive behaviors that lead to their being diagnosed with the problem (Gaub & Carlson, 1997; Silver, 1992). Some children with ADHD outgrow their early problems, but most continue to have difficulties into adolescence and adulthood. They are considerably more likely than other children to drop out of high school later and to commit reckless criminal acts (Green, Biederman, Fargone, Sienna, & Garcia-Jetton, 1997; Wender, 1995).

The causes of ADHD are quite varied. Biology clearly plays a role. If one identical twin has ADHD, the odds are about 50% that the other twin also does, a rate roughly 10 times that among children in general (Goodman & Stevenson, 1989). In addition, ADHD in adopted children is associated with ADHD in the biological parent but not in the rearing parent (Zametkin, 1995). Another finding implicating biological factors is that in children with ADHD, the prefrontal cortex, the part of the brain that is most involved in regulation of attention and inhibition of action, often exhibits abnormal activity (Riccio, Hynd, Cohen, & Gonzalez, 1993).

Environments also influence development of ADHD. Some of these environmental effects are direct. For example, prenatal exposure to alcohol, which can affect brain development, is associated with children later developing ADHD (Silver, 1992). Other environmental factors contribute to ADHD indirectly. Parents and teachers often punish children with ADHD because of their inattentive and/or disruptive behavior, and peers frequently reject them for the same reason (Bernier & Siegel, 1994). These reactions, unfortunately, only exacerbate the problem (Hinshaw et al., 1997).

At the same time, several environmental factors that are often cited in newspaper and magazine articles as causes of ADHD actually do not contribute to it. Consumption of food additives and sugar, for example, has not been shown to be related to ADHD (Hynd, Horn, Voeller, & Marshall, 1991). Similarly, despite concerns that fast-paced, jump-cut television programs such as *Sesame Street* might reduce children's attention span, there is no evidence that this occurs (Huston & Wright, 1998).

The most common treatment for children with ADHD is stimulant medications, such as Ritalin. Although it seems paradoxical that a stimulant could help children who are already overly active, Ritalin helps about 70% of children for whom it is prescribed. The medication allows children with ADHD to focus their attention better and become less distractible. This leads to improved academic achievement, better relationships with classmates, and reduced activity levels (Cantwell, 1996; Silver, 1992). The benefits, however, continue only as long as children continue to take the stimulants. Longer-lasting gains require behavioral treatments, such as teaching children strategies for screening out disruptions, as well as medication (Barkley, 1994). The most effective behavioral interventions also include working with those who are involved with the children on a daily basis, namely teachers and parents (Pelham & Hoza, 1996). Encouraging teachers to allow children with ADHD to alternate between studying and moving around the classroom, and helping parents muster the patience needed to deal with these challenging children, seem especially effective. Combined, these behavioral interventions and medications help a great many children with ADHD.

DAVID YOUNG-WOLFF / PHOTOEDIT

The short attention spans of children with attention-deficit disorder often lead them to distract not only themselves but also other children in their classroom.

Mathematics

As discussed in Chapter 7, from early in their first year, infants display a rudimentary sense of number, but one that is limited to sets of 1, 2, and 3 objects. By the time they are 3 or 4 years old, they supplement this initial competence with skill at counting and with knowledge of the relative sizes of single-digit numbers. These early-emerging numerical competencies provide a base from which children can learn arithmetic and other more advanced mathematical skills.

Arithmetic

One of the most striking characteristics of children's arithmetic is the variety of overt strategies that they use to solve problems. Most children acquire their first overt arithmetic strategy, counting from 1 (e.g., solving 2 + 2 by putting up two fingers on each hand and counting "1, 2, 3, 4"), when they are 4 or 5 years old (Geary, 1994; Siegler & Robinson, 1982). Very quickly, they begin to use the strategy of retrieval (recalling answers from memory) to answer a few simple problems, such as 2 + 2. In first grade, when children begin to do arithmetic on a daily basis, they add several new strategies. The most common is *counting from the larger addend* (e.g., solving 3 + 9 by counting, "9, 10, 11, 12"). Another common strategy is *decomposition,* which involves dividing a problem into two easier ones (e.g, solving 3 + 9 by thinking "3 + 10 is 13; 13 – 1 = 12"). Similar use of varied strategies is also present in other arithmetic operations (Siegler, 1987, 1988a). For example, to solve a multiplication problem such as 3 × 4, children sometimes write three 4s and add them, sometimes make three bundles of four hatch marks and count them, and sometimes retrieve 12 from memory.

Just as children's choices among word-identification strategies are highly adaptive, so are their choices among arithmetic strategies (Geary, 1994; Siegler & Shrager, 1984). Even 4-year-olds choose in sensible ways, solving easy problems quickly and accurately by using retrieval and solving harder problems less quickly but still accurately by counting (Figure 8.10). As children gain experience with arithmetic, their strategy choices shift toward increasing use of retrieval. The

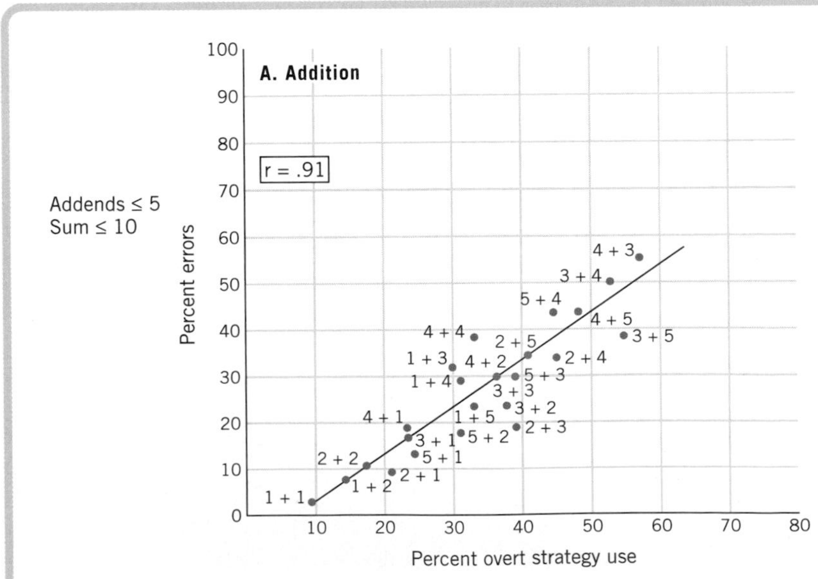

FIGURE 8.10 Young children's strategy choices in addition, subtraction, and multiplication As was illustrated previously with reading (Figure 8.7), there is a strong positive correlation between the difficulty of a problem, as defined by the percentage of errors it elicits, and the frequency of using an overt strategy, such as counting on one's fingers. Thus, on problems that 4- and 5-year-olds found easy, such as 2 + 2, they usually used retrieval. On problems they found difficult, such as 4 + 3, they usually used overt strategies such as counting from 1. (Siegler, 1986)

learning process seems to be the same as with the corresponding shift toward visually based retrieval in reading. The more often children generate the correct answer to a problem, regardless of the strategy they use to generate it, the more often they will be able to retrieve that answer, thereby avoiding the need to use a slower process such as counting.

Again as with reading, children show substantial individual differences in learning arithmetic. Differences are present both in children's rate of learning and in their cognitive style. Learners can be divided into three groups: *good students, not-so-good students,* and *perfectionists* (Siegler, 1988b). Good students answer quickly and accurately and retrieve answers to many problems. Not-so-good students answer more slowly and less accurately and retrieve answers to fewer problems. Perfectionists are like good students in answering quickly and accurately; however, they use retrieval no more often than not-so-good students, reserving it for problems on which they are very sure of the answer. On problems for which they think they know the answer but are not 100% sure, they use other strategies to check. The same three groups are evident among children from middle-income and low-income families, among African-American and Euro-American children, and in reading as well as arithmetic (Kerkman & Siegler, 1993). These individual differences in strategy choices reflect differences in knowledge (good students and perfectionists can retrieve answers to more problems than not-so-good students) and differences in criteria for stating retrieved answers (perfectionists need to be more sure than good or not-so-good students do). (As noted in Box 8.5, the poor knowledge and frequent incorrect retrievals that characterize not-so-good students are also characteristic of children who suffer from the more general difficulty known as mathematical disability.)

Conceptual understanding Understanding arithmetic involves more than memorizing answers and problem-solving procedures. It also requires a grasp of underlying concepts and principles. Unfortunately, many children learn procedures that are effective on typical problems without understanding why the procedures are appropriate. Such shallow understanding leads to difficulty when these children

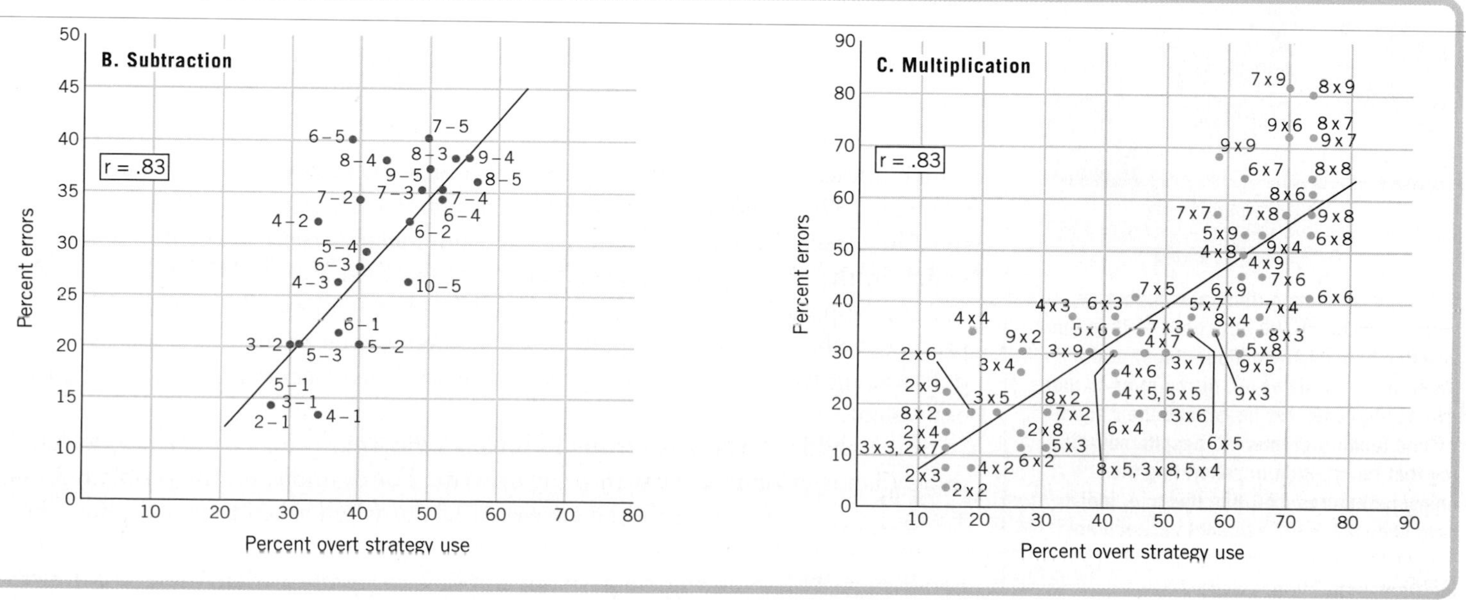

individual differences 8.5

Mathematical Disabilities

Approximately 6% of children perform so poorly in math that they are classified as having mathematical disabilities. David Geary, a psychologist who has intensively studied such children, has noted that they tend to be slow and inaccurate in solving arithmetic problems and to use retrieval rarely, much like the not-so-good students described previously (Geary, 1993; Hoard, Geary, & Hamson, 1999). Their performance improves with experience, but most continue to be slow at arithmetic even as adults (Geary & Brown, 1991; Goldman, Pellegrino, & Mertz, 1988; Jordan, Levine, & Huttenlocher, 1995). They also have difficulty with the many mathematical skills that build on single-digit arithmetic, such as word problems, multidigit arithmetic, and algebra (Ostad, 1998; Zawaiza & Gerber, 1993; Zentall & Ferkis, 1993).

Several specific problems contribute to these children's difficulties. Many children with mathematical disabilities are from poor backgrounds and come to school with little previous exposure to numbers. This leads to their lacking key concepts and skills that other children bring with them to school and that are crucial for further learning (Griffin, in press; Hitch & McAuley, 1991). Other causes of mathematical disabilities include poor working-memory capacity for numbers, slow processing of numerical information, poor teaching, and anxiety about mathematics (Ashcraft, Kirk, & Hopko, 1998; Hoard et al., 1999).

A variety of programs have been designed to help such children. Among the most promising is **Project Rightstart,** a curriculum designed to prepare kindergartners from low-income backgrounds for elementary school mathematics (Griffin & Case, 1996). To achieve this goal, Project Rightstart presents the kindergartners with a variety of board games in which the children roll dice or draw number cards that require them to add or subtract to determine the number of spaces they can move their token toward the goal. Through playing the games, children acquire mathematical skills, such as counting and reading numbers, and mathematical concepts, such as the relation of addition and subtraction. Board games that convey such lessons are common in middle-income homes but less common in low-income ones.

Underlying Project Rightstart is the theory that such everyday family experiences lay the foundation for later learning of mathematics. Consistent with this theory, participation in Project Rightstart has raised the mathematical skills and conceptual understanding of low-income kindergartners from diverse ethnic and racial groups to levels as high as those of typical middle-income peers. The program leads to substantial gains in teacher ratings and standardized math-achievement test scores that persist at least through the end of second grade. Thus, programs such as Project Rightstart that improve preschoolers' mathematical skills and conceptual understanding can reduce the number of children who have trouble with mathematics, at least in the early grades.

MICHAEL NEWMAN / PHOTOEDIT

This child's pointing illustrates a gesture–speech mismatch. He answered "17" to this problem because he added all four of the other numbers. However, his pointing to the two 4s suggests that he noticed their equality and found it of interest, despite not utilizing that recognition in generating his answer. Gestures that, like this one, indicate knowledge not evident in speech are associated with a high probability of learning from instruction.

encounter novel problems that build on the same underlying concepts but that require different solution procedures.

A good example of this experience involves the concept of **mathematical equality,** the idea that the values on the two sides of the equal sign must balance. The overwhelming majority of cases in which young children encounter the equal sign have numbers only to the left of it (e.g., 3 + 4 = ______; 3 + 4 + 5 = ______). For purposes of solving such problems, the equal sign can be treated as a kind of signal to start adding. Eventually, however, children encounter problems with numbers on both sides of the equal sign, such as 3 + 4 + 5 = ______ + 5. Susan Goldin-Meadow, Martha Alibali, and their colleagues have found that as late as fourth grade, most children in the United States answer such problems incorrectly (Alibali, 1999; Goldin-Meadow, 2001; Graham & Perry, 1993). The most common incorrect approach is to add all the numbers to the left of the equal sign, which in the above problem would generate the final answer "12." Children who use this approach are extending a procedure that works on typical problems to problems where it does not apply. More generally, such errors reveal a lack of understanding that the equal sign means that the values on the two sides must be equivalent.

Some children who answer such problems incorrectly may actually understand more than is evident in what they say or write. For example, on the problem 3 + 4 + 5 = ______ + 5, these children answer "12," but when asked to explain how they solved it, they point to all four numbers rather than just to the three preceding the equal sign. This pointing suggests an implicit recognition that there is a fourth number to be considered, even though their stated answer of "12" and their verbal explanation of their solution procedure ignored it (Alibali, 1999; Goldin-Meadow, Alibali, & Church, 1993). Children who initially show such **gesture–speech mismatches,** in which their gesturing conveys different information than their verbal statements, learn more from instruction than peers whose gesturing and speech are consistent (that is, those who say "12" and point only to the three numbers preceding the equal sign). Similarly, children whose explanations of their answer on a pretest are vague and incorrect subsequently learn more from instruction than do children whose pretest explanations are clear and incorrect (Graham & Perry, 1993). These findings illustrate a common conclusion: Increasing variability of thought and action (for example, diverging gestures and speech) often indicates heightened readiness to learn (Church, 1999; Perry & Elder, 1997; Siegler, 1994: Thelen, 2001).

Project Rightstart a curriculum designed to prepare kindergartners from low-income backgrounds for elementary school mathematics

mathematical equality the concept that the values on each side of the equal sign must be equivalent

gesture–speech mismatches a phenomenon in which hand movements and verbal statements convey different ideas

Cultural context Arithmetic performance, like other skills, varies with the context in which it occurs. Sometimes, children who are unskilled at arithmetic in the classroom context add and subtract much more skillfully in everyday contexts that are familiar and important to them. A particularly dramatic illustration of this phenomenon comes from a study of Brazilian children who supplemented their family's meager incomes by selling sweets, soft drinks, and fruit on street corners (Nunes, Schliemann, & Carraher, 1993). The children ranged in age from 9 to 15 and had attended school—often sporadically—between one and eight years.

These children showed excellent understanding of arithmetic when problems were presented in the context of street vending but poor understanding when the same problems were presented in the conventional school format. They also used different strategies in the two situations. For example, when the interviewer posed as a customer at one child's stand and asked the cost of 4 coconuts at 35 cruzeiros per coconut, the child said "Three will be 105, plus 30, that's 135 . . . one coconut is 35 . . . that is . . . 140" (Nunes & Bryant, 1996, p. 106). Thus, the child skillfully used the strategy of decomposition to solve the problem. In contrast, when the same child was asked "What is 35 times 4," he wrote the 35 above the 4 and then said, "4 times 5, 20, carry the 2; 2 plus 3 is 5, times 4 is 20" (p. 106). He then wrote down 20 next to his earlier 0, which resulted in the incorrect answer, 200. Although the two problems were identical mathematically, the differing contexts made them seem quite different to this child. The same was true for the other child vendors: when the problem was presented in the context of vending, it was meaningful to them, and they solved it in a way that reflected its meaning; when the problem was presented as a formal problem, such as 35×4, it was meaningless to them, and they tried to solve it by using an algorithm that they did not understand. Making mathematics meaningful to children, and ensuring that they understand underlying concepts as well as procedures, is one of the largest challenges that teachers face.

Cross-national comparisons of students' mathematical knowledge indicate that some educational systems fare far better than others in helping children understand fundamental concepts. For example, the most comprehensive recent international comparison, the Third International Mathematics and Science Study (Martin, et al., 1997), indicated that eighth graders in Japan, Hong Kong, Hungary, and the Netherlands all show much greater conceptual understanding than do

Brazilian children who sell candy, fruit, and other small items at street stands, and who therefore often need to make change for their customers, acquire excellent informal arithmetic skills, despite not attending school. However, the same children do far less well when problems are presented in standard classroom fashion, such as "What is 35 times 4?"

DAVID RAZIER / THE IMAGE WORKS

their peers in the United States. Prior studies of fourth and twelfth graders showed similar patterns (Stigler & Hiebert, 1999). There seem to be two main reasons. One is that in the countries with the highest math achievement, teachers and students spend much more time on mathematics than they do in the United States. The other is that in the countries with the highest math achievement, instruction tends to emphasize understanding of concepts, rather than memorization of procedures (Stigler & Hiebert, 1999). In Japan, students often spend the entire class period discussing a single problem: they first try to solve the problem independently, then they write alternative ways of solving it on the board, and then the whole class discusses why each of several correct approaches is correct and why each of several incorrect approaches is incorrect. This instructional technique seems to contribute to the superior understanding of mathematics shown by Japanese students.

Algebra

Learning algebra greatly extends the range of problems that children can solve mathematically. Again, however, lack of conceptual understanding hinders learning. The problem is that many students treat algebra as an exercise in following arbitrary rules of symbol manipulation rather than as a system for representing problems in meaningful ways and finding solutions to them. For example, when asked to write an equation to represent the statement "There are six times as many students as professors at this university," a high percentage of engineering students at a respected university wrote 6S = P (Clement, 1982). At first glance, this equation may look reasonable—but only until the realization sets in that it means that multiplying the larger number (the number of students) by 6 yields a result equal to the smaller number (the number of professors).

Two processes appear to be central to learning algebra: schema formation and automatization of basic procedures (Cooper & Sweller, 1987). **Schemas** are strategies that can be applied to solving any problem within a class of situations. For example, children learn that given any two values from among time, speed, and distance, they can compute the third value by multiplying or dividing the other two. Thus, if asked how long it takes a train to travel 200 miles at an average speed of 50 miles per hour, they know to divide the distance by the speed. The other key process in learning algebra is automatizing widely applicable procedures, such as adding equal quantities to each side of an equation in order to eliminate the quantity on one side. Automatizing such common procedures frees cognitive resources for thinking about less-routine aspects of problems.

Intelligent computer-based tutors, such as PAT (Practical Algebra Tutor) (Koedinger, Anderson, Hadley, & Mark, 1997), teach algebra in a way that meets both objectives. PAT focuses on how algebra can be used to solve everyday problems, such as choosing between alternative phone company plans or rental car rates. For example, one problem that PAT presents requires students to decide whether it would be cheaper to rent a truck from Hertz or Avis. To solve the problem, students construct a spreadsheet within which they identify the relevant quantities (cost per day, cost per mile, number of days, etc.), label the columns with the name of the variables, enter algebraic expressions, and derive an answer. They also construct graphs of the solution, to show how the answer might change depending on the length of the rental.

One of the strengths of computer-based tutors is that they can provide immediate, individualized feedback to each student. PAT includes not only a model of

schemas strategies that can be applied for solving any problem within a class of situations how students generate correct algebraic rules but also models of how they generate common erroneous rules. For example, PAT anticipates that some students will analogize from the rule "$a(b + c) = ab + ac$" and erroneously conclude that $a + (bc) = ab + ac$. Thus, if a student is working with the expression $a + (bc)$ and makes an error that would follow from treating the expression as equal to $ab + ac$, PAT asks the student if that is what he or she was thinking. If the answer is "yes," the program explains why the approach is wrong and then provides hints about the correct way to think about the problem; if the first, relatively general hint does not allow the student to solve the problem, PAT provides increasingly specific hints until the student succeeds. Students also can ask PAT for help whenever they get stuck. Moreover, PAT keeps records of each student's strengths and weaknesses, and uses the records to provide extra practice in areas of difficulty until the student masters them. The problems presented by the tutor include the main schemas needed to solve ninth-grade algebra problems; PAT also provides ample practice in applying them, thus allowing students to automatize their use.

This intelligent computer-based system has achieved impressive results. One test of PAT involved presenting it to 470 ninth graders in twenty algebra classrooms in the inner city of Pittsburgh (Koedinger et al., 1997). Students in these classrooms did better on both standardized algebra achievement tests and relevant SAT problems than did other students at the same high schools and from similar backgrounds who were taught algebra through conventional means. Comparable success has been reported with a geometry tutor developed by the same team of investigators (Anderson & Lebiere, 1998). By providing carefully thought-out problems, immediate, individualized feedback, and extensive practice, intelligent computer-based tutors promise to enhance students' learning of algebra, geometry, and other areas of mathematics.

review:

Learning to read begins in preschool, when many children come to recognize the letters of the alphabet and gain phonemic awareness. Early in elementary school, children learn to identify words through two main processes—phonological recoding and visually based retrieval—and they choose adaptively between these strategies. Reading comprehension improves through automatization of word identification, development of strategies, and acquisition of metacognition and content knowledge. How much children read and how much their parents read to them also influence reading development.

Learning to write well is difficult. It requires focusing simultaneously on low-level goals (proper spelling, punctuation, and capitalization) and high-level goals (making arguments clear and persuasive). Many Western children enter school knowing that writing proceeds in a horizontal sequence from left to right, that the text on one line continues on the next, and that words are separated by small spaces. Improvements in writing with age and experience reflect automatization of low-level goals, new organizational strategies, growing metacognitive understanding of what readers need to be told, and increasing content knowledge.

Mathematical development follows a similar general pattern. Most children enter school with some useful knowledge, such as counting and knowing how to count from 1 to solve addition problems. Once in school, children learn a wide range of strategies for solving arithmetic and other mathematical problems, and they generally choose among these strategies in sensible ways. Learning mathematics also requires a grasp of underlying concepts and principles, which many students find elusive. Computer tutors that diagnose the sources of incorrect answers and provide hints for overcoming them have proved successful in helping children acquire understanding of essential concepts and problem-solving skills in geometry, algebra, and other areas of mathematics.

Chapter Summary

- Alfred Binet and his colleague Théophile Simon developed the first widely used intelligence test. Its purpose was to identify children who were unlikely to benefit from standard instruction in the classroom. Modern intelligence tests are descendants of the Binet-Simon test.
- One of Binet's key insights was that intelligence includes diverse capabilities, which need to be assessed in order to measure intelligence accurately.

What Is Intelligence?

- Intelligence can be viewed as a single trait, such as *g;* as a few separate abilities, such as Thurstone's primary mental abilities; or as a very large number of specific processes, such as those described in information-processing analyses.
- Intelligence is often measured through use of IQ tests, such as the Stanford-Binet and the WISC. These tests examine general information, vocabulary, arithmetic, language comprehension, spatial reasoning, and variety of other intellectual abilities.

Measuring Intelligence

- A person's overall score on an intelligence test, the person's IQ score, is a measure of general intelligence. It reflects the individual's intellectual ability relative to age peers.
- Most children's IQ scores are quite stable over periods of years, though scores do vary somewhat over time.

IQ Scores as Predictors of Important Outcomes

- IQ scores correlate positively with long-term educational and occupational success.
- Other factors, such as social understanding, creativity, and motivation also influence success in life.

Genes, Environment, and the Development of Intelligence

- Development of intelligence is influenced by the child's own qualities, by the immediate environment, and by the broader societal context.
- Genetic inheritance is one important influence on IQ. This influence tends to grow larger with age, in part due to some genes not expressing themselves until late childhood or adolescence, and in part due to genes influencing children's choices of environments.
- Gender is unrelated to average IQ, though boys and girls differ somewhat in particular abilities.
- A child's family environment, as measured by the HOME, is related to the child's IQ score. The relation reflects within-family influences, such as parents' intellectual and emotional support for the particular child, as well as between-family influences, such as differences in parental wealth and education.
- Schooling positively influences IQ and school achievement.
- Broader societal factors, such as poverty and discrimination against racial and ethnic minorities, also influence children's IQs.
- To alleviate the harmful effects of poverty, the United States has undertaken both small-scale preschool intervention programs and the much larger Project Head Start. Both have initial positive effects on intelligence and school achievement, though the effects fade over time. On the other hand, the programs have enduring positive effects on the likelihood of not being held back in a grade and the likelihood of completing high school.
- Intensive intervention programs, such as the Carolina Abecedarian Project, that begin in the child's first year and provide optimal child-care circumstances and structured academic curricula have produced increases in intelligence that continue into adolescence and adulthood.

Alternative Perspectives on Intelligence

- New approaches to intelligence, such as Gardner's multiple intelligence theory and Sternberg's theory of successful intelligence, are attempts to broaden traditional conceptions of intelligence.

Aquisition of Academic Skills: Reading, Writing, and Mathematics

- Many children learn letter names and gain phonemic awareness before they start school. Both are correlated with later reading achievement, and phonemic awareness is causally related to it.
- Word identification is achieved by two main strategies: phonological recoding and visually based retrieval.
- Reading comprehension benefits from automatization of word identification, because the automatization frees cognitive resources for understanding the text. Use of strategies, metacognitive understanding, and content knowledge also influence reading comprehension, as does the amount that parents read to their children and the amount that children read themselves.
- Although many children begin to write during the preschool period, writing well remains difficult for many years for most

children. Much of the difficulty comes from the fact that writing requires children to attend simultaneously to low-level processes, such as punctuation and spelling, and to high-level processes, such as anticipating what readers will and will not know.

- As with reading, automatization of basic processes, use of strategies, metacognitive understanding, and content knowledge influence development of writing.
- Attention-deficit disorder, a difficulty in inhibiting impulses to act, adversely influences acquisition of reading and writing skills. Both brain abnormalities and environmental factors, such as prenatal exposure to alcohol, contribute to the syndrome.
- Most children use several strategies to learn arithmetic, such as counting fingers and retrieving answers from memory. They choose among them in adaptive ways, using the more time-consuming and effortful strategies only on the more difficult problems where they are needed to generate correct answers.
- As children encounter more advanced math, conceptual understanding becomes increasingly important. Many children master familiar procedures but do not understand the meaning of these procedures.
- Computer-based tutors offer a promising way of gaining understanding both of procedures and of underlying mathematical concepts.

Critical Thinking Questions

1. Intelligence can be viewed as one thing, several things, or many things. List the characteristics that you think are important components of intelligence and explain their relevance.
2. Individual differences in intelligence are more stable than individual differences in other areas of psychological functioning such as emotional regulation or aggression. Why do you think this is so?
3. Do you think that in the future, broader theories of intelligence such as Gardner's or Sternberg's will replace the more narrowly focused approaches to intelligence that are currently dominant? Or do you think that the latter approaches will remain dominant? Explain.
4. Participation in Head Start does not lead to higher IQ or achievement test scores by the end of high school, but it does lead to lower rates of dropping out or being placed in special-education classes. Why do you think this is the case?
5. Explain Chall's (1979) statement: "In the primary grades, children learn to read; in the higher grades, they read to learn."

Key Terms

g (general intelligence), p. 289
crystallized intelligence, p. 289
fluid intelligence, p. 289
primary mental abilities, p. 290
three-stratum theory of intelligence, p. 290
Wechsler Intelligence Scale for Children (WISC), p. 292
IQ (intelligence quotient), p. 293
normal distribution, p. 293
standard deviation, p. 293
Carolina Abecedarian Project, p. 307
multiple intelligence theory, p. 308
theory of successful intelligence, p. 310
phonemic awareness, p. 311
phonological recoding, p. 312
visually based retrieval, p. 313
strategy-choice process, p. 313
mental model, p. 314
dyslexia, p. 315
phonological processing, p. 315
comprehension monitoring, p. 316
ADHD (attention-deficit hyperactivity disorder), p. 319
Project Rightstart, p. 322
mathematical equality, p. 322
gesture–speech mismatches, p. 323
schemas, p. 324

CHAPTER 9

Theories of Social Development

DOROTHEA SHARP, *Building a Sandcastle*

THEMES

- Nature and Nurture
- The Active Child
- Continuity/Discontinuity
- Mechanisms of Change
- The Sociocultural Context
- Individual Differences
- Research and Children's Welfare

On a late summer afternoon, the two children pictured on the next page were playing in the backyard of the boy's home as their mothers, who had been best friends for many years, were having tea on the deck. Five-year-old Colin and 4½-year-old Catherine had played together since infancy, despite the many differences between them. For example, Catherine hated movies with any violent or scary content; as a toddler she wouldn't even watch *Sesame Street* because she was frightened of Oscar the Grouch. In contrast, Colin loved action films full of car chases, fires, and explosions. His rifle and helmet testify to his fascination with guns and the military.

On this particular afternoon, the children had been playing happily until Colin's mother asked them to stop so she could take their photographs. As is evident, Catherine was happy to comply with the adult's request. She eagerly struck a stereotypic feminine pose, one a starlet might assume for the paparazzi. Colin did not want his picture taken and was distinctly uncooperative. His resentment of his mother's intrusion into his play is reflected in his aggressive stance and expression.

What accounts for the very different behavior of these two children? Why do they have such markedly distinct preferences for activities? What makes them respond so differently to an adult's intrusion in their play? At the most basic level, of course, they are genetically different. And being of different sexes, they are subject to various hormonal and other biological differences associated with being male and female. Of primary importance to this chapter, however, Colin and Catherine have disparate life histories. They have been raised by different sets of parents, and they have spent time with different siblings and friends. Although they have lived in the same neighborhood and attended the same preschool, they have had different neighbors and teachers. In trying to explain the differences that are so salient in the photographs of these two children, the fundamental question from the perspective of this chapter is, What is the role of the social environment in Colin's and Catherine's development?

In this chapter, we review some of the most important and influential general theories of social development, theories that attempt to account for how children's development is affected by the people and social institutions around them. In Chapter 4, "Theories of Cognitive Development," we discussed some of the reasons that theories are important (p. 126); those reasons apply equally well to the theories of social development discussed in this chapter.

Theories of social development attempt to account for many important aspects of development, including emotion, personality, attachment, self, peer relationships, morality, and gender. In the first half of this chapter, we describe four types of theories—psychoanalytic, learning, social cognitive, and ecological. We discuss the basic tenets of each, as well as some of the evidence relevant to them. In the second half of the chapter, we highlight the kinds of contributions these theories make by examining the insights each has provided about a single topic—gender development. Because gender is such a salient and important category of human development, psychologists have devoted a great deal of attention to studying how gender-related behavior, attitudes, and values develop. Examining how the major theories address a specific area of social development should help clarify both the ways in which the theories differ and the ways in which they complement each other.

Every one of our seven themes appears in this chapter, although three are particularly prominent. The theme that pervades this chapter is *individual differences:* the first half of the chapter is concerned with how the individual child's social

BOTH: COURTESY OF JUDY DELOACHE

world affects his or her development; the second half focuses on how and why males and females differ. The theme of *nature and nurture* appears repeatedly, as the theories vary in the degree to which they emphasize biological factors. The *active child* theme is also a major focus: some of the theories emphasize children's active participation in, and effect on, their own socialization, whereas others view children's development as shaped primarily by external forces.

Psychoanalytic Theories

No psychological theory has had greater impact on Western culture and on thinking about personality and social development than the psychoanalytic theory of Sigmund Freud. A successor to Freud's theory, the life-span developmental theory of Erik Erikson, has also been quite influential.

View of Children's Nature

In both Freud's and Erikson's theories, development is very much driven by biological maturation. For Freud, behavior is motivated by the need to satisfy basic drives. These drives, and the various motives that arise from them, are largely unconscious, and individuals often have only the dimmest understanding of why they do what they do. The dominant metaphor in the Freudian view is an individual buffeted about by many forces, both internal and external, that the individual doesn't understand and can't control. In Erikson's theory, development is driven by a series of age-related developmental crises, or tasks, that the individual must resolve in order to achieve healthy development.

Central Developmental Issues

Three of our seven themes—*continuity/discontinuity, individual differences,* and *nature and nurture*—play prominent roles in psychoanalytic theory. The developmental accounts of Freud and Erikson are, like Piaget's theory that you encountered in Chapter 4, stage theories that stress discontinuity in development. However, within the framework of discontinuous development, psychoanalytic theories stress the continuity of individual differences, maintaining that children's early experiences shape their subsequent development. The interaction of nature and nurture arises in terms of Freud's and Erikson's emphasis on the biological underpinnings of developmental stages and how they interact with the child's experience.

Freud's Theory of Psychosexual Development

CULVER PICTURES

Sigmund Freud, the father of psychoanalysis, had a lasting impact on developmental psychology through his emphasis on the lifelong impact of early relationships.

Sigmund Freud (1856–1939), the founder of psychoanalytic theory, was encouraged by his Viennese parents in his academic pursuits: while the rest of the family made do with candles, young Sigmund had an oil lamp to light his studies (Crain, 1985). As a neurologist, Freud became interested in the origins and treatment of mental illness. His interest in psychological development grew as he became increasingly convinced that the majority of his patients' emotional problems originated early in childhood, particularly in their very early relationships with their parents.

Freud made fundamental, lasting contributions to developmental psychology. They include, first, his emphasis on the role of *early experience* in the development of personality and psychopathology. The importance of early experience seems obvious today, but it had been ignored before Freud shone his theoretical spotlight on it. Second was his recognition of the importance of *subjective* experience; how a person understands or feels about his or her experience is more crucial to development than is objective reality. A third major contribution was Freud's discovery of the *unconscious,* the mental activity that goes on without awareness but that nevertheless influences many aspects of one's functioning. Unconscious processes play a major role in contemporary cognitive and emotion research and theory. Finally, Freud's emphasis on the importance of close, emotional *relationships* has had an enormous impact on the field of developmental psychology.

In our discussion of Freud's theoretical views, we focus primarily on the developmental aspects of his theory, especially the broad themes that remain influential today. One thing you will see in the quotations from Freud's work is what an interesting and provocative writer he was.

Basic Features of Freud's Theory

Freud's theory of development includes three major components: (1) five biologically determined stages of development; (2) motivation springing from drives and the reduction of those drives; and (3) basic structures of personality. This theory is referred to as a theory of *psychosexual* development because it posits a series of universal developmental stages in which **psychic energy**—the biologically based, instinctual drives that energize behavior, thoughts, and feelings—becomes focused in different **erogenous zones** of the body, that is, areas of the body that are erotically sensitive. Initially, all the instinctual drives are based on bodily needs, but during development, some psychic energy is diverted and transformed into psychological needs and desires.

The Developmental Process

In Freud's view, development starts with a helpless infant beset by instinctual drives whose satisfaction is vital for survival. Foremost among them is the need for nourishment. Hunger creates tension. The young infant has no knowledge of how to reduce it, so the arousal and distress associated with hunger are expressed through crying, which prompts the mother to breast-feed the baby. (In Freud's day, virtually all babies were breast-fed.) The resulting satisfaction of the infant's hunger, as well as the experience of nursing, is a source of intense pleasure for the infant.

The biological drives with which the infant is born constitute the **id**—the earliest and most primitive of the three personality structures. The id, which is totally unconscious, is the source of psychic energy. It is the "dark, inaccessible part of our personality . . . a cauldron full of seething excitations" in need of satisfaction (Freud, 1933/1964). The id is ruled by the pleasure principle—the goal of achieving maximal pleasure maximally quickly. A hungry baby wants food *now.* The id remains the source of psychic energy throughout life. Its operation is most apparent in selfish or impulsive behavior in which immediate gratification is sought with little or no regard for consequences, or in dreams, which are free from the constraints of reality.

During the first year of life, the infant is in Freud's first stage of psychosexual development, the **oral stage**, so called because the primary source of gratification and pleasure is oral activity, such as sucking and eating. "If the infant could express itself, it would undoubtedly acknowledge that the act of sucking at its mother's breast is far and away the most important thing in life" (Freud, 1920/1965). The pleasure associated with breast feeding is so intense that other oral activities—sucking on a thumb or pacifier, for instance—also provide pleasure. For Freud, the baby's feelings for his or her mother are "unique, without parallel," and through them the mother is "established unalterably for a whole lifetime as the first and strongest love-object and as the prototype for all later love-relations" (1940/1964).

The infant's mother is also a source of security. However, this security is not free. As always with Freud, there is a dark side: infants "pay for this security by a fear of loss of love" (Freud, 1940/1964). For Freud, common fearful reactions to being alone or in the dark are based on "missing someone who is loved and longed for" (1926/1959).

Later in the first year, the second personality structure, the **ego,** begins to emerge. The ego is the mind's link to reality, to the external world. "The id stands for the untamed passions," whereas the ego "stands for reason and good sense" (1933/1964). The ego operates under the reality principle, trying to hold the id's demands in check in order to perceive reality accurately, remember relevant previous situations, and make plans for effective action. Over time, as the ego continually seeks resolution between the demands of the id and the demands of the real world, it becomes stronger and more differentiated, eventually developing into the individual's sense of self. Nevertheless, the ego is never fully in control:

> The ego's relation to the id might be compared with that of a rider to his horse. The horse supplies the locomotive energy, while the rider has the privilege of deciding on the goal and of guiding the powerful animal's movement. But only too often . . . the rider [is] obliged to guide the horse along the path by which it itself wants to go.
>
> (Freud, 1933/1964, p. 77)

During the infant's second year, maturation makes possible the development of control over some bodily processes, including urination and defecation. At this point, the infant enters Freud's second stage, the **anal stage,** which lasts until

psychic energy Freud's term for the biologically based instinctual drives that he believed energize behavior, thoughts, and feelings

erogenous zones in Freud's theory, areas of the body that become erotically sensitive in successive stages of development

id in psychoanalytic theory, the earliest and most primitive personality structure. It is unconscious and operates with the goal of seeking pleasure.

oral stage the first stage in Freud's theory, occurring in the first year, in which the primary source of satisfaction and pleasure is oral activity

ego in psychoanalytic theory, the second personality structure to develop. It is the rational, logical, problem-solving component of personality.

anal stage the second stage in Freud's theory, lasting roughly from 1 to 3 years of age, in which the primary source of pleasure comes from defecation

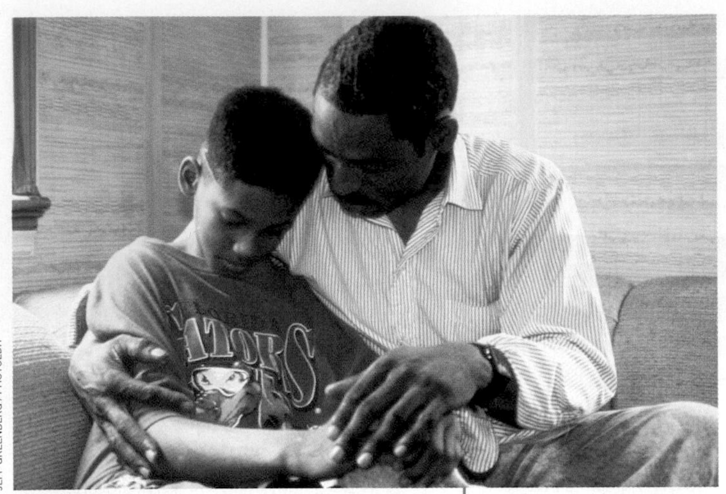

JEFF GREENBERG / PHOTOEDIT

Through identifying with his father, this young boy should, according to Freud's theory, develop a strong superego.

roughly age 3. In this stage, the anal area becomes the focus of the child's erotic interests—specifically the pleasurable relief of the tension derived from defecation. Conflict ensues when, for the first time, the infant's parents begin to make specific demands on him or her, most notably their insistence on toilet training. In the years to come, parents and others will increase their demands on the child to control his or her impulses and to delay gratification.

Freud's third stage of development, the **phallic stage,** spans the ages of 3 to 6. In this stage, the focus of sexual pleasure again migrates, as children become interested in their own genitalia and curious about those of parents and playmates. Both boys and girls derive pleasure from masturbation, an activity that the parents of Freud's time and place often severely punished.

During this stage, the third personality structure, the **superego,** emerges. The superego is essentially what we think of as conscience. It enables the child to control his or her own behavior on the basis of beliefs about right and wrong. The superego is based on the child's identification with his or her parents and the child's **internalization,** or adoption, of their rules and standards for acceptable and unacceptable behavior. The superego guides the child to avoid actions that would result in guilt, which the child experiences when violating these internalized rules and standards.

The fourth developmental stage, the **latency period,** lasts from about age 6 to age 12. It is, as its name implies, a time of relative calm. Sexual desires are safely hidden away in the unconscious, and psychic energy gets channeled into constructive, socially acceptable activities, including both intellectual and social pursuits. As a result, both the ego and superego continue to develop.

The fifth and final stage, the **genital stage,** begins with the advent of sexual maturation. The sexual energy that had been kept in check for several years reasserts itself with full force, although it is now directed toward opposite-sex peers. Ideally, the individual has developed a strong ego that facilitates coping with reality and a superego that is neither too weak nor too strong.

Freud thought that healthy development culminates in the ability to invest oneself in, and derive pleasure from, both love and work. This outcome can be sabotaged in a multitude of ways, however. If fundamental needs are not met during any stage, children may become *fixated* on those needs, continually attempting to satisfy them and to resolve the issues and conflicts relevant to the stage in question. For example, if the mother does not adequately satisfy her infant's needs for oral gratification, later in life the individual may repeatedly engage in substitute oral activities, such as excessive eating, nail-biting, smoking, and so on. Similarly, toddlers subjected to very harsh toilet training during the anal stage might remain preoccupied with cleanliness and either become compulsively tidy and rigid or extremely sloppy and lax. Thus, in Freud's view, the nature of the child's passage through the stages of psychosexual development shapes the individual's personality for life.

phallic stage the third stage in Freud's theory, lasting from age 3 to age 6, in which sexual pleasure is focused on the genitalia

superego in psychoanalytic theory, the third personality structure consisting of internalized moral standards

internalization the process of adopting as one's own the attributes, beliefs, and standards of another person

latency period the fourth stage in Freud's theory, lasting from age 6 to age 12, in which sexual energy gets channeled into socially acceptable activities

genital stage the fifth and final stage in Freud's theory, beginning in adolescence, in which sexual maturation is complete and sexual intercourse becomes a major goal

Erikson's Theory of Psychosocial Development

Of the many followers of Freud, none has had greater influence in developmental psychology than Erik Erikson (1902–1994). Erikson accepted the basic elements of Freud's theory, but he enlarged its scope to include other factors that shape development, including culture and contemporary issues, such as juvenile delinquency, changing sexual roles, and the generation gap. Hence, Erikson's is a theory of *psychosocial* development.

TED STRESHINSKY / CORBIS

Erik Erikson, who was born in Germany, took a long time to settle into a career. Instead of attending college, he wandered around Europe pursuing his interest in art for several years. Eventually he was hired as an art instructor in a school run by Anna Freud, Sigmund Freud's daughter, and became an analyst. He moved to the United States in the early 1930s, when fascism was on the rise in Germany.

The Developmental Process

Erikson proposed eight age-related stages of development that span infancy to old age. We will discuss only the first five stages, which focus on development in infancy, childhood, and adolescence. Each of Erikson's stages is characterized by a specific *crisis*, or set of developmental issues, that the individual must resolve. If the dominant issue of a given stage is not successfully resolved before maturation and social pressures usher in the next stage, the person will continue to struggle with it.

1. Basic Trust vs. Mistrust (the first year). In Erikson's first stage (which corresponds to Freud's oral stage), the crucial issue for the infant is developing a sense of basic trust—"an essential trustfulness of others as well as a fundamental sense of one's own trustworthiness" (Erikson, 1969, p. 96). If the mother is warm, consistent, and reliable in her caregiving, the infant learns that she can be trusted. More generally, the baby comes to feel good and reassured by being close to other people. If the ability to trust others when it is appropriate to do so is not developed, the individual will have difficulty forming intimate relationships later in life.

2. Autonomy vs. Shame and Doubt (ages 1 to 3½). The challenge for the child between ages 1 and 3½ (Freud's anal stage) is to achieve a strong sense of autonomy while adjusting to increasing social demands. Going well beyond Freud's focus on toilet training, Erikson pointed out that during this period dramatic increases in every realm of children's real-world competence, including motor skills, cognitive abilities, and language, foster children's desires to make choices and decisions for themselves. Infants' new ability to explore the environment changes the family dynamics (as we discussed in Chapter 5), initiating a long-running battle of wills in which parents try to restrict the child's freedom and teach the child what behaviors are acceptable and unacceptable. If parents provide a supportive atmosphere that allows children to achieve self-control without the loss of self-esteem, children gain a sense of autonomy. In contrast, if children are subjected to severe punishment, ridicule, or shame, they may come to doubt their abilities or to feel a general sense of shame.

NANCY RICHMOND / THE IMAGE WORKS

This child's parents have not yet succeeded in training her to behave in the socially appropriate way with respect to eating. Once they do, she would feel ashamed to finish a meal looking like this.

3. Initiative vs. Guilt (ages 4 to 6). Like Freud, Erikson saw the time between ages 4 and 6 years as a period during which children come to identify with and learn from their parents: "[the child] hitches his wagon to nothing less than a star: he wants to be like his parents, who to him appear very powerful and very beautiful" (Erikson, 1994). The child in this third stage of life is constantly setting goals (building a high tower of blocks, learning the alphabet) and working to achieve them. Like Freud, Erikson believed that a crucial attainment is the development of conscience, the internalization of the parents' rules and standards, and the experiencing of guilt when failing to uphold them. The challenge for the child is to achieve a balance between initiative and guilt. If parents are not highly controlling or punitive, children can develop high standards and the initiative to meet them without being crushed by worry about not being able to measure up.

4. Industry vs. Inferiority (age 6 to puberty). Erikson's fourth stage, which lasts from age 6 to puberty (Freud's latency period), is crucial for ego development. During this stage, children master cognitive and social skills that are important in their culture, and they learn to work industriously and to play well with peers.

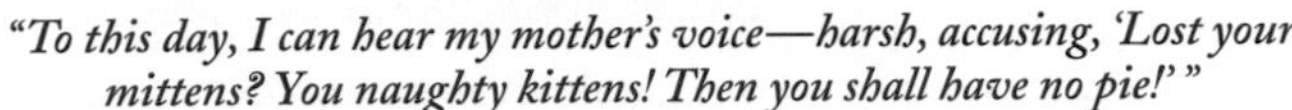

"To this day, I can hear my mother's voice—harsh, accusing, 'Lost your mittens? You naughty kittens! Then you shall have no pie!'"

"You've got to want to connect the dots, Mr. Michaelson."

The vast abundance of cartoons about Freud and psychoanalysis testifies to his enormous impact on society.

Successful experiences give the child a sense of competence, but failure can lead to excessive feelings of inadequacy or inferiority. Erikson (1959) pointed out that teachers can be very helpful in this stage: "Again and again, I have observed in the lives of especially gifted and inspired people that one teacher, somewhere, was able to kindle the flame of a hidden talent" (p. 87).

5. Identity vs. Role Confusion (adolescence to early adulthood). Erikson accorded great importance to adolescence, seeing it as a critical stage for the achievement of a core sense of *identity.* Adolescents change so rapidly in so many ways that they can hardly recognize themselves, either in the mirror or in their minds. The dramatic physical changes of puberty and the emergence of strong sexual urges are accompanied by new social pressures, including a need to make educational and occupational decisions. Caught between their past identity as a child and the many options and uncertainties of their future, adolescents must resolve the question of who they really are or live in confusion about what roles they should play as adults. As you will see in Chapter 11, the idea of the search for identity is particularly relevant for young people in modern multicultural societies, and developmentalists have devoted a good deal of attention to the stage of identity versus role confusion.

Current Perspectives

The most significant of Freud's contributions to developmental psychology were his emphasis on the importance of early experience and emotional relationships and his recognition of the role of subjective experience and unconscious mental activity. Erikson's emphasis on the quest for identity in adolescence has had a lasting impact, providing the foundation for a wealth of research on this aspect of adolescence.

The signal weakness of Freud's and Erikson's theories is that their major theoretical claims are stated too vaguely to be testable. As a consequence, although the broad themes of Freud's and Erikson's theories continue to be important, the specifics of these theories are regarded by most developmentalists as highly questionable. Nevertheless, there is no question that Freud's theory has been one of the most influential psychological theories ever.

review: The psychoanalytic theories of Sigmund Freud and Erik Erikson propose that social and emotional development proceed in a series of stages, with each stage characterized by a particular task or crisis that must be resolved for subsequent healthy development. A healthy personality involves an appropriate balance between the three structures of personality—id, ego, and superego. Maturational factors play a key role, and psychic energy and sexual impulses are seen, especially by Freud, as being major forces in development. Early experience in the context of the family is considered to have a lasting impact on the individual's relationships with other people. These theories have had enormous, continuing impact on Western culture.

Learning Theories

I imagine the mind of children as easily turned, this or that way as water itself.

John Locke

As you may recall from Chapter 1, the empiricist philosopher John Locke believed that experience shapes the nature of the human mind. The intellectual descendants of Locke are psychologists who consider learning from experience to be the primary factor in social and personality development.

View of Children's Nature

In contrast to Freud's emphasis on the role of internal forces and subjective experience, most learning theorists have emphasized the role of external factors in shaping personality and social behavior. They have often made very bold claims about the extent to which development could be guided by how people treat children, rewarding or reinforcing certain behaviors and punishing or ignoring others. John Watson's went so far as to assert that by controlling a child's environment, he could train any child to "become any type of specialist I might select." More contemporary learning theorists have emphasized the importance of cognitive factors and the active role children play in their own development.

Central Developmental Issues

The primary developmental question on which learning theories take a unanimous stand is that of *continuity/discontinuity:* they all emphasize continuity, proposing that the same principles control learning and behavior throughout life and that therefore there are no qualitatively different stages in development. Like information-processing theorists, learning theorists focus on the role of specific *mechanisms of change*—learning principles, such as reinforcement and observational learning. They believe that children become different from one another primarily because they have different histories of reinforcement and observational learning. The theme of *research and children's welfare* is also relevant here in that therapeutic approaches based on learning principles have been widely used to treat children with a variety of problems.

Watson's Behaviorism

John B. Watson (1878–1958), the founder of behaviorism (whom you encountered in Chapters 1 and 5), believed that all behavior can be understood as responses to events in the environment and that psychologists should study only objectively verifiable behaviors, not the "mind." He believed that children's development is determined by their social environment—most especially, how their parents treat them. Having placed responsibility for children's development squarely on the shoulders of their parents, Watson offered them advice, even going so far as to write a child-rearing manual, *Psychological Care of Infant and Child* (1928). One piece of this advice that was widely adopted in the United States was to put infants on a strict feeding schedule. The idea was that the baby would become conditioned to expect a feeding at regular intervals and would not cry for attention in between. To implement such a strict regimen, Watson advised parents to achieve distance and objectivity in their dealings with their offspring (just as he exhorted psychologists to be objective in their research).

Watson's ignoring of mental states and his almost exclusive emphasis on conditioning is now regarded as simplistic. However, his famous study of classical conditioning of fear in 11-month-old Little Albert (Watson & Rayner, 1920), which we discussed in Chapter 5, laid the foundation for treatment procedures based on the opposite process—the deconditioning, or elimination, of fear. A student of Watson's (Jones, 1924), treated 2-year-old Peter, who was deathly afraid of white rabbits (as well as white rats, white fur coats, white feathers, and a variety of other white things). To decondition his fear, the experimenter first gave him a favorite snack. Then, as Peter ate, a white rabbit in a cage was very slowly brought closer and closer to him—but never close enough to make him afraid. After repeatedly experiencing the feared object in a context in which he experienced no fear but did have the positive experience of his snack, Peter got over his fear. Eventually, he was even able to pet the rabbit. This approach, now known as **systematic desensitization,** has been widely used to rid people of fears and phobias of everything from dogs to dentists.

Skinner's Operant Conditioning

B. F. Skinner (1904–1990) was just as strong a proponent as Watson of environmental control of behavior, once claiming that "a person does not act upon the world, the world acts upon him" (Skinner, 1971, p. 211). As described in Chapter 5, a major tenet of Skinner's theory of *operant conditioning* is that we tend to repeat behaviors that lead to favorable outcomes (reinforcement) and suppress those that result in unfavorable outcomes (punishment). Skinner believed that everything we do in life—every act—is an operant response influenced by the outcomes of past behavior.

Skinner's research on the nature and function of reinforcement led to many discoveries, including two that are of particular interest to parents and teachers. One is the fact that *attention* can by itself serve as a powerful reinforcer: children often do things "just to get attention" (Skinner, 1953, p. 78). Thus, the best strategy for discouraging a child from throwing further temper tantrums is to ignore that behavior whenever it occurs. The popular behavior-management strategy of *time-out,* or temporary isolation, involves systematically withdrawing attention and thereby removing the reinforcement for inappropriate behavior, with the goal of extinguishing it. A second important discovery is the great difficulty of extin-

systematic desensitization a form of therapy based on classical conditioning, in which positive responses are gradually conditioned to stimuli that initially elicit a highly negative response; especially useful in the treatment of fears and phobias

behavior modificiation a form of therapy based on principles of operant conditioning in which reinforcement contingencies are changed to encourage more adaptive behavior guishing behavior that has been *intermittently reinforced,* that is, behavior that has sometimes been followed by reward and sometimes not. As Skinner discovered in his research with animals, intermittent reinforcement makes behaviors resistant to extinction; if the reward is totally withdrawn, the behavior persists longer than it would if it had always been reinforced.

To the detriment of their child-rearing goals, parents often apply intermittent reinforcement inadvertently. They valiantly try not to reward their children's whiny or aggressive demands, but—being human—they sometimes give in. Such intermittent reinforcement is very powerful: if a parent who had occasionally given in to whining never did it again, the child would nevertheless continue to resort to whining for a long time, assuming that because it worked in the past, it might work again. The intermittent-reinforcement effect is one reason most parents have children with at least a few persistent bad habits.

NINA LEEN, LIFE MAGAZINE © TIME WARNER, INC

B. F. Skinner, who once appeared in fortieth place in a popular magazine's list of the 100 most important people who ever lived (Miller, 1993), believed that children's development is primarily a matter of their reinforcement history.

Skinner's work on reinforcement has also led to a form of therapy known as **behavior modification,** which has proven quite useful for changing undesirable behaviors. A simple example of this approach involved a preschool child who spent too much of his time in solitary activities. Observers noticed that the boy's teachers were reinforcing his withdrawn behavior: they talked to him and comforted him when he was alone but tended to ignore him when he played with other children. The boy's withdrawal was modified by reversing the reinforcement contingencies: the teachers began paying attention to the boy whenever he joined a group and ignoring him whenever he withdrew. Soon the child was spending most of his time playing with his classmates (Harris, Wolf, & Baer, 1967).

Social Learning Theory

Social learning theory, like other learning theories, attempts to account for personality and other aspects of social development in terms of learning mechanisms. However, in assessing the influence of the environment on children's development, social learning theory emphasizes observation and imitation, rather than reinforcement, as the primary mechanisms of development. Albert Bandura (1977, 1986), for example, has argued that most human learning is inherently *social* in nature and is based on observation of the behavior of other people. Children learn most rapidly and efficiently simply from watching what other people do and then imitating them. Reinforcement can increase the likelihood of imitation but it is

A good example of observational learning.

a closer look

Bandura and Bobo

A series of classic studies by Albert Bandura and his colleagues (Bandura, 1965; Bandura, Ross, & Ross, 1963) will give you a good sense of the kind of questions and methods that typify social learning theory research. The investigators began by having preschool children individually watch a short film in which an adult model performed highly unusual aggressive actions on a Bobo doll (an inflatable toy, with a weight in the bottom so it pops back up as soon as it's knocked down; see photos on p. 341). The model punched the doll, hit it with a mallet while shouting "sockeroo," threw balls at it while shouting "bang bang," and so on.

In one study, three groups of children observed the model receive different consequences for this aggressive behavior. A third of them saw the model be rewarded (an adult gave the model candy and soda and praised the "championship performance"). Another third saw the model scolded and spanked for the aggressive behavior. The remaining children saw the model experience no consequences. The question was whether **vicarious reinforcement**—observing someone else receive a reward or a punishment—would affect the children's subsequent reproduction of the behavior. After viewing the film, each child was left alone in a playroom with a Bobo doll, and hidden observers recorded whether the child imitated what he or she had seen the model do. Later, whether or not they had imitated the model, the children were offered juice and prizes to reproduce all the model's actions that they could remember.

The results are shown in the figure. The children who had seen the model punished imitated the behavior less than did those in the other two groups. However, the children in all conditions had *learned* from observing the model's behavior and remembered what they had seen; when offered rewards to reproduce the aggressive actions, they did so, even if they had not spontaneously performed them in the initial test.

One particularly interesting feature of this research is the gender differences that emerged: boys were more physically

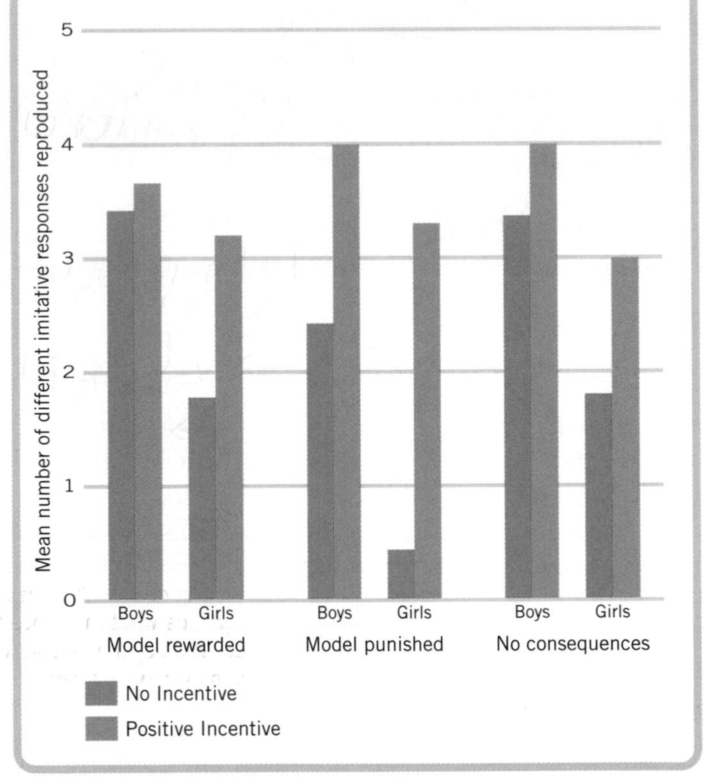

The average number of aggressive behaviors children imitated after seeing a model rewarded, punished, or receiving no consequences for her behavior. In the no-incentive test, the children were simply left alone in the room with the Bobo doll but were given no instructions. In the positive-incentive test, they were offered a reward to do what they had seen the model do. The results clearly show that the children had learned from what they observed and that they had learned more than they initially showed. (Adapted from Bandura, 1965)

not necessary for learning. Because direct reinforcement is not required for learning, children can learn from symbolic models, that is, from reading books and from watching TV or movies (see Box 9.1).

Over time, Bandura increasingly emphasized the cognitive aspects of observational learning, eventually renaming his view "social cognitive theory." Observational learning clearly depends on basic cognitive processes of *attention* to others' behavior, *encoding* what is observed, *storing* the information in memory, and *retrieving* it at some later time in order to reproduce the behavior observed earlier. Thanks to observational learning, many young children know quite a bit about activities such as driving a car—you insert the key in the ignition, press on the accelerator, turn the steering wheel—long before being allowed to get behind the wheel themselves.

vicarious reinforcement observing someone else receive a reward or punishment

reciprocal determinism Bandura's concept that child–environment influences operate in both directions; children are affected by aspects of their environment, but they also influence the environment

9.1

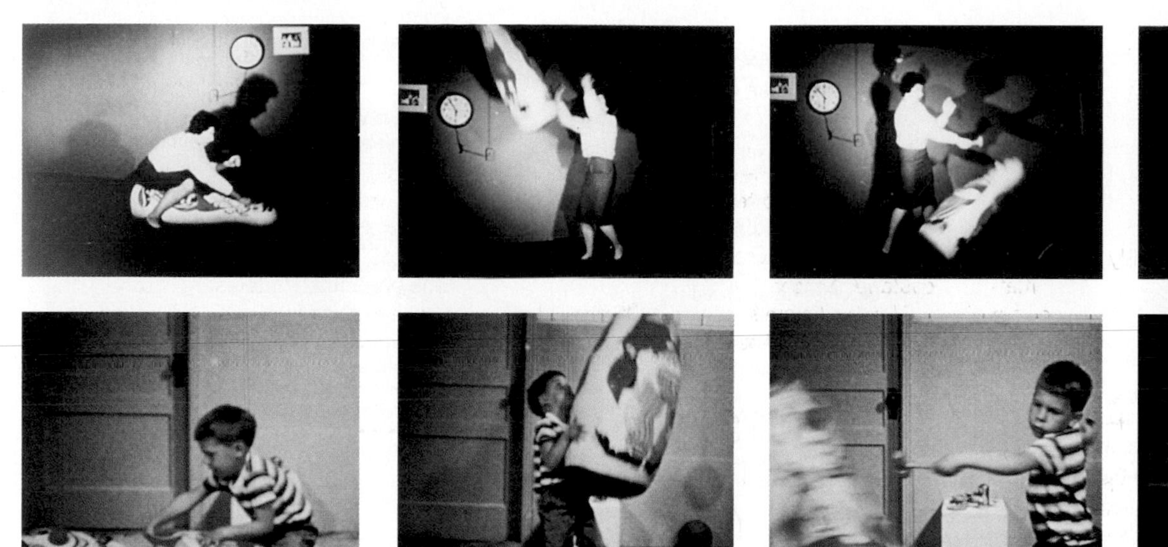

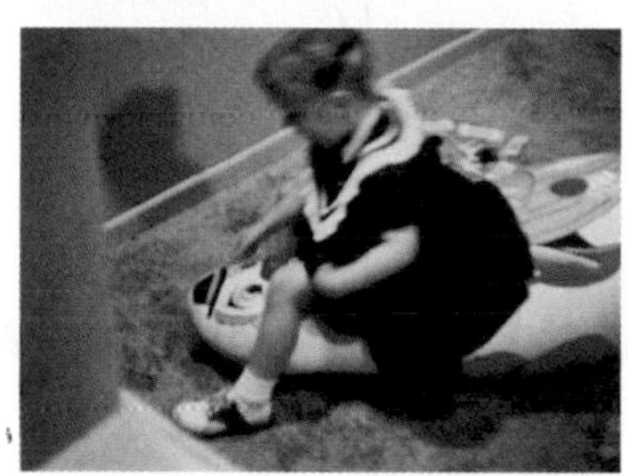

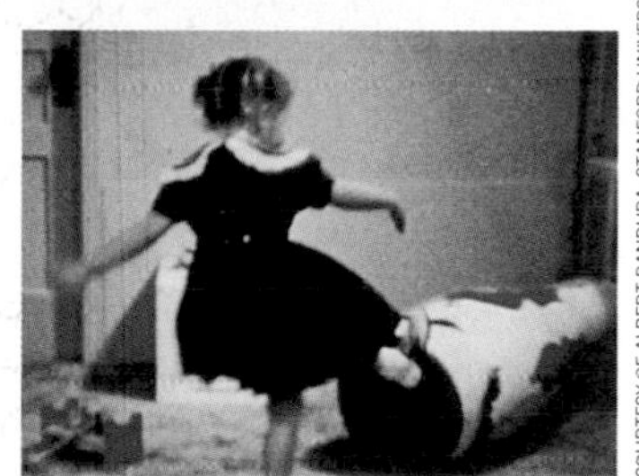

COURTESY OF ALBERT BANDURA, STANFORD UNIVERSITY

aggressive toward the Bobo doll than girls were. However, the girls had learned as much about the modeled behaviors as the boys, as shown by their increased level of imitation when offered a reward. Presumably, boys and girls generally learn a great deal about the behaviors considered appropriate to both sexes but inhibit those they believe to be inappropriate for their own sex.

This classic research thus demonstrates that children can quickly acquire new behaviors simply as a result of observing others, that their tendency to reproduce what they have learned depends on whether the person whose actions they observed was rewarded or punished, and that what children learn from watching others is not necessarily evident in their behavior.

These photographs show an adult performing a series of aggressive actions on a Bobo doll. The boy who had observed the adult's behavior subsequently imitated it when left alone in the room with the Bobo doll. The girl, who did not initially reproduce the model's aggressive actions, did imitate the model's behavior when offered a reward to do so.

Unlike most learning theorists, Bandura emphasized the active role of children in their own development, describing development as a **reciprocal determinism** between children and their social environment. This idea is illustrated in Figure 9.1 (p. 342), which depicts a case in which a child's aggressive tendencies have an impact on his playmates and are in turn shaped by how those playmates respond.

Current Perspectives

In contrast to the psychoanalytic theories, learning theories are based on principles derived from empirical research. As a result, they make clear, explicit predictions that can be empirically tested. In part for this reason, an enormous amount of

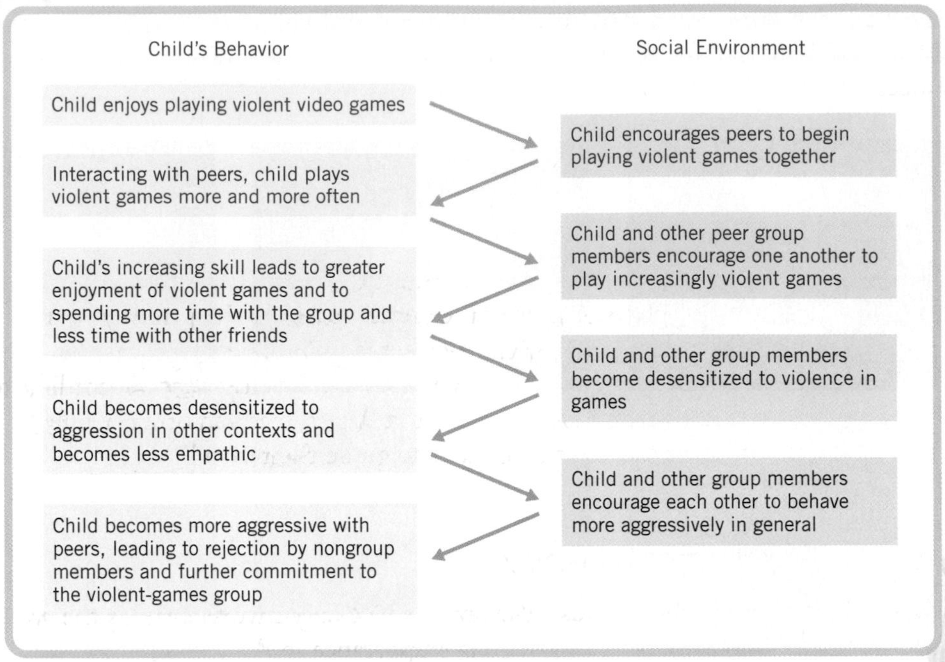

Child's Behavior	Social Environment
Child enjoys playing violent video games →	Child encourages peers to begin playing violent games together
← Interacting with peers, child plays violent games more and more often →	Child and other peer group members encourage one another to play increasingly violent games
← Child's increasing skill leads to greater enjoyment of violent games and to spending more time with the group and less time with other friends →	Child and other group members become desensitized to violence in games
← Child becomes desensitized to aggression in other contexts and becomes less empathic →	Child and other group members encourage each other to behave more aggressively in general
← Child becomes more aggressive with peers, leading to rejection by nongroup members and further commitment to the violent-games group	

FIGURE 9.1 Reciprocal determinism A hypothetical example showing how a child both influences and is influenced by the social environment. (Based on data from Anderson & Bushman, 2001)

research has been inspired by them, and we have learned a great deal about parental socialization practices and how children learn social behaviors in many domains. Important practical applications have resulted, including clinical procedures of systematic desensitization and behavior modification. The primary weakness of the learning approach is its lack of attention to biological influences and, except for Bandura's theory, to the impact of cognition.

review: Learning theorists assume that social development is in large part attributable to what children learn through their interactions with other people. Early behaviorists such as Watson and Skinner emphasized the reinforcement history of the individual, believing that children's social behavior is shaped by the pattern of rewards and punishments they receive from others. Social learning theorists, most notably Albert Bandura, emphasize the role of cognition in social learning, noting that children learn a great deal simply from observing the behavior of other people. Learning approaches have inspired a variety of treatment methods useful for a wide range of behavioral problems in children.

Theories of Social Cognition

Developmental theories of social cognition have to do with children's ability to think and reason about their own and other people's thoughts, feelings, motives, and behaviors. Like adults, children are active processors of social information. They pay attention to what other people do and say, and they are constantly drawing inferences, forming interpretations, and constructing explanations, or attributions, for what they observe. They process information about their own behavior and experiences in the same way.

The complexity of children's thinking and reasoning about the social world is related to, and limited by, the complexity of their thought processes in general.

After all, the same mind that solves arithmetic and conservation problems also solves problems of how to make friends and resolve moral dilemmas. With advances in cognitive development in general, the way that children think about themselves and other people deepens and becomes more abstract.

View of Children's Nature

Social cognitive theories provide a sharp contrast to the emphasis that psychoanalytic and social learning theories place on external forces as the primary source of development. Instead, social cognitive theories emphasize the process of **self-socialization**—children's active shaping of their own development. According to this view, children's knowledge and beliefs about themselves and other people lead them to adopt particular goals and standards to guide their own behavior.

Central Developmental Issues

Obviously, the central theme most relevant to social cognitive theories is the *active child. Individual differences* are also of great importance in the area of social cognition; comparisons are often drawn between the thinking and behavior of males and females, aggressive and nonaggressive children, and so on. *Continuity/discontinuity* is another important issue for theories of social cognition. Taking a discontinuity perspective, some theorists, such as Robert Selman and Lawrence Kohlberg, have formulated stage theories that emphasize age-related qualitative changes in how children think about the social world. Others, such as Kenneth Dodge, have applied information-processing concepts to social development, stressing continuity in the processes involved in social reasoning. We next consider these two types of social cognitive theories.

Selman's Stage Theory of Role Taking

In formulating his theory of social cognition, Selman (1980; Yeates & Selman, 1989) focused on the development of **role taking**—the ability to adopt the perspective of another person, to think about something from another's point of view. He proposed that being able to assume the perspective of another person is necessary to understand that person's thoughts, feelings, or motives. If you cannot take another's viewpoint, you cannot possibly understand that person.

According to Selman, young children's social cognition is quite limited because they lack the ability to role-take. Indeed, Selman, like Piaget, suggested that before the age of 6, children are virtually unaware that there is any perspective other than their own; they assume that whatever they think, others will think as well. Perhaps failure to recognize the discrepant view of someone else underlies those endless sibling arguments of the familiar form "'Did,' 'Did not,' 'Did so,' 'Did not'" and so on.

Selman proposed that children go through four increasingly complex and abstract stages in their thinking about other people. In Stage 1 (roughly ages 6 to 8), children come to appreciate that someone else can have a perspective different from their own, but they assume that the person's different view is due to that person's not possessing the same information they do. In Stage 2 (ages 8 to 10), children not only realize that someone else can have a different view but they also are able to think about the other person's point of view. However, it is not until Stage 3

self-socialization the idea that children play a very active role in their own socialization through their activity preferences, friendship choices, and so on

role taking being aware of the perspective of another person, thereby better understanding that person's behavior, thoughts, and feelings (ages 10 to 12) that children can systematically compare their own and another person's point of view. At this stage, they can also take the perspective of a third party and assess the points of view of two other people. In Stage 4 (age 12 and older), adolescents attempt to understand another's perspective by comparing it to a "generalized other," assessing whether the person's view is the same as that of most people in their social group.

Notice that in Selman's stages of role taking, children become less egocentric in their reasoning, and they thus become increasingly capable of considering multiple perspectives simultaneously (e.g., their own, another person's, and "most people's"). Both of these changes in social cognition mirror the cognitive changes identified by Piaget (and discussed in Chapter 4). Not surprisingly, children's progress through Selman's stages of role taking is strongly related to their progress through Piaget's stages (Keating & Clark, 1980).

Dodge's Information-Processing Theory of Social Problem Solving

The information-processing approach to social cognition emphasizes the crucial role of cognitive processes in social behavior. This approach is exemplified by Kenneth Dodge's analysis of children's use of aggression as a problem-solving strategy (Crick & Dodge, 1994; Dodge, 1986). Dodge and his colleagues propose that in solving social problems, children go through six steps. They *encode* a problematic event, *interpret* the social cues involved in it, *formulate a goal* to resolve the incident in some way, *generate* strategies to achieve the goal, *evaluate* the likely success of those potential strategies, and then *enact* a behavior. In carrying out such an analysis, children bring to bear their preexisting knowledge, concepts, and attitudes, including their past social experiences, their general social expectancies, and their knowledge of social rules.

In the research on which Dodge's theory is based, children are presented stories in which one child suffers because of the actions of another, but the situation is ambiguous with respect to the intent of the perpetrator. For example, in one story, a child is working hard to assemble a puzzle when a peer bumps into the table, causing the puzzle pieces to scatter, and merely says "oops." Children are asked to imagine themselves as the victim in this scenario and to describe what they would do and why. Some children, for example, might interpret the other child's knocking into the puzzle as an accident and simply ignore the event. Others might conclude that the peer bumped the table on purpose, decide to get even, and punch the offender as a way of achieving that end.

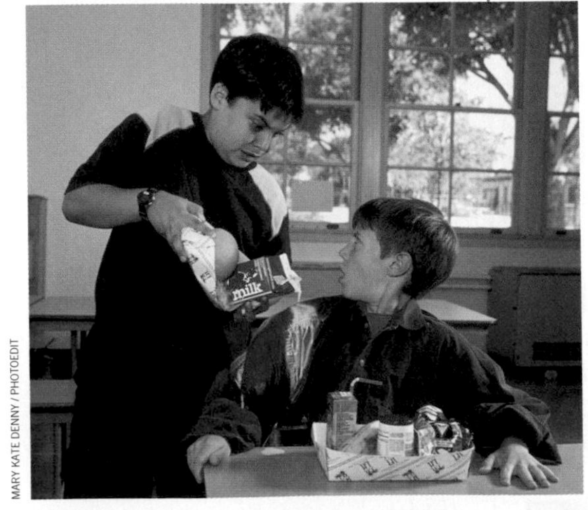

MARY KATE DENNY / PHOTOEDIT

The boy who was spilled on by the other boy seems to have a hostile attributional bias. Because he readily assumes that other people have the intent to harm him, he attributes a hostile intention to the other boy, which leads to a hostile response on his part.

Using this model, Dodge and his colleagues have found that aggressive children respond differently to ambiguous scenarios than nonaggressive children do. Many highly aggressive children seem to have a **hostile attributional bias,** that is, a general expectation that others are hostile to them (Crick & Dodge, 1994; Dodge, 1980; Graham & Hudley, 1994). This bias leads these children to search for evidence of hostile intent on the part of the peer in the scenario and to attribute to the peer a desire to harm them. They are likely to conclude that retaliation is the appropriate response to the peer's behavior. Hostile attributional biases become self-fulfilling prophecies: a child's aggressive retaliation to the presumed hostile act of a peer elicits counterattacks and rejection by his or her peers, further fueling the child's belief in the hostility of others.

Current Perspectives

Social cognitive theorists have made several important contributions to the study of social development. One is their strong emphasis on children as active seekers of information about the social realm rather than as passive recipients of others' social acts. Another contribution is the theoretical insight that the effect of children's social experience depends on their interpretation of those experiences. Thus, children who make different attributions about a given social event, such as someone's causing them harm, will respond differently to it. In addition, a large amount of research has supported the social cognitive position. Although these theories have provided a very healthy antidote to social theories that left children's cognition out of the picture, they provide a similarly incomplete account. Most notably, they have very little to say about biological factors in social development.

hostile attributional bias in Dodge's theory, the tendency to assume that other people's ambiguous actions stem from a hostile intent

review: Theories of social cognition stress the role of cognitive processes—attention, knowledge, interpretation, reasoning, explanation—in children's social development. A key aspect of these theories is an emphasis on the process of self-socialization, through which children actively shape their own development. Robert Selman's theory of role taking proposes that children go through stages in terms of their ability to appreciate that different people can have different points of view. The information-processing approach taken by Kenneth Dodge to the study of aggression emphasizes the role of children's interpretation of the behavior of other people. Aggressive children often have a hostile attributional bias, a general expectation that other people will be hostile to them.

Ecological Theories of Development

We now turn to a set of theories united by the fact that they take a very broad view of the context of social development. Virtually all psychological theories, and certainly all that we have reviewed thus far in this chapter, emphasize the role of the environment in the development of individual children. However, the "environment" in many of these theories is often narrowly construed as immediate contexts—family, peers, schools. The first approach discussed here—the bioecological model—considers multiple levels of environmental influence that simultaneously affect development. The other two approaches—ethological and evolutionary psychology views—relate children's development to the grand context of the evolutionary history of our species.

View of Children's Nature

Although the bioecological model stresses the effects of context on development, it also emphasizes the child's active role in selecting and influencing those contexts. Children's personal characteristics—temperament, intellectual ability, athletic skill, and so on—lead them to choose certain environments and also influence the people around them. Ethological and evolutionary theories view children as inheritors of genetically based abilities and predispositions that underlie most aspects of their behavior. The focus of these theories is largely on aspects of behavior that serve, or once served, an adaptive function.

Central Developmental Issues

The developmental issue that is front and center in ecological theories is the interaction of *nature and nurture*. The importance of the *sociocultural context* and the *continuity* of development are other implicit emphases in all these theories. The *active role* of children in their own development is another central focus, primarily of the bioecological approach.

The Bioecological Model

The most encompassing model of the general context of development is Urie Bronfenbrenner's bioecological model (Bronfenbrenner, 1979; Bronfenbrenner & Morris, 1998). Bronfenbrenner conceptualizes the environment as "a set of nested structures, each inside the next, like a set of Russian dolls" (1979, p. 22). Each structure represents a different level of influence on development (Figure 9.2). Embedded in the center of the multiple levels of influences is the individual child, with his or her particular constellation of characteristics (gender, age, temperament, health, intelligence, physical attractiveness, and so on) that, over the course of development, interact with the environmental forces that each level comprises. The different levels vary in how immediate their effects are, but Bronfenbrenner emphasizes that *every* level, from the intimate context of a child's nuclear family to the general culture in which the family lives, has an impact on that child's development. Note that each of the levels depicted in Figure 9.2 is labeled as a "system," emphasizing the complexity and interconnectedness of what goes on in each one.

The first level in which the child is embedded is the **microsystem**—the activities, roles, and relationships in which the child directly participates over time. The child's family is a crucial component of the microsystem, and its influence is predominant in infancy and early childhood. The microsystem becomes richer and more complex as the child grows older and interacts increasingly often with peers, teachers, and others in settings such as school, neighborhood, organized sports, clubs, religious activities, and so on. Bronfenbrenner stresses the *bidirectional* nature of all relationships within the microsystem. For example, the parents' marital relationship can affect their children, and their children's behavior can have an impact on the marital relationship. A good, supportive marital relationship helps parents interact more sensitively and effectively with their children (Cowan, Powell, & Cowan, 1998; Cox, Owen, Lewis, & Henderson, 1989), but a chronically fussy baby can create friction and even damage the relationship between parents (Belsky, Rosenberger, & Crnic, 1995).

The second level in Bronfenbrenner's model is the **mesosystem,** which encompasses the *connections* among various microsystems, such as family, peers, and schools. Supportive relations among these contexts can benefit the child. For example, children's academic success at school is facilitated when their parents value scholastic endeavors and have positive contact with their teachers (Luster & McAdoo, 1996; Stevenson, Chen, & Lee, 1993) and when their peers encourage academic achievement (Steinberg, Darling, & Fletcher, 1995). When connections in the mesosystem are nonsupportive, negative outcomes are more likely.

The third level of social context, the **exosystem,** comprises settings that children may not directly be a part of but that can still influence their development. Their parents' workplaces, for example, can affect children in many ways, from the employer's policies about flexible work hours, parental leave, and on-site child care to the general atmosphere in which parents work. Parents' enjoyment or dislike of their work can affect the emotional relationships within the family (Greenberger, O'Neil,

microsystem in bioecological theory, the immediate environment that an individual personally experiences

mesosystem in bioecological theory, the interconnections among immediate, or microsystem, settings

exosystem in bioecologocal theory, environmental settings that a person does not directly experience but that can affect the person indirectly

macrosystem in bioecological theory, the larger cultural and social context within which the other systems are embedded

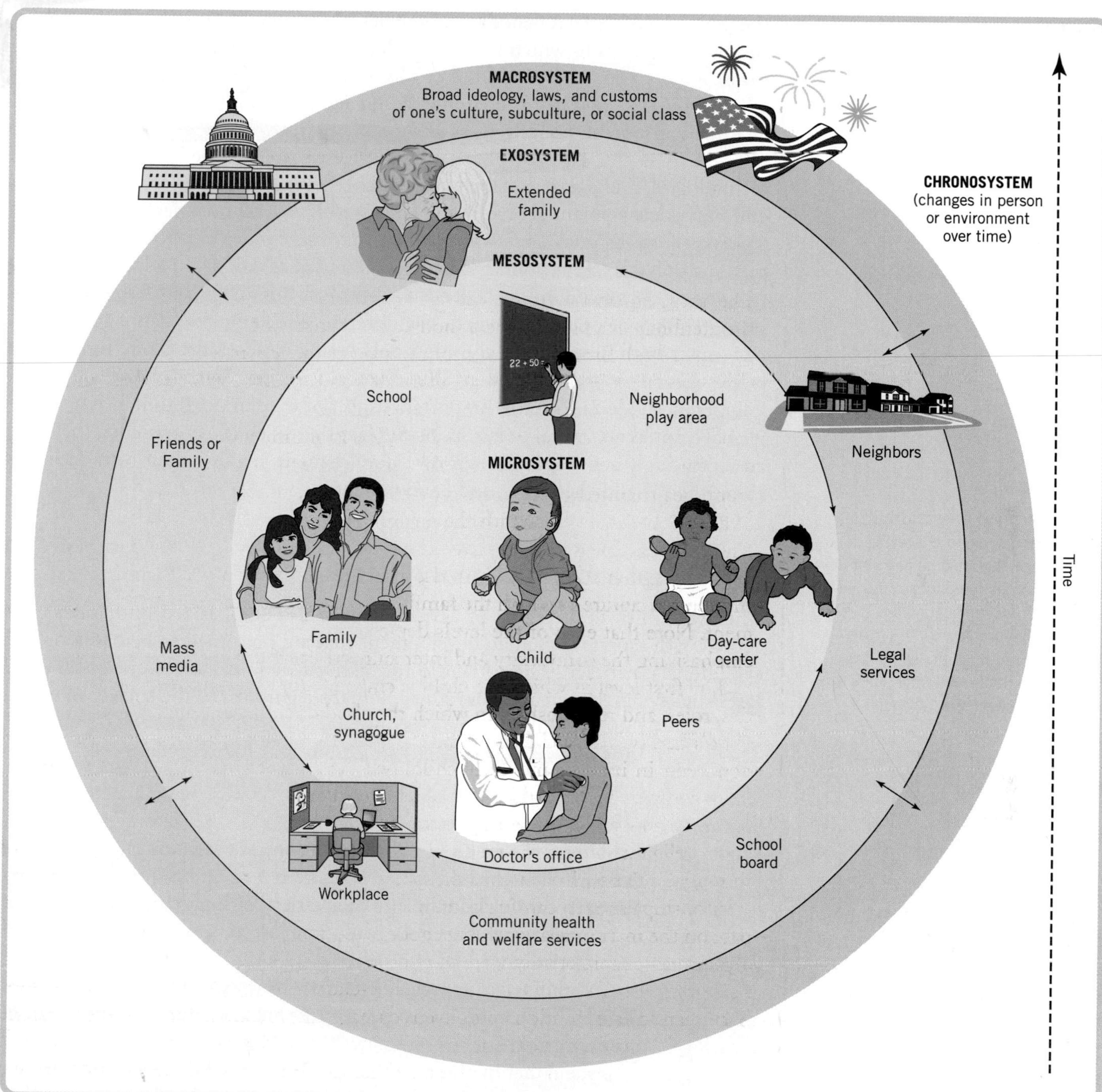

FIGURE 9.2 The bioecological model Urie Bronfenbrenner thinks of the child's environment as composed of a series of nested structures, including the microsystem (the immediate environment with which the child directly interacts), the mesosystem (the connections that exist among microsystems), the exosystem (social settings the child is not a part of but that still affect him or her), and the macrosystem (the general cultural context in which all the other systems are embedded). This figure illustrates the environment of a child living in the United States. (Adapted from Bronfenbrenner, 1979)

& Nagel, 1994). Even something as seemingly remote from the child as the financial success or failure of a parent's employer can be crucial: job loss, for example, is related to abusive or neglectful parenting (Emery & Laumann-Billings, 1998).

The outer level of Bronfenbrenner's model is the **macrosystem,** which consists of the general beliefs, values, customs, and laws of the larger society in which all

chronosystem in bioecological theory, historical changes that influence the other systems

the other levels are embedded. It includes the general cultural, subcultural, or social-class groups to which the child belongs. Cultural and class differences permeate almost every aspect of children's lives, including differences in beliefs about what qualities should be fostered in children and how best to foster them.

Finally, Bronfenbrenner's model also has a temporal dimension, which he has referred to as the **chronosystem.** In any given society, beliefs, values, customs, technologies, and social circumstances change over time, with consequences for children's development. For example, as a result of technological advances that gave rise to the "digital age," children today have access to a vast realm of information and entertainment unimaginable to previous generations. In addition, the impact of environmental events depends on another chronological variable—the age of the child. For example, divorce has different effects on toddlers and teens; it may make both of them unhappy, but only young children are likely to have the extra burden of thinking that the divorce is their fault (Hetherington & Clingempeel, 1992). Another important aspect of the temporal dimension, which we have noted on several occasions, is the fact that as children get older, they take an increasingly active role in their own development, making their own decisions about their friends, activities, and environments.

Ethological and Evolutionary Theories

The broad, historical context of development is also emphasized in theories concerned with aspects of human development that are presumed to be based on our evolutionary heritage. These theories primarily focus on species-specific behaviors—behaviors that are common to all humans regardless of the society in which they live. In these theories, the shared context is the evolutionary history of the species rather than common cultural experiences.

THOMAS D. MCAVOY / TIMEPIX

This famous photograph shows Konrad Lorenz (1952) and a gaggle of Greylag goslings who were imprinted on him and followed him all over his farm. Lorenz discovered that mallard ducklings are more discriminating: they would imprint on him only if he squatted low and dragged himself around, quacking all the while, for hours on end. He was a very dedicated scientist.

Ethology

Ethology, the study of behavior within an evolutionary context, attempts to understand behavior in terms of its adaptive or survival value. According to ethologists, a variety of innate behavior patterns in animals were shaped by evolution just as surely as their physical characteristics were (Crain, 1985).

An ethological approach has often been applied to developmental issues. The prototypical, and best-known, example is the study of imprinting made famous by Konrad Lorenz (1903–1989), often referred to as the father of modern ethology (Lorenz, 1935, 1952). **Imprinting** is a process in which newborn birds and mammals of some species become attached to their mother at first sight and follow her everywhere, a behavior that ensures the baby will stay near a source of protection and food. For imprinting to occur, the infant has to encounter its mother during a specific *critical period* very early in life.

The basis for imprinting is not actually the baby's mother per se; rather, the infants of some species are genetically predisposed to follow the first moving object with particular characteristics that they see after emerging into the world. In chickens, for example, imprinting is elicited specifically by the sight of a bird's head and neck regions (Johnson, 1992). Which particular object the individual will dutifully trail after is thus a matter of experience, a case of experience-expectant learning (discussed in Chapter 3). Typically, the first moving object any chick sees *is* its mother, so everything works out just fine.

Although human newborns do not "imprint," they do have a strong tendency to visually follow a stimulus that has two blobs horizontally placed in the top third of an oval shape—in other words, a face shape with eyes (see Chapter 5). Thus, right from birth, infants work to maintain visual contact with other humans. One of the most influential applications of ethology to human development, which we discuss in Chapter 11, is Bowlby's (1969) application of the concept of imprinting to the process by which infants form emotional attachments to their mother.

ethology the study of the evolutionary bases of behavior

imprinting a form of learning in which the young of some species of newborn birds and mammals become attached to and follow adult members of the species (usually their mother)

parental-investment theory a theory that stresses the evolutionary basis of many aspects of parental behavior, including the extensive investment parents make in their offspring

Evolutionary Psychology

A relatively new branch of psychology that is closely related to ethology is evolutionary psychology, which applies the Darwinian concepts of natural selection and adaptation to human behavior. The basic idea of this approach is that in the evolutionary history of our species, certain genes predisposed individuals to behave in ways that solved the adaptive problems they faced (obtaining food, avoiding predators) and hence increased the likelihood that they would survive, mate, and reproduce. Through natural selection, those genes became increasingly common and were passed down to modern humans. According to this view, many of the ways we behave today are a legacy from our prehistoric ancestors (Geary, 1999).

A major premise of evolutionary psychology is that organisms, including humans, are motivated to behave in ways that preserve their genes in the gene pool of the species (a concept we encountered in the genetics section of Chapter 3). For this reason, evolutionary psychologists have been very interested in issues of sexual attraction, mating, and reproduction. They are also interested in parenting, since a person's genes will be perpetuated in the gene pool only if his or her offspring survive long enough to pass those genes on to the next generation. According to **parental-investment theory,** this fact accounts for why parents spend the enormous amount of time, energy, and resources that they do in raising their children (Bjorklund & Shackelford, 1999; Trivers, 1972). Parental-investment theory also points to a possible dark side of the evolutionary picture. As Figure 9.3 shows, estimates of the rate of murder committed by stepfathers against children residing with them is hundreds of times higher than the rate for fathers and their biological children. Further, in families in which both natural and stepchildren reside, abusive parents typically target their abuse toward their stepchildren (Daly & Wilson, 1996). Although there are clearly many factors that contribute to these patterns,

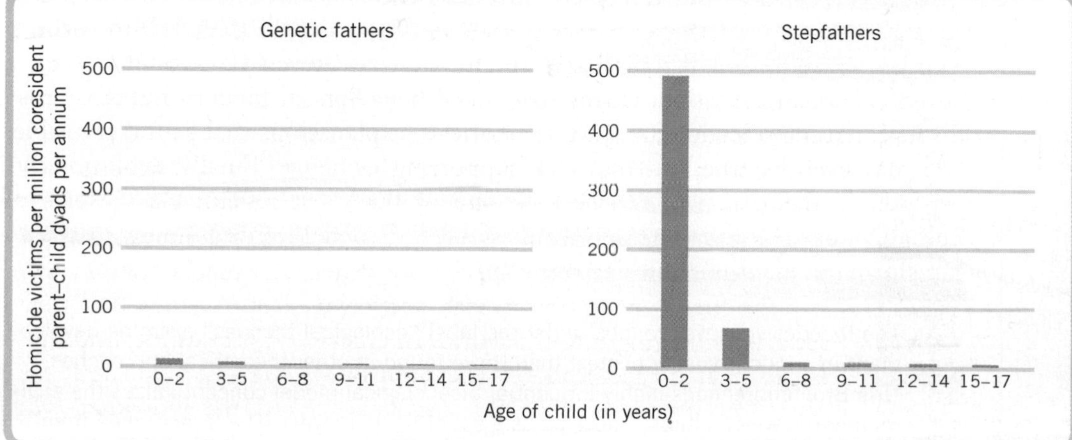

FIGURE 9.3 Estimated rates of child homicide commited by genetic fathers versus stepfathers in Canada from 1974 to 1990 As is shockingly clear, stepchildren, especially very young ones, are much more likely to be victims of violent abuse than are biological children. (Adapted from Daly & Wilson, 1966)

they are consistent with parent-investment theory; that is, because parenting is so costly, it is not, from an evolutionary point of view, worth investing in children who cannot contribute to the perpetuation of one's own genes.

Another modern-day phenomenon that has captured the attention of evolutionary psychologists is the lengthy period of human children's immaturity and dependence. David Bjorklund (1997), for example, argues that this extended immaturity has adaptive benefits:

> A prolonged period of youth is necessary for humans [who,] more than any other species, must survive by their wits; human communities are more complex and diverse than those of any other species, and this requires that they have not only a flexible intelligence to learn the conventions of their societies but also a long time to learn them.
>
> (p. 153)

Many evolutionary theorists have suggested that *play,* which is one of the most salient forms of behavior during the period of immaturity of most mammals, is an ideal platform for learning. Children develop motor skills racing and wrestling one another, playing jacks, throwing toy spears, or kicking a ball into a goal. They try out and practice a variety of roles (as mentioned in Chapter 7), enacting what they know about being a bus driver or a shepherd. One of the main virtues of play is that children can experiment in a situation with minimal consequences; no one gets hurt if a baby doll is accidentally dropped on its head or a cap gun is fired at a "bad guy's" chest.

Current Perspectives

The three theoretical positions discussed in this section have all made a valuable contribution to developmental science by placing individual development in a much broader context than is typically done in mainstream psychology. All of them challenge researchers to look beyond the lab—far beyond it.

Bronfenbrenner's bioecological model can be criticized for not really having much to say about specific biological factors in development. In contrast, the primary contribution of ethology and evolutionary psychology comes from their emphasis on all children's biological nature, including genetic tendencies grounded in evolution.

Evolutionary psychology has come in for serious criticism. One frequent complaint is that, like psychoanalytic theories, many of the claims of evolutionary psychologists are impossible to test. Often, a behavioral pattern that is consistent with an evolutionary account is at least equally consistent with accounts from social learning or some other perspective. In the view of Steven Jay Gould (1978), a noted expert on evolution, claims that social behaviors in modern humans arose through natural selection are "just-so" stories—explanations that sound plausible, and may even be true, but that lack supporting evidence. Finally, evolutionary-psychology theories tend to overlook one of the most remarkable features of human beings, a feature strongly emphasized by Bronfenbrenner—our capacity to transform our environments and ourselves.

review:

The theories we have grouped under the label "ecological theories" examine development in a much broader context than those found in other theoretical approaches. Urie Bronfenbrenner's highly influential bioecological model conceptualizes the environment in which children develop as a set of nested layers. The layers range from aspects of the environment that the individual child directly experiences on a daily basis to the broader society and historical time in which the child lives. Theories of development based on ethology and evolutionary psychology emphasize the influence of the evolutionary history of the human species on the development of individual children. Parental-investment theory proposes that the perpetuation of one's genes underlies the enormous effort that parents invest in raising their children. Other evolutionary theories emphasize that the play of human children, like the play of other immature mammals, serves an adaptive function.

Social Theories and Gender Development

For a variety of reasons, people everywhere care greatly about gender. Indeed, it typically is the first thing about a newborn to be announced to the parents. It is also one of the first things people notice about any stranger they encounter, and, on the relatively rare occasions when it is difficult to tell a person's gender, they typically put some effort into trying to figure it out.

All the major theories we have reviewed in this chapter devote substantial attention to the topic of gender. In this section we consider what each of these theories has to say about it, including how children develop a sense of gender and how gender affects behavior. As noted earlier, seeing how the major theories address gender not only provides a variety of insights into gender development but also highlights how the theories differ from and, often, complement one another.

Before discussing the applications of these theories to gender development, we need to briefly consider what is known about sex differences. Clearly, males and females are anatomically, physiologically, and hormonally different in many ways. When it comes to psychological variables, however, sex differences are less marked. (Although some developmentalists use the terms *sex* and *gender* differently when describing male/female differences, others do not. We use them interchangeably.)

People generally think they know a lot about sex differences, and they think there are a lot of differences to know about. However, the number of stereotypes about sex differences that most of us hold is far greater than the number of sex differences that actually exist. Table 9.1 (p. 352) presents a list of sex differences for which there is considerable evidence based on surveys of very large numbers of studies comparing males and females. We want to emphasize two important points about these findings. First, the list is fairly short—only nine consistently documented differences are included. Second, even for the sex differences that are well documented, the differences are almost always quite small. Figure 9.4 depicts the usual pattern, in which the average performance of one sex on a given psychological measure is *slightly* higher than that of the other sex. The most salient feature of the graph is the extreme overlap in the distribution of scores for females and males. Males and females are much more similar psychologically than they are different.

"Congratulations! It's a baby."

Think how unsatisfying this announcement would be. Parents want to know their baby's sex right away.

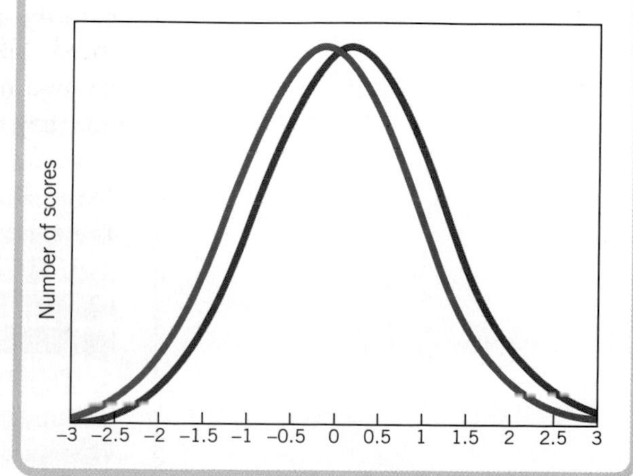

FIGURE 9.4 A typical distribution of scores **This graph depicts a typical distribution of scores for males and females on some hypothetical dimension. Although there is a statistically significant difference in average performance, the difference is very small and there is considerable overlap between the scores of the two groups. This is the typical pattern when sex differences are found on psychological variables.**

TABLE 9.1

Documented Psychological Differences Between the Sexes

Verbal ability	Girls develop verbal skills earlier and continue to have a small advantage throughout childhood and adolescence.
Visual/spatial abilities	From middle childhood on, males perform slightly better than females on spatial tests of mental rotation and spatial inferences.
Mathematical ability	From adolescence on, males have a small advantage over females on mathematical reasoning (but not on computation). A larger advantage for males is apparent among high math achievers.
Aggression	From very early in life, males are more aggressive than females and, as adolescents and adults, more likely to be involved in violent crime.
Activity level	Boys are more physically active than girls, beginning before birth.
Fear, timidity, risk taking	From the first year of life, boys are less fearful and less cautious than girls and more willing to take risks.
Emotional expressivity	From early in life, females are more emotionally expressive than males.
Compliance	From the preschool years, girls are more compliant than boys to the requests and demands of adults.
Developmental vulnerability	From conception, boys are more vulnerable to a wide range of developmental problems.

Sources: Eaton & Enns, 1986; Feingold, 1994; Halpern, 1997; Maccoby & Jacklin, 1974; Ruble & Martin, 1998

We turn now to a summary of the views on gender development offered by psychoanalytic, social learning, social cognitive, and ecological theories.

Psychoanalytic Theory

"Biology is destiny," Freud proclaimed in one of his most famous and provocative statements. By this he meant that an individual's psychological development is to a great extent determined by his or her biological sex, by the very fact of being male or female. He thought that even very young children have a sexual nature that influences their behavior and their relationships with other people. No aspect of Freud's theory has been more hotly contested than his view on childhood sexuality and its consequences for gender development, including his belief that there are sex differences in superego strength.

Freud thought that gender differences in attitudes and behavior originate in children's identification with their same-sex parent. This identification begins with children's discovery, during the phallic period (around 3 to 6 years), of the vital difference between having and lacking a penis. At this time, a boy takes a strong interest in his penis, "so easily excitable and changeable, and so rich in sensations" (Freud, 1923/1960, p. 246). Freud supposed that girls notice and resent the fact that they do not have one, experiencing what he called *penis envy*.

Freud also believed that young children experience intense sexual desires during the phallic stage. This belief stemmed from the fact that, in his therapeutic practice, he heard many recollections by adult women of sexual abuse in childhood by their fathers—too many, he eventually decided, to be credible. He concluded that his patients must be reporting fantasies based on sexual desires and feelings they had experienced in childhood.

Coping with childhood sexual desires is, according to Freud, the path to the development of the superego. For boys, the path is through the resolution of the **Oedipus complex**, a psychosexual conflict in which a boy experiences a form of sexual desire for his mother and wants an exclusive relationship with her. (As a product of his time and society, Freud focused on males as the prototype and viewed females as secondary.) Freud named this complex after the king in Greek legend who (unknowingly) killed his father and (again unknowingly) married his mother. Freud believed that, in an abstract way, this classic tragedy is reenacted in the lives of every family. Although this idea may seem outlandish, most families have experienced episodes that are consistent with it. For example, when one of our sons was a 5-year-old, he told his mother that he wanted to marry her someday. She said that she was sorry, but she was already married to Daddy, so he would have to marry someone else. The boy replied, "I have a good idea. I'll put Daddy in a big box and mail him away somewhere. Then we can get married!"

Oedipus complex Freud's term for the conflict experienced by boys in the phallic period because of their sexual desire for their mother and their fear of retaliation by their father

Electra complex Freud's term for the conflict experienced by girls in the phallic stage when they develop unacceptable romantic feelings for their father and see their mother as a rival

In Freud's account of the Oedipal conflict, the son comes to see his father as an all-powerful rival for his mother's affections. He feels hostility toward his father and fears retaliation—the loss of his penis (castration)—at the hands of his father. (In the Austria of Freud's time, parents often made explicit threats of castration to prevent masturbation.) A boy's desire for his mother and hostility toward his father are so threatening that the boy's ego acts to protect him through repression, banishing his anxiety-producing thoughts and impulses to the unconscious. In addition, the boy increases his *identification* with his father: instead of seeking to challenge his father, he tries to be more like him, transforming himself from rival to protégé. The most important outcome of the Oedipus complex is that through striving to be like his father, the boy *internalizes* his father's values, beliefs, and attitudes—forming the basis for a conscience. Hence, the boy's successful resolution of the Oedipus complex is his development of a strong conscience and ego ideal.

Freud thought that girls experience a similar but less intense conflict in the phallic stage. As part of an **Electra complex** (also named after a figure in Greek mythology), a daughter develops erotic feelings toward her father, seeing her mother as a rival. Although she does not experience the intense fear of sexual mutilation that boys do, concern about the loss of parental love leads her to repress her unacceptable feelings toward her father. However, because girls do not experience as much conflict as boys do, Freud thought they would have less motivation to identify with their mother and for that reason would develop a weaker superego than boys do.

Like many of his ideas, Freud's "Oedipal" explanation of superego and gender development was greatly influential throughout much of the twentieth century. However, no empirical support for Freud's theory was ever produced, and it is now regarded as an intriguing misstep. Nevertheless, Freud's views on gender development are important as a historical backdrop to more contemporary perspectives.

Social Learning Theory

Social learning theorists hold that children have a multitude of experiences through which they learn behaviors, beliefs, and values considered by their society to be desirable or appropriate for their sex (Bandura, 1977; Bandura & Walters, 1963; Mischel, 1970; Perry & Bussey, 1984). In this view, children are socialized for gender through both *observational* and *direct* learning.

Observational Learning

Social learning theory emphasizes that simply by observing other people, children have lots of opportunity for gathering information about gender and what is considered appropriate behavior for their own sex. Those opportunities come not only in their direct interactions with other people, but also through a variety of media, as discussed in Box 9.2.

Because all societies differentially assign certain work roles to males and females, all children see their parents, as well as other adults and children, engaging in gender-typed activities. For example, throughout the world, regardless of what behavior is typical for men, children see their mothers serving as the primary caregiver in the family and the person responsible for food preparation (Rossi, 1977). In addition, children observe the behavior of their own sex more than that of the other sex because they tend to spend more time with people of their own sex. Naturalistic observations conducted in public settings revealed that boys were more often in the company of men, whereas girls were more often with women (Hoffman & Teyber, 1985), and throughout childhood, children spend much more time in the company of same-sex peers (Maccoby, 1998).

Are children influenced by what they observe in the behavior of males and females? Laboratory studies have established that children pay more attention to same-sex adult models and consequently remember better what they saw them do. In addition, children more often imitate same-sex models (Bussey & Bandura, 1984; Perry & Bussey, 1979). Although this preference is true for both boys and girls, girls are more willing to imitate male models than boys are to imitate females.

Modeling effects are also apparent in everyday life, beginning with the family. In general, children who are raised in less conventional families tend to be less strongly sex-typed than are children growing up in more traditional families. For example, maternal employment outside the home, egalitarian division of labor within the home, rearing by the mother only, and nontraditional values on the part of parents have all been associated with lower levels of sex-typing in their children (see Ruble & Martin, 1998).

Children are also strongly influenced by peer models for gender-appropriate behaviors. For example, in an observational study conducted in a preschool classroom, boys were influenced by the number and proportion of same-sex children who were playing with a set of toys: they approached toys that were being played with primarily by boys, shunning those popular mainly with girls (Shell & Eisenberg, 1990).

Direct Teaching

Social learning theorists propose that in addition to learning gender-typed behaviors through observation, children also learn them through direct teaching. There are consistent differences in how parents treat their sons and daughters, systematically encouraging and rewarding "gender-appropriate" behaviors in boys and girls. American parents, for example, consistently provide their children—even infants—with gender-appropriate toys (Fisher-Thompson, 1993). They purchase toy tools and trucks for their boys, kitchen utensils and dolls for their girls. The Christmas presents that parents buy for their children are generally either gender-appropriate or neutral, and boys are especially unlikely to receive any girl toys (Robinson & Morris, 1986). These purchases may, of course, stem not just from the parents' proclivities to socialize their children into appropriate gender roles but also from the children's own preferences. Indeed, a study of 750 letters to Santa Claus from 5- to 9-year-olds showed that most requests were clearly gender-typed: many more boys than girls asked for a vehicle, whereas almost a third of the girls, but virtually no boys, wanted Santa to bring them a doll (Robinson & Morris, 1986). Many a parent's firm resolve never to buy a GI Joe or Barbie has been thwarted by their son's or daughter's persistent pleading.

applications 9.2

Where Are Mrs. Rogers and Curious Jane?

Before reading further, take a moment to list your five favorite television programs. Now count the number of major characters in them who are male and female. Which characters are highly active and/or have positions of power on the show? How would you characterize the general nature of your programs—action-packed adventure, romantic comedy, sports shows, soap operas? What would be different if you made a list of the programs you liked best as a child?

We'd be willing to bet that your list of characters includes more males than females, probably by a substantial degree (except for daytime soap operas). We also suspect that more of our male readers would list action and sports as favorite programs, whereas more women would have romantic shows or soap operas on their lists. We're also pessimistic that the imbalance of male over female characters would be any different for your current favorite shows versus those you watched in your youth; indeed, it would probably be even greater. The reason we feel such confidence in our predictions is that these differences in the gender representation of characters on TV have been very well documented, are very large, and have changed relatively little over the past three decades (Huston, 1983; Huston & Wright, 1998; Signorielli, 1993).

How many of these *Sesame Street* characters can you name? More importantly, how many are male?

The differential treatment of the sexes in the media is not limited to numerical representations. Portrayals of males and females tend to be highly stereotypical in terms of appearance, personal characteristics, occupations, and the nature of the roles they play. On average, male characters tend to be older and in more powerful roles; females tend to be young, attractive, and provocatively dressed (Calvert & Huston, 1987; Signorielli, 1993; Signorielli, McLeod, & Healy, 1994).

Does it matter that there are large differences in both the number and nature of the portrayals of the sexes on TV? Keep in mind that the average American child between ages 3 and 11 watches 2 to 4 hours of TV a day (Huston & Wright, 1998). From a social learning theory, gender schema, or bioecological perspective, the fact that children have so much exposure to highly stereotyped gender models should matter a great deal.

There is some evidence for such a supposition. For example, children who watch a lot of TV have more highly stereotypic beliefs about males and females and prefer gender-typed activities to a greater extent than do children who are less avid viewers (McGhee & Frueh, 1980; Signorielli & Lears, 1992). But since the evidence is correlational, it is difficult to know how to interpret it. Does TV watching influence children to form more rigid gender stereotypes, or do children who already have such stereotypes find TV more appealing?

Some evidence suggesting that TV watching causes stereotyping comes from a study of what ensued in the early 1980s when television was introduced to an isolated town in Canada. Beforehand, the children of the town, referred to as "Notel," held less stereotyped views of gender than did children from comparison towns that did have access to TV. A few years after Notel began tuning in, the children of the town showed a substantial increase in their gender stereotyping (Williams, 1986).

Children are, of course, exposed to media other than television, but similar gender disparities have been documented in them as well. For example, children's books still contain far more male than female characters, and characters of both sexes are portrayed in gender-stereotypic ways. Males are depicted as active and effective in the world at large, whereas females are passive, typically found indoors, and creating problems that require the help of males to solve (Kortenhaus & Demorest, 1993; Tognoli, Pullen, & Lieben, 1994; Turner-Bowker, 1996). One way to address this imbalance in children's picture books might be to use gender-neutral characters—animals or fantasy creatures of ambiguous gender. However, such an approach might run into difficulties. In one study of mother–child picture-book reading, the gender of the bear characters in the book was not identified in the text or pictures; they were not clothed, there were no hair bows or neckties, and they were not shown doing gender-typed activities. With no cues to gender, the mothers referred to almost all the depicted bears as male (DeLoache, Cassidy, & Carpenter, 1987).

One other medium in which gender differences abound is video games. The games themselves typically feature a high-action format and violent themes, and they are replete with gender stereotypes, as male heroes with bulging biceps rescue scantily clad heroines with bulging bosoms. Partly because of these characteristics, boys are much more avid video game players than girls are, and this difference is cause for some concern. Because *some* videogames that involve speeded action and divided attention improve children's attentional and spatial skills (Greenfield, deWinstanley, Kilpatrick, & Kaye, 1994; Okagaki & Frensch, 1996; Subrahmanyam & Greenfield, 1996), the fact that boys spend more time playing them could widen the gap between male and female spatial abilities.

Of greater concern has been a gender gap in computer competence. As computer skills become ever more vital in the modern world, girls would be at an increasing disadvantage if they were less skilled than boys at using computers. Fortunately, recent surveys have revealed that the gap has essentially closed in the United States. Girls and boys now have equal exposure to computers, computer skills, and confidence in their skills (Subrahmanyam, Kraut, Greenfield, & Gross, 2000).

Another consistent difference in parents' treatment of boys and girls is that they are more responsive and supportive of sex-appropriate play themes and activities than of cross-sex play (e.g., Fagot & Hagan, 1991; Lytton & Romney, 1991; Roopnarine, 1986). Probably most fathers would more enthusiastically join their son in a game of catch than a tea party, and some would actively discourage or even belittle the boy for being interested in such a feminine activity as serving tea and cookies (see Box 9.3).

A relatively subtle form of gender-typing has been noted in conversations between parents and children. As discussed in Chapter 10, for example, when talking with girls, mothers discuss feelings more often, and talk about a greater variety of emotions, than they do when conversing with boys. In turn, girls talk about feeling states more often than boys do (Dunn, Bretherton, & Munn, 1987; Kuebli, Butler, & Fivush, 1995). A not-so-subtle difference in how parents talk to boys and girls has been observed in natural conversations in a science museum. While using interactive exhibits, parents were three times more likely to offer explanations about what they were observing to boys than to girls (Crowley, Callanan, Tenenbaum, & Allen, 2001).

Thus, parents do treat their sons and daughters differently to some degree. However, several comprehensive reviews of research on parental socialization practices in natural settings have revealed fewer differences and more similarities in parents' treatment of their children than the social learning position would lead one to expect (Huston, 1983; Lytton, 2000; Lytton & Romney, 1991; Maccoby & Jacklin, 1974; Leaper, Anderson, & Sanders, 1998). For example, parents do not behave differently toward sons and daughters in terms of the amount of affection and warmth they display, the amount of time they interact with their children, their responsiveness to their offspring, or the degree to which they restrict their children's activities.

There is no doubt that, as social learning theorists have noted, children learn a great deal about gender-appropriate behavior through both direct teaching and observing same-sex models of various ages. However, the current consensus among researchers is that parents do not play as extensive a role in shaping their children's gender development through differential reinforcement as social learning theorists originally believed. Research has shown that 12- to 18-month-old infants already differ in their preference for toys considered appropriate for their gender (Caldera, Huston, & O'Brien, 1989; Snow, Jacklin, & Maccoby, 1983). Thus, the encouragement parents offer for gender-appropriate toy preferences may primarily reinforce existing preferences rather than create new ones. In other words, a child's genotype may somehow lead to toy preferences that then elicit differential responses from his or her parents (an example of a genotype–environment effect like those described in Chapter 3) (Lytton, 2000). In addition, it has been shown that after the preschool years, parents become less likely to differentially reinforce gender-typed attitudes and behaviors, and, as we will see later in this chapter, peers become more likely to do so (e. g., Carter & McCloskey, 1984).

Social Cognitive Theories

Imitating same-sex models, which is a basic mechanism for sex-role acquisition in social learning theories, depends upon children's knowing what sex they are in the first place. Where does this knowledge come from, and how do it and other forms of knowledge contribute to gender-role development? Two theories that attempt to answer this question are Kohlberg's cognitive developmental theory and gender schema theory.

individual differences 9.3

Asymmetries in Sex-Typing

Recall the children in the photos at the beginning of this chapter. If they were your children, which would you find less acceptable—for the girl to don the helmet and pick up the gun or for the boy to strike the starlet pose? Would you be more upset to hear another child call your daughter a "tomboy" or to hear someone refer to your son as a "sissy"? Suppose your spouse dressed your baby boy in a pink outfit with ruffles or put blue overalls on your infant girl? Would you be more likely to change the child's wardrobe in one case than in the other?

The point we are making is that there is an asymmetry in the extent to which most people find it acceptable for boys and girls to engage in activities deemed more appropriate for the other sex. Generally, parents, peers, and teachers all respond more negatively to boys who do "girl things" than vice versa. One of our children attended preschool with a girl who spent most of her time in the block-building area and a boy who, almost every day, selected a pink tutu from the dress-up corner to wear over his clothes. The teachers, parents, and other adults who observed these two children were concerned about the boy's behavior but not the girl's.

There is also an asymmetry in how parents respond to gender-typed behavior in their children. This unevenness is dramatically exemplified in contrasting reactions of this mother and father to a toddler's falling and hurting himself:

> *Mother:* "Come here, honey. I'll kiss it better."
> *Father:* "Oh toughen up. Quit your bellyaching."
>
> (Gable, Belsky, & Crnic, 1993, p. 32)

As this example suggests, mothers tend to behave less differentially toward their sons and daughters, allowing both sexes more latitude, than fathers do. Fathers play a particularly active role in instilling male behaviors in their sons (Jacklin, DiPietro, & Maccoby, 1984; Leve & Fagot, 1997; Turner & Gervai, 1995). They generally react negatively to their son for doing anything, such as crying, that they think of as "feminine." Fathers show less disapproval of their daughter for doing something "masculine." Thus, a son who plays with dolls is much more likely to elicit a strong negative response from his father than is a daughter playing with a truck. Similar patterns of differentiation are evident in children and appear early: elementary school boys reject cross-gender behavior in others more than girls do (Bussey & Perry, 1982).

A third form of asymmetry in sex-typing presumably results from the first two: boys are more strongly or rigidly sex-typed than girls are (Carter & McClosky, 1984). At all ages, boys (and men) engage in a relatively narrow range of activities, almost exclusively those considered to be either masculine or neutral. Compared with boys, girls have a wider range of interests, and they are more likely to do things considered appropriate for boys (Bussey & Bandura, 1992; Fagot & Leinbach, 1993). The difference seems to stem in large part from male *avoidance* of feminine activities, not just a preference for masculine ones (Bussey & Bandura, 1992; Martin et al., 1995; Powlishta, Serbin, & Moller, 1993). By age 5, boys are more likely than girls to say that they *dislike* other-sex toys (Bussey & Bandura, 1992; Eisenberg, Murray, & Hite, 1982). The preference for objects and activities deemed appropriate for one's own sex and the bias against those deemed appropriate for the other sex decline during the school years, although much more so for girls than boys (Serbin et al., 1993).

CORBIS IMAGES / PICTUREQUEST

This father is facilitating the development of a gender-appropriate behavior in his son. He would be likely to react negatively if the boy did something his father thought was inappropriate for boys.

Kohlberg's Cognitive Developmental Theory

Reflecting a Piagetian framework, Lawrence Kohlberg's (1966) cognitive developmental theory of sex-role development proposes that children actively construct gender knowledge in the same way they construct other knowledge about the world. And, just as young children's understanding of the physical world is limited, so is their understanding of the social world, including their knowledge of the meaning and immutability of gender.

gender identity awareness of one's own gender

gender stability awareness that gender is stable over time

gender constancy realization that gender is invariant in spite of superficial changes in appearance or activities (also known as gender consistency)

The limitedness of young children's understanding of gender is revealed by an experience a boy named Jeremy had when he went to preschool one day wearing barrettes. As reported by his mother, Sandra Bem, a developmental psychologist,

> several times that day, another little boy insisted that Jeremy must be a girl because "only girls wear barrettes." After repeatedly asserting that "wearing barrettes doesn't matter; being a boy means having a penis and testicles," Jeremy finally pulled down his pants as a way of making his point more convincingly. The boy was not impressed. He simply said, "Everybody has a penis; only girls wear barrettes."
>
> (Bem, 1989, p. 662)

How do young children like Jeremy's classmate get beyond their very superficial ideas about gender? Kohlberg specified three stages in the development of a mature understanding of gender. First, young children establish **gender identity:** by about 30 months of age, they learn that they are members of one gender category or the other and begin labeling themselves as either a girl or a boy (Fagot & Leinbach, 1989) (e.g., "I'm a girl"). However, they do not yet realize that gender is permanent (they think a girl could grow up to be a father) (Slaby & Frey, 1975). The next stage, **gender stability,** begins at around 3 or 4 years of age, as children come to realize that gender is stable over time. ("I'm a girl, and I'll always be a girl.") However, they are still not clear that gender is independent of superficial appearance and think that a boy who dons a dress and now looks like a girl has become a girl.

The basic understanding of gender is completed in the third stage (at around 5 to 7 years of age), when children achieve **gender constancy,** the understanding that gender is *consistent* across situations ("I'm a girl, and nothing I do will change that"). Kohlberg noted that this is the same age at which children begin to succeed on Piagetian conservation problems (see Chapter 4) and argued that both achievements reflect the same stage of thinking. Kohlberg maintained that children's understanding that gender remains constant even when superficial changes occur is similar to their understanding that the amount of a substance is conserved even when its appearance is altered (a ball of clay that has been mashed flat is still the same amount of clay; a girl chewing tobacco while wearing a baseball uniform is still a girl).

Once gender constancy is attained, according to Kohlberg, children begin to seek out and attend to same-sex models in order to learn how to behave. ("Since I'm a girl, I should like to do girl things, so I need to find out what those are.") Thus, imitation of the behavior of same-sex models is an important component in cognitive developmental theory, just as it is in social learning theory, but modeling occurs as a consequence of cognitive change. The extremely masculine and feminine poses of Colin and Catherine in the photos at the beginning of this chapter suggest that both children have achieved gender constancy and have been studying same-sex adult models.

Children's understanding of gender does, in fact, develop in the sequence Kohlberg described, and the attainment of gender constancy occurs at more or less the same age as success on conservation problems (e.g., Marcus & Overton, 1978; Munroe, Shimmin, & Munroe, 1984). However, a major problem for the theory is the fact that young children begin showing gender-based preferences for toys, activities, and playmates long before they have a mature understanding of gender constancy or have begun attending selectively to same-sex models. In addition, it is clear that factors other than general cognitive development underlie progress through Kohlberg's stages. For example, knowledge of the genital differences between the sexes (presumably from having seen other people naked) helps children appreciate that gender is not based on superficial appearance (Bem, 1989). Another influential social cognitive theory of gender development that specifically addresses these problems is gender schema theory.

gender schema organized mental representations (concepts, beliefs, memories) about gender, including stereotypes about gender

gender self-socialization the process through which children's bias to behave in accord with their gender identity leads them to acquire greater knowledge and expertise with gender-consistent entities

Gender Schema Theory

Gender schema theory (Bem, 1981; Martin, 1993; Martin & Halverson, 1981) offers a view of gender development that is similar to Kohlberg's but is also different in several important ways. To begin with, it proposes that children's intrinsic motivation to acquire gender-consistent interests, values, and behavior emerges as soon as children can *identify* their own gender, sometime in the third year—much earlier than Kohlberg thought. It also proposes that children's understanding of gender develops through their construction of **gender schemas**—mental representations incorporating everything they know about gender, including memory representations of their own experience with males and females, gender stereotypes transmitted directly by adults and peers ("boys don't cry," "girls like to be neat and tidy"), and messages conveyed indirectly through the media. These schemas are dynamic, changing constantly as children acquire additional gender-related concepts (Ruble & Martin, 1998).

Young children begin with a simple *in-group/out-group* gender schema that they use to classify other people as being either "the same as me" or not. A natural motivation for cognitive consistency leads them to prefer, pay attention to, and remember more about others of their sex. As a consequence, an *own-sex schema* is formed, consisting of detailed knowledge about how to do things that are consistent with one's own gender.

Strong evidence suggests that children tend to prefer and to learn more about entities designated as appropriate for their sex. For example, simply learning that an unfamiliar object is "for my sex" makes children like it more. In one study, an experimenter showed 4- to 5-year-olds unfamiliar, gender-neutral objects and told the children either that the objects were "for boys" or that they were "for girls." (Each of the objects was labeled in one way for some of the children and the opposite way for the others.) Girls reported liking the "girl" objects more than boys did, and vice versa. Girls also believed that other girls would like the "girl" items better than boys would (Martin, Eisenbud, & Rose, 1995). In another study, 4- to 9-year-olds were given boxes of unfamiliar gender-neutral objects described as either "boy" or "girl" things. The children spent more time exploring whichever toys had been labeled as being for their own sex, and a week later, they remembered more about the same-sex items (Bradbard, Martin, Endsley, & Halverson, 1986).

Figure 9.5 illustrates this process of **gender self-socialization** through which children's bias to behave in accord with their gender identity leads them to acquire greater knowledge and expertise with gender-consistent entities. Imagine a young girl presented with the choice between a toy truck and a doll. Her selection will depend on both her gender identity and her knowledge about these specific toys. If she knows that she is a girl (i.e., has gender identity) and knows that trucks are "boy toys" and dolls are "girl toys," she is likely to choose the doll for herself. Through her subsequent exploration of the doll, she will learn more about dolls, how to play with them, what others think about her playing with dolls, and so on. Avoiding the truck, she will learn nothing further about trucks. The power of children's gender self-socialization is familiar to many parents who have tried but failed to get their children to develop in more gender-neutral ways. Despite their parents' efforts, many little boys show no interest in nurturing baby dolls, and many little girls are devoted to pink clothing and Barbie dolls.

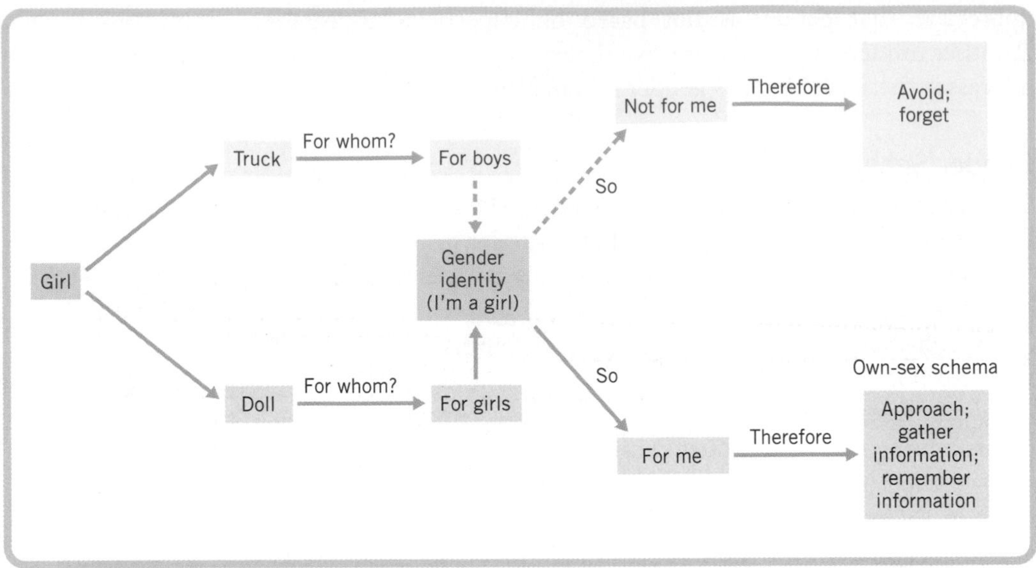

FIGURE 9.5 Gender schema theory According to gender schema theory, children first classify new objects and activities according to an in-group/out-group schema as "for boys" or "for girls." Objects or activities believed to be for the other sex are ignored, whereas those for one's own sex are investigated, and what is learned is incorporated into the child's own-sex schema. (Adapted from Martin & Halverson, 1987)

As cognitive structures, gender schemas are also responsible for a bias in processing and remembering information about gender. Children tend to remember more about what they see members of their own sex do than what other-sex individuals do (Signorella, Bigler, & Liben, 1997; Stangor & McMillan, 1992). Further, they are likely to accurately encode and remember information about story characters who behave in gender-consistent ways and to forget or distort gender-inconsistent information (Liben & Signorella, 1993; Martin & Halverson, 1983). For example, children who heard a story that featured a girl sawing wood often remembered it later as a story about a boy sawing wood, and children who saw commercials that showed a boy playing with a doll and a girl playing with a truck tended to misremember the sex of the children performing the actions (Martin & Halverson, 1983; Stangor & Ruble, 1989). The twin tendencies to retain schema-consistent and ignore or distort schema-inconsistent information help to perpetuate gender stereotypes that have little or no basis in reality.

ESBIN-ANDERSON / THE IMAGE WORKS

JIM PICKERELL / STOCK BOSTON

Young children who see these photographs would probably remember that they saw a boy playing with a truck and a girl playing with a doll, illustrating the power of gender schemas to distort memories for schema-inconsistent information.

Ecological Theories

The topic of gender development is highly compatible with Bronfenbrenner's bioecological model and evolutionary psychology. The theories provide a very useful framework for considering the multitude of differential influences on how boys and girls develop the preferences, attitudes, and behaviors typical of their sex.

The Bioecological Model

Gender differences show up at every level of Bronfenbrenner's bioecological model, interacting with aspects of the child's genetic and biological makeup that are characteristic of his or her sex. At the *microsystem* level, one difference that can be easily seen is the physical environment in which very young children live. Many American parents construct masculine or feminine living spaces for their children (Pomerleau, Bolduc, Malcuit, & Cossette, 1990; Rheingold & Cook, 1975). How hard would it be to guess the sex of the occupant of a pastel-painted room with a doll collection displayed on a bed covered in a pink, ruffly bedspread?

Also at the microsystem level, U.S. classrooms are the site of a great deal of differential treatment of boys and girls. For example, preschool and elementary school teachers tend to value the stereotypically "feminine" behavior of obedience and to discourage "masculine" assertiveness (Fagot, 1985). In addition, boys receive more disapproval and criticism from their teachers than girls do (Huston, 1983). This situation has been referred to as a "feminine bias" in American schools. However, this bias does not necessarily work in favor of girls, because it reinforces conformity and sitting quietly in class (Serbin, Powlishta, & Gulko, 1973), possibly at the expense of achievement and independence.

Other aspects of U.S. schools, however, can be seen as evidence of a "masculine bias." Boys dominate classrooms. For example, when elementary school children eagerly wave their hands for a chance to answer a teacher's question, the teacher is more likely to call on a boy than a girl, so boys get more time in the spotlight (Sadker & Sadker, 1994). However, one reason boys get called on more often is that more of them are waving their hands (Altermatt, Jovanovic, & Perry, 1998).

The *mesosystem* level of Bronfenbrenner's bioecological model encompasses interactions among microsystems such as home and school. Research on parents' beliefs and expectations about academic achievement has shown that parents and teachers think that elementary school girls are better at reading than boys are but that boys are better at math (Eccles, Jacobs, & Harold, 1990; Meece, Parsons, Kaczala, Goff, & Futterman, 1982). These beliefs are relatively independent of children's actual performance in these subjects. The similar stereotypes held by their parents and teachers are probably communicated to children, thereby providing consistent messages across two microsystems.

Children seem to be listening to these messages. Research by Jacqueline Eccles and her colleagues (Eccles et al., 1993; Jacobs, Lanza, Osgood, Eccles, & Wigfield, 2002) reveals that girls perceive themselves as less competent at math, see it as a less valuable subject, and are less interested in taking more math classes in the future. They tend to attribute their successes in mathematics classes to *external* factors and their failures to *internal* ones. Thus, a girl who has done well on a math test thinks, "Wow, I was lucky that time" or "I guess the teacher likes me." When she does poorly, she concludes, "I'm just no good at math." Boys tend to show the opposite pattern of self-perceptions, interests, and attributions.

At the *exosystem* level, the occupational roles that are available for men and women in a given society are quite different. Children in North America, for example, are exposed, on average, to more female nurses and more male doctors, and they see that secretaries are usually women and that the majority of CEOs are men. They also see that most of their teachers are women, and many young children come to believe that education is a female-only profession. Indeed, a colleague of ours, a college professor, reported that his 4-year-old son vehemently denied his father's claim to be a teacher, insisting that all teachers are women. Thus, the child at the center of the bioecological model is affected by the distribution of gender roles in the society.

The *macrosystem,* which includes the general culture in which the child lives, is a crucial source of gender differentiation, starting with the basic extent to which males and females are valued in the society. In many, if not most, societies, males have been valued more highly than females (Durkin, 1995). Throughout history, female infanticide has been practiced to make room for male offspring and, as noted in Chapter 2, continues even today in some parts of the world (Hrdy, 1999). The Western world shows the same bias in favor of males, although not in such extreme ways. According to polls in the United States, for example, most people hope that their first child is a boy, especially if they plan to have only one child (Frenkiel, 1993). In some societies, the higher value of males is explicitly communicated to children. For example, Muslim boys in Turkish villages are taught from an early age to experience and display "male pride." By school age, they are expected to act with decorum—to know and value their maleness (Delaney, 2000).

Finally, Bronfenbrenner's *chronosystem* is also relevant to gender development. Consider the dramatic changes in social attitudes about gender roles that have occurred in Western societies over the past few decades. One domain in which this is especially apparent is career opportunities. When the authors of this book were children, the range of jobs open to females was vastly narrower than it is today. We never saw a woman shinny up a telephone pole, haul a fire hose, or fly a military plane. There were also many fewer women lawyers, doctors, and college professors than there are today.

GETTY IMAGES

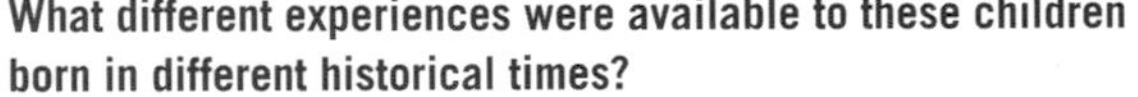

What different experiences were available to these children born in different historical times?

BETTMANN / CORBIS

RICHARD HUTCHINGS / PHOTOEDIT

Inherent in the bioecological model is the existence of complex interactions among levels. An excellent example of such an interaction involving gender comes from research by Glen Elder and his colleagues on adults who had been children during the Great Depression in the 1930s (Elder, Van Nguyen, & Caspi, 1985). The economic hardship that was experienced by so many families during the depression era adversely affected the psychological well-being of girls more than that of boys. The effect was due to their fathers' rejecting and punitive behavior toward them. However, not all girls were treated in this way; highly attractive girls rarely suffered paternal rejection, no matter how severe the economic pressures on the family. Thus, working from the outside to the inside of Bronfenbrenner's model, we see a particular historical time (chronosystem) in which government and business policies (macrosystem) caused widespread financial collapse leading to massive unemployment (exosystem) of family breadwinners (mesosystem). In turn, the resulting financial and other strains increased fathers' rejecting behavior toward certain of their children (microsystem).

Evolutionary Psychology

Evolutionary psychology and parental-investment theory have a great deal to say about sex differences in childhood, as well as in adolescence and adulthood. Consider, for example, the marked gender differences that are common in play. One of the most readily observed of those differences across a wide range of cultures is the prevalence of "rough-and-tumble" play among boys. Taking an evolutionary perspective, David Geary (1999) proposes that the play fighting of boys may represent "an evolved tendency to practice the competencies that were associated with male-male competition during human evolution" (p. 31). In contrast, play parenting, including play with dolls, is much more common among girls than boys in all cultures in which children's play has been studied. This makes sense from an evolutionary point of view. Until quite recently, maternal care in the form of breast feeding was required for infants' survival, so mothers had no alternative

According to evolutionary psychology, gender differences in play probably have their origin in the evolutionary history of the human species. Gender-stereotypic play is assumed to have prepared children for their differential roles in society.

MARLEEN FERGUSON CATE / PHOTOEDIT

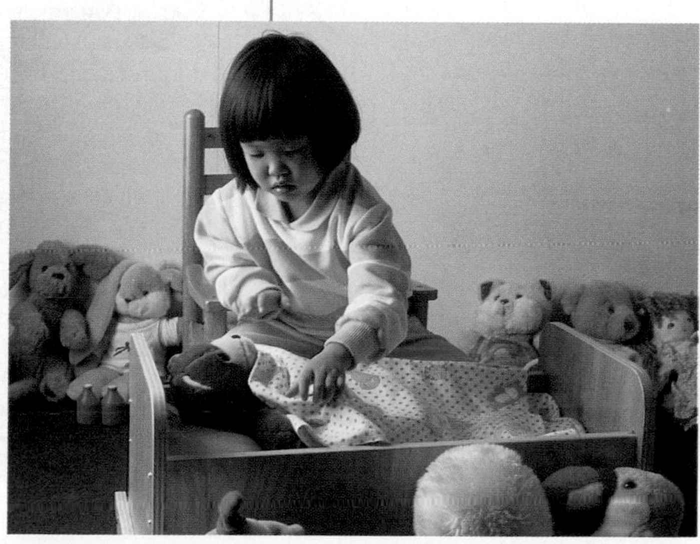

JULIE HOUCK / STOCK BOSTON

to the investment of considerable time, effort, and energy in caring for their young children. Mothers today still do more child care than fathers do in all the cultures in which child care has been examined (Geary, 1998). The fact that parenting play has also been observed in young female primates and is subsequently related to improved survival rates in their offspring leads Geary to view this form of play as "an evolved tendency to seek out activities that will enhance later parenting skills" (Geary, 1999, p. 31).

Parental-investment theory claims that following the onset of puberty, gender differences arise in how males and females approach the task of mating. For a woman, it is important to have a mate who will invest in her and in the long-term care of her children, ensuring the survival of her children to pass on her genes. Thus, her best interests are served by being selective and holding out for a mate who has achieved cultural success and hence can provide valuable resources, whether in the form of cash, cows, or cowrie shells. Men, on the other hand, can have children at no other cost than the investment of their sperm, so the goal of perpetuating their genes is best served by short-term relationships and mating with multiple partners who are fertile and young enough to produce healthy children. Consistent with this view is research reporting that women tend to be attracted to men who appear to be mature and culturally successful (i.e., potential mates with resources to contribute), whereas men focus more on youth and physical attractiveness (i.e., signs of fertility) (Buss, 1994).

The interesting and provocative accounts offered by parental-investment theorists for sex differences in behavior have not gone unchallenged. The general criticisms of evolutionary psychology noted earlier apply equally well in this area, and many specific criticisms, both empirical and theoretical, have also been raised (e.g., Miller, Putcha-Bhagavatula, & Pedersen, 2002). For example, the idea that women have an evolutionary-based preference for men who can provide lots of resources is undermined by the fact that this preference primarily typifies cultures in which women have little power (Eagly & Wood, 1999).

review:

Gender is a topic of major concern for all the general theories of social development. Although the similarities between the sexes far outweigh the differences, the way males and females differ has been the focus of great theoretical interest. Freud's view was premised on his assumptions about childhood sexuality and differences between boys and girls in the development of the superego to control sexual impulses. According to social learning theory, males and females learn gender-typed behavior by paying more attention to and imitating same-sex models more often than opposite-sex models. In addition, social learning theories emphasize that parents and other adults often directly encourage sex-typing in their children by differentially reinforcing them for gender-appropriate behavior. Gender schema theory is a social cognitive approach to gender development that grew out of Lawrence Kohlberg's view that sex-role development begins with children's identification of their own gender. Children then construct gender schemas, or mental representations, of everything they know about gender, including gender stereotypes. They are intrinsically motivated to acquire gender-consistent interests, values, and behavior—to socialize themselves to behave in accord with their gender identity.

In Bronfenbrenner's bioecological model, there are influences on gender development operating at every level of the system, from schoolteachers' differential treatment of boys and girls to cultural and historical differences in the value placed on male and female offspring. Evolutionary psychologists suggest that sex differences in children's play—the rough-and-tumble play of boys and the play parenting of girls—may be related to evolution-based social roles.

An Integrative Theory: Maccoby's Account of Gender Segregation

gender segregation children's tendency to associate with same-sex peers and to avoid opposite-sex peers

In our discussion of the major theories of social development and their perspectives on gender development, we have considered the theories more or less separately from one another. However, as Eleanor Maccoby (1998, 2002) has demonstrated, elements from these general theoretical positions can be successfully integrated. Social learning, social cognitive, and evolutionary psychology views all play a part in her account of **gender segregation**—the strong tendency of children to seek out and interact with peers of their own sex and to actively avoid children of the other sex. Maccoby's theory is based on an array of research findings that testify to how natural gender segregation is to elementary school children. This naturalness is clearly reflected in the following interviews.

> *Interviewer:* In your class, do the boys mix more with the boys or the girls?
> *Harry:* The boys!
> *Interviewer:* Why?
> *Harry:* Well, there's boy talk and girl talk.
>
> *Interviewer:* I've noticed in the lunchroom that very often boys sit together and girls sit together. Why do you think that is?
> *Bob:* So they can talk. The boys talk about football and sports and girls talk about whatever they talk about.
>
> *Sandra:* If you talk with boys they [other girls] say that you're almost going with him.
> *Interviewer:* What does the boy think?
> *Sandra:* I don't know. I can't tell what a boy thinks. It's hard.
> *Interviewer:* You mentioned that you have deep conversations with your girlfriends. Do you ever have conversations like that with boys?
> *Sandra:* Never. I mean, it never crossed my mind.
>
> (Schofield, 1981, quoted in Maccoby, 1998, pp. 61–62)

Gender segregation is observable quite early. American toddlers in day care or play groups begin to prefer same-sex playmates, with girls showing the preference somewhat earlier than boys. The tendency becomes increasingly strong until, by grade school, it is quite pronounced (LaFreniere, Strayer, & Gauthier, 1984; Maccoby & Jacklin, 1987; Serbin, Moller, Gulko, Powlishta, & Colburne, 1994; Sippola, Bukowski, & Noll, 1997). Figure 9.6 shows the results of one study in which preschool children spent nearly three times as much time playing with same-sex peers as with other-sex children. By first grade, the ratio was 11 to 1 (Maccoby & Jacklin, 1987). Gender segregation peaks at around 8 to 11 years of age and then declines slowly, especially as adolescents become romantically interested in the other sex.

The general tendency toward gender segregation that is shown by children in the United States appears to be virtually universal (Ruble & Martin, 1998). Whiting and Edwards (1988) observed same-sex preferences in several small societies around the world, including villages and neighborhoods in Africa, India, Mexico, the Philippines, and the United States. In all of them, children chose same-sex playmates and spent more of their playtime interacting with other children of their own sex. Between 6 and 10 years of age, children initiated social acts five times as often with same-sex peers as they did with other-sex peers.

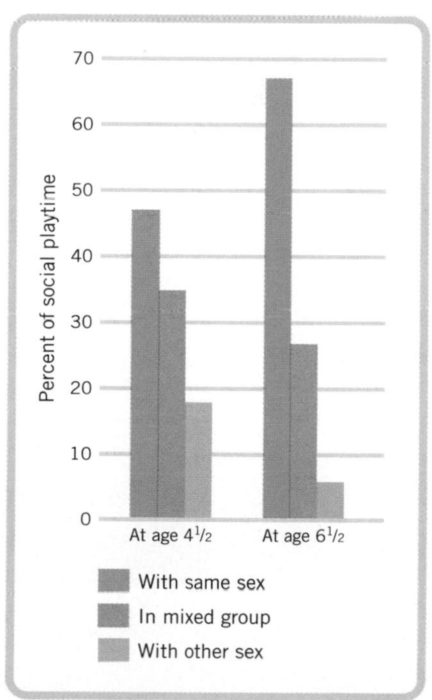

FIGURE 9.6 Gender segregation in play Percent of social playtime that preschool and first-grade children spent with children of their own or the other gender. (Adapted from Maccoby, 1990)

SUSIE FITZHUGH

Boys sit with boys, girls sit with girls, This standard lunchroom scene illustrates gender segregation.

The separation of children into same-sex groups is for the most part initiated by children themselves. Thus, it constitutes another example of gender self-socialization. The degree to which children themselves enforce gender segregation is clearly illustrated in the following description of an event in an American elementary school:

> In the lunchroom, when the two second-grade tables were filling, a high-status boy walked by the inside table, which had a scattering of both boys and girls, and said loudly, "Oooo, too many girls," as he headed for a seat at the far table. The boys at the inside table picked up their trays and moved, and no other boys sat at the inside table, which the pronouncement had effectively made taboo.
>
> (Thorne, 1986, quoted in Maccoby, 1998, p. 24)

The strength of the tendency toward gender segregation is also reflected in the difficulty of changing it. Intervention programs designed to increase cross-sex play have not been notably effective or had long-lasting effects (Lockheed & Harris, 1984; Serbin, Tonick, & Sternglanz, 1977; Theokas, Ramsey, & Sweeney, 1993). Indeed, efforts by teachers to increase children's interaction with members of the other sex often meet strong resistance: as one 11-year-old girl expressed it, teachers who try to get boys and girls to play together more often are "geeky ughs" (Maccoby, 1998, p. 26).

Why are children so motivated so early to stick to their "own kind"? Maccoby (1998) proposes that same-sex playmate choices originate in children's discovery, through their early interactions with both boys and girls, that the play styles of same-sex peers are more compatible with their own play preferences. Specifically, they learn that boys frequently engage in physically active rough-and-tumble play, tend to play in relatively large groups, and devote considerable effort to jockeying for dominance and "grandstanding" in an attempt to impress their peers. Direct mutual confrontations are common in their interactions, and rough play can easily lead to aggression. In addition, boys zealously guard their separateness: they actively separate themselves from adults, testing the limits of adult rules and sanctions, and they actively exclude girls from their groups.

Children also learn that girls devote much effort to establishing and maintaining positive social relations. They spend more time with just one or a few other girls and avoid open conflict in their interactions, expressing hostility indirectly. Self-disclosure is an important component of girls' interactions, which are reciprocal and sustained. Unlike boys, girls tend to maintain communication with adults.

Maccoby believes that multiple factors contribute to differences in the interaction styles of boys and girls and hence to the self-initiated segregation of the sexes. Some may have an evolutionary origin, including the male agenda of establishing dominance hierarchies. Similar differences in male and female play styles and the tendency toward sex segregation are found in some nonhuman primates. Physiological (hormonal) factors also appear to contribute, including the exposure to androgens (male hormones) that male fetuses normally have. Evidence for the role of androgens comes from research showing that female monkeys who are prenatally administered androgens engage in more rough-and-tumble play than do normal females. Similar observations have been made for girls who were accidentally exposed to androgen prenatally.

Cognitive factors also play a part in Maccoby's view of gender segregation. Although knowledge about gender stereotypes does not seem to be strongly related to gender segregation, knowledge of one's own gender, as well as of the gender of others, obviously is. Socialization pressures also contribute to gender segregation, although the pressure comes primarily from children's peers rather than from adults, as in the lunchroom example quoted earlier. Children of both sexes who attempt to interact with a child of the other sex are teased for "liking" or "loving" that child. Adults' contribution to gender segregation comes primarily from their encouragement of differences in the interaction styles of boys and girls. As we discussed earlier, parents play more gently with girls and encourage them to talk about feelings, and they play more roughly with boys and discourage crying or showing fear or weakness.

Gender segregation is thus a very strong tendency consistently observed across societies and even species. It is to a great degree initiated and enforced by children themselves. Because of their preference for different kinds of play and other interactions, children derive more pleasure and comfort from staying primarily with their "own kind." In turn, this voluntary sex segregation promotes further self-socialization of gender differences.

review:

The theory of gender segregation proposed by Eleanor Maccoby brings together elements from all the major social development theories in an attempt to understand the strong tendency that children throughout the world have to associate with peers of their own sex and to avoid children of the other sex. Self-socialization plays a prominent role in her theory, since it is primarily children themselves who initiate and enforce gender segregation. The impetus for gender-segregated groups stems in large part from basic differences in interaction styles, which are themselves the result of multiple factors, including gender knowledge and socialization pressures, as well as biological factors with a presumably evolutionary origin.

Chapter Summary

Four major types of social development theories present contrasting views of the social world of children, as well as different perspectives on gender development.

Psychoanalytic Theories

- The psychoanalytic theory of Sigmund Freud has had an enormous impact on developmental psychology and psychology as a whole, primarily through Freud's emphasis on the importance of early experience for personality and social development, his depiction of unconscious motivation and processes, and his emphasis on the importance of close relationships.
- Freud posited five biologically determined stages of psychosexual development (oral, anal, phallic, latency, genital) in which psychic energy becomes focused in different areas of the body. Children face specific conflicts at each stage, and these conflicts must be resolved for healthy development to occur. Freud also posited three structures of personality—id (unconscious urges), ego (rational thought), and superego (conscience).
- Erik Erikson extended Freud's theory by identifying eight stages of psychosocial development extending across the entire life span. In each stage, a developmental crisis is experienced that, if not successfully resolved, will continue to trouble the individual.

Learning Theories

- John Watson believed strongly in the power of environmental factors, especially reinforcement, to influence children's development.
- B. F. Skinner held that all behavior can be explained in terms of operant conditioning. He discovered the importance of intermittent reinforcement and the powerful reinforcing value of attention.
- Albert Bandura's social learning theory originally emphasized imitation as a prime source of learning. His research established that children can learn simply by observing other people. Bandura has increasingly stressed the importance of cognition in social learning.

Theories of Social Cognitition

- Social cognitive theories assume that children's knowledge and beliefs are vitally important in social development.
- Robert Selman's theory proposes that children go through four stages in the development of the ability to take the role or perspective of another person. They progress from the simple appreciation that someone can have a view different from their own to being able to think about the view of a "generalized other."
- The social information-processing approach to social cognition emphasizes the importance of children's attributions regarding their own and others' behavior. The role of such attribution is clearly reflected in a hostile attributional bias, which leads children to assume hostile intent on the part of others and to respond aggressively in situations in which the intention of others is ambiguous.

Ecological Theories of Development

- Bronfenbrenner's bioecological model conceptualizes the environment as a set of nested contexts, with the child at the center. These contexts range from the microsystem, which includes the activities, roles, and relationships in which a child directly participates on a regular basis, to the macrosystem, the general cultural context in which the child lives.
- Ethological theories examine behavior within the evolutionary context, trying to understand its adaptive or survival value. The research of Konrad Lorenz on imprinting is particularly relevant to social development in children.
- Evolutionary psychologists apply Darwinian concepts of natural selection to human behavior. Characteristic of their approach are parental-investment theory and the idea that the long period of immaturity and dependence in human infancy enables young children to learn and practice many of the skills needed later in life.

Social Theories and Gender Development

- Freud believed that the Oedipus complex and the Electra complex form the basis for superego (conscience) development, as the child, fearing retaliation for loving and desiring his or her other-sex parent, identifies with and adopts the values of their same-sex parent. Freud thought that girls experience less fear than boys do, leading them to identify less strongly with their same-sex parent and hence to develop a weaker conscience.
- Social learning theorists believe that children learn "gender-appropriate" behavior through imitation, direct reinforcement, and observational learning.
- Self-socialization is a primary feature of social cognitive theories of gender development, including Kohlberg's cognitive developmental theory and gender schema theory. Children's knowledge of their own gender and gender stereotypes motivates them to adopt the preferences and behaviors considered appropriate for their own sex.
- Ecological theorists take into account the larger context of gender development. According to the bioecological model, social influences at many levels play a role in gender development. According to parental-investment theory, many gender differences in sexual behavior are based on genetically inherited strategies for mating and producing offspring that will survive to pass on their parents' genes.

An Integrative Theory: Maccoby's Account of Gender Segregation

- Eleanor Maccoby's account of gender segregation, the voluntary and self-enforced separation of children into all-girl and all-boy groups, integrates elements of other theories. Evolution-based tendencies toward rough play make boys less satisfactory play partners for girls, who prefer quieter activities. Spending most of their time with others of the same sex reinforces the natural tendencies of both boys and girls.

Critical Thinking Questions

1. The concept of self-socialization plays a prominent role in social cognitive theories. Explain what is meant by this term. To what extent and in what ways do the other major theories reviewed in the chapter allow for the possibility of self-socialization?
2. Look again at the pictures of Colin and Catherine at the beginning of the chapter and the obvious sex differences displayed in their behavior. Think of one claim about these differences that would be made by each of the four classes of theories covered in this chapter.
3. Suppose you wanted to raise your own children to be as minimally sex-typed as possible. What have you learned in this chapter that you could apply toward this goal? Which of the four types of theories would you rely on most?
4. Thinking back over your childhood, what did girls and boys do to establish and enforce gender segregation? In what ways did adults (parents, teachers) contribute to separation of the sexes?
5. What message do you think is delivered to children by the huge imbalance in the number and power of male and female characters on the major mass medium of the Western world—television?

Key Terms

psychic energy, p. 332
erogenous zones, p. 332
id, p. 333
oral stage, p. 333
ego, p. 333
anal stage, p. 333
phallic stage, p. 334
superego, p. 334
internalization, p. 334
latency period, p. 334
genital stage, p. 334
systematic desensitization, p. 338
behavior modification, p. 339
vicarious reinforcement, p. 340
reciprocal determinism, p. 341
self-socialization, p. 343
role taking, p. 343
hostile attributional bias, p. 344
microsystem, p. 346
mesosystem, p. 346
exosystem, p. 346
macrosystem, p. 347
chronosystem, p. 348
ethology, p. 348
imprinting, p. 348
parental-investment theory, p. 349
Oedipus complex, p. 352
Electra complex, p. 353
gender identity, p. 358
gender stability, p. 358
gender constancy, p. 358
gender schema, p. 359
gender self-socialization, p. 359
gender segregation, p. 365

CHAPTER 10

Emotional Development

PHILIP EVERGOOD, *Her World,* 1948

Imagine the following situation. A young girl is taken to a room in preschool where an experimenter shows her some tasty treats such as M&Ms, marshmallows, or pretzels. Then the experimenter tells the girl that he is going to leave the room "for a while" and that she has two choices. If she waits until he returns to the room, she can have two of the treats, or if she wishes, she can ring a bell and the experimenter will return immediately—but she will get only one treat. The child is then left alone for a considerable period of time, say 15 to 20 minutes, or until she rings the bell.

Walter Mischel and his colleagues used this procedure in numerous studies with preschoolers and young school-age children to study their ability to delay immediate gratification in order to obtain larger rewards. Videotaping what the children did during the time they were alone with the treats, they found that the children used different strategies. Some distracted themselves by talking to themselves, singing, trying to sleep, or making up games to play. Others kept looking at the rewards or the bell.

Which children do you think were most successful at curbing their desire for the treat and holding out for the larger reward? Of course, the children who distracted themselves (Mischel, 1981; Rodriguez, Mischel, & Shoda, 1989). More important, the amount of time children were able to delay requesting the treat proved to be a remarkably good predictor of their social and cognitive competence and their coping skills at an older age. For example, ten years after the experiment, the children were rated by their parents with regard to their academic and social competence, as well as their verbal fluency, rational thinking, attentiveness, planfulness, and ability to deal with frustration. Those who had waited the longest in Mischel's experiment were rated higher on these dimensions than were those who had summoned the experimenter back after shorter periods of time (Mischel, Shoda, & Peake, 1988; Peake, Hebl, & Mischel, 2002). They also obtained higher SAT scores (Shoda, Mischel, & Peake, 1990). In addition, in their late 20s, they were found to be more socially competent, planful, and self-regulated, and had higher self-esteem. Men in this group also were less likely to have used cocaine or crack in the past year (Ayduk, Mendoza-Denton, Downey, Peake, & Rodriguez, 2000; Mischel, 2000; Peake & Mischel, 2000).

The fact that children's ability to delay gratification in one situation in preschool predicted their social, emotional, and academic competence so many years later illustrates the importance of what has been labeled "emotional intelligence,"

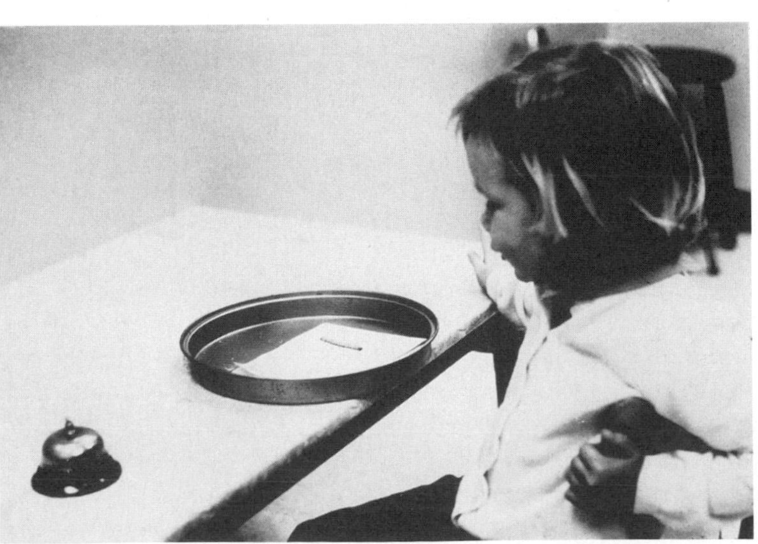

This girl was in one of Mischel's studies of preschoolers' delay of gratification. Children can delay longer if they avert their attention from the desirable object (a pretzel in this study).

BASED ON MISCHEL, W. EBBESON, E.B., & ZEISS, A.R. (1972). COGNITIVE & ATTENTIONAL MECHANISMS IN DELAY OF GRATIFICATION. JOURNAL OF PERSONALITY AND SOCIAL PSYCHOLOGY, 21, 204–218 or "affective social competence." **Emotional intelligence** refers to a set of abilities that are key to competent social functioning. These abilities include being able to motivate oneself and persist in the face of frustration, control impulses and delay gratification, identify and understand one's own and others' feelings, regulate one's moods, regulate the expression of emotion in social interactions, and empathize with others' emotions (Goleman, 1995; Halberstadt, Denham, & Dunsmore, 2001; Saarni, 1990).

The importance of emotional intelligence is reflected in the fact that, more than IQ, it predicts how well people do in life, especially in their social lives. For example, in a study in which 450 boys from impoverished neighborhoods were followed up in middle age, how well these boys had done at work or in the rest of their lives had relatively little relation to their IQs. Rather, how well they had done corresponded with their ability to manage their frustration, control their emotions, and get along with others (Felsman & Vaillant, 1987). The similarity between the results of this study and the findings of Mischel and his colleagues underscores the point that our emotions, and how we deal with them, play a huge role in the quality of our lives and in our relationships with others.

In this chapter, we examine the development of emotions as well as the development of children's ability to regulate their emotions and the behavior associated with them. In addition, we discuss the development of children's understanding of emotion, which affects what children feel and how well they can control their emotions and behavior. In the course of our discussion, we will give particular emphasis to several of our themes. Key among them will be the theme of *individual differences* as we examine differences among children in various aspects of their emotional functioning. We also discuss the origins of these differences, including heredity, parental socialization practices, and cultural beliefs related to emotion. Thus, the themes of *nature and nurture* and the *sociocultural context* will also be prominent.

emotional intelligence a set of abilities that contribute to competence in the social and emotional domains, including being able to motivate oneself and persist in the face of frustration, control impulses and delay gratification, identify and understand one's own and others' feelings, regulate one's moods, regulate the expression of emotion in social interactions, and empathize with others' emotions

emotion emotion is characterized by a motivational force or action tendency and by changes in physiology, subjective experience, and overt behavior. It is defined by functionalists as the attempt or readiness to establish, maintain, or change one's relation with the environment on matters of importance.

The Development of Emotions in Childhood

Most people take the idea of **emotion** for granted and just equate the term with "feelings." However, developmentalists have a much more complex view of emotions. They see emotions in terms of several components: (1) the desire to take action, including the desire to escape, approach, or change people or things in the environment; (2) physiological correlates, including heart and breath rate, hormone levels, and the like; (3) subjective feelings; and (4) the cognitions that may elicit or accompany them. A simple example illustrates these components in combination: When people experience fear in response to a growling dog, they typically have the motivation to get away from the dog, experience heightened physiological arousal, have the subjective experience of fearfulness, and probably are thinking about the ways in which the dog might hurt them. Because of the assumed importance of their motivational component, emotions sometimes are defined as an individual's attempt or readiness to establish, maintain, or change their relation with the environment on matters of importance to them (Saarni, Mumme, & Campos, 1998).

Although most psychologists share this general view of emotions, they often do not agree on the relative importance of its key components (Saarni et al., 1998; Sroufe, 1995). For example, some theorists believe that cognitions play a much more important role in the experience of emotion than do others. Moreover, there is considerable debate about the basic nature of emotions—that is, whether they

discrete emotions theory a theory about emotions discussed by Tomkins, Izard, and others in which emotions are viewed as innate and discrete from one another from very early in life, and each emotion is believed to be packaged with a specific and distinctive set of bodily and facial reactions

functionalist approach a theory of emotion proposed by Campos and others that argues that the basic function of emotions is to promote action toward achieving a goal. In this view, emotions are not discrete from one another and vary somewhat based on the social environment.

are innate or partly learned—and about when and in what form different emotions emerge during infancy.

Before considering the development of specific emotions in childhood, we first need to examine some of the major views that have been proposed regarding the nature and emergence of emotions.

Theories on the Nature and Emergence of Emotion

The debate about the nature and emergence of emotions in children has deep roots. In *The Expression of the Emotions in Man and Animals*, published in 1872, Charles Darwin argued that there is a direct link between certain inner emotional states and their facial expression, and that these associations are unlearned and found even in very young babies. Darwin believed that human emotional expressions are based on a limited set of basic emotions that are mostly innate to the species and therefore similar across all people. A corresponding view held by some current investigators such as Silvan Tomkins and Carroll Izard is **discrete emotions theory,** which argues that emotions are innate, that each emotion is packaged with a specific and distinctive set of bodily and facial reactions, and that distinct emotions are evident from very early in life (Izard, 1991; Tomkins, 1962).

Other researchers maintain that emotions are not distinct from one another at the beginning of life and that environmental factors play an important role in the emergence of feelings and the expression of emotion. Some of these researchers, for example, argue that infants experience only excitement and distress in the first weeks of life, and that other emotions emerge at later ages as a function of experience (Sroufe, 1979). According to Alan Sroufe (1979, 1995), there are three basic affect systems—joy/pleasure, anger/frustration, and wariness/fear—and these systems undergo developmental change from primitive to more advanced forms during the early years of life. For example, wariness/fear is first expressed as a startle or pain reaction. At a few months of age, infants start to show wariness of novel situations, and a few months later show clear signs of fear in novel situations. In Sroufe's view, such changes are largely due to infants' accumulating social interaction and experience and their expanding ability to understand their experiences. As one example, infants go through a period in which they often exhibit a fear of strangers. However, this fear does not emerge until around the age of 6 or 7 months, presumably because by that age infants have had enough social experience to realize that strangers and familiar people are not interchangeable.

Theorists who take a **functionalist approach** to understanding emotional development also emphasize the role of the environment in emotional development and propose that the basic function of emotions is to promote action toward achieving a goal (Campos, Mumme, Kermoian, & Campos, 1994; Saarni et al., 1998). The emotion of fear, for instance, often causes one to flee or otherwise avoid a stimulus that represents a threat. This action helps achieve the goal of self-preservation. (See Table 10.1 for other examples.) Functionalists such as Joseph Campos have also argued that because humans are social beings, their understanding of, and goals in, various situations—and hence their emotional reactions in these situations—are affected by significant others. For example, young children's experience of emotions such as shame and guilt is related to both the values and standards communicated to them by their parents and the manner in which they are communicated.

Research supports all the aforementioned perspectives to some degree, and no one theory has emerged as definitive. As you will see in the next section, young in-

TABLE 10.1

Characteristics of Some Families of Emotion

Emotion type	Goal connected with the emotion	Meaning regarding the self	Meaning regarding others	Action tendency
Disgust	Avoiding contamination or illness	This stimulus may contaminate me or make me ill	—	Active rejection of the thing causing disgust
Fear	Maintaining one's own physical and psychological integrity	This stimulus is threatening to me	—	Flight or withdrawal
Anger	Attaining the end state that the individual currently is invested in	There is an obstacle to my obtaining my goal	—	Forward movement especially to eliminate obstacles to one's goal
Sadness	Attaining the end state that the individual currently is invested in	My goal is unattainable	—	Disengagement and withdrawal
Shame	Maintaining others' respect and affection; preserving self-esteem	I am bad (my self-esteem is damaged)	Others notice how bad I am	Withdrawal; avoiding others, hiding oneself
Guilt	Meeting one's own internalized values	I have done something contrary to my values	Someone has been injured by my actions	Movement to make reparation, to inform others, or to punish self

Adapted from Saarni et al. (1998), p. 239

fants show a variety of emotions, with partial or complete facial expressions of interest, smiling, and disgust appearing soon after birth and expressions of anger and sadness appearing as early as 2 months of age (Izard, Hembree, & Huebner, 1987; Rosenstein & Oster, 1988). However, as you will also see, it is not very clear to what degree these facial expressions, especially negative facial expressions, can be reliably differentiated or occur in expected situations. It also is not clear to what degree young children's basic emotions are innate or develop as a consequence of experience. No doubt, both heredity and experience play a part.

The Emergence of Emotion in the Early Years and Childhood

Parents are likely to think that they see many emotions in their infants, including joy and interest, anger, fear, and sadness—even in their 1-month-olds. However, parents' identification of the emotion their infant is experiencing at any given moment is somewhat subjective: parents often read into their infant's emotional reaction the emotion that would seem appropriate in the immediate situation. For example, a parent may assume that an infant's negative reaction to being given a novel toy is fear, when it could just as well be anger or upset at being overstimulated or at having a current activity disrupted.

To make their own interpretations of infants' emotions more objective, researchers have devised highly elaborate systems for coding and classifying the emotional meaning of infants' facial expressions. These systems identify emotions first by coding dozens of facial cues—whether the eyebrows are raised or knitted together; whether the eyes are wide open, tightly closed, or narrowed; whether lips are pursed, softly rounded, or retracted straight back; and so on—and then by analyzing the combination in which these cues are present. Nonetheless, it is often hard to determine exactly what

As is evident from this infant's expression, it often is difficult to identify what negative emotion a young infant is feeling.

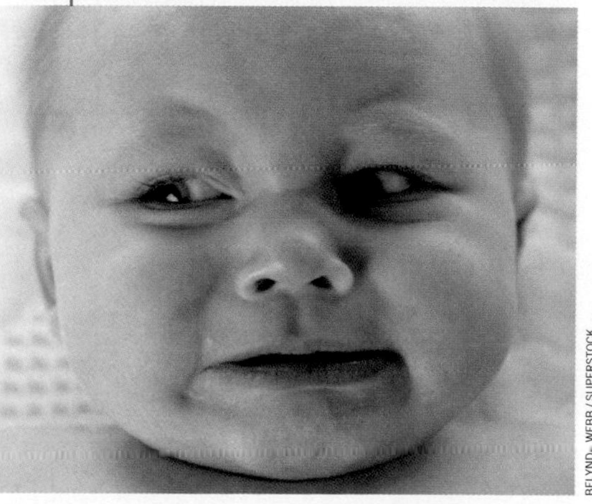
BELYND. WEBB / SUPERSTOCK

social smiles smiles that are directed at people. They first emerge as early as 6 to 7 weeks of age.

emotions infants are experiencing, and it is particularly difficult to differentiate among the various negative emotions that young infants express. Correspondingly, getting a clear picture of early emotional development is a more difficult task when it comes to negative emotions than it is with regard to positive emotions.

We begin our examination of the emergence of emotions with the easier task—tracing the early development of positive emotions.

Positive Emotions

The first clear sign of happiness that infants express is smiling. Young infants smile from their earliest days, but the meaning of their smiles appears to change with age. During the first month of life, infants exhibit fleeting smiles, primarily during the REM phase of sleep, in which dreams occur. After the first month of life, infants sometimes smile when they are stroked gently. These early smiles may be reflexive and seem to be evoked by some biological state rather than by social interaction (Sroufe & Waters, 1976; Wolff, 1987).

During the third month of life, but perhaps as early as 6 or 7 weeks of age, babies exhibit a strikingly important development—the emergence of **social smiles,** that is, smiles directed toward people (White, 1985). Social smiles frequently occur during interactions with a parent (Malatesta, Culver, Tesman, & Shephard, 1989) and tend to elicit the parent's delight, interest, and affection (Huebner & Izard, 1988; Malatesta & Haviland, 1982). In turn, this response usually further inspires the infant's social smiling. Thus, the infant's early social smiles likely promote care from parents and other adults and enhance the quality of the infant's relationships with other people.

Smiles that arise as a function of social interactions, as contrasted with those associated with strictly biological stimuli, typically first appear during the infant's third month.

DOROTHY LITTELL GRECO / THE IMAGE WORKS

The social basis of social smiles is highlighted by the fact that although young infants sometimes smile at interesting objects, humans are much more likely to make them smile. This difference was demonstrated in a study in which 3-month-old infants smiled and vocalized much more at people, even strangers, than at puppetlike foam balls that resembled people, were animated, and "talked" to the infant (Ellsworth, Muir, & Hains, 1993).

When infants are at least 2 months of age, they also show happiness in both social and nonsocial contexts in which they can control a particular event. In one study that showed this, researchers divided infants into two groups and attached a string to an arm of each infant. Observing the infants individually, they arranged for infants in one group to hear music whenever they pulled the string and for infants in the other group to hear music at random intervals. The infants who "caused" the music to play by pulling on the string showed more interest and smiling when the music came on than did the infants whose string-pulling had no connection to the music's being played (Lewis, Alessandri, & Sullivan, 1990). This pleasure in controlling events is evident in infants' delight when they can consistently make a noise by shaking their rattle or banging a toy on the floor.

At about 7 months of age, infants start to smile primarily at *familiar* people, rather than at people in general. (In fact, as you will see, unfamiliar people often elicit distress at this age.) These selective smiles are likely to elicit delight and motivate parents to continue interacting with the infant. In turn, infants of this age often respond to parents' playfulness and smiles with excitement and joy, which also prolongs their positive social interactions (Weinberg &

Tronick, 1994). Such exchanges of positive affect, especially when they occur with parents and not strangers, make parents feel special to the infant and strengthen the bond between them.

After about 3 or 4 months of age, infants laugh as well as smile during a variety of activities. For example, they are likely to laugh when a parent tickles them or blows on their tummy, bounces them on a knee or swings them around in the air, or shares a favorite activity such as bathing with them. By late in the first year of life, children's cognitive development allows them to take pleasure from unexpected or discrepant events such as Mom making a funny noise or wearing a funny hat (Kagan, Kearsley, & Zelazo, 1978).

During the second year of life, children start to clown around themselves and are delighted when they can make other people laugh—as in the case of this 18-month-old who, fully clothed, sits on his potty and looks at his mother:

> *Child.* Poo (grunts heavily). Poo! (grunts). Poo! (gets up, looks at Mother, picks up empty potty, and waves it at Mother, laughing)
>
> (Dunn, 1988, p. 154)

Incidents like this are common in the second year of life and demonstrate infants' desires to share positive emotion and activities with parents.

Negative Emotions

The first negative emotion that is discernible in infants is generalized distress, which can be evoked by a variety of stressful experiences ranging from hunger and pain to overstimulation. Often expressed with piercing cries and a face screwed up in a tight grimace, this type of distress is unmistakable.

The emergence and development of other negative emotions in infancy are, as noted, more difficult to pin down. Nevertheless, investigators have been able to differentiate among some negative emotions in fairly young infants. By 2 months of age, facial expressions of what appears to be anger or sadness have been observed and reliably differentiated from one another and from distress/pain in *some* contexts, such as when infants are being given an injection during a medical procedure (Izard et al., 1987). Moreover, analysis of the facial reactions of 2½- to 6-month-olds provides some evidence of congruence between infants' experience of common negative situations and the facial expressions children exhibit in those situations. For example, negative situations (e.g., mothers' expressions of sadness or anger) evoke more anger and sadness and blends of these emotions from infants than do positive situations (e.g., infants' play with their mother or their mother expressing joy) (Izard et al., 1995).

However, the interpretation of negative emotions is complicated by the fact that infants sometimes display negative emotions that seem incongruent with the situation they are experiencing (Camras, 1992). In the string-pulling study cited earlier, for example, the infants who could "control" the music by pulling the string attached to their arms fussed and sometimes expressed anger when pulling the string no longer turned on the music. Other times, however, these infants showed fear when pulling the string no longer produced music (Lewis et al., 1990). Incongruities such as this highlight the difficulty of knowing for certain what emotion an infant may be experiencing in certain situations.

Some theorists believe that young infants can experience sadness and anger, whereas others believe that they only experience an undifferentiated state of distress.

MICHAEL KRASOWITZ / FPG INTERNATIONAL / GETTY IMAGES

separation anxiety feelings of distress that children, especially infants and toddlers, experience when they are separated, or expect to be separated, from individuals to whom they are attached

One way to examine this issue is to see if infants show specific negative emotions in the situations in which they might be expected to and not in other situations. For example, in fear-inducing situations, do infants show fear more often than other emotions such as surprise? Also, do they show more fear in fear-inducing situations than in situations expected to elicit emotions other than fear? One group of investigators (Hiatt, Campos, & Emde, 1979) examined these issues by putting 10- to 12-month-old infants in six situations designed to elicit happiness, fear, or surprise. The happy situations were playing peekaboo and playing with an attractive toy. Fear situations were crawling over a visual cliff (the laboratory platform, described in Chapter 5, that gives the illusion of dropping off like a cliff in the middle) and being approached by a stranger (a common source of fear at this age). The surprise situations were seeing an object vanish (an illusion created by the experimenter) and seeing a toy hidden in a particular location and then witnessing a different toy emerge from the same location. In happy situations, babies showed more happiness than other emotions and more happiness than in fear-inducing or surprising situations. In contrast, in the fear contexts, infants generally showed no more fear than other negative reactions. In surprising situations, surprise reactions occurred more frequently than happiness or fear, but surprise was shown as frequently in the fear and happiness situations as in the situations expected to evoke surprise. Thus, it was not clear that infants' fear and surprise reactions were distinct from other emotional responses.

On the basis of other studies of this sort, it has also been suggested that young infants are experiencing undifferentiated distress when they evidence negative emotion (Oster, Hegley, & Nagel, 1992), and that anger and distress/pain are especially likely to be undifferentiated in most contexts (Camras, 1992). As far as parents are concerned, it may not be important that they cannot distinguish whether their infant is experiencing distress or anger or fear; the important thing is that they know something is wrong. Mothers are likely to pick up their infants quickly when they show any of these emotions (Huebner & Izard, 1988). However, as children grow, it probably becomes more important that other people understand whether one is experiencing pain, distress, or anger (Camras, 1992).

Fear and distress As you have seen, there is little firm evidence of distinct fear reactions in infants during the first months of life (Witherington, Campos, & Hertenstein, 2001). Then, at around the age of 6 or 7 months, clear signs of fear begin to appear, most notably the fear of strangers in many circumstances. Consider the following contrast: At the age of 10 weeks, Janine was whimpering in her crib, when a stranger came over and smiled and talked to her. Janine stopped fussing and smiled at the stranger. At the age of 8 months, Janine is playing on her mother's knee when her mother has to put her down and leave the room to answer the door. A moment later the visitor, a stranger, enters the room without Janine's mother.

> When the visitor enters, Janine cries. The visitor tries to comfort Janine by picking her up and talking softly to her, but she cries still more frantically until her mother returns and holds her. Then Janine calms down and smiles when mother lifts her high in the air in play.
>
> (Bronson, 1972)

Thus, by 6 or 7 months of age, unfamiliar people no longer provide comfort and pleasure similar to that provided by familiar people. This change in infants' behavior likely reflects their growing attachment to parents.

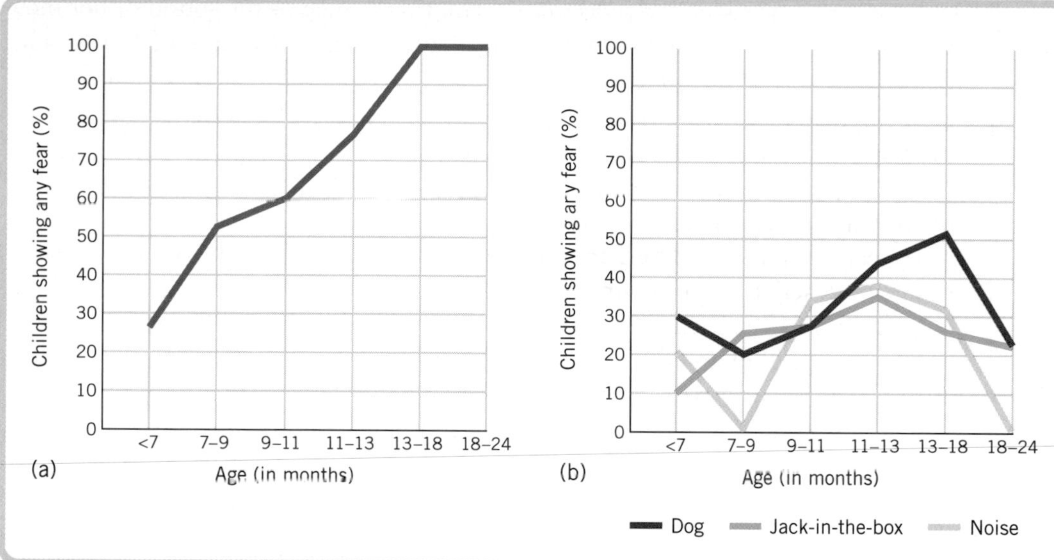

FIGURE 10.1 Percentages of young children showing fear of (a) the visual cliff and (b) dogs, noises, and a jack-in-the-box Children 1½ to 2 years of age show the most fear of the visual cliff. Children show the most fear of the jack-in-the-box and loud noises at about 1 year of age and the most fear of dogs at 1 to 1½ years of age. (Adapted from Scarr & Salapatek, 1970)

In general, the fear of strangers intensifies and lasts until about age 2. However, it should be noted that the fear of strangers is quite variable, depending on both the infant's temperament (i.e., how fearful the infant is in general) and the specific context, such as whether a parent is present and the manner in which the stranger approaches (e.g., abruptly and excitedly or slowly and calmly).

Other fears also are evident at around the age of 7 months, including fear of novel toys, loud noises, and sudden movements by people or objects, all of which tend to decline after 12 months of age, as shown in Figure 10.1 (Kagan et al., 1978; Scarr & Salapatek, 1970). The emergence of such fears is clearly adaptive. Because babies often do not have the ability to escape from potentially dangerous situations, they must rely on their parents to protect them, and expressions of fear and distress are powerful tools for bringing help and support when they are needed.

An especially salient and important type of fear or distress that begins at about 8 months of age is **separation anxiety**—distress due to separation from the parent that is the child's primary caregiver. When infants experience separation anxiety, they typically whine, cry, or otherwise express fear and upset. However, the degree to which children exhibit distress when separated from their parents varies with the context. For example, infants show much less distress when they crawl or walk away from their parent than when their parent does the departing (Rheingold & Eckerman, 1970). Separation anxiety tends to increase from 8 to 13 or 15 months of age, and then begins to decline (Kagan, 1976).

This pattern of separation anxiety occurs across many cultures, displayed by infants reared in environments as disparate as the United States, Israeli kibbutzim (communal farming communities), and !Kung San hunting-and-gathering groups in the Kalahari Desert in Africa (Kagan, 1976) (see Figure 10.2). Blind children also show separation anxiety, albeit a few months later than children

FIGURE 10.2 Percentages of Chinese and Euro-American children at different ages displaying fretting or crying at the departure of mother Children exhibit the most evidence of separation anxiety at about 13 months of age, and Chinese children have been found to display somewhat more anxiety and distress than Euro-American children. (Adapted from Kagan, Kearsley, & Zelanzo, 1978)

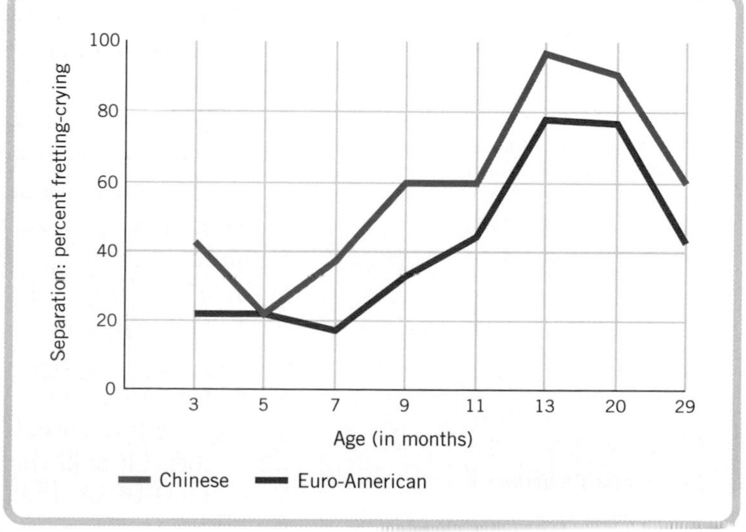

who can see. The sudden absence of their mother's voice or the sound of her moving away may elicit separation anxiety in them. Typical is the case of Karen, who, at about the age of 11 months,

> let herself down to the floor and started to creep to the box which was about 2 feet away from her. She was somewhat hesitant or cautious but she was curious. At this moment mother got up to go to Debby (the younger baby sister) to give her the pacifier because she was fussing. Karen immediately started to whimper, reversed direction, and went back to cling to the mother's chair, and when mother sat down again reached to touch mother's arm.
>
> (Fraiberg, 1975, p. 330)

Anger and sadness By the second year of life, differentiating between infants' anger and other negative emotions is no longer difficult (Camrus, Oster, Campos, Miyake, & Bradshaw, 1992): 1-year-olds clearly and frequently express anger, often toward other people (Radke-Yarrow & Kochanska, 1990). Displays of anger increase in the second year of life, as children are better able to control their environments and are likely to be upset when control is taken away from them or when they are otherwise frustrated (see Figure 10.3) (Goodenough, 1931).

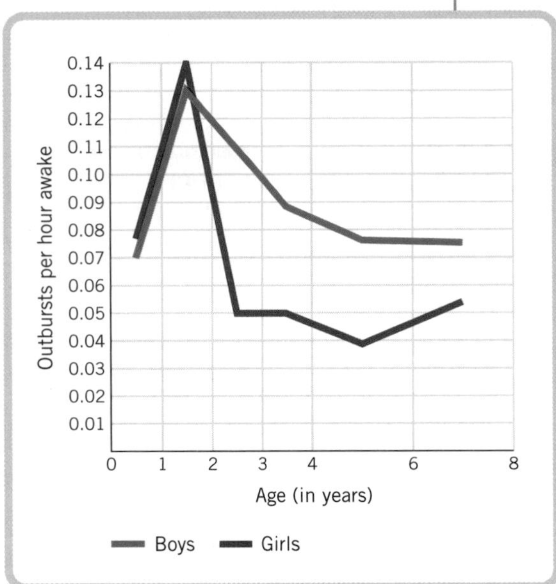

FIGURE 10.3 Frequency of angry outbursts in the home Children display the most anger at home during the second year of life. Displays of anger drop sharply thereafter, especially for girls. (Adapted from Goodenough, 1931)

Infants often exhibit sadness in the same types of situations in which they show anger, such as after a painful event, when they cannot control outcomes in their environment, and when they are separated from parents, although displays of sadness appear to be somewhat less frequent than displays of anger or distress (Izard et al., 1987, 1995; Lewis et al., 1990; Shiller, Izard, & Hembref, 1986). However, when older infants or young children are separated from their parents for extended periods of time and are not given sensitive care during this period, they often show intense and prolonged displays of sadness (Bowlby, 1973; Robertson & Robertson, 1971).

The Self-Conscious Emotions: Embarrassment, Pride, Guilt, and Shame

During the second year of life, children begin to show a range of new emotions: embarrassment, pride, guilt, and shame (Stipek, Gralinski, & Kopp, 1990; Zahn-Waxler & Robinson, 1995). These emotions often are called **self-conscious emotions** because they relate to our sense of self and our consciousness of others' reactions to us. Some investigators such as Michael Lewis believe that these emotions do not emerge until the second year because they depend on young children's understanding that they themselves are entities distinct from other people, an understanding that is gradually emerging in the first years of life (Lewis, 1998).

At about 15 to 24 months of age, some children start to show embarrassment when they are made the center of attention. Asked to show off an ability or a new piece of clothing, for example, they lower their eyes, hang their head, blush, or hide their face in their hands (Lewis, 1995).

The first signs of pride are evident in children's smiling glances at others when they have successfully met a challenge or achieved something new, like taking their first step. By 3 years of age, children's pride is increasingly tied to the level of their performance. Children express more pride, for example, when they succeed on difficult tasks than on easy ones (Lewis, Alessandri, & Sullivan, 1992).

self-conscious emotions emotions such as guilt, shame, embarrassment, and pride that relate to our sense of self and our consciousness of others' reactions to us

The two other self-conscious emotions, guilt and shame, are sometimes mistakenly thought of as roughly equivalent, but they are actually quite distinct. Guilt is associated with empathy for others and involves feelings of remorse and regret about one's behavior and the desire to undo the consequences of that behavior (Hoffman, 1998). When children feel guilty, they focus on the consequences of their wrongdoing and may try to make it up to those affected by their behavior. In contrast, shame does not seem to be related to concern about others (Eisenberg, 2000; Tangney, 1998). When children feel shame, their focus is on themselves: they feel that they are exposed and they often feel like hiding.

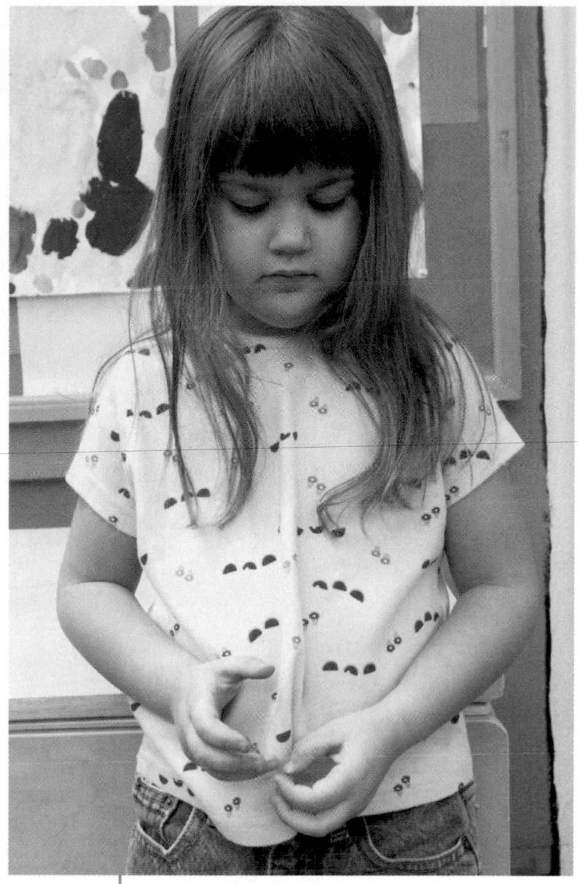
ELLEN B. SENISI

Children in the preschool years often exhibit shame or guilt when they do something wrong.

Shame and guilt can be distinguished fairly early. In one study, researchers arranged for 2-year-olds to play with a rag doll belonging to an adult (the experimenter). The doll had been specially rigged so that one leg would fall off during the course of play, while the adult was out of the room. When the "accident" occurred, some toddlers displayed a pattern of behavior that seemed to reflect shame—that is, they avoided the adult when she returned to the room and delayed telling her about the mishap. Other children showed a pattern of behavior that seemed to reflect guilt—that is, they repaired the doll quickly, told the adult about the mishap shortly after she returned to the room, and showed relatively little avoidance of her (Barrett et al., 1993).

Although some situations may be more likely to elicit shame than guilt, the same situation often elicits shame in some people and guilt in others. Whether children experience guilt or shame partly depends on parental practices. Children are more likely to experience guilt than shame if, when they have done something wrong, their parents emphasize the "badness" of the behavior rather than of the child—saying, for example, "John, you *did* a bad thing when you. . . " as opposed to "John, you're a bad *boy*" or "John, you're so *stupid* [or careless, or mean]" (Tangney & Dearing, 2002). In addition, children are more likely to feel guilt rather than shame if parents help them to understand the consequences their actions have for others, teach them the need to repair the harm they have done, avoid publicly humiliating them or using derisive humor to induce shame, and communicate respect and love of their children even in disciplinary situations (Hoffman, 2000; Tangney & Dearing, 2002).

The situations likely to induce self-conscious emotions in children vary somewhat across cultures. For example, among traditional Zuni Indians, standing out from others is discouraged; thus, Zuni children who achieve an individual success, such as doing better than peers on a project, are likely to feel embarrassment or shame (Benedict, 1934). Similarly, the Japanese tend to avoid bestowing praise because they believe that it engenders a focus on the self rather than on the needs of the larger social group (Lewis, 1992); thus, Japanese children, in comparison with U.S. children, are less likely to experience pride as a consequence of personal success. Moreover, in cultures that emphasize the welfare of the group rather than the individual—such as in Java, Indonesia—the violation of cultural standards that benefit others in the group is likely to result in feelings of shame (Lewis, 1992).

The appearance of the social emotions in the second and third year of life is based not only on the emergence of self-awareness but also on children's growing awareness of adults' reactions and expectations (Lewis, 1998). Pride and shame, in particular, are likely to be stronger when the child understands what behaviors are likely to elicit adult approval or condemnation. Although people can feel pride or shame without someone else's knowing about their actions, it is likely that these emotions initially occur in situations in which young children are interacting with people whose opinions of them matter.

It is common for children to experience a modest increase in negative emotions as they move into adolescence. Often this increase is evidenced in family interactions.

Emotional Development in Childhood

The causes of emotions continue to change in childhood. For example, as the basis of children's self-esteem or self-evaluation changes with cognitive development and experience (see Chapter 11), events that make them feel happiness and pride are likely to change. From early to middle childhood, for instance, acceptance by peers and achieving goals become increasingly important sources of happiness and pride. What makes children smile and laugh also changes with age. As their language skills develop along with their understanding of people and events, children in the preschool years begin to find verbal jokes funny (Dunn, 1988).

Similar examples can be seen in regard to children's negative emotions. For instance, as children's cognitive ability to represent imaginary phenomena develops in the preschool years, they often start to fear imaginary creatures such as ghosts or monsters. Such fears are uncommon in elementary school children (Silverman, La Greca, & Wasserstein, 1995), probably because children of this age have a better understanding of reality than do younger children. Instead, school-age children's anxieties and fears are generally related to important, real-life issues (albeit sometimes exaggerated), such as challenges at school (tests and grades, being called on in class, and pleasing teachers), health (their parents' and their own), and personal harm (being robbed, mugged, or shot). In one study of U.S. second to fifth graders, 56% of the children reported worries about being physically attacked or otherwise harmed by someone (Silverman et al., 1995).

The causes of anger also change as children develop a better understanding of others' intentions and motives in the early school years. For example, in the early preschool years, whether or not a child feels anger when pushed by a peer is not likely to depend on whether the push was intentional. However, by the early school years, children are less likely to be angered if they believe that harm done to them by others was unintentional or that the motive for harmful action was benign rather than malicious (Dodge, Murphy, & Buchsbaum, 1984).

The frequency of experiencing specific emotions also may change in childhood and adolescence. In the preschool and early school years, there is some evidence that, overall, children become less intense and less emotionally negative with age (Guerin & Gottfried, 1994; Murphy, Eisenberg, Fabes, Shepard, & Guthrie, 1999). There also is some support for the common assumption that adolescence is a time of greater negative emotion than is middle childhood. The typical adolescent experiences a mild increase in the frequency or intensity of negative emotions, or a mild decrease in positive emotion, in early to mid-adolescence (Greene, 1990; Larson & Lampman-Petraitis, 1989). At the same time, a minority of adolescents experience a major increase in the occurrence of negative emotions, often in their relations with their parents (Collins, 1990; see Chapter 13). In addition, serious bouts of depression are much more common in adolescence than previously. Only about 1% of 11-year-olds are diagnosed as clinically depressed, that is, in need of treatment (Figure 10.4) (Hankin & Abramson), although reports of subclinical depression and anxiety are considerably higher (Esser, 1990; Weems, Silverman, & La Greca, 2000). In adolescence, the rate of depression increases dramatically—to between 15% and 20% according to one study (Hankin et al., 1998)—

FIGURE 10.4 Development of overall rates of clinical depression by gender and age **Rates of depression increase in early adolescence and increase dramatically at age 15 to 18, especially for girls. (Adapted from Hankin et al., 1998)**

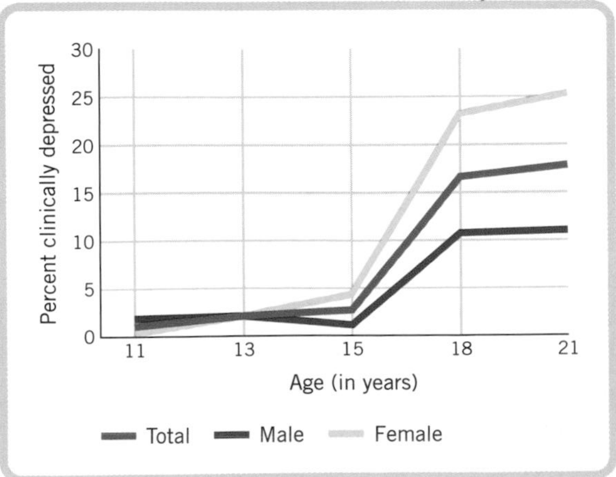

individual differences 10.1

Gender Differences in Adolescent Depression

One of the most striking features of adolescent depression is the sex-related difference in its occurrence. Starting at age 13 to 15 in the United States, girls begin exhibiting higher rates of depression than do boys (Garber, Kelley, & Martin, 2002; Hankin & Abramson, 1999; Nolen-Hoeksema & Girgus, 1994). This difference increases over time and is quite large by about age 18 (see Figure 10.4). Similar gender differences in the patterns of adolescent depression have been found in numerous countries (Hankin et al., 1998; Nolen-Hoeksema, 1990; Wichstrom, 1999).

Why are females more likely to experience depression? Evidence for the role of hormones or, more generally, heredity is fairly weak (Hankin & Abramson, 1999). Rather, the key factor may be the greater stress that adolescence represents for females (Petersen, Sarigiani, & Kennedy, 1991), at least in certain cultures. One important stressor can be concerns about one's body and appearance. As discussed in Chapter 3, adolescent females in the United States report greater dissatisfaction with their bodies than males report with theirs; this dissatisfaction, fueled by a cultural obsession with an "ideal" body type attainable only by a few, seems to contribute substantially to low self-esteem and depression (Hankin & Abramson, 1999; Wichstrom, 1999).

Another stressor for girls can be early or late puberty, which represents a clear risk for depression. Early maturity may create stress for girls because males are likely to pressure them to engage in behaviors typical of older adolescents, including sexual activity, drinking, and delinquency, and many younger girls may not be cognitively and socially mature enough to cope with these pressures (Ge, Conger, & Elder, 1996). Being a late maturer may be related to depression in girls because their "unwomanly" physical appearance is different from that of their peers (Wichstrom, 1999). In either case, concerns about acceptance by others are likely to arise, and girls appear to be more likely than boys to be upset and depressed by problems in their peer relationships (Nolen-Hoeksema, 2001).

It is also likely that adolescent girls, like young women, are more prone than their male peers to ruminate—that is, to repeatedly focus on symptoms of their distress ("I'm so fat" or "I'm so tired") and on the meaning of their distress ("What's wrong with my life?") (Nolen-Hoeksema, Larson, & Grayson, 1999). Such thinking appears to increase the chances of females' becoming depressed (Hankin & Abramson, 1999).

and subclinical depression increases dramatically as well (Wichstrom, 1999). These changes in emotionality in adolescence likely reflect a combination of the physiological changes of puberty and increases in stressful peer or familial interactions. (Box 10.1 discusses gender differences in adolescent depression.)

review:

Emotions are fundamental to much of human functioning and undergo change in the early months and years of life. Smiles emerge early but do not become social until the second to third month of life, and what makes children smile and laugh changes with age and cognitive development. Distress in newborns involves hunger and various other discomforts; by 6 to 7 months of age, it is often caused by a stranger's approach; and by approximately 8 months of age, it is likely to be triggered by a separation from parents. Separation distress develops in similar ways in various cultures and in blind children.

It is hard to know exactly when anger emerges because distress/pain and anger are difficult to differentiate early in life. Children may experience anger by the second month of life in response to loss of control. In the first months, it is similarly difficult to differentiate fear from distress, but fear likely has emerged by 6 or 7 months of age, when children appear to feel fear of strangers. Young children also exhibit sadness, especially when they are separated from loved ones for extended periods of time.

The self-conscious emotions—embarrassment, pride, shame, and guilt—emerge somewhat later than most emotions, probably in the second year of life. Their emergence is tied in part to the development of a rudimentary sense of self and to an appreciation of others' reactions to the self. Situations that evoke these emotions vary across cultures.

Emotions continue to change in their occurrence and causes in childhood and adolescence. Age-related cognitive, biological, and experiential factors likely account for these changes.

emotional self-regulation the process of initiating, inhibiting, or modulating internal feeling states, emotion-related physiological processes, and emotion-related cognitions or behaviors in the service of accomplishing one's goals

Regulation of Emotion

Throughout life, being able to regulate one's emotions is crucial to achieving one's goals. This is no simple task. Indeed, **emotional self-regulation** is a complex process that involves initiating, inhibiting, or modulating several components in the service of accomplishing one's goals. These components include (1) *internal feeling states* (the subjective experience of emotion); (2) *emotion-related physiological processes* (e.g., heart rate, hormonal, or other physiological reactions associated with emotions); (3) *emotion-related cognitions* (e.g., thoughts about what one wants or how to interpret a situation); and (4) *emotion-related behavior* (e.g., facial expressions of feelings or aggression due to anger).

The emergence of emotional regulation in childhood is a long, slow process. Obviously, young infants are not very good at controlling their emotional reactions. They are easily overwhelmed by loud noises, abrupt movements, hunger, or pain and must rely on their caregivers to settle them down. Older infants also have difficulty dealing with intense emotions such as fear of strangers or of being left alone, and they often run to parents for comfort. Indeed, it takes years for children to develop the abilities to reliably regulate their emotions and control the behaviors associated with them.

The Development of Emotional Regulation

The development of emotional regulation is characterized by three general age-related patterns of change. The first pattern involves the transition from infants' relying almost totally on other people to help them regulate their emotions to their increasing ability to self-regulate during early childhood. The second related pattern involves the use of cognitive strategies to control negative emotions. The third pattern involves the selection of appropriate regulating strategies.

The Shift from Caregiver Regulation to Self-Regulation

In the first months of life, parents help infants regulate their emotional arousal by controlling their exposure to stimulating events (Gianino & Tronick, 1988). When an infant is distressed, frustrated, or frightened, parents typically try to soothe or distract the baby. For example, they often calm a crying infant by talking to the infant in a soft, reassuring tone of voice or, after the infant is a few months old, by diverting his or her attention to an interesting object.

However, young infants' reliance on adults' efforts to regulate them starts to change quickly. By 6 months of age, infants can reduce their distress by averting their gaze in arousing or uncertain situations. Occasionally 6-month-olds can also *self-soothe*—that is, engage in stylized or repetitive rubbing or stroking of their bodies or clothing—or distract themselves by specifically looking at neutral or positive objects rather than at upsetting persons or objects. Between ages 1 and 2, infants increasingly avert their attention to nondistressing objects or people to distract themselves from distressing stimuli (Grolnick, Bridges, & Connell, 1996; Mangelsdorf, Shapiro, & Marzolf, 1995; Parritz, 1996). Such changes in young children's behavior probably are made possible by their growing ability to control both their own attention and their movements.

Over the course of the early years, children develop and improve their ability to distract themselves when distressed by playing on their own, and they become less likely to seek comfort from their parents when they must delay gratification or are upset (Bridges & Grolnick, 1995). In addition, because they are better able to use language with age, when they do seek comfort, children are more likely to discuss upsetting emotional situations with parents rather than simply cry (Kopp, 1992). With age, children's ability to regulate their expression of negative emotion also improves. Instead of disobeying parents or throwing a temper tantrum, children can increasingly manage their negative emotional arousal by talking to others and negotiating ways to resolve situations that at least partially meet their own needs (Klimes-Dougan & Kopp, 1999; Kopp, 1992). For example, if a preschooler is unhappy about being told by a parent to stop playing immediately and to clean up his or her room, the child may verbally protest and lobby for extra play time rather than crying or throwing a tantrum.

LAURA DWIGHT

Parents often help young children to regulate themselves by physically calming them or distracting them with an object.

Children's improving self-regulation may be due not only to age-related increases in their control of their attention and movements but also to changes in what adults expect of children. As children age, adults increasingly expect them to manage their own emotional arousal and behavior. Once children are capable of crawling, for example, they are viewed as more responsible for their behavior and for complying with parental expectations (Campos, Kermoian, & Zumbahlen, 1992). At about 9 to 12 months of age, children start to show awareness of adults' demands and begin to regulate themselves accordingly. For example, they are increasingly likely to comply with simple instructions, such as to not touch dangerous objects. In the second year of life, they also show increases in the ability to inhibit their motor behavior—such as slowing down their walking when asked to do so (Kochanska, Murray, & Harlan, 2000). Although these abilities are quite limited in the toddler years, they improve considerably in the fourth year of life (Reed, Pien, & Rothbart, 1984) and further improve in the school years (Williams, Ponesse, Schacher, Logan, & Tannock, 1999). As a result, children are increasingly able to conform to adults' expectations, such as not hurting others when angered and staying seated at school when they would much prefer to get up and talk or play.

The Use of Cognitive Strategies to Control Negative Emotion

Whereas younger children most often regulate negative emotions by using behavioral strategies, such as distracting themselves with play, older children also are able to use cognitive strategies such as mentally distracting themselves from negative or stressful events or trying to see things in a positive light (Altshuler, Genevro, Ruble, & Bornstein, 1995; Mischel & Mischel, 1983). In the delay-of-gratification studies discussed at the beginning of the chapter, for example, Mischel found that 5-year-olds were more aware than preschool children that focusing their attention away from the desired food would help them to delay gratification and obtain an extra treat. By sixth grade, children recognized that thinking about desirable treats in an abstract manner unrelated to their desirability helps in resisting temptation (Mischel & Mischel, 1983). To resist pretzels, for example, they would have been able to think about how the pretzels could be used to make a toy log cabin rather than about how good they would taste.

As children age, they are also better able, when necessary, to use cognitive strategies to adjust to emotionally difficult situations. Finding themselves caught in unpleasant or threatening circumstances, they may think about their goals or the meaning of events in a different light so they can adapt gracefully to the situation. This ability helps children avoid acting in ways that might be counterproductive. When children are teased by peers, for example, they may be able to defuse the situation by downplaying the importance of the teasing and not reacting to it in a way that would provoke more teasing.

social competence the ability to achieve personal goals in social interactions while simultaneously maintaining positive relationships with others

The Selection of Appropriate Regulatory Strategies

In dealing with emotion, children, over time, are increasingly able to select cognitive or behavioral strategies that are appropriate for the particular situation and stressor (Brenner & Salovey, 1997). One reason for this is that, with age, children are more aware that whether or not a particular coping behavior is appropriate depends on the individual's specific needs and goals, as well as on the nature of the problem. In one demonstration of this increasing ability, fifth, eighth, and eleventh graders were presented with everyday problem situations—such as not getting into a computer class that they really wanted to take—and were asked to rate how good various responses would be for dealing with the particular situation. Responses to the computer-class dilemma included such possibilities as "Find out why you did not get into the computer class," "Spend some time after school each day on the computer working through a book you bought about computers," and "Decide not to learn how to use the computers." On this dilemma as well as on the others presented, the children's selection of coping solutions deemed most appropriate by teachers increased with age (Berg, 1989).

Children's improving ability to select appropriate strategies for dealing with negative situations is also aided by their increasing ability to distinguish between stressors that can be controlled (such as homework) and those that cannot be (such as painful medical procedures), as well as choosing the most effective strategies for managing their reactions to these stressors. Older children, for example, are more aware than younger children that in situations they cannot control, it is easier to manage their emotion by simply adapting to the situation rather than trying to change it (e.g., Altshuler et al., 1995; Hoffner, 1993; Rudolph, Dennig, & Weisz, 1995). Faced with having to undergo major surgery, for instance, older children may adapt by trying to think about the positive consequences of having the surgery, such as being in better health afterward, or by distracting themselves by thinking about or engaging in enjoyable activities. Younger children, in contrast, are more likely to insist that they don't need the operation.

The Relation of Emotional Regulation to Social Competence and Adjustment

As we noted earlier, the development of emotional regulation has important consequences for children, especially with regard to their social competence. **Social competence** is a set of skills that help individuals achieve their personal goals in social interactions while maintaining positive relationships with others (Rubin et al., 1998). Children who are better able to inhibit inappropriate behaviors, delay gratification, and use cognitive methods of controlling their emotion and behavior tend to be socially competent overall, liked by their peers, and well adjusted (Calkins & Dedmon, 2000; Gilliom, Shaw, Beck, Schonberg, & Lukon, 2002; Lemery, Essex, & Snider, 2002; Lengua, 2002).

Similarly, children who are able to deal constructively with stressful situations—negotiating with others to settle conflicts, planning strategies to resolve upsetting situations, seeking social support, and so on—generally are more socially competent overall than are children who avoid dealing with stressful situations altogether (Compas, Saltzman, Thomsen, & Wadsworth, 2001). Children and adolescents who know how to solicit social support when they need help, or to share their concerns or anxieties, also are likely to deal relatively well with the many stressors that most children face (Bryant, 1987; Rutter, 1987).

review:

Children's efforts to regulate their emotions and emotionally driven behavior change with age. Whereas young infants must rely on adults to manage their emotions, older infants and young children increasingly develop means to regulate their own emotions and behavior through methods such as averting their attention, self-soothing, and distracting themselves with other activities. Their ability to inhibit their actions also improves with age. Improvements in children's regulatory capacities likely are based on increases in their abilities to control their attention and their own bodies, as well as on changes in adults' expectations of them.

In contrast to young children, who often try to cope with their emotions by taking direct action, older children also are able to use cognitive modes of coping, such as trying to think about something else or focusing on positive aspects of a negative situation. In addition, they are increasingly able to select ways of regulating themselves and coping with stress that are appropriate to the requirements of specific situations.

The abilities to regulate one's emotions and related behavior, and to deal constructively with stressful situations, are associated with high social competence and low levels of problem behavior.

Individual Differences in Emotion and Its Regulation

Although there are similarities among children in the overall development of their emotions and self-regulatory capabilities, there also are very large individual differences in their emotional functioning. Some infants and children are relatively mellow; they do not become upset easily and are better able than other children their own age to calm down when they are upset. Other children are quite emotional; they get upset quickly, and their negative emotion persists for a long time, with the result that others find it difficult to interact with them. Moreover, children differ in their timidity, in their expression of positive emotion, and in the ways they deal with their emotions. Compare these two 3-year-old children, Maria and Bruce, as they react to Teri, an adult female stranger:

> When Teri walks over to Maria and starts to talk with her, Maria smiles and is eager to show Teri what she is doing. When Teri asks Maria if she would like to go down the hall to the play room (where experiments are conducted), Maria jumps up and takes Teri's hand.
>
> In contrast, when Teri walks over to Bruce, Bruce turns away. He doesn't talk to her and averts his eyes. When Teri asks him if he wants to play a game, Bruce moves away, looks timid, and softly says "no."
>
> (Eisenberg, laboratory observations)

Children also vary in the speed with which they express their emotions, as illustrated by the differences in these two preschool boys:

> When someone crosses Taylor, his wrath is immediate. There is no question how he is feeling, no time to correct the situation before he erupts. Douglas, though, seems almost to consider the ongoing emotional situation. One can almost see annoyance building until he finally sputters, "Stop that!"
>
> (Denham, 1998, p. 21)

A number of explanations have been suggested for the differences among children in their emotionality and regulation of emotion, as well as in their tendencies to react to others with timidity. Some explanations emphasize biologically based

temperament constitutionally based individual differences in emotional, motor, and attentional reactivity and self-regulation that demonstrate consistency across situations, as well as relative stability over time

differences in children as reflected in their temperaments; others highlight the role of socialization in the development of children's personalities. Almost certainly, both biological and environmental factors contribute to the differences we see in children's emotions and related behaviors.

Temperament

Because infants differ so much in their emotional reactivity, even from birth, it is commonly assumed that children are born with different emotional characteristics. Differences in various aspects of children's emotional reactivity that emerge early in life are labeled as dimensions of **temperament.** Mary Rothbart and John Bates, two leaders in the study of temperament, define temperament as

> constitutionally based individual differences in emotional, motor, and attentional reactivity and self-regulation. Temperamental characteristics are seen to demonstrate consistency across situations, as well as relative stability over time.
>
> (Rothbart & Bates, 1998, p. 109)

The phrase "constitutionally based" in this definition means biologically based and refers to both heredity and to aspects of biological functioning such as neural development and hormonal responding that can be affected by the environment during the prenatal period and after birth. Thus, the construct of temperament is highly relevant to our themes of *individual differences* and the role of *nature and nurture* in development.

The pioneering work in the field of temperament research was the New York Longitudinal Study, conducted by Stella Chess and Alexander Thomas (Thomas, Chess, & Birch, 1963; Thomas & Chess, 1977). These researchers began by interviewing a sample of parents repeatedly and in depth about their infants' specific behaviors. To reduce the possibility of bias in the parents' reports, the researchers asked the parents to provide detailed descriptions of their infant's behavior rather than interpretive characterizations; and to promote parental candor, they attempted to remain completely nonjudgmental. From those interviews, nine aspects of infants' temperament were identified: activity level, rhythmicity, approach/withdrawal, adaptability, intensity of reaction, threshold of responsiveness, quality of mood, distractability, and attention span (see Table 10.2). On the basis of these characteristics, infants were classified into three groups: easy, difficult, and slow-to-warm-up.

1. *Easy babies* adjusted easily to new situations, quickly established routines, and generally were cheerful in mood and easy to calm.
2. *Difficult babies* were slow to adjust to new experiences, likely to react negatively and intensely to stimuli and events, and irregular in their bodily functions.
3. *Slow-to-warm-up babies* were somewhat difficult at first but became easier over time.

In the initial study, 40% of the infants were classified as easy, 10% as difficult, and 15% as slow-to-warm-up. The rest did not fit into one of these categories. Of particular importance, some dimensions of children's temperament showed relative stability over time, with temperament in infancy predicting how children were doing years later. For example, difficult infants tended to have problems with adjustment and at school, whereas few of the easy children had difficulties of these sorts. (We return to the issue of stability of temperament and its social and emotional correlates shortly.)

TABLE 10.2

Examples of Thomas and Chess's Temperament Dimensions at Different Ages

Temperamental Quality	Rating	2 Months	2 Years	10 Years
Activity level	High	Moves often in sleep. Wriggles when diaper is changed.	Climbs furniture. Explores. Gets in and out of bed while being put to sleep.	Plays ball and engages in other sports. Cannot sit still long enough to do homework.
	Low	Does not move when being dressed or during sleep.	Enjoys quiet play with puzzles. Can listen to records for hours.	Likes chess and reading. Eats very slowly.
Rhythmicity	Regular	Has been on four-hour feeding schedule since birth. Regular bowel movement.	Eats a big lunch each day. Always has a snack before bedtime.	Eats only at mealtimes. Sleeps the same amount of time each night.
	Irregular	Awakes at a different time each morning. Size of feedings varies.	Nap time changes from day to day. Toilet training is difficult because bowel movement is unpredictable.	Food intake varies. Falls asleep at a different time each night.
Distractability	Distractable	Will stop crying for food if rocked. Stops fussing if given pacifier when diaper is being changed.	Will stop tantrum if another activity is suggested.	Needs absolute silence for homework. Has a hard time choosing a shirt in a store because they all appeal to him.
	Not distractable	Will not stop crying when diaper is changed. Fusses after eating, even if rocked.	Screams if refused some desired object. Ignores mother's calling.	Can read a book while television is at high volume. Does chores on schedule.
Approach/ withdrawal	Positive	Smiles and licks washcloth. Has always liked bottle.	Slept well the first time he stayed overnight at grandparents' house.	Went to camp happily. Loved to ski the first time.
	Negative	Rejected cereal the first time. Cries when strangers appear.	Avoids strange children in the playground. Whimpers first time at beach. Will not go into water.	Severely homesick at camp during first days. Does not like new activities.
Adaptability	Adaptive	Was passive during first bath; now enjoys bathing. Smiles at nurse.	Obeys quickly. Stayed contentedly with grandparents for a week.	Likes camp, although homesick during first days. Learns enthusiastically.
	Not adaptive	Still startled by sudden, sharp noise. Resists diapering.	Cries and screams each time hair is cut. Disobeys persistently.	Does not adjust well to new school or new teacher. Comes home late for dinner even when punished.
Attention span and persistence	Long	If soiled, continues to cry until changed. Repeatedly rejects water if he wants milk.	Works on a puzzle until it is completed. Watches when shown how to do something.	Reads for two hours before sleeping. Does homework carefully.
	Short	Cries when awakened but stops almost immediately. Objects only mildly if cereal precedes bottle.	Gives up easily if a toy is hard to use. Asks for help immediately if undressing becomes difficult.	Gets up frequently from homework for a snack. Never finishes a book.
Intensity of reaction	Intense	Cries when diapers are wet. Rejects food vigorously when satisfied.	Yells if he feels excitement or delight. Cries loudly if a toy is taken away.	Tears up an entire page of homework if one mistake is made. Slams door of room when teased by younger brother.
	Mild	Does not cry when diapers are wet. Whimpers instead of crying when hungry.	When another child hit her, she looked surprised, did not hit back.	When a mistake is made in a model airplane, corrects it quietly. Does not comment when reprimanded.
Threshold of responsiveness	Low	Stops sucking on bottle when approached.	Runs to door when father comes home. Must always be tucked tightly into bed.	Rejects fatty foods. Adjusts shower until water is at exactly the right temperature.
	High	Is not startled by loud noises. Takes bottle and breast equally well.	Can be left with anyone. Falls asleep easily on either back or stomach.	Never complains when sick. Eats all foods.
Quality of mood	Positive	Smacks lips when first tasting new food. Smiles at parents.	Plays with sister; laughs and giggles. Smiles when he succeeds in putting shoes on.	Enjoys new accomplishments. Laughs aloud when reading a funny passage.
	Negative	Fusses after nursing. Cries when carriage is rocked.	Cries and squirms when given haircut. Cries when mother leaves.	Cries when he cannot solve a homework problem. Very "weepy" if he does not get enough sleep.

Adapted from Thomas, Chess, and Birch (1970)

ALFRED EISENSTAEDT / TIMEPIX

Due partly to variations in temperament, children often show very different reactions to the same situation.

Since the ground-breaking efforts of Thomas and Chess, extensive work has been devoted to determining how best to conceptualize and measure various aspects of temperament (see Box 10.2). In contrast to Thomas and Chess's approach, many contemporary theorists and researchers believe that it is important to assess positive and negative emotion as separate components of temperament, to differentiate among types of negative emotionality, and to assess different types of regulatory capacities. Recent research that has taken this approach suggests that infant temperament is captured by six dimensions (Rothbart & Bates, 1998):

1. *Fearful distress*—distress and withdrawal in new situations and how long it takes a child to adjust
2. *Irritable distress*—fussiness, anger, and frustration, especially if the child is not allowed to do what he or she wants
3. *Attention span and persistence*—duration of orienting toward objects or events of interest
4. *Activity level*—how much an infant moves (e.g., kicks, crawls)
5. *Positive affect*—smiling and laughter, approach to people, degree of cooperativeness and manageability
6. *Rhythmicity*—the regularity and predictability of the child's bodily functions such as eating and sleeping

In childhood, only the first five aspects of temperament are particularly important in classifying children and predicting their behavior (Rothbart & Bates, 1998). The terms used by investigators to refer to these dimensions vary somewhat—for example, irritable distress may be called frustration or anger—but these dimensions generally include most of the aspects of temperament that have been studied extensively.

Stability of Temperament Over Time

As we have seen, temperament, by definition, involves traits that remain relatively stable over time. One example of such stability can be seen in the research described in Box 10.2, in which children who as infants showed behavioral inhibition, or fearful distress, with novel stimuli also showed elevated levels of fear in novel situations at age 2 and elevated levels of social inhibition at age 4½. In similar patterns of stability, children who at age 3 are more prone to negative emotion than are their peers tend to be more negative than their peers at age 6 or 8 (Guerin & Gottfried, 1994; Rothbart, Derryberry, & Hershey, 2000). Children who are high in the ability to focus attention in the preschool years are also high in this ability at age 11 to 12 (Murphy et al., 1999). Some aspects of temperament show a degree of consistency even from the prenatal period into the postnatal period. In one longitudinal study, for example, fetuses who were very active in the womb after 20 weeks of gestation tended to be more active, difficult, unpredictable, and nonadaptive at 3 months and 6 months of age (DiPietro, Hodgson, Costigan, & Johnson, 1996).

JON FEINGERSH / CORBIS STOCK MARKET

A fetus's activity level in the womb appears to be related to some aspects of postnatal temperament. Fetuses who are more active tend to be active, difficult, and nonadaptive in the first half-year of life.

It is important to note, however, that some aspects of temperament tend to be more stable than others. Over the course of infancy, activity level, for example, may be less stable than positive emotionality, fear, and distress/anger (Lemery, Goldsmith, Klinnert, & Mrazek, 1999), and there is considerable change during childhood in the degree to which children are extremely high or low in reactivity when confronted with unfamiliar situations, people, or objects (Kagan, Snidman, & Arcus, 1998).

The Role of Temperament in Children's Social Skills and Adjustment

One of the reasons for researchers' deep interest in temperament is that it plays an important role in determining children's social adjustment. Consider a boy who is prone to negative emotions such as anger and often has difficulty controlling them. Compared with other boys, he is likely to sulk, yell at others, be defiant with adults, and be aggressive with peers. Such behaviors often lead to long-term problems in adjustment and in getting along with others. Consequently, it is not surprising that differences among children in aspects of their temperament such as anger/irritability, positive emotion, and the ability to inhibit behavior—aspects reflected in the difference between difficult and easy temperament—have been associated with differences in children's social competence and adjustment (Eisenberg, Fabes, Guthrie, & Reiser, 2000; Guerin, Gottfried, & Thomas, 1997; Rothbart & Bates, 1998).

Such differences are highlighted by a large longitudinal study in New Zealand conducted by Avshalom Caspi, Terrie Moffitt, and their colleagues. These researchers found that children who were negative, impulsive, and unregulated as young children tended as adolescents or young adults to have more problems with adjustment, such as not getting along with others, than did peers with other temperaments. They also were more likely to engage in illegal behaviors and to get in trouble with the law (Caspi, Henry, McGee, Moffitt & Silva, 1995; Caspi & Silva, 1995; Henry, Caspi, Moffitt, & Silva, 1994). In addition, at age 21, they reported getting along less well with whomever they were living with (e.g., roommates) and experiencing more unemployment. Furthermore, in their intimate relationships at age 21, they reported fewer mutual interests, more unequal balance of power, and less intimacy and trust. As adults, they tended to have few people from whom they could get social support (Caspi, 2000).

Researchers also have found that behaviorally inhibited children are more likely than other children to have problems such as anxiety, depression, phobias, and social withdrawal at older ages (Biederman et al., 1990; Rothbart & Bates, 1998). Thus, different problems with adjustment seem to be associated with different temperaments.

However, how children ultimately adjust depends not only on their temperament but also on how their temperament fits with the particular environment they

a closer look

Measurement of Temperament

Currently a number of different methods are used to assess temperament. In one method, similar to that used by Thomas and Chess, parents or other adults (often teachers or observers) periodically report on aspects of a child's temperament, such as fearfulness, anger/frustration, and positive affect. These reports, based on observations of the children in various contexts, tend to be fairly stable over time and predict general later development in such areas as behavioral problems, anxiety disorders, and social competence (see table) (Rothbart, Ahadi, & Evans, 2000; Rothbart & Bates, 1998).

Laboratory observations have also been used to assess temperament, often with respect to a dimension called **behavioral inhibition.** Behaviorally inhibited children tend to be high in fearful distress and are particularly fearful and restrained when dealing with novel or stressful situations. In a longitudinal study conducted by Jerome Kagan, investigators observed young children's reactions to a variety of novel sights and experiences. The observations were conducted in early infancy, at age 2, and at age 4½. About 20% of the children were consistently quite inhibited and reactive when exposed to the unfamiliar stimuli. As infants, these children cried and thrashed about when brightly colored toys were moved back and forth in front of their faces or when cotton swabs dipped in dilute alcohol were applied to their noses. At age 2 years, one-third of these inhibited children were highly fearful in unfamiliar laboratory situations—such as being exposed to a loud noise, the smell of alcohol, and an unfamiliar woman dressed in a clown outfit—and nearly all showed at least some fear in these situations.

Other children were less reactive: as infants, they rarely fussed when they encountered the novel experiences, and at age 2, most showed little or no fear in the unfamiliar situations. At the age of 4½ years, the children who had been reactive to unfamiliar situations were more subdued, less social, and less positive in their behavior than were the uninhibited children, who were relatively spontaneous, asked questions of the researchers when being evaluated, commented on events happening around them, and smiled and laughed more (Kagan, 1997; Kagan, Snidman, & Arcus, 1998). Thus, laboratory observations appear to be good measures of children's reactions to unfamiliarity, an aspect of temperament that is quite evident for some youngsters.

Physiological measures also have proved useful for assessing some aspects of children's temperament. For example, Kagan (1998) has found differences in the variability of heart rate in high-reactive and low-reactive children. Heart rate variability—how much an individual's heart rate normally fluctuates—is believed to reflect, in part, the way the central nervous system responds to novel situations and the individual's ability to regulate emotion (Porges, 1991; Porges, Doussard-Roosevelt, & Maiti, 1994). Children who have heart rates that are constantly high and vary little as a function of breathing tend to be highly reactive and inhibited in response to novel situations. In contrast, children who have variable and often lower heart rates tend to exhibit high positive emotions and low negative reactions in stressful situations, such as when toddlers are confronted with barriers that prevent them from reaching desirable objects (Calkins, 1997; Porges et al., 1994).

Children's emotional responses to new situations and their negative and positive emotionality also appear to be reflected in the electroencephalographic brain-wave patterns produced by the left and right lobes of their frontal cortex (see Chapter 3, p. 106) (Davidson & Fox, 1982; Fox, 1994). Activation of the left frontal lobe as measured with an electroencephalogram (EEG) has been associated with approach behavior, positive affect, exploration, and sociability. Activation of the

behavioral inhibition a temperamentally based style of responding. Behaviorally inhibited children tend to be high in fearful distress and are particularly fearful and restrained when dealing with novel or stressful situations.

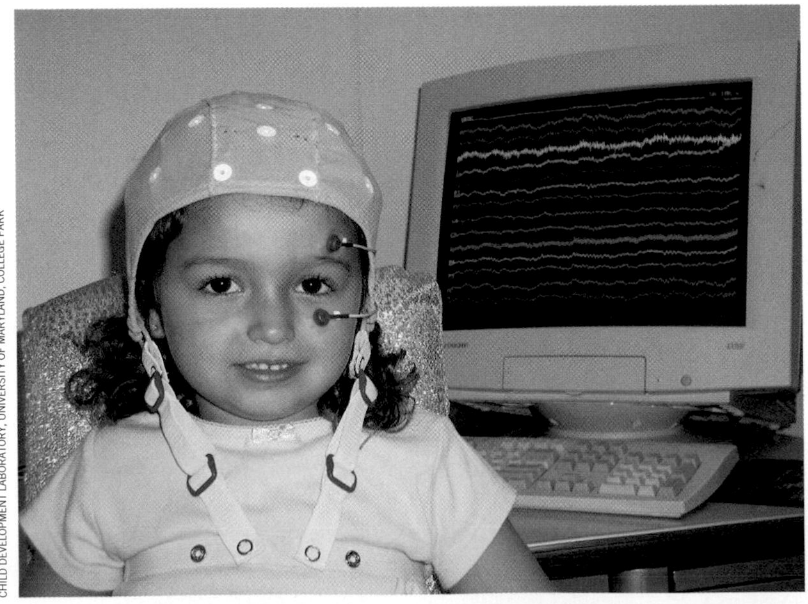

COURTESY OF SEAN FLANAGAN & STACEY BARTON, CHILD DEVELOPMENT LABORATORY, UNIVERSITY OF MARYLAND, COLLEGE PARK

Nathan Fox and his colleagues have found that children who tend to experience positive emotions and approach new situations show a different pattern of EEG activation than children who tend to experience negative emotions and are more inhibited in their behavior. However, it is unclear if EEG patterns change as a function of children's behavior or if brain waves reflect an aspect of physiological functioning that causes these patterns in behavior.

right frontal lobe has been linked to withdrawal, negative affect, fear, and anxiety. Of particular interest, infants who are highly reactive to novel stimuli (that is, who show high levels of negative emotion and motor activity) show greater activation of the right frontal cortex in novel situations than do less reactive infants (Calkins, Fox, & Marshall, 1996). EEG patterns of frontal lobe activation also have been linked with emotionality and social competence in preschool-age children. For example, in a study of 4-year-olds interacting with three same-sex peers, children who showed social initiative and positive affect exhibited greater relative activation in the left hemisphere. In contrast, children who tended to withdraw from social interactions—playing alone, for example, or doing nothing during play sessions with peers—exhibited greater activation of the right frontal lobe (Fox et al., 1995). Research of this type indicates that aspects of children's temperament and brain activity are interrelated.

Each type of measure of temperament has advantages and disadvantages, and there is considerable debate regarding the merits of the various methods (Kagan, 1998; Rothbart & Bates, 1998). The key advantage of parents' reports of temperament is that parents have extensive knowledge of their children's behavior in many different situations. One important disadvantage of parents' reports is that they may not always be objective, as suggested by the fact that they sometimes do not correspond with what is found with laboratory measures (Seifer, Sameroff, Barrett, & Kraufchuk, 1994). Another disadvantage is that many parents do not have wide knowledge of other children's behavior to use as a basis for comparison when reporting on their own children (what is irritability to some parents, for example, may be near-placidness to others).

The key advantage of laboratory observational data is that such data are less likely to be biased than is an adult's personal view of the child. A key disadvantage is that children's behavior usually is observed in only a limited set of circumstances. Consequently, laboratory observational measures may reflect a child's mood or behavior at a given moment, in a particular context, rather than reflecting the child's general temperament. Physiological measures such as an EEG are also relatively objective and unlikely to be biased, but there is no way to tell whether the processes reflected by physiological measures are a cause or consequence of the child's emotion and behavior in the specific situation. It is unclear, for example, whether left and right frontal lobe activity triggers, or is triggered by, a particular emotional response. Thus, no measure of temperament is foolproof, and it is prudent to measure temperament with a variety of different measures.

10.2

Examples of Items in Mary Rothbart's Temperament Scales

Response scale for items:

1 Never	2 Very rarely	3 Less than half the time	4 About half the time	5 More than half the time	6 Almost always	7 Always	X Does not apply

Temperament dimension	Sample items in infant scale	Sample items in child scale
Fearful distress	How often during the last week did the baby: —cry or show distress at a loud sound (blender, vacuum cleaner, etc.)? —cry or show distress at a change in parents' appearance (glasses off, shower cap on, etc.)?	—Is not afraid of large dogs and/or other animals. —Is afraid of loud noises.
Irritability (or distress at limitations in infancy and anger/frustration in childhood)	When having to wait for food or liquids during the last week, how often did the baby: —seem not bothered? —show mild fussing? —cry loudly?	—Has temper tantrums when s/he doesn't get what s/he wants. —Gets mad when even mildly criticized.
Attention span	How often during the last week did the baby: —look at pictures in books and/or magazines for 5 minutes or longer at a time? —play with one toy or object for 10 minutes or longer?	—When drawing or coloring in a book, shows strong concentration. —When building or putting something together, becomes very involved in what s/he's doing, and works for long periods.
Activity level	During feeding (during the last week), how often did the baby: —lie or sit quietly? —squirm or kick? —wave arms?	—Tends to run, rather than walk, from room to room. —When outside, often sits quietly.
Positive affectivity	When tossed around playfully (during the last week), how often did the baby: —smile? —laugh?	—Smiles and laughs during play with parents. —Usually has a serious expression, even during play.

Adapted from Rothbart Infant Behavior Questionnaire and Child Behavior Questionnaire (unpublished documents)

goodness of fit the degree to which an individual's temperament is compatible with the demands and expectations of his or her social environment

are in—what is often called **goodness of fit.** For example, if children with difficult temperaments have parents who are supportive and consistent in their parenting, their outcomes are more favorable than if their parents are punitive, rejecting, or inconsistent in their parenting. Drawing on their New York Longitudinal Study, Thomas and Chess described a case in which a girl with a difficult temperament had parents who initially did not deal well with her temperament but who learned to do so with help from the researchers.

> Ellen . . . had a difficult temperament as a child. Her parents were intelligent and well-meaning, but they did not understand Ellen's behavior and responded to her inconsistently and with frequent scolding. As a result of this poorness of fit, the child developed a mild behavior disorder with excessive resistance and crying to any criticism, even if given gently, overreaction to her younger sister's teasing, with loud screams and shouts of "leave me alone," similar intense negative responses to any change in family plans, and a strong tendency to be a worrier and apprehensive. The parents came for advice, and were quickly responsive to an explanation of Ellen's temperament and the need for firm but quiet, patient, and consistent management. The girl's symptoms disappeared within a year, and her social and academic development progressed smoothly thereafter. When interviewed recently in our current follow-up, she was launched successfully on a professional career, was happily married, and functioning well socially. She continued to be intensely expressive, but it was now predominantly positive instead of negative. Ellen explained that she is afraid of expressing anger. "I'm afraid it will come out violently. I put the cork on and it simmers." . . . . In summary, Ellen, as a young adult, retains some features of difficult temperament, including intensity of expression. She also still has discomfort with new situations ("I was always that way") but does not let this interfere with her involvement and mastery of any important situation or demand.
>
> (Chess & Thomas, 1990, pp. 214–215)

Thus, children's adjustment and social competence are predicted by the combination of their temperament and their parents' child-rearing practices. Moreover, the child's temperament and parents' socialization efforts seem to affect one another over time (Cook, Kenny, & Goldstein, 1991; Eisenberg, Fabes, et al. 1999). For example, parents of negative, unregulated children may eventually become less patient and more punitive with their children, and this intensification of disciplining may cause their children to become even more negative and unregulated. Thus, temperament plays a role in the development of children's social and psychological adjustment, but that role is complex and varies as a function of the child's social environment.

review:

Temperament refers to individual differences in various aspects of children's emotional reactivity, regulation, and other characteristics such as behavioral inhibition and activity level. Temperament is believed to have a constitutional basis, but it is also is affected by experiences in the environment, including social interactions. Temperament tends to be somewhat stable over time, although the degree of its stability varies across the dimensions of temperament and individuals.

Temperament plays an important role in adjustment. A difficult and unmanageable temperament in childhood tends to predict problem behaviors in childhood and adulthood, and children who as infants are fearful and reactive to novel objects, places, and people sometimes have later difficulties in interactions with other people, including peers. However, children whose temperaments put them at risk for poor adjustment often do well if they receive sensitive and appropriate parenting and if there is a good fit between their temperament and their social environment.

Children's Emotional Development in the Family

It is clear that the dimensions of temperament related to emotional development are linked to heredity. Twin and adoption studies show that identical twins are more similar than are fraternal twins in the intensity of their emotional reactions, shyness, and sociability, as well as in other aspects of **personality.** Furthermore, biological siblings tend to be more similar to one another in some aspects of temperament than do siblings who are not biologically related. On the basis of such studies, it is estimated that genes account for a substantial portion of the variation in some aspects of temperament (McCrae et al., 2000; Robinson, Kagan, Reznick, & Corley, 1992; Saudino, McGuire, Reiss, Hetherington, & Plomin, 1995).

However, some aspects of temperament may be more genetically based than others. For example, studies of toddler twins suggest that heredity plays a moderate role in individual variation in negative emotions such as anger and social fearfulness but a much smaller role in positive emotion (Emde et al., 1992; Goldsmith, Buss, & Lemery, 1997).

Findings in behavioral genetics research also suggest that several environmental factors play an important role in shaping individual differences in temperament, including those related to children's emotionality (Caspi, 1998; Goldsmith et al., 1997). Chief among these factors are children's relationships with their parents and their parents' socialization practices.

personality the pattern of behavioral and emotional propensities, beliefs and interests, and intellectual capacities that characterize an individual. Personality has its roots in temperament (and thus has a constitutional basis) but is shaped by interactions with the social and physical world.

socialization the processes by which individuals, through experience with others, develop the skills and ways of thinking and feeling, as well as standards and values, that allow them to adapt to their group and live with other people. Parents, teachers, and other adults are important socializers for children, although other children, the media, and social institutions can play a role in socialization.

Quality of the Child's Relationships with Parents

The quality of children's relationships with their parents can influence their emotional development in several ways. As is discussed fully in Chapter 11, the quality of children's relationships with their parents seems to influence their sense of security and how they feel about themselves and other people. In turn, these feelings affect children's emotionality. For example, children who have secure relationships with their parents tend to show more positive emotion and less social anxiety than do children who are insecurely attached to their parents (e.g., Bohlin, Hagekull, & Rydell, 2000). In addition, children with a close, secure relationship with their parents tend to be more advanced in their understanding of emotion, perhaps because their parents tend to discuss feelings with them more than do parents of less securely attached children (Laible & Thompson, 1998, 2000). This enhanced understanding of emotion is likely to help these children to recognize when and how to regulate their emotion. Finally, the quality of children's early relationships with parents provides them with cognitive prototypes of how relationships are conducted and thus influences their emotional responses to people and events in their world.

Parental Socialization of Children's Emotional Responding

Parents' **socialization** of their children—that is, their direct and indirect influence on their children's standards, values, and ways of thinking and feeling—includes the socialization of their children's emotional response. Parents socialize their children's emotional development through (1) their expression of emotion with their children and other people, (2) their reactions to their children's expression of emotion, and (3) the discussions they have with their children about emotion and emotional regulation.

Parents' Expression of Emotion

The expression of emotion by parents may affect children's social competence and psychological well-being in a variety a ways. First, the emotions expressed in the home may influence children's views about themselves and others in their social world (Dunsmore & Halberstadt, 1997). For example, children exposed to a lot of anger and hostility may come to view themselves as individuals who anger people and may come to believe that most people are hostile. Second, parental expression of emotion provides children with a model of when and how to express emotion (Denham, Zoller, & Couchoud, 1994; Dunn & Brown, 1994) and also may affect children's understanding of what types of emotional expressions are appropriate and effective in interpersonal relations (Halberstadt, Cassidy, Stifter, Parke, & Fox, 1995). If parents do not talk about emotions but express their feelings nonverbally, for example, their children may come to believe that it is not appropriate to discuss their feelings directly with others. They also may get the message that emotions are basically bad and should be avoided or inhibited. Finally, the emotions to which children are exposed may affect their level of distress and arousal, which can influence how they process information about ongoing social interactions.

Whatever the underlying process, it is clear that the consistent and open expression of positive or negative emotion in the home is associated with specific outcomes for children. In a review of existing studies, Amy Halberstadt and her colleagues found that when positive emotion is prevalent in the home, children tend to express positive emotion themselves. They are socially skilled, able to understand others' emotions (at least in childhood), are low in aggression, well adjusted, and tend to have high self-esteem (Halberstadt, Crisp, & Eaton, 1999). In contrast, when negative emotion is predominant in the family, especially intense and hostile emotion, children tend to exhibit low levels of social competence and to express negative emotion themselves (Eisenberg et al., 2001; Halberstadt et al., 1999). Even when the conflict and anger in the home involve the adults and not the children directly, there is an increased likelihood that the children will develop behavior problems and deficits in social competence (Davies & Cummings,

BROOKLYN PRODUCTIONS / THE IMAGE BANK / GETTY IMAGES

Children who are exposed to relatively high levels of positive emotion in the family tend to express more positive emotion and are more socially skilled and adjusted than children who are exposed to high levels of negative emotion.

1994; Grych & Fincham, 1990). These outcomes are also more likely when children are exposed to high levels of parental depression (Downey & Coyne, 1990; Spieker, Larson, Lewis, Keller, & Gilchrist, 1999).

Of course, parental expression of emotion is not always the cause of positive or negative outcomes in children; children undoubtedly influence the expression of emotion in the home. For example, children who have difficult temperaments or are unmanageable are likely to evoke negative emotion from their parents. Moreover, genetic factors may contribute to some of the associations between parental emotion and children's emotions or behavior. That is, due to heredity, both parent and child may be prone to anger and impulsive behavior. Thus, both heredity and the kinds of emotions children see and experience in the home undoubtedly play roles in children's emotional and social development.

Parents' Reactions to Children's Emotions

Parents' reactions to children's negative emotions also seem to affect children's emotional expressivity, as well as their social competence and adjustment. Consider the different message a child receives when parents act as if his or her sorrowful or fearful emotions are meaningful and worthy of attention and when they criticize or minimize their child's emotional experience:

> Jeremy . . . watched the movie *Jaws*, against his mother's better judgment. He fearfully, animatedly asked many questions about the movie afterwards, and anxiously discussed it in great detail (e.g., "What was that red stuff?") His mother and father answered all the questions and supported him as he resolved these things in his mind. Jeremy's emotions were accepted, and he was able to regulate them, as well as to learn about what makes things "scary."
>
> (Denham, 1998, p. 106)

> Scott's parents, who are punitive socializers, show disregard and even contempt when his best friend moves away. These parents tease Scott for his tender feelings, so that in the end he is let down not only by the disappearance of his friend, but by their reactions as well. . . . [H]e is very lonely and still feels very bad.
>
> (Denham, 1998, p. 120)

Parents who respond to their children's sadness and anxiety by dismissing or criticizing their feelings communicate to their children that their feelings are not valid. In turn, their children tend be less emotionally and socially competent than children whose parents are emotionally supportive. For example, they tend to be lower in sympathy for others, less skilled at coping with stress, and more prone to negative emotions and problem behaviors such as aggression (Eisenberg, Cumberland, & Spinrad, 1998; Eisenberg, Fabes, et al., 1999; McDowell & Parke, 2000). In contrast, parents who react in a supportive way when their children are upset help their children to regulate their emotional arousal and to find ways to express their emotions constructively. In turn, their children tend to be more competent both with peers and academically (Gottman, Katz, & Hoover, 1997).

Parental Discussion of Emotion

As you will shortly see, children's emotional understanding is a key part of their emotional development and self-regulation. Thus, family conversations about emotion are an important aspect of children's emotional socialization. Parents who discuss emotions with their children teach them about the meanings of emotions,

individual differences 10.3

Gender Differences in the Expression of Emotion

Today the notion that girls are more emotional than boys—as reflected in the expression "Boys don't cry"—is considered by many to be a dated gender-role stereotype. Yet there probably is some truth to this stereotype. In certain respects, boys and girls express, and possibly even experience, emotions differently (Brody & Hall, 1993). Although there seem to be few consistent dfferences between girls' and boys' displays of emotion in infancy (Brody, 1999), by the toddler or preschool years, boys tend to begin a pattern of displaying more anger than girls do (Birnbaum & Croll, 1984; Fabes, Eisenberg, Nyman, & Michealieu, 1991; Kochanska, 2001). There also is some evidence that girls exhibit more fear, distress, and embarrassment than boys do (Cummings, Iannotti, & Zahn-Waxler, 1985; Kochanska, 2001; Lewis, Sullivan, Stanger, & Weiss, 1989), although certainly not in all contexts.

How do we explain gender differences of this sort? Are they based primarily on biological differences between males and females? Although sex differences in infancy are subtle, at best (Brody, 1985), there are some data indicating that male newborns are more irritable and reactive than female newborns (e.g., Phillips, King, & DuBois, 1978). Such sex differences at an early age suggest that the differences in emotionality between girls and boys are due to biology. However, if biological differences were the main influence on the differences in boys' and girls' emotional expression, one would expect considerable cross-cultural consistency in these differences. Instead, differences in boys' and girls' emotional expression are somewhat variable across cultures. For example, on measures of emotional expression, girls in the United States score somewhat higher in sadness than do boys, whereas in China, boys score higher than do girls (Ahadi, Rothbart, & Ye, 1993). Thus, it is highly likely that differences in socialization at many levels—in the home, the schools, the peer group, and the larger community—play an important role in the expression of emotion.

The influence of the home is clear from the fact that parents in the United States report that they are more likely to instruct older sons than daughters not to show fear (Casey & Fuller, 1994). Similarly, parents of boys in the United States and in some countries in northern Europe report that they are more likely to socialize their sons than their daughters not to cry or express feelings (Block, 1978), and parents in Western cultures may allow boys to express anger more than they allow girls to (Birnbaum & Croll, 1984). Correspondingly, girls and boys in these cultures expect different reactions from parents when they display emotion. School-aged boys are more likely than girls to expect their parents to disapprove of their expression of sadness (Fuchs & Thelen, 1988), whereas girls are more likely than boys to expect adult disapproval and negative consequences if they express anger (Perry, Perry, & Weiss, 1989; Zeman & Shipman, 1996).

Parents also display emotion differently to sons and daughters. During mother–child interactions, North American mothers express more emotion with daughters, especially positive emotion (Brody, 1993; Garner, Robertson, & Smith, 1997; Malatesta et al., 1989). There is also some evidence that North American parents express more anger or general negative emotion toward their sons (e.g., Garner et al., 1997).

Finally, mothers discuss emotions differently with sons than they do with daughters. Judy Dunn and her colleagues found that mothers mentioned feelings more frequently to 18-month-old girls than to boys, and by 24 months of age, girls referred to feelings more often than did boys (Dunn, Bretherton, & Munn, 1987). Similar findings were obtained in another longitudinal study of children observed from age 40 months to 70 months (Kuebli, Butler, & Fivush, 1995) and in research on 4-year-old Mexican-American children and their mothers (Eisenberg, 1999). To some degree, mothers may also talk about different emotions with sons and daughters, discussing positive emotions and sadness more with daughters and discussing certain negative emotions, particularly anger and disgust, more with sons (Brody & Hall, 1993; Fivush, 1989; Kuebli & Fivush, 1992; Kuebli et al., 1995). Because of such differences, girls may learn that they are not supposed to express anger and may become more attuned than boys to emotions such as sadness.

Another factor has been suggested by Leslie Brody (1993), who argues that gender differences in the expression of negative emotion may be partly attributable to girls' earlier and superior language development. Because girls use language earlier than boys do and are exposed to more parental discussion of emotion, it may be that they learn to curb behavioral expressions of negative emotions more readily than boys and to express their negative emotions through verbal and facial communication. In fact, girls report using language to communicate negative emotion, whereas boys cite using mild aggression for the same purpose (Zeman & Shipman, 1996).

Thus, it is likely that both biological and socialization factors contribute to differences in how and when boys and girls express emotion. These differences in children, in turn, contribute to differences in the quality of their social behavior and perhaps in their adjustment.

the circumstances in which they should and should not be expressed, and the consequences of expressing or not expressing them (Eisenberg, Cumberland, et al. 1998). They can also coach their children about ways of coping with their emotions and expressing them appropriately (Gottman et al., 1997). As a result, their children tend to display better emotional understanding than do children whose parents do not discuss emotions with them. A longitudinal study by Judy Dunn and her colleagues found, for example, that the degree to which children are exposed to, and participate in, discussions of emotions with family members at ages 2 and 3 predicts their understanding of others' emotions seven months later and at age 6 (Brown & Dunn, 1996; Dunn, Brown, & Beardsall, 1991; Dunn, Brown, Slomkowski, Tesla, & Youngblade, 1991).

Not surprisingly, family discussions of emotion are especially likely to occur when a family member is experiencing a negative emotion, and they are more likely to foster children's understanding of emotion if they are supportive rather than hostile (Dunn & Brown, 1994; Eisenberg, Cumberland, et al., 1998). It also benefits children's emotional understanding if parents discuss emotions with their children in terms of everyday situations and don't talk about emotions just during those situations involving conflict and anger (Dunn & Brown, 1994; Laird, Pettit, Mize, Brown, & Lindsey, 1994). For example, parents can talk with the child about how a younger sibling gets upset if he or she is very tired or is teased too much, or how the child feels and reacts after he or she is excluded from play by peers.

Of course, children's own characteristics may play a role in the degree to which family members talk about emotion. Parents are more likely to discuss emotions with children who have some initial understanding of emotions and are interested in them. In addition, family members may discuss emotions more with children who are having problems in regard to their social competence or fearfulness (Denham & Auerbach, 1995; Denham, Mitchell-Copeland, Strandberg, Auerbach, & Blair, 1997). Thus, as with parents' expression of emotion, children's individual characteristics—including some with a hereditary basis (as described in Box 10.3)—can have an impact on the nature of parental discussion of emotion.

review:

Children's emotional development is influenced by their relationship with their parents: children who have secure relations with their parents tend to show more positive emotion and greater emotional understanding than children whose relations with their parents are insecure. Another influence on children's emotional development is their parents' socialization of emotional responding, including what emotions parents express with their children and others and how they express them; how parents respond to their children's negative emotions; and whether and how parents discuss emotions with their children.

Culture and Children's Emotional Development

Although people in all cultures likely experience many similar emotions, research shows that the degree to which different emotions are expressed varies considerably across cultures. One reason for cultural differences in emotional expression may be genetic, in that people in different racial or ethnic groups may tend, on average, to have somewhat different temperaments. Some research with infants suggests that this is the case. There is evidence, for example, that 11-month-old Euro-American infants are more reactive in general than are Chinese or Chinese-American babies and cry or smile more in response to evocative events (e.g., scary toys, a vanishing object) (Freedman & Freedman, 1969). American infants also respond more quickly than do Chinese infants to emotion-inducing events such as having their arm held down (Kisilevsky et al., 1998).

Cultural differences in parenting practices may also contribute to cross-cultural differences in infants' expression of emotion. In Central Africa, the infants in a Ngandu community fuss and cry more than do infants in an Aka community. This may be attributable to differences in caregiving practices related to the contrasting lifestyles of these two groups. The Aka are hunters and gatherers; in their daily foraging activities, carried out by women and children together, children are almost always within arm's reach of someone who can feed or hold them when the need arises. The Ngandu, on the other hand, are farmers; their infants are left alone more often. Thus, Aka infants may cry and fuss less because they have more physical contact with caregivers and their needs are met more quickly. Of course, genetic factors related to temperament could also contribute to the differences (Hewlett, Lamb, Shannon, Leyendecker, & Scholmerich, 1998).

The influence of cultural factors on emotional expression is strikingly revealed by a comparison of Japanese and American children. In one study, Japanese and American preschoolers were asked to say what they would do in hypothetical situations of conflict and distress, such as being hit, hearing parents argue, or seeing a peer knock down a tower of blocks they had just built. American preschoolers expressed more anger and aggression in response to these vignettes than did Japanese children. This difference may have to do with the fact that American mothers appear to be more likely than Japanese mothers to encourage their children's emotional expressiveness (Zahn-Waxler, Friedman, Cole, Mizuta, & Hiruma, 1996). This is in keeping with the high value Euro-American culture places on self-assertion and emotional expression, even the expression of negative emotion (Zahn-Waxler et al., 1996). In contrast, Japanese culture emphasizes interdependence, the subordination of oneself to one's group, and, correspondingly, the importance of maintaining harmonious interpersonal relationships. Thus, Japanese mothers often may discourage their children from expressing negative emotion (Markus & Kitayama, 1991; Matsumoto, 1996; Mesquita & Frijda, 1992).

Interviews with children in remote villages in Nepal allowed Pamela Cole and her colleagues to examine how Buddhist and Hindu values, as well as social class, contribute to children's understanding of emotion.

COURTESY OF PAMELA COLE

Cultures also differ in the degree to which they value and promote specific emotions, and these differences are often reflected in parents' socialization of emotion, as well as in their children's subsequent emotional behavior and adjustment. A striking example of this is provided by the Tamang in rural Nepal. The Tamang are Buddhists who place great value on keeping one's *sem* (mind-heart) calm and clear of emotion, and they believe that people should not express much negative emotion because of its disruptive effects on interpersonal relationships. Consequently, although Tamang parents are responsive to the distress of infants, they often ignore or scold children older than age 2 when they express negative emotion, and they seldom offer explanations or support to reduce children's negative emotional arousal. Yet despite the fact that comparable nonsupportive behavior in U.S. parents has been associated with low social competence in children, it does not seem to have a negative effect on the social competence of Tamang children. Because of the value placed on controlling the expression of emotion in Tamang culture, parental behaviors that would seem dismissive and punitive to American parents likely take on a different meaning for Tamang parents and children and probably have different consequences (Cole & Dennis, 1998).

Parents' ideas about the usefulness of various emotions also vary in different subcultures within the United States. In a study of African-American mothers living in a dangerous neighborhood, mothers valued and promoted their daughters' readiness to express anger and aggressiveness in situations related to self-protection because they wanted their daughters to act quickly and decisively to defend themselves when necessary. One way they did this was to play-act the role of an adversary, teasing, insulting, or challenging their daughters in the midst of everyday interactions. An example of this is provided by Beth's mother, who initiated a teasing event by challenging Beth (27 months) to fight:

> "Hahahaha, Hahaha. Hahahahah. [Provocative tone:] You wanna fight about it?" Beth laughed. Mother laughed. Mother twice reiterated her challenge and then called Beth an insulting name, "Come on, then, chicken." Beth retorted by calling her mother a chicken. The two proceeded to trade insults through the next 13 turns, in the course of which Beth marked three of her utterances with teasing singsong intonation and aimed a shaming gesture (rubbing one index finger across the other) at her mother. The climax occurred after further mock provocation from the mother, when Beth finally raised her fists (to which both responded with laughter) and rushed toward her mother for an exchange of ritual blows.
>
> (Miller & Sperry, 1987, pp. 20–21)

It is unlikely that mothers in a less difficult and dangerous neighborhood would try to promote the readiness to express aggression in their children, especially in their daughters. Thus, the norms, values, and circumstances of a culture or subcultural group likely contribute substantially to differences among groups in their expression of emotion.

review:

Children's emotionality and emotional regulation are influenced not only by heredity but also by the quality of the parent–child relationship and parents' emotional socialization of their children. In addition, children's emotional functioning is affected by expectations and perceptions about themselves and others that they develop based on viewing others' emotions, others' reactions to their emotions, and discussions of emotion.

Children's tendencies in regard to experiencing and regulating emotions may be affected by differences in temperament among different groups of people, as well as by cultural differences in beliefs about what emotions are valued and when and where emotions should be expressed. In addition, girls and boys differ somewhat in their expression of emotion, and these differences are likely due to socialization in the family and culture.

Children's Understanding of Emotion

Another key influence on children's emotional reactions and regulation of emotion is their understanding of emotion—that is, their understanding of how to identify emotions, what they mean, their social functions, and what factors affect emotional experience. Because an understanding of emotion affects social behavior, it is critical to the development of social competence. Children's understanding of emotions is primitive in infancy but develops rapidly over the course of childhood.

Identifying the Emotions of Others

The first step in the development of emotional knowledge is the recognition of different emotions in others. By 4 to 7 months of age, infants can distinguish certain emotional expressions, such as happiness and surprise (Serrano, Iglesias, &

social referencing infants' use of a parent's facial, gestural, or vocal cues to decide how to deal with novel, ambiguous, or possibly threatening situations

Loeches, 1993; Walker-Andrews & Dickson, 1997). If, for example, they are habituated to pictures of happy faces and then are presented with a picture of a face depicting surprise, they show renewed interest; that is, they look longer at the new picture. However, it is not until infants are about 7 months of age that they start to perceive others' emotional expressions as meaningful. For example, if infants at this age are shown a videotape in which a person's facial expression and voice are consistent in their emotional expression (e.g., a smiling face and a bubbly voice) and a videotape in which a person's facial expression and voice are emotionally discrepant (e.g., a sad face and a bubbly voice), they will attend more to the matching presentation (Walker-Andrews & Dickson, 1997). Infants much younger than 7 months generally do not seem to notice the difference between the two presentations.

At about 8 to 12 months of age, children begin to demonstrate that they can relate facial expressions of emotion and emotional tones of voice to events in the environment. These skills are evident in children's **social referencing**—that is, their use of a parent's facial or vocal cues to decide on how to deal with novel, ambiguous, or possibly threatening situations (see Chapter 5, p. 191). For example, at the approach of an unfamiliar dog, a young child may read the expression on the parent's face to see if the parent thinks the dog is something to be greeted or avoided. In laboratory studies of this phenomenon, infants are typically exposed to novel people or toys while their mother, at the experimenter's direction, shows a happy, fearful, or neutral facial expression. In studies of this type, 12-month-olds tend to stay near their mother when she shows fear; to move toward the novel person or object if she expresses positive emotion; and to move partway toward the object or person if her emotion is neutral (Moses, Baldwin, Rosicky, & Tidball, 2001; Saarni et al., 1998). In one study in which the novel event was the visual cliff (described in Chapter 5, p. 190), 74% of 12-month-olds crossed over the cliff to their mother if she showed happiness, whereas none did if the mother exhibited fear (Sorce, Emde, Campos, & Klinnert, 1985). Related research has demonstrated 12-month-olds' ability to read their mother's tone of voice: when infants who were prevented from seeing their mother's face were presented with novel toys, they were more cautious and exhibited more fear when the mother's voice was fearful than when it was neutral (Mumme, Fernald, & Herrera, 1996). Thus, by the end of the first year of life, infants generally use parents' emotional signals to guide their interpretation of, and reactions to, potentially upsetting or dangerous events and objects.

By the age of 3, children in laboratory studies demonstrate a rudimentary ability to label a fairly narrow range of emotional expressions displayed in pictures or on puppets' faces (Bullock & Russell, 1985; Denham, 1986; Russell & Bullock, 1986). Young children are best at labeling happiness, with their ability to distinguish among different negative emotions—anger, fear, and sadness—gradually appearing in the late preschool and early school years (Eisenberg, Murphy, & Shepard, 1997; Smith & Walden, 1998; Wiggers & van Lieshout, 1985). (African-American children from disadvantaged backgrounds appear to recognize fear expressions earlier than do Euro-American children, perhaps because they are exposed to more fear-inducing situations in their daily lives [Smith & Walden, 1998]). Most children cannot label more complex emotions such as pride, shame, and guilt until early to mid-elementary school.

Interestingly, young children also are relatively skilled at identifying others' emotions solely on the basis of their expressive body movements. In a study that included 4-, 5-, and 8-year-olds, children viewed adults dancing, some in ways that reflected sadness, others in ways that reflected fear, anger, or happiness. Four-year-olds had some understanding that dancers performing the sad dance were sadder than other dancers. Five-year-olds showed better-than-chance levels of accuracy in identifying sad, fearful, and happy dancers, although they were best at identifying sadness. Eight-year-olds were skilled at identifying all four emotions exhibited in the dancing (Boone & Cunningham, 1998).

The ability to discriminate and label different emotions helps children to respond appropriately to their own and others' emotions. If a child understands that he or she is experiencing guilt, for example, the child may understand the need to make reparation to diminish the guilt. Similarly, a child who can see that a peer is angry can devise ways to avoid or appease that peer. In fact, children who are more skilled than their peers at interpreting others' displays of emotion are also higher in social competence (Feldman, Philippot, & Custrini, 1991; Walden & Field, 1990).

Understanding the Causes of Emotion

Knowledge of the causes of emotions also is important for understanding one's own and others' behavior and motives. It likewise is key for regulating one's own behavior. Consider, for example, a child who is being rebuffed or insulted by a friend whom the child has just beaten in a game or on an exam. If the child understands that, in such a situation, the friend may be lashing out in this manner not because the friend is nasty or a sore loser but because the friend feels threatened and inadequate, the child may be much better able to control his or her own response.

A variety of studies have shown rapid development over the preschool and school years in children's understanding of the kinds of situations that typically evoke different emotions in others. In a typical study of this understanding, children are told short stories, often accompanied by pictures, about characters in situations such as having a birthday party or losing a pet. Children are then asked how the character in the story feels. Even 2-year-olds are fairly accurate at identifying happy situations, indicating their answer by selecting a picture of a happy face from an array of faces depicting a variety of emotions (Figure 10.5) (Michalson & Lewis, 1985). By age 3, children are quite good at identifying happy situations. However, in line with their initial limited ability to identify negative emotions, they are not accurate at identifying sad situations until age 4 (Borke, 1971; Denham & Couchoud, 1990). Young children have even more difficulty identifying fear- and anger-inducing situations, but their ability to do so increases with age in the preschool and elementary school years (Eisenberg, Murphy, et al., 1997; Smith & Walden, 1998). Children's ability to understand the circumstances that evoke complex social emotions such as pride, guilt, shame, and jealousy often emerges after age 7 and, according to cross-cultural research that involved children from Western nations and a remote Himalayan village, is considerable by late elementary school and early adolescence (Harris, Olthof, Terwogt, & Hardman, 1987; Thompson, 1987; Wiggers & van Lieshout, 1985).

However, it is not altogether clear how accurately this type of story-telling method measures young children's ability to identify others' emotions from situational cues. The correct identification of the emotion may simply reflect how the children themselves would feel in the given situation rather than their ability to evaluate how others feel (Chandler & Greenspan, 1972).

Another way to assess children's understanding of the causes of emotions is to record what they say about emotions in their everyday conversations and to ask

FIGURE 10.5 Illustrations for a measure of children's ability to label others' emotions Pictures such as these are used in tasks in which children are told short stories and asked to identify others' emotions. With age children become better able to indicate what emotion the story characters feel. (Adapted from Michaelson & Lewis, 1985)

them to discuss and explain others' emotions. Even 28-month-olds mention emotions such as happiness, sadness, anger, fear, crying, and hurting in appropriate ways in their conversations (e.g., "You sad, Daddy?" or "Don't be mad") and sometimes even mention their causes (e.g., "Santa will be happy if I pee in the potty" or "Grandma mad. I wrote on wall") (Bretherton & Beeghly, 1982). By age 4 to 6, children's explanations for why peers experience negative emotions in real-life situations in their preschool are somewhat similar to those of adults (Fabes et al., 1988). Children get more skilled at explaining the causes of emotion across the preschool and school years (Fabes, Eisenberg, Nyman, & Michealieu, 1991; Strayer, 1986). For example, third and sixth graders are more likely than kindergartners to believe that someone caught being dishonest will be scared (Barden, Zelko, Duncan, & Masters, 1980).

With age, children also come to understand that people can feel emotions based on reminders of past events. For example, in one study, 3- to 5-year-olds were told stories about children who experience a negative event and then see reminders of that event. One story was about a girl named Mary who has a pet rabbit that lives in a typical rabbit cage (Figure 10.6). One day Mary's rabbit is chased away by a dog and is never seen again. In different versions of the story, Mary later encounters one of three reminders of her loss—the same dog, her rabbit's cage, or a photograph of her rabbit. At this point the children were told that Mary started to feel sad and were asked, "Why did Mary start to feel sad right now?" On stories such as these, 39% of 3-year-olds, 83% of 4-year-olds, and 100% of 5-year-olds understood that the story characters were sad because a memory cue had made them think about a previous unhappy event (Lagattuta, Wellman, & Flavell, 1997). Understanding that memory cues can trigger emotions associated with past events helps children to explain their own and others' emotional reactions in situations that in themselves seem emotionally neutral.

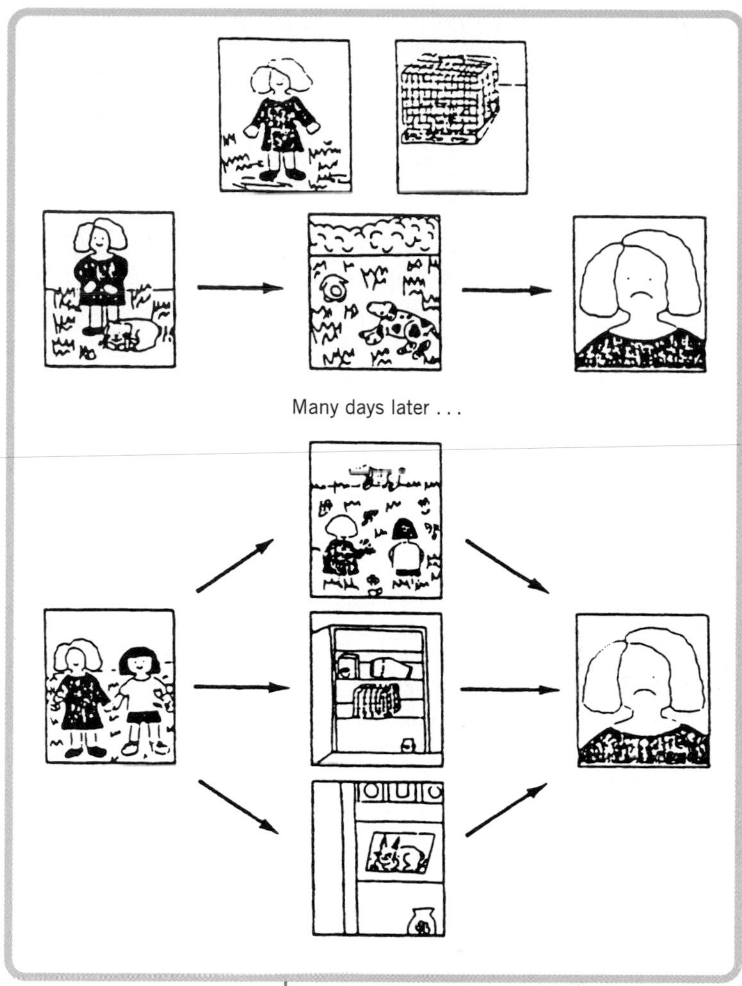

FIGURE 10.6 Pictures in a task used to test children's understanding that emotions can stem from reminders of past experiences This story is about a girl named Mary, who has a pet rabbit that lives in a typical rabbit cage. One day Mary's rabbit is chased away by a dog and never seen again. (Adapted from Lagattuta, Wellman, & Flavell, 1997)

Children's Understanding of Real and False Emotions

An important component in the development of emotional understanding is the realization that the emotions people express do not necessarily reflect their true feelings (Figure 10.7). The beginnings of this realization are seen in 3-year-olds' occasional (and usually transparent) attempts to mask their emotions when they receive a disappointing gift or prize. However, 3- and 4-year-olds seldom refer to the control of facial displays of emotion when they are questioned about similar disappointing situations involving hypothetical children (Cole, 1986).

By age 5, children's understanding of the difference between real and false emotion has improved considerably, as demonstrated in a study that used six stories such as the following:

> Michelle is sleeping over at her cousin Johnny's house today. Michelle forgot her favorite teddy bear at home. Michelle is really sad that she forgot her teddy bear. But, she doesn't want Johnny to see how sad she is because Johnny will call her a baby. So, Michelle tries to hide how she feels.
>
> (Banerjee, 1997)

After children were questioned to ensure that they understood the story, they were asked questions such as "Show me the picture for how Michelle really feels. How does Michelle really feel?" "Show me the picture for how Michelle will try to look on her face. How will Michelle try to look?" Whereas about half of 3- and 4-year-olds gave correct responses on four or more of the stories, over 80% of 5-year-olds gave correct responses. Studies with both Japanese and Western children also confirm that between 4 and 6 years of age, children's understanding that people can be misled by others' facial expressions increases (Gardner, Harris, Ohmoto, & Hamazaki, 1988; Gross & Harris, 1988).

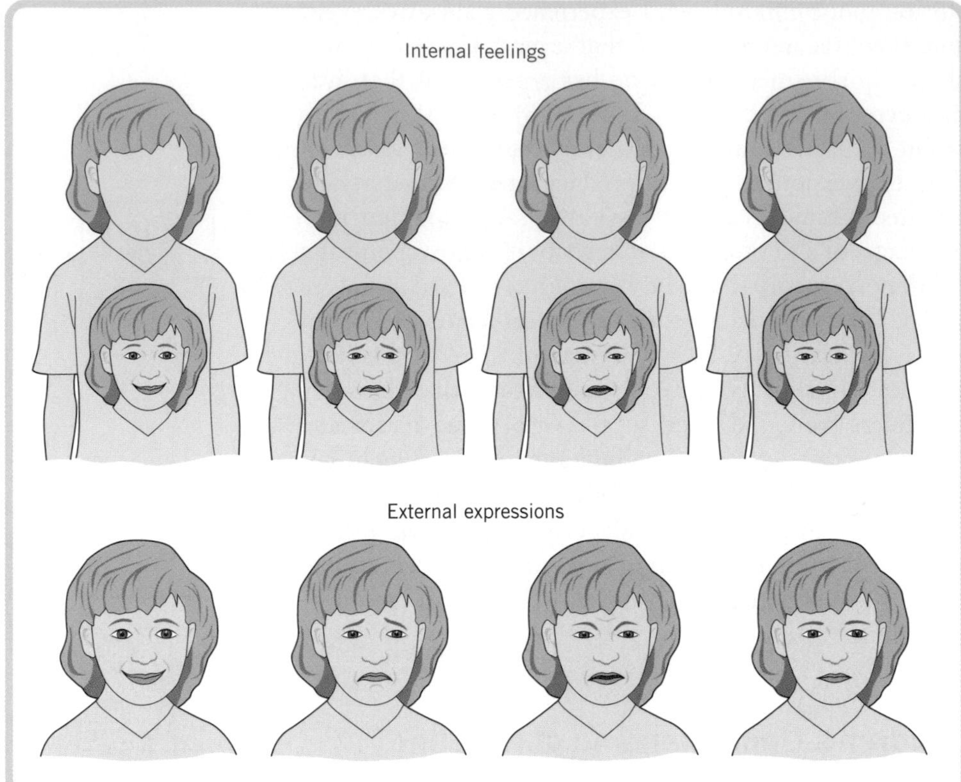

FIGURE 10.7 Facial display figures used in the assessment of expression regulation The figures on the girl's chest indicate how she feels inside. Children select from the different pictures of facial expressions to indicate what expression the girl would show externally, that is, on her face. (Adapted from Jones, Abbey, & Cumberland, 1998)

Part of the improvement in understanding false emotion involves an increasing understanding of **display rules**—a social group's informal norms about when, where, and how much one should show emotions and when and where displays of emotion should be suppressed or masked. Over the preschool and elementary school years, children develop a more refined understanding of when and why display rules are used (Banerjee, 1997; Rotenberg & Eisenberg, 1997; Saarni, 1979). They increasingly understand, for example, that people use verbal and facial display rules to protect others' feelings or their own, as when they pretend to like someone's cooking so as not to hurt the cook's feelings (labeled a *prosocial motive*) or hide their emotions when they themselves are being teased or lose a contest (labeled a *self-protective motive*) (Gnepp & Hess, 1986). (Figure 10.8 shows age-related changes in these types of motives.)

These age-related increases in children's understanding of real versus false emotion and display rules are apparently related to increases in children's cognitive capacities (Flavell, 1986). For example, children who are higher than their peers in reasoning on Piagetian preoperational and concrete operational conservation tasks (see Chapter 4, pp. 137–138) exhibit greater understanding of emotions (Carroll & Steward, 1984).

Social factors also seem to affect children's understanding of display rules. For example, display rules are somewhat different for males and females and reflect societal beliefs about how males and females should feel and behave. Elementary school girls in the United States are more likely than their male counterparts to feel that it is acceptable for them to express emotions such as pain (Zeman & Garber, 1996). Girls also are somewhat more attuned than boys to the need to inhibit emotional displays that might hurt others' feelings (Cole, 1986; Saarni, 1984). This is expecially true for girls from cultures such as India, in which females are expected to be deferential and highly alert to expressing only socially appropriate emotions

display rules a social group's informal norms about when, where, and how much one should show emotions and when and where displays of emotion should be suppressed or masked by displays of other emotions

(Joshi & MacLean, 1994). These findings obviously are consistent with the gender stereotypes that girls are more likely both to try to protect others' feelings and to be more emotional than boys.

Parents' beliefs and behaviors—which often reflect cultural beliefs—likely contribute to children's understanding and use of display rules. Various Nepalese subcultures, for example, differ in the emphasis they place on controlling emotional displays. Correspondingly, the degree to which Nepalese children report masking negative emotions varies with the degree to which mothers in different Nepalese subcultures report teaching their children about how to manage emotions (Cole & Tamang, 1998). In addition, cultural beliefs stemming from social status and religion, which undoubtedly are partly learned from parents, seem to affect the degree to which Nepalese children express emotions such as anger and shame (Cole, Bruschi, & Tamang, 2002). A less benign example of parents' influence on children's understanding and use of display rules is the fact that U.S. children are more likely to display knowledge of self-protective display rules if they are frequently exposed to hostility in the home (Jones et al., 1998). Thus, children seem to be attuned to display rules if they are valued in their culture or if an awareness of them serves an important function in the family.

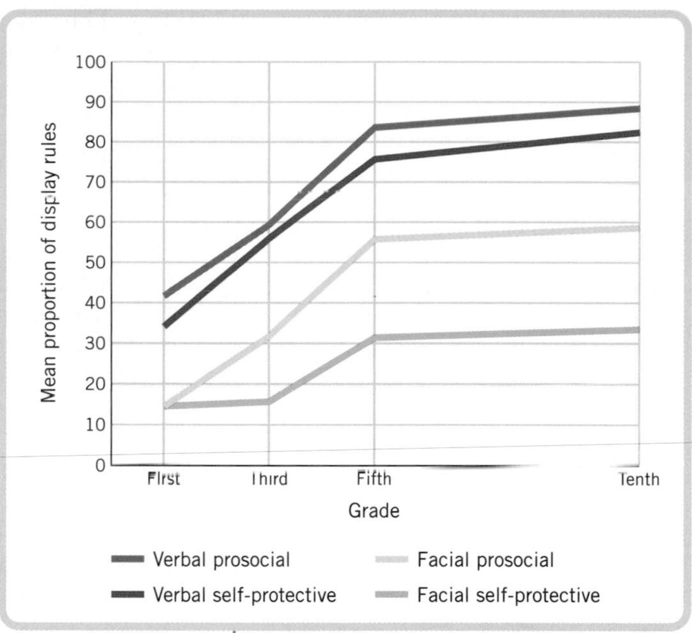

FIGURE 10.8 Mean proportion of display rules as a function of mode of expression (verbal or facial), story type (prosocial or protective), and grade Children in first, third, fifth, and tenth grade listened to stories designed to elicit display rules. Then they were asked to predict and explain what the story protagonists would say and what facial expressions the protagonists would show in the emotion-laden situations. Children's knowledge of how and when to control emotional displays increased between first and fifth grade and then leveled off. Their understanding was greater for verbal display rules, whereby children monitor, falsify, and inhibit their speech, than for facial display rules. Children also understood prosocial display rules (used to protect another's feelings) better than self-protective display rules (used for personal gain). (Adapted from TK)

Understanding Simultaneous and Ambivalent Emotions

One of the most difficult basic emotion-related concepts for children to grasp is that people can feel several emotions at once, including ambivalent emotions. Most young children tend to report that, in a given situation, their emotions are all of a kind, all positive or all negative (Harter, 1999). Four- and five-year-olds tend either not to realize that multiple feelings can exist or to view conflicting emotions as occurring at different times in reaction to different events (Donaldson & Westerman, 1986; Reissland, 1985).

Sometime between the ages of 5 and 7, children come to realize that they can feel two compatible emotions simultaneously: "I'm happy and excited when I have a birthday party and expect gifts" (Harter, 1999). In the next few years, they further recognize that they can simultaneously feel two positive emotions or two negative emotions toward the same person—for example, that they can feel both fearful and angry toward someone, such as a parent or teacher. They also understand that they can simultaneously experience positive and negative emotions that are related to different sources (Harter & Buddin, 1987; Wintre & Vallance, 1994). This understanding was expressed by a child who said, "I was sitting in school feeling worried about all of the responsibilities of a new pet but I was happy that I had gotten straight A's on my report card" (Harter, 1998, p. 51).

By mid- to late childhood, children realize that they (and others) can simultaneously experience positive and negative emotions related to the same source. For example, a girl who received a gift she did not like might remark, "I was happy that I got a present but mad that it wasn't what I wanted" (Harter, 1999, p. 52). At around age 10, children also begin to understand emotional ambivalence, recognizing that positive and negative emotions can interact with one another and that people can have mixed feelings (Donaldson & Westerman, 1986; Reissland,

1985). Thus, with increasing age, children better understand the complexity of their own and others' emotions, a skill that is likely to be reflected in both their self-understanding and in their social interactions with others.

review:

Children's understanding of emotions plays an important role in their emotional functioning. Although infants can detect differences in different emotional expressions such as happiness and surprise by 4 to 7 months of age, it is not until they are about 7 months of age that they start to treat others' emotional expressions as meaningful. At about 8 to 12 months of age, children begin to connect facial expressions of emotion or an emotional tone of voice with other events in the situation, as evidenced by their use of social referencing. By age 3, children demonstrate a rudimentary ability to label facial expressions and understand simple situations that are likely to cause happiness.

As children move through the preschool and elementary school years, their understanding of emotions and situations that cause emotions grows in range and complexity. They increasingly appreciate that the emotions people show may not reflect their true feelings. In addition, with age, children increasingly understand that they and others can feel more than one emotion at the same time and that different emotions may interact and affect one another.

Chapter Summary

Development of Emotions in Childhood

- Discrete-emotions theorists believe that each emotion is packaged with a specific set of bodily and facial reactions and that distinct emotions are evident from very early in life. In contrast, functionalists believe that emotions reflect what individuals are trying to do in specific situations—that is, their concerns and goals at the moment—and that there is not a set of innate, discrete emotions but many emotions based on people's many different interactions with the social world.
- From early in life, emotions play an important role in both survival and social communication. Although infants show negative and positive affect from birth, it is not clear if young infants experience different types of negative emotions such as anger, fear, and sadness.
- Emotions undergo change in the early months and years of life. Smiles become social around the second to third month of life, and what makes children smile and laugh changes with cognitive development.
- Newborns exhibit distress due to discomfort and hunger. By 6 to 7 months of age they often are distressed when strangers approach them, and by approximately 8 months of age they tend to get distressed when separated from their parents.
- The social emotions—embarrassment, pride, shame, and guilt—emerge in the second year of life. Their emergence is tied in part to the development of a rudimentary sense of self and to an appreciation of others' reactions to the self.
- In childhood, children's emotional reactions are increasingly influenced by their growing cognitive understandings of events and emotions. For some children, there is an increase in the experience of negative emotion from childhood to adolescence. Rates of clinical and subclinical depression are much higher in adolescence than at younger ages, especially for girls.

Regulation of Emotion

- Emotional self-regulation involves the process of initiating, inhibiting, or modulating internal feeling states, emotion-related physiological processes, emotion-related cognitions, and emotion-related behavior in the service of accomplishing one's goals.
- Young infants are not very skilled at regulating themselves and must rely on adults to manage their emotions. However, children's self-regulation improves with age as they increasingly use cognitive strategies and more appropriate and effective means of managing their emotions and behavior. Improvements in children's regulatory capacities are based on increases in their abilities to control their own bodies and their cognitive development, as well as changes in adults' expectations.
- Emotional self-regulation generally is associated with high social competence and low problem behavior.

Individual Differences in Emotion and Its Regulation

- Both biological and environmental factors contribute to the differences we see in children's emotions and related behaviors. Temperament, which is believed to have a constitutional basis but also is affected by social experiences, predicts adjustment in childhood and adulthood. However, children with difficult temperaments often do well if they receive sensitive and appropriate parenting.

Children's Emotional Development in the Family

- Children's emotional development is affected by the quality of their early social relationships and their parents' discussion of emotion. High levels of positive emotion in the home are associated with favorable outcomes for children, whereas high levels of negative emotion and punitive reactions to children's displays of negative emotion often are linked to negative developmental outcomes. Parental discussion of emotion may promote children's understanding of emotion and their social competence.
- Girls and boys differ somewhat in their expression of emotion, and these differences are likely due to socialization in the family and culture.

Culture and Children's Emotional Development

- There may be differences in temperament across some cultures, which affect children's tendencies to experience and regulate emotions.
- There are cultural differences in beliefs about what emotions are valued and when emotions should be expressed, and these shape children's expression of emotion.

Children's Understanding of Emotion

- To interact with others effectively, a person must be able to identity others' emotions and have some knowledge of their causes and significance. At about 7 months of age, infants start to treat others' emotional expressions as meaningful. At 8 to 12 months of age, children start to exhibit social referencing.
- By age 2 to 3 years, children demonstrate a rudimentary ability to label facial expressions and simple situations associated with happiness. Children's understanding of facial expressions, the situations that cause emotions, display rules, and mixed emotions increases in the preschool and elementary school years.

Critical Thinking Questions

1. How might differences in children's intelligence contribute to (a) the emotions they display and (b) their understanding of emotions? What other factors might contribute to children's understanding of their own and others' emotions?
2. List at least five aspects of temperament. What aspects of adults' personality might each predict?
3. Suppose you wanted to assess changes with age in children's regulation of emotion. Think of five different tasks you could use to assess age-related changes. Which would be best to use in early childhood and which would better reflect changes at older ages?
4. Recall from Chapter 7 the development of children's theory of mind. How might advances in children's understanding of theory of mind relate to their understanding of emotion?

Key Terms

emotional intelligence, p. 373
emotion, p. 373
discrete emotions theory, p. 374
functionalist approach, p. 374
social smiles, p. 376
separation anxiety, p. 379
self-conscious emotions, p. 380
emotional self-regulation, p. 384
social competence, p. 386
temperament, p. 388
behavioral inhibition, p. 392
goodness of fit, p. 394
personality, p. 395
socialization, p. 395
social referencing, p. 402
display rules, p. 406

CHAPTER 11

Attachment to Others and Development of Self

ENDRE RODER, *The New Born,* 1992

Between 1937 and 1943, numerous child-care professionals in both the United States and Europe reported a disturbing phenomenon: children who seemed to have no concern or feeling for anyone but themselves. Some of the children were withdrawn and isolated; others were overactive, distractible, and abusive toward other children. By adolescence, they often had histories of persistent stealing, violence, and sexual misdemeanors. Many of these children had been reared in institutions in which they received adequate physical care but experienced little social interaction; others had been shifted from foster home to foster home in infancy and early childhood (Bowlby, 1953).

At about the same time, similar disturbances were being observed among children who had been orphaned or separated from their parents during World War II and were in refugee camps or other institutional settings. John Bowlby, an English psychoanalyst who worked with many of these children, reported that they were very listless, depressed or otherwise emotionally disturbed, and mentally stunted. Older refugee children often seemed to have lost all interest in life and were possessed by feelings of emptiness (Bowlby, 1953). These children tended not to develop normal emotional attachments with other people.

On the basis of such observations, René Spitz, a French psychoanalyst who had worked with Freud, conducted a series of classic studies of the effects of deprivation of mothering (Spitz, 1945, 1946, 1949). He filmed infants (a methodological innovation) residing in orphanages, most of whom had been born out of wedlock and were awaiting adoption. The films were extremely poignant and painful to watch. They documented the fact that, despite receiving good institutional care, the infants were generally sickly and physically and developmentally retarded. In many cases, the infants seemed unmotivated to live: their death rate was about 37% over two years, compared with no deaths in an institution where children had daily contact with their mothers. The films' most important contribution, however, was their evidence of intense and prolonged grief and depressive reactions in infants who had been separated from their mothers after developing a loving relationship with them. Developmentalists of the time did not believe that infants could suffer such grief syndromes (Emde, 1994).

These early observations also challenged the more central belief, then held by many child-care professionals, that if children in institutions such as orphanages received good physical care, including proper nourishment and health care, they would develop normally. These professionals placed little emphasis on the emotional dimensions of caregiving. As a result of these studies of children who lost their parents in the 1940s, it became generally recognized that institutions like orphanages, no matter how hygienic and competently managed, put babies at high risk because they did not provide the kind of caregiving that enables infants to form close socioemotional bonds. Adoption—the earlier the better—came to be viewed as a far better option.

More important, the observations and writings of John Bowlby and others involved with institutionalized children led to more systematic study of how the quality of parent–child interactions affects children's development in families, especially their development of emotional attachments to other people. This work, which continues today, has led to a much deeper understanding of the ways in which the early parent–child emotional bond can influence children's social and emotional development. Indeed, many investigators now believe that children's early relationships with parents influence the nature of their interactions with others from infancy into adulthood, as well as their feelings about their own worth.

In this chapter, we will first explore how children develop **attachments,** or close, enduring emotional bonds to parents or other primary caregivers. Then we will examine the ways in which the development of attachments to others seems to set the stage for the child's near- and long-term development. As you will see, the attachment process appears to be biologically based yet unfolds in different ways depending on the familial and cultural context. Thus, the themes of *nature and nurture* and the *sociocultural context* will be important in our discussion of this topic. You will also see that although most children in normal social circumstances do develop attachments to their parents, the quality of these attachments differs in important ways and has implications for each child's social and emotional development. The theme of *individual differences* will therefore figure prominently in our discussion as well.

attachment an emotional bond with a specific person that is enduring across space and time. Usually, attachments are discussed in regard to the relation between infants and specific caregivers, although they can also occur in adulthood.

Next we will examine a related issue—the development of children's sense of self—that is, their self-understanding, self-identity, and self-esteem. Although many factors influence these areas of development, the quality of children's early attachments lays the foundation for how children feel about themselves, including their sense of security and well-being. Over time, children's self-understanding, self-esteem, and self-identity are also shaped by how others perceive and treat them, by biologically based characteristics of the child (such as attractiveness), and by children's developing abilities to think about and interpret their social worlds. Thus, the themes of *nature and nurture, individual differences,* the *sociocultural context,* and the *active child* will be evident in our discussion of the development of self.

The Caregiver–Child Attachment Relationship

Following the very disturbing observations of the 1930s and 1940s regarding children separated from their parents early in life, researchers began to conduct systematic studies of this phenomenon. Much of the early research, such as that conducted by Spitz, focused on how the development of young children who had been orphaned or otherwise separated from their parents was affected by the quality of the caregiving they subsequently received.

Another line of research involved experimental work with monkeys. In some of the best-known research in the whole of psychology, Harry Harlow and his colleagues (Harlow & Harlow, 1965; Young, Suomi, Harlow, McKinney, 1973; Harlow & Zimmerman, 1959) reared infant rhesus monkeys in isolation from birth, comparing their development with that of monkeys reared normally with their mothers. The isolated babies were well fed and kept healthy, but they had no exposure to other monkeys. When they finally were placed with other monkeys six months later, they exhibited severe social disturbances. They compulsively bit and rocked themselves and avoided other monkeys completely, apparently incapable of communicating with, or learning from, others. As adults, formerly isolated females had no interest in sex. If they were artificially impregnated, they did not know what to do with their babies. At best, they tended to ignore or reject them; at worst, they attacked and killed them. This research, although examining the effects of the lack of all early social interaction (and not just that with parents), strongly supported the view that children's healthy social and emotional development is rooted in their early social interactions with adults.

Harlow's female monkeys who were raised in isolation were poor mothers as adults. This outcome suggested that "mother love" is essential to normal social and emotional development.

HARLOW PRIMATE LABORATORY, UNIVERSITY OF WISCONSIN

Attachment Theory

The findings from observations of children and monkeys separated from their parents were so dramatic that psychiatrists and psychologists were compelled to rethink their ideas about early development. Foremost in this effort was John Bowlby, who proposed **attachment theory,** and his student, Mary Ainsworth, who extended and tested Bowlby's ideas.

Bowlby's Attachment Theory

Bowlby's theory of attachment was strongly influenced by several key tenets of Freud's theory, especially the idea that infants' earliest relationships with their mothers shape their later development. However, Bowlby replaced the psychoanalytic notion of a "needy, dependent infant motivated by drive reduction" with the idea of a "competence-motivated infant" who uses his or her primary caregiver as a **secure base** (Waters & Cummings, 2000). The general idea of the secure base is that the presence of a trusted caregiver provides the infant or toddler with a sense of security that allows the child to explore the environment and hence to become generally knowledgeable and competent. In addition, the primary caregiver serves as a haven of safety when the infant feels threatened or insecure, and the child derives comfort and pleasure from being near the caregiver.

Bowlby's idea of the primary caregiver as a secure base for offspring was directly influenced by ethological theory, particularly the ideas of Konrad Lorenz (see Chapter 9, p. 000). Bowlby proposed the existence of an attachment process between infant and caregiver that is rooted in evolution. Just like imprinting, this attachment process develops from the interaction between species-specific learning biases (such as infants' strong tendency to look at faces) and the infant's experience with his or her caregiver; and like imprinting, attachment increases the infant's chance of survival. Thus, the attachment process is viewed as having an innate basis, but the development and quality of infants' attachments are highly dependent on the nature of their experiences with caregivers.

According to Bowlby, the initial development of attachment takes place in four phases.

1. *Preattachment* (birth to 6 weeks). In this phase, the infant produces innate signals, most notably crying, that bring others to his or her side, and the infant is comforted by the ensuing interaction.

2. *Attachment-in-the-making* (6 weeks to 6–8 months). During this phase, infants begin to respond preferentially to familiar people. Typically they smile, laugh, or babble more frequently in the presence of their primary caregiver and are more easily soothed by that person. Like Freud and Erikson, Bowlby saw this phase as a time when infants form expectations about how their caregivers will respond to their needs and, accordingly, do or do not develop a sense of trust in them.

3. *Clear-cut attachment* (between 6–8 months and 1½–2 years). In this phase, infants actively seek contact with their regular caregivers. They happily greet their mother when she appears and, correspondingly, may exhibit *separation protest or distress* when she departs (see Chapter 10, p. 379). For most children, the mother now serves as a secure base, facilitating the infant's exploration and mastery of the environment.

4. *Reciprocal relationships* (from 1½ or 2 years on). During this final phase, toddlers' rapidly increasing cognitive and language abilities enable them to under-

attachment theory theory based on John Bowlby's work that posits that children are biologically predisposed to develop attachments with caregivers as a means of increasing the chances of their own survival

secure base Bowlby's term for when an attachment figure's presence provides an infant or toddler with a sense of security that makes it possible for the infant to explore the environment

internal working model of attachment the child's mental representation of the self, of attachment figure(s), and of relationships in general that is constructed as a result of experiences with caregivers. The working model guides children's interactions with caregivers and other people in infancy and at older ages.

Strange Situation a procedure developed by Mary Ainsworth to assess infants' attachment to their primary caregiver stand their parents' feelings, goals, and motives and to use this understanding to organize their efforts to be near their parents. As a result, separation distress declines, and a more mutually regulated relationship gradually emerges as the child takes an increasingly active role in developing a working partnership with his or her parents (Bowlby, 1969).

The usual outcome of these phases is an enduring emotional tie uniting the infant and caregiver. In addition, the child develops an **internal working model of attachment,** a mental representation of the self, of attachment figures, and of relationships in general. This internal working model is based on the child's early experiences with his or her caregiver, in which the child discovered the extent to which the caregiver could be depended upon to satisfy the child's needs and provide a sense of security. Bowlby believed that this internal working model continues to guide the individual's expectations about relationships throughout life. If caregivers are accessible and responsive, young children come to expect interpersonal relationships to be gratifying and feel that they themselves are worthy of receiving care and love. As adults, they look for, and expect to find, satisfying and security-enhancing relationships similar to the ones they had with their attachment figures in childhood. If children's attachment figures are unavailable or unresponsive, children develop negative perceptions of relationships with other people and of themselves (Bowlby, 1973, 1980; Bretherton & Munholland, 1999). Thus, children's internal working models of attachment are believed to influence their overall adjustment, social behavior, and the development of their self-esteem and sense of self (Thompson, 2000).

Ainsworth's Research

Mary Ainsworth, who began working with John Bowlby in 1950, provided empirical support for Bowlby's theory and extended it in important ways. Her first study, conducted in Uganda in 1954, involved extensive naturalistic observations of everyday infant–mother interactions in twenty-eight homes. She observed, for example, how children in Uganda used their mothers as a secure base for exploration and how they reacted to separations from their mothers (Ainsworth, 1967). On the basis of her research in Uganda and her later observations of families in Baltimore, Maryland, Ainsworth came to the conclusion that the extent to which an infant is able to use his or her primary caregiver as a secure base, and how the infant reacts to brief separations from and reunions with the caregiver, provide insight into the quality of the infant's attachment to the caregiver.

Measurement of Attachment Security

In addition to her observational research, Ainsworth designed a laboratory test for measuring the security of an infant's attachment to his or her parent. This test is called the **Strange Situation** because it is conducted in a context that is unfamiliar to the child and likely to heighten the child's need for his or her parent. Typically, the infant, accompanied by the parent, is placed in a laboratory playroom outfitted with interesting toys. After the experimenter introduces the parent and child to the room, the child is exposed to seven episodes, including two separations from and reunions with the parent and interactions with a stranger when alone and when the parent is in the room (see Table 11.1). Each episode lasts approximately 3 minutes, although some are shorter if the child becomes upset. Observers rate

TABLE 11.1

Episodes in Ainsworth's Strange Situation Procedure

Episode	Events	Aspect of Attachment Behavior Assessed
1	Experimenter introduces caregiver and infant to the unfamiliar room, shows parent where to sit and shows baby toys; then leaves.	None
2	Caregiver and child are alone; caregiver is told not to initiate interaction but to respond to baby as appropriate.	Exploration and use of parent as a secure base
3	Stranger enters and is seated quietly for 1 minute; then talks to caregiver for 1 minute; then tries to interact with baby the last minute.	Reaction to the stranger
4	Mother leaves child alone with the stranger, who lets baby play but offers comfort if needed. Segment is shortened if the baby becomes too distressed.	Separation distress and reaction to stranger's comforting
5	Caregiver calls to baby from outside door; enters the room, and pauses by the door. Stranger leaves. Caregiver lets infant play or may comfort infant if distressed.	Reaction to reunion with parent
6	Parent leaves infant alone in the room. Segment is ended if infant is too distressed.	Separation distress
7	Stranger enters room, greets infant, and pauses. She sits or comforts infant if the infant is upset. Segment is ended if the infant is very upset.	Ability to be soothed by stranger
8	Caregiver calls from outside the door, enters and greets infant and pauses. Caregiver sits if infant is not upset but may provide comfort if infant is distressed. Caregiver allows infant to return to play if interested.	Reaction to reunion

Adapted from Ainsworth et al. (1978)

the infant's behaviors, including their attempts to seek closeness and contact with the parent, their resistance to or avoidance of the parent, and their interactions with the parent from a distance using language or gestures.

Although this minimelodrama is a highly artificial situation, it has proven extremely useful in understanding the nature and importance of early parent–child relationships. As Jay Belsky observed of the Strange Situation:

> It may be artificial, but so is a treadmill test for the heart. That's a physical stress test—this is an emotional stress test. They're both artificial, but they're both diagnostic too.
>
> (quoted in Talbot, 1998, p.46)

In her work with the Strange Situation, Ainsworth (1973) discerned three distinct patterns in infants' behavior that seemed to indicate the quality or security of their attachment bond. These patterns—which are reflected in the infant's behavior throughout the Strange Situation, but especially during the *reunions* with the parent—have been replicated many times in research with mothers, and sometimes with fathers. On the basis of these patterns, Ainsworth identified three attachment categories.

The first attachment category—the one into which the majority of infants fall—is **securely attached.** Babies in this category use their mother as a secure base during the initial part of the session, leaving her side to explore the many toys available in the room. As they play with the toys, these infants occasionally look back to check on their mother or bring a toy over to show her. They are usually, but by no means always, distressed to some degree when their mother leaves the room, especially when they are left totally alone. However, when their mother returns, they make it clear that they are glad to see her, either by simply greeting her with a happy smile or, if they have been upset during her absence, by moving over to her to be picked up and comforted. If they have been upset, their mother's presence comforts and calms them, often enabling them to again explore the room. About 65% of middle-class children in the United States fall into this category (see Figure 11.1); for infants from lower socioeconomic groups, the rate is significantly lower (Thompson, 1998).

secure attachment a pattern of attachment in which an infant or child has a high-quality, relatively unambivalent relationship with his or her attachment figure. In the Strange Situation, a securely attached infant, for example, may be upset when the caregiver leaves but may be happy to see the caregiver return, recovering quickly from any distress. When children are securely attached, they can use caregivers as a secure base for exploration.

insecure attachment a pattern of attachment in which children have a less positive attachment to their caregiver than do securely attached children. Insecurely attached children can be classified as insecure/resistant (ambivalent), insecure/avoidant, or disorganized/disoriented.

insecure/resistant (or ambivalent) attachment a type of insecure attachment in which infants or young children are clingy and stay close to their caregiver rather than exploring their environment. In the Strange Situation, insecure/resistant infants tend to get very upset when the caregiver leaves them alone in the room, and are not readily comforted by strangers. When their caregiver returns, they are not easily comforted and both seek comfort and resist efforts by the caregiver to comfort them.

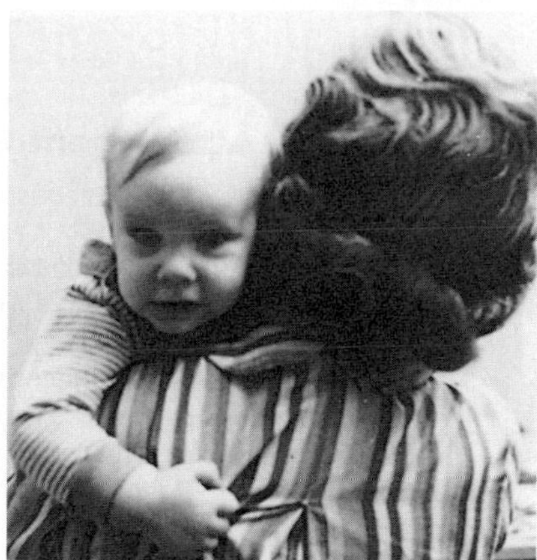

In the Strange Situation, this securely attached child explores the environment when his mother is in the room, cries and stops exploring when she leaves, and is easily calmed by his mother when she returns.

The other two attachment categories that Ainsworth originally identified involve children who are rated as **insecurely attached.** Insecurely attached children have less positive attachment to their caregivers than do securely attached children. One type of insecurely attached infant is classified as **insecure/resistant,** or **ambivalent.** These infants are often clingy from the beginning of the Strange Situation, staying close to the mother instead of exploring the toys. When the mother leaves the room, the infant tends to get very upset, often crying intensely. In the reunion, the infant typically reestablishes contact with the mother, only to then resist her efforts at offering comfort. For example, the infant may rush to the mother bawling, with outstretched arms, signaling the wish to be picked up, and then, as soon as he or she is picked up, may arch away from the mother or begin squirming to get free from her embrace. About 15% of typical middle-class children in the United States fall into the insecure/resistant category.

The other type of insecurely attached infant noted by Ainsworth is classified as **insecure/avoidant**. Insecure/avoidant children tend to avoid their mother in the Strange Situation. For example, they often fail to greet her during the reunions and ignore her or turn away while she is in the room. Approximately 20% of typical middle-class children fall into the insecure/avoidant category (Thompson, 1998).

Subsequent to Ainsworth's original research, attachment investigators found that the reactions of a small percent of children in the Strange Situation did not fit well into any of Ainsworth's three categories. To accommodate these reactions, they developed a fourth category—**disorganized/disoriented** (Main & Solomon, 1990). Infants in this category seem to have no consistent way of coping with the stress of the Strange Situation. Their behavior is often confused or even contradictory. For example, they may exhibit fearful smiles and look away while approaching their mother, or they may seem quite calm and contented and then suddenly display angry distress. They also frequently appear dazed or disoriented and may freeze in their movements or exhibit undirected and incomplete movements. These infants seem to have an unsolvable problem—they want to approach their mother, but they also seem to regard her as a source of fear from which they want to withdraw (Main & Hesse, 1990). Less than 5% of middle-class American infants fall into this category. However, this percentage may be considerably higher in samples in which parents are having serious difficulties with their own working models of attachment (van IJzendoorn, 1995; see Box 11.1).

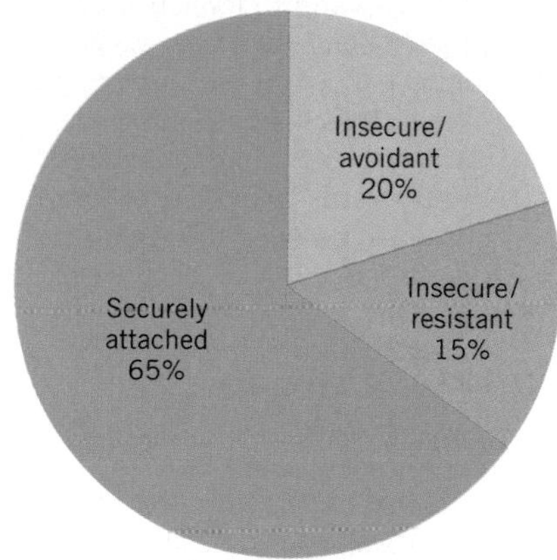

FIGURE 11.1 Percents of middle-class American children in secure and insecure attachment groups About two-thirds of middle-class American children are securely attached. In addition to the insecurely attached children depicted in the chart, less than 5% of children—those who previously were designated as insecure/avoidant or insecure/resistant or were unclassified—are now categorized as disorganized/disoriented children. (Adapted from Thompson, 1998)

insecure/avoidant attachment a type of insecure attachment in which infants or young children seem somewhat indifferent toward their caregiver and may even avoid the caregiver. In the Strange Situation, they seem indifferent toward their caregiver before the caregiver leaves the room and indifferent or avoidant when the caregiver returns. If they get upset when left alone, they are as easily comforted by a stranger as by a parent.

disorganized/disoriented attachment a type of insecure attachment in which infants have no consistent way of coping with the stress of the Strange Situation. Their behavior is often confused or even contradictory, and they often appear dazed or disoriented.

individual differences

Parental Attachment Status

According to attachment theorists, parents have "working models" of attachment relationships that guide their actions with their children and thereby influence the security of their children's attachment. These **adult attachment models** are based on adults' perceptions of their own childhood relationships with their parents and of the continuing influence of those relationships (Main, Kaplan, & Cassidy, 1985).

Parental models of attachment usually are measured with the Adult Attachment Interview (AAI), developed by Mary Main, Carol George, and their colleagues. In this interview, adults are asked to discuss their early childhood attachments and to evaluate them from their current perspective (Hesse, 1999). For example, they are asked to describe their relationship to each parent in childhood; what their parents did for them when they were hurt or upset; what they remember about separations from parents; if they ever felt rejected by their parents; and how their adult personalities were shaped by these experiences. These descriptions are used to classify the adults into four major attachment groups—autonomous, or secure; dismissing; preoccupied; and unresolved/disorganized.

Adults who are rated *autonomous,* or *secure,* are those whose descriptions are coherent, consistent, and relevant to the questions. Generally, autonomous adults describe their past in a balanced manner, recalling both positive and negative features of their parents and of their relationships with them. They also report that their early attachments were influential in their development. Autonomous adults discuss their past in a consistent and coherent manner even if they did not have supportive parents.

Adults in the other three categories are considered to be insecure in their attachment status. *Dismissing* adults often insist that they cannot remember interactions with parents related to their attachment, or they minimize the impact that these experiences had on them. They may also contradict themselves when describing their attachment-related experiences, and seem unaware of their inconsistencies. For example, they may describe their mother in glowing terms and later talk about how she got angry at them whenever they hurt themselves (Hesse, 1999). *Preoccupied* adults are intensely focused on their parents and tend to provide confused and angry accounts of attachment-related experiences. A prototypical response is "I got so angry [at my mother] that I picked up the soup bowl and threw it at her" (Hesse, 1999, p. 403). Preoccupied adults often seem to be so caught up in their attachment memories that they cannot provide a coherent description of them. *Unresolved/disorganized* adults appear to be suffering the aftermath of past traumatic experiences of loss or abuse. Their descriptions of their childhood show striking lapses in reasoning and may not make sense. For example, an unresolved/disorganized adult may indicate that he or she believes that a dead parent is still alive or that the parent died because of negative thoughts that the adult had about him or her (Hesse, 1999).

Parents' classification as autonomous, dismissing, or preoccupied predict both their sensitivity toward their own children and their children's attachment to them. Autonomous (secure) parents tend to be sensitive, warm parents, and their infants usually are securely attached to them (Magai, Hunziker, Mesias, & Culver, 2000; Steele, Steele, & Fonagy, 1996; van IJzendoorn, 1995). Correspondingly, preoccupied and dismissive parents tend to have insecurely attached infants, although this relation is not very strong for preoccupied parents (see figure). This general pattern of findings has been obtained in studies in a number of different Western cultures (Hesse, 1999). Moreover, mothers' attachment scores have been associated not only with those of their infants but also with their own mothers' scores on the AAI (Benoit & Parker, 1994).

Although there clearly is a relation between parents' attachment models and the security of their children's attachments, the reason for this association is

adult attachment models working models of attachment in adulthood that are believed to be based upon adults' perceptions of their own childhood experiences—especially their relationships with their parents—and of the influence of these experiences on them as adults. The four major attachment groups in adulthood are autonomous (or secure), dismissing, preoccupied, and unresolved/disorganized.

A key question, of course, is whether there is some similarity between infants' behavior in the Strange Situation and their behavior at home. The answer is yes (Solomon & George, 1999). For example, in comparison with infants who are insecurely attached, 12-month-olds who are securely attached exhibit more enjoyment of physical contact and less fussy or difficult behavior, and they are better able to use their mothers as a secure base for exploration at home (Pederson & Moran, 1996). Thus, they are more likely to learn about their environments and to enjoy doing so. As you will shortly see, attachment measurements derived from the Strange Situation also correlate with later behavior patterns.

Cultural Variations in Attachment

Because human infants are believed to be biologically predisposed to form attachments with their caregivers, one might expect attachment behaviors to be similar in different cultures. In fact, in large measure, infants' behaviors in the Strange Situation are similar across numerous cultures, including those of China, western

11.1

not clear. There is little doubt that autonomous parents are more sensitively attuned to their children and that this contributes to their children's being securely attached (Pederson, Gleason, Moran, & Bento, 1998). And it may very well be that autonomous adults, who tend to have been securely attached as infants or children (Hamilton, 2000; Waters, Merrick, Trebouz, Cromwell, & Albersheim, 2000), are more sensitive parents because of their own early experiences with sensitive parents. But it is not clear what adults' responses on the AAI actually represent. Although attachment theorists claim that the content and coherence of adults' discussions of their own early childhood experiences reflect the effects of these early experiences, there is little evidence to prove (or disprove) this theory (Fox, 1995; Thompson, 1998). Rather than reflecting their own childhood experiences, adults' discussions of them may instead reflect their personal theories about development and child rearing, their current level of psychological functioning, or their personality, all of which also may affect their parenting. Regardless of the reason, the relation between parents' attachment models and their infants' attachment suggests that parents' beliefs about parenting and about relationships have a powerful influence on the bond between them and their children (Thompson, 1998).

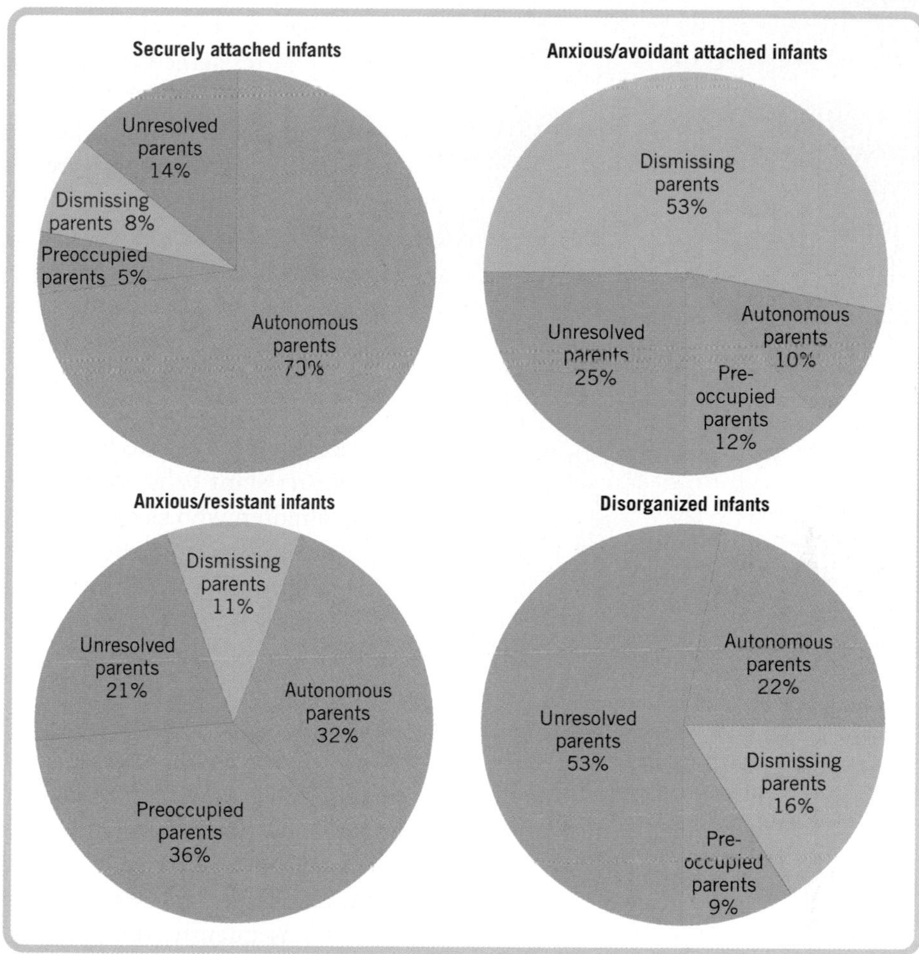

Parents with secure adult attachments tend to have securely attached children. (Adapted from van IJzendoorn, 1995)

Europe, and various parts of Africa. In all these cultures, there are securely attached, insecure/resistant, and insecure/avoidant infants (van IJzendoorn & Sagi, 1999). (Relatively little is known about disorganized/disoriented babies in other cultures because they have seldom been studied and appear to be relatively uncommon.)

However, some interesting and important differences in behavior in the Strange Situation also have been noted in certain other cultures (van IJzendoorn & Kroonenberg, 1988; Zevalkink, Riksen-Walraven, & Van Lieshout, 1999). For example, while Japanese infants in one study showed roughly the same percentage of secure attachment in the Strange Situation as middle-class U.S. infants do (about 68%), there was a notable difference in the types of insecure attachment they displayed. All the insecurely attached Japanese infants were classified as insecure/resistant; none exhibited insecure/avoidant behavior (Takahashi, 1986). This difference may be due to the fact that Japanese culture exalts the idea of oneness between mother and child, and child-rearing practices in Japan, compared with those in the United States, foster greater closeness and physical intimacy between

DON STEVENSON / INDEX STOCK IMAGERY / PICTUREQUEST

The degree to which children are encouraged to be independent varies across cultures and can affect whether children are categorized as insecure/resistant or securely attached.

mothers and infants, as well as infants' dependency on their mothers (Rothbaum, Pott, Azuma, Miyake, & Weisz, 2000). Thus, in the Strange Situation, Japanese children may desire more bodily contact and reassurance than do U.S. children and therefore may be more likely to exhibit anger and resistance to their mother after being denied contact with her (Mizuta, Zahn-Waxler, Cole, & Hiruma, 1996). The Japanese emphasis on dependence and closeness between infant and mother may also explain the fact that Japanese infants are less likely to show exploratory behaviors in the Strange Situation (Rothbaum et al., 2000).

Child-rearing practices also seem to explain an intriguing cultural difference between Israeli children who attend day care and sleep at home and Israeli children raised in a kibbutz—a communal arrangement in which children from different families are raised together and sometimes sleep together in a dormitory. Although the children raised in a kibbutz with communal sleeping arrangements are involved with their parents daily, they are somewhat less likely to be securely attached and are more likely to show insecure/resistant behavior than are Israeli children in day care or even kibbutz children who sleep in their own homes. This may be because children who sleep away from their parents receive less consistent and sensitive caregiving from their nighttime caregivers than do children who are home with their parents at night (van IJzendoorn & Kroonenberg, 1988; van IJzendoorn & Sagi, 1999).

It is important to note that how young children react to separations from and reunions with caregivers in the Strange Situation can also be affected by their prior experience with unfamiliar situations and people. For example, children who are in day care tend to react less negatively and seek less comfort in the Strange Situation than children who are at home every day with the same caregiver. Thus part of the difference in the reaction of Japanese and U.S. infants to the Strange Situation may be due to the fact that very few infants in Japan are enrolled in day care. Consequently, group differences in children's behaviors in the Strange Situation may reflect not only real differences in the security of their attachments but also differences in their everyday experiences.

Factors Associated with the Security of Children's Attachments

One obvious question in trying to explain differences in attachment patterns is whether the parents of securely attached and insecurely attached children differ in the way they interact with their children. Evidence suggests that they do and that, on the average, the differences in their interactions with their children are related to differences in the quality of young children's attachments. Although much less is known about father–child interactions than about mother–child interactions, this seems to be true for fathers as well as mothers.

Parental Sensitivity

parental sensitivity an important factor contributing to the security of an infant's attachment. Parental sensitivity can be exhibited in a variety of ways, including responsive caregiving when children are distressed or upset and helping children to engage in learning situations by providing just enough, but not too much, guidance and supervision.

Attachment theorists have argued that **parental sensitivity** in child rearing is the most crucial parental factor contributing to the development of a secure attachment (Ainsworth, Blehar, Waters, & Wall, 1978). One key aspect of parental sensitivity is responsive caregiving when children are distressed or upset. The mothers of securely attached 1-year-olds tend to read their babies' signals accurately, responding quickly to the needs of a crying baby and smiling readily and happily back at a smiling one. Positive exchanges between mother and child—such as smiling and laughing, making sounds at one another, or coordinated play—may be a particularly important aspect of sensitive parenting that promotes secure attachment (De Wolff & IJzendoorn, 1997).

ELIZABETH CREWS

The mothers of securely attached infants generally respond warmly to their offspring and are sensitive to their needs.

In contrast, the mothers of anxious/resistant infants have been found to be inconsistent in their early caregiving; they sometimes respond promptly to their infants' distress, but sometimes they do not. These mothers often seem highly anxious and overwhelmed themselves. Mothers of anxious/avoidant infants tend to be indifferent and emotionally unavailable, sometimes rejecting their baby's attempts at physical closeness (Isabella, 1993). Disorganized/distressed infants often appear to be confused or frightened by the behavior of their mothers, perhaps because this attachment category is often associated with a history of parental abuse (Carlson, 1998; Cicchetti & Toth, 1998).

Maternal sensitivity has been associated with the quality of children's attachment in numerous cultural groups and across a number of studies. In these studies, infants whose mothers are insensitive show only a 38% rate of secure attachment, which is much lower than the typical rate of 68% for middle-class U.S. children (Posada et al., 1999; van IJzendoorn & Sagi, 1999; Valenzuela, 1997). A similar but somewhat weaker relation has been found between fathers' sensitivity and the security of their children's attachment (van IJzendoorn & De Wolff, 1997).

In all the research discussed above, the investigators were examining correlations between parental sensitivity and children's attachment status. Consequently, it is impossible to determine from these studies whether parents' sensitivity was actually responsible for their children's security of attachment or was merely associated with it due to some other factor, such as the child's temperament (see next section), that affected both the parent's sensitivity and the child's security of attachment. However, evidence that parental sensitivity does in fact have a causal effect on infants' attachment has been provided by short-term experimental interventions designed to enhance the sensitivity of mothers' caregiving. These interventions, discussed in Box 11.2 (p. 423), have been found to increase not only mothers' sensitivity with their infants but also the security of their infants' attachment (Bakermans-Kranenburg, van IJzendoorn, & Juffer, in press; van IJzendoorn, Juffer, & Duyvesteyn, 1995).

Children's Temperament

As we discussed in Chapter 10, some children are warm, friendly, and responsive to adults, whereas others tend to be irritable, unmanageable, or difficult to console. Such differences in temperament might be expected to influence both the way parents behave with their children and the security of a child's attachment. If a child is difficult, for example, parents may become frustrated and less sensitive in their caregiving over time. Similarly, children who are problematically abnormal in their abilities or in their responses to adults may elicit more negative responses from their parents, and these children are more likely to be insecurely attached than are other children (Mangelsdorf et al., 1996; Vaughn et al., 1994).

Nevertheless, a number of studies suggest that temperament likely plays only a small role in children's security of attachment (Seifer, Schiller, Sameroff, Resnick, & Riordan, 1996; Solomon & George, 1999).

Does Security of Attachment Have Long-Term Effects?

The reason that developmentalists are so interested in the security of children's attachment is that securely attached infants appear to grow up to be better adjusted and more socially skilled than insecurely attached children. One explanation for this may be that children with a secure attachment are more likely to develop positive and constructive internal working models of attachment. (Recall that children's working models of attachment are believed to shape their self-perceptions, their expectations about other people, and their social behavior.) In addition, children who experience the sensitive, supportive parenting that is associated with secure attachment are likely to learn that it is acceptable to express emotions in an appropriate way and that emotional communication with others is important (Cassidy, 1994; Sroufe, 1995). In contrast, insecure/avoidant children, whose parents tend to be nonresponsive to their signals of distress, are likely to learn to inhibit emotional expressiveness and to not seek comfort from other people (Bridges & Grolnick, 1995).

Consistent with these patterns, children who were securely attached as infants seem to have closer, more harmonious relationships with peers than do insecurely attached children. For example, as toddlers and preschoolers, they are somewhat more regulated, sociable, and socially competent with peers (Fagot, 1997; Troy & Sroufe, 1987; Vondra, Shaw, Swearingen, Cohen, & Owens, 2001). They are also better able to understand other people's emotions (Laible & Thompson, 1998; Steele, Steele, Croft, & Fonagy, 1999), display more helping, sharing, and concern for peers (Iannotti, Cummings, Pierrehumbert, Milano, & Zahn-Waxler, 1992; Kestenbaum, Farber, & Sroufe, 1989; van IJzendoorn, 1997), and are less aggressive and antisocial (DeMulder, Denham, Schmidt, & Mitchell, 2000; Lyons-Ruth, Easterbrooks, & Cibelli, 1997). Children who were securely attached after infancy tend to have more and higher-quality close friendships and are somewhat more sociable and well liked, even in middle childhood and adolescence (Schneider, Atkinson, & Tardif, 2001). There is also some evidence that although securely and insecurely attached children do not differ in terms of intelligence (Thompson, 1998), securely attached children tend to earn higher grades than insecurely attached children and to be more attentive and involved at school (Jacobsen & Hofmann, 1997).

Securely attached infants are more likely as toddlers to engage in prosocial behavior, such as trying to comfort someone who is sad, than are those who were insecurely attached.

MARY KATE DENNY / PHOTOEDIT

Clearly, then, children's security of attachment is related to their later psychological, social, and cognitive functioning. Nevertheless, experts disagree on the meaning of this relationship. While recognizing that development is always a product of both a child's current circumstances *and* his or her developmental history, some theorists believe that the security of attachment in the earliest years has important effects on later development (Bowlby, 1973; Sroufe, Egeland, & Kreutzer, 1990). Others believe that security of attachment in the early years predicts later

applications 11.2

Interventions and Attachment

To determine if parental sensitivity is *causally* related to differences in security of attachment, researchers have designed special intervention studies. In these studies, parents in an experimental group are first trained to be more sensitive in their caregiving. Later, the attachment statuses of their infants are compared with those of children whose parents, as members of a control group, experienced no intervention (van IJzendoorn, Juffer, & Duyvesteyn, 1995).

An intervention study of this sort was conducted in the Netherlands by Daphna van den Boom (1994). Infants who were rated as irritable shortly after their birth were selected for the study because irritable infants are at risk for insecure attachments. When the infants were about 6 months of age, half of their mothers were randomly chosen to be in the experimental group for three months. The mothers in this group were taught to be attuned to their infants' cues and to respond to them in a manner that fostered positive exchanges between mother and child.

At the end of the intervention, mothers in the experimental group were more attentive and responsive to their infants, as well as more stimulating, than were mothers who did not receive the intervention. In turn, their infants were more sociable, explored the environment more, were better able to soothe themselves, and cried less than did infants whose mothers did not receive the intervention. Especially significant, the rates of secure attachment were notably higher for infants whose mothers were in the intervention group than for those whose mothers were not—62% compared with 22%.

In a longitudinal follow-up, the infants and mothers were evaluated again when the children were 18 months, 24 months, and 3½ years of age. At 18 months of age, 72% of the children in the intervention group were securely attached, compared with 26% of the children in the control group. When their infants were 24 months old, mothers in the intervention group were, as earlier, more accepting, accessible, cooperative, and sensitive with their infants than were the control-group mothers, and their children were more cooperative. Similar findings were obtained when the children were 3½ years old. Some, but not all, of the intervention's effects appeared to be due to the intervention's affecting the quality of the mother–child attachment at age 1 or 2, which in turn affected the quality of mothers' behavior with their infants six or more months later (van den Boom, 1995). Based on evidence from experimental studies such as this, it seems clear that parenting sensitivity contributes to infants' and young children's security of attachment.

development *only* to the degree that the child's environment—including the quality of parent–child interactions—does not change (Lamb, Thompson, Gardner, & Charnov, 1985). According to this view, early security of attachment predicts children's functioning at an older age because "good" parents remain good parents and "bad" parents remain bad parents. If the parent–child relationship and family circumstances change due to divorce, financial stress, or other factors, including positive ones, the child's attachment and development are likely to change as well.

Empirical findings support both perspectives to some degree. One study reported that even if they functioned poorly during the preschool years, children who had a secure attachment and adapted well during infancy and toddlerhood were more socially and emotionally competent in middle childhood than their peers who had been insecurely attached (Sroufe et al., 1990). This suggests that a child's early attachment has some effects over time. However, there also is evidence that children's security of attachment changes somewhat as their environment changes—for example, with stress and conflict in the home (Frosch, Mangelsdorf, & McHale, 2000; Lewis, Feiring, & Rosenthal, 2000)—and that parent–child interactions or parenting behavior at a given age predicts the child's social and emotional competence at that age better than measures of attachment taken at younger ages (Thompson, 1998; Youngblade & Belsky, 1992). Thus, it is likely that children's development can be predicted better from the combination of both their early attachment status and the quality of subsequent parenting than from either factor alone. Finally, it is important to keep in mind that most of the research on attachment is correlational, so it is difficult to pin down causal relations.

review:

Evidence of the poor development of infants who are deprived of caring, consistent relationships with an adult led to extensive interest in infants' early attachments. John Bowlby proposed that a secure attachment provides children with a secure base for exploration and contributes to a positive internal working model of relationships in general. According to attachment research, pioneered by Mary Ainsworth, children's attachment relationships with caregivers can be classified as secure, insecure/avoidant, insecure/resistant, and disorganized/disoriented. Children in the first three of these categories display similarities across cultures, although the percentage of children in different attachment groups sometimes varies across cultures or subcultures.

Factors that appear to influence the security of attachment include caregivers' sensitivity and responsiveness to a child's needs, parents' attachment status, and, to a modest degree, the child's temperament. Children's security of attachment to their caregivers predicts the quality of their relationships with family members and peers and their academic skills, all of which are likely to affect how children feel about and evaluate themselves. These relations may hold not only because the sensitivity of parenting in the early years of life has long-term effects but also because sensitive parents usually continue to provide effective parenting, whereas less sensitive parents continue to interact with the children in ways that undermine children's optimal development.

Conceptions of the Self

As we have noted, children's security of attachments to caregivers affects their feelings about themselves, especially in regard to their relationships with other people. Thus, attachment experiences early in life likely color the sense of self that emerges in infancy. However, the development of a sense of self is an ongoing, very complex process that involves much more than notions of the self that formed in infancy.

When we speak of **self,** we are referring to a conceptual system made up of one's thoughts and attitudes about oneself. An individual's conceptions about the self can include thoughts about one's own physical being (body, possessions), social characteristics (e.g., relationships, personality, social roles), and "spiritual" or internal characteristics (e.g., thoughts and psychological functioning). It also may include notions about how the self changes or remains the same over time, beliefs about one's own role in shaping these processes, and even reflections on one's own consciousness of selfhood (Damon & Hart, 1988). The development of the self is important because individuals' self-conceptions, including the ways they view themselves and how they feel about themselves, appear to influence their overall feelings of well-being and competence.

The Development of Conceptions of Self

Children's sense of self emerges in the early years of life, especially in their interactions with people of importance to them, and continues to develop into adulthood, becoming more complex as the individual's emotional and cognitive development deepens.

self a conceptual system made up of one's thoughts and attitudes about oneself

The Self in Infancy

There is compelling evidence that infants have a rudimentary sense of self in the first months of life. As we saw in Chapter 5, by 2 to 4 months of age, infants have a sense of their ability to control objects outside of themselves; this is evidenced by their enthusiastic reactions to controlling the movement of a mobile, by pulling a string attached to an arm, and their anger when they no longer have control (Lewis, Alessandri, & Sullivan, 1990). They also seem to have some understanding of their own bodily movements. For example, when viewing live video images of their own leg movements, 3- to 5-month-old infants looked longer and moved their legs more when the video showed their leg movements from a perspective other than their own (e.g., when the right and left legs were reversed in the image) than when the video showed leg movements as they themselves saw them (Rochat & Morgan, 1995). Perhaps their longer looking reflected their surprise at, or interest in, seeing the reversal of their limbs (Rochat & Striono, 2002).

Infants' sense of self becomes much more distinct at about 8 months of age, when infants respond to separation from their mother with separation distress. Further indications that children view others as beings different from themselves, at least in regard to their actions, are apparent by age 1. As discussed in Chapter 4, around their first birthday, infants begin to show joint attention with others to objects in the environment. For example, they will visually follow the direction of a caregiver's pointing finger to find the object that the caregiver is pointing at, and then turn back to the caregiver to confirm that they are indeed looking at the intended object (Harter, 1998; Stern, 1985). They sometimes will also give objects to an adult in an apparent effort to engage the adult in their activities (West & Rheingold, 1978).

Infants' emerging recognition of the self becomes more directly apparent by 18 to 20 months of age, when many children can look into a mirror and realize that the image they see there is themselves (Asendorpf, Warkentin, & Baudonniere, 1996; Lewis & Brooks-Gunn, 1979). In studies that test this ability, a dot of rouge is surreptitiously put on a child's face, and then the child is placed in front of a mirror. The child is then asked who the person with the red spot is, or is asked to clean the spot off the person in the mirror. Children younger than 18 months old often try to touch the child in the mirror, or they do nothing. By about the age of 18 months, many children make movements toward the rouge on their own face, so it is assumed that they realize that the mirror image is a self-reflection.

DR. MICHAEL LEWIS, INSTITUTE FOR THE STUDY OF CHILD DEVELOPMENT, ROBERT WOOD JOHNSON MEDICAL SCHOOL, UNIVERSITY OF MEDICINE AND DENTISTRY OF NEW JERSEY, EAST BRUNSWICK, N.J.

In this photo from the original research of Lewis and Brooks-Gunn, the girl recognizes that the child in the mirror with a spot on her cheek is herself.

There is other evidence that young children recognize themselves by age 2. In one study, 63% of a group of 20- to 25-month-olds picked themselves out when they were presented with pictures of themselves and two same-sex, same-age children. By approximately age 30 months, 97% of the children immediately picked their own photograph (Bullock & Lutkenhaus, 1990).

During their third year, children's self-awareness becomes quite clear. As we saw in Chapter 10, 2-year-olds exhibit embarrassment and shame—emotions that involve concern about how others view oneself (Lewis, 1995, 1998). The strength of 2-year-olds' self-awareness is even more evident in their notorious self-assertion, which has caused the period between ages 2 and 3 to be called the "terrible twos."

During this time, children frequently try to determine their activities and goals independently of parents, often in direct opposition to what their parents (and other adults) want them to do (Bullock & Lutkenhaus, 1990). They frequently become frustrated and upset when they realize that they cannot get what they want and cannot control their caregivers.

Two-year-olds' self-awareness is also evident in, and enhanced by, their use of language. They can, for example, use pronouns to refer to themselves ("me," "mine") and can label themselves by name (e.g., "Daddy take Julia's book") (Bates, 1990). Young children can also use language to store in memory their own experiences and behavior, giving them access to information about themselves and their past. Thus, language makes it possible for children to construct a narrative of their own "life story" and develop a more enduring picture of the self (Harter, 1998).

Parents contribute to the child's expanding self-image by providing descriptive information about the child ("You're such a big boy"), evaluative descriptions of the child ("You're so smart"), and information about the degree to which the child has met rules and standards ("Big girls don't hit their baby sisters"). Parents also collaborate in children's construction of autobiographical memory by reminding them of their past experiences (Snow, 1990).

The Self in Childhood

As children progress through childhood, their conceptions of themselves—and the characteristics in terms of which they define themselves—become increasingly complex and encompassing. This developmental pattern in self-understanding has been vividly illustrated by Susan Harter, a leading researcher on children's emerging sense of self. Combining statements made by a wide array of children in a number of empirical studies, Harter has constructed composite examples of children's typical self-descriptive statements at different ages. The following is a composite example of how 3- to 4-year-olds describe themselves.

> I'm three years old and I live in a big house with my mother and father and my brother, Jason, and my sister, Lisa. I have blue eyes and a kitty that is orange and a television in my room. I know all of my ABC's, listen: A, B, C, D, E, F, G, H, J, L, K, O, M, P, Q, X, Z. I can run real fast. I like pizza and I have a nice teacher at preschool. I can count up to 10, want to hear me? I love my dog Skipper. I can climb to the top of the jungle gym—I'm not scared! I'm never scared! I'm always happy. . . . I'm really strong. I can lift this chair, watch me!
>
> (Harter, 1999, p. 37)

In describing themselves, young children often make reference to their preferences and possessions such as a family pet.

SUPERSTOCK

As this composite example demonstrates, at age 3 to 4, children understand themselves in terms of concrete, observable characteristics related to physical attributes ("I have blue eyes"), physical activities and abilities ("I can run real fast"), social relationships ("my brother, Jason, and my sister, Lisa"), and psychological traits ("I am always happy") (Damon & Hart, 1988; Harter, 1999). Their focus on observable features is further reflected by the fact that the prototypical child in the composite example above bragged about particular skills such as running fast and did not make generalizations about his/her overall ability as an athlete. Even when the child made a general statement about himself/herself ("I'm really strong"), this statement was closely tied to actual behavior (lifting a chair). Young children also describe themselves in terms of their preferences ("I love my dog Skipper") and possessions ("I have . . . a kitty . . . and a television").

The composite example reflects another characteristic typical of children's self-concept during the preschool years: their self-evaluations are unrealistically positive. Young children seem to think they are really like what they want to be (Harter &

Pike, 1984; Stipek, Roberts, & Sanborn, 1984). For example, the child in the composite example claimed mastery of the ABCs but clearly lacked it. Maintaining positive illusions about themselves is relatively easy for young children because they generally do not compare their performance with that of others and thus do not recognize relative deficits in their abilities. In addition, they usually do not consider their own prior successes and failures when assessing their abilities. Even if they have failed at a task several times, they are likely to believe that they will succeed on the next try (Ruble, Grosovsky, Frey, & Cohen, 1992).

social comparison the process of comparing aspects of one's own psychological, behavioral, or physical functioning to that of others in order to evaluate oneself

Children begin to refine their conceptions of self in elementary school, in part because they increasingly engage in **social comparison,** comparing themselves with others in terms of their characteristics, behaviors, and possessions ("He can kick the ball farther than I can"), and increasingly pay attention to discrepancies between their own and others' performance on tasks ("She got an A on the test and I got only a C") (Frey & Ruble, 1985). By middle to late elementary school, children's conceptions of self have begun to become integrated and more broadly encompassing, as is illustrated by the following composite self-description that would be typical of a child between the ages of 8 and 11:

> I'm pretty popular, at least with the girls. That's because I'm nice to people and helpful and can keep secrets. Mostly I am nice to my friends, although if I get in a bad mood I sometimes say something that can be a little mean. . . . At school, I'm feeling pretty smart in certain subjects like Language Arts and Social Studies. . . . But I'm feeling pretty dumb in Math and Science, especially when I see how well a lot of the other kids are doing. Even though I'm not doing well in those subjects, I still like myself as a person, because Math and Science just aren't that important to me. How I look and how popular I am are more important. I also like myself because I know my parents like me and so do other kids. That helps you like yourself.
>
> (Harter, 1999, p. 48)

The developmental changes in older children's conceptions of self reflect cognitive advances in their ability to use higher-order concepts that integrate more specific behavioral features of the self. For example, the child in the preceding self-description was able to relate being "popular" to several behaviors, such as being "nice to others," being "helpful," and being able to "keep secrets." The newfound cognitive capacity to form higher-order conceptions of the self allows older children to construct more global views of themselves and to evaluate themselves as a person overall.

In addition, older children can coordinate opposing self-representations ("smart" and "dumb") that, at a younger age, they would have considered mutually exclusive (Harter, 1999; Marsh, Craven, & Debus, 1998). Older children are also inclined to compare themselves with others on the basis of objective performance information (such as test scores) in formulating their self-evaluations (Ruble & Flett, 1988; Ruble & Frey, 1991). These abilities result in a more balanced and realistic assessment of the self, although they also can result in feelings of inferiority and helplessness (see Box 11.3).

In elementary school, children's self-concepts increasingly are based on their relationships with others, especially peers, and others' evaluations of them. As a result, their self-descriptions often contain a pronounced social element and focus on any personality traits or physical characteristics that may influence their place in their social networks (Damon & Hart, 1988):

> WHAT ARE YOU LIKE? I am friendly. WHY IS THAT IMPORTANT? Other kids won't like you if you aren't.
>
> (Damon & Hart, 1988, P. 60)

helpless pattern of motivation a response to failure in which individuals feel badly, blame themselves for their failure, and do not persist at the task because they feel that they cannot succeed

mastery-oriented pattern of motivation a response to failure in which individuals do not evaluate themselves negatively and increase their efforts to master the task

WHAT KIND OF PERSON ARE YOU? I am very smart. WHY IS THAT IMPORTANT? My friends only like smart kids.

(Damon & Hart, 1988, P. 60)

Because older school-aged children's conceptions of self are strongly influenced by the opinions of others, children at this age are vulnerable to low self-esteem if others view them negatively or as less competent than their peers.

a closer look 11.3

Conceptions of the Self and Children's Achievement Motivation

How children think and feel about themselves plays a role in how they respond to their successes and failures. When some children fail on a task, they show what is labeled a **helpless pattern of motivation:** they feel badly, blame themselves for their failure, and do not persist at the task. In contrast, when other children fail on a task, they show a **mastery-oriented pattern of motivitation:** they do not evaluate themselves negatively and increase their efforts to succeed on the task. Helpless responses to tasks have been found in children as young as 4 or 5 years old and are quite evident in some children by the mid- to late-elementary school years (Cain & Dweck, 1995; Harter, 1983).

What accounts for this difference in achievement motivation? Carol Dweck suggested that the differences reflect children's different personal theories about intelligence and how one succeeds. Older children who show a helpless response to failure tend to think that intelligence is a fixed trait and cannot be changed. When evaluating their own performance, they tend to focus on outcomes (that is, success or failure) rather than on the processes (such as effort) that lead to success (Heyman & Dweck, 1998). Therefore, they think that if they have failed, it is because they simply are not very smart and that there is nothing they can do about it. Believing that their failure is beyond their control, they are unlikely to change their approach or to try harder to succeed in the future. In contrast, children who show a mastery-oriented response attribute their failures to modifiable factors such as insufficient effort or lack of preparation. They focus on the processes involved in learning rather than on the immediate outcomes and tend to believe that they can succeed if they only try harder.

For younger children who do not fully understand the notion of enduring traits, all that may be necessary to develop a helpless orientation is the tendency to evaluate themselves on the basis of their successes and failures on tasks (e.g., scores they get on a test) and on others' evaluations of their outcomes (Burhans & Dweck, 1995). Children who have these tendencies are less likely to develop an internal or intrinsic desire to learn than are children who focus on effort and other processes involved in learning (Harter, 1983).

Whether children develop a helpless or mastery orientation toward learning depends in part on adults' reactions to children's successes and failures. For example, children who are regularly praised for their intelligence when they succeed on a task (e.g., "You must be smart at these problems") tend to think of intelligence as something that cannot be changed and are relatively likely to show a helpless reaction to failure. In contrast, children who are regularly praised for their effort or use of effective strategies when they succeed on tasks (e.g., "You must have worked hard at these problems") tend to believe that intelligence is a characteristic that can be improved through effort, and they are more likely to be motivated to master tasks they have failed at (Kamins & Dweck, 1999; Mueller & Dweck, 1998).

Research conducted with children at risk for depression suggests that it is possible to change children's helpless reactions. Children at risk for depression, like children with a helpless orientation, tend to be pessimistic, to attribute the causes of failure to internal factors, and to feel powerless to change negative events. In one study, 13-year-olds at risk for depression met in groups of ten to twelve children for 18 hours over 12 weeks. They were taught to identify negative beliefs about themselves, to evaluate these beliefs by examining evidence for and against them, and to generate more realistic and optimistic alternative beliefs. To encourage them to take a more positive and active approach to managing events, they also were taught social skills such as taking others' perspectives (so that they could act in ways that were appropriate and had the desired effect), setting goals before acting, generating a variety of possible solutions for problems, and weighing the pros and cons when making decisions. Children who received this training exhibited fewer problem behaviors six months later and were less depressed six months and two years later than children who were equally at risk for depression but did not participate in the groups (Jaycox, Reivich, Gillham, & Seligman, 1994). Most important for the question of preventing or overcoming children's helpless achievement orientations, these improvements appear due in large measure to changes in how optimistic the children were in explaining their positive and negative experiences (Gillham, Reivich, Jaycox, & Seligman, 1995). Thus, it would seem that getting children with a helpless orientation to change views about the reasons for their failures would help them begin to develop a mastery orientation.

The Self in Adolescence

Children's conceptions of self change in fundamental ways across adolescence, due in part to the emergence of abstract thinking during this stage of life (see Chapter 4). The ability to use abstract thinking allows adolescents to think of themselves in terms of abstract characteristics that encompass a variety of concrete characteristics and behaviors. Consider the following prototypical composite self-description of a young adolescent:

> I'm an extrovert with my friends: I'm talkative, pretty rowdy, and funny. . . . All in all, around people I know pretty well I'm awesome, at least I think my friends think I am. I'm usually cheerful when I'm with my friends, happy and excited to be doing things with them. . . . With my parents, . . . I feel sad as well as mad and also hopeless about ever pleasing them. . . . At school, I'm pretty intelligent, I know that because I'm smart when it comes to how I do in classes, I'm curious about learning new things, and I'm also creative when it comes to solving problems. My teacher says so. . . . I can be a real introvert around people I don't know well—I'm shy, uncomfortable, and nervous. Sometimes I'm simply an airhead, I act really dumb and say things that are just plain stupid. . . .
>
> (Harter, 1999, p. 60)

As is evident in this composite example, young people's concern over their social competence and their social acceptance, especially by peers, intensifies in early adolescence (Damon & Hart, 1988). The example also illustrates young adolescents' ability to arrive at higher-level, abstract self-descriptions such as "extrovert" by combining personal traits such as "talkative," "rowdy," and "funny."

Particularly notable is the fact that adolescents can conceive of themselves in terms of a variety of selves, depending on the context. The adolescent in the composite, for instance, describes himself/herself as a somewhat different person with friends and with parents, as well as in familiar and unfamiliar settings. Most young adolescents do not seem particularly troubled by their awareness that the person they appear to be can vary according to the context. In part, this may be because young adolescents tend to think about each of their abstract representations of the self separately from other abstractions and cannot integrate them (Higgins, 1991). Consequently, in terms of their overall sense of themselves, it does not overly concern young adolescents that they may be both intelligent and an airhead, or extroverted and introverted (see Figure 11.2). As one young adolescent put it when accounting for the fact that he had described himself as both "caring" and "rude":

> Well, you are caring with your friends and rude to people who don't treat you nicely. There's no problem. I guess I just think about one thing about myself at a time and don't think about the other until the next day.
>
> (quoted in Harter, 1999, p. 64)

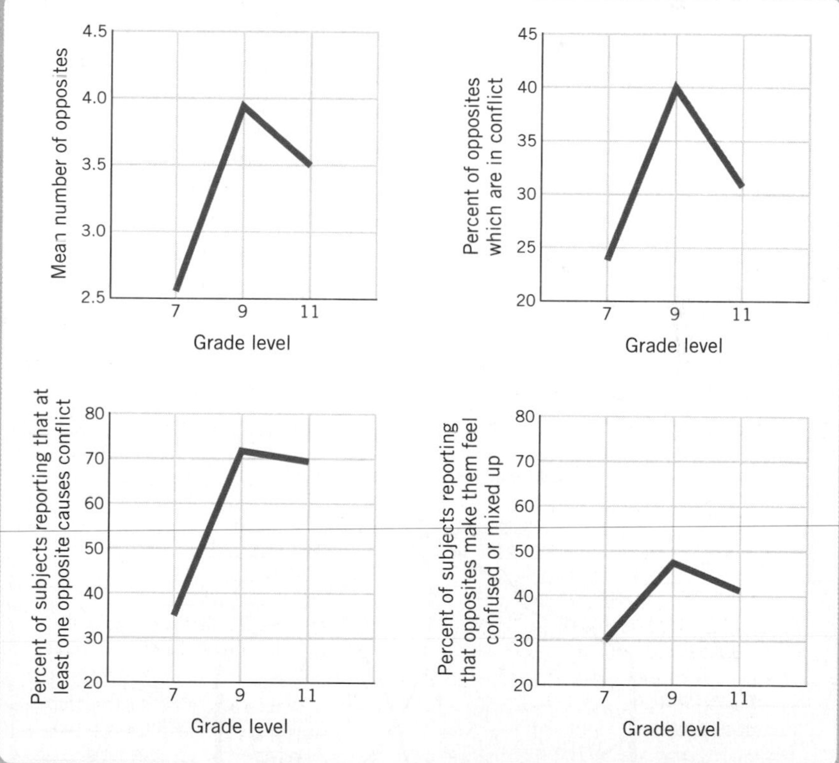

FIGURE 11.2 Developmental differences in adolescents' perceptions of opposing and conflicting self-attributes When asked about their characteristics, seventh graders were much less likely than older adolescents to report contradictions in their characteristics and that these contradictions caused them to feel internal conflict such as confusion or negative emotion. (Adapted from Harter & Monsour, 1992)

personal fable a story that adolescents tell about themselves that involves beliefs in the uniqueness of their own feelings and their immortality

imaginary audience the belief, stemming from adolescent egocentrism, that everyone else is focused on the adolescent's appearance and behavior

According to David Elkind (1967), thinking about the self in early adolescence is characterized by a form of egocentrism called the **personal fable,** in which adolescents overly differentiate their feelings from those of others and come to regard themselves, and especially their feelings, as unique and special. They may believe that only they can experience whatever misery or rapture or confusion they are currently feeling. This belief is typified in the adolescent assertion "But you don't know how it feels," or "My parents don't understand me, what do *they* know about what it's like to be a teenager?" (Elkind, 1967; Harter, 1999, p. 76).

The kind of egocentrism that forms the basis for adolescents' personal fables also causes many adolescents to be preoccupied with what others think of them (Elkind, 1967; Harter, 1999; Rosenberg, 1979). This preoccupation is exhibited in what David Elkind (1967) has labeled as the adolescent's belief in an **imaginary audience,** that is, the belief that everyone else is focused on the adolescent's appearance and behavior. According to Elkind, because adolescents are so concerned with their own appearance and behavior, they assume that wherever they are, all eyes are upon them, scrutinizing their every blemish or social misstep.

In their middle teens, adolescents often begin to agonize over the contradictions in their behavior and characteristics. They tend to become introspective and concerned with the question of "Who am I?" (Broughton, 1978). Consider this prototypical self-description of a 15-year-old:

> What am I like as a person? You're probably not going to understand. I'm complicated! With my really *close* friends, I am very tolerant, I mean I'm understanding and caring. With a *group* of friends I'm rowdier. I'm also usually friendly and cheerful but I can be pretty obnoxious and intolerant if I don't like how they're acting. I'd *like* to be friendly and tolerant all the time, that's the kind of person I *want* to be, and I'm disappointed in myself when I'm not. At school, I'm serious, even studious every now and then, but on the other hand, I'm a goof-off too, because if you're *too* studious, you won't be popular. . . . I really don't understand how I can switch so fast from being cheerful with my friends, then coming home and feeling anxious, and then getting frustrated and sarcastic with my parents. Which one is the *real* me?
>
> (quoted in Harter, 1999, p. 67)

FIGURE 11.3 The multiple selves of a prototypical 15-year-old girl This girl viewed herself as being different in different contexts or with different people. For example, she described herself as open with her mother but not her father, and as quiet with her best friend but rowdy with a group of friends. (Adapted from Harter, 1999)

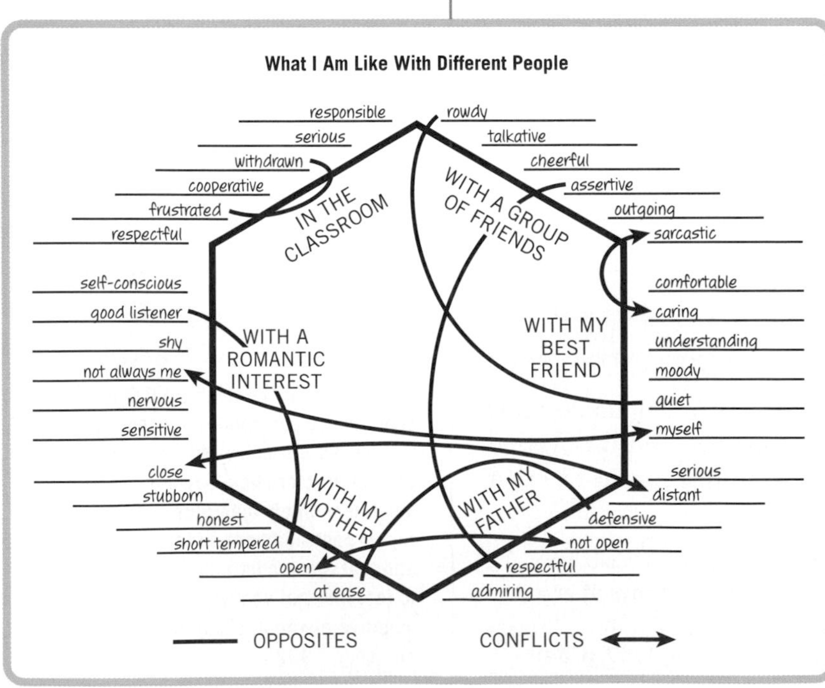

Although adolescents in their middle teens are better than younger adolescents at identifying contradictions in themselves (see Figure 11.3) and often feel conflicted about these inconsistencies, most still do not have the cognitive skills needed to integrate their recognition of these contradictions into a coherent conception of self. As a consequence, adolescents of this age often feel confused and concerned about who they really are. As one teen put it, "It's not right, it should all fit together in one piece!" (Harter, 1999, p. 71; Harter, Bresnick, Bouchey, & Whitsell, 1998).

In late adolescence and early adulthood, the individual's conception of self becomes both more integrated and less determined by what others think. Both of these shifts are captured by Harter's composite representation of a high school senior:

> I'd like to be an ethical person who treats other people fairly. That's the kind of lawyer I'd like to be, too. I don't always live up to that standard; that is, sometimes I do something that doesn't feel that ethical. When that happens I get a little depressed because I don't like myself as a person. But I tell myself that its natural to make mistakes, so I don't really question the fact that deep down inside, the real me is a moral person. Basically, I like who I am. . . . Being athletic isn't that high on my own list of what is important, even though it is for a lot of the kids in our school. But I don't really care what they think anymore. I *used* to, but now what *I* think is what counts. After all, I have to live with myself as a person and to respect that person, which I do now, more than a few years ago.
>
> (quoted in Harter, 1999, p. 78)

As in the case of this senior, older adolescents' conceptions of self frequently reflect internalized personal values, beliefs, and standards (Damon & Hart, 1988). Many of these values, beliefs, and standards have been established by others in the child's life, but they are now internally accepted and generated. Thus, older adolescents place less emphasis on what other people think than at younger ages and are more concerned with meeting their own standards and with their future self—what they are becoming or going to be (Harter, 1999; Higgins, 1991).

Like the senior in the composite example, older adolescents are also more likely to have the cognitive capacity to integrate opposites or contradictions in the self that occur in different contexts or at different times (Higgins, 1991). They may explain contradictory characteristics in terms of the need to be flexible, and may view variations in their behavior with different people as "adaptive" because one cannot act the same with everyone. Similarly, they may integrate changes in emotion under the characteristic "moody." Moreover, contradictions are likely to be viewed as a normal part of being human. Adolescents who can integrate their opposing attributes in this manner are less conflicted and upset by them.

However, whether older adolescents are able to successfully integrate contradictions in themselves likely depends not only on their own cognitive capacities but also on help from parents, teachers, and other people in understanding the complexity of personalities. The support and tutelage of others in this regard allows adolescents to internalize values, beliefs, and standards that they feel committed to and to feel comfortable with who they are (Hart & Fegley, 1995; Harter, 1999).

FRANCISCO CRUZ / SUPERSTOCK

Feelings of self-worth develop partly from the child's feelings of acceptance in the family.

Identity in Adolescence

Clearly, the question "Who am I?" is a central and often disturbing one for many adolescents. It is also a question that, for many older adolescents, expands well beyond the issue of multiple selves and inconsistent behavior. As they begin to approach adulthood, adolescents must begin to develop a sense of personal identity that incorporates numerous aspects of self, including their values and their goals for the future. For example, adolescents in contemporary societies are faced with thinking about and preparing for possible career choices, so they have to start constructing a sense of who they will be in the adult work world. For some, this includes the decision of whether work or some other pursuit, such as child rearing or advancing their education or seeking adventure, will be the factor that organizes life in early adulthood.

TONY FREEMAN / PHOTOEDIT

During late adolescence, reexamination of one's value system is common; renewed commitment to previously held beliefs on the one hand, or total rejection on the other, are not unusual outcomes.

In addition, adolescents tend to increasingly think about political or religious systems of beliefs and values, and often feel the need to figure out who they are in terms of these belief and value systems. Many adolescents and young adults make commitments to religious or political ideologies after exploring various options. Others may have difficulty figuring out what they believe in and may struggle with belief systems that they had accepted unquestioningly as children. Adolescents must also sort through beliefs and values that guide sexual behavior, such as those regarding whether or not premarital sex is acceptable. Some adolescents and young adults also have to deal with their sexual identity—that is, acknowledging whether they are heterosexual, gay or lesbian, or bisexual. Achieving a sense of identity in all these contexts is especially difficult in modern "wired" cultures in which youth have access to far more information and role choices than their counterparts in the past ever did.

Erikson's Theory of Identity Formation

As discussed briefly in Chapter 9, Erik Erikson argued that the resolution of these many identity issues is the chief developmental task in adolescence. He referred to the resolution of these issues as the crisis of **identity versus identity confusion.** In his view, the challenge is as follows: "From among all possible and imaginable relations, [the person] must make a series of ever-narrowing selections of personal, occupational, sexual, and ideological commitments" (1968, p. 245). Successful resolution of this crisis involves the construction of a coherent identity—that is, an identity that is an integration of various aspects of the self into a consistent whole that is stable over time and across events.

According to Erikson, adolescents who fail to achieve an identity can experience one of several negative outcomes. One such outcome is **identity confusion,** an incomplete and sometimes incoherent sense of self. Adolescents in a state of identity confusion often feel lost, isolated, and depressed, as well as uncertain about who they are. Erikson suggested that some form of identity confusion is very common in adolescence and that it generally lasts for a relatively short time, although it can persist and turn into a more severe psychological disturbance.

Another negative outcome related to the struggle for identity can arise if adolescents commit themselves prematurely to an identity without adequately considering their choices. This identity choice is called **identity foreclosure.** Included in

identity versus identity confusion Erikson's psychosocial stage of development that occurs during adolescence. During this stage, the adolescent or young adult either develops an identity or experiences an incomplete and sometimes incoherent sense of self.

identity confusion an incomplete and sometimes incoherent sense of self that often occurs in Erikson's stage of identity versus identity confusion

identity foreclosure premature commitment to an identity without adequate consideration of other options

negative identity identity that stands in opposition to what is valued by people around the adolescent. Some adolescents form a negative identity while trying to construct an identity during Erikson's stage of identity versus identity confusion.

this category might be a 17-year-old who quits school and goes to work in a dead-end job because he or she does not envision any other options, or a young adolescent who decides to become a doctor simply because his or her parent is one, never considering any other options during high school, college, or medical school.

A different self-defeating outcome of the search for an identity is a **negative identity,** an identity that represents the opposite of what is valued by people around the adolescent. A typical example would be a minister's daughter who repeatedly gets into trouble with the law or is sexually promiscuous, or a professor's child who drops out of high school and has no occupational goal. Erikson suggested that for some adolescents, taking on a negative identity is one way to get noticed by their parents or other people important to them when more conventional attempts have failed.

Due to the complexity of achieving an identity in modern society, and because of the negative consequences of failing to do so, Erikson argued for the importance of a **psychosocial moratorium**—a time-out period during which the adolescent is not expected to take on adult roles and can pursue activities that lead to self-discovery. During this period, adolescents can try out new looks, new ways of acting, new ideas about what they want to do for a living, and so forth.

Although Erikson argued that this period of experimentation is important to adolescents' finding the best identity for themselves, a moratorium of this sort is possible or acceptable only in some cultures. Even then, it often is a luxury reserved for the middle and upper classes (i.e., those can who afford the moratorium provided by the college years). If adolescents must work full time to help support their families and themselves, many identity options will be closed to them because of limits on their time and schooling. In addition, in traditional societies a moratorium is unheard of and unnecessary: children know from a very young age what their adult identity will be because there are few role choices available, and people generally live their lives in the same manner as their parents have.

MICHAEL NEWMAN / PHOTOEDIT

Trying out various "looks" can be an aspect of the self-discovery that occurs among many adolescents in some cultures.

Research on Identity Formation

Following up on Erikson's depiction of identity formation, a number of researchers looked for ways to measure the identity status of adolescents and to trace the outcome of the various statuses proposed by Erikson. The method most often used for this purpose was devised by James Marcia (1980). In this method, adolescents or young adults are typically asked questions designed to reveal the extent of their exploration of, and commitment to, issues related to occupation, ideology (e.g., religion, politics), and sexual behavior. The answers to these questions are used to classify the individual into one of the following four identity-status categories (see Table 11.2 for the criteria of each status):

1. Identity-diffusion status. The individual does not have firm commitments regarding the issues in question and is not making progress toward them.

2. Foreclosure status. The individual has not engaged in any identity experimentation and has established a vocational or ideological identity based on the choices or values of others.

3. Moratorium status. The individual is exploring various occupational and ideological choices and has not yet made a clear commitment to them.

4. Identity-achievement status. The individual has achieved a coherent and consolidated identity based on personal decisions regarding occupation, ideology, and the like. The individual believes that these decisions were made autonomously and is committed to them.

psychosocial moratorium a time-out during which the adolescent is not expected to take on adult roles and can pursue activities that lead to self-discovery

identity-diffusion status a category of identity status in which the individual does not have firm commitments and is not making progress toward them

foreclosure status a category of identity status in which the individual is not engaged in any identity experimentation and has established a vocational or ideological identity based on the choices or values of others

moratorium status a category of identity status in which the individual is in the phase of experimentation with regard to occupational and ideological choices and has not yet made a clear commitment to them

identity-achievement status a category of identity status in which, after a period of exploration, the individual has achieved a coherent and consolidated identity based on personal decisions regarding occupation, ideology, and the like. The individual believes that these decisions were made autonomously and is committed to them.

LAURA ZITO

In some traditional cultures, adolescents have few role options and, consequently, know from a young age what their adult identity will be.

Researchers generally have found that, at least in modern Western societies, the identity status of adolescents and young adults is related to their adjustment, social behavior, and personality. On the whole, adolescents and young adults who have attained identity-achievement status are socially more mature and higher in achievement motivation than are their peers. In contrast, individuals who have an identity-diffusion status tend to be apathetic, to lack intimate relationships with peers, and to be most at risk for drug abuse (Damon, 1983; Grotevant, 1998; Jones, 1992; Marcia, 1980). Individuals with a foreclosure status are the most authoritarian in their attitudes (that is, they strongly believe in obeying authority) (Damon, 1983; Marcia & Friedman, 1970; Podd, Marcia, & Rubin, 1970) and are likely to rely on others to make important life decisions for them (Orlofsky, 1978; Waterman & Waterman, 1971). Those with a moratorium status are relatively high in self-esteem, high in anxiety, and low in authoritarian attitudes. Perhaps because they are in a period of experimentation, they also are more likely to have engaged in unprotected sex or to have tried drugs such as marijuana (Damon, 1983; Hernandez & DiClemente, 1992; Jones, 1992; Marcia, 1980). In the course of adolescence and early adulthood, people in identity-diffusion and moratorium statuses tend to move into identity-achievement status, whereas those in a foreclosed state often remain there (Berzonsky & Adams, 1999; Meeus, Iedem, Heisen, & Vollebergh, 1999).

TABLE 11.2

Criteria for the Identity Statuses

	Identity Status			
Position on Occupation and Ideology	**Foreclosure**	**Identity Diffusion**	**Moratorium**	**Identity Achievement**
Crisis	Absent	Present or absent	In crisis	Has occurred
Commitment	Present	Absent	Present but vague	Has occurred

Adapted from Marcia (1980)

Influences on Identity Formation

A number of factors influence adolescents' identity formation. One key factor is the approach parents take with their offspring. Adolescents are more likely to have a foreclosed identity status if their parents are overly protective or employ an *authoritarian* parenting style (that is, a style that is cold and controlling; see Chapter 12) (Berzonsky & Adams, 1999). In contrast, adolescents are more likely to explore identity options if they have at least one parent who encourages in them both a sense of connection with the parent and a striving for autonomy and individuality (Grotevant, 1998).

Another factor affecting identity formation is the individual's own behavior. The early use of drugs, for example, appears to undermine adolescents' abilities to develop healthy identities, perhaps because it diverts their attention from school and other activities, such as hobbies and clubs, that provide opportunities for learning and self-exploration (Jones, 1992).

Identity formation is also influenced by both the larger social context and the historical context (Bosma & Kunnen, 2001). Adolescents from poor communities, for example, may have fewer career options due to low-quality schooling, financial limitations, and a lack of career information and role models. Such limitations likely affect some aspects of these adolescents' identity formation.

The role of the historical context in identity formation is most clearly seen in the changes it brings about in identity options over time. Until a few decades ago, for instance, most adolescent girls focused their search for identity on the goal of marriage and family. Even in developed societies, few career opportunities were available to females, and young women who chose a career path instead of, or even in addition to, raising a family were generally regarded as "selfish" by the society at large. Today, women in many cultures are more likely to base their identity on both family and career. Thus, familial, individual, socioeconomic, historical, and cultural factors all contribute to identity development.

review:

Children's self-conceptions change greatly with age. In childhood, they move from being very concrete and based on physical characteristics and overt behavior to being based more on internal qualities and the nature of their relationships with others. Young children tend to view themselves in uniformly positive ways and overestimate their abilities. Older children are more likely than younger children to evaluate themselves on their general level of competence and to assess their own strengths and weaknesses realistically. In late childhood, children increasingly incorporate others' perceptions of themselves into their self-image, and their conceptions of self also become much more complex and integrated with age.

Adolescents think of themselves in more abstract terms than do younger children and are better able to conceive of different selves in different contexts. When young adolescents perceive discrepancies in their behavior and characteristics across contexts, they usually are not upset by them. According to Elkind, many young adolescents develop a form of egocentrism that expresses itself as the "personal fable" and the "imaginary audience." In mid-adolescence, teenagers often agonize over the discrepancies they see in themselves and tend to become concerned with the question of "Who am I?" and with what others think of them. In late adolescence and early adulthood, concepts of the self become much more integrated and are more likely to include personal attributes that reflect internalized personal values, beliefs, and standards.

According to Erikson, adolescence is the time of the crisis of identity versus identity confusion, in which the young person must form an identity by making a series of ever-narrowing selections of personal, occupational, sexual, and ideological commitments. A psychological moratorium, a time of experimenting with different identities, appears to be healthy in Western cultures but may not be a viable option in some cultures and subcultures. The premature choice of an identity, called identity foreclosure, may prevent the individual from obtaining his or her full potential, as may identity diffusion or the taking on of a negative identity. How and when young people construct their identity are affected by a variety of influences, ranging from personal and familial factors to cultural and historical ones.

Ethnic Identity

The development of identity can present special challenges for minority-group adolescents because it often involves complications related to ethnicity *and/or* race. In certain contexts a legitimate distinction can be drawn between the concept of ethnicity (which refers to shared cultural traditions) (Spencer & Markstrom-Adams, 1990) and the concept of race (which refers to a shared biological ancestry). In the context of identity formation, however, the two concepts are, for

ethnic identity individuals' sense of belonging to an ethnic group, including the degree to which they associate their thinking, perceptions, feelings, and behavior with membership in that ethnic group

practical purposes, quite similar. Thus, for the present discussion, we use the term **ethnic identity** to refer to an individual's sense of belonging to an ethnic or racial group, including the degree to which the individual associates his or her thinking, perceptions, feelings, and behavior with membership in that ethnic or racial group (Rotheram & Phinney, 1987).

Ethnic Identity in Childhood

Children's ethnic identity is viewed as having five components (Bernal, Knight, Ocampo, Garza, & Cota, 1993):

PAUL CHELSEY/STONE/GETTY IMAGES

Much of young children's learning about their ethnic group takes place in the family. Parents teach their children the specific practices associated with their group, and can instill pride in their ethnic heritage.

1. *Ethnic knowledge.* Children's knowledge that their ethnic group has certain distinguishing characteristics—behaviors, traits, values, customs, styles, and language—that set it apart from other groups.
2. *Ethnic self-identification.* Children's categorization of themselves as members of their ethnic group.
3. *Ethnic constancy.* Children's understanding that the distinguishing characteristics of their ethnic group that they carry in themselves do not change across time and place and that they will always be a member of their ethnic group.
4. *Ethnic-role behaviors.* Children's engagement in the behaviors that reflect the distinguishing characteristics of their ethnic group.
5. *Ethnic feelings and preferences.* Children's feelings about belonging to their ethnic group and their preferences for the characteristics that distinguish it and for its members.

Ethnic identity develops gradually during childhood, although it does not develop for all ethnic-minority children. Preschool children do not really understand the significance of being a member of an ethnic group, although they may be able to label themselves as "Mexican," "American Indian," "African-American", or the like. Even if they engage in behaviors that characterize their ethnic group and have some simple knowledge about the group, they do not understand that ethnicity is a lasting feature of the self (Bernal et al., 1993) (see Table 11.3).

By the early school years, ethnic-minority children know the common characteristics of their ethnic group, start to have feelings about being members of the group, and may have begun to form ethnically based preferences regarding foods, traditional holiday activities, language use, and the like (Ocampo, Bernal, & Knight, 1993). Children tend to identify themselves according to their ethnic group at about age 7 to 10 (Ocampo et al., 1993) and at approximately 8 to 11 begin to understand that their race or ethnicity is a constant, unchanging feature of themselves.

The family and the larger social environment play a major role in the development of children's ethnic identity. Parents and other family members and adults can be instrumental in teaching their children about the strengths and unique features of their ethnic culture and instilling them with ethnic pride. Such instruction can be especially important for the development of a positive ethnic identity when the child's racial or ethnic group is the object of prejudice and discrimination in the larger society (Spencer & Markstrom-Adams, 1990).

TABLE 11.3

Examples of Components of Ethnic Identity in Preschool and the Early School Years

Ethnic-Identity Components	Preschool Level	Early School Level
Ethnic knowledge	Simple, global knowledge.	More complex and specific knowledge, including cultural traits.
Ethnic self-identification	Empty labels. "I'm Mexican because my mother said so."	Meaningful labels. "I'm Mexican because my parents come from Mexico."
Ethnic constancy	Don't understand.	Understand permanence of their ethnicity.
Ethnic-role behaviors	Engage in and describe behaviors; may not know why behaviors are ethnic.	Engage in more role behaviors; know more about their ethnic relevance.
Ethnic feelings and preferences	Undeveloped; do as their families do.	Have feelings and preferences.

Adapted from Bernal, Knight, Ocampo, Garza, & Cota (1993)

Ethnic Identity in Adolescence

The issue of ethnic identity often becomes much more central in adolescence, as young people try to forge their overall identity. Minority-group members in particular may be faced with difficult and painful decisions as they try to decide the degree to which they will adopt the values of their ethnic group or those of the dominant culture (Phinney, 1993a; Spencer & Markstrom-Adams, 1990).

One difficulty for ethnic-minority adolescents is that they are more likely than they were at younger ages to be aware of discrimination against their group and consequently may feel ambivalent about the group and their own ethnic status. Ethnic-minority children may also be faced with basic conflicts between the values of their ethnic group and those of the dominant culture (Parke & Buriel, 1998). For example, many ethnic groups place a premium on respect for elders and on dedication and service to one's family. These values may stand in direct opposition to the emphasis that Western cultures place on autonomy and self-interest. Adolescents in traditional Mexican-American families, for example, may be expected to spend after-school time helping take care of elderly or young family members or earning money for the family. At the same time, the majority culture may be urging them to participate in school-related activities, such as sports, clubs, or study groups, that can lead to expanded opportunities. Such a clash of values can cause conflict in the family and within adolescents as they attempt to build an identity and develop their values and goals for the future.

Ethnic-minority youth also may experience special peer pressures. African-American and Hispanic-American students who do well in school, for example, are sometimes viewed negatively by peers as trying to move into the Euro-American culture and thus may feel pressure to slack off in school. Similarly, ethnic-minority adolescents whose dress, speech, aspirations, or choice of friends is perceived by peers to reflect the dominant culture are sometimes branded with the label "oreo," "banana," or "apple"—black, yellow, or red on the outside but white on the inside. These adolescents often feel forced to conform to the ways of their ethnic group or face being ostracized (Spencer & Markstrom-Adams, 1990).

Family or peer pressures such as these may help explain why the rate of foreclosed identity is higher among ethnic-minority adolescents than it is among majority adolescents (Spencer & Markstrom-Adams, 1990; Streitmatter, 1988). Indeed, in some minority groups such as certain American Indian tribes, traditional values and activities may be so valued that it is adaptive for youth to simply adhere to them without exploring their identities in any way (Parke & Buriel, 1998; Spencer & Markstrom-Adams, 1990). For these young people, abandoning the accustomed ways of family and community to "make it" in an unfamiliar culture carries a high risk of loneliness and depression.

In contrast, for some minority youth who had previously accepted their ethnic identity without much thought, adolescence is a time when they start to explore the meaning of their ethnicity and its role in their identity. Extending the work of Erikson, Jean Phinney (Phinney & Kohatsu, 1997) has identified three phases of ethnic-identity development that many such individuals go through. In the first phase, *ethnic-identity diffusion/foreclosure,* many ethnic-minority adolescents have not examined their ethnicity and are not particularly interested in it. Others, a minority, have internalized the majority society's negative views of their ethnic group. The second phase, *ethnic-identity search/moratorium,* is characterized by an interest in learning about one's ethnic or racial culture, a consideration of the effects of ethnicity on one's life in the present and future, and often an awareness of prejudice and its effects. In some cases, this exploration eventually leads to the third phase, *ethnic-identity achievement,* which is characterized by a more conscious awareness of, and commitment to, one's ethnic group and ethnic identity (Spencer & Markstrom-Adams, 1990). This phase is associated with high self-esteem, optimism, and a sense of mastery (Phinney, Cantu, & Kurtz, 1997; Roberts et al., 1999). As one Asian-American male expressed it, "My culture is important and I am proud of what I am. Japanese people have so much to offer" (quoted in Phinney, 1993b, p. 72).

The exploration of ethnic identity does not always follow this pattern, however. For some ethnic-minority adolescents, an identity search leads to exploration of majority identities and a lessening of commitment to the ethnic group. In still other cases, ethnic-minority youth develop a *bicultural identity* that includes a comfortable identification with both the majority culture and their own ethnic culture. There is some initial research indicating that minority-group members who are bicultural tend to have better physical and psychological health than those who are not (LaFromboise, Coleman, & Gerton, 1993).

review:

The development of identity may be especially complicated for many ethnic-minority youth because it involves incorporating ideas and feelings about their ethnicity and/or race. The development of an ethnic identity begins in childhood and involves acquiring knowledge about one's ethnic group, identifying oneself as a member of that group, developing an understanding of ethnic constancy, engaging in ethnic-role behaviors, and developing feelings and preferences with regard to belonging to one's ethnic group. Family and community influence these aspects of development.

The achievement of an identity during adolescence can be difficult and painful for minority youth due to their awareness of prejudice against their group and to possible clashes between the values and goals of the group and those of the majority culture. In adolescence, minority youth who previously accepted their ethnic identity without much thought often start to explore the meaning of their ethnicity and its role in their identity. As a result of this exploration, some adolescents come to accept their ethnicity and even embrace it (ethnic identity achievement), others gravitate toward the majority culture, and still others become bicultural.

Sexual Identity or Orientation

In childhood and especially adolescence, an individual's identity includes his or her **sexual orientation**—that is, a person's preference in regard to males or females as objects of erotic feelings. The majority of youth are attracted to individuals of the other sex; a sizable minority are not. Dealing with new feelings of sexuality can be a difficult experience for many adolescents, although the issue of establishing a sexual identity is much harder for some adolescents than for others.

sexual orientation a person's preference in regard to males or females as objects of erotic feelings

sexual-minority youth people who experience same-sex attractions and for whom the question of personal sexual identity is often confusing and painful

The Origins of Youths' Sexual Identity

At puberty, when there are large rises in gonadal hormones (Buchanan, Eccles, & Becker, 1992; Halpern, Udry, & Suchindran, 1997), adolescents are more likely than at younger ages to experience feelings of sexual attraction to others. Most current theorists believe that whether those feelings are inspired by members of the other sex or one's own is based primarily on biological factors, although the environment may also be a contributing factor. Twin and adoption studies, as well as DNA studies, indicate that a person's sexual orientation is at least partly hereditary: identical twins, for example, are more likely to exhibit similar sexual orientations than are fraternal twins (Bailey & Pillard, 1991; Bailey, Pillard, Neale, & Agyes, 1993; Hamer, Hu, Magnuson, Hu, & Pattatucci, 1993). However, biological factors may not directly determine an individual's sexual orientation; rather, they may predispose children to experiences that contribute to their sexual orientation (Bem, 1996).

Sexual Identity in Sexual-Minority Youth

For the majority of youth everywhere, the question of personal sexual orientation never arises, at least at a conscious level. They feel themselves to be unquestioningly heterosexual. For a minority of youth, however, the question of personal sexual identity is a vital one that, initially at least, is often confusing and painful. These are the **sexual-minority youth,** who experience same-sex attractions.

It is difficult to know precisely how many youths are in this category. Although current estimates indicate that only 1% to 2% of high school students in the United States identify themselves as gay, lesbian, or bisexual (Rotheram-Borus & Langabeer, 2001), the number of youths with same-sex attractions is considerably larger because many do not identify themselves as such until early adulthood or later.

In most ways, sexual-minority children and adolescents are indistinguishable from their heterosexual peers; they deal with many of the same family and identity issues in adolescence and generally function just as well. However, they do face some special challenges. Because being gay, lesbian, or bisexual is viewed negatively by many members of society, it often is difficult for sexual-minority youth to recognize or accept their own sexual preferences and disclose this information to others—that is, to "come out." However, with the media's increasing attention to, and positive portrayals of, sexual-minority people, more sexual-minority youths in the United States are coming out today, and are doing so at earlier ages, than did any previous cohort (Savin-Williams, 1998a).

The Process of Coming Out

For many sexual-minority youth, the coming-out process involves several developmental milestones. It begins with the *first recognition*—an initial cognitive and emotional realization that one is somewhat different from others, along with a feeling of alienation from oneself and others. At this point, there generally is some awareness that same-sex attractions may be the relevant issue, but the individual does not disclose this information. Many sexual-minority youth have some awareness of their sexual attractions by middle childhood. In a recent study, initial same-sex attractions typically were found to occur at age 8 or 9 (see Table 11.4). As one gay male reported:

> Maybe it was the third grade and there was an ad in the paper about an all-male cast for a movie. This confused me but fascinated—intrigued—me, so I asked the librarian and she looked all flustered, even mortified, and mumbled that I ought to ask my parents.
>
> (quoted in Savin-Williams, 1998a, p. 24)

However, there is great variability in the age at which same-sex attractions are first noticed. Some recall these attractions as part of their earliest memories, whereas others recall not having these feelings until young adulthood (Savin-Williams & Diamond, 2000). Moreover, whereas most sexual-minority men feel that they were always gay and were born that way, a number of sexual-minority women (16% in one study) feel that they were initially heterosexual and in midlife, after falling in love with a woman, became lesbian (Schneider, 2001).

The next milestone is *test and exploration,* a period in which the individual feels ambivalent about his or her same-sex attractions but eventually has limited contact with gay or lesbian individuals or communities and starts to feel alienated from heterosexuality. At the third milestone, *identity acceptance,* there is a preference for social interaction with other sexual-minority individuals. During this period the

TABLE 11.4

Ages of Identity Milestones for Gay/Bisexual Male Youth in Savin-Williams's Study (all are gay youth who have acknowledged their sexual-minority identity)

Event	Mean Age in Years	Age Range	Percent Who Had Not Experienced the Event
Awareness of same-sex attractions	8	3–17	0%
Knew meaning of *homosexuality*	10	4–19	0%
Applied the term *homosexual* to own attractions	13	5–20	0%
First gay sex	14	5–24	7%
First heterosexual sex	15	5–22	48%
Recognized self as gay/bisexual	17	8–24	0%
First disclosed to another	18	13–25	0%
First same-sex romance	18	11–25	29%
First disclosed to:			
Sibling	19	13–25	38%
Father	19	13–25	44%
Mother	19	13–25	31%
Developed positive sexual identity	19	10–25	23%

These numbers do not apply to samples of young men who have not acknowledged their same-sex attractions.
Adapted from Table 1.2 in R. Savin-Williams, . . . *And Then I Became Gay.* New York: Routledge, 1998, p. 15.

person comes to feel more positive about his or her sexual identity and for the first time discloses it to heterosexuals (e.g., family or friends).

The average age at which sexual-minority youth privately label themselves as gay, lesbian, or bisexual is about 15 to 18 years of age (D'Augelli, 1996; D'Augelli & Hershberger, 1993; Savin-Williams, 1998a). Males tend to engage in sexual activity with same-sex partners before identifying themselves as gay, whereas females are more likely to identity themselves as lesbian before engaging in same-sex sexual activities (Savin-Williams & Diamond, 2000). Many gay, lesbian, or bisexual youth and young adults, especially females, engage in heterosexual activities prior to, or overlapping with, same-sex activities, sometimes to hide or deny their same-sex attractions (Diamond, Savin-Williams, & Dube, 1999). In fact, many females who identify themselves as lesbian report that they still have some sexual attraction to males (Diamond, 1998).

VINCENT DEWITT / STOCK, BOSTON

Sexual-minority youth deal with many of the same family and identity issues as other adolescents, and generally are as adjusted as other teens. However, they face special challenges if their peers and family do not accept their sexual identity.

The final step is *identity integration,* in which gay, lesbian, and bisexual individuals firmly view themselves as such, feel pride in themselves and their particular sexual community, and publicly come out to many people. Often, arrival at this milestone is accompanied by anger over society's prejudice against members of sexual minorities (Savin-Williams, 1996; Sophie, 1985/1986).

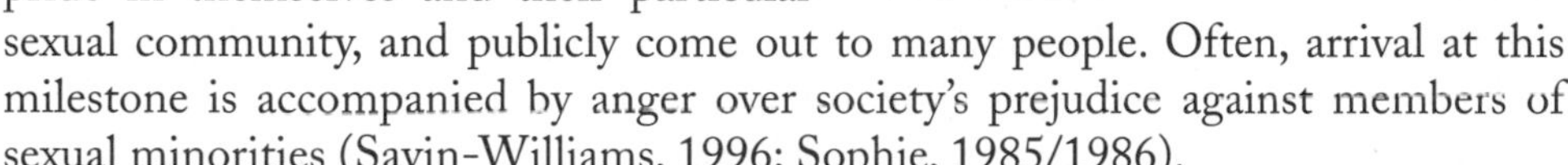

Of course, not all individuals go through all of these steps; some never fully accept their own sexuality or discuss it with others. Others—about a third in one study—are "discovered" by their parents and do not disclose their sexual identity by choice (Rotheram-Borus & Langabeer, 2001).

Consequences of Coming Out

Sexual-minority youth typically do not disclose their same-sex preferences to peers or siblings until about 16½ to 19 years of age (D'Augelli & Hershberger, 1993; Herdt & Boxer, 1993; Savin-Williams, 1998; Savin-Williams & Diamond, 2000) and do not tell their parents until a year or two later, if at all (Savin-Williams, 1998b). If they are from communities or religious or ethnic backgrounds that are relatively low in acceptance of same-sex attractions, they are probably less likely than other sexual-minority youth to disclose their sexual preference to family members. For example, there is some evidence that Latino and Asian-American families are less accepting of same-sex attractions than are Euro-American families (Dube, Savin-Williams, & Diamond, 2001). The effects of such low cultural acceptance are reflected in this statement from a young Asian-American man:

> I am first generation from Southeast Asia. I am still very culturally bound and my . . . mother can't fathom homosexuality, and many of our friends are the same. So I can't express myself to my culture or to my family. It probably delayed my coming out. I wish I could have done it in high school like other kids.
>
> (quoted in Savin-Williams, 1998, pp. 216–217)

There is good reason for many sexual-minority youth to fear disclosing their sexual identity to their family: many parents initially respond with anger and especially disappointment. Often parents feel that they are somehow responsible for their children's same-sex attractions and that these attractions violate their religious principles (Savin-Williams, 2001). Surveys indicate that about 20% to 40% of sexual-minority youth are insulted or threatened by relatives after they reveal their sexual identity, and 5% or so experience physical violence (Berrill, 1990; D'Augelli, 1998). Mothers tend to be somewhat more accepting of their child's same-sex attractions than are fathers (D'Augelli, Hershberger, & Pilkington, 1998), which may explain why sexual-minority youth are more likely to reveal their same-sex attractions to their mothers than to their fathers. Sexual-minority youth who disclose their sexual identity at a relatively early age and those whose are publicly open about their sexual identity are most often subjected to abuse in the home or community (Pilkington & D'Augelli, 1995).

Fears of being harassed or rejected outside the home cause many sexual-minority youth to hide their sexual identity from peers. In fact, most heterosexual adolescents are not very accepting of same-sex preferences in their peers, and many sexual-minority youth report losing at least one friend as a result of disclosing their sexual orientation (Pilkington & D'Augelli, 1995). In most cases, sexual-minority youth disclose their sexual identity first to a sexual-minority friend, and many sexual-minority youth report that having one or more sexual-minority friends is important in providing social support and acceptance (Savin-Williams, 1994, 1998a).

Presumably due to the pressures of coping with their sexuality, sexual-minority youth have higher reported rates of attempted suicide than do other youth, with the estimated attempt rates ranging from about 20% to over 50% (D'Augelli, 1998; D'Augelli, Hershberger, & Pilkington, 2001; Rotheram-Borus & Langabeer, 2001). However, these high rates may be misrepresentative because they are derived mostly from studies of youth at risk rather than of typical sexual-minority adolescents. Although there is some evidence that sexual-minority youth are more likely than other youth to have school-related problems and problems with substance abuse and the law (Savin-Williams, 1994), there is debate about how representative these data are as well (Rotheram-Borus & Langabeer, 2001). Regardless of the statistics, it is clear that having to adjust to being gay, or lesbian, or bisexual often makes it all the more difficult for youth as they attempt to establish their personal and social identities.

review:

Although in most respects sexual-minority youth differ little from other youth, they may face special challenges in regard to their identity and disclosing their same-sex preferences to others. Typically, but not always, they move through the milestones of *first recognition, test and exploration, identity acceptance,* and *identity integration.* Many sexual-minority youth have some awareness of their sexual attractions by middle childhood, although some individuals do not report same-sex sexual attractions until middle adulthood. Because many sexual-minority youth have some difficulty accepting their sexuality and fear revealing their attractions to others, they often do not tell anyone else about their same-sex attractions until age 16 to 19.

Parents sometimes have difficulty accepting their children's same-sex orientation, and a minority of parents abuse or reject their children for this reason. Although sexual-minority youth usually come out first to a friend, they often fear harassment from peers. Perhaps because of rejection or harassment by family and peers, sexual-minority youth appear to be more likely than other youth to attempt suicide.

Self-Esteem

A key element of self-concept is **self-esteem,** or one's overall evaluation of the self and the feelings engendered by that evaluation (Crocker, 2001). Self-esteem is important because it is related to how satisfied people are with their lives and their overall outlook. Individuals with high self-esteem tend to feel good about themselves and hopeful in general. Individuals with low self-esteem tend to feel worthless, depressed, and hopeless (Harter, 1999). Self-esteem starts to develop early in life, although a variety of factors can affect an individual's level of self-esteem throughout his or her life.

self-esteem one's overall evaluation of the worth of the self and the feelings that this evaluation engenders

Sources of Self-Esteem

A number of factors are related to children's self-esteem. These include their genetic inheritance, the quality of their relationships with others, their appearance and competence, their school and neighborhood, and various cultural factors that impinge on their lives. In addition, how children think about themselves contributes to their feelings of self-worth. Thus, the development of self-esteem offers a highly transparent example of the interaction of *nature and nurture,* including the *sociocultural context.* Moreover, it is a domain of functioning marked by *large individual differences.*

To measure children's self-esteem, researchers ask children, verbally or with questionnaires, about their perceptions of themselves. As reflected in Table 11.5, they assess children's sense of their own physical attractiveness, athletic competence, social acceptance, scholastic ability, and the appropriateness of their behavior. In addition, they ask children about their global self-esteem—how they feel about themselves in general (Harter, 1998).

TABLE 11.5

Sample Items from Susan Harter's Self-Perception Profile for Children, a Commonly Used Measure of Self-Esteem and Self-Perceptions

Really True for me	Sort of True for me				Sort of True for me	Really True for me
			Scholastic Competence			
☐	☐	Some kids feel that they are very *good* at their school work	BUT	Other kids *worry* about whether they can do the school work assigned to them.	☐	☐
			Social Acceptance			
☐	☐	Some kids find it *hard* to make friends	BUT	Other kids find it's pretty *easy* to make friends.	☐	☐
			Athletic Competence			
☐	☐	Some kids do very *well* at all kinds of sports	BUT	Other kids *don't* feel that they are very good when it comes to sports.	☐	☐
			Physical Appearance			
☐	☐	Some kids are *happy* with the way they look	BUT	Others kids are *not* happy with the way they look.	☐	☐
			Behavioral Conduct			
☐	☐	Some kids often do *not* like the way they *behave*	BUT	Other kids usually *like* the way they behave.	☐	☐
			Global Self-Esteem			
☐	☐	Some kids are often *unhappy* with themselves	BUT	Other kids are pretty *pleased* with themselves.	☐	☐

Adapted from Harter (1985)

Heredity

Heredity contributes to differences among children in their sense of self-worth in several ways. The most obvious, of course, are in terms of physical appearance and athletic ability, both of which are strongly related to self-esteem. In addition, genetically based intellectual abilities and aspects of personality, such as sociability and proneness to negative emotionality, no doubt play a part in academic and social self-esteem. The hereditary contribution to self-esteem is underscored by the fact that on all these dimensions, self-esteem is more similar in siblings who are closer genetically (e.g., identical twins are more similar in self-esteem than are fraternal twins, and nontwins are more similar than stepsiblings) (McGuire, Neiderhiser, Reiss, Hetherington, & Plomin, 1994).

Social Contributions to Self-Esteem

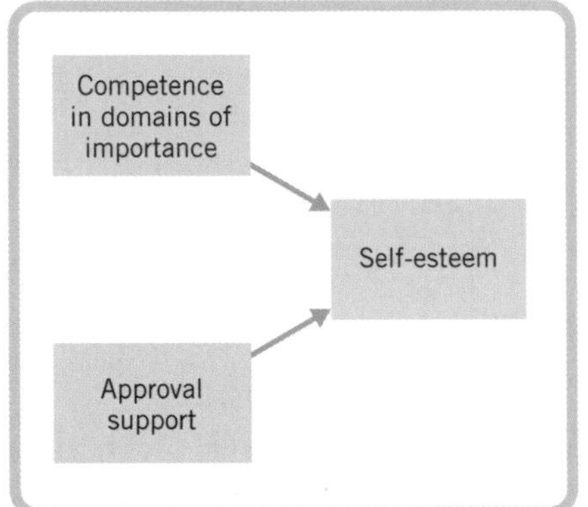

FIGURE 11.4 Factors contributing to children's self-esteem Children's self-esteem is affected by the approval and support they receive from parents, friends, and other people in their communities, as well as by their physical, social, behavioral, and academic competence, which are affected by both environmental and genetic factors. (Adapted from Harter, 1999)

One of the most important influences on children's self-esteem is the approval and support they receive from others. This idea goes back a full century to Charles Cooley's (1902) proposal of the "looking glass self"—the concept that people's self-esteem is a reflection of what others think of them (see Figure 11.4). More specifically, Cooley maintained that self-esteem is the internalized evaluations of others who are important to the individual. Similar ideas were proposed by Erikson (1950) and Bowlby (1969), who argued that children's sense of self is grounded in the quality of their relations with others. If, at a young age, children feel loved, they come to believe that they are lovable and worthy of others' love. If, to the contrary, they feel unloved as children, they come to believe the opposite. This view is supported by the evidence presented in our earlier discussion of attachment (Verschueren, Marcoen, & Schoefs, 1996).

Children begin to become concerned about winning their parents' love and approval at about age 2 (Stipek, Recchia, & McClinic, 1992). Thereafter, whether and how parents communicate or withhold their love and approval affects whether children see themselves as competent and lovable or incompetent and unlovable. Parents who tend to be accepting and involved with their child and who use supportive yet firm child-rearing practices tend to have children with high self-esteem (Feiring & Taska, 1996; Lamborn, Mounts, Steinberg, & Dornbusch, 1991). Parents who regularly belittle or reject their *children* for unacceptable behavior—rather than condemning the specific *behavior*—are likely to instill their children with a sense of worthlessness and of being loved only to the extent that they meet parental standards (Harter, 1999).

CINDY CHARLES / PHOTOEDIT

Although far from the sole factor in shaping a child's self-esteem, the quality and nature of interactions with parents and other caregivers is among the more important influences.

Over the course of childhood, children's self-esteem is increasingly affected by peer acceptance (Harter, 1999). Indeed, in late childhood, children's feelings of competence about their appearance, athletic ability, and likability may be affected more by peers' evaluations than by parents'. At the same time, it is likely that children's self-esteem is not only affected by, but also affects, how peers respond to them. For example, a child with low self-esteem is a likely candidate for being teased, rejected, or ignored. In contrast, a child with high self-esteem is likely to be well liked.

Although the approval of others is a major factor in children's self-esteem, as most children approach adolescence, they increasingly rely on internalized standards to evaluate themselves (Connell & Wellborn, 1991; Higgins, 1991). Thus, their self-esteem becomes less tied to the approval of others. Experts agree that adolescents who do not follow this pattern, and instead continue to base their self-evaluations on others' standards and approval, are at risk for psychological problems, at least in Western industrialized cultures, where an internalized, relatively stable sense of self provides the foundation for healthy identity formation (Damon & Hart, 1988; Higgins, 1991).

Appearance and Competence

In childhood and adolescence, attractive individuals are much more likely to report high self-esteem than are those who are less attractive (Erkut, Marx, Fields, & Sing, 1998; Harter, 1993; Verkuyten, 1990). This is not surprising, since attractive people are viewed more positively, and are treated better by others, than are unattractive people. Perhaps as a consequence, they also behave in more socially competent ways and have more desirable traits (such as being well-adjusted and popular), which likely enhances their appeal to others (Langlois et al., 2000). The association between self-esteem and attractiveness may be stronger for girls than for boys, particularly in late childhood and adolescence, because girls are much more likely to report concerns about their appearance (see Figure 11.5). This gender difference may partly explain why males report slightly higher self-esteem than do females, especially in late adolescence (Kling, Hyde, Showers, & Buswell, 1999).

As might be expected, children who are successful academically tend to have higher self-esteem with respect to their intellect and academic competence than do their less successful peers, and they tend to feel more optimistic about the outcomes of their future efforts (Harter, 1983; Skinner, Zimmer-Gembeck, & Connell, 1998). Although the evidence is not conclusive (Byrne, 1996), it appears that academic achievement affects children's self-esteem more than self-esteem affects academic achievement (Harter, 1983). Feeling competent in academics and athletics appears to be an especially important aspect of self-esteem for boys (Harter, 1999).

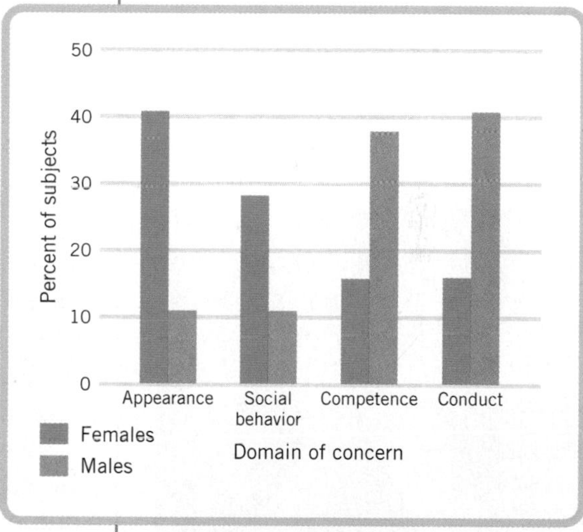

FIGURE 11.5 Gender differences in adolescents' concerns about their appearance, social behavior, competence, and conduct Girls report more concerns about their appearance and social behavior, whereas boys report more concerns about their competence and conduct. (Adapted from Harter, 1999)

School and Neighborhood

Children's and adolescents' self-esteem can also be affected by their school and neighborhood environments. The effect of the school environment is most apparent in the decline in self-esteem that is associated with the transition from elementary school into junior high (Eccles et al., 1989; Seidman, Allen, Aber, Mitchell, & Feinman, 1994). As discussed in Chapter 1, the junior high environment often is not a good developmental match for 11- and 12-year-olds because it is difficult for children of that age to make the switch from having one teacher whom they know well and who is well acquainted with their skills and weaknesses to having many teachers who know little about them. In addition, the transition to junior high forces students to enter a new group of peers and to go from the top of

EMMANUEL FAURE / SUPERSTOCK

Impoverished environmental and economic situations appear to place a child at greater risk for developing low self-esteem.

one school pecking order to the bottom of another. Especially in poor, overcrowded, urban schools, young adolescents often do not receive the attention, support, and friendship they need to do well and to feel good about themselves (Eccles & Midgley, 1989; Seidman et al., 1994).

That children's self-esteem can be affected by their neighborhood is suggested by the evidence that living in poverty in an urban environment is associated with lower self-esteem among adolescents in the United States (Paschall & Hubbard, 1998). This may be due to high levels of stress that undermine the quality of parenting, prejudice from more affluent peers and adults, and inadequate material and psychological resources (Walker, Taylor, McElroy, Phillip, & Wilson, 1995).

Self-Esteem in Minority Children

Minority children in the United States generally are more likely than majority (Euro-American) children to live in "undesirable," impoverished neighborhoods and to be subjected to prejudice from both adults and peers. Because children's self-esteem is strongly influenced by the evaluations of others, it often is assumed that minority children, especially African-American and Latino children, have lower self-esteem than do Euro-American children.

In fact, this is not always true. Young Euro-American children do tend to have higher self-esteem than their African-American peers, but after age 10, the trend reverses slightly. This shift most likely occurs because (1) African-Americans tend to identify more with their racial group than do Euro-Americans, and (2) African-American culture, more than Euro-American culture, emphasizes desirable aspects of the group's distinctiveness (as reflected in the popular slogan from the 1960s and 1970s, "Black is beautiful"). Because ethnic identity is an important aspect of self-concept for many African-Americans, this emphasis on the positive features of being African-American may enhance African-American adolescents' and adults' self-esteem (Gray-Little & Hafdahl, 2000).

MARY KATE DENNY / PHOTOEDIT

Children who do poorly at school tend to have lower self-esteem than do their more successful peers. However, children's perceptions of their academic competence tend to be less important to their overall self-esteem than are their perceptions of their appearance.

Less is known about the self-esteem of Latino and other minority children. Because of the poverty and prejudice that many Latino-Americans experience, one might expect their self-esteem to be consistently much lower than that of Euro-Americans at all ages. However, although Latinos score significantly lower on measures of self-esteem in elementary school than do Euro-Americans, this difference is much smaller in adolescence (Twenge & Crocker, 2002). In part, this change may be due to the fact that Latino (e.g., Mexican-American) parents encourage their children's identification with the family and with the larger ethnic group (Parke & Buriel, 1998), which can provide a buffer against some of the negative effects that poverty and prejudice often have on self-esteem. Especially in communities where Latinos are in the majority, Latino youth who identify with their ethnic group tend to have higher self-esteem (Umaña, Taylor, Diversi, & Fine, 2002).

Other minority groups in the United States show different patterns of self-esteem. Asian-American children, for example, report higher self-esteem than do Euro- and African-Americans in elementary school, but by high school their reported self-esteem is lower than that of Euro-Americans (Twenge & Crocker, 2002). As we discuss in the next section, cultural factors may contribute to the lower levels of self-esteem reported in some ethnic-minority groups.

How children and adolescents think about themselves is influenced much more strongly by acceptance from their family, neighbors, and friends than by reactions from strangers and the society at large. Thus, minority-group parents can help their children to develop high self-esteem and a sense of well-being by instilling them with pride in their culture, by being supportive, and by helping them to deal with prejudice. Having positive peer and adult role models from their own ethnic group also contributes to children's positive feelings about themselves and their ethnicity (Fischer & Shaw, 1999; Walker et al., 1995).

Culture and Self-Esteem

In various cultures, the sources of self-esteem, as well as its form and function, may be different, and the criteria that children use to evaluate themselves may vary accordingly. It is not surprising, then, that scores on standard measures of self-esteem vary considerably across cultures. Except perhaps in the area of social competence, for example, self-esteem scores tend to be lower in China, Japan, and Korea than in the United States, Canada, Australia, and some parts of Europe (Harter, 1999; Sakurai, 1983; Stigler, Smith, & Mao, 1985). Although these differences could be partly due to the greater emphasis that the Asian cultures place on humility and self-effacement, this probably is not the whole explanation. There appear to be fundamental differences between Asian and Western cultures that affect the very meaning of self-esteem.

In Western cultures, and the United States in particular, self-esteem is related to individual accomplishments and self-promotion. In contrast, in Asian societies such as Japan and China, which traditionally have had a collectivist or group orientation, self-esteem is related to contributing to the welfare of the larger group and affirming the norms of social interdependence. In this cultural context, self-criticism and efforts at self-improvement are viewed as evidence of commitment to the group, and self-criticism may actually lead to positive feelings about the self (Heine, Lehman, Markus, & Kitayama, 1999). Given this motivation toward self-criticism, Chinese and Japanese children are likely to have a lower self-evaluation than Western children do on measures of self-esteem designed in the United States. Thus, it cannot be assumed that factors that lead to high self-esteem in the United States or other Western countries necessarily are associated with high self-esteem in non-Western societies. The same holds true with regard to subcultures in the United States that have maintained traditional non-Western ideas about the self and its relation to other people.

review:

Many factors affect children's and adolescents' self-esteem. Genetic predispositions, the support and approval of parents and peers, physical attractiveness, academic competence, and social factors such as the neighborhood and school environments all affect how children and youth feel about themselves. Although minority children in the United States often are exposed to prejudice and poverty, supportive families and communities can buffer and even enhance their self-esteem. The sources of self-esteem, as well as its form and functon, may differ across cultures, and self-evaluations may differ accordingly.

Chapter Summary

The Caregiver–Child Attachment Relationship

- According to Bowlby's theory, attachment is a biologically based process that is rooted in evolution and increases the helpless infant's chance of survival. A secure attachment also provides children with a secure base for exploration. An outcome of early parent–caregiver interactions is an internal working model of relationships.
- The quality of children's attachment with their primary caregiver has been assessed with Ainsworth's Strange Situation. Children typically are categorized as securely attached or as insecurely attached (insecure/resistant, insecure/avoidant, or disorganized/disoriented). Children are more likely to be securely attached if their caregivers are sensitive and responsive to their needs.
- There are similarities in children's attachments across many cultures, although the percents of children in different attachment categories sometimes vary across cultures or subcultures.
- Parents' attachment status and their working models of relationships are related to the quality of their attachment with their infants. There appears to be some continuity in attachment from childhood to adulthood, unless hardships such as divorce, illness, child maltreatment, or maternal depression occur between childhood and adulthood.
- Intervention programs demonstrate that parents can be trained to be more sensitive, attentive, and stimulating in their parenting and that these changes are associated with increases in infants' sociability, exploration, ability to soothe themselves, and security of attachment.
- Children's security of attachment to their caregivers predicts interpersonal relationships and adjustment.

Conceptions of the Self

- Young children's conceptions of themselves are very concrete—based on physical characteristics and overt behavior—and uniformly positive. With age, conceptions of self increasingly are based on internal qualities and the quality of relationships with others and are more realistic, integrated, abstract, and complex.
- According to Elkind, because of their focus on what others think of them, young adolescents think about an "imaginary audience" and develop "personal fables."
- According to Erikson, the crisis of identity versus identity confusion occurs in adolescence. The individual's attempt to construct an identity—as well as whether and when the individual experiences a psychological moratorium, identity foreclosure, identity diffusion, or identity achievement—is influenced by personal characteristics and familial and cultural factors.

Ethnic Identity

- In childhood, the development of an ethnic identity involves self-identification as a member of an ethnic group, developing an understanding of ethnic constancy, engaging in ethnic-role behaviors, acquiring knowledge about one's ethnic group, and developing a sense of belonging to the ethnic group. Family and community influence these aspects of development.
- In adolescence, minority youth who previously accepted their ethnic identity without much thought often start to explore the meaning of their ethnicity and its role in their identity. Many ethnic-minority youth initially tend to be diffused or foreclosed in regard to their identities; then they become increasingly interested in exploring their ethnicity (search/moratorium). Some come to accept their ethnicity and even embrace it (ethnic-identity achievement); others gravitate toward the majority culture; still others become bicultural.

Sexual Identity or Orientation

- Sexual-minority (gay, lesbian, or bisexual) youth are similar to other youth in their development of identity and self, although they face special difficulties. Many, but not all, have some awareness of their same-sex attractions by middle childhood. Developmental milestones in the process of self-labeling and disclosure among sexual-minority youth include (1) first recognition, (2) test and exploration, (3) identity acceptance, and (4) identity integration. However, not all individuals go through all these steps, and many have difficulty accepting their sexuality and revealing it to others.

Self-Esteem

- Children's self-esteem is affected by many factors, including genetic predispositions, the quality of parent–child and peer relationships, physical attractiveness, academic competence, and various social factors.
- Although minority children in the United States often are exposed to prejudice and poverty, supportive families and communities can buffer and even enhance their self-esteem.
- Concepts of what a person should be like differ across cultures, with the consequence that self-evaluations and self-esteem scores differ in different cultures.
- When children fail on a task, some show a "helpless" pattern of motivation, whereas others show a mastery-oriented pattern of response. Children who show a helpless response to failure tend to think about people in terms of fixed traits and are at risk for continued failure and depression. Children's styles of thinking about themselves can be affected by prevention programs.

Critical Thinking Questions

1. Some theorists believe that early attachment relationships have enduring long-term effects. Others think that such effects depend on the quality of the ongoing parent–child relationship, which tends to be correlated with the security of children's early attachment to parents. How do you think researchers might go about examining this issue?
2. Based on what you have read about attachment and the development of the self, what might be some of the negative effects on children of being put in a series of different foster care homes? How might these effects vary with the age of the child?
3. What are the similarities and differences in the stages or phases of identity development as discussed Erikson or Marcia (general identity development), Phinney (ethnic identity), and Savin-Williams (sexual-minority identity)? What factors might contribute to similarities and differences? What variables might be especially relevant for ethnic identity, and for identity in regard to sexual orientation?
4. What are some of the practical and conceptual difficulties of determining when children first recognize that they prefer same-sex or other-sex individuals (i.e., are physically attracted to them)?
5. Recall Erikson's psychosocial stages of development (Chapter 9). How might a person's self-esteem be affected by the events and outcomes associated with each of the stages?

Key Terms

attachment, p. 412
attachment theory, p. 414
secure base, p. 414
internal working model of attachment, p. 415
Strange Situation, p. 415
secure atttachment, p. 416
insecure atttachment, p. 417
insecure/resistant (or ambivalent) attachment, p. 417
insecure/avoidant attachment, p. 417
disorganized/disoriented attachment, p. 417
adult attachment models, p. 418
parental sensitivity, p. 420
self, p. 424
social comparison, p. 427
helpless pattern of motivation, p. 428
mastery-oriented pattern of motivation, p. 428
personal fable, p. 430
imaginary audience, p. 430
identity versus identity confusion, p. 432
identity confusion, p. 432
identity foreclosure, p. 432
negative identity, p. 433
psychosocial moratorium, p. 433
identity-diffusion status, p. 433
foreclosure status, p. 433
moratorium status, p. 433
identity-achievement status, p. 433
ethnic identity, p. 436
sexual orientation, p. 439
sexual-minority youth, p. 439
self-esteem, p. 443

CHAPTER 12

The Family

JACOB LAWRENCE, *In a Free Government, the Security of Civil Rights Must Be the Same as That for Religious . . . ,* 1976

THEMES

- Nature and Nurture
- The Active Child
- Continuity/Discontinuity
- Mechanisms of Change
- The Sociocultural Context
- Individual Differences
- Research and Children's Welfare

In 1979, the People's Republic of China announced a sweeping new policy that was to affect Chinese families dramatically. Due to the myriad problems associated with the country's overpopulation, the Chinese government decided to initiate and strictly enforce a limit of one child per family, especially in urban populations. Backed up by a system of economic rewards for those who complied and financial and social sanctions against those who did not, this policy was quite effective, especially in urban areas. For example, in Shanghai in 1985, 98% of births were first births; across the country, the figure was 68% (Poston & Falbo, 1990).

The controversial nature of this policy aside, for developmental psychologists it represented a natural experiment for studying how the structure of the family affects children's development. Think about the differences in upbringing that might occur when parents have one child as opposed to two or more. To begin with, an only child is likely to receive more individual attention from parents and more of the family's resources. In addition, an only child does not have to cooperate and share with siblings. Because of differences such as these, many people predicted that the new generation of single children raised in the People's Republic of China would be overindulged and have little experience in compromising and cooperating with others. Thus, there was concern that these single children (called "onlies") would become spoiled "little emperors" (Falbo & Poston, 1993). Such a concern was not confined to China. An increase of one-child families in the United States likewise raised worries that single children would become spoiled brats (Falbo & Polit, 1986).

In general, however, there is no consistent support for these concerns. It is clear that onlies in China, especially in urban areas, were actually doing better on tests of academic performance and intelligence than children from families with more than one child (Falbo & Poston, 1993; Falbo, Poston, & Jiao, 1989; Jiao, Ji, & Jing, 1996). And although some initial studies found that only children in China were viewed by peers as more self-interested and less cooperative than children with siblings, and were less liked (e.g., Jiao, Ji, & Jing, 1986), more recent studies have found little evidence that only children have more problem behaviors (Wang et al., 2000; Zhang, 1997). In fact, there appears to be little difference between onlies and other children in regard to personality or social behavior, including positive behaviors needed for getting along with others and negative behaviors such as aggression and lying (Falbo & Poston, 1993; Poston & Falbo, 1990). The difference between the early and later findings may be due to the possibility that parents' behaviors toward only children have changed as one-child families have become more common and expected, with the consequence that onlies are less likely to be spoiled. The

ADRIAN BRADWHAW / NEWSMAKERS / GETTY IMAGES

The one-child policy in China provided an opportunity to assess the effects of being an only child. In general, only children in China are as well-adjusted as children from larger families and tend to do better in school.

more recent findings in China are similar to those in the United States and other countries (Doh & Falbo, 1999; Falbo & Polit, 1986).

One unintended negative consequence of the one-child policy was a marked drop in the recorded birth rate of girls—from the normally occurring 100 females for every 106 males to 100 females for every 117 males (BBC News Online, 2001). This drop, related to higher valuing of males in Chinese culture, was largely the result of selective abortion or female infanticide or abandonment.

The one-child policy in China is a good example of how the nature of families can change and of how, consistent with Bronfenbrenner's model discussed in Chapter 9, the larger world affects what goes on within families. Culture, as well as social and economic events, can have a tremendous effect on the nature of families and interactions among family members. In industrialized Western societies as well, a variety of social changes in the past fifty years have had marked effects on the structure of the family. For example, families are smaller than in the past, and many more people are choosing to have children outside of wedlock (Ventura, Martin, Curtin, & Mathews, 1997). In addition, it is not uncommon today for children to be reared by one biological parent or to live in a family in which there have been one or more divorces. Such changes in the family can affect the resources available to the child, as well as the parents' child-rearing practices and behavior.

In this chapter, we examine many developmental aspects of family interaction, including the ways in which parents' approach to parenting can influence their children's development, the ways in which children can influence their parents' parenting, and the ways in which siblings may influence one another. In addition, we consider a number of social changes that have occurred in the United States over the past half century—from the age of first-time parenthood to increased rates of divorce, remarriage, and maternal employment—and examine the implications they may have for family functioning and children's development. We will also consider some of the ways in which factors such as poverty and culture may influence developmental outcomes.

As you will see, the theme of *nature and nurture* is central in the study of the role of the family because a child's heredity and rearing influence each other and jointly affect the child's development. In addition, the theme of *the active child* is evident in our discussion of how children influence the way their parents socialize them. The theme of *sociocultural context* is also key, in that parenting practices are

EYEWIRE / GETTY IMAGES

MONIKA GRAFF / THE IMAGE WORKS

Among the many changes that have occurred in the American family over the past half century is a rise in the age of first marriage.

strongly influenced by cultural beliefs, biases, and goals and are related to different outcomes for children in different cultures. Further, the issue of *individual differences* is a major theme in this chapter because different styles of parenting, child-rearing practices, and family structures are associated with differences among children in their social and emotional functioning. Finally, because parenting influences the quality of children's day-to-day experience, as well as children's beliefs and behaviors, information about families and parenting has relevance for our theme of *research and children's welfare.*

The Nature and Functions of the Family

What is considered a family varies across individuals and cultures. In some places, for example, a family typically includes several generations and married siblings living together; in the United States, it often includes just a single parent living alone with his or her children. What are the characteristics of most families around the world and how do most families function?

Functions of Families

No matter what their structure or size, families in all societies serve several functions related to child rearing (LeVine, 1988):

1. **Survival of offspring.** Families help to ensure that children survive to maturity by attending to their physical needs, health needs, and safety.
2. **Economic function.** Families provide the means for children to acquire the skills and other resources they need to be economically productive in adulthood.
3. **Cultural training.** Families teach children the basic values in their culture.

The first function is obviously the most fundamental; the goals of the economic and cultural functions are of little importance if children do not survive. Thereafter, however, if children are to fare well, they must learn the skills needed to make a living and the values and norms of the society they live in. Thus, families serve functions that are of fundamental importance for the development of their children.

survival of offspring a function of the family; pertains to ensuring the survival of offspring by providing for their needs

economic function a function of the family; pertains to providing the means for children to acquire the skills and other resources they need to be economically productive as adults

cultural training a function of the family; pertains to teaching children the basic values in their culture

family dynamics the way in which the family operates as a whole

Family Dynamics

How well a family fulfills its basic child-rearing functions depends on a great many factors, not the least of which is **family dynamics,** that is, how the family operates as a whole. In subsequent sections we discuss the ways in which individual family members contribute to a child's development. However, it is important to approach these discussions with a clear appreciation of the overall impact of family dynamics. No member of a family functions in isolation. Families are complex social units whose members are all interdependent and reciprocally influence each other. Consider the diverse ways in which family members affect one another in the following scenario.

A man loses his job due to company cutbacks. He becomes very stressed and irritable with both his wife and children. His wife, in turn, has to work more hours to make ends meet, and she becomes less patient with the children. The mother's increased workload also means that the couple's 8-year-old daughter, Terese, is expected to do more of the chores in the home; and Terese is angry because her brother, Thomas, is not required to help her out. Thus, Terese is hostile to both her parents and Thomas. In reaction, Thomas starts to complain about Terese and fight with her, further upsetting his parents. Over time, tension and conflict among all family members increase, adding to the stress created by the family's economic situation.

As researchers have increasingly recognized the complexity of family dynamics, they have come to a number of conclusions (Parke & Buriel, 1998). First, as is clear from the foregoing example, family members—mothers, fathers, and children—all influence one another, both directly and indirectly, through their behaviors. Second, family functioning is influenced by the social support that parents receive from kin, friends, neighbors, and social institutions such as schools and churches (Parke & Kellam, 1994; Taylor & Roberts, 1995). Thus, the sociocultural context is important for understanding family dynamics and their possible effects on children. Finally, family dynamics must be looked at developmentally. As children grow older, the nature of parent–child interactions changes. For example, as we saw in Chapter 5, when infants begin to walk, parents start to discipline them more because they can get into more trouble and more easily defy their parents' wishes and commands. Thus, as children become increasingly mobile, emotional exchanges between parents and children often include more anger (Campos, Kermoian, & Zumbahlen, 1992). Similarly, when children reach adolescence, there sometimes is increased conflict between them and their parents over the children's activities or friends (Steinberg, 1988). (See Box 12.1.)

Family dynamics may also be altered by changes in parents (for example, in their beliefs about parenting and the family), in the marital relationship (for example, how well parents are getting along), or in the relationships of other family members (for example, if the level of conflict between siblings increases). Modifications in the family structure due to births, deaths, divorce, remarriage, or other factors can also influence family members' interactions and may affect family routines, norms, and activities. In many cases, family dynamics promote more or less gradual, continuous change in a child's development; however, a single event such as a traumatic divorce or the death of a parent may cause a fairly dramatic change in a child's behavior and emotional adjustment.

In thinking about family dynamics, it is also important to keep in mind that both biological characteristics of children (e.g., their attractiveness and temperament) and parental behaviors contribute to the nature of parent–child interactions (Collins, Maccoby, Steinberg, Hetherington, & Bornstein, 2000; Deater-Deckard, 2000). Thus, family dynamics are affected by the hereditary characteristics of the various family members as well as by the social behaviors and attitudes that parents and children have acquired through learning.

With this larger framework of family dynamics in mind, we now turn to the role that parents play in the socialization of their children.

review: Families are complex social units that serve diverse functions, including helping offspring survive, teaching them skills in order to be economically productive adults, and teaching them the values of the culture. Family members' behaviors influence one another and can alter the functioning of the entire family. Moreover, family dynamics are affected by a number of factors, including changes in the parents, changes in the child with development, and changes in family circumstances.

a closer look 12.1

Parent–Child Relationships in Adolescence

As noted in Chapter 1, a common stereotype about adolescence is that conflict between parents and their children inevitably escalates dramatically and that parents and their adolescent children typically become alienated from each other. However, a good deal of research has shown that this simply is not true in most families (Laursen & Collins, 1994). For example, in a study of approximately 1,000 U.S. adolescents from immigrant and native-born families of Mexican, Chinese, Filipino, and European backgrounds, there was little increase in reported conflict with parents between the sixth and the tenth grades (Fuligni, 1998).

This pattern holds true despite the fact that as children advance through adolescence, they become more willing to disagree openly with their parents and feel that their parents should have less authority over them in personal matters (Fuligni, 1998; Youniss & Smollar, 1985). For the most part, however, disagreements between parents and adolescents, though fairly frequent, typically are over mundane topics such as attire and hair style. Moreover, the increase in mild conflict and bickering between adolescents and their parents in early adolescence is typically followed by the establishment of a relationship that is less contentious and volatile, and more egalitarian (Steinberg, 1990; Steinberg & Morris, 2001).

In a minority of families, however, parent–child conflict in adolescence runs hotter and deeper, often involving issues such as sex, drugs, and choice of friends (Arnett, 1999; Papini & Sebby, 1988). Higher levels of conflict seem especially likely when children attain puberty earlier than their peers (Hill, 1988; Steinberg, 1987, 1988). This may be because in the case of early-maturing adolescents, there is likely to be a wider gap between how much autonomy parents are willing to grant their children and how much autonomy the adolescents themselves think they deserve.

Although most parents and their adolescents are not alienated, feelings of closeness and support between parents and children often decline, especially at the beginning of puberty (Collins, 1990; Fuligni, 1998; Steinberg, 1988; Stemmler & Petersen, 1999), and adolescents spend less time with their parents than do younger children (Larson & Richards, 1991). This decline in feelings of closeness is likely due in part to the desire by adolescents to be more autonomous and to an increase in their activities outside the home. Nonetheless, although peers are important confidants for adolescents (see Chapter 13), parents remain their primary source of support.

MONIKA GRAFF / THE IMAGE WORKS

Most adolescents and their parents do not experience high levels of conflict.

The Influence of Parental Socialization

Socialization is the process through which children acquire the values, standards, skills, knowledge, and behaviors that are regarded as appropriate for their present and future role in their particular culture. Parents can influence their children's development through socialization in at least three different ways (Parke & Buriel, 1998):

socialization the process through which children acquire the values, standards, skills, knowledge, and behaviors that are regarded as appropriate for their present and future role in their particular culture

1. *Parents as direct instructors.* Parents may directly teach their children skills, rules, and strategies and explicitly inform or advise them on various issues.
2. *Parents as indirect socializers.* Parents provide indirect socialization in the course of their day-to-day interactions with their children. Through their

own behaviors, for example, parents unintentionally demonstrate skills and communicate information and rules. They also model attitudes and behaviors toward others, such as helpfulness or aggression.

3. *Parents as providers and controllers of opportunities.* Parents manage children's experiences and social lives, including their exposure to positive or negative experiences, their opportunities to play with certain toys and children, and their exposure to various kinds of information. This managerial role is especially prominent and influential when children are young. If parents decide to place their child in day care, for example, the child's daily experience with peers and adult caregivers will likely differ dramatically from that of young children whose daily care is provided at home by a parent.

Parents use all these ways of socializing their children's behavior and development. However, as you will see, parents differ considerably in how they do so.

Parenting Style and Practices

As you undoubtedly recognize from your own experience, parents in different families exhibit quite different **parenting styles,** that is, parenting behaviors and attitudes that set the emotional climate of parent–child interactions. Some parents, for example, are strict rule setters who expect complete and immediate compliance from their children. Others are more likely to allow their children some leeway in following the standards they have set for them. Still others seem oblivious to what their children do. Parents also differ in the overall emotional tone they bring to their parenting, especially with regard to the warmth and support they convey to their children.

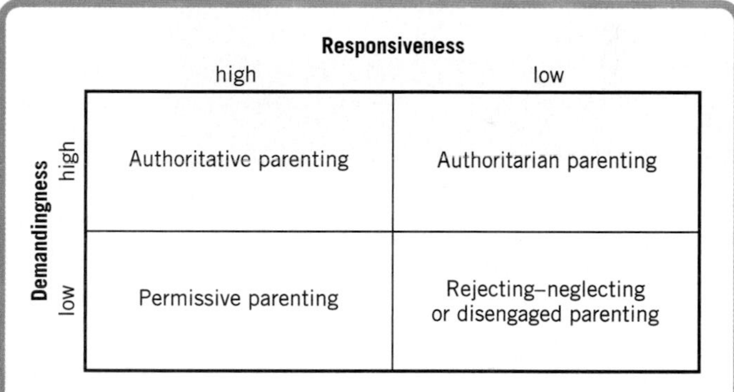

FIGURE 12.1 Parental demandingness and responsiveness The relations of parental demandingness and responsiveness to Baumrind's typology of parenting styles.

In trying to understand the impact that parents can have on children's development, researchers have identified two dimensions of parenting style that are particularly important: (1) the degree of parental warmth, support, and acceptance versus parental rejection and nonresponsiveness; and (2) the degree of parenting control and demandingness (Maccoby & Martin, 1983). As you will see, these aspects of parenting—which reflect individual differences in parents—appear to play an important role in shaping individual differences in children.

The pioneering research on parenting style was conducted by Diana Baumrind (1973), who differentiated among four styles of parenting related to the dimensions of support and control: authoritative, authoritarian, permissive, and rejecting-neglecting (Baumrind, 1973, 1991b) (Figure 12.1). The differences in these parenting styles are reflected in the following examples, in which four different children take away another child's toy.

Authoritative. When Kareem takes away Troy's toy, Kareem's mother takes him aside, points out that the toy belongs to Troy and that Kareem has made Troy upset. She also says, "Remember our rule about taking others' things. Now think about how to make things right with Troy." Her tone is firm but not hostile, and she waits to see if Kareem returns the toy.

Authoritarian. When Elene takes Mark's toy, Elene's mother comes over, grabs her arm, and says in an angry voice, "Haven't I warned you about taking others' things? Return that toy now or you will not be able to watch TV tonight. I'm tired of you disobeying me!"

parenting styles parenting behaviors and attitudes that set the emotional climate in regard to parent–child interactions, such as parental responsiveness and demandingness

TONY FREEMAN / PHOTOEDIT

Positive social and academic outcomes seem more likely when levels of parental warmth and control are both high.

Permissive. When Jeff takes away Angelina's toy, Jeff's mother does not intervene. She doesn't like to discipline her son and usually does not try to control his actions, even though she is very affectionate with him in other situations.

Rejecting-Neglecting. When Heather takes away Alonzo's toy, Heather's mother, as she does in most situations, pays no attention. She generally is not very involved with her child and would prefer that her husband deal with disciplining Heather. Even when Heather behaves well, her mother rarely hugs her or expresses approval of Heather or her behavior.

According to Baumrind, **authoritative** parents, like Kareem's mother, tend to be demanding but also warm and responsive. They set clear standards and limits for their children, monitor their children's behavior, and are firm about enforcing important limits. However, they allow their children considerable autonomy within those limits, are not restrictive or intrusive, and are able to engage in calm conversation and reasoning with their children. They are attentive to their children's concerns and needs, communicate openly with their children about them, and are measured and consistent rather than harsh or arbitrary in disciplining. Authoritative parents usually want their children to be socially responsible, assertive, and self-controlled. Baumrind found that children of authoritative parents tend to be competent, self-assured, popular with peers, able to control their own behavior in accordance with adults' expectations, and low in antisocial behavior. As adolescents, they tend to be relatively high in social and academic competence, self-reliance, and positive behavior, and relatively low in drug use and problem behavior (Baumrind, 1991a, 1991b; Lamborn, Mounts, Steinberg, & Dornbusch, 1991).

Authoritarian parents exhibit behaviors similar to those of Elene's mother. They tend to be cold and unresponsive to their children's needs. They also are high in control and demandingness, and expect their children to comply with their demands without question or explanation. Authoritarian parents tend to enforce their demands through the exercise of parental power and the use of threats and punishment. Children of authoritarian parents tend to be relatively low in social and academic competence, unhappy and unfriendly, and low in self-confidence, with boys affected more negatively than girls in early childhood (Baumrind, 1991b). In adolescence, children with authoritarian parents tend to be lower in social and academic competence than those with authoritative parents (Lamborn et al., 1991).

In studies by Baumrind and many others, parents' control of children's behavior has been measured mostly in terms of the setting and enforcing of limits. Another type of control is psychological control—control that constrains, invalidates, and manipulates children's psychological and emotional experience and expression. Examples include parents' cutting off children when they want to express themselves, threatening to withdraw love and attention if they do not behave as expected, exploiting children's sense of guilt, belittling their worth, and discounting or misinterpreting their feelings. These kinds of psychological control are more likely to be reported by children in relatively poor families. Their use by parents predicts children's depression in late middle childhood and adolescence and delinquent behavior in early adolescence (Barber, 1996; Pettit, Laird, Dodge, Bates, & Criss, 2001).

Permissive parents are responsive to their children's needs and wishes and are lenient with them. Like Jeff's mother, they are nontraditional and do not require their children to regulate themselves or act in appropriate ways. Their children tend to be impulsive, lacking in self-control, and low in school achievement (Baumrind, 1973, 1991a, 1991b), and, in adolescence, engage in more school misconduct and drug use than do adolescents with authoritative parents (Lamborn et al., 1991).

Rejecting-neglecting parents, such as Heather's mother, are disengaged parents, low in both demandingness and responsiveness to their children. They do not set limits for them or monitor their behavior and are not supportive of them. Sometimes they are rejecting or neglectful of their children altogether. These parents are focused on their own needs rather than their children's. Children who experience rejecting-neglecting parenting tend to have disturbed attachment relationships when they are infants or toddlers and problems with peer relationships as children (Parke & Buriel, 1998; Thompson, 1998). In adolescence, they tend to exhibit antisocial behavior, poor self-regulation, internalizing problems (e.g., depression, social withdrawal), substance abuse, risky or promiscuous sexual behavior, and fairly low academic and social competence (Baumrind, 1991a, 1991b; Lamborn et al., 1991). The negative effects of this type of parenting continue to accumulate and worsen over the course of adolescence (Steinberg, Lamborn, Darling, Mounts, & Dornbusch, 1994).

In addition to the broad effects that different parenting styles seem to have for children, they also establish an emotional climate that affects the impact of whatever specific parenting practices parents may employ (Darling & Steinberg, 1993). For example, children are more likely to view punishment as being justified and indicating serious misbehavior when it comes from an authoritative parent than when it comes from a parent who generally is punitive and hostile. Moreover, parenting style affects children's receptiveness to parents' practices. Children are more likely to listen to, and care about, their parents' preferences and demands if their parents are supportive and generally reasonable than if they are distant, neglectful, or expect obedience in all situations. Thus, parenting practices and parenting style jointly influence children's behavior and development.

authoritative parenting a parenting style that is high in demandingness and supportiveness. Authoritative parents set clear standards and limits for their children and are firm about enforcing them; at the same time, they allow their children considerable autonomy within those limits, are attentive and responsive to their children's concerns and needs, and respect and consider their child's perspective.

authoritarian parenting a parenting style that is high in demandingness and low in responsiveness. Authoritarian parents are nonresponsive to their children's needs and tend to enforce their demands through the exercise of parental power and the use of threats and punishment. They are oriented toward obedience and authority and expect their children to comply with their demands without question or explanation.

permissive parenting a parenting style that is high in responsiveness but low in demandingness. Permissive parents are responsive to their children's needs and do not require their children to regulate themselves or act in appropriate or mature ways.

rejecting-neglecting (disengaged) parenting a parenting style that is low in both responsiveness and demandingness. Rejecting-neglecting parents do not set limits for or monitor their children's behavior, are not supportive of them, and sometimes are rejecting or neglectful. They tend to be focused on their own needs rather than their children's.

Ethnic and Cultural Influences

In keeping with our theme of the *sociocultural context*, it is important to note that the effects of different parenting styles and practices in the United States vary somewhat as a function of ethnic or racial group. In Baumrind's original study (1972), for example, authoritarian parenting was not associated with negative outcomes for African-American adolescent girls, although it was for Euro-American adolescent girls. Similar findings were reported in a more recent study. In this research, for African-American adolescents at all levels of family affluence, parents' unilateral decision making, an aspect of authoritarian control, was associated with positive outcomes such as lower levels of deviant behavior and higher levels of academic competence (Lamborn, Dornbusch, & Steinberg, 1996). One possible explanation for these findings is that caring parents of African-American adolescents, more than other parents, feel the need to use authoritarian control in order to protect their children from danger, whether that danger be from prejudice in predominantly Euro-American, affluent communities or from the risks in living in a disadvantaged neighborhood. African-American adolescents may recognize that their parents' controlling practices often are due to concern for their well-being and, consequently, respond relatively positively to their parents' demands.

Particular parenting styles and practices may also have different meanings, and different effects, in different cultures. For example, authoritative parenting seems

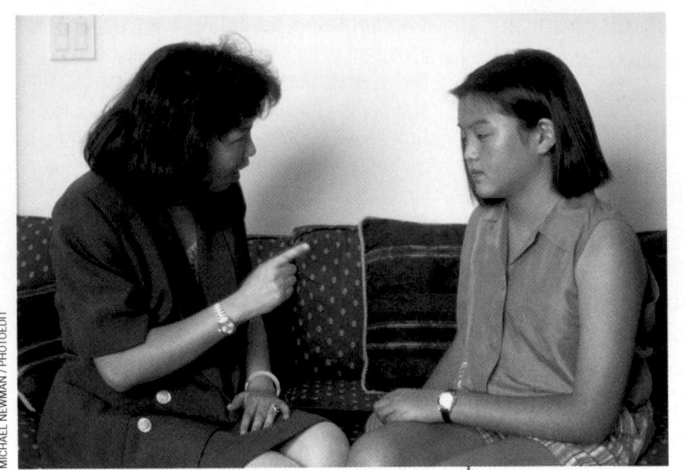
MICHAEL NEWMAN / PHOTOEDIT

The meaning of parental discipline varies depending on the culture or subculture. For example, authoritarian child-rearing practices seem to be associated with less negative consequences in Chinese and first-generation Chinese-American families than in Euro-American families.

to be associated with a close relationship between parent and child and with children's academic success in Euro-American families, but in the case of first-generation (though not second-generation) Chinese-American children, these outcomes seem unrelated to authoritative parenting. Perhaps this is because Chinese-American mothers, compared with Euro-American mothers, are more likely to believe that children owe unquestioning obedience to parents and thus use scolding and guilt to control their children (Chao, 1994). Although such a pattern of parental control is generally viewed as authoritarian, it appears to have few negative effects for Chinese-American children, at least prior to adolescence. One possible explanation is that in Chinese culture, children (but perhaps not adolescents [Yau & Smetana, 1996]) may view parental strictness and emphasis on obedience as signs of parental involvement and caring, and as important for family harmony (Chao, 1994). In contrast, research in the People's Republic of China shows that when authoritarian parenting includes harsh physical punishment, it is associated with negative effects for children, such as aggression, low social competence, and low academic performance (Chen, Dong, & Zhou, 1997; Zhou, 2001).

Because of variations such as these, findings regarding parenting in U.S. families cannot automatically be generalized to other cultures or subcultures, especially if the findings involve primarily Euro-American middle-class families. It is thus essential that the relation of parenting to children's development be considered in terms of the cultural context in which it occurs.

The Child as an Influence on Parenting

Among the strongest influences on parents' parenting style and practices are the characteristics of their children, such as their appearance, behavior, and attitudes. Thus, *individual differences* in children contribute to the parenting they receive, which in turn contributes to differences among children in their behavior and personalities.

Attractiveness

As unfair as it may seem, some of children's influence on their parents is due to their degree of physical attractiveness. For example, mothers of very attractive infants are more affectionate and playful with their infants than are mothers of infants with unappealing faces. Mothers of unappealing infants are more likely than other mothers to attend to other people who are in the vicinity rather than to their infants and to report that their infants interfere with their lives (Langlois, Ritter, Casey, & Sawin, 1995). Thus, from the first months of life, unattractive infants may experience somewhat different parenting than attractive infants. And this pattern continues, with attractive children, like attractive infants, tending to elicit more positive responses from adults (Langlois et al., 2000).

It is not clear why attractive children receive preferential treatment. However, an evolutionary explanation would propose that parents are motivated to invest more time and energy in offspring who are healthy and genetically fit and therefore likely to survive, and it may be that attractiveness is seen as an indicator of these characteristics (Langlois et al., 2000).

Children's Behaviors and Temperaments

The influence that children have on parenting because of their appearance is a passive contribution. Consistent with the theme of *the active child,* children are active contributors to the parenting process as well. Children who are disobedient, angry, and challenging, for example, make it more difficult for parents to use authoritative parenting than do children who are compliant and positive in their behavior (Brody & Ge, 2001; Cook, Kenny, & Goldstein, 1991).

Differences in children's behavior with their parents—including the degree to which they are emotionally negative, unregulated, and disobedient—can be due to a number of reasons. The most prominent of these are genetic factors related to temperament (Emde et al., 1992; Goldsmith, Buss, & Lemery, 1997). Children can also learn to be noncompliant through interactions with their parents that reinforce their negative behavior. In resisting their parents' demands, for example, they may become so whiny, aggressive, or hysterical that their parents back down, leading the children to resort to the same behavior to resist future demands (Patterson, 1982). To further complicate matters, children's behavior with their parents can be affected by their *perceptions* of their parents' attitudes toward them. Even if inaccurate, children's perceptions that their parents are hostile toward them increases the likelihood of their becoming antisocial or depressed (Neiderhiser, Pike, Hetherington, & Reiss, 1998). Thus, children not only elicit positive and negative behaviors from parents but also filter, and react to, parental behaviors based on their own view of those behaviors.

Over time, the **bidirectionality of parent–child interactions** reinforces and perpetuates each party's behavior. One study, for example, found that children's low self-regulation at age 6 to 8 (which may have been influenced by maternal behaviors at an earlier age) predicted mothers' punitive reactions (e.g., scolding and rejection) to their children's expressions of negative emotion two years later (at age 8 to 10). In turn, mothers' punitive reactions when their children were age 8 to 10 predicted low levels of self-regulation in the children two years later, at ages 10 to 12 (Eisenberg et al., 1999) (Figure 12.2). A similar self-reinforcing and escalating negative pattern is common when parents are hostile and inconsistent in enforcing standards of conduct with their adolescent children, and their children, in turn, are insensitive, disruptive, and inflexible with them (Rueter & Conger, 1998). (See Box 12.2.)

bidirectionality of parent–child interactions the idea that parents affect children's characteristics and behaviors and vice versa; both processes occur during parent–child interactions

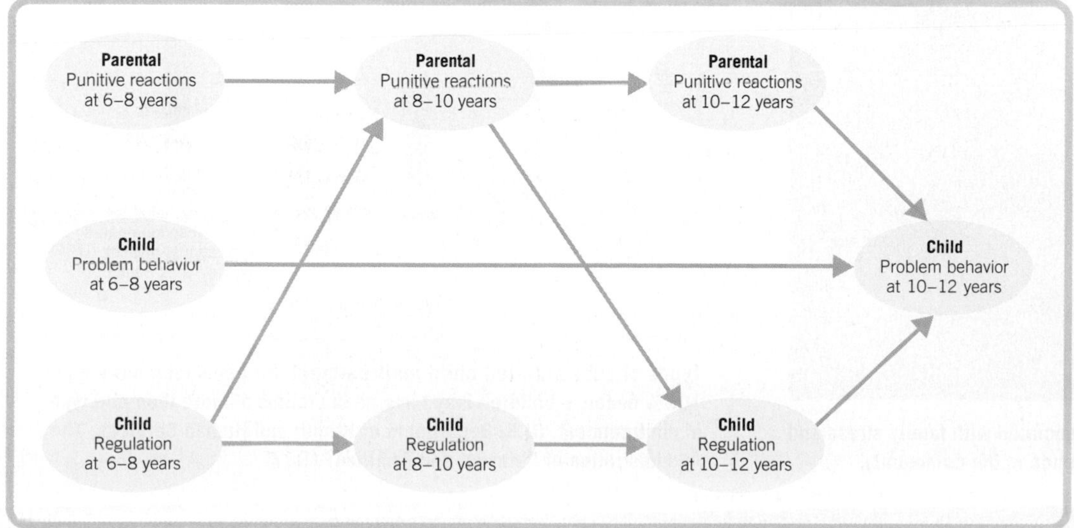

FIGURE 12.2 Bidirectional parent–child interactions In a study of elementary school children, children's self-regulation at ages 6 to 8 predicted parents' punitive reactions when the children were 8 to 10 years of age, which in turn predicted children's self-regulation at ages 10 to 12. Both parental punitive reactions and children's self-regulation at ages 10 to 12, as well as their problem behavior at a younger age, predicted externalizing problem behavior at ages 10 to 12. (Adapted from Eisenberg et al. ,1997)

applications

Child Maltreatment by Parents

One of the most serious threats to children's development in the United States is **child maltreatment,** defined as intentional abuse or neglect that endangers the well-being of anyone under the age of 18. In 1999, an estimated 2.9 million children were reported to child protection agencies as alleged victims of child maltreatment. About one-third of those cases were substantiated—a rate of 11.8 children per 1,000—with many others seeming credible but lacking in evidence sufficient to warrant action by authorities (Department of Health and Human Services, 1999; Wang & Daro, 1997). Slightly over half of the substantiated cases were instances of child neglect in which children were not given adequate physical care; the remaining instances involved physical, sexual, or emotional abuse and other types of maltreatment such as abandonment or educational or medical neglect (Department of Health and Human Services, 1999) (see figure below). More tragic still, over 1,000 children—most of them under the age of 6—are killed each year by a parent or parent figure (Department of Health and Human Services, 1999; Emery & Laumann-Billings, 1998).

In about 75% of cases of maltreatment, the perpetrators are parents, most often the mother (Department of Health and Human Services, 1999). Although it is tempting to view child maltreatment in these instances as due solely to psychologically disturbed parents, a variety of factors, including characteristics of the parent, the community, and the child, may contribute to its occurrence. Parents who maltreat their children often have poor impulse control, low self-esteem, and high levels of negative emotions and negative reactions to stress, all of which increase the likelihood of family violence (Emery & Laumann-Billings, 1998). They also are likely to feel that they have relatively little control over their children, a feeling that, in mothers at least, may lead to physiological arousal and punitive reactions (Bugental & Johnston, 2000; Bugental, Mantyla, & Lewis, 1989). Parental alcohol and drug dependence also increase the probability of abuse, as does abuse of the mother by her partner (Emery & Laumann-Billings, 1998; McCloskey, Figueredo, & Koss, 1995).

When maltreatment occurs, such personal characteristics are usually found in combination with other factors, many of which are related to low family income: high levels of parental stress, unemployment, inadequate housing, and community violence (Emery & Laumann-Billings, 1998; Lynch & Cicchetti, 1998). In fact, maltreatment relates directly to level of family income (see figure on the next page).

Another factor that contributes to child maltreatment is a family's social isolation and lack of social support. Typically, such isolation results from mistrust of other people, a lack of the social skills needed to maintain positive relationships, frequent moves from place to place due to economic factors, or living in a commu-

child maltreatment intentional abuse or neglect that endangers the well-being of anyone under the age of 18

BOB KALMAN / THE IMAGE WROKS

Physical abuse of children is associated with family stress and economic stress, as well as violence in the community.

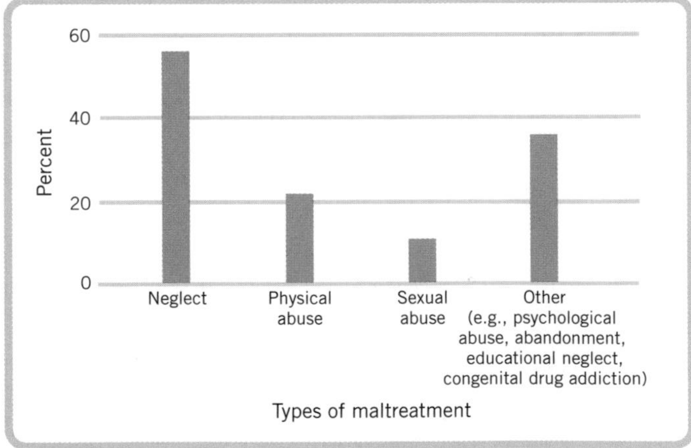

Types of substantiated child maltreatment **Percents total more than 100% because children may have been victims of more than one type of maltreatment. (U.S. Department of Health and Human Services, The Administration of Children and Families, 1997)**

12.2

nity characterized by violence and transience. The importance of social support is highlighted by the fact that impoverished parents are less likely to maltreat their children if they live in a neighborhood with relatively low turnover of residents, a sense of community, and mutual caring among neighbors (Belsky, 1993; Coulton, Korbin, Su, & Chow, 1995; Garbarino & Kostelny, 1992).

In certain instances, the personality or behavior of the child may be a contributing factor to maltreatment. This is not in any way to suggest that maltreated children are to blame for their maltreatment. However, victims of maltreatment do tend to share some common features, such as poor physical or mental health and a difficult temperament (Belsky, 1993; Cicchetti & Toth, 1998). The combination of a child who, in one way or another, is "difficult" and a parent who does not have the psychological resources to deal with stress is particularly dangerous.

The developmental costs that maltreatment can have for children are great, although it sometimes is difficult to know if the negative characteristics and behaviors often exhibited by maltreated children are the consequence of maltreatment or preceded it. In comparison with other children, maltreated children are more likely to have insecure attachments, especially disorganized/disoriented attachments, to caregivers. They also tend to be distractible, aggressive, prone to negative emotion, and low in self-esteem (Cicchetti & Toth, 1998; Smith & Walden, 1999). In addition, maltreated children, on average, are low in prosocial behaviors such as sharing and in feeling empathy toward others. As young children, for example, when they observe a peer who is crying or frightened, they tend to respond with inappropriate emotion or behavior, including anger and aggression (George & Main, 1979; Main & George, 1985). In elementary school, maltreated children are more likely than their peers to engage in conflict with their friends and to be aggressive (Bolger & Patterson, 2001; McCloskey & Stuewig, 2001); and in adolescence and adulthood, they are at risk for developing serious psychopathologies, including depression, anxiety, substance abuse, eating disorders, sexual dysfunction, hyperactivity, and defiance of authority (Cicchetti & Toth, 1998; Keiley, Howe, Dodge, Bates, & Pettit, 2001; Kilpatrick et al., 2000). Given this pattern of characteristics and behavior, it is no surprise that maltreated children—especially those maltreated at a young age and over many years—are relatively likely to have difficulties with peer relationships and in maintaining friendships (Parker & Herrera, 1996; Rogosch, Cicchetti, & Aber, 1995; Salzinger, Feldman, Ng-Mak, Mojica, & Stockhammer, 2001).

Maltreated children also have difficulties in school. In comparison with other children, physically abused children have the most disciplinary problems at school (Eckenrode, Laird, & Doris, 1993); neglected children and sexually abused children are often anxious and inattentive, have difficulty understanding their class work, and are overly dependent on their teachers for help, approval, and support (Erickson et al., 1989). Not surprisingly, maltreated children often get poorer grades than their peers and are more than twice as likely to fail a grade (Eckenrode et al., 1993).

A wide variety of interventions have been used to try to prevent or stop maltreatment of children. Unfortunately, the effectiveness of these treatments often is unknown because outcomes have not been systematically evaluated. However, evidence does suggest that early interventions that provide parent training and stress-management skills may be helpful. One type of early intervention that has shown promise is home-visitor programs that are designed for low-income, and often unmarried, new mothers who are considered at risk for maltreating their children. These programs, which provide the parents with assistance in meeting their physical, psychological, and material needs, sometimes have been associated with reduced rates of chronic maltreatment (Eckenrode et al., 2001; Emery & Laumann-Billings, 1998; Olds, Henderson, & Tatelbaum, 1986), and are leading to increased hopes of finding effective approaches. Until the problem is brought under control, developing successful programs for the prevention of child maltreatment will be a major priority for both researchers and policy makers.

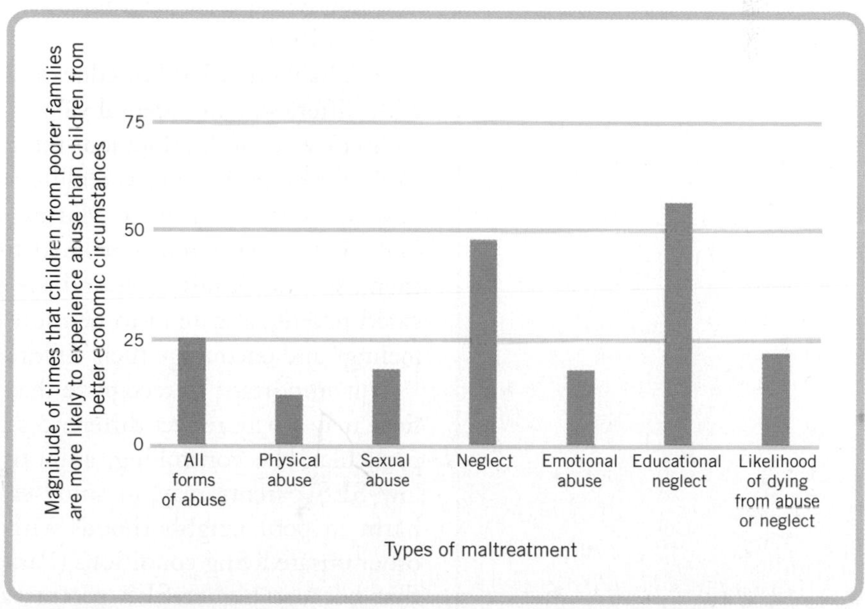

Likelihood of children to experience maltreatment, by income level Children in families earning less than $15,000 a year, in comparison with families earning $30,000 a year or more, were 25 times more likely to experience all forms of abuse and 48 times more likely to experience neglect. (Adapted from Sedlak & Broadhurt, 1996)

Socioeconomic Influences on Parenting

Another factor that is associated with parenting styles and practices is socioeconomic status (SES). Parents with low SES are more likely than higher-SES parents to use an authoritarian and punitive child-rearing style; higher-SES parents tend to use a style that is more accepting and democratic (Hoff-Ginsberg & Tardif, 1995; Kelley, Sanchez-Hucles, & Walker, 1993). Higher-SES mothers, for example, are less likely than low-SES mothers to be controlling, restrictive, and disapproving in their interactions with their young children. In addition, higher-SES mothers talk more with, and elicit more talk from, their children. They also name more objects for them and follow up more directly on what their children say. This greater use of language by higher-SES mothers may foster better communication between parent and child, and it may promote the child's verbal skills (Hart & Risley, 1992; Hoff-Ginsberg & Tardif, 1995).

Some of the SES differences in parenting style and practices are related to differences in parental beliefs and values (Skinner, 1985). Both in the United States and in other Western countries, parents from lower-SES families often value conformity in children's behavior, whereas higher-SES parents are more likely to want their children to become self-directed and autonomous (Alwin, 1984; Luster, Rhoades, & Haas, 1989). Some investigators have suggested that adults come to value the qualities required in their jobs and, accordingly, train their children to behave in a manner consistent with their own job-related experience. Blue-collar workers have jobs that require little self-direction and reward conformity, whereas white-collar workers and professionals are expected to be self-starters and are rewarded for initiative (Kohn, 1969). However, it is unclear whether occupational values or other factors associated with low SES (such as stress that reduces parents' patience) contribute to the degree of controllingness that low-SES parents exhibit with their children (Alwin, 1989; Hoff-Ginsberg & Tardif, 1995).

It is likely that level of education is also an important aspect of SES associated with differences in parental values. Highly educated parents tend to hold a more complex view of development than do parents with less education. They are more likely, for example, to view children as active participants in their own learning and development (Johnson & Martin, 1985; Skinner, 1985). Such a view may make high-SES parents more inclined to allow children a say in matters that involve them, such as family rules and the consequences for breaking them. Highly educated parents also tend to be more concerned with their children's thoughts and feelings and encourage their children to express them.

It is important to recognize that SES differences in parenting styles and practices may partly reflect differences in the environments in which families live. In particular, the controlling, authoritarian parenting style that is more typical of low-SES parents may, in some cases, be adaptive for protecting children from harm in poor neighborhoods with high rates of violence, substance abuse, and other unsafe living conditions (Parke & Buriel, 1998). At the same time, it may be that because higher-SES parents are less stressed about economic matters and concerns over protecting their children from violence, they have more time and energy to commit to thinking about complex issues in child rearing and may be better able to interact with their children in a controlled yet stimulating manner (Hoff-Ginsberg & Tardif, 1995).

Economic Stress and Parenting

Protracted economic stress is a strong predictor of quality of parenting, familial interactions, and children's adjustment—and the outcome is generally negative (McLoyd, 1998; Valenzuela, 1997). For example, economic pressures tend to increase the likelihood of marital conflict, which in turn makes parents more likely to be uninvolved with, or hostile to, their children (Conger et al., 1993; Conger, Ge, Elder, Lorenz, & Simons, 1994; Conger et al., 2002). Marital conflict also makes parents less likely to cooperate and support each other in regard to parenting (Floyd, Gilliom, & Costigan, 1998; Margolin, Gordis, & John, 2001). In children and adolescents, nonsupportive, inconsistent parenting associated with economic hardship correlates with increased risk for depression, loneliness, unregulated behavior, delinquency, and substance use (Brody et al., 1994; Conger et al., 1994; Lempers, Clark-Lempers, & Simons, 1989).

The quality of parenting and family interactions is especially likely to be compromised for families at the poverty level, which in 1997 included 32% of U.S. single-parent families headed by mothers and 5% of families headed by married adults (U.S. Bureau of the Census, 1998). All told, about 17% of children under 18 years of age live in poverty in the United States, the highest rate of child poverty among industrialized, Western countries (U.S. Bureau of the Census, 2000) (see Figures 12.3 and 12.4). At one time or another, a substantial number of families in poverty experience homelessness, which obviously makes effective parenting extremely difficult (see Box 12.3).

One factor that can help moderate the potential impact of economic stress on parenting is having supportive relationships with relatives, friends, neighbors, or others who can provide material assistance, child care, advice, approval, or a sympathetic ear. Such positive connections can help people feel successful as parents and actually be better parents. In one study of low-income Latino, American Indian, and Euro-American parents of young children, those who reported that they received sufficient social support had more confidence in their parenting skills, and more satisfaction in the parenting role, than did those who reported insufficient

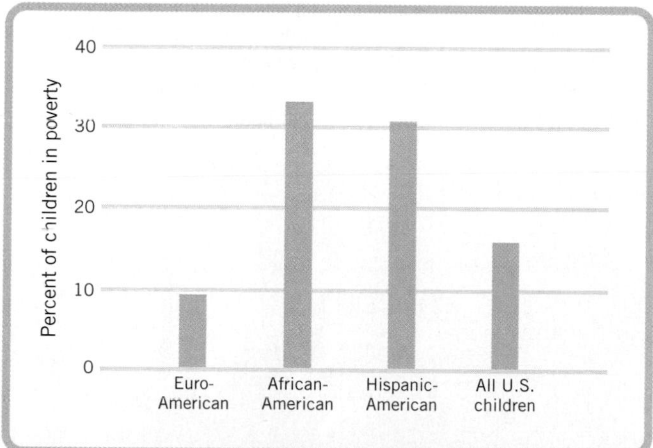

FIGURE 12.3 Child poverty rates in 1999 in the United States Minority children in the United States—especially African-American and Hispanic-American children—are more than 3 times as likely to live in poverty than are Euro-American children. (U.S. Bureau of the Census, 2000)

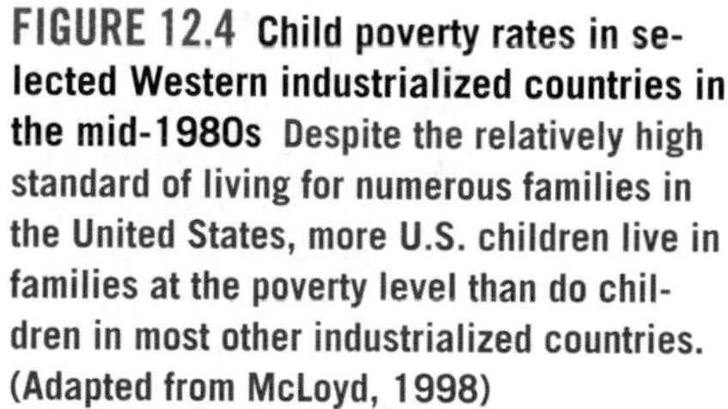

FIGURE 12.4 Child poverty rates in selected Western industrialized countries in the mid-1980s Despite the relatively high standard of living for numerous families in the United States, more U.S. children live in families at the poverty level than do children in most other industrialized countries. (Adapted from McLoyd, 1998)

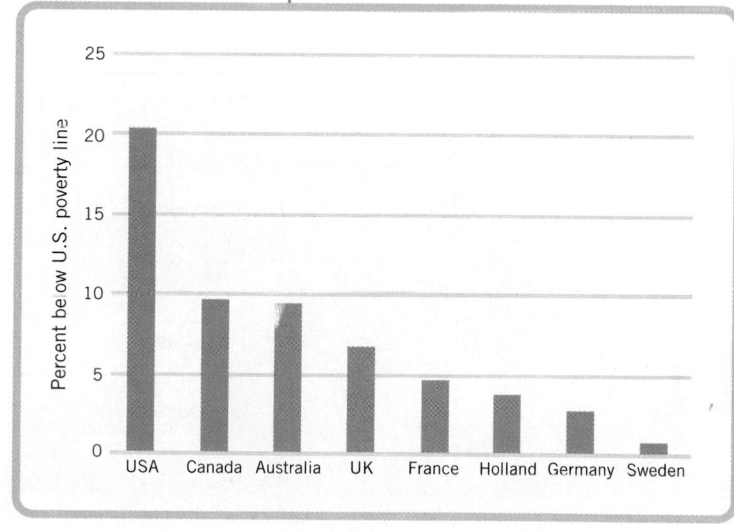

a closer look 12.3

Homelessness

It is impossible to know the precise number of homeless children and families in the United States, much less in the world. In some countries, such as India and Brazil, the figure is in the millions (Diversi, Filho, & Morelli, 1999; Verma, 1999). In the United States, it is estimated that over 700,000 people are homeless on any given night and that 2 million people are homeless sometime over the course of a given year. One-fourth of the estimated homeless people in the United States are children (U.S. Conference of Mayors, 1998), many of whom live with at least one parent, usually the mother.

Homeless children are at risk in a variety of ways. They are often malnourished and lack adequate medical care, and are exposed to numerous other hazards to their well-being, including the chaotic and unsafe conditions found in many shelters. Homeless children tend to exhibit delays in language and motor development and are also prone to cognitive and social deficits such as short attention spans, aggression, and inappropriate social behavior (Rafferty & Shinn, 1991). As might be expected, poor school performance and absenteeism from school are common among homeless children, as are serious behavioral problems at school (Masten et al., 1997). Homeless children also experience more internalizing problems, such as depression, social withdrawal, and low self-esteem, than do poor children who are not homeless (Buckner, Bassuk, Weinreb, & Brooks, 1999; DiBiase & Waddell, 1995; Rafferty & Shinn, 1991). The most serious behavioral, cognitive, and academic problems occur in homeless children whose parents—homelessness aside—experience a great deal of stress in regard to parenting and who have experienced major life stressors in the prior year (Danseco & Holden, 1998).

When they were young, mothers of homeless families often experienced stressors such as physical and sexual abuse, living on the street, and living in foster care or in an institution (Shinn, Knickman, & Weitzman, 1991). Many homeless men appear to have similar backgrounds (Interagency Council on the Homeless, 1999). In turn, their children are at increased risk both of being sexually abused (Buckner et al., 1999) and of ending up in foster care (Zlotnick, Kronstadt, & Klee, 1998). Thus, the cycle of deprivation, abuse, and disruption of social relationships that contributes to homelessness is likely self-perpetuating.

In adolescence, numerous youths choose to leave their homes or are kicked out, and many of them live on the streets. Estimates of homeless, runaway, or "thrown away" adolescents in the United States (many of whom may not be included in homeless statistics) range from about 575,000 to over 1 million (Wolfe, Toro, & McCaskill, 1999). These homeless youths, in comparison with housed adolescents from the same neighborhoods, generally report having experienced more conflict with, and rejection by, their parents and more parental maltreatment, including physical abuse. These differences in experience seem to be based in part on differences in the parents' behavior or in levels of stress in the home; they do not seem to be due merely to the homeless children's having had more problems of adjustment and alcohol abuse (Wolfe et al., 1999). Once on the streets, over a third of adolescents are likely to be affiliated with gangs and involved in illegal activities such as dealing drugs, stealing, and prostitution (Unger et al., 1998).

In many third-world countries, homeless children often live with other children on the streets and report doing so because of the loss of their parents or because of sexual, mental, or physical abuse at home (Aptehar & Ciano-Federoff, 1999). In many cases, children living on the streets reside at least part of the time with a parent or other relative (Diversi et al., 1999; Verma, 1999). Some youths report that they stay on the streets in order to enjoy freedom with their friends (Campos et al., 1994; Sampa, 1997).

Life on the streets in most third-world countries is even riskier than it is in the United States. In one study of Brazilian street youth, 75% were engaged in illegal activities such as stealing and prostitution (Campos et al., 1994). The longer these children were on the streets, the more likely they were to be involved in illegal activities. Street children also were at risk for drug abuse and had begun sexual activities at a younger age than their peers who hung out on the street but usually slept in homes. Thus, it is clear that homelessness, wherever it occurs, takes a tremendous toll on the welfare of children and on the larger society.

TONY FREEMAN / PHOTOEDIT

Children in homeless families are at risk for depression, behavioral problems, and academic failure.

DMITRI SHALGANOV / PPI / NEWSMAKERS / GETTY IMAGES

Homeless youth are at high risk for becoming involved in drugs and prostitution.

social support. In turn, their use of optimal parenting practices (such as setting limits while using little punishment) was greater than that of the parents who were less satisfied with their social support (MacPhee, Fritz, & Miller-Heyl, 1996).

review::

Styles of parenting are associated with important developmental outcomes. Researchers have delineated four basic parenting styles varying in parental warmth and control: authoritative (relatively high in control but supportive); authoritarian (high in control but low in warmth); permissive (high in warmth and low in control); and rejecting-neglecting (low in both warmth and control). Particular styles of parenting can affect the meaning and impact of specific parenting practices, as well as children's receptiveness to these practices. In addition, the significance and effects of different parenting styles or practices may vary somewhat across cultures.

Education and income are associated with variations in parenting. Economic stressors can undermine the quality of marital and parent–child interactions. Children in poor and homeless families are more at risk for serious adjustment problems, such as depression, academic failure, disruptive behavior at school, and drug use.

Mothers, Fathers, and Siblings

As part of their focus on family dynamics, developmentalists have examined differences in children's interactions with mothers, fathers, and siblings. Two questions that they have been particularly interested in are: How do mothers and fathers differ in their parenting? and How do siblings affect one another?

Differences in Mothers' and Fathers' Interactions with Their Children

It will come as no surprise that there is a great deal of difference, both quantitative and qualitative, between mothers' and fathers' interactions with their children. Although in most Western cultures today spouses share child-care responsibilities to some degree, in the majority of families, mothers—including those who work outside the home—still spend considerably more time with their children than do fathers (Parke & Buriel, 1998). In this United States, this seems to be true in Latino-American, African-American, and Euro-American families, continuing from the early years into adolescence (Parke & Buriel, 1998).

Fathers' participation in child care differs not only in amount but in kind. Fathers in Western industrialized cultures spend a greater proportion of their available time playing with their children than do mothers, both in infancy and childhood, and the type of play they engage in differs from mothers' play (Parke & Buriel, 1998). In an Australian study, for example, fathers were more likely to engage their children in physical and outdoor play activities (e.g., rough-and-tumble play and playing ball) than were mothers (Russell & Russell, 1987) (Table 12.1). In contrast, mothers tended to play more reserved games (e.g., peekaboo), to teach and read to their children, and to play more with toys indoors (Parke, 1996; Russell & Russell, 1987).

Although these general patterns prevail in many cultures, there are also some cultural variations. Fathers in Sweden, Malaysia, and India, for example, do not report much play at all with their children (Hwang,

Fathers tend to engage in more physical play with their children than do mothers.

JIM SUGAR / STOCKPHOTO

TABLE 12.1

Self-Reported Frequencies of Interactions of Mothers and Fathers with Their Boys and Girls

Parental participation in tasks related to the child's needs were rated on a 5-point scale from "never" (1) to "always" (5). Parent–child interactions were rated on a 5-point scale from "never" (1) to "almost everyday" (5). Categories with asterisks differed significantly across parents.

	Boys		Girls	
	Fathers	**Mothers**	**Fathers**	**Mothers**
Participates in tasks related to the child's needs				
Responsibility for bedtime*	4.4	4.8	4.4	4.5
Health needs*	3.5	4.9	2.9	4.6
Daily school needs*	1.5	4.9	1.8	5.0
Responsibility for dressing*	1.9	4.9	2.1	4.9
Parent–child interaction*				
Go over schoolwork*	4.2	4.8	4.1	4.8
Read to child*	4.0	4.3	4.1	4.8
Play with toys indoors	3.6	3.9	3.2	3.7
Play rough-and-tumble games*	4.2	3.1	3.7	2.8
Take to/watch sports	2.9	2.8	1.7	2.0
Go over a child's day*	4.7	5.0	4.4	4.7
Sit and talk	4.6	4.9	4.6	4.7
Go to park/beach	3.3	3.5	3.3	3.4

Adapted from Russell & Russell (1987)

1987; Roopnarine, Lu, & Ahmeduzzaman, 1989). Indeed, both mothers and fathers in some cultures simply play less with their children than do American parents (Goncu, Mistry, & Mosier, 2000; Roopnarine & Hossain, 1992). In a study of Gusii infants and parents in Kenya, fathers were seldom seen within 5 feet of their infants, and mothers spent 60% less time playing with infants than American mothers typically do (LeVine et al., 1996). The degree of maternal and paternal involvement in parenting and the nature of parents' interactions with children doubtlessly vary as a function of cultural practices and such factors as the amount of time parents work away from home and children spend at home.

Sibling Relationships

Siblings influence each other's development and the functioning of the larger family system in many ways, both positive and negative. They serve not only as playmates for one another but also as sources of support, instruction, security, assistance, and caregiving (Brody, Stoneman, MacKinnon, & MacKinnon, 1985; Herrera & Dunn, 1997; Whiting & Edwards, 1988). On the other hand, they also can be rivals and sources of mutual conflict and irritation (Vandell, 1987); and they can contribute to the development of a sibling's undesirable behaviors, such as noncompliance with parents' rules, delinquency, and drinking (Bank, Patterson, & Reid, 1996; McGue, Sharma, & Benson, 1996; Slomkowski, Rende, Conger, Simons, & Conger, 2001). The degree to which sibling relations are positive or negative in these regards can obviously have a major impact on siblings' depression and problem behavior (Stocker, Burwell, & Briggs, 2002), as well as on the family as a whole.

Numerous factors affect whether or not siblings get along with each other. On the whole, sibling relationships usually get off to a rocky start, with most children showing some negative reactions to the birth of a sibling, especially if they receive much less attention once the new baby arrives. However, parents can help older children accept a new sibling by preparing them for the sibling's arrival, explaining the care that a newborn requires and outlining the changes that will occur in the family's daily routines. Parents can further aid a child's acceptance of a new sibling by involving the child in activities with the newborn, such as holding or feeding the baby (Vandell, 1987).

TARO YAMASAKI / TIMEPIX

The quality of parents' relationships with their children is related to how well siblings interact.

One factor that is key to how well siblings ultimately get along is the similarity of their temperament. In early and middle childhood, siblings seem to get along better if they are temperamentally alike—that is, unless they both have difficult temperaments (Munn & Dunn, 1989; Stoneman & Brody, 1993). Indeed, if either sibling has a difficult temperament—for example, is highly active, emotionally intense, and difficult to manage—the sibling relationship is likely to suffer (Brody, Stoneman, & McCoy, 1994).

Siblings' relationships tend to be less hostile and more supportive when their parents are warm and accepting of them (Ingoldsby, Shaw, & Garcia, 2001; MacKinnon-Lewis, Starnes, Volling, & Johnson, 1997). Siblings also have closer, more positive relationships if their parents treat them similarly (Brody, Stoneman, McCoy, & Forehand, 1992; McHale, Crouter, McGuire, & Updegraff, 1995). Parents' differential treatment of their children can be very upsetting to the less-favored child (O'Connor, Hetherington, & Reiss, 1998) and is associated with problems in adjustment, especially if the less-favored child does not have a positive relationship with his or her parents (Feinberg & Hetherington, 2001). Consider the following situation involving a 30-month-old boy and his 14-month-old sister:

> Andy was a rather timid and sensitive child, cautious, unconfident, and compliant. His younger sister, Susie, was a striking contrast—assertive, determined, and a handful for her mother, who was nevertheless delighted by her boisterous daughter. . . . Susie persistently attempted to grab a forbidden object on a high kitchen counter, despite her mother's repeated prohibitions. Finally, she succeeded, and Andy overheard his mother make a warm, affectionate comment on Susie's action: "Susie, you are a determined little devil." Andy, sadly, commented to his mother, "I'm not a determined little devil." His mother replied, laughing, "No! What are you? A poor old boy!"
>
> (Dunn, 1992, p. 6)

Repeated instances like this one are likely to make Andy jealous of his sister and may hurt his relationship with her, not to mention making Andy feel badly about himself. Differential treatment by parents is more influential in early and middle childhood, with less-favored siblings being more likely to be worried, anxious, or depressed than their more-favored siblings (Dunn, 1992). By early adolescence, however, children often view differential treatment by parents as justified because of differences they perceive between themselves and their siblings in age, needs, and personal characteristics. When children view differential treatment by parents as justified, they report more positive relationships with their sibling than when they feel that differential parental treatment is unfair (Kowal & Kramer, 1997).

Another factor that can affect the quality of siblings' interactions is the nature of the parents' relationships with each other. Siblings get along better if their parents are getting along with each other (McGuire, McHale, & Updegraff, 1996). In part, this may be because the parents model positive behavior. Correspondingly, parents who fight with one another model negative behavior for their children. They also may be less sensitive and appropriate in their efforts to manage their children's interactions with each other, which is likely to affect the level of hostility in siblings' interactions (Howe, Aquan-Assee, & Bukowski, 2001).

Rivalry and conflict between siblings tend to be higher in divorced families and in remarried families than in nondivorced families, even between biological siblings. Although some siblings turn to one another for support when their parents divorce or remarry (Jenkins, 1992), they also may compete for parental affection and attention, which often are scarce in these situations. As members of a new family, biologically related siblings are generally more involved with one another and higher in support—as well as in conflict and rivalry—than are unrelated stepsiblings. Relationships between half siblings may be especially emotionally charged, perhaps because the older sibling may resent the younger sibling who is born to both parents in the new marital relationship (Hetherington, 1999).

Thus, the quality of sibling relationships differs across families depending on the personalities of the siblings, the ways that parents interact with each child and one another, and children's perceptions of their treatment by other family members. Such differences highlight the fact that families are complex, dynamic social systems, and that all members contribute to one another's functioning.

review:

Mothers typically interact with their children much more than fathers do. The nature of mother–child and father–child interactions also tends to differ, with fathers engaging in more physical play with their children. Parent–child interactions differ across cultures; for example, in some cultures, parents play little or not at all with their children.

Siblings are important contributors to one another's socialization and development. They can be sources of learning and support for each other, as well as rivalry and conflict. Siblings get along better with one another if they have good relationships with their parents and if they do not feel that their parents treat them differentially. Sibling relationships are, on the average, more hostile and conflicted in divorced and remarried families than in nondivorced families. Thus, sibling relationships, like all family relationships, must be viewed in the context of the larger family system.

Changes in Families in the United States

The family in the United States changed dramatically in the second half of the twentieth century. For one thing, from the 1950s to the end of the century, the median age at which people first married rose from age 20 to 25 for women and from age 23 to 26.7 for men (Coltrane, 1996; U.S. Bureau of the Census, 1999). The economic arrangement of the U. S. family also changed quite strikingly. In 1940, the father was the breadwinner and the mother was a full-time homemaker in 52% of nonfarm families. By 1989, only 25% of American nonfarm families fit this description (Figure 12.5). Thus, in most families, mothers and fathers were employed outside the home.

A third change that occurred in the family, partly as a result of the two just mentioned, was that the average age at which women bore children increased, especially within marriages. In the late 1970s, fewer than one in five births in the United States were to women over age 30. By 1990, one out of three births were to women 30 and older (Coltrane, 1996; U.S. Bureau of the Census, 1991), and this rate held through the 1990s (U.S. Bureau of the Census, 1999).

Two of the most far-reaching changes in the U.S. family in the past half century have been the upsurge in divorce and the increase in the number of children born to unwed mothers. The divorce rate more than doubled between 1960 and 1980, with about one out of two marriages ending in divorce. This rate has held fairly steady ever since (Coltane, 1996; Monthly Vital Statistics Report, 1995, 1999; Youth Indicators, 2001). The rise in out-of-wedlock births began in the 1980s. Between 1980 and 1994, the number of births among unmarried women between the ages of 15 and 44 increased from 29 to 47 per 1,000 women and has decreased only slightly since (National Center for Health Statistics, 1999) (see Figure 12.6).

Due both to the increase in divorce and the increase in the birth rate among unmarried women, the number of single-parent households in the United States more than doubled between 1970 and 1990. In 2000, only 69% of children lived with two parents (not necessarily their biological parents), including 75% percent of Euro-American children, 35% of African-American children, and 63% of Latino children (ChildStats.gov, 2001; U.S. Bureau of the Census, March 1998). Thus, about 20 million children under age 18 lived with only one parent in 1998 (U. S. Census Bureau, 1998). If current trends continue, about half of the children born in the 1990s will spend some time in a single-parent family before the age of 18, with an increasing number of them living in father-headed single-parent households (Coltrane, 1996).

Although people are more likely to divorce than in the past, most divorced people also remarry. About 40% of marriages in the United States involve at least one person who was married previously, and often that person already has children.

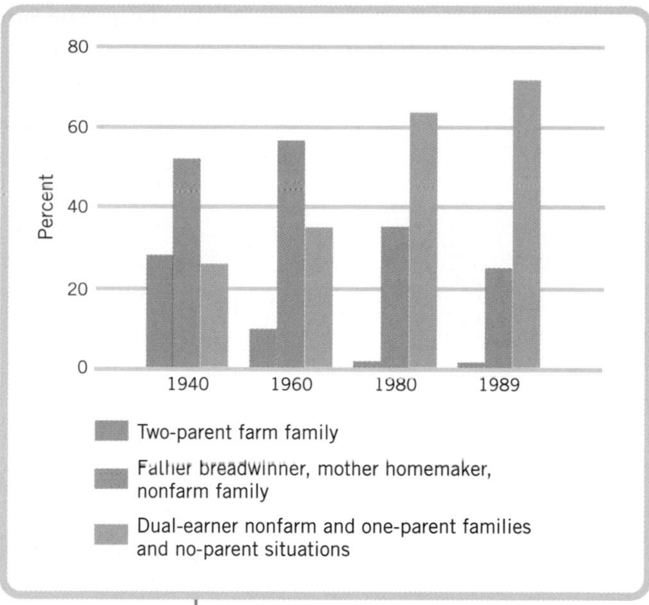

FIGURE 12.5 Economic arrangement of the U.S. family, 1940–1989 Over about fifty years (starting in 1940), the percent of two-parent families including a stay-at-home mother or two-parent farming families dropped substantially, whereas the percent of dual-earner, single-parent, and no-parent families increased to about 70%. (Adapted from Hernandez, 1993)

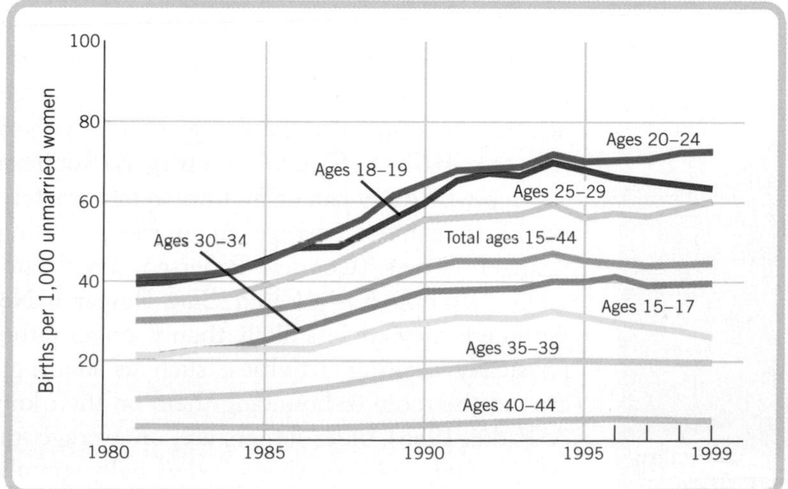

FIGURE 12.6 Birth rates for unmarried women Between 1980 and 1994, the birth rate among unmarried women ages 15 to 44 increased from 29 to 47 per 1,000. The rate has since stabilized; between 1994 and 1997–1999, the rate fell slightly to 44 per 1,000. During the 1980–1994 period, birth rates increased sharply for unmarried women in all age groups. (Adapted from ChildStats.gov, 2001)

Thus, the number of families including children from one or both parents' prior marriages has increased substantially (Coltrane, 1996).

All these changes in the structure and composition of families have vast implications for an understanding of child development and family life. In the following sections we will consider in detail the impact of age on parenting, the effects of both divorce and remarriage on children's development, and the issues surrounding maternal employment and child care. We will also consider an additional change in family structure that has recently received a good deal of public attention: the increase in the number of lesbian and gay parents.

Older Parents

The age at which parents have children can affect their parenting in a number of ways. Within limits, having children at a later age has decided parenting advantages. As discussed in Box 12.4, adolescents, whether married or not, are generally less psychologically or financially equipped to deal with having children than are people past adolescence. Their parenting skills and knowledge of how to obtain and use medical and educational resources also are often inferior to those of older parents, and their children consequently are at risk in many aspects of their development.

Even parents in their early 20s lack the resources of older first-time parents, who tend to have more education, higher-status occupations, and higher incomes. Older parents also are more likely to have planned the birth of their children and to have fewer children overall. Thus, they have more financial resources for raising a family. An additional benefit for mothers who delay childbearing is that they tend to perform fewer hours of housework, either because they are able to afford household help or because their husbands, also being older and having similar or higher SES characteristics, are more likely than the husbands of young mothers to believe that housework should be shared (Coltrane, 1996). Taken together, these factors help reduce the overall stresses of parenting for mothers.

Older parents also tend to be more positive in their parenting of infants than younger parents—unless they already have several children. In one study of mothers aged 16 to 38 who had recently given birth, the older the mother, the more she expressed satisfaction with parenting and commitment to the parenting role. Older mothers also reported greater gratification from their interactions with the baby, displayed more positive emotion toward the baby, and showed greater sensitivity to the baby's cues. However, these positive outcomes did not extend to mothers who already had two or more children. These mothers tended to exhibit less positive affect and sensitive behavior with their infants than did younger mothers with two or more other children, perhaps because the former had less energy to deal with so many children (Ragozin, Basham, Crnic, Greenberg, & Robinson, 1982).

Men who delay parenting until approximately age 30 or later are likewise more positive about the parenting role than are younger fathers (Cooney, Pedersen, Indelicato, & Palkovitz, 1993; NICHD Early Child Care Research Network, 2000a). Although they are less likely than younger fathers to engage in physically exciting activities, such as chasing their children around the room or bouncing them on their knee (MacDonald & Parke, 1986), older fathers are, on average, more responsive, affectionate, and cognitively and verbally stimulating with their infants, and are more likely to provide a moderate amount of

On average, older fathers engage in more verbal interactions with their preschool-age children than do younger fathers.

MICHAEL NEWMAN / PHOTOEDIT

individual differences 12.4

Adolescents as Parents

Childbearing in adolescence is a common occurrence in the United States. Among 15- to 19-year-olds in 1998, the rate of births was 39 per 1,000 females. True, this rate was substantially below the 1960 rate of 89 births per 1,000 females in this age range (ChildStats.gov, 2001; Ventura et al., 1997), probably due in part to the greater availability of birth control and abortions. Nevertheless, the current rate is still much higher than that in other industrialized countries. For example, U.S. adolescent birth rates are twice those in Great Britain (which is second highest), about seven times those in Denmark and the Netherlands, and fifteen times those in Japan (Coley & Chase-Lansdale, 1998). In contrast to the rate of births for all adolescent females, the rate of births to *unmarried* adolescents aged 15 to 17 increased over 50% from 1980 to 1994, but then fell 16% between 1994 and 1998 (ChildStats.gov, 2001; Ventura et al., 1997). Thus, births to teens have been decreasing in the recent past.

A number of factors affect U.S. teenage girls' risk for childbearing during adolescence. Two factors that reduce the risk are living with both biological parents and being involved in school activities and religious organizations (Moore, Manlove, Glei, & Morrison, 1998). Factors that substantially increase the risk include being raised in poverty by single or adolescent mothers (Coley & Chase-Lansdale, 1998; Hardy, Astone, Brooks-Gunn, Shapiro, & Miller, 1998) and having an older sibling who is sexually active or a teen parent (East & Jacobson, 2001; Miller, Benson, & Galbraith, 2001). For young adolescent girls, having a mother who is cold and uninvolved may increase the risk of their becoming pregnant in later adolescence. In part, this may be because girls whose mothers fit this pattern tend to do poorly in school and hang out with peers who get into trouble, which leads to risk taking and pregnancy (Scaramella, Conger, Simons, & Whitbeck, 1998). In fact, girls who are at risk for becoming mothers as teenagers tend to have many friends who are sexually active (East, Felice, & Morgan, 1993; Scaramella et al., 1998). It is likely that girls' willingness to engage in sex is influenced by its acceptability in their group of friends.

Having a child in adolescence is associated with many negative consequences for both the adolescent mother and the child (Jaffe, 2002). Motherhood curtails the mother's opportunities for education, career development, and normal relationships with peers. Even if teenage mothers marry, they are very likely to get divorced and to spend many years as single mothers (Coley & Chase-Lansdale, 1998; Lamb & Teti, 1991). In addition, adolescent mothers often have poor parenting skills and are more likely than older mothers to provide low levels of verbal stimulation to their infants, to expect their children to behave in ways beyond their years, and to neglect and abuse them (Culp, Appelbaum, Osofsky, & Levy, 1988; Lamb & Ketterlinus, 1991).

Given these deficits in parenting, it is not surprising that children of teenage mothers are more likely than children of older mothers to exhibit low impulse control, problem behaviors, and delays in cognitive development in the preschool years and thereafter. As adolescents themselves, children born to teenagers have higher rates of academic failure, delinquency, incarceration, and early sexual activity than do adolescents born to older mothers (Coley & Chase-Lansdale, 1998; Wakschlag et al., 2001). This does not mean that all children born to adolescent mothers are destined to poor developmental outcomes. Adolescent mothers who have more knowledge about child development and parenting, in comparison with their less knowledgeable peers, have children who display fewer problem behaviors and better intellectual development in early childhood (Miller, Miceli, Whitman, & Borkowski, 1996).

Adolescent males are more at risk for becoming fathers if they are poor, prone to substance abuse and behavioral problems, and have a police record (Fagot, Pears, Capaldi, Crosby, & Leve, 1998; Lerman, 1993; Moore & Florsheim, 2001). Many young unmarried or absent fathers see their children regularly, at least during the first few years, but rates of contact decrease over time (Corey & Chase-Lansdale, 1998). In one study, 40% of 2-year-old children had no contact with their adolescent fathers (Fagot et al., 1998). Fathers remain more involved with their children if they have a warm, supportive relationship with the mother in the weeks after delivery and if the mother does not experience many stressful life events (particularly financial problems) during and soon after the pregnancy (Cutrona, Hessling, Bacon, & Russell, 1998). Children of adolescent mothers fare better in their own adolescence if they have a strong attachment to their biological father or to a stepfather, especially if he lives with the child. However, exposure to a fathering figure may have little beneficial effect on children of adolescent mothers if the father–child relationship is not positive (Furstenberg & Harris, 1993).

JOHN BERRY / SYRACUSE NEWSPAPERS / THE IMAGE WORKS

Teenage mothers tend to be daughters of teenage mothers and to have sexually active sisters and friends.

child care (Neville & Parke, 1997; NICHD Early Child Care Research Network, 2000a; Volling & Belsky, 1991). These differences may be partly due to older fathers' being better established in their careers, allowing them to focus on their role as father and to be more flexible in their beliefs about acceptable roles and activities for fathers (Coltrane, 1996; Parke & Buriel, 1998).

Divorce

Each year in the United States, approximately 1 million children experience the divorce of their parents (U.S. Bureau of the Census, 1992). About half of these children acquire a stepparent within four years of their biological parents' separation, and 10% experience at least two divorces before the age of 16 (Furstenberg, 1988). Thus, the effects of divorce and remarriage on children are of great concern.

The Potential Impact of Divorce

Most experts agree that children of divorce are at greater risk for short- and long-term psychological, behavioral, academic, and relationship problems than are most children who are living with both their biological parents. Compared with the majority of their peers in intact families, for example, they are more likely to experience depression and sadness, to have lower self-esteem, and to be less socially responsible and competent (Amato, 2001; Amato & Keith, 1991; Hetherington, Bridges, & Insabella, 1998). Adolescents whose parents divorce exhibit a greater tendency toward dropping out of school, engaging in delinquent activities and substance abuse, and having children out of wedlock (Amato & Keith, 1991; Hetherington et al., 1998; Simons & Associates, 1996).

As adults, children from divorced and remarried families are at greater risk for divorce themselves (Bumpass, Martin, & Sweet, 1991; Rodgers, Power, & Hope, 1997). Being less likely to have completed high school or college, they often earn lower incomes in early adulthood than do their peers from intact families (Hetherington, 1999). They are also at slightly greater risk for serious emotional disorders such as depression, anxiety, and phobias (Chase-Lansdale, Cherlin, & Kiernan, 1995).

Clearly, divorce can have negative effects for some children. Nevertheless, most children whose parents divorce do not suffer significant, enduring problems as a consequence. Although some experts estimate that 20% to 25% of children from divorced families exhibit significant problems, compared with 10% of children in intact families (Hetherington et al., 1998), the estimates of other experts are more modest (Amato & Keith, 1991). In fact, although divorce usually is a very painful experience for children, the differences between children from divorced families and children from intact families in terms of their psychological and social functioning are small overall. In addition, these differences often reflect an extension of differences in the children's and/or their parents' psychological functioning that existed for years prior to the divorce (Clarke-Stewart, Vandell, McCartney, Owen, & Booth, 2000; Emery & Forehand, 1994).

BRUCE AYRES / STONE / GETTY IMAGES

Divorced parents who are single often have to deal with increased levels of stress, which can affect the quality of their parenting.

Factors Affecting the Impact of Divorce

A variety of interacting factors seem to predict whether or not the painful experiences of divorce and remarriage will cause children significant or lasting problems. The question here is one of *individual differences:* Why do some children of divorce do better than others?

The level of parental conflict appears to be an important factor that influences a child's adjustment to divorce.

Parental conflict One influence on children's adjustment to divorce is the level of parental conflict prior to, during, and subsequent to a divorce. Indeed, levels of parental conflict may predict the outcomes for children more than divorce itself. Not only is parental conflict distressing for children to observe but it also may cause them to feel insecure about their own relationships with their parents (Davies & Cummings, 1994; Grych & Fincham, 1997). For example, children may fear that their parents will desert them or stop loving them. Conflict between parents often increases when the divorce is being negotiated and may continue for years after the divorce. Especially if it includes violence witnessed by children, it may not only be extremely upsetting for the children but may also increase the chances that they will use violence with partners when they themselves are older (Andrews, Foster, Capaldi, & Hops, 2000; Wallerstein & Blakeslee, 1989).

Parental conflict is more likely to have negative effects on children if they feel caught in the middle of it, as when they are forced to act as intermediaries between their parents or to inform one parent about the other's activities. Similar pressures may arise if children feel the need to hide from one parent information about, or their loyalty to, the other. Adolescents who feel that they are caught up in their divorced parents' conflict are at increased risk for being depressed or anxious and for engaging in problematic behavior such as drinking, stealing, cheating at school, cutting class, fighting, carrying a weapon, or using drugs (Buchanan, Maccoby, & Dornbusch, 1991).

Stress A second factor that affects children's adjustment to divorce is the stress experienced by the custodial parent and children in the new family arrangement. Not only must custodial parents juggle household, child-care, and financial responsibilities that usually are shared by two parents, but they often must do so isolated from those who might otherwise help. This isolation typically occurs when custodial parents have to change their residence and lose access to established social networks, or when friends and relatives—especially in-laws—take sides in the divorce and turn against them. In addition, custodial mothers usually experience a substantial drop in their income, and only a minority of mothers receive full child-support payments (U.S. Bureau of the Census, 1998a; U.S. Bureau of the Census, 1991b). All this may occur on top of the conflicts mentioned above. Not surprisingly, custodial parents, usually mothers, often are not only stressed but angry, hurt, or depressed as well.

As a result of all these factors, the parenting of newly divorced mothers often tends to be characterized by more irritability and coercion, and less warmth, consistency, and monitoring of children, than that of mothers in two-parent families (Hetherington, 1993; Hetherington et al., 1998; Simons & Johnson, 1996). This is unfortunate because children tend to be most adjusted during and after the divorce if their custodial parent is supportive and uses authoritative parenting (Hetherington, 1993; Simons & Associates, 1996; Steinberg, Mounts, Lamborn, & Dornbush, 1991). Making parenting even more difficult for the mother, noncustodial fathers often are permissive and indulgent with their children (Hetherington, 1989; Parke & Buriel, 1998), increasing the likelihood that children will resent and resist their mother's attempts to control their behavior.

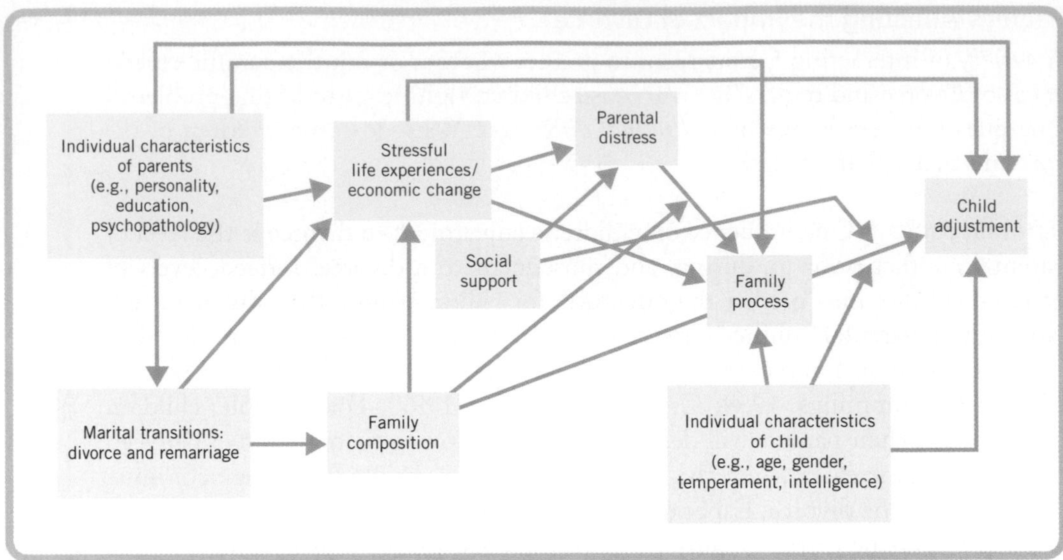

FIGURE 12.7 A model of the predictors of children's adjustment following divorce and remarriage Children's adjustment to parental divorce depends on many interrelated factors. These include characteristics of the parent and children, factors such as remarriage and economic changes, family composition (e.g., who is living in the home), degree of social support, parental distress in response to stressful events, and family processes that reflect these dynamics.

Thus, stressful life experiences during and after divorce often undermine the quality of parenting and of family interactions, which affects children's adjustment. These stressful life experiences can also have a direct effect on the child's adjustment (Figure 12.7). Having to move because of reduced household income, for example, may mean that at a time of high emotional vulnerability, a child also has to go through a wrenching transition to a new residence, neighborhood, school, and peer group.

Age of the child An additional factor that influences the impact of divorce is the child's age at the time of the divorce. Compared with older children and adolescents, younger children may have more trouble understanding the causes and consequences of divorce, may be more anxious about abandonment by their parents, and may be more likely to blame themselves for the divorce (Hetherington, 1989). As an 8-year-old boy explained, a year after his parents' divorce:

> My parents didn't get along. . . . They used to argue about me all the time when they were married. I guess I caused them a lot of trouble by not wanting to go to school and all. I didn't mean to make them argue. . . .
>
> (Wallerstein & Blakeslee, 1989, p. 73)

This boy firmly believed that he caused the divorce.

The following clinical report presents a picture of how divorce often affects young children:

> When we first saw seven-year-old Ned, he brought his family album to the office. He showed us picture after picture of himself with his father, his mother, and his little sister. Smiling brightly, he said, "It's going to be all right. It's really going to be all right." A year later, Ned was a sad child. His beloved father was hardly visiting and his previously attentive mother was angry and depressed. Ned was doing poorly in school, was fighting on the playground, and would not talk much to his mother.
>
> (Wallerstein & Blakeslee, 1989, p. xvi)

Although older children and adolescents are better able to understand a divorce than are younger children, they are nonetheless particularly at risk for problems with adjustment, including poor academic achievement and negative relationships with their parents. Adolescents who live in neighborhoods characterized by a high crime rate, poor schools, and an abundance of antisocial peers are at especially high risk (Hetherington et al., 1998), most likely because the opportunities to get into trouble are amplified when there is only one parent—who often must work—to monitor the child's activity. College students are less reactive to their parents' divorce, probably because of their maturity and relative independence from the family (Amato & Keith, 1991).

With regard to their parents' remarriage, young adolescents appear to be more negatively affected than younger children. One possible explanation for this is that young adolescents' struggles with the issues of autonomy and sexuality are heightened by the presence of a new parent who has authority to control them and is a sexual partner of their biological parent (Hetherington, 1993; Hetherington et al., 1992). An additional problem for young adolescent males whose parents remarry is that they tend to be monitored less by their parents than are their peers in intact families, which may partly explain the higher rate of delinquent behavior among these boys (Pagani, Tremblay, Vitaro, Kerr, & McDuff, 1998).

Contact with noncustodial fathers Contrary to popular wisdom, the frequency of children's contact with their noncustodial father is not, in itself, a significant factor in their adjustment after divorce (Amato & Keith, 1991). Sadly, this is probably good news, because some data indicate that less than 50% of noncustodial fathers have contact with their children more than once a year (Parke & Buriel, 1998). What does affect children's adjustment after divorce is the quality of the contact with the noncustodial father: children who have contact with competent, supportive, authoritative noncustodial fathers show better adjustment than children who have frequent but superficial or disruptive contact with their noncustodial fathers (Hetherington, 1989; Hetherington et al., 1998; Whiteside & Becker, 2000).

The contribution of parents' characteristics As noted earlier, it is important to recognize that the greater frequency of problem behaviors in children in divorced and remarried families may not be solely due to the divorce and remarriage. Rather, it sometimes may be related to characteristics of the parents that existed long before the divorce and that increase the likelihood of inept parenting. For example, the parents may have difficulty coping with stress or forming social relationships that promote well-being, as suggested by the fact that parents who divorce are more likely than undivorced parents to be neurotic, depressed, alcoholic, or antisocial, to hold dysfunctional beliefs about relationships, or to lack skills for regulating conflict and negative emotion (Emery, Waldron, Kitzmann, & Aaron, 1999; Jochlin, McGue, & Lykken, 1996; Kurdek, 1993). Any one of these characteristics would be likely to undermine the quality of their parenting. Of course, many factors contribute to whether or not people get divorced; dysfunctional behaviors and personality characteristics are just one factor that can contribute to problems among children of divorce.

The contribution of children's characteristics The greater frequency of problem behaviors in children of divorce may also be related to characteristics of the children themselves. Children whose parents divorce tend to be more poorly adjusted prior to the divorce than are children from nondivorced families (Amato & Keith,

1991; Block, Block, & Gjerde, 1986). This difference may be due to stress in the home, poor parenting, or parental conflict prior to divorce. Alternatively or additionally, it may be due to inherited characteristics such as a lack of self-regulation or a predisposition to negative emotion (O'Connor, Caspi, DeFries, & Plomin, 2000). Such characteristics would not only underlie children's adjustment problems but, when expressed in both children and their parents, would also increase the likelihood of divorce (Hetherington et al., 1998; Jochlin et al., 1996). Consistent with the idea of *the active child,* children with difficult personalities and limited coping capacities may also react more adversely to the negative events associated with divorce than do other children.

Positive outcomes of divorce Finally, it should be noted that parental divorce can have positive consequences for children, especially if their exposure to parental conflict decreases as a consequence. In fact, following their parents' divorce, some girls in mother-headed families become exceptionally resilient individuals who are able to deal well with adversity and problems, apparently due to their successfully confronting the changes and responsibilities that follow divorce (Hetherington, 1989; Hetherington et al., 1998).

Custody of Children After Divorce

In 1998, children living with one divorced parent were more than four times as likely to live with their mothers as with their fathers (U.S. Bureau of the Census, March 1998). However, parents sometimes have joint custody of their children. Custody can be joint in terms of legal decision making, actual residence of the child, or both. In joint legal custody, parents share the responsibility of making decisions regarding their children's lives. Joint physical custody involves children's alternately residing with each parent on a regular basis. According to one study, 21% of custodial parents (1.3 million) with formal child-support agreements had joint-custody arrangements, most of which (about 80%) involved joint legal custody only (Nord & Zill, 1997).

Children in joint legal or physical custody generally are better adjusted than are children in sole custody (Bauserman, 2002). However, the effects of joint custody on children likely depend in part on the degree of cooperation between ex-spouses. When parents cooperate with each other and keep the children's best interests in mind, children are unlikely to feel caught in the middle if their parents are in conflict (Maccoby, Buchanan, Mnookin, & Dornbusch, 1993). Unfortunately, mutually helpful parenting is not the norm. One study found that once parents had been separated for a year and a half or more, most engaged in conflict or did not deal much with each other (Maccoby et al., 1993).

An Alternative to Divorce: Ongoing Marital Conflict

On the basis of the publicity given to the negative effects that divorce can have on children, some people have argued that it would be better for families if it were more difficult for parents to obtain a divorce. When considering this argument, it is important to realize that sustained conflict between parents who are not separated has negative effects on children at all ages (Emery, 1982). Infants can be harmed by marital conflict because it may cause mothers to be less warm and supportive, which can undermine the security of the early parent–child attachment (Frosch, Mangelsdorf, & McHale, 2000). Young children are especially likely to feel threatened and helpless when there is ongoing parental conflict—even more so if the conflict involves high levels of verbal and physical aggression (Grych, 1998). Children and adolescents exposed to sustained marital conflict tend to be more aggressive and engage in more delinquent behavior than do their peers from less combative family environments. Sustained marital conflict also can make children hostile, depressed, and anxious, particularly if it leads—as it frequently does—to parental hostility toward them (Buehler et al., 1997; Harold & Conger, 1997).

Stepparenting

In 1996, roughly 6% of U.S. children lived in a household with a stepparent—in 80% of these cases, a stepfather (ChildStats.gov, 2001). Because many children who were not living with a stepparent in 1996 had done so in the past, or might do so in the future, it was estimated that the number of children who would experience living with a stepparent by the age of 18 would actually be considerably higher, perhaps 17% (Hetherington et al., 1998).

The entry of a stepparent into the family is often a very threatening event for children. As described by one long-term study, the world is suddenly full of anxious questions:

> What will this new man do for me? Will he threaten my position in the family? Will he interfere with my relationship with Mom and Dad? . . . Is he good for my mom? Will she be in a better mood? Will she treat me better? . . . Will my dad be angry? Will having a stepfather around make Dad want to visit me more or less? Will he fade out of the picture? Will Mom be nicer to Dad now? Will Mom and Dad ever get remarried now that someone else is in the picture?
>
> (Wallerstein & Blakeslee, 1989, p. 246)

The answers to specific questions like these obviously vary by the individual case. Neverthcless, investigators have found some general patterns in the adjustments that are required of both children and adults when a remarriage occurs.

Stepfathers

Stepfathers often find it difficult to assume the role of being a father to their stepchildren. Although most stepfathers want their new families to thrive, they generally feel less close to their stepchildren than do fathers in intact families (Hetherington, 1993). At first, they tend to be polite and ingratiating toward their stepchildren and are not as involved in monitoring or controlling them as are fathers in nondivorced families (Kurdek & Fine, 1993). Perhaps due to conflict with, and lack of acceptance by, their stepchildren, over time many stepfathers become emotionally distant and disengaged parents, even after five years or more (Hetherington, Henderson, & Reiss, 1999; Mekos, Hetherington, & Reiss, 1996).

Conflict between stepfathers and stepchildren tends to be greater than that between fathers and their biological offspring (Bray & Berger, 1993; Hetherington et al., 1992, 1999). To take the extreme case, violence by stepfathers toward their stepchildren is many times higher than violence perpetrated by biological fathers (Daly & Wilson, 1996). Stepchildren often contribute to conflict with their stepfathers by expressing defiance and hostility toward them. Because of the conflict and resulting stress that are common in stepfamilies, it is not surprising that children with stepfathers tend to have higher rates of depression, withdrawal, and disruptive problem behaviors than do children in intact families (Hetherington & Stanley Hagan, 1995).

complex stepfamilies families that contain stepsiblings or half siblings

The adjustment of an adolescent to a stepparent depends in part on the nature of the reconstituted family and the length of time the new family has existed. In simple stepfamilies, which contain only one parent's children, adolescents' adjustment is little different from that in intact families if the stepfather has been part of the family for many years. In contrast, adolescents exhibit more acting-out behaviors and lack of social responsibility in **complex stepfamilies,** which contain stepsiblings or half siblings (Hetherington et al., 1999).

Having an involved stepfather can bring some benefits. Remarriage can improve family finances substantially and provide a source of emotional support and assistance for the custodial parent. A new stepfather may be especially helpful both in controlling his stepson and in providing a male role model (Parke & Buriel, 1998). Stepfathers' contribution to the supervision of their stepsons is particularly important because custodial remarried mothers tend to become lax in monitoring their sons' behavior (Hetherington & Stanley-Hagen, 1995, 2002).

Stepmothers

Because there are decidedly fewer stepmothers than stepfathers, much less research has been devoted to them and much less is known about them. However, it appears that stepmothers generally have more difficulty with their stepchildren than do stepfathers. Often fathers expect stepmothers to take an active role in parenting, including monitoring and disciplining the child. However, children frequently resent the stepmother's taking the role of disciplinarian. Nonetheless, when it is possible for stepmothers to use authoritative parenting successfully, stepchildren may be better adjusted (Hetherington et al., 1998).

Factors Affecting Children's Adjustment in Stepfamilies

The adjustment of children living with a stepparent is influenced by a number of other factors, including the child's age at the time of the remarriage and the sex of the child. Very young children tend to accept stepparents more easily than do older children and adolescents, and the presence of a competent, supportive stepfather, in comparison with having no father, may decrease the likelihood of problems in young boys. Girls are more inclined than boys to have problems with their stepparents and to exhibit problems in adjustment and low achievement (Amato & Keith, 1991; Hetherington, 1989; Hetherington et al., 1998). Often the difficulty girls have with their stepfathers arises from the fact that prior to the remarriage, divorced mothers frequently have had a close, confiding relationship with their daughters, and the entry of the stepfather into the family disrupts this relationship. These changes can lead to resentment in the daughter and conflict with both her mother and the stepfather (Hetherington et al., 1992; Hetherington & Stanley-Hagen, 1995).

Children of both sexes are most adjusted in stepfamilies when their custodial parent is authoritative in his or her parenting style. Children are also likely to do better in stepfamilies if the stepparent is warm and involved and supports the custodial parent's decisions rather than trying to exert control over the children independently (Bray & Berger, 1993; Hetherington et al., 1998).

Finally, the ease or difficulty that a stepparent has integrating into the family is influenced not only by the stepparent's and stepchildren's behaviors but also by the attitudes and behavior of the custodial parent. For example, support from custodial fathers for stepmothers' parenting may be important in fostering effective parenting by stepmothers (Brand, Clingempeel, & Bowen-Woodward, 1988). The attitude of the noncustodial biological parent toward the stepparent is also likely to be important. If the noncustodial parent has hostile feelings toward the new stepparent and communicates these feelings to the child, the child is likely to feel caught in the middle, increasing his or her adjustment problems (Buchanan et al., 1991). The noncustodial parent's hostile feelings may also encourage the child to behave in a hostile or distant manner with the stepparent. Thus, the success or failure of stepfamilies is affected by the behavior and attitudes of all involved parties.

Lesbian and Gay Parents

Another way that U.S. families have changed in recent decades is that more lesbian and gay adults are parents. The numbers of lesbian and gay parents cannot be estimated with confidence because many conceal their sexual orientation. Estimates that have been offered range from 1 to 5 million for lesbian mothers and from 1 to 3 million for gay fathers (Gottman, 1990). It is estimated that there are no fewer than 6 million children of lesbian or gay parents (Patterson, 1995b).

Most children of lesbian or gay parents are born when their parents are involved in a heterosexual marriage or relationship. In many cases, the parents divorce when one parent comes out as lesbian or gay; in other cases, the parents decide not to divorce. In addition, an increasing number of single and coupled lesbians are choosing to give birth to children, often through the use of artificial insemination. Other lesbians choose to become foster or adoptive mothers. For gay men, becoming an adoptive or foster parent is often quite difficult due to legal barriers and prejudice in many states, although they have somewhat fewer problems in cases involving difficult-to-place children, such as those who are older, ill, or disabled. In some cases, gay men have opportunities to act as stepfathers to the biological children of their partners (Patterson & Chan, 1997).

The question that concerns many people is whether children raised by gay parents grow up to be different from other children. According to a growing body of research, children of gay parents are, in fact, very similar in their development to children of heterosexual parents in terms of adjustment, personality, and relationships with peers (Flaks, Ficher, Masterpasqua, & Joeseph, 1995; Golombak, Spencer, & Rutter, 1983; Patterson, 1997). They are also similar in the degree to which their behavior is gender-typed and in their sexual orientation (Bailey, Bobrow, Wolfe, & Mikach, 1995; Gottman, 1990; Patterson, Fulcher, & Wainright, in press). Perhaps surprisingly, children of lesbian parents do not appear to be teased more than other children (Tasker & Golombok, 1995). However, this may be partly because children of lesbians or gays often are not open with their friends about their parents' sexual orientation. In fact, children of gay men often try to hide their fathers' sexual preference from their friends, in part because they fear being labeled by peers as gay or lesbian themselves (Bozett, 1980, 1987; Crosbie-Burnett & Helmbrecht, 1993).

As in families with heterosexual parents, whether or not children of lesbian and gay parents do well seems to depend on family dynamics. Children of lesbian parents are better adjusted when their mother and her partner are getting along and are not highly stressed (Chan, Raboy, & Patterson, 1998), when they report sharing child-care duties evenly (Patterson, 1995a), and when they are satisfied with the division of labor in the home (Chan, Brooks, Raboy, & Patterson, 1998). In families with a gay father and his

Although more study is needed, research to date suggests that the development of children of lesbian and gay parents differs little, if at all, from that of children of heterosexual parents.

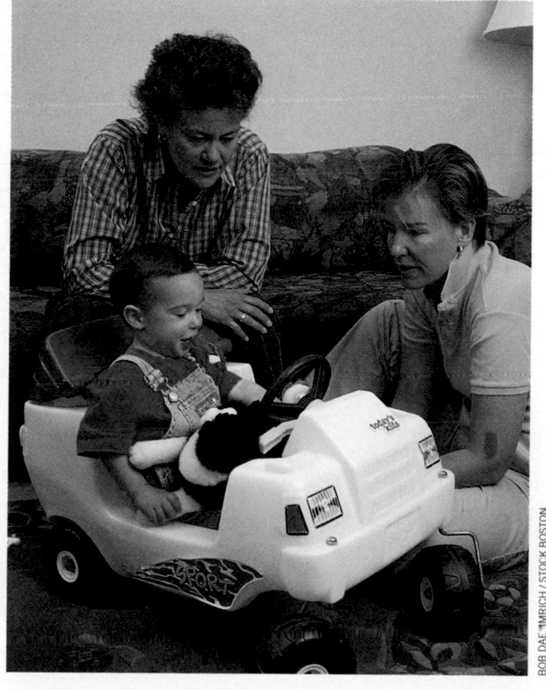

BOB DAEMMRICH / STOCK BOSTON

partner, sons' happiness with their family life is related to the inclusion of the partner in family activities and the son's having a good relationship with the partner as well as with his father (Crosbie-Burnett & Helmbrecht, 1993).

review:

The American family has changed dramatically in recent decades. Adults are marrying later and having children later; more children are born to single mothers; and divorce and remarriage are common occurrences.

Adolescent parents come disproportionately from impoverished backgrounds and are more likely than other teens to have behavioral and academic problems. Adolescent mothers tend to be less effective parents than older mothers, and their children are at risk for behavioral and academic problems and early sexual activity. In contrast, mothers who delay childbearing tend to be more responsive with their children than mothers who have their first children at a younger age.

Parental divorce and remarriage have been associated with enduring negative outcomes, such as behavioral problems, for only a minority of children. The major factor contributing to negative outcomes for children of divorce is dysfunctional family interactions in which parents deal with each other in hostile ways and children feel caught in the middle. Parental depression and upset, as well as economic pressures and other types of stress associated with single parenting, often compromise the quality of parents' interactions with each other and with their children.

Stepfamilies present special challenges. Conflict is common in stepfamilies, especially when the children are adolescents, and stepparents usually are less involved with their stepchildren than are biological parents. Children do best if all parents are supportive and use an authoritative parenting style.

An increasing number of children live in families in which at least one parent is openly lesbian or gay. There is no evidence that children raised by lesbian or gay parents are more likely to be lesbian or gay themselves or to differ from children of heterosexual parents in their adjustment.

Maternal Employment and Child Care

Paralleling many of the other changes that have occurred in the family over the past half century in the United States, the employment rate for mothers increased more than fourfold. In 1955, only 17% of mothers with children under the age of 18 were in the workforce; in 1998, 72% were. More striking to developmentalists, in 1955, only 18% of mothers with children under the age of 6 were employed outside the home; in 1998, 64% were, including 58% of mothers with children under the age of 1 (Bureau of Labor Statistics, 1999). (Currently, the majority of first-time mothers who are employed at the time of their pregnancy return to their jobs before their child is a year old, with most returning to work full time three months after the birth [Bureau of Labor Statistics, 1999; Coltrane, 1996]). These changes in the rates of maternal employment reflect a variety of factors, including greater acceptance of mothers' working outside the home, more opportunities in the workplace for women, and increased financial need, often brought about by single motherhood or divorce.

Not surprisingly, the dramatic rise in the number of mothers working outside the home raised a variety of concerns about the possible effects of maternal employment on children's development. Some experts on development and some social critics predicted that maternal employment would seriously diminish the quality of maternal caregiving and that the mother–child relationship would suffer accordingly. Others worried that latchkey children who were left to their own devices after school would get into serious trouble, academically and socially. Over the past two decades, much research has been devoted to addressing such concerns. For the most part, the findings have been reassuring.

The Effects of Maternal Employment

Taken as a whole, research has found little evidence that maternal employment per se has negative effects on children's development. There is little consistent evidence, for example, that the quality or even the quantity of mothers' interactions with their children necessarily diminishes as a result of their employment (Hoffman, 1989; Paulson, 1996). Some working mothers spend less time with their children than do nonworking mothers; other working mothers make a point of spending extra time with their children. What the evidence does suggest is that maternal employment may be associated with negative outcomes for children under certain circumstances and with positive outcomes under other circumstances. For example, if employed mothers are involved with their children, and if their children's activities are supervised after school, their children tend to do as well at school as children of mothers who are not employed outside the home (Beyer, 1995). However, if children are not adequately supervised and monitored after school, their academic performance may suffer (Muller, 1995).

Recent research indicates that there may be an important exception to this general pattern of findings. This research found that infants whose mothers were working by the time the infants were 9 months old tended to score lower on a school-readiness scale at 36 months. This pattern of findings was especially pronounced when mothers worked long hours (30 hours or more per week) and when mothers were not sensitive caregivers. The pattern was also more pronounced for children with married rather than single parents, and for boys. Although mothers who decided to work by the time the infant was 9 months of age may have differed in some unmeasured characteristics from those who did not, these findings suggest that long hours of maternal employment early in an infant's life may have some negative effects on early cognitive development (Brooks-Gunn, Han, & Waldfogel, 2002).

Contextual variation in the effects of maternal employment on children's development is also evident in studies of older children. In a large study of elementary school children, sons and daughters of employed mothers displayed higher academic competence than did children of full-time homemakers; for example, they had higher scores on math and reading tests (Hoffman & Youngblade, 1999). They also were somewhat more assertive and independent. In addition, girls of employed mothers exhibited higher social adjustment and competence. These positive outcomes seemed to be due, in part, to the fact that employed mothers—especially working-class employed mothers—used more optimal child-rearing practices: they were less permissive, coercive, or authoritarian, and more authoritative, in their style of parenting. One negative outcome was noted in the findings, however: boys who were from middle-class families in which both parents worked exhibited more problem behavior, such as aggression, than did middle-class boys with stay-at-home mothers—perhaps because they had less supervision.

There also appear to be costs and benefits of maternal employment for low-income families, depending on the circumstances. Adolescents in low income,

Some research suggests that African-American daughters of working mothers are less likely to quit school than are African-American daughters of mothers who are not employed.

single-parent, mother-headed families report feeling more positive emotions and higher self-esteem if their mothers are employed full time (Duckett & Richards, 1995). Perhaps this is because maternal employment is an important factor in pulling mother-headed, poor families out of poverty (Harvey, 1999; Lichter & Lansdale, 1995). Moreover, African-American daughters of working mothers are more likely to stay in school than are African-American daughters of unemployed working-class mothers (Wolfer & Moen, 1996). However, there is also some evidence that unmarried mothers with poor-paying jobs may become less supportive of their children and provide a less stimulating home environment after they start working than when they were at home full time (Menaghan & Parcel, 1995). This drop in supportiveness is no doubt linked to the fact that single mothers with low-paying jobs are particularly likely to be stressed, unhappy with their jobs, and unable to afford child care or other services to assist them with child rearing.

Maternal employment may have specific benefits for girls. Children of employed mothers are more likely than children of nonemployed mothers to reject aspects of traditional gender roles that are confining, and they are more likely to believe that women, like men, can be competent (Hoffman, 1984, 1989). Children of employed mothers are also more likely to be exposed to egalitarian parental roles in the family, and this experience seems to affect girls' feelings of effectiveness (Hoffman & Youngblade, 1999).

The effects that maternal employment—or the lack thereof—can have on children also depends in part on how the mother is affected by her employment status. In general, outcomes are likely to be better for both mothers and children if the mother's employment status is consistent with her desire to be either employed or a full-time homemaker (Beyer, 1995; Parke & Buriel, 1998). Mothers who want to work but do not, for example, sometimes are depressed (Gove & Zeiss, 1987), which can undermine the quality of their parenting. For mothers who want to work and do, employment can have a positive effect on their self-perceptions. In a study of working-class mothers, those who were employed were less depressed than those who were not, apparently because work increased their morale and sense of effectiveness (Hoffman & Youngblade, 1999). Mothers who feel effective and who have high morale are likely to be less punitive and more supportive in their parenting than are demoralized mothers (Bugental & Johnston, 2000).

Another factor that is key to how maternal employment affects children's development is the nature and quality of the day care children receive. But there, too, as you will see, the effects vary as a function of the context and the individuals involved.

The Effects of Child Care

Because so many mothers work outside the home, a large number of infants and young children receive care on a regular basis from someone besides their parents. In 1995 in the United States, 45% of infants under the age of 1 year and 78% of 4-year-olds were in child care on a regular basis. This child care takes a variety of

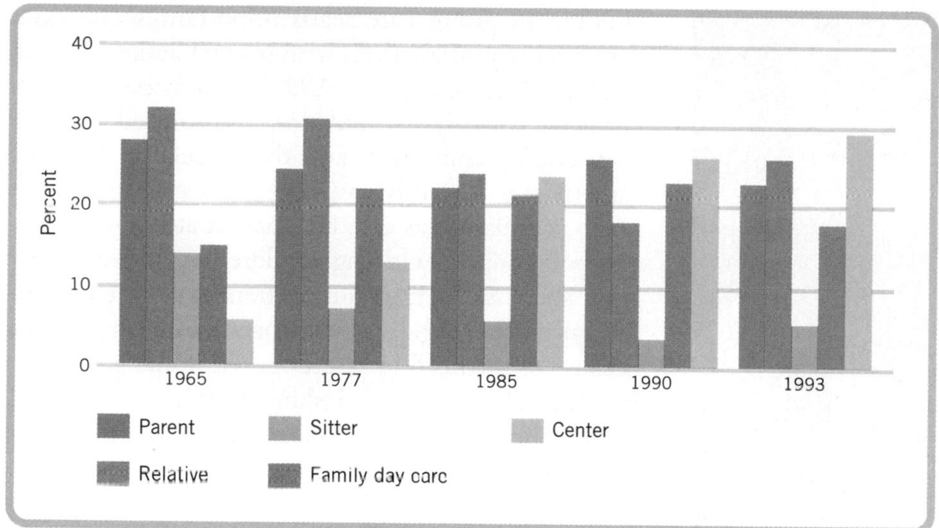

FIGURE 12.8 Primary care for youngest preschool child of employed mothers, 1965–1993 The use of center care for preschoolers increased dramatically from 1965 into the 1990s. (Adapted from Hofferth, 1996)

forms. In 1995, for example, 21% of the children under the age of 6 received child care from relatives; 18% were in the care of a nonrelative; and 31% were enrolled at a day-care center (National Center for Education Statistics, 1996) (Figure 12.8).

Child care provided by day-care centers has increased sharply since 1965, when only 6% of young preschoolers were cared for in day-care centers (Hofferth, 1996). Center care is especially common for children aged 3 to 6 who are not yet in kindergarten (see Figure 12.9).

Of all the concerns that have been raised over the possible effects that maternal employment might have on children's development, those related to nonparental child care have been the most hotly debated. Some experts have argued that, especially for children from deprived backgrounds, group care, with its wide variety of activities, can provide greater cognitive stimulation than care at home (Consortium for Longitudinal Studies, 1983). Some have also suggested that

FIGURE 12.9 Percentages of children in different types of child care In 1999, 54% of children from birth through third grade received some form of child care from persons other than their parents. This translates to close to 20 million children. The type of child care received is related to the age of the child. Children from birth through age 2 were more likely to be in home-based care, either with a relative or nonrelative, than to be in center-based care. Children ages 3 to 6 who are not yet in kindergarten are more likely to be in a center-based child-care arrangement, which includes nursery schools and other early childhood education programs. Kindergartners were more likely to be in home-based care. Among children attending first through third grade, children were more likely to be in home-based care with a relative than in a center or at home with a nonrelative. (Adapted from ChildStats.gov, 2001)

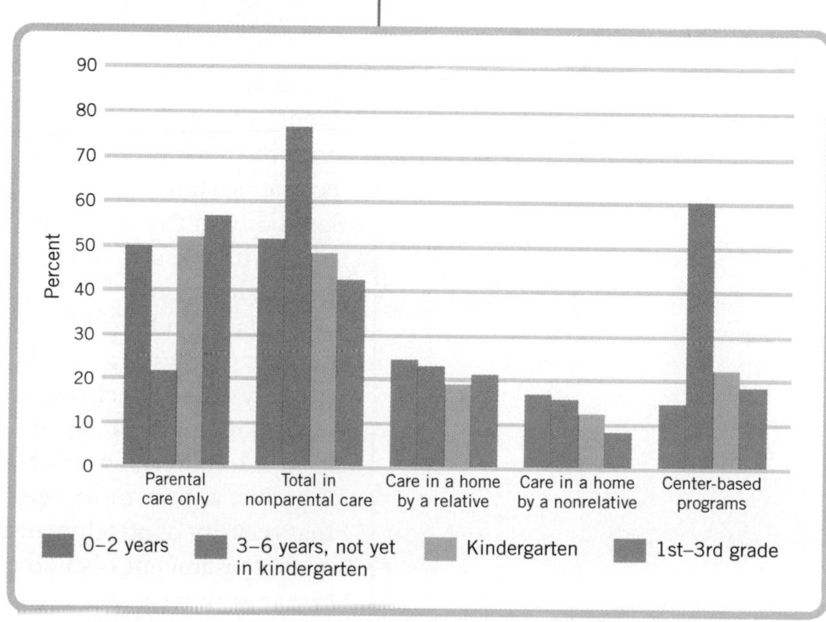

LAURA DWIGHT

A little more than three-fourths of 4-year-olds in this country are regularly in child care.

children in group care learn important social skills through their interactions with peers (Clarke-Stewart, 1981; Volling & Feagans, 1995). Critics counter that enriched cognitive stimulation is provided only by high-quality child care, and that much of the child care that is currently available does not provide as much stimulation as care by a parent at home. Critics also point out that although children in child care may learn social skills from interactions with their peers, they also learn negative behaviors, such as aggression, because of the need to assert oneself in the group setting (Bates et al., 1994; Haskins, 1985).

Probably the greatest concern about child care has been that it might undermine the early mother–child relationship (e.g., Belsky, 1986). For example, based on attachment theory (see Chapter 11), it has been argued that young children who are separated from their mothers on a frequent basis are more likely to develop insecure attachments to their mothers than are children whose daily care is provided by their mothers.

Attachment and the Parent–Child Relationship

The issue of whether nonparental child care in the early years interferes with children's attachments to their parents, especially the primary caregiving parent, has been examined in many studies. Some of the early research indicated that young children in child care might be prone to insecure attachment (Belsky, 1986). However, a variety of subsequent studies involving infants and preschoolers show no evidence overall that children in child care are less securely attached than other children or display less positive behavior in interactions with their mothers (Erel, Oberman, & Yirmiya, 2000). Other research indicates that in a very small minority of cases, extensive child care is associated with negative effects on attachment, but that these cases tend to involve other risk factors, such as frequent turnover in outside caregivers and poor-quality care at home (Lamb, 1998).

Similar findings are emerging from a major in-depth study funded by the National Institute of Child Health and Development (NICHD) that is following the development of approximately 1,300 children in various child-care arrangements and in elementary school. This study, begun in 1991, includes families who are from ten locations around the United States and who vary considerably in their economic status, ethnicity, and race. The study measures (1) characteristics of the families and the child-care setting and (2) children's attachment to, and interactions with, their mothers, as well as their social behavior, cognitive development, and health status.

To date, findings for infancy and early childhood are available. The most important of these is that how children in nonmaternal care fare is much more strongly related to characteristics of the family—such as level of income, maternal education, maternal sensitivity, and the like—than to the nature of the child care itself. Moreover, any effects that child care might have on development, positive or negative, appear to be very limited in magnitude. For example, the study found that security of attachment in the first 15 months of life was not predicted by the quality or amount of child care, the age at which child care began, the provider of care (e.g., a relative, a nonrelative in the child's or caregiver's home, or at a child-care center), or caregiver turnover. Indeed, insecure attachments of a notable degree were predicted only when two conditions existed simultaneously—that is,

(1) when the children experienced poor-quality child care, or had 10 or more hours of child care per week, or had more than one child-care arrangement; and (2) when the mothers were not very sensitive or responsive to their children (NICHD Early Child Care Research Network, 1997c). When children were 24 and 36 months old, the quality of mother–child interaction was, to a slight degree, predicted by the number of hours in child care. Mothers of children who were in day care for longer hours, compared with mothers who did not use child care or put their child in care for fewer hours, tended to be less sensitive with their children, and their children tended to be less positive in interactions with them (NICHD Early Child Care Research Network, 1999). Even in these circumstances, the magnitudes of the effects were small.

ELLEN E. SENISI

The education and stability of day care staff are important factors affecting children's development.

Self-Regulation and Social Behavior

The possible effects of child care on children's self-control, compliance, and social behavior have also been a focus of much concern and research. Here, the findings are mixed. A number of investigators have found that children who are in child care do not differ in problem behavior from those reared at home (Erel et al., 2000; Lamb, 1998). However, findings from the NICHD study suggest that, depending on their age, children who are in child care for many hours a day or who experience a number of changes in caregivers may tend to have more problem behaviors. Specifically, more time in child care or more changes in caregivers in the first two years of life predicted lower social competence and more problem behavior or noncompliance with adults at age 2 but not at age 3 (NICHD Early Child Care Research Network, 1998a). However, by 4½ years of age, children in extensive child care had more externalizing problems, such as aggression and noncompliance, particularly if they were attending a child-care center. Of the children in this study who were in day care more than 30 hours a week, 17% showed aggressive behaviors between the ages of 4½ and 6, whereas only 6% of those who spent less than 10 hours a week in day care showed such behavior (Douglas, 2001). The amount of child care over time was likewise associated with levels of internalizing problems, such as anxiety and social withdrawal. This pattern of findings was still evident in kindergarten (NICHD Early Child Care Research Network, 2001b, 2001c).

Thus, although many children in child care never develop significant behavior problems, the risk of their exhibiting problem behaviors increases the longer they are in child care, especially center care. However, it must be remembered that the family circumstances of those children who are in day care for long hours likely differ in a variety of ways (e.g., income and parental education, parental personality) from the circumstances of those in day care for fewer hours, so cause-and-effect relations cannot be assumed (Bolger & Scarr, 1995; NICHD Early Child Care Research Network, 1997d). Moreover, although children in day care may learn negative behaviors, they also tend to learn positive social skills, especially if their caregivers are sensitive and responsive with them (NICHD Early Child Care Research Network, 2001a).

Cognitive and Language Development

The possible effects of child care on children's cognitive and language performance are of particular concern to educators as well as to parents. For the most part, findings in this area are not highly consistent across studies and may vary as a function

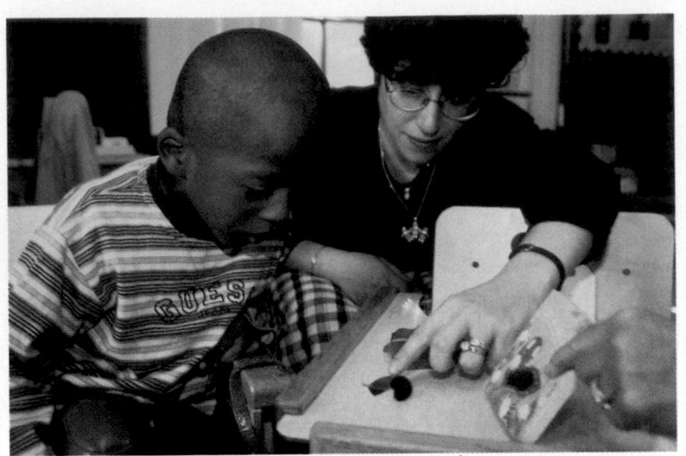

GREENBERG / FOLIO, INC.

For low-income students, some positive academic outcomes that are associated with high-quality preschool child care have been found to persist into elementary grades.

of the age of the children studied and the quality of care provided to them. The NICHD study found that, overall, the number of hours in child care did not correlate with cognitive or language development when demographic variables such as family income were taken into account. However, higher-quality child care that included specific efforts to stimulate children's language development was linked to better cognitive and language development in the first three years of life (NICHD Early Child Care Research Network, 2000b). By age 4½, children in higher-quality child care (especially center care) scored higher on tests of pre-academic skills and language than did those in lower-quality care (NICHD Early Child Care Research Network, 2001b).

Other research suggests that child care may have positive effects on cognition beyond infancy. For example, in Sweden and the United States, a number of researchers have found that children enrolled in out-of-home child care perform better on cognitive tasks, even in elementary school (Erel et al., 2000; Lamb, 1998). High-quality child care that involves preschool programs designed to promote children's later success at school may be especially beneficial for disadvantaged children. As in the case of Head Start, discussed in Chapter 8, children who experience such programs show improvements in their social competence and declines in conduct problems (Lamb, 1998; Reynolds, Mavrogenes, Bezruczko, & Hagemann, 1996; Webster-Stratton, 1998).

Quality of Child Care

It is not surprising that the quality of child care children receive is related to some aspects of their development. Unfortunately, most child-care centers in the United States do not meet the recommended minimal standards established by such organizations as the American Academy of Pediatrics and the American Public Health Association. These minimum standards include:

1. A child-to-caregiver ratio of 3:1 for children aged 6 to 15 months, 4:1 for 2-year-olds, and 7:1 for 3-year-olds
2. Maximum group sizes of six for children aged 6 to 15 months old, eight for 2-year-olds, and fourteen for 3-year-olds
3. Formal training for caregivers (including certification or a college degree) in child development, early childhood education, or a related field

In the NICHD study, children in a form of day care that met more of these guidelines tended to score higher on language comprehension and readiness for school, and had fewer behavior problems at age 36 months. The more standards that were met, the better the children performed at 3 years of age (NICHD Early Child Care Research Network, 1998b). (See Table 12.2 for standards set by an education association for quality child care.)

However, some research studies in several other countries as well as in the United States have found the quality of child care to have little effect on the development of children from typical families (Scarr, 1998). Studies may differ in their findings because they do not equally assess a wide range of quality in child-care programs, because they differ in the types of families included in the research, or because they differ in the degree to which more concerned parents choose higher-quality centers.

TABLE 12.2

Characteristics of Good Child-Care Programs

Experts in early education suggest that parents visit child-care programs before selecting one for their children. Here are some of the indicators of high-quality child care, set by the National Association for the Education of Young Children (1986).

Characteristics of the Staff

1. The adults caring for children enjoy observing and understand how young children learn and grow. They are considerate to children, and their expectations vary according to children's ages and interests. Staff also continue to learn about young children through conferences and other forms of education.
2. The staff continually foster children's emotional and social development. They listen and talk to the children; are consistent and gentle, yet firm, in discipline; help children learn to consider others' feelings and rights; and assist them in learning how to deal with negative emotions constructively.
3. There are enough adults available to work with groups of children and to meet their individual needs. For infants, there should be no more than eight children in the care of at least two adults. Two- and 3-year-olds should be in groups of no more than 16, with two adults. Four- and 5-year-olds should be in groups of no more than 20 children, with at least two adults.
4. All staff members work together cooperatively. They meet regularly to plan and evaluate the program, and they will adjust daily activities to accommodate children's individual needs and interests.
5. The staff observe and keep records of each child's progress and development. They stress children's accomplishments, use their records to educate parents, and are responsive to parents' concerns about their child's progress.

Program Activities and Equipment

1. The environment fosters children's working and playing together. Staff provide opportunities for both vigorous outdoor play and quiet indoor play, for children to select their own activities, and for children to work alone as well as in small groups. Children also are encouraged to develop self-help skills when they are ready.
2. A quality program provides opportunities for a wide range of activities and sufficient equipment and play materials, which are readily available to children. There is a range of materials, such as climbing equipment, blocks, balls, dramatic play props, materials for art projects (e.g., sand, clay, wood, paint), puzzles, small manipulatable toys, books, and plants or animals and other natural science objects for children to care for or to observe. In addition, there are opportunities for activities involving music and movement, such as dance.
3. Children are assisted in increasing their language skills and their understanding of the world. Children talk freely among themselves and with adults, and staff talk with children about objects, feelings, experiences, and events. Children are encouraged to solve their own problems and to think independently. Trips and visitors enhance children's learning experiences.
4. The health of the children, staff, and parents is promoted and protected. The staff are alert to health issues—for example, with regard to food, room temperature, and cleanliness—and medical records and emergency information are kept for each child.
5. The facility is safe for children and staff; for example, the facility is free of hazards, toxic materials are locked away, and indoor and outdoor surfaces are cushioned with materials such as carpeting or wood chips.
6. The environment is large enough to allow a variety of activities and equipment. There should be at least 35 square feet of usable playroom floor space indoors per child and 75 square feet of play space outdoors for each child. There is also space for adults to walk between sleeping children's cots and for children's personal items.

Staff Relations with the Community

1. A good program considers and supports the needs of entire families. Parents are welcome to observe the children, discuss policies, and participate in center activities. Staff members share highlights of a child's experiences with parents and are alert to family matters that might affect a child. The staff also respect family members from diverse cultures and backgrounds.
2. Staff are aware of and contribute to community resources. For example, they refer family members to appropriate services when needed, share information on community recreational and educational opportunities, and collaborate with other professional groups to provide high-quality child care.

Good centers encourage parents who are interested in their programs to observe and ask questions about the facilities, staff, and program philosophy and activities. If staff are not open about these matters, it is likely that the facility does not provide optimal care. (Note that the standards discussed on page 488 are even more stringent than the standards of this professional association.)

review:

The bulk of recent research on maternal employment indicates that it often benefits children and mothers and that it has few negative effects on children if they are in child care of acceptable quality and are supervised and monitored. Unfortunately, however, in low-income families, especially those headed by a single parent, adequate child care and supervision may not always be possible.

Because so many mothers work, a large proportion of children receive some care from adults other than their parents. Recent research on child care indicates that, on the whole, children's receiving nonmaternal care has small, if any, effect on the quality of the mother–child relationship or on children's social behavior and cognitive and language development. It also indicates that child-care experiences need not have harmful effects on any part of children's development, although they can have negative effects under certain circumstances. Whether child care has positive or negative effects on children's functioning probably depends on the characteristics of the child, the child's relationship with his or her mother, and the care situation.

Chapter Summary

The Nature and Functions of the Family

- Families serve at least three goals with respect to child rearing: helping offspring survive, teaching them the skills they will need to be economically productive as adults, and teaching them the values of the culture.
- How well a family fulfills its functions depends on its family dynamics: all the family members influence one another and the nature of their interactions shapes childrens development.
- Parents socialize their children's development through direct instruction, through their modeling of skills, attitudes, and behavior, and through their managing of children's experiences and social lives.
- Researchers have identified several types of parenting style related to the dimensions of warmth and control. Authoritative parents are supportive and relatively high in control; their children tend to be socially and academically competent. Authoritarian parents are low in warmth and high in control; their children tend to be relatively low in social and academic competence, unhappy, and low in self-confidence. Permissive parents are responsive to their children's needs and wishes and low on control; their children tend to be low in self-control and in school achievement. Rejecting-neglecting parents are low in demandingness, support, and control; their children tend to have disturbed attachment relationships during infancy, poor peer relations during childhood, and poor adjustment in adolescence.
- The significance and effects of different parenting styles or practices may vary somewhat across cultures.
- Parenting style and practices are affected by characteristics of the children, including their attractiveness, behavior, and temperament.
- Parents' beliefs and values tend to differ across social class, such that lower socioeconomic status tends to be associated with authoritarian parenting (except perhaps in low-SES African-American families).
- Economic stressors can undermine the quality of marital and parent–child interactions, increasing children's risk for depression, academic failure, disruptive behavior, and drugs use.
- Parental maltreatment of children is usually related to a combination of factors, beginning with parental characteristics like poor impulse control, low self-esteem, and high levels of negative emotion and including additional contributors like high stress levels, unemployment, inadequate housing, drug abuse, and community violence. Children who have difficult temperaments, are in poor health, or exhibit abnormal behavior are more likely to be abused. Maltreated children tend to have problems in regulation, adjustment, and academic performance.
- Homeless children are more likely than other children to show delays in cognitive and language development, to have academic difficulties, and to show problems in adjustment.

Mothers, Fathers, and Siblings

- Mothers typically interact with their children much more than fathers do, and fathers' play tends to be more physical than is mothers'. However, the nature of parent-child interactions differs across cultures.
- Siblings learn from one another, can be sources of support for children, and sometimes engage in conflict. Siblings get along better with one another if they have good relationships with their parents and if they do not feel that they are treated worse than their siblings by their parents.

Changes in Families in the United States

- In the United States today, adults are marrying later, more children are being born to single mothers, and divorce and remarriage are common occurrences.
- Mothers who delay childbearing tend to be more responsive with their children and to enjoy motherhood more than mothers who have their first children at a younger age.
- Adolescent parents come disproportionately from impoverished backgrounds and families with cold, uninvolved parents. Adolescent mothers tend to be less effective parents than older parents, and their children are at risk for behavioral and academic problems, delinquency, and early sexual activity. Children of adolescent mothers fare better if their mothers have more knowledge about parenting and if the children themselves have a warm, involved relationship with their fathers.
- Parental divorce and remarriage have been associated with enduring negative outcomes such as behavioral problems for a minority of children. The major factor contributing to negative outcomes for children of divorce is hostile, dysfunctional family interactions, including continuing conflict between ex-spouses.
- Parental depression and upset, as well as other types of stress associated with single parenting, often compromise the quality of parents' interactions with their children.
- Conflict is common in stepfamilies. Children often are hostile toward stepparents, and stepparents usually are less involved with their stepchildren than are biological parents. Children do best if all parents are supportive and use an authoritative parenting style.

- There is no evidence that children raised by lesbian or gay parents differ from children of heterosexual parents in their sexual orientation or adjustment.

Maternal Employment and Child Care

- Children and mothers reap some benefits from maternal employment, and maternal employment has few negative effects on children if they are in child care of acceptable quality and are supervised and monitored by parents.
- Experience with nonmaternal care has small, if any, effects on the quality of the mother–child relationship. Child care is associated with a small increase in negative problem behavior. It is not consistently related to cognitive and language development, although young infants in child care for long hours before the age of 9 months may score lower on a school-readiness scale at age 36 months. Children in high-quality care do better in their cognitive and language development than children in low-quality care. Whether child care has positive or negative effects on children's functioning probably depends in part on the characteristics of the child, the child's relationship with his or her mother, and the quality of the child-care situation.

Critical Thinking Questions

1. It often is assumed that parental socialization of children's behavior is a bidirectional process with the parent affecting the child's behavior and the child's behavior also evoking some socialization practices or behaviors. Provide examples of bidirectional causality in regard to (a) the relation between parental punitive practices and children's aggression, and (b) the relation between parental use of punitive control and children's self-regulation.
2. In some cultures, respect of authorities, including parents, and the authority of parents in general are valued more than in many Western industrialized countries. How might this cultural variation affect interactions between parents and children and the relation of parenting styles to children's social and emotional development? Similarly, how might living in a culture in which men and women often are separated (e.g., do not eat together) and women are discouraged from going out in public effect parent–child relationships and interactions?
3. Think about the ways your parents interacted with you when you were a child. Based on Baumrind's categories of parenting style, which type of parenting did your mother and/or father display? What specific behaviors did you use to classify their parenting?
4. Make a list of the advantages and disadvantages of joint custody for children of divorce. How would the advantages and disadvantages vary for families in which the parents (a) argue a lot versus do not argue a lot, and (b) live 50 miles apart versus 5 miles apart after the divorce?
5. What factors might make it difficult to study children's development in families with gay parents?

Key Terms

survival of offspring, p. 454
economic function, p. 454
cultural training, p. 454
family dynamics, p. 454
socialization, p. 456
parenting styles, p. 457
authoritative parenting, p. 458
authoritarian parenting, p. 458
permissive parenting, p. 458
rejecting-neglecting (disengaged) parenting, p. 459
bidirectionality of parent–child interactions, p. 461
child maltreatment, p. 462
complex stepfamilies, p. 480

CHAPTER 13

Peer Relationships

ANTONIO BERNI, *La Gallina Ciega*

THEMES

- Nature and Nurture
- The Active Child
- Continuity/Discontinuity
- Mechanisms of Change
- The Sociocultural Context
- Individual Differences
- Research and Children's Welfare

In Chapters 1 and 11, we described the plight of institutionalized orphans who, lacking consistent interaction with a caring adult, developed social, emotional, and cognitive deficits. After World War II, an interesting exception to this pattern was noted by Anna Freud—the daughter of Sigmund Freud—and Sophie Dann (1972/1951). They observed six young German-Jewish children who had been victims of the Hitler regime. Soon after these children were born, their parents were deported to Poland and killed. The children were subsequently moved from one refuge to another until, between the ages of approximately 6 and 12 months, they were placed in a ward for motherless children in a concentration camp. The care they received in this ward was undoubtedly compromised by the fact that their caregivers were themselves prisoners who were undernourished and overworked. Moreover, the rates of deportation and death among the prisoners were high, so it is likely that the children's caregivers changed very frequently.

In 1945, approximately two to three years after the children's arrival at the concentration camp, the camp was liberated, and within a month, the six children were sent to Britain. After spending two months in a reception facility, the children, as a group, were sent to various shelters, and then, finally, to a country house that had been converted to accommodate orphans.

Given the conditions of their early lives, it is not surprising that these children initially showed a variety of problem behaviors in their new home:

> During the first days after arrival they destroyed all the toys and damaged much of the furniture. Toward the staff they behaved either with cold indifference or with active hostility, making no exception for the young assistant Maureen who had accompanied them from Windermere and was their only link with the immediate past. At times they ignored the adults so completely that they would not look up when one of them entered the room. . . . In anger, they would hit the adults, bite or spit . . . shout, scream, and use bad language.
>
> (Freud & Dann, 1972, p. 452)

These children behaved quite differently with each other, however. They obviously were deeply attached to one another, sensitive to each others' feelings, and exhibited almost a complete lack of envy, jealousy, and rivalry. They shared possessions and food, helped and protected one another, and admired one another's abil-

BETTMANN / CORBIS

Anna Freud's study of children who lived together in a concentration camp provided evidence of the importance of early peer relationships.

ities and accomplishments. The children's closeness is reflected in this brief selection from Freud and Dann's daily observations:

> November 1945—John cries when there is no cake left for a second helping for him. Ruth and Miriam offer him what is left of their portions. While John eats their pieces of cake, they pet him and comment contentedly on what they have given him. . . .
>
> December 1945—Paul loses his gloves during a walk. John gives him his own gloves, and never complains that his hands are cold. . . .
>
> April 1946—On the beach in Brighton, Ruth throws pebbles into the water. Peter is afraid of the waves and does not dare to approach them. In spite of his fear, he suddenly rushes to Ruth, calls out: "Water coming, water coming," and drags her back to safety. . . .

Freud and Dann concluded that the children, although aggressive and difficult for adults to handle, were "neither deficient, delinquent nor psychotic" (p. 473) and that their relationships with one another helped them to master their anxiety and develop the capacity for social relationships.

This naturally occurring experiment provided early evidence that relationships with peers can help very young children develop some of the social and emotional capacities that usually emerge in the context of adult–child attachments. Two decades later, similar findings were obtained in research with monkeys. As was discussed in Chapter 10, Stephen Suomi and Harry Harlow raised laboratory monkeys in isolation from other monkeys from birth to 6 months of age. By the end of this period, the isolate monkeys had developed significant abnormalities in behavior such as compulsive rocking and reluctance to explore. Some of the isolate monkeys were subsequently placed with one or two normal, playful monkeys who were three months younger. Over the course of the next several months, the isolate monkeys' abnormal behaviors diminished greatly, and they began to explore their environment and engage in social interactions, demonstrating that peers can provide some of the social and emotional experiences required for normal development in monkeys (Suomi & Harlow, 1972).

Findings such as these do not suggest that peers alone can produce optimal development in young children. However, they do suggest that peers can contribute to children's development in meaningful ways. In fact, in Western societies, children's relationships with other children—their friends and acquaintances at school and in the neighborhood—usually play a very important role in their lives. By middle childhood in the United States, for example, more than 30% of children's social interactions involve peers (Rubin, Bukowski, & Parker, 1998). As they grow older, children spend increasingly more time with peers and interact with a greater number of them. Thus, peer interactions are a context in which children develop social skills and test new behaviors—both good and bad.

In this chapter, we consider the special nature of peer interactions and their implications for children's social development. First, we discuss theoretical views on what makes peer interactions special. Then we look at friendships, the most intimate form of peer relationships, and consider questions such as: How do children's interactions with friends differ from those with other peers (nonfriends)? How do friendships change with age? What do children get out of friendships and how do they think about them?

Next, we consider children's interactions with children in the larger peer group. These relationships are discussed separately from friendships because they appear to play a somewhat different role in children's development, particularly in regard to the provision of intimacy. We try to answer questions such as, What are the differences between children who are liked, disliked, or not noticed by their peers? Does children's acceptance or rejection by peers have long-term implications for their behavior and psychological adjustment?

In our discussions of both friendships and more general peer relationships, we will examine *individual differences* among children in their relationships with peers and the ways in which these differences may cause differences in development. In addition, we will focus on the influence that the *sociocultural context* has on peer relationships, the contributions that both *nature and nurture* make to the quality of children's peer relationships, the role of the *active child* in choosing friends and activities with peers, and the question of whether changes in children's thinking about friendships exhibits *continuity or discontinuity.* Finally, interventions to improve children's interactions with other children are examined as an example of *research and children's welfare.*

What Is Special About Peer Relationships?

Many theorists have argued that peer relationships provide special opportunities for children's development. To begin with, **peers** are, by definition, individuals who are close in age to one another, closer usually than siblings. Thus, in contrast with their status in most of their other relationships, especially those with adults, children are relatively equal in terms of power when they interact with their peers (Furman & Buhrmester, 1985).

Piaget (1932/1965) suggested that because of this relative equality, children tend to be more open and spontaneous with peers when expressing their ideas and beliefs than they are with adults. As Piaget noted, children often accept adults' beliefs and rules on the basis of mere obedience rather than on the basis of understanding or agreement (Youniss, 1980). With peers, on the other hand, children are more likely to openly criticize another's ideas, clarify and elaborate their own ideas, and ask for feedback (Kruger & Tomasello, 1986). In this way, peers jointly construct their own rules, ideas, and explanations for why or how things work or should work.

Similarly, Vygotsky (1978) suggested that children learn new skills and develop their cognitive capacities in peer interactions. However, unlike Piaget, Vygotsky highlighted the role of cooperation between peers. In particular, he emphasized the ways in which children's working together helps to build new skills and abilities, as well as to convey the knowledge and skills valued by the culture.

Both disagreement and cooperation within the context of peer relationships have been emphasized by theorists as important contributors to children's cognitive development.

SUSIE FITZHUGH

Other researchers have emphasized the social and emotional gains provided by peer interaction. In the preschool and school years, peers are an important source of companionship and assistance with problems and tasks (Youniss, 1980). As children become older, peers may become more important as a source of emotional support. Harry Stack Sullivan (1953) believed that friendships are essential for older children's sense of well-being. He noted that in early adolescence, children begin to develop close, intimate relationships with same-sex peers—what he called "chumships." According to Sullivan, chumships provide children with their first experience of an intimate interpersonal relationship based on reciprocity and exchange between equals. In this relationship, young adolescents become concerned about what they can do to make their chums feel good about themselves and happy. Sullivan suggested that children who are not liked by peers develop feelings of inferiority and loneliness, as well as concerns about their own abilities. As we will discuss later, there is some support for Sullivan's view, although the contribution of friends to children's development is somewhat more complicated than Sullivan's depiction suggests.

In summary, theorists such as Piaget, Vygotsky, and Sullivan have argued that peer relationships provide a unique context for cognitive, social, and emotional development. In their view, the equality, reciprocity, cooperation, and intimacy that can develop in peer relationships enhance children's reasoning ability and their concern for others. The equality and closeness between peers discussed by theorists is most often found in children's friendships. We will therefore examine children's friendships first, focusing particularly on what friendships are like, how they change with age, and what possible benefits and costs they carry with them.

peers people of approximately the same age and status

friendships intimate, reciprocated positive relationships between two people

Friendships

> "Kay and Sarah are my *best* friends—we talk and share secret things . . . and we sometimes do things with Jo and Kerry and Sue. Then there's all the rest of the girls—some are nice. But the boys—yuk!"
>
> (Annie, aged 8, cited by Dunn, personal communication, 1999)

Annie, the speaker above, a typical 8-year-old, filled in the chart in Figure 13.1 to describe her relationships with the children in her class. She is very good friends with the girls in the inner circle, Kay and Sarah. They play together, share toys, problems, and secrets, and also quarrel. The three girls in the next circle are part of a larger friendship group that includes Annie and her closest friends. Then there are the other children in the class, represented in the outer two circles. As her comments clearly indicate, Annie is closer to the girls than to the boys in this group and undoubtedly plays and talks with the girls more than with the boys. Although Annie does not have close relationships with these girls, she cares about what they think of her, and she and her close friends are interested in, and likely to gossip about, what goes on in the larger group.

The children in Annie's inner circle no doubt share characteristics that are common among most close friends. Researchers generally agree that friends are people who like to spend time together and feel affection for one another. In addition, their interactions are characterized by *reciprocities;* that is, friends have mutual regard for one another, exhibit give-and-take in their behavior (such as cooperation and negotiation), and benefit in comparable ways from their social exchanges (Bukowski, Newcomb, & Hartup, 1996). In brief, a **friendship** is an intimate, reciprocated positive relationship between two people.

The degree to which the conditions of friendship become evident in peer interactions increases with age during

FIGURE 13.1 A graphic representation of Annie's peer social world Annie's close friends are all girls, and nearly all of the children she socializes with are girls. Most girls in the United States show similar relationship patterns at Annie's age.

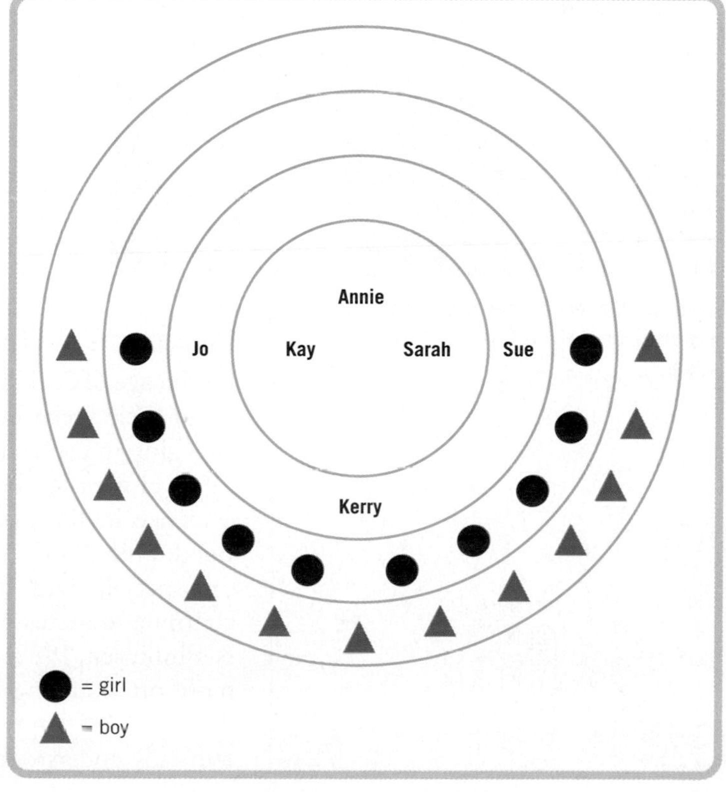

childhood. As you will see, it is not clear if, by the definition just given, very young children have relationships that qualify as friendships. By the preschool years, however, children often proclaim who their friends are, and the truth of their sentiment is obvious from their interactions with them. We will start our discussion of friendship by examining the nature of relationships between young children and then consider the nature of friendship in the school years.

Early Peer Interactions and Friendships

Very young children usually cannot verbally indicate who they like, so researchers must make inferences about children's friendships from observing their behavior with peers. In doing so, researchers have focused particularly on such issues as the age at which friendships first develop, the nature of early friendships, and age-related changes in friendships.

Do Very Young Children Have Friends?

Some investigators have argued that children can have friends by or before the age of 2 (Howes, 1996). Consider the following example:

> Anna and Suzanne are not yet 2 years old. Their mothers became acquainted during their pregnancies and from their earliest weeks of life the little girls have visited each other's houses. When the girls were 5 months old they were enrolled in the same child-care center. They now are frequent play partners, and sometimes insist that their naptime cots be placed side by side. Their greetings and play are often marked by shared smiles. Anna and Suzanne's parents and teachers identify them as friends.
>
> (Howes, 1996, p. 66)

ELIZABETH CREWS

Some researchers believe that friendships may begin as early as 2 years of age or before.

Even 12- to 18-month-olds seem to select and prefer some children over others, touching them, smiling at them, and engaging in positive interactions with them more than they do with other peers (Howes, 1983). In addition, when a preferred peer shows distress, toddlers are three times more likely to respond by offering comfort or by alerting an adult than they are when a nonpreferred peer is upset (Howes & Farver, 1987). Starting at around 20 months of age, children also increasingly initiate more interactions with some children than with others and contribute more in games with them (Ross & Lollis, 1989).

Differences in Children's Interactions with Friends and Nonfriends

By the age of 2, children begin to develop several skills that allow greater complexity in their social interactions, including imitating other people's social behavior, engaging in cooperative problem solving, and reversing roles during play (Howes, 1996; Howes & Matheson, 1992). These more complex skills tend to be in greater evidence in the play of friends than of nonfriends (acquaintances) (Werebe & Baudonniere, 1991).

Especially with friends, cooperation and coordination in children's interactions continue to increase substantially from the toddler to the preschool years (Howes & Phillipsen, 1988). This is especially evident in shared pretend play, which occurs more often among friends than among nonfriends (Howes & Unger, 1989). As discussed in Chapters 6 and 7, pretend play involves symbolic actions that must be mutually understood by the play partners, as in the following example:

> Johnny, 30 months, joins his friend Kevin who is pretending to go on a picnic. Johnny, on instruction from 3-year-old Kevin, fills the car with gas, "drives" the car, then gets the food out, pretends to eat it, saying he doesn't like it! Both boys pretend to spit out the food, saying "yuk!", laughing. . . .
>
> (Dunn, personal communication, 1999)

Pretend play may occur more often among friends because friends' experiences with one another allow them to trust that their partner will work to interpret and share the meaning of symbolic actions (Howes, 1996).

While the rate of cooperation and positive interactions among young friends is higher than among nonfriends, so is the rate of conflict. Preschool friends quarrel as much or more with one another as do nonfriends and also more often express hostility by means of assaults, threats, and refusing requests (Fabes, Eisenberg, Smith, & Murphy, 1996; Hartup, Laursen, Stewart, & Eastenson, 1988). The higher rate of conflict for friends is likely due, in part, to the greater amount of time friends spend together.

Although preschool friends are more likely than nonfriends to fight, they also are more likely to resolve conflicts in controlled ways, such as by negotiating, asserting themselves nonaggressively, acquiescing, or simply ceasing the activity that is causing the conflict (Fabes et al., 1996; Hartup et al., 1988) (see Table 13.1). Moreover, friends are more likely than nonfriends to resolve conflicts in ways that result in equal outcomes rather than in one child's winning and another's losing. Thus, after a conflict, friends are more likely than nonfriends to continue their interactions and to maintain positive regard for one another.

TABLE 13.1

Strategies Chosen by Schoolchildren When a Peer Says Something Mean to, or About, Them

Percent of Children Selecting Each Strategy When the Peer Is:

	Their Best Friend	Classmate (Neither a Friend nor Enemy)
Talk to friend/classmate	43%	19%
Think about what to do	24%	14%
Hit, kick, yell	9%	10%
Hold anger in	8%	5%
Quit thinking about it	6%	20%
Get away from what happened	4%	17%
Talk to someone else about it	4%	11%
Do nothing	1%	4%

Adapted from Whitesell & Harter, 1996

Developmental Changes in Friendship

In the school years, many of the patterns apparent in the interactions among preschool-age friends and nonfriends persist and become more sharply defined. As earlier, friends, in comparison with nonfriends, communicate more and better with each other and cooperate and work together more effectively (Hartup, 1996). They also fight more often, but again, they also are more likely to negotiate their way out of the conflict (Laursen, Finkelstein, & Betts, 2001). In addition, they now have the maturity to take responsibility for the conflict and to give reasons for their disagreement, increasing the likelihood of their maintaining the friendship (Fonzi, Schneider, Tani, & Tomada, 1997; Hartup, French, Laursen, Johnston, & Ogawa, 1993; Whitesell & Harter, 1996).

While children's friendships remain similar in many aspects as the children grow older, they do change in one important dimension: the level and importance of intimacy. The change is reflected both in the nature of friends' interactions with each other and in the way children conceive of friendship. Between ages 6 and 8, for example, children define friendship primarily on the basis of actual activities with their peers and tend to define "best" friends as peers with whom they play all the time and share everything (Youniss, 1980). At this age, children also tend to view friends in terms of rewards and costs (Bigelow, 1977). Friends are rewarding to be with: they are close by, have interesting toys, and have similar expectations about play activities. Nonfriends tend to be uninteresting or difficult to get along

TABLE 13.2

Dimensions on Which Elementary School Children Often Evaluate Their Friendships

Validation and Caring
Makes me feel good about my ideas.
Tells me I am good at things.

Conflict Resolution
Make up easily when we have a fight.
Talk about how to get over being mad at each other.

Conflict and Betrayal
Argue a lot.
Doesn't listen to me.

Help and Guidance
Help each other with schoolwork a lot.
Loan each other things all the time.

Companionship and Recreation
Always sit together at lunch.
Do fun things together alot.

Intimate Exchange
Always tell each other our problems.
Tell each other secrets.

Adapted from Parker & Asher, 1993

with. Thus, in the early school years, children's views of friendship are instrumental and concrete (Rubin et al., 1998).

In contrast, between the early school years and adolescence, children increasingly experience and define their friendships in terms of mutual liking, closeness, and loyalty (Newcomb & Bagwell, 1995; Furman & Buhrmester, 1992). At about 9 years of age, children seem to become more sensitive to the needs of others and to the inequalities among people. Children define friends in terms of taking care of one another's physical and material needs, providing general assistance and help with schoolwork, reducing loneliness and the sense of being excluded, and sharing feelings. The following descriptions of friends are typical:

> *female, 10:* If you're hurt, they come over and visit.
> *male, 9:* Help someone out. If the person is stuck, show them the answer but tell them why it's the answer.
> *female, 9:* Being nice to each other. If something happened to you, they run over to help you.
> *male, 9:* You're lonely and your friend on a bike joins you. You feel a lot better because he joined you.
>
> (Youniss, 1980, pp. 177–178)

When children are about 10 years old, loyalty, mutual understanding, and self-disclosure become important components of children's conceptions of friendship (Bigelow, 1977). In addition, both preadolescents and adolescents emphasize cooperative reciprocity (doing the same things for one another), equality, and trust between friends (Youniss, 1980). The following descriptions are indicative of how children in this age range view their friends:

> *male, 10:* You exchange kindness for a long time, not just for a day.
> *female, 10:* Somebody you can keep your secrets with together. Two people who are really good to each other.
> *male, 12:* A person you can trust and confide in. Tell them what you feel and you can be yourself with them.
> *female, 13:* They'll understand your problems. They won't always be the boss. Sometimes they'll let you decide; they'll take turns. If you did something wrong, they'll share the responsibility.
> *male, 14:* They have something in common. You hang around with him. . . . We're more or less the same; the same personalities.
>
> (Youniss, 1980, pp. 180–182)

More than younger friends, adolescent friends use friendship as a context for self-exploration and working out personal problems (Gottman & Mettetal, 1986). Thus, friendships become an increasing source of intimacy and disclosure with age, as well as a source of honest feedback. It may be for these reasons that friendships are so valued by adolescents and are believed to be so important by psychologists.

What accounts for the various age-related changes that occur in children's friendships, particularly with regard to their conception of friendship? Some researchers have argued that the changes in children's thinking about friendship are qualitative, or *discontinuous*. For example, Selman (1980) suggested that changes in children's reasoning about friendships are a consequence of age-related qualitative changes in their ability to take others' perspectives (see Chapter 9, p. 343). In the view of Selman, as well as of Piaget and others, young children have limited awareness that others may feel or think about things differently than they themselves do. Consequently, their thinking about friendships is limited in the degree to which they consider issues beyond their own needs. As children begin to understand others' thoughts and feelings, they realize that friendships involve consideration of both parties' needs so that the relationship is mutually satisfying.

Adolescent friends are more likely to share confidences with one another than are younger friends.

Other researchers argue that the age-related changes in children's conceptions of friendships reflect differences in how children think and express their ideas rather than age-related differences in the basic way they view friendships. Hartup and Stevens (1997) maintain that children of all ages consider their friendships "to be marked by reciprocity and mutuality—the giving and taking, and returning in kind or degree" (p. 356). What differs with age is merely the complexity with which children view friendship and describe its dimensions. Nonetheless, these differences likely have important effects on children's behavior with friends and on their reactions to friends' behavior. For example, because sixth graders are more likely than second graders to report that intimacy and support are important features of friendships (Furman & Bierman, 1984), they are more likely to evaluate their own and their friends' behaviors in terms of these dimensions.

The Functions of Friendships

As is clear from their statements about the meaning of friendships, having friends provides numerous potential benefits for children. The most important of these, noted by Piaget, Vygotsky, Sullivan, and others, are emotional support and the validation of one's own thoughts, feelings, and worth, as well as opportunities for the development of important social and cognitive skills.

Support and Validation

Friends can provide a source of emotional support and security, even at an early age. Consider the following fantasy play interaction between Eric and Naomi, two 4-year-olds who have been best friends for some time. In the course of their play, Eric expresses his ongoing fear that other children don't like him and think he's stupid:

> *Eric:* I'm the skeleton! Whoa! [screams] A skeleton, everyone! A skeleton!
> *Naomi:* I'm our friend, the dinosaur.
> *Eric:* Oh, hi Dinosaur. [subdued] You know, no one likes me.
> *Naomi:* [reassuringly] But I like you. I'm your friend.
> *Eric:* But none of my other friends like me. They don't like my new suit. They don't like my skeleton suit. It's really just me. They think I'm a dumb-dumb.
> *Naomi:* I know what. He's a good skeleton.
> *Eric:* [yelling] I am not a dumb-dumb!
> *Naomi:* I'm not calling you a dumb-dumb. I'm calling you a friendly skeleton.
> (Parker & Gottman, 1989, p. 95)

In this fantasy play situation, Naomi clearly served as a source of support and validation for Eric. She not only reassured Eric when he expressed concern that others do not like him but when Eric confessed that the other children think he, not the skeleton, is dumb, she shifted the focus from him to the fantasy skeleton character. Moreover, she praised the fantasy skeleton character to make Eric feel competent ("He's a good skeleton") (Gottman, 1986).

reciprocated best friendship a friendship in which two children view one another as best or close friends

Friends also can provide support when a child feels lonely. School-age children with best friends and with intimate, supportive friendships experience less loneliness than children without a best friend or with friends who are less caring and intimate (Erdley, Nangle, Newman, & Carpenter, 2001; Parker & Asher, 1993).

The support of friends can be particularly important during difficult periods of transition that involve peers. For example, young children have more positive initial attitudes toward school if they begin school with a large number of established friends as classmates (Ladd & Coleman, 1996; Ladd & Kochenderfer, 1996). In part, this may be because the presence of established friends in the early weeks of school reduces the strangeness of the new environment. Similarly, as sixth graders move into junior high, they are more likely to increase in their level of sociability and leadership if they have stable, high-quality, intimate friendships during this period (Berndt, Hawkins, & Jiao, 1999).

Friendships may also serve as a buffer against unpleasant experiences, such as being yelled at by the teacher or picked on by peers (Ladd & Kochenderfer, 1996; Ladd, Kochenderfer, & Coleman, 1996). This buffering effect was made especially clear by a study of elementary school children who were reported to be verbally or physically victimized by their peers. Among this group, the children who showed an increase a year later in adjustment problems (e.g., sadness, loneliness, fearfulness, aggression, and lying or stealing) were those who did not have a **reciprocated best friendship,** that is, a friendship in which two children are best friends to each other (Hodges, Boivin, Vitaro, & Bukowski, 1999). Victimized children also fare better if they have a number of friendships and if their friends are liked by peers and capable of defending them (Hodges, Malone, & Perry, 1997). Moreover, children with early problem behaviors—who are at risk for peer rejection—are less likely to be victimized by peers if they have a mutual friendship than are children without a reciprocated best friendship (Schwartz, McFadyen-Ketchum, Dodge, Pettit, & Bates, 1999).

As was noted previously, the degree to which friends provide caring and support generally increases from childhood into adolescence (Hunter & Youniss, 1982). Adolescents view friends as being trustworthy and a very important source of emotional support and understanding (Youniss, 1980). Indeed, adolescents report that friends are more important confidants and providers of support than are parents (Furman & Buhrmester, 1992; Hunter & Youniss, 1982) (Figure 13.2).

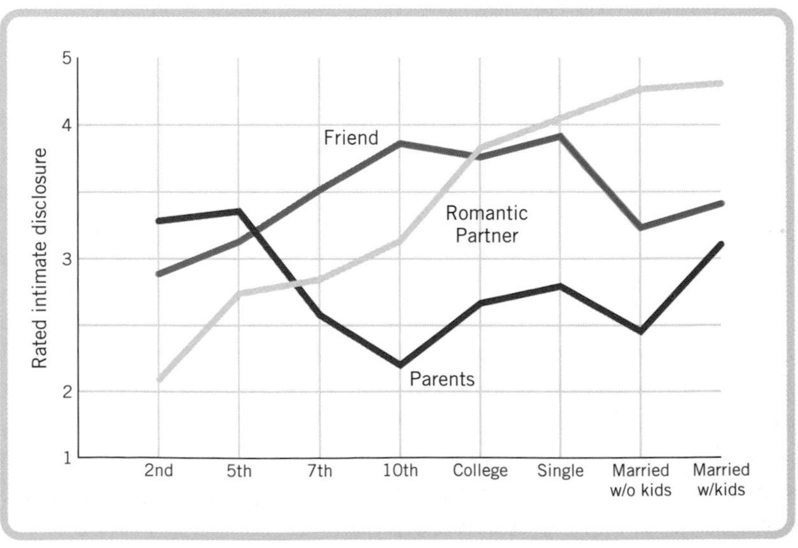

FIGURE 13.2 Age trends in reports of self-disclosure to parents and peers By early adolescence, children disclose more to friends than to their parents. Young adults continue to disclose much more to friends than to their parents, but by college age they disclose most to romantic partners. (Adapted from Burmeister, 1996)

Even though friends provide support in regard to experiences at school and general feelings of loneliness, it is unclear if they can have a buffering effect on children's adjustment to major stressful life experiences such as parental divorce, the death of a parent, or a breakup with a boyfriend or girlfriend (Windle, 1992; Wolchik, Ruchlman, Braver, & Sandler, 1989). In highly stressful situations, support from adults may be more important for children's well-being than support from friends (Wolchik et al., 1989).

TONY FREEMAN / PHOTOEDIT

Interactions with friends provide children with opportunities to get constructive feedback regarding their behavior and ideas.

The Development of Social and Cognitive Skills

Friendships provide a context for the development of social skills and knowledge that children need to form positive relationships with other people. As previously noted, young children seem to first develop more complex play in interactions with friends, and throughout childhood, cooperation, negotiation, and the like are all more common among friends than among nonfriends. In addition, young children who discuss emotions with their friends and interact in positive ways with them develop a better understanding of others' mental and emotional states than do children whose peer relationships are less close (Hughes & Dunn, 1998; Maguire & Dunn, 1997).

Friendship provides other avenues to social and cognitive development as well. Through gossip with friends about other children, for example, children learn about peer norms and learn how, why, and when to display or control the expression of emotions (Gottman, 1986; Ladd & Kochenderfer, 1996). As Piaget pointed out, friends are more likely than nonfriends to criticize and elaborate on each other's ideas and to elaborate and clarify their own ideas (Azmitia & Montgomery, 1993; Nelson & Aboud, 1985). This kind of openness promotes cognitive skills and enhances performance on creative tasks (Miell, 2000). One demonstration of this was provided by a study in which teams of 10-year-olds, half of them made up of friends and the other half made up of nonfriends, were assigned to write a story about rain forests. The teams consisting of friends engaged in more constructive conversations (e.g., they posed alternative approaches and provided elaborations more frequently) and were more focused on the task than were teams of nonfriends. In addition, the stories written by friends were of higher quality than those written by nonfriends (Hartup, 1996).

Sex Differences in the Functions of Friendships

As children grow older, sex differences emerge in what girls and boys feel they get from their friendships. By late elementary school, girls feel that their friendships are more intimate and provide more validation, caring, help, and guidance than do boys (Eisenberg, Martin, & Fabes, 1996; Lempers & Clark-Lempers, 1993; Parker & Asher, 1993). For instance, girls are more likely than boys to report that they rely on their friends for advice or help with homework, that they and their friends share confidences and stick up for one another, and that their friends tell them that they are good at things and make them feel important and special.

Girls and boys are less likely to differ in terms of the amount of conflict and betrayal in their best friendships; for example, they report similar amounts of fighting, saying mean things about the friend to other people, or bugging one another. However, girls report less difficulty than boys in resolving conflict with friends, particularly with regard to being able to talk about how to get over being mad at each other. Boys' and girls' friendships also do not differ much in terms of the companionship and recreational opportunities they provide (e.g., doing things together, going to each other's houses) (Parker & Asher, 1993), although they may differ in the time spent together in various activities (e.g., sports).

Effects of Friendships on Psychological Functioning and Behavior over Time

Because friendships fill important needs for children, it might be expected that having friends enhances children's social and emotional health. In fact, having close, reciprocated friendships in elementary school has been linked to a variety of positive psychological and behavioral outcomes for children, not only during the school years but also years later in early adulthood. However, there also may be costs to having friends, if the friends engage in negative behaviors.

The Possible Long-Term Benefits of Having Friends

Longitudinal research provides the best data concerning the possible long-term effects of having friends in elementary school. Because this research is generally correlational, however, it is difficult to determine if having friends influences long-term outcomes such as psychological adjustment or if characteristics of the child such as psychological adjustment affect whether the child has friends.

In one longitudinal study of the effects of friendships, researchers looked at children when they were fifth graders and when they were young adults. They found that, compared with their peers who did not have reciprocated best friendships, fifth graders who did have them were viewed by classmates as more mature and competent, less aggressive, and more socially prominent (e.g., they were liked by everyone or were picked for such positions as class president or team captain). At approximately age 23, those individuals who had had reciprocated best friendships in fifth grade reported doing better in college and in their family and social life than did individuals who had not had a reciprocated best friendship. They also reported having fewer problems with the law and exhibiting less psychopathology (e.g., depression). Finally, those who had had reciprocated best friends as fifth graders had greater feelings of self-worth (Bagwell, Newcomb, & Bukowski, 1998). Thus, having a reciprocated best friend in preadolescence relates not only to positive social outcomes in middle childhood but also to self-perceived competence and adjustment in adulthood.

The Possible Costs of Friendships

Although friendships are usually associated with positive outcomes, sometimes they are not. Friends who have behavioral problems may exert a detrimental influence, contributing to the likelihood of a child's or adolescent's engaging in violence, using drugs, or exhibiting other negative behaviors.

Aggression and disruptiveness In late elementary school or early adolescence, children who have antisocial and aggressive friends tend to exhibit antisocial and aggressive tendencies themselves (Berndt et al., 1999; Brendgen, Vitaro, & Bukowski, 2000; Tremblay, Masse, Vitaro, & Dobkin, 1995). However, because this finding is based on correlational evidence, it is unclear to what degree having aggressive friends actually *causes* children and adolescents to behave aggressively or is merely a correlate of being aggressive (and does not necessarily induce aggressive behavior). As was discussed in Chapter 3, children's characteristics, such as their activity level or quickness to anger, may affect the environments they choose, including their friends. Thus, aggressive children may gravitate toward aggressive peers for friendship, thereby taking an active role in creating their own peer group. The effect may also be bidirectional: through their talk and behavior, boys who are aggressive may socialize and reinforce aggression and deviance in one another by making them seem acceptable (Dishion, Eddy, Haas, Li, & Spracklen, 1997; Greenberger, Chen, Beam, Whang, & Dong, 2000).

Whether having an aggressive friend affects a child's own behavior over time may depend on the child's baseline level of aggression. This possibility was suggested by a longitudinal study that followed three groups of boys who had been assessed as *nondisruptive, highly disruptive,* or *moderately disruptive* (that is, somewhat, but not highly, above average in aggressive and disruptive behavior). The boys who had been assessed as moderately disruptive *and* who also had aggressive, disruptive friends at ages 11 and 12 reported more delinquent acts at age 13 than did boys who were moderately disruptive but did not have disruptive friends. At the same time, boys who had been assessed as either highly aggressive and disruptive or nonaggressive and nondisruptive did not change their behavior, regardless of their friends' behavior (Vitaro, Tremblay, Kerr, Pagani, & Bukowski, 1997). Thus, young adolescents who are somewhat aggressive and disruptive, but who do not yet exhibit a high level of such behavior, seem to be the most vulnerable to the negative influence of aggressive and disruptive friends.

Alcohol and substance abuse As in the case of aggression, adolescents who abuse alcohol or drugs tend to have friends who do so also (Mounts & Steinberg, 1995; Urberg et al., 1997). And as in the case of aggression, it is not clear if friends' substance abuse is a cause or merely a correlate of adolescents' substance abuse, or if the relation between the two is bidirectional. On the one hand, there is some evidence that adolescents who are especially susceptible to peer pressure to misbehave select friends who drink and use drugs, which then contributes to their own alcohol and substance use (Schulenberg et al., 1999). At the same time, there is some evidence for a more direct causal link: adolescents who start drinking or smoking during the school year tend to have a close friend who was already using alcohol or tobacco (Urberg, Degirmencioglu, & Pilgrim, 1997; Windle, 1994). There is also evidence that adolescents' drinking and their friends' alcohol use appear to mutually affect one another over time so that drinking often escalates among friends (Curran, Stice, & Chassin, 1997). Regardless of the precise sequence of events, hanging out with friends who engage in substance abuse appears to put adolescents at risk.

The extent to which friends' use of drugs and alcohol may put an adolescent at risk seems to depend, in part, on the nature of the child–parent relationship. An adolescent with a drug-using close friend is at risk primarily if the adolescent's parents are cold, detached, and uninclined to monitor and supervise the adolescent's activities (Mounts & Steinberg, 1995; Pilgrim, Luo, Urberg, & Fang, 1999). If the adolescent's parents are authoritative in their parenting, monitoring their child's behavior and setting firm limits but also being warm and receptive to the adolescent's viewpoint (see p. 458), the adolescent is more likely to be protected against peer pressure to use drugs (Mounts, 2002).

Peers can encourage youth to use alcohol, although those prone to such behavior may seek friends who also like to drink.

BOB DAEMMRICH / THE IMAGE WORKS

individual differences

Culture and Children's Peer Experience

Young children's contact with unrelated peers varies considerably around the world. In some communities, such as one in Okinawa, Japan, Beatrice Whiting and Carolyn Edwards (1988) found that children were free to wander in the streets and public areas of town and had extensive contact with peers. In contrast, in some sub-Saharan African societies, children were confined primarily to the yard and therefore had relatively little contact with peers other than their siblings.

As might be expected, Whiting and Edwards found that children's access to the wider community, including peers, increased with age. However, even when children were aged 6 to 10, there were marked differences in the extent to which their social interactions extended beyond the family. In large measure, these differences were based on parents' attitudes toward childhood peer relationships. For example, in kin-based societies such as Kenya, peer interactions were discouraged:

> Parents feared the inherent potential for competition and conflict; they did not want their children to fight with outsiders and engender spiteful relations or become vulnerable to aggression and sorcery. Moreover, as their children did not attend school, they had no need for them to easily acquire skills of affiliating, negotiating, and competing with nonfamily agemates.
>
> (Edwards, 1992, p. 305)

However, Edwards noted that the situation in Kenya is changing as the economy modernizes and literacy has become a valued skill. Parents usually want their children to be educated, and education involves contact with peers.

Even across industrialized cultures, there are differences in the nature of peer interaction. For example, Korean-American children at preschool are less likely than Euro-American children to engage in direct social interaction with peers, such as talking, smiling, or pretend play. Even when they engage in a joint activity, they are more likely to do so without talking or looking at one another. This difference may occur because Euro-American mothers, in contrast to Korean-American mothers, view play as more important for learning and development and encourage more direct peer interaction (Farver, Kim, & Lee, 1995).

There are also cultural differences in the degree to which parents expect their children to develop such social skills as negotiating, taking the initiative, and standing up for their rights. Euro-American and Euro-Australian mothers, for example, expect their children to develop such skills earlier than do Japanese mothers (Hess, Kashiwagi, Azuma, Price, & Dickson, 1980) and Lebanese-Australian mothers (Goodnow, Cashmore, Cotton, & Knight, 1984). This probably is because the Euro-American and Euro-Australian mothers are influenced by their respective culture's emphasis on personal autonomy and independence and believe that the aforementioned skills are important for success. Japanese mothers and

Children's Choice of Friends

What factors influence which of their peers children become friends with? For young children, proximity is an obvious key factor. Preschoolers tend to become friends with peers who are nearby physically, as neighbors or playgroup members. (As Box 13.1 points out, young children's access to peers can vary widely by culture.) Although proximity becomes less important with age, it continues to play a role in individuals' choice of friends in adolescence and even into adulthood (Clarke-McLean, 1996; Dishion, Andrews, & Crosby, 1995).

In most industrialized countries, similarity in age also is a major factor in friendship, with most children tending to make friends with age-mates (Aboud & Mendelson, 1996; Dishion et al., 1995). In part, this may be due to the fact that in most industrialized societies, children are segregated by age in school: in societies where children do not attend school or otherwise are not segregated by age, they are more likely to develop friendships with children of different ages.

Another powerful factor in friend selection is sex: girls tend to be friends with girls, and boys, with boys (Maccoby, 2000; see Chapter 9). The preference for same-sex friends emerges in preschool and continues through childhood (Hartup, 1983), although liking of other-sex peers increases from childhood into early adolescence (Sippola, Bukowski, & Noll, 1997). To a lesser degree, children tend to be friends with peers of the same race, although this tendency varies across groups (Graham & Cohen, 1997). In the United States, for example, African-American

13.1

Australian mothers of Lebanese heritage are likely to be similarly influenced by their respective cultures' emphasis on the interdependence of family members, and therefore may be more likely to accept or even encourage dependency in young children (Johnson, 1993; White & LeVine, 1986). Thus, differences in parents' expectations regarding what social skills their children will develop and when likely influence what parents teach their children about social interactions with peers.

MORTON BEEBE / CORBIS

In some groups in Kenya, children are discouraged from forming relationships with peers who are not related. Thus, children interact primarily with siblings and adult relatives.

and other minority children are more likely to show attraction and friendship toward Euro-American children than vice versa, especially when Euro-Americans are in the majority in a given community (Aboud & Mendelson, 1996).

Beyond these basic factors, a key determinant of liking and friendship is similarity of interests and behavior. By age 7, children tend to like peers who are similar to themselves in the cognitive maturity of their play (Rubin, Lynch, Coplan, Rose-Krasnor, & Booth, 1994) and in the level of their aggressive behavior (Poulin et al., 1997). Fourth- to eighth-grade friends are more similar than nonfriends in their cooperativeness, helping behavior, antisocial behavior, acceptance by peers, and shyness (Haselager, Hartup, van Lieshout, & Riksen-Walraven, 1998), as well as in their level of academic motivation (Kindermann, 1993). Adolescent friends tend to be similar in their interests, attitudes, and behavior (Gavin & Furman, 1996). Adolescents also tend to hang out and be friends with peers who are similar in their susceptibility to experiencing negative emotions such as distress and depression (Haselager et al., 1998; Hogue & Steinberg, 1995).

Thus, birds of a feather *do* tend to flock together. Similarity probably initially attracts children to each other and then serves to maintain their friendships. The fact that friends tend to be similar on a number of dimensions underscores the difficulty of knowing whether friends actually affect one another's behavior or whether children simply seek out peers who think, act, and feel as they do.

review:

Peers, especially friends, provide intimacy, support, and rich opportunities for the development of play and for the exchange of ideas. Children engage in more complex and cooperative play and in more conflict with friends than with nonfriends, and tend to resolve conflicts with friends in more appropriate ways. With age, the dimensions of children's friendships change somewhat. Whereas young children define friendship primarily on the basis of actual activities with their peers and on the rewards and costs, older children increasingly rely on their friends to provide a context for self-disclosure, intimacy, self-exploration, and problem solving. As was suggested by Piaget and Vygotsky, friends also provide opportunities for the development of important social and cognitive skills. However, friends can have negative effects on children if they engage in problematic behaviors such as aggression or substance abuse.

Children tend to become friends with peers who are similar in age, sex, race, and social behavior. This makes it especially difficult to distinguish between characteristics that children bring to friendships and the effects of friends on one another.

Peers in Groups

Let's go back to Annie for a moment. Recall that she not only had a couple of close friends, Kay and Sarah, but she also had a group of friends—Jo, Kerry, and Sue—with whom she "did things" (see Figure 13.1) and to whom she felt closer than she did to other children in her peer group. This pattern of social relationships is typical. Like Annie, most children usually have one or a few very close friends and some less close additional friends with whom they spend time and share activities. These groups tend to exist within a larger social network of peers that hangs together loosely. Developmentalists have been especially interested in how these peer groups emerge and change with age and how they affect the development of their members.

The Nature of Young Children's Groups

When in a setting with a number of their peers, very young children, including toddlers, sometimes interact in small groups. One striking feature of these first peer groups is the early emergence of status patterns within them, with some children being more dominant and central to group activities than others (Rubin et al., 1998).

By the time children are preschool age, there is a clear dominance hierarchy among the members of a peer group. It is evident which children are likely to prevail over other group members when there is conflict, and there is a consistent pattern of winners and losers in physical confrontations. Some ethological theorists believe that dominance hierarchies serve a valuable purpose because they reduce overt aggression among children. In fact, children who lose in conflicts over objects tend to back off and avoid further conflict with the victorious child (Strayer & Strayer, 1976).

As we will discuss shortly, by middle childhood, status in the peer groups involves much more than dominance, and children become very concerned about their peer-group standing. Before examining peer status, however, we need to examine the nature of social groups in middle childhood and early adolescence.

Cliques and Social Networks in Middle Childhood and Early Adolescence

cliques friendship groups that children voluntarily form or join themselves

Starting in middle childhood, most children are part of a stable social group or clique. **Cliques** are friendship groups that children voluntarily form or join themselves. In middle childhood, cliques tend to include three to nine children, and the members usually are of the same sex and race (Rubin et al., 1998). By age 11, many of children's social interactions—from gatherings in the school lunchroom to outings at the mall—occur within the clique (Crockett, Losoff, & Peterson, 1984). Although friends tend to be members of the same clique, many members of a clique do not view each other as close friends (Cairns, Leung, Buchanan, & Cairns, 1995).

A key feature that underlies cliques and binds their members together is the similarities the members share. Members of cliques, like friends, tend to be similar in their degree of academic motivation (Cairns, Cairns, & Neckerman, 1989; Kindermann, 1993), in their aggressive behavior (Cairns, Cairns, Neckerman, Gest, & Gariepy, 1988), and in their shyness, attractiveness, popularity, and adherence to conventional values such as politeness and cooperativeness (Leung, 1996).

Despite the social glue of similarity, the membership of cliques tends to be stable for only a few weeks (Cairns et al., 1995). A study of fourth and fifth graders, for example, found the turnover rate of cliques to be about 50% over eight months (Kindermann, 1993). Over a year's time, only about 30% of fourth and seventh graders' social groups maintained at least half of their members; the degree to which groups were stable was much greater if children were assigned to the same classroom from one year to the next (Neckerman, 1996).

As in early childhood, some children play a more important role in children's social groups than do others. However, whereas the central figures in young children's groups tend to be dominant, during the school years, with both girls and boys, children who are central to the peer group are likely to be popular, athletic, cooperative, seen as leaders, and studious relative to other peers (Farmer & Rodkin, 1996). However, especially in the case of boys, they sometimes are also aggressive and viewed by peers as "tough" or "cool" (Estell, Cairns, Farmer, & Cairns, 2002; Rodkin, Farmer, Pearl, & Van Acker, 2000).

Cliques in middle childhood serve a variety of functions: they provide a ready-made pool of peers for socializing; they offer validation of the characteristics that the group members have in common; and, perhaps most important, they provide a sense of belonging. By middle childhood, children are quite concerned about being accepted by peers, and issues of peer status become a common topic of children's conversation and gossip (Gottman, 1986; Kanner, Feldman, Weinberger, & Ford, 1987; Rubin et al., 1998). Being accepted by others who are similar to oneself in various ways may provide a sense of personal affirmation, as well as of being a welcomed member of the larger peer group.

Cliques and Social Networks in Adolescence

From age 11 to 18, there is a marked drop in the number of students who belong to a single clique and an increase in the number of adolescents who have ties to many cliques or to students at the margins of cliques (Shrum & Cheek, 1987). There also is an increase in the stability of cliques. In a study of sixth, eighth, and tenth graders, 60% of members in a clique during the fall semester were still

DONNA DAY / IMAGE STATE

Children and adolescents in cliques tend to spend a lot of time together and often dress similarly.

together in a clique in the spring (Degirmencioglu, Urberg, Tolson, & Richard, 1998).

The dynamics of cliques also vary at different ages in adolescence. During early and middle adolescence, children report placing a high value on being in a popular group and in conforming to the group's norms regarding dress and behavior. Failure to conform—even something as trivial-seeming as wearing the wrong brand or style of jeans or belonging to an afterschool club that is viewed as uncool—can result in being ridiculed or shunned by the group. In comparison with older adolescents, younger adolescents also report more interpersonal conflict with members of the group as well as with those in other groups. In later adolescence, the importance of belonging to a clique and of conforming to its norms appears to decline, as does the friction and antagonism within and between groups of adolescents. With increasing age, adolescents are not only more autonomous but they also tend to look more to individual relationships than to group relationships to fulfill their social needs (Gavin & Furman, 1989; Rubin et al., 1998).

Although older adolescents seem less tied to cliques, they still often belong to crowds. **Crowds** are groups of people who have similar stereotyped reputations. Among American high school students, typical crowds may include the "brains," "jocks," "loners," "burnouts," "druggies," "populars," "freaks," or "losers" (Brown, 1990; Eckert, 1989; La Greca, Prinstein, & Fetter, 2001). Which crowd adolescents belong to often is not their choice; it is assigned to the individual by the consensus of the peer group, even though the individual may actually spend little time with other members of his or her designated crowd (Brown, 1990).

Being associated with a crowd may enhance or hurt adolescents' reputations and influence how they are treated by peers. Someone labeled a loser or freak, for example, may be ignored or ridiculed by people in groups such as the jocks or populars. Being labeled as part of a particular crowd also may limit adolescents' options with regard to exploring their identities (see Chapter 11, pp. 432–433). This is because crowd membership may "channel" adolescents into relationships with other members of the same crowd rather than with a diverse group of peers (Eckert, 1989; Rubin et al., 1998). Thus, adolescents in one crowd may be exposed to the acceptance of violence or drugs by peers, whereas members of another crowd may find that their peers value success in academics or sports rather than involvement in illegal or violent activities (La Greca et al., 2001).

Boys and Girls in Cliques and Crowds

In adolescence, girls are more likely than boys to be integrated into cliques and to draw a large percentage of their friends from their own clique (Urberg, Degirmencioglu, Tolson, & Halliday-Scher, 1995). Perhaps because of their tighter connection to a single peer group, girls seem to be more upset than boys are by the arguments and negative interactions that sometimes go on within cliques (Gavin & Furman, 1989). And perhaps because of their looser connection to a single peer group, boys appear to have a greater diversity of friends (Urberg et al., 1995).

As discussed previously, children tend to affiliate with same-sex peers throughout childhood and into adolescence (Benenson, 1990; see Chapter 9). However, by seventh grade, about 10% of cliques contain both boys and girls (Cairns et al.,

crowds groups of adolescents who have similar stereotyped reputations. Among American high school students, typical crowds may include the "brains," "jocks," "loners," "burnouts," "druggies," "populars," "freaks," "nonconformists," or "losers."

gangs loosely organized groups of adolescents or young adults that identify as a group and often engage in illegal activities

1995). Thereafter, girls and boys tend to associate with one another more, and dyadic dating relationships become increasingly common (Dunphy, 1963; Richards, Crowe, Larson, & Swarr, 1998). Consequently, by high school, cliques of friends often include adolescents of both sexes (Fischer, Sollie, & Morrow, 1986).

Negative Influences of Cliques and Social Networks

Like close friends, members of the clique or the larger peer network can sometimes lead the child or adolescent astray. Preadolescents and adolescents are more likely to smoke, drink, or use drugs, for example, if members of their peer group do so and if they hang out with peers who have been in trouble (Dishion, Capaldi, Spracklen, & Li, 1995; Rose, Chassin, Presson, & Sherman, 1999; Urberg et al., 1995). Adolescents who have an extreme orientation to peers—that is, who are willing to do anything to be liked by peers—are particularly at risk to be aggressive, use illegal substances or alcohol, and do poorly in school if such behavior secures peer acceptance (Fuligni, Eccles, Barber, & Clements, 2001).

Perhaps the greatest potential for negative peer-group influence is represented by membership in **gangs,** which are loosely organized groups of adolescents or young adults that identify as a group and often engage in illegal activities. Gang members often say that they join or stay in a gang for protection from other gangs. One male gang member explained that "being cool with a gang" meant that "you don't have to worry about nobody jumping you. You don't got to worry about getting beat up" (quoted in Decker, 1996, p. 253). Gangs also provide members with a sense of belonging and a way to spend their time. Gang members frequently report that the most common gang activities are "hanging out" together and engaging in fairly innocuous behaviors (e.g., drinking beer, playing sports, cruising, looking for girls, and having parties) (Decker & van Winkle, 1996). Nonetheless, many gang members frequently engage in antisocial and illegal activities such as selling drugs, stealing cars, and fighting (see Chapter 14, pp. 558–559). In fact, adolescent males and females tend to engage in more illegal activities such as delinquency and drug abuse when they are in a gang than when they are not (Bjerregaard & Smith, 1993; Esbensen & Huizinga, 1993).

Negative peer-group influences can also exist among college students. For example, students involved in athletics and fraternities or sororities are more likely than are other students to engage in binge drinking, in part because the practice tends to be positively sanctioned by those groups as a regular part of their social activities (Carter & Kahnweiler, 2000; Meilman, Leichliter, & Presley, 1999). In fact, intervention programs designed to reduce binge drinking on campuses sometimes try to address the role of these peer groups in the process (Bishop, 2000; Nelson & Wechsler, 2001).

The potential for peer-group influence to promote problem behavior is affected by family and cultural influences. As noted in our discussion of friendship, having authoritative, involved parents helps protect adolescents from peer pressure to use drugs, whereas having authoritarian, detached parents increases their susceptibility to such pressure. Adolescents who do not live with their father or a stepfather and who have a poor relationship with their mother may be especially vulnerable to such pressure (Farrell & White, 1998). Use of drugs in the peer group may have somewhat less of an effect on the drug use of American Indian youths who live on a reservation than on that of Euro-American youths, perhaps because among the former, family sanctions regarding the use of alcohol and drugs play a greater role than the peer group in whether or not they use drugs (Swain, Oetting,

Thurman, Beauvais, & Edwards, 1993). Similarly, among adolescents in mainland China and in Taiwan, peer-group influence seems to play a somewhat weaker role in promoting problem behavior (including drinking, antisocial behavior, and school misconduct) than it does for Euro- and Chinese-American adolescents (Chen, Greenberger, Lester, Dong, & Guo, 1998). Although the precise reasons for all these differences in peer-group influence are not yet known, it is clear from findings such as these that family and cultural factors can affect the degree to which peers' behaviors are associated with adolescents' problem behavior.

review:

Very young children often interact with peers in groups, and dominance hierarchies emerge in these groups by preschool age. By middle childhood, most children belong to cliques of same-sex peers who often are similar in their aggressiveness and orientation toward school.

In adolescence, the importance of cliques tends to diminish, and adolescents typically belong to more than one group. The degree of conformity to the norms of the peer group regarding dress, talk, and behavior decreases over the high school years. Nonetheless, adolescents often are members of "crowds" such as the jocks, loners, or brains—that is, groups of people with similar reputations. Even though adolescents often do not choose what crowd they belong to, belonging to a particular crowd may affect adolescents' reputations, their treatment by peers, and their exploration of identities.

Peer groups sometimes contribute to the development of antisocial behavior, alcohol consumption, and substance use. Membership in a gang is particularly likely to encourage problem behavior. The degree to which the peer group influences adolescents' antisocial behavior or drug abuse appears to vary according to family and cultural factors.

Status in the Peer Group

As noted in the preceding section, older children and adolescents often are extremely concerned with their peer status: being popular is of great importance, and peer rejection can be a devastating experience. Rejection by peers is associated with a range of developmental outcomes for children, such as dropping out of school and problem behaviors, and these relations can hold independent of any effects of having, or not having, close friends (Gest, Graham-Berman, & Hartup, 2001). Because of the central role that peer relations play in children's lives, developmental researchers have devoted a good deal of effort to studying the concurrent and long-term effects associated with peer status.

In this section, we will examine children's status in the peer group, including how it is measured, its stability, the characteristics that determine it, and the long-term implications of being popular with, or rejected by, peers.

Measurement of Peer Status

The most common method developmentalists use to assess peer status is to ask children to rate how much they like or dislike each of their classmates. Alternatively, they may ask children to nominate some of those whom they like the most and the least or whom they do or don't like to play with. The information from these procedures is used to calculate the children's **sociometric status,** that is, the degree to

TABLE 13.3

Common Sociometric Categories

Popular—Children are designated as *popular* if they receive many positive nominations (e.g., for being liked) and few negative nominations (e.g., for being disliked).

Rejected—Children are designated as *rejected* if they receive many negative nominations and few positive nominations.

Neglected—Children are designated as *neglected* if they are low in social impact—that is, if they receive few positive or negative nominations. These children are not especially liked or disliked by peers; they simply go unnoticed.

Average—Children are designated as *average* if they receive an average number of both positive and negative nominations.

Controversial—Children are designated as *controversial* if they receive many positive and many negative nominations. They are noticed by peers and are liked by a quite a few children and disliked by quite a few others.

sociometric status a measurement that reflects the degree to which children are liked or disliked by their peers as a group

popular peer status a category of sociometric status that refers to children or adolescents who are viewed positively (liked) by many peers and are viewed negatively (disliked) by few peers

which the children are liked or disliked by their peers as a group. The most commonly used sociometric system classifies children into five groups (Coie & Dodge, 1988): popular, rejected, neglected, average, or controversial (see Table 13.3).

Characteristics Associated with Sociometric Status

Why are some children liked better than others? One obvious factor is physical attractiveness. Attractive children are much more likely to be popular than are children who are unattractive (Langlois et al., 2000). This pattern, which emerges in early childhood, is particularly apparent in adolescence. Indeed, physical attractiveness in adolescence may be more important than sociability in contributing to both peer acceptance in a new setting and the development of positive friendships (Hanna, 1998). Another largely physical factor contributing to peer status is athletic ability, especially for boys. "Jocks" generally are perceived as popular by peers (Rodkin et al., 2000). Peer status is also affected by the status of one's friends: having popular friends appears to boost one's own popularity (Eder, 1985; Sabongui, Bukowski, & Newcomb, 1998). Beyond these simple determiners, sociometric status also seems to be affected by a variety of other factors, including children's social behavior, personality, cognitions about themselves and others, and goals when interacting with peers.

Although it may seem unfair, physically attractive children and teens tend to be more popular than their less attractive peers.

KERI PICKETT / TIMEPIX

Popular Children

Popular children tend have a number of social skills that contribute to their being well liked. To begin with, they tend to be skilled at initiating interaction with peers and at maintaining positive relationships with others (Rubin et al., 1998). For example, when popular children enter a group of children who are already talking or playing, they first try to see what is going on in the group and then join in by talking about the same topic or engaging in the same activity as the group (Putallaz, 1983). In keeping with this approach, popular

ELLEN B. SENISI

Children who are accepted by peers tend to find ways to enter into a group without disrupting its activities.

children are relatively unlikely to draw unwarranted attention to themselves when entering a group (Dodge, Schlundt, Schocken, & Delugach, 1983). At a broader level, popular children tend to be cooperative, friendly, sociable, and sensitive to others, and are perceived that way by their peers, teachers, and adult observers (Dodge, Lochman, Harnish, Bates, & Pettit, 1997; Newcomb, Bukowski, & Pattee, 1993; Rubin et al., 1998). They also are not prone to intense negative emotions and regulate themselves well (Eisenberg et al., 1993).

Although popular children often are less aggressive overall than are rejected children (Newcomb et al., 1993), in comparison with children designated as *average* (i.e., those who receive an average number of both positive and negative nominations), they are less aggressive only with respect to aggression that is driven by generalized anger, vengefulness, or satisfaction in hurting others (Dodge, Coie, Pettit, & Price, 1990). With respect to assertive aggressiveness, including pushing and fighting, popular children often do not differ from average children (Newcomb et al., 1993).

Rejected Children

A majority of **rejected** children tend to fall into one of two categories: those who are overly aggressive and those who are withdrawn.

Aggressive-rejected children According to reports from peers, teachers, and adult observers, 40% to 50% of rejected children tend to be aggressive. These **aggressive-rejected** children are especially prone to hostile and threatening behavior, physical aggression, disruptive behavior, and delinquency (Hinshaw, Zupan, Simmel, Nigg, & Melnick, 1997; Kupersmidt, Burchinal, & Patterson, 1995; Newcomb et al., 1993). When they are angry or want their own way, many rejected children also engage in **relational aggression,** spreading rumors about peers, withholding friendship to inflict harm, and ignoring and excluding other children (Crick, Casas, & Mosher, 1997; Tomada & Schneider, 1997).

Most of the research on the role of aggression in peer status is correlational, so it is impossible to know for certain if aggression causes peer rejection or results from it. However, some research supports the view that aggressive behavior often underlies rejection by peers. For example, observation of unfamiliar peers getting to know one another has shown that those who are aggressive become rejected over time (Coie & Kupersmidt, 1983). Other longitudinal research has shown that children who are aggressive, negative, and disruptive tend to become increasingly disliked by peers across the school year (Little & Garber, 1995; Maszk, Eisenberg, & Guthrie, 1999).

Nonetheless, not all aggressive children are rejected by their peers: some develop a network of aggressive friends and are not rejected in their peer group. As noted earlier, some preadolescent boys who start fights and get into trouble are viewed as "cool" and are at the center of social activity in their own and the larger peer group (Rodkin et al., 2000). Many of these boys may fall into the group of *controversial* children—those who are liked by some children and disliked by others. Some aggressive adolescents also fall into this category, and although they may be less popular than other children overall, they are as likely as nonaggressive peers to have friends in their own social circle (Cairns et al., 1988).

rejected peer status a category of sociometric status that refers to children or adolescents who are liked by few peers and disliked by many peers

aggressive-rejected children a category of sociometric status that refers to children who are especially prone to physical aggression, disruptive behavior, delinquency, and negative behavior such as hostility and threatening others

relational aggression a kind of aggression that involves exclusion from the social group or attempting to do harm to another's relationships with others. It includes spreading rumors about peers, withholding friendship to inflict harm, and ignoring and excluding peers when a child is angry or wants his or her own way.

withdrawn-rejected children a category of sociometric status that refers to rejected children who are socially withdrawn, wary, and often timid

Withdrawn-rejected children The second group of rejected children, those who are **withdrawn-rejected,** make up about 10% to 20% of the rejected category. These children are socially withdrawn and wary, and, according to some research, often timid (Cillessen, van IJzendoorn, van Lieshout, & Hartup, 1992; Rubin et al., 1998). Many feel isolated and lonely.

ELIZABETH CREWS

Children who are socially withdrawn miss opportunities to learn social skills and may eventually be rejected by peers, especially if they behave in negative ways.

However, research suggests that not all socially withdrawn children are rejected. In one study of different types of socially withdrawn children, observers kept track of the times kindergarten children played alone or wandered around aimlessly or merely watched other children (Harrist, Zaia, Bates, Dodge, & Pettit, 1997). In addition, teachers provided information on the children's tendencies to isolate themselves and to exhibit negative emotions and a range of negative behaviors. Assessing the children's sociometric status in kindergarten and over the next few years, the researchers found that *active-isolates*—children who were socially isolated and displayed immature, unregulated, or angry, defiant behavior such as bullying, boasting, and meanness—were particularly likely to be rejected by peers. In kindergarten, 59% of these children were rejected, and only about 14% were popular. In contrast, children who interacted with peers at a low rate but were viewed by teachers as relatively socially competent were simply neglected—that is, they were not nominated as liked or disliked by peers. Finally, children who were very high in isolated behavior and were viewed by teachers as timid and anxious tended to be average in their sociometric status. Thus, withdrawn behavior in itself was not associated with being rejected by peers; rather, it was withdrawn behavior combined with negative actions or emotions that correlated with rejection. However, as you will shortly see, this pattern may change with age.

Social cognition and social rejection Rejected children, particularly those who are aggressive, tend to differ from more popular children in their social motives and their processing of information related to social situations. For example, rejected children are more likely than better-liked peers to be motivated by goals such as "getting even" with others or showing them up (Crick & Dodge, 1994; Rubin et al., 1998). As discussed in Chapter 9 (p. 344), they also are relatively likely to attribute malicious intent to others in negative social situations, even when the intent of others is uncertain (Crick & Dodge, 1994). For example, when asked how they would react to a peer's bumping into them, rejected children tend to respond with answers like "I'd hit him because he did it on purpose" and "Get a teacher, because he was mean"—even though they have been given no indication of whether or not the bumping was intentional.

Moreover, rejected children have more difficulty than other children finding constructive solutions to difficult social situations, such as wanting a turn on a swing when someone else is using it. When asked how they would deal with such situations, rejected children suggest fewer and more hostile strategies than do their more popular peers (Rubin et al., 1998). In the study of withdrawn-rejected children discussed previously (Harrist et al., 1997), for example, the strategies suggested by the active isolates were relatively unlikely to include constructive approaches—such as a polite request to use the swing—and were more likely to include demands or threats. (Box 13.2 discusses programs designed to help rejected children gain peer acceptance.)

applications 13.2

Fostering Children's Peer Acceptance

Given the difficult and often painful outcomes commonly associated with a child's being aggressive-rejected or withdrawn-rejected, a number of researchers have designed programs to help children in these categories gain acceptance from peers. Their approaches have varied according to what they believe the causes of social rejection to be, but a number of approaches have proved to be useful, at least to some degree.

One common approach involves **social skills training.** The assumption behind this approach is that rejected children lack social skills that promote positive peer relations. These deficits are viewed as occurring at three levels (Mize & Ladd, 1990):

1. *Lack of social knowledge*—Rejected children lack social knowledge regarding the goals, strategies, and normative expectations that apply in specific peer contexts. For example, children engaged in a joint activity usually expect a newcomer to the group to blend in slowly and not to begin immediately pushing his or her own ideas or wishes. Lacking an understanding of this, aggressive-rejected children are likely to barge into a conversation or to try to control the group's choice of activities. In contrast, a withdrawn-rejected child may not know how to start a conversation or contribute to the group's activities when the opportunity arises.
2. *Performance problems*—Some rejected children possess the social knowledge required for being successful in various peer contexts, but they may still act inappropriately because they are unable or unmotivated to use their knowledge to guide their performance.
3. *Lack of appropriate monitoring and self-evaluation*—To behave in a way that is consistent with the interests and actions of their peers, children need to monitor their own and others' social behavior. Such monitoring requires them to accurately interpret social cues regarding what is occurring, what others are feeling and thinking, and how their own behavior is being perceived. Rejected children often cannot engage in such monitoring and thus cannot modify their behavior in appropriate ways.

To help children overcome such deficits, some social skills training programs teach children to pay attention to what is going on in a group of peers, to rehearse skills related to participating with peers, to cooperate, and to communicate in positive ways. Interventions may include coaching and rehearsing children on how to start a conversation with an unfamiliar peer, how to compliment a peer, how to smile and offer help, and how to take turns and share materials (Oden & Asher, 1977). In some interventions, the emphasis is primarily on teaching children to think about alternative ways to achieve a goal, evaluate the consequences of each alternative, and then select an appropriate strategy. Children may be asked to think about or act out a situation in which they are excluded or teased by peers and to come up with various strategies for handling the situation. The children are then helped to evaluate the strategies and to understand their specific costs and benefits (e.g., Coleman, Wheeler, & Webber, 1993).

For aggressive-rejected children, some training programs include a focus on problematic perceptions. As discussed earlier, aggressive-rejected children tend to mistrust peers and misinterpret their actions as hostile, even when peers' intentions are ambiguous. Thus, in some interventions children are trained to think about the range of possible causes for others' behaviors and to try to accurately assess whether others' negative actions are intentional. Often children are asked to role-play or discuss hypothetical situations involving negative social encounters with a peer (e.g., a peer's cutting into line ahead of them or stepping on their foot). This kind of activity helps them learn to identify a peer's intent by reading his or her facial cues (e.g., a look of surprise or chagrin, or one that is indifferent or challenging) (Hudley & Graham, 1993).

Not all interventions are successful, but some do improve certain children's social behavior and their relationships with peers (Asher & Rose, 1997; Coleman et al., 1993). One program designed to promote aggressive-rejected children's use of deliberate, nonimpulsive problem solving was effective in both reducing aggressive behavior and in increasing peer acceptance immediately subsequent to the intervention, as well as a year later (Lochman, Coie, Underwood, & Terry, 1993). Other interventions designed to promote children's problem-solving skills and use of socially appropriate strategies have had some success in reducing the degree to which children associate with deviant peers (Vitaro, Brendgen, Pagani, Tremblay, & McDuff, 1999). Still other procedures devised to reduce adolescents' hostile interpretations of peers' intentions have been successful and have also led to reductions in boys' verbally hostile behavior (Hudley & Graham, 1993). Because friendships and peer acceptance are so important to the social and psychological well-being of children, researchers are continuing to search for ways to help rejected children become more accepted by their peers.

Social rejection and self-evaluations Perhaps due to their deficits in social behavior, withdrawn-rejected children, in comparison with other children, have less confidence in their social skills and report being more anxious in peer contexts (Hymel, Bowker, & Woody, 1993). In contrast, although aggressive-rejected children often lack important social skills, they tend to overestimate their social competence with peers (Hymel, Bowker, & Woody, 1993; Patterson, Kupersmidt, & Griesler, 1990). This tendency may create additional problems for them, leading them to jump into social situations that they cannot handle well and to fail to monitor the outcomes of their actions.

Neglected Children

As noted earlier, some withdrawn children are categorized as **neglected** children because they are not nominated by peers as either liked or disliked. These children tend to be less sociable, aggressive, and disruptive than average children (Rubin et al., 1998) and to back away from peer interactions that involve aggression (Coie & Dodge, 1988). Although these children interact less frequently with peers than do children who are average in sociometric status, they are not particularly anxious about social interactions (Hatzichristou & Hopf, 1996; Rubin et al., 1998). In fact, neglected children display relatively few behaviors that differ greatly from those of many other children (Bukowski, Gauze, Hoza, & Newcomb, 1993). They appear to be neglected primarily because they are not noticed by their peers.

Controversial Children

In some ways, the most intriguing group of children are **controversial** children, those who are liked by some peers and disliked by others. Controversial children tend to have characteristics of both popular and rejected children (Rubin et al., 1998). For example, they tend to be aggressive, disruptive, and prone to anger, but they also tend to be cooperative, sociable, good at sports, and humorous (Bukowski et al., 1993; Coie & Dodge, 1988). They are very socially active and tend to be group leaders (Coie, Dodge, & Kupersmidt, 1990). Controversial children also tend to be viewed by peers as arrogant and snobbish (Hatzichristou & Hopf, 1996), which could explain why they are disliked by some peers.

Stability of Sociometric Status

Do popular children always remain at the top of the social heap? Do rejected children sometimes become better liked? In other words, how stable is a child's sociometric status in the peer group? The answer to this question depends in part on the particular time span and sociometric status that are in question.

Over relatively short time periods such as weeks or a few months, children who are popular or rejected tend to remain so, whereas children who are neglected or controversial are highly likely to change their status (Asher & Dodge, 1986; Chen, Rubin, & Li, 1995b; Newcomb & Bukowski, 1984). The lack of stability for neglected and controversial children may be because these children, especially neglected children, are quite similar in their behavior to many of their peers.

Over longer periods of time, children's sociometric status is more likely to change. In one study in which children were rated by their peers in fifth grade and again two years later, only children who had initially been rated average maintained their status overall, whereas nearly two-thirds of those who had been rated popular, rejected, or controversial received a different rating (Newcomb & Bukowski, 1984). Over time, sociometric stability for rejected children is generally higher than for popular, neglected, or controversial children (Harrist et al., 1997; Parke et al., 1997) and may increase with the age of the child (Coie & Dodge, 1983; Rubin et al., 1998).

social skills training training programs designed to help rejected children gain peer acceptance that are based on the assumption that rejected children lack important knowledge and skills that promote positive interaction with peers

neglected peer status a category of sociometric status that refers to children or adolescents who are infrequently mentioned as liked or disliked; they simply are not noticed much by peers.

controversial peer status a category of sociometric status that refers to children or adolescents who are liked by quite a few peers and are disliked by quite a few others

Developmental Trends in Predictors of Children's Sociometric Status

Do the same characteristics and behaviors that predict peer status at one age also predict it at another age? Or are the predictors of peer status different at different ages? Researchers have noted three patterns of findings that are relevant to this question (Coie et al., 1990; Rubin et al., 1998).

First, the major predictors of popularity do not seem to change substantially with age. At all ages, children who are selected as popular by their peers tend to be viewed by others as helpful, friendly, and considerate. However, it is interesting that over time, some children who are labeled as "popular" may no longer exhibit these behaviors. By the middle-school years, children with the reputation of being popular sometimes start to shun less popular peers. As a result, they are considered "stuck up" and start to be viewed with ambivalence by their peers and sometimes even become resented or disliked (Eder, 1985; Merton, 1997). Eventually such children would probably no longer obtain the status of popular when measured by sociometric techniques, although they might be stereotyped and described by peers as being popular (LaFontana & Cillessen, 1998).

A second developmental trend is that although aggression is a frequent predictor of rejection in childhood, overt aggression appears to play a less important role in peer rejection in adolescence (Coie et al., 1990). This may be because overt aggression occurs much less frequently among adolescents and older children than among younger children.

The third developmental trend is that withdrawn behavior seems to become a more important predictor of peer rejection with increasing age in childhood. As we have noted, many younger withdrawn children who simply are not sociable or are timid and anxious are not rejected by peers. However, by the middle to late elementary school years, children who are quite withdrawn stand out and are disliked more than are sociable children. In addition, withdrawn children seem to become increasingly alienated from the group as time goes on.

As they progress through school, social isolation may also be forced on some children (Bowker, Bukowski, Zargarpour, & Hoza , 1998). That is, children who are disliked and rebuffed by peers, often because of their disruptive or aggressive behavior, may increasingly isolate themselves from the group even if they initially were not withdrawn (Coie et al., 1990; Rubin et al., 1998).

Little is known about developmental changes in the characteristics and behaviors of controversial and neglected children because such children have been studied primarily between the ages of 8 to 12 (Coie et al., 1990). Nonetheless, it seems likely that some controversial children become members of groups of adolescents who are aggressive and come into conflict with other peers and with adults, such as teachers (Cairns et al., 1988).

Cross-Cultural Similarities and Differences in Factors Related to Peer Status

Most of the research on behaviors associated with being liked or disliked by peers has been conducted in the United States, but findings similar to those we have discussed have been obtained in other countries as well. In a variety of countries ranging from Canada, Italy, and Greece to Indonesia and China, for example, socially rejected children tend to be aggressive and disruptive; and, in most countries, popular children tend to be described as prosocial and as having leadership skills

(Attili, Vermigli, & Schneider, 1997; Chen, Rubin, & Li, 1995a; Chen, Rubin, & Sun, 1992; French, Setiono, & Eddy, 1999; Hatzichristou & Hopf, 1996; Tomada & Schneider, 1997). Similar cross-cultural parallels have been found with regard to withdrawal and rejection. Various studies done with schoolchildren in Germany and Italy, for example, have shown that, as in the United States, withdrawal becomes linked with peer rejection in elementary school (Asendorpf, 1990; Attili et al., 1997; Casiglia, Lo Coco, & Zappulla, 1998).

Research has also demonstrated that there are certain cultural differences in the characteristics associated with children's sociometric status. One notable example is the status associated with shyness among Chinese children. Rather than being neglected or rejected like their Western counterparts, Chinese children who are shy, have sensitive feelings, and are cautious and inhibited in their behavior are viewed by teachers as socially competent and as leaders, and they are liked by their peers (Chen et al., 1995a, 1995b; Chen, Rubin, Li, & Li, 1999; Chen et al., 1992). A likely explanation for this difference is that Chinese culture values self-effacing, withdrawn behavior, and Chinese children are encouraged to behave accordingly (Ho, 1986). In contrast, Western cultures place great value on independence and self-assertion. In these cultures, withdrawn children are likely to be viewed as weak, needy, and socially incompetent. Thus, cultural norms play an important role in determining what types of behavior and characteristics children like or dislike in their peers.

Peer Status as a Predictor of Risk

Having an undesirable peer status has been associated with a variety of near- and long-term risks and negative outcomes for children, including inferior academic performance, loneliness, delinquency, and poor adjustment.

Academic Performance

Research in a variety of places, including North America, China, and Indonesia, indicates that rejected children, especially those who are aggressive, are more likely than their peers to have difficulties in the academic domain (Chen, Rubin, & Li, 1997; French et al., 1999). They have higher rates of school absenteeism than their peers (DeRosier, Kupersmidt, & Patterson, 1994) and lower grade-point averages (Wentzel & Caldwell, 1997). Those who are aggressive are especially likely to be uninterested in school and to be viewed by peers and teachers as poor students (Hymel et al., 1993; Wentzel & Asher, 1995).

Longitudinal research indicates that the tendency of rejected children to do more poorly in school worsens across time (Coie, Lochman, Terry, & Hyman, 1992; Ollendick, Weist, Borden, & Greene, 1992). In one study that followed children from fifth grade through the high school years, rejected children were much more likely than other children, especially popular children, to be required to repeat a grade or to be suspended from school, to be truants, or to drop out (Kupersmidt & Coie, 1990) (Figure 13.3). They were also more likely to have difficulties with the law, in many cases, no doubt, deepening their academic difficulties. All told, approximately 25% to 30% of rejected children drop out of school compared with approximately 8% or less of other children (Parker & Asher, 1987; Rubin et al., 1998). Children who feel isolated and lonely at school and believe they feel that way due to rejection by peers may be especially likely to drop out of school (Hymel, Comfort, Schonert-Reichl, & McDougall, 1996).

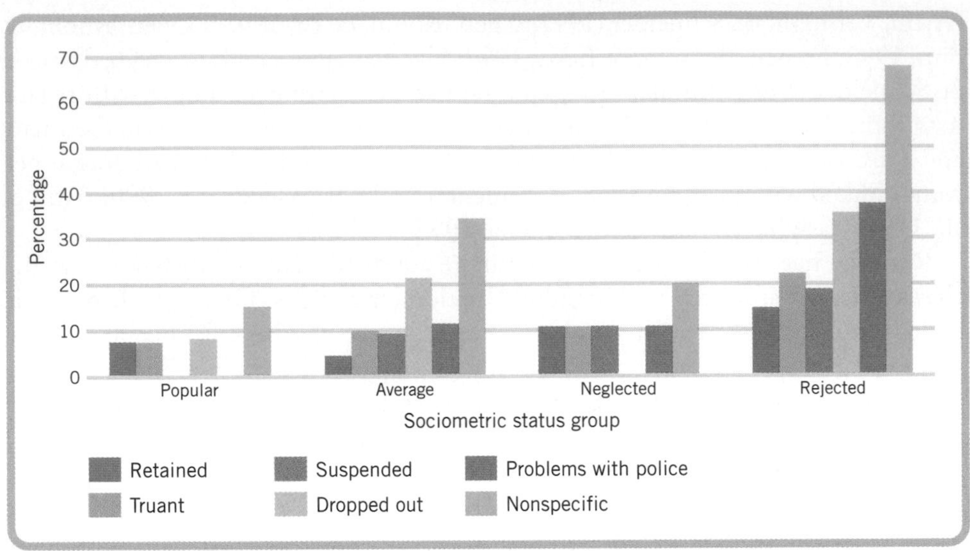

FIGURE 13.3 The relation of children's sociometric status to academic and behavioral problems Children's sociometric status is related to their future problem behaviors. Rejected children are far more likely to be held back in, or suspended from, school, to be truants, to drop out, and to have problems with the police. The occurrence of any of these problems is labeled as "nonspecific" in this figure. (Adapted from Kupersmidt & Coie, 1990)

Problems with Adjustment

Children who are rejected in the elementary school years—especially aggressive-rejected boys—are at risk for externalizing symptoms, that is, outwardly expressed behavior problems such as aggression, delinquency, hyperactivity and attention-deficit disorders, conduct disorder, and substance abuse (Bierman & Wargo, 1995; Coie, Terry, Lenox, Lochman, & Hyman, 1995; Ollendick et al., 1992). In one study that followed over 1,000 children from third to tenth grade (Coie et al., 1995), boys and girls who were assessed as rejected in third grade were, according to parent reports, higher than their peers in externalizing symptoms three years and seven years later. In addition, aggressive boys (both rejected and nonrejected) increased in parent-reported externalizing symptoms between grades six and ten, whereas other boys did not; and by tenth grade, aggressive-rejected boys were especially high in externalizing symptoms (Figure 13.4). By tenth grade, aggressive-rejected boys themselves reported an average of over twice the number of symptoms as did all other boys (Figure 13.5).

This same study provides evidence that peer rejection may also be associated with internalizing problems, that is, internally expressed problems such as loneliness, depression, withdrawn behavior, and obsessive-compulsive behavior. Girls and boys who were rejected in third grade were, as reported by parents, higher than their peers in internalizing symptoms by sixth grade and tenth grade. Moreover, the aggressive-rejected boys increased markedly in self-reported internalizing symptoms from sixth to tenth grade, whereas all other boys reported a drop in these symptoms (Figure 13.6). Aggressive-rejected girls were viewed by parents as most prone to internalizing problems by grade ten. Thus, both boys and girls who were assessed as rejected in third grade—especially if they also were aggressive—were at risk for developing internalizing problems years later.

Also at risk for internalizing problems in Western cultures are children who are very withdrawn but nonaggressive with their peers. As we have seen, although these children tend to become rejected by the middle to late elementary school years, they are generally not at risk for the kinds of psychological and behavioral problems that aggressive-rejected children often experience. However, a consistent pattern of social withdrawal, reticence, social anxiety, and wariness with familiar

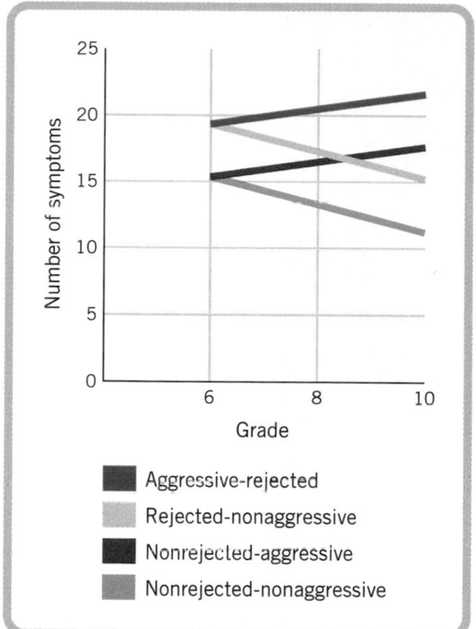

FIGURE 13.4 Rates of parent-reported externalizing symptoms in adolescent males as a function of third-grade rejection and aggression Boys who were assessed as rejected in third grade were reported by parents years later to be higher than their peers in externalizing symptoms. Aggressive boys (both rejected and nonrejected) increased in parent-reported externalizing symptoms between grades 6 and 10, whereas other boys did not; by tenth grade, aggressive-rejected boys were especially high in externalizing symptoms. (Adapted from Coie et al., 1995)

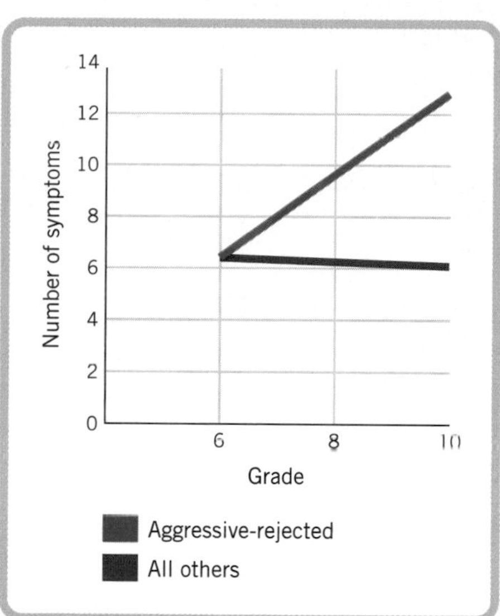

FIGURE 13.5 Rates of boys' self-reported externalizing symptoms as a function of third-grade rejection and aggression Although aggressive-rejected boys did not differ from other boys in reported externalizing symptoms in sixth grade, by tenth grade, aggressive-rejected boys reported an average of over twice the number of symptoms as did all other boys. (Adapted from Coie et al., 1995)

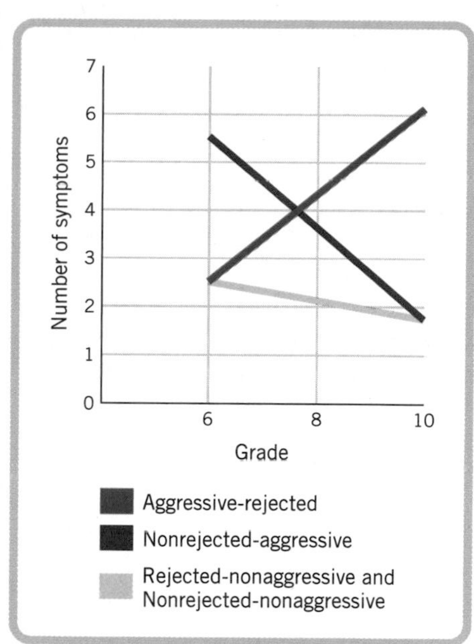

FIGURE 13.6 Rates of boys' self-reported internalizing symptoms as a function of third-grade rejection and aggression Aggressive-rejected boys' reports of internalizing problems increased from sixth to tenth grade, whereas such reports decreased over the same period of time for all other boys. (Adapted from Coie et al., 1995)

people, including peers, is associated with symptoms such as depression, low self-worth, and loneliness in childhood and at older ages (Bowker et al., 1998; Hoza, Molina, Bukowski, & Sippola, 1995). Such a pattern is also associated with less support from peers (La Greca & Lopez, 1998). Indeed, it may be that children who withdraw from their peers suffer feelings of isolation and insecurity in part because they do not feel they can count on peers for support (Rubin, Chen, McDougall, Bowker, & McKinnon, 1995).

Children who are socially withdrawn with familiar peers may differ in important ways from their peers even in adulthood. In a longitudinal study of American children born in the late 1920s, boys who were rated by their teachers as reserved and unsociable were less likely to have been married and to have had children than were less reserved boys. They also tended to begin their careers at later ages, had less success in their careers, and were less stable in their jobs. Reserved men who were late in establishing stable careers had twice the rate of divorce and marital separation by midlife as did their less reserved peers. In contrast, reserved girls were more likely than their less reserved peers to have a conventional lifestyle of marriage, parenthood, and homemaking rather than working outside the home. Thus, a reserved style of interaction at school in childhood was associated with more negative outcomes for men than for women, perhaps because in the United States, especially several decades ago, a reserved style was more compatible with

SCOTT BARROW, INC. / SUPERSTOCK

Children who are shy with familiar peers are at risk for loneliness and feelings of insecurity. Boys who are shy with familiar peers may also be at risk for negative outcomes as adults.

the feminine homemaker role than with the demands of achieving outside the home (Caspi, Elder, & Bem, 1988).

A final group of rejected children who may be especially at risk for loneliness and other internalizing problems is **victimized** children, children who are targets of their peers' aggression and demeaning behavior. These children tend to be aggressive as well as withdrawn and anxious (Hodges et al., 1997; Schwartz, McFadyen-Ketchum, Dodge, Pettit, & Bates, 1998). Although the sequence of events is not entirely clear, it appears that children in this group are more likely to be rejected first and then victimized rather than the reverse (Hanish & Guerra, 2000a; Schwartz et al., 1999). Victimization by peers, in turn, likely increases children's aggression, withdrawal, depression, and loneliness (Hanish & Guerra, 2002; Hodges & Perry, 1999; Schwartz et al., 1998), leading to problems at school and avoidance of school (Juvonen, Nishina, & Graham, 2000; Kochenderfer & Ladd, 1996).

Unfortunately, peer victimization is not an uncommon event. Approximately one-fifth of kindergartners in one study in the United States were repeatedly victimized by peers (Kochenderfer & Ladd, 1996). Although this rate appears to be lower among older children (Olweus, 1994), peer victimization is a serious problem that warrants concern, especially since the same children tend to be victimized again and again (Hanish & Guerra, 2000b).

Paths to Risk

Clearly, children who are rejected by peers are at risk for academic and adjustment problems. The key question is whether peer rejection actually causes problems at school and in adjustment, or whether children's maladaptive behavior (e.g., aggression) leads to both peer rejection and problems in adjustment (Parker, Rubin, Price, & DeRosier, 1995; Woodward & Fergusson, 1999). Although conclusive evidence is not yet available, findings suggest that peer status and the quality of children's social behavior have partially independent effects on subsequent adjustment (Coie et al., 1992; DeRosier et al., 1994). Thus, it is likely that children's maladaptive behavior and their peer status both play a causal role in their future adjustment—separately and in combination (Fergusson, Woodward, & Horwood, 1999).

Once children are rejected by peers, they may be denied opportunities for positive peer interactions and thus for learning social skills. Moreover, cut off from desirable peers, they may be forced to associate with other rejected children, and rejected children may teach one another, and mutually reinforce, deviant norms and behaviors. The lack of social support from peers also may render rejected children more vulnerable than other children to the effects of stressful life experiences

victimized peer status with respect to peer relations, this term refers to children who are targets of their peers' aggression and demeaning behavior (e.g., poverty, parental conflict, divorce), negatively influencing their social behavior even further, which in turn affects both their peer status and adjustment.

review:

Peers' sociometric status is assessed by peers' reports of their liking and disliking of one another. On the basis of such reports, children typically have been classified as popular, rejected, average, neglected, or controversial.

Popular children tend to be attractive, socially skilled, prosocial, well regulated, and low in aggression that is driven by anger, vengefulness, or satisfaction in hurting others. Some rejected children tend to be relatively aggressive, disruptive, and low in social skills; they also tend to make hostile attributions about others' intentions and have difficulty dealing with difficult social situations in a constructive manner. Withdrawn children who are aggressive and hostile as well are also rejected by peers by kindergarten age. In contrast, most children who are withdrawn from their peers but are not hostile and aggressive are at somewhat less risk, although they sometimes become rejected later in elementary school.

Neglected children interact less frequently with peers than do children who are average in sociometric status, and they display relatively few behaviors that differ greatly from those of many other children. Controversial children display characteristics of both popular and rejected children and tend to be very socially active. Children who are neglected or controversial, unlike rejected children, are particularly likely to change their status, even over short periods of time.

Rejection by peers in childhood—especially rejection due to aggression—predicts relatively high levels of subsequent academic problems and externalizing behaviors. Rejected children also tend to become more withdrawn and are prone to loneliness and depression. It is likely that children's maladaptive behavior as well as their low status with peers contribute to these negative developmental outcomes.

The Role of Parents in Children's Peer Relationships

> Cliff is having a hard time, . . . he just doesn't have any good friends, says he has no one to do things with . . . he's just not part of the gang. . . . I hate to see him having troubles with the other kids—I keep wondering if I should do something about it, or if he just has to sort it out hisself. . . . And it reminds me of *my* troubles at school.
>
> (quoted in Dunn, unpublished)

The speaker, the mother of 8-year-old Cliff, not only worries about Cliff's problems with his peers but also feels that she may have contributed to them—a common reaction of parents of lonely and rejected children. The idea that parents influence children's ability to relate to peers has a long history, beginning with Freud's emphasis on the importance of the mother–child relationship as a foundation for later personality development and interpersonal relationships. Moreover, both attachment theorists (see Chapter 11) and social learning theorists (see Chapter 9) have asserted that early parent–child interactions are linked to children's peer interactions at an older age. It also seems likely that children's ongoing relationships with their parents can affect their relationships with their peers.

Relations Between Attachment and Competence with Peers

Attachment theory maintains that whether a child's attachment to the parent is secure or insecure affects the child's future social competence and the quality of the child's relationships with others, including peers. Attachment theorists have suggested that a secure attachment between parent and child promotes competence with peers in at least three ways (Elicker, Englund, & Sroufe, 1992). First, children with a secure attachment develop positive social expectations. They thus are inclined to interact readily with other children and expect these interactions to be positive and rewarding. Second, because of their experience with a sensitive and responsive caregiver, they develop the foundation for understanding reciprocity in relationships. Consequently, they learn to give and take in relationships and to be empathic to others. Finally, children who are securely attached are likely to be confident, enthusiastic, and emotionally positive—characteristics that are attractive to other children and facilitate social interaction.

BOB DAEMMRICH / STOCK BOSTON

Children who have secure attachment relationships with their parents tend to develop better social skills than do their peers who are not securely attached.

Conversely, attachment theorists argue, an insecure attachment is likely to impair a child's competence with peers. If parents are rejecting and hostile or neglectful, young children are likely to become hostile themselves and to expect little good from other people. They may be predisposed to perceive peers as hostile and, consequently, are likely to be aggressive toward them. These children also may expect rejection from other people and may try to avoid experiencing it by withdrawing from peer interaction (Furman, Simon, Shaffer, & Bouchey, 2002; Renken, Egeland, Marvinney, Sroufe, & Mangelsdorf, 1989).

There is a good deal of evidence to support these theoretical views. Children who do not experience sensitive, responsive parenting and who are not securely attached do, in fact, tend to have difficulties with peer relationships (Fagot, 1997; Pastor, 1981). Toddlers and preschoolers who were insecurely attached as infants tend to be aggressive, whiny, socially withdrawn, and low in popularity in elementary school (Bohlin, Hagekull, & Rydell, 2000; Erickson, Sroufe, & Egeland, 1985; LaFreniere & Sroufe, 1985). Throughout childhood, these children, in comparison with securely attached children, express less positive emotion with peers, as well as less sympathy and prosocial behavior, and demonstrate poorer skills in resolving conflicts (Elicker et al., 1992; Fox & Calkins, 1993; Kestenbaum, Farber, & Sroufe, 1989).

Securely attached children, on the other hand, have been shown to exhibit positive emotions and good social skills, and, not surprisingly, to be relatively popular with peers, both as preschoolers (La Freniere & Sroufe, 1985) and in elementary school (Elicker et al., 1992; Kerns, Klepac, & Cole, 1996; Schneider, Atkinson, & Tardif, 2001). Even in late elementary school, children with a greater number of close, supportive, and lasting friendships tend to be those children with a history of a secure attachment to their parents (Freitag, Belsky, Grossman, Grossman, & Scheuerer-Englisch, 1996; Kerns et al., 1996; Schneider et al., 2001).

Thus, security of the parent–child relationship is linked with quality of peer relationships. This link probably arises from both the early and the continuing effect that parent–child attachment has on the quality of the child's overall social behavior. However, it is also possible that characteristics of children, such as sociability, influence both the quality of their attachments and the quality of their relationships with peers.

Quality of Ongoing Parent–Child Interactions and Peer Relationships

Not surprisingly, ongoing parent–child interactions are associated with peer relations in much the same way that attachment patterns are. Mothers of socially competent and popular children, for example, are more likely than mothers of less competent children to discuss feelings with their children and to use warm control, positive verbalizations, reasoning, and explanations (Denham & Grout, 1992; Hart, DeWolf, Wozniak, & Burts, 1992; Leve & Fagot, 1997). Unpopular children, on the other hand, often experience harsh, authoritarian discipline, and their activities tend to go relatively unmonitored (Dishion, 1990; Hart, Ladd, & Burleson, 1990).

In general, fathers' parenting practices appear to be somewhat less closely related to children's social competence and sociometric status than are those of mothers (Eisenberg, Fabes, & Murphy, 1996; Hart et al., 1992). However, the degree to which fathers are affectionate and express positive rather than negative emotions toward their children does predict the positiveness of preschoolers' interactions with close friends (Kahen, Katz, & Gottman, 1994; Youngblade & Belsky, 1992). Moreover, boys whose fathers play with them are liked better by peers than are boys whose fathers do not play with them, perhaps because the rough-and-tumble nature of typical father–son play helps boys learn to interpret others' emotions, and to regulate their own, in physically arousing play (MacDonald & Parke, 1984; Pettit, Brown, Mize, & Lindsey, 1998).

In considering findings such as these, it is generally assumed that quality of parenting influences the degree to which children behave in socially competent ways, which in turn affects whether or not children are accepted by peers. But as in the case of attachment, it is difficult to prove that quality of parenting actually has a causal influence on children's social behavior with peers. It may be that children who are unregulated and disruptive because of constitutional factors (e.g., genetics, prenatal influences) elicit both negative parenting and negative peer responses (Rubin, Nelson, Hastings, & Asendorpf, 1999) (see Chapters 3 and 12); or it may be that both harsh parenting and the children's negative behavior with peers are due to heredity. The most likely possibility is that the causal links are bidirectional—that parents' behavior affects their children's peer competence and vice versa—and that both environmental and biological factors play a role in the development of children's social competence with peers.

Parental Beliefs and Behaviors

Parents of children who are socially competent with peers think about parenting and their children somewhat differently than do parents of children with low social competence. For one thing, they are more likely to believe that they should play an active role in teaching their children social skills and in providing opportunities for peer interaction. They also tend to believe that when their children display inappropriate or maladaptive behavior with a peer (e.g., aggression, hostility, social withdrawal), it is because of the circumstances of the *specific situation,* such as provocation by the peer or a mutual misunderstanding. In contrast, parents of less socially competent children tend to believe that when their children behave in socially inappropriate ways, the reason for the problematic behavior lies in the child's nature and that it would thus be very hard to alter the child's behavior (Rubin et al., 1998). In other words, they tend to believe that the child "was born that way." Of course, it is difficult to know the degree to which parents' beliefs about their children's social competencies are based on realistic perceptions of their offspring or on their own belief systems and personal history (such as the troubles Cliff's mother experienced when she was a schoolchild).

Parents' beliefs about their children's social competence often are reflected in the way they respond to their children. Mothers of children who are socially withdrawn with peers tend to attribute their children's withdrawal to immaturity or character traits, and they react by being protective and trying to solve their children's social problems for them (Mills & Rubin, 1993). Whenever a peer tries to take a toy from their child, for instance, they may scold the peer or remove their child from the play situation. In contrast, mothers of socially competent children would be more likely to give their children a chance to deal with the peer by themselves. Thus, parents often may promote their children's socially adaptive or maladaptive behavior with peers as a result of their beliefs about their children's social competencies.

Gatekeeping, Coaching, and Modeling by Parents

Several other dimensions of parent–child interactions may influence children's competencies in peer relationships. These include parents' gatekeeping role in their children's social life, their coaching of social skills, and their modeling of social behavior.

Gatekeeping

As noted in Chapter 12, parents, especially those of young children, act as gatekeepers, controlling where their children go, with whom they interact, and how much time they spend with peers doing various activities. However, some parents are more thoughtful and active in this role than are others (Mounts, 2002). Preschoolers whose parents arrange and oversee opportunities for them to interact with peers tend to be more positive and social with peers, have a larger number of play partners, more easily initiate social interactions with peers, and have a more stable set of companions than do other children—so long as their parents are not overly controlling during the interaction (Ladd & Golter, 1988; Ladd & Hart, 1992).

MICHAEL NEWMAN / PHOTOEDIT

Parents may contribute to their children's development of social competence by arranging opportunities for their children to interact with peers.

Coaching

Preschool children also tend to be more popular if their parents effectively coach them in how to deal with unfamiliar peers. Mothers of accepted children tend to teach their children group-oriented strategies for gaining entry into a group of peers: they may make suggestions about what to say when entering the group, for example, or they may discourage the child from disrupting the group's current activities. In contrast, mothers of children who are low in sociometric status often try to direct the group's activity themselves or urge their child to initiate activities that are inconsistent with what the group is currently doing (Finnie & Russell, 1988; Russell & Finnie, 1990). For reasons that are not yet clear, mothers' coaching may be especially important for enhancing girls' social skills (Pettit et al., 1998).

Modeling

Another way that parents influence their children's competence with peers is by modeling socially competent and incompetent behaviors, such as how to influence other people and deal with conflicts (Russell, Pettit, & Mize, 1998). In the way they communicate with their children, for example, parents appear to influence the communication style their children adopt with peers. Parents of rejected children tend to talk to them at length, to talk when the child is trying to talk, and to respond in ways that are unrelated to what the child has just said. Such a parent might ask, "Do you want to go to the park today?" and then say something like— "Oh, did the teacher like your picture?" in response to the child's answer. Rejected children, in turn, tend to converse with their peers in a similar manner, talking at the same time as their peers and saying things that do not maintain the thread of the conversation. In contrast, popular children, like their parents, are more likely to engage in turn taking and to stay on the topic in their conversations with peers (Black & Logan, 1995). Thus, children's imitation of their parents' style of conversation may affect the quality of their interactions with, and acceptance by, peers. Children's imitation of parents' behaviors with their friends may account for the fact that the quality of parents' friendships and those of their children tend to be similar (Simpkins & Parke, 2001).

TONY FREEMAN / PHOTOEDIT

Children who frequently observe their parents express negative emotion—especially hostile, assertive, negative emotion—tend to express more negative emotion themselves and to be less socially skilled than their peers.

Family Stress and Children's Social Competence

As discussed in Chapter 12 (p. 465), parents who are preoccupied and distressed by problems related to poverty are less likely to be warm and supportive and to monitor their children's behavior (McLoyd, 1998; McLoyd, Jayaratne, Ceballo, & Borquez, 1994). Thus, it is not surprising that children from families with fewer economic resources and higher levels of stress (e.g., unemployment, health problems) are more likely than other children to be rejected by their peers (Dishion, 1990; Patterson, Griesler, Vaden, & Kupersmidt, 1992). This pattern of findings is illustrated by the data in Figure 13.7, which is from a longitudinal study. In this study, elementary school children from low-income families were considerably more likely to be rejected than were children from middle-class families (boys also were rejected more than girls). A similar association between family economic status and children's social competence with peers has been observed in China (Chen & Rubin, 1994). Of course, prejudice toward children from lower social classes may partly account for this pattern of findings (Eder, 1985). However, it is also likely that the effects of poverty and stress on parenting are reflected in children's compromised social competence.

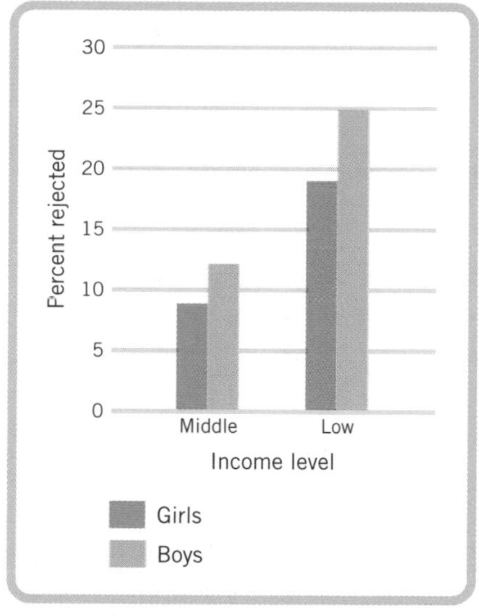

FIGURE 13.7 Percentages of children rejected by peers as a function of gender and family income As can be seen in these data from a longitudinal study, elementary school children from families with low incomes are considerably more likely to be rejected than are children from middle-class families. (Adapted from Patterson, Griesler, Vaden, & Kupersmidt, 1992)

review:

Although differences in children's social behavior likely are based in part on constitutional factors that influence temperament and personality, parents appear to influence children's competence with peers. Attachment theorists have suggested that a secure attachment between parent and child promotes peer competence because securely attached children develop positive social expectations, the foundation for understanding reciprocity in relationships, and a sense of self-worth and self-efficacy. In fact, securely attached children tend to be more positive in their behavior and affect, more socially skilled, and better liked than insecurely attached children. Ongoing parent–child interactions show similar associations with peer relations.

Parents can also influence their children's competence with peers through their beliefs, their role as gatekeepers, and the social behaviors they teach and model for their children. It is probable that the causal links between quality of parenting and children's social competence are bidirectional and that both environmental (e.g., parenting, divorce, poverty) and biological factors play a role in the development of children's social competence with peers.

Chapter Summary

What Is Special About Peer Relationships?

- Theorists such as Piaget, Vygotsky, and Sullivan have argued that the equality, reciprocity, cooperation, and intimacy that characterize many peer relationships enhance children's ability to reason and their concern for others.

Friendships

- Consistent with theorists' arguments, peers, especially friends, provide intimacy, support, and rich opportunities for the development of play and for exchange of ideas.
- Even very young children prefer some children over others. Toddlers engage in more complex and cooperative play with friends than with nonfriends, and those who engage in such play exhibit more positive and social behavior with peers when they are older.
- As children grow, friends rely on each other and increasingly provide a context for self-disclosure and intimacy. Adolescent friends, more than younger friends, use friendship as a context for self-exploration and personal problem solving, and as a source of honest feedback.
- Children's conceptions of friends change with age. Young children define friendship primarily on the basis of actual activities with their peers. With age, issues such as loyalty, mutual understanding, trust, cooperative reciprocity, and self-disclosure become important components of friendship.
- As was suggested by Piaget, Vygotsky, and Sullivan, friends provide emotional support; validation or confirmation of the legitimacy of one's own thoughts, feelings, and worth; and opportunities for the development of important social and cognitive skills.
- Having friends is associated with positive developmental outcomes, such as social competence and adjustment. However, friends also may have negative effects on children if they engage in problematic behaviors such as violence or substance abuse.
- Intervention programs can be helpful in teaching children social skills. One common approach, social skills training, involves teaching children skills related to three types of deficits: lack of social knowledge, problems in performing appropriate behaviors, and a lack of appropriate monitoring and self-evaluation.
- Children tend to become friends with peers who are similar in age, sex, and race, and who are similar in behaviors such as aggression, sociability, and cooperativeness.
- The degree to which adults encourage children to play with unrelated peers varies greatly in different cultures, as does the degree to which parents expect their children to develop social skills with peers (e.g., negotiating, taking initiative, standing up for their rights).

Peers in Groups

- The size of very young children's playgroups increases with age, and dominance hierarchies emerge by preschool age.
- By middle childhood, most children belong to cliques of same-sex peers, and members of cliques often are similar in their aggressiveness and orientation toward school. Membership in these cliques is not very stable over time.
- In adolescence, the importance of cliques tends to diminish, and adolescents tend to belong to more than one group. With increasing age, adolescents are not only more autonomous, but also tend to look more to individual relationships rather than to a social group to fulfill their social needs. Nonetheless, adolescents often are members of crowds. In adolescence, girls and boys associate with one another more with increasing age, both as members of social groups and in dyadic relationships.
- In some circumstances, the peer group may contribute to the development of antisocial behavior, alcohol consumption, and substance use.

Status in the Peer Group

- On the basis of their sociometric ratings, children typically have been classified as popular, rejected, neglected, average, or controversial.
- Children's status in the larger peer group varies as a function of their social behavior and thinking about their social interactions, as well as their physical attractiveness.
- Popular children tend to be socially skilled, prosocial, and well regulated in their expression of emotion and behavior.
- Children who are rejected by their peers often (but not always) are aggressive and/or socially withdrawn. Rejected-aggressive children are low in social skills, tend to make hostile attributions about others' intentions, and have difficulty coming up with constructive strategies for dealing with difficult social situations. Withdrawn children who are rejected during preschool tend to be aggressive and hostile. In contrast, children who are withdrawn from their peers but are not hostile or aggressive are at less risk for rejection during the early school years, although they tend to become rejected later in elementary school.
- Neglected children—those who are not nominated by peers as either liked or disliked—tend to be less sociable, aggressive, and disruptive than average children. They display relatively few behaviors that differ greatly from those of many other children.
- Controversial children tend to have characteristics of both popular and rejected children: they tend to be aggressive, disruptive, and prone to anger, as well as helpful, cooperative, sociable, good at sports, and humorous.

- Although children's status with their peers frequently changes over time, those children who are rejected frequently remain rejected. Children who are neglected or controversial are particularly likely to change their status, even over short periods of time.
- The major predictors of popularity do not seem to change substantially with age. Overt aggression appears to play a less important role in peer rejection in adolescence than at younger ages. Withdrawn behavior seems to become a more important predictor of peer rejection with increasing age in childhood.
- In general, in numerous cultures, children who are popular or rejected share similar characteristics. However, reticent behavior is valued in some East Asian cultures, and Chinese children who are sensitive and shy in their behavior are viewed as socially competent by teachers and peers.
- Rejection by peers in childhood—especially rejection due to aggression—predicts subsequent academic problems, delinquency, substance abuse, social withdrawal, and loneliness and depression. Children who are consistently withdrawn, reticent, and wary with familiar people, including peers, are more likely than less withdrawn children to experience internalizing problems such as depression, low self-worth, and loneliness concurrently and at older ages. It is likely that children's maladaptive behavior and their peer status both play a causal role in their future adjustment—separately and in combination.

The Role of Parents in Children's Peer Relationships

- Consistent with the predictions of attachment theorists, securely attached children tend to be more positive in their behavior and affect, more socially skilled, and better liked than insecurely attached children.
- Parents of socially competent and popular children are more likely than parents of less competent children to use warm control, positive verbalizations, reasoning, and explanations in interactions with their children, and hold more positive beliefs about their children's abilities. It is likely that the causal links between quality of parenting and children's social competence are bidirectional and that both environmental and biological factors play a role in the development of children's social competence with peers.
- Parents are the gatekeepers of young children's peer interactions in the sense that they organize and control their children's social experiences.
- Parents explicitly teach and model behaviors that children can adopt in their social interactions with peers—such as methods of influencing others and dealing with conflicts.
- Stressors such as poverty appear to have a negative effect on the quality of parenting, which in turn is linked to low peer competence in children.

Critical Thinking Questions

1. What are some of the ways in which same-aged peer relationships and relationships with older or younger siblings might differ? On what dimensions are they typically the same? What might Piaget and Vygotsky say about the different costs and benefits of interactions with same-aged friends and differently aged siblings?
2. What procedures and methods might someone use to assess which 2-year-old playmates in a group are close friends? How would these methods be the same or different if one were assessing close friendships at ages 6, 11, and 17?
3. List at least five ways in which interactions among boys and among girls in elementary school likely differ (e.g., type of activities, style of interaction). In what ways might such differences, if they exist, influence children's socioemotional development?
4. Consider a child who is growing up in an isolated area with few peers nearby and being schooled at home. In what ways might his or her daily experience differ from that of children attending school? How might this affect his or her development, positively or negatively? What factors might mitigate or increase these effects?

Key Terms

peers, p. 496
friendships, p. 497
reciprocated best friendship, p. 502
cliques, p. 509
crowds, p. 510
gangs, p. 511
sociometric status, p. 512
popular peer status, p. 513
rejected peer status, p. 514
aggressive-rejected children, p. 514
relational aggression, p. 514
withdrawn-rejected children, p. 515
social skills training, p. 516
neglected peer status, p. 517
controversial peer status, p. 517
victimized peer status, p. 522

CHAPTER 14

Moral Development

ANDREW MACARA, *Cricket, Sri Lanka,* 1998

THEMES

- Nature and Nurture
- The Active Child
- Continuity/Discontinuity
- Mechanisms of Change
- The Sociocultural Context
- Individual Differences
- Research and Children's Welfare

In April 1999, Eric Harris and Dylan Klebold, two students at Columbine High School in Littleton, Colorado, killed a dozen students and a teacher and injured twenty-three other persons. As terrible as this incident was, it could have been much worse. The two adolescents, who had planned the massacre carefully for months, had actually prepared ninety-five explosive devices, which did not go off due to an electronic failure. One set of explosives was placed a few miles from school and was supposed to explode to distract the police while Harris and Klebold carried out the attack at the school. The second set was supposed to go off in the cafeteria, killing many students and forcing others to flee into the schoolyard, where Harris and Klebold were to hide in wait and gun them down. The third set of explosives was planted in the killers' cars in the school parking lot. It was timed to explode after the police and paramedics arrived on the scene, causing more death and chaos. In videotapes made weeks before the attacks, the boys gleefully predicted that they would kill 250 people and bragged about the publicity they would get for their actions. They also made it clear that their attack was payback for having been humiliated and rejected by their peers: on one videotape, Harris, holding a sawed-off shotgun, declared, "Isn't it fun finally to get the respect that we are going to deserve?" (quoted in Aronson, 2000, p. 86).

One might think that Harris and Klebold had suffered terrible childhoods. Yet, from all reports, their parents were probably more supportive than the average. And although they did endure considerable peer rejection at Columbine, before Harris moved to Littleton, he was a fairly popular student in his school in Plattsburgh, New York. Explanations for why Harris and Klebold did what they did are not as simple as it might initially seem.

In striking contrast to the lethally self-centered actions of Harris and Klebold, in the midst of the carnage, some students stayed with and tried to assist a teacher and other students who were shot. One boy running for his life helped a badly wounded girl get to an exit. Another boy draped himself over his sister and her friend so that he would be the one to be shot (Gibbs, 1999). These students were concerned with others' lives even when their own were at risk.

The Columbine tragedy, and subsequent incidents like it, are the latest additions to a long list of incidents that raise questions about why some adolescents become involved in antisocial and illegal behavior, ranging from vandalism and other forms of delinquency to horrific violent crime. The starting point for finding

GARY CASKEY / REUTERS NEW MEDIA INC. / CORBIS

Although many contributing factors to the Columbine tragedy have been identified, the precise reasons for the actions of Harris and Klebold may never be known. As you will discover in this chapter, moral development—and whether an individual is inclined to prosocial or aggressive, antisocial behavior—depends on the interaction of a great many variables.

answers to these questions is understanding aspects of children's thinking and behavior that contribute to morality.

To act in moral ways on a regular basis, children must have an understanding of right and wrong and the reasons that actions are moral or immoral. In addition, they must have a conscience, that is, they must be concerned about acting in a moral manner and feel guilty when they don't. When studying moral development, researchers have focused on a number of different questions related to these requirements. How do children think about moral issues and how does this thinking change with age? Does children's reasoning about moral issues relate to their behavior? How early do caring and sharing, or aggression and cruelty, first appear in children? What factors contribute to differences among children in the degree to which they display helpful and caring behaviors, aggression, and a sense of conscience? Can steps be taken to help children develop caring and helpful behavior and to reduce the likelihood of their developing immoral or antisocial behaviors?

We start our discussion of moral development by examining children's moral judgment—that is, how children think about situations involving moral decisions. Then we examine findings on the early emergence of conscience and the development of *prosocial* behaviors—behaviors such as helping and sharing that benefit others. Next, we turn to aggression and other antisocial behaviors such as stealing. As you will see, children's moral development is influenced by advances in their social and cognitive capacities, as well as by genetic factors and environmental factors, including family and cultural influences. Therefore, the themes of *individual differences, nature and nurture,* and the *sociocultural context* will be prominent. In addition, theory and research on moral judgment grew out of Piaget's work in this area, which, like his theory on cognitive development (see Chapter 4), involves stages of development and assumes that children actively try to understand the world around them. Consequently, the themes of *continuity/discontinuity, mechanisms of change,* and *the active child* are evident in our consideration of the development of moral judgment.

Moral Judgment

The morality of a given action cannot be determined at face value. Consider a girl who steals food to feed her starving sister. Stealing usually is regarded to be an antisocial behavior, but obviously the morality of this girl's behavior is not so clear. Or consider an adolescent male who offers to help a peer fix his bike but does so because he wants to know the location of the bike in order to steal it later. Although this adolescent's behavior may appear altruistic, clearly it is not. These examples illustrate that the morality of a behavior is based partly on the cognitions—including conscious intentions and goals—that underlie the behavior.

Indeed, some psychologists (as well as philosophers and educators) believe that the reasoning behind a behavior is critical for determining whether a given behavior is moral or immoral and that changes in moral reasoning form the basis of moral development. As a consequence, much of the research on children's moral development has focused on how children resolve moral conflicts and how their reasoning about moral issues changes with age. The most important contributors to the current understanding of the development of children's moral reasoning are Piaget and Lawrence Kohlberg, both of whom took a cognitive developmental approach to studying the development of morality.

TONY FREEMAN / PHOTOEDIT

Piaget (1932/1965) argued that in games such as marbles, children learn that rules are a creation of human beings—that they are not absolute but are interpreted, and can be changed, by the consensus of the peer group.

Piaget's Theory of Moral Judgment

The foundation of cognitive theories about the origin of morality is Piaget's work *The Moral Judgment of the Child* (1932/1965). In this book, Piaget described how children's moral reasoning changes from a rigid acceptance of the dictates and rules of authorities to an appreciation that moral rules are a product of social interaction and hence are modifiable. Piaget believed that interactions with peers, more than adult influence, account for advances in children's moral reasoning.

Piaget initially studied children's moral reasoning by observing them playing games, such as marbles, in which they often deal with issues related to rules and fairness. In addition, Piaget conducted open-ended interviews with children to examine their thinking about issues such as transgressions of rules, the role of intentionality in morality, fairness of punishment, and justice when distributing goods among people. In these interviews, he typically presented them with pairs of short vignettes such as the following:

> A little boy who is called John is in his room. He is called to dinner. He goes into the dining room. But behind the door there was a chair, and on the chair there was a tray with fifteen cups on it. John couldn't have known that there was all this behind the door. He goes in, the door knocks against the tray, bang go the fifteen cups, and they all get broken!
>
> Once there was a little boy whose name was Henry. One day when his mother was out he tried to get some jam out of the cupboard. He climbed up on to a chair and stretched out his arm. But the jam was too high up and he couldn't reach it and have any. But while he was trying to get it he knocked over a cup. The cup fell down and broke.
>
> (Piaget, 1932/1965, p. 122)

After children heard these stories, they were asked which boy was naughtier and why. Children younger than 6 years old typically said that the child who broke fifteen cups was naughtier. In contrast, older children believed that the child who was trying to sneak jam was naughtier, even though he broke only one cup. Based partly on children's responses to such vignettes, Piaget concluded that there are two stages of development in children's moral reasoning, as well as a transitional period between the stages.

The Stage of the Morality of Constraint

The first stage of moral reasoning, referred to as the *morality of constraint,* is most characteristic of children who have not achieved the cognitive stage of concrete operations—that is, children younger than 7 or 8 years old (see Chapter 4). Children in this stage regard rules and duties to others as unchangeable "givens." In their view, justice is whatever authorities (adults, rules, or laws) say is right, and authorities' punishments are always justified. Acts that are not consistent with rules and authorities' dictates are "bad"; acts that are consistent with them are "good." It is in this stage that children believe that what determines whether an action is good or bad is the consequences of the action, not the motives or intentions behind it.

Piaget suggested that young children's belief that rules are unchangeable is due to two factors, one social and one cognitive. First, Piaget argued that parental control of children is coercive and unilateral, leading to children's unquestioning respect for adults and for their rules. Second, children's cognitive immaturity causes them to believe that rules are "real" things, like chairs or gravity, that exist outside people and are not the product of the human mind.

The Transitional Period

According to Piaget, the period from about age 7 or 8 to age 10 represents a transition from the morality of constraint to the next stage. During this transitional period, children typically interact more with peers than previously, and these interactions are more egalitarian and involve more give-and-take than their interactions with adults. In games with peers, children learn that rules can be constructed and changed by the group. They also increasingly learn to take one another's perspective and to cooperate. As a consequence, children start to value fairness and equality and begin to become more autonomous in their thinking about moral issues. Piaget viewed children as taking an active role in this transition, using information from their social interactions to figure out how moral decisions are made and how rules are constructed.

The Stage of Autonomous Morality

By about age 11 or 12, Piaget's second stage of moral reasoning emerges. In this stage, referred to as the stage of *autonomous morality* (also called *moral relativism*), children no longer accept blind obedience to authority as the basis of moral decisions. They fully understand that rules are the product of social interaction and agreement and can be changed if the majority of a group agrees to do so. In addition, they consider fairness and equality among people as important factors to consider when constructing rules. Children at this stage also believe that punishments should "fit the crime" and that punishment delivered by adults is not necessarily fair. They also consider individuals' motives and intentions when evaluating their behavior; thus, they view breaking one cup while sneaking jam as worse than accidentally breaking fifteen cups.

According to Piaget, all normal children progress from the morality of constraint to autonomous moral reasoning. Individual differences in the rate of their progress are due to numerous factors, including differences in children's cognitive maturity, in their opportunities for interactions with peers and for reciprocal role taking, and in how authoritarian and punitive their parents are.

Evaluation of Piaget's Theory

Piaget's general vision of moral development has been supported by empirical research. Studies of children from many countries and various racial or ethnic groups have shown that with age, boys and girls increasingly take motives and intentions into account when judging the morality of actions (Berg & Mussen, 1975; Lickona, 1976). In addition, parental punitiveness, which would be expected to reinforce a morality of constraints, has been associated with less mature moral reasoning and moral behavior (Hoffman, 1983). Consistent with Piaget's belief that cognition plays a role in the development of moral judgment, children's performance on tests of perspective-taking skills, Piagetian logical tasks, and IQ tests have all been associated with their level of moral judgment (Berg & Mussen, 1975; Lickona, 1976).

Some aspects of Piaget's theory, however, have been soundly criticized and have not held up well to scrutiny. For example, there is little evidence that peer interaction per se stimulates moral development (Lickona, 1976), and it seems likely that the quality of peer interactions—for example, whether or not they involve cooperative interactions—is more important than mere quantity of interaction with peers. In addition, Piaget underestimated young children's ability to appreciate the role of intentionality in morality. When Piagetian moral vignettes are presented in ways that make the individuals' intentions more obvious—such as by using videotaped dramas—preschoolers and early elementary school children recognize that individuals with bad intentions are naughtier than those with benign intentions (Chandler, Greenspan, & Barenboim, 1973; Grueneich, 1982; Yuill & Perner, 1988). (It is likely that in Piaget's research, young children focused primarily on the consequences of the individuals' actions because consequences were emphasized and very salient in his stories.) Moreover, as you will see later in the chapter, it is clear that young children do not believe that some actions, such as hurting others, are right even when adults say they are.

Piaget's theory and stage approach provided the basis for more recent thinking and research on the development of moral judgment. The most notable example is the more complex and differentiated theory of moral development formulated by Lawrence Kohlberg.

Kohlberg's Theory of Moral Judgment

LEE LOCKWOOD / TIMEPIX

Kohlberg, like Piaget, argued that stages of moral reasoning involve a qualitative change in reasoning and that each stage represents a new way of thinking that replaces the child's thinking at prior, lower levels.

Because his thinking was heavily influenced by the ideas of Piaget, Kohlberg (1976; Colby & Kohlberg, 1987a) was primarily interested in the sequences through which children's moral reasoning develops. On the basis of a longitudinal study in which he assessed the moral reasoning of children of various ages, Kohlberg proposed that moral development proceeds through a specific series of stages that are discontinuous and hierarchical. That is, each new stage reflects a qualitatively different, more adequate way of thinking than the one before it (see Table 14.1).

Kohlberg assessed moral judgment by presenting children with hypothetical moral dilemmas and then questioning them about the issues these dilemmas involved. The most famous dilemma is about Heinz, whose wife was dying from a special kind of cancer. A drug that might save her had been discovered by a local pharmacist, but he was charging ten times what the drug cost him to make, far more money than Heinz had. Heinz

> went to everyone he knew to borrow the money but he could only get together about . . . half of what it [the drug] cost. He told the druggist his wife was dying, and asked him to sell it cheaper or let him pay later. But the druggist said, "No, I discovered the drug and I'm going to make money from it." So Heinz got desperate and broke into the man's store to steal the drug for his wife.

After relating this dilemma to children, Kohlberg asked them questions such as: Should Heinz have done that? Was it actually wrong or right? Why? Is it a husband's duty to steal the drug for his wife if he can get it no other way? For Kohlberg, the reasoning behind children's decisions, rather than their choice of what to do in the dilemma, is what reflects the quality of their moral reasoning. For example, the response that "Heinz should steal the drug because he probably won't get caught and put in jail" was considered less advanced than "Heinz should steal the drug because he wants his wife to feel better and to live."

TABLE 14.1

Kohlberg's Levels and Stages of Moral Reasoning

Preconventional Level

Stage 1: Punishment and Obedience Orientation. At Stage 1, what is seen as right is obedience to authorities. Children's "conscience" (what makes them decide what is right or wrong) is fear of punishment, and their moral action is motivated by avoidance of punishment. The child does not consider the interests of others or recognize that they differ from his or her own interests. Examples of reasoning for (pro) and against (con) Heinz's stealing the drug for his wife are as follows:

Pro: If you let your wife die, you will get in trouble. You'll be blamed for not spending the money to save her and there'll be an investigation of you and the druggist for your wife's death.

Con: You shouldn't steal the drug because you'll be caught and sent to jail if you do. If you do get away, your conscience would bother you thinking how the police would catch up with you at any minute (Kohlberg, 1969, p. 381).

Stage 2: Instrumental and Exchange Orientation. At Stage 2, what is right is what is in one's own best interest or involves equal exchange between people (tit-for-tat exchange of benefits).

Pro: If you do happen to get caught you could give the drug back and you wouldn't get much of a sentence. It wouldn't bother you much to serve a little jail term, if you have your wife when you get out.

Con: He may not get much of a jail term if he steals the drug, but his wife will probably die before he gets out so it won't do him much good. If his wife dies, he shouldn't blame himself, it wasn't his fault she has cancer (Kohlberg, 1969, p. 381).

Conventional Level

Stage 3: Mutual Interpersonal Expectations, Relationships, and Interpersonal Conformity ("Good Girl, Nice Boy") Orientation. In Stage 3, good behavior is doing what is expected by people who are close to the person or what people generally expect of someone in a given role (e.g., "a son"). Being "good" is important in itself and means having good motives, showing concern about others, and maintaining good relationships with others.

Pro: No one will think you're bad if you steal the drug, but your family will think you're an inhuman husband if you don't. If you let your wife die, you'll never be able to look anybody in the face again.

Con: It isn't just the druggist who will think you're a criminal, everyone else will too. After you steal it, you'll feel bad thinking how you've brought dishonor on your family and yourself; you won't be able to face anyone again (Kohlberg, 1969, p. 381).

Stage 4: Social System and Conscience ("Law and Order") Orientation. Right behavior in Stage 4 involves fulfilling one's duties, upholding laws, and contributing to society or one's group. The individual is motivated to keep the social system going and to avoid a breakdown in its functioning.

Pro: In most marriages, you accept the responsibility to look after one another's health and after their life and you have the responsibility when you live with someone to try and make it a happy life (Colby & Kohlberg, 1987b, p. 43).

In the revised coding manual, Colby and Kohlberg (1987b) provide virtually no examples of Stage 4 reasoning supporting the decision that Heinz should not steal the drug for his wife. However, they provide reasons for not stealing the drug for a pet: Heinz should not steal for a pet because animals cannot contribute to society (p. 37).

Postconventional or Principled Level

Stage 5: Social Contract or Individual Rights Orientation. At Stage 5, right behavior involves upholding rules that are in the best interest of the group ("the greatest good for the greatest number"), are impartial, or were agreed upon by the group. However, some values and rights, such as life and liberty, are universally right and must be upheld in any society, regardless of majority opinion. It is difficult to construct a Stage 5 reason that justifies not stealing the drug.

Pro: Heinz should steal the drug because the right to life supersedes or transcends the right to property (Colby & Kohlberg, 1987b, p. 11).

Pro: Heinz is working from a hierarchy of values, in which life (at least the life of his wife) is higher than honesty. . . . Human life and its preservation—at last as presented here—must take precedence over other values, like Heinz's desire to be honest and law abiding, or the druggist's love of money and his rights. All values stem from the ultimate value of life (Colby & Kohlberg, 1987b, p. 54).

Stage 6: Universal Ethical Principles. Right behavior in Stage 6 is commitment to self-chosen ethical principles that reflect universal principles of justice (e.g., equality of human rights, respect for the dignity of each human being). When laws violate these principles, the individual should act in accordance with these universal principles rather than the law.

Kohlberg's Stages

On the basis of the reasoning underlying children's responses, Kohlberg proposed three levels of moral judgment—preconventional, conventional, and postconventional, or principled. Preconventional moral reasoning is self-centered: it focuses on getting rewards and avoiding punishment. Conventional moral reasoning is centered on social relationships: it focuses on compliance with social duties and laws. Postconventional moral reasoning is centered on ideals: it focuses on moral principles. Each of these three levels involves two stages of moral judgment (see Table 14.1, p.537). However, so few people ever attained Stage 6 (Universal Ethical Principles) that Kohlberg (1978) eventually stopped scoring it as a separate stage, and many theorists consider it an elaboration of Stage 5.

Kohlberg argued that people in all parts of the world move through his stages in the same order, although they differ in how far they progress through the stages. As in Piaget's theory, age-related advances in cognitive skills, especially perspective taking, are believed to underlie the development of higher-level moral judgment. Consistent with Kohlberg's theory, people who have higher-level cognitive skills and are better educated exhibit higher-level moral judgment (Colby, Kohlberg, Gibbs, & Lieberman, 1983; Mason & Gibbs, 1993; Rest, 1983; Walker, 1980). Children who exhibit higher levels of perspective taking than their peers also score higher in their moral judgment.

BILL E. BARNES / PHOTOEDIT

Delinquents tend to use lower-level reasoning than do nondelinquents (Nelson, Smith, & Dodd, 1990). For example, they tend to justify their choice of action in moral conflicts with reasoning based on punishment for "getting caught" or self-gain.

In their initial research, Kohlberg and his colleagues (Colby et al., 1983) studied only boys, whom they followed into adulthood. As shown in Figure 14.1, moral judgment changed systematically with age. When the boys were 10 years old, they used primarily Stage 1 reasoning (blind obedience to authority) and Stage 2 reasoning (self-interest). Thereafter, reasoning in these stages dropped off markedly. For most adolescents aged 14 and older, Stage 3 reasoning (being "good" to earn approval or maintain relationships) was the primary mode of reasoning, although some adolescents occasionally used Stage 4 reasoning (fulfilling duties and upholding laws to maintain social order). Only a small number of participants, even by age 36, ever achieved Stage 5 (upholding the best interests of the group while recognizing life and liberty as universal values).

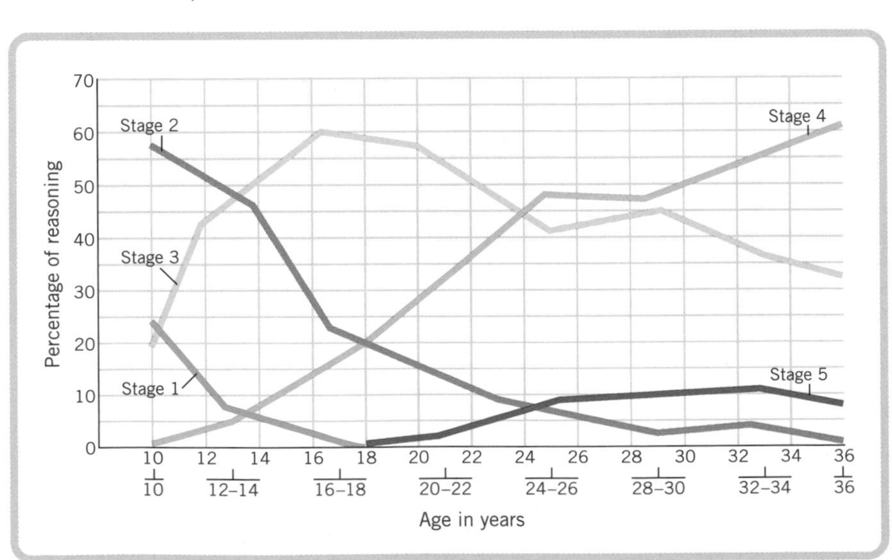

FIGURE 14.1 Mean percentage of moral reasoning at each stage for each age group This graph shows age trends in moral reasoning in Kohlberg's longitudinal sample.

There appears to be a modest degree of association between the level of moral reasoning used by people and how moral their behavior is. For example, people with higher-level moral reasoning are more likely to assist others (Blasi, 1980), are less likely to engage in delinquent activities (Jurkovic, 1980; Lee & Prentice, 1988; Palmer & Hollin, 1998), and more likely to behave in a moral manner (Kohlberg & Candee, 1984).

Critique of Kohlberg's Theory

Kohlberg's work is very important because it demonstrated that there are relatively systematic changes with age in children's moral judgment. In addition, because individuals' levels of moral judgment have been related to their moral behavior, especially for people reasoning at higher levels (e.g., Kutnick, 1985; Underwood & Moore, 1982), Kohlberg's thinking has been useful in understanding how cognitive processes contribute to moral behavior. Prior to Kohlberg, morality was a domain of behavior that many believed to be shaped primarily by social and emotional factors, rather than by a combination of cognitive, social, and emotional development.

Kohlberg's theory and findings also produced a flurry of controversy and criticism. One controversial issue pertains to cultural differences. Although children in many non-Western, nonindustrialized cultures start out reasoning much the way Western children do in Kohlberg's scoring system, their moral judgment generally does not advance as far as that of their Western peers (e.g., Kohlberg, 1969; Nisan & Kohlberg, 1982; Snarey, 1985). This finding has led to the criticism that Kohlberg's stories and scoring system reflect a biased, intellectualized Western conception of morality that is not applicable to non-Western societies (Simpson, 1974). In societies in which most conflicts of interest are worked out through face-to-face contact and in which the goal of preserving group harmony is of critical importance, issues of individual rights and civil liberties may not be viewed as especially relevant. Moreover, in some societies, obedience to authorities, elders, and religious dictates are valued more than principles of freedom and individual rights.

Another criticism has to do with Kohlberg's argument that change in moral development is discontinuous. Kohlberg asserted that because each stage is more advanced than the previous one, once individuals attain a new stage, they seldom use characteristics of a lower stage. However, research has shown that children and adults often use both higher and lower stages at the same time. Thus, their reasoning does not go through an orderly, upward progression without regression to lower stages of reasoning (Rest, 1979). As a consequence, it is not clear that the development of moral reasoning is discontinuous (qualitative). Rather, children and adolescents may gradually acquire the cognitive skills to use increasingly higher stages of moral reasoning but also may use lower stages when it is consistent with their goals, motives, or beliefs in a particular situation. For example, even an adolescent who is capable of using Stage 4 reasoning may well use Stage 2 reasoning to justify a decision to break the law for personal gain.

The most hotly debated issue regarding Kohlberg's theory is whether there are sex differences in moral judgment. As noted previously, Kohlberg developed his stages on the basis of interviews with a sample of boys. Carol Gilligan (1977, 1982) argued that Kohlberg's classification of moral judgment is biased against females because it does not adequately recognize differences in the way males and females reason morally. Gilligan suggested that because of differences in their socialization, males tend to value principles of justice and rights, whereas females value caring, responsibility for others, and avoidance of exploiting or hurting others

(Gilligan & Attanucci, 1988). This difference in moral orientation, according to Gilligan, causes males to score higher on Kohlberg's dilemmas than females do.

Contrary to Gilligan's theory, there is little evidence that boys and girls, or men and women, score differently on Kohlberg's stages of moral judgment (Turiel, 1998; Walker, 1984, 1991). However, consistent with Gilligan's arguments, during adolescence and adulthood, females focus somewhat more on issues of caring about other people in their moral judgment (Garmon, Basinger, Gress, & Gibbs, 1996; Jaffee & Hyde, 2000; Wark & Krebs, 1996). Differences in males' and females' moral reasoning seem to be most evident when individuals report on moral dilemmas in their own lives (Jaffee & Hyde, 2000). Thus, Gilligan's work has been very important in broadening the focus of research on moral reasoning and in demonstrating that males and females differ somewhat in the issues they focus upon when confronting moral issues.

Although Kohlberg's stages probably are not as invariant in sequence nor as universal as he claimed, they do describe changes in children's moral reasoning that are observed in many Western societies. These changes are important because people who reason at higher stages are somewhat more likely to behave in moral ways—such as helping others. Thus, understanding developmental changes in moral judgment provides insight into why, as children grow older, they tend to engage in more prosocial behavior.

Prosocial Moral Judgment

When children respond to Kohlberg's dilemmas, they must choose between two acts that are wrong, for example, stealing or allowing someone to die. However, there are other types of moral dilemmas in which the choice is between personal advantage or convenience and fairness to, or the welfare of, others (Damon, 1977; Eisenberg, 1986; Eisenberg, Carlo, Murphy, & Van Court, 1995; Skoe, 1998).

To determine how children resolve these dilemmas, researchers present children with stories in which the characters must choose between helping someone or meeting their own needs. These dilemmas are called *prosocial* moral dilemmas; they concern **prosocial behavior**—that is, voluntary behavior intended to benefit another, such as helping, sharing, and comforting of others. The following story illustrates the type of dilemma that has been used with children age 4 and older:

> One day a boy named Eric was going to a friend's birthday party. On his way he saw a boy who had fallen down and hurt his leg. The boy asked Eric to go to his house and get his parents so the parents could come and take him to a doctor. But if Eric did run and get the child's parents, he would be late to the birthday party and miss the ice cream, cake and all the games.
>
> What should Eric do? Why?
>
> (Eisenberg-Berg & Hand, 1979, p. 358)

On these tests, children and adolescents use five stages of prosocial moral reasoning, delineated by Eisenberg (1986), that resemble Kohlberg's stages (see Table 14.2). Preschool children express primarily hedonistic reasoning (Level 1) in which their own needs are central. They typically indicate that Eric should go to the party because he wants to. However, preschoolers also often mention others' physical needs, which suggests that some preschoolers are concerned about other people's welfare (Level 2). (For example, they may indicate that Eric should help because the other boy is bleeding or hurt.) Such labeling of others' needs increases in the elementary school years. In addition, in elementary school, children increasingly express concern about social approval and acting in a manner that is viewed

prosocial behavior voluntary behavior intended to benefit another, such as helping, sharing, and comforting of others

TABLE 14.2

Levels of Prosocial Behavior

Level 1: Hedonistic, self-focused orientation. The individual is concerned with his or her own interests rather than with moral considerations. Reasons for assisting or not assisting another include direct personal gain, future reciprocation, and concern for the other based on need or affection. (Predominant mode primarily for preschoolers and younger elementary school children.)

Level 2: Needs-based orientation. The individual expresses concern for the physical, material, and psychological needs of others even when those needs conflict with his or her own. This concern is expressed in the simplest terms, without clear evidence of self-reflective role taking, verbal expressions of sympathy, or reference to such emotions as pride or guilt. (Predominant mode for many preschoolers and many elementary school children.)

Level 3: Approval and/or stereotyped orientation. The individual justifies engaging or not engaging in prosocial behavior on the basis of others' approval or acceptance and/or on stereotyped images of good and bad persons and behavior. (Predominant mode for some elementary school and high school students.)

Level 4a: Self-reflective empathic orientation. The individual's judgments include evidence of self-reflective sympathetic responding or role taking, concern with the other's humanness, and/or guilt or positive emotion related to the consequences of one's actions. (Predominant mode for a few older elementary school children and many high school students.)

Level 4b: Transitional level: The individual's justifications for helping or not helping involve internalized values, norms, duties, or responsibilities. They may also reflect concerns for the condition of the larger society or refer to the necessity of protecting the rights and dignities of other persons. These ideals, however, are not clearly or strongly stated. (Predominant mode for a minority of people of high school age or older.)

Level 5: Strongly internalized stage: The individual's justifications for helping or not helping are based on internalized values, norms, or responsibilities; the desire to maintain individual and societal contractual obligations or improve the condition of society; and the belief in the rights, dignity, and equality of all individuals. This level is also characterized by positive or negative emotions related to whether or not one succeeds in living up to one's own values and accepted norms. (Predominant mode for only a small minority of high school students.)

Adapted from Eisenberg (1986)

as "good" or "nice" by other people and society (e.g., they indicate that Eric should help "to be nice"; Level 3). In late childhood and adolescence, children's judgments begin to be based, in varying degrees, on (Level 4a) perspective taking (e.g., "Eric should think about how he would feel in that situation") and morally relevant affect such as sympathy, guilt, and positive feelings due to the real or imagined consequences of performing beneficial actions (e.g., "Eric would feel bad if he didn't help and the boy was in pain"). The judgments of a minority of older adolescents reflect (Levels 4b and 5) internalized values and affect related to not living up to those values (e.g., self-censure).

This pattern of changes in prosocial moral reasoning has been found for children in Brazil, Germany, Israel, and Japan (Carlo, Koller, Eisenberg, Da Silva, & Frohlich, 1996; Eisenberg, Boehnke, Schuhler, & Silbereisen, 1985; Fuchs, Eisenberg, Hertz-Lazarowitz, & Sharabang, 1986; Munekata & Ninomiya, 1985). However, children from different cultures do vary somewhat in their prosocial moral reasoning. For example, older children (and adults) in some traditional societies in Papua New Guinea exhibit higher-level reasoning less often than do people in Western cultures. However, the types of reasoning they frequently use—reasoning that pertains to others' needs and the relationship between people—are consistent with the values of a culture in which people must cooperate with one another in face-to-face interactions in order to survive (Tietjen, 1986). In nearly all cultures, reasoning that reflects the needs of others and global concepts of good and bad behavior (Kohlberg's Stage 3 and Eisenberg's Level 3) emerges at somewhat younger ages on prosocial dilemmas than on Kohlberg's moral dilemmas.

With age, children's prosocial moral judgment, like their reasoning on Kohlberg's moral dilemmas, becomes more abstract and based more on internalized principles and values (Eisenberg, 1986; Eisenberg et al., 1995; Eisenberg, Miller, Shell, McNalley, & Shea, 1991). Moreover, paralleling the case with moral reasoning on

In response to the story about a child on the way to a party who sees an injured boy, a typical response of many 9- or 10-year-olds is, "Help because the boy's leg is hurt and he needs to go to a doctor."

MICHAEL NEWMAN / PHOTOEDIT

Kohlberg's measure, children using higher-level prosocial moral reasoning tend to be more sympathetic and prosocial in their behavior than children who use lower-level prosocial moral judgment (Eisenberg, 1986; Eisenberg et al., 1991; Janssens & Dekovic, 1997).

Domains of Social Judgment

In everyday life, children make decisions about many kinds of actions, including whether to follow rules and laws or break them, whether to fight or walk away from conflict, whether to dress formally or informally, whether to study or goof off after school, and so on. Some of these decisions involve moral judgments; others involve social conventional judgments; still others involve personal judgments (Nucci, 1981; Turiel, 1978, 1998).

Moral judgments pertain to issues of right and wrong, fairness, and justice. **Social conventional judgments** pertain to customs or regulations intended to ensure social coordination and social organization, such as choices about modes of dress, table manners, and forms of greeting (e.g., using "Sir" when addressing a male teacher). **Personal judgments** refer to actions in which individual preferences are the main consideration. For example, within Western culture, the choice of friends or recreational activities usually is considered a personal choice (Nucci & Weber, 1995; Turiel, 1998). Whether children perceive particular judgments as moral, social conventional, or personal affects the importance they accord them.

Children's Use of Social Judgment

In many cultures, children begin to differentiate between moral and social conventional issues at an early age (Miller & Bersoff, 1992; Nucci, Camino, & Sapiro, 1996; Tisak, 1995). By age 3, they generally believe that moral violations (e.g., stealing another child's possession or hitting another child) are more wrong than social conventional violations (e.g., not saying "please" when asking for something or a boy's wearing nail polish). By age 4, they believe that moral transgressions, but not social conventional transgressions, are wrong even if an adult does not know about them and even if adult authorities have not said they are wrong (Smetana & Braeges, 1990). This distinction is reflected in the following excerpt from an interview with a 5-year-old boy:

> *Interviewer:* This is a story about Park School. In Park School the children are allowed to hit and push others if they want. It's okay to hit and push others. Do you think it is all right for Park School to say children can hit and push others if they want to?
> *Boy:* No. It is not okay.
> *Interviewer:* Why not?
> *Boy:* Because that is like making other people unhappy. You can hurt them that way. It hurts other people, hurting is not good.

This boy is firm in his belief that hurting others is wrong, even if adults say it is acceptable. Compare that reasoning with the boy's response to a question about the acceptability of a school policy that allows children to take off their clothes in hot weather.

> *Interviewer:* I know another school in a different city. . . . Grove School. . . . At Grove School the children are allowed to take their clothes off if they want to. Is it okay or not okay for Grove School to say children can take their clothes off if they want to?

moral judgments decisions that pertain to issues of right and wrong, fairness, and justice

social conventional judgments decisions that pertain to customs or regulations intended to secure social coordination and social organization

personal judgments decisions that refer to actions in which individual preferences are the main consideration

Boy: Yes. Because this is the rule.
Interviewer: Why can they have that rule?
Boy: If that's what the boss wants to do, he can do that. . . . He is in charge of the school.

(Turiel, 1987, p. 101)

With regard to both moral and social conventional issues in the family, children—even adolescents—believe that parents have authority, although somewhat less authority over the latter (Smetana, 1988, 1995). With respect to matters of personal judgment, however, even preschoolers tend to believe that they themselves should have control, and older children and adolescents are quite firm in their belief that they should control choices in the personal domain (e.g., their appearance, how they spend their money, and their choice of friends) at home and school. Because parents often feel that they should have some authority over their children's personal choices, parents and adolescents frequently do battle in this domain—battles that parents often lose (Smetana, 1988; Smetana & Asquith, 1994).

Cultural and Socioeconomic Differences

People in different cultures sometimes vary in whether they view decisions as moral, social conventional, or personal (Shweder, Mahapatra, & Miller, 1987). Take the question of one's obligation to attend to the minor needs of parents or the moderate needs of friends or strangers. Hindu Indians view this question as one of clear moral obligation (Miller, Bersoff, & Harwood, 1990). In contrast, Americans appear to consider it a matter of personal choice or a combination of moral and personal choice. This difference in perceptions may be due to the strong cultural emphasis on individual rights in the United States and the emphasis on duties to others in India (Killen & Turiel, 1998; Miller & Bersoff, 1995).

Differences in religious beliefs can also underlie variation within and across cultures with regard to which events are considered moral, social conventional, or personal (Turiel, 1998; Wainryb & Turiel, 1995). For example, Hindus in India believe that if a widow eats fish, she has committed an immoral act. In Hindu society, fish is viewed as a "hot" food, and eating "hot" food is believed to stimulate the sexual appetite. Consequently, traditional Hindus assume that a widow who eats fish will behave immorally and offend her husband's spirit. Underlying this belief is the obligation that Hinduism places on a widow to seek salvation and be reunited with the soul of her husband rather than initiating another relationship (Shweder et al., 1987). Of course, for most other people in the world, a widow's eating fish would be considered a matter of personal choice. Thus, beliefs regarding the significance and consequences of various actions in different cultures can influence the designation of behaviors as moral, social conventional, or personal.

Socioeconomic class can also influence the degree to which children differentiate among moral, social conventional, and personal choices. Research in the United States and Brazil indicates that children of lower-income families are somewhat less likely than middle-class children to differentiate sharply between moral and social conventional actions. Moreover, prior to adolescence, children of lower socioeconomic status are less likely than middle-class children to view personal issues as a matter of choice. These differences may be due to the tendency of individuals of low socioeconomic status to both place a greater emphasis on submission to authority and to allow their children less autonomy (Nucci, 1997).

Children in India are much more likely than in the United States to say that helping other people is a moral obligation, not a matter of personal choice.

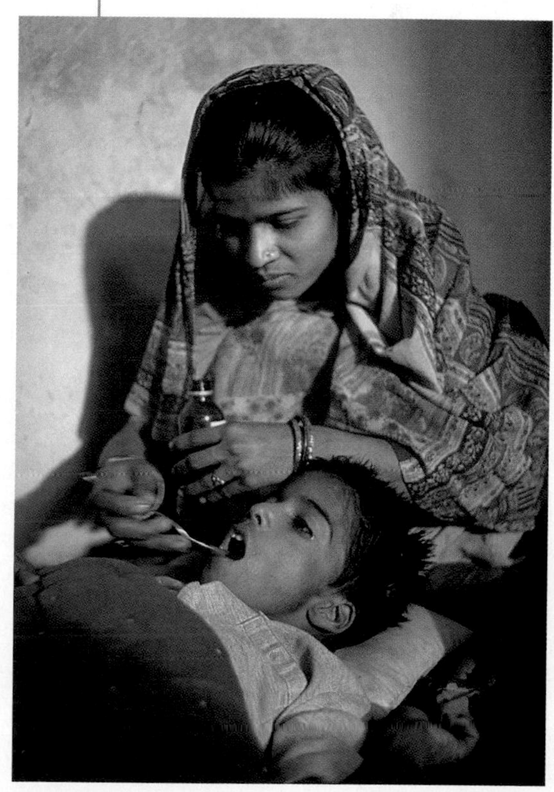

review:

How children think about moral issues provides one basis for their moral or immoral behavior. Piaget delineated two moral stages—morality of constraint and autonomous morality—separated by a transitional stage. In the first stage, children regard rules as fixed and tend to weigh consequences more than intentions in evaluating actions. According to Piaget, a combination of cognitive growth and egalitarian, cooperative interactions with peers brings children to the autonomous stage, in which they recognize that rules can be changed by group consent and judge the morality of actions on the basis of intentions more than consequences. Aspects of Piaget's theory have not held up well to criticism—for example, children use intentions to evaluate behavior at a younger age than he believed—but his theory provided the foundation for Kohlberg's work on stages of moral reasoning.

Kohlberg outlined three levels of moral judgment—preconventional, conventional, and postconventional—each initially containing two stages (Stage 6 was subsequently dropped). He hypothesized that his sequence of stages reflected discontinuous (qualitative) changes in moral reasoning with age and that children in all parts of the world go through the same stages (although they may stop development at different points). There is debate regarding whether children's moral reasoning moves through discontinuous stages of development; whether Kohlberg's approach is valid in all cultures; and whether there are gender differences in moral judgment. Research on other types of moral judgment such as prosocial moral judgment suggests that children's concerns about the needs of others emerge at a younger age than Kohlberg's work indicates. However, prosocial moral reasoning, like Kohlberg's justice-oriented moral reasoning, seems to become more abstract and based on internalized principles with age.

There are important differences among the moral, social conventional, and personal domains of behavior and judgment—differences that even children know. For example, young children believe that moral transgressions, but not social conventional or personal violations, are wrong regardless of whether adults say they are unacceptable. There are some cultural differences in whether a given behavior is viewed as having moral implications, but it is likely that people in all cultures differentiate among moral, social conventional, and personal domains of functioning.

The Early Development of Conscience

We all are familiar with the notion of a conscience—that voice inside us that pushes us to behave in moral ways and makes us feel guilty if we don't. Stated more formally, **conscience** is an internal regulatory mechanism that increases the individual's ability to conform with standards of conduct accepted in his or her culture. Consistent with Freud's theory (Chapter 9), it is likely that the conscience of a young child reflects primarily internalized parental standards (although probably the standards of both parents, not just of the same-sex parent). The conscience restrains antisocial behavior or destructive impulses and promotes a child's compliance with adults' rules and standards, even when no one is monitoring the child's behavior (Kochanska, 1993, 2002). The conscience also can promote prosocial behavior by causing the child to feel guilty when he or she engages in uncaring behavior or does not live up to internalized values about helping others (Eisenberg, 1986, 2000; Hoffman, 1982).

Factors Affecting the Development of Conscience

conscience an internal regulatory mechanism that increases the individual's ability to conform with standards of conduct accepted in his or her culture

Although Freud maintained that the conscience emerges as an outcome of identification with the same-sex parent at about age 4 to 6, children actually develop a conscience slowly over time. By age 2, toddlers start to show an appreciation for moral standards and rules and begin to exhibit signs of guilt when they do something wrong (Kopp, 2001; Zahn-Waxler & Kochanska, 1990; Zahn-Waxler & Robinson, 1995). As they mature, children are more likely to take on their parents' moral values if their parents use disciplinary practices that deemphasize parental power, including rational explanations that help children understand and learn the parents' values (Hoffman, 1983; Kochanska, Padavich, & Koenig, 1996). Children's adoption of their parents' values is also facilitated by a secure, positive parent–child relationship, in part because such a relationship inclines children to be open to their parents' communication of their values (Bretherton, Golby, & Cho, 1997; Kochanska & Murray, 2000; Thompson, 1998).

Children may develop a conscience in different ways according to their temperament. For infants who are prone to fear (e.g., who are fearful of unfamiliar people or situations), the development of conscience seems to be promoted by the mother's use of gentle discipline that includes reasoning with the child, making polite suggestions, and providing nonmaterial incentives for compliance. When mothers use gentle discipline, fearful children do not become so apprehensive and anxious that they tune out their mother's messages about desired behavior. Gentle discipline arouses fearful children just enough that they attend to and remember what their mother tells them (Kochanska, 1993). In contrast, gentle discipline seems to be unrelated to the development of conscience in fearless young children, perhaps because it is insufficient to arouse their attention (Kochanska, 1995, 1997a). What does seem to foster the development of conscience in fearless children is a positive parent–child relationship in which there is cooperation and a secure attachment. Fearless children appear motivated by the desire to please their mother more than by fear of her (Kochanska, 1997b). Unfortunately, research on this topic seldom has been conducted with fathers, so it is not known if the findings for mothers' discipline generalize to fathers' discipline.

The early development of conscience doubtlessly contributes to whether children come to accept parental and societal values concerning moral and immoral behavior. Therefore, the nature of early parent–child disciplinary interactions sets the stage for children's subsequent moral development.

SUSIE FITZHUGH

If disciplined in a harsh manner, children who are temperamentally fearful are likely to become too distressed to get their parents' disciplinary message. For such children, parental reasoning is more likely to promote the development of guilt and internalized (i.e., willing and eager) compliance with parental rules and demands.

review: The conscience is believed to reflect internalized moral standards; it restrains the child from engaging in immoral behavior and involves feelings of guilt for misbehavior. Contrary to Freud's beliefs, the conscience emerges slowly over time, beginning before age 2. Children are more likely to internalize parental standards if they have secure attachments with their parents and if their parents use rational explanations in their discipline rather than excessive parental power. Factors that promote the development of conscience differ somewhat for children with different temperaments.

Prosocial Behavior

As we noted earlier, moral behavior is as important for moral development as are moral cognitions (such as those reflected in moral judgment) and moral emotions, such as guilt. The same is true for prosocial behavior; all children are capable of prosocial behaviors, but children differ in how often they engage in these behaviors and in their reasons for doing so. Consider the behavior of the following three preschool children:

> Sara is drawing a picture and has a box of crayons. Erin is sitting across from her, and wants to draw. But Erin has only a single crayon and all the rest are in use by other children. She looks around for crayons of other colors. After a short time, Erin looks somewhat distressed. Sara notices that Erin is looking for crayons and is distressed, so she smiles and hands Erin a few of her own crayons, saying, "Here, do you want to use these?"
>
> Marc is sitting at a table drawing with crayons when Manuel comes over and wants to draw. Manuel can't find any crayons and shows signs of upset. Marc looks at Manuel and then returns to his own drawing. Finally, Manuel asks Marc, "Can I have some crayons?" At first Marc ignores Manuel. After Manuel asks for crayons again, Marc hands Manuel three crayons without any comment or display of emotion.
>
> Sakina is drawing when Darren comes to the table, picks up a piece of paper, and looks around for crayons. When Darren can't find any, he exhibits mild distress and then asks Sakina for some crayons. Sakina just ignores him. When Darren tries to take a crayon that Sakina is not using, Sakina angrily pushes him away.
>
> (Eisenberg, laboratory observations)

ELIZABETH CREWS

Most toddlers in their second year share objects with their parents and with other children (Hay, Castle, Stimson, & Davies, 1995).

In response to observing that someone else is sad or in distress, Sara shares without even being asked and with a show of goodwill. Marc shares only if asked repeatedly. Sakina does not share at all and does not seem to care if other children are upset. Do these differences in patterns of behavior forecast consistent differences among Sara, Marc, and Sakina in their positive moral behavior as they are growing up?

The answer is yes; there is some developmental consistency in children's readiness to engage in prosocial behaviors, such as sharing, helping, and comforting (Eisenberg & Fabes, 1998; Eisenberg, Miller, et al., 1991). In fact, children like Sara who share spontaneously with peers tend to be more concerned with others' needs throughout childhood and adolescence, and even in early adulthood. In comparison with their peers, for example, they are more likely to assist other people even when doing so involves a cost to themselves; and they are viewed by their mothers as helpful in adolescence. As young adults, they report that they feel responsible for the welfare of others and that they try to suppress aggression toward others when angered (Eisenberg, Guthrie, et al., 1999, 2002). In contrast, children like Sakina are unlikely to be concerned with others' needs and feelings when they are older.

Of course, not all prosocial behaviors are of equal worth. Compare Qing's sharing of crayons, for instance, with Sara's:

> Qing is drawing and has lots of crayons. Michael sits down, wants to draw, and looks for crayons. He is upset when he can't find any. When he asks Qing for some of her crayons, she says, "I'll give you some crayons if you give me some of your paper."
>
> (Eisenberg, laboratory observations)

Qing is willing to share, but only for a price. Similarly, some children may help or share to gain social acceptance from peers or to avoid their anger ("I'll share my doll if you'll be my friend"). Most parents and teachers do not want to encourage children to perform prosocial behaviors primarily in exchange for rewards or social approval. Rather, adults generally want children to help others for altruistic motives. **Altruistic motives** initially include empathy or sympathy for others and, at later ages, the desire to act in ways consistent with one's own conscience and moral principles (Eisenberg, 1992).

altruistic motives helping others for reasons that initially include empathy or sympathy for others and, at later ages, the desire to act in ways consistent with one's own conscience and moral principles

empathy an emotional reaction to another's emotional state or condition that is similar to that other person's state or condition

sympathy the feeling of concern for another person (or animal) in reaction to that other person's (or animal's) emotional state or condition; often an outcome of empathizing with another's negative emotion or situation

The Development of Prosocial Behavior

The origins of altruistic prosocial behavior are rooted in the capacity to feel empathy and sympathy. **Empathy** is an emotional reaction to another's emotional state or condition (e.g., poverty) that is highly similar to (or consistent with) the other person's state or condition (Eisenberg, 1986; Feshbach, 1978). For example, if a girl sees another child who is sad or injured and, as a consequence, feels sad herself, she is experiencing empathy. To experience empathy, children must be able to identify the emotions of others (at least to some degree) and understand that another person is feeling an emotion or is in some kind of need.

Sympathy often is an outcome of empathizing with another's negative emotion or negative situation. It is the feeling of concern for another person (or animal) in reaction to the other's emotional state or condition. What distinguishes sympathy from empathy is the element of concern: people who experience sympathy for another person are not merely feeling the same emotion as the other person.

RICK RICKMAN / MATRIX

This group of boys shaved their heads to show their sympathy, support, and solidarity with their friend (middle) who was being treated for cancer. Children's ability to sympathize with others appears to increase somewhat with age in early and middle childhood.

ELIZABETH CREWS

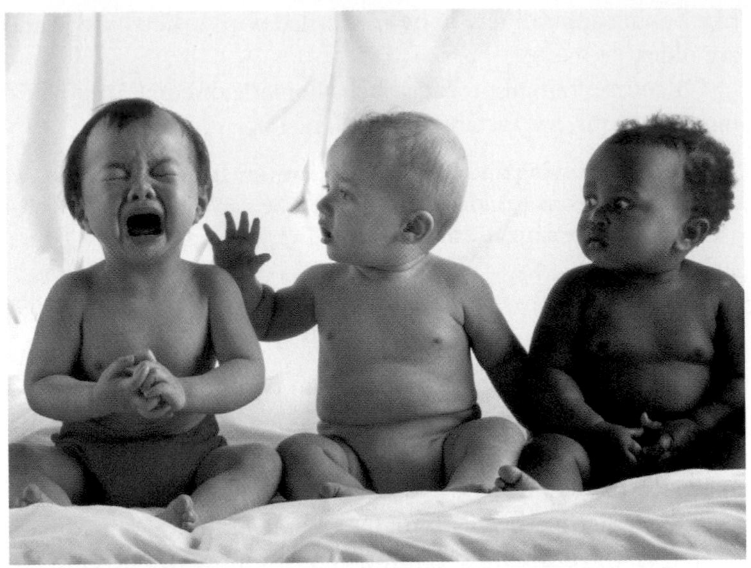

ANDY COX / GETTY IMAGES

Young children who view another child's distress sometimes respond with looks of concern or attempts to console or help the distressed peer—about 20% of the time in a study of 16- to 33-month-olds (Howes & Farver, 1987). Even young infants sometimes show interest in a peer's distress.

An important factor contributing to empathy or sympathy is, obviously, the ability to take the perspective of others. Although early theorists such as Piaget believed that children are unable to do this until age 6 to 7 (Piaget & Inhelder, 1956), it is now clear that children have some ability to understand others' perspectives much earlier. Some children as young as 6 months old show interest in a peer's distress by leaning or gesturing toward, or touching, the distressed peer (Hay, Nash, & Pedersen, 1981). By 10 to 14 months of age, children sometimes become disturbed and upset when they view other people who are upset:

> Jenny [a 14-month-old] observed a crying 6-month old baby. She watched; tears welled in her eyes; she began to cry.
>
> (Radke-Yarrow & Zahn-Waxler, 1984)

Of course, it may be that infants are not really concerned about others' distress; they may merely become upset when they see others who are sad, distressed, and fearful because they do not differentiate clearly between another's emotional distress and their own (Hoffman, 1990). Indeed, young children such as Jenny sometimes seek comfort from a parent when they see someone else upset. Or children may be both upset for another person and for themselves. For example, when one 12-month-old boy viewed another person in distress, he alternated between gently touching the distressed person and himself (Zahn-Waxler, Radke-Yarrow, & King, 1979).

As they approach age 2, children start to differentiate more clearly between another's emotional distress and their own. They are less likely to become distressed when other people are upset and are more likely to try to comfort them, indicating that they know who it is that is suffering. Consider the following example:

> A neighbor's baby cries. Jenny (18 months old) looked startled, her body stiffened. She approached and tried to give the baby cookies. She followed him around and began to whimper herself. She then tried to stroke his hair, but he pulled away.

Later, she approached her mother, led her to the baby, and tried to put mother's hand on the baby's head. He calmed down a little, but Jenny still looked worried. She continued to bring him toys and to pat his head and shoulders.

(Radke-Yarrow & Zahn-Waxler, 1984, p. 89)

Martin Hoffman (1990, 2000) has argued that although young children may be able to take others' perspective in terms of feelings of distress, their efforts to help or comfort are often egocentric. That is, young children have difficulty differentiating between their own and others' thoughts, so they are apt to help others in ways that they themselves would like, not in ways that are most helpful to the other person. For example, a young boy who sees a friend in distress may fetch his own mother to help, even if the friend's mother is available. However, as children become better able to understand how others think and feel, their helping behavior becomes more sensitive and appropriate for the other person's needs.

In the second and third years of life, the frequency and variety of young children's prosocial behaviors increase. Children not only comfort others (see Table 14.3) and share objects, but also help adults with various household tasks such as sweeping, holding the dustpan, or helping set the table (Dunn & Munn, 1986; Levitt, Weber, Clark, & McDonnell, 1985; Rheingold, 1982). Moreover, their prosocial behaviors at home often seem to be motivated by concern for others because they frequently show expressions of concern when they help or comfort others (Radke-Yarrow & Zahn-Waxler, 1984; Zahn-Waxler, Radke-Yarrow, Wagner, & Chapman, 1992). As is shown in Table 14.3, 25% of 23- to 25-month-olds showed concern when they observed someone in distress that they had not caused themselves.

As should be clear from the table, young children do not regularly act in prosocial ways (Lamb & Zakhireh, 1997). Between the ages of 2 and 3, children most often ignore their siblings' distress or need, or they simply watch without intervening. Occasionally, they even make the situation worse with teasing or aggression (Dunn, 1988; see "aggressive behavior" in Table 14.3). In one study of children in a play-group setting, 16- to 33-month-olds responded to peers' distress only 22% of time, usually with attempts to intervene on the peer's behalf, comfort the peer, or bring a distressing situation to the attention of the caregiver. Consistent with our discussion in Chapter 13, these children were much more likely to help a friend than a child who was not a friend (Howes & Farver, 1987).

Children's prosocial behaviors such as helping, sharing, and donating increase in frequency from the preschool years to adolescence. Older adolescents (e.g., 16-year-olds) are more likely than younger children to share and donate toys or money at a cost to themselves (Eisenberg & Fabes, 1998). Thus, in general, children engage in more prosocial behavior with age.

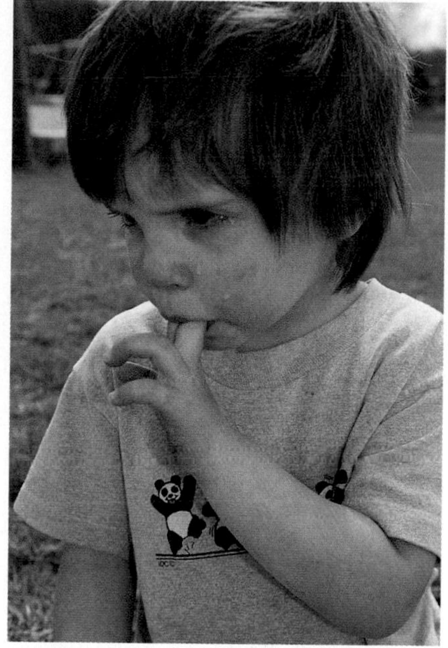

MARGARET ROSS / STOCK BOSTON

Young children sometimes respond to another's distress with self-focused discomfort or anxiety. Children who experience such personal distress tend to be motivated to make themselves, not the other person, feel better.

TABLE 14.3

Mothers' Reports of the Proportion of Times Children Responded to Others' Distress During the Second Year of Life

	When the child witnesses another's distress			When the child caused another's distress		
	13–15 months	18–20 months	23–25 months	13–15 months	18–20 months	23–25 months
Prosocial behavior	.09	.21	.49	.07	.10	.52
Empathy or sympathy	.09	.10	.25	.03	.03	.14
Aggressive behavior	.01	.01	.03	.01	.04	.19
Self-distress (personal distress)	.15	.12	.07	.34	.41	.33

Adapted from Zahn-Waxler, Radke-Yarrow, Wagner, & Chapman (1992)

The Origins of Individual Differences in Prosocial Behavior

Although children's prosocial behaviors and the factors that might contribute to them change with age, consistent with the theme of *individual differences,* there is great variation among children of the same age in their propensity to help, share with, and comfort others. Recall the behaviors of Sara, Marc, and Sakina, the three children described earlier in this chapter. Why do children of the same ages differ so much in their prosocial behavior? To identify the origins of these individual differences, we must consider the themes of *nature and nurture* and *sociocultural context.*

Biological Factors

Many biologists and psychologists have proposed that humans are biologically predisposed to be prosocial. They believe that humans have evolved the capacity for empathy and altruism because these traits increase the likelihood of an individual's genes being passed on to the next generation (Hoffman, 1981). According to this view, people who help others are more likely than less helpful people to be assisted when they themselves are in need and, thus, are more likely to survive and reproduce (Trivers, 1983). In addition, people who assist those with whom they share genes are more likely than less helpful people to have relatives who reproduce and pass on those genes to the next generation (Wilson, 1975). Evolutionary explanations for prosocial behavior, however, pertain to the human species as a whole and do not explain individual differences in empathy, sympathy, and prosocial behavior.

Nonetheless, genetic factors do seem to contribute to individual differences in these characteristics. In twin studies with adults, twins' reports of their own empathy and prosocial behavior are considerably more similar for identical twins than for fraternal twins (Matthews, Batson, Horn, & Rosenman, 1981; Rushton, Fulker, Neale, Nias, & Eysenck, 1986). In one of the few twin studies of children's prosocial behavior, researchers observed young twins' reactions to adults' simulations of distress in the home and in the laboratory. In addition, mothers of the twins reported on their toddlers' prosocial behavior. On the basis of heritability estimates derived from this study, it appears that genetic factors contributed modestly to the children's prosocial actions and the degree to which toddlers exhibited concern for others. However, heredity appeared to play a smaller role in the toddlers' prosocial behavior and sympathy than it seems to play in adults' (Zahn-Waxler, Robinson, & Emde, 1992).

How do genetic factors affect empathy, sympathy, and prosocial behavior? Most likely their effects are related to differences in temperament. For example, differences in children's tendencies to experience negative emotion and their ability to regulate emotion are related to children's empathy and sympathy. Children who tend to experience emotion without getting overwhelmed by it are especially likely to experience sympathy (Eisenberg, Fabes, et al., 1996, 1998). Another partly genetic factor that affects children's enactment of prosocial behavior is their assertiveness: perspective taking is more likely to lead to prosocial action if children are assertive enough to intervene when they understand that another person needs help. For example, once a child understands that a peer cannot tie the sash of his or her painting apron, the observing child must be confident enough to approach the peer and offer assistance. Nonassertive children may not act prosocially even if they understand the other person's problem and would like to help (Barrett & Yarrow, 1977; Denham & Couchoud, 1991). This is a good example of how children's cognitive functioning and their personality characteristics jointly affect their social behavior.

The Socialization of Prosocial Behavior

The primary environmental influence on children's development of prosocial behavior probably is their socialization in the family. Researchers have identified three ways in which parents socialize prosocial behavior in their children: (1) through their modeling and teaching prosocial behavior; (2) through their arranging opportunities for their children to engage in prosocial behavior; and (3) through their methods of disciplining their children and eliciting prosocial behavior from them. Another socializing influence is the other people whose behavior children imitate, including those on television.

CHRIS ANDERSON / AURORA

Children are more likely to donate to charity if they see others donate and if adults explain to them how donating helps others.

Modeling and the communication of values Just as they imitate many other behaviors, children tend to imitate other people's helping and sharing behavior, including even that of peers or unknown adults (Eisenberg & Fabes, 1998; Rushton, 1975). Children are especially likely to imitate the prosocial behavior of adults with whom they have a positive relationship (Hart & Fegley, 1995; Yarrow, Scott, & Zahn-Waxler, 1973). This may help explain the fact that parents and children tend to be similar in their levels of prosocial behavior and sympathy (Clary & Miller, 1986; Eisenberg, Fabes, Schaller, Carlo, & Miller, 1991; Rheingold, 1982), although heredity may also contribute to the similarity between parent and child in sympathy and helpfulness.

In a particularly interesting study, individuals who had risked their lives to rescue Jews from the Nazis in Europe during World War II were interviewed many years later, along with "bystanders" from the same communities who had not been involved in rescue activities (Oliner & Oliner, 1988). When recalling the values that they had learned from their parents and other influential adults, 44% of the rescuers mentioned generosity and caring for others; only 21% of bystanders mentioned the same values. As shown in Table 14.4, bystanders were almost twice as likely as rescuers to cite economic competence as a value learned from their parents. Rescuers and bystanders differed little on values of fairness that pertained to getting what one merits (equity).

Bystanders also reported that their parents emphasized ethical obligations to family, community, church, and country, but not to other groups of people. In contrast, rescuers were seven times more likely than bystanders to report that their parents taught them that values related to caring should be applied to all human beings (28% of rescuers; 4% of bystanders):

> "They taught me to respect all human beings."
> "He taught me to love my neighbor—to consider him my equal whatever his nationality or religion."
>
> (Oliner & Oliner, 1988, p. 165)

Thus, the values parents convey to their children may influence not only whether children are prosocial but also toward whom they are prosocial.

One effective way for parents to teach their children prosocial values and behaviors is to have discussions with them that appeal to their ability to sympathize. In laboratory studies, when elementary school children heard adults explicitly point out the positive consequences of prosocial actions for others (e.g., "poor children . . . would be so happy and excited if they could buy food and toys"), they were relatively likely to donate money anonymously to help other people (Eisenberg-Berg &

TABLE 14.4

Values Learned from Parents by Rescuers and Bystanders (Percent of Rescuers and Bystanders Who Reported Learning a Given Type of Value from Parents)

Type of Value	Rescuers (%)	Bystanders (%)
Economic competence	19	34
Independence	6	8
Fairness/equity (including reciprocity)	44	48
Fairness/equity applied universally	14	10
Caring	44	21
Caring applied universally	28	4

Adapted from Oliner & Oliner (1988)

Geisheker, 1979; Perry, Bussey, & Freiberg, 1981). Children were less likely to donate anonymously if adults simply said that helping is "good" or "nice" and did not provide sympathy-arousing rationales for helping or sharing (Bryan & Walbek, 1970).

Opportunities for prosocial activities Providing children with opportunities to engage in helpful activities can increase their willingness to take on prosocial tasks at a later time (Eisenberg, Cialdini, McCreath, & Shell, 1987; Staub, 1979). In the home, opportunities to help others include household tasks that are performed on a routine basis and benefit others (Richman, Berry, Bittle, & Himan, 1988; Whiting & Whiting, 1975), although performance of household tasks may foster prosocial actions primarily toward family members (Grusec, Goodnow, & Cohen, 1996). For adolescents, voluntary community service such as working in homeless shelters or other community agencies also can be a way of gaining experience in helping others and increasing their feelings of prosocial commitment (Johnson, Beeke, Mortimer, & Snyder, 1998; Yates & Youniss, 1996). Participation in prosocial activities may provide children and adolescents with opportunities to experience emotional rewards for helping, to take others' perspectives, and to increase their confidence that they are competent to assist others.

Discipline and parenting style Parents who are constructive and supportive in their parenting tend to have children who are high in prosocial behavior and sympathy (Eisenberg & Fabes, 1998; Spinrad et al., 1999). In contrast, a parenting style that involves physical punishment, threats, and an authoritarian approach (see Chapter 12) tends to be associated with a lack of sympathy and prosocial behavior in children (Dekovic & Janssens, 1992; Hastings, Zahn-Waxler, Robinson, Usher, & Bridges, 2000; Krevans & Gibbs, 1996; Robinson, Zahn-Waxler, & Emck, 1994).

The way in which parents attempt to directly elicit prosocial behavior from their children is also important. If children are regularly punished for failing to engage in prosocial behavior, they may start to believe that the reason for helping others is primarily to avoid punishment (Dix & Grusec, 1983; Hoffman, 1983). Similarly, although giving children material rewards for prosocial behaviors may induce them to help in the immediate situation, it may reduce their long-term willingness to help people in general (Fabes, Fultz, Eisenberg, Max-Plumlee, & Christopher, 1989; Szynal-Brown & Morgan, 1983). Children who are rewarded for prosocial actions may believe that they helped solely for the rewards and, thus, may be less motivated to help when no rewards are offered.

In contrast to harsh discipline or material inducements, discipline involving reasoning fosters voluntary prosocial behavior, especially when the reasoning points out the consequences of the child's behavior for others (Krevans & Gibbs, 1996; Miller, Eisenberg, Fabes, & Shell, 1989) and is used by parents who generally are warm and supportive (Hoffman, 1963). Reasoning may help children understand the consequences of their behavior, provide reasons that children can use to guide their behavior in future situations, and encourage children to sympathize with others (Henry, Sager, & Plunkett, 1996; Hoffman, 1983). Maternal use of reasoning (e.g., "Can't you see that Tim is hurt?") seems to

When adults point out the consequences of a child's transgressions for others, children are more likely to respond with sympathy and prosocial behavior in other situations (Eisenberg & Fabes, 1998; Krevans & Gibbs, 1996).

SUSIE FITZHUGH

applications 14.1

School-Based Interventions for Promoting Prosocial Behavior

Knowledge about the socialization of helping and sharing behavior has been used to design school interventions aimed at fostering such behavior. Perhaps the most ambitious of these interventions was the Child Development Project in the East Bay area of San Francisco (Battistich, Solomon, Watson, & Schaps, 1997; Battistich, Watson, Solomon, Schaps, & Solomon, 1991). The primary component of this longitudinal intervention, which followed children across elementary school, was training teachers how to provide opportunities for children to develop a prosocial orientation toward their classmates and the community. The training focused on getting children to:

1. collaborate with others in the pursuit of common academic and social goals;
2. develop and practice important social competencies such as understanding of others' thoughts and feelings;
3. provide meaningful help to others and receive help when it was needed;
4. discuss and reflect upon the degree to which their own and others' behavior reflects fairness, concern and respect for others, and social responsibility;
5. participate in decision making about classroom norms, rules, and activities and take on responsibility for appropriate aspects of classroom life.

Teachers often used everyday events and story characters to discuss others' motives, feelings, and needs, as well as prosocial values and behaviors. They also used reasoning in their disciplinary actions whenever possible. In addition, teachers encouraged students to participate in school and community service and to help peers.

The program has led to increases in spontaneous prosocial behavior, conflict-resolution skills, and prosocial moral reasoning among students in elementary grades (Solomon, Battistich, & Watson, 1993; Solomon, Watson, Delucchi, Schaps, & Battistich, 1988). Initially, the program was used primarily with advantaged Euro-American children so its usefulness with more disadvantaged children was unknown. However, similar intervention programs that have since been used with impoverished children have shown similar success (Solomon, Battistich, Watson, Schaps, & Lewis, 2000).

In recent years, the concept of the school as a caring community has become a central part of similar interventions. The caring school community is one in which teachers and students care about and support one another; share common values, norms, goals, and a sense of belonging; and participate in and influence group decisions. Programs designed to promote caring schools included many of the components of the initial Child Development Project. Initial findings suggest that enhancing a sense of community promotes children's concern for others, prosocial behavior, conflict-resolution skills, ethical attitudes and values, academic motivation, and liking of school, and is associated with fewer problem behaviors and less use of drugs (Battistich, Schaps, Watson, Solomon, & Lewis, 2000; Battistich et al., 1997; Solomon et al., 2000).

increase prosocial behavior even for 1- to 2-year-olds, as long as mothers state their reasoning in an emotional tone of voice (Zahn-Waxler et al., 1979). Emotion in the mother's voice likely catches her toddler's attention and communicates that she is very serious about what she is saying.

The combination of parental warmth and parenting practices—not parental warmth by itself—seems to be especially effective for fostering prosocial tendencies in children. Thus, children tend to be more prosocial when their parents are not only warm and supportive but also model prosocial behavior, include reasoning and references to moral values and responsibilities in their discipline, and expose their children to prosocial models and activities (Dekovic & Janssens, 1992; Janssens & Dekovic, 1997; Yarrow et al., 1973).

Because most of the research on the socialization of prosocial responding is correlational in design, it is impossible to draw firm conclusions about cause-and-effect relations from much of the research. However, some school interventions have been effective at promoting prosocial behavior in children. Thus, environmental factors must contribute to its development (see Box 14.1). Intervention research provides evidence that experience in helping and cooperating with others, exposure to prosocial values and behaviors, and adults' use of reasoning in discipline jointly contribute to the development of prosocial behavior.

Television Given children's tendencies to imitate what they see others do, there has been considerable concern about the socializing effects of television viewing, especially because children spend so much time watching TV and so much of what

a closer look 14.2

Cultural Contributions to Children's Prosocial and Antisocial Tendencies

Culture influences the amount of prosocial and antisocial behavior that children display (Graves & Graves, 1983; Rohner, 1975; Turnbull, 1972). For example, children from traditional communities and subcultures (e.g., Mexicans and Mexican-Americans) are more likely to cooperate on laboratory tasks than are children from urban, Westernized groups (Eisenberg & Mussen, 1989; Knight, Cota, & Bernal, 1993). Moreover, when children were observed interacting at home and in their neighborhoods, children in traditional societies in Kenya, Mexico, and the Philippines helped, shared, and offered support to others in their families and communities more than did children in the United States, India, and Okinawa. In the more prosocial cultures, children often lived in extended families with many relatives. At a young age, they were assigned chores that were very important for the welfare of other family members, such as caring for younger children and tending herds (Whiting & Edwards, 1988; Whiting & Whiting, 1975). As a result of taking on these duties, children may have learned that they were responsible for others and that their helping behavior was expected and valued by adults.

The same study revealed cultural differences in aggression. Children's tendencies to assault, berate, and scold others were related primarily to family structure and interactions among parents. Children with lower rates of assaulting and reprimanding tended to live in cultures in which fathers were closely involved with their wives and children, helped their wives with the care of infants, and were relatively unlikely to assault their wives. In such family circumstances, children may have learned nonaggressive modes of social interaction from their fathers and were relatively unlikely to have been exposed to aggressive adult models.

Even in various industrial societies today, there are differences in cultural values regarding prosocial and antisocial behavior. For example, the incidence of kindergartners' sharing, helping, and comforting is higher in Taiwan and Japan than in the United States (Stevenson, 1991). Chinese and Japanese cultures traditionally place great emphasis on teaching children to share and to be responsible for the needs of others in the group (the family, class, or community). In Japan, there also is an emphasis on creating a "community of learners" in the elementary school classroom—that is, teaching children to respond supportively to one another's thoughts and feelings (Lewis, 1995). However, the traditional emphasis on prosocial behavior in many Asian cultures seems to be eroding (Lee & Zhan, 1991), perhaps due to increasing industrialization and exposure to Western culture and values, which are less likely to emphasize the welfare of the larger group.

CATHERINE URSILLO / PHOTO RESEARCHERS, INC.

Cross-cultural research has shown that girls who live in societies where they are expected to take care of younger children are more prosocial than are girls who live in societies that do not have this expectation.

they watch contains violence. As you will see in our discussion of antisocial behavior, this concern is well-founded. However, some content on television—albeit relatively little—includes prosocial behaviors, and children sometimes imitate this behavior (Hearold, 1986; Huston & Wright, 1998). For example, children who view prosocial behaviors on shows such as *Mr. Rogers' Neighborhood* tend to engage in more prosocial behavior immediately after and sometimes later in time (Friedrich & Stein, 1973). However, the positive effects of viewing prosocial television often do not last long. Parents can increase their children's imitation of televised prosocial behavior if they get them to role-play the prosocial situations they saw in the television program (Friedrich & Stein, 1975) and if children are provided with play materials for acting out the prosocial themes in the television show (Friedrich-Cofer, Huston-Stein, Kipnis, Susman, & Clewett, 1979).

review::

Prosocial behaviors emerge by the second year of life and increase in frequency during the toddler years. Prosocial behavior continues to increase in frequency and sensitivity in the preschool years and elementary school years. Early individual differences in prosocial behavior predict differences among children in these types of behaviors years later.

Increases with age in prosocial behavior may be partly due to children's developing abilities to sympathize and take others' perspectives. Differences among children in their empathy, sympathy, personal distress, and perspective taking also contribute to individual differences in children's prosocial behavior. Furthermore, biological factors, which may contribute to differences among children in temperament, likely affect how empathic and prosocial children become.

The development of prosocial behavior also is related to children's upbringing. In general, a positive relationship between parents and children is linked to prosocial moral development, especially when supportive parents use effective parenting practices. Authoritative, positive discipline, including the use of reasoning by parents and teachers, and exposure to prosocial models, values, and activities are associated with the development of sympathy and prosocial behavior. In addition, viewing prosocial television can foster prosocial behavior. Cultures differ in the degree to which they value and teach prosocial behavior, and these differences are reflected in how much children help, share with, and are concerned about other people.

Intervention programs in schools designed to foster prosocial behavior have been found to increase children's prosocial behavior and prosocial moral reasoning. Such findings convincingly demonstrate that social factors (as well as heredity) contribute to the development of prosocial tendencies.

Antisocial Behavior

Pick up any newspaper and you are inevitably reminded of the violence that is commonplace among youth in urban, industrial countries, especially in Western societies. In 1998, in the United States, juveniles under age 18 were involved in 12% of murder arrests, 14% of aggravated assault arrests, 27% of robbery arrests, and 24% of weapons arrests (Snyder, 1999). Statistics like these, along with incidents like the Columbine tragedy described at the beginning of the chapter, raise questions such as: Are youth who commit violent acts already aggressive in childhood? How do levels of aggression change with development? What factors contribute to individual differences in children's antisocial behavior? As we address these issues, the themes of *individual differences, nature and nuture, the sociocultural context*, and *applications of research* will be most salient.

The Development of Aggression and Other Antisocial Behaviors

Aggression is behavior aimed at harming or injuring others (Parke & Slaby, 1983), and it is behavior that emerges quite early. How early? Although conflicts between infants are very common at 12 to 18 months of age, most do not involve aggression (Coie & Dodge, 1998; Hay & Ross, 1982). However, at around 18 months of age, physical aggression such as hitting and pushing begins and increases in frequency until about age 2. Then it decreases in frequency, and, with the growth of language skills, verbal aggression such as insults and taunting increases (Coie & Dodge, 1998).

aggression behavior aimed at harming or injuring others

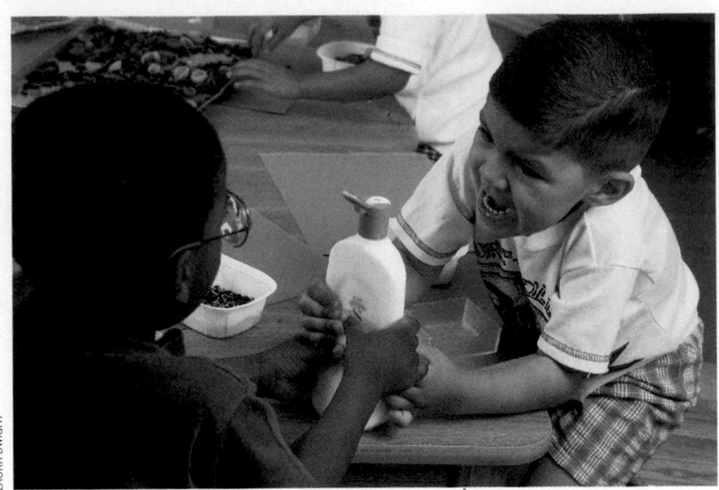

LAURA DWIGHT

Aggressive conflicts over objects are very common in young children.

Among the most frequent causes of aggression in the preschool years are conflicts between peers over possessions (Fabes & Eisenberg, 1992; Shantz, 1987) and conflict between siblings over most anything (Abramovitch, Corter, & Lando, 1979). Conflict over possessions often is an example of **instrumental aggression,** that is, aggression motivated by the desire to obtain a concrete goal, such as gaining a toy or a better place in line. Preschool children also sometimes use relational aggression as a means to control or hurt their peers (Crick, Casas, & Mosher, 1997). **Relational aggression** is aggression that harms others by damaging their peer relationships, such as by excluding them from a play activity or a social group or spreading negative rumors about them.

instrumental aggression aggression motivated by the desire to obtain a concrete goal

relational aggression aggression that harms others by damaging their peer relationships

The drop in physical aggression in the preschool years is likely due to a variety of factors, including not only children's increasing ability to use verbal and relational aggression but also their developing ability to use language to resolve conflicts and to control their own emotions and actions (Coie & Dodge, 1998). Thus, overt physical aggression continues to decline in frequency for most children during elementary school, although some children develop frequent and serious problems with aggression and antisocial behavior at this age (Cairns, Cairns, Neckerman, Ferguson, & Gariepy, 1989; Loeber & Hay, 1993).

Whereas aggression in young children usually is motivated by the desire to achieve instrumental goals, elementary school children's aggression often is based on hostility, the desire to hurt another person, or the need to protect against a perceived threat to self-esteem (Dodge, 1980; Hartup, 1974). At this age, covert types of antisocial behaviors such as stealing, lying, and cheating occur with considerable frequency and begin to be characteristic of some children with behavioral problems (Loeber & Schmaling, 1985).

In adolescence, the frequency of overt aggression decreases for most teenagers (Loeber, 1982), although serious acts of violence increase markedly. As is illustrated in Figure 14.2, adolescent violent crime peaks at age 17, when 29% of males and

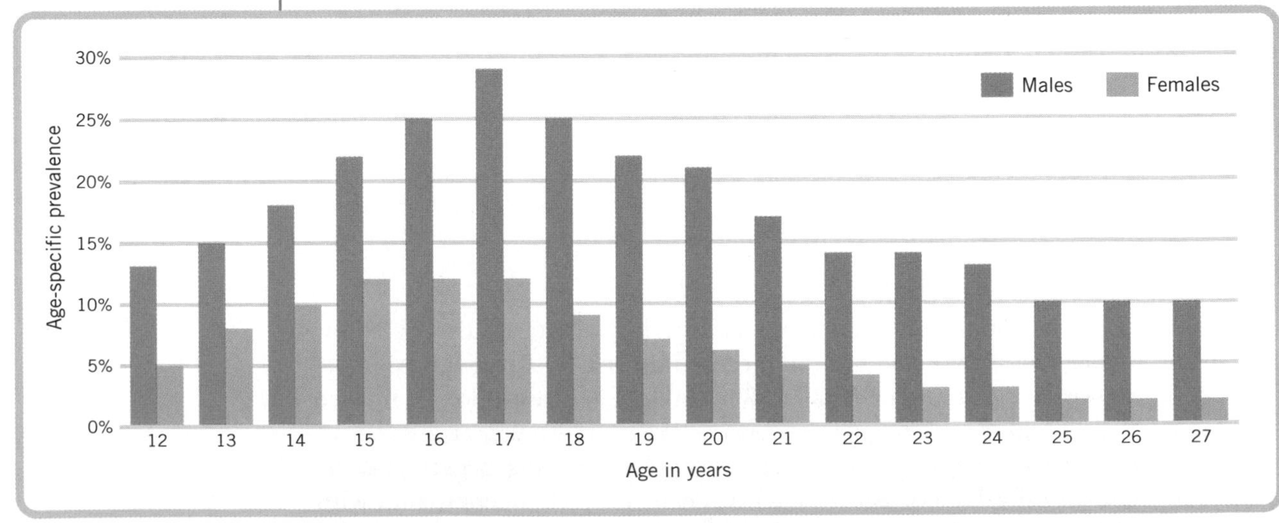

FIGURE 14.2 Prevalence of self-reported violence for males and females at different ages At all ages, males report enacting more violence than do females. (Adapted from Coie & Dodge, 1998)

a closer look 14.3

Gender Differences in Prosocial and Antisocial Behavior

A common gender stereotype asserts that females are more empathic, caring, and prosocial, and less aggressive, than males. Is there any truth to this stereotype? The answer is yes, although the actual gender differences are not as great as most people believe. For example, girls help and share more than boys and are perceived as more concerned about others. However, in laboratory research in which they view empathy-inducing film scenes (e.g., an injured child being teased, a sad hospitalized child), girls and boys do not differ in their physiological reactions (e.g., heart rate) or facial reactions (e.g., looks of distress or concerned attention) (Eisenberg & Fabes, 1998; Eisenberg, Fabes, Schaller, & Miller, 1989). Thus, it may be that boys are more likely than girls to suppress, ignore, or deny their emotional reactions to the plights of others.

Girls' tendencies to experience or acknowledge more empathy and sympathy than boys may be one of many factors contributing to the fact that boys generally are higher than girls in both verbal and physical aggression (Knight, Fabes, & Higgins, 1996). This sex difference, which emerges by the preschool years, is present across varied socioeconomic groups and cultures (Hyde, 1984; Whiting & Whiting, 1975) and increases with age in childhood (Knight et al., 1996). Biological factors such as the amount of testosterone in the bloodstream may also contribute to the gender difference in aggression (Coie & Dodge, 1998; Collaer & Hines, 1995). At the same time, gender segregation in children's peer groups (see Chapter 9) may heighten the gender difference in aggression because boys' interactions are rougher and more oriented to dominance and competition than are those of girls (Leaper, 1994; Maccoby, 1988).

There is, however, one type of aggression that is more common among girls than boys—relational aggression (Crick & Bigbee, 1998; Crick, Caras, & Ku, 1999). During both the preschool and elementary school years, girls are more likely to both commit and be victims of relational aggression, such as exclusion from the social group or being made the target of nasty rumors. One reason that girls use more relational aggression may be that intimate relationships with peers are particularly important to girls (Crick & Grotpeter, 1995). Thus, when they feel threatened or slighted, they tend to try to hurt one another by disrupting those relationships (Crick, Bigbee, & Howes, 1996; Galen & Underwood, 1997).

SW PRODUCTION / INDEX STOCK IMAGERY / PICTUREQUEST

Relational aggression is more common among girls than boys in both the preschool and school years. Children who are the victims of relational aggression are more likely than their peers to be rejected by the peer group and to have problems with adjustment such as depression and loneliness (Crick & Grotpeter, 1996).

12% of females report committing at least one serious violent offense. As the figure also shows, male adolescents and adults engage in much more violent behavior and crime than do females (Coie & Dodge, 1998; Elliott, 1994) (see Box 14.3).

Consistency of Aggressive and Antisocial Behavior

There is considerable consistency in both girls' and boys' aggression across childhood and adolescence. Children who are aggressive and prone to conduct problems such as stealing in middle childhood tend to be aggressive and delinquent in adolescence (Olweus, 1979; White, Moffitt, Earls, Robins, & Silva, 1990), more so than children who develop conduct disorders at a later age (Lahey, Goodman, et al., 1999). In one study, children who had been identified as aggressive by their peers when they were 8 years old had more criminal convictions and engaged in more

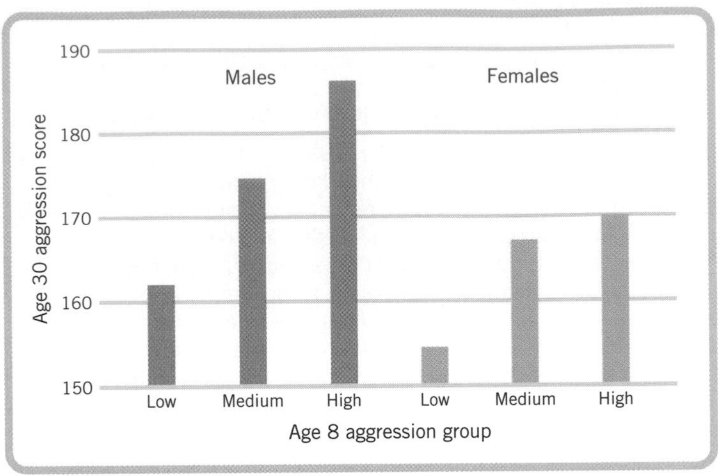

FIGURE 14.3 The relation of peer-nominated aggression at age 8 to self-reported aggression at age 30 Boys and girls who were nominated as high in aggression at age 8 were higher in self-reported aggression at age 30 than were those of their peers who had been nominated as lower in aggression. (Adapted from Eron, Huesmann, Dubow, Romanoff, & Yarmel, 1987)

serious criminal behavior at age 30 than those who had not been identified as aggressive (see Figure 14.3; Eron, Huesmann, Dubow, Romanoff, & Yarmel, 1987).

Adolescents most at risk for serious problem behaviors are those who, as elementary school children, engaged in both aggression *and* other antisocial behaviors such as lying and stealing (Loeber, 1982). However, aggression is not a necessary ingredient for later problem behavior. Some children who are not overtly aggressive in childhood simply move from lying, stealing, and property damage in childhood to more serious crimes such as stealing cars, robbery, and selling drugs in adolescence (Loeber et al., 1993).

Many children who are aggressive from early in life have neurological deficits (i.e., brain dysfunctions) that underlie such problems as difficulty in paying attention and hyperactivity (Moffitt, 1993a; Speltz, DeKlyen, Calderon, Greenberg, & Fisher, 1999). These deficits may result in troubled relations with parents, peers, and teachers, further fueling the child's aggressive, antisocial pattern of behavior. Problems with attention are particularly likely to have this effect because they make it difficult for these children to carefully consider all the relevant information in a social situation before deciding how to act; thus, their behavior often is inappropriate for the situation.

It should be noted that these patterns are separate from those related to the overall problem of "juvenile delinquency." Adolescents with a long childhood history of troubled behavior represent only a minority of adolescents who engage in antisocial behavior (Hamalainen & Pulkkinen, 1996). Most adolescents who perform delinquent acts have no history of aggression or antisocial behavior before age 11 (Elliott, 1994). These adolescents may engage in antisocial behavior in response to the normal pressures of adolescence; for example, their antisocial behavior may be an attempt to assert their autonomy from adults or to be accepted by their peers. These adolescents typically stop engaging in antisocial behavior later in adolescence or early adulthood (Moffitt, 1990, 1993a).

Characteristics of Aggressive-Antisocial Children and Adolescents

Aggressive-antisocial children and adolescents differ, on average, from their nonaggressive peers in a variety of characteristics. These include their temperament and personality and their processing of social information.

Temperament and Personality

Children who develop problems with aggression and antisocial behavior tend to exhibit a difficult temperament from a very early age (Rothbart & Bates, 1998). Longitudinal studies have shown, for example, that infants and toddlers who frequently express intense negative emotion and demand much attention tend to have higher levels of problem behaviors such as aggression in the preschool, elementary, and high school years (Bates, Bayles, Bennett, Ridge, & Brown, 1991; Olson, Bates, Sandy, & Lanthier, 2000). Similarly, preschoolers who exhibit lack of control, impulsivity, high activity level, irritability, and distractibility are prone to fighting, delinquency, and other antisocial behavior at ages 9 through 15, aggression and criminal behavior in late adolescence, and, in the case of males, violent crime in adulthood (Caspi, Henry, McGee, Moffitt, & Silva, 1995; Caspi & Silva, 1995; Tremblay, Pihl, Vitaro, & Dobkin, 1994). Some of these children and adolescents tend not to feel guilt, empathy, or sympathy for others. They are often charming but insincere and callous (Cohen & Strayer, 1996; Hastings et al., 2000). The combination of impulsivity, problems with attention, and callousness in childhood is especially likely to predict antisocial behavior and run-ins with the police in adolescence (Christian, Frick, Hill, Tyler, & Frazer, 1997; Frick, 1998), and perhaps in adulthood as well (Lynam, 1996, 1997).

Social Cognition

In addition to their differences in temperament, aggressive children differ from nonaggressive children in their social cognition. This difference is important because social cognition is involved in children's interpretations of their interactions with others and affects their reactions to them.

As discussed in Chapter 9, aggressive children tend to interpret the world through an "aggressive" lens. They are more likely than nonaggressive children to attribute hostile motives to others in contexts in which the other person's motives and intentions are unclear (the "hostile attributional bias") (Graham & Hudley, 1994; Shahinfar, Kupersmidt, & Matza, 2001). Moreover, compared with those of nonaggressive peers, their goals in social encounters are more likely to be hostile and inappropriate to the situation. Consequently, in specific encounters, they are likely to construct negative, hostile goals such as intimidating or getting back at a peer (Crick & Dodge, 1994; Slaby & Guerra, 1988). Moreover, when constructing possible reactions in a negative social situation, aggressive children tend to come up with fewer options than nonaggressive children do, and these options are more likely to involve aggressive or disruptive behavior (Deluty, 1985; Slaby & Guerra, 1988).

In line with these tendencies, aggressive children are also inclined to evaluate aggressive responses more favorably, and competent, prosocial responses less favorably, than do nonaggressive children (Crick & Dodge, 1994; Dodge, Pettit, McCloskey, & Brown, 1986; Quiggle, Garber, Panak, & Dodge, 1992). They do so in part because they expect aggressive behavior to result in positive outcomes (e.g., getting their way) and to reduce negative treatment by others (Dodge et al., 1986; Perry, Perry & Rasmussen, 1986). In addition, aggressive children feel more confident of their ability to perform acts of physical and verbal aggression (Quiggle et al., 1992), which may increase the probability of their selecting aggressive responses. Given all this, it is not surprising that aggressive children are predisposed toward choosing aggressive behaviors (Crick & Dodge, 1994; Waldman, 1996).

It is important to note, however, that although all these aspects of functioning contribute to the prediction of children's aggression, not all aggressive children exhibit the same deficits. Children who are prone to emotionally driven, hostile aggression—labeled **reactive aggression**—are particularly likely to perceive others' motives as hostile (Crick & Dodge, 1996), to generate aggressive responses to provocation, and to evaluate them as morally acceptable (Dodge, Lochman, Harnish, Bates, & Pettit, 1997). In contrast, children who are prone to unemotional aggression aimed at fulfilling a need or desire (labeled **proactive aggression**) tend to anticipate more positive social consequences for aggression (Crick & Dodge, 1996; Dodge et al., 1997).

BOB DAEMMRICH / STOCK BOSTON

Proactive aggression (purposeful aggression not evoked by emotion) is used by children to bully others and to get what they want from them.

The Origins of Aggression

What are the causes of aggression in children? Key contributors include genetic makeup, socialization by family members, the influence of peers, and cultural factors.

Biological Factors

Biological factors undoubtedly contribute to individual differences in aggression, but their precise role is not very clear. According to twin studies, antisocial behavior runs in families and is partially due to genetic factors (Coie & Dodge, 1998; Lahey, Waldman, & McBurnett, 1999; Slutske et al., 1997), especially when such behavior emerges in childhood rather than adolescence (Taylor, Iacono, & McGue, 2001). We have already noted one manifestation of genetic effects in aggression—the fact that many aggressive children have a difficult temperament. Hormonal factors are also assumed to play a role in aggression. For example, testosterone levels seem to be related to activity level and responses to provocation, and high testosterone levels sometimes have been linked to aggressive behavior (Archer, 1991). As noted earlier, neurological deficits that affect attention and regulatory capabilities also may contribute to aggression and antisocial behavior (Moffitt, 1993b): children who are not well regulated are likely to have difficulty controlling their tempers and inhibiting aggressive impulses.

Whatever their specific role, the biological correlates of aggression probably are neither necessary nor sufficient to cause aggressive behavior in most children. Genetic, neurological, or hormonal characteristics may put a child at risk for developing aggressive and antisocial behavior, but whether or not the child becomes aggressive will depend on numerous factors, including experiences in the social world (Coie & Dodge, 1998). Moreover, heredity is not equally related to all types of aggression and antisocial behavior. For example, heredity appears to play a stronger role in aggression in early childhood and adulthood than in adolescence, when environmental factors are a major contributor to aggression (Miles & Carey, 1997; Rende & Plomin, 1995).

Socialization of Aggression and Antisocial Behavior

Many people, including some legislators and judges, feel that the development of aggression can be traced back to socialization in the home. In fact, the quality of parenting experienced by antisocial children is poorer than that experienced by

reactive aggression emotionally driven, antagonistic aggression sparked by one's perception that other people's motives are hostile

proactive aggression unemotional aggression aimed at fulfilling a need or desire other children (Scarmella, Conger, Spoth, & Simmons, 2002). However, the degree to which poor parenting rather than other factors accounts for antisocial behavior is unclear.

Parental punitiveness Many children whose parents often use harsh but nonabusive physical punishment are prone to problem behaviors in the early years, aggression in childhood, and criminality in adolescence and adulthood (DeKlyen, Biernbaum, Speltz, & Greenberg, 1998; McCord, 1991; Rothbaum & Weisz, 1994). This is especially true when parents are cold and punitive in general (Deater-Deckard & Dodge, 1997).

It is important to note, however, that the relation between physical punishment and children's antisocial behavior varies across groups. As discussed in Chapter 12, in some cultures and subcultures, physical punishment and controlling parental behaviors are viewed as part of responsible parenting when coupled with parental support and normal demands for compliance. When this is the case, parental punishment tends not to be associated with antisocial behavior. This may explain in part why the relation between physical punishment and antisocial behavior is weaker for African-American children than it is for Euro-American children (Deater-Deckard & Dodge, 1997; Deater-Deckard, Dodge, Bates, & Pettit, 1996), because African-American children may tend to see authoritarian parenting as protective.

In contrast, abusive punishment is likely to be associated with the development of antisocial tendencies regardless of the racial, ethnic, or cultural group in question (Coie & Dodge, 1998; Deater-Deckard, Dodge, Bates, & Pettit, 1995; Luntz & Widom, 1994; Weiss, Dodge, Bates, & Pettit, 1992). Very harsh physical discipline appears to lead to the kinds of social cognition that are associated with aggression, such as assuming that others have hostile intentions, generating aggressive solutions to problems, and expecting aggressive behavior to result in positive outcomes (Dodge, Pettit, Bates, & Valente, 1995).

In addition, parents who use abusive punishment provide their children with salient models of aggressive behavior for their children to imitate. Ironically, children who are subjected to such punishment are likely to be anxious or angry and therefore are unlikely to attend to their parents' instructions or demands or to be motivated to behave as their parents wish them to (Hoffman, 1983).

There likely is a reciprocal relation between children's behavior and their parents' punitive discipline (Cohen & Brook, 1995; Eisenberg, Fabes, et al., 1999). That is, children who are high in antisocial behavior or low in self-regulation tend to elicit harsh parenting; in turn, harsh parenting increases the children's problem behavior. Although research findings with adolescents are not all that consistent (Cohen & Brook, 1995; Feldman & Weinberger, 1994; Stice & Barrera, 1995), it is likely that parents' punitive behaviors and adolescents' antisocial behavior also influence one another in a way that continues this vicious cycle.

It is important to realize that genetic factors may contribute to the relation between punitive parenting and children's aggression. Parents who are genetically prone to anger and violence will tend to have children with a genetic predisposition toward the same characteristics, and these same parents are more likely than other parents to engage in harsh or punitive parenting. Thus, it is very difficult to separate the effects of genetics and socialization in determining the cause of children's aggression.

Ineffective discipline and family coercion Another factor that can increase children's antisocial behavior is ineffective parenting. Parents who are inconsistent in administering discipline and in following through on punishments are more likely than other parents to have aggressive and delinquent children (Dumka, Roosa, & Jackson, 1997; Frick, Christian, & Wooten, 1999; Laub & Sampson, 1994). In contrast, parents who monitor their children's behavior and activities generally rear children with relatively few behavior problems (Frick et al., 1999; Pettit, Laird, Dodge, Bates & Criss, 2001). In a study of adolescent Mexican-Americans, youths who were acculturated—that is, whose families had been in the United States for more than a generation and spoke English at home—were more delinquent than nonacculturated peers, and reduced parental monitoring and inconsistent discipline appeared to partly account for the relation between acculturation and delinquency (Samaniego & Gonzales, 1999). One reason parental monitoring may be important is that it reduces the likelihood that older children and adolescents will associate with deviant, antisocial peers (Barrera, Biglan, Ary, & Li, 2001; Patterson, Capaldi, & Bank, 1991). It also makes it more likely that parents will know if their children are engaging in antisocial behavior.

Ineffective discipline is often evident in the pattern of family interaction described by Patterson (1982, 1995) and discussed in Chapter 1. In this pattern, the aggression of children who are out of control is often unintentionally reinforced by parents when they give in to their children's temper and demands (Snyder & Patterson, 1995). This may be especially true for problem boys, who are much more likely than other boys to react negatively to their mother's scolding or attempts to discipline them (Patterson, Reid, & Dishion, 1992). Whether or not maternal coercion elicits the same pattern of response from girls as from boys is not yet known because most of the relevant research has been done with boys, but there is some reason to believe that it does not (McFadyen-Ketchum, Bates, Dodge, & Pettit, 1996).

Parental conflict Children who are frequently exposed to verbal and physical violence between their parents tend to be more antisocial and aggressive than other children (Davies & Cummings, 1994; Fantuzzo et al., 1991; Ingoldsby, Shaw, Owens, & Winslow, 1999). One obvious reason for this is that embattled parents often model aggressive behavior. Another is that children whose mothers are physically abused tend to believe that violence is an acceptable and even necessary part of family interactions (Graham-Bermann & Brescoll, 2000). Compared with spouses who get along well with each other, embattled parents also tend to be less skilled at parenting and more hostile with their children, and their children are prone to behavioral problems and depression (Emery, 1989; Gonzales, Pitts, Hill, & Roosa, 2000).

As noted in Chapter 12, even when marital conflict results in divorce, the problems do not end: the more children must contend with family transitions such as divorce and remarriage, the more antisocial and delinquent behavior they exhibit (Capaldi & Patterson, 1991; Pagani, Tremblay, Vitaro, Kerr, & McDuff, 1998). Furthermore, for a period of time after a divorce, mothers tend to become less supportive toward

BOB DAEMMRICH / THE IMAGE WORKS

Children are more likely to develop aggressive and antisocial behavior if they are exposed to marital conflict, especially violence. Parents who are in unhappy marriages tend to be withdrawn and nonsupportive with their children, which appears to contribute to their children's problems with adjustment.

their children, and to be more inconsistent and authoritarian, and less effective, in controlling their children. Such ineffective parenting can lead to a coercive cycle of parenting (Hetherington, Hagen & Anderson, 1989). Thus, parental conflict and its aftermath can increase children's antisocial behavior in a number of different ways.

Socioeconomic status and children's antisocial behavior Children from low-income families tend to be more antisocial and aggressive than children from more prosperous homes (Bolger, Patterson, Thompson, & Kupersmidt, 1995; Keiley, Bates, Dodge, & Pettit, 2000). What might account for this difference? There are many reasons.

One major reason is the greater amount of stressors experienced by children in poor families, including stress in the family (illness, domestic violence, divorce, legal problems) and neighborhood violence. Stressors of these sorts are linked to increased aggression and antisocial behavior (Dodge, Pettit, & Bates, 1994; Guerra, Huesmann, Tolan, Van Acker, & Eron, 1995; Halliday, Boykins, & Graham, 2001; Linares et al., 2001). Moreover, low socioeconomic status is associated with living in a single-parent family or being an unplanned child of a teenage parent, both of which are linked to children's aggressive behavior (Deater-Deckard, Dodge, Bates, & Pettit, 1998).

Because of the many poverty-related stressors faced by their parents, children living in poverty are also frequently exposed to parenting deficits that predict children's antisocial, aggressive behavior. Their parents are more likely than other parents to use erratic, threatening, and harsh discipline, and tend to be lax in supervising their children. They also model more aggression and are more likely to reject their children than are parents who do not face the stresses associated with poverty (Conger, Ge, Elder, Lorenz, & Simons, 1994; Dodge et al., 1994; Sampson & Laub, 1994).

In addition to all these risk factors, other factors such as the presence of gangs, the lack of jobs for juveniles, and few opportunities to engage in constructive activities such as clubs and sports likely contribute to the antisocial behavior of many youth in poor neighborhoods.

Peer Influence

Peers are an important influence on children's aggression and other antisocial behaviors. Having antisocial friends or being part of an antisocial peer group, especially a gang, can contribute to antisocial activities.

Friends and the peer group As we discussed in Chapter 13, aggressive children tend to socialize with other aggressive children, and boys who initially are moderately aggressive become more delinquent over time if they have close friends who are aggressive. Although highly aggressive friends may not directly cause one another's aggressive behavior, they certainly may spur each other on.

The larger peer group with whom older children and adolescents socialize may influence aggression even more than their close friends do (Coie & Dodge, 1998). In one study, boys whose companions were involved in covert problem behavior such as theft and selling drugs were over four times more likely to engage in similar behavior themselves than were boys without antisocial companions. They also were twice as likely to start engaging in covert antisocial behaviors if they had not already done so. Similarly, boys exposed to peers involved in *overt* antisocial behaviors, such as violence and the use of a weapon, were over three times as likely as other boys to engage in such acts themselves (Keenan, Loeber, Zhang, Southamer-Loeber, & Van Kammen, 1995). Associating with delinquent peers tends to increase delinquency because these peers model and reinforce antisocial behavior in the peer group. At the same time, participating in delinquent activities brings adolescents into contact with more delinquent peers (Thornberry, Lizotte, Krohn, Farnworth, & Jang, 1994).

Although research findings vary somewhat, it appears that children's susceptibility to peer pressure to become involved in antisocial behavior increases in the elementary school years, peaks at about eighth or ninth grade, and declines thereafter (Berndt, 1979; Brown, Clasen, & Eicher, 1986; Steinberg & Silverberg, 1986). However, there are exceptions to this pattern that appear to be related to cultural factors. Mexican-American immigrants, for example, who are less acculturated and less comfortable using the English language, appear to be less susceptible to peer pressure toward antisocial behavior than are Mexican-American children who are more acculturated. Peers may play less of a role in promoting antisocial behavior for adolescents embedded in a traditional culture oriented toward adults' expectations (e.g., deference and courtesy toward adults and adherence to adult values; Wall, Power, & Arbona, 1993).

Gangs An important peer influence on antisocial behavior can be membership in a gang. It has been estimated that there were 28,700 gangs with 780,000 members active in the United States in 1998 (Moore & Cook, 1999). These gangs tend to be composed of young people, mainly males, who are similar in ethnic and racial background. Most gangs are loosely organized, and most members do not join until their teen years. Although gangs are associated with conflict between ethnic groups, much gang violence takes place between gangs of the same ethnicity (generally Hispanic/Latino or African-American) rather than between gangs of different ethnicities. Drug use and drug selling are common in many gangs, but drugs are not a part of some gangs, and only a minority of gang members sell drugs (Decker & van Winkle, 1996; Esbensen & Huizinga, 1993; Short, 1996).

Adolescents who join gangs tend to engage in antisocial activities and to have delinquent friends prior to joining a gang. However, being in a gang appears to increase adolescents' delinquent behavior over and above the effects of their prior delinquency and association with delinquent peers (Battin, Hill, Abbott, Catalano, & Hawkins, 1998; Lahey, Gordon, Loeber, Stouthamer-Loeber, & Farrington,

A. RAMEY / STOCK BOSTON

Gangs often provide youth with a sense of belonging, underscored with specific gang signs.

1999). Not surprisingly, the longer adolescents remain in a gang, the more likely they are to engage in delinquent and aggressive behavior (Craig, Vitaro, Gagnon, & Tremblay, 2002)

Violence in gangs has become more and more deadly over the years, although there is considerable variability in the levels of violence within and between gangs. Much of the violence involves gang members' attempts to gain or preserve status in the group. Violence also often occurs due to competition with, and retaliation against, other gangs. Moreover, gang members sometimes engage in acts of violence together as a means of increasing group solidarity (Decker, 1996; Short, 1996).

Because many gang members do not have a high school education or do poorly in school, they are likely to have few opportunities to earn money through legitimate employment. Thus, involvement in illegal gang activities may be the most attractive means they know for obtaining money. As a result, many inner-city gang members continue their membership in gangs rather than entering into conventional adult roles (Short, 1996). Indeed, the financial benefits that accrue from illegal activities such as robberies and drug sales are cited by many gang members as a reason for staying in a gang (Decker & van Winkle, 1996).

Television and Video Games

Children's popular culture in the United States is awash in violence, especially its television programming. From 1973 to 1993, 71% of prime-time network programs and 92% of Saturday morning dramatic programs targeted at children contained scenes of violence, ranging from minor instances of hitting in cartoons to gory murders. The average number of violent scenes per hour was 5.3 during prime time and 23 on Saturday mornings (Huston & Wright, 1998). In addition, children often view violent evening shows that are supposedly intended only for adults. Does all this exposure to violence on television have an effect on children? The answer is yes.

There is strong evidence that the more children watch television—especially violence on television—the more violent they are likely to become (Hearold, 1986; Huston & Wright, 1998; Wood, Wong, Chachere, 1991). For example, in a large longitudinal study that followed children from age 8 into adulthood, television viewing at age 8 predicted boys' (but not girls') aggression and severity of criminal arrests in adulthood. This was true even when the effects of intelligence, parenting, and levels of aggression in childhood were taken into consideration (Eron, Huesmann, Lefkowitz, & Warler, 1972; Huesmann, 1986). In longitudinal research conducted over shorter periods of time, similar findings have been obtained in other countries and for girls as well as boys (Huesmann & Eron, 1986). Because viewing television violence predicts later aggression even when taking into account children's initial level of aggression, it is likely that violent television is a causal factor in later aggression. At the same time, aggressive children watch more violent television, so it is also likely that a cycle develops in which both violent television increases children's aggression and aggressive children watch more violent television (Huston & Wright, 1998).

THE EVERETT COLLECTION

Children's cartoons often contain a lot of explicit violence. Although the characters are not real, children may still imitate the violent acts they portray.

The effects of TV violence may be compounded by exposure to violence in movies, video games, and popular songs. Consistent with the general finding that playing violent video games is associated with increases in aggression and aggressive thoughts and feelings (Anderson & Bushman, 2001), it is interesting to note that Harris and Klebold, the killers at Columbine, were obsessed with the violent

applications 14.4

The Fast Track Intervention

Psychologists interested in the prevention of antisocial behavior and violence have designed numerous school-based intervention programs. One of the most intensive is Fast Track—a large federally funded study that is currently being tested in high-risk schools in four U.S. cities (Conduct Problems Prevention Research Group, 1999a,b). This program was initially implemented for three successive years with almost 400 first-grade classes, half of which received the intervention and half of which served as a control group. The children in both groups tended to come from low-income families, about half of which were minority families.

There were two major parts of the intervention. In the first part, all children in the intervention classes were trained with a special curriculum designed to promote understanding and communication of emotions, positive social behavior, self-control, and social problem solving (Greenberg, Kusche, Cook & Quamma, 1995). The children were taught to recognize emotional cues in themselves and to distinguish appropriate and inappropriate behavioral reactions to emotions. They were also taught how to make and keep friends, how to share, how to listen to others, and how to calm themselves down and to inhibit aggressive behavior when they became upset or frustrated.

In the second part of the program, children with the most serious problem behaviors (about 10% of the group) participated in a more intensive intervention. In addition to the school intervention, they attended special meetings throughout the year, receiving social skills training similar to what they experienced in the classroom. They were also tutored in their schoolwork. Their parents participated in group sessions and received training that was designed to build their self-control and promote developmentally appropriate expectations for their child's behavior. In addition, the program sought to develop parenting skills that would improve parent–child interaction, decrease children's disruptive behavior, and establish a positive relationship between parents and the child's school.

The program has been quite successful. In the classrooms as a whole, there was less aggression and disruptive behavior and a more positive classroom atmosphere than in the control classes. More important, the children in the intervention group improved in their social and emotional skills (such as recognizing and coping with emotions), as well as in academic skills. They had more positive interactions with peers, were liked more by their classmates, and exhibited fewer conduct problems than the control children. Their parents improved in their parenting skills and were more involved with their children's school.

In a recent follow-up at the end of third grade, 37% of the children in the intervention group were found to be free of serious conduct problems, whereas only 27% of the children who did not receive the intervention were free of problems (Conduct Problems Prevention Research Group, 2002). Teachers' and parents' reports, as well as information from school records, indicated that there was a modest effect at both home and school. As the study continues, it will be important to assess whether the positive effects persist as the children move into early adolescence. Moreover, this intervention program is quite expensive, so it will be necessary to identify the parts of the intervention that are the most effective.

Target high-risk schools
and
Select first graders with pervasive conduct problems

Promote competency in:
- Academic achievement
- Child coping/Problem solving
- Peer relations
- Parenting and socialization
- Home–school partnership
- Classroom atmosphere

Reduce adolescent rates in:
- Antisocial activity
- Substance abuse
- Psychological problems
- School drop-out

Objectives of the Fast Track project.

videogame Doom—a realistic game in which players hold the power of life and death—and played it every day (Bai, 1999). It is not surprising that a society that promotes and glamorizes violence for commercial purposes should have high rates of violence among its youth.

Biology and Socialization: Their Joint Influence on Children's Antisocial Behavior

As should be clear by now, it is very difficult to separate out the specific biological, cultural, peer, and familial factors that affect the development of children's antisocial behavior (Vanden Oord, Boomsma, & Verhalst, 2000). As we have noted, for example, antisocial children sometimes have biologically based characteristics that tend to elicit negative reactions from others, which in turn increases the children's probability of becoming antisocial. This is especially the case when children's negative behavior elicits harsh punishment.

The relation between socialization and biology is further complicated by the fact that parents whose children are antisocial and aggressive often are that way themselves and predisposed to punitive parenting. Moreover, the effects of parenting on children's aggression sometimes differ depending on the children's temperament—for example, how difficult, active, or unmanageable they are (Bates, Pettit, Dodge, & Ridge, 1998; Colder, Lochman, & Wells, 1997).

Nonetheless, parental treatment of children clearly affects children's antisocial behavior. Direct evidence of the role of parental effects can be found in intervention studies. When parents are trained to deal with their children in an effective manner, there are improvements in their children's conduct problems (Dishion & Andrews, 1995; Kazdin, Siegel, & Bass, 1992). Similar effects have been obtained in intervention studies in schools (see Box 14.4). Moreover, aggressive children exposed to inept, harsh parenting tend to show more antisocial behavior over time. Effects such as these indicate that socialization in and of itself plays a role in the development of antisocial behavior.

review:

Aggressive behavior emerges by the second year of life and increases in frequency during the toddler years. Physical aggression starts to decline in frequency in the preschool years; in elementary school, children tend to exhibit more nonphysical aggression (e.g., relational aggression) than at younger ages, and some children increasingly engage in antisocial behaviors such as stealing. Early individual differences in aggression and conduct problems predict antisocial behavior in later childhood, adolescence, and adulthood. Children who first engage in aggressive, antisocial acts in early to mid-adolescence are less likely than children who are aggressive and antisocial at a younger age to continue their antisocial behavior after adolescence.

Biological factors, including those related to temperament and neurological problems, likely affect how aggressive children become. Social cognition is also associated with aggressiveness in a variety of ways, including the attribution of hostile motives to others, having hostile goals, constructing and enacting aggressive responses in difficult situations, and evaluating aggressive responses favorably.

Children's aggression is affected by a range of environmental factors, as well as by heredity. In general, low parental support, poor monitoring, or the use of disciplinary practices that are abusive or inconsistent are related to high levels of children's antisocial behavior. Parental conflict in the home and many of the stresses associated with family transitions (e.g., divorce) and poverty can increase the likelihood of children's aggression. In addition, involvement with antisocial peers and viewing violent television likely contribute to antisocial behavior, although aggressive children also seek out antisocial peers and violent television. Intervention programs can be used to reduce aggression, which provides evidence of the role of environmental factors in children's aggression.

There are wide individual differences in aggression and other forms of antisocial behavior. From preschool on, boys are more physically aggressive than girls and more likely to engage in delinquent behavior. However, girls are more likely than boys to engage in one type of aggression—attempts to hurt another person's social relationships (relational aggression). Cultural values and practices, as communicated in the child's social world, also contribute to differences among people in aggressive behavior.

Chapter Summary

Moral Judgment

- Piaget delineated two age-related moral stages and a transitional period. In the first stage, morality of constraint, young children tend to believe that rules are unchangeable and to weigh consequences more than intentions in evaluating the morality of actions. In the autonomous stage, children realize that rules are social products that can be changed, and they consider motives and intentions when evaluating behavior. Several aspects of Piaget's theory have not held up well to criticism, but his theory has provided the foundation for subsequent work on moral reasoning.
- Kohlberg outlined three levels of moral judgment—preconventional, conventional, and postconventional—each originally containing two stages (Stage 6 was eventually dropped from Kohlberg's scoring procedure). Kohlberg hypothesized that his sequence of stages reflects age-related discontinuous (qualitative) changes in moral reasoning that are universal. According to Kohlberg, these changes stem from cognitive advances, particularly in perspective taking. Although there is support for the idea that higher levels of moral reasoning are related to cognitive growth, it is not clear that children's moral reasoning moves through discontinuous stages of development or develops the same way in all cultures and for all kinds of moral issues (e.g., prosocial moral reasoning).
- There are important differences among the moral, social conventional, and personal domains of behavior and judgment. Young children, like older children, differentiate among different domains of social judgment. Which behaviors are considered matters of moral, social conventional, or personal judgment varies somewhat across cultures.

The Early Development of Conscience

- The conscience involves internalized moral standards and feelings of guilt for misbehavior: it restrains the individual from engaging in unacceptable behavior. The conscience develops slowly over time, beginning before age 2. Children are more likely to internalize parental standards if they are securely attached and if their parents do not rely on excessive parental power in their discipline.

Prosocial Behavior

- Prosocial behavior is voluntary behavior intended to benefit another, such as helping, sharing, and comforting others. Young children who are prosocial, especially those who spontaneously engage in sharing that is costly to themselves, tend to be prosocial when older.
- Prosocial behaviors emerge by the second year of life and increase in frequency with age, probably due to age-related increases in children's abilities to sympathize and take others' perspectives. Differences among children in these abilities contribute to individual differences in children's prosocial behavior.
- Heredity, which contributes to differences among children in temperament, likely affects how empathic and prosocial children are.
- A positive parent–child relationship, authoritative parenting, the use of reasoning by parents and teachers, and exposure to prosocial models, values, activities, and TV programming are associated with the development of sympathy and prosocial behavior.
- School-based intervention programs designed to promote cooperation, perspective taking, helping, prosocial values, and the exercise of autonomy are associated with increased prosocial tendencies in children.

Antisocial Behavior

- Aggressive behavior emerges by the second year of life and increases in frequency during the toddler years; physical aggression starts to decline in frequency in the preschool years. In elementary school, children tend to exhibit more nonphysical aggression (e.g., relational aggression) than at younger ages, and some children increasingly engage in antisocial behaviors such as stealing.
- From preschool on, boys are more physically aggressive than girls and more likely to engage in delinquent behavior, whereas girls are more likely than boys to engage in relational aggression.
- Early individual differences in aggression and conduct problems predict antisocial behavior in later childhood, adolescence, and adulthood.
- Biological factors that contribute to differences among children in temperament and neurological problems likely affect how aggressive children become. Social cognition also affects aggression: aggressive children tend to attribute hostile motives to others and to have hostile goals themselves.
- Children's aggression is promoted by a range of environmental factors, including low parental support; poor monitoring; abusive, coercive, or inconsistent disciplining; and stress or conflict in the home. In addition, involvement with antisocial peers and exposure to violent TV programs and video games likely contribute to antisocial behavior, although it is also likely that aggressive children seek out antisocial peers and violent entertainment.
- Interventions in high-risk schools designed to promote understanding and communication of emotions, positive social behavior, self-control, and social problem solving and skills can reduce the likelihood that children will develop behavior problems, including aggression.

Critical Thinking Questions

1. Think of a recent moral dilemma in your own life. What sorts of reasoning did you use when thinking about the dilemma? On what dimensions does it differ from Kohlberg's Heinz dilemma? How might these differences affect reasoning about this dilemma?
2. How would you design a study to determine why aggressive children and adolescents have aggressive friends? How would you determine whether aggressive youth simply chose aggressive friends, or whether aggressive friends tend to make youth become more aggressive?
3. Suppose you wanted to assess children's helping behavior that was altruistic and not due to factors such as the expectation of personal gain or concern about others' approval. How would you design a study to assess altruistic helping in 5-year-olds? Might the procedure differ if you wanted to assess altruistic helping in 16-year-olds?
4. Freud believed that morality does not emerge until the child develops a superego at around 4 to 6 years of age. What evidence contradicts his theory?
5. Using the tenets of social learning theory (see Chapter 9), outline ways that parents might deter the development of aggression in their children.

Key Terms

prosocial behavior, p. 540
moral judgments, p. 542
social conventional judgments, p. 542
personal judgments, p. 542
conscience, p. 544
altruistic motives, p. 547
empathy, p. 547
sympathy, p. 547
aggression, p. 555
instrumental aggression, p. 556
relational aggression, p. 556
reactive aggression, p. 560
proactive aggression, p. 560

CHAPTER 15

Conclusions

PABLO PICASSO, *Paul Drawing, Françoise and Paloma,* 1954

THEMES

- Nature and Nurture
- The Active Child
- Continuity/Discontinuity
- Mechanisms of Change
- The Sociocultural Context
- Individual Differences
- Research and Children's Welfare

In the preceding fourteen chapters, we have presented you with a great deal of information about how children develop. You have learned about the development of perception, attachment, conceptual understanding, language, intelligence, emotional regulation, peer relations, aggression, morality, and a host of other vital human characteristics. Although these are all important parts of child development, the sheer amount of information may seem daunting; getting lost in the trees, and losing a sense of the forest, is a real danger. We therefore devote this final chapter to providing you with an overview of the forest, tying together the many specifics that you have learned into an integrative framework. A likely side benefit of reading this chapter is that you probably will discover that you understand much more about child development than you realized.

The integrative framework that organizes this chapter consists of the seven themes that were introduced in Chapter 1 and highlighted throughout the book. As we have noted, most child-development research is ultimately aimed at understanding fundamental issues related to these themes. This is true regardless of the type of development that the research addresses and regardless of whether the research focuses on prenatal events, infants, toddlers, preschoolers, school-age children, or adolescents. Beneath the myriad details, the seven themes emerge again and again.

Theme 1: Nature and Nurture: All Interactions, All the Time

When people think of a child's nature, they typically focus on the biological characteristics with which the child enters the world. When they think of the child's nurture, they focus on the child-rearing experiences provided by parents, caretakers, and other adults. Within this view, nurture is like a sculptor, shaping the raw material provided by the child's nature into closer and closer approximations of its final form.

Although this metaphor is appealing, the reality is much more complex. One source of complexity is children's active participation in their own development. Children, unlike marble or clay, seek out their own experiences, based on their inclinations and interests. They also influence other people's behavior toward them; from birth onward, their nature influences the nurture they receive. Another source of complexity is timing. Rather than nature doing its work before birth and nurture doing its work after, nurture influences development even before birth, and nature is at least as influential in adolescence and adulthood as earlier. In this section, we review how nature and nurture interact to produce development.

LAURA DWIGHT

Rather than sitting back passively, waiting for parents and others to teach them, infants and toddlers actively explore their world. Even the most mundane explorations, such as pulling a shoelace, provide them not only with entertainment but also with information about the environment around them.

Nature and Nurture Begin Interacting Before Birth

When prenatal development proceeds normally, it is easy to think of it as a simple unfolding of innate potential, one in which the environment matters little. When things go wrong, however, the interaction of nature and nurture is all too evident. Consider the effects of teratogens. Prenatal exposure to these potentially harmful substances—among them cigarettes, alcohol, and illegal drugs—can cause a wide variety of physical and cognitive impairments. However, whether a given baby will actually be affected depends on innumerable interactions among the genetics of the mother, the genetics of the fetus, and a host of environmental factors such as the particular teratogen and the timing and amount of exposure.

The interaction of nature and nurture during the prenatal period is also evident in fetal learning. Fetuses in the womb hear their mother's voice; this leads to their learning to prefer her voice over that of other women, a preference that is apparent from the day of birth. Fetuses also develop taste preferences related to their mother's diet during pregnancy. Thus, even qualities that are present at birth, which we usually think of as being determined purely by nature, sometimes reflect the fetus's experience as well.

Infants' Nature Elicits Nurture

Nature equips babies with a host of qualities that elicit appropriate nurture from parents and other caregivers. One big factor in babies' favor is that they are cute; most people enjoy watching and interacting with them. Their looking and smiling at other people motivates others to feel warmly toward them and to care for them. Their emotional expressions—cries, coos, and smiles—guide caregivers' efforts to figure out what to do to make them happy and comfortable. In addition, their attentiveness to sights and sounds that they find interesting encourages others to talk to them and to provide the stimulation necessary for further learning.

Timing Matters

The effects of a given kind of nurture, helpful or harmful, depend on the nature of the organism at the time of the experience. As already noted, timing of exposure to teratogens greatly influences their effects on prenatal development. For example, if a pregnant woman comes down with rubella early in pregnancy, when the developing visual and auditory systems are at a particularly sensitive point, her baby may be born deaf or blind; if she has the same disease later in pregnancy, no damage will occur.

Timing also influences the effects of innumerable experiences that occur in the months and years following birth. Perceptual capabilities present numerous illustrations of the importance of appropriate experience at the appropriate time. The general rule is "use it or lose it"; for normal development to occur, children must encounter the relevant experience during a certain window of time.

Binocular depth perception provides a good example. For normal depth perception, both eyes must focus on the same point. By age 4 months, most infants' eyes do this; however, some infants are born with strabismus (they are cross-eyed), and each of their eyes focuses on a different point, preventing them from obtaining binocular cues to depth. Cross-eyedness is correctable through surgery, but depth perception develops normally only if the surgery is done early. Performing the operation before age 4 months virtually guarantees development of normal depth perception, because it allows normal development of relevant neural pathways in the brain. In contrast, performing the surgery after age 3 years does no good.

Auditory development involves similar sensitive periods. Until 8 months of age, infants can discriminate between phonemes regardless of whether they appear in the language the infants hear daily. By age 12 months, however, infants lose the ability to hear the difference between similar sounds that they do not ordinarily encounter or that are not meaningfully different in their native language.

Similar sensitive periods occur in grammatical development. Children from East Asia who begin to learn English as a second language before age 7 acquire grammatical competence in English that eventually matches that of native-born American children. Those who emigrate at later ages to an English-speaking country rarely gain comparable mastery of English grammar, even after many years of hearing and speaking the language in their adopted land. Deaf children's learning of American Sign Language shows a similar pattern: early exposure results in more complete grammatical mastery.

The importance of normal early experience is also evident in social and emotional development. Infants and toddlers who do not receive love from any caregiver, such as those who spent their first years in the horrible orphanages in Romania in the 1980s or in concentration camps during World War II, often continue to interact abnormally with other people, even after being placed in loving homes. Thus, in many aspects of the development of perception, language, emotions, and social behavior, the timing of experience is crucial: normal early experience is vital for successful later development.

Nature Does Not Reveal Itself All at Once

Many genetically influenced properties do not become evident until middle childhood, adolescence, or adulthood. One obvious example is the physical changes that occur at puberty. A less obvious example involves nearsightedness. Many children are born with genes that predispose them to become nearsighted, but most do not become so until late childhood or early adolescence. The more close work they do during childhood, the more likely that the genetic predisposition will eventually be realized.

DAVID YOUNG-WOLFF / PHOTOEDIT

Differences in running speeds are partially attributable to genetic differences that are present at birth, but nature takes time to reveal itself: who could have looked at these children when they were newborns and predicted which would be the best runners?

The development of schizophrenia follows a similar path. Schizophrenia is highly influenced by genes inherited at conception, but most people who become schizophrenic do not do so until late adolescence or early adulthood. As with other aspects of development, the emergence of schizophrenia reflects a complex interplay between nature and nurture. Children with a schizophrenic biological parent who are raised by nonschizophrenic parents are more likely to become schizophrenic themselves than are the biological children of the nonschizophrenic parents. Children who are raised in troubled homes are also more likely than others to become schizophrenic. However, in a study of adopted children, the only ones with a substantial likelihood of becoming schizophrenic were those whose biological mothers were schizophrenic and who also grew up in troubled families. The interaction between the children's nature and the nurture they received was crucial.

Everything Influences Everything

One common reaction to learning about the complex interactions between nature and nurture is "It sounds like everything influences everything else." This conclusion is basically accurate. Consider some of the factors that influence children's and adolescents' self-esteem. Genes matter; the closer the biological relation between two children or adolescents, the more similar their degree of self-esteem is likely to be. A large part of the reason for this genetic influence on self-esteem is that genes influence a wide range of other characteristics that themselves influence self-esteem. For example, genes strongly affect attractiveness, athletic talent, and academic success, all of which contribute to self-esteem.

Factors other than genes also play large roles in the development of self-esteem. Support from one's family and peers contribute in a positive way; poverty and unpopularity contribute in a negative way. Values of the broader society also are influential. East Asian societies emphasize the importance of self-criticism, and children and adolescents in those societies express less self-esteem than do peers in Western societies. The ways that institutions are organized also interact with characteristics of the child. For example, in the United States, physically mature girls show increased resistance to authority during junior high school, apparently because they chafe under the tight discipline characteristic of junior high schools. Thus, children's nature—their genes, personal characteristics, and behavioral tendencies—interact with the nurture they receive from parents, teachers, peers, and the broader society in ways that shape their self-esteem and other qualities.

Theme 2: Children Play Active Roles in Their Own Development

Children are physically active even before they leave the womb; the kicking that thrills prospective parents is just the most obvious example. Less obvious is how early children become mentally active: even as newborns, they selectively focus on objects and events that interest them, rather than passively gazing at whatever appears before their eyes. Infants' and older children's actions also produce reactions in other people, which further shape the children's development. In this section, we examine four ways in which children contribute to their own development: through physically interacting with the environment, interpreting their experience, regulating their behavior, and eliciting reactions from other people.

Self-Initiated Activity

Even in the womb, normal development depends on the fetus's being active. Fetuses must wiggle their fingers to strengthen their muscles, make breathing movements to strengthen their lungs, push against the uterus to elicit the contractions that expel them into the world, and so on.

COURTESY OF ALICE & ROBERT SIEGLER

Children's choices of activities shape their development. This child's interest in print led him to learn to read and write at age 3; the fact that he was one of the authors' children also probably had something to do with his early interest in these skills.

From the day they are born, children's active nature is apparent in their choosing to look at some things rather than others. They like looking at faces, especially their mother's face. They like looking at objects rather than at blank fields. They like looking at moving objects rather than at stationary ones and at the edges of objects rather than at their interiors. These looking preferences guide babies' attention to the most informative aspects of the environment and thus enhance their learning.

Infants' ability to interact with the environment expands greatly during the first year. At around 3 months, most infants become able to follow moving objects fairly smoothly with their eyes, which improves their ability to follow the actions occurring around them. At 6 or 7 months, most become able to crawl on their bellies and soon after, on their hands and knees; as a result, they no longer have to wait for the world to come to them. By 8 or 9 months, most can hold up their heads, which allows them to reach accurately for objects even when they are not being supported. And by 13 or 14 months, most begin to walk independently, opening a new era in their exploration of the world.

As development proceeds, children's self-initiated activity extends to new domains such as language. Toddlers delight in telling their parents the names of objects for no apparent reason beyond the joy of doing so. They also practice talking in their cribs, even when nobody else is present to hear them. They and older children, both deaf and hearing, invent gestures and words to represent objects and events. As their language proficiency develops, children become skilled at initiating conversations that bring them information, allow them to express their feelings and desires, and help them regulate their emotions.

Similar patterns are seen at older ages in other areas, such as antisocial behavior. For example, in later childhood and adolescence, children's choices of friends and peer groups become increasingly important influences on their aggression, drinking, drug use, and so on. Thus, from before birth through adolescence, children's self-initiated activities contribute to their development.

Active Interpretation of Experience

Children also contribute to their development by trying to understand what they see and hear. Even in the first year, infants form a sense of what is possible. Thus, they show surprise when an impossible event seems to occur, such as one solid object appearing to move through another. Toddlers' and preschoolers' continuous "why" questions attest particularly clearly to their eagerness to understand the world.

This desire to understand also motivates young children to construct informal theories concerning inanimate objects, living things, and people. These theories allow them to go beyond the data provided by their senses to infer underlying causes. For example, preschoolers reason that there must be something inside animals that causes them to grow, breathe, have babies, get sick, and so on, even though they do not know what that something is. They also reason that inanimate objects must have different material inside them than living things do. Children also generate informal theories of more mundane activities: recall the young fisherman who claimed that not looking hungry when fishing would make the fish more likely to bite.

Children's and adolescents' interpretation of experience extends to inferences about themselves as well as about the external world. When some children fail on a task, for example, they feel sad and question their ability. Other children who fail on the same task interpret the failure as a challenge and view it as an opportunity to improve their performance. Similarly, in negative situations, children who are aggressive tend to attribute hostile intentions to others even when the motives of others are unclear; this interpretation leads the aggressive children to lash out before the other person can hurt them. Thus, subjective interpretations of experiences, as well as objective reality, shape development.

Self-Regulation

Another way in which children contribute to their development is by regulating their behavior. Consider how they regulate their emotions. In the first months after they are born, infants rely almost totally on parents and other caregivers to help them cope with fright and frustration. By age 6 months, they learn to cope with fear by turning away from scenes that frighten them and by rubbing their bodies to soothe themselves. During the toddler and preschool periods, children become increasingly adept at using various strategies, such as distracting themselves, when faced with stressors or temptation. During elementary school, they increasingly regulate their expression of emotions and use cognitive strategies to cope with negative situations. During adolescence, they become increasingly able to deal with emotional stress by discussing their problems with peers. At all ages, children who successfully regulate their emotions tend to be more popular and more socially competent than those who are less skilled at emotional regulation.

Over the course of development, there is also a considerable increase in the range of areas in which children regulate their own activities, rather than having others regulate them. Whether 6-year-olds go to sports events, for example, or the movies or the library or religious services, depends mainly on whether their parents take them there. Whether 16-year-olds engage in the same activities depends mainly on whether they want to do so. Selecting moral values, choosing a romantic partner, pursuing an occupation, and deciding whether to have children are just a few of the major decisions that face adolescents and young adults. As noted in Sternberg's theory of intelligence, the wisdom with which people make these choices is an important determinant of their success in life.

Eliciting Reactions from Other People

From the first days of life, children act differently from each other and evoke different reactions from other people. For example, babies with easy temperaments elicit more positive reactions from their parents than do cranky or fussy babies. Similarly, attractive babies receive more affectionate and playful mothering than do less attractive ones. As children develop, their interests and abilities also begin to influence their parents' interactions with them. For example, mothers are more likely to entrust children with helping to care for a younger sibling if they are relatively responsible and sympathetic to the younger child.

The effects that children's initial inclinations have on their parents' behavior toward them tend to multiply over time. Most parents of children who are disobedient, angry, and challenging initially try to be supportive but firm. However, if the bad behavior and defiance continue, many parents give up and become hostile and punitive in return. Other parents, faced with belligerence and aggression, back down from confrontations and increasingly give in to their children's demands. Once such negative cycles are established, they are difficult to stop. If teenagers act

It is all too easy for relations between parents and children to spiral downward, with disobedience and anger from children eliciting anger and hostility from parents, which then elicits more disobedience and anger from children, and so on.

disruptively, and parents respond with hostility, problems generally worsen over the course of adolescence.

Children's characteristics and behavior influence not just their parents' reactions but also those of their peers. At all ages, children who are cooperative, friendly, sociable, and sensitive to others tend to be popular with their peers, whereas those who are aggressive or disruptive tend to be disliked and rejected. These peer reactions have long-term as well as near-term consequences. Rejected children are more likely than popular children to have later difficulty in school and are at higher risk for later criminal activity. Thus, children actively influence their development not only by physically interacting with the environment, interpreting their experiences, and regulating their behavior, but also by eliciting different reactions from other people.

Theme 3: Development Is Both Continuous and Discontinuous

Long before there was a scientific discipline of child development, philosophers and others interested in human nature were already arguing about whether development is continuous or discontinuous. Current disputes between those who believe that development is continuous, such as social learning theorists, and those who believe it is discontinuous, such as stage theorists, are part of the same tradition. There is a good reason why both positions have endured so long: each captures important truths about development. The continuity/discontinuity issue includes two more specific issues: continuity/discontinuity of individual differences and continuity/discontinuity of the standard course of development with age.

Continuity/Discontinuity of Individual Differences

One sense of continuity/discontinuity involves stability of individual differences over time. The basic question is whether children who initially are higher or lower than most peers in some quality continue to be higher or lower in that quality years later. It turns out that many individual differences in psychological properties are moderately stable over the course of development, but the stability is always far from 100%.

Consider the development of intelligence. Some stability is present from infancy onward. For example, the faster that infants habituate to repeated presentation of the same display, the higher their IQ scores tend to be ten or more years later. Similarly, infants' patterns of electrical brain activity (EEGs) are related to their speed of processing and attention regulation at age 12 years. The amount of stability increases with age. IQ scores show some stability from age 3 to age 13, considerable stability from age 5 to age 15, and great stability from age 8 to age 18. However, even at older ages, IQ scores vary somewhat from occasion to occasion. For example, when the same children take IQ tests at ages 8 and 17, the two scores differ on average by 9 points. Part of this variability reflects random fluctuations in how sharp the person is on the particular day of testing and in the person's knowledge of the particular questions on each test. Another part of the variability reflects the fact that even if two children start out with equal intelligence, one may show greater intellectual growth over time.

Individual differences in social and personality characteristics also show some continuity over time. Shy toddlers tend to grow into shy children, aggressive children tend to grow into aggressive adolescents, generous children tend to grow into generous adults, and so on. However, although there is some continuity of individual differences in social, emotional, and personality development, the degree of continuity is generally lower than in intellectual development. For example, whereas children who are high in reading and math achievement in fifth grade generally remain so in seventh grade, children who are popular in fifth grade may or may not be popular in seventh grade. In addition, aspects of temperament such as fearfulness and shyness often change considerably over early and middle childhood.

Regardless of whether the focus is on intellectual, social, or emotional development, the stability of individual differences is influenced by the stability of the relevant aspects of the environment. For example, an infant's attachment to his or her mother correlates positively with the infant's long-term security, but the correlation is higher if the home environment stays consistent than if serious disruptions occur. Similarly, IQ scores are more stable if the home environment remains stable. Thus, continuities in individual differences reflect continuities in children's environments as well as continuities in their genes.

Continuity/Discontinuity over Age: The Question of Stages

Many of the most prominent theories of development divide childhood and adolescence into a small number of discrete stages: Piaget's and Case's theories of cognitive development, Freud's theory of psychosexual development, Erikson's theory of psychosocial development, and Kohlberg's theory of moral development all describe development in this way. The enduring popularity of these stage approaches is easy to understand. They simplify the enormously complicated process of development by dividing it into a few distinct periods. They point to important characteristics of behavior during each period. They impart an overall sense of coherence to the developmental process.

Although stage theories differ in their particulars, they share five key assumptions: (1) development progresses through a series of qualitatively distinct stages; (2) when children are in a given stage, a fairly broad range of their behavior exhibits the features characteristic of that stage; (3) all children go through each stage; (4) the stages occur in the same order for all children; and (5) transitions between stages occur quickly.

Development turns out to be considerably less tidy than stage approaches imply, however. Children who exhibit preoperational reasoning on some tasks often exhibit concrete operational reasoning on others; children who reason in a preconventional way about some moral dilemmas often reason in a conventional way about others; and so on. Rarely is a sudden change evident across a broad range of tasks.

In addition, developmental processes often show a great deal of continuity. Throughout childhood and adolescence, there are continuous increases in the ability to regulate emotions, make friends, understand social norms, take other people's perspectives, inhibit physical aggression, use language, remember events, solve problems, and engage in many other activities.

This does not mean that there are no sudden jumps. When we consider specific tasks and processes, rather than broad domains, we see a number of discontinuities. Three-month-olds move from having almost no binocular depth perception to having adultlike levels within a week or two. Before age 7 months, infants rarely fear strangers; after this time, wariness develops quickly. Many toddlers move in a single day from being unable to walk without support to walking unsupported for a number of steps. After acquiring about one word per week between ages 12 and 18 months, toddlers undergo a vocabulary explosion in which they learn roughly ten words per day for years thereafter. Girls do not menstruate until the month of menarche, but then menstruate every month for the next thirty-five or forty years. Thus, although broad domains rarely show discontinuous changes, specific activities fairly often do.

Whether development appears to be continuous or discontinuous often varies with whether the focus is on behavior or on underlying processes. Behaviors that emerge or disappear quite suddenly may reflect continuous underlying processes. Recall the case of infants' stepping reflex. For the first two months after birth, if infants are supported in an upright position with their feet touching the ground, they will first lift one leg and then the other in a pattern similar to walking. At around age 2 months, however, this reflex suddenly disappears. Underlying the abrupt change in behavior, however, are gradual changes in two dimensions that underlie the behavioral change—infants' weight and leg strength. As babies grow, their weight gain outstrips their gain in leg strength, and they become unable to lift their legs without help. Thus, when babies who have stopped stepping are supported in a tank of water, making it easier for them to lift their legs, the stepping reflex reappears.

Whether development appears continuous or discontinuous also depends on the time scale being considered. Recall that when a child's height was measured every 6 months from birth to 18 years, the growth looked continuous (see Figure 1.2, p. 16). When height was measured daily, however, development looked discontinuous, with occasional "growth days" sprinkled among numerous days without growth.

One way of integrating developmental continuities and discontinuities within a unified framework is to envision development as a road trip through a series of distinct regions. Imagine driving a car across the United States from New York to San Francisco. In one sense, the drive is a continuous progression westward along Interstate 80. In another sense, the drive starts in the East and then proceeds (in an invariant order, without the possibility of skipping a region) through the Midwest and the Rocky Mountains before reaching its end point in California. The East includes the Atlantic Coast and the Appalachians, and it tends to be hilly, cloudy, and green; the Midwest tends to be flatter, dryer, and sunnier; the Mountain States are dryer and sunnier still, with extensive mountainous areas; and most of California is dry and sunny, with both extensive flat and extensive mountainous areas. The differences between regions in climate, color, and topography are large and real, but the boundaries between them are arbitrary. Is Ohio the westernmost Eastern state or the easternmost Midwestern state? Is eastern Colorado part of the Midwest or part of the Rocky Mountain area?

The continuities and discontinuities in development are a lot like those on the road trip. Consider children's conceptions of the self. At one level of analysis, the development of the self is continuous. Over the course of development, children (and adults) understand more and more about themselves. At another level of analysis, milestones characterize each period of development. During infancy, children come to distinguish between themselves and other people, but they rarely if ever take another person's perspective on themselves. During the toddler period, children increasingly view themselves as others might, which allows them to feel such emotions as shame and embarrassment. During the preschool period, children realize that certain of their personal characteristics, such as their gender, are fundamental and permanent, and they use this knowledge to guide their behavior. During the elementary school years, children increasingly think of themselves in terms of their competencies relative to other children (intelligence, athletic skill, popularity, etc.). During adolescence, children come to recognize that, to an extent, who we are as individuals reflects our own choices.

Thus, any statement about when a given competency emerges is somewhat arbitrary, much like a statement about where a geographic region begins. Nonetheless, identifying the milestones helps us understand where we are on the map.

Theme 4: Mechanisms of Developmental Change

As with so many issues, contemporary thinking about developmental change owes a large debt to the ideas of Jean Piaget. Within Piaget's theory, change occurs through the interaction of assimilation and accommodation. Through assimilation, children interpret new experiences in terms of their existing mental structures; through accommodation, they revise their existing mental structures in accord with the new experiences. Thus, when we hear a truly unfamiliar type of music (for most of us, Javanese twelve-tone music would fit this description), we assimilate the sounds to more familiar musical patterns, to the extent we can. At the same time, our understanding accommodates to the experience, so that when we next encounter the unfamiliar music, it will be a little easier to grasp and will feel a little less strange.

A great deal has been learned about developmental mechanisms since Piaget formulated his theory. Some of the advances have come in understanding change at the biological level, others in understanding it at the behavioral level, and yet others in understanding it at the level of cognitive processes.

Biological Change Mechanisms

Biological change mechanisms come into play from the moment a sperm unites with an egg. Each of these cells contains half of the DNA that will constitute the child's genotype throughout life. The genotype contains instructions that specify the rough outline of development, but all particulars are filled in by subsequent interactions between the genotype and the environment.

The way in which the brain forms following conception illustrates the complexity of change at the biological level. The first key process in brain development is *neurogenesis*, which by the third or fourth week after conception is producing roughly 10,000 brain cells *per minute*. About 100 days later, the brain contains just about all of the neurons it ever will have. As neurons form, a process of *cell migration* causes many of them to travel from where they were produced to their long-term location.

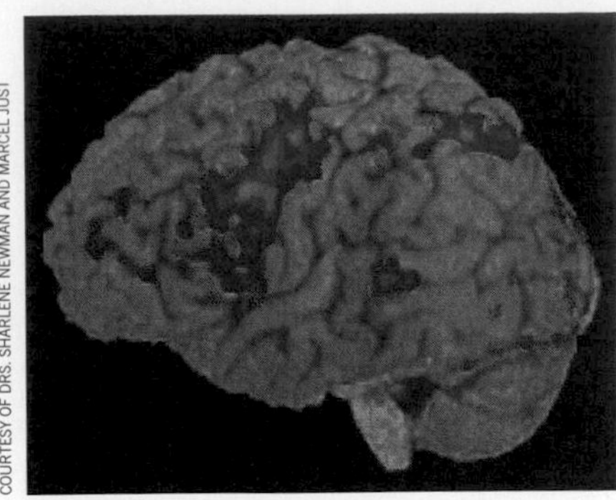
COURTESY OF DRS. SHARLENE NEWMAN AND MARCEL JUST

This fMRI image, taken while a person in a scanner was reading a sentence projected on a screen, shows that diverse areas of the brain contribute to reading comprehension. The large cluster of red toward the front of the brain (the middle of the scan) includes Broca's area, which tends to be especially active in the processing of grammar and meaning. The smaller cluster of red at the back of the brain (the rightmost area of the scan) likely is involved in visual processing of the text. The red area located low and central in the scan corresponds to Wernicke's area, which is particularly involved in processing the meaning of words and sentences. The red area in the upper right part of the image probably reflects processing of the spatial location of the text on the screen.

Once neurons reach their destination, they undergo a process of *differentiation*, in which dendrites and axons grow out from the original cell body. Later in the prenatal period, the process of *myelination* adds an insulating sheath over certain axons, which speeds up the rate of transmission of electrical signals along them. Myelination continues through childhood and into adolescence in some parts of the brain.

Yet another process, *synaptogenesis*, involves formation of synapses at the end of axons and at the beginning of dendrites that allow neurotransmitters to transmit signals from neuron to neuron. From the prenatal period to early or middle childhood (depending on the particular part of the brain), the number of synapses increases rapidly. By the end of this period of explosive growth, the number of synapses in the area far exceeds the number in the brains of adults. A process of *pruning* then reduces the number of synapses in the area. The greatest pruning occurs at characteristic times in each part of the brain but at different times in different parts of the brain. Those synapses that are frequently used are maintained; those that are not are eliminated ("use it or lose it" at the biological level). The pruning of unneeded synapses makes information processing more efficient.

The brain includes a number of areas that are specialized for particular psychological functions. This specialization makes possible rapid and universal development of these functions. Some of them are closely linked to sensory and motor systems. The visual cortex and lateral geniculate are particularly active in processing sights, the auditory cortex is particularly active in processing sounds, the motor cortex is particularly active in motor activity, and so on.

Other brain areas are specialized for altogether different functions. The limbic system is particularly prominent in producing emotions. Certain areas of the occipital and temporal lobes of the cortex are especially crucial for recognizing faces. Broca's and Wernicke's areas are especially active in processing speech. Certain areas toward the back of the right hemisphere are especially active in processing spatial configurations. Each of these areas is involved in numerous other types of processing, and all types of processing involve numerous brain areas, but each of the areas mentioned above is especially active in processing the type of information associated with it. Thus, biological mechanisms underlie both very specific and very general changes.

Behavioral Change Mechanisms

Behavioral change mechanisms describe environmental contingencies and responses to them that contribute to development. These mechanisms shape behavior from extremely early in development.

Habituation and Conditioning

The capacity to habituate to familiar stimuli begins before fetuses leave the womb. When simple syllables such as "ba-by" are spoken into a microphone close to the belly of a woman in her ninth month of pregnancy, her fetus's heart beats faster. The fetus's heart rate changes less and less as the same pair of syllables is repeated in the same order several times. However, when the order of syllables is reversed, so that "by-ba" is presented, the fetus's heart rate again increases, thus demonstrating that the fetus habituated to the original "word" and dishabituated to the novel one. Similar habituation is seen following birth as well; for example, when a picture of a face is shown repeatedly, infants reduce their looking, but they show renewed interest when a different face appears. Habituation helps babies learn by motivating them to seek new stimulation as they lose interest in familiar sights and sounds.

From their first days in the outside world, infants also can learn through classical conditioning. If an initially neutral stimulus is repeatedly presented just before an unconditioned stimulus, it comes to elicit a similar response to that elicited by the unconditioned stimulus. Recall Little Albert, who, after repeatedly seeing a harmless white rat and then hearing a frightening loud noise immediately after, came to fear the white rat (as well as doctors and nurses wearing white lab coats).

The fact that an infant would become afraid not only of the white rat but also of the doctors and nurses illustrates the functioning of another key learning ability that is present from infancy: generalization. Although infants' learning tends to be less general than that of older children, it is never completely literal. Infants generalize the lessons of their past experience to new situations that differ at least in certain details from the original ones.

Like older children, infants also learn through instrumental conditioning; behaviors that are rewarded become more frequent, and behaviors that do not lead to rewards become less frequent. In the first few months after birth, infants learn from instrumental conditioning only when the reinforcement occurs immediately after the relevant behavior; over the next several months, infants become able to learn when delays are longer as well. Thus, basic behavioral learning mechanisms—habituation, generalization, classical conditioning, and instrumental conditioning—allow children to learn from their interactions with the environment from the first days onward.

Social Learning

Children (and adults) learn a great deal from observing and interacting with other people. This social learning pervades our life to such an extent that it is difficult to think of it as a specific learning capability. However, when we compare humans with other animals, even close relatives such as apes and chimpanzees, the omnipresence of social learning in people's lives becomes apparent. Humans are far more skillful than any other animal in learning what others are trying to teach them, and also are far more inclined to teach others what they know. Among the crucial contributors to this social learning are imitation, social referencing, language, and guided participation.

The first discernible form of social learning is imitation. At first, the imitation seems limited to behaviors that infants sometimes produce on their own, such as sticking out their tongue. However, by age 6 months, infants sometimes imitate novel behaviors that they never make spontaneously. By 15 months, toddlers not only learn novel behaviors but remember them and can continue to produce them for at least a week. This imitation isn't just "monkey-see, monkey-do." When children of this age see a model try to do something but fail, they imitate what the model was trying to do rather than what the model actually did.

Social learning influences socioemotional development as well as acquisition of actions and knowledge. When an unfamiliar person enters the room, 12-month-olds look to their mothers for guidance. If the mother's face or voice shows fear, the baby tends to stay close to her; if the mother smiles, the baby is more likely to approach the stranger. Similarly, a baby of this age will cross the visual cliff if the mother smiles but not if she looks apprehensive. Social learning also shapes children's standards and values. From the second year of life, toddlers internalize their parents' values and standards and use them to guide and evaluate their own conduct.

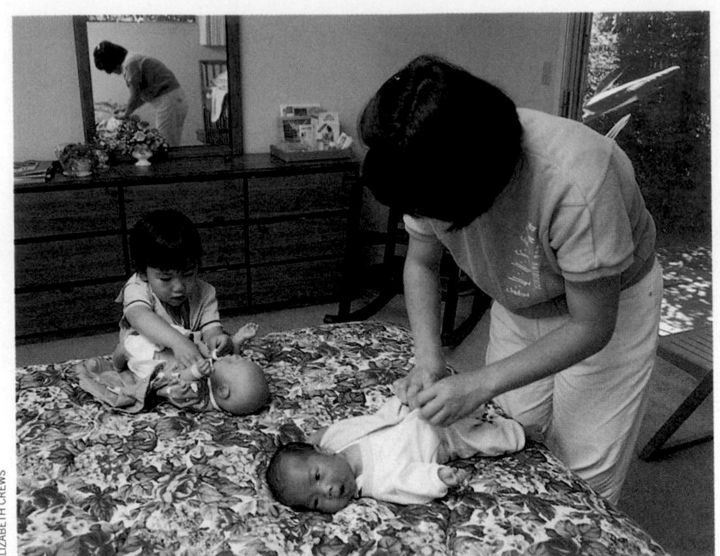

ELIZABETH CREWS

Changing the doll's diapers while Mom changes the baby's is a common activity among children in many homes. Such imitation of parents usually reflects a positive parent–child relationship.

Later in development, peers, teachers, and other adults also influence children's standards and values through the process of social learning. Peers, in particular, play a steadily increasing role over the course of childhood and adolescence.

The amount of social learning varies with the quality of the relationship between the child and the other person. Children are more likely to imitate the behavior of adults with whom they have positive relationships than the behavior of other adults. They also are more likely to imitate friends' behaviors than those of other children who they see doing the same thing; even 1-year-olds prefer to imitate their friends.

Imitation is not the only mechanism of social learning. Another pervasive and effective approach is social scaffolding. In this approach, an older and more knowledgeable person provides a learner with an overview of the task, demonstrates how to do the most difficult parts of it, and hints what the learner should do next. Such scaffolding allows a beginner to do more than would be possible on his or her own. Then, as the learner masters the basics of the task, the scaffolder transfers increasing responsibility until the learner is doing the entire task without assistance. Thus, adults and children work together to produce social learning.

Cognitive Change Mechanisms

Many of the most compelling analyses of developmental change are at the level of cognitive processes. Both general and specific information-processing mechanisms play important roles.

General Information-Processing Mechanisms

Many cognitive mechanisms can be applied to all kinds of information. These general information-processing mechanisms fall into four main categories: basic processes, strategy formation, metacognition, and content knowledge.

Basic processes are the simplest, most broadly applicable, and earliest-developing general information-processing mechanisms. One important basic process is automatization. As children execute a mental process increasingly often, they do so with increasing efficiency. For example, when toddlers begin to speak, pronouncing a word is a slow, effortful process. With practice, pronunciation becomes automatized, which allows children to say words quickly and effortlessly. This frees the mental resources needed to generate longer, more complex sentences. Another basic process, encoding, involves identifying the key features in a situation and mentally representing them. Much of the reason that novel styles of art and music are so confusing is that we do not know what we need to encode to make sense of them. As we learn to encode the crucial information, the previously incoherent sights and sounds come into focus, and we experience them as being sensible, memorable, and even beautiful.

Strategy formation also contributes to many types of development. Toddlers, for example, form strategies for achieving such goals as obtaining a toy that is out of reach or descending a steep surface, preschoolers form strategies for counting and solving arithmetic problems, school-age children form strategies for playing games and getting along with others, and so on. Often, children form multiple strategies for solving a single kind of problem—for example, strategies for approaching unfamiliar children on a playground and joining the game or for solving arithmetic problems. Knowing multiple strategies allows children to adapt to the demands of different problems and situations.

Metacognition is a third general process that contributes to development in large ways. For example, part of the reason why children increasingly rely on memory strategies is that they come to realize that they are unlikely to remember large amounts of material verbatim without using such strategies. Among the most important applications of metacognition is adaptive choice among alternative strategies. The memory strategy of rehearsal presents one clear example. Children often rehearse when they need to remember information verbatim, as with remembering a phone number or a locker combination. However, they almost never rehearse when the literal information does not matter, as with summarizing a story.

Content knowledge is a fourth general contributor to cognitive change. The more children know about any topic, whether it be chess, soccer, dinosaurs, or language, the better able they are to learn and remember new information about it.

TOPHAM / THE IMAGE WORKS

Exceptional content knowledge can outweigh all of adults' usual intellectual advantages over children. On the day this photograph was taken, this 8-year-old boy became the youngest person ever to defeat a Chess Grand Master (the ranking awarded to the greatest chess players in the world).

Domain-Specific Learning Mechanisms

Children acquire some complex competencies surprisingly rapidly. For example, virtually all infants become skilled perceivers within the first six months, despite the fact that visual perception poses extremely difficult problems that to date have not been solved by even the most sophisticated computer systems. What seems to unite the complex capabilities that children acquire especially rapidly, such as perception, language, production and interpretation of emotions, and attachment to caregivers, is their clear evolutionary importance. Evolution seems to have provided us with specialized learning mechanisms that ensure that virtually everyone will quickly and easily acquire abilities that are important to survival.

One type of mechanism that enhances learning in these areas is accurate assumptions about the experiences that the world will provide. Even infants in their first year seem to assume that bigger moving objects will produce stronger effects than smaller moving objects. Similarly, toddlers' word learning is aided by the whole-object assumption (the idea that words that are used to label objects refer to the whole object rather than to a part of it) and the mutual exclusivity assumption (the idea that each object has a single name). These assumptions are usually correct for the words that young children hear and thus help them learn what the words mean and communicate with others.

Children's informal theories about the main types of entities in the world—inanimate objects, people, and other living things—also facilitate their learning about them. The value of learning rapidly about the properties of people, plants and animals, and inanimate objects once again is clear; for example, saying "More juice" to another person is considerably more likely to be successful than is saying it to the family dog. Crucial in children's informal theories, as in scientists' formal ones, are causal relations that explain a large number of observations in terms of a few basic concepts. Possessing basic understanding of key concepts such as forces and solidity for inanimate objects, goal-directed movement and growth for living things, and beliefs and desires for people helps children act appropriately in new situations. For example, when preschoolers meet an unfamiliar child, they assume that the child will have beliefs and desires, which helps them understand the other child's actions and act appropriately. Autistic children, who often do not understand that they and other people have beliefs and desires, have a much harder time interacting appropriately with others. Thus, both general and domain-specific cognitive learning mechanisms help children understand the world around them.

Theme 5: The Sociocultural Context Shapes Development

Children develop within a personal context of other people: families, friends, neighbors, teachers, and classmates. They also develop within an impersonal context of historical, economic, technological, and political forces, as well as societal beliefs, attitudes, and values. The impersonal context is as important as the personal one in shaping development. There is little reason to think that parents in developed societies today care more about their children's development than parents of the past did. Yet their children less often die in infancy, have fewer diseases, eat a more varied and nutritious diet, obtain more years of formal schooling, and see more of the world than did children from the wealthiest families 200 years ago. Thus, when and where children grow up profoundly influences their lives.

Growing Up in Societies with Different Values

Values and practices that people within a society take for granted as the "natural" way often vary substantially among societies. These variations considerably influence the rate and form of development. In previous chapters, you encountered examples of this in every aspect of development, including in domains that are commonly thought of as governed by maturation. For example, it is generally assumed that the timing of walking and other motor skills in infancy is determined solely by biology. However, babies who grow up in African tribes that strongly encourage infants' motor development tend to walk and reach other motor milestones earlier than do infants in the United States. Conversely, babies who grow up in South American tribes that discourage early motor activity reach the motor milestones later than infants in the United States.

Emotional reactions provide another example of how cultural attitudes and values influence behavior even when we might not expect them to do so. Infants in all societies that have been studied show the same attachment patterns, but the frequency of each pattern varies with the values of the society. Relative to babies in the United States and Germany, for instance, Japanese babies who are placed in the Strange Situation more often become very upset, thus showing the insecure-resistant attachment pattern. Babies from northern Germany, on the other hand, are more likely than babies from the United States or Japan to ignore their mother when she reenters the room in the Strange Situation, thus showing the insecure-avoidant attachment pattern. These differences in attachment patterns appear to be due to differing cultural values and practices. Japanese mothers encourage dependence in children and rarely leave their babies alone, which may lead to the babies' becoming especially upset when they are left alone in the Strange Situation. In contrast, northern German parents emphasize early independence and self-sufficiency, which may lead babies in the Strange Situation not to approach the mother when she reenters the room after the separation.

The culture of Mexican villages successfully encourages cooperation and caring among children.

WESLEY BOCKE / PHOTO RESEARCHERS, INC.

Cultural influences such as these continue well beyond infancy. Japanese culture, for example, places a higher value on hiding negative emotions than does American culture; correspondingly, Japanese preschoolers express negative emotions less often than do American preschoolers. American mothers encourage more peer interaction between preschoolers than do Korean mothers; correspondingly, American preschoolers interact more with peers than do Korean children. Child rearing in Mexican villages emphasizes cooperation and caring about others; children raised in these areas are more likely to share their goods than are children from Mexican cities or the United States, a pattern that continues among Mexican-American children whose parents moved from Mexican villages to the United States.

DAVID HARRY STEWART / STONE / GETTY IMAGES

Although authoritarian parenting is generally associated with negative outcomes for adolescents in the United States, the negative outcomes do not generally hold for African-American adolescents.

Culture influences not only parents' actions but also children's interpretations of the actions. For example, Chinese-American mothers use a great deal of scolding and guilt to control their children. In the broader U.S. population, use of this disciplinary approach is associated with negative outcomes, but the association is not present among first-generation Chinese-American children. Similarly, authoritarian parenting is generally associated with negative outcomes for adolescents, but it does not seem to have this effect on African-American adolescents. In both cases, the differing effectiveness of the disciplinary approaches may reflect children's interpretations of the parents' behavior. If children believe that scolding or authoritarian parenting is in their best interest, the behaviors can be effective. However, if children see such disciplinary approaches as reflecting negative parental feelings toward them, the discipline will be ineffective or harmful.

Sociocultural differences exert a similar influence on cognitive development. They help determine which skills and knowledge children acquire—for example, whether children learn to operate abacuses or pocket calculators. They also influence how well children learn skills that everyone acquires to some degree; Australian Aboriginal children, whose lives will eventually depend on their ability to trek through the desert to distant oases, develop spatial skills superior to those of urban Australian children. Finally, cultural values influence the educational system, which in turn influences what and how deeply children learn. For example, students in community-of-learners classrooms learn about fewer scientific topics than do children in traditional classrooms, but they learn about them in greater depth.

Growing Up in Different Times and Places

When and where children grow up profoundly influences their development. As noted earlier, in modern societies, many aspects of children's lives are greatly improved over what they were in the past. Not all of the historical changes in these societies have helped children, however. For example, in North America and Europe, there are far more children of divorce than in the past, and these children are at risk for many problems. On average, they are more prone to sadness and depression, have lower self-esteem, and are less socially competent than peers who live in intact families. Although most children from divorced families do not have serious problems, about 20% to 25% do: engaging in delinquent activities, dropping out of school, and having children out of wedlock are all more common among children whose parents are divorced.

Other historical changes may result in children's lives being different, but neither better nor worse. The great expansion of child care outside the home represents one such case. In the United States, about half of infants and three-fourths of 4-year-olds currently receive child care outside their homes, five times the rates in 1965. As this change was occurring, many people feared that such care would weaken attachment between babies and mothers. Others expressed hopes that such care would greatly stimulate cognitive development, especially of children from impoverished backgrounds, because of the greater opportunities for interaction with other children and adults. In fact, the data indicate that neither the fears nor the exaggerated hopes were justified. Overall, children who receive care outside the home tend to develop very similarly, both emotionally and cognitively, to those who do not. Thus, some of the effects of growing up now rather than in the past are positive, others are negative, and yet others make life different but neither better nor worse.

Growing Up in Different Circumstances Within a Society

Even among children growing up at the same time in the same society, differences in economic circumstances, family relationships, and peer groups lead to large differences in children's lives.

Economic Influences

In every society, the economic circumstances of a child's family considerably influence the child's life. However, the degree of income inequality within each society influences just how large a difference the economic circumstances make. In societies with large income inequalities, such as the United States, poor children's academic achievement is far lower than that of children from wealthier families. In societies with smaller inequalities, such as Japan and Sweden, children from affluent families also do better academically than children from poorer families, but the differences are smaller.

It is not just academic achievement that is influenced by economic circumstances; all aspects of development are. Infants from impoverished families more often are insecurely attached to their mothers. Children and adolescents from impoverished families more often are rejected as friends and more often say they are lonely. Illegal substance use, crime, and depression are more common among poor adolescents than among peers from wealthier backgrounds.

A major reason for these problems is the pressure that poverty places on parents. Poverty is related to marital conflict, which often leads parents to be uninvolved with, or hostile toward, their children and unsupportive of each other's disciplinary techniques. It also is related to authoritarian and punitive child rearing. Poor families also have a considerably higher rate of divorce, which usually further reduces the children's economic circumstances. Indeed, a large part of the harmful effect of divorce on children stems from the economic pressures it creates.

This evocative photograph makes us wonder how the severe poverty this Depression Era family faced affected the children's subsequent lives.

Influences of Family and Peers

Every child's family and peer group is unique, and the ways in which families and peer groups differ have a substantial influence on development. In some families, regardless of income, parents are sensitive to babies' needs and form close attachments with them; in others, this does not occur. In some families, again regardless of income, parents read to their children each night; in others, they do not.

Friends, other peers, teachers, and other adults also are important parts of children's sociocultural environment. Friends play a particularly large role. They can provide companionship and feedback, contribute to self-esteem, and serve as a buffer against stress. During adolescence, friends often become particularly important sources of sympathy and support. On the other hand, friends sometimes have a negative influence, drawing children and adolescents into reckless and aggressive behavior, including crime, drinking, and drug use. Thus, for better and worse, personal relationships, like economic circumstances, history, and culture, play crucial roles in shaping development.

Theme 6: How Do Children Become So Different from One Another?

Children differ among themselves on an infinite number of dimensions: demographic characteristics (gender, race, ethnicity, SES), psychological characteristics (intellect, personality, artistic ability), experiences (where they grow up, whether their parents are divorced, whether they participate in organized sports), and so on. How can we tell which individual differences are the crucial ones?

As illustrated in Figure 15.1, three properties seem most important in determining the importance of a dimension of individual differences. First, as shown by the dotted arrows, children's status on the most important dimensions is related to their status at that time on other important dimensions. Thus, one reason why intelligence is considered a central individual difference is that the higher a child's IQ at a given age, the higher the child's grades, achievement test scores, and general knowledge tend to be at the same time. A second key characteristic is stability over time (the solid arrows). A dimension of individual differences is of greater interest if the higher that children score on it early in development, the higher they

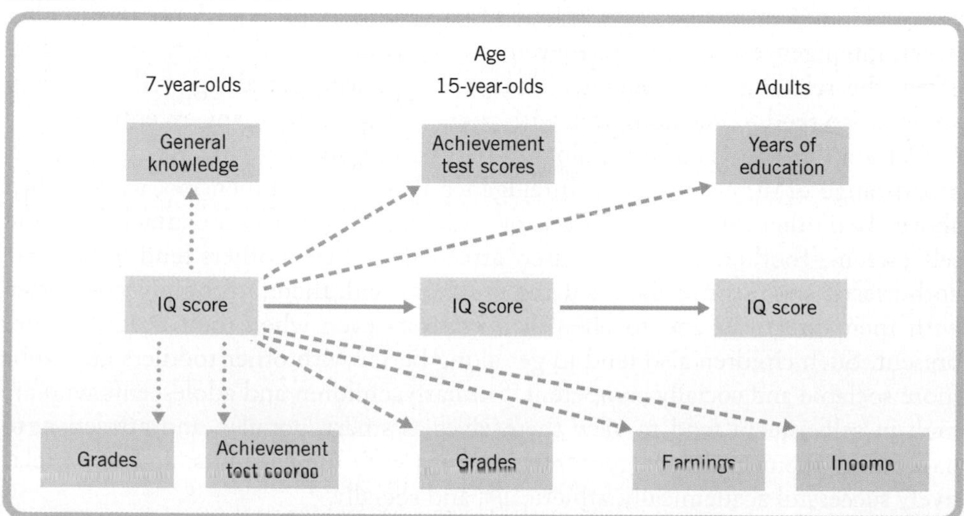

FIGURE 15.1 Intelligence and individual differences Intelligence is considered a crucial dimension of individual differences because IQ scores (1) show considerable continuity over age (solid arrows); (2) correlate with other conceptually related dimensions such as general knowledge and grades at any one age (dotted arrows extending from IQ to other outcomes at age 7); and (3) predict future outcomes, such as years of education and income in adulthood (dashed arrows connecting IQ score at age 7 to later outcomes).

are likely to score on it later. Thus, another reason for interest in IQ is that children with high IQs usually grow into adults with high IQs. A third characteristic of major dimensions of individual differences is that a child's status on the dimension predicts outcomes on other important dimensions in the future (dashed arrows). Thus, a third reason for interest in children's IQ scores is that they predict earnings, occupational status, and years of education in adulthood.

These three criteria make clear why demographic variables such as gender, race, ethnicity, and SES are studied so often. Such variables are related to a wide range of other differences at the time they are measured, they are highly or completely stable over time, and they predict individual differences on other dimensions in the future. Consider differences related to gender, for example. Boys tend to be larger, stronger, more physically active, and more aggressive; to play in larger groups; to be better at visuospatial thinking; and to more often have attention-deficit hyperactivity disorder (ADHD) and math or reading disabilities. Girls tend to be more verbal, quicker perceptually, better at writing, more likely to comfort others, and more likely to express sympathy and empathy for people in distress. Part of the reason for these differences is that children's gender influences how other people act toward them. For example, both mothers and fathers more often encourage girls to play with dolls and to wash dishes, and more often encourage boys to play with tools and wash the family car. Gender also influences the way that children react to a given experience. For example, when a divorced parent remarries, girls tend to have more conflicts with stepparents than boys do.

Below we consider the extent to which several other variables show the three characteristics of major individual differences—associations with a broad range of qualities measured at the same time, stability over time, and long-term relations to other behavioral characteristics.

Breadth of Individual Differences at a Given Time

Individual differences on different dimensions are not randomly distributed. Children who are high on one dimension also tend to be high on other, conceptually related dimensions. Thus, children who do well on one measure of intellect—language, memory, conceptual understanding, problem solving, reading, or mathematics—tend to do well on others. Similarly, children who do well on one measure of social or emotional functioning—relations with parents, relations with peers, relations with teachers, self-esteem, prosocial behavior, and lack of aggression and lying—also tend to do well on others. Sometimes, as with the relation between intelligence and school achievement, the connections are very strong. More often, the relations are moderate. Thus, children who get along well with their parents also tend to get along well with peers, but there are many exceptions.

Certain dimensions of psychological functioning seem crucial for an especially broad range of other outcomes. Intelligence is one such dimension, as described above. Two other crucial dimensions of individual differences are attachment and self-esteem. Toddlers who are securely attached to their mothers tend to be more enthusiastic and positive about solving problems with them, to comply more often with their directives, and to obey their requests even when their mother is not present. Such children also tend to get along better with other toddlers and to be more sociable and socially competent. Similarly, children and adolescents who are high in self-esteem tend to view themselves as smart, popular, and attractive; to have many friends; to have good relationships with their parents; and to be relatively successful academically, athletically, and socially.

Stability over Time

Many individual differences show moderate stability over time. For example, infants with easy temperaments tend to continue to have easy temperaments in middle and later childhood. Children who show strong consciences relative to peers at age 1 usually continue to do so at least through age 5. Elementary school children with attention-deficit disorder, reading disabilities, or mathematics disabilities usually continue to have difficulties in those areas into adulthood.

The reasons for such stability of psychological characteristics are to be found in the stability of both genes and environment. A child's genotype remains identical over the course of development (though particular genes switch on and off at different times). Most children's environments remain fairly stable as well. Families that are middle class when a child is born tend to remain middle class; families that value education when the child is born usually continue to value education; families that are sensitive and supportive generally remain that way; and so on. Major changes, such as divorce and unemployment, do occur, and they affect children's happiness, self-esteem, and other variables. Nonetheless, the relative stability of children's environments, like the stability of their genes, contributes to the stability over time of their psychological functioning.

Predicting Future Individual Differences on Other Dimensions

Individual differences on some dimensions are related not only to future status on that dimension but also to future status on other dimensions. For example, infants who are securely attached tend as toddlers and preschoolers to have more social ties to their peers than do insecurely attached children. When they reach school age, they tend to understand other children's emotions relatively well and to be relatively skilled in resolving conflicts. When they reach adolescence and adulthood, they tend to form close attachments with romantic partners. All of these outcomes are consistent with the view that secure early attachment provides a working model that influences subsequent relationships with other people.

As with stability over time of a single dimension, the relative stability of most children's environment contributes to these long-term relations. If children's environments change in important ways, the typical continuities also may be broken. Thus, stressful events such as divorce reduce the likelihood that children who were securely attached during infancy will continue to show the positive relations with peers usually associated with secure attachment.

Determinants of Individual Differences

Individual differences, like all aspects of development, are ultimately attributable to children's genes and the environments they encounter.

Genetics

For a number of important characteristics—including IQ, prosocial behavior, and empathy—about 50% of the differences among individuals are attributable to differences in genetic inheritance. The degree of genetic influence on individual differences tends to increase over the course of development. For example, correlations between the IQs of adopted

Genetic similarities sometimes produce striking physical resemblance between parent and child. We can only wonder whether this baby, as she develops, will come to resemble her father in other ways as well.

COURTESY OF BETHANY RITTLE-JOHNSON

children and their biological parents, whom the children never see, steadily increase over the course of childhood and adolescence. One reason is that many genes do not exercise their effects until late childhood or adolescence. Another reason is that over the course of development, children become increasingly free to choose environments that are in accord with their genetic predispositions.

Experience

Individual differences reflect children's experiences as well as their genes. Consider just one major environmental influence: one's parents. The more speech that parents address to their toddlers, the more rapidly the toddlers learn new words. The more that parents read to their toddlers, the better readers the children become. The more stimulating and responsive the home intellectual environment, the higher children's IQ and school achievement tend to be. Parents exert at least as large an influence on their children's social and emotional development as on their intellectual development. For example, the likelihood that children will adopt their parents' standards and values appears to be influenced by the type of discipline their parents use with them. Similarly, parents influence their children's willingness to share, especially if the parents discuss the reasons for such prosocial activities and have good relationships with the children.

Parenting, like all of children's other experiences, does not occur in a vacuum; different kinds of parenting work best for different children. This is evident in the development of conscience. For fearful children, the key factor determining whether the child internalizes the parents' moral values is gentle discipline. Fearful children may become so anxious in the face of rigorous discipline that they cannot focus on the moral values that the parents are trying to instill. For fearless children, on the other hand, the key factor is a positive relationship with one's parents. Such fearless children often do not respond to gentle discipline; they tend to internalize the parents' values only if they feel positively toward them. As an old adage states, "It's a wise parent who knows his child."

Theme 7: Child-Development Research Can Improve Children's Lives

One of the few goals shared by virtually everyone is that children be as happy and healthy as possible. Understanding how children develop can lead to progress toward this goal. Theories of development provide general principles for interpreting children's behavior and for analyzing their problems. Empirical studies yield specific lessons regarding how to promote children's physical well-being, their relationships with other people, and their learning. In this section, we examine practical implications of child-development research for raising, educating, and helping children.

Implications for Parenting

Several principles of good parenting are so obvious it might seem as though they hardly need to be pointed out. Yet the number of children who experience difficulties related to poor parenting make it clear that these principles cannot be emphasized enough.

Pick a Good Partner

The practical lessons of child-development research for parents begin even before they become parents. Given the importance of genetics, pick a partner whose physical, intellectual, and emotional characteristics suggest that he or she will provide your child with good genes. Given the importance of the environment, pick a partner who will be a good mother or father. In terms of long-term impact on your child, this choice almost certainly will be the most important decision you ever make.

Ensure a Healthy Pregnancy

An expectant mother should maintain a healthy diet, have regular checkups, and keep stress levels low to increase the likelihood of a successful pregnancy. Equally important is avoiding teratogens such as tobacco, alcohol, and illegal drugs.

Know Which Decisions Are Likely to Have a Long-Term Impact

In addition to the joy they feel when their baby is born, new parents face a daunting number of decisions. Fortunately, babies are quite resilient. In the context of a loving and supportive home, a wide range of choices work out about equally well. Some decisions that seem minor, however, can have important effects. One such decision involves the baby's sleeping position: having a baby sleep on his or her back, rather than on his or her stomach, reduces the possibility of SIDS (sudden infant death syndrome).

In other cases, the lesson of child-development research is that early problems are often transitory, so there is no reason to worry about them. Colic, which affects about 10% of babies, is one such problem; the frequent, high-pitched, grating, sick-sounding cries are difficult for parents to bear, but they have no long-term implications for the babies' development. Given a colicky baby, the best path for parents is to relax, seek social support, and obtain babysitting help to allow some time off from caregiving.

Form a Secure Attachment

Most parents have no difficulty forming a secure attachment with their baby. Some parents and babies, however, do not form such bonds. Parents can maximize the likelihood of their baby's becoming securely attached by maintaining a positive approach in their caregiving and by being responsive to the baby's needs. This is easier said than done, of course, and the baby's temperament, as well as the parents' attitude and responsiveness, influence the likelihood of a secure attachment. However, even when babies are initially irritable and difficult, programs that teach parents how to be responsive and positive with them can lead to more secure attachments.

Prepare Older Siblings for the Baby's Arrival

Another complex problem that confronts many parents is how to treat earlier-born children after the arrival of a new baby. Older siblings often are less than thrilled with the presence of the interloper. However, this transition can be eased if, during the pregnancy, parents discuss with the brothers and sisters where the baby will sleep, what kind of attention infants need, and how family routines will change. Once the baby is born, parents can help older siblings develop a positive

RICHARD HUTCHINGS / PHOTO RESEARCHERS, INC.

Family activities, such as looking at photo albums and reminiscing about the people and settings they depict, provide both stimulation and warm, positive feelings for many children.

attitude by involving them in holding, rocking, and feeding the baby and by making sure that they do not feel neglected.

Provide a Stimulating Environment

The home environment has a great deal to do with children's learning, particularly in early childhood. One good example involves reading acquisition. Telling stories to toddlers and preschoolers, being responsive when they tell stories to you, and reading to them all are positively related to later reading achievement. One reason is that such activities promote phonological awareness (the ability to identify the component sounds within words). Nursery rhymes seem to be particularly effective in this regard; any child who hears *Green Eggs and Ham* sufficiently often learns to appreciate the similarities and differences in *Sam, ham, am,* and related words. Phonological awareness helps children learn to sound out words, which, in turn, helps them learn to retrieve the words' identities quickly and effortlessly. Successful early reading leads children to read more, which helps them improve their reading further over the course of schooling. More generally, the more stimulating the environment, the more eager children will be to learn.

Educational Implications

Theories and research on child development hold a number of further lessons for how to educate children most effectively. Each of the major theories of cognitive development has useful instructional implications.

Piaget's theory emphasizes the importance of the child's active involvement, both mental and physical, in the learning process. This active involvement is especially important in helping children master counterintuitive ideas. For example, the physical experience of walking around a pivot while holding a long metal rod at points close to and far from the pivot allowed children to overcome a widely held misconception that previous classroom physics had failed to correct—the idea that all parts of an object must move at the same speed. Indeed, even high school level science instruction usually fails where this hands-on experience succeeded.

Information-processing theories suggest methods for identifying the sources of children's misunderstandings. The basic idea is to choose problems on which children with systematic misconceptions will generate distinctive patterns of errors. Then, if a child shows a particular misconception, instruction can be directed at the source of the difficulty. (Recall the example of identifying "bugs" in long-subtraction strategies.)

Core-knowledge approaches emphasize children's informal theories. Knowing about these theories can help teachers interpret children's comments and correct their confusions. For example, young children's relatively advanced knowledge of human beings plays a central role in their initial theories of biology and leads them to draw both correct and incorrect inferences about plants and animals. First and second graders, for instance, often believe that water provides nutrition for plants, just as food does for people. This view makes it difficult for them to understand that plants actually create food through photosynthesis. When teachers understand the source of children's confusion, they can explain both the similarities and differences in the way that people and plants obtain nutrition.

Sociocultural theories emphasize the need to turn classrooms into communities of learners in which children cooperate with each other in their pursuit of knowledge. Rather than following the traditional model of instruction in which teachers lecture and children take notes, community-of-learners classrooms follow an alternative approach in which teachers provide the minimum guidance needed for children to learn and gradually decrease their own role relative to that of the children. Such programs also encourage children to make use of the resources of the broader community—children and teachers at other schools, outside experts, Web sites, reference books, and so on. The approach can be effective not only in building intellectual skills but also in promoting desirable values, such as personal responsibility and mutual respect.

Helping Children at Risk

Several principles that have emerged from empirical research offer valuable guidance for helping children at risk for serious developmental problems

The Importance of Timing

Providing treatment at the optimal time is crucial, not only in the earlier-noted case of strabismus but in a variety of other developmental contexts as well. Treatments for low-birth-weight (LBW) babies are one important example. About 6% of babies in the United States, and as many as 50% of babies in poor countries such as Bangladesh, are born weighing 5½ pounds or less. Relative to babies of normal size, babies born this small have higher rates of many problems: poor hearing, language impairments, hyperactivity, and learning disabilities among them. However, the number of LBW babies who develop such problems can be

LAURA DWIGHT

The intellectual stimulation children receive and the academic skills they acquire in Head Start classrooms such as this one boost their IQ and achievement test scores not only at program completion but for several years thereafter.

reduced through stimulation techniques, such as massaging, stroking, and moving the babies' arms and legs. Starting such gentle stimulation soon after birth is crucial to the success of the approach.

Timing also is important in helping children at risk for learning difficulties. All theories of cognitive development indicate that learning difficulties should be addressed early, before children lose confidence in their ability to learn or become resentful toward schools and teachers. This realization, together with research documenting the difficulty that many children from impoverished backgrounds have in school, laid the groundwork for Project Head Start and a variety of smaller experimental preschool programs. Evaluations of the programs' effects indicate that both the experimental programs and Head Start increase children's IQs and achievement test scores by the end of the programs and for several years thereafter. Subsequently, the positive effects on IQ and academic achievement usually fade, but other positive effects continue. Fewer children who participate in such programs are ever held back in school or assigned to special-education classes, and more graduate from high school.

Even greater positive effects of early educational programs are possible, as illustrated by the Abecedarian Project. Designed to show what could be achieved through an optimally staffed, carefully designed program that started during infancy and lasted through age 5, the Abecedarian Project produced gains in both academic achievement and social skills that continued throughout childhood and adolescence. Its results demonstrate that it is possible for intensive programs that start early to have substantial, lasting benefits on poor children's academic achievement.

Early detection of child maltreatment, and intervention to put an end to it, is also crucial. In the United States, roughly 4% of children age 17 and younger are abused or neglected each year. Inadequate care, physical abuse, and sexual abuse are the three most common problems. Parents who are stressed economically have poor impulse control, use alcohol and illegal drugs, are socially isolated, and themselves are being abused by their partner are the most likely to maltreat their children.

Knowing the characteristics of abused and neglected children can help teachers and others who come into contact with children recognize potential problems early and alert social service agencies so that they can investigate and remedy the problems. Children who are maltreated tend to have difficult temperaments, to have few friends, to be in poor physical or mental health, to do poorly in school, and to show abnormal aggressiveness or passivity. Adolescents who are maltreated may be depressed or hyperactive, use drugs or alcohol, and have sexual problems such as promiscuity or abnormal fearfulness. Early recognition of the signs of abuse can literally save a child's life.

Biology and Environment Work Together

Another principle with important practical implications is that biology and environment work together to produce all behavior. This principle has proved important in designing treatments for ADHD. Although stimulant drugs such as Ritalin are the best-known treatment for this problem, research has shown that when medications are used alone, their benefits usually end as soon as children stop taking them. Longer-lasting benefits require behavioral therapy as well as medication. One effective behavioral treatment is to teach the children strategies

ELIZABETH CREWS

In addition to their traditional mission of helping children learn, teachers in contemporary classrooms also need to be aware of signs of children being maltreated, so that they can alert the proper authorities to potential cases of abuse and neglect.

for screening out distractions. The medications calm children with ADHD sufficiently that they can benefit from the therapy; the therapy helps them learn effective ways for dealing with their problems and interacting with other people.

Every Problem Has Many Causes

An additional principle that has proved useful for helping children with developmental problems is that trying to identify *the* cause of any particular problem is futile; problems invariably have multiple causes. Accordingly, providing effective treatment often requires addressing many different difficulties. This principle has provided useful guidance for intervening with children who are rejected by other children. Helping these children gain better social skills requires increasing their understanding of other people. It also requires helping them learn new strategies, such as how to enter an ongoing group interaction unobtrusively and how to resolve conflicts without resorting to violence. It also requires helping them learn from their own experience, for example, by monitoring the success of the different strategies they try. Together, these approaches can help rejected children make friends and become better accepted.

Improving Social Policy

Even if you do not have children of your own and rarely interact with them, your actions as a citizen can influence their lives. Votes in elections and referenda, opinions expressed in informal discussions, and participation in advocacy organizations all can make a difference. Knowledge of child-development research can inform your stances on many issues relevant to children. The conclusions that you reach will, and should, reflect your values as well as the evidence. For example, research indicates that in California, a statewide reduction in maximum class size from thirty-three to twenty raised third graders' average test scores from the fiftieth to the fifty-third percentile on a nationally normed achievement test (Carlos &

Howell, 1999). Research cannot indicate, however, whether this gain was worth the cost of hiring the number of teachers that were needed to reduce the number of pupils in each classroom by this amount. That conclusion depends on values as well as data. Nonetheless, as the example illustrates, knowing the scientific evidence can help us, as citizens, make better-informed decisions.

Maternity Leave

Should society require employers to grant maternity leave in the months after a baby is born? Knowing that long hours of maternal employment before an infant is 9 months old may have negative effects on early cognitive development argues in favor of society making it easier for parents to take maternity leave. However, other considerations such as economic costs are also important; as noted above, the scientific evidence alone can never be decisive.

Day Care

Similar debates have arisen about whether the general society should subsidize day-care payments for parents of young children. One argument against such a policy has been the claim that children develop more successfully if they stay at home than if they attend day care. This argument has turned out to be false, however. Children who attend day care develop extremely similarly to children who receive care at home from their parents.

Eyewitness Testimony

Understanding child development also is vital for deciding whether children should be allowed to testify in court cases and for obtaining the most accurate testimony possible from them. Each year, more than 100,000 children in the United States testify in court, many of them in trials involving allegations of abuse. Often, the child and the accused are the only ones who witnessed the events. Research indicates that, in general, the accuracy of testimony increases with age; 8-year-olds recall more than 6-year-olds, and 6-year-olds recall more than 4-year-olds. However, when children are shielded from misleading and repeated questioning, even 4- and 5-year-olds usually provide accurate testimony about the types of

ELIZABETH CREWS

Children are naturally curious about the world; encouraging this curiosity, and channeling it in fruitful directions, is among the most vital goals facing parents and society alike.

issues that are central in court cases. Asking children to draw what happened increases the amount of relevant information that they correctly remember. Presenting them with anatomically correct dolls decreases accuracy and increases false claims, perhaps because it blurs the boundaries between fact and imagination. Given the high stakes in such cases, using the lessons of research to elicit the most accurate possible testimony from children is essential for justice to be done.

Child-development research holds lessons for numerous other social problems as well. Research on the causes of aggression has led to programs such as Fast Track, which are designed to teach aggressive children to manage their anger and avoid violence. Research on the roots of morality has led to programs such as the Child Development Project, designed to encourage students to help others who are in need. Research on the effects of poverty has provided the basis for the Abecedarian Project and other early education efforts. There is no end of social problems that need to be addressed. Understanding child development can help us address them more effectively.

Critical Thinking Questions

1. What qualities of children influence the way that other people act toward them, and how do these actions influence their development?
2. Individual differences show some stability over time. How do both genes and environment contribute to this stability?
3. How would growing up in one developed society rather than another, for example, the United States rather than Japan, be expected to influence a child's development?
4. How have the changes that have taken place in the United States over the past century influenced children's development? Has the overall effect of the changes been predominantly beneficial or predominantly harmful?
5. What practical lessons have you learned from this course that will influence the way that you raise your children if you have them?

GLOSSARY

A-Not-B error the tendency to reach where objects have been found before, rather than where they were last hidden (p. 133)

accommodation the process by which people adapt current knowledge structures in response to new experiences (p. 129)

adaptation the tendency to respond to the demands of the environment in ways that meet one's goals (p. 129)

ADHD (attention-deficit hyperactivity disorder) a syndrome that involves difficulty in sustaining attention (p. 319)

adult attachment models working models of attachment in adulthood that are believed to be based upon adults' perceptions of their own childhood experiences—especially their relationships with their parents—and of the influence of these experiences on them as adults. The four major attachment groups in adulthood are autonomous (or secure), dismissing, preoccupied, and unresolved/disorganized. (p. 418)

affordances the possibilities for action offered by objects and situations (p. 194)

aggression behavior aimed at harming or injuring others (p. 555)

aggressive-rejected children a category of sociometric status that refers to children who are especially prone to physical aggression, disruptive behavior, delinquency, and negative behavior such as hostility and threatening others (p. 514)

alleles two or more different forms of a gene for a particular trait (p. 89)

altruistic motives helping others for reasons that initially include empathy or sympathy for others and, at later ages, the desire to act in ways consistent with one's own conscience and moral principles (p. 547)

amniotic sac a membrane that is filled with a clear, watery fluid in which the fetus floats and that acts as a protective buffer for the fetus in several ways (p. 50)

anal stage the second stage in Freud's theory, lasting roughly from 1 to 3 years of age, in which the primary source of pleasure comes from defecation (p. 333)

anorexia nervosa an eating disorder in which individuals starve themselves because of an extremely distorted body image (p. 118)

apoptosis programmed cell death (p. 49)

appearance-reality problems problems in which appearances and reality diverge (p. 263)

assimilation the process by which people translate incoming information into a form that they can understand (p. 129)

association areas parts of the brain which lie between the major sensory and motor areas that process and integrate input from those areas (p. 102)

attachment an emotional bond with a specific person that is enduring across space and time. Usually, attachments are discussed in regard to the relation between infants and specific caregivers, although they can also occur in adulthood. (p. 412)

attachment theory theory based on John Bowlby's work that posits that children are biologically predisposed to develop attachments with caregivers as a means of increasing the chances of their own survival (p. 414)

auditory localization perception of the location in space of a sound source (p. 179)

authoritarian parenting a parenting style that is high in demandingness and low in responsiveness. Authoritarian parents are nonresponsive to their children's needs and tend to enforce their demands through the exercise of parental power and the use of threats and punishment. They are oriented toward obedience and authority and expect their children to comply with their demands without question or explanation. (p. 458)

authoritative parenting a parenting style that is high in demandingness and supportiveness. Authoritative parents set clear standards and limits for their children and are firm about enforcing them; at the same time, they allow their children considerable autonomy within those limits, are attentive and responsive to their children's concerns and needs, and respect and consider their child's perspective. (p. 458)

autism a syndrome that tends to produce a number of intellectual and emotional limitations, particularly in understanding and relating to other people (p. 263)

autostimulation theory the idea that brain activity during REM sleep in the fetus and newborn makes up for natural deprivation of external stimuli and facilitates the early development of the visual system (p. 71)

axons neural fibers that conduct electrical signals away from the cell body to connections with other neurons (p. 101)

basic level the middle level, and often the first level learned, within a category hierarchy; for example, dog in the animal/dog/poodle example (p. 256)

basic processes the simplest and most frequently used mental activities (p. 146)

behavior modificiation a form of therapy based on principles of operant conditioning in which reinforcement contingencies are changed to encourage more adaptive behavior (p. 339)

behavioral genetics the science concerned with how variation in behavior and development results from the combination of genetic and environmental factors (p. 94)

behavioral inhibition a temperamentally based style of responding. Behaviorally inhibited children tend to be high in fearful distress and are particularly fearful and restrained when dealing with novel or stressful situations. (p. 392)

bidirectionality of parent–child interactions the idea that parents affect children's characteristics and behaviors and vice versa; both processes occur during parent–child interactions (p. 461)

bilingualism the ability to use two languages (p. 217)

binocular disparity the difference between the retinal image of an object in each eye that results in two slightly different signals being sent to the brain (p. 177)

blastocyst the hollow sphere of cells into which the zygote arranges itself at around the 4th day of development (p. 49)

body image how an individual perceives and feels about his or her physical appearance (p. 114)

bulimia an eating disorder that is characterized by eating binges followed by self-induced vomiting, fasting, and other drastic efforts to avoid gaining weight (p. 118)

Carolina Abecedarian Project a comprehensive and successful enrichment program for children from low-income families (p. 307)

categorical perception the perception of speech sounds as belonging to discrete categories (p. 220)

category hierarchy categories that are related by set–subset relations, such as animal/dog/poodle (p. 254)

cell body a component of the neuron that contains the basic biological material that keeps the neuron functioning (p. 101)

centration the tendency to focus on a single, perceptually striking feature of an object or event (p. 136)

cephalocaudal development the pattern of growth in which areas near the head develop earlier than areas farther away from the head (p. 50)

cerebral cortex the "gray matter" of the brain that plays a primary role in what is thought to be particularly human-like functioning, from seeing and hearing to writing to feeling emotion (p. 102)

cerebral hemispheres the two halves of the cortex. For the most part, sensory input from one side of the body goes to the opposite hemisphere of the brain. (p. 103)

cerebral lateralization the phenomenon that each hemisphere of the brain is specialized for different modes of processing (p. 103)

child maltreatment intentional abuse or neglect that endangers the well-being of anyone under the age of 18 (p. 462)

chromosomes long, threadlike molecules that transmit genetic information. Chromosomes are made up of DNA. (p. 87)

chronosystem in bioecological theory, historical changes that influence the other systems (p. 348)

classical conditioning a form of learning that consists of associating an initially neutral stimulus with a stimulus that always evokes a particular reflexive response (p. 195)

clinical interview a procedure in which questions are adjusted in accord with the answers the interviewee provides (p. 27)

cliques friendship groups that children voluntarily form or join themselves (p. 509)

colic excessive crying for no apparent reason (p. 73)

collective monologues young children's talk with one another that often tends to be a series of nonsequiturs, with the content of each child's turn having little or nothing to do with what the other child has just said (p. 236)

complex stepfamilies families that contain stepsiblings or half siblings (p. 480)

comprehension monitoring the process of keeping track of one's understanding of a verbal description or text (p. 316)

conception the union of an egg and sperm (p. 45)

concepts general ideas or understandings that can be used to group together objects, events, qualities, or abstractions that are similar in some way (p. 252)

concrete operational stage the period (7 to 12 years) within Piaget's theory in which children become able to reason logically about concrete objects and events (p. 131)

conditioned response (CR) in classical conditioning, an originally reflexive response that comes to be elicited by the conditioned stimulus (p. 195)

conditioned stimulus (CS) in classical conditioning, the neutral stimulus that is repeatedly paired with the unconditioned stimulus (p. 195)

connectionist theories a type of information-processing approach that emphasizes the simultaneous activity of numerous, interconnected processing units (p. 151)

conscience an internal regulatory mechanism that increases the individual's ability to conform with standards of conduct accepted in his or her culture (p. 544)

conservation concept the idea that merely changing the appearance of objects does not change their key properties (p. 137)

continuous development the idea that changes with age occur gradually, in small increments, like that of a pine tree growing taller and taller (p. 14)

contrast sensitivity the ability to detect differences in light and dark areas in a visual pattern (p. 173)

control group the group of children in an experimental design who are not presented the experience of interest (p. 32)

controversial peer status a category of sociometric status that refers to children or adolescents who are liked by quite a few peers and are disliked by quite a few others (p. 517)

core-knowledge theories approaches that emphasize the sophistication of infants' and young children's thinking in areas that have been important throughout human evolutionary history (p. 155)

corpus callosum a dense tract of nerve fibers that enable the two hemispheres of the brain to communicate (p. 103)

correlation the association between two variables (p. 30)

correlation coefficient a statistic that indicates the direction and strength of a correlation (p. 30)

correlational designs studies intended to indicate how variables are related to each other (p. 30)

critical period the time during which language develops readily and after which (sometime between age 5 and puberty) language acquisition is much more difficult and ultimately less successful (p. 215)

crossing over the process by which sections of DNA switch from one chromosome to the other. Crossing over promotes variability among individuals. (p. 88)

cross-sectional design a research method in which children of different ages are compared on a given behavior or characteristic over a short period of time (p. 34)

crowds groups of adolescents who have similar stereotyped reputations. Among American high school students, typical crowds may include the "brains," "jocks," "loners," "burnouts," "druggies," "populars," "freaks," "nonconformists," or "losers." (p. 510)

crystallized intelligence factual knowledge about the world (p. 289)

cultural tools the innumerable products of human ingenuity that enhance thinking (p. 160)

cultural training a function of the family; pertains to teaching children the basic values in their culture (p. 454)

dead reckoning the ability to keep track continuously of one's location relative to the starting point and thus to go directly back to it (p. 273)

deferred imitation the repetition of other people's behavior a substantial time after it originally occurred (p. 134)

dendrites neural fibers that receive input from other cells and conduct it toward the cell body in the form of electrical impulses (p. 101)

dependent variable a behavior that is measured to determine whether it is affected by exposure to the independent variable (p. 32)

developmental resilience successful development in the face of multiple and seemingly overwhelming developmental hazards (p. 79)

differentiation the extraction from the constantly changing stimulation in the environment of those elements that are invariant, or stable (p. 194)

direction-of-causation problem the concept that a correlation between two variables does not indicate which, if either, variable is the cause of the other (p. 31)

discontinuous development the idea that changes with age include occasional large shifts, like the transition from caterpillar to cocoon to butterfly (p. 14)

discrete emotions theory a theory about emotions discussed by Tomkins, Izard, and others in which emotions are viewed as innate and discrete from one another from very early in life, and each emotion is believed to be packaged with a specific and distinctive set of bodily and facial reactions (p. 374)

disorganized/disoriented attachment a type of insecure attachment in which infants have no consistent way of coping with the stress of the Strange Situation. Their behavior is often confused or even contradictory, and they often appear dazed or disoriented. (p. 417)

display rules a social group's informal norms about when, where, and how much one should show emotions and when and where displays of emotion should be suppressed or masked by displays of other emotions (p. 406)

distributional properties the phenomenon that in any language, certain sounds are more likely to appear together than are others (p. 223)

DNA (deoxyribonucleic acid) molecules that carry all the biochemical instructions involved in the formation and functioning of an organism (p. 87)

domain specific limited to a particular area, such as living things or people (p. 156)

dominant allele the allele that, if present, gets expressed (p. 89)

dose–response relation the fact that the greater the exposure to a potential teratogen the fetus receives, the more likely it is that a defect will occur and the more severe the defect is likely to be (p. 60)

dual representation the idea that the use of a symbolic artifact can only be achieved if it is represented mentally in two ways at the same time: both as a real object and as a symbol for something other than itself (p. 244)

dynamic-systems theories an information-processing approach that emphasizes how varied aspects of the child function as a single, integrated whole (p. 152)

dyslexia inability to read well despite normal intelligence (p. 315)

economic function a function of the family; pertains to providing the means for children to acquire the skills and other resources they need to be economically productive as adults (p. 454)

ego in psychoanalytic theory, the second personality structure to develop. It is the rational, logical, problem-solving component of personality. (p. 333)

egocentric representations coding of spatial locations relative to one's own body, without regard to the surroundings (p. 270)

egocentrism the tendency to perceive the world solely from one's own point of view (p. 135)

Electra complex Freud's term for the conflict experienced by girls in the phallic stage when they develop unacceptable romantic feelings for their father and see their mother as a rival (p. 353)

embryo the name given to the developing organism from the 3rd to 8th week of prenatal development (p. 49)

embryology the study of prenatal development (p. 43)

emotion emotion is characterized by a motivational force or action tendency and by changes in physiology, subjective experience, and overt behavior. It is defined by functionalists as the attempt or readiness to establish, maintain, or change one's relation with the environment on matters of importance. (p. 373)

emotional intelligence a set of abilities that contribute to competence in the social and emotional domains, including being able to motivate oneself and persist in the face of frustration, control impulses and delay gratification, identify and understand one's own and others' feelings, regulate one's moods, regulate the expression of emotion in social interactions, and empathize with others' emotions (p. 373)

emotional self-regulation the process of initiating, inhibiting, or modulating internal feeling states, emotion-related physiological processes, and emotion-related cognitions or behaviors in the service of accomplishing one's goals (p. 384)

empathy an emotional reaction to another's emotional state or condition that is similar to that other person's state or condition (p. 547)

encoding the process of representing in memory information that draws attention or is considered important (p. 146)

environment every aspect of the individual and his or her surroundings other than genes (p. 86)

epigenesis the idea that there is an emergence of new structures and functions rather than there simply being growth of smaller structures into larger ones (p. 43)

equilibration the process by which children (or other people) balance assimilation and accommodation to create stable understanding (p. 129)

erogenous zones in Freud's theory, areas of the body that become erotically sensitive in successive stages of development (p. 332)

essentialism the view that living things have an essence inside them that makes them what they are (p. 267)

ethology the study of the evolutionary bases of behavior (p. 348)

exosystem in bioecological theory, environmental settings that a person does not directly experience but that can affect the person indirectly (p. 346)

experience-dependent plasticity the process through which neural connections are created and reorganized throughout life as a function of an individual's experiences (p. 110)

experience-expectant plasticity the process through which the normal wiring of the brain occurs in part as a result of the kinds of general experiences that every human who inhabits any reasonably normal environment will have (p. 109)

experimental control the ability of the researcher to determine the specific experiences that children have during the course of an experiment (p. 32)

experimental designs a group of approaches that allow inferences about causes and effects to be drawn (p. 31)

experimental group a group of children in an experimental design who are presented the experience of interest (p. 32)

expressive (holistic) style children who use this speech strategy give more attention to the overall sound of language—its rhythmic and intonational patterns—than to the phonetic elements of which it is composed (p. 228)

external validity the degree to which results can be generalized beyond the particulars of the research (p. 26)

failure-to-thrive (nonorganic) — (FTT) a condition in which infants become malnourished and fail to grow or gain weight for no obvious medical reason (p. 115)

false-belief problems tasks that test a child's understanding that other people will act in accord with their own beliefs even when the child knows that those beliefs are incorrect (p. 262)

family dynamics the way in which the family operates as a whole (p. 454)

fast mapping the process of rapidly learning a new word simply from the contrastive use of a familiar and an unfamiliar word (p. 230)

fetal alcohol syndrome (FAS) the effects of maternal alcoholism on a fetus, including facial deformity, varying degrees of mental retardation, attention problems, hyperactivity, and organ defects (p. 62)

fluid intelligence ability to think on the spot to solve novel problems (p. 289)

foreclosure status a category of identity status in which the individual is not engaged in any identity experimentation and has established a vocational or ideological identity based on the choices or values of others (p. 433)

formal operational stage the period (12 years and beyond) within Piaget's theory in which people become able to think about abstractions and hypothetical situations (p. 131)

fovea the central region of the retina (p. 173)

fraternal twins twins that result when two eggs happen to be released into the fallopian tube at the same time and are fertilized by two different sperm. Fraternal twins share only half their genetic makeup. (p. 49)

friendships intimate, reciprocated positive relationships between two people (p. 497)

frontal lobe the lobe of the brain associated with organizing behavior and the one that is thought responsible for the human ability to plan ahead (p. 102)

functionalist approach a theory of emotion proposed by Campos and others that argues that the basic function of emotions is to promote action toward achieving a goal. In this view, emotions are not discrete from one another and vary somewhat based on the social environment. (p. 374)

***g* (general intelligence)** the part of intelligence that is common to all intellectual tasks (p. 289)

gametes (germ cells) reproductive cells that contain only half the genetic material of all other normal cells in the body (p. 44)

gangs loosely organized groups of adolescents or young adults that identify as a group and often engage in illegal activities (p. 511)

gastrulation the process by which cells start to differentiate after the zygote implants into the uterine lining; the inner cell mass becomes the embryo, and the rest of the cells become its support system (p. 49)

gender constancy realization that gender is invariant in spite of superficial changes in appearance or activities (also known as gender consistency) (p. 358)

gender identity awareness of one's own gender (p. 358)

gender schema organized mental representations (concepts, beliefs, memories) about gender, including stereotypes about gender (p. 359)

gender segregation children's tendency to associate with same-sex peers and to avoid opposite-sex peers (p. 365)

gender self-socialization the process through which children's bias to behave in accord with their gender identity leads them to acquire greater knowledge and expertise with gender-consistent entities (p. 359)

gender stability awareness that gender is stable over time (p. 358)

generativity the idea that by using the finite set of words in our vocabulary, we can put together an infinite number of sentences and express an infinite number of ideas (p. 211)

genes sections of chromosomes that are the basic unit of heredity in all living things (p. 87)

genital stage the fifth and final stage in Freud's theory, beginning in adolescence, in which sexual maturation is complete and sexual intercourse becomes a major goal (p. 334)

genome the complete set of genes that an organism possesses (p. 86)

genotype the genetic material an individual inherits (p. 86)

gesture–speech mismatches a phenomenon in which hand movements and verbal statements convey different ideas (p. 323)

glial cells cells in the brain that provide a variety of critical supportive functions (p. 101)

goodness of fit the degree to which an individual's temperament is compatible with the demands and expectations of his or her social environment (p. 394)

guided participation a process in which more knowledgeable individuals organize situations in ways that allow less knowledgeable people to learn (p. 159)

habituation a simple form of learning that is shown by a decrease in response to repeated or continued stimulation (p. 57)

helpless pattern of motivation a response to failure in which individuals feel badly, blame themselves for their failure, and do not persist at the task because they feel that they cannot succeed (p. 428)

heritability a statistical estimate of the proportion of the measured variance on a given trait among individuals in a given population that is attributable to genetic differences among those individuals (p. 97)

heritable anything (characteristics, traits, etc.) influenced by heredity (p. 94)

heterozygous a description of a person who inherits two different alleles for a trait (p. 89)

holophrastic period the period when children begin using the words in their small productive vocabulary one word at a time (p. 227)

homozygous a description of a person who inherits two of the same allele for a trait (p. 89)

hostile attributional bias in Dodge's theory, the tendency to assume that other people's ambiguous actions stem from a hostile intent (p. 344)

hypotheses educated guesses (p. 24)

id in psychoanalytic theory, the earliest and most primitive personality structure. It is unconscious and operates with the goal of seeking pleasure (p. 333)

identical twins twins that result from the splitting in half of the inner cell mass at the zygote stage, which gives each zygote exactly the same genetic makeup (p. 49)

identity-achievement status a category of identity status in which, after a period of exploration, the individual has achieved a coherent and consolidated identity based on personal decisions regarding occupation, ideology, and the like. The individual believes that these decisions were made autonomously and is committed to them. (p. 433)

identity confusion an incomplete and sometimes incoherent sense of self that often occurs in Erikson's stage of identity versus identity confusion (p. 432)

identity-diffusion status a category of identity status in which the individual does not have firm commitments and is not making progress toward them (p. 433)

identity foreclosure premature commitment to an identity without adequate consideration of other options (p. 432)

identity versus identity confusion Erikson's psychosocial stage of development that occurs during adolescence. During this stage, the adolescent or young adult either develops an identity or experiences an incomplete and sometimes incoherent sense of self. (p. 432)

imaginary audience the belief, stemming from adolescent egocentrism, that everyone else is focused on the adolescent's appearance and behavior (p. 430)

imprinting a form of learning in which the young of some species of newborn birds and mammals become attached to and follow adult members of the species (usually their mother) (p. 348)

independent variable the experience that children in the experimental group receive and that children in the control group do not receive (p. 32)

infant-directed speech (IDS) the distinctive mode of speech that adults adopt when talking to babies and very young children (p. 218)

inner cell mass the bulge of cells on the inside of the blastocyst that eventually forms into the embryo (p. 49)

insecure attachment a pattern of attachment in which children have a less positive attachment to their caregiver than do securely attached children. Insecurely attached children can be classified as insecure/resistant (ambivalent), insecure/avoidant, or disorganized/disoriented. (p. 417)

insecure/avoidant attachment a type of insecure attachment in which infants or young children seem somewhat indifferent toward their caregiver and may even avoid the caregiver. In the Strange Situation, they seem indifferent toward their caregiver before the caregiver leaves the room and indifferent or avoidant when the caregiver returns. If they get upset when left alone, they are as easily comforted by a stranger as by a parent. (p. 417)

insecure/resistant (or ambivalent) attachment a type of insecure attachment in which infants or young children are clingy and stay close to their caregiver rather than exploring their environment. In the Strange Situation, insecure/resistant infants tend to get very upset when the caregiver leaves them alone in the room, and are not readily comforted by strangers. When their caregiver returns, they are not easily comforted and both seek comfort and resist efforts by the caregiver to comfort them. (p. 417)

instrumental aggression aggression motivated by the desire to obtain a concrete goal (p. 556)

instrumental conditioning *(operant conditioning)* learning the relation between one's own behavior and the consequences that result (p. 196)

intention the goal of acting in a certain way (p. 259)

intermodal perception the combining of information from two or more sensory systems (p. 182)

internal validity the degree to which effects observed within experiments can be attributed to the variables that the researcher intentionally manipulated (p. 26)

internal working model of attachment the child's mental representation of the self, of attachment figure(s), and of relationships in general that is constructed as a result of experiences with caregivers. The working model guides children's interactions with caregivers and other people in infancy and at older ages. (p. 415)

internalization the process of adopting as one's own the attributes, beliefs, and standards of another person (p. 334)

interrater reliability the amount of agreement in the observations of different raters who witness the same behavior (p. 25)

intersubjectivity the sharing of a common focus of attention by two or more people (p. 225)

IQ (intelligence quotient) a summary measure used to indicate a child's intelligence relative to others of the same age (p. 293)

joint attention a process in which social partners intentionally focus on a common referent in the external environment (p. 162)

kwashiorkor malnutrition brought about by inadequate protein (p. 119)

language comprehension understanding what others say (or sign or write) (p. 211)

language production actually speaking (or signing or writing) to others (p. 211)

latency period the fourth stage in Freud's theory, lasting from age 6 to age 12, during which sexual energy gets channeled into socially acceptable activities (p. 334)

lobes major areas of the cortex (p. 102)

longitudinal design a method of study in which the same children are studied twice or more over a substantial period of time (p. 34)

low birth weight (LBW) a birth weight of less than 5½ pounds (2,500 grams) (p. 75)

macrosystem in bioecological theory, the larger cultural and social context within which the other systems are embedded (p. 347)

marasmus malnutrition brought about by the ingestion of too few calories (p. 119)

mastery-oriented pattern of motivation a response to failure in which individuals do not evaluate themselves negatively and increase their efforts to master the task (p. 428)

mathematical equality the concept that the values on each side of the equal sign must be equivalent (p. 322)

means–end problem solving the process of using an action (the means) to achieve a goal (the end) (p. 204)

meiosis specialized cell division necessary for reproduction that produces cells (gametes) that have only half of the normal complement of chromosomes (p. 44)

menarche the onset of menstruation (p. 114)

mental model processes used to represent a situation or sequence of events (p. 314)

mesosystem in bioecological theory, the interconnections among immediate, or microsystem, settings (p. 346)

metalinguistic knowledge an understanding of the properties and function of language—that is, an understanding of language as language (p. 212)

microgenetic design a method of study in which the same children are studied repeatedly over a short period of time (p. 35)

microsystem in bioecological theory, the immediate environment that an individual personally experiences (p. 346)

modularity hypothesis the idea that the human brain contains an innate, self-contained language module that is separate from other aspects of cognitive functioning (p. 238)

monocular or pictorial cues the perceptual cues of depth that can be perceived by one eye alone. Examples are relative size and interposition. (p. 177)

moral judgments decisions that pertain to issues of right and wrong, fairness, and justice (p. 542)

moratorium status a category of identity status in which the individual is in the phase of experimentation with regard to occupational and ideological choices and has not yet made a clear commitment to them (p. 433)

morphemes the smallest units of meaning in a language, composed of one or more phonemes (p. 212)

multifactorial refers to the involvement of many factors in any outcome (p. 94)

multiple intelligence theory Gardner's theory of intellect, based on the view that people possess at least eight types of intelligence (p. 308)

mutation a change in a section of DNA. Mutations can contribute to genetic diversity among people, but most have a deleterious effect on the individual. (p. 88)

myelin sheath a fatty sheath that forms around certain axons in the body and increases the speed and efficiency of information transmission in the nervous system (p. 101)

myelination the formation of myelin (a fatty sheath) around the axons of neurons that speeds and increases information-processing abilities (p. 103)

naive psychology a commonsense level of understanding of other people and oneself (p. 258)

narratives descriptions of past events that have the basic structure of a story (p. 236)

naturalistic experiments a type of experimental design in which data are collected in everyday settings (p. 33)

naturalistic observation examination of how children behave in their usual environments—schools, playgrounds, homes, and so on (p. 28)

nature our biological endowment; the genes we receive from our parents (p. 10)

negative identity identity that stands in opposition to what is valued by people around the adolescent. Some adolescents form a negative identity while trying to construct an identity during Erikson's stage of identity versus identity confusion. (p. 433)

neglected peer status a category of sociometric status that refers to children or adolescents who are infrequently mentioned as liked or disliked; they simply are not noticed much by peers (p. 517)

neural-network approach a synonym for connectionist theories (p. 151)

neural tube a U-shaped groove formed from the top layer of differentiated cells in the embryo that eventually becomes the brain and spinal cord (p. 50)

neurogenesis the proliferation of neurons through cell division (p. 103)

neurons cells that are specialized for sending and receiving electrical messages between the brain and all parts of the body, as well as within the brain itself (p. 101)

non-REM sleep a quiet or deep sleep state characterized by the absence of motor activity or eye movements and regular, slow brain waves, breathing, and heart rate (p. 70)

norm of reaction the concept that encompasses all the phenotypes that can theoretically result from a given genotype in relation to all the environments in which it can survive and develop (p. 91)

normal distribution a pattern of data in which scores fall symmetrically around a mean value, with most scores falling close to the mean and fewer and fewer scores farther from it (p. 293)

numerical equality the realization that all sets of *N* objects have something in common (p. 278)

nurture the environments, both physical and social, that influence our development (p. 10)

object permanence the knowledge that objects continue to exist even when they are out of view (p. 132)

object segregation the identification of separate objects in a visual array (p. 176)

object substitutions a form of pretense in which an object is used as something other than itself (p. 245)

occipital lobe the lobe of the brain that is primarily involved in processing visual information (p. 102)

Oedipus complex Freud's term for the conflict experienced by boys in the phallic period because of their sexual desire for their mother and their fear of retaliation by their father (p. 352)

optical expansion a depth cue in which an object occludes increasingly more of the background, indicating that the object is approaching (p. 177)

oral stage the first stage in Freud's theory, occurring in the first year, in which the primary source of satisfaction and pleasure is oral activity (p. 333)

organization the tendency to integrate particular observations into coherent knowledge (p. 129)

overextension the use of a given word in a broader context than is appropriate (p. 228)

overlapping-waves theories an information-processing approach that emphasizes the variability of children's thinking (p. 152)

overregularization speech errors in which children treat irregular forms of words as if they were regular (p. 234)

parallel processing thinking that occurs simultaneously (p. 151)

parental-investment theory a theory that stresses the evolutionary basis of many aspects of parental behavior, including the extensive investment parents make in their offspring (p. 349)

parental sensitivity an important factor contributing to the security of an infant's attachment. Parental sensitivity can be exhibited in a variety of ways, including responsive caregiving when children are distressed or upset and helping children to engage in learning situations by providing just enough, but not too much, guidance and supervision. (p. 420)

parenting styles parenting behaviors and attitudes that set the emotional climate in regard to parent–child interactions, such as parental responsiveness and demandingness (p. 457)

parietal lobe the lobe of the brain that governs spatial processing as well as integrating sensory input with information stored in memory (p. 102)

peers people of approximately the same age and status (p. 496)

perception the process of organizing and interpreting sensory information (p. 171)

perceptual categorization the grouping together of objects with similar appearances (p. 255)

perceptual constancy the perception of objects as being of constant size, shape, color, etc., in spite of physical differences in the retinal image of the object (p. 174)

permissive parenting a parenting style that is high in responsiveness but low in demandingness. Permissive parents are responsive to their children's needs and do not require their children to regulate themselves or act in appropriate or mature ways. (p. 458)

personal judgments decisions that refer to actions in which individual preferences are the main consideration (p. 542)

personal fable a story that adolescents tell about themselves that involves beliefs in the uniqueness of their own feelings and their immortality (p. 430)

personality the pattern of behavioral and emotional propensities, beliefs and interests, and intellectual capacities that characterize an individual. Personality has its roots in temperament (and thus has a constitutional basis) but is shaped by interactions with the social and physical world. (p. 395)

personification generalizing knowledge about people to infer properties of other animals (p. 158)

personify to attribute qualities of human beings to other entities (p. 265)

phallic stage the third stage in Freud's theory, lasting from age 3 to age 6, in which sexual pleasure is focused on the genitalia (p. 334)

phenotype the observable expression of the genotype, including both body characteristics and behavior (p. 86)

phenylketonuria (PKU) a disorder related to a defective recessive gene on chromosome 12 that prevents metabolism of phenylalanine. Without early diagnosis and a properly restricted diet, PKU can lead to severe mental retardation. (p. 92)

phonemes the elementary units of meaningful sound used to produce languages (p. 212)

phonemic awareness ability to identify component sounds within words (p. 311)

phonological development the acquisition of knowledge about the sound system of a language (p. 212)

phonological processing ability to discriminate and remember sounds within words (p. 315)

phonological recoding skills ability to translate letters into sounds and to blend sounds into words (p. 312)

phylogenetic continuity the idea that because of our common evolutionary history, humans share some characteristics and developmental processes with other animals, especially mammals (p. 48)

placenta an organ with an extraordinarily rich network of blood vessels that permits the exchange of materials between the bloodstreams of the fetus and its mother while keeping the two circulatory systems separate (p. 50)

plasticity the capacity of the brain to be affected by experience (p. 108)

polygenic inheritance inheritance in which traits are governed by more than one gene (p. 90)

popular peer status a category of sociometric status that refers to children or adolescents who are viewed positively (liked) by many peers and are viewed negatively (disliked) by few peers (p. 513)

positive reinforcement a reward that reliably follows a behavior and increases the likelihood that the behavior will be repeated (p. 196)

pragmatic cues aspects of the social context used for word learning (p. 231)

pragmatic development the acquisition of knowledge about how language is used (p. 212)

preferential-looking technique a method for studying visual attention in infants that involves showing infants two patterns or two objects at a time to see if the infants have a preference for one over the other (p. 172)

premature any child born at 35 weeks after conception or earlier, as opposed to the normal term of 38 weeks (p. 75)

preoperational stage the period (2 to 7 years) within Piaget's theory in which children become able to represent their experiences in language, mental imagery, and symbolic thought (p. 131)

prereaching movements clumsy swiping movements by young infants toward the general vicinity of objects they see (p. 188)

pretend play make-believe activities in which children often create new symbolic relations—for example, using a broom to represent a horse (p. 245)

primary mental abilities seven abilities said by Thurstone to be crucial to intelligence (p. 290)

proactive aggression unemotional aggression aimed at fulfilling a need or desire (p. 560)

problem solving the process of attaining a goal by using a strategy to overcome an obstacle (p. 144)

Project Rightstart a curriculum designed to prepare kindergartners from low-income backgrounds for elementary school mathematics (p. 322)

prosocial behavior voluntary behavior intended to benefit another, such as helping, sharing, and comforting of others (p. 540)

prosody the characteristic rhythm, tempo, cadence, melody, intonational patterns, and so forth with which a language is spoken (p. 219)

psychic energy Freud's term for the biologically based instinctual drives that he believed energize behavior, thoughts, and feelings (p. 332)

psychological constructs ideas used to understand human behavior, such as desires, beliefs, and actions (p. 258)

psychosocial moratorium a time-out during which the adolescent is not expected to take on adult roles and can pursue activities that lead to self-discovery (p. 433)

puberty the developmental stage marked by the ability of the body to reproduce. This stage is accompanied by dramatic bodily changes. (p. 114)

random assignment a procedure in which each child has an equal chance of being assigned to each group within an experiment (p. 32)

reactive aggression emotionally driven, antagonistic aggression sparked by one's perception that other people's motives are hostile (p. 560)

recessive allele the allele that is not expressed if a dominant allele is present (p. 89)

reciprocal determinism Bandura's concept that child–environment influences operate in both directions; children are affected by aspects of their environment, but they also influence the environment (p. 341)

reciprocated best friendship a friendship in which two children view one another as best or close friends (p. 502)

reference in language and speech, the associating of words and meaning (p. 226)

referential (analytic) style speech strategy that analyzes the speech stream into individual phonetic elements and words; the first utterances of children who adopt this style tend to use isolated, often monosyllabic words (p. 228)

reflexes innate, fixed patterns of action that occur in response to particular stimulation (p. 183)

regulator genes genes that control the activity of other genes (p. 88)

rehearsal the process of repeating information over and over to aid memory (p. 149)

rejected peer status a category of sociometric status that refers to children or adolescents who are liked by few peers and disliked by many peers (p. 514)

rejecting-neglecting (disengaged) parenting a parenting style that is low in both responsiveness and demandingness. Rejecting-neglecting parents do not set limits for or monitor their children's behavior, are not supportive of them, and sometimes are rejecting or neglectful. They tend to be focused on their own needs rather than their children's. (p. 459)

relational aggression aggression that harms others by damaging their peer relationships (p. 556)

reliability the degree to which independent measurements of a given behavior are consistent (p. 25)

REM (rapid eye movement) an active sleep state that is associated with dreaming in adults and is characterized by quick, jerky eye movements under closed lids (p. 70)

retina the back surface of the eye containing the light-sensitive neurons, the rods and cones, that translate light into messages that are sent to the brain (p. 173)

role taking being aware of the perspective of another person, thereby better understanding that person's behavior, thoughts, and feelings (p. 343)

schemas strategies that can be applied for solving any problem within a class of situations (p. 324)

scientific method an approach to testing beliefs that involves choosing a question, formulating a hypothesis, testing the hypothesis, and drawing a conclusion (p. 24)

script the way in which some type of everyday event usually goes (p. 150)

secular trends marked changes in physical development that have occurred over generations (p. 114)

secure attachment a pattern of attachment in which an infant or child has a high-quality, relatively unambivalent relationship with his or her attachment figure. In the Strange Situation, a securely attached infant, for example, may be upset when the caregiver leaves but may be happy to see the caregiver return, recovering quickly from any distress. When children are securely attached, they can use caregivers as a secure base for exploration. (p. 416)

secure base Bowlby's term for when an attachment figure's presence provides an infant or toddler with a sense of security that makes it possible for an infant to explore the environment (p. 414)

selection the more frequent survival and reproduction of organisms that are well adapted to their environment (p. 18)

selective attention the process of intentionally focusing on the information that is most relevant to the current goal (p. 149)

self a conceptual system made up of one's thoughts and attitudes about oneself (p. 424)

self-conscious emotions emotions such as guilt, shame, embarrassment, and pride that relate to our sense of self and our consciousness of others' reactions to us (p. 380)

self-esteem one's overall evaluation of the worth of the self and the feelings that this evaluation engenders (p. 443)

self-locomotion the ability to move oneself around in the environment (p. 189)

self-socialization the idea that children play a very active role in their own socialization through their activity preferences, friendship choices, and so on (p. 343)

semantic development the learning of the system for expressing meaning in a language, including word learning (p. 212)

sensation the processing of basic information from the external world by the sensory receptors in the sense organs (eyes, ears, skin, etc.) and brain (p. 171)

sensitive period the period of time during which a developing organism is most vulnerable to damage by outside agents (p. 59)

sensorimotor stage the period (birth to 2 years) within Piaget's theory in which intelligence is expressed through sensory and motor abilities (p. 131)

separation anxiety feelings of distress that children, especially infants and toddlers, experience when they are separated, or expect to be separated, from individuals to whom they are attached (p. 379)

sequential processing thinking that occurs one thought after another (p. 151)

sex chromosomes the chromosomes that determine an individual's gender (p. 87)

sexual-minority youth people who experience same-sex attractions and for whom the question of personal sexual identity is often confusing and painful (p. 439)

sexual orientation a person's preference in regard to males or females as objects of erotic feelings (p. 439)

SIDS (sudden infant death syndrome) the unexpected death of an infant less than 1 year of age that has no identifiable cause (p. 63)

small for gestational age (SGA) babies that weigh substantially less than is normal for whatever their gestational age (p. 75)

social comparison the process of comparing aspects of one's own psychological, behavioral, or physical functioning to that of others in order to evaluate oneself (p. 427)

social competence the ability to achieve personal goals in social interactions while simultaneously maintaining positive relationships with others (p. 386)

social conventional judgments decisions that pertain to customs or regulations intended to secure social coordination and social organization (p. 542)

social referencing infants' use of a parent's facial, gestural, or vocal cues to decide how to deal with novel, ambiguous, or possibly threatening situations (p. 402)

social scaffolding a process in which more competent people provide a temporary framework that supports children's thinking at a higher level than children could manage on their own (p. 162)

social skills training training programs designed to help rejected children gain peer acceptance that are based on the assumption that rejected children lack important knowledge and skills that promote positive interaction with peers (p. 516)

social smiles smiles that are directed at people. They first emerge as early as 6 to 7 weeks of age. (p. 376)

socialization the process through which children acquire the values, standards, skills, knowledge, and behaviors that are regarded as appropriate for their present and future role in their particular culture (p. 456)

sociocultural context the physical, social, cultural, economic, and historical circumstances that make up any child's environment (p. 19)

sociocultural theories approaches that emphasize the contribution to children's development of other people and the surrounding culture (p. 159)

socioeconomic status a measure of social class based on income and education (p. 21)

sociometric status a measurement that reflects the degree to which children are liked or disliked by their peers as a group (p. 512)

spines formations on the dendrites of neurons that increase the dendrites' capacity to form connections with other neurons (p. 103)

stage theories approaches that propose that development involves a series of discontinuous, age-related phases (p. 15)

standard deviation a measure of the variability of scores in a distribution; in a normal distribution, 68% of scores fall within 1 standard deviation of the mean and 95% of scores fall within 2 standard deviations (p. 293)

state refers to an infant's level of arousal and engagement in the environment, ranging from deep sleep to intense activity. State is an important mediator of young infants' experience of the world. (p. 69)

stepping reflex a neonatal reflex in which an infant lifts first one leg and then the other in a coordinated pattern like walking (p. 187)

stereopsis the process by which the visual cortex combines the differing neural signals, caused by binocular disparity, resulting in the perception of depth (p. 177)

Strange Situation a procedure developed by Mary Ainsworth to assess infants' attachment to their primary caregiver (p. 415)

strategy-choice process procedure for selecting among alternative ways of solving problems (p. 313)

structured interview a research procedure in which all participants are asked to answer the same questions (p. 27)

structured observation a procedure that involves presenting an identical situation to each child and recording the child's behavior (p. 29)

style the strategies that young children enlist in beginning to speak (p. 228)

subitizing a process by which adults and children can look at a few objects and almost immediately know how many objects are present (p. 281)

subordinate level the most specific level within a category hierarchy; for example, poodle in the animal/dog/poodle example (p. 256)

superego in psychoanalytic theory, the third personality structure consisting of internalized moral standards (p. 334)

superordinate level the most general level within a category hierarchy; for example, animal in the animal/dog/poodle example (p. 256)

survival of offspring a function of the family; pertains to ensuring the survival of offspring by providing for their needs (p. 454)

swaddling a soothing technique, used in many cultures, which involves wrapping a baby tightly in cloths or a blanket, thereby restricting limb movement (p. 72)

symbolic representation the use of one object to stand for another (p. 135)

symbols systems for representing our thoughts, feelings, and knowledge and for communicating them to other people (p. 210)

sympathy the feeling of concern for another person (or animal) in reaction to that other person's (or animal's) emotional state or condition; often an outcome of empathizing with another's negative emotion or situation (p. 547)

synapses microscopic junctions between the axon terminal of one neuron and the dendritic branches or cell body of another. Synapses are where the communication between neurons happens. (p. 101)

synaptogenesis the process by which neurons form synapses with other neurons, resulting in trillions of connections (p. 107)

syntactic bootstrapping the strategy of using the grammatical structure of whole sentences to figure out meaning (p. 232)

syntactic development the learning of the syntax of a language (p. 212)

syntax rules in a language that specify how words from different categories (nouns, verbs, adjectives, etc.) can be combined (p. 212)

systematic desensitization a form of therapy based on classical conditioning, in which positive responses are gradually conditioned to stimuli that initially elicit a highly negative response; especially useful in the treatment of fears and phobias (p. 338)

task analysis the research technique of identifying goals, relevant information in the environment, and potential processing strategies for a problem (p. 143)

telegraphic speech the term describing children's first sentences that are generally two-word utterances (p. 233)

temperament constitutionally based individual differences in emotional, motor, and attentional reactivity and self-regulation that demonstrate consistency across situations, as well as relative stability over time (p. 388)

temporal lobe the lobe of the brain that is associated with memory, visual recognition, and the processing of emotion and auditory information (p. 102)

teratogens environmental agents that have the potential to cause harm during prenatal development. The harm can range from easily correctible problems to death. (p. 59)

test–retest reliability the degree of similarity of a child's performance on two or more occasions (p. 26)

theory of mind a basic understanding of how the mind works and how it influences behavior (p. 260)

theory of mind module (TOMM) a hypothesized brain mechanism devoted to understanding other human beings (p. 264)

theory of successful intelligence Sternberg's theory of intellect, based on the view that intelligence is the ability to achieve success in life (p. 310)

third-variable problem the concept that a correlation between two variables may stem from both being influenced by some third variable (p. 31)

three-stratum theory of intelligence Carroll's model of intelligence, including *g* at the top of the hierarchy, eight moderately general abilities in the middle, and many specific processes at the bottom (p. 290)

umbilical cord a tube that contains the blood vessels that travel from the placenta to the developing organism and back again (p. 50)

unconditioned response (UCR) in classical conditioning, a reflexive response that is elicited by the unconditioned stimulus (p. 195)

unconditioned stimulus (UCS) in classical conditioning, a stimulus that evokes a reflexive response (p. 195)

universal grammar the idea that using a language requires knowledge of a set of highly abstract, unconscious rules and that these rules are common to all languages (p. 238)

utilization deficiency the phenomenon that initial uses of strategies do not improve memory as much as later uses (p. 149)

validity the degree to which a test measures what it is intended to measure (p. 26)

variables attributes that vary across individuals and situations, such as age, gender, and expectations (p. 30)

variation differences in thought and behavior within and among individuals (p. 18)

vicarious reinforcement observing someone else receive a reward or punishment (p. 340)

victimized peer status with respect to peer relations, this term refers to children who are targets of their peers' aggression and demeaning behavior (p. 522)

violation-of-expectancy a procedure used to study infant cognition in which infants are shown an event that should evoke surprise or interest if it violates something the infant knows or assumes to be true (p. 200)

visual acuity the sharpness of visual discrimination (p. 172)

visually based retrieval proceeding directly from the visual form of a word to its meaning (p. 313)

voice onset time (VOT) the length of time between when air passes through the lips and when the vocal cords start vibrating (p. 220)

wait-and-see style the children who use this speech strategy often begin to speak very late but then have a large vocabulary and quickly acquire more words (p. 228)

Wechsler Intelligence Scale for Children (WISC) a widely used test designed to measure the intelligence of children 6 years and older (p. 292)

withdrawn-rejected children a category of sociometric status that refers to rejected children who are socially withdrawn, wary, and often timid (p. 515)

zone of proximal development (ZPD) the range of performance between what children can do unsupported and what they can do with optimal support (p. 164)

zygote the fertilized egg formed from the union of an egg cell and a sperm cell (p. 46)

REFERENCES

Aboud, F. E., & Mendelson, M. J. (1996). Determinants of friendship selection and quality: Developmental perspectives. In W. M. Bukowski, A. F. Newcomb, & W. W. Hartup (Eds.), *The company they keep: Friendship in childhood and adolescence* (pp. 87–112). Cambridge, England: Cambridge University Press.

Abramovitch, R., Corter, C., & Lando, B. (1979). Sibling interaction in the home. *Child Development, 4*, 997–1003.

Achenbach, T. M., Phares, V., Howell, C. T., Rauh, V. A., & Nurcombe, B. (1990). Seven-year outcome of the Vermont intervention program for low-birthweight infants. *Child Development, 61*, 1672–1681.

Acredolo, C., & Schmidt, J. (1981). The understanding of relative speeds, distances, and durations of movement. *Developmental Psychology, 17*, 490–493.

Acredolo, L. P. (1978). The development of spatial orientation in infancy. *Developmental Psychology, 14*, 224–234.

Acredolo, L. P., Adams, A., & Goodwin, S. W. (1984). The role of self-produced movement and visual tracking in infant spatial orientation. *Journal of Experimental Child Psychology, 38*, 312–327.

Acredolo, L. P., & Goodwyn, S. W. (1990). Sign language in babies: The significance of symbolic gesturing for understanding language development. In R. Vasta (Ed.), *Annals of child development: A research annual* (Vol. 7, pp. 1–42). London: Jessica Kingsley.

Adams, M. J. (1990). *Beginning to read: Thinking and learning about print.* Cambridge, MA: MIT Press.

Adams, M. J., Treiman, R., & Pressley, M. (1998), Reading, writing, and literacy. In W. Damon (Series Ed.) and I. E. Sigel & K. A. Renninger (Vol. Eds.), *Handbook of child psychology: Vol.4. Child psychology in practice.* (5th ed., pp. 275–355). New York: Wiley.

Adams, R. J. (1995). Further exploration of human neonatal chromatic-achromatic discrimination. *Journal of Experimental Child Psychology, 60*, 344–360.

Adamson, L. B., & Bakeman, R. (1991). The development of shared attention during infancy. In R. Vasta (Ed.), *Annals of child development* (Vol. 8, pp. 1–41). London: Kingsley.

Adolph, K. E. (1997). Learning in the development of infant locomotion. *Monographs of the Society for Research in Child Development, 62*(3, Serial No. 251).

Adolph, K. E. (2000). Specificity of learning: Why infants fall over a veritable cliff. *Psychological Science, 11*, 290–295.

Adolph, K. E., Eppler, M., & Gibson, E. (1993). Crawling versus walking infants' perception of affordances for locomotion over sloping surfaces. *Child Development, 64*, 1158–1174.

Adolph, K. E., Vereijken, B., & Denny, M. A. (1998). Learning to crawl. *Child Development, 69*, 1299–1312.

Aguiar, A., & Baillargeon, R. (2000). Perseveration and problem solving in infancy. In H. W. Reese (Ed.). *Advances in child development and behavior* (Vol. 27, pp. 135–180). San Diego, CA: Academic Press.

Ahadi, S. A., Rothbart, M. K., & Ye, R. (1993). Children's temperament in the U.S. and China: Similarities and differences. *European Journal of Personality, 7*, 359–377.

Ahmed, A., & Ruffman, T. (1998). Why do infants make A not B errors in a search task, yet show memory for the location of hidden objects in a nonsearch task? *Developmental Psychology, 34*, 441–453.

Ainsworth, M. D. S. (1967). *Infancy in Uganda: Infant care and the growth of attachment.* Baltimore, MD: Johns Hopkins Press.

Ainsworth, M. D. S. (1973). The development of infant-mother attachment. In B. Caldwell & H. Ricciuti (Eds.), *Review of child development research* (Vol. 3, pp. 1–94). Chicago: University of Chicago Press.

Ainsworth, M. D. S., Blehar, M. C., Waters, E., & Wall, S. (1978). *Patterns of attachment: A psychological study of the strange situation.* Hillsdale, NJ: Erlbaum.

Alexander, K. L., & Entwistle, D. R. (1996). Schools and children at risk. In A. Booth & J. F. Dunn (Eds.), *Family-school links: How do they affect educational outcomes?* (pp. 67–88). Mahwah, NJ: Erlbaum.

Alibali, M. W. (1999). How children change their minds: Strategy change can be gradual or abrupt. *Developmental Psychology, 35*, 127–145.

Allison, D. B., & Pi-Sunyer, F. X. (1994, May/June). Fleshing out obesity. *The Sciences*, 38–43.

Altermatt, E. R., Jovanovic, J., & Perry, M. (1998). Bias or responsivity? Sex and achievement-level effects on teachers' classroom questioning practices. *Journal of Educational Psychology, 90*, 516–527.

Altshuler, J. L., Genevro, J. L., Ruble, D. N., & Bornstein, M. H. (1995). Children's knowledge and use of coping strategies during hospitalization for elective surgery. *Journal of Applied Developmental Psychology, 16*, 53–76.

Alwin, D. F. (1984). Trends in parental socialization: Detroit, 1958–1983. *American Journal of Sociology, 90*, 359–381.

Alwin, D. F. (1989). Social stratification, conditions of work, and parental socialization values. In N. Eisenberg, J. Reykowski, & E. Staub (Eds.), *Social and moral values: Individual and societal perspectives* (pp. 327–346). Hillsdale, NJ: Erlbaum.

Amato, P. R. (2001). Children of divorce in the 1990s; An update of the Amato and Keith (1991) meta-analysis. *Journal of Family Psychology, 15*, 355–370.

Amato, P. R., & Keith, B. (1991). Parental divorce and the well-being of children: A meta-analysis. *Psychological Bulletin, 110*, 26–46.

American Psychiatric Association. (1994). *Diagnostic and statistical manual of mental disorders.* Washington, DC: Author.

Anderman, E. M., & Midgley, C. (1997). Changes in achievement goal orientations, perceived academic competence, and grades across the transition to middle-level schools. *Contemporary Educational Psychology, 22*, 269–298.

Anderson, C. A., & Bushman, B. J. (2001). Effects of violent video games on aggressive behavior, aggressive cognition, aggressive affect, physiological arousal, and prosocial behavior: A meta-analytic review of the scientific literature. *Psychological Science, 12*, 353–359.

Anderson, J. R., & Lebiere, C. (1998). *Atomic components of thought.* Mahwah, NJ: Erlbaum.

Anderson, M. (1992). *Intelligence and development: A cognitive theory.* Oxford, England: Blackwell.

Anderson, R. C., Wilson, P. T., & Fielding, L. G. (1988). Growth in reading and how children spend their time outside school. *Reading Research Quarterly, 23,* 285–303.

Andrews, J., Foster, S., Capaldi, D., & Hops, H. (2000). Adolescent and family predictors of physical aggression, communication, and satisfaction in young adult couples: A prospective analysis. *Journal of Consulting and Clinical Psychology, 68,* 195–208.

Anglin, J. M. (1993). Vocabulary development: A morphological analysis. *Monographs of the Society for Research in Child Development, 58*(10, Serial No. 238).

Anisfeld, M., Turkewitz, G., Rose, S. A., Rosenberg, F. R., Sheiber, F. J., Couturier-Fagan, D. A., et al. (2001). No compelling evidence that newborns imitate oral gestures. *Infancy, 1,* 111–122.

Aptehar, L., & Ciano-Federoff, L. M. (1999). Street children in Nairobi: Gender differences in mental health. *New Directions in Child Development, 85,* 35–46.

Archer, J. (1991). The influence of testosterone on human aggression. *British Journal of Psychology, 81,* 1–28.

Arduini, D., Rizzo, G., & Romanini, C. (1995). Fetal behavioral states and behavioral transitions in normal and compromised fetuses. In J. Lecanuet, W. P. Fifer, N.A. Krasnegor, & W.P. Smotherman (Eds.), *Fetal development: A psychobiological perspective.* Hillsdale, NJ: Erlbaum.

Aristotle. (1954). *Nicomachean ethics* (D. Ross, Trans.). London: Oxford University Press.

Arnett, J. J. (1999). Adolescent storm and stress, a reconsideration. *American Psychologist, 54,* 317–328.

Aronson, E. (2000). *Nobody left to hate: Teaching compassion after Columbine.* New York: Worth.

Asendorpf, J. B. (1990). Development of inhibition during childhood: Evidence for situational specificity and a two-factor model. *Developmental Psychology, 26,* 721–730.

Asendorpf, J. B., Warkentin, V, & Baudonniere, P.-M. (1996). Self-awareness and other-awareness: II. Mirror self-recognition, social contingency awareness, and synchronic imitation. *Developmental Psychology, 32,* 313–321.

Ashcraft, M. H., Kirk, E. P., & Hopko, D. (1998). On the cognitive consequences of mathematics anxiety. In C. Donlan (Ed.), *The development of mathematical skills* (pp. 175–196). East Sussex: Psychology Press.

Asher, S. R., & Dodge, K. A. (1986). Identifying children who are rejected by their peers. *Developmental Psychology, 22,* 444–449.

Asher, S. R., & Rose, A. J. (1997). Promoting children's social-emotional adjustment with peers. In P. Salovey & D. J. Sluyter (Eds.), *Emotional development and emotional intelligence* (pp.196–224). New York: Basic Books.

Aslin, R. N. (1981). Development of smooth pursuit in human infants. In D. F. Fisher, R. A. Monty & J. W. Senders (Eds.), *Eye movements: Cognition and visual perception* (pp. 31–51). Hisllsdale, NJ: Erlbaum.

Aslin, R. N., Jusczyk, P. W., & Pisoni, D. B. (1998). Speech and auditory processing during infancy: Constraints on and precursors to language. In W. Damon (Series Ed.), D. Kuhn, & R. S. Siegler (Vol. Eds.), *Handbook of child psychology: Vol. 2. Cognition, perception, and language* (5th ed., pp. 147–198). New York: Wiley.

Aslin, R. N., Saffran, J. R., & Newport, E. L. (1998). Computation of conditional probability statistics by 8-month-old infants. *Psychological Science, 9,* 321–324.

Astington, J. W. (1993). *The child's discovery of the mind.* Cambridge, MA: Harvard University Press.

Atran, S. (1990). *Cognitive foundations of natural history.* Cambridge, England: Cambridge University Press.

Atran, S. (1994). Causal constraints on categories and categorical constraints on biological reasoning across cultures. In S. Sperber, D. Premack, & A. J. Premack (Eds.), *Causal cognition: A multidisciplinary debate.* New York: Oxford University Press.

Attie, I., Brooks-Gunn, J., & Petersen, A. C. (1990). A developmental perspective on eating disorders and eating problems. In M. Lewis & S. Miller (Eds.), *Handbook of developmental psychopathology* (pp. 409–420). New York: Plenum Press.

Attili, G., Vermigli, P., & Schneider, B. H. (1997). Peer acceptance and friendship patterns among Italian schoolchildren within a cross-cultural perpective. *International Journal of Behavioral Development, 21,* 277–288.

Augusta, D., & Hakuta, K. (1998). *Educating language-minority children.* Washington, DC: National Academy Press.

Avis, J., & Harris, P. L. (1991). Belief-desire reasoning among Baka children: Evidence for a universal conception of mind. *Child Development, 62,* 460–467.

Ayduk, O., Mendoza-Denton, R., Downey, G., Peake, P. K., & Rodriguez, M. (2000). Regulating the interpersonal self: Strategic self-regulation for coping with rejection sensitivity. *Journal of Personality and Social Psychology, 79,* 776–792.

Azmitia, M., & Montgomery, R. (1993). Friendship, transactive dialogues, and the development of scientific reasoning. *Social Development, 2,* 202–221.

Backscheider, A. G., Shatz, M., & Gelman, S. A. (1993). Preschoolers' ability to distinguish living kinds as a function of regrowth. *Child Development, 64,* 1242–1257.

Baenninger, M., & Newcombe, N. (1989). The role of experience in spatial test performance: A meta-analysis. *Sex Roles, 20,* 327–344.

Baffes, P., & Mooney, R. (1996). Refinement-based student modeling and automated bug library construction. *Journal of Artificial Intelligence in Education, 7,* 75–116.

Bagwell, C. L., Newcomb, A. F., & Bukowski, W. M. (1998). Preadolescent friendship and peer rejection as predictors of adult adjustment. *Child Development, 69,* 140–153.

Bahrick, L. E. (1994). The development of infants' sensitivity to arbitrary intermodal relations. *Ecological Psychology, 6,* 111–123.

Bahrick, L. E., & Watson, J. S. (1985). Detection of intermodal proprioceptive-visual contingency as a potential basis of self-perception in infancy. *Developmental Psychology, 21,* 963–973.

Bai, D., & Bertenthal, B. I. (1992). Locomotor status and the development of spatial search skills. *Child Development, 63,* 215–226.

Bai, M. (1999, May 3). Anatomy of a massacre. *Newsweek.*

Bailey, J. M., Bobrow, D., Wolfe, M., & Mikach, S. (1995). Sexual orientation of adult sons and gay fathers. *Developmental Psychology, 31,* 124–129.

Bailey, J. M., & Pillard, R. C. (1991). A genetic study of male sexual orientation. *Archives of General Psychiatry, 43,* 808–812.

Bailey, J. M., Pillard, R. C., Neale, M. C., & Agyes, Y. (1993). Heritable factors influence sexual orientation in women. *Archives of General Psychiatry, 50,* 217–223.

Baillargeon, R. (1987a). Object permanence in 3.5- and 4.5-month-old infants. *Developmental Psychology, 23,* 655–664.

Baillargeon, R. (1987b). Representing the existence and the location of hidden objects: Object permanence in 6- and 8-month old infants. *Cognition, 23,* 21–41.

Baillargeon, R. (1991). Reasoning about the height and location of a hidden object in 4.5- and 6.5-month-old infants. *Cognition, 38,* 13–42.

Baillargeon, R. (1993). The object concept revisited: New directions in the investigation of infants' physical knowledge. In C. E. Granrud (Ed.), *Visual perception and cognition in infancy.* Hillsdale, NJ: Erlbaum.

Baillargeon, R. (1994). How do infants learn about the physical world? *Current Directions in Psychological Science, 3,* 133–140.

Baillargeon, R. (1995). A model of physical reasoning in infancy. In C. Rovee-Collier & L. P. Lipsitt (Eds.), *Advances in Infancy Research* (Vol 9). Norwood, NJ: Ablex.

Baillargeon, R. & DeVos, J. (1991). Object permanence in 3.5- and 4.5-month-old infants: Further evidence. *Child Development, 62,* 1227–1246.

Baillargeon, R., DeVos, J., & Graber, M. (1989). Location memory in 8-month-old infants in a non-search AB task: Further evidence. *Cognitive Development, 4,* 345–367.

Baillargeon, R. & Graber, M. (1987). Where's the rabbit? 5.5-month-old infants' representation of the height of a hidden object. *Cognitive Development, 2,* 375–392.

Baillargeon, R., Kotovsky, L., & Needham, A. (1995). The acquisition of physical knowledge in infancy. In G. Lewis, D. Premack, & D. Sperber (Eds.), *Causal understandings in cognition and culture.* Oxford, England: Oxford University Press.

Baillargeon, R., Needham, A., & DeVos, J. (1992). The development of young infants' intuitions about support. *Early Development and Parenting, 1,* 69–78.

Baillargeon, R., Spelke, E. S., & Wasserman, S. (1985). Object permanence in 5-month-old infants. *Cognition, 20,* 191–208.

Baker, L. (1994). Fostering metacognitive development. In H. Reese (Ed.), *Advances in child development and behavior* (Vol. 25). San Diego, CA: Academic Press.

Bakermans-Kranenburg, M. J., van IJzendoorn, M. H., & Juffer, F. (in press). Less is more: Meta-analyses of sensitivity and attachment interventions in early childhood. *Psychological Bulletin.*

Balaban, M. T., Anderson, L. M., & Wisniewski, A. B. (1998). Lateral asymmetries in infant melody perception. *Developmental Psychology, 34,* 39–48.

Baldwin, D. A. (1991). Infants' contribution to the achievement of joint reference. *Child Development, 62,* 875–890.

Baldwin, D. A. (1993a). Early referential understanding: Infants' ability to recognize referential acts for what they are. *Developmental Psychology, 29,* 832–843.

Baldwin, D. A. (1993b). Infants' ability to consult the speaker for clues to word reference. *Journal of Child Language, 20,* 395–419.

Baldwin, D. A., Markman, E. M., & Mellartin, R. L. (1993). Infants' ability to draw inferences about nonobvious object properties: Evidence from exploratory play. *Child Development, 64,* 711–728.

Baldwin, D. A., & Moses, L. J. (1994). Early understanding of referential intent and attentional focus: Evidence from language and emotion. In C. Lewis & P. Mitchell (Eds.). *Children's early understanding of mind.* Hove, England: Erlbaum.

Ball, W., & Tronick, E. (1971). Infant responses to impending collision: Optical and real. *Science, 171,* 818–820.

Bandura, A. (1965). Influence of models: Reinforcement contingencies on the acquitition of imitative behaviors. *Journal of Personality and Social Psychology, 1,* 589–595.

Bandura, A. (1977). *Social learning theory.* Upper Saddle River, NJ: Prentice-Hall.

Bandura, A. (1986). *Social foundations of thought and action.* Upper Saddle River, NJ: Prentice-Hall.

Bandura, A., Ross, D., & Ross, S. A. (1963). Imitation of film-mediated aggressive models. *Journal of Abnormal Social Psychology, 66,* 3–11.

Bandura, A., & Walters, R. H. (1963). *Social learning and personality development.* New York: Holt, Rinehart, & Winston.

Banerjee, M. (1997). Hidden emotions: Preschoolers' knowledge of appearance-reality and emotion display rules. *Social Cognition, 15,* 107–132.

Banich, M. T. (1997). *Neuropsychology: The neural bases of mental function.* New York: Houghton Mifflin.

Banich, M. T., Levine, S., Kim, H., & Huttenlocher, P. (1990). The effects of developmental factors on IQ in hemiplegic children. *Neuropsychologia, 28,* 35–47.

Banigan, R. L., & Mervis, C. B. (1988). Role of adult input in young children's category evolution: An experimental study. *Journal of Child Language, 15,* 493–504.

Bank, L., Patterson, G. R., & Reid, J. B. (1996). Negative sibling interaction patterns as predictors of later adjustment problems in adolescent and young adult males. In G. H. Brody (Ed.), *Sibling relationships: Their causes and consequences* (pp. 197–229). Norwood, NJ: Ablex Press.

Banks, M. S., & Dannemiller, J. L. (1987). Infant visual psychophysics. In P. Salapatek & L. Cohen (Eds.), *Handbook of infant perception. Vol. 1. From sensation to perception* (pp. 115–184). Orlando, FL: Academic Press.

Banks, M. S., & Shannon, E. S. (1993). Spatial and chromatic visual efficiency in human neonates. In C. Granrud (Ed.), *Visual perception and cognition in infancy.* Hillsdale, NJ: Erlbaum.

Barber, B. K. (1996). Parental psychological control: Revisiting a neglected construct. *Child Development, 67,* 3296–3319.

Barden, R. C., Zelko, F. A., Duncan, S. W., & Masters, J. C. (1980). Children's consensual knowledge about the experiential determinants of emotion. *Journal of Personality and Social Psychology, 39,* 968–976.

Barinaga, M. (2000). A new clue to how alcohol damages brains. *Science, 287,* 947–948.

Barkley, R. A. (1994). Impaired delayed responding: A unified theory of attention-deficit hyperactivity disorder. In R. A. Barkley (Ed.), *Disruptive behavior disorders in childhood* (pp. 11–57). New York: Plenum Press.

Barkley, R. A. (1997). Behavioral inhibition, sustained attention, and executive functions. Constructing a unifying theory of ADHD. *Psychological Bulletin, 121,* 65–94.

Barnard, K. E., Bee, H. L., & Hammond, M. A. (1984). Home environment and cognitive development in a healthy, low-risk sample: The Seattle study. In A. W. Gottfried (Ed.), *Home environment and early cognitive development* (pp. 117–150). New York: Academic Press.

Baron-Cohen, S. (1991). The development of a theory of mind in autism: Deviance and delay? *Psychiatric Clinics of North America, 14*, 33–51.

Baron-Cohen, S. (1993). From attention-goal psychology to belief-desire psychology: The development of a theory of mind, and its dysfunction. In S. Baron-Cohen, H. Tager-Flusberg, & D. J. Cohen (Eds.), *Understanding other minds: Perspectives from autism.* Oxford, England: Oxford University Press.

Barr, R., Dowden, A., & Hayne, H. (1996). Developmental changes in deferred imitation by 6- to 24-month-old infants. *Infant Behavior and Development, 19*, 159–170.

Barr, R., & Hayne, H. (1999). Developmental changes in imitation from television during infancy. *Child Development, 70*, 1067–1081.

Barr, R. G., Quek, V. S., Cousineau, D., Oberlander, T. F., Brian, J. A., & Young, S. N. (1994). Effects of intra-oral sucrose on crying, mouthing and hand-mouth contact in newborn and six-week-old infants. *Developmental Medicine & Child Neurology, 36*, 608–618.

Barr, R. G., Rotman, A., Yaremko, J., Leduc, D., & Francoeur, T. E. (1992). The crying of infants with colic: A controlled empirical description. *Pediatrics, 90*, 14–21.

Barrera, M., Jr., Biglan, A., Ary, D., & Li, F. (2001). Replication of a problem behavior model with American Indian, Hispanic, and Caucasian youth. *Journal of Early Adolescence, 21*, 133–157.

Barrett, D. E., & Yarrow, M. R. (1977). Prosocial behavior, social inferential ability, and assertiveness in young children. *Child Development, 48*, 475–481.

Barrett, K. C., Zahn-Waxler, C., & Cole, P. M. (1993). Avoiders versus amenders—implication for the investigation of guilt and shame during toddlerhood? *Cognition and Emotion, 7*, 481–505.

Bartsch, K., & Wellman, H. M. (1995). *Children talk about the mind.* New York: Oxford University Press.

Bates, E. (1990). Language about me and you: Pronominal reference and the emerging concept of self. In D. Cicchetti & M. Beeghly (Eds.), *The self in transition: Infancy to childhood* (pp. 165–182). Chicago: University of Chicago Press.

Bates, E., Dale, P. S., & Thal, D. (1995). Individual differences and their implications for theories of language development. In P. Fletcher & B. MacWhinney (Eds.), *The handbook of child language* (pp. 96–151). Oxford, England: Basil Blackwell.

Bates, E., & Elman, J. L. (1993). Connectionism and the study of change. In M. H. Johnson (Ed.), *Brain development and cognition: A reader* (pp. 623–642). Cambridge, MA: Blackwell.

Bates, J. E., Bayles, K., Bennett, D. S., Ridge, B., & Brown, M. M. (1991). Origins of externalizing behavior problems at eight years of age. In D. Pepler & K. Rubin (Eds.), *Development and treatment of childhood aggression* (pp. 93–120). Hillsdale, NJ: Erlbaum.

Bates, J. E., Marvinney, D., Kelly, T., Dodge, K. A., Bennett, D. S., & Pettit, G. S. (1994). Child-care history and kindergarten adjustment. *Developmental Psychology, 30*, 690–700.

Bates, J. E., Pettit, G. S., Dodge, K. A., & Ridge, B. (1998). Interaction of temperamental resistance to control and restrictive parenting in the development of externalizing behavior. *Developmental Psychology, 34*, 982–995.

Battin, S. R., Hill, K. G., Abbott, R. D., Catalano, R. F., & Hawkins, J. D. (1998). The contribution of gang membership to delinquency beyond delinquent friends. *Criminology, 36*, 93–115.

Battistich, V., Schaps, E., Watson, M., Solomon, D., & Lewis, C. (2000). Effects of the Child Development Project on students' drug use and other problem behaviors. *Journal of Primary Prevention, 21*, 75–99.

Battistich, V., Solomon, D., Watson, M., & Schaps, E. (1997). Caring school communities. *Educational Psychologist*, 32, 137–151.

Battistich, V., Watson, M., Solomon, D., Schaps, E., & Solomon, J. (1991). The Child Development Project: A comprehensive program for the development of prosocial character. In W. M. Kurtines & J. L. Gerwirtz (Eds.), *Handbook of moral behavior and development. Vol. 3. Application* (pp. 1–34). New York: Erlbaum.

Bauer, P. J. (1995). Recalling past events: From infancy to early childhood. *Annals of Child Development, 11*, 25–71.

Bauer, P., J., & Fivush, R. (1992). Constructing event representations: Building on a foundation of variation and enabling relations. *Cognitive Development, 7*, 381–401.

Baumrind, D. (1972). An exploratory study of socialization effects on black children: Some black-white comparisons. *Child Development, 43*, 261–267.

Baumrind, D. (1973). The development of instrument competence through socialization. In A. D. Pick (Ed.), *Minnesota symposia on child psychology* (Vol. 7, pp. 3–46). Minneapolis: University of Minnesota Press.

Baumrind, D. (1991a). The influence of parenting style on adolescent competence and substance use. *Journal of Early Adolescence, 11*, 56–95.

Baumrind, D. (1991b). Parenting styles and adolescent development. In R. M. Lerner, A. C. Petersen, & J. Brooks-Gunn (Eds.), *Encyclopedia of adolescence. Vol. 11* (pp. 746–758). New York: Garland.

Bauserman, R. (2002). Child adjustment in joint-custody versus sole-custody arrangements: A meta-analytic review. *Journal of Family Psychology, 16*, 91–102.

Bayley, N. (1993). *Bayley scales of infant development: Birth to two years* (2nd ed.). New York: The Psychological Corporation.

BBC News Online. (2001, March 28). China's population growth "slowing." Retrieved from http://news.bbc.co.uk/hi/english/world/asia-pacific/newsid 1246000/1246731.stm.

Beal, C. R. (1994). *Boys and girls: The development of gender roles.* New York: McGraw-Hill.

Beal, C. R., Garrod, A. C., & Bonitatibus, G. J. (1990). Fostering children's revision skills through training in comprehension monitoring. *Journal of Educational Psychology, 82*, 275–280.

Beardsall, L., & Dunn, J. (1989). *Life events in childhood: Shared and non-shared experiences of siblings.* Unpublished manuscript.

Becker, H. J. (2000). Who's wired and who's not: Children's access to and use of computer technology. *The Future of Children, 10*, 44–75.

Becker-Bryant, J., & Polkosky, M. D. (2001, April). *Parents' responses to preschoolers' lexical innovations.* Paper presented at the biennial meeting of the Society for Research in Child Development, Minneapolis, MN.

Beckwith, L., & Rodning, C. (1991). Intellectual functioning in children born preterm: Recent research. In L. Okagaki & Robert J. Sternberg (Eds.), *Directors of development: Influences on the development of children's thinking.* Hillsdale, NJ: Erlbaum.

Behl-Chadha, G. (1996). Basic-level and superordinate-like categorical representations in early infancy. *Cognition, 60*, 105–141.

Behrend, D. A., Rosengren, K. S., & Perlmutter, M. (1992). The relation between private speech and parental interactive style. In R. M. Diaz & L. E. Berk (Eds.), *Private speech: From social interaction to self-regulation* (pp. 85–100). Hillsdale, NJ: Erlbaum.

Bell, S. M., & Ainsworth, M. D. S. (1972). Infant crying and maternal responsiveness. *Child Development, 43*, 1171–1190.

Bellugi, U., Poizner, H., & Klima, E. S. (1989). Language, modality and the brain. *Trends in Neurosciences, 12,* 380–388.

Belsky, J. (1986). Infant day care: A cause for concern? *Zero to Three, 6*, 1–9.

Belsky, J. (1993). Etiology of child maltreatment: A developmental-ecological analysis. *Psychological Bulletin, 114,* 413–433.

Belsky, J., Rosenberger, K., & Crnic, K. (1995). Maternal personality, marital quality, social support and infant temperament: Their significance for infant-mother attachment in human families. In C. R. Pryce & R. D. Martin (Eds.), *Motherhood in human and nonhuman primates: Biosocial determinants* (pp. 115–124). Basel, Switzerland: Karger.

Bem, D. (1996). Exotic becomes erotic: A developmental theory of sexual orientation. *Psychological Review, 103,* 320–335.

Bem, S. I. (1981). Gender schema theory: A cognitive account of sex typing. *Psychological Review, 88*, 354–364.

Bem, S. I. (1989). Genital knowledge and gender constancy in preschool children. *Child Development, 60*, 649–662.

Benbow, C. P. (1988). Sex differences in mathematical reasoning ability in intellectually talented preadolescents: Their nature, effects, and possible causes. *Behavioral and Brain Sciences, 11*, 169–183.

Benbow, C. P. (1992). Academic achievement in mathematics and science of students between ages 13 and 23: Are there differences among students in the top one percent of mathematical ability? *Journal of Educational Psychology, 84*, 51–61.

Benbow, C. P., & Minor, L. L. (1990). Cognitive profiles of verbally and mathematically precocious students: Implications for identification of the gifted. *Gifted Child Quarterly, 34*, 21–26.

Benedict, H. (1979). Early lexical development: Comprehension and production. *Journal of Child Language, 6*, 183–200.

Benedict, R. (1934). *Patterns of culture.* Boston: Houghton Mifflin.

Benenson, J. F. (1990). Gender differences in social networks. *Journal of Early Adolescence, 10*, 472–495.

Benoit, D., & Parker, K. C. H. (1994). Stability and transmission of attachment across three generations. *Child Development, 65,* 1444–1456.

Benson, J. B., & Uzgiris, I. C. (1985). Effect of self-initiated locomotion on infant search activity. *Developmental Psychology, 21*, 923–931.

Bereiter, C., & Scardamalia, M. (1982). From conversation to composition: The role of instruction in a developmental process. In R. Glaser (Ed.), *Advances in instructional psychology* (Vol. 2, pp. 1–64). Mahwah, NJ: Erlbaum.

Berg, C. A. (1989). Knowledge of strategies for dealing with everyday problems from childhood through adolescence. *Developmental Psychology, 25,* 607–618.

Berg, C. A., Strough, J., Calderone, K., Meegan, S. P., & Sansone, C. (1997). Planning to prevent everyday problems from occurring. In S. L. Friedman & E. K. Scholnick (Eds.), *The developmental psychology of planning: Why, how and when do we plan?* (pp. 209–236). Mahwah, NJ: Erlbaum.

Berg, N.E., & Mussen, P. (1975). Origins and development of concepts of justice. *Journal of Social Issues, 31*, 183–201.

Berg, W. K., & Berg, K. M. (1987). Psychophysiologic development in infancy: State, startle and attention. In J. Osofsky (Ed.), *Handbook of infancy* (2nd ed.). New York: Wiley.

Berko, J. (1958). The child's learning of English morphology. *Word, 14,* 150–177.

Bernal, M. E., Knight, G. P., Ocampo, K. A., Garza, C.A., & Cota, M. K. (1993). Development of Mexican American identity. In M. E. Bernal & G. P. Knight (Eds.), *Ethnic identity: Formation and transmission among Hispanics and other minorities* (pp. 31–46). Albany: State University of New York Press.

Berndt, T. J. (1979). Developmental changes in conformity to peers and parents. *Developmental Psychology, 15*, 608–616.

Berndt, T. J., Hawkins, J. A., & Jiao, Z. (1999). Influences of friends and friendships on adjustment to junior high school. *Merrill-Palmer Quarterly, 45*, 13–41.

Bernier, J. C., & Siegel, D. H. (1994). Attention-deficit hyperactivity disorder: A family ecological systems perspective. *Families in Society, 75*, 142–150.

Berrill, K. T. (1990). Anti-gay violence and victimization in the United States: An overview. *Journal of Interpersonal Violence, 5,* 274–294.

Bertenthal, B. I. (1993). Infants' perception of biomechanical motions: Intrinsic image and knowledge-based constraints. In C. Granrud (Ed.), *Visual perception and cognition in infancy* (pp. 175–214). Hillsdale, NJ: Erlbaum.

Bertenthal, B. I., & Campos, J. J. (1990). A systems approach to the organizing effects of self-produced locomotion during infancy. In C. Rovee-Collier & L. P. Lipsitt (Eds.), *Advances in infancy research* (pp. 1–60). Norwood, NJ: Ablex.

Bertenthal, B. I., Campos, J. J., & Haith, M. M. (1980). Development of visual organization: The perception of subjective contours. *Child Development, 51,* 1077–1080.

Bertenthal, B. I., Campos, J. J., & Kermoian, R. (1994). An epigenetic perspective on the development of self-produced locomotion and its consequences. *Current Directions in Psychological Science, 5*, 140–145.

Bertenthal, B. I., & Clifton, R. K. (1998). Perception and action. In W. Damon (Series Ed.), D. Kuhn, & R. Siegler (Vol. Eds.), *Handbook of child psychology: Vol. 2. Cognition, perception and language* (5th ed., pp. 51–102). New York: Wiley.

Bertenthal, B. I., Proffitt, D. R., & Kramer, S. J. (1987). Perception of biomechanical motions by infants: Implementation of various processing constraints. *Journal of Experimental Psychology, 13,* 577–585.

Berzonsky, M. D., & Adams, G. R. (1999). Reevaluating the identity status paradigm: Still useful after 35 years. *Developmental Review, 19,* 557–590.

Beyer, S. (1995). Maternal employment and children's academic achievement: Parenting styles as mediating variables. *Developmental Review, 15,* 212–253.

Bialystok, E., Shenfield, T., & Codd, J. (2000). Languages, scripts, and the environment: Factors in developing concepts of print. *Developmental Psychology, 36,* 66–76.

Biederman, J., Rosenbaum, J. F., Hirshfeld, D. R., Faraone, S. V., Bolduc, E. A., Gersten, M., et al. (1990). Psychiatric correlates of behavioral inhibition in young children of parents with and without psychiatric disorders. *Archives of General Psychiatry, 47,* 21–26.

Bierman, K. L., & Wargo, J. B. (1995). Predicting the longitudinal course associated with aggressive-rejected, aggressive (nonrejected), and rejected (nonaggressive) status. *Development and Psychopathology, 7*, 669–682.

Bigelow, B. J. (1977). Children's friendship expectations: A cognitive developmental study. *Child Development, 48*, 246–253.

Birch, L. L., & Fisher, J. A. (1996). The role of experience in the development of children's eating behavior. In E. D. Capaldi (Ed.), *Why we eat what we eat: The psychology of eating* (pp. 113–141). Washington, DC: American Psychological Association.

Biringen, Z., Emde, R. N., Campos, J. J., & Appelbaum, M. I. (1995). Affective reorganization in the infant, the mother, and the dyad: The role of upright locomotion and its timing. *Child Development, 66*, 499–514.

Birnbaum, D. W., & Croll, W. L. (1984). The etiology of children's stereotypes about sex differences in emotionality. *Sex Roles, 10*, 677–691.

Bisanz, J., Morrison, F. J., & Dunn, M. (1995). Effects of age and schooling on the acquisition of elementary quantitative skills. *Developmental Psychology, 31*, 221–236.

Bishop, J. B. (2000). An environmental approach to combat binge drinking on college campuses. *Journal of College Student Psychotherapy, 15*, 15–30.

Bithoney, W. G., & Newberger, E. H. (1987). Child and family attributes of failure-to-thrive. *Journal of Developmental and Behavioral Pediatrics, 8*, 32–36.

Bjerregaard, B., & Smith, C. (1993). Gender differences in gang participation, delinquency, and substance use. *Journal of Quantitative Criminology, 9*, 329–355.

Bjorklund, D. F. (1997). The role of immaturity in human development. *Psychological Bulletin, 122*, 153–169.

Bjorklund, D. F., Miller, P. H., Coyle, T. R., & Slawinsky, J. L. (1997). Instructing children to use memory strategies: Evidence of utilization deficiencies in memory training studies. *Developmental Review, 17*, 411–442.

Bjorklund, D., & Shackelford, T. K. (1999). Differences in parental investment contribute to important differences between men and women. *Current Directions in Psychological Science, 8*, 86–89.

Black, B., & Logan, A. (1995). Links between communication patterns in mother-child, father-child, and child-peer interactions and children's social status. *Child Development, 66*, 255–271.

Blasi, A. (1980). Bridging moral cognition and moral action: A critical review of the literature. *Psychological Bulletin, 88*, 1–45.

Blass, E. M. (1990). Suckling: Determinants, changes, mechanisms, and lasting impressions. *Developmental Psychology, 26*, 520–533.

Blass, E. M., & Ciaramitaro, V. (1994). A new look at some old mechanisms in human newborns: Taste and tactile determinants of state, affect, and action. *Monographs of the Society for Research in Child Development, 59*, v–81.

Blass, E. M., Ganchrow, J.R., & Steiner, J.E. (1984). Classical conditioning in newborn humans 2–48 hours of age. *Infant Behavior and Development, 7*, 223–235.

Blass, E. M., & Hoffmeyer, L. B. (1991). Sucrose as an analgesic in newborn humans. *Pediatrics, 87*, 215–218.

Blass, E. M., & Teicher, M. H. (1980). Suckling. *Science, 210*, 15–22.

Block, J. H. (1978). Another look at sex differentiation in the socialization behaviors of mothers and fathers. In J. Sherman & F. L. Denmark (Eds.), *Psychology of women: Future of research* (pp. 29–87). New York: Psychological Dimensions.

Block, J. H., Block, J., & Gjerde, P. F. (1986). The personality of children prior to divorce: A prospective study. *Child Development, 57*, 827–840.

Bloom, L. (1970). *Language development: Form and function in emerging grammars.* Cambridge, MA: MIT Press.

Bloom, L. (1975). Language development. In F. Horowitz (Ed.), *Review of child development research* (Vol. 4, pp. 245–303). Chicago: University of Chicago Press.

Bloom, L. (1991). *Language development from two to three.* Cambridge, England: Cambridge University Press.

Bloom, L. (1998). Language acquisition in its developmental context. In D. Kuhn & R. S. Siegler (Eds.), *Handbook of child psychology,. Vol. 2. Cognition, perception, and language.* (5th ed.) New York: Wiley.

Bloom, L., Rocissano, L., & Hood, L. (1976). Adult-child discourse: Developmental interaction between information processing and linguistic knowledge. *Cognitive Psychology, 8*, 521–552.

Bloom, L., & Tinker, E. (2001). The intentionality model and language acquisition: Engagement, effort, and the essential tension in development. *Monographs of the Society for Research in Child Development, 66*(4, Serial No. 267).

Bohlin, G., Hagekull, B., & Rydell, A-M. (2000). Attachment and social functioning: A longitudinal study from infancy to middle childhood. *Social Development, 9*, 24–39.

Boismeyer, J. D. (1977). Visual stimulation and wake-sleep behavior in human neonates. *Developmental Psychobiology, 10*, 219–227.

Bolger, K. E., & Patterson, C. J. (2001). Developmental pathways from child maltreatment to peer rejection. *Child Developmental, 72*, 549–568.

Bolger, K. E., Patterson, C. J., Thompson, W. W., & Kupersmidt, J. B. (1995). Psychosocial adjustment among children experiencing persistent and intermittent family economic hardship. *Child Development, 66*, 1107–1129.

Bolger, K. E., & Scarr, S. (1995). Not so far from home: How family characteristics predict child care quality. *Early Development and Parenting, 4*, 103–112.

Boone, R. T., & Cunningham, J. G. (1998). Children's decoding of emotion in expressive body movement: The development of cue attunement. *Developmental Psychology, 34*, 1007–1016.

Borke, H. (1971). Interpersonal perception of young children: Egocentrism or empathy? *Developmental Psychology, 5*, 263–269.

Bornstein, M. H. (1975). Qualities of color vision in infancy. *Journal of Experimental Child Psychology, 19*, 401–419.

Bornstein, M. H., Kessen, W., & Weiskopf, S. (1976). Color vision and hue categorization in young human infants. *Journal of Experimental Psychology: Human Perceptions and Performance, 2*, 115–129.

Bornstein, M. H., & Sigman, M. D. (1986). Continuity in mental development from infancy. *Child Development, 57*, 251–274.

Borstelmann, L. J. (1983). Children before psychology: Ideas about children from antiquity to the late 1800s. In P. H. Mussen (Series Ed.) & W. Kessen (Vol. Ed.), *Handbook of child psychology: Vol. 1. History, theory, and methods* (4th ed., pp. 1–40). New York: Wiley.

Boscolo, P. (1995). The cognitive approach to writing and writing instruction: A contribution to a critical appraisal. *CPC, 14*, 343–366.

Bosma, H. A., & Kunnen, E. S. (2001). Determinants and mechanisms in ego identity development: A review and synthesis. *Developmental Review, 21*, 39–66.

Bouchard, T. J., Jr., Lykken, D. T., McGue, M., Segal, N. L., & Tellegen, A. (1990). Sources of human psychological differences: The Minnesota Study of Twins Reared Apart. *Science, 250,* 223–228.

Bower, T. G. R., & Wishart, J. G. (1972). The effects of motor skill on object permanence. *Cognition, 1,* 165–172.

Bowerman, M. (1978). The acquisition of word meaning: An investigation into some current conflicts. In N. Waterson & C. Snow (Eds.), *The development of communication.* Chichester, England, Wiley.

Bowerman, M. (1979). The acquisition of complex sentences. In P. Fletcher & M. Garman (Eds.), *Language acquisition* (pp. 285–306). Cambridge: Cambridge University Press.

Bowker, A., Bukowski, W. M., Zargarpour, S., & Hoza, B. (1998). A structural and functional analysis of a two-dimensional model of social isolation. *Merrill-Palmer Quarterly, 44,* 447–463.

Bowlby, J. (1953). *Child care and the growth of love.* London: Penguin Books.

Bowlby, J. (1969). *Attachment and loss: Vol. 1. Attachment.* New York: Basic Books.

Bowlby, J. (1973). *Attachment and loss: Vol. 2. Separation.* New York: Basic Books.

Bowlby, J. (1980). *Attachment and loss: Vol. 3. Loss: Sadness and depression.* New York: Basic Books.

Boysson-Bardies, B. de (1999). *How language comes to children: From birth to two years* (M. DeBevoise, Trans.). Cambridge, MA: MIT Press. (Original work published 1996.)

Boysson-Bardies, B. de, Sagart, L., & Durant, C. (1984). Discernable differences in the babbling of infants according to target language. *Journal of Child Language, 11,* 1–15.

Bozett, F. W. (1980). *A secure base: Parent-child attachment and healthy human development.* New York: Basic Books.

Bozett, F. W. (1987). Children of gay fathers. In F. W. Bozett (Ed.), *Gay and lesbian parents* (pp. 39–57). New York: Praeger.

Brachfeld, S., Goldberg, S., & Sloman, J. (1980). Parent-infant interaction in free play at 8 and 12 months: Effects of prematurity and immaturity. *Infant Behavior and Development, 3,* 289–305.

Brackbill, Y., McManus, K., & Woodward, L. (1985). *Medication in maternity: Infant exposure and maternal information.* Ann Arbor: University of Michigan Press.

Bradbard, M. R., Martin, C. L., Endsley, R. C., & Halverson, C. F. (1986). Influence of sex stereotypes on children's exploration and memory: A complete versus performance distinction. *Developmental Psychology, 22,* 481–486.

Bradley, L., & Bryant, P. E. (1983). Categorizing sounds and learning to read—a causal connection. *Nature, 301,* 419–421.

Bradley, R. H. (1989). The use of the HOME inventory in longitudinal studies of child development. In M. H. Bornstein & N. A. Krasnegor (Eds.), *Stability and continuity in mental development: Behavioral and biological perspectives* (pp. 191–215). Mahwah, NJ: Erlbaum.

Bradley, R. H. (1994). The HOME Inventory: Review and reflections. In H. W. Reese (Ed.), *Advances in child development and behavior* (Vol. 25, pp. 241–288). San Diego, CA: Academic Press.

Bradley, R. H., & Caldwell, B. M. (1984). The relation of infants' home environments to achievement test performance in first grade: A follow-up study. *Child Development, 55,* 803–809.

Braine, M. D. S. (1963). The ontogeny of English phrase structure. *Language, 39,* 1–13.

Braine, M. D. S. (1976). Review of *The acquisition of phonology* by N. V. Smith. *Language, 52,* 489–498.

Brand, E., Clingempeel, W. G., & Bowen-Woodward, K. (1988). Family relationships and children's psychosocial adjustment in stepmother and stepfather families. In E. M. Hetherington & J. D. Arasteh (Eds.), *Impact of divorce, single-parenting, and stepparenting on children* (pp. 299–324). Hillsdale, NJ: Erlbaum.

Brasington, R. (1990). Nintendinitis. *New England Journal of Medicine, 322,* 1473–1474.

Bray, J. H., & Berger, S. H. (1993). Developmental issues in Stepfamilies Research Project: Family relationships and parent-child interactions. *Journal of Family Psychology, 7,* 76–90.

Brazelton, T. B. (1990). Saving the bathwater. *Child Development, 61,* 1661–1671.

Brazelton, T. B., Nugent, J. K., & Lester, B. M. (1987). Neonatal Behavioral Assessment Scale. In J.D. Osofsky (Ed.), *Handbook of infant development* (2nd ed., pp. 780–817). New York: Wiley.

Bremner, J. G. (1978). Spatial errors made by infants: Inadequate spatial cues or evidence of egocentrism? *British Journal of Psychology, 69,* 77–84.

Bremner, J. G., & Knowles, L. S. (1984). Piagetian stage 4 search errors with an object that is directly accessible both visually and manually. *Perception, 13,* 307–314.

Bremner, J. G., Knowles, L., & Andreasen, G. (1994). Processes underlying young children's spatial orientation during movement. *Journal of Experimental Child Psychology, 57,* 355–376.

Brendgen, M., Vitaro, F., & Bukowski, W. M. (2000). Deviant friends and early adolescents' emotional and behavioral adjustment. *Journal of Research on Adolescence, 10,* 173–189.

Brendgen, M., Vitaro, F., Bukowski, W. M., Boyle, A. B., & Markiewicz, C. (2001). Developmental profiles of peer social preference over the course of elementary school: Associations with trajectories of externalizing and internalizing behavior. *Developmental Psychology, 37,* 308–320.

Brenner, E. M., & Salovey, P. (1997). Emotion regulation during childhood: Developmental, interpersonal, and individual considerations. In P. Salovey & D. Sluyter (Eds.), *Teaching in the heart of the classroom: Emotional development, emotional literacy, and emotional intelligence* (pp. 168–192). New York: Basic Books.

Bretherton, I., & Beeghly, M. (1982). Talking about internal states: The acquisition of an explicit theory of mind. *Developmental Psychology, 18,* 906–921.

Bretherton, I., Golby, B., & Cho, E. Y. (1997). Attachment and the transmission of values. In J. E. Grusec & L. Kuczynski (Eds.), *Parenting and children's internalization of values* (pp. 103–134). New York: Wiley.

Bretherton, I., & Munholland, K. A. (1999). Internal working models in attachment relationships: A construct revisited. In J. Cassidy & P. R. Shaver (Eds.), *Handbook of attachment: Theory, research, and clinical implications* (pp. 89–111). New York: Guilford Press.

Bridges, L. J., & Grolnick, W. S. (1995). The development of emotional self-regulation in infancy and early childhood. In N. Eisenberg (Ed.), *Review of personality and psychology: Vol. 15. Social development* (pp. 185–211). Thousand Oaks, CA: Sage.

Bril, B., & Sabatier, C. (1986). The cultural context of motor development: Postural manipulations in the daily life of Bambara babies (Mali). *International Journal of Behavioral Development, 9,* 439–453.

Brody, G. H., & Ge, X. (2001). Linking parenting processes and self-regulation to psychological functioning and alcohol use during early adolescence. *Journal of Family Psychology, 15,* 82–94.

Brody, G. H., Stoneman, Z., Flor, D., McCrary, C., Hastings, L., & Conyers, O. (1994). Financial resources, parent psychological functioning, parent co-caregiving, and early adolescent competence in rural two-parent African-American families. *Child Development, 65,* 590–605.

Brody, G. H., Stoneman, Z., MacKinnon, C. E., & MacKinnon, R. (1985). Role relationships and behavior between preschool-aged and school-aged sibling pairs. *Developmental Psychology, 21,* 124–129.

Brody, G. H., Stoneman, Z., & McCoy, J. K. (1994). Forecasting sibling relationships in early adolescence from child temperament and family processes in middle childhood. *Child Development, 65,* 771–784.

Brody, G. H., Stoneman, Z., McCoy, J. K., & Forehand, R. (1992). Contemporaneous and longitudinal associations of sibling conflict with family relationship assessments and family discussions about sibling problems. *Child Development, 63,* 391–400.

Brody, L. R. (1985). Gender differences in emotional development: A review of theories and research. *Journal of Personality, 53,* 102–149.

Brody, L. R. (1993). On understanding gender differences in the expression of emotion. In S. L. Ablon, D. Brown, E. J. Khantzian, & J. E. Mack (Eds.), *Human feelings: Explanations in affect development and meaning* (pp. 87–121). Hillsdale, NJ: Analytic Press.

Brody, L. R. (1999). *Gender, emotion, and the family.* Cambridge, MA: Harvard University Press.

Brody, L. R., & Hall, J. A. (1993). On understanding gender differences in the expression of emotion: Gender roles, socialization, and language. In S.L. Ablon, D. Brown, E.J. Khantzian, & J.E. Mack (Eds.), *Human feelings: Explorations in affect development and meaning* (pp. 87–121). Hillsdale, NJ: Analytic Press.

Brody, N. (1992). *Intelligence* (2nd ed.). San Diego, CA: Academic Press.

Bronfenbrenner, U. (1979). *The ecology of human development: Experiments by nature and design.* Cambridge, MA: Harvard University Press.

Bronfenbrenner, U. (1993). The ecology of cognitive development: Research models and fugitive findings. In R. H. Wozniak & K. W. Fisher (Eds.), *Development in context* (pp. 3–44). Hilldsdale, NJ: Erlbaum.

Bronfenbrenner, U., & Morris, P. A. (1998). The ecology of developmental processes. In R. M. Lerner (Ed.), *Handbook of child psychology: vol. 1. Theoretical models of human development* (5th ed., pp. 535–584). New York: Wiley.

Bronson, G. W. (1972). Infants' reactions to unfamiliar persons and novel objects. *Monographs of the Society for Research in Child Development, 37*(3, Serial No. 148).

Brooks-Gunn, J. (1987). Pubertal processes and girls' psychological adaptation. In R. M. Lerner & T. L. Foch (Eds.), *Biological psychosocial interactions in early adolescence.* Hillsdale, NJ: Erlbaum.

Brooks-Gunn, J., Han, W.-J., & Waldfogel, J. (2002). Maternal employment and child cognitive outcomes in the first three years of life: The NICHD study of early child care. *Child Development, 73,* 1052–1072.

Broughton, J. M. (1978). The development of the concepts of self, mind, reality, and knowledge. In W. Damon (Ed.), *New directions for child development: Social cognition* (pp. 75–100). San Francisco: Jossey-Bass.

Brown, A. L. (1997). Transforming schools into communities of thinking and learning about serious matters. *American Psychologist, 52,* 300–413.

Brown, A. L., Kane, M. J., & Echols, K. (1986). Young children's mental models determine analogical transfer across problems with a common goal structure. *Cognitive Development, 1,* 103–122.

Brown, B. B. (1990). Peer groups and peer cultures. In S. S. Feldman & G. R. Elliott (Eds.), *At the threshold: The developing adolescent* (pp. 171–196). Cambridge, MA: Harvard University Press.

Brown, B. B., Clasen, D. R., & Eicher, S. A. (1986). *Developmental Psychology, 22,* 521–530.

Brown, J. L., & Pollitt, E. (1996, February). Malnutrition, poverty, and intellectual development. *Scientific American,* 38–43.

Brown, J. R., & Dunn, J. (1996). Continuities in emotion understanding from three to six years. *Child Development, 67,* 789–802.

Brown, J. S., & Burton, R. B. (1978). Diagnostic models for procedural bugs in basic mathematical skills. *Cognitive Science, 2,* 155–192.

Brown, R. (1957). Linguistic determinism and the part of speech. *Journal of Abnormal and Social Psychology, 55,* 1–5.

Brown, R. (1973). *A first language: The early stages.* Cambridge, MA: Harvard University Press.

Brown, R., & Fraser, C. (1963). The acquisition of syntax. In C. N. Cofer & B. S. Musgrave (Eds.), *Verbal behavior and learning* (pp. 158–196). New York: McGraw-Hill.

Brown, R., & Hanlon, C. (1970). Derivational complexity and order of acquisition in child speech. In J. R. Hayes (Ed.), *Cognition and the development of language* (pp. 11–53). New York: Wiley.

Bruck, M. (1992). Persistence of dyslexics' phonological awareness deficits. *Developmental Psychology, 28,* 874–886.

Bruck, M., Ceci, S. J., Francoeur, E., & Renick, A. (1995). Anatomically detailed dolls do not facilitate preschoolers' reports of a pediatric examination involving genital touching. *Journal of Experimental Psychology, 1,* 95–109.

Bruner, J. S. (1973). *Beyond the information given: Studies in the psychology of knowing.* New York: Norton.

Bruner, J. S. (1975). The ontogenesis of speech acts. *Journal of Child Language, 2,* 1–19.

Bruner, J. S. (1977). Early social interaction and language acquisition. In H. R. Schaffer (Ed.), *Studies in mother-infant interaction* (pp. 271–289). London: Academic Press.

Bruner, J. S. (1996). *The culture of education.* Cambridge, MA: Harvard University Press.

Bryan, J. H., & Walbek, N. H. (1970). Preaching and practicing generosity: Children's actions and reactions. *Child Development, 41,* 329–353.

Bryant, B. K. (1987). Mental health, temperament, family, and friends: Perspectives on children's empathy and social perspective taking. In N. Eisenberg & J. Strayer (Eds.), *Empathy and its development* (pp. 245–270). Cambridge, England: Cambridge University Press.

Bryant, P. (1974). *Perception and understanding in young children: An experimental approach.* London: Methuen.

Buchanan, C. M., Eccles, J. S., & Becker, M. B. (1992). Are adolescents the victims of raging hormones: Evidence for activational effects of hormones on moods and behavior at adolescence. *Psychological Bulletin, 111,* 62–107.

Buchanan, C. M., Maccoby, E. E., & Dornbusch, S. M. (1991). Caught between parents: Adolescents' experience in divorced families. *Child Development, 62*, 1008–1029.

Buckner, J. C., Bassuk, E. L., Weinreb, L. F., & Brooks, M. G. (1999). Homelessness and its relation to the mental health and behavior of low-income school-age children. *Developmental Psychology, 35*, 246–257.

Buehler, C., Anthony, C., Krishnakumar, A., Stonge, G., Gerard, J., & Pemberton, S. (1997). Interparental conflict and youth problem behaviors: A meta-analysis. *Journal of Child and Family Studies, 6*, 233–247.

Bugental, D. B., & Johnston, C. (2000). Parental and child cognitions in the context of the family. In S. T. Fiske, D. L. Schacter, & C. Zahn-Waxler (Eds.), *Annual Review of Psychology, 51*, 315–344.

Bugental, D. B., Mantyla, S. M., & Lewis, J. (1989). Parental attributions as moderators of affective communication to children at risk for physical abuse. In D. Cicchetti & V. Carlson (Eds.), *Child maltreatment: Theory and research on the causes and consequences of child abuse and neglect* (pp. 254–279). New York: Cambridge University Press.

Bukowski, W. M., Gauze, C., Hoza, B., & Newcomb, A. F. (1993). Differences and consistency between same-sex and other-sex peer relationships during early adolescence. *Developmental Psychology, 29*, 255–263.

Bukowski, W. M., Newcomb, A. F., & Hartup, W. W. (1996). Friendship and its significance in childhood and adolescence: Introduction and comment. In W. M. Bukowski, A. F. Newcomb, & W. W. Hartup (Eds.), *The company they keep: Friendship in childhood and adolescence* (pp. 1–15). Cambridge, England: Cambridge University Press.

Bullock, M., & Lutkenhaus, P. (1990). Who am I? Self-understanding in toddlers. *Merrill-Palmer Quarterly, 36*, 217–238.

Bullock, M., & Russell, J. A. (1985). Further evidence on preschoolers' interpretation of facial expressions. *International Journal of Behavioral Development, 8*, 15–38.

Bumpass, L. L., Martin, T. C., & Sweet, J. A. (1991). The impact of family background and early marital factors on marital disruption. *Journal of Family Issues, 12*, 22–42.

Burchinal, M. R., Campbell, F. A., Bryant, D. M., Wasik, B. H., & Ramey, C. T. (1997). Early intervention and mediating processes in cognitive performance of children of low-income African American families. *Child Development, 68*, 935–954.

Bureau of Labor Statistics. (1999). Labor force statistics from the Current Population Survey. Washington, DC: U.S. Department of Labor. Retrieved from: www.stats.lbs.gov/news.release/famee.t06.htm.

Burhans, K. K., & Dweck, C. S. (1995). Helplessness in early childhood: The role of contingent worth. *Child Development, 66*, 1719–1738.

Burmeister, D. (1996). Need fulfillment, interpersonal competence, and the developmental contexts of early adolescent friendship. In W. M. Bukowski, A. F. Newcomb, & W. W. Hartup (Eds), *The company they keep. Friendship in childhood and adolescence* (pp. 66–86). Cambridge, England: Cambridge University Press.

Bus, A. G., van IJzendoorn, M. H., & Pellegrini, A. D. (1995). Joint book reading makes for success in learning to read: A meta-analysis on intergenerational transmission of literacy. *Review of Educational Research, 65*, 1–21.

Bushman, B. J., & Huesmann, L. R. (2001). Effects of televised violence on aggression. In D. G. Singer & J. L. Singer (Eds.), *Handbook of children and the media* (pp. 223–254). Thousand Oaks, CA: Sage.

Bushnell, E. W., & Boudreau, J. P. (1991). The development of haptic perception during infancy. In M. A. Heller & W. Schiff (Eds.), *The psychology of touch* (pp. 139–161). Hillsdale, NJ: Erlbaum.

Bushnell, E. W., McKenzie, B. E., Lawrence, D. A., & Connell, S. (1995). The spatial coding strategies of 1-year-old infants in a locomotor search task. *Child Development, 66*, 937–958.

Bushnell, I. W. R. (1998). The origins of face perception. In F. Simion & G. Butterworth (Eds.), *The development of sensory, motor, and cognitive capacities in early infancy: From perception to cognition* (pp. 69–86). Hove, England: Psychology Press.

Bushnell, I. W. R., Sai, F., & Mullin, J. T. (1989). Neonatal recognition of the mother's face. *British Journal of Developmental Psychology, 7*, 3–15.

Buss, D. M. (1994). *The evolution of desire.* New York: Basic Books.

Bussey, K., & Bandura, A. (1984). Gender constancy, social power, and sex-linked modeling. *Journal of Personality and Social Psychology, 47*, 1292–1302.

Bussey, K., & Bandura, A. (1992). Self-regulatory mechanisms governing gender development. *Child Development, 63*, 1236–1250.

Bussey, K., & Perry, D. G. (1982). Same-sex imitation: The avoidance of cross-sex models or the acceptance of same-sex models? *Sex Roles, 8*, 773–784.

Butterworth, G. E. (1998). What is special about pointing in babies? In F. Simion & G. Butterworth (Eds.), *The development of sensory, motor and cognitive capacities in early infancy: From perception to cognition* (pp. 171–190). Hove, England: Psychology Press/Erlbaum.

Butterworth, G. E., & Grover, L. (1988). The origins of referential communication in human infancy. In L. Weiskrantz (Ed.), *Thought without language* (pp. 5–24). Oxford, England: Clarendon Press.

Byrne, B. M. (1996). Academic self-concept: Its structure, measurement, and relation to academic achievement. In B. A. Bracken (Ed.), *Handbook of self-concept: Developmental, social, and clinical considerations* (pp. 287–316). New York: Wiley.

Byrne, B., & Fielding-Barnsley, R. (1995). Evaluation of a program to teach phonemic awareness to young children: A 2- and 3-year follow-up and a new preschool trial. *Journal of Educational Psychology, 87*, 488–503.

Caen, H. (1996, February 4). So far, so what? *San Francisco Chronicle*, p. A1.

Cahan, S., & Cahan, N. (1989). Age versus schooling effects on intelligence development. *Child Development, 60*, 1239–1249.

Cain, K. M., & Dweck, C. S. (1995). The relation between motivational patterns and achievement cognitions through the elementary school years. *Merrill-Palmer Quarterly, 41*, 25–52.

Cairns, R. B., Cairns, B. D., & Neckerman, H. J. (1989). Early school dropout: Configurations and determinants. *Child Development, 60*, 1437–1452.

Cairns, R. B., Cairns, B. D., Neckerman, H. J., Ferguson, L. L., & Gariepy, J. L. (1989). Growth and aggression: 1. Childhood to early adolescence. *Developmental Psychology, 25*, 320–330.

Cairns, R. B., Cairns, B. D., Neckerman, H. J., Gest, S. D., & Gariepy, J. L. (1988). Social networks and aggressive behavior: Peer support or peer rejection. *Developmental Psychology, 24*, 815–823.

Cairns, R. B., Leung, M-C., Buchanan, L., & Cairns, B. D. (1995). Friendships and social networks in childhood and adolescence: Fluidity, reliability, and interrelations. *Child Development, 66*, 1330–1345.

Caldera, Y. M., Huston, A. C., & O'Brien, M. (1989). Social interactions and play patterns of parents and toddlers with feminine, masculine, and neutral toys. *Child Development, 60,* 70–76.

Caldwell, B. M., & Bradley, R. (1979). *Home observation for measurement of the environment.* Unpublished manuscript, University of Arkansas, Little Rock.

Calkins, S. D. (1997). Cardiac vagal tone indices of temperamental reactivity and behavioral regulation in young children. *Developmental Psychobiology, 31,* 125–135.

Calkins, S. D., & Dedmon, S. E. (2000). Physiological and behavioral regulation in two-year-old children with aggressive/destructive behavior problems. *Journal of Abnormal Child Psychology, 28,* 103–118.

Calkins, S. D., Fox, N. A., & Marshall, T. R. (1996). Behavioral and physiological antecedents of inhibited and uninhibited behavior. *Child Development, 67,* 523–540.

Callanan, M. A. (1985, April). Object labels and young children's acquisition of categories. Paper presented at the Society for Research in Child Development Conference, Toronto, Ontario. Canada.

Callanan, M. A. (1990). Parents' descriptions of objects: Potential data for children's inferences about category principles. *Cognitive Development, 5,* 101–122.

Calvert, S. L., & Huston, A. C. (1987). Television and children's gender schemata. In L. S. Liben & M. L. Signorella (Eds.), *Children's gender schemata* (pp. 75–88). San Francisco: Jossey-Bass.

Campbell, F. A., & Ramey, C. T. (1994). Effects of early intervention on intellectual and academic achievement: A follow-up study of children from low-income families. *Child Development, 65,* 684–698.

Campbell, F. A., & Ramey, C. T. (1995). Cognitive and school outcomes for high risk African-American students at middle adolescence: Positive effects of early intervention. *American Educational Research Journal, 32,* 743–772.

Campbell, S. B., Cohn, J. F., & Meyers, T. (1995). Depression in first-time mothers: Mother-infant interaction and depression chronicity. *Developmental Psychology, 31,* 349–357.

Campos, J. J., Anderson, D. I., Barbu-Roth, M. A., Hubbard, E. M., Hertenstein, M. J., & Witherington, D. (2000). Travel broadens the mind. *Infancy, 1,* 149–220.

Campos, J. J., Bertenthal, B. I., & Kermoian, R. (1992). Early experience and emotional development: The emergence of wariness of heights. *Psychological Science, 3,* 61–64.

Campos, J. J., Kermoian, R., & Zumbahlen, M. R. (1992). Socio-emotional transformations in the family system following infant crawling onset. In N. Eisenberg & R. A. Fabes (Eds.), *New directions for child development: No. 55. Emotion and its regulation in early development* (pp. 25–40). San Francisco: Jossey-Bass.

Campos, J. J., Langer, A., & Krowitz, A. (1970). Cardiac responses on the visual cliff in prelocomotor human infants. *Science, 170,* 196–197.

Campos, J. J., Mumme, D. L., Kermoian, R., & Campos, R. G. (1994). A functionalist perspective on the nature of emotion. *Monographs of the Society for Research in Child Development, 59*(2-3, Serial No. 240), 284–303.

Campos, J. J., & Stenberg, C. R. (1981). Perception, appraisal, and emotion: The onset of social referencing. In M. E. Lamb & L. R. Sherrod (Eds.), *Infant social cognition: Empirical and theoretical considerations* (pp. 273–314). Hillsdale, NJ: Erlbaum.

Campos, R. G. (1989). Soothing pain-elicited distress in infants with swaddling and pacifiers. *Child Development, 60,* 781–792.

Campos, R., Raffaelli, M., Ude, W., Greco, M., Ruff, A., Rolf, J., et al. (1994). Social networks and daily activities of street youth in Belo Horizonte, Brazil. *Child Development, 65,* 319–330.

Camras, L. A. (1992). Expressive development and basic emotions. *Cognition and Emotion, 6,* 269–283.

Camras, L. A., Oster, H., Campos, J. J., Miyake, K., & Bradshaw, D. (1992). Japanese and American infants' responses to arm restraint. *Developmental Psychology, 28,* 578–583.

Canfield, R. L., & Haith, M. M. (1991). Active expectations in 2- and 3-month-old infants: Complex event sequences. *Developmental Psychology, 27,* 198–208.

Cantwell, D. P. (1996). Attention deficit disorder: A review of the past 10 years. *Journal of the American Academy of Child and Adolescent Psychiatry, 35,* 978–987.

Capaldi, D. M., & Patterson, G. R. (1991). Relation of parental transitions to boys' adjustment problems: I. A linear hypothesis. II. Mothers at risk for transitions and unskilled parenting. *Developmental Psychology, 27,* 489–504.

Cardoso-Martins, C. (1991). Awareness of phonemes and alphabetic literacy acquisition. *British Journal of Educational Psychology, 61,* 164–173.

Carey, S. (1978). The child as a word learner. In M. Halle, J. Bresnan, & G. A. Miller (Eds.), *Linguistic theory and psychological reality* (pp. 264–293). Cambridge, MA: MIT Press.

Carey, S. (1985). *Conceptual change in childhood.* Cambridge, MA: MIT Press.

Carey, S. (1999). Sources of conceptual change. In In E. K. Scholnick, K. Nelson, S. A. Gelman, & P. H. Miller (Eds.), *Conceptual development: Piaget's legacy* (pp. 293–326). Mahwah, NJ: Erlbaum.

Carey, S., & Bartlett, E. (1978). Acquiring a single new word. *Papers and Reports on Child Language Development, 15,* 17–29.

Carey, S., & Spelke, E. S. (1994). Domain-specific knowledge and conceptual change. In L. S. Hirschfeld & S. A. Gelman (Eds.), *Mapping the mind: Domain specificity in cognition and culture* (pp. 169–220). Cambridge, England: Cambridge University Press.

Carlo, G., Koller, S. H., Eisenberg, N., DaSilva, M. S., & Frohlich, C. B. (1996). A cross-national study on the relations among prosocial moral reasoning, gender role orientations, and prosocial behaviors. *Developmental Psychology, 32,* 231–240.

Carlos, L., & Howell, P. (1999). *Class size reduction in California 1996–98: Early findings signal promise and concerns.* CSR Research Consortium. Retrieved from: www.classize.org.

Carlson, E. A. (1998). A prospective longitudinal study of attachment disorganization/disorientation. *Child Development, 69,* 1107–1128.

Carlson, S., Hyvarinen, L., & Raninen, A. (1986). Persistent behavioral blindness after early visual deprivation and active visual rehabilitation: A case report. *British Journal of Ophthalmology, 70,* 607–611.

Carpenter, M., Nagell, K., & Tomasello, M. (1998). Social cognition, joint attention, and communicative competence from 9 to 15 months of age. *Monographs of the Society for Research in Child Development, 63*(4, Serial No. 255).

Carpenter, P. A., Just, M. A., & Shell, P. (1990). What one intelligence test measures: A theoretical account of the processing in the Raven Progressive Matrices Test. *Psychological Review, 97,* 404–431.

Carroll, J. B. (1993). *Human cognitive abilities: A survey of factor-analytic studies.* New York: Cambridge University Press.

Carroll, J. J., & Steward, M. S. (1984). The role of cognitive development in children's understandings of their own feelings. *Child Development, 55,* 1486–1492.

Carter, C. A., & Kahnweiler, W. M. (2000). The efficacy of the social norms approach to substance abuse prevention applied to fraternity men. *Journal of American College Health, 49,* 66–71.

Carter, D. B., & McClosky, L. A. (1984). Peers and maintenance of sex-typed behavior: The development of children's conceptions of cross-gender behavior in their peers. *Social Cognition, 2,* 294–314.

Case, R. (1992). The role of the frontal lobes in the regulation of cognitive development. *Brain and Cognition, 20,* 51–73.

Case, R., Griffin, S., & Kelley, W. M. (1999). Socioeconomic gradients in mathematical ability and their responsiveness to intervention during early childhood. In D. P. Keating & C. Hertzman (Eds.), *Developmental health and the wealth of nations: Social, biological, and educational dynamics* (pp. 125–149). New York: Guilford Press.

Casey, B. J., Cohen, J. D., Jezzard, P., Turner, R., Noll, D. C., Trainor, R. J., et al. (1995). Activation of prefrontal cortex in children during a non-spatial working memory task with functional MRI. *NeuroImage, 2,* 221–229.

Casey, R. J. & Fuller, L. L. (1994). Maternal regulation of children's emotions. *Journal of Nonverbal Behavior, 18,* 57–89.

Casiglia, A. C., Lo Coco, A., & Zappulla, C. (1998). Aspects of social reputation and peer relationships in Italian children: A cross-cultural perspective. *Developmental Psychology, 34,* 723–730.

Caspi, A. (1998). Personality development across the life course. In W. Damon (Series Ed.) & N. Eisenberg (Vol. Ed.), *Handbook of child psychology: Vol. 3. Social, emotional, and personality development* (5th ed., pp. 311–388). New York: Wiley.

Caspi, A. (2000). The child is father of the man: Personality continuities from childhood to adulthood. *Journal of Personality and Social Psychology, 78,* 158–172.

Caspi, A., Elder, G., Jr., & Bem, D. (1988). Moving away from the world: Lifecourse patterns of shy children. *Developmental Psychology, 24,* 824–831.

Caspi, A., Henry, B., McGee, R. O., Moffitt, T. E., & Silva, P. A. (1995). Temperamental origins of child and adolescent behavior problems: From age three to age fifteen. *Child Development, 66,* 55–68.

Caspi, A., & Silva, P. A. (1995). Temperamental qualities at age 3 predict personality traits in adulthood: Longitudinal evidence from a birth cohort. *Child Development, 66,* 486–498.

Cassidy, J. (1994). Emotion regulation: Influences of attachment relationships. *Monographs of the Society for Research in Child Development, 59*(2-3, Serial No. 240), 228–249.

Cattell, R. B. (1987). *Intelligence: Its structure, growth and action.* Amsterdam: North-Holland.

Caudill, W., & Plath, D. (1966). Who sleeps by whom? Parent-child involvement in urban Japanese families. *Psychiatry, 29,* 344–366.

Ceci, S. J. (1991). How much does schooling influence general intelligence and its cognitive components? A reassessment of the evidence. *Developmental Psychology, 27,* 703–722.

Ceci, S. J. (1993). Contextual trends in intellectual development. *Developmental Review, 13,* 403–435.

Ceci, S. J. (1996). *On intelligence: A biological treatise on intellectual development* (Expanded ed.). Cambridge, MA: Harvard University Press.

Ceci, S. J., & Bruck, M. (1998). Children's testimony: Applied and basic issues. In W. Damon (Series Ed.), I. Sigel & K. A. Renninger (Vol. Eds.), *Handbook of child psychology: Vol. 4. Child psychology in practice* (5th ed., pp. 713–774). New York: Wiley.

Ceci, S. J., Leichtman, M., & White, T. (1999). Interviewing preschoolers: Remembrance of things planted. In D. P. Peters (Ed.), *The child witness in context: Cognitive, social, and legal perspectives.* Dordrecht, The Netherlands: Kluwer.

Centers for Disease Control and Prevention. (1999, November 17). *Physical activity and health: Adolescents and young adults.* Retrieved August 5, 2002, from: http://www.cdc.gov/nccdphp/sgr/adoles.htm.

Chabris, C. F., & Kosslyn, S. M. (1998). How do the cerebral hemispheres contribute to encoding spatial relations? *Current Directions in Psychological Science, 7,* 8–14.

Chall, J. S. (1979). The great debate: Ten years later, with a modest proposal for reading stages. In L. B. Resnick & P. A. Weaver (Eds.), *Theory and practice of early reading* (Vol. 1, pp. 29–55). Mahwah, NJ: Erlbaum.

Chalmers, D., & Lawrence, J. (1993). Investigating the effects of planning aids on adults' and adolescents' organization of a complex task. *International Journal of Behavioral Development, 16,* 191–214.

Chan, R. W., Brooks, R. C., Raboy, B., & Patterson, C. J. (1998). Division of labor among lesbian and heterosexual parents: Associations with children's adjustment. *Journal of Family Psychology, 12,* 402–419.

Chan, R. W., Raboy, B., & Patterson, C. J. (1998). Psychosocial adjustment among children conceived via donor insemination by lesbian and heterosexual mothers. *Child Development, 69,* 443–457.

Chandler, M., Fritz, A. S., & Hala, S. (1989). Small-scale deceit: Deception as a marker of two-, three-, and four-year-olds' early theories of mind. *Child Development, 60,* 1263–1277.

Chandler, M. J., & Greenspan, S. (1972). Ersatz egocentrism: A reply to H. Borke. *Developmental Psychology, 7,* 104–106.

Chandler, M. J., Greenspan, S., & Barenboim, C. (1973). Judgments of intentionality in response to videotaped and verbally presented moral dilemmas: The medium is the message. *Child Development, 44,* 315–320.

Chang, H. W., & Trehub, S. E. (1977). Auditory processing of relational information by young infants. *Journal of Experimental Child Psychology, 24,* 324–331.

Changeux, J. P. (1985). *Neuronal man: The biology of mind.* Princeton, NJ: Princeton University Press.

Changeux, J. P., & Danchin, A. (1976). Selective stabilization of developing synapses as a mechanism for the specification of neuronal networks. *Nature, 264,* 705–712.

Changeux, J.-P., & Dehaene, S. (1989). Neuronal models of cognitive functions. *Cognition, 33,* 63–109.

Chao, R. K. (1994). Beyond parental control and authoritarian parenting style: Understanding Chinese parenting through the cultural notion of training. *Child Development, 65,* 1111–1119.

Chao, R. K. (2001). Extending research on the consequences of parenting style for Chinese Americans and European Americans. *Child Development, 72,* 1832–1843.

Chase-Lansdale, P. L., Cherlin, A. J., & Kiernan, K. E. (1995). The long-term effects of parental divorce on the mental health of young adults: A developmental perspective. *Child Development, 66,* 1614–1634.

Chen, C., Greenberger, E., Lester, J., Dong, Q., & Guo, M-S. (1998). A cross-cultural study of family and peer correlates of adolescent misconduct. *Developmental Psychology, 34*, 770–781.

Chen, X., & Rubin, K. H. (1994). Family conditions, parental acceptance, and social competence and aggression in Chinese children. *Social Development, 3*, 269–290.

Chen, X., Rubin, K. H., & Li, B. (1995a). Social functioning and adjustment in Chinese children: A longitudinal study. *Developmental Psychology, 31*, 531–539.

Chen, X., Rubin, K. H., & Li, B. (1995b). Social and school adjustment of shy and aggressive children in China. *Development and Psychopathology, 7*, 337–349.

Chen, X., Rubin, K. H., & Li, D. (1997). Relations between academic achievement and social adjustment: Evidence from Chinese children. *Developmental Psychology, 33*, 518–525.

Chen, X., Rubin, K. H., Li, B., & Li, D. (1999). Adolescent outcomes of social functioning in Chinese children. *International Journal of Behavioral Development, 23*, 199–223.

Chen, X., Rubin, K. H., & Sun, Y. (1992). Social reputation and peer relationships in Chinese and Canadian children: A cross-cultural study. *Child Development, 63*, 1336–1343.

Chen, Z. & Siegler, R. S. (2000). Across the great divide: Bridging the gap between understanding of toddlers' and older children's thinking. *Monographs of the Society for Research in Child Development, 65*(2, Serial No. 261).

Chen, Z., Dong, Q., & Zhou, H. (1997). Authoritative and authoritarian parenting practices and social and school performance in Chinese children. *International Journal of Behavioral Development, 21*, 855–873.

Chen, Z., Sanchez, R. P., & Campbell, T. (1997). From beyond to within their grasp: The rudiments of analogical problem solving in 10- and 13-month olds. *Developmental Psychology, 33,* 790–801.

Chess, S., & Thomas, A. (1990). Continuities and discontinuities in temperament. In L. Robins & M. Rutter (Eds.), *Straight and devious pathways from childhood to adulthood* (pp. 182–220). Cambridge, England: Cambridge University Press.

Chi, M. T. H. (1978). Knowledge structures and memory development. In R. S. Siegler (Ed.), *Children's thinking: What develops?* (pp. 73–96).Hillsdale, NJ: Erlbaum.

Chi, M. T. H. (1981). Knowledge development and memory performance. In J. P. Das & N. O'Conner (Eds.), *Intelligence and learning*. New York: Plenum Press.

Chi, M., Hutchinson, J., & Robin, A. (1989). How inferences about novel domain-related concepts can be constrained by structured knowledge. *Merrill-Palmer Quarterly, 35*, 27–62.

ChildStats. (2001). *America's children 2001*. Retrieved from http:///www.ChildStats.gov.

Chisolm, J. S. (1963). *Navajo infancy: An ethological study of child development*. New York: Aldine.

Chomsky, N. (1957). *Syntactic structures*. The Hague: Mouton.

Chomsky, N. (1959). Review of B. F. Skinner's *Verbal behavior. Language, 35,* 26–129.

Chomsky, N. (1988). *Language and problems of knowledge*. Cambridge, MA: MIT Press.

Christian, R. E., Frick, P. J., Hill, N. L., Tyler, L., & Frazer, D. R. (1997). Psychopathy and conduct problems in children: II. Implications for subtyping children with conduct problems. *Journal of the American Academy of Child and Adolescent Psychiatry, 36*, 233–241.

Chugani, H. T., Phelps, M. E., & Mazziotta, J. C. (1987). Positron emission tomography study of human brain functional development. *Annals of Neurology, 22,* 487–497.

Church, R. B. (1999). Using gesture and speech to capture transitions in learning. *Cognitive Development, 14*, 313–342.

Cicchetti, D., & Toth, S. L. (1998). Perspectives on research and practice in developmental psychopathology. In W. Damon (Series Ed.) and I. E. Sigel & K. A. Renninger (Vol. Eds.), *Handbook of child psychology, Vol. 4: Child psychology in practice* (5th ed., pp. 479–583). New York: Wiley.

Cillessen, A. H., van IJzendoorn, H. W., van Lieshout, C. F., & Hartup, W. W. (1992). Heterogeneity among peer-rejected boys: Subtypes and stabilities. *Child Development, 63*, 893–905.

Clark, E. V. (1979). Building a vocabulary: Words for objects, actions, and relations. In P. Fletcher & M. Garman (Eds.), *Language acquisition* (pp. 149–160). Cambridge, England: Cambridge University Press.

Clark, E. V. (1993). *The lexicon in acquisition*. Cambridge, England: Cambridge University Press.

Clark, J. E., & Phillips, S. J. (1993). A longitudinal study of interlimb coordination in the first year of independent walking: A dynamical systems analysis. *Child Development, 64,* 1143–1157.

Clarke-McLean, J. (1996). Social networks among incarcerated juvenile offenders. *Social Development, 5*, 203–217.

Clarke-Stewart, K. A. (1981). Observation and experiment: Complementary strategies for studying day care and social development. In S. Kilmer (Ed.), *Advances in early education and day care* (Vol. 2, pp. 227–250). Greenwich, CT: JAI Press.

Clarke-Stewart, K. A., Vandell, D. L., McCartney, K., Owen, M. T., & Booth, C. (2000). Effects of parental separation and divorce on very young children. *Journal of Family Psychology, 14*, 304–326.

Clarkson, M. G., & Clifton, R. K. (1991). Acoustic determinants of newborn orienting. In M. J. S. Weiss & P. R. Zelazo (Eds.), *Newborn attention: Biological constraints and the influence of experience* (pp. 99–119). Stamford, CT: Ablex.

Clary, E. G., & Miller J. (1986). Socialization and situational influences on sustained altruism. *Child Development, 57*, 1358–1369.

Clearfield, M. W., & Mix, K. S. (1999). Number versus contour length in infants' discrimination of small visual sets. *Psychological Science, 10*, 408–411.

Clement, J. (1982). Algebra word problem solutions: Thought processes underlying a common misconception. *Journal for Research in Mathematics Education, 13*, 16–30.

Clifton, R. K., Muir, D. W., Ashmead, D. H., & Clarkson, M. G. (1993). Is visually guided reaching in early infancy a myth? *Child Development, 64*, 1099–1110.

Clifton, R. K., Rochat, P., Litovsky, R. Y., & Perris, E. E. (1991). Object representation guides infants' reaching in the dark. *Journal of Experimental Psychology: Human Perception and Performance, 17,* 323–329.

Clore, G. (1981). *The wit and wisdom of Benjamin Clore*. Unpublished manuscript.

Cohen, D., & Strayer, J. (1996). Empathy in conduct-disordered and comparison youth. *Developmental Psychology, 32*, 988–998.

Cohen, L. B., & Oakes, L. M. (1993). How infants perceive a simple causal event. *Developmental Psychology, 29*, 421–433.

Cohen, P., & Brook, J. S. (1995). The reciprocal influence of punishment and child behavior disorder. In J. McCord (Ed.), *Coercion and punishment in long-term perspectives* (pp. 154–164). Cambridge, England: Cambridge University Press.

Coie, J. D., & Dodge, K. A. (1983). Continuities and changes in children's social status: A five-year longitudinal study. *Merrill-Palmer Quarter, 29*, 261–282.

Coie, J. D., & Dodge, K. A. (1988). Multiple sources of data on social behavior and social status in the school: A cross-age comparison. *Child Development, 59*, 815–829.

Coie, J. D., & Dodge, K. A. (1998). Aggression and antisocial behavior. In W. Damon (Series Ed.) and N. Eisenberg (Vol. Ed.), *Handbook of child psychology. Vol. 3. Social, emotional, and personality development* (pp. 779–862). New York: Wiley.

Coie, J. D., Dodge, K. A., & Kupersmidt, J. B. (1990). Peer group behavior and social status. In S. R. Asher & J. D. Coie (Eds.), *Peer rejection in childhood* (pp. 17–59). Cambridge, England: Cambridge University Press.

Coie, J. D., & Kupersmidt, J. (1983). A behavioral analysis of emerging social status in boys' groups. *Child Development, 54*, 1400–1416.

Coie, J. D., Lochman, J. E., Terry, R., & Hyman, C. (1992). Predicting early adolescent disorder from childhood aggression and peer rejection. *Journal of Consulting and Clinical Psychology, 60*, 783–792.

Coie, J. D., Terry, R., Lenox, K., Lochman, J., & Hyman, C. (1995). Childhood peer rejection and aggression as predictors of stable patterns of adolescent disorder. *Development and Psychopathology, 7*, 697–713.

Colby, A., & Kohlberg, L. (1987a). *The measurement of moral judgment. Vol. 1.* Cambridge, England: Cambridge University Press.

Colby, A., & Kohlberg, L. (1987b). *The measurement of moral judgment. Vol. 2.* Cambridge, England: Cambridge University Press.

Colby, A., Kohlberg, L., Gibbs, J., & Lieberman, M. (1983). A longitudinal study of moral judgment. *Monographs of the Society for Research in Child Development, 48* (Serial No. 200), 1–124.

Colder, C. R., Lochman, J. E., & Wells, K. C. (1997). The moderating effects of children's fear and activity level of relations between parenting practices and childhood symptomatology. *Journal of Abnormal Child Psychology, 25*, 251–263.

Cole, M. (1996). *Cultural psychology: A once and future discipline.* Cambridge, MA: Harvard University Press.

Cole, P. M. (1986). Children's spontaneous control of facial expression. *Child Development, 57*, 1309–1321.

Cole, P. M., Bruschi, C. J., & Tamang, B. L. (2002). Cultural differences in children's emotional reactions to difficult situations. *Child Development, 73*, 983–996.

Cole, P. M., & Dennis, T. A. (1998). Variations on a theme: Culture and the meaning of socialization practices and child competence. *Psychological Inquiry, 9*, 276–278.

Cole, P. M., & Tamang, B. L. (1998). Nepali children's ideas about emotional displays in hypothetical challenges. *Developmental Psychology, 34*, 640–646.

Coleman, M., Wheeler, L., & Webber, J. (1993). Research on interpersonal problem-solving training: A review. *Remedial and Special Education, 14*, 25–37.

Coley, J. D. (1993). *Emerging differentiation of folkbiology and folkpsychology: Similarity judgments and property attributions.* Doctoral dissertation, University of Michigan, Departmentof Psychology, Ann Arbor.

Coley, R. L., & Chase-Lansdale, P. L. (1998). Adolescent pregnancy and parenthood: Recent evidence and future directions. *American Psychologist, 53*, 152–166.

Collaer, M. L., & Hines, M. (1995). Human behavioral sex differences: A role for gonadal hormones in early development? *Psychological Bulletin, 118*, 55–107.

Collie, R., & Hayne, H. (1999). Deferred imitation by 6- and 9-month-old infants: More evidence for declarative memory. *Developmental Psychobiology, 35*, 83–90.

Collins, W. A. (1990). Parent-child relationships in the transition to adolescence: Continuity and change in interaction, affect, and cognition. In R. Montemayor, G. R. Adams, & T. P. Gullotta (Eds.), *From childhood to adolescence: A transitional period?* (pp. 85–106). Newbury Park, CA: Sage.

Collins, W. A. (1997). Relationships and development during adolescence: Interpersonal adaptation to individual change. *Personal Relationships, 4*, 1–14.

Collins, W. A., Maccoby, E. E., Steinberg, L., Hetherington, E. M., & Bornstein, M. H. (2000). Contemporary research on parenting: The case for nature and nurture. *American Psychologist, 55*, 218–232.

Colombo, J. (1993). *Infant cognition: Predicting childhood intellectual function.* Newbury Park, CA: Sage.

Colombo, J. (1995). On the neural mechanisms underlying developmental and individual differences in visual fixation in infancy: Two hypotheses. *Developmental Review, 15*, 97–135.

Coltrane, S. (1996.) *Family man.* New York: Oxford University Press.

Colwell, J., Grady, C., & Rhiati, S. (1995). Computer games, self esteem, and gratification of needs in adolescents. *Journal of Community and Applied Social Psychology, 5*, 195–206.

Compas, B. E., Connor, J. K., Saltzman, H., Thomsen, A. H., & Wadsworth, M. E. (2001). Coping with stress during childhood and adolescence: Problems, progress, and potential in theory and research. *Psychological Bulletin, 127*, 87–127.

Conduct Problems Prevention Research Group. (1999a). Initial impact of the Fast Track Prevention Trial for conduct problems: I. The high-risk sample. *Journal of Consulting and Clinical Psychology, 67*, 619–647.

Conduct Problems Prevention Research Group. (1999b). Initial impact of the Fast Track Prevention Trial for conduct problems: II. Classroom effects. *Journal of Consulting and Clinical Psychology, 67*, 648–657.

Conduct Problems Prevention Research Group. (2002). Evaluation of the first 3 years of the Fast Track Prevention trial with children at high risk for adolescent conduct problems. *Journal of Abnormal Child Psychology, 30*, 19–35.

Conger, R. D., Conger, K. J., Elder, G. H., Jr., Lorenz, F. O., Simons, R. L., & Whitbeck, L. B. (1993). Family economic stress and adjustment of early adolescent girls. *Developmental Psychology, 29*, 206–219.

Conger, R. D., Ge, X., Elder, G. H. Jr., Lorenz, F. O., & Simons, R. L. (1994). Economic stress, coercive family process, and developmental problems of adolescents. *Child Development, 65*, 541–561.

Conger, R. D., Wallace, L. E., Sun, Y., Simmons, R. L., McLoyd, V. C., & Brody, G. H. (2002). Economic pressure in African American families: A replication and extension of the family stress model. *Developmental Psychology, 38*, 179-193.

Connell, J. P., & Wellborn, J. G. (1991). Competence, autonomy, and relatedness: A motivational analysis of self-system processes. In M. R. Gunnar & L. A. Sroufe (Eds.), *The Minnesota Symposium on Child Development: Vol. 23. Self processes and development* (pp. 43–78). Hillsdale, NJ: Erlbaum.

Conner, D. B., Knight, D. K., & Cross, D. R. (1997). Mothers' and fathers' scaffolding of their 2-year-olds during problem solving and literacy interactions. *British Journal of Developmental Psychology, 15,* 323–338.

Consortium for Longitudinal Studies (1983). *As the twig is bent: Lasting effects of preschool programs.* Hillsdale, NJ: Erlbaum.

Cook, W. L., Kenny, D. A., & Goldstein, M. J. (1991). Parental affective style risk and the family system: A social relations model analysis. *Journal of Abnormal Psychology, 100,* 492–501.

Cooley, C. H. (1902). *Human nature and the social order.* New York: Scribner's.

Cooney, T. M., Pedersen, F. A., Indelicato, S., & Palkovitz, R. (1993). Timing of fatherhood: Is "on-time" optimal? *Journal of Marriage and the Family, 55,* 205–215.

Cooper, G., & Sweller, J. (1987). Effects of schema acquisition and rule automation on mathematical problem-solving transfer. *Journal of Educational Psychology, 79,* 347–362.

Cooper, H. M., Charlton, K., Valentine, J. C., & Muhlenbruck, L. (2000). Making the most of summer school: A meta-analytic and narrative review. *Monographs of the Society for Research in Child Development, 65*(1, Serial No. 260), 1–11.

Cooper, R. P., & Aslin, R. N. (1994). Developmental differences in infant attention to the spectral properties of infant-directed speech. *Child Development, 65,* 1663–1677.

Corballis, M. C. (1999). The gestural origins of language. *American Scientist, 87,* 138–145.

Cornell, E. H., Heth, C. D., Kneubuhler, Y., & Sehgal, S. (1996). Serial position effects in children's route reversal errors: Implications for police search operations. *Applied Cognitive Psychology, 10,* 301–326.

Corrigan, R., & Denton, P. (1996). Causal understanding as a developmental primitive. *Developmental Review, 16,* 162–202.

Coulton, C. J., Korbin, J. E., Su, M., & Chow, J. (1995). Community level factors and child maltreatment rates. *Child Development, 66,* 1262–1276.

Cowan, P. A., Powell, D., & Cowan, C. P. (1998). Parenting interventions: A family systems perspective. In I. E. Sigel & K. A. Renninger (Eds.), *Handbook of child psychology: Vol. 4. Child psychology in practice* (5th ed., pp. 3–72). New York: Wiley.

Cowan, W. M. (1979). The development of the brain. *Scientific American, 241,* 112–133.

Cox, M. J., Owen, M. T., Lewis, J. M., & Henderson, V. K. (1989). Marriage, adult adjustment, and early parenting. *Child Development, 60,* 1015–1024.

Craig, W. M., Vitaro, F., Gagnon, G., & Tremblay, R. E. (2002). The road to gang membership: Characteristics of stable and unstable male gang members from ages 10 to 14. *Social Development, 11,* 53–68.

Crain, W. C. (1985). *Theories of development: Concepts and applications* (2nd ed.). Upper Saddle River, NJ: Prentice-Hall.

Cramer, P., & Steinwert, T. (1998). Thin is good, fat is bad: How early does it begin? *Journal of Applied Developmental Psychology, 19,* 429–451.

Crawford, J. (1997). *Best evidence: Research foundations of the Bilingual Education Act.* Washington, DC: National Clearinghouse for Bilingual Education.

Crick, N. R., & Bigbee, M. A. (1998). Relational and overt forms of peer victimization: A multiinformant approach. *Journal of Consulting and Clinical Psychology, 66,* 337–347.

Crick, N. R., Bigbee, M. A., & Howes, C. (1996). Gender differences in children's normative beliefs about aggression: How do I hurt thee? Let me count the ways. *Child Development, 67,* 1003–1014.

Crick, N. R., Casas, J. F., & Ku, H.-C. (1999). Relational and physical forms of peer victimization in preschool. *Developmental Psychology, 35,* 376–385.

Crick, N. R., Casas, J. F., & Mosher, M. (1997). Relational and overt aggression in preschool. *Developmental Psychology, 33,* 579–588.

Crick, N. R., & Dodge, K. A. (1994). A review and reformulation of social information-processing mechanisms in children's social adjustment. *Psychological Bulletin, 115,* 74–101.

Crick, N. R., & Dodge, K. A. (1996). Social information-processing mechanisms in reactive and proactive aggression. *Child Development, 67,* 993–1002.

Crick, N. R., & Grotpeter, J. K. (1995). Relational aggression, gender, and social-psychological adjustment. *Child Development, 66,* 710–722.

Crick, N. R., & Grotpeter, J. K. (1996). Children's treatment by peers: Victims of relational and overt aggression. *Development and Psychopathology, 8,* 367–380.

Crocker, J. (2001). Self-esteem in adulthood. In N. Smelser & P. Baltes (Eds.), *International Encyclopedia of the Social and Behavioral Sciences.* Oxford, England: Elsevier.

Crockett, L., Losoff, M., & Peterson, A. C. (1984). Perceptions of the peer group and friendship in early adolescence. *Journal of Early Adolescence, 4,* 155–181.

Crosbie-Burnett, M., & Helmbrecht, L. (1993). A descriptive empirical study of gay male stepfamilies. *Family Relations,* 42, 256–262.

Crowley, K., Callanan, M. A., Tenenbaum, H. R., & Allen, E. (2001). Parents explain more often to boys than to girls during shared scientific thinking. *Psychological Science, 12,* 258–261.

Culp, R. E., Appelbaum, M. I., Osofsky, J. D., & Levy, J. A. (1988). Adolescent and older mothers: Comparison between prenatal maternal variables and newborn interaction measures. *Infant Behavior and Development, 11,* 353–362.

Cummings, E. M., Iannotti, R. J., & Zahn-Waxler, C. (1985). Influence of conflict between adults on the emotions and aggression of young children. *Developmental Psychology, 21,* 495–507.

Curran, P. J., Stice, E., & Chassin, L. (1997). The relation between adolescent alcohol use and peer alcohol use: A longitudinal random coefficients model. *Journal of Consulting and Clinical Psychology, 65,* 130–140.

Curtiss, S. (1977). *Genie: A psycholinguistic study of a modern-day "wild child."* London: Academic Press.

Curtiss, S. (1989). The independence and task-specificity of language. In M. H. Bornstein & J. S. Bruner (Eds.), *Interaction in human development* (pp. 105–138). Hillsdale, NJ: Erlbaum.

Cutrona, C. E., Hessling, R. M., Bacon, P. L., & Russell, D. W. (1998). Predictors and correlates of continuing involvement with the baby's father among adolescent mothers. *Family Psychology, 12,* 369–387.

Daly, M., & Wilson, M. I. (1996). Violence against stepchildren. *Current Directions in Psychological Science, 5*, 77–81.

Damasio, A. (1999). *The feeling of what happens: Body and emotion in the making of consciousness.* New York: Harcourt Brace & Company.

Damon, W. (1977). *The social world of the child.* San Francisco: Jossey-Bass.

Damon, W. (1983). *Social and personality development: Infancy through adolescence.* New York: Norton.

Damon, W., & Hart, D. (1988). *Self-understanding in childhood and adolescence.* Cambridge, England: Cambridge University Press.

Danseco, E. R., & Holden, E. W. (1998). Are there different types of homeless families? A typology of homeless families based on cluster analysis. *Family Relations, 47*, 159–165.

Dantzig, T. (1967). *Number: The language of science.* New York: Free Press.

Darling, N., & Steinberg, L. (1993). Parenting style as context: An integrative model. *Psychological Bulletin, 113*, 487–496.

Darwin, C. (1877). A biographical sketch of an infant. *Mind, 2*, 285–294.

Darwin, C. (1965). *The expression of the emotions in man and animals.* Chicago: University of Chicago Press. (Original work published in 1872)

D'Augelli, A. R. (1996). Lesbian, gay, and bisexual development during adolescence. In R. P. Cabaj & T. S. Stein (Eds.), *Textbook of homosexuality and mental health* (pp. 267–288). Washington, DC: American Psychiatric Press.

D'Augelli, A. R. (1998). Developmental implications of victimization of lesbian, gay, and bisexual youth. In G. M. Herek (Ed.), *Stigma and sexual orientation: Understanding prejudice against lesbians, gay men, and bisexuals* (pp. 187–210). Thousand Oaks, CA: Sage.

D'Augelli, A. R., & Hershberger, S. L. (1993). Lesbian, gay, and bisexual youth in community settings: Personal challenges and mental health problems. *American Journal of Community Psychology, 21*, 421–448.

D'Augelli, A. R., Hershberger, S. L., & Pilkington, N. W. (1998). Lesbian, gay, and bisexual youth and their families: Disclosure of sexual orientation and its consequences. *American Journal of Orthopsychiatry, 68*, 361–371.

D'Augelli, A. R., Hershberger, S. L., & Pilkington, N. W. (2001). Suicidality patterns and sexual orientation-related factors among lesbian, gay, and bisexual youth. *Suicide and Life-threatening Behavior, 31*, 250–265.

Davidson, R. J., & Fox, N. A. (1982). Asymmetrical brain activity discriminates between positive and negative affective stimuli in human infants. *Science, 218*, 1235–1237.

Davies, P. T., & Cummings, E. M. (1994). Marital conflict and child adjustment: An emotional security hypothesis. *Psychological Bulletin, 116*, 387–411.

Davis, B. E., Moon, R. Y., Sachs, H. C., & Ottolini, M. C. (1998). Effects of sleep position on infant motor development. *Pediatrics, 102*, 1135–1140.

Dawkins, R. (1996). *The blind watchmaker.* New York: Norton.

Dawson, G., Klinger, L. G., Panagiotides, H., Spieker, S., & Frey, K. (1992). Infants of mothers with depressive symptoms: Electrophysiological and behavioral findings related to attachment status. *Development and Psychopathology, 4*, 67–80.

Deary, I. J. (1995). Auditory inspection time and intelligence: What is the direction of causation? *Developmental Psychology, 31*, 237–250.

Deater-Deckard, K. (2000). Parenting and child behavioral adjustment in early childhood: A quantitative genetic approach to studying family processes. *Child Development, 71*, 468–484.

Deater-Deckard, K., & Dodge, K. A. (1997). Externalizing behavior problems and discipline revisited: Nonlinear effects and variation by culture, context, and gender. *Psychological Inquiry, 8*, 161–175.

Deater-Deckard, K., Dodge, K. A., Bates, J. E., & Pettit, G. S. (1995, March-April). *Risk factors for the development of externalizing behavior problems: Are there ethnic group differences in process?* Paper presented at the biennial meeting of the Society for Research in Child Development, Indianapolis, IN.

Deater-Deckard, K., Dodge, K. A., Bates, J. E., & Pettit, G. S. (1996). Physical discipline among African American and European American mothers: Links to children's externalizing behaviors. *Developmental Psychology, 32*, 1065–1072.

Deater-Deckard, K., Dodge, K. A., Bates, J. E., & Pettit, G. S. (1998). Multiple risk factors in the development of externalizing behavior problems: Group and individual differences. *Development and Psychopathology, 10*, 469–493.

Deater-Deckard, K., & O'Connor, T. G. (2000). Parent-child mutuality in early childhood: Two behavioral genetic studies. *Developmental Psychology, 36*, 1–10.

DeCasper, A. J., & Fifer, W. P. (1980). Of human bonding: Newborns prefer their mothers' voices. *Science, 208*, 1174–1176.

DeCasper, A. J., Lecanuet, J. P., Busnel, M. C., Granier-Deferre, C., & Maugeais, R. (1994). Reactions to recurrent maternal speech. *Infant Behavior and Development, 17*, 159–164.

DeCasper, A. J., & Spence, M. J. (1986). Prenatal maternal speech influences newborns' perception of speech sounds. *Infant Behavior and Development, 9*, 133–150.

Decker, S. H. (1996). Collective and normative features of gang violence. *Justice Quarterly, 13*, 243–264.

Decker, S. H., & van Winkle, B. (1996). *Life in the gang: Family, friends, and violence.* Cambridge, England: Cambridge University Press.

DeFries, J. C., & Gillis, J. J. (1993). Genetics of reading disability. In R. Plomin & G. E. McClearn (Eds.), *Nature, nurture, and psychology* (pp. 121–145). Washington, DC: American Psychological Association.

DeFries, J. C., Plomin, R., & LaBuda, M. C. (1987). Genetic stability of cognitive development from childhood to adulthood. *Developmental Psychology, 23*, 4–12.

Degirmencioglu, S. M., Urberg, K. A., Tolson, J. M, & Richard, P. (1998). Adolescent friendship networks: Continuity and change over the school year. *Merrill-Palmer Quarterly, 44*, 313–337.

deHouwer, A. (1995). Bilingual language acquisition. In P. Fletcher & B. MacWhinney (Eds.), *The handbook of child language* (pp. 219–250). Oxford, England: Basil Blackwell.

DeKlyen, M., Biernbaum, M. A., Speltz, M. L., & Greenberg, M. T. (1998). Fathers and preschool behavior problems. *Developmental Psychology, 34*, 264–275.

Dekovic, M., & Janssens, J. M. A. M. (1992). Parents' child-rearing style and children's sociometric status. *Developmental Psychology, 28*, 925–932.

Delaney, C. (2000). Making babies in a Turkish village. In J. S. DeLoache & A. Gottlieb (Eds.), *A world of babies: Imagined childcare guides for seven societies.* New York: Cambridge University Press.

DeLoache, J. S. (1987). Rapid change in the symbolic functioning of very young children. *Science, 238,* 1556–1557.

DeLoache, J. S. (1995). Early understanding and use of symbols. *Current Directions in Psychological Science, 4,* 109–113.

DeLoache, J. S. (2000). Dual representation and young children's use of scale models. *Child Development, 71,* 329–338.

DeLoache, J. S. (2002). The symbol-mindedness of young children. In W. Hartup & R. Weinberg (Eds.), *The Minnesota Symposium on Child Psychology* (Vol. 32). Mahwah, NJ: Erlbaum.

DeLoache, J. S., Cassidy, D. J., & Carpenter, C. J. (1987). The three bears are all boys: Mothers' labelling of gender-neutral picture book characters. *Sex roles, 17,* 163–178.

DeLoache, J. S., & Gottlieb, A. (Eds.). (2000). *A world of babies: Imagined childcare guides for seven societies.* Cambridge, England: Cambridge University Press.

DeLoache, J. S., & Marzolf, D. P. (1995). The use of dolls to interview young children. *Journal of Experimental Child Psychology, 60,* 155–173.

DeLoache, J. S., Miller, K. F., & Rosengren, K. S. (1997). The credible shrinking room: Very young children's performance with symbolic and non-symbolic relations. *Psychological Science, 8,* 308–313.

DeLoache, J. S., Pierroutsakos, S. L., Uttal, D. H., Rosengren, K. S., & Gottlieb, A. (1998). Grasping the nature of pictures. *Psychological Science, 9,* 205–210.

DeLoache, J. S., & Smith, C. M. (1999). The early understanding and use of symbolic representations. In I. E. Sigel (Ed.), *Theoretical perspectives in the development of representational (symbolic) thought* (pp. 61–86). Hillsdale, NJ: Erlbaum.

DeLoache, J. S., Strauss, M. S., & Maynard, J. (1979). Picture perception in infancy. *Infant Behavior and Development, 2,* 77–89.

Deluty, R. H. (1985). Cognitive mediation of aggressive, assertive, and submissive behavior in children. *International Journal of Behavioral Development, 8,* 355–369.

DeMarie-Dreblow, D., & Miller, P. H. (1988). The development of children's strategies for selective attention: Evidence for a transitional period. *Child Development, 59,* 1504–1513.

Dempster, F. N. (1993). Resistance to interference: Developmental changes in a basic processing mechanism. In R. Pasnak & M. L. Howe (Eds.), *Emerging themes in cognitive development* (Vol. 1). New York: Springer.

Dempster, F. N. (1995). Interference and inhibition in cognition: An historical perspective. In F. N. Dempster & C. J. Brainerd (Eds.), *Interference and inhibition in cognition* (pp. 3–26). San Diego, CA: Academic Press.

DeMulder, E. K., Denham, S., Schmidt, M., & Mitchell, J. (2000). Q-sort assessment of attachment security during the preschool years: Links from home to school. *Developmental Psychology, 36,* 274–282.

Denham, S. A. (1986). Social cognition, prosocial behavior, and emotion in preschoolers: Contextual validation. *Child Development, 57,* 194–201.

Denham, S. A. (1998). *Emotional development in young children.* New York: Guilford Press.

Denham, S. A., & Auerbach, S. (1995). Mother-child dialogue about emotions and preschoolers' emotional competence. *Genetic, Social, and General Psychology Monographs, 121,* 311–337.

Denham, S. A., & Burton, R. (1996). A social-emotional intervention program for at-risk four-year-olds. *Journal of School Psychology, 34,* 225–245.

Denham, S. A., & Couchoud, E. A. (1990). Young preschoolers' understanding of emotions. *Child Study Journal, 20,* 171–192.

Denham, S. A., & Couchoud, E. A. (1991). Social-emotional predictors of preschoolers' responses to adult negative emotion. *Journal of Child Psychology and Psychiatry, 32,* 595–608.

Denham, S. A., & Grout, L. (1992). Mothers' emotional expressiveness and coping: Relations with preschoolers' social-emotional competence. *Genetic, Social, and General Psychology Monographs, 118,* 73–101.

Denham, S. A., Mitchell-Copeland, J., Strandberg, K., Auerbach, S., & Blair, K. (1997). Parental contributions to preschoolers' emotional competence: Direct and indirect effects. *Motivation and Emotion, 21,* 65–86.

Denham, S. A., Zoller, D., & Couchoud, E. A. (1994). Socialization of preschoolers' emotion understanding. *Developmental Psychology, 30,* 928–936.

Dennis, S. (1992). Stage and structure in the development of children's spatial representations. In R. Case (Ed.), *The mind's staircase: Exploring the conceptual underpinnings of children's thought and knowledge.* Hillsdale, NJ: Erlbaum.

Dennis, W., & Najarian, P. (1957). Infant development under environmental handicap. *Psychological Monographs, 71*(7, Whole No. 436).

Department of Health and Human Services. (1999). *Highlights of findings.* Retrieved from: http://www/acf.dhhs.gov/programs/cb/publications/cm99.

DeRosier, M. E., Kupersmidt, J. B., & Patterson, C. J. (1994). Children's academic and behavioral adjustment as a function of the chronicity and proximity of peer rejection. *Child Development, 65,* 1799–1813.

Detterman, D. K. (1993). Giftedness and intelligence: One and the same. In G. R. Bock & K. Ackrill (Eds.), *The origins and development of high ability* (pp. 22–31). New York: Wiley.

deVilliers, J. G., & deVilliers, P. A. (1973). A cross-sectional study of the acquisition of grammatical morphemes in child speech. *Journal of Psycholinguistic Research, 2,* 267–278.

De Vries, J. I. P., Visser, G. H. A., & Prechtl, H. F. R. (1982). The emergence of fetal behavior: I. Qualitative aspects. *Early Human Development, 7,* 301–322.

DeVries, M. W. (1984). Temperament and infant mortality among the Masai of East Africa. *American Journal of Psychiatry, 141,* 1189–1194.

De Wolff, M. S., & van IJzendoorn, M. H. (1997). Sensitivity and attachment: A meta-analysis on parental antecedents of infant attachment. *Child Development, 68,* 571–591.

Diamond, A. (1985). Development of the ability to use recall to guide action, as indicated by the infant's performance on AB. *Child Development, 56,* 868–883.

Diamond, A. (1991). Neuropsychological insights into the meaning of object concept development. In S. Carey & R. Gelman (Eds.), *The epigenesis of mind: Essays on biology and cognition* (pp. 67–110). Hillsdale, NJ: Erlbaum.

Diamond, A., & Gilbert, J. (1989). Development as progressive inhibitory control of action: Retrieval of a contiguous object. *Cognitive Development, 4,* 223–249.

Diamond, L. M. (1998). Development of sexual orientation among adolescent and young adult women. *Developmental Psychology, 34,* 1085–1095.

Diamond, L. M., Savin-Williams, R. C., & Dube, E. M. (1999). Sex, dating, passionate friendships and romance: Intimate peer relations among lesbian, gay, and bisexual adolescents. In W. Furman, B. B. Brown, & C. Feiring (Eds.), *The development of romantic relationships in adolescence* (pp. 175–210). Cambridge, England: Cambridge University Press.

DiBiase, R., & Waddell, S. (1995). Some effects of homelessness on the psychological functioning of preschoolers. *Journal of Abnormal Child Psychology, 23*, 783–792.

Dichtelmiller, M., Meisels, S. J., Plunkett, J. W., Bozynski, M. E., & Mangelsdorf, S. (1992). The relationship of parental knowledge to the development of extremely low birth weight infants. *Journal of Early Intervention, 16*, 210–220.

Diener, M. (2000). Gift from the Gods: A Balinese guide to early child rearing. In J. DeLoache & A. Gotlieb (Eds.), *A world of babies: Imagined childcare guides for seven societies*. Cambridge, England: Cambridge University Press.

DiPietro, J. A., Costigan, K. A., Shupe, A. K., Pressman, E. K., & Johnson, T. R. B. (1998). Fetal neurobehavioral development: Associations with socioeconomic class and fetal sex. *Developmental Psychobiology, 33*, 79–91.

DiPietro, J. A., Hodgson, D. M., Costigan, K. A., & Johnson, T. R. B. (1996). Fetal antecedents of infant temperament. *Child Development, 67*, 2568–2583.

DiPietro, J. A., Hodgson, D. M., Costigan, K., Hilton, S., & Johnson, T. R. (1996). Fetal neurobehavioral development. *Child Development, 67*, 2553–2567.

DiPietro, J. A., Suess, P. A., Wheeler, J. S., Smouse, P. H., & Newlin, D. B. (1995). Reactivity and regulation in cocaine-exposed infants. *Infant Behavior and Development, 18*, 407–414.

Dirks, J., & Gibson, E. (1977). Infants' perception of similarity between live people and their photographs. *Child Development, 48*, 124–130.

Dishion, T. J. (1990). The family ecology of boys' peer relations in middle childhood. *Child Development, 61*, 874–892.

Dishion, T. J., & Andrews, D. W. (1995). Preventing escalation in problem behaviors with high-risk young adolescents: Immediate and 1-year outcomes. *Journal of Consulting and Clinical Psychology, 63*, 538–548.

Dishion, T. J., Andrews, D. W., & Crosby, L. (1995). Antisocial boys and their friends in early adolescence: Relationship characteristics, quality, and interactional process. *Child Development, 66*, 139–151.

Dishion, T. J., Capaldi, D., Spracklen, K. M., & Li, F. (1995). Peer ecology of male adolescent drug use. *Development and Psychopathology, 7*, 803–824.

Dishion, T. J., Eddy, J. M., Haas, E., Li, F., & Spracklen, K. (1997). Friendships and violent behavior during adolescence. *Social Development, 6*, 207–223.

Diversi, M., Filho, N. M., & Morelli, M. (1999). Daily reality on the streets of Campinas, Brazil. *New Directions in Child Development, 85*, 19–34.

DiVitto, B., & Goldberg, S. (1979). The effects of newborn medical status on early parent-infant interaction. In T. M. Field, A. M. Sostch, S. Goldberg, & H. H. Shuman (Eds.), *Infants born at risk: Behavior and development* (pp. 311–332). New York: Spectrum.

Dix, T., & Grusec, J. E. (1983). Parental influence techniques: An attributional analysis. *Child Development, 54*, 645–652.

Dobson, V. (1983). Clinical applications of preferential looking measures of visual acuity. *Behavioral Brain Research, 10*, 25–38.

Dobzhansky, T. (1955). *Evolution, genetics, and man.* New York: Wiley.

Dodge, K. A. (1980). Social cognition and children's aggressive behavior. *Child Development, 51*, 162–170.

Dodge, K. A. (1986). A social information processing model of social competence in children. In M. Perlmutter (Ed.), *Minnesota Symposium on Child Psychology: Vol. 18. Cognitive perspectives on children's social and behavioral development* (pp. 77–125). Mahwah, NJ: Erlbaum.

Dodge, K. A., Coie, J. D., Pettit, G. S., & Price, J. M. (1990). Peer status and aggression in boys' groups: Developmental and contextual analyses. *Child Development, 61*, 1289–1309.

Dodge, K. A., Lochman, J. E., Harnish, J. D., Bates, J. E, & Pettit, G. S. (1997). Reactive and proactive aggression in school children and psychiatrically impaired chronically assaultive youth. *Journal of Abnormal Psychology, 106*, 37–51.

Dodge, K. A., Murphy, R. R., & Buchsbaum, K. (1984). The assessment of intention-cue detection skills in children: Implications for developmental psychopathology. *Child Development, 55,* 163–173.

Dodge, K. A., Pettit, G. S., & Bates, J. E. (1994). Socialization mediators of the relation between socioeconomic status and child conduct problems. *Child Development, 65*, 649–665.

Dodge, K. A., Pettit, G. S., Bates, J. E., & Valente, E. (1995). Social information processing patterns partially mediate the effect of early physical abuse on later conduct problems. *Journal of Abnormal Psychology, 104*, 632–643.

Dodge, K. A., Pettit, G. S., McClaskey, C. L., & Brown, M. M. (1986). Social competence in children. *Monographs of the Society for Research in Child Development, 51*(2, Serial No. 213), 1–85.

Dodge, K. A., Schlundt, D. G., Schocken, I., & Delugach, J. D. (1983). Social competence and children's social status: The role of peer group entry strategies. *Merrill-Palmer Quarterly, 29*, 309–336.

Doh, H. S., & Falbo, T. (1999). Social competence, maternal attentiveness, and overprotectiveness: Only children in Korea. *International Journal of Behavioral Development, 23*, 149–162.

Donaldson, S. K., & Westerman, M. A. (1986). Development of children's understanding of ambivalence and causal theories of emotions. *Developmental Psychology, 22*, 655–662.

Dorval, B., & Eckerman, C. O. (1984). Developmental trends in the quality of conversation achieved by small groups of acquainted peers. *Monographs of the Society for Research in Child Development, 49* (Serial No. 206).

Dougherty, T. M., & Haith, M. M. (1997). Infant expectations and reaction time as predictors of childhood speed of processing and IQ. *Developmental Psychology, 33,* 146–155.

Douglas, E. (2001, July/August). The ABCs of early child care research: Keeping Congress accurately informed. *Psychological Science Agenda, 14*, 10–11.

Downey, G., & Coyne, J. C. (1990). Children of depressed parents: An integrative review. *Psychological Bulletin, 108*, 50–76.

Drillien, C. M. (1964). *The growth and development of the prematurely born infant.* Edinburgh & London: Livingstone.

Dromi, E. (1987). *Early lexical development.* London: Cambridge University Press.

Drotar, D. (1992). Personality development, problem solving, and behavior problems among preschool children with early histories of nonorganic failure-to-thrive: A controlled study. *Developmental and Behavioral Pediatrics, 13*, 266–273.

Drotar, D., Eckerle, D., Satola, J., Pallotta, J., & Wyatt, B. (1990). Maternal interactional behavior with nonorganic failure-to-thrive infants: A case comparison study. *Child Abuse and Neglect, 14*, 41–51.

Dube, E. M., Savin-Williams, R. C., & Diamond, L. M. (2001). Intimacy development, gender, and ethnicity among sexual-minority youth. In A. R. D'Augelli & C. Patterson (Eds.), *Lesbian, gay and bisexual identities among youth: Psychological perspectives* (pp. 129–152). New York: Oxford University Press.

Duckett, E., & Richards, M. H. (1995). Maternal employment and the quality of daily experience for young adolescents of single mothers. *Journal of Family Psychology, 9*, 418–432.

Dumka, L. E., Roosa, M. W., & Jackson, K. M. (1997). Risk, conflict, mothers' parenting, and children's adjustment in low-income, Mexican immigrant and Mexican American families. *Journal of Marriage and the Family, 59*, 309–323.

Duncan, G. J. (1991). The economic environment of children. In A. C. Huston (Ed.), *Children in poverty: Child development and public policy* (pp. 23–50). New York: Cambridge University Press.

Duncan, G. J., & Brooks-Gunn, J. (2000). Family poverty: Welfare reform, and child development. *Child Development, 71*, 188–196.

Duncan, G. J., Brooks-Gunn, J., & Klebanov, P. K. (1994). Economic deprivation and early childhood development. *Child Development, 65*, 296–318.

Duncan, O. D., Featherman, D. L., & Duncan, B. (1972). *Socioeconomic background and achievement*. New York: Seminar Press.

Dunn, J. (1988). *The beginnings of social understanding*. Cambridge, MA: Harvard University Press.

Dunn, J. (1992). Siblings and their development. *Current Directions in Psychological Science, 1*, 6–9.

Dunn, J., & Brown, J. (1994). Affect expression in the family, children's understanding of emotions, and their interactions with others. *Merrill-Palmer Quarterly, 40*, 120–137.

Dunn, J., Bretherton, I., & Munn, P. (1987). Conversations about feeling states between mothers and their young children. *Developmental Psychology, 23*, 132–139.

Dunn, J., Brown, J., & Beardsall, L. (1991). Family talk about feeling states and children's later understanding of others' emotions. *Developmental Psychology, 27*, 448–455.

Dunn, J., Brown, J., Slomkowski, C., Tesla, C., & Youngblade, L. (1991). Young children's understanding of other people's feelings and beliefs: Individual differences and their antecedents. *Child Development, 62*, 1352–1366.

Dunn, J., & Munn, P. (1986). Siblings and the development of prosocial behavior. *International Journal of Behavioral Development, 9*, 265–284.

Dunphy, D. C. (1963). The social structure of urban adolescent peer groups. *Sociometry, 26*, 230–246.

Dunsmore, J. C., & Halberstadt, A. G. (1997). How does family emotional expressiveness affect children's schemas? *New Directions for Child Development, 77*, 45–68.

Eagly, A. H., & Wood, W. (1999). The origins of sex differences in human behavior: Evolved dispositions versus social roles. *American Psychologist, 54*, 408–423.

East, P. L., Felice, M. E., & Morgan, M. C. (1993). Sisters' and girlfriends' sexual and childbearing behavior: Effects on early girls' sexual outcomes. *Journal of Marriage and the Family, 55*, 953–963.

East, P. L., & Jacobson, L. J. (2001). The younger siblings of teenage mothers: A follow-up of their pregnancy risk. *Developmental Psychology, 37*, 254–264.

Easterbrooks, M. A., Davidson, C. E., & Chazan, R. (1993). Psychosocial risk, attachment, and behavior problems among school-aged children. *Development and Psychopathology, 5*, 389–402.

Eaton, W. O., & Enns, L. R. (1986). Sex differences in human motor activity level. *Psychological Bulletin, 100*, 19–28.

Eaton, W. O., & Ritchot, K. F. M. (1995). Physical maturation and information processing speed in middle childhood. *Developmental Psychology, 31*, 967–972.

Eaton, W. O., & Saudino, K. J. (1992). Prenatal activity level as a temperament dimension? Individual differences and developmental functions in fetal movement. *Infant Behavior and Development, 15*, 57–70.

Eccles, J. S., Jacobs, J. E., & Harold, R. D. (1990). Gender role stereotypes, expectancy effects, and parents' socialization of gender differences. *Journal of Social Issues, 46*, 183–201.

Eccles, J. S., Lord, S., & Buchanan, C. M. (1996). School transitions in early adolescence: What are we doing to our young people? In J. A. Graber, J. Brooks-Gunn, & A. C. Petersen (Eds.), *Transitions through adolescence* (pp. 251–284). Mahwah, NJ: Erlbaum.

Eccles, J. S., & Midgley, C. (1989). Stage/environment fit: Developmentally appropriate classrooms for early adolescents. In R. Ames & C. Ames (Eds.), *Research on motivation in education* (Vol. 3, pp. 139–181). Orlando, FL: Academic Press.

Eccles, J. S., Midgley, C., Wigfield, A., Buchanan, C. M., Reuman, D., Flanagan, C., & MacIver, D. (1993). Development during adolescence: The impact of stage-environment fit on young adolescents' experiences in schools and in families. *American Psychologist, 48*, 90–101.

Eccles, J. S., Wigfield, A., Flanagan, C., Miller, C., Reuman, D., & Yee, D. (1989). Self-concepts, domain values, and self-esteem: Relations and changes at early adolescence. *Journal of Personality, 57*, 283–310.

Eckenrode, J., Laird, M., & Doris, J. (1993). School performance and disciplinary problems among abused and neglected children. *Developmental Psychology, 29*, 53–62.

Eckenrode, J., Zielinski, D., Smith, E., Marcynyszyn, L. A., Henderson, C. R., Jr., Kitzman, H., et al. (2001). Child maltreatment and the early onset of problem behaviors: Can a program of nurse home visitation break the link? *Development and Psychopathology, 13*, 873–890.

Eckert, P. (1989). *Jocks and burnouts: Social categories and identity in the high school*. New York: Teachers' College Press.

Edelman, G. M. (1987). *Neural Darwinism: The theory of neuronal group selection*. New York: Basic Books.

Eder, D. (1985). The cycle of popularity: Interpersonal relations among female adolescents. *Sociology of Education, 58*, 154–165.

Edwards, C. P. (1992). Cross-cultural perspective on family-peer relations. In R. D. Parke & G. W. Ladd (Eds.), *Family-peer relationships: Modes of linkage* (pp. 285–316). Hillsdale, NJ: Erlbaum.

Ehri, L. C. (1986). Sources of difficulty in learning to spell and read. In M. L. Wolraich & D. Routh (Eds.), *Advances in developmental and behavioral pediatrics* (Vol. 7, pp. 121–195). Greenwich, CT: JAI Press.

Eimas, P. D., & Quinn, P. C. (1994). Studies on the formation of perceptually based basic-level categories in young infants. *Child Development, 65*, 903–917.

Eimas, P. D., Siqueland, E. R., Jusczyk, P., & Vigorito, J. (1971). Speech perception in infants. *Science, 171*, 303–306.

Eisenberg, A. R. (1999). Emotion talk among Mexican American and Anglo American mothers and children from two social classes. *Merrill-Palmer Quarterly, 45*, 267–284.

Eisenberg, N. (1986). *Altruistic emotion, cognition, and behavior.* Hillsdale, N.J: Erlbaum.

Eisenberg, N. (2000). Emotion, regulation, and moral development. In S. T. Fiske, D. L. Schacter, & C. Zahn-Waxler (Eds.), *Annual review of psychology* (Vol. 51; pp. 665–697). Palo Alto, CA: Annual Reviews.

Eisenberg, N., Boehnke, K., Schuhler, P., & Silbereisen, R.K. (1985). The development of prosocial behavior and cognitions in German children. *Journal of Cross-Cultural Psychology, 16,* 69–82.

Eisenberg, N., Carlo, G., Murphy, B., & Van Court, P. (1995). Prosocial development in late adolescence: A longitudinal study. *Child Development, 66,* 911–936.

Eisenberg, N., Cialdini, R., McCreath, H., & Shell, R. (1987). Consistency-based compliance: When and why do children become vulnerable? *Journal of Personality and Social Psychology, 52,* 1174–1181.

Eisenberg, N., Cumberland, A., & Spinrad, T. L. (1998). Parental socialization of emotion. *Psychological Inquiry, 9,* 241–273.

Eisenberg, N., & Fabes, R. A. (1998). Prosocial development. In W. Damon (Series Ed.) & N. Eisenberg (Vol. Ed), *Handbook of child psychology: Vol. 3. Social, emotional, and personality development* (5th ed., pp. 701–778). New York: Wiley.

Eisenberg, N., Fabes, R. A., Bernzweig, J., Karbon, M., Poulin, R., & Hanish, L. (1993). The relations of emotionality and regulation to preschoolers' social skills and sociometric status. *Child Development, 64,* 1418–1438.

Eisenberg, N., Fabes, R. A., Guthrie, I. K., & Reiser, M. (2000). Dispositional emotionality and regulation: Their role in predicting quality of social functioning. *Journal of Personality and Social Psychology, 78,* 136–157.

Eisenberg, N., Fabes, R. A., & Murphy, B. C. (1996). Parents' reactions to children's negative emotions: Relations to children's social competence and comforting behavior. *Child Development, 67,* 2227–2247.

Eisenberg, N., Fabes, R. A., Murphy, B., Karbon, M., Smith, M., & Maszk, P. (1996). The relations of children's dispositional empathy-related responding to their emotionality, regulation, and social functioning. *Developmental Psychology, 32,* 195–209.

Eisenberg, N., Fabes, R. A., Schaller, M., Carlo, G., & Miller, P. A. (1991). The relations of parental characteristics and practices to children's vicarious emotional responding. *Child Development, 62,* 1393–1408.

Eisenberg, N., Fabes, R. A., Schaller, M., & Miller, P. A. (1989). Sympathy and personal distress: Development, gender differences, and interrelations of indexes. *New Directions in Child Development, 44,* 107–126.

Eisenberg, N., Fabes, R. A., Shepard, S. A., Guthrie, I. K., Murphy, B. C., & Reiser, M. (1999). Parental reactions to children's negative emotions: Longitudinal relations to quality of children's social functioning. *Child Development 70,* 513–534.

Eisenberg, N., Fabes, R. A., Shepard, S. A., Murphy, B. C., Jones, J., & Guthrie, I. K. (1998). Contemporaneous and longitudinal prediction of children's sympathy from dispositional regulation and emotionality. *Developmental Psychology, 34,* 910–924.

Eisenberg, N., Gershoff, E. T., Fabes, R. A., Shepard, S. A., Cumberland, A. J., Lososya, et al. (2001). Mothers' emotional expressivity and children's behavior problems and social competence: Mediation through children's regulation. *Developmental Psychology, 37,* 475–490.

Eisenberg, N., Guthrie, I. K., Murphy, B. C., Shepard, S. A., Cumberland, A., & Carlo, G. (1999). Consistency and development of prosocial dispositions: A longitudinal study. *Child Development, 70,* 1360–1372.

Eisenberg, N., Martin, C. L., & Fabes, R. A. (1996). Gender development and gender differences. In D. C. Berliner & R. C. Calfee (Eds.), *The handbook of educational psychology* (pp. 358–396). New York: Macmillan.

Eisenberg, N., Miller, P. A., Shell, R., McNalley, S., & Shea, C. (1991). Prosocial development in adolescence: A longitudinal study. *Developmental Psychology, 27,* 849–857.

Eisenberg, N., Murphy, B., & Shepard, S. (1997). The development of empathic accuracy. In W. Ickes (Eds.), *Empathic accuracy* (pp. 73–116). New York: Guilford Press.

Eisenberg, N., Murray, E., & Hite, T. (1982). Children's reasoning regarding sex-typed toy choices. *Child Development, 53,* 81–86.

Eisenberg, N., & Mussen, P. (1989). *The roots of prosocial behavior in children.* Cambridge, England: Cambridge University Press.

Eisenberg-Berg, N., & Geisheker, E. (1979). Content of preachings and power of the model/preacher. The effects on children's generosity. *Developmental Psychology, 15,* 168–175.

Eisenberg-Berg, N., & Hand, M. (1979). The relationship of preschooler's reasoning about prosocial moral conflicts to prosocial behavior. *Child Development, 50,* 356–363.

Elbert, T., Pantev, C., Wienbruch, C., Rockstroh, B., & Taub, E. (1995). Increased cortical representation of the fingers of the left hand in string players. *Science, 270,* 305–307.

Elder, G. H., Jr., Van Nguyen, T., & Caspi, A. (1985). Linking family hardship to children's lives. *Child Development, 56,* 361–375.

Elicker, J., Englund, M., & Sroufe, L. A. (1992). Predicting peer competence and peer relationships in childhood from early parent-child relationships. In R. D. Parke & G. W. Ladd (Eds.), *Family-peer relationships: Modes of linkage* (pp. 77–106). Hillsdale, NJ: Erlbaum.

Elkind, D. (1967). Egocentrism in adolescence. *Child Development, 38,* 1025–1034.

Ellemberg, D., Lewis, T. L., Maurer, D., & Brent, H. P. (2000). Influence of monocular deprivation during infancy on the later development of spatial and temporal vision. *Vision Research, 40,* 3283–3295.

Elliott, D. S. (1994). Serious violent offenders: Onset, developmental course, and termination: The American Society of Criminology 1993 Presidential Address. *Criminology, 32,* 1–21.

Ellis, S. A., & Rogoff, B. (1986). Problem solving in children's management of instruction. In E. Mueller & C. Cooper (Eds.), *Process and outcome in peer relationships.* Orlando, FL: Academic Press.

Ellis, S. A., & Siegler, R. S. (1997). Planning as a strategy choice. Why don't children plan when they should? In S. Friedman & E. Scholnick (Eds.), *Why, how, and when do we plan? The developmental psychology of planning* (pp. 183–208. Hillsdale, NJ: Erlbaum

Ellsworth, C., Muir, D., & Hains, S. (1993). Social competence and person-object differentiation: An analysis of the still-face effect. *Developmental Psychology, 29,* 63–73.

Elman, J. L., Bates, E. A., Johnson, M. H., Karmiloff-Smith, A., Parisi, D., & Plunkett, K. (1996). *Rethinking innateness: A connectionist perspective on development.* Cambridge, MA: MIT Press.

Ely, R., & McCabe, A. (1994). The language play of kindergarten children. *First Language, 14,* 19–35.

Emde, R. N. (1994). Individual meaning and increasing complexity: Contributions of Sigmund Freud and René Spitz to developmental psychology. In R. D. Parke, P. A. Ornstein, J. J. Rieser, & C. Zahn-Waxler (Eds.), *A century of developmental psychology* (pp. 203–231). Washington, DC: American Psychological Association.

Emde, R. N., Plomin, R., Robinson, J., Corley, R., DeFries, J., Fulker, D. W., et al. (1992). Temperament, emotion, and cognition at fourteen months: The MacArthur Longitudinal Twin Study. *Child Development, 63*, 1437–1455.

Emery, R. E. (1982). Interparental conflict and the children of discord and divorce. *Psychological Bulletin, 92*, 310–330.

Emery, R. E. (1989). Family violence. *American Psychologist, 44*, 321–328.

Emery, R. E., & Forehand, R. (1994). Parental divorce and children's well-being: A focus on resilience. In R. J. Haggerty, L. R. Sherrod, N. Garmezy, & M. Rutter (Eds.), *Stress, risk, and resilience in children and adolescents: Processes, mechanisms, and interventions* (pp. 64–99). Cambridge, England: Cambridge University Press.

Emery, R. E., & Laumann-Billings, L. (1998). An overview of the nature, causes, and consequences of abusive family relationships. *American Psychologist, 53,* 121–135.

Emery, R. E., Waldron, M., Kitzmann, K. M., & Aaron, J. (1999). Delinquent behavior, future divorce or nonmarital childrearing, and externalizing behavior among offspring: A 14-year prospective study. *Journal of Family Psychology, 13*, 568–579.

Entwistle, D., & Alexander, K. (1992). Summer setback: Pace, poverty, school composition, and mathematics achievement in the first two years of school. *American Sociological Review, 57*, 72–84.

Eppler, M. A., Adolph, K. E., & Weiner, T. (1996). The developmental relationship between infants' exploration and action on sloping surfaces. *Infant Behavior and Development, 19,* 259–264.

Epstein, L. H., Valoski, A., Wing, R. R., & McCurley, J. (1994). Ten-year outcomes of behavioral family-based treatment for childhood obesity. *Health Psychology, 13,* 373–383.

Erdley, C. A., Nangle, D. W., Newman, J. E., & Carpenter, E. M. (2001). Children's friendship experiences and psychological adjustment: Theory and research. *New Directions for Child and Adolescent Development, 91*, 5–24.

Erel, O., Oberman, Y., & Yirmiya, N. (2000). Maternal versus nonmaternal care and seven domains of children's development. *Psychological Bulletin, 126*, 727–747.

Erickson, M., Egeland, B., & Pianta, R. (1989). The effects of maltreatment on the development of young children. In D. Cicchetti & V. Carlson (Eds.), *Child maltreatment: Theory and research on the causes and consequences of child abuse and neglect* (pp. 647–684). New York: Cambridge University Press.

Erickson, M. F., Sroufe, L. A., & Egeland, B. (1985). The relationship between quality of attachment and behaviour problems in preschool in a high-risk sample. In I. Bretherton & E. Waters (Eds.), *Growing points of attachment theory and research. Monographs of the Society of Research in Child Development, 50* (1-2, Serial No. 209), 147–166.

Erikson, E. H. (1950). *Childhood and society*. New York: Norton.

Erikson, E. H. (1959). Identity and the life cycle. *Psychological issues* (Monograph 1). New York: International Universities Press.

Erikson, E. H. (1968). *Identity: Youth and crisis.* New York: Norton.

Erikson, E. H. (1969). *Gandhi's truth*. New York: Norton.

Erikson, E. H. (1976). Reflections on Dr. Borg's life cycle. *Daedalus, 105*, 1–28.

Erikson, E. H. (1994). *Identity and the life cycle.* New York: Norton.

Erkut, S., Marx, F., Fields, J. P., & Sing, R. (1998). Raising confident and competent girls: One size does not fit all. In L. A. Peplau, S. C. DeBro, R. Veniegas, & P. L. Taylor (Eds.), *Gender, culture, and ethnicity: Current research about women and men*. Mountain View, CA: Mayfield.

Eron, L. D., Huesmann, L. R., Dubow, E., Romanoff, R., & Yarmel, P. W. (1987). Aggression and its correlates over 22 years. In D. H. Crowell, I. M., Evans, & C. R. O'Donnell (Eds.), *Childhood aggression and violence: Sources of influence, prevention, and control* (pp. 249–262). New York: Plenum Press.

Eron, L. D., Huesmann, L. R., Lefkowitz, M. M., & Warler, L. O. (1972). Does television violence cause aggression? *American Psychologist, 27*, 253–263.

Esbensen, F.-A., & Huizinga, D. (1993). Gangs, drugs, and delinquency in a survey of urban youth. *Criminology, 31*, 565–589.

Esser, G. (1990). Epidemiology and course of psychiatric disorders in school aged children: Results of a longitudinal study. *Journal of Child Psychology and Psychiatry, 31,* 243–263.

Estell, D. B., Cairns, R. B., Farmer, T. W., & Cairns, B. D. (2002). Aggression in inner-city early elementary classrooms: Individual and peer group configurations. *Merrill-Palmer Quarterly, 48,* 52–76.

Eveleth, P. B., & Tanner, J. M. (1990). *Worldwide variation in human growth* (2nd ed.). Cambridge, England: Cambridge University Press.

Fabes, R. A., & Eisenberg, N. (1992). Young children's coping with interpersonal anger. *Child Development, 63*, 116–128.

Fabes, R. A., Eisenberg, N., McCormick, S. E., & Wilson, M. S. (1988). Preschoolers' attributions of the situational determinants of others' naturally occurring emotions. *Developmental Psychology, 24*, 376–385.

Fabes, R. A., Eisenberg, N., Nyman, M., & Michealieu, Q. (1991). Young children's appraisals of others' spontaneous emotional reactions. *Developmental Psychology, 27,* 858–866.

Fabes, R. A., Eisenberg, N., Smith, M. C., & Murphy, B. (1996). Getting angry at peers: Associations with liking of the provocateur. *Child Development, 67*, 942–956.

Fabes, R. A., Fultz, J., Eisenberg, N., May-Plumlee, T., & Christopher, F. S. (1989). The effects of reward on children's prosocial motivation: A socialization study. *Developmental Psychology, 25*, 509–515.

Fagot, B. I. (1985). Stages in thinking about early sex role development. *Developmental Review, 5*, 83–98.

Fagot, B. I. (1997). Attachment, parenting, and peer interactions of toddler children. *Developmental Psychology, 33*, 489–499.

Fagot, B. I., & Hagan, R. I. (1991). Observations of parent reactions to sex-stereotyped behaviors: Age and sex effects. *Child Development, 62*, 617–628.

Fagot, B. I., & Leinbach, M. D. (1989). The young child's gender schema: Environmental input, internal organization. *Child Development, 60,* 663–672.

Fagot, B. I., & Leinbach, M. D. (1993). Gender-role developments in young children: From discrimination to labeling. *Developmental Review, 13*, 205–224.

Fagot, B. I., Pears, K. C., Capaldi, D. M., Crosby, L., & Leve, C. S. (1998). Becoming an adolescent father: Precursors and parenting. *Developmental Psychology, 34*, 1209–1219.

Fairburn, C. O., Welch, S. L., Doll, H. A., Davies, B. A., O'Connor, M. E. (1997). Risk factors for bulimia nervosa: A community-based case control study. *Archives of General Psychiatry, 54,* 509–517.

Falbo, T., & Polit, D. F. (1986). A quantitative review of the only-child literature: Research evidence and theory development. *Psychological Bulletin, 100,* 176–189.

Falbo, T., & Poston, D. L. (1993). The academic, personality, and physical outcomes of only children in China. *Child Development, 64,* 18–35.

Falbo, T., Poston, D. L., & Jiao, S. (1989). Physical achievement and personality characteristics of Chinese children. *Journal of Biosocial Science, 21,* 483–495.

Fantuzzo, J. W., DePaola, L. M., Lambert, L., Martino, T., Anderson, G., & Sutton, S. (1991). Effects of interparental violence on the psychological adjustment and competencies of young children. *Journal of Consulting and Clinical Psychology, 59,* 258–265.

Fantz, R. L. (1961). The origin of form perception. *Scientific American, 204,* 66–72.

Fantz, R. L., Fagan, J. F., III, & Miranda, S. B. (1975). Early visual selectivity as a function of pattern variables, previous exposure, age from birth and conception, and expected cognitive deficit. In L.B. Cohen & P. Salapatek (Eds.), *Infant perception: From sensation to cognition: Vol 1. Basic visual processes* (pp. 249–345). New York: Academic Press.

Farmer, T. W., & Rodkin, P. C. (1996). Antisocial and prosocial correlates of classroom social positions: The social network centrality perspective. *Social Development, 5,* 174–188.

Farrant, K., & Reese, E. (2002). *Attachment security and mother-child reminiscing: Reflections on a shared past.* Unpublished manuscript.

Farrell, A. D., & White, K. S. (1998). Peer influences and drug use among urban adolescents: Family structure and parent-adolescent relationship as protective factors. *Journal of Consulting and Clinical Psychology, 66,* 248–258.

Farver, J. A., Kim, Y. K., & Lee, Y. (1995). Cultural differences in Korean- and Anglo-American preschoolers' social interaction and play behaviors. *Child Development, 66,* 1088–1099.

Farver, J. A., & Wimbarti, S. (1995). Indonesian children's play with their mothers and older siblings. *Child Development, 66,* 1493–1503.

Feigenson, L., Carey, S., & Spelke, E. (2002). Infants' discrimination of number vs. continuous extent. *Cognitive Psychology, 44,* 33–66.

Feinberg, M., & Hetherington, E. M. (2001). Differential parenting as a within-family variable. *Journal of Family Psychology, 15,* 22–37.

Feingold, A. (1988). Cognitive gender differences are disappearing. *American Psychologist, 43,* 95–103.

Feingold, A. (1994). Gender differences in personality: A meta-analysis. *Psychological Bulletin, 116,* 429–456.

Feiring, C., & Taska, L. S. (1996). Family self-concept: Ideas on its meaning. In B. A. Bracken (Ed.), *Handbook of self-concept: Developmental, social, and clinical considerations* (pp. 317–373). New York: Wiley.

Feitelson, D., & Goldstein, Z. (1986). Patterns of book ownership and reading to young children in Israeli school-oriented and nonschool-oriented families. *The Reading Teacher, 39,* 924–930.

Feldman, D. H. (1986). *Nature's gambit: Child prodigies and the development of human potential.* New York: Basic Books.

Feldman, H., Goldin-Meadow, S., & Gleitman, L. R. (1978). Beyond Herodotus: The creation of language by linguistically deprived deaf children. In A. Locke (Ed.), *Action, gesture, and symbol: The emergence of language* (pp. 351–414). London: Academic Press

Feldman, R. S., Philippot, P., & Custrini, R. J. (1991). Social competence and nonverbal behavior. In R. S. Feldman & B. Rime (Eds.), *Fundamentals of nonverbal behavior* (pp. 329–350). Cambridge, England: Cambridge University Press.

Feldman, S. S., & Weinberger, D. A. (1994). Self-restraint as a mediator of family influences on boys' delinquent behavior. *Child Development, 65,* 195–211.

Felsman, J. K., & Vaillant, G. E. (1987). Resilient children as adults: a 40-year study. In E. J. Anderson & B. J. Cohler (Eds.), *The invulnerable child* (pp. 211–228). New York: Guilford.

Fenson, L., Dale, P. S., Reznick, J. S., Bates, E., Thal, D. J., & Pethick, S. J. (1994). Variability in early communicative development. *Monographs of the Society for Research in Child Development, 59*(Serial No. 242).

Fergusson, D. M., Woodward, L. J., & Horwood, L. J. (1999). Childhood peer relationship problems and young people's involvement with deviant peers in adolescence. *Journal of Abnormal Child Psychology, 27,* 357–370.

Fernald, A. (1985). Four-month-old infants prefer to listen to motherese. *Infant Behavior and Development, 8,* 181–195.

Fernald, A. (1989). Intonation and communicative intent in mothers' speech to infants: Is the melody the message? *Child Development, 60,* 1497–1510.

Fernald, A., & McRoberts, G. (1995). *Infants' developing sensitivity to language-typical word order patterns.* Paper presented at the 20th annual Boston University Conference on Child Language Development, Boston.

Fernald, A., & Morikawa, H. (1993). Common themes and cultural variations in Japanese and American mothers' speech to infants. *Child Development, 64,* 637–656.

Fernald, A., Taeschner, T., Dunn, J., Papousek, M., Boysson-Bardies, B. de, & Fukui, I. (1989). A cross-language study of modifications in mothers' and fathers' speech to preverbal infants. *Journal of Child Language, 16,* 477–501.

Ferrier, L. J. (1978). Some observations of error in context. In N. Waterson & C. Snow (Eds.), *The development of communication* (pp. 301–309). Chichester: Wiley.

Feshbach, N. D. (1978). Studies of empathic behavior in children. In B. A. Maher (Ed.), *Progress in experimental personality research* (Vol. 8, pp. 1–47). New York: Academic Press.

Field, D. (1987). A review of preschool conservation training: An analysis of analyses. *Developmental Review, 7,* 210–251.

Field, T. M. (1990). Alleviating stress in newborn infants in the intensive care unit. In B. M. Lester & E. Z. Tronick (Eds.), *Stimulation and the preterm infant: The limits of plasticity.* Philadelphia: Saunders.

Field, T. M., Grizzle, N., Scafidi, F., Abrams, S., Richardson, S., Kuhn, C., & Schanberg, S. (1996). Massage therapy for infants of depressed mothers. *Infant Behavior and Development, 19,* 107–112.

Field, T. M., Scafidi, R., & Schanberg, S. (1987). Massage of preterm newborns to improve growth and development. *Pediatric Nursing, 13,* 385–387.

Fifer, W. P., & Moon, C. M. (1995). The effects of fetal experience with sound. In J. P. Lecanuet, W. P. Fifer, N. A. Krasnegor, & W. P. Smotherman (Eds.), *Fetal development: A psychobiological perspective.* Hillsdale, NJ: Erlbaum.

Finnie, V., & Russell, A. (1988). Preschool children's social status and their mothers' behavior and knowledge in the supervisory role. *Developmental Psychology, 24,* 789–801.

Fischer, A. R., & Shaw, C. M. (1999). African Americans' mental health and perceptions of racist discrimination: The moderating effects of racial socialization experiences and self-esteem. *Journal of Counseling Psychology, 46,* 395–407.

Fischer, J. L., Sollie, D. L., & Morrow, K. B. (1986). Social networks in male and female adolescents. *Journal of Adolescent Research, 1,* 1–14.

Fisher, C. (2000). From form to meaning: A role for structural alignment in the acquisition of language. *Advances in Child Development and Behavior, 27,* 1–53.

Fisher, C., Gleitman, H., & Gleitman, L. R. (1991). On the semantic content of subcategorization frames. *Cognitive Psychology, 23,* 331–392.

Fisher, E. P. (1992). The impact of play on development: A meta-analysis. *Play and Culture, 5,* 159–181.

Fisher-Thompson, D. (1993). Adult toy purchase for children: Factors affecting sex-typed toy selection. *Journal of Applied Developmental Psychology, 14,* 385–406.

Fitzgerald, J. (1992). Variant views about good thinking during composing: Focus on revision. In M. Pressley, K. R. Harris, & J. T. Guthrie (Eds.), *Promoting academic competence and literacy in school* (pp. 337–358). San Diego, CA: Academic Press.

Fivush, R. (1989). Exploring sex differences in the emotional content of mother-child conversations about the past. *Sex Roles, 20,* 675–691.

Fivush, R. (1991). The social construction of personal narratives. *Merrill-Palmer Quarterly, 37,* 59–81.

Fivush, R., & Hammond, N. R. (1990). Autobiographical memory across the preschool years: Toward reconceptualizing childhood amnesia. In R. Fivush & J. A. Hudson (Eds.) *Knowing and remembering in young children* (pp. 223–248). Cambridge, England: Cambridge University Press.

Flaks, D. E., Ficher, I., Masterpasqua, F., & Joseph, G. (1995). Lesbians choosing motherhood: A comparative study of lesbian and heterosexual parents and their children. *Developmental Psychology, 31,* 105–114.

Flavell, J. H. (1971). Stage-related properties of cognitive development. *Cognitive Psychology, 2,* 421–453.

Flavell, J. H. (1982). On cognitive development. *Child Development, 53,* 1–10.

Flavell, J. H. (1986). The development of children's knowledge about the appearance-reality distinction. *American Psychologist, 41,* 418–425.

Flavell, J. H., Flavell, E. R., & Green, F. L. (1983). Development of the appearance-reality distinction. *Cognitive Psychology, 15,* 95–120.

Flavell, J. H., Zhang, X.-D., Zou, H., Dong, Q., & Qi, S. (1983). A comparison between the development of the appearance-reality distinction in the People's Republic of China and the United States. *Cognitive Psychology, 15,* 459–466.

Floyd, F. J., Gilliom, L. A., & Costigan, C. L. (1998). Marriage and the parenting alliance: Longitudinal prediction of change in parenting perceptions and behavior. *Child Development, 69,* 1461–1479.

Fodor, J. A. (1992). A theory of the child's theory of mind. *Cognition, 44,* 283–296.

Fodor, J. A. (1983). *The modularity of mind.* Cambridge, MA: MIT Press.

Fonzi, A., Schneider, B. H., Tani, F., & Tomada, G. (1997). Predicting children's friendship status from their dyadic interaction in structured situations of potential conflict. *Child Development, 68,* 496–506.

Fox, N. A. (1994). Dynamic cerebral processes underlying emotion regulation. *Monographs of the Society for Research in Child Development, 59*(2-3, Serial No. 240), 152–166.

Fox, N. A. (1995). Of the way we were: Adult memories about attachment experiences and their role in determining infant-parent relationships: A commentary on van IJzendoorn (1995). *Psychological Bulletin, 117,* 404–410.

Fox, N. A., & Calkins, S. D. (1993). Pathways to aggression and social withdrawal: Interactions among temperament, attachment, and regulation. In K. H. Rubin & J. Asendorpf (Eds.), *Social withdrawal, inhibition, and shyness in childhood* (pp. 81–100). Hillsdale, NJ: Erlbaum.

Fox, N. A., Rubin, K. H., Calkins, S. D., Marshall, T. R., Coplan, R. J., Porges, et al. (1995). Frontal activation asymmetry and social competence at four years of age. *Child Development, 66,* 1770–1784.

Fraiberg, S. (1975). The development of human attachments in infants blind from birth. *Merrill-Palmer Quarterly, 21,* 315–334.

Fraisse, P. (1982). The adaptation of the child to time. In W. J. Friedman (Ed.), *The developmental psychology of time.* New York: Academic Press.

Frazier, J. A., & Morrison, F. J. (1998). The influence of extended-year schooling on growth of achievement and perceived competence in early elementary school. *Child Development, 69,* 495–517.

Freedman, D. G., & Freedman, N. C. (1969). Behavioral differences between Chinese-American and European-American newborns. *Nature, 224,* 1227.

Freitag, M. K., Belsky, J., Grossmann, K., Grossmann, K. E., & Scheuerer-Englisch, H. (1996). Continuity in parent-child relationships from infancy to middle childhood and relations with friendship competence. *Child Development, 67,* 1437–1454.

French, D. C., Setiono, K., & Eddy, J. M. (1999). Bootstrapping through the cultural comparison minefield: Childhood social status and friendship in the United States and Indonesia. In W. A. Collins & B. Laursen (Eds.), *Relationships as developmental contexts: The Minnesota Symposia on Child Psychology. Vol. 30*(pp. 109–131). Mahwah, NJ: Erlbaum.

French, L. A., Lucariello, J., Seidman, S., & Nelson, K. (1985). The influence of discourse content and context on preschoolers' use of language. In L. Galda & A. Pellegrini (Eds.), *Play, language and stories.* Norwood, NJ: Albex.

Frenkiel, N. (1993, November 11). Planning a family, down to a baby's sex. *New York Times,* B1, B4.

Freud, A., & Dann, S. (1951/1972). An experiment in group upbringing. In U. Bronfenbrenner (Ed.), *Influences on human development* (pp. 449–473). Hinsdale, IL: Dryden Press. (Original work published 1951 in *The Psychoanalytic Study of the Child,* Vol. 6, pp. 127–168).

Freud, S. (1920/1965). *A general introduction to psychoanalysis* (J. Riviere, trans.). New York: Washington Square Press. (Original work published 1920.)

Freud, S. (1923/1960). *The ego and the id* (J. Riviere, trans.) New York: W. W. Norton & Co. (Original work published 1923.)

Freud, S. (1926/1959). Inhibitions, symptoms and anxiety. In J. Strachey (Ed. & Trans.), *The standard edition of the complete works of Sigmund Freud* (Vol. 12, pp. 145–156). London: Hogarth Press. (Original work published 1926.)

Freud, S. (1933/1964). *New introductory lectures on psychoanalysis* (J. Strachey, trans.). New York: W. W. Norton & Co. (Original work published 1933.)

Freud, S. (1940/1964). An outline of psychoanalysis. In J. Strachey (Ed. & Trans.), *The standard edition of the complete psychological works of Sigmund Freud* (Vol. 23). London: Hogarth Press. (Original work published 1940.)

Freund, L. S. (1990). Maternal regulation of children's problem-solving behavior and its impact on children's performance. *Child Development, 61,* 113–126.

Frey, K. S., & Ruble, D. N. (1985). What children say when the teacher is not around: Conflicting goals in social comparison and performance assessment in the classroom. *Journal of Personality and Social Psychology, 48,* 550–562.

Frick, P. J. (1998). Callous-unemotional traits and conduct problems: Applying the two-factor model of psychopathy to children. In D. J. Cooke et al. (Eds.), *Psychopathy: Theory, research and implications for society* (pp. 161–187). Amsterdam: Kluwer Academic Publishers.

Frick, P. J., Christian, R. E., & Wooten, J. M. (1999). Age trends in the association between parenting practices and conduct problems. *Behavior Modification, 23,* 106–128.

Friedman, M. A., & Brownell, K. D. (1995). Psychological correlates of obesity: Moving to the next research generation. *Psychological Bulletin, 117,* 3–20.

Friedman, S. L., & Scholnick, E. K. (1997). An evolving "Blueprint" for planning: Psychological requirements, task characteristics, and social-cultural influences. In S. L. Friedman & E. K. Scholnick (Eds.), *The developmental psychology of planning: Why, how, and when do we plan?* (pp. 3–22). Mahwah, NJ: Erlbaum.

Friedman, W. J. (1991). The development of children's memory for the time of past events. *Child Development, 62,* 139–155.

Friedman, W. J. (2000). The development of children's knowledge of the times of future events. *Child Development, 71,* 913–932.

Friedman, W. J., Gardner, A. G., & Zubin, N. R. E. (1995). Children's comparisons of the recency of two events from the past year. *Child Development, 66,* 970–983.

Friedrich, L. K. & Stein, A. H. (1973). Aggressive and prosocial television programs and the natural behavior of preschool children. *Monographs of the Society for Research in Child Development, 38*(4, Serial No. 151), 1–64.

Friedrich, L. K., & Stein, A. H. (1975). Prosocial television and young children: The effects of verbal labeling and role playing on learning and behavior. *Child Development, 46,* 27–38.

Friedrich-Cofer, L., Huston-Stein, A., Kipnis, D. M., Susman, E. J., & Clewett, A. S. (1979). Environmental enhancement of prosocial television content: Effects on interpersonal behavior, imaginative play, and self-regulation in a natural setting. *Developmental Psychology, 15,* 637–646.

Frith, U. (1989). *Autism: Explaining the enigma.* Oxford, England: Basil Blackwell.

Frodi, A. M., & Lamb, M. E. (1980). Child abusers' responses to infant smiles and cries. *Child Development, 51,* 238–241.

Frosch, C. A., Mangelsdorf, S. C., & McHale, J. L. (2000). Marital behavior and the security of preschooler-parent attachment relationships. *Journal of Family Psychology, 14,* 144–161.

Frye, D., Braisby, N., Lowe, J., Maroudas, C., & Nicholls, J. (1989). Young children's understanding of counting and cardinality. *Child Development, 60,* 1158–1171.

Frye, D., Zelazo, P. D., Brooks, P. J., & Samuels, M. C. (1996). Inference and action in early causal reasoning. *Developmental Psychology, 32,* 120–131.

Fuchs, D., & Thelen, M. H. (1988). Children's expected interpersonal consequences of communicating their affective state and reported likelihood of expression. *Child Development, 58,* 1314–1322.

Fuchs, I., Eisenberg, N., Hertz-Lazarowitz, R., & Sharabany, R. (1986). Israeli city and American children's moral reasoning about prosocial moral conflicts. *Merrill-Palmer Quarterly, 32,* 37–50.

Fuligni, A. J. (1998). Authority, autonomy, and parent-adolescent conflict and cohesion: A study of adolescents from Mexican, Chinese, Filipino, and European backgrounds. *Developmental Psychology, 34,* 782–792.

Fuligni, A. J., Eccles, J. S., Barber, B. L., & Clements, P. (2001). Early adolescent peer orientation and adjustment during high school. *Developmental Psychology, 37,* 28–36.

Furman, W., & Bierman, K. L. (1984). Children's conceptions of friendship: A multimethod study of developmental changes. *Developmental Psychology, 20,* 925–931.

Furman, W., & Buhrmester, D. (1985). Children's perceptions of the personal relationships in their social networks. *Developmental Psychology, 21,* 1016–1024.

Furman, W., & Buhrmester, D. (1992). Age and sex differences in perceptions of networks of personal relationships. *Child Development, 63,* 103–115.

Furman, W., Simon, V. A., Shaffer, L., & Bouchey, H. A. (2002). Adolescents' working models and styles for relationships with parents, friends, and romantic partners. *Child Development, 73,* 241–255.

Furstenberg, F. F., Jr. (1988). Child care after divorce and remarriage. In E. M. Hetherington & J. D. Arasteh (Eds.), *Impact of divorce, single parenting, and stepparenting on children* (pp. 245–261). Hillsdale, NJ: Erlbaum.

Furstenberg, F. F., Jr., & Harris, K. M. (1993). When and why fathers matter: Impacts of father involvement on children of adolescent mothers. In R. I. Lerman & T. J. Ooms (Eds.), *Young unwed mothers* (pp. 117–138). Philadelphia: Temple University Press.

Gable, S., Belsky, J., & Crnic, K. (1993, March). *Coparenting in the child's second year: Stability and change from 15 to 21 months.* Paper presented at the biennial meeting of the Society for Research in Child Development, New Orleans, LA.

Galen, B. R., & Underwood, M. K. (1997). A developmental investigation of social aggression among children. *Developmental Psychology, 33,* 589–600.

Gallistel, C. R. (1990). *The organization of learning.* Cambridge, MA: MIT Press.

Gallistel, C. R., Brown, A. L., Carey, S., Gelman, R., & Keil, F. C. (1991). Lessons from animal learning for the study of cognitive development. In S. Carey & R. Gelman (Eds.), *The epigenesis of mind: Essays on biology and cognition.* Hillsdale, NJ: Erlbaum.

Gallup, G. H., & Newport, F. (1991). Belief in paranormal phenomena among adult Americans. *Skeptical Inquirer, 15,* 137–146.

Galton, F. (1962). *Hereditary genius: An inquiry into its laws and consequences.* London: Macmillan. Cleveland, OH: World. (Original work published 1869.)

Gandelman, R. (1992). *The psychobiology of behavioral development.* Oxford: Oxford University Press.

Garbarino, J. (1992). The meaning of poverty in the world of children. *American Behavioral Scientist, 35,* 220–237.

Garbarino, J., & Kostelny, K. (1992). Child maltreatment as a community problem. *Child Abuse and Neglect, 16,* 455–467.

Garber, J., Keiley, M. K., & Martin, N. C. (2002). Developmental trajectories of adolescents' depressive symptoms: Predictors of change. *Journal of Consulting and Clinical Psychology, 70,* 79–95.

Gardner, D., Harris, P. L., Ohmoto, M., & Hamazaki, T. (1988). Japanese children's understanding of the distinction between real and apparent emotion. *International Journal of Behavioral Development, 11,* 203–218.

Gardner, H. (1993). *Multiple intelligences: The theory in practice.* New York: Basic Books.

Gardner, R. A., & Gardner, B. T. (1969). Teaching sign language to a chimpanzee. *Science, 165,* 664–672.

Garmezy, N. (1983). Stressors of childhood. In N. Garmezy & M. Rutter (Eds.), *Stress, coping, and development in children* (pp. 43–84). New York: McGraw-Hill.

Garmon, L. C., Basinger, K. S., Gress, V. R., & Gibbs, J. C. (1996). Gender differences in stage and expression of moral judgment. *Merrill-Palmer Quarterly, 42,* 418–437.

Garner, P. W., Robertson, S., & Smith, G. (1997). Preschool children's emotional expressions with peers: The roles of gender and emotional socialization. *Sex Roles, 36,* 675–691.

Gaub, M., & Carlson, C. L. (1997). Gender differences in ADHD: A meta-analysis and critical review. *Journal of the American Academy of Child and Adolescent Psychiatry, 36,* 1036–1045.

Gauvain, M. (2001). *The social context of cognitive development.* New York: The Guilford Press.

Gavin, L. A., & Furman, W. (1989). Age differences in adolescents' perceptions of their peer groups. *Developmental Psychology, 25,* 827–834.

Gavin, L. A., & Furman, W. (1996). Adolescent girls' relationships with mothers and best friends. *Child Development, 67,* 375–386.

Ge, X., Conger, R. D., & Elder, G. H., Jr. (1996). Coming of age too early: Pubertal influences on girls' vulnerability to psychological distress. *Child Development, 67,* 3386–3400.

Geary, D. C. (1993). Mathematical disabilities: Cognitive, neuropsychological, and genetic components. *Psychological Bulletin, 114,* 345–362.

Geary, D. C. (1994). *Children's mathematical development: Research and practical implications.* Washington, DC: American Psychological Association.

Geary, D. C. (1996). International differences in mathematical achievement: Their nature, courses, and consequences. *Current Directions in Psychological Science, 5,* 133–137.

Geary, D. C. (1998). *Male, female: The evolution of human sex differences.* Washington, DC: American Psychological Association.

Geary, D. C. (1999). Evolution and developmental sex differences. *Current Directions in Psychological Science, 8,* 115–120.

Geary, D. C., & Bjorklund, D. F. (2000). Evolutionary developmental psychology. *Child Development, 71,* 57–65.

Geary, D. C., & Brown, S. C. (1991). Cognitive addition: Strategy choice and speed-of-processing differences in gifted, normal, and mathematically disabled children. *Developmental Psychology, 27,* 398–406.

Gelman, R., & Gallistel, C. R. (1978). *The child's understanding of number.* Cambridge, MA: Harvard University Press.

Gelman, R., Meck, E., & Merkin, S. (1986). Young children's numerical competence. *Cognitive Development, 1,* 1–29.

Gelman, R., & Williams, E. (1998). Enabling constraints for cognitive development and learning: Domain specificity and epigenesis. In W. Damon (Series Ed.), D. Kuhn, & R. Siegler (Vol. Eds.), *Handbook of child psychology: Vol. 2. Cognition, perception, and language* (5th ed., pp. 575–630). New York: Wiley.

Gelman, S. (in press). *The essential child.* New York: Oxford University Press.

Gelman, S. A., Coley, J. D., & Gottfried, G. M. (1994). Essentialist beliefs in children: The acquisition of concepts and theories. In L. A. Hirschfeld & S. A. Gelman (Eds.) *Mapping the mind: Domain specificity in cognition and culture.* New York: Cambridge University Press.

Gelman, S. A., Coley, J. D., Rosengren, K. S., Hartman, E., & Pappas, A., (1998). Beyond labeling: The role of maternal input in the acquisition of richly structured categories. *Monographs of the Society for Research in Child Development, 63*(1, Serial No. 253).

Gelman, S., & Gottfried, G. M. (1996). Children's causal explanations of animate and inanimate motion. *Child Development, 67,* 1970–1987.

Gentner, D. (1982). Why nouns are learned before verbs: Linguistic relativity versus natural partitioning. In S. A. Kuczaj (Ed.), *Language development: Syntax and semantics.* Hillsdale, NJ: Erlbaum.

Gentner, D. (1989). The mechanisms of analogical transfer. In S. Vosniadou & A. Ortony (Eds.), *Similarity and analogical reasoning.* London: Cambridge University Press.

Gentner, D., Ratterman, M. J., Markman, A., & Kotovsky, L. (1995). Two forces in the development of relational similarity. In T. J. Simon & G. S. Halford (Eds.), *Developing cognitive competence: New approaches to process modeling* (pp. 263–313). Hillsdale, NJ: Erlbaum.

George, C., & Main, M. (1979). Social interactions of young abused children: Approach, avoidance, and aggression. *Child Development, 50,* 306–318.

Gerken, L. A. (1994). Child phonology: Past research, present questions, future directions. In M. A. Gernsbacher (Ed.), *Handbook of psycholinguistics* (pp. 781–820). New York: Academic Press.

Gesell, A., & Thompson, H. (1938). *The psychology of early growth including norms of infant behavior and a method of genetic analysis.* New York: Macmillan.

Gest, S. D., Graham-Bermann, S. A., & Hartup, W. W. (2001). Peer experience: Common and unique features of number of friendships, social network centrality, and sociometric status. *Social Development, 10,* 23–40.

Gewirtz, J. L., & Boyd, E. F. (1977). Does maternal responding imply reduced infant crying? A critique of the 1972 Bell and Ainsworth report. *Child Development, 48,* 1200–1207.

Ghim, H.-R. (1990). Evidence for perceptual organization in infants: Perception of subjective contours by young infants. *Infant Behavior and Development, 13,* 221–248.

Gianino, A., & Tronick, E. Z. (1988). The mutual regulation model: The infant's self and interactive regulation, coping, and defense. In T. Field, P. McCabe, & N. Schneiderman (Eds.), *Stress and coping* (pp. 47–68). Hillsdale, NJ: Erlbaum.

Gibbs, N. (1999, May 3). In sorrow and disbelief. *Time.*

Gibson, E. J. (1988). Exploratory behavior in the development of perceiving, acting, and the acquiring of knowledge, *Annual Review of Psychology, 39,* 1–41.

Gibson, E. J. (1994). Has psychology a future? *Psychological Science, 5,* 69–76.

Gibson, E. J., & Schmuckler, M. A. (1989). Going somewhere: An ecological and experimental approach to the development of mobility. *Ecological Psychology, 1,* 3–25.

Gibson, E. J., Riccio, G., Schmuckler, M. A., Stoffgren, T. A., Rosenberg, D., & Taormina, J. (1987). Detection of the traversability of surfaces by crawling and walking infants. *Journal of Experimental Psychology: Human Perception and Performance, 13,* 533–544.

Gibson, E. J., & Walk, R. D. (1960). The "visual cliff." *Scientific American, 202,* 64–71.

Gillham, J. E., Reivich, K. J., Jaycox, L. H., & Seligman, M. E. P. (1995). Prevention of depressive symptoms in schoolchildren: Two-year follow-up. *Psychological Science, 6,* 343–350.

Gilligan, C. (1977). In a different voice: Women's conceptions of self and morality. *Harvard Educational Review, 47,* 481–517.

Gilligan, C. (1982). *In a different voice: Psychological theory and women's development.* Cambridge, MA: Harvard University Press.

Gilligan, C., & Attanucci, J. (1988). Two moral orientations: Gender differences and similarities. *Merrill-Palmer Quarterly, 34,* 223–238.

Gilliom, M., Shaw, D. S., Beck, J. E., Schonberg, M. A., & Lukon, J. L. (2002). Anger regulation in disadvantaged preschool boys: Strategies, antecedents, and the development of self-control. *Developmental Psychology, 38,* 222–235.

Ginsburg, H. P., & Opper, S. (1988). *Piaget's theory of intellectual development* (3rd ed.). Englewood Cliffs, NJ: Prentice Hall.

Gleitman, L., Gleitman, H., Landau, B., & Wanner, E. (1988). Where the learning begins: Initial representations for language learning. In F. Newmeyer (Ed.), *The Cambridge Linguistic Survey* (Vol. 3, pp. 150–193). Cambridge, MA: Harvard University Press.

Gnepp, J., & Hess, D. L. R. (1986). Children's understanding of verbal and facial display rules. *Development Psychology, 22,* 103–108.

Goldfield, B. A., & Reznick, J. S. (1990). Early lexical acquisition: Rate, content, and the vocabulary spurt. *Journal of Child Language, 17,* 171–184.

Goldin-Meadow, S. (1999). The role of gesture in communication and thinking. *Trends in Cognitive Sciences, 3,* 419–429.

Goldin-Meadow, S. (2001). Giving the mind a hand: The role of gesture in cognitive change. In J. L McClelland, & R. S. Siegler, (Eds.), Mechanisms of cognitive development: Behavioral and neural perspectives (pp. 5–31). Mahwah, NJ: Erlbaum.

Goldin-Meadow, S., Alibali, M. W., & Church, R. B. (1993). Transitions in concept acquisition: Using the hand to read the mind. *Psychological Review, 100,* 279–297.

Goldin-Meadow, S., & Mylander, C. (1998). Spontaneous sign systems created by deaf children in two cultures. *Nature, 391,* 279–281.

Goldin-Meadow, S., Seligman, M. E. P., & Gelman, R. (1976). Language in the two-year-old. *Cognition, 4,* 189–202.

Goldman, S. R., Pellegrino, J. W., & Mertz, D. L. (1988). Extended practice of basic addition facts: Strategy changes in learning disabled students. *Cognition and Instruction, 5,* 223–265.

Goldsmith, H. H., Buss, K. A., & Lemery, K. S. (1997). Toddler and childhood temperament: Expanded content, stronger genetic evidence, new evidence for the importance of environment. *Developmental Psychology, 33,* 891–905.

Goldson, E. (1996). Prematurity: Discussion. *International Journal of Behavioral Development, 19,* 465–475.

Goleman, D. (1995). *Emotional intelligence.* New York: Bantam Books.

Golinkoff, R. M., & Alioto, A. (1995). Infant-directed speech facilitates lexical learning in adults hearing Chinese: Implications for language acquisition. *Journal of Child Language, 22,* 703–726.

Golinkoff, R. M., Alioto, A., & Hirsh-Pasek, K. (1996). Infants' word learning is facilitated when novel words are presented in infant-direct speech and in either sentence-medial or sentence-final position. In D. Cahana-Arnitay, L. Hughes, A. Stringfellow, & A. Zukowske (Eds.), *Proceedings of the 20th Boston University Conference on Language Development.* Somerville, MA: Cascadilla Press.

Golinkoff, R. M., Mervis, C. B., & Hirsh-Pasek, K. (1994). Early object labels: The case for a developmental lexical principles framework. *Journal of Child Language, 21,* 125–156.

Golombok, S., Spencer, A., & Rutter, M. (1983). Children in lesbian and single-parent households: Psychosexual and psychiatric appraisal. *Journal of Child Psychology and Psychiatry, 24,* 551–572.

Goncu, A. (1993). Development of intersubjectivity in the dyadic play of preschoolers. *Early Childhood Research Quarterly, 8,* 99–116.

Goncu, A., Mistry, J., & Mosier, C. (2000). Cultural variations in the play of toddlers. *International Journal of Behavioral Development, 24,* 321–329.

Gonzales, N. A., Pitts, S. C., Hill, N. E., & Roosa, M. W. (2000). A mediational model of the impact of interparental conflict on child adjustment in a multiethnic, low-income sample. *Journal of Family Psychology, 14,* 365–379.

Good, T. L., & Brophy, J. E. (1996). *Looking in classrooms* (7th ed.). New York: Addison-Wesley.

Goodenough, F. C. (1931). *Anger in young children.* Minneapolis: University of Minnesota Press.

Goodglass, H. (1979). Effect of aphasia on the retrieval of lexicon and syntax. In C. J. Fillmore, D. Kempler, & W. S.-Y. Wang (Eds.), *Individual differences in language ability and language behavior* (pp. 253–260). New York: Academic Press.

Goodglass, H. (1993). *Understanding aphasia.* San Diego, CA: Academic Press.

Goodman, G. S., & Aman, C. (1990). Children's use of anatomically detailed dolls to recount an event. *Child Development, 61,* 1859–1871.

Goodman, R., & Stevenson, J. (1989). A twin study of hyperactivity: II. The aetiological role of genes, family relationships, and perinatal adversity. *Journal of Child Psychology and Psychiatry, 30,* 691–709.

Goodnow, J. J. (1977). *Children drawing.* Cambridge, MA: Harvard University Press.

Goodnow, J. J., Cashmore, J., Cotton, S., & Knight, R. (1984). Mothers' developmental timetables in two cultural groups. *International Journal of Psychology, 19,* 193–205.

Goodwyn, S. W., Acredolo, L. P., & Brown, C. A. (2000). Impact of symbolic gesturing on early language development. *Journal of Nonverbal Behavior, 24,* 81–103.

Gopnik, A., & Astington, J. W. (1988). Children's understanding of representational change and its relation to the understanding of false belief and the appearance-reality distinction. *Child Development, 59,* 26–37.

Gopnik, A., & Meltzoff, A. N. (1997). *Words, thoughts, and theories.* Cambridge, MA: MIT Press.

Gopnik, A., & Slaughter, V. (1991). Young children's understanding of changes in their mental states. *Child Development, 62,* 98–110.

Gortmaker, S. L., Must, A., Perrin, J. M., Sobol, A. M., & Dietz, W. H. (1993). Social and economic consequences of overweight in adolescence and young adulthood. *New England Journal of Medicine, 329,* 1008–1012.

Gortmaker, S. L., Must, A., Sobol, A. M., Peterson, K., Colditz, G. A., & Dietz, W. H. (1996). Television viewing as a cause of increasing obesity among children in the United States, 1986–1990. *Archives of Pediatrics & Adolescent Medicine, 150,* 356–362.

Goswami, U. (1995). Transitive relational mappings in 3- and 4-year-olds: The analogy of Goldilocks and the Three Bears. *Child Development, 66,* 877–892.

Gottesman, I. I. (1991). *Schizophrenia genesis: The origins of madness.* New York: Freeman.

Gottesman, I. I., & Goldsmith, H. H. (1994). Developmental psychopathology of antisocial behavior: Inserting genes into its ontogenesis and epigenesis. In C. Nelson (Ed.), *Minnesota Symposium on Child Psychology: Vol. 27. Threats to optimal development: Integrating biological, psychological, and social risk factors* (pp. 69–104). Hillsdale, NJ: Erlbaum.

Gottlieb, A. (2000). Luring your child into this life: A Beng path for infant care. In J. S. DeLoache & A. Gottlieb (Eds.), *A world of babies: Imagined childcare guides for seven societies.* Cambridge, England: Cambridge University Press.

Gottlieb, G. (1992). *Individual development and evolution.* New York: Oxford University Press.

Gottlieb, G., Wahlsten, D., & Lickliter, R. (1997). The significance of biology for human development: A developmental psychobiological systems view. In W. Damon (Series Ed.) & R. M. Lerner (Vol. Ed.), *Handbook of child psychology: Vol. 1. Theoretical models of human development* (5th ed., pp. 233–273). New York: Wiley.

Gottman, J. M. (1986). The world of coordinated play: same- and cross-sex friendship in young children. In J. M. Gottman & J. G. Parker (Eds.), *Conversations of friends: Speculations on affective development* (pp. 139–191). Cambridge University Press: Cambridge, England.

Gottman, J. M., Katz, L. F., & Hooven, C. (1996). Parental meta-emotion philosophy and the emotional life of families: Theoretical models and preliminary data. *Journal of Family Psychology, 10,* 243–268.

Gottman, J. M., & Mettetal, G. (1986). Speculations about social and affective development: friendship and acquaintanceship through adolescence. In J. M. Gottman & J. G. Parker (Eds.), *Conversations of friends: Speculations on affective development* (pp. 192–237). Cambridge University Press: Cambridge, England.

Gottman, J. S. (1990). Children of gay and lesbian parents. In F. W. Bozett & M. B. Sussman (Eds.), *Homosexuality and family relations* (pp. 177–196). New York: Harrington Park Press.

Goubet, N., & Clifton, R. K. (1998). Object and event representation in 6-½-month-old infants. *Developmental Psychology, 34,* 63–76.

Gould, J. (1978). Sociobiology: The art of story telling. *New Scientist, 80,* 530–533.

Gould, S. J. (1992, February). Mozart and modularity. *Natural History,* pp. 8–14.

Gove, W. R., & Zeiss, C. (1987). Multiple roles and happiness. In F. Crosby (Ed.), *Spouse, parent, worker* (pp. 125–137). New Haven, CT: Yale University Press.

Graber, J. A., Brooks-Gunn, J., Paikoff, R. L., & Warren, M. P. (1994). Prediction of eating problems: An 8-year study of adolescent girls. *Developmental Psychology, 30,* 823–834.

Graham, J. A., & Cohen, R. (1997). Race and sex as factors in children's sociometric ratings and friendship choices. *Social Development, 6,* 355–372.

Graham, S., & Harris, K. R. (1992). Self-regulated strategy development: Programmatic research in writing. In B. Y. L. Wong (Ed.), *Contemporary intervention research in learning disabilities: An international perspective* (pp. 47–64). New York: Springer-Verlag.

Graham, S., & Hudley, C. (1994). Attributions of aggressive and non-aggressive African-American male early adolescents: A study of construct accessibility. *Developmental Psychology, 28,* 731–740.

Graham, T., & Perry, M. (1993). Indexing transitional knowledge. *Developmental Psychology, 29,* 779–788.

Graham-Bermann, S. A., & Brescoll, V. (2000). Gender, power, and violence: Assessing the family stereotypes of the children of batterers. *Journal of Family Psychology, 14,* 600–612.

Granrud, C. E. (1987). Size constancy in newborn human infants. *Investigative Ophthalmology and Visual Science, 28*(Suppl.), 5.

Graves, N. B., & Graves, T. D. (1983). The cultural context of prosocial development: An ecological model. In D. L. Bridgeman (Ed.), *The nature of prosocial development* (pp. 243–264). New York: Academic Press.

Gray, E. (1993). *Unequal justice: The prosecution of child sexual abuse.* New York: Macmillan.

Gray-Little, B., & Hafdahl, A. R. (2000). Factors influencing racial comparisons of self-esteem: A quantitative review. *Psychological Bulletin, 126,* 26–54.

Green, J. A., Jones, L. E., & Gustafson, G. E. (1987). Perception of cries by parents and nonparents: Relation to cry acoustics. *Developmental Psychology, 23,* 370–382.

Green, R. W., Biederman, J., Faraone, S. V., Sienna, M., & Garcia-Jetton, J. (1997). Adolescent outcome of boys with attention-deficity/hyperactivity disorder and social disability: Results from a 4-year longitudinal follow-up study. *Journal of Consulting and Clinical Psychology, 65,* 758–767.

Greenberg, M. T., Kusche, C. A., Cook, E. T., & Quamma, J. P. (1995). Promoting emotional competence in school-aged children: The effects of the PATHS curriculum. *Development and Psychopathology, 7,* 117–136.

Greenberger, E., Chen, C., Beam, M., Whang, S-M., & Dong, Q. (2000). The perceived social context of adolescents' misconduct; A comparative study of youths in three cultures. *Journal of Research on Adolescence, 10,* 365–388.

Greenberger, E., O'Neil, R., & Nagel, S. K. (1994). Linking workplace and homeplace: Relations between the nature of adults' work and their parenting behaviors. *Developmental Psychology, 30,* 990–1002.

Greene, A. L. (1990). Patterns of affectivity in the transition to adolescence. *Journal of Experimental Child Psychology, 50,* 340–356.

Greene, J. G., Fox, N. A., & Lewis, M. (1983). The relationship between neonatal characteristics and three-month mother-infant interaction in high risk infants. *Child Development, 54,* 1286–1296.

Greenfield, P. M., deWinstanley, P., Kilpatrick, H., & Kaye, D. (1994). Action video games and informal education: Effects on strategies for dividing visual attention. *Journal of Applied Developmental Psychology, 15,* 105–123.

Greenough, W. T., & Black, J. E. (1992). Induction of brain structure by experience: Substrates for cognitive development. In M. Gunnar & C. Nelson (Eds.), *Minnesota Symposia on Child Psychology: Vol. 24. Developmental behavioral neuroscience* (pp. 155–200). Hillsdale, NJ: Erlbaum.

Greenough, W. T., Larson, J. R., & Withers, G. S. (1985). Effects of unilateral and bilateral training in a reaching task on dendritic branching of neurons in the rat motor-sensory forelimb cortex. *Behavioral and Neural Biology, 44,* 301–314.

Griffin, S. A. (in press). Evaluation of a program designed to teach number sense to children at risk for school failure. *Journal of Mathematics Education.*

Griffin, S. A., & Case, R. (1996). Evaluating the breadth and depth of training effects, when central conceptual structures are taught. In R. Case & Y. Okamoto (Eds.), The role of central conceptual structures in the development of children's thought. *Monographs of the Society for Research in Child Development, 61*(1/2, Serial No. 246).

Grilo, C. M., & Pogue-Geile, M. F. (1991). The nature of environmental influences on weight and obesity: A behavior genetic analysis. *Psychological Bulletin, 10,* 520–537.

Grolnick, W. S., Bridges, L. J., & Connell, J. P. (1996). Emotion regulation in two-year-olds: Strategies and emotional expression in four contexts. *Child Development, 67,* 928–941.

Groome, L. J., Swiber, M. J., Atterbury, J. L., Bentz, L. S., & Holland, S. B. (1997). Similarities and differences in behavioral state organization during sleep periods in the perinatal infant before and after birth. *Child Development, 68,* 1–11.

Gross, D., & Harris, P. L. (1988). False beliefs about emotion: Children's understanding of misleading emotional displays. *International Journal of Behavioral Development, 11,* 475–488.

Gross, R. T., Spiker, D., & Haynes, C. W. (1997). *Helping low birth weight, premature babies: The infant health and development program.* Stanford, CA: Stanford University Press.

Grotevant, H. D. (1998). Adolescent development in family contexts. In W. Damon (Series Ed.) & N. Eisenberg (Vol. Ed.), *Handbook of child psychology: Vol. 3. Social, emotional, and personality development* (5th ed., pp. 1097–1149). New York: Wiley.

Grueneich, R. (1982). Issues in the developmental study of how children use intention and consequence information to make moral evaluations. *Child Development, 53,* 29–43.

Grusec, J. E., Goodnow, J. J., & Cohen, L. (1996). Household work and the development of concern for others. *Developmental Psychology, 32,* 999–1007.

Grych, J. H. (1998). Children's appraisals of interparental conflict: Situational and contextual influences. *Journal of Family Psychology, 12,* 437–453.

Grych, J. H., & Fincham, F. D. (1990). Marital conflict and children's adjustment: A cognitive-contextual framework. *Psychological Bulletin, 108,* 267–290.

Grych, J. H., & Fincham, F. D. (1997). Children's adaptation to divorce: From description to explanation. In S. A. Wolchik & I. N. Sandler (Eds.), *Handbook of children's coping: Linking theory and intervention* (pp. 159–193). New York: Plenum Press.

Guerin, D. W., & Gottfried, A. W. (1994). Developmental stability and change in parent reports of temperament: A ten-year longitudinal investigation from infancy through preadolescence. *Merrill-Palmer Quarterly, 40,* 334–355.

Guerin, D. W., Gottfried, A. W., & Thomas, C. W. (1997). Difficult temperament and behaviour problems: A longitudinal study from 1.5 to 12 years of age. *International Journal of Behavioral Development, 21,* 71–90.

Guerra, N. G., Huesmann, L. R., Tolan, P. H., Van Acker, R. & Eron, L. D. (1995). Stressful events and individual beliefs as correlates of economic disadvantage and aggression among urban children. *Journal of Consulting and Clinical Psychology, 63,* 518–528.

Gustafson, G. (1984). Effects of the ability to locomote on infants' social and exploratory behaviors: An experimental study. *Developmental Psychology, 20,* 397–405.

Gustafson, G. E., & Green, J. A. (1988, April). *A role of crying in the development of prelinguistic communicative competence.* Paper presented at the International Conference on Infant Studies, Washington, DC.

Guthrie, J. T., Wigfield, A., Metsala, J. L., & Cox, K. E. (1999). Motivational and cognitive predictors of text comprehension and reading amount. *Scientific Studies of Reading, 3,* 231–256.

Guttentag, R. E. (1984). The mental effort requirement of cumulative rehearsal: A developmental study. *Journal of Experimental Child Psychology, 37,* 92–106.

Guttentag, R. E. (1985). Memory and aging: Implications for theories of memory development during childhood. *Developmental Review, 5,* 56–82.

Guyer B., Hoyer D. L., Martin J. A., Ventura S. J., MacDorman M. R., Strobino D. (1999, December). Annual summary of vital statistics—1998. *Pediatrics, 104,* 1229–1246.

Gwiazda, J., Brill, S., Mohindra, I., & Held, R. (1980). Preferential looking acuity in infants from 2–58 weeks of age. *American Journal of Optometry and Physiological Optics, 57,* 428–432.

Haith, M. M. (1980). *Rules that babies look by: The organization of newborn visual activity.* Hillsdale, NJ: Erlbaum.

Haith, M. M., & Benson, J. B. (1998). Infant cognition. In W. Damon (Series Ed.), D. Kuhn, & R. S. Siegler (Vol. Eds.), *Handbook of child psychology: Vol. 2. Cognition, perception, and language* (5th ed., pp. 199–254). New York: Wiley.

Haith, M. M., Bergman, T., & Moore, M. J. (1977). Eye contact and face scanning in early infancy. *Science, 198,* 853–855.

Haith, M. M., Hazen, C., & Goodman, G. S. (1988). Expectation and anticipation of dynamic visual events by 3.5-month-old babies. *Child Development, 59,* 467–479.

Haith, M. M., Wentworth, N., & Canfield, R. L., (1993). The formation of expectations in early infancy. In C. Rovee-Collier & L. P. Lipsitt (Eds.), *Advances in infancy research.* Norwood, NJ: Ablex.

Hakuta, K. (1999). The debate on bilingual education. *Journal of Developmental & Behavioral Pediatrics, 20,* 36–37.

Hakuta, K., Ferdman, B. M., & Diaz, R. M. (1987). Bilingualism and cognitive development: Three perspectives. In S. Rosenberg (Ed.), *Advances in applied psycholinguistics: Vol. 2. Reading, writing, and language learning* (pp. 284–319). New York: Cambridge University Press.

Halberstadt, A. G., Cassidy, J., Stifter, C. A., Parke, R. D., & Fox, N. A. (1995). Self-expressiveness within the family context: Psychometric support for a new measure. *Psychological Assessment, 7,* 93–103.

Halberstadt, A. G., Crisp, V. W., & Eaton, K. L. (1999). Family expressiveness: A retrospective and new directions for research. In P. Philippot, R. S. Feldman, & E. Coats (Eds.), *The social context of nonverbal behavior*. New York: Cambridge University Press.

Halberstadt, A. G., Denham, S. A., & Dunsmore, J. C. (2001). Affective social competence. *Social Development, 10,* 79–119.

Hale, S., Frye, A. F., & Jessie, K. A. (1993). Effects of practice on speed of information processing in children and adults: Age sensitivity and age invariants. *Developmental Psychology, 29,* 880–892.

Halford, G. S., Smith, S. B., Dickson, J. C., Maybery, M. T., Kelly, M. E., Bain, J. D., & Stewart, J. E. M. (1995). Modeling the development of reasoning strategies: The roles of analogy, knowledge, and capacity. In T. J. Simon & G. S. Halford (Eds.), *Developing cognitive competence: New approaches to process modeling* (pp. 77–156). Hillsdale, NJ: Erlbaum.

Hall, D. G., Waxman, S. R., & Hurwitz, W. R. (1993). How two- and four-year-old children interpret adjectives and count nouns. *Child Development, 64,* 1651–1664.

Halliday-Boykins, C. A., & Graham, S. (2001). At both ends of the gun: Testing the relationship between community violence exposure and youth violent behavior. *Journal of Abnormal Child Psychology, 29,* 383–402.

Halpern, C.T., Udry, J. R., & Suchindran, C. M. (1997), Testosterone predicts initiation of coitus in adolescent females, *Psycohosomatic Medicine, 50,* 161–171.

Halpern, D. F. (1992). *Sex differences in cognitive abilities* (2nd ed.). Mahwah, NJ: Erlbaum.

Halpern, D. F. (1997). Sex differences in intelligence: Implications for education. *American Psychologist, 52,* 1091–1102.

Halpern, L. F., Anders, T. F., Garcia-Coll, C., & Hua, J. (1994). Infant temperament: Is there a relation to sleep-wake states and maternal nighttime behavior? *Infant Behavior and Development, 17,* 255–263.

Hamalainen, M., & Pulkkinen, L. (1996). Problem behavior as a precursor of male criminality. *Development and Psychopathology, 8,* 443–455.

Hamer, D. H., Hu, S., Magnuson, V. L., Hu, N., & Pattatucci, A. M. L. (1993). A linkage between DNA markers on the X chromosome and male sexual orientation. *Science, 261,* 311–327.

Hamilton, C. E. (2000). Continuity and discontinuity of attachment from infancy through adolescence. *Child Development, 71,* 690–694.

Hanish, L. D., & Guerra, N. G. (2000a). Predictors of peer victimization among urban youth. *Social Development, 9,* 521–543.

Hanish, L. D., & Guerra, N. G. (2000b). The roles of ethnicity and school context in predicting children's victimization by peers. *American Journal of Community Psychology, 28,* 201–223.

Hanish, L. D., & Guerra, N. G. (2002). A longitudinal analysis of patterns of adjustment following peer victimization. *Development and Psychopathology, 14,* 69–89.

Hankin, B. L., & Abramson, L. Y. (1999). Development of gender differences in depression: description and possible explanations. *Annals of Medicine, 31,* 372–379.

Hankin, B. L., Abramson, L. Y., Moffitt, T. E., Silva, P. A., McGree, R., & Angell, K. E. (1998). Development of depression from preadolescence to young adulthood: Emerging gender differences in a 10-year-longitudinal study. *Journal of Abnormal Psychology, 107,* 128–140.

Hanna, E., & Meltzoff, A. N. (1993). Peer imitation by toddlers in laboratory, home, and day-care contexts: Implications for social learning and memory. *Developmental Psychology, 29,* 701–710.

Hanna, N. A. (1998). Predictors of friendship quality and peer group acceptance at summer camp. *Journal of Early Adolescence, 18,* 291–318.

Hardy, J. B., Astone, N. M., Brooks-Gunn, J., Shapiro, S., & Miller, T. L. (1998). Like mother, like child: Intergenerational patterns of age at first birth and association with childhood and adolescent characteristics and adult outcomes in the second generation. *Developmental Psychology, 34,* 1220–1232.

Harkness, S., & Super, C. (1995). Culture and parenting. In M. Bornstein (Ed.), *Handbook of parenting* (Vol. 2, pp. 211–234). Hillsdale, NJ: Erlbaum.

Harkness, S., Super, C., Keefer, C. H., Raghavan, C. S., & Campbell, E. K. (1996). Ask the doctor: The negotiation of cultural models in American parent-pediatrician discourse. In S. Harkness & C. M. Super (Eds.), *Parents' cultural belief systems: Their origins, expressions, and consequences*. New York: Guilford.

Harlow, H. F., & Harlow, M. K. (1965). The affectional systems. In A. M. Schrier, H. F. Harlow, & F. Stollnitz (Eds.), *Behavior of nonhuman primates: Vol. 2*. New York: Academic Press.

Harlow, H. F., & Zimmerman, R. (1959). Affectional responses in the infant monkey. *Science, 130,* 421–432.

Harman, C., Rothbart, M. K., & Posner, M. I. (1997). Distress and attention interactions in early infancy. *Motivation & Emotion, 21,* 27–43.

Harnishfeger, K. K., & Bjorklund, D. F. (1993). The ontogeny of inhibition mechanisms: A renewed approach to cognitive development. In M. L. Howe & R. Pasnak (Eds.), *Emerging themes in cognitive development: Vol 1. Foundations*. New York: Springer-Verlag.

Harold, G. T., & Conger, R. D. (1997). Marital conflict and adolescent distress: The role of adolescent awareness. *Child Development, 68,* 333–350.

Harris, F. R., Wolf, M. M., & Baer, D. M. (1967). Effects of adult social reinforcement on child behavior. In W. W. Hartup and N. L. Smothergill (Eds.), *The young child: Reviews of research*. Washington, DC: National Association for the Education of Young Children.

Harris, J. F. (1995). Where is the child's environment? A group socialization theory of development. *Psychological Review, 102,* 458–489.

Harris, K. R., & Graham, S. (1992). Self-regulated strategy development: A part of the writing process. In M. Pressley, K. R. Harris, & J. T. Guthrie (Eds.), *Promoting academic competence and literacy in school* (pp. 277–309). San Diego, CA: Academic Press.

Harris, P. L. (1974). Perseverative search at a visibly empty place by young infants. *Journal of Experimental Child Psychology, 18,* 535–542.

Harris, P. L. (1991). The work of the imagination. In A. Whiten (Ed.), *Natural theories of mind*. Oxford, England: Basil Blackwell.

Harris, P. L. (1992). From simulation to folk psychology: The case for development. *Mind & Language, 7,* 120–144.

Harris, P. L., Olthof, T., Terwogt, M. M., & Hardman, C. E. (1987). Children's knowledge of the situations that provoke emotion. *International Journal of Behavioral Development, 10,* 319–343.

Harris, R. T. (1991, March-April). Anorexia nervosa and bulimia nervosa in female adolescents. *Nutrition Today, 26,* 30–34.

Harrist, A. W., Zaia, A. F., Bates, J. E., Dodge, K. A., & Pettit, G. S. (1997). Subtypes of social withdrawal in early childhood: Sociometric status and social-cognitive differences across four years. *Child Development, 68,* 278–294.

Hart, B., & Risley, T. R. (1992). American parenting of language-learning children: Persisting differences in family-child interactions observed in natural home environments. *Developmental Psychology, 28,* 1096–1105.

Hart, B., & Risley, T. R. (1994). *Meaningful differences in the everyday experience of young American children.* Baltimore: Paul H. Brookes.

Hart, C. H., DeWolf, D. M., Wozniak, P., & Burts, D. C. (1992). Maternal and paternal disciplinary styles: Relations with preschoolers' playgroup behavioral orientations and peer status. *Child Development, 63,* 879–892.

Hart, C. H., Ladd, G. W., & Burleson, B. R. (1990). Children's expectations of the outcomes of social strategies: Relations with sociometric status and maternal disciplinary styles. *Child Development, 61,* 127–137.

Hart, D., & Fegley, S. (1995). Altruism and caring in adolescence: Relations to self-understanding and social judgment. *Child Development, 66,* 1346–1359.

Harter, S. (1983). Developmental perspectives on the self-system. In P. H. Mussen (Series Ed.) & E. M. Hetherington (Vol. Ed.), *Handbook of child psychology: Vol. 4. Socialization, personality, and social development* (pp. 275–385). New York: Wiley.

Harter, S. (1985). *Manual for the self-perception profile for children.* Unpublished manuscript, University of Denver, Denver, CO.

Harter, S. (1993). Causes and consequences of low self-esteem in children and adolescents. In R. F. Baumeister (Ed.), *Self-esteem: The puzzle of low self-regard* (pp. 87–116). New York: Plenum Press.

Harter, S. (1998). The development of self-representations. In W. Damon (Series Ed.) & N. Eisenberg (Vol. Ed.), *Handbook of child psychology: Vol. 3. Social, emotional, and personality development* (5th ed., pp. 553–617). New York: Wiley.

Harter, S. (1999). *The cognitive and social construction of the developing self.* New York: Guilford Press.

Harter, S., Bresnick, S., Bouchey, H. A., & Whitsell, N. R. (1998). The development of multiple role-related selves during adolescence. *Development and Psychopathology, 9,* 835–854.

Harter, S., & Buddin, B. J. (1987). Children's understanding of the simultaneity of two emotions: A five-stage developmental acquisition sequence. *Developmental Psychology, 23,* 388–399.

Harter, S., & Monsour, A. (1992). Developmental analysis of conflict caused by opposing attributes in the adolescent self-portrait. *Developmental Psychology, 28,* 251–260.

Harter, S., & Pike, R. (1984). The Pictorial Scale of Perceived Competence and Social Acceptance for young children. *Child Development, 55,* 1969–1982.

Hartshorn, K., & Rovee-Collier, C. (1997). Infant learning and long-term memory at 6 months: A confirming analysis. *Developmental Psychology, 30,* 71–85.

Hartup, W. W. (1974). Aggression in childhood: Developmental perspectives. *American Psychologist, 27,* 336–341.

Hartup, W. W. (1983). Peer relations. In P. H. Mussen (Ed.), *Handbook of child development: Vol. 4. Socialization personality and social development* (4th ed., pp. 103–196, 4th ed.). New York: Wiley.

Hartup, W. W. (1996). The company they keep: Friendships and their developmental significance. *Child Development, 67,* 1–13.

Hartup, W. W., & Stevens, N. (1997). Friendships and adaptation in the life course. *Psychological Bulletin, 121,* 355–370.

Hartup, W. W., French, D. C., Laursen, B., Johnston, M. K., & Ogawa, J. R. (1993). Conflict and friendship relations in middle childhood: Behavior in a closed-field situation. *Child Development, 64,* 445–454.

Hartup, W. W., Laursen, B., Stewart, M. A., & Eastenson, A. (1988). Conflicts and the friendship relations of young children. *Child Development, 59,* 1590–1600.

Harvey, E. (1999). Short-term and long-term effects of early parental employment on children of the National Longitudinal Survey of youth. *Developmental Psychology, 35,* 445–459.

Haselager, G. J. T., Hartup, W. W., van Lieshout, C. F. M., & Riksen-Walraven, J. M. A. (1998). Similarities between friends and nonfriends in middle childhood. *Child Development, 69,* 1198–1208.

Hasher, L., & Zacks, R. T. (1984). Automatic processing of fundamental information: The case of frequency of occurrence. *American Psychologist, 39,* 1372–1388.

Haskins, R. (1985). Public school aggression among children with varying day care experience. *Child Development, 56,* 689–703.

Haskins, R. (1989). Beyond metaphor: The efficacy of early childhood education. *American Psychologist, 44,* 274–282.

Hastings, P. D., Zahn-Waxler, C., Robinson, J., Usher, B., & Bridges, D. (2000). The development of concern for others in children with behavior problems. *Developmental Psychology, 35,* 531–546.

Hatano, G., & Inagaki, K. (1996). Cognitive and cultural factors in the acquisition of intuitive biology. In D. R. Olson & N. Torrance (Eds.), *Handbook of education and human development: New models of learning, teaching and schooling.* Cambridge, England: Blackwell.

Hatano, G., & Osawa, K. (1983). Digit memory of grand experts in abacus-derived mental calculation. *Cognition, 15,* 95–110.

Hatano, G., Siegler, R. S., Richards, D. D., Inagaki, K., Stavy, R., & Wax, N. (1993). The development of biological knowledge: A multinational study. *Cognitive Development, 8,* 47–62.

Hatzichristou, C., & Hopf, D. (1996). A multiperspective comparison of peer sociometric status groups in childhood and adolescence. *Child Development, 67,* 1085–1102.

Hawley, T. L., & Disney, E. R. (1992, Winter). Crack's children: The consequences of maternal cocaine abuse. *Social Policy Report: Society for Research in Child Development, 6.*

Hay, D. F., Castle, J., Stimson, C. A., & Davies, L. (1995). The social construction of character in toddlerhood. In M. Killen & D. Hart (eds.), *Moral in everyday life* (pp. 23–51). Cambridge, England: Cambridge University Press.

Hay, D. F., Nash, A., & Pedersen, J. (1981). Responses of six-month-olds to the distress of their peers. *Child Development, 52,* 1071–1075.

Hay, D. F., & Ross, H. S. (1982). The social nature of early conflict. *Child Development, 53,* 105–113.

Hayes, K. J., & Hayes, C. (1951). The intellectual development of a home-raised chimpanzee. *Proceedings of the American Philosophical Society, 95,* 105–109.

Hearold, S. (1986). A synthesis of 1043 effects of television on social behavior. In G. Comstock (Ed.), *Public communication and behavior* (Vol. 1, pp. 65–133). New York: Academic Press.

Hedges, L. V., & Nowell, A. (1995). Sex differences in mental test scores, variability, and numbers of high-scoring individuals. *Science, 269,* 41–45.

Heine, S.J., Lehman, D. R., Markus, H. R., & Kitayama, S. (1999). Is there a universal need for positive self-regard? *Psychological Review, 106,* 766–794.

Held, R., Birch, E. E., & Gwiazda, J. (1980). Stereoacuity of human infants. *Proceedings of the National Academy of Sciences of the USA, 77,* 5572–5574.

Henry, B., Caspi, A., Moffitt, T. E., & Silva, P. A. (1994). Temperamental and familial predictors of violent and non-violent criminal convictions: From age 3 to age 18. *Developmental Psychology, 32,* 614–623.

Henry, C. S., Sager, D. W., & Plunkett, S. W. (1996). Adolescents' perceptions of family system characteristics, parent-adolescent dyadic behaviors, adolescent qualities, and adolescent empathy. *Family Relations, 45*, 283–292.

Hepper, P. (1988). Adaptive fetal learning: Prenatal exposure to garlic affects postnatal preferences. *Animal Behaviour, 36*, 935–936.

Herdt, G., & Boxer, A. M. (1993). *Child of horizons: How gay and lesbian teens are leading a new way out of the closet*. Boston: Beacon Press.

Hernandez, D. J. (1993). America's children: Resources for family, government and the economy. New York: Russell Sage Foundation.

Hernandez, J. T., & DiClemete, R. J. (1992). Self control and ego identity development as predictors of unprotected sex in late adolescent males. *Journal of Adolescence, 15,* 437–447.

Herrera, C., & Dunn, J. (1997). Early experiences with family conflict: Implications for arguments with a close friend. *Developmental Psychology, 33*, 869–881.

Hertsgaard, L., & Bauer, P. (1990). *Thirteen- and sixteen-month olds' long-term recall of event sequences.* Poster presented at the Society for Research in Child Development, Seattle.

Hess, R. D., Kashiwagi, K., Azuma, H., Price, G. G., & Dickson, W. P. (1980). Maternal expectations for mastery of developmental tasks in Japan and the United States. *International Journal of Psychology, 15*, 259–271.

Hesse, E. (1999). The adult attachment interview: Historical and current perspectives. In J. Cassidy & P. R. Shaver (Eds.), *Handbook of attachment: Theory, research, and clinical applications* (pp. 395–433). New York: Guilford Press.

Hetherington, E. M. (1989). Coping with family transitions: Winners, losers, and survivors. *Child Development, 60*, 1–14.

Hetherington, E. M. (1993). An overview of the Virginia Longitudinal Study of Divorce and Remarriage with a focus on early adolescent. *Journal of Family Psychology, 7*, 39–56.

Hetherington, E. M. (1999). Social capital and the development of youth from nondivorced, divorced, and remarried families. In W. A. Collins & B. Laursen (Eds.), *Relationships as developmental contexts. The Minnesota Symposia on Child Psychology* (Vol. 30, pp. 177–209). Mahwah, NJ: Lawrence Erlbaum Assoc.

Hetherington, E. M., Bridges, M., & Insabella, G. M. (1998). What matters? What does not? Five perspectives on the association between marital transitions and children's adjustment. *American Psychologist, 53,* 167–184.

Hetherington, E. M., & Clingempeel, W. G. (1992). Coping with marital transitions: A family systems perspective. *Monographs of the Society for Research in Child Development, 57* (Serial No. 227), 1–242.

Hetherington, E. M., Clingempeel, W. G., Anderson, E. R., Deal, J. E., Stanley-Hagen, M., Hollier, E. A., & Lindner, M. S. (1992). Coping with marital transitions: A family systems perspective. *Monographs of the Society for Research in Child Development, 57*(2–3, Serial No. 227).

Hetherington, E. M., Hagan, M. S., & Anderson, E. R. (1989). Marital transitions: A child's perspective. *American Psychologist, 44*, 303–312.

Hetherington, E. M., Henderson, S. H., & Reiss, D. (1999). Adolescent siblings in stepfamilies: Family functioning and adolescent adjustment. *Monographs of the Society for Research in Child Development, 64* (4, Serial No. 259), iv–209.

Hetherington, E. M., & Stanley-Hagan, M. S. (1995). Parenting in divorced and remarried families. In M. Bornstein (Ed.), *Handbook of parenting* (Vol. 3, pp. 233–255). Hillsdale, NJ: Erlbaum.

Hetherington, E. M., & Stanley-Hagan, M. S. (2002). Parenting in divorced and remarried families. In M. Bornstein (Ed.), *Handbook of parenting*, Vol. 3 (2nd ed., pp. 287–315). Mahwah, NJ: Erlbaum.

Hewlett, B. S., Lamb, M. E., Shannon, D., Leyendecker, B., & Scholmerich, A. (1998). Culture and early infancy among central African foragers and farmers. *Developmental Psychology, 34,* 651–661.

Heyman, G. D., & Dweck, C. S. (1998). Children's thinking about traits: Implications for judgments of the self and others. *Child Development, 64,* 391–403.

Heyns, B. (1978). *Summer learning and the effects of schooling*. San Diego, CA: Academic Press.

Hiatt, S. W., Campos, J. J., & Emde, R. N. (1979). Facial patterning and infant emotional expression: Happiness, surprise, and fear. *Child Development, 50,* 1020–1035.

Hickling, A. K., & Gelman, S. A. (1995). How does your garden grow? Early conceptualization of seeds and their place in the plant growth cycle. *Child Development, 66*, 856–876.

Higgins, E. T. (1991). Development of self-regulatory and self-evaluative processes: Costs, benefits, and tradeoffs. In M. R. Gunnar & L. A. Sroufe (Eds.), *The Minnesota Symposia on Child Development: Vol. 23. Self processes and development* (pp. 125–166). Hillsdale, NJ: Erlbaum.

Hill, J. O., & Peters, J. C. (1998). Environmental contributions to the obesity epidemic. *Science, 280,* 1371–1373.

Hill, J. P. (1988). Adapting to menarche: Familial control and conflict. In M. R. Gunnar & W. A. Collins (Eds.), *Minnesota symposia on child psychology* (Vol. 21, pp. 43–77). Hillsdale, NJ: Erlbaum.

Hinshaw, S. P., Zupan, B. A., Simmel, C., Nigg, J. T., & Melnick, S. (1997). Peer status in boys with and without attention-deficit hyperactivity disorder: Predictions from overt and covert antisocial behavior, social isolation, and authoritative parenting beliefs. *Child Development, 68*, 880–896.

Hirsh-Pasek, K., & Golinkoff, R. M. (1991). Language comprehension: A new look at some old themes. In N. A. Krasnegor, D. M. Rumbaugh, R. I. Schiefelbusch, & M. Studdert-Kennedy (Eds.), *Biological and behavioral determinants of language development* (pp. 301–320). Hillsdale, NJ: Erlbaum.

Hitch, G. J., & McAuley, E. (1991). Working memory in children with specific arithmetical learning disabilities. *British Journal of Psychology, 82*, 375–386.

Ho, D. Y. F. (1986). Chinese patterns of socialization: A critical review. In M. H. Bond (Ed.), *The psychology of Chinese people* (pp. 1–37). New York: Oxford University Press.

Hoard, M. K., Geary, D. C., & Hamson, C. O. (1999). Numerical and arithmetical cognition: Performance of low- and average-IQ children. *Mathematical Cognition, 5*, 65–91.

Hochberg, J., & Brooks, V. (1962). Pictorial recognition as an unlearned ability: A study of one child's performance. *American Journal of Psychology, 75,* 624–628.

Hodges, E. V. E., Boivin, M., Vitaro, F., & Bukowski, W. M. (1999). The power of friendship: Protection against an escalating cycle of peer victimization. *Developmental Psychology, 35,* 94–101.

Hodges, E. V. E., Malone, M. J., & Perry, D. G. (1997). Individual risk and social risk as interacting determinants of victimization in the peer group. *Developmental Psychology, 33,* 1032–1039.

Hodges, E. V. E., & Perry, D. G. (1999). Personal and interpersonal antecedents and consequences of victimization by peers. *Journal of Personality and Social Psychology, 76,* 677–685.

Hoff, E. (2001). *Language development* (2nd ed.). Belmont, CA: Wadsworth.

Hofferth, S. (1996). Child care in the United States today. *The Future of Children, 6,* 41–61.

Hoff-Ginsberg, E. (1993). *Early syntax is robust, but learning object labels depends on input.* Paper presented at the 6th International Congress for the Study of Child Language, Trieste, Italy.

Hoff-Ginsberg, E. (1994). Influences of mother and child on maternal talkativeness. *Discourse Processes, 18,* 105–117.

Hoff-Ginsberg, E., & Tardif, T. (1995). Socioeconomic status and parenting. In M. H. Bornstein (Ed.), *Handbook of parenting. Vol. 2. Biology and ecology of parenting* (pp. 161–188). Mahwah, NJ: Erlbaum.

Hoffman, C. D., & Teyber, E. C. (1985). Naturalistic observations of sex differences in adult involvement with girls and boys of different ages. *Merrill-Palmer Quarterly, 31,* 93–97.

Hoffman, L. W. (1984). Work, family, and the socialization of the child. In R. D. Parke (Ed.), *The family: Review of child development research* (Vol. 7, pp. 223–282). Chicago: University of Chicago Press.

Hoffman, L. W. (1989). Effects of maternal employment in the two-parent family. *American Psychologist, 44,* 283–292.

Hoffman, L. W., & Youngblade, L. (1999). *Mothers at work: Effects on children's well-being.* Cambridge England: Cambridge University Press.

Hoffman, M. L. (1963). Parent discipline and the child's consideration for others. *Child Development, 34,* 573–588.

Hoffman, M. L. (1981). Is altruism part of human nature? *Journal of Personality and Social Psychology, 40,* 121–137.

Hoffman, M. L. (1982). Development of prosocial motivation: Empathy and guilt. In N. Eisenberg (Ed.), *The development of prosocial behavior* (pp. 281–313). New York: Academic Press.

Hoffman, M. L. (1983). Affective and cognitive processes in moral internalization. In E. T. Higgins, D. N. Ruble, & W. W. Hartup (Eds.), *Social cognition and social development: A sociocultural perspective* (pp. 236–274). Cambridge, MA: Cambridge University Press.

Hoffman, M. L. (1990). Empathy and justice motivation. *Motivation and Emotion, 14,* 151–171.

Hoffman, M. L. (1998). Varieties of empathy-based guilt. In J. Bybee (Ed.), *Guilt and children* (pp. 91–112). San Diego, CA: Academic Press.

Hoffman, M. L. (2000). *Empathy and moral development: Implications for caring and justice.* Cambridge, England: Cambridge University Press.

Hoffner, C. (1993). Children's strategies for coping with stress: Blunting and monitoring. *Motivation and Emotion, 17,* 91–106.

Hofstadter, M., & Reznick, J. S. (1996). Response modality affects human infant delayed-response performance. *Child Development, 67,* 646–658.

Hogue, A., & Steinberg, L. (1995). Homophily of internalized distress in adolescent peer groups. *Developmental Psychology, 31,* 897–906.

Holden, C. (1980). Identical twins reared apart. *Science, 207,* 1323–1325.

Honzik, M. P., MacFarlane, J. W., & Allen, L. (1948). The stability of mental test performance between two and eighteen years. *Journal of Experimental Education, 17,* 309–329.

Hood, B., & Willatts, P. (1986). Reaching in the dark to an objects' remembered position: Evidence for object permanence in 5-month-old infants. *British Journal of Developmental Psychology, 4,* 57–65

Hopkins, B., & Westra, T. (1988). Maternal handling and motor development: An intracultural study. *Genetic, Social, and General Psychology Monographs, 14,* 377–420.

Horn, J. L., Donaldson, G., & Engstrom, R. (1981). Apprehension, memory and fluid intelligence decline in adulthood. *Research on Aging, 3,* 33–84.

Howe, M. L., & Courage, M. L. (1997). The emergence and early development of autobiographical memory. *Psychological Review, 104,* 499–523.

Howe, N., Aquan-Assee, J., & Bukowski, W. M. (2001). Predicting sibling relations over time: Synchrony between maternal management styles and sibling relationship quality. *Merrill-Palmer Quarterly, 47,* 121–141.

Howes, C. (1983). Patterns of friendship. *Child Development, 54,* 1041–1053.

Howes, C. (1996). The earliest friendships. In W. M. Bukowski, A. F. Newcomb, & W. W. Hartup (Eds.), *The company they keep. Friendship in childhood and adolescence* (pp. 66–86). Cambridge, England: Cambridge University Press.

Howes, C., & Farver, J. (1987). Toddlers' responses to the distress of their peers. *Journal of Applied Developmental Psychology, 8,* 441–452.

Howes, C., & Matheson, C. C. (1992). Sequences in the development of competent play with peers: Social and social pretend play. *Developmental Psychology, 28,* 961–974.

Howes, C., & Phillipsen, L. (1998). Continuity in children's relations with peers. *Social Development, 7,* 340–349.

Howes, C., & Unger, O. A. (1989). Play with peers in child care settings. In M. Bloch & A. Pelligrini (Eds.), *The ecological contexts of children's play* (pp. 104–119). Norwood, NJ: Ablex.

Hoza, B., Molina, B. S. G., Bukowski, W. M., & Sippola, L. K. (1995). Peer variables as predictors of later childhood adjustment. *Development and Psychopathology, 7,* 787–802.

Hrdy, S. B. (1999). *Mother nature: A history of mothers, infants, and natural selection.* New York: Pantheon.

Hubbard, F. O. A., & van IJzendoorn, M. H. (1991). Maternal unresponsiveness and infant crying across the first 9 months: A naturalistic longitudinal study. *Infant Behavior and Development, 14,* 299–312.

Hudley, C., & Graham, S. (1993). An attributional intervention to reduce peer-directed aggression among African-American boys. *Child Development, 64,* 124–138.

Hudson, J. A., Sosa, B. B., & Shapiro, L. R. (1997). Scripts and plans: The development of preschool children's event knowledge and event planning. In S. L. Friedman & E. K. Scholnick (Eds.), *The developmental psychology of planning: Why, how, and when do we plan?* (pp. 77–102). Mahwah, NJ: Erlbaum.

Huebner, R. R., & Izard, C. E. (1988). Mothers' responses to infants' facial expressions of sadness, anger, and physical distress. *Motivation and Emotion, 12,* 185–196.

Huesmann, L. R. (1986). Psychological processes promoting the relation between exposure to media violence and aggressive behavior by the viewer. *Journal of Social Issues, 42*, 125–139.

Huesmann, L. R., & Eron, L. D. (1986). *Television and the aggressive child: A cross-national perspective*. Hillsdale, NJ: Erlbaum.

Hughes, C., & Dunn, J. (1998). Understanding mind and emotion: Longitudinal associations with mental-state talk between young friends. *Developmental Psychology, 34*, 1026–1037.

Humphreys, L. G. (1989) Intelligence: Three kinds of instability and their consequences for policy. In R. L. Linn (Ed.), *Intelligence* (pp. 193–216). Urbana: University of Illinois Press.

Hunt, E. (1978). Mechanics of verbal ability. *Psychological Review, 85*, 109–130.

Hunt, E., Streissguth, A. P., Kerr, B., & Olson, H. C. (1995). Mothers' alcohol consumption during pregnancy: Effects on spatial-visual reasoning in 14-year-old children. *Psychological Science, 6*, 339–342.

Hunt, J. (1961). *Intelligence and experience*. New York: Ronald Press.

Hunter, F. T., & Youniss, J. (1982). Changes in functions of three relationships during adolescence. *Developmental Psychology, 18*, 806–811.

Hunter, J. E. (1986). Cognitive ability, cognitive aptitudes, job knowledge, and job performance. *Journal of Vocational Behavior, 29*, 340–362.

Hunziker, U. A., & Barr, R. G. (1986). Increased carrying reduces infant crying: A randomized control trial. *Pediatrics, 77*, 641–648.

Huston, A. C. (1983). Sex-typing. In P. H. Mussen (Ed.), *Handbook of child psychology: Vol. 4. Socialization, personality, and social development* (4th ed., pp. 387–467). New York: Wiley.

Huston, A. C., & Wright, J. C. (1998). Mass media and children's development. In W. Damon (Series Ed.) and I. E. Sigel & K. A. Renninger (Vol. Eds), *Handbook of child psychology. Vol. 4. Child psychology in practice* (5th ed., pp. 999–1058). New York: Wiley.

Huttenlocher, J., Haight, W., Bryk, A., Seltzer, M., & Lyons, T. (1991). Early vocabulary growth: Relation to language input and gender. *Developmental Psychology, 27*, 236–248.

Huttenlocher, J., & Higgins, E. T. (1978). Issues in the study of symbolic development. In W. A. Collins (Ed.), *Minnesota Symposia on Child Psychology* (Vol. 11, pp. 98–140). Hillsdale, NJ: Erlbaum.

Huttenlocher, J., Jordan, N. C., & Levine, S. C. (1994). A mental model for early arithmetic. *Journal of Experimental Psychology: General, 123*, 284–296.

Huttenlocher, J., Levine, S., & Vevea, J. (1998). Environmental input and cognitive growth: A study using time-period comparisons. *Child Development, 69*, 1012–1029.

Huttenlocher, P. R. (1994). Synaptogenesis in human cerebral cortex. In G. Dawson & K. W. Fischer (Eds.), *Human behavior and the developing brain* (pp. 137–152). New York: Guilford Press.

Huttenlocher, P. R., & Dabholkar, A. S. (1997). Regional differences in synaptogenesis in human cerebral cortex. *Journal of Comparative Neurology, 387*, 167–178.

Huttunen, M., & Niskanen, P. (1978). Prenatal loss of father and psychiatric disorders. *Archives of General Psychiatry, 35*, 429–431.

Hwang, P. (1987). The change role of Swedish fathers. In M. E. Lamb (Ed.), *The father's role: Cross-cultural perspectives* (pp. 197–226). Hillsdale, NJ: Erlbaum.

Hyde, J. S. (1984). How large are gender differences in aggression? A developmental meta-analysis. *Developmental Psychology, 20*, 722–736.

Hyde, J. S., & McKinley, N. M. (1997). Gender differences in cognition: Results from meta-analyses. In P. J. Caplan, M. Crawford, J. S. Hyde, & J. T. E. Richardson (Eds.), *Gender differences in human cognition* (pp. 30–51). New York: Oxford University Press.

Hymel, S., Bowker, A., & Woody, E. (1993). Aggressive versus withdrawn unpopular children: Variations in peer and self-perceptions in multiple domains. *Child Development, 64*, 879–896.

Hymel, S., Comfort, C., Schonert-Reichl, & McDougall, P. (1996). Academic failure and school dropout: The influence of peers. In J. Juvonen & K. R. Wentzel (Eds.), *Social motivation: Understanding children's social adjustment* (pp. 313–345). New York: Cambridge University Press.

Hynd, G. W., Horn, K. L., Voeller, K. K., & Marshall, R. M. (1991). Neurobiological basis of attention-deficit hyperactivity disorder (ADHD). *School Psychology Review, 20*, 174–186.

Iannotti, R. J., Cummings, E. M., Pierrehumbert, B., Milano, M. J., & Zahn-Waxler, C. (1992) Parental influences on prosocial behavior and empathy in early childhood. In J. M. A. M. Janssens & J. R. M. Gerris (Eds.), *Child rearing: Influence on prosocial and moral development* (pp. 77–100). Amsterdam: Swets & Zeitlinger.

Inagaki, K., & Hatano, G. (1991). Constrained person analogy in young children's biological inference. *Cognitive Development, 6*, 219–231.

Inagaki, K., & Hatano, G. (1993). Young children's understanding of the mind-body distinction. *Child Development, 64*, 1534–1549.

Inagaki, K., & Hatano, G. (1996). Young children's recognition of commonalities between animals and plants. *Child Development, 67*, 2823–2840.

Ingoldsby, E. M., Shaw, D. S., & Garcia, M. M. (2001). Intrafamily conflict in relation to boys' adjustment at school. *Development and Psychopathology, 13*, 35–52.

Ingoldsby, E. M., Shaw, D. S., Owens, E.B., & Winslow, E. B. (1999). A longitudinal study of interparental conflict, emotional and beahvioral reactivity, and preschoolers' adjustment problems among low-income families. *Journal of Abnormal Child Psychology, 27*, 343–356.

Inhelder, B., & Piaget, J. (1958). *The growth of logical thinking from childhood to adolescence*. New York: Basic Books.

Interagency Council on the Homeless (Department of Housing and Urban Development). (1999). *Homelessness: Programs and the people they serve*. The Urban Institute. Retrieved from: http://www/huduser.org/publications/homeless/homelessness.

Isabella, R. A. (1993). Origins of attachment: Maternal interactive behavior across the first year. *Child Development, 64*, 605–621.

Iverson, J. M., & Goldin-Meadow, S. (1998). Why people gesture when they speak. *Nature, 396*, 228.

Izard, C. E. (1991). *The psychology of emotions*. New York: Plenum Press.

Izard, C. E., Fantauzzo, C. A., Castle, J. M., Haynes, O.M., Rayias, M. F., & Putnam, P. H. (1995). The ontogeny and significance of infants' facial expressions in the first 9 months of life. *Developmental Psychology, 31*, 997–1013.

Izard, C. E., Hembree, E. A., & Huebner, R. R. (1987). Infants' emotional expressions to acute pain: Developmental change and stability of individual differences. *Developmental Psychology, 23*, 105–113.

Jacklin, C. N., DiPietro, J. A., & Maccoby, E. E. (1984). Sex-typing behavior and sex-typing in pressure in child/parent interactions. *Archives of Sexual Behavior, 13*, 413–425.

Jacobs, J. E., Lanza, S., Osgood, D. W., Eccles, J. S., & Wigfield, A. (2002). Changes in children's self-competence and values: Gender and domain differences across grades one through twelve. *Child Development, 73*, 509–527.

Jacobsen, T., & Hofmann, V. (1997). Children's attachment representations: Longitudinal relations to school behavior and academic competency in middle childhood and adolescence. *Developmental Psychology, 33*, 703–710.

Jacobson, J. L., & Jacobson, S. W. (1996). Intellectual impairment in children exposed to polychlorinated biphenyls in utero. *New England Journal of Medicine, 335*, 783–789.

Jacobson, J. L., Jacobson, S. W., Padgett, R. J., Brumitt, G. A., & Billings, R. L. (1992). Effects of prenatal PCB exposure on cognitive processing efficiency and sustained attention. *Developmental Psychology, 28*, 297–306.

Jaffee, S. R. (2002). Pathways to adversity in young adulthood among early childbearers. *Journal of Family Psychology, 16*, 38–49.

Jaffee, S., & Hyde, J. S. (2000). Gender differences in moral orientation: A meta-analysis. *Psychological Bulletin, 126*, 703–726.

Jakobson, R. (1941). *Child language, aphasia and phonological universals*. The Hague: Mouton. (English translation 1968)

James, D., Pillai, M., & Smoleniec, J. (1995). Neurobehavioral development in the human fetus. In J. Lecanuet, W. P. Fifer, N. A. Krasnegor, & W. P. Smotherman (Eds.), *Fetal development: A psychobiological perspective*. Hillsdale, NJ: Erlbaum.

Janssens, J. M. A. M., & Dekovic, M. (1997). Child rearing, prosocial moral reasoning, and prosocial behaviour. *International Journal of Behavioral Development, 20*, 509–527.

Jaswal, V. K., & Fernald, A. (2002). Learning to communicate. In A. Slater & M. Lewis (Eds.), *Introduction to Infant Development* (pp. 244–265). Oxford: Oxford University Press.

Jaycox, L. H., Reivich, K. J., Gillham, J., & Seligman, M. E. (1994). Prevention of depressive symptoms in school children. *Behavior Research and Therapy, 32*, 801–816.

Jegalian, K., & Lahn, B. T. (2001, February). Why the Y is so weird. *Scientific American, 284*(2), 56–61.

Jencks, C. (1979). *Who gets ahead? The determinants of economic success in America*. New York: Basic Books.

Jenkins, J. (1992). Sibling relationships in disharmonious homes: Potential difficulties and protective effects. In F. Boer & J. Dunn (Eds.), *Children's sibling relationships: Developmental and clinical issues* (pp. 125–138). Hillsdale, NJ: Erlbaum.

Jenkins, J. M., & Astington, J. W. (1996). Cognitive factors and family structure associated with theory of mind development in young children. *Developmental Psychology, 32*, 70–78.

Jensen, A. R. (1973). *Educability and group differences*. New York: Harper & Row.

Jiao, S., Ji, G., & Jing, Q. (1986). Comparative study of behavioral qualities of only children and sibling children. *Child Development, 57*, 367–361.

Jiao, S., Ji, G., & Jing, Q. (1996). Cognitive development of Chinese urban only children and children with siblings. *Child Development, 67*, 387–395.

Jochlin, V., McGue, M., & Lykken, D. T. (1996). Personality and divorce: A genetic analysis. *Journal of Personality and Social Psychology, 71*, 288–299.

Johnson, F. A. (1993). *Dependence and Japanese socialization: Psychoanalytic and anthropological investigation into amae*. New York: New York University Press.

Johnson, J. E., & Martin, C. (1985). Parents' beliefs and home learning environments: Effects on cognitive development. In I. E. Sigel (Ed.), *Parental belief systems: The psychological consequences for children* (pp. 25–50). Hillsdale, NJ: Erlbaum.

Johnson, J., & Newport, E. L. (1989). Critical period effects in second language learning: The influence of maturational state on the acquisition of English as a second language. *Cognitive Psychology, 21*, 60–99.

Johnson, K. E., Mervis, C. B., & Boster, J. S. (1992). Developmental changes within the structure of the mammal domain. *Developmental Psychology, 28*, 74–83.

Johnson, M., Beebe, T., Mortimer, J., & Snyder, M. (1998). Volunteerism in adolescence: A process perspective. *Journal of Research on Adolescence, 8*, 309–330.

Johnson, M. H. (1992). Imprinting and the development of face recognition: From chick to man. *Current Directions in Psychological Science, 1*, 52–55.

Johnson, M. H. (1998). The neural basis of cognitive development. In W. Damon (Series Ed.), D. Kuhn, & R. S. Siegler (Vol. Eds.), *Handbook of child psychology: Vol. 2. Cognition, perception, and language* (5th ed., pp. 1–49). New York: Wiley.

Johnson, M. H., Dziurawiec, S., Ellis, H. D., & Morton, J. (1991). Newborns' preferential tracking of face-like stimuli and its subsequent decline. *Cognition, 40*, 1–19.

Johnson, M. H., & Morton, J. (1991). *Biology and cognitive development: The case of face recognition*. Oxford, England: Blackwell.

Johnson, S. C., & Solomon, G. E. A. (1996). Why dogs have puppies and cats have kittens: The role of birth in young children's understanding of biological origins. *Child Development, 68*, 404–419.

Johnson, S. L., & Birch, L. L. (1994). Parents' and children's adiposity and eating style. *Pediatrics, 94*, 653–661.

Johnson, S. P., & Aslin, R. N. (1995). Perception of object unity in 2-month-old infants. *Developmental Psychology, 31*, 739–745.

Johnson-Laird, P. N. (1983). *Mental models: Towards a cognitive science of language, inference, and consciousness*. Cambridge, England: Cambridge University Press.

Jones, D. C., Abbey, B. B., & Cumberland, A. (1998). The development of display rule knowledge: Linkages with family expressiveness and social competence. *Child Development, 69*, 1209–1222.

Jones, K. L., & Smith, D. W. (1973). Recognition of the fetal alcohol syndrome in early infancy. *Lancet, 2*, 99–100.

Jones, M. (1990). Children's writing. In R. Grieve and M. Hughes (Eds.), *Understanding children: Essays in honor of Margaret Donaldson* (pp. 94–120). Oxford, England: Blackwell.

Jones, M. C. (1924). A laboratory study of fear: The case of Peter. *Pedagogical Seminary, 31*, 308–315.

Jones, R. M. (1992). Ego identity and adolescent problem behavior. In G. R. Adams, T. P. Gulotta, & R. Montemayor (Eds.), *Advances in adolescent development: Vol. 4. Adolescent identity formation* (pp. 216–233). Newbury Park, CA: Sage.

Jordan, N. C., Levine, S. C., & Huttenlocher, J. (1995). Calculation abilities in young children with different patterns of cognitive functioning. *Journal of Learning Disabilities, 28*, 53–64.

Joshi, M. S., & MacLean, M. (1994). Indian and English children's understanding of the distinction between real and apparent emotion. *Child Development, 65*, 1372–1384.

Juel, C. (1988). Learning to read and write: A longitudinal study of 54 children from first through fourth grades. *Journal of Educational Psychology, 80*, 417–447.

Juel, C. (1994). *Learning to read and write in one elementary school.* New York: Springer-Verlag.

Juraska, J. M., Henderson, C., & Muller, J. (1984). Differential rearing experience, gender and radial maze performance. *Developmental Psychobiology, 17*, 209–215.

Jurkovic, G. J. (1980). The juvenile delinquent as a moral philosopher: A structural-developmental perspective. *Psychological Bulletin, 88*, 709–727.

Jusczyk, P. W. (1997). *The discovery of spoken language.* Cambridge, MA: MIT Press.

Jusczyk, P. W., & Aslin, R. N. (1995). Infants' detection of sound patterns of words in fluent speech. *Cognitive Psychology, 29*, 1–23.

Jusczyk, P. W., Cutler, A., & Redanz, N. (1993). Preference for the predominant stress patterns of English words. *Child Development, 64*, 675–687.

Jusczyk, P. W., & Hohne, E. A. (1997). Infants' memory for spoken words. *Science, 277*, 1984–1986.

Juvonen, J., Nishina, A., & Graham, S. (2000). Peer harassment, psychological adjustment, and school functioning in early adolescence. *Journal of Educational Psychology, 92*, 349–359.

Kagan, J. (1972). Do infants think? *Scientific American, 226*, 74–82.

Kagan, J. (1976). Emergent themes in human development. *American Scientist, 64*, 186–196.

Kagan, J. (1996). Three pleasing ideas. *American Psychologist, 51*, 901–908.

Kagan, J. (1997). Temperament and the reactions to unfamiliarity. *Child Development, 68*, 139–143.

Kagan, J. (1998). Biology and the child. In W. Damon (Series Ed.) & N. Eisenberg (Vol. Ed.), *Handbook of child psychology: Vol. 3. Social, emotional, and personality development* (5th ed., pp. 177–235). New York: Wiley.

Kagan, J., Kearsley, R. B., & Zelazo, P. (1978). *Infancy: Its place in human development.* Cambridge, MS: Harvard University Press.

Kagan, J., Snidman, N., & Arcus, D. (1998). Childhood derivatives of high and low reactivity in infancy. *Child Development, 69*, 1483–1493.

Kahen, V., Katz, L. F., & Gottman, G. M. (1994). Linkages between parent-child interaction and conversations of friends. *Social Development, 3*, 238–254.

Kail, R. (1984). *The development of memory in children* (2nd ed.). New York: Freeman.

Kail, R. (1991). Developmental changes in speed of processing during childhood and adolescence. *Psychological Bulletin, 109*, 490–501.

Kail, R. (1997). Processing time, imagery, and spatial memory. *Journal of Experimental Child Psychology, 64*, 67–78.

Kalish, C. W. (1996). Preschoolers' understanding of germs as invisible mechanism. *Cognitive Development, 11*, 83–106.

Kalish, C. W. (1997). Preschoolers' understanding of mental and bodily reactions to contamination: What you don't know can hurt you, but cannot sadden you. *Developmental Psychology, 33*, 79–91.

Kalmar, M. (1996). The course of intellectual development in preterm and fullterm children: An 8-year longitudinal study. *International Journal of Behavioral Development, 19*, 491–516.

Kamins, M. L., & Dweck, C. S. (1999). Person versus process praise and criticism: Implications for contingent self-worth and coping. *Developmental Psychology, 35*, 835–847.

Kanner, A. D., Feldman, S. S., Weinberger, D. A., & Ford, M. E. (1987). Uplifts, hassles, and adaptational outcomes in early adolescents. *Journal of Early Adolescence, 7*, 371–394.

Kaplan, H., & Dove, H. (1987). Infant development among the Ache of Eastern Paraguay. *Developmental Psychology, 23*, 190–198.

Kaplan, P. S., Zarlengo-Strouse, P., Kirk, L. S., & Angel, C. L. (1997). Selective and nonselective associations between speech segments and faces in human infants. *Developmental Psychology, 33*, 990–999.

Karmel, B. Z., & Gardner, J. M. (1996). Prenatal cocaine exposure effects on arousal-modulated attention during the neonatal period. *Developmental Psychobiology, 19*, 463–480.

Kaye, K. L., & Bower, T. G. R. (1994). Learning and intermodal transfer of information in newborns. *Psychological Science, 5*, 286–288.

Kazdin, A. E., Siegel, T. C., & Bass, D. (1992). Cognitive problem-solving skills training and parent management training in the treatment of antisocial behavior in children. *Journal of Consulting and Clinical Psychology, 60*, 733–747.

Kearins, J. M. (1981). Visual spatial memory in Australian aboriginal children of desert regions. *Cognitive Psychology, 13*, 434–460.

Keating, D., & Clark, L. V. (1980). Development of physical and social reasoning in adolescence. *Developmental Psychology, 16*, 23–30.

Keating, D. P., & Hertzman, C. (Eds.) (1999). *Developmental health and the wealth of the nations: Social, biological, and educational dynamics.* New York: Guilford Press.

Kee, D. W., & Howell, S. (1988, April). *Mental effort and memory development.* Paper presented at the meeting of the American Educational Research Association, New Orleans, LA.

Keel, P. K., & Mitchell, J. E. (1997). Outcome in bulimia nervosa. *American Journal of Psychiatry, 154*, 313–321.

Keenan, K., Loeber, R., Zhang, Q., Stouthamer-Loeber, M., & Van Kammen, W. B. (1995). The influence of deviant peers on the development of boys' disruptive and delinquent behavior: A temporal analysis. *Development and Psychopathology, 7*, 715–726.

Keil, F. C. (1979). *Semantic and conceptual development: An ontological perspective.* Cambridge, MA: Harvard University Press.

Keil, F. C. (1992). The origins of an autonomous biology. *Minnesota Symposium on Child Psychology, 25*, 103–138.

Keil, F. C. (1995). The birth and nurturance of concepts by domains: The origins of concepts of living things. In L. A. Hirschfeld & S. Gelman (Eds.), *Mapping the mind: Domain specificity in cognition and culture* (pp. 234–254). Cambridge, England: Cambridge University Press.

Keil, F. C. (1998). Cognitive science and the origins of thought and knowledge. In W. Damon (Series Ed.) & R. M. Lerner (Vol. Ed.), *Handbook of child psychology: Vol 1. Theoretical models of human development* (5th ed., pp. 341–414.). New York: Wiley.

Keiley, M. K., Bates, J. E., Dodge, K. A., & Pettit, G. (2000). A cross-domain growth analysis: Externalizing and internalizing behaviors during 8 years of childhood. *Journal of Abnormal Child Psychology, 28*, 161–179.

Keiley, M., Howe, T. R., Dodge, K. A., Bates, J. E., & Pettit, G. S. (2001). The timing of child physical maltreatment: A cross-domain growth analysis of impact on adolescent externalizing and internalizing problems. *Development and Psychopathology, 13*, 891–912.

Kelley, M. L., Sanchez-Hucles, J., & Walker, R. (1993). Correlates of disciplinary practices in working- to middle-class African-American mothers. *Merrill-Palmer Quarterly, 39*, 252–264.

Kellman, P. J., & Arterberry, M. E. (1998). *The cradle of knowledge: Development of perception in infancy.* Cambridge, MA: MIT Press.

Kellman, P. J., & Banks, M. S. (1997). Infant visual perception. In W. Damon (Series Ed.), R. Siegler, & D. Kuhn (Vol. Eds.), *Handbook of child psychology: Vol. 2. Cognition, perception, and language* (5th ed., pp. 103–146). New York: Wiley.

Kellman, P. J., & Spelke, E. S. (1983). Perception of partly occluded objects in infancy. *Cognitive Psychology, 15*, 483–524.

Kellman, P. J., Spelke, E. S., & Short, K. (1986). Infant perception of object unitary from translatory motion in depth and vertical translation. *Child Development, 57*, 72–86.

Kellogg, R. T. (1994). *The psychology of writing.* New York: Oxford University Press.

Kerkman, D. D., & Siegler, R. S. (1993). Individual differences and adaptive flexibility in lower-income children's strategy choices. *Learning and Individual Differences, 5*, 113–136.

Kerns, K. A., Klepac, L., & Cole, A. (1996). Peer relationships and preadolescents' perceptions of security in the child-mother relationship. *Developmental Psychology 32*, 457–466.

Kessen, W. (1965). *The child.* New York: Wiley.

Kestenbaum, R., Farber, E.A., & Sroufe, L.A. (1989). Individual differences in empathy among preschoolers: Relation to attachment history. In N. Eisenberg (Ed.), *Empathy and related emotional responses: New directions for child development: Vol. 44* (pp. 51–64). San Francisco: Jossey-Bass.

Kety, S. S., Wender, P. H., Jacobsen, B., Ingraham, L. J., Jansson, L., Faber, B., & Kinney, D. K. (1994). Mental illness in the biological and adoptive relatives of schizophrenic adoptees: Replication of the Copenhagen study in the rest of Denmark. *Archives of General Psychiatry, 51*, 442–455.

Killen, M., & Turiel, E. (in press). Adolescents' and young adults' evaluations of helping and sacrificing for others. *Journal of Research on Adolescence.*

Kilpatrick, D. G., Acierno, R., Saunders, B., Resnick, H. S., Best, C. L., & Schnurr, P. P. (2000). Risk factors for adolescent substance abuse and dependence: Data from a national sample. *Journal of Consulting and Clinical Psychology, 68*, 19–30.

Kim, K., & Spelke, E.S. (1992). Infants' sensitivity to effects of gravity on visible object motion. *Journal of Experimental Psychology: Human Perception and Performance, 18*, 385–393.

Kimura, D., & Hampson, E. (1994). Cognitive pattern in men and women is influenced by fluctuations in sex hormones. *Psychological Science, 3*, 57–61.

Kindermann, T. A. (1993). Natural peer groups as contexts for individual development: The case of children's motivation in school. *Developmental Psychology, 29*, 970–977.

Kisilevsky, B. S., Fearon, I., & Muir, D. W. (1998). Fetuses differentiate vibroacoustic stimuli. *Infant Behavior and Development, 21*, 25–46.

Kisilevsky, B. S., Hains, S. M. J., Leen, K., Muir, D. W., Xu, F., Fu, G., et al. (1998). The still-face effect in Chinese and Canadian 3- and 6-month-old infants. *Developmental Psychology, 34*, 629–639.

Kisilevsky, B. S., & Muir, D. W. (1991). Human fetal and subsequent newborn responses to sound and vibration. *Infant Behavior and Development, 14*, 1–26.

Klahr, D. (1978). Goal formation, planning, and learning by preschool problem solvers or: "My socks are in the dryer." In R. S. Siegler (Ed.), *Children's thinking: What develops?* Hillsdale, NJ: Erlbaum.

Klahr, D., & MacWhinney, B. (1998). Information processing. In W. Damon (Series Ed.) & D. Kuhn & R. S. Siegler (Vol. Eds.), *Handbook of child psychology: Vol. 2. Cognition, perception, and language.* (5th ed., pp. 631–678.) New York: Wiley.

Klima, E. S., & Bellugi, U. (1967). Syntactic regularities in the speech of children. In J. Lyons & R. Wales (Eds.), *Psycholinguistic papers. Proceedings of the Edinburgh Conference* (pp. 183–208). Edinburgh: Edinburgh University Press.

Klimes-Dougan, B., & Kopp, C. B. (1999). Children's conflict tactics with others: A longitudinal investigation of the toddler and preschool years. *Merrill-Palmer Quarterly, 45*, 226–241.

Kling, K. C., Hyde, J. S., Showers, C. J. & Buswell, B. N. (1999). Gender differences in self-esteem: A meta-analysis. *Psychological Bulletin, 125*, 470–500.

Klonoff-Cohen, H. S., Edelstein, S. L., Lefkowitz, E. S., Srinivasan, I. P., Kaegi, D., Chang, J. C., & Wiley, K. J. (1995). The effect of passive smoking and tobacco exposure through breast milk on sudden infant death syndrome. *Journal of the American Medical Association, 273*, 795–798.

Kluender, K. R., Diehl, R. L., & Killeen, P. R. (1987). Japanese quail can learn phonetic categories. *Science, 237*, 1195–1197.

Knight, G. P., Cota, M. K., & Bernal, M. E. (1993). The socialization of cooperative, competitive, and individualistic preferences among Mexican American children: The mediating role of ethnic identity. *Hispanic Journal of Behavioral Sciences, 15*, 291–309.

Knight, G. P., Fabes, R. A., & Higgins, D. A. (1996). Concerns about drawing causal inferences from meta-analyses: An example in the study of gender differences in aggression. *Psychological Bulletin, 119*, 410–421.

Kobasigawa, A., Ransom, C. C., & Holland, C. J. (1980). Children's knowledge about skimming. *Alberta Journal of Educational Research, 26*, 169–182.

Kochanska, G. (1993). Toward a synthesis of parental socialization and child temperament in early development of conscience. *Child Development, 64*, 325–347.

Kochanska, G. (1995). Children's temperament, mothers' discipline, and security of attachment: Multiple pathways to emerging internalization. *Child Development, 66*, 597–615.

Kochanska, G. (1997a). Multiple pathways to conscience for children with different temperaments: From toddlerhood to age five. *Developmental Psychology, 33*, 228–240.

Kochanska, G. (1997b). Mutually responsive orientation between mothers and their young children: Implications for early socialization. *Child Development, 68*, 94–112.

Kochanska, G. (2001). Emotional development in children with different attachment histories: The first three years. *Child Development, 72*, 474–490.

Kochanska, G. (2002). Committed compliance, moral self, and internalization: A mediational model. *Developmental Psychology, 38,* 339–351.

Kochanska, G., Coy, K. C., & Murray, K. T. (2001). The development of self-regulation in the first four years of life. *Child Development, 72,* 1091–1111.

Kochanska, G., & Murray, K. T. (2000). Mother-child mutually responsive orientation and conscience development: From toddler to early school age. *Child Development, 71,* 417–431.

Kochanska, G., Murray, K. T., & Harlan, E. T. (2000). Effortful control in early childhood: Continuity and change, antecedents, and implications for social development. *Developmental Psychology, 36,* 220–232.

Kochanska, G., Padavich, D. L., & Koenig, A. L. (1996). Children's narratives about hypothetical moral dilemmas and objective measures of their conscience: Mutual relations and socialization antecedents. *Child Development, 67,* 1420–1436.

Kochenderfer, B. J., & Ladd, G. W. (1996). Peer victimization: Cause or consequence of school maladjustment? *Child Development, 67,* 1305–1317.

Kodama, H., Shinagawa, F., & Motegi, M. (1978). *WISC-R manual: Standardized in Japan.* New York: Psychological Corporation.

Koedinger, K. R., Anderson, J. R., Hadley, W. H., & Mark, M. (1997). Intelligent tutoring goes to school in the big city. *International Journal of Artificial Intelligence in Education, 8,* 30–43.

Kohlberg, L. (1966). A cognitive-developmental analysis of children's sex-role concepts and attitudes. In E. E. Maccoby (Ed.), *The development of sex differences* (pp. 82–173). Stanford, CA: Stanford University Press.

Kohlberg, L. (1969). Stage and sequence: The cognitive-developmental approach to socialization. In D. A. Goslin (Ed.), *Handbook of socialization theory and research* (pp. 325–480). New York: Rand McNally.

Kohlberg, L. (1976). Moral stage and moralization: The cognitive-developmental approach. In T. Lickona (Ed.), *Moral development and behavior: Theory, research, and social issues* (pp. 84–107). New York: Holt, Rinehart, & Winston.

Kohlberg, L. (1978). Revisions in the theory and practice of moral development. *New Directions for Child Development, 2,* 83–88.

Kohlberg, L., & Candee, D. (1984). The relationship of moral judgment to moral action. In W. M. Kurtines & J. L. Gewirtz (Eds.), *Morality, moral behavior, and moral development* (pp. 52–73). New York: Wiley.

Kohn, M. L. (1969). *Class and conformity: A study in values.* Homewood, IL: Dorsey Press.

Kolata, G. (1987). Associations or rules in learning language? *Science, 237,* 133–134.

Kolb, B. (1995). *Brain plasticity and behavior.* Hillsdale, NJ: Erlbaum.

Kolb, B., & Whishaw, I. Q. (1996). *Fundamentals of human neuropsychology* (4th ed.). New York: Freeman.

Kopp, C. B. (1990). Risks in infancy: Appraising the research. *Merrill-Palmer Quarterly, 36,* 117–139.

Kopp, C. B. (1992). Emotional distress and control in young children. In N. Eisenberg & R. A. Fabes (Eds.), *Emotion and its regulation in early development (New Directions in Child Development)* (pp. 41–56). San Francisco: Jossey-Bass.

Kopp, C. B. (2001). Self regulation in childhood. *International Encyclopedia of the Social and Behavioral Sciences.* London: Elsevier.

Kopp, C. B., & Kaler, S. R. (1989). Risk in infancy: Origins and implications. *American Psychologist, 44,* 224–230.

Koren, G., Nulman, I., Rovet, J., Greenbaum, R., Loebstein, M., & Einarson, T. (1998). Long-term neurodevelopmental risks in children exposed in utero to cocaine. The Toronto Adoption Study. *Annals of the New York Academy of Sciences, 846,* 306–313.

Korner, A. F., & Thoman, E. (1970). Visual alertness in neonates as evoked by maternal care. *Journal of Experimental Child Psychology, 10,* 67–78.

Korner, M. (1991). Universals of behavioral development in relation to brain myelination. In K. R. Gibson & A. C. Petersen (Eds.), *Brain maturation and cognitive development: Comparative and cross-cultural perspectives.* New York: de Gruyter.

Kortenhaus, C. M., & Demorest, J. (1993). Gender role stereotyping in children's literature: An update. *Sex Roles, 28,* 219–232.

Kotovsky, L., & Baillargeon, R. (1994). Calibration-based reasoning about collision events in 11-month-old infants. *Cognition, 51,* 107–129.

Kowal, A., & Kramer, L. (1997). Children's understanding of parental differential treatment. *Child Development, 68,* 113–126.

Krascum, R. M., & Andrews, S. (1998). The effects of theories on children's acquisition of family-resemblance categories. *Child Development, 69,* 333–346.

Krevans, J., & Gibbs, J. C. (1996). Parents' use of inductive discipline: Relations to children's empathy and prosocial behavior. *Child Development, 67,* 3263–3277.

Kruger, A. C., & Tomasello, M. (1986). Transactive discussions with peers and adults. *Developmental Psychology, 22,* 681–685.

Krumhansl, C. L., & Jusczyk, P. W. (1990). Infants' perception of phrase structure in music. *Psychological Science, 1,* 70–73.

Kuczaj, S. A., II (1977). The acquisition of regular and irregular past tense forms. *Journal of Verbal Learning and Verbal Behavior, 16,* 589–600.

Kuebli, J., Butler, S., & Fivush, R. (1995). Mother-child talk about past emotions: Relations of maternal language and child gender over time. *Cognition and Emotion, 9,* 265–283.

Kuebli, J., & Fivush, R. (1992). Gender differences in parent-child conversations about past emotions. *Sex Roles, 27,* 683–698.

Kuhl, P. K. (1991). Human adults and human infants show a "perceptual magnet effect" for the prototypes of speech categories, monkeys do not. *Perception and Psychophysics, 50,* 93–107.

Kuhl, P. K., & Meltzoff, A.N. (1982). The bimodal perception of speech in infancy. *Science, 218,* 1138–1141.

Kuhl, P. K., & Meltzoff, A. N. (1984). The intermodal representation of speech in infants. *Infant Behavior and Development, 7,* 361–381.

Kuhl, P. K., & Miller, J. D. (1978). Speech perception by the chinchilla: Identification functions for synthetic VOT stimuli. *Journal of the Acoustical Society of America, 63,* 905–917.

Kuhl, P. K., & Padden, D. M. (1983). Enhanced discriminability at the phonetic boundaries for the place feature in macaques. *Journal of the Acoustical Society of America, 73,* 1003–1010.

Kuhl, P. K., Williams, K. A., Lacerda, F., Stevens, K. N., & Lindbloom, B. (1992). Linguistic experiences alter phonetic perception in infants by 6 months of age. *Science, 255,* 606–608.

Kuhn, D. (1995). Microgenetic study of change: What has it told us? *Psychological Science, 6,* 133–139.

Kuhn, D., Garcia-Mila, M., Zohar, A., & Andersen, C. (1995). Strategies of knowledge acquisition. *Monographs of the Society for Research in Child Development, 60*(4, Serial No. 245).

Kunzinger, E. L., & Wittryol, S. L. (1984). The effects of differential incentives on second-grade rehearsal and free recall. *Journal of Genetic Psychology, 144,* 19–30.

Kupersmidt, J. B., Burchinal, M., & Patterson, C. J. (1995). Developmental patterns of childhood peer relations as predictors of externalizing behavior problems. *Development and Psychopathology, 7,* 825–843.

Kupersmidt, J. B., & Coie, J. D. (1990). Preadolescent peer status, aggression, and school adjustment as predictors of externalizing problems in adolescence. *Child Development, 61,* 1350–1362.

Kurdek, L. A. (1993). Predicting marital dissolution: A 5-year prospective longitudinal study of newlywed couples. *Journal of Personality and Social Psychology, 64,* 221–242.

Kurdek, L. A., & Fine, M. A. (1993). Parent and nonparent residential family members as providers of warmth, support, and supervision to young adolescents. *Journal of Family Psychology, 7,* 245–249.

Kutnick, P. (1985). The relationship of moral judgment and moral action: Kohlberg's theory, criticism and revision. In S. Modgil & C. Modgil (Eds.), *Lawrence Kohlberg: Consensus and controversy* (pp. 125–148). Philadelphia: Falmer Press.

La Greca, A. M., & Lopez, N. (1998). Social anxiety among adolescents: Linkages with peer relations and friendships. *Journal of Abnormal Child Psychology, 26,* 83–94.

La Greca, A. M., Prinstein, M. J., & Fetter, M. D. (2001) Adolescent peer crowd affiliation: Linkages with health-risk behaviors and close friendships. *Journal of Pediatric Psychology, 26,* 131–143.

Ladd, G. W., & Coleman, C. C. (1997). Children's classroom peer relationships and early school attitudes: Concurrent and longitudinal associations. *Early Education and Development, 8,* 51-66.

Ladd, G. W., & Golter, B. S. (1988). Parents' management of preschooler's peer relations: Is it related to children's social competence? *Developmental Psychology, 24,* 109–117.

Ladd, G. W., & Hart, C. H. (1992). Creating informal play opportunities: Are parents' and preschoolers' initiations related to children's competence with peers? *Developmental Psychology, 28,* 1179–1187.

Ladd, G. W., & Kochenderfer, B. J. (1996). Linkages between friendship and adjustment during early school transition. In W. M. Bukowski, A. F. Newcomb, & W. W. Hartup (Eds.), *The company they keep. Friendship in childhood and adolescence* (pp. 322–345). Cambridge, England: Cambridge University Press.

Ladd, G. W., Kochenderfer, B. J., & Coleman, C. C. (1996). Friendship quality as a predictor of young children's early school adjustment. *Child Development, 67,* 1103–1118.

LaFontana, K. M., & Cillessen, A. H. N. (1998). The nature of children's stereotypes of popularity. *Social Development, 7,* 301–320.

LaFreniere, P. J., & Sroufe, L. A. (1985). profiles of peer competence in the preschool: Interrelations between measures, influence of social ecology, and relations to attachment history. *Developmental Psychology, 21,* 56–69.

LaFreniere, P., Strayer, F. F., & Gauthier, R. (1984). The emergence of same-sex affiliative preferences among preschool peers: A developmental ethological perspective. *Child Development, 55,* 1958–1965.

LaFromboise, T., Coleman, H. L. K., & Gerton, J. (1993). Psychological impact of biculturalism: Evidence and theory. *Psychological Bulletin, 125,* 470–500.

Lagattuta, K. H., Wellman, H. M., & Flavell, J. H. (1997). Preschoolers' understanding of the link between thinking and feeling: Cognitive cuing and emotional change. *Child Development, 68,* 1081–1104.

Lagercrantz, H., & Slotkin, T. A. (1986). The "stress" of being born. *Scientific American,* 100–107.

Lahey, B. B., Goodman, S. H., Waldman, I. D., Bird, H., Canino, G., Jensen, P., er al. (1999). Relation of age of onset to the type and severity of child and adolescent conduct problems. *Journal of Abnormal Child Psychology, 27,* 247–260.

Lahey, B. B., Gordon, R. A., Loeber, R., Stouthamer-Loeber, M., & Farrington, D. P. (1999). Boys who join gangs: A prospective study of predictors of first gang entry. *Journal of Abnormal Child Psychology, 27,* 261–276.

Lahey, B. B., Waldman, I. D., & McBurnett, K. (1999). Annotation: The development of antisocial behavior: An integrative causal model. *Journal of Child Psychology and Psychiatry, 40,* 669–682.

Laible, D. J., & Thompson, R. A. (1998). Attachment and emotional understanding in preschool children. *Developmental Psychology, 24,* 1038–1045.

Laible, D. J., & Thompson, R. A. (2000). Mother-child discourse, attachment security, shared positive affect, and early conscience development. *Child Development, 71,* 1424–1440.

Laird, R. D., Pettit, G. S., Mize, J., Brown, E. G., & Lindsey, E. (1994). Mother-child conversations about peers: Contributions to competence. *Family Relations, 43,* 425–532.

Lamb, B., & Lang, R. (1992). Aetiology of cerebral palsy. *British Journal of Obstetrics and Gynecology, 99,* 176–178.

Lamb, M. E. (1998). Nonparental child care: Context, quality, correlates, and consequences. In W. Damon (Series Ed.) and I. E. Sigel & K. A. Renninger (Vol. Eds.), *Handbook of child psychology: Vol. 4. Child psychology in practice* (5th ed., pp. 73–133). New York: Wiley.

Lamb, M. E., & Ketterlinus, R. D. (1991). Parental behavior, adolescent. In R. M. Lerner, A. C. Petersen, & J. Brooks-Gunn (Eds.), *Encyclopedia of adolescence* (pp. 735–738). New York: Garland.

Lamb, M. E., & Teti, D. M. (1991). Parenthood and marriage in adolescence: Associations with educational and occupational attainment. In R. M. Lerner, A. C. Petersen, & J. Brooks-Gunn (Eds.), *Encyclopedia of adolescence* (pp. 742–745). New York: Garland.

Lamb, M. E., Thompson, R. A., Gardner, W., & Charnov, E. L. (1985). *Infant-mother attachment: The origins and developmental significance of individual differences in Strange Situation behavior.* Hillsdale, NJ: Erlbaum.

Lamb, S., & Zakhireh, B. (1997). Toddlers' attention to the distress of peers in a daycare setting. *Early Education and Development, 8,* 105–118.

Lamborn, S. D., Dornbusch, S. M., & Steinberg, L. (1996). Ethnicity and community context as moderators of the relations between family decision making and adolescent adjustment. *Child Development, 67,* 283–301.

Lamborn, S. D., Mounts, N. S., Steinberg, L., & Dornbusch, S. M. (1991). Patterns of competence and adjustment among adolescents from authoritative, authoritarian, indulgent, and neglectful families. *Child Development, 62,* 1049–1065.

Lampl, M., Veldhuis, J. D., & Johnson, M. L. (1992). Saltation and stasis: A model of human growth. *Science, 258,* 801–803.

Landau, B., & Gleitman, L. R. (1985). *Language and experience: Evidence from the blind child.* Cambridge, MA: Harvard University Press.

Landau, B., Smith, L. B., & Jones, S. S. (1988). The importance of shape in early lexical learning. *Cognitive Development, 3,* 299–321.

Landau, B., Smith, L., & Jones, S. (1998) Object perception and object naming in early development. *Trends in Cognitive Sciences, 2,* 19–24.

Landau, S., Lorch, E. P., & Milich, R. (1992). Visual attention to and comprehension of television in attention-deficit hyperactivity disordered and normal boys. *Child Development, 63,* 928–937.

Landry, S. H., Chapieski, M. L., Richardson, M. A., Palmer, J., & Hall, S. (1990). The social competence of children born prematurely: Effects of medical complications. *Child Development, 61,* 1605–1616.

Lane, H. (1976). *The wild boy of Aveyron.* Cambridge, MA: Harvard University Press.

Langlois, J. H., Kalakanis, L., Rubenstein, A. J., Larson, A., Hallam, M., & Smoot, M. (2000). Maxims or myths of beauty? A meta-analytic and theoretical review. *Psychological Bulletin, 126,* 390–423.

Langlois, J. H., Ritter, J. M., Casey, R. J., & Sawin, D. B. (1995). Infant attractiveness predicts maternal behaviors and attitudes. *Developmental Psychology, 31,* 464–472.

Langlois, J. H., Ritter, J. M., Roggman, L. A., & Vaughn, L. S. (1991). Facial diversity and infant preferences for attractive faces. *Developmental Psychology, 27,* 79–84.

Langlois, J. H., Roggman, L. A., Casey, R. J., Ritter, J. M., Rieser-Danner, L. A., & Jenkins, V. Y. (1987). Infant preferences for attractive faces: Rudiments of a stereotype? *Developmental Psychology, 23,* 363–369.

Langlois, J. H., Roggman, L. A., & Rieser-Danner, L. A. (1990). Infants' differential social responses to attractive and unattractive faces. *Developmental Psychology, 26,* 153–159.

Largo, R. H., Pfister, D., Molinari, L., Kundu, S., Lipp, A., & Duc, G. (1989). Significance of prenatal, perinatal and postnatal factors in the development of AGA preterm infants at five to seven years. *Developmental Medicine and Child Neurology, 31,* 440–456.

Larson, R., & Lampman-Petraitis, C. (1989). Daily emotional states as reported by children and adolescents. *Child Development, 60,* 1250–1260.

Larson, R. W., & Richards, M. H. (1991). Daily companionship in late childhood and early adolescence: Changing developmental contexts. *Child Development, 62,* 284–300.

Larson, R. W., & Richards, M. H. (1994). *Divergent realities: The emotional lives of mothers, fathers, and adolescents.* New York: Basic Books.

Laub, J. H., & Sampson, R. J. (1988). Unraveling families and delinquency: A reanalysis of the Glueck's data. *Criminology, 26,* 355–379.

Laursen, B., & Collins, W. A. (1994). Interpersonal conflict during adolescence. *Psychological Bulletin, 115,* 197–209.

Laursen, B., Finkelstin, B. D., & Betts, N. T. (2001). A developmental meta-analysis of peer conflict resolution. *Developmental Review, 21,* 423–449.

Lazar, I., Darlington, R., Murray, H., Royce, J., & Snipper, A. (1982). Lasting effects of early education: A report from the Consortium for Longitudinal Studies. *Monographs of the Society for Research in Child Development, 47*(Serial No. 195).

Le, H. N. (2000). Never leave your little one alone: Raising an Ifaluk child. In J. S. DeLoache & A. Gottlieb (Eds.). *A world of babies: Imagined childcare guides for seven societies.* Cambridge, England: Cambridge University Press.

Leaper, C. (1994). Exploring the correlates and consequences of gender segregation: Social relationships in childhood, adolescence, and adulthood. In W. Damon (Series Ed.) & C. Leaper (Vol. Ed.), *New directions for child development. The development of gender relationships.* San Francisco: Jossey-Bass.

Leaper, C., Anderson, K. J., & Sanders, P. (1998). Moderators of gender effects on parents' talk to their children. *Developmental Psychology, 34,* 3–27.

Lecanuet, J. P., Granier-Deferre, C., & Busnel, M. C. (1995). Human fetal auditory perception. In J. P. Lecanuet, W. P. Fifer, N. A. Krasnegor, & W. P. Smotherman (Eds.), *Fetal development: A psychobiological perspective.* Hillsdale, NJ: Erlbaum.

Lecours, A. R. (1975). Myelogenetic correlates of the development of speech and language. In E. H. Lenneberg & E. Lenneberg (Eds.), *Foundations of language development: A multidisciplinary approach.* New York: Academic Press.

Lee, H., & Barratt, M. (1993). Cognitive development of preterm low birth weight cildren at 5 to 8 years old. *Journal of Developmental and Behavioral Pediatrics, 14,* 242–249.

Lee, L. C., & Zhan, G. Q. (1991). Political socialization and parental values in the People's Republic of China. *International Journal of Behavioral Development, 14,* 337–373.

Lee, M., & Prentice, N. M. (1988). Interrelations of empathy, cognition, and moral reasoning with dimensions of juvenile delinquency. *Journal of Abnormal Child Psychology, 16,* 127–139

Lee, V. E., Brooks-Gunn, J., Schnur, E., & Liaw, F.-R. (1990). Are Head Start effects sustained? A longitudinal follow-up comparison of disadvantaged children attending Head Start, no preschool, and other preschool programs. *Child Development, 61,* 495–507.

Lemaire, P., & Siegler, R. S. (1995). Four aspects of strategic change: Contributions to children's learning of multiplication. *Journal of Experimental Psychology: General, 124,* 83–97.

Lemery, K. S., Essex, M. J., & Smider, N. A. (2002). Revealing the relationship between temperament and behavior problem symptoms by eliminating measurement confounding: Expert ratings and factor analyses. *Child Development, 73,* 867–882.

Lemery, K. S., Goldsmith, H. H., Klinnert, M. D., & Mrazek, D. A. (1999). Developmental models of infant and childhood temperament. *Developmental Psychology, 35,* 189–204.

Lempers, J. D., & Clark-Lempers, D. S. (1993). A functional comparison of same-sex and opposite-sex friendships during adolescence. *Journal of Adolescent Research, 8,* 89–108.

Lempers, J. D., Clark-Lempers, D., & Simons, R. L. (1989). Economic hardship, parenting, and distress in adolescence. *Child Development, 60,* 25–39.

Lengua, L. J. (2002). The contribution of emotionality and self-regulation to the understanding of children's response to multiple risk. *Child Development, 73,* 144–161.

Lenneberg, E. H. (1967). *Biological foundations of language.* New York: Wiley.

Lerman, R. I. (1993). A national profile of young unwed fathers. In R. I. Lerman & T. J. Ooms (Eds.), *Young unwed fathers* (pp. 27–51). Philadelphia: Temple University Press.

Lerner, I. M., & Libby, W. J. (1976). *Heredity, evolution, and society.* (2nd ed.). San Francisco: Freeman.

Lerner, R. (1995). The limits of biological influence: Behavioral genetics as the Emperor's New Clothes. *Psychological Inquiry, 6,* 145–156.

Leslie, A. M. (1987). Pretense and representation: The origins of "theory of mind." *Psychological Review, 94,* 412–426.

Leslie, A. M. (1991). The theory of mind impairment in autism: Evidence for a modular mechanism of development? In A. Whiten (Ed.), *Natural theories of mind: Evolution, development and simulation of everyday mindreading.* Oxford, England: Basil Blackwell.

Leslie, A. M. (1994). ToMM, ToBy, and agency: Core architecture and domain specificity in cognition and culture. In L. Hirschfeld & S. Gelman (Eds.), *Mapping the mind: Domain specificity in cognition and culture.* New York: Cambridge University Press.

Lester, B. M. (1998). The maternal lifestyles study. *Annals of the New York Academy of Sciences, 846,* 296–305.

Lester, B. M., & Tronick, E. Z. (1994). The effect of prenatal cocaine exposure and child outcome. *Infant Mental Health Journal, 15,* 107–120.

Lester, B. M., & Zeskind, P. S. (1978). Brazelton scale and physical size correlates of neonatal cry features. *Infant Behavior and Development, 49,* 589–599.

Lester, B. M., Anderson, L. T., Boukydis, C. F. Z., Garcia-Coll, C. T., Vohr, B., & Peucker, M. (1989). Early detection of infants at risk for later handicap through acoustic cry analysis. *Birth Defects: Original Article Series, 26,* 99–118.

Lester, B. M., Boukydis, C. F. Z., Garcia-Coll, C. T., Hole, W., & Peucker, M. (1992). Infantile colic: Acoustic cry characteristics, maternal perception of cry, and temperament. *Infant Behavior and Development, 15,* 15–26.

Leung, M.-C. (1996). Social networks and self enhancement in Chinese children: A comparison of self reports and peer reports of group membership. *Social Development, 5,* 146–157.

Leve, L. D., & Fagot, B. I. (1997a). Gender-role socialization and discipline processes in one- and two-parent families. *Sex Roles, 36,* 1–21.

Leve, L. D., & Fagot, B. I. (1997b). Prediction of positive peer relations from observed parent-child interactions. *Social Development, 6,* 254–269.

Levin, I. (1982). The nature and development of time concepts in children: The effects of interfering cues. In W. J. Friedman (Ed.), *The developmental psychology of time.* New York: Academic Press.

Levin, I. (1989). Principles underlying time measurement: The development of children's constraints on counting time. In I. Levin & D. Zakay (Eds.), *Time and human cognition: A life-span perspective.* Amsterdam: Elsevier.

Levin, I., & Korat, O. (1993). Sensitivity to phonological, morphological, and semantic cues in early reading and writing in Hebrew. *Merrill-Palmer Quarterly, 39,* 213–232.

Levin, I., Siegler, R. S., & Druyan, S. (1990). Misconception about motion: Development and training effects. *Child Development, 61,* 1544–1557.

Levine, J., & Suzuki, D. (1993). *The secret of life.* Boston: WGBH Educational Foundation.

LeVine, R. A. (1988). Human parental care: Universal goals, cultural strategies, individual behavior. In R. A. Le Vine, P. M. Miller, & M. M. West (Eds.). *Parental behavior in diverse societies: New directions for child development, Vol. 40* (pp. 3–12). San Francisco: Jossey-Bass.

LeVine, R. A., Dixon, S., LeVine, S., Richman, A., Leiderman, P. H., Keefer, C. H., & Brazelton, T. B. (1996). *Childcare and culture: Lessons from Africa.* Cambridge, England: Cambridge University Press.

Levitt, M. J., Weber, R. A., Clark, M. C., & McDonnell, P. (1985). Reciprocity of exchange in toddler sharing behavior. *Developmental Psychology, 21,* 122–123.

Lewis, C. C. (1995). *Educating hearts and minds.* Cambridge, England: Cambridge University Press.

Lewis, M. (1992). *Shame: The exposed self.* New York: The Free Press.

Lewis, M. (1995). Embarrassment: The emotion of self-exposure and evaluation. In J. P. Tangney & K. W. Fischer (Eds.), *Self-conscious emotions* (pp. 198–218). New York: Guilford Press.

Lewis, M. (1998). Emotional competence and development. In D. Pushkar, W. M. Bukowski, A. E. Schwartzman, D. M. Stack, & D. R. White (Eds.), *Improving competence across the lifespan* (pp. 27–36). New York: Plenum Press.

Lewis, M., Alessandri, S. M., & Sullivan, M. W. (1990). Violation of expectancy, loss of control, and anger expressions in young infants. *Developmental Psychology, 26,* 745–751.

Lewis, M., Alessandri, S. M., & Sullivan, M. W. (1992). Differences in shame and pride as a function of children's gender and task difficulty. *Child Development, 63,* 630–638.

Lewis, M., & Brooks-Gunn, J. (1979). *Social cognition and the acquisition of self.* New York: Plenum Press.

Lewis, M., Feiring, C., & Rosenthal, S. (2000). Attachment over time. *Child Development, 71,* 707–720.

Lewis, M., Sullivan, M. W., Stanger, C. & Weiss, M. (1989). Self-development and self-conscious emotions. *Child Development, 60,* 146–156.

Lewkowicz, D. J., Karmel, B. Z., & Gardner, J. M. (1998). Effects of prenatal cocaine exposure on responsiveness to multimodal information in infants between 4 and 10 months of age. *Annals of the New York Academy of Sciences, 846,* 408–411.

Lewontin, R. (1982). *Human diversity.* New York: Scientific American Books.

Liaw, F. R., & Brooks-Gunn, J. (1993). Patterns of low birth weight on children's cognitive development. *Developmental Psychology, 29,* 1024–1035.

Liben, L. S. (1999). Developing an understanding of external spatial representations. In I. E. Sigel (Ed.), *Development of mental representation: Theories and applications* (pp. 297–321). Mahwah, NJ: Erlbaum.

Liben, L. S., & Signorella, M. L. (1993). Gender-schematic processing in children: The role of initial interpretations of stimuli. *Developmental Psychology, 29,* 141–149.

Lichter, D. T., & Lansdale, N. S. (1995). Parental work, family structure, and poverty among Latino children. *Journal of Marriage and the Family,57,* 346–354.

Lickona, T. (1976). Research on Piaget's theory on moral development. In T. Lickona (Ed.), *Moral development and behavior: Theory, research, and social issues* (pp. 219–240). New York: Holt, Rinehart, and Winston.

Liebert, R. M., & Sprafkin, J. (1988). *The early window: Effects of television on children and youth* (3rd ed.). New York: Pergamon Press.

Lieven, E. V. M. (1994). Crosslinguistic and crosscultural aspects of language addressed to children. In C. Gallaway & B. J. Richards (Eds.), *Input and interaction in language acquisition* (pp. 56–73). Cambridge, England: Cambridge University Press.

Lillard, A. S. (1998). Wanting to be it: Children's understanding of intentions underlying pretense. *Child Development, 69,* 981–993.

Lillard, A. S., & Flavell, J. H. (1992). Young children's understanding of different mental states. *Developmental Psychology, 28*, 626–634.

Limber, J. (1973). The genesis of complex sentences. In T. Moore (Ed.), *Cognitive development and the acquisition of language* (pp. 169–186). New York: Academic Press.

Linares, L. O., Heeren, T., Bronfman, E., Zuckerman, B., Augustyn, M., & Tronick, E. (2001). A mediational model for the impact of exposure to community violence on early child behavior problems. *Child Development, 72*, 639–652.

Lindberg, M. A. (1980). Is knowledge base development a necessary and sufficient condition for memory development? *Journal of Experimental Child Psychology, 30,* 401–410.

Lindberg, M. A. (1991). A taxonomy of suggestibility and eyewitness memory: Age, memory process, and focus of analysis. In J. L. Doris (Ed.), *The suggestibility of children's recollections*. Washington, DC: American Psychological Association.

Lindell, S. G. (1988). Education for childbirth: A time for change. *Journal of Obstetrics, Gynecology, and Neonatal Nursing, 17*, 108–112.

Linkletter, A. (1957). *Kids say the darndest things*. Englewood Cliffs, NJ: Prentice-Hall.

Lipsitt, L. P. (1977). Taste in human neonates: Its effect on sucking and heart rate. In J. M. Weiffenbach (Ed.), *Taste and development: The genesis of sweet preference* (DHEW Publication No. NIH 77-1068, pp. 125–141). Washington, DC: U. S. Government Printing Office.

Little, S. A., & Garber, J. (1995). Aggression, depression, and stressful life events predicting peer rejection in children. *Development and Psychopathology, 7*, 845–856.

Lochman, J. E., Coie, J. D., Underwood, M. K., & Terry, R. (1993). Effectiveness of a social relations intervention program for aggressive and nonaggressive, rejected children. *Journal of Consulting and Clinical Psychology, 61*, 1053–1058.

Locke, J. L. (1983). *Phonological acquisition and change.* New York: Academic Press.

Lockheed, M., & Harris, A. M. (1984). Cross-sex collaborative learning in elementary classrooms. *American Educational Research Journal, 21*, 275–294.

Lockman, J. J. (1984). The development of detour ability during infancy. *Child Development, 55,* 482–491.

Lockman, J. J., Ashmead, D., & Bushnell, E. (1984). The development of anticipatory hand orientation during infancy. *Journal of Experimental Child Psychology, 37,* 176–186.

Lockman, J. J., & McHale, J. P. (1989). Object manipulation in infancy: Developmental and contextual determinants. In J. J. Lockman & N. L. Hazen (Eds.), *Action in social context: Perspectives on early development* (pp. 129–167). New York: Plenum Press.

Lockman, J. J., & Thelen, E. (1993). Developmental biodynamics: Brain, body, behavior connections. *Child Development, 64,* 953–959.

Loeber, R. (1982). The stability of antisocial and delinquent child behavior: A review. *Child Development, 53*, 1431–1446.

Loeber, R., & Hay, D. F. (1993). Developmental approaches to aggression and conduct problems. In M. Rutter & D. F. Hay (Eds.), *Development through life: A handbook for clinicians* (pp. 488–516). Oxford, England: Blackwell.

Loeber, R., & Schmaling, K. B. (1985). Empirical evidence for overt and covert patterns of antisocial conduct problems: A meta-analysis. *Journal of Abnormal Child Psychology, 13*, 315–336.

Loeber, R., Wung, P., Keenan, K., Giroux, B., Stouthamer-Loeber, M., Van Kammen, W. B., & Maughan, B. (1993). Developmental pathways in disruptive child behavior. *Development and Psychopathology, 5*, 103–133.

Loehlin, J. C. (1989). Partitioning environmental and genetic contributions to behavioral development. *American Psychologist, 44*, 1285–1292.

Loomis, J. M, Klatzky, R. L., Golledge, R. G., Cicinelli, J. G., Pellegrino, J. W., & Fry, P. A. (1993). Nonvisual navigation by blind and sighted: Assessment of path integration ability. *Journal of Experimental Psychology: General, 122*, 73–91.

Lorenz, K. Z. (1935). Der Kumpan in der Umwelt das Vogels. *Journal of Ornithology, 83*, 137–213.

Lorenz, K. Z. (1952). *King Solomon's ring*. New York: Crowell.

Lovett, M. W., Borden, S. L., DeLuca, T., Lacerenza, L., Benson, N. J., & Blackstone, D. (1994). Treating the core deficits of developmental dyslexia: Evidence of transfer of learning after phonologically- and strategy-based reading training programs. *Developmental Psychology, 30*, 805–822.

Lozoff, B. (1989). Nutrition and behavior. *American Psychologist, 44*, 231–236.

Lubinski, D., & Humphreys, L. G. (1997). Incorporating general intelligence into epidemiology and the social sciences. *Intelligence, 24*, 159–202.

Luntz, B. K., & Widom, C. S. (1994). Antisocial personality disorders in abused and neglected children grown up. *American Journal of Psychiatry, 151*, 670–674.

Luster, T., & Dubow, E. (1992). Home environment and maternal intelligence as predictors of verbal intelligence: A comparison of preschool and school-age children. *Merrill Palmer Quarterly, 38*, 151–175.

Luster, T., & McAdoo, H. (1996). Family and child influences on educational attainment: A secondary analysis of the High/Scope Perry Preschool data. *Developmental Psychology, 32*, 26–39.

Luster, T., Rhoades, K., & Haas, B. (1989). The relation between parental values and parenting behavior: A test of the Kohn hypothesis. *Journal of Marriage and the Family, 51*, 139–147.

Lynam, D. R. (1996). Early identification of chronic offenders: Who is the fledgling psychopath? *Psychological Bulletin, 120*, 209–234.

Lynam, D. R. (1997). Pursuing the psychopathy: Capturing the fledgling psychopath in a nomological net. *Journal of Abnormal Psychology, 106*, 425–438.

Lynch, M. & Cicchetti, D. (1998). An ecological-transactional analysis of children and contents: The longitudinal interplay among child maltreatment, community violence, and children's symptomatology. *Development and Psychopathology, 10,* 235–257.

Lynn, R. and Hampson, S.L. (1986) The rise of national intelligence: Evidence from Britain, Japan and the USA. *Personality and Individual Differences, 7,* 323–332.

Lyon, G. R. (1995). Toward a definition of dyslexia. *Annals of Dyslexia, 45*, 20–45.

Lyons-Ruth, K., Easterbrooks, M. A., & Cibelli, C. D. (1997). Infant attachment strategies, infant mental lag, and maternal depressive symptoms: Predictors of internalizing and externalizing problems at age 7. *Developmental Psychology, 33,* 681–692.

Lytton, H. (2000). Toward a model of family-environmental and child-biological influences on development. *Developmental Review, 20,* 150–179.

Lytton, H., & Romney, D. M. (1991). Parents' differential socialization of boys and girls: A meta-analysis. *Psychological Bulletin, 109*, 267–296.

Maccoby, E. E. (1988). Gender as a social category. *Developmental Psychology, 24*, 755–765.

Maccoby, E. E. (1998). *The two sexes: Growing up apart, coming together.* Cambridge, MA: Harvard University Press.

Maccoby, E. E. (2000). Perspectives on gender development. *International Journal of Behavioral Development, 24*, 398–496.

Maccoby, E. E. (2002). Gender and group process: A developmental perspective. *Current Directions in Psychological Science, 11,* 54–58.

Maccoby, E. E., Buchanan, C. M., Mnookin, R. H., & Dornbusch, S. M. (1993). Postdivorce roles of mothers and fathers in the lives of their children. *Journal of Family Psychology, 7*, 24–38.

Maccoby, E. E., & Jacklin, C. N. (1974). *The psychology of sex differences.* Stanford, CA: Stanford University Press.

Maccoby, E. E., & Jacklin, C. N. (1987). Gender segregation. In H. W. Reese (Ed.), *Advances in child development and behavior* (Vol. 20). Orlando, FL: Academic Press.

Maccoby, E. E., & Martin, J. A. (1983). Socialization in the context of the family: Parent-child interaction. In P. H. Mussen (Ed.) & E. M. Hetherington (Vol. Ed.), *Handbook of child psychology. Vol 4. Socialization, personality, and social development* (pp. 1–101). New York: Wiley.

MacDonald, K., & Parke, R. D. (1984). Bridging the gap: Parent-child play interaction and peer interactive competence. *Child Development, 55*, 1265–1277.

MacDonald, K., & Parke, R. D. (1986). Parent-child physical play: The effects of sex and age of children and parents. *Sex Roles*, 15, 367–378.

MacFarlane, A. (1975). Olfaction in the development of social preferences in the human neonate. *Parent-infant interaction* (CIBA Foundation Symposium, No. 33, pp. 103–117). Amsterdam: Elsevier.

MacKinnon-Lewis, C., Starnes, R., Volling, B., & Johnson, S. (1997). Perceptions of parenting as predictors of boys' sibling and peer relations. *Developmental Psychology, 33*, 1024–1031.

Maclean, M., Bryant, P., & Bradley, L. (1987). Rhymes, nursery rhymes and reading in early childhood. *Merrill-Palmer Quarterly, 33*, 255–281.

MacPhee, D., Fritz, J., & Miller-Heyl, J. (1996). Ethnic variations in personal social networks and parenting. *Child Development, 67*, 3278–3295.

MacWhinney, B., & Chang, F. (1995). Connectionism and language learning. In C. Nelson (Ed.), *The Minnesota Symposium on Child Psychology: Vol. 28. Basic and applied perspectives on learning, cognition, and development* (pp. 33–57). Mahwah, NJ: Erlbaum.

Madole, K. L., & Cohen, L. B. (1995). The role of object parts in infants' attention to form-function correlations. *Developmental Psychology, 31*, 637–648.

Magai, C., Hunziker, J., Mesias, W., & Culver, L. C. (2000). Adult attachment styles and emotional biases. *International Journal of Behavioral Development, 24,* 301–309.

Maguire, M. C., & Dunn, J. (1997). Friendships in early childhood and social understanding. *International Journal of Behavioral Development, 21*, 669–686.

Mahler, M. S., Pine, F., & Bergman, A. (1975). *The psychological birth of the human infant: Symbiosis and individuation.* New York: Basic Books.

Mahoney, J. L. (2000). School extracurricular activity participation as a moderator in the development of antisocial patterns. *Child Development, 71*, 502–516.

Main, M., & George, C. (1985). Responses of abused and disadvantaged toddlers to distress in agemates: A study in the day care setting. *Developmental Psychology, 21*, 407–412.

Main, M., & Hesse, E. (1990). Parents' unresolved traumatic experiences are related to infant disorganized attachment status: Is disorganized and/or frightening parental behavior the linking mechanism? In M. T. Greenberg, D. Cicchetti, & E. M. Cummings (Eds.), *Attachment in the preschool years* (pp. 161–182). Chicago: University of Chicago Press.

Main, M., Kaplan, N., & Cassidy, J. (1985). Security infancy, childhood and adulthood: A move to the level of representation. *Monographs of the Society for Research in Child Development, 50*(1-2, Serial No. 209).

Main, M., & Solomon, J. (1990). Procedures for identifying infants as disorganized/disoriented during the Ainsworth Strange Situation. In M. T. Greenberg, D. Cicchetti, & E. M. Cummings (Eds.), *Attachment in the preschool years* (pp. 121–160). Chicago: University of Chicago Press.

Malatesta, C. Z., Culver, C., Tesman, J. R., & Shepard, B. (1989). The development of emotion expression during the first two years of life. *Monographs of the Society for Research in Child Development, 54*(1-2, Serial No. 219), 1–104.

Malatesta, C. Z., & Haviland, J. M. (1982). Learning display rules: The socialization of emotion expression in infancy. *Child Development, 53,* 991–1003.

Maldonado-Duran, J. M. (2000). A new perspective on failure to thrive. *Bulletin of Zero to Three, 21,* 14.

Malina, R. M. (1975). *Growth and development: The first twenty years in man.* Minneapolis: Burgess Publishing.

Malina, R. M., & Bouchard, C. (1991). *Growth, maturation, and physical activity.* Champaign, IL: Human Kinetics Academic.

Mandel, D. R., Jusczyk, P. W., & Pisoni, D. B. (1995). Infants' recognition of the sound patterns of their own names. *Psychological Science, 6,* 315–318.

Mandler, J. M., & McDonough, L. (1998). Studies in inductive inference in infancy. *Cognitive Psychology, 37,* 60–96.

Mangelsdorf, S. C., Plunkett, J. W., Dedrick, C. F., Berlin, M., Meisels, S. J., McHale, J. L., & Dichtellmiller, M. (1996). Attachment security in very low birth weight infants. *Developmental Psychology, 32,* 914–920.

Mangelsdorf, S. C., Shapiro, J. R., & Marzolf, D. (1995). Developmental and temperamental differences in emotion regulation in infancy. *Child Development, 66*, 1817–1828.

Manis, F. R., Seidenberg, M. S., Doi, L. M., McBride-Chang, C., & Peterson, A. (1996). On the bases of two subtypes of developmental dyslexia. *Cognition, 58*, 157–195.

Maratsos, M. (1998). The acquisition of grammar. In D. Kuhn & R. S. Siegler (Eds.), *Handbook of child psychology: Vol. 2. Cognition, perception, and language* (5th ed., pp. 421–466). New York: Wiley.

Marchman, V. (1992). Constraint on plasticity in a connectionist model of the English past tense. *Journal of Cognitive Neuroscience, 5,* 215–234.

Marcia, J. E. (1980). Identity in adolescence. In J. Adelson (Ed.), *Handbook of adolescent psychology* (pp. 159–187). New York: Wiley.

Marcia, J. E., & Friedman, M. L. (1970). Ego identity status in college women. *Journal of Personality, 38,* 249–263.

Marcovitch, S., & Zelazo, P. D. (1999). The A-not-B error: Results from a logistic meta-analysis. *Child Development, 70,* 1297–1313.

Marcus, D. E., & Overton, W. F. (1978). The development of cognitive gender constancy and sex role preferences. *Child Development, 49,* 434–444.

Marcus, G. F. (1996). Why do children say "breaked"? *Current Directions in Psychological Science, 5,* 81–85.

Marcus, G. F., Pinker, S., Ullman, M., Hollander, M., Rosen, T. J., & Zu, F. (1992). Overregularization in language acquisition. *Monographs of the Society for Research in Child Development, 57*(4, Serial No. 228).

Margolin, G., Gordis, E. B., & John, R. S. (2001). Coparenting: A link between marital conflict and parenting in two-parent families. *Journal of Family Psychology, 15,* 3–21.

Mark, M. A., & Greer, J. E. (1995). The VCR tutor: Effective instruction for device operation. *Journal of the Learning Sciences, 4,* 209–246.

Markman, E. M. (1989). *Categorization and naming in children.* Cambridge, MA: MIT Press.

Markman, E. M., & Hutchinson, J. E. (1984). Children's sensitivity to constraints on word meaning: Taxonomic vs. thematic relations. *Cognitive Psychology, 16,* 1–27.

Markman, E. M., & Wachtel, G. A. (1988). Children's use of mutual exclusivity to constrain the meanings of words. *Cognitive Psychology, 20,* 121–157.

Markus, H. R., & Kitayama, S. (1991). Culture and the self: Implications for cognition, emotion, and motivation. *Psychological Review, 98,* 224–253.

Marler, P. (1970). Birdsong and speech development: Could there be parallels? *American Scientist, 58,* 669–673.

Marler, P. (1991). The instinct to learn. In S. Carey & R. Gelman (Eds.), *The epigenesis of mind: Essays on biology and cognition.* Hillsdale, NJ: Erlbaum.

Marlier, L., Schaal, B., & Soussignon, R. (1998). Neonatal responsiveness to the odor of amniotic and lacteal fluids: A test of perinatal chemosensory continuity. *Child Development, 69,* 611–623.

Marsh, H. W., Craven, R., & Debus, R. (1998). Structure, stability, and development of young children's self-concepts: A multicohort-multioccasion study. *Child Development, 69,* 1030–1053.

Martin, C. L. (1993). New directions of investigating children's gender knowledge. *Developmental Review, 13,* 184–204.

Martin, C. L., & Halverson, C. F., Jr. (1981). A schmetic processing model of sex typing and stereotyping in children. *Child Development, 52,* 1119–1134.

Martin, C. L., & Halverson, C. F., Jr. (1983). The effects of sex-typing schemas on young children's memory. *Child Development, 54,* 563–574.

Martin, C. L., Eisenbud, L., & Rose, H. (1995). Children's gender-based reasoning about toys. *Child Development, 66,* 1453–1471.

Martin, G. B., & Clark, R. D., III. (1982). Distress crying in neomates: Species and peer specificity. *Developmental Psychology, 38,* 3–9.

Martin, M. O., Mullis, I. V. A., Beaton, A. E., Gonzalez, E. J., Smith, T. A., & Kelly, D. L. (1997). *Science achievement in the primary school years: IEA's third international mathematics and sciences study (TIMSS).* Boston, MA: Center for the Study of Testing, Evaluation, and Education Policy, Boston College.

Masataka, N. (1992). Motherese in a signed language. *Infant Behavior and Development, 15,* 453–460.

Mason, M. G., & Gibbs, J. C. (1993). Social perspective taking and moral judgment among college students. *Journal of Adolescent Research, 8,* 109–123.

Masten, A., Best, K., & Garmezy, N. (1990). Resilience and development: Contributions from the study of children who overcame adversity. *Development and Psychopathology, 2,* 425–444.

Masten, A. S., & Coatsworth, J. D. (1998). The development of competence in favorable and unfavorable environments: Lessons from research on successful children. *American Psychologist, 53,* 205–220.

Masten, A. S., Sesma, A., Si-Asar, R., Lawrence, C., Miliotis, D., & Dionne, J. A. (1997). Educational risks for children experiencing homelessness. *Journal of School Psychology, 35,* 27–46.

Masters, M. S., & Sanders, B. (1993). Is the gender difference in mental rotation disappearing? *Behavior Genetics, 23,* 337–341.

Masur, E. (1982). Mothers' responses to infants' object-related gestures: Influences on lexical development. *Journal of Child Language, 9,* 23–30.

Maszk, P., Eisenberg, N., & Guthrie, I. K. (1999). Relations of children's social status to their emotionality and regulation: A short-term longitudinal study. *Merrill-Palmer Quarterly, 45,* 468–492.

Matheny, A. P., Jr. (1990). Developmental behavior genetics: Contributions from the Louisville Twin Study. In M. E. Hahn, J. K. Hewitt, N. D. Henderson, & R. H. Benno (Eds.), *Developmental behavior genetics: Neural, biometrical, and evolutionary approaches* (pp. 25–39). New York: Oxford University Press.

Matheny, A. P., Jr., Wilson, R. S., Dolan, A. B., & Krantz, J. Z. (1981). Behavioral contrasts in twinships: Stability and patterns of differences in childhood. *Child Development, 52,* 579–598.

Mathews, T. J., MacDorman, M. F., Menacker, F. (2002). Infant mortality statistics from the 1999 period linked birth/infant death data set. *National Vital Statistics Reports, 50,* 1–27.

Matsumoto, D. (1996). *Unmasking Japan.* Stanford, CA: Stanford University Press.

Matthews, K. A., Batson, C. D., Horn, J., Rosenman, R. H. (1981). Principles in his nature which interest him in the fortune of others: The heritability of empathic concern for others. *Journal of Personality, 49,* 237–247.

Mattson, S. N., Riley, E. P., Delis, D. C., & Jones, K. L. (1998). Neuropsychological comparison of alcohol-exposed children with or without physical features of fetal alcohol syndrome. *Neuropsychology, 12,* 146–153.

Maurer, D. (1985). Infant's perception of facedness. In T. M. Field & N. A. Fox (Eds.), *Social perception in infants.* Norwood, NJ: Ablex.

Maurer, D., Lewis, T. L., Brent, H. P., & Levin, A. V. (1999). Rapid improvement in the acuity of infants after visual input. *Science, 286,* 108–110.

Maurer, D., & Maurer, C. (1988). *The world of the newborn.* New York: Basic Books.

Maurer, D. & Salapatek, P. (1976). Developmental changes in the scanning of faces by young infants. *Child Development, 47,* 523–527.

McCabe, A., & Peterson, C. (1991). Getting the story: A longitudinal study of parental styles in eliciting narratives and developing narrative skill. In A. McCabe & C. Peterson (Eds.), *Developing narrative structure* (pp. 217–253). Hillsdale, NJ: Erlbaum.

McCall, R. B., Applebaum, M. I., & Hogarty, P. S. (1973). Developmental changes in mental performance. *Monographs of the Society for Research in Child Development, 38*(Serial No. 150).

McCall, R. B., & Carriger, M. S. (1993). A meta-analysis of infant habituation and recognition memory performance as predictors of later IQ. *Child Development, 64,* 57–79.

McCall, R. B., Eichorn, D. H., & Hogarty, P. S. (1977). Transitions in early mental development. *Monographs of the Society for Research in Child Development, 42*(3, Serial No. 171).

McCarton, C. M., Brooks-Gunn, J., Wallace, I. F., & Bauer, C. R. (1997). Results at age 8 years of intervention for low-birth-weight premature infants: The infant health and development program. *Journal of the American Medical Association*, *277*, 126–132.

McClelland, J. L., Rumelhart, D. E., & The PDP Research Group. (1986). *Parallel distributed processing: Explorations in the microstructure of cognition: Vol. 2. Psychological and biological models.* Cambridge, MA: MIT Press.

McClintock, M. K., & Herdt, G. (1996). Rethinking puberty: The development of sexual attraction. *Current Directions, 5,* 178–183.

McCloskey, L. A., Figueredo, A. J., & Koss, M. P. (1995). The effects of systematic family violence on children's mental health. *Child Development, 66*, 1239–1261.

McCloskey, L. A., & Stuewig, J. (2001). The quality of peer relationships among children exposed to family violence. *Development and Psychopathology, 13*, 83–96.

McCord, J. (1991). The cycle of crime and socialization practices. *Journal of Criminal Law and Criminology, 82*, 211–228.

McCrae, R. R., Costa, P. T., Jr., Ostendorf, F., Angleitner, A., Hrebickova, M., Avia, M. D., et al. (2000). Nature over nurture: Temperament, personality, and life-span development. *Journal of Personality and Social Psychology, 78,* 173–186.

McCune, L. (1995). A normative study of representational play in the transition to language. *Developmental Psychology, 31,* 198–206.

McDowell, D. J., & Parke, R. D. (2000). Differential knowledge of display rules for positive and negative emotions: Influences from parents, influences on peers. *Social Development, 9,* 415–432.

McEwen, B. S., & Schmeck, H. M. (1994). *The hostage brain.* New York: Rockefeller University Press.

McFadyen-Ketchum, S. A., Bates, J. E., Dodge, K. A., & Pettit, G. S. (1996). Patterns of change in early childhood aggressive-disruptive behavior: Gender differences in predictions from early coercive and affectionate mother-child interactions. *Child Development, 67*, 2417–2433.

McGhee, P. E., & Frueh, T. (1980). Television viewing and the learning of sex-role stereotypes. *Sex Roles, 6*, 179–188.

McGilly, K., & Siegler, R. S. (1990). The influence of encoding and strategic knowledge on children's choices among serial recall strategies. *Developmental Psychology, 26,* 931–941.

McGraw, M. B. (1943). *Neuromuscular maturation of the human infant.* New York: Hafner.

McGue, M., Bouchard, T. J., Jr., Iacono, W. G., & Lykken, D. T. (1993). Behavioral genetics of cognitive ability: A life-span perspective. In R. Plomin & G. E. McClearn (Eds.), *Nature, nurture, and psychology* (pp. 59–76). Washington, DC: American Psychological Association.

McGue, M., & Lykken, D. T. (1992). Genetic influence on risk of divorce. *Psychological Science, 3,* 368–373.

McGue, M., Sharma, A., & Benson, P. (1996). Parent and sibling influences on adolescent alcohol use and misuse: Evidence in a U.S, adoption cohort. *Journal of Studies on Alcohol*, *57*, 8–18.

McGuire, S., McHale, S. M., & Updegraff, K. (1996). Children's perceptions of the sibling relationship in middle childhood: Connections within and between family relationships. *Personal Relationships, 3*, 229–239.

McGuire, S., Neiderhiser, J. M., Reiss, D., Hetherington, E. M., & Plomin, R. (1994). Genetic and environmental influences on perceptions of self-worth and competence in adolescence: A study of twins, full siblings, and step-siblings. *Child Development, 65,* 785–799.

McHale, S. M., Crouter, A. C., McGuire, S. A., & Updegraff, K. A. (1995). Congruence between mothers' and fathers' differential treatment of siblings: Links with family relations and children's well being. *Child Development, 66*, 116–128.

McKey, R. H., Condelli, L., Ganson, H., Barrett, B. J., McConkey, C., & Plantz, M. C. (1985). *The impact of Head Start on children, families, and communities*. Washington, DC: U. S. Government Printing Office.

McLoyd, V. C. (1998). Children in poverty: Development, public policy, and practice. In W. Damon (Series Ed.) & I. E. Sigel & K. A. Renninger (Vol. Eds), *Handbook of child psychology: Vol. 4. Child psychology in practice* (5th ed., pp. 135–208). New York: Wiley.

McLoyd, V. C., Jayaratne, T. E., Ceballo, R., & Borquez, J. (1994). Unemployment and work interruption among African American single mothers: Effects on parenting and adolescent socioemotional functioning. *Child Development, 65*, 562–589.

Meece, J. L., Parsons, J. E., Kaczala, C. M., Goff, S. B., & Futterman, R. (1982). Sex differences in math achievement: Toward a model of academic choice. *Psychological Bulletin, 91*, 324–348.

Meeus, W., Iedema, J., Helsen, M., & Vollebergh, W. (1999). Patterns of adolescent identity development: Review of literature and longitudinal analyses. *Developmental Review, 19,* 419–461.

Mehler, J., Jusczyk, P., Lambertz, G., Halsted, N., Bertoncini, J., & Amiel-Tison, C. (1988). A precursor of language acquisition in young infants. *Cognition, 29*, 143–178.

Meilman, P., Leichliter, J. S., & Presley, C. A. (1999). Greeks and athletes: Who drinks more? *Journal of American College Health, 47*, 187–190.

Meisels, S. J., & Plunkett, J. W. (1988). Developmental consequences of preterm birth: Are there long-term effects? In P. B. Baltes, D. L. Featherman, & R. M. Lerner (Eds.), *Life-span development and behavior* (Vol. 9). Hillsdale, NJ: Erlbaum.

Mekos, D., Hetherington, E. M., & Reiss, D. (1996). Sibling differences in problem behavior and parental treatment in nondivorced and remarried families. *Child Development, 67*, 2148–2165.

Meltzoff, A. N. (1988a). Imitation of televised models by infants. *Child Development, 59,* 1221–1229.

Meltzoff, A. N. (1988b). Infant imitation and memory: Nine-month-olds in immediate and deferred tests. *Child Development, 59,* 217–225

Meltzoff, A. N. (1995a). Apprehending the intentions of others: Re-enactment of intended acts by 10-month-old children. *Developmental Psychology, 31,* 838–850.

Meltzoff, A. N. (1995b). What infant memory tells us about infantile amnesia: Long-term recall and deferred imitation. *Journal of Experimental Child Psychology, 59*, 497–515.

Meltzoff, A. N., & Borton, R. W. (1979). Intermodal matching by human neonates. *Nature, 282,* 403–404.

Meltzoff, A. N., & Moore, M. K. (1977). Imitation of facial and manual gestures by human neonates. *Science, 198,* 75–78.

Meltzoff, A. N., & Moore, M. K. (1983). Newborn infants imitate adult facial gestures. *Child Development, 54,* 702–709.

Meltzoff, A. N., & Moore, M. K. (1994). Imitation, memory, and the representation of persons. *Infant Behavior and Development, 17,* 83–99.

Menaghan, E. G., & Parcel, T. L. (1995). Social sources of change in children's home environments: The effects of parental occupational experiences and family conditions. *Journal of Marriage and the Family, 57,* 69–84.

Menella, J. A., & Beauchamp, G. K. (1993a). Beer, breast feeding, and folklore. *Developmental Psychobiology, 26,* 459–466.

Menella, J. A., & Beauchamp, G. K. (1993b). The effects of repeated exposure to garlic-flavored milk on the nursling's behavior. *Pediatric Research, 34,* 805–808.

Menella, J. A., & Beauchamp, G. K. (1996). The human infant's response to vanilla flavor in mother's milk and formula. *Infant Behavior and Development, 19,* 13–19.

Mennella, J. A., Jagnow, C. P., & Beauchamp, G. K. (2001). Prenatal and postnatal flavor learning by human infants. *Pediatrics, 107,* e88.

Mennella, J. A., Johnson, A., & Beauchamp, G. K. (1995). Garlic ingestion by pregnant women alters the odor of amniotic fluid. *Chemical Senses, 20,* 207–209.

Merton, D. E. (1997). The meaning of meanness: Popularity, competition, and conflict among junior high school girls. *Sociology of Education, 70,* 175–191.

Mervis, C. B. (1987). Child-basic object categories and early lexical development. In U. Neisser (Ed.), *Concepts and conceptual development: Ecological and intellectual factors in categorization.* Cambridge, MA: Cambridge University Press.

Merzenrich, M. M. (2001). Cortical plasticity contributing to child development. In J. L. McClelland & R. S. Siegler (Eds.), *Mechanisms of cognitive development: Behavioral and neural perspectives* (pp. 67–96). Mahwah, NJ: Erlbaum.

Mesquita, B., & Frijda, N. H. (1992). Cultural variations in emotions: A review. *Psychological Bulletin, 112,* 179–204.

Michalson, L., & Lewis, M. (1985). What do children know about emotions and when do they know it. In M. Lewis & C. Saarni (Eds.), *The socialization of emotions* (pp. 117–139). New York: Plenum.

Miell, D. (2000). Children's creative collaborations: The importance of friendship when working together on a musical composition. *Social Development, 9,* 348–369.

Miles, D. R., & Carey,G. (1997). Genetic and environmental architecture of human aggression. *Journal of Personality and Social Psychology, 72,* 207–217.

Milewski, A. E. (1976). Infants' discrimination of internal and external pattern elements. *Journal of Experimental Child Psychology, 22,* 229–246.

Millar, W. S. (1990). Span of integration for delayed-reward contingency learning in 6- to 8-month-old infants. In A. Diamond (Ed.), *The development and neural bases of higher cognitive functions* (pp. 239–259). New York: New York Academy of Sciences.

Miller, B. C., Benson, B., & Galbraith, K. A. (2001). Family relationships and adolescent pregnancy risk: A research synthesis. *Developmental Review, 21,* 1–38.

Miller, C. L., Miceli, P. J., Whitman, T. L., & Borkowski, J. G. (1996). Cognitive readiness to parent and intellectual-emotional development in children of adolescent mothers. *Developmental Psychology, 32,* 533–541.

Miller, G. A. (1977). *Spontaneous apprentices: Children and language.* New York: Seabury.

Miller, J. G., & Bersoff, D. M. (1995). Development in the context of everyday family relationships: Culture, interpersonal morality, and adaptation. In M. Killen & D. Hart (Eds.), *Morality in everyday life: Developmental perspectives* (pp. 259–282). Cambridge, England: Cambridge University Press.

Miller, J. G., Bersoff, D. M., & Harwood, R. L. (1990). Perceptions of social responsibilities in India and in the United States: Moral imperatives or personal decisions? *Journal of Personality and Social Psychology, 58,* 33–47.

Miller, K. (1989). Measurement as a tool for thought: The role of measuring procedures in children's understanding of quantitative invariance. *Developmental Psychology, 25,* 589–600.

Miller, K. F., Smith, C. M., Zhu, J., & Zhang, H. (1995). Preschool origins of cross-national differences in mathematical competence: The role of number-naming systems. *Psychological Science, 6,* 56–60.

Miller, L. C., Putcha-Bhagavatula, A., & Pedersen, W. C. (2002). Men's and women's mating preferences: Distinct evolutionary mechanisms? *Current Directions in Psychological Science, 11,* 88–93.

Miller, L. T., & Vernon, P. A. (1997). Developmental changes in speed of information processing in young children. *Developmental Psychology, 33,* 549–554.

Miller, P. A., & Eisenberg, N. (1988). The relation of empathy to aggression and externalizing/antisocial behavior. *Psychological Bulletin, 103,* 324–344.

Miller, P. A., Eisenberg, N., Fabes, R. A., & Shell, R. (1989). Socialization of empathic and sympathetic responding. In N. Eisenberg (Ed.), *The development of empathy and related vicarious responses. New Directions in Child Development* (pp. 65–83). San Francisco: Jossey-Bass.

Miller, P. H. (2002). *Theories of developmental psychology* (4th ed.). New York: Worth.

Miller, P. H., & Coyle, T. R. (1999). Developmental change: Lessons from microgenesis. In E. K. Scholnick, K. Nelson, S. A. Gelman, & P. H. Miller (Eds.), *Conceptual development: Piaget's legacy* (pp. 209–239). Mahwah, NJ: Erlbaum.

Miller, P. H., & Seier, W. (1994). Strategy utilization deficiencies in children: When, where, and why. In H. Reese (Ed.), *Advances in child development and behavior* (Vol. 25). New York: Academic Press.

Miller, P. J., & Sperry, L. L. (1987). The socialization of anger and aggression. *Merrill-Palmer Quarterly, 33,* 1–31.

Miller, P. J., & Sperry, L. L. (1988). Early talk about the past: The origins of conversational stories of personal experience. *Journal of Child Language, 15,* 293–315.

Mills, D. L., Coffey-Corina, S., & Neville, H. J. (1997). Language comprehension and cerebral specialization from 13 to 20 months. *Developmental Neuropsychology, 13,* 397–445.

Mills, R. S. L., & Rubin, K. H. (1993). Socialization factors in the development of social withdrawal. In K. H. Rubin & J. Asendorpf (Eds.), *Social withdrawal, inhibition and shyness in childhood* (pp. 117–150). Hillsdale, NJ: Erlbaum.

Minde, K. (1993). Prematurity and illness in infancy: Implications for development and intervention. In C. H. Zeanah Jr. (Ed.), *Handbook of infant development.* New York: Guilford Press.

Mischel, H. N., & Mischel, W. (1983). The development of children's knowledge of self-control strategies. *Child Development, 54,* 603–619.

Mischel, W. (1970). Sex typing and socialization. In P. H. Mussen (Ed.), *Carmichael's handbook of child psychology* (Vol. 2, pp. 3–72). New York: Wiley.

Mischel, W. (1981). Metacognition and the rules of delay. In J. H. Flavell & L. Ross (Eds.), *Social cognitive development* (pp. 240–271). Cambridge, England: Cambridge University Press.

Mischel, W. (2000, June). *Attention control in the service of the self: Harnessing willpower in goal pursuit.* Paper presented at the Self Workshop, National Institutes of Mental Health, Bethesda, MD.

Mischel, W., Shoda, Y., & Peake, P. K. (1988). The nature of adolescent competencies predicted by preschool delay of gratification. *Journal of Personality and Social Psychology, 54,* 687–696.

Mitchell, E. (1985). The dynamics of family interaction around home video games. *Marriage and Family Review, 8,* 121–135.

Mize, J., & Ladd, G. W. (1990). Toward the development of successful skills training for preschool children. In S. R. Asher & J. D. Coie (Eds.), *Peer rejection in childhood* (pp. 338–361). Cambridge, England: Cambridge University Press.

Mizuta, I., Zahn-Waxler, C., Cole, P. M., & Hiruma, N. (1996). A cross-cultural study of preschoolers' attachment: Security and sensitivity in Japanese and US Dyads. *International Journal of Behavioral Development, 19,* 141–159.

Moffitt, T. E. (1990). Juvenile delinquency and attention deficit disorder: Boys' developmental trajectories from age 3 to age 15. *Child Development, 61,* 893–910.

Moffitt, T. E. (1993a). Adolescence-limited and life-course-persistent antisocial behavior: A developmental taxonomy. *Psychological Review, 100,* 674–701.

Moffitt, T. E. (1993b). The neuropsychology of conduct disorder. *Development and Psychopathology, 5,* 135–151.

Molfese, D. L., & Betz, J. (1988). Electrophysiological indices of the early development of lateralization for language and cognition, and their implications for predicting later development. In D. L. Molfese & S. J. Segalowitz (Eds.), *Brain lateralization in children: Developmental implications* (pp. 171–190). New York: Guilford Press.

Molfese, D. L., & Molfese, V. J. (1994). Short-term and long-term developmental outcomes: The use of behavioral and electrophysiological measures in early infancy as predictors. In G. Dawson & K. W. Fischer (Eds.), *Human behavior and the developing brain* (pp. 493–517). New York: Guilford Press.

Molfese, D. L., Freeman, R. B., & Palermo, D. S. (1975). The ontogeny of brain lateralization for speech and nonspeech stimuli. *Brain and Language, 2,* 356–368.

Monthly Vital Statistics Report (National Center for Health Statistics). (1995, March 22). Vol. 43, No. 9.

Moon, C., Cooper, R. P., & Fifer, W. P. (1993). Two-day-olds prefer their native language. *Infant Behavior and Development, 16*(4), 495–500.

Moore, C., & D'Entremont, B. (2001). Developmental changes in pointing as a function of attentional focus. *Journal of Cognition and Development, 2,* 109–129.

Moon, C., & Fifer, W. (1990, April). *Newborns prefer a prenatal version of mother's voice.* Presented at the biannual meeting of the International Society of Infant Studies, Montreal, Canada.

Moore, D. R., & Florsheim, P. (2001). Interpersonal processes and psychopathology among expectant and nonexpectant adolescent couples. *Journal of Consulting and Clinical Psychology, 69,* 101–111.

Moore, J. P., & Cook, I. L. (1999, December). Highlights of the 1998 National Young Gang Survey. Office of Juvenile Justice and Delinquency Prevention. *OJJDP Fact Sheet* (http://www.ncjrs.org/txtfiles1/ojjdp/fs99123.txt).

Moore, K. A., Manlove, J., Glei, D., & Morrison, D. R. (1998). Nonmarital school-age motherhood: Family, individual, and school characteristic. *Journal of Adolescent Research, 13,* 433–457.

Moore, K. L., & Persaud, T. V. N. (1993). *Before we are born* (4th ed.). Philadelphia: Saunders.

Morelli, G. A., Rogoff, B., Oppenheim, D., & Goldsmith, D. (1992). Cultural variation in infants' sleeping arrangements: Questions of independence. *Developmental Psychology, 28,* 604–613.

Morrongiello, B. A., Fenwick, K. D., Hillier, L., & Chance, G. (1994). Sound localization in newborn human infants. *Developmental Psychobiology, 27,* 519–538.

Moses, L. J., Baldwin, D. A., Rosicky, J. G., & Tidball, G. (2001). Evidence for referential understanding in the emotions domain at twelve and eighteen months. *Child Development, 72,* 655–948.

Moskowitz, S. (1983). *Love despite hate.* New York: Schocken.

Mounts, N. S. (2002). Parental management of adolescent peer relationships in context: The role of parenting style. *Journal of Family Psychology, 16,* 58–69.

Mounts, N. S., & Steinberg, L. (1995). An ecological analysis of peer influence on adolescent grade point average and drug use. *Developmental Psychology, 31,* 915–922.

Mueller, C. M., & Dweck, C. S. (1998). Praise for intelligence can undermine children's motivation and performance. *Journal of Personality and Social Psychology, 75,* 33–52.

Muller, C. (1995). Maternal employment, parent involvement, and mathematics achievement among adolescents. *Journal of Marriage and the Family, 57,* 85–100.

Muller, M., & Wehner R. (1988). Path integration in desert ants. Cataglyphis fortis *Proceedings of the National Academy of Sciences, 85,* 5287–5290.

Mumme, D. L., Fernald, A., & Herrera, C. (1996). Infants' responses to facial and vocal emotional signals in a social referencing paradigm. *Child Development, 67,* 3219–3237.

Munakata, Y., McClelland, J. L., Johnson, M. H., & Siegler, R. S. (1997). Rethinking infant knowledge: Toward an adaptive process account of successes and failures in object permanence tasks. *Psychological Review, 104,* 686–713.

Munekata, H., & Ninomiya, K. (1985). Development of prosocial moral judgments. *Japanese Journal of Educational Psychology, 33,* 157–164.

Munn, D., & Dunn, J. (1989). Temperament and the developing relationship between siblings. *International Journal of Behavioral Development, 12,* 433–451.

Munroe, R. H., Shimmin, H. S., & Munroe, R. L. (1984). Gender understanding and sex role preference in four cultures. *Developmental Psychology, 20,* 673–682.

Murphy, B. C., Eisenberg, N., Fabes, R. A., Shepard, S., & Guthrie, I. K. (1999). Consistency and change in children's emotionality and regulation: A longitudinal study. *Merrill-Palmer Quarterly, 45,* 413–444.

Murray, L., & Trevarthen, C. (1985). Emotional regulation of interactions between two-month-olds and their mothers. In T. M. Field & N. A. Fox (Eds.), *Social perception in infants* (pp. 177–197). Norwood, NJ: Ablex.

Myers, B. J., Olson, H. C., & Kaltenbach, K. (1992). Cocaine-exposed infants: Myths and misunderstandings. *Zero-to-Three, 13,* 1–5.

Myers, J., Jusczyk, P. W., Kemler-Nelson, D. G., Luce, J. C., Woodward, A. L., & Hirsh-Pasek, K. (1996). Infants' sensitivity to word boundaries in fluent speech. *Journal of Child Language, 23,* 1–30.

Naigles, L. (1990). Children use syntax to learn verb meanings. *Journal of Child Language, 17,* 357–374.

Naigles, L., & Gelman, S. A. (1995). Overextensions in comprehension and production revisited: Preferential looking in a study of dog, cat, and cow. *Journal of Child Language, 22,* 19–46.

Namy, L. L. (2001). What's in a name when it isn't a word? 17-month-olds' mapping of nonverbal symbols to object categories. *Infancy, 2,* 73–86.

Namy, L. L., & Waxman, S. R. (1998). Words and gestures: Infants' interpretations of different forms of symbolic reference. *Child Development, 69,* 295–308.

Nanez, J., Sr., & Yonas, A. (1994). Effects of luminance and texture motion on infant defensive reactions to optical collision. *Infant Behavior and Development, 17,* 165–174.

Nathanielsz, P. W. (1994). *A time to be born.* Oxford: Oxford University Press.

National Association for the Education of Young Children. (1986). Washington DC: Author.

National Center for Children in Poverty. (2001). *Child Poverty Fact Sheet.* Retrieved from http://cpmcnet.columbia.edu/dept/nccp/ycpf-01.html.

National Center for Health Statistics. (1998). *Health, United States, 1998: With socioeconomic status and health chartbook.* Retrieved from http://www.cdc.gov/nchs/data/hus/hus98.pdf

National Center for Health Statistics. (1999a). *America's children 1999. Part 1. Population and family characteristics.* Retrieved from: http://www/childstats.gov/ac1999/poptxt.asp.

National Center for Health Statistics. (1999b). *Prevalence of overweight among children and adolescents: United States, 1999.* Washington, DC: U. S. Department of Health and Human Services.

National Center for Health Statistics. (2001). *Smoking during pregnancy—rates drop steadily in the 1990's, but among teen mothers progress has stalled.* Retrieved from http://www.cdc.gov/nchs/releases/01news/smokpreg.htm

National Clearinghouse for Alcohol and Drug Information. (1995). *Birth defects and adverse birth outcomes.* Retrieved from http://quitsmoking.about.com/gi/dynamic/offsite.htm?site=http:%2F%2Fwww.health.org%2F

National Federation of State High School Associations. (1997). *High school athletic participation survey.* Kansas City, MO: Author.

Neckerman, H. J. (1996). The stability of social groups in childhood and adolescence: The role of the classroom social environment. *Social Development, 5,* 131–145.

Needham, A. (1997). Factors affecting infants' use of featural information in object segregation. *Current Directions in Psychological Science, 6*(2), 26–33.

Needham, A., & Baillargeon, R. (1993). Intuitions about support in 4.5-month-old infants. *Cognition, 47,* 121–148.

Needham, A., & Baillargeon, R. (1997). Object segregation in 8-month-old infants. *Cognition, 62,* 121–149.

Needham, A., Baillargeon, R., & Kaufman, L. (1997). Object segregation in infancy. In C. Rovee-Collier & L. Lipsitt (Eds.), *Advances in infancy research* (Vol. 11, pp. 1–44). Norwood, NJ: Ablex.

Neiderhiser, J. M., Pike, A., Hetherington, E. M., & Reiss, D. (1998). Adolescent perceptions as mediators of parenting: Genetic and environmental contributions. *Developmental Psychology, 34,* 1459–1469.

Nelson, C. A. (1987). The recognition of facial expressions in the first two years of life: Mechanisms of development. *Child Development, 58,* 889–909.

Nelson, C. A., & de Haan, M. (1996). Neural correlates of infants' visual responsiveness to facial expressions of emotion. *Developmental Psychobiology, 29,* 577–595.

Nelson, J., & Aboud, F. E. (1985). The resolution of social conflict between friends. *Child Development, 56,* 1009–1017.

Nelson, J. R., Smith, D. J., & Dodd, J. (1990). The moral reasoning of juvenile delinquents: A meta-analysis. *Journal of Abnormal Child Psychology, 18,* 231–239.

Nelson, K. E. (1973). Structure and strategy in learning to talk. *Monographs of the Society for Research in Child Development, 38*(1–2, Serial No. 149).

Nelson, K. E. (1993). The psychological and social origins of autobiographical memory. *Psychological Science, 4,* 7–14.

Nelson, K. E., Denninger, M. M., Bonvillian, J. D., Kaplan, B. J., & Baker, N. D. (1984). Maternal input adjustments and nonadjustments as related to children's linguistic advances and to language acquisition theories. In A. D. Pellegrini & T. D. Yawkey (Eds.), *The development of oral and written languages: Readings in developmental and applied linguistics* (pp. 31–56). New York: Ablex.

Nelson, K. E., & Gruendel, J. M. (1979). At morning it's lunchtime: A scriptal view of children's dialogues. *Discourse Processes, 2,* 73–94.

Nelson, K. E., & Hudson, J. (1988). Scripts and memory: Functional relationships in development. In F. E. Weinert & M. Perlmutter (Eds.), *Memory development: Universal changes and individual differences* (pp. 147–167). Hillsdale, NJ: Erlbaum.

Nelson, T. F., & Wechsler, N. (2001). Alcohol and college athletes. *Medicine and Science in Sports and Exercise, 33,* 43–47.

Neville, B., & Parke, R. D. (1997). Waiting for paternity: Interpersonal and contextual implications of the timing of fatherhood. *Sex Roles, 37,* 45–89.

Neville, H. J. (1990). Intermodal competition and compensation in development: Evidence from studies of the visual system in congenitally deaf adults. *Annals of the New York Academy of Sciences, 608,* 71–91.

Neville, H. J., & Bavelier, D. (1999). Specificity and plasticity in neurocognitive development in humans. In M. S. Gazzaniga (Ed.), *The cognitive neurosciences* (2nd ed., pp. 83–98). Cambridge, MA: MIT Press.

Newcomb, A. F., & Bagwell, C. L. (1995). Children's friendship relations: A meta-analytic review. *Psychological Bulletin, 117,* 306–347.

Newcomb, A. F., & Bukowski, W. M. (1984). A longitudinal study of the utility of social preference and social impact sociometric classification schemes. *Child Development, 55,* 1434–1447.

Newcomb, A. F., Bukowski, W. M., & Pattee, L. (1993). Children's peer relations: A meta-analytic review of popular, rejected, neglected, controversial, and average sociometric status. *Psychological Bulletin, 113,* 99–128.

Newcombe, N. S., & Huttenlocher, J. (2000). *Making space: The development of spatial representation and reasoning.* Cambridge, MA: MIT Press.

Newell, K. M., Scully, D. M., McDonald, P. V., & Baillargeon, R. (1989). Task constraints and infant grip configurations. *Developmental Psychobiology, 22,* 817–832.

Newman, J. (1995, December). How breast milk protects newborns. *Scientific American, 273*(6), 76–79.

Newport, E. L. (1990). Maturational constraints on language learning. *Cognitive Science, 14,* 11–28.

Newport, E. L. (1991). Contrasting concepts of the critical period for language. In S. Carey & R. Gelman (Eds.), *The epigenesis of mind: Essays on biology and cognition. The Jean Piaget Symposium series* (pp. 111–130). Hillsdale, NJ: Erlbaum.

Newport, E. L., Gleitman, H., & Gleitman, L. (1977). Mother, I'd rather do it myself: Some effects and noneffects of maternal speech style. In C. E. Snow & C. A. Ferguson (Eds.), *Talking to children: Language input and acquisition* (pp. 109–150). Cambridge, England: Cambridge University Press.

NICHD Early Child Care Research Network. (1997a). The effects of infant child care on infant-mother attachment security: Results of the NICHD study of early child care. *Child Development, 68,* 860–879.

NICHD Early Child Care Research Network. (1997b). Familial factors associated with the characteristics of nonmaternal care for infants. *Journal of Marriage and the Family, 59,* 389–408.

NICHD Early Child Care Research Network. (1998a). Early child care and self-control, compliance, and problem behavior at 24 and 36 months. *Child Development, 69,* 1145–1170.

NICHD Early Child Care Research Network. (1998b). *When child-care classrooms meet recommended guidelines for quality.* Paper submitted for publication.

NICHD Early Child Care Research Network. (1999). Child care and mother-child interaction in the first three years of life. *Developmental Psychology, 35,* 1399–1413.

NICHD Early Child Care Research Network. (2000a). Factors associated with fathers' caregiving activities and sensitivity with young children. *Journal of Family Psychology, 14,* 200–219.

NICHD Early Child Care Research Network. (2000b). The relation of child care to cognitive and language development. *Child Development, 71,* 960–980.

NICHD Early Child Care Research Network. (2001a). Child care and children's peer interactions at 24 and 36 months: The NICHD Study of Early Child Care. *Child Development, 72,* 1478–1500.

NICHD Early Child Care Research Network. (2001b, April). Early child care and children's development prior to school entry. Paper presented at the biennial meeting of the Society for Research in Child Development, Minneapolis.

NICHD Early Child Care Research Network. (2001c, April). Further explorations of the detected effects of quantity of early child care on socioemotional development. Paper presented at the biennial meeting of the Society for Research in Child Development, Minneapolis.

Nisan, M., & Kohlberg, L. (1982). Universality and variation in moral judgment: A longitudinal and cross-sectional study in Turkey. *Child Development, 53,* 865–876.

Nisbett, R. E., & Wilson, T. D. (1977). Telling more than we can know: Verbal reports on mental processes. *Psychological Review, 84,* 231–259.

Nolen-Hoeksema, S. (1990). *Sex differences in depression.* Stanford, CA: Stanford University Press.

Nolen-Hoeksema, S. (2001). Gender differences in depression. *Current Directions in Psychological Science, 10,* 173–176.

Nolen-Hoeksema, S., & Girgus, J. S. (1994). The emergence of gender differences in depression during adolescence. *Psychological Bulletin, 115,* 424–443.

Nolen-Hoeksema, S., Larson, J., & Grayson, C. (1999). Explaining the gender differences in depressive symptoms. *Journal of Personality and Social Psychology, 77,* 1061–1072.

Nord, C. W., & Zill, N. (1997). Noncustodial parents' participation in their children's lives. Washington, DC: Department of Health and Human Services. Retrieved from: http//www.dhhs.gov/programs/cse/new/csr9708.htm#9708a.

Nucci, L. P. (1981). Conceptions of personal issues: A domain distinct from moral or societal concepts. *Child Development, 52,* 114–121.

Nucci, L. P. (1997). Culture, universals, and the personal. *New Directions in Child Development, 76,* 5–22.

Nucci, L. P., Camino, C., & Sapiro, C. M. (1996). Social class effects on northeastern Brazilian children's conceptions of areas of personal choice and social regulation. *Child Development, 67,* 1223–1242.

Nucci, L. P., & Weber, E. K. (1995). Social interactions in the home and the development of young children's conceptions of the personal. *Child Development, 66,* 1438–1452.

Nunes, T., & Bryant, P. (1996). *Children doing mathematics.* Cambridge, MA: Blackwell.

Nunes, T., Schliemann, A.-L., and Carraher, D. (1993). *Street mathematics and school mathematics.* New York: Cambridge University Press.

Oakes, L. M., & Cohen, L. B. (1995). Infant causal perception. In C. Rovee-Collier & L. P. Lipsitt (Eds.), *Advances in infancy research* (Vol. 9). Norwood, NJ: Ablex.

Oakhill, J. V., & Cain, K. E. (2000). Children's difficulties in text comprehension: Assessing casual issues. *Journal of Deaf Studies & Deaf Education, 5,* 51–59.

Oakhill, J. V., & Cain, K. E. (2002). The development of comprehension skills. To appear in P. E. Bryant & T. Nunes (Eds.), *Handbook of children's literacy* (title pending). Dordrecht, The Netherlands: Kluwer Academic Publishers..

Ocampo, K. A., Bernal, M. E., & Knight, G. P. (1993). Gender, race, and ethnicity: The sequencing of social constancies. In M. E. Bernal & G. P. Knight (Eds.), *Ethnic identity: Formation and transmission among Hispanics and other minorities* (pp. 11–30). Albany: State University of New York Press.

O'Connor, T. G., Caspi, A., DeFries, J. C., & Plomin, R. (2000). Are associations between parental divorce and children's adjustment genetically mediated? An adoption study. *Developmental Psychology, 36,* 429–437.

O'Connor, T. G., Hetherington, E. M., & Reiss, D. (1998). Family systems and adolescent development: Shared and nonshared risk and protective factors in nondivorced and remarried families. *Development and Psychopathology, 10,* 353–375.

O'Connor, T. G., & Rutter, M. (2000). Attachment disorder behavior following early severe deprivation: Extension and longitudinal follow-up. *Journal of the American Academy of Child and Adolescent Psychiatry, 39,* 703–712.

O'Connor, T. G., Rutter, M., Beckett, C., Keaveney, L., Kreppner, J. M., & The English and Romanian Adoptees Study Team. (2000). The effects of global severe privation on cognitive competence: Extension and longitudinal follow-up. *Child Development, 71,* 376–390.

O'Reilly, A. W., & Bornstein, M. H. (1993). Caregiver-child interaction in play. In M. H. Bornstein & A. W. O'Reilly (Eds.), *The role of play in the development of thought* (New Directions for Child Development, No. 59). San Francisco: Jossey–Bass.

Oden, S., & Asher, S. R. (1977). Coaching children in social skills for friendship making. *Child Development, 48,* 498–506.

Okagaki, L., & Frensch, P. A. (1996). Effects of video game playing on measures of spatial performance: Gender effects in late adolescence. In P. M. Greenfield & R. R. Cocking (Eds.), *Interacting with video* (pp. 115–140). Norwood, NJ: Ablex.

Olds, D. L., Henderson, C. R., & Tatelbaum, R. (1986). Preventing abuse and child neglect: A randomized trial of nurse home visits. *Pediatrics, 78,* 65–78.

Oliner, S. P. & Oliner, P. M. (1988). *The altruistic personality: Rescuers of Jews in Nazi Europe.* New York: Free Press.

Ollendick, T. H., Weist, M. D., Borden, M. C., & Greene, R. W. (1992). Sociometric status and academic, behavioral, and psychological adjustment: A five-year longitudinal study. *Journal of Consulting and Clinical Psychology, 60,* 80–87.

Oller, D. K., & Eilers, R. E. (1988). The role of audition in infant babbling. *Child Development, 59,* 441–449.

Oller, D. K., & Pearson, B. Z. (2002). Assessing the effects of bilingualism. In D. K. Oller (Ed.), *Language and literacy in bilingual children.* Clevedon, UK: Multilingual Matters.

Olson, R. K., Forsberg, H., & Wise, B. (1994). Genes, environment, and the development of orthographic skills. In V. W. Berninger (Ed.), *The varieties of orthographic knowledge I: Theoretical and developmental issues.* Dordrecht, The Netherlands: Kluwer Academic Publishers.

Olson, S. L., Bates, J. E., & Kaskie, B. (1992). Caregiver-infant interaction antecedents of children's schoolage cognitive ability. *Merrill-Palmer Quarterly, 38,* 309–330.

Olson, S. L., Bates, J. E., Sandy, J. M., & Lanthier, R. (2000). Early developmental precursors of externalizing behavior in middle childhood and adolescence. *Journal of Abnormal Child Psychology, 28,* 119–133.

Olson, S. L., Schilling, E. M., & Bates, J. E. (1999). Measurement of impulsivity: Construct coherence, longitudinal stability, and relationship with externalizing problems in middle childhood and adolescence. *Journal of Abnormal Child Psychology, 27,* 151–165.

Olweus, D. (1979). Stability and aggressive reaction patterns in males: A review. *Psychological Bulletin, 86,* 852–875.

Olweus, D. (1994). Annotation: Bullying at school: Basic facts and effects of a school based intervention program. *Journal of Child Psychology and Psychiatry, 35,* 1171–1190.

Opfer, J. E. (2001). *Teleological action speaks louder than words: A microgenetic analysis of conceptual change in naive biology.* Poster presented at the biennial meeting of the Cognitive Development Society, Virginia Beach, VA.

Opfer, J. E., & Gelman, S. A. (2001). Children's and adults' models of teleological action: The development of biology-based models. *Child Development, 72,* 1367–1381.

Orlofsky, J. L. (1978). Identity formation: Achievements and fear of success in college mean and women. *Journal of Youth and Adolescence, 7,* 49–62.

Ornstein, P. A., & Naus, M. J. (1985). Effects of the knowledge base on children's memory strategies. In H. W. Reese (Ed.), *Advances in child development and behavior* (Vol. 19). New York: Academic Press.

Ornstein, P. A., Shapiro, L. R., Clubb, P. A., Follmer, A., & Baker-Ward, L. (1997). The influence of prior knowledge on children's memory for salient medical experiences. In N. L. Stein, P. A. Ornstein, B. Tversky, & C. Brainerd (Eds.), *Memory for everyday and emotional events.* Mahwah, NJ: Erlbaum.

Osborne, L. (1999, October 24). A linguistic big bang. *The New York Times Magazine*, pp. 84–89.

Ostad, S. A. (1998). Developmental differences in solving simple arithmetic word problems and simple number-fact problems: A comparison of mathematically normal and mathematically disabled children. *Mathematical Cognition, 4*, 1–19.

Oster, H., Hegley, D., & Nagel, L. (1992). Adult judgments and fine-grained analysis of infant facial expressions: Testing the validity of a priori coding formulas. *Developmental Psychology, 28,* 1115–1131.

Otake, M., & Schull, W. J. (1984). In utero exposure to A-bomb radiation and mental retardation: A reassessment. *British Journal of Radiology, 57,* 409–414.

Overman, W. H., Pate, B. J., Moore, K., & Peleuster, A. (1996). Ontogeny of place learning in children as measured in the radial arm maze, Morris search task, and open field task. *Behavioral Neuroscience, 110,* 1205–1228.

Pacifici, C., & Bearison, D. J. (1991). Development of children's self-regulations in idealized and mother-child interactions. *Cognitive Development, 6,* 261–277.

Pagani, L., Tremblay, R. E., Vitaro, F., Kerr, M., & McDuff, P. (1998). The impact of family transition on the development of delinquency in adolescent boys: A 9-year longitudinal study. *Journal of Child Psychology and Psychiatry, 39,* 489–499.

Paley, V. G. (1981). *Wally's stories.* Cambridge, MA: Harvard University Press.

Palincsar, A. S., & Magnusson, S. J. (2001). The interplay of first-hand and text-based investigations to model and support the development of scientific knowledge and reasoning. In D. Klahr & S. Carver (Eds.), *Cognition and instruction: 25 years of progress.* Mahwah, NJ: Erlbaum.

Palmer, C. F. (1989). The discriminating nature of infants' exploratory actions. *Developmental Psychology, 25,* 885–893.

Palmer, E. J., & Hollin, C. R. (1998). A comparison of patterns of moral development in young offenders and non-offenders. *Legal and Criminological Psychology, 3*, 225–235.

Papert, S. (1996). *The connected family: Bridging the digital generation gap.* Atlanta: Longstreet Press.

Papini, D. R., & Sebby, R. A. (1988). Variations in conflictual family issues by adolescent pubertal status, gender, and family member. *Journal of Early Adolescence, 8*, 1–15.

Parke, R. D. (1996). *Fatherhood.* Cambridge: MA: Harvard University Press.

Parke, R. D., & Buriel, R. (1998). Socialization in the family: Ethnic and ecological perspectives. In W. Damon (Series Ed.) and N. Eisenberg (Vol. Ed.), *Social, emotional and personality development. Vol. 3. Handbook of child psychology* (pp. 463–552). New York: Wiley.

Parke, R. D., & Collmer, C. (1975). Child abuse: An interdisciplinary review. In E. M. Hetherington (Ed.), *Review of child development research* (Vol. 5). Chicago: University of Chicago Press.

Parke, R. D., & Kellam, S. (Ed.). (1994). *Advances in family research. Vol. 4. Family relationships with other social systems.* Hillsdale, NJ: Erlbaum.

Parke, R. D., O'Neil, R., Spitzer, S., Isley, S., Welsh, M., Wang, S., et al. (1997). A longitudinal assessment of sociometric stability and the behavioral correlates of children's social status. *Merrill-Palmer Quarterly, 43,* 635–662.

Parke, R. D., & Slaby, R. G. (1983). The development of aggression. In P. H. Mussen (Series Ed.) and E. M. Hetherington (Vol. Ed.), *Handbook of child psychology, Vol. 4. Socialization, personality, and social development* (pp. 547–641). New York: Wiley.

Parker, J. G., & Asher, S. R. (1987). Peer relations and later personal adjustment: Are low-accepted children at risk. *Psychological Bulletin, 102,* 357–389.

Parker, J. G., & Asher, S. R. (1993). Friendship and friendship quality in middle childhood: Links with peer group acceptance and feelings of loneliness and social dissatisfaction. *Developmental Psychology, 29,* 611–621.

Parker, J. G., & Gottman, J. M. (1989). Social and emotional development in a relational context. In T. J. Berndt & G. W. Ladd (Eds.), *Peer relationships in child development* (pp. 95–131). New York: Wiley.

Parker, J. G., & Herrera, C. (1996). Interpersonal processes in friendship: A comparison of maltreated and nonmaltreated children's experience. *Developmental Psychology, 32,* 1025–1038.

Parker, J. G., Rubin, K. H., Price, J. M., & DeRosier, M. E. (1995). In D. Cicchetti & D. Cohen (Eds.), *Developmental psychopathology. Vol. 2: risk, disorder, and adaptation* (pp. 96–161). New York: Wiley.

Parmelee, A. H., Sigman, M., Garbanati, J., Cohen, S., Beckwith, L., & Asarnow, R. (1994). Neonatal encephalographic organization and attention in early adolescence. In G. Dawson & K. W. Fischer (Eds.), *Human behavior and the developing brain* (pp. 537–554). New York: Guilford Press.

Parritz, R. H. (1996). A descriptive analysis of toddler coping in challenging circumstances. *Infant Behavior and Development, 19,* 171–180.

Paschall, M. J., & Hubbard, M. L. (1998). Effects of neighborhood and family stressors on African American male adolescents' self-worth and propensity for violent behavior. *Journal of Consulting and Clinical Psychology, 66,* 825–831.

Pascual-Leone, A., Cammarota, A., Wasserman, E. M., Brasil-Neto, J. P., Cohen, L. G., & Hallett, M. (1993). Modulation of motor cortical outputs to the reading hand of braille readers. *Annals of Neurology, 34,* 33–37.

Pastor, D. (1981). The quality of mother-infant attachment and its relationship to toddler's initial sociability with peers. *Developmental Psychology, 17*(3), 326–335.

Patterson, C. J. (1995a). Families of the lesbian baby boom: Parents' division of labor and children's adjustment. *Developmental Psychology, 31,* 115–123.

Patterson, C. J. (1995b). Lesbian and gay parenthood. In M. H. Bornstein (Ed.), *Handbook of parenting. Vol. 3. Status and social conditions of parenting* (pp. 255–274). Mahwah, NJ: Erlbaum.

Patterson, C. J. (1997). Children of lesbian and gay parents. In T. H. Ollendick & R. J. Prinz (Eds.), *Advances in clinical child psychology* (Vol. 19, pp. 235–282). New York: Plenum Press.

Patterson, C. J., & Chan, R. W. (1997). Gay fathers. In M. Lamb (Ed.), *The role of the father in child development* (3rd ed., pp. 245–260). New York: Wiley.

Patterson, C. J., Fulcher, M., & Wainright, J. (in press). Children of lesbian and gay parents: Research, law and policy. In B. L. Bottoms, M. B. Kovera, & B. D. McAuliff (Eds.), *Children and the law: Social science and policy.* Cambridge, England: Cambridge University Press.

Patterson, C. J., Griesler, P. C., Vaden, N. A. & Kupersmidt, J. B. (1992). Family economic circumstances, life transitions, and children's peer relations. In R. D. Parke & G. W. Ladd (Eds.), *Family-peer relationships: Modes of linkage.* Hillsdale, NJ: Erlbaum.

Patterson, C. J., Kupersmidt, J. B., & Griesler, P. C. (1990). Children's perceptions of self and of relationships with others as a function of sociometric status. *Child Development, 61,* 1335–1349.

Patterson, F., & Linden, E. (1981). *The education of Koko.* New York: Holt, Rinehart, & Winston.

Patterson, G. R. (1982). *Coercive family processes.* Eugene, OR: Castilla Press.

Patterson, G. R. (1995). Coercion—A basis for early age of onset for arrest. In J. McCord (Ed.), *Coercion and punishment in long-term perspective* (pp. 81–105). New York: Cambridge University Press.

Patterson, G. R., Capaldi, D., & Bank, L. (1991). An early starter model for predicting delinquency. In D. J. Pepler & K. H. Rubin (Eds.), *The development and treatment of childhood aggression* (pp. 139–168). Hillsdale, NJ: Erlbaum.

Patterson, G. R., Reid, J. B., & Dishion, T. J. (1992). *A social learning approach: Vol. 4. Antisocial boys.* Eugene, OR: Castalia Press.

Patteson, D. M., & Barnard, K. E. (1990). Parenting of low birth weight infants: A review of issues and interventions. *Infant Mental Health Journal, 11,* 37–56.

Paulson, S. E. (1996). Maternal employment and adolescent achievement revisited: An ecological perspective. *Family Relations, 45,* 201–208.

Peake, P. K., Hebl, M., & Mischel, W. (2002). Strategic attention deployment for delay of gratification in working and waiting situations. *Developmental Psychology, 38,* 313–326.

Peake, P. K., & Mischel, W. (2000). *Adult correlates of preschool delay of gratification.* Unpublished data. Smith College, Northampton, MA.

Peal, E., & Lambert, W. E. (1962). The relation of bilingualism to intelligence. *Psychological Monographs, 76*(546), 1–23.

Pearson, B. Z., & Fernández, S. C. (1994). Patterns of interaction in the lexical growth in two languages of bilingual infants and toddlers. *Language Learning, 44,* 617–653.

Pedersen, N. L., Plomin, R., Nesselroade, J. R., & McClearn, G. E. (1992). A quantitative genetic analysis of cognitive abilities during the second half of the life span. *Psychological Science, 3,* 346–353.

Pedersen, P. A., & Blass, E. M. (1982). Prenatal and postnatal determinants of the 1st suckling episode in albino rats. *Developmental Psychobiology, 15,* 349–355.

Pederson, D. R., Gleason, K. E., Moran, G., & Bento, S. (1998). Maternal attachment representations, maternal sensitivity, and the infant-mother attachment relationship. *Developmental Psychology, 34,* 925–933.

Pederson, D. R., & Moran, G. (1996). Expressions of attachment relationship outside of the Strange Situation. *Child Development, 67,* 915–927.

Pegg, J. E., Werker, J. F., & McLeod, P. J. (1992). Preference for infant-directed over adult-directed speech: Evidence from 7-week-old infants. *Infant Behavior and Development, 15,* 325–345.

Pelaez-Nogueras, M., Field, T. M., Hossain, Z., & Pickens, J. (1996). Depressed mothers' touching increases infants' positive affect and attention in still-face interactions. *Child Development, 67*, 1780–1792.

Pelham, W. E., & Hoza, B. (1996). Intensive treatment: A summer treatment program for children with ADHD. In E. D. Hibbs & P. S. Jensen (Eds.), *Psychosocial treatments for child and adolescent disorders: Empirically based strategies for clinical practice* (pp. 311–340). Washington, DC: American Psychological Association.

Pellegrini, A. D., & Smith, P. K. (1998). Physical activity play: The nature and function of a neglected aspect of play. *Child Development, 69*, 577–598.

Perner, J., Ruffman, T., & Leekham, S. R. (1994). Theory of mind is contagious: You catch it from your sibs. *Child Development, 65*, 1228–1238.

Perris, E. E., & Clifton, R. K. (1988). Reaching in the dark toward sound as a measure of auditory localization in infants. *Infant Behavior and Development, 11*, 473–492.

Perry, D. G., & Bussey, K. (1979). The social learning theory of sex differences: Imitation is alive and well. *Journal of Personality and Social Psychology, 37*, 1699–1712.

Perry, D. G., & Bussey, K. (1984). *Social development.* Upper Saddle River, NJ: Prentice-Hall.

Perry, D. G., Bussey, K., & Freiberg, K. (1981). Impact of adults' appeals for sharing on the development of altruistic dispositions in children. *Journal of Experimental Child Psychology, 32*, 127–138.

Perry, D. G., Perry, L. C., & Rasmussen, P. (1986). Cognitive social learning mediators of aggression. *Child Development, 57*, 700–711.

Perry, D. G., Perry, L. C., & Weiss, R. (1989). Sex differences in the consequences that children anticipate for aggression. *Developmental Psychology, 25*, 312–319.

Perry, M., Church, R. B., & Goldin-Meadow, S. (1988). Transitional knowledge in the acquisition of concepts. *Cognitive Development, 3*, 359–400.

Perry, M., & Elder, A. D. (1997). Knowledge in transition: Adults' developing understanding of a principle of physical causality. *Cognitive Development, 12*, 131–157.

Petersen, A. C., Compas, B. E., Brooks-Gunn, J., Stemmler, M., Ey, S., & Grant, K. E. (1993). Depression in adolescence. *American Psychologist, 48*, 155–168.

Petersen, A. C., Sarigiani, P. A., & Kennedy, R. E. (1991). Adolescent depression: Why more girls? *Journal of Youth and Adolescence, 20*, 247–271.

Peterson, C. L., & McCabe, A. (1988). The connective "and" as discourse glue. *First Language, 8*, 19–28.

Petitto, L. A., Holowka, S., Sergio, L. E., & Ostry, D. (2001). Language rhythms in baby hand movements. *Nature, 413*, 35–36.

Petitto, L. A., & Marentette, P. F. (1991). Babbling in the manual mode: Evidence for the ontogeny of language. *Science, 251*, 1493–1496.

Pettit, G. S., Brown, E. G., Mize, J., & Lindsey, E. (1998). Mothers' and fathers' socializing behavior in three contexts: Links with children's peer competence. *Merrill-Palmer Quarterly, 44*, 173–193.

Pettit, G. S., Laird, R. D., Dodge, K. A., Bates, J. E., & Criss, M. M. (2001). Antecedents and behavior-problem outcomes of parental monitoring and psychological control in early adolescence. *Child Development, 72*, 583-598.

Phillips, S., King, S., & DuBois, L. (1978). Spontaneous activities of female versus male newborns. *Child Development, 49*, 590–597.

Phinney, J. S. (1993a). Multiple group identities: differentiation, conflict, and integration. In J. Kroger (Ed.), *Discussions on ego identity* (pp. 47–73). Hillsdale, NJ: Erlbaum.

Phinney, J. S. (1993b). A three-stage model of ethnic identity development in adolescence. In M. E. Bernal & G. P. Knight (Eds.), *Ethnic identity: Formation and transmission among Hispanics and other minorities* (pp. 61–79). Albany: State University of New York Press.

Phinney, J. S., Cantu, C. L., & Kurtz, D. A. (1997). Ethnic and American identity as predictors of self-esteem among African American, Latino, and White adolescents. *Journal of Youth and Adolescence, 26*, 165–185.

Phinney, J. S., & Kohatsu, E. L. (1997). Ethnic and racial identity development and mental health. In J. Schulenberg, J. L. Maggs, & K. Hurrelmann (Eds.), *Health risks and developmental transitions during adolescence* (pp. 420–443). Cambridge, England: Cambridge University Press.

Piaget, J. (1926). *The language and thought of the child.* New York: Harcourt, Brace & World. (Original work published 1923)

Piaget, J. (1928/1959). *Judgment and reasoning in the child.* Patterson, NJ: Littlefield, Adams. (Original work published in 1928 by Routledge & Kegan Paul, London.)

Piaget, J. (1932/1965). *The moral judgment of the child.* New York: Free Press.

Piaget, J. (1946). *The development of children's concept of time.* Paris: Presses Universitaires de France.

Piaget, J. (1951). *Play, dreams, and imitation in childhood.* New York: Norton.

Piaget, J. (1952a). *The child's concept of number.* New York: Norton.

Piaget, J. (1952b). *The origins of intelligence in children.* New York: Int. University Press.

Piaget, J. (1954). *The construction of reality in the child.* New York: Basic Books.

Piaget, J. (1969). *The child's conception of time.* New York: Ballantine.

Piaget, J. (1970). *Psychology and epistemology.* New York: W. W. Norton.

Piaget, J. (1971). *The construction of reality in the child.* New York: Ballantine.

Piaget , J., & Inhelder, B. (1956). *The child's conception of space* (F. J. Langdon & J. L. Lunzer, Trans.). Atlantic Highlands, NJ: Humanities Press. (Reprinted in *The essential Piaget: An interpretive reference and guide*, pp. 576–642, by H. E. Gruber & J. J. Voneche, Eds., 1977, New York: Basic Books.)

Piaget, J., & Inhelder, B. (1964). *The early growth of logic in the child.* New York: Norton.

Pierroutsakos, S. L., & DeLoache, J. S. (2002). Why do infants grasp pictured objects? *Infancy, 3.*

Pilgrim, C., Luo, Q., Urberg, K. A. & Fang, X. (1999). Influence of peers, parents, and individual characteristics on adolescent drug use in two cultures. *Merrill-Palmer Quarterly, 45*, 85–107.

Pilkington, N. W., & D'Augelli, A. R. (1995). Victimization of lesbian, gay, and bisexual youth in community settings. *Journal of Community Psychology, 23*, 33–56.

Pillow, B. H. (1988). The development of children's beliefs about the mental world. *Merrill-Palmer Quarterly, 34*, 1–32.

Pine, J. M. (1994). Environmental correlates of variation in lexical style: Interactional style and the structure of the input. *Applied Psycholinguistics, 15,* 355–370.

Pinker, S. (1994). *The language instinct: The new science of language and mind.* Harmondsworth, Middlesex: Alan Lane, Penguin.

Pinker, S. (1997). *How the mind works.* New York: W. W. Norton.

Plato. (1980). *The laws of Plato* (T. L. Pangle, Trans.). New York: Basic Books.

Plomin, R. (1990). *Nature and nurture.* Belmont, CA: Brooks/Cole.

Plomin, R., & Bergeman, C. S. (1991). The nature of nurture: Genetic influence on "environmental" measures. *Behavioral and Brain Sciences, 14,* 373–427.

Plomin, R., Corley, R., Caspi, A., Fulker, D. W., & DeFries, J. (1998). Adoption results for self-reported personality: Evidence for nonadditive genetic effects? *Journal of Personality and Social Psychology, 75,* 211–218.

Plomin, R., Corley, R., DeFries, J. C., & Fulker, D. W. (1990). Individual differences in television viewing in early childhood: Nature as well as nurture. *Psychological Science, 6,* 371–377.

Plomin, R., & Daniels, D. (1987). Why are children in the same family so different from each other? *Behavioral and Brain Sciences, 10,* 1–16.

Plomin, R., DeFries, J. C., McClearn, G. E., & Rutter, M. (1997). *Behavioral genetics* (3rd ed.). New York: Freeman.

Plumert, J. M. (1995). Relation between children's overestimation of their physical abilities and accident proneness. *Developmental Psychology, 31,* 866–876.

Podd, M. H., Marcia, J. E., & Rubin, B. M. (1970). The effects of ego identity and partner perception on a prisoner's dilemma game. *Journal of Social Psychology, 82,* 117–126.

Polka, L., & Werker, J. F. (1994). Developmental changes in perception of non-native vowel contrasts. *Journal of Experimental Psychology: Human Perception and Performance, 20,* 421–435.

Pollak, S. D., Cicchetti, D., Klorman, R., & Brumaghim, J. T. (1997). Cognitive brain event-related potentials and emotion processing in maltreated children. *Child Development, 68,* 773–787.

Pollitt, E., Golub, M., Grantham-McGregor, S., Levitsky, D., Schurch, B., Strupp, B., & Wachs, T. (1996). A reconceptualization of the effects of undernutrition on children's biological, psychosocial, and behavioral development. *SRCD Social Policy Report, 10*(5), 1–21.

Pollitt, E., Gorman, K. S., Engle, P., Martorell, R., & Rivera, J. (1993). Early supplementary feeding and cognition: Effects over two decades. *Monographs of the Society for Research in Child Development, 58*(7, Serial No. 238), 1–99.

Pomerleau, A., Bolduc, D., Malcuit, G., & Cossette, L. (1990). Pink or blue: Environmental gender stereotypes in the first tyo years of life. *Sex Roles, 22,* 359–367.

Poole, D. A., & Lindsay, D. S. (1995). Interviewing preschoolers: Effects of nonsuggestive techniques, parental coaching, and leading questions on reports of nonexperienced events. *Journal of Experimental Child Psychology, 60,* 129–154.

Popkin, B. M., & Doan, R. M. (1990). Women's roles, time allocation and health. In J. Caldwell, S. Findley, P. Caldwell, G. Santow, W. Cosford, J. Braid, & D. Broers-Freeman (Eds.), *What we know about health transition: The cultural, social, and behavioral determinants of health transition* (Vol. 2, No. 2, pp. 683–706). Canberra: Australian National University Press.

Porges, S. W. (1991). Vagal tone: An autonomic mediator of affect. In J. Garber & K. A. Dodge (Eds.), *The development of emotion regulation and dysregulation* (pp. 111–128). Cambridge, England: University of Cambridge Press.

Porges, S. W., Doussard-Roosevelt, J. A., & Maiti, A. K. (1994). Vagal tone and the physiological regulation of emotion. *Monographs of the Society for Research in Child Development, 59*(2-3, Serial No. 240), 167–186.

Porter, R. H., Makin, J. W., Davis, L. B., & Christensen, K. M. (1991). An assessment of the salient olfactory environment of formula-fed infants. *Physiology & Behavior, 50,* 907–911.

Porter, R. H., Makin, J. W., Davis, L. B., & Christensen, K. M. (1992). Breast-fed infants respond to olfactory cues from their own mother and unfamiliar lactating females. *Infant Behavior & Development, 15,* 85–93.

Posada, G., Jacobs, A., Carbonell, O., Alzate, G., Bustemante, M., & Arenas, A. (1999). Maternal care and attachment security in ordinary and emergency contexts. *Developmental Psychology, 35,* 1379–1388.

Posner, M. I., Rothbart, M. K., Farah, M., & Bruer, J. (Eds.). (2001). The developing human brain [Special issue]. *Developmental Science, 4*(3).

Poston, D. L., Jr., & Falbo, T. (1990). Academic performance and personality traits of Chinese children: "Onlies" versus others. *American Journal of Sociology, 96,* 433–451.

Poulin, F., Cillessen, A. H. N., Hubbard, J. A., Coie, J. D., Dodge, K. A., & Schwartz, D. (1997). Children's friends and behavioral similarity in two social contexts. *Social Development, 6,* 224–236.

Poulin-Dubois, D. (1999). Infants' distinction between animate and inanimate objects: The origins of naive psychology. P. Rochat (Ed.), *Early social cognition: Understanding others in the first months of life* (pp. 257–280). Mahwah, NJ: Erlbaum.

Powell, G. F., Brasel, J. A., & Blizzard, R. M. (1967). Emotional deprivation and growth retardation simulating idiopathic hypopituitarism: I. Clinical evaluation of the syndrome. *New England Journal of Medicine, 276,* 1272–1278.

Powlishta, K. K., Serbin, L. A., & Moller, L. C. (1993). The stability of individual differences in gender typing: Implications for understanding gender segregation. *Sex Roles, 29,* 723–737.

Pratt, M. W., Kerig, P., Cowan, P. A., & Cowan, C. P. (1988). Mothers and fathers teaching 3-year-olds: Authoritative parenting and adult scaffolding of young children's learning. *Developmental Psychology, 24,* 832–839.

Pressley, M., El-Dinary, P. B., Stein, S., Marks, M. B., & Brown, R. (1992). Good strategy instruction is motivating and interesting. In A. Renninger, S. Hidi, & A. Krapp (Eds.), *The role of interest in learning and development* (pp. 333–358). Mahwah, NJ: Erlbaum.

Pressley, M., Levin, J. R., & McDaniel, M. A. (1987). Remembering versus inferring what a word means: Mnemonic and contextual approaches. In M. G. McKeown & M. E. Curtis (Eds.), *The nature of vocabulary acquisition* (pp. 107–128). Cambridge, MA: MIT Press.

Putallaz, M. (1983). Predicting children's sociometric status from their behavior. *Child Development, 54,* 1417–1426.

Querleu, D., Renard, X., Boutteville, C., & Crèpin, G. (1989). Hearing by the human fetus? *Seminars in Perinatology, 13*(5), 409–420.

Quiggle, N. L., Garber, J., Panak, W. F., & Dodge, K. A. (1992). Social information processing in aggressive and depressed children. *Child Development, 63,* 1305–1320.

Quine, W. V. O. (1960). *Word and object.* Cambridge, England: Cambridge University Press.

Quinn, P. C., & Eimas, P. D. (1996). Peceptual organization and categorization. In C. Rovee-Collier & L. P. Lipsitt (Eds.), *Advances in infancy research:* Vol. 10, pp. 1–36. Norwood, NJ: Ablex.

Radke-Yarrow, M., & Kochanska, G. (1990). Anger in young children. In N. L. Stein, B. Leventhal, & T. Trabasso (Eds.), *Psychological and biological approaches to emotion* (pp. 297–310). Hillsdale, NJ: Erlbaum.

Radke-Yarrow, M., & Zahn-Waxler, C. (1984). Roots, motives, and patterns in children's prosocial behavior. In E. Staub, D. Bar-Tal, J. Karylowski, & J. Reykowski (Eds.), *Development and maintenance of prosocial behavior: International perspectives on positive behavior* (pp. 81–99). New York: Plenum Press.

Radziszewska, B., & Rogoff, B. (1988). Influence of adult and peer collaborators on the development of children's planning skills. *Developmental Psychology, 24,* 840–848.

Rafferty, Y., & Shinn, M. (1991). The impact of homelessness on children. *American Psychologist, 46,* 1170–1179.

Ragozin, A. S., Basham, R. B., Crnic, K. A., Greenberg, M. T., & Robinson, N. M. (1982). Effects of maternal age on parenting roles. *Developmental Psychology, 18,* 627–634.

Rakic, P. (1995). Corticogenesis in human and nonhuman primates. In M. S. Gazzaniga (Ed.), *The cognitive neurosciences* (pp. 127–145). Cambridge, MA: MIT Press.

Rakison, D. H., & Butterworth, G. (1998). Infants' use of parts in early categorization. *Developmental Psychology, 34,* 49–62.

Rakison, D. H., & Poulin-Dubois, D. (2001). The developmental origin of the animate-inanimate distinction. *Psychological Bulletin, 2,* 209–238.

Ramey, C. T., & Campbell, F. A. (1992). Poverty, early childhood education, and academic competence: The Abecedarian experiment. In A. C. Huston (Ed.), *Children in poverty: Child development and public policy.* Cambridge, England: Cambridge University Press.

Ramey, C. T., Campbell, F. A., Burchinal, M., Skinner, M. L., Gardner, D. M., & Ramey, S. L. (2000). Persistent effects of early childhood education on high-risk children and their mothers. *Applied Developmental Science, 4,* 2–14.

Ramey, C. T., Yates, K. O., & Short, E. J. (1984). The plasticity of cognitive performance: Insights from preventive intervention. *Child Development, 55,* 1913–1925.

Ratner, N., & Bruner, J. (1978). Games, social exchange and the acquisition of language. *Journal of Child Language, 5,* 391–401.

Rayner, K., & Pollatsek, A. (1989). *The psychology of reading.* Englewood Cliffs, NJ: Prentice-Hall.

Reardon, P., Bushnell, E. W. (1988). Infants' sensitivity to arbitrary pairings of color and taste. *Infant Behavior and Development, 11,* 245–250.

Reed, M. A., Pien, D. P., & Rothbart, M. K. (1984). Inhibitory self-control in preschool children. *Merrill-Palmer Quarterly, 30,* 131–147.

Reese, E., & Fivush, R. (1993). Parental styles of talking about the past. *Developmental Psychology, 29,* 596–606.

Reinisch, J. M., & Sanders, S. A. (1992). Prenatal hormonal contributions to sex differences in human cognitive and personality development. In A. A. Gerall, M. Moltz, & I. I. Ward (Eds.), *Sexual differentiation: Vol. 11. Handbook of behavioral neurobiology* (pp. 221–243). New York: Plenum Press.

Reissland, N. (1985). The development of concepts of simultaneity in children's understanding of emotions. *Journal of Child Psychology and Psychiatry, 26,* 811–824.

Rende, R., & Plomin, R. (1995). Nature, nurture, and the development of psychopathology. In D. Ciccetti & D. J. Cohen (Eds.), *Developmental psychopathology. Vol. 1. Theory and methods* (pp. 291–314). New York: Wiley.

Renken, B., Egeland, B., Marvinney, D., Sroufe, L. A., & Mangelsdorf, S. (1989). Early childhood antecedents of aggression and passive-withdrawal in early elementary school. *Journal of Personality, 57,* 257–281.

Rescorla, L. A. (1980). Overextension in early language. *Journal of Child Language, 7,* 321–335.

Rest, J. R. (1979). *Development in judging moral issues.* Minneapolis: University of Minnesota Press.

Rest, J. R. (1983). Morality. In P. Mussen (Ed.), *Handbook of child psychology. Vol. 3. Cognitive development* (pp. 556–629). New York: Wiley.

Reynolds, A. J., Mavrogenes, N. A., Bezruczko, N., & Hagemann, M. (1996). Cognitive and family-support mediators of preschool effectiveness: A confirmatory analysis. *Child Development, 67,* 1119–1140.

Rheingold, H. L. (1982). Little children's participation in the work of adults, a nascent prosocial behavior. *Child Development, 53,* 114–125.

Rheingold, H. L., & Cook, K. (1975). The contents of boys' and girls' rooms as an index of parents' behavior. *Child Development, 46,* 459–463.

Rheingold, H. R., & Eckerman, C. O. (1970). The infant separates himself from his mother. *Science, 168,* 78–90.

Ricard, M., & Allard, L. (1993). The reaction of 9- to 10-month-old infants to an unfamiliar animal. *The Journal of Genetic Psychology, 154,* 5–16.

Riccio, C. A., Hynd, G. W., Cohen, M. J., & Gonzalez, J. J. (1993). Neurological basis of attention deficit hyperactivity disorder. *Exceptional Children, 60,* 118–124.

Richards, D. D., & Siegler, R. S. (1984). The effects of task requirements on children's life judgments. *Child Development, 55,* 1687–1696.

Richards, M. H., Crowe, P. A., Larson, R., & Swarr, A. (1998). Developmental patterns and gender differences in the experience of peer companionship during adolescence. *Child Development, 69,* 154–163.

Richman, C. L., Berry, C., Bittle, M., & Himan, M. (1988). Factors related to helping behavior in preschool-age children. *Journal of Applied Developmental Psychology, 9,* 151–165.

Ridderinkhof, K. R., & Molen, M. W. (1997). Mental resources, processing speed, and inhibitory control: A developmental perspective. *Biological Psychology, 45,* 241–261.

Roberts, D. F., Foehr, U. G., Rideout, V. J., & Brodie, M. (1999). *Kids and media at the new millennium.* Menlo Park, CA: Kaiser Family Foundation.

Roberts, R. E., Phinney, J. S., Masse, L. C., Chen, Y. R., Roberts, C. R., & Romero, A. (1999). The structure of ethnic identity of young adolescents from diverse ethnocultural groups. *Journal of Early Adolescence, 19,* 301–322.

Robertson, J., & Robertson, J. (1971). *Young children in brief separation: Thomas, 2 years 4 months, in fostercare for 10 days* [Film]. London: Tavistock Institute of Human Relations.

Robertson, S. S. (1990). Temporal organization in fetal and newborn movement. In H. Bloch & B. I. Bertenthal (Eds.), *Sensory-motor organizations and development in infancy and early childhood* (pp. 105–122). Dordrecht, The Netherlands: Kluwer Academic Publishers.

Robin, D. J., Berthier, N. E., & Clifton, R. K. (1996). Infants' predictive reaching for moving objects in the dark. *Developmental Psychology, 32,* 824–835.

Robinson, C. C., & Morris, J. T. (1986). The gender-stereotyped nature of Christmas toys received by 36-, 48-, and 60-month-old children: A comparison between nonrequested vs. requested toys. *Sex Roles, 15,* 21–32.

Robinson, J. L., Kagan, J., Reznick, J. S., & Corley, R. (1992). The heritability of inhibited and uninhibited behavior: A twin study. *Developmental Psychology, 28,* 1030–1037.

Robinson, J. L., Zahn-Waxler, C., & Emde, R. N. (1994). Patterns of development in early empathic behavior: Environmental and child constitutional influences. *Social Development, 3,* 125–145.

Robinson, N. M., & Robinson, H. B. (1992). The use of standardized tests with young gifted children. In P. S. Klein & A. Tannenbaum (Eds.), *To be young and gifted* (pp. 141–170). Norwood, NJ: Ablex.

Rochat, P. (1989). Object manipulation and exploration in 2- to 5-month-old infants. *Developmental Psychology, 25,* 871–884.

Rochat, P. (1992). Self-sitting and reaching in 5- to 8-month-old infants: The impact of posture and its development on early eye-hand coordination. *Journal of Motor Behavior, 24,* 210–220.

Rochat, P., & Goubet, N. (1995). Development of sitting and reaching in 5- to 6-month-old infants. *Infant Behavior and Development, 18,* 53–68.

Rochat, P., & Morgan, R. (1995). Spatial determinants in the perception of self-produced leg movements by 3- to 5-month-old infants. *Developmental Psychology, 31,* 626–636.

Rochat, P., & Striano, T. (2002). Who's in the mirror? Self-other discrimination in specular images by four- and nine-month-old infants. *Child Development, 73,* 35–46.

Rodgers, B., Power, C., & Hope, S. (1997). Parental divorce and adult psychological distress: Evidence from a national birth cohort: A research note. *Journal of Child Psychology and Psychiatry, 38,* 867–872.

Rodkin, P. C., Farmer, T. W., Pearl, R., & Van Acker, R. (2000). Heterogeneity of popular boys: Antisocial and prosocial configurations. *Developmental Psychology, 36,* 14–24.

Rodriguez, M. L., Mischel, W., & Shoda, Y. (1989). Cognitive person variables in the delay of gratification of older children at risk. *Journal of Personality and Social Psychology, 57,* 358–367.

Roffwarg, H. P., Muzio, J. N., & Dement, W. C. (1966). Ontogenetic development of the human sleep-dream cycle. *Science, 152,* 604–619.

Rogers, F. (1996). *Dear Mr. Rogers, does it ever rain in your neighborhood? Letters to Mister Rogers.* New York: Penguin Books.

Rogoff, B. (1990). *Apprenticeship in thinking.* New York: Oxford University Press.

Rogoff, B. (1998). Cognition as a collaborative process. In W. Damon (Series Ed.), D. Kuhn & R. S. Siegler (Vol. Eds.), *Handbook of child psychology: Vol. 2. Cognition, perception, and language* (5th ed., pp. 679–744). New York: Wiley.

Rogosch, F., Cicchetti, D., & Aber, J. L. (1995). The role of child maltreatment in early deviations in cognitive and affective processing abilities and later relationship problems. *Development and Psychopathology, 7,* 591–609.

Rohner, R. P. (1975). *They love me, they love me not.* HRAF Press.

Rommetveit, R. (1985). Language acquisition as increasing linguistic structuring of experience and symbolic behavior control. In J. V. Wertsch (Ed.), *Culture, communication, and cognition: Vygotskian perspectives* (pp. 183–204). Cambridge, England: Cambridge University Press.

Roopnarine, J. L. (1986). Mothers' and fathers' behaviors toward the toy play of their infant sons and daughters. *Sex Roles, 14,* 59–68.

Roopnarine, J. L., & Hossain, Z. (1992). Parent-child interaction patterns in urban Indian families in New Delhi: Are they changing? In J. L. Roopnarine & D. B. Carter (Eds.), *Parent-child socialization in diverse cultures. Annual advances in applied developmental psychology.* (Vol. 5, pp. 1–16). Norwood, NJ: Ablex Publishing.

Roopnarine, J. L., Lu, M., & Ahmeduzzaman, M. (1989). Parental reports of early patterns of caregiving play and discipline in India and Malaysia. *Early Child Development and Care, 50,* 109–120.

Rosch, E., Mervis, C. B., Gray, W. D., Johnson, D. M. & Boyes-Braem, P. (1976). Basic objects in natural categories. *Cognitive Psychology, 8,* 382–439.

Rose, J. S., Chassin, L., Presson, C. C., & Sherman, S. J. (1999). Peer influences on adolescent cigarette smoking: A prospective sibling analysis. *Merrill-Palmer Quarterly, 45,* 62–84.

Rose, S. A., & Feldman, J. F. (1995). Prediction of IQ and specific cognitive abilities at 11 years from infancy measures. *Developmental Psychology, 31,* 531–539.

Rose, S. A., & Feldman, J. F. (1997). Memory and speed: Their role in the relation of infant information processing to later IQ. *Child Development, 68,* 630–641.

Rosen, W. D., Adamson, L. B., & Bakeman, R. (1992). An experimental investigation of infant social referencing: Mothers' messages and gender differences. *Developmental Psychology, 28,* 1172–1178.

Rosenberg, M. (1979). *Conceiving the self.* New York: Basic Books.

Rosengren, K. S., Gelman, S. A., Kalish, C. W., & McCormick, M. (1991). As time goes by: Children's early understanding of growth in animals. *Child Development, 62,* 1302–1320.

Rosengren, K. S., & Hickling, A. K. (1994). Seeing is believing: Children's explorations of commonplace, magical, and extraordinary transformations. *Child Development, 65,* 1605–1626.

Rosengren, K. S., Kalish, C. W., Hickling, A. K., and Gelman, S. A. (1994). Exploring the relation between preschool children's magical beliefs and causal thinking. *British Journal of Developmental Psychology, 12,* 69–82.

Rosenshine, B., & Meister, C. (1994). Reciprocal teaching: A review of nineteen experimental studies. *Review of Educational Research, 64,* 479–530.

Rosenstein, D., & Oster, H. (1988). Differential facial responses to four basic tastes in newborns. *Child Development, 59,* 1555–1568.

Ross, H. S., & Lollis, S. (1989). A social relations analysis of toddler peer relations. *Child Development, 60,* 1082–1091.

Rossi, A. S. (1977). A biosocial perspective on parenting. *Daedalus, 106,* 1–31.

Rotenberg, K., & Eisenberg, N. (1997). Developmental differences in the understanding of and reaction to others' inhibition of emotional expression. *Developmental Psychology, 33,* 526–537.

Rothbart, M. K., & Bates, J. E. (1998). Temperament. In W. Damon (Series Ed.) & N. Eisenberg (Vol. Ed.), *Handbook of child psychology: Vol. 3. Social, emotional, and personality development* (5th ed., pp. 105–176). New York: Wiley.

Rothbart, M. K., Ahadi, S. A., & Evans, D. E. (2000). Temperament and personality: Origins and outcomes. *Journal of Personality and Social Psychology, 78,* 122–135.

Rothbart, M. K., Derryberry, D., & Hershey, K. (1999). Stability of temperament in childhood: Laboratory infant assessment to parent report at seven years. In V. J. Molfese & D. L. Molfese (Eds.), *Temperament and personality development across the life span* (pp. 85–119). Hillsdale, NJ: Erlbaum.

Rothbaum, F., & Weisz, J. R. (1994). Parental caregiving and child externalizing behavior in nonclinical samples: A meta-analysis. *Psychological Bulletin, 116,* 55–74.

Rothbaum, F., Pott, M., Azuma, H., Miyake, K., & Weisz, J. (2000). The development of close relationships in Japan and the United States: Paths of symbiotic harmony and generative tension. *Child Development, 71,* 1121–1142.

Rotheram, M. J., & Phinney, J. S. (1987). Introduction: Definitions and perspectives in the study of children's ethnic socialization. In J. S. Phinney & M. J. Rotheram (Eds.), *Children's ethnic socialization* (pp. 10–28). Newbury Park: CA: Sage.

Rotheram-Borus, M. J., & Langabeer, K. A. (2001). Developmental trajectories of gay, lesbian, and bisexual youths. In A. R. D'Augelli, & Patterson, C. (Eds.), *Lesbian, gay and bisexual identities among youth: Psychological perspectives* (pp. 97–128). New York: Oxford University Press.

Rovee-Collier, C. (1997). Dissociations in infant memory: Rethinking the development of implicit and explicit memory. *Psychological Review, 104,* 467–498.

Rowe, D. C. (1994). *The limits of family influence: Genes, experience, and behavior.* New York: Guilford Press.

Rubenstein, A. J., Kalakanis, L., & Langlois, J. H. (1999). Infant preferences for attractive faces: A cognitive explanation. *Developmental Psychology, 35,* 848–855.

Rubin, K. H., Bukowski, W., & Parker, J. G. (1998). Peer interactions, relationships, and groups. In W. Damon (Series Ed.) & N. Eisenberg (Vol. Ed.), *Handbook of Child Psychology: Vol. 3. Social, emotional, and personality development* (5th ed.). New York: Wiley.

Rubin, K. H., Chen, X., McDougall, P., Bowker, A.,& McKinnon, J. (1995). The Waterloo Longitudinal Project: Predicting internalizing and externalizing problems in adolescence. *Development and Psychopathology, 7,* 751–764.

Rubin, K. H., Lynch, D., Coplan, R., Rose-Krasnor, L., & Booth, C. L. (1994). "Birds of a feather...": Behavioral concordances and preferential personal attraction in children. *Child Development, 65,* 1778–1785.

Rubin, K. H., Nelson, L. J., Hastings, P., & Asendorpf, J. (1999). The transaction between parents' perceptions of their children's shyness and their parenting styles. *International Journal of Behavioral Development, 23,* 937–957.

Ruble, D. N., & Flett, G. L. (1988). Conflicting goals in self-evaluative information seeking: Developmental and ability level analyses. *Child Development, 59,* 97–106.

Ruble, D. N., & Frey, K. S. (1991). Changing patterns of comparative behavior as skills are acquired: A functional model of self-evaluation. In J. Suls & T. A. Wills (Eds.), *Social comparison: Contemporary theory and research* (pp. 70–112). Hillsdale, NJ: Erlbaum.

Ruble, D. N., Grosovsky, E. H., Frey, K. S., & Cohen, R. (1992). Developmental changes in competence assessment. In A. K. Boggiano & T. S. Pittman (Eds.), *Achievement and motivation: A social developmental perspective.* New York: Cambridge University Press.

Ruble, D. N., & Martin, C. L. (1998). Gender development. In N. Eisenberg (Ed.), *Handbook of child psychology: Vol. 3, Social emotional, and personality development* (5th ed., pp. 933–1016.). New York: Wiley.

Rudolph, K. D., Dennig, M. D., & Weisz, J. R. (1995). Determinants and consequences of children's coping in the medical setting: Conceptualization, review, and critique. *Psychological Bulletin, 118,* 328–357.

Rueter, M. A., & Conger, R. D. (1998). Reciprocal influences between parenting and adolescent problem-solving behavior. *Developmental Psychology, 34,* 1470–1482.

Ruff, H. A. (1986). Components of attention during infants' manipulative exploration. *Child Development, 57,* 105–114.

Ruffman, T., Perner, J., Naito, M., Parkin, L., & Clements, W. A. (1998). Older (but not younger) siblings facilitate false belief understanding. *Developmental Psychology, 34,* 161–174.

Rumelhardt, D. E., & McClelland, J. L. (1986). On learning the past tense of English verbs. In J. L. McClelland, D. E. Rumelhardt, & the PDP Research Group (Eds.), *Parallel distributed processing: Explorations in the microstructure of cognition: Vol. 2. Psychological and biological models.* Cambridge, MA: Bradford Books/MIT Press.

Rushton, J. P. (1975). Generosity in children: Immediate and long term effects of modeling, preaching, and moral judgment. *Journal of Personality and Social Psychology, 31,* 459–466.

Rushton, J. P., Fulker, D. W., Neale, M. C., Nias, D. K. B., & Eysenck, H. J. (1986). Altruism and aggression: The heritability of individual differences. *Journal of Personality and Social Psychology, 50,* 1192–1198.

Russell, A., & Finnie, V. (1990). Preschool children's social status and maternal instructions to assist group entry. *Developmental Psychology, 26,* 603–611.

Russell, A., Pettit, G. S., & Mize, J. (1998). Horizontal qualities in parent-child relationships: Parallels with and possible consequences for children's peer relationships. *Developmental Review, 18,* 313–352.

Russell, G,. & Russell, A. (1987). Mother-child and father-child relationships in middle childhood. *Child Development, 58,* 1573–1585.

Russell, J. A., & Bullock, M. (1986). On dimensions preschoolers use to interpret facial expressions of emotion. *Developmental Psychology, 22,* 97–102.

Rutter, M. (1979). Protective factors in children's responses to stress and disadvantage. In M. W. Kent & J. E. Rolf (Eds.), *Primary prevention of psychopathology: Social competence in children* (Vol. 3). Hanover: University of New England.

Rutter, M. (1987). Psychosocial resilience and protective mechanisms. *American Journal of Orthopsychiatry, 57,* 316–331.

Rutter, M., & The English and Romanian Adoptees Study Team. (1998). Developmental catch-up, and deficit, following adoption after severe global early privation. *Journal of Child Psychology and Psychiatry, 39,* 465–476.

Rymer, R. (1993). *Genie: An abused child's flight from silence.* New York: HarperCollins.

Saarni, C. (1979). Children's understanding of display rules for expressive behavior. *Developmental Psychology, 15,* 424–429.

Saarni, C. (1984). An observational study of children's attempts to monitor their expressive behavior. *Child Development, 55,* 1504–1513.

Saarni, C. (1990). Emotional competence: How emotions and relationships become integrated. In R. A. Thompson (Ed.), *Socioemotional development* (pp. 115–182). Lincoln, NE: University of Nebraska Press.

Saarni, C., Mumme, D. L., & Campos, J. J. (1998). Emotional development: Action, communication, and understanding. In W. Damon (Series Ed.) & N. Eisenberg (Vol. Ed.), *Handbook of child psychology: Vol. 3. Social, emotional, and personality development* (5th ed., pp. 237–309). New York: Wiley.

Saarnio, D. A., Oka, E. R., & Paris, S. G. (1990). Developmental predictors of children's reading comprehension. In T. H. Carr & B. A. Levy (Eds.), *Reading comprehension difficulties: Processes and intervention.* Mahwah, NJ: Erlbaum.

Sabongui, A. G., Bukowski, W. M., & Newcomb, A. F. (1998?). The peer ecology of popularity: The network embeddedness of a child's friend predicts the child's subsequent popularity. *New Directions in Child Development*, 83–91.

Sachs, J., & Devin, J. (1976). Young children's use of age appropriate speech styles in social interaction and role-playing. *Journal of Child Language, 3,* 81–98.

Sadker, M., & Sadker, D. (1994). *Failing at fairness: How America's schools cheat girls.* New York: Scribner.

Saffran, J. R., Aslin, R. N., & Newport, E. L. (1996). Statistical learning by 8-month-old infants. *Science, 274,* 1926–1928.

Saffran, J. R., Johnson, E. K., Aslin, R. N., & Newport, E. L. (1999). Statistical learning of tone sequences by human infants and adults. *Cognition, 70,* 27–52.

Sakurai, S. (1983). Development of the Japanese version of Harter's Perceived Competence Scale for Children. *Japanese Journal of Educational Psychology, 31,* 245–249.

Salapatek, P., & Kessen, W. (1966). Visual scanning of triangles by the human newborn. *Journal of Experimental Child Psychology, 3,* 155–167.

Salzinger, S., Feldman, R. S., Ng-Mak, D. S., Mojica, E., & Stockhammer, T. F. (2001). The effect of physical abuse on children's social and affective status: A model of cognitive and behavioral processes explaining the association. *Developmental and Psychopathology, 13,* 805–825.

Samaniego, R. Y., & Gonzales, N. A. (1999). Multiple mediators of the effects of acculturation status on delinquency for Mexican American adolescents. *American Journal of Community Psychology, 27,* 189–210.

Sameroff, A. J. (1986). Environmental context of child development. *Journal of Pediatrics, 109,* 102–200.

Sameroff, A. J., & Chandler, M. J. (1975). Reproductive risk and the continuum of caretaking casualty. In F. Horowitz (Ed.), *Review of child development research* (Vol. 4). Chicago: University of Chicago Press.

Sameroff, A. J., Seifer, R., Baldwin, A., & Baldwin, C. (1993). Stability of intelligence from preschool to adolescence: The influence of social and family risk factors. *Child Development, 64,* 80–97.

Sameroff, A. J., Seifer, R., Zax, M., & Barocas, R. (1987). Early indicators of developmental risk: The Rochester Longitudinal Study. *Schizophrenia Bulletin, 13,* 383–394.

Sampa, A. (1997). Street children of Lusaka: "A case of the Zambia Red Cross drop-in centre." *Journal of Psychology in Africa; South of the Sahara, the Caribbean and Afro-Latin-America, 2,* 1–23.

Sampson, R. J., & Laub, J. H. (1994). Urban poverty and the family context of delinquency: A new look at structure and process in a classic study. *Child Development, 65,* 523–540.

Sandman, C. A., Wadhwa, P., Hetrick, W., Porto, M., & Peeke, H. V. S. (1997). Human fetal heart rate dishabituation between thirty and thirty-two weeks gestation. *Child Development, 68,* 1031–1040.

Santrock, John. (1998). *Child development.* New York: McGraw-Hill.

Saudino, K. J., & Eaton, W. O. (1991). Infant temperament and genetics: An objective twin study of motor activity level. *Child Development, 62,* 1167–1174.

Saudino, K., McGuire, S., Reiss, D., Hetherington, E. M., & Plomin, R. (1995). Parent ratings of EAS temperaments in twins, full siblings, half siblings, and step siblings. *Journal of Personality and Social Psychology, 68,* 723–733.

Savage-Rumbaugh, E. S., Murphy, J., Sevcik, R. A., Brakke, K. E., Williams, S. L., & Rumbaugh, D. M. (1993). Language comprehension in ape and child. *Monographs of the Society for Research in Child Development, 58*(3–4, Serial No. 233).

Savin-Williams, R. C. (1994). Verbal and physical abuse as stressors in the lives of lesbian, gay male, and bisexual youths: Associations with school problems, running away, substance abuse, prostitution, and suicide. *Journal of Consulting and Clinical Psychology, 62,* 261–269.

Savin-Williams, R. C. (1996) Self-labeling and disclosure among gay, lesbian, and bisexual youths. In J. Laird & R-J. Green (Eds)., *Lesbians and gays in couples and families* (pp. 153–182). San Francisco: Jossey-Bass.

Savin-Williams, R. C. (1998a). *". . . And then I became gay": Young men's stories.* New York: Routledge.

Savin-Williams, R. C. (1998b). The disclosure to families of same-sex attractions by lesbian, gay, and bisexual youths. *Journal of Research on Adolescence, 8,* 49–68.

Savin-Williams, R. C. (2001). *Mom, Dad, I'm gay: How families negotiate coming out.* Washington, DC: American Psychological Association Press.

Savin-Williams, R. C., & Diamond, L. M. (2000). Sexual identity trajectories among sexual-minority youths: Gender comparisons. *Archives of Sexual Behavior, 29,* 419–440.

Saxe, G. B., Guberman, S. R., & Gearhart, M. (1987). Social processes in early number development. *Monographs of the Society for Research in Child Development, 52*(2, Serial No. 216).

Scaife, M., & Bruner, J. S. (1975). The capacity for joint visual attention in the infant. *Nature, 253,* 265–266.

Scaramella, L. V., Conger, R. D., Simons, R. L., & Whitbeck, L. B. (1998). Predicting risk for pregnancy by late adolescence: A social contextual perspective. *Developmental Psychology, 34,* 1233–1245.

Scaramella, L. V., Conger, R. D., Spoth, R., & Simons, R. L. (2002). Evaluation of a social contextual model of delinquency: A cross-study replication. *Child Development, 73,* 175–195.

Scarborough, H. S., & Dobrich, W. (1994). On the efficacy of reading to preschoolers. *Development Review, 14,* 245–302.

Scardamalia, M., & Bereiter, C. (1984). Written composition. In M. Wittrock, (Ed.), *Handbook of research on teaching* (3rd ed.). New York: Macmillan.

Scarr, S. (1992). Developmental theories for the 1990s: Development and individual differences. *Child Development, 63,* 1–19.

Scarr, S. (1998). American child care today. *American Psychologist, 53,* 95–108.

Scarr, S., & McCartney, K. (1983). How people make their own environments: A theory of genotype-environment effects. *Child Development, 54,* 424–435.

Scarr, S., & Salapatek, P. (1970). Patterns of fear development during infancy. *Merrill-Palmer Quarterly, 16,* 53–90.

Scarr, S., & Weinberg, R. A. (1976). I. Q. test performance of black children adopted by white families. *American Psychologist, 31,* 726–739.

Scarr, S., & Weinberg, R. A. (1983). The Minnesota Adoption Studies: Genetic differences and malleability. *Child Development, 54,* 260–267.

Schaal, B., Orgeur, P., & Rognon, C. (1995). Odor sensing in the human fetus: Anatomical, functional, and chemoecological bases. In J. P. Lecanuet, W. P. Fifer, N. A. Krasnegor, & W. P. Smotherman (Eds.), *Fetal development: A psychobiological perspective.* Hillsdale, NJ: Erlbaum.

Schauble, L. (1996). The development of scientific reasoning in knowledge-rich contexts. *Developmental Psychology, 32,* 102–119.

Schellenberg, E. G., & Trehub, S. E. (1996). Natural musical intervals: Evidence from infant listeners. *Psychological Science, 7,* 272–277.

Scheper-Hughes, N. (1992). *Death without weeping: The violence of everyday life in Brazil.* Los Angeles: University of California Press.

Schieffelin, B. B., & Ochs, E. (1987). *Language socialization across cultures.* New York: Cambridge University Press.

Schmuckler, M. A. (1996). Visual-proprioceptive intermodal perception in infancy. *Infant Behavior and Development, 19,* 221–232.

Schneider, B. H., Atkinson, L., & Tardif, C. (2001). Child-parent attachment and children's peer relations: A quantitative review. *Developmental Psychology, 37,* 86–100.

Schneider, M. S. (2001). Toward a reconceptualization of the coming-out process for adolescent females. In A. R. D'Augelli & C. Patterson (Eds.), *Lesbian, gay and bisexual identities among youth: Psychological perspectives* (pp. 71–96). New York: Oxford University Press.

Schneider, W. (1998). Performance prediction in young children: Effects of skill, metacognition and wishful thinking. *Developmental Science, 1,* 291–297.

Schneider, W., Korkel, J., & Weinert, F. E. (1989). Domain-specific knowledge and memory performance: A comparison of high- and low-aptitude children. *Journal of Educational Psychology, 81,* 306–312.

Schneider, W., & Pressley, M. (1997). *Memory development between 2 and 20* (2nd ed). New York: Springer-Verlag.

Schoeber-Peterson, D., & Johnson, C. J. (1991). Non-dialogue speech during preschool interactions. *Journal of Child Language, 18,* 153–170.

Scholl, B. J., & Leslie, A. M. (1999). Modularity, development and 'theory of mind.' *Mind & Language, 14,* 131–153.

Scholnick, E. K., Friedman, S. L., & Wallner-Allen, K. E. (1997). What do they really mean? A comparative analysis of planning tasks. In S. L. Friedman & E. K. Scholnick (Eds.), *The developmental psychology of planning: Why, how, and when do we plan?* (pp. 127–156). Mahwah, NJ: Erlbaum.

Schulenberg J., Maggs, J. L., Dielman, T. E., Leech, S. L., Kloska, D. D., Shope, J. T., & Laetz, V. B. (1999). On peer influences to get drunk: A panel study of young adolescents. *Merrill-Palmer Quarterly, 45,* 108–142.

Schult, C. A., & Wellman, H. M. (1997). Explaining human movements and actions. *Cognition, 62,* 291–324.

Schwartz, D., McFadyen-Ketchum, S. A., Dodge, K. A., Pettit, G. S., & Bates, J. E. (1998). Peer group victimization as a predictor of children's behavior problems at home and in school. *Development and Psychopathology, 10,* 87–99.

Schwartz, D., McFadyen-Ketchum, S., Dodge, K. A., Pettit, G. S., & Bates, J. E. (1999). Early behavior problems as a predictor of later peer group victimization: Moderators and mediators in the pathways of social risk. *Journal of Abnormal Child Psychology, 27,*191–201.

Schwartz, S., & Johnson, J. J. (1985). *Psychopathology of childhood.* New York: Pergamon.

Sedlak, A. J., & Broadhurst, D. D. (1996, September). Executive summary of the third national incidence study of child abuse and neglect. National Clearinghouse on Child Abuse and Neglect Information. U.S. Department of Health and Human Services. Retrieved from: http://www.calib.com/nccanch/pubs/statinfo/nis3.cfm.

Seidman, E., Allen, L., Aber, J. L., Mitchell, C., & Feinman, J. (1994). The impact of school transitions in early adolescence on the self-system and perceived social context of poor urban youth. *Child Development 65,* 507–522.

Seifer, R., Sameroff, A. J., Barrett, L. C., & Krafchuk, E. (1994). Infant temperament measured by multiple observations and mother report. *Child Development, 65,* 1478–1490.

Seifer, R., Schiller, M., Sameroff, A. J., Resnick, S., & Riordan, K. (1996). Attachment, maternal sensitivity, and infant temperament during the first year of life. *Developmental Psychology, 32,* 12–25.

Selfe, L. (1995). Nadia reconsidered. In C. Golomb (Ed.), *The development of artistically gifted children: Selected case studies* (pp. 197–236). Hillsdale, NJ: Erlbaum.

Selman, R. L. (1980). *The growth of interpersonal understanding: Developmental and clinical analysis.* New York: Academic Press.

Senghas, A., & Coppola, M. (2001). Children creating language: How Nicaraguan sign language acquired a spatial grammar. *Psychological Science, 12,* 323–328.

Serbin, L. A., Moller, L. C., Gulko, J., Powlishta, K. K., & Colburne, K. A. (1994). The emergence of gender segregation in toddler playgroups. In C. Leaper (Ed.), *Childhood gender segregation: Causes and consequences. New directions for child development,* (Vol. 65, pp. 7–17). San Francisco, CA: Jossey-Bass.

Serbin, L. A., Powlishta, K. K., & Gulko, J. (1993). The development of sex typing in middle childhood. *Monographs of the Society for Research in Child Development, 58*(2, Serial No. 232).

Serbin, L. A., Tonick, I. J., & Sternglanz, S. H. (1977). Shaping cooperative cross-sex play. *Child Development, 48,* 924–929.

Serrano, J. M., Iglesias, J., & Loeches, A. (1993). Visual discrimination and recognition of facial expressions of anger, fear and surprise in four- to six-month-old infants. *Developmental Psychobiology, 25,* 411–425.

Seyfarth, R. M., & Cheney, D. L. (1993). Meaning, reference, and intentionality in the natural vocalizations of monkeys. In H. L. Roitblat, L. M. Herman, & P. E. Nachtigall (Eds.), *Language and communication: Comparative perspectives* (pp. 195–220). Hillsdale, NJ: Erlbaum.

Shahinfar, A., Kupersmidt, J. B., & Matza, L. S. (2001). The relation between exposure to violence and social information processing among incarcerated adolescents. *Journal of Abnormal Psychology, 110,* 136–141.

Shankweiler, D., Crain, S., Katz, L., Fowler, A. E., Liberman, A. M., Brady, S. A., et al. (1995). Cognitive profiles of reading-disabled children: Comparison of language skills in phonology, morphology, and syntax. *Psychological Science, 6*, 149–156.

Shantz, C. U. (1987). Conflicts between children. *Child Development, 58*, 283–305.

Shapiro, L. R., & Hudson, J. A. (1991). Tell me a make-believe story: Coherence and cohesion in young children's picture-elicited narratives. *Developmental Psychology, 27*, 960–974.

Shatz, M., & Gelman, R. (1973). The development of communication skills: Modifications in the speech of young children as a function of listener. *Monographs of the Society for Research in Child Development, 38*, 1–37.

Shaywitz, B. A., Shaywitz, S. E., Pugh, K. R., Constable, R., Skudlarski, P., Fulbright, R. K. (1995). Sex differences in the functional organization of the brain for language. *Nature, 373*, 607–609.

Shaywitz, S. E., Shaywitz, B. A., Pubh, K. R., Fulbright, R. K., Constable, R. T., Mencl, W. E., Shankweiler, D. P., Liberman, A. M., Skudlarski, P., Fletcher, J. M., Katz, L., Marchione, K. E., Lacadie, C., Gatenby, C., & Gore, J. C. (1998). Functional disruption in the organization of the brain for reading in dyslexia. *Proceedings of the National Academy of Science USA, 95*, 2636–2641.

Shell, R., & Eisenberg, N. (1990). The role of peers' gender in children's naturally occurring interest in toys. *International Journal of Behavioral Development, 13*, 373–388.

Shiller, V., Izard, C. E., & Hembref, E. A. (1986). Patterns of emotion expression during separation in the Strange Situation. *Developmental Psychology, 22*, 378–382.

Shinn, M., Knickman, J. R., & Weitzman, B. C. (1991). Social relationships and vulnerability to becoming homeless among poor families. *American Psychologist, 46*, 1180 1187.

Shoda, Y., Mischel, W., & Peake, P. K. (1990). Predicting adolescent cognitive and self-regulatory competencies from preschool delay of gratification: Identifying diagnostic conditions. *Journal of Personality and Social Psychology, 26*, 978–986.

Shrager, J., & Siegler, R. S. (1998). SCADS: A model of children's strategy choices and strategy discoveries. *Psychological Science, 9*, 405–410.

Shrum, W., & Cheek, N. H. (1987). Social structure during the school years: Onset of the degrouping process. *American Sociological Review, 52*, 218–223.

Shulman, S., Eliker, J., & Sroufe, L. A. (1994). Stages of friendship growth in preadolescence as related to attachment history. *Journal of Social and Personal Relationships, 11*, 341–361.

Shultz, T. R., Schmidt, W. C., Buckingham, D., & Mareschal, D. (1995). Modeling cognitive development with a generative connectionist algorithm. In T. Simon & G. Halford (Eds.), *Developing cognitive competence: New approaches to process modeling*. Hillsdale, NJ: Erlbaum.

Shweder, R. A., Balle-Jensen, L., & Goldstein, W. (1995). Who sleeps by whom revisited: A method for extracting the moral goods implicit in praxis. In J. J. Goodnow, P. J. Miller, & F. Kessell (Eds.), *Cultural practices as contexts for development: New directions for child development*. San Francisco: Jossey-Bass.

Shweder, R. A., Mahapatra, M., & Miller, J. G. (1987). Culture and moral development. In J. Kagan & S. Lamb (Eds.), *The emergence of morality in young children* (pp. 1–83). Chicago: University of Chicago Press.

Siegal, M. (1991). *Knowing children: Experiments in conversation and cognition*. Hove, England: Erlbaum.

Siegel, L. S. (1984). Home environment influences on cognitive development in preterm and full-term children during the first 5 years. In A. W. Gottfried (Ed.), *Home environment and early cognitive development*. New York: Academic Press.

Siegel, L. S. (1993). The cognitive basis of dyslexia. In R. Pasnak & M. L. Howe (Eds.), *Emerging themes in cognitive development: Vol. 2. Competencies*. New York: Springer-Verlag.

Siegel, L.S. (1985). A risk index to predict learning problems in preterm and fullterm children. In W. K. Frankenburg, R. N. Emde, & J. W. Sullivan (Eds.), *Early identification of children at-risk: An international perspective* (pp. 231–244). New York: Plenum Press.

Siegler, R. S. (1976). The effects of simple necessity and sufficiency relationships on children's causal inferences. *Child Development, 47*, 1058–1063.

Siegler, R. S. (1981). Developmental sequences within and between concepts. *Society for Research in Child Development Monographs, 46*(2, Serial No. 189).

Siegler, R. S. (1986). Unities in strategy choices across domains. In M. Perlmutter (Ed.), *Minnesota symposium on child psychology*, (Vol. 19). Mahwah, NJ: Erlbaum, 1–48.

Siegler, R. S. (1987a). Strategy choices in subtraction. In J. Sloboda and D. Rogers (Eds.), *Cognitive process in mathematics* (pp. 81–106). Oxford: Oxford University Press.

Siegler, R. S. (1987b). The perils of averaging data over strategies: An example from children's addition. *Journal of Experimental Psychology: General, 116*(3), 250–264.

Siegler, R. S. (1988a). Individual differences in strategy choices: Good students, not-so-good students, and perfectionists. *Child Development, 59*, 833–851.

Siegler, R. S. (1988b). Strategy choice procedures and the development of multiplication skill. *Journal of Experimental Psychology: General, 117*, 258–275.

Siegler, R. S. (1994). Cognitive variability: A key to understanding cognitive development. *Current Directions in Psychological Science, 3*, 1–5.

Siegler, R. S. (1995). How does change occur: A microgenetic study of number conservation. *Cognitive Psychology, 28*, 225–273.

Siegler, R. S. (1996). *Emerging minds: The process of change in children's thinking*. New York: Oxford University Press.

Siegler, R. S. (2000). The rebirth of children's learning. *Child Development, 71*, 26–35.

Siegler, R. S., & Jenkins, E. A. (1989). *How children discover new strategies*. Hillsdale, NJ: Erlbaum.

Siegler, R. S., & McGilly, K. (1989). Strategy choices in children's time-telling. In I. Levin and D. Zakay (Eds.) *Time and human cognition: A life span perspective*, (pp. 185–218). The Netherlands: Elsevier Science Publishers.

Siegler, R. S., & Robinson, M. (1982). The development of numerical understandings. In H. W. Reese & L. P. Lipsitt (Eds.), *Advances in child development and behavior* (Vol. 16). New York: Academic Press.

Siegler, R. S., & Shrager, J. (1984). Strategy choices in addition and subtraction: How do children know what to do? In C. Sophian (Ed.), *The origins of cognitive skills* (pp. 229–293). Mahwah, NJ: Erlbaum.

Sigman, M. (1995). Nutrition and child development: More food for thought. *Current Directions in Psychological Science, 4,* 52–55.

Sigman, M., Cohen, S. E., & Beckwith, L. (1997). Why does infant attention predict adolescent intelligence? *Infant Behavior and Development, 20,* 133–140.

Signorella, M. L., Bigler, R. S., & Liben, L. S. (1997). A meta-analysis of children's memories for own-sex and other-sex information. *Journal of Applied Developmental Psychology, 18,* 429–445.

Signorielli, N. (1993). Television, the portrayal of women, and children's attitudes. In G. Berry & J. K. Asmen (Eds.), *Children and television: Images in a changing sociocultural world.* Newbury Park, CA: Sage.

Signorielli, N. & Lears, M. (1992). Children, television, and conceptions about chores: Attitudes and behaviors. *Sex Roles, 27,* 157–170.

Signorielli, N., McLeod, D., & Healy, E. (1994, winter). Gender stereotypes in MTV commercials: The beat goes on. *Journal of Broadcasting & Electronic Media, 38,* 91–101.

Silver, L. B. (1992). *Attention-deficit hyperactivity disorder.* Washington, DC: American Psychiatric Association.

Silverman, W. K., La Greca, A. M., & Wasserstein, S. (1995). What do children worry about? Worries and their relation to anxiety. *Child Development, 66,* 671–686.

Simion, F., Valenza, E., Umilta, C., & Barba, B. D. (1998). Preferential orienting to faces in newborns: A temporal-nasal asymmetry. *Journal of Experimental Psychology: Human Perception and Performance, 24,* 1399–1405.

Simmons, R. G., & Blyth, D. A. (1987). *Moving into adolescence: The impact of pubertal change and school context.* Hawthorne, NY: de Gruyter.

Simon, T. J. (1997). Reconceptualizing the origins of number knowledge: A "non-numerical" account. *Cognitive Development, 12,* 349–372.

Simon, T. J., Hespos, S. J., & Rochat, P. (1995). Do infants understand simple arithmetic: A replication of Wynn (1992). *Cognitive Development, 10,* 253–269.

Simons, R. L., & Associates (Eds.). (1996). *Understanding differences between divorced and intact families: Stress, interaction, and child outcome* (pp. 81–93). Thousand Oaks, CA: Sage.

Simons, R. L., & Johnson, C. (1996). Mother's parenting. In R. L. Simons & Associates (Eds.), *Understanding differences between divorced and intact families: Stress, interaction, and child outcome* (pp. 81–93). Thousand Oaks, CA: Sage.

Simonton, D. K. (1991). Emergence and realization of genius: The lives and works of 120 classical composers. *Journal of Personality and Social Psychology, 61,* 829–840.

Simpkins, S. D., & Parke, R. D. (2001). The relations of parental friendships and children's friendships: Self-report and observational analysis. *Child Development, 72,* 569–582.

Simpson, E. L. (1974). Moral development research: A case study of scientific cultural bias. *Human Development, 17,* 81–106.

Singer, J. L., & Singer, D. G. (1981). *Television, imagination, and aggression: A study of preschoolers.* Mahwah, NJ: Erlbaum.

Singleton, J. L., & Newport, E. L. (in press). When learners surpass their models: The acquisition of American Sign Language from inconsistent input. *Cognitive Psychology.*

Sippola, L. K., Bukowski, W. M., & Noll, R. B. (1997). Dimensions of liking and disliking underlying the same-sex preference in childhood and early adolescence. *Merrill-Palmer Quarterly, 43,* 591–609.

Sippola, L. K., Bukowski, W. M., & Noll, R. B., (1997). Dimensions of liking and disliking underlying the same-sex preference in childhood and early adolescence. *Merrill-Palmer Quarterly, 43,* 591–609.

Siqueland, E. R., & DeLucia, C. A. (1969). Visual reinforcement of non-nutritive sucking in human infants. *Science, 165,* 1144–1146.

Siqueland, E. R., & Lipsitt, L. P. (1966). Conditioned head-turning in the human newborn. *Journal of Experimental Child Psychology, 3,* 356–376.

Skinner, B. F. (1953). *Science and human behavior.* New York: Macmillan.

Skinner, B. F. (1971). *Beyond freedom and dignity.* New York: Bantam.

Skinner, E. A. (1985). Determinants of mother-sensitive and contingent-responsive behavior: The role of childbearing beliefs and socioeconomic status. In I. E. Sigel (Ed.), *Parental belief systems: The psychological consequences for children* (pp. 51–82). Hillsdale, NJ: Erlbaum.

Skinner, E. A., Zimmer-Gembeck, M. J., & Connell, J. P. (1998). Individual differences and the development of perceived control. *Monographs of the Society for Research in Child Development, 63*(2-3, Serial No. 254).

Skoe, E. E. A. (1998). The ethic of care: Issues in moral development. In E. E. A. Skoe, & A. L. von der Lippe (Eds.), *Personality development in adolescence: A cross national and life span perspective* (pp. 143–171). London: Routledge.

Slaby, R. G., & Frey, K. S. (1975). Development of gender constancy and selective attention to same-sex models. *Child Development, 46,* 849–856.

Slaby, R. G., & Guerra, N. G. (1988). Cognitive mediators of aggression in adolescent offenders: Assessment. *Developmental Psychology, 24,* 580–588.

Slater, A. M., Bremner, G., Johnson, S. P., Sherwood, P., Hayes, R., & Brown, E. (2000). Newborn infants' preference for attractive faces: The role of internal and external facial features. *Infancy, 1,* 265–274.

Slater, A. M., Johnson, S. P., Brown, E., & Badenoch, M. (1996). Newborn infants' perception of partly occluded objects. *Infant Behavior and Development, 19,* 145–148.

Slater, A. M., Mattock, A., & Brown, E. (1990). Size constancy at birth: Newborn infants' responses to retinal and real size. *Journal of Experimental Child Psychology, 49,* 314–322.

Slater, A. M., & Morison, V. (1985). Shape constancy and slant perception at birth. *Perception, 14,* 337–344.

Slater, A. M., Rose, D., & Morison, V. (1984). New-born infants' perception of similarities and differences between two- and three-dimensional stimuli. *British Journal of Developmental Psychology, 2,* 287–294.

Slater, A. M., Von der Schulenburg, C., Brown, E., Badenoch, M., Butterworth, G., Parsons, S., & Samuels, C. (1998). Newborn infants prefer attractive faces. *Infant Behavior and Development, 21,* 345–354.

Slaughter, V., Jaakkola, R., & Carey, S. (1999). Constructing a coherent theory: Children's biological understanding of life and death. In M. Siegal & C. C. Peterson (Eds.), *Children's understanding of biology and health* (pp. 71–96). Cambridge, England: Cambridge University Press.

Slobin, D. I. (Ed.). (1985). *The crosslinguistic study of language acquisition* (Vols. 1–2). Hillsdale, NJ: Erlbaum.

Slomkowski, C., Rende, R., Conger, K. J., Simons, R. L., & Conger, R. D. (2001). Sisters, brothers, and delinquency: Evaluating social influence during early and middle adolescence. *Child Development, 72,* 271–283.

Slutske, W. S., Heath, A. C., Dinwiddie, S. H., Madden, P. A. F., Bucholz, K. K., Dunne, M. P., Statham, D. J., & Martin, N. G. (1997). Modeling genetic and environmental influences in the etiology of conduct disorder: A study of 2,682 adult twin pairs. *Journal of Abnormal Psychology, 106,* 266–279.

Smetana, J. G. (1988). Adolescents' and parents' conceptions of parental authority. *Child Development, 59*, 321–335.

Smetana, J. G. (1995). Context, conflict, and constraint in adolescent-parent authority relationships. In M. Killen & D. Hart (Eds.), *Morality in everyday life: Developmental perspectives* (pp. 225–255). Cambridge, England: Cambridge University Press.

Smetana, J. G., & Asquith, P. (1994). Adolescents' and parents' conceptions of parental authority and personal autonomy. *Child Development, 65*, 1147–1162.

Smetana, J. G., & Braeges, J. L. (1990). The development of toddlers' moral and conventional judgments. *Merrill-Palmer Quarterly, 36*, 329–346.

Smith, B. A., & Blass, E. M. (1996). Taste-mediated calming in premature, preterm, and full-term human infants. *Developmental Psychology, 32*, 1084–1089.

Smith, L. B. (1999). Do infants possess innate knowledge structures? The con side. *Developmental Science, 2*, 133–144.

Smith, L. B., Jones, S., & Landau, B. (1992). Count nouns, adjectives and perceptual properties in novel word interpretations. *Developmental Psychology, 28*, 273–288.

Smith, L. B., Thelen, E., Titzer, R., & McLin, D. (1999). Knowing in the context of acting: The task dynamics of the A-not-B error. *Psychological Review, 106*, 235–260.

Smith, M., & Walden, T. (1998). Developmental trends in emotion understanding among a diverse sample of African-American preschool children. *Journal of Applied Developmental Psychology, 19*, 177–197.

Smith, M., & Walden, T. (1999). Understanding feelings and coping with emotional situations: A comparison of maltreated and nonmaltreated preschoolers. *Social Development, 8*, 93–116.

Smotherman, W. P., & Robinson, S. R. (1987). Psychobiology of fetal experience in the rat. In N. A. Krasnegor, E. M. Blass, M. A. Hofer, & W. P. Smotherman (Eds.), *Perinatal development: A psychobiological perspective* (pp. 39–60). Orlando, FL: Academic Press.

Snarey, J. R. (1985). Cross-cultural universality of socio-moral development: A critical review of Kohlbergian review. *Psychological Bulletin, 97*, 202–232.

Snow, C. (1999). Social perspectives on the emergence of language. In B. MacWhinney (Ed.), *The emergence of language* (pp. 257–276). Mahwah, NJ: Erlbaum.

Snow, C. E. (1990). Building memories: The ontogeny of autobiography. In D. Cicchetti & M. Beeghly (Eds.), *The self in transition: Infancy to childhood* (pp. 213–242). Chicago: University of Chicago Press.

Snow, M. E., Jacklin, C. N., & Maccoby, E. E. (1983). Sex-of-child differences in father-child interaction at one year of age. *Child Development, 54*, 227–232.

Snyder, H. N. (1999). *Juvenile Justice Bulletin: Juvenile arrests 1998*. Washington, DC: Office of Juvenile Justice and Delinquency Prevention.

Snyder, J. J., & Patterson, G. R. (1995). Individual differences in social aggression: A test of a reinforcement model of socialization in the natural environment. *Behavior Therapy, 26*, 371–391.

Society for Research in Child Development. (1999). *Directory of members, 1999–2000*. Ann Arbor, MI: Author.

Soken, N. H., & Pick, A. D. (1992). Intermodal perception of happy and angry expressive behaviors by seven-month-old infants. *Child Development, 63*, 787–795.

Solomon, D., Battistich, V., & Watson, M. (1993, March). *A longitudinal investigation of the effects of a school intervention program on children's social development*. Paper presented at the biennial meeting of the Society for Research in Child Development. New Orleans, LA.

Solomon, D., Battistich, V., Watson, M., Schaps, E., & Lewis, C. (2000). A six-district study of educational change: Direct and mediated effects of the child development project. *Social Psychology of Education, 4*, 3–51.

Solomon, D., Watson, M. S., Delucchi, K. L., Schaps, E., & Battistich, V. (1988). Enhancing children's prosocial behavior in the classroom. *American Educational Research Journal, 25*, 527–554.

Solomon, J., & George, C. (1999). The measurement of attachment security in infancy and childhood. In J. Cassidy & P. R. Shaver (Eds.), *Handbook of attachment: Theory, research, and clinical applications* (pp. 287–316). New York: Guilford Press.

Sophian, C., & Yengo, L. (1985). Infants' search for visible objects: Implications for the interpretation of early search errors. *Journal of Experimental Child Psychology, 40*, 260–278.

Sophie, J. (1985–1986). A critical examination of stage theories of lesbian identity development. *Journal of Homosexuality, 12*, 39–51.

Sorce, J. F., Emde, R. N., Campos, J. J., & Klinnert, M. D. (1985). Maternal emotional signaling: Its effect on the visual cliff behavior of 1-year-olds. *Developmental Psychology, 21*, 195–200.

Spearman, C. (1927). *The abilities of man: Their nature and measurement*. New York: Macmillan.

Spelke, E. S. (1976). Infants' intermodal perception of events. *Cognitive Psychology, 8*, 553–560.

Spelke, E. S. (1979). Perceiving bimodally specified events in infancy. *Developmental Psychology, 15*, 626–636.

Spelke, E. S. (1988). The origins of physical knowledge. In L. Weiskrantz (Ed.), *Thought without language*. New York: Oxford University Press.

Spelke, E. S. (1994). Initial knowledge: Six suggestions. *Cognition, 50*, 431–445.

Spelke, E. S. (2000). Core knowledge. *American Psychologist, 55*, 1233–1243.

Spelke, E. S., Breinlinger, K., Macomber, J., & Jacobson, K. (1992). Origins of knowledge. *Psychological Review, 99*, 605–632.

Spelke, E. S., & Cortelyou, A. (1980). Perceptual aspects of social knowing: Looking and listening in infancy. In M. E. Lamb & L. R. Sherrod (Eds.), *Infant social cognition* (pp. 61–84). Hillsdale, NJ: Erlbaum.

Spelke, E. S., & Newport, E. L. (1998). Nativism, empiricism, and the development of knowledge. In W. Damon (Series Ed.) & R. M. Lerner (Vol. Ed.), *Handbook of child psychology: Vol. 1. Theoretical models of human development* (5th ed., pp. 275–340). New York: Wiley.

Spelke, E. S., & Owsley, C. (1979). Intermodal exploration and knowledge in infancy. *Infant Behavior and Development, 2*, 13–17.

Speltz, M. L., DeKlyen, M., Calderon, R., Greenberg, M. T., & Fisher, P. A. (1999). Neuropsychological characteristics and test behaviors of boys with early onset conduct problems. *Journal of Abnormal Psychology, 108*, 315–325.

Spence, M. J., & Freeman, M. S. (1996). Newborn infants prefer the maternal low-pass filtered voice, but not the maternal whispered voice. *Infant Behavior and Development, 19*, 199–212.

Spencer, J. P., Smith, L. B., & Thelen, E. (2001). Tests of a dynamic systems account of the A-not-B error: The influence of prior experience on the spatial memory abilities of two-year-olds. *Child Development, 72,* 1327–1346.

Spencer, J. P., & Thelen, E. (2000). Spatially specific changes in infants' muscle coactivity as they learn to reach. *Infancy, 1,* 275–302.

Spencer, J. P., Vereijken, B., Diedrich, F. J., & Thelen, E. (2000). Posture and the emergence of manual skills. *Developmental Science, 3,* 216–233.

Spencer, M. B., & Markstrom-Adams, C. (1990). Identity processes among racial and ethnic minority children in America. *Child Development, 61,* 290–310.

Spieker, S. J., Larson, N. C., Lewis, S. M., Keller, T. E., & Gilchrist, L. (1999). Developmental trajectories of disruptive behavior problems in preschool children of adolescent mothers. *Child Development, 70,* 443–458.

Spinrad, T., Losoya, S. H., Eisenberg, N., Fabes, R. A., Shepard, S. A., Cumberland, A., et al. (1999). The relations of parental affect and encouragement to children's moral emotions and behaviour. *Journal of Moral Education, 28,* 323–337.

Spitz, R. A. (1945). Hospitalism: An inquiry into the genesis of psychiatric conditions in early childhood. *The Psychoanalytic Study of the Child, 1,* 53–74.

Spitz, R. A. (1946). Hospitalism, a follow-up report. *The Psychoanalytic Study of the Child, 2,* 113–117.

Spitz, R. A. (1949). Motherless infants. *Child Development, 20,* 145–155.

Springer, K. (1996). Young children's understanding of a biological basis for parent-offspring relations. *Child Development, 67,* 2841–2856.

Springer, K. (1999). How a naive theory of biology is acquired. In M. Siegal & C. C. Peterson (Eds.), *Children's understanding of biology and health* (pp. 45–70). Cambridge, England: Cambridge University Press.

Springer, K., & Keil, F. C. (1991). Early differentiation of causal mechanisms appropriate to biological and nonbiological kinds. *Child Development, 62,* 767–781.

Springer, K., Nguyen, T., & Samaniego, R. (1996). Early understanding of age- and environment-related noxiousness in biological kinds: Evidence for a naive theory. *Cognitive Development, 11,* 65–82.

Sroufe, L. A. (1979). Socioemotional development. In J. Osofsky (Ed.), *The handbook of infant development* (pp. 462–516). New York: Wiley.

Sroufe, L. A. (1995). *Emotional development: The organization of emotional life in the early years.* Cambridge, England: Cambridge University Press.

Sroufe, L. A., Egeland, B., & Kreutzer, T. (1990). The fate of early experience following developmental change: Longitudinal approaches to individual adaptation in childhood. *Child Development, 61,* 1363–1373.

Sroufe, L. A., & Waters, E. (1976). The ontogenesis of smiling and laughter: A perspective on the organization of development in infancy. *Psychological Review, 83,* 173–189.

St. James-Roberts, I., & Halil, T. (1991). Infant crying patterns in the first year: Normal community and clinical findings. *Journal of Child Psychology and Psychiatry, 32,* 951–968.

St. James-Roberts, I., Conroy, S., & Wilsher, C. (1998). Stability and outcome of persistent infant crying. *Infant Behavior and Development, 21,* 411–435.

Stack, D. M., & Arnold, S. L. (1998). Changes in mothers' touch and hand gestures influence infant behavior during face-to-face interchanges. *Infant Behavior and Development, 21,* 451–468.

Stack, D. M., & Muir, D. W. (1990). Tactile stimulation as a component of social interchange: New interpretations for the still-face effect. *British Journal of Developmental Psychology, 8,* 131–145.

Stack, D. M., & Muir, D. W. (1992). Adult tactile stimulation during face-to-face interactions modulates five-month-olds' affect and attention. *Child Development, 63,* 1509–1525.

Stack, D., Muir, D., Sherriff, F., & Roman, J. (1989). Development of infant reaching in the dark to luminous objects and "invisible sounds." *Perception, 18,* 69–82.

Stanger, J. D., and Gridina, N. (1999). *Media in the home 1999: The fourth annual survey of parents and children.* Philadelphia: Annenberg Public Policy Center, University of Pennsylvania.

Stangor, C., & McMillan, D. (1992). Memory for expectancy-congruent and expectancy-incongruent information: A review of the social and social developmental literatures. *Psychology Bulletin, 111,* 42–61.

Stangor, C., & Ruble, D. N. (1989). Differential influences of gender schemata and gender constancy on children's information processing and behavior. *Social Cognition, 7,* 353–372.

Stanovich, K. E. (1992). Speculations on the causes and consequences of individual differences in early reading acquisition. In P. B. Gough, L. C. Ehri, & R. Treiman (Eds.), *Reading acquisition* (pp. 307–342). Mahwah, NJ: Erlbaum.

Stanovich, K. E., & Siegel, L. S. (1994). Phenotypic performance profile of children with reading disabilities: A regression-based test of the phonological-core variable-difference model. *Journal of Educational Psychology, 86,* 24–53.

Stark, R. I., & Myers, M. M. (1995). Breathing and hiccups in the fetal baboon. In J. P. Lecanuet, W. P. Fifer, N. A. Krasnegor, & W. P. Smotherman (Eds.), *Fetal development: A psychobiological perspective.* Hillsdale, NJ: Erlbaum.

Starkey, P. (1992). The early development of numerical reasoning. *Cognition, 43,* 93–126.

Starkey, P., Spelke, E. S., & Gelman, R. (1990). Numerical abstraction by human infants. *Cognition, 36,* 97–128.

Staub, E. (1979). *Positive social behavior and morality: Vol 2: Socialization and development.* New York: Academic Press.

Steele, H., Steele, M., Croft, C., & Fonagy, P. (1999). Infant-mother attachment at one year predicts children's understanding of mixed emotions at six years. *Social Development, 8,* 161–178.

Steele, H., Steele, M., & Fonagy, P. (1996). Associations among attachment classifications of mothers, fathers, and their infants. *Child Development, 67,* 541–555.

Stein, N. L. (1988). The development of children's storytelling skill. In M. B. Franklin & S. Barten (Eds.), *Child language: A book of readings* (pp. 282–297). New York: Oxford University Press.

Stein, Z., Susser, M., Saenger, G., & Marolla, F. (1975). *Famine and human development: The Dutch hunger winter of 1944–1945.* New York: Oxford University Press.

Steinberg, L. (1987). Impact of puberty on family relations: Effects of pubertal status and pubertal timing. *Developmental Psychology, 23,* 451–460.

Steinberg, L. (1988). Reciprocal relation between parent-child distance and pubertal maturation. *Developmental Psychology, 24,* 122–128.

Steinberg, L. (1990). Autonomy, harmony, and conflict in the family relationship. In S. S. Feldman & G. R. Elliott (Eds.), *At the threshold: The developing adolescent* (pp. 54–89). Cambridge, MA: Harvard University Press.

Steinberg, L. D., Darling, N. E., & Fletcher, A. C. (1995). Autoritative parenting and adolescent development: An ecological journey. In P. Moen, G. H. Elder, & K. Luscher (Eds.), *Examining lives in context* (pp. 423–466). Washington, DC: American Psychological Association.

Steinberg, L., Lamborn, S. D., Darling, N., Mounts, N. S., & Dornbusch, S. M. (1994). Over time changes in adjustment and competence among adolescents from authoritative, authoritarian, indulgent, and neglectful families. *Child Development, 65*, 754–770.

Steinberg, L., & Morris, A. S. (2001). Adolescent development. *Annual Review of Psychology, 52,* 83–110.

Steinberg, L., Mounts, N. S., Lamborn, S. D., & Dornbush, S. M. (1991). Authoritative parenting and adolescent adjustment across varied ecological niches. *Journal of Research on Adolescence, 1*, 19–36.

Steinberg, L., & Silverberg, S. B. (1986). The vicissitudes of autonomy in early adolescence. *Child Development, 57*, 841–851.

Steiner, J. E. (1979). Human facial expressions in response to taste and smell stimulation. In H. Reese & L. Lipsitt (Eds.), *Advances in child development and behavior* (Vol. 13, pp. 257–295). New York: Academic Press.

Stemmler, M., & Petersen, A. C. (1999). Reciprocity and change within the affective family environment in early adolescence. *International Journal of Behavioral Development, 23*, 185–198.

Stenberg, C., Campos, J., & Emde, R. (1983). The facial expression of anger in seven-month-old infants. *Child Development, 54*, 178–184.

Stern, D. (1985). *The interpersonal world of the infant.* New York: Basic Books.

Sternberg, R. J. (2000). The theory of successful intelligence. *Review of General Psychology, 3,* 292–316.

Steuer, F. B., Applefield, J. M., & Smith, R. (1971). Televised aggression and the interpersonal aggression of preschool children. *Journal of Experimental Child Psychology, 11,* 442–447.

Stevenson, H. W. (1991). The development of prosocial behavior in large-scale collective societies: China & Japan. In R. A. Hinde & J. Groebel (Eds.), *Cooperation and prosocial behaviour* (pp. 89–105). Cambridge: Cambridge University Press.

Stevenson, H. W., Chen, C., & Lee, S-Y. (1993). Mathematics achievement of Chinese, Japanese, and American children: Ten years later. *Science, 259*, 53–58.

Stevenson, H. W., & Stigler, J. W. (1992). *The learning gap: Why our schools are failing and what we can learn from Japanese and Chinese education.* New York: Summit Books.

Stice, E., & Barrera, M. (1995). A longitudinal examination of the reciprocal relations between perceived parenting and adolescents' substance use and externalizing behavior. *Developmental Psychology, 31*, 322–334.

Stifter, C. A., & Braungart, J. (1992). Infant colic: A transient condition with no apparent effects. *Journal of Applied Developmental Psychology, 13,* 447–462.

Stigler, J. W. (1984). "Mental abacus": The effect of abacus training on Chinese children's mental calculation. *Cognitive Psychology, 16,* 145–176.

Stigler, J. W., & Hiebert, J. (1999). *The teaching gap.* New York: Free Press.

Stigler, J. W., Smith, S., & Mao, L.-W. (1985). The self-perception of competence by Chinese children. *Child Development, 56,* 1259–1270.

Stipek, D., Gralinski, H., & Kopp, C. (1990). Self-concept development in the toddler years. *Developmental Psychology, 26,* 972–977.

Stipek, D. J., Recchia, S., & McClinic, S. (1992). Self-evaluation in young children. *Monographs of the Society for Research in Child Development, 57*(1, Serial No. 226), 1–79.

Stipek, D. J., Roberts, T. A., & Sanborn, M. E. (1984). Preschool-age children's performance expectations for themselves and another child as function of the incentive value of success and the salience of past performance. *Child Development, 55,* 1982–1989.

Stocker, C. M., Burwell, R. A., & Briggs, M. L. (2002). Sibling conflict in middle childhood predicts children's adjustment in early adolescence. *Journal of Family Psychology, 16,* 50–57.

Stone, J. L., & Church, J. (1957). *Childhood and adolescence: A psychology of the growing person.* New York: Random House.

Stoneman, Z., & Brody, G. H. (1993). Sibling temperaments, conflict, warmth, and role asymmetry. *Child Development, 64,* 1786–1800.

Strauss, M. S., & Curtis, L. E. (1984). Development of numerical concepts in infancy. In C. Sophian (Ed.), *Origins of cognitive skills* (pp. 131–155). Mahwah, NJ: Erlbaum.

Strayer, F. F., & Strayer, J. (1976). An ethological analysis of social agonism and dominance relations among preschool children. *Child Development, 47,* 980–989.

Strayer, J. (1986). Children's attributions regarding the situational determinants of emotion in self and others. *Developmental Psychology, 22,* 649–654.

Streeter, L. A. (1976). Language perception of 2-month old infants shows effects of both innate mechanisms and experience. *Nature, 259,* 39–41.

Streissguth, A. P., Barr, H. M., & Martin, D. C. (1983). Maternal alcohol use and neonatal habituation assessed with the Brazelton scale. *Child Development, 54*, 1109–1118.

Streissguth, A. P., Bookstein, F. L., Sampson, P. D., & Barr, H. M. (1993). *The enduring effects of prenatal alcohol exposure on child development: Birth through seven years, a partial least squares solution.* Ann Arbor: University of Michigan Press.

Streitmatter, J. L. (1988). Ethnicity as a mediating variable of early adolescent identity development. *Journal of Adolescence, 11,* 335–346.

Streri, A., & Spelke, E. S. (1988). Haptic perception of objects in infancy. *Cognitive Psychology, 20,* 1–23.

Stunkard, A. J., Foch, T. T., & Hrubeck, Z. (1986). A twin study of human obesity. *Journal of the American Medical Association, 256,* 51–54.

Stunkard, A. J., Sorenson, T. I. A., Hanis, C., Teasdale, T. W., Chakraborty, R., Schull, W. J., & Schulsinger, F. (1986). An adoption study of human obesity. *New England Journal of Medicine, 314,* 193–198.

Subbotsky, E. B. (1993). *Foundations of the mind: Children's understanding of reality.* Cambridge, MA: Harvard University Press.

Subbotsky, E. B. (1994). Early rationality and magical thinking in preschoolers: Space and time. *British Journal of Developmental Psychology, 12*, 97–108.

Subrahmanyam, K., & Greenfield, P. M. (1994). Effect of video game practice on spatial skills in girls and boys. *Journal of Applied Developmental Psychology, 15,* 13–32.

Subrahmanyam, K., & Greenfield, P. M. (1996). Effect of video game practice on spatial skills in girls and boys. In P. M. Greenfield & R. R. Cocking (Eds.), *Interacting with video* (pp. 95–114). Norwood, NJ: Ablex.

Subrahmanyam, K., Kraut, R. E., Greenfield, P. M., & Gross, E. F. (2000). The impact of home computer use on children's activities and development. *The Future of Children, 10,* 123–144.

Sue, S., & Okazaki, S. (1990). Asian-American educational achievements: A phenomenon in search of an explanation. *American Psychologist, 45,* 913–920.

Sullivan, H. S. (1953). *The interpersonal theory of psychiatry.* New York: Norton.

Sullivan, K., & Winner, E. (1993). Three-year-olds' understanding of mental states: The influence of trickery. *Journal of Experimental Child Psychology, 56,* 135–148.

Sullivan, M. W., Lewis, M., & Alessandri, S. M. (1992). Cross-age stability in infant emotional expressions during learning and extinction. *Developmental Psychology, 28,* 58–63.

Sulloway, F. J. (1996). *Born to rebel: Birth order, family dynamics, and creative lives.* New York: Pantheon Books.

Suomi, S., & Harlow, H. F. (1972). Social rehabilitation of isolate-reared monkeys. *Developmental Psychology, 6,* 487–496.

Super, C. (1976). Environmental effects on motor development: The case of "African infant precocity." *Developmental Medicine and Child Neurology, 18,* 561–567.

Super, C. M., & Harkness, S. (1986). The developmental niche: A conceptualization at the interface of child and culture. *International Journal of Behavioral Development, 9,* 545–569.

Sutton, S. K., & Davidson, R. J. (1997). Prefrontal brain asymmetry: A biological substrate of the behavioral approach and inhibition systems. *Psychological Science, 8,* 204–210.

Suzuki, L. A., & Valencia, R. R. (1997). Race-ethnicity and measured intelligence: Educational implications. *American Psychologist, 52,* 1103–1114.

Swain, R. C., Oetting, E. R., Thurman, P. J., Beauvais, F., & Edwards, R. (1993). American Indian adolescent drug use and socialization characteristics. *Journal of Cross-Cultural Psychology, 24,* 53–70.

Szynal-Brown, C., & Morgan, R. R. (1983). The effects of reward on tutor's behaviors in a cross-age tutoring context. *Journal of Experimental Child Psychology, 36,* 196–208.

Tager-Flusberg, H. (1992). Autistic children's talk about psychological states: Deficits in the early acquisition of a theory of mind. *Child Development, 63,* 161–172.

Takahashi, K. (1986). Examining the Strange-Situation procedure with Japanese mothers and 12-month-old infants. *Developmental Psychology, 22,* 265–270.

Talbot, M. (1998, May 24). Attachment theory: The ultimate experiment. *New York Times Magazine,* 24–30, 38, 46, 50, 54.

Tallal, P., Miller, S. L., Bedi, G., Byma, G., Wang, X., Nagarajan, S. S., et al. (1996). Language comprehension in language-learning impaired children improved with acoustically modified speech. *Science, 271,* 81–84.

Tamis-LeMonda, C. S., & Bornstein, M. H. (1994). Specificity in mother-toddler language-play relations across the second year. *Developmental Psychology, 30,* 283–292.

Tangney, J. P. (1998). How does guilt differ from shame? In J. Bybee (Ed.), *Guilt and children* (pp. 1–17). San Diego, CA: Academic Press.

Tangney, J., & Dearing, R. (2002). *Shame and guilt.* New York: Guilford Press.

Tannenbaum, A. J. (1986). Giftedness: A psychosocial approach. In J. Sternberg & J. E. Davidson (Eds.), *Conceptions of giftedness* (pp. 21–52). Cambridge, England: Cambridge University Press.

Tanner, J. M. (1961). *Education and physical growth: Implications of the study of children's growth for educational theory and practice.* New York: International Universities Press.

Tasker, F., & Golombok, S. (1995). Adults raised as children in lesbian families. *American Journal of Orthopsychiatry, 65,* 203–215.

Taylor, J., Iacono, W. G., & McGue, M. (2001). Evidence for a genetic etiology of early-onset delinquency. *Journal of Abnormal Behavior, 109,* 634–643.

Taylor, M. (1999). *Imaginary companions and the children who create them.* New York: Oxford University Press.

Taylor, M., & Carlson, S. M. (1997). The relation between individual differences in fantasy and theory of mind. *Child Development, 68,* 436–455.

Taylor, M., Cartwright, B. S., & Carlson, S. M. (1993). A developmental invertigation of children's imaginary companions. *Developmental Psychology, 29,* 276–285.

Taylor, M., & Gelman, S. A. (1989). Incorporating new words into the lexicon: Preliminary evidence for language hierarchies in two-year-old children. *Cognitive Development, 60,* 625–636.

Taylor, M. G. (1993). *Children's beliefs about the biological and social origins of gender differences.* Unpublished doctoral dissertation, University of Michigan, Ann Arbor.

Taylor, R. D., & Roberts, D. (1995). Kinship support and maternal and adolescent well-being in economically disadvantaged African-American families. *Child Development, 66,* 1585–1597.

Taylor, R. L., & Richards, S. B. (1991). Patterns of intellectual differences of Black, Hispanic, and White children. *Psychology in the Schools, 28,* 5–8.

Teasdale, T. W., & Owen, O. R. (1984). Heredity and familial environment in intelligence and educational level: A sibling study. *Nature, 309,* 620–622.

Teller, D. Y., McDonald, M. A., Preston, K., Sebris, S. L., & Dobson, V. (1986). Assessment of visual acuity in infants and children: The acuity card procedure. *Developmental Medicine and Child Neurology, 28,* 779–789.

Temple, E., & Posner, M. I. (1998). Brain mechanisms of quantity are similar in 5-year-old children and adults. *Proceedings of the National Academy of Sciences of the USA, 95,* 7836–7841.

Terrace, H. S., Petitto, L. A., Sanders, R. J., & Bever, T. G. (1979). Can an ape create a sentence? *Science, 206,* 891–902.

Tesman, J. R., & Hills, A. (1994). Developmental effects of lead exposure in children. *Social Policy Report, Society for Research in Child Development, 8*(3).

Thatcher, R.W. (1992) Cyclic cortical reorganization during childhood. *Brain & Cognition, 20,* 24–50.

Thelen, E. (1986). Treadmill-elicited stepping in seven-month-old infants. *Child Development, 57,* 1498–1506.

Thelen, E. (1995). Motor development: A new synthesis. *American Psychologist, 50,* 79–95.

Thelen, E. (2001). Dynamic mechanisms of change in early perceptual-motor development. In J. L. McClelland & R. S. Siegler, (Eds.), *Mechanisms of cognitive development: Behavioral and neural perspectives* (pp. 161–184). Mahwah, NJ: Erlbaum.

Thelen, E., Corbetta, D., Kamm, K., Spencer, J. P., Schneider, K., & Zernicke, R. F. (1993). The transition to reaching: Mapping intention and intrinsic dynamics. *Child Development, 64,* 1058–1098.

Thelen, E., & Fisher, D. M. (1982). Newborn stepping: An explanation for the "disappearing reflex." *Developmental Psychology, 18,* 760–775.

Thelen, E., Fisher, D. M., & Ridley-Johnson, R. (1984). The relationship between physical growth and a newborn reflex. *Infant Behavior and Development, 7,* 479–493.

Thelen, E., & Smith, L. B. (1994). *A dynamic systems approach to the development of cognition and action.* Cambridge, MA: MIT Press/Bradford Books.

Thelen, E., & Smith, L. B. (1998). Dynamic systems theory. In W. Damon (Series Ed.) & R. M. Lerner (Vol. Ed.), *Handbook of child psychology: Vol. 1. Theoretical models of human development* (5th ed., pp. 563–634). New York: Wiley.

Theokas, C., Ramsey, P. G., & Sweeney, B. (1993, March). *The effects of classroom interventions on young children's cross-sex contacts and perceptions.* Paper presented at the biennial meeting of the Society for Research in Child Development, New Orleans, LA.

Thinus-Blanc, C., & Gaunet, F. (1997). Representation of space in blind persons: Vision as a spatial sense? *Psychological Bulletin, 121,* 20–42.

Thomas, A., & Chess, S. (1977). *Temperament and development.* New York: Brunner/Mazel.

Thomas, A., Chess, S., & Birch, H. G. (1963) *Temperament and behavior disorders in children.* New York: New York University Press.

Thomas, A., Chess, S., & Birch, H. G. (1970). The origin of personality. *Scientific American, 223*(2), 102–109.

Thompson, J. R., & Chapman, R. S. (1977). Who is "Daddy" revisited: The status of two-year-olds' over-extended words in use and comprehension. *Journal of Child Language, 4,* 359–375.

Thompson, R. A. (1987). Development of children's inferences of the emotions of others. *Developmental Psychology, 23,* 124–131.

Thompson, R. A. (1998). Early sociopersonality development. In W. Damon (Series Ed.) & N. Eisenberg (Vol. Ed), *Handbook of child psychology: Vol. 3. Social, emotional, and personality development* (5th ed., pp. 23–104). New York: Wiley.

Thompson, R. A. (2000). The legacy of early attachments. *Child Development, 71,* 145–152.

Thompson, R. F. (2000). *The brain: A neuroscience primer* (3rd ed.). New York: Worth.

Thompson, R. F., & Spencer, W. A. (1966). Habituation: A model for the study of neuronal substrates of behavior. *Psychological Review, 73,* 16–43.

Thornberry, T. P., Lizotte, A. J., Krohn, M. D., Farnworth, M., & Jang, S. J. (1994). Delinquent peers beliefs and delinquent behavior: A longitudinal test of interactional theory. *Criminology, 32,* 47–83.

Thorne, B. (1986). Girls and boys together . . . but mostly apart: Gender arrangements in elementary schools. In W. W. Hartup & Z. Rubin (Eds.), *Relationships and development.* Mahwah, NJ: Erlbaum.

Thurstone L. L. (1938). *Primary mental abilities.* Chicago: University of Chicago Press.

Tienari, P. L., Lahti, I., Sorri, A., Naarala, M., Moring, J., Kaleva, M., et al. (1990). Adopted away offspring of schizophrenics and controls. In L. Robins & M. Rutter (Eds.), *Straight and devious pathways from childhood to adulthood.* Cambridge, England: Cambridge University Press.

Tietjen, A. (1986). Prosocial reasoning among children and adults in a Papua New Guinea society. *Developmental Psychology, 22,* 861–868.

Time. (1998, June 1). The boy who loved bombs.

Tincoff, R., & Jusczyk, P. W. (1999). Some beginnings of word comprehension in 6-month-olds. *Psychological Science, 10,* 172–175.

Tisak, M. S. (1995). Domains of social reasoning and beyond. In R. Vista (Ed.), *Annals of child development* (Vol. 11, pp. 95–130). London: Jessica Kingsley.

Tognoli, J., Pullen, J., & Lieber, J. (1994). The privilege of place: Domestic and work locations of characters in children's books. *Children's Environments Quarterly, 11,* 272–280.

Tolchnisky-Landsmann, L., & Levin, I. (1985). Writing in preschoolers: An age-related analysis. *Applied Psycholinguistics, 6,* 319–339.

Tomada, G., & Schneider, B. H. (1997). Relational aggression, gender, and peer acceptance: Invariance across culture, stability over time, and concordance among informants. *Developmental Psychology, 33,* 601–609.

Tomasello, M. (1988). Learning to use prepositions: A case study. *Journal of Child Language, 14,* 79–98.

Tomasello, M. (1992). The social bases of language acquisition. *Social Development, 1,* 68–87.

Tomasello, M. (1994). Can an ape understand a sentence? A review of *Language comprehension in ape and child* by E. S. Savage-Rumbaugh et al. *Language & Communication, 14,* 377–390.

Tomasello, M. (1995). Language is not an instinct. *Cognitive Development, 10,* 131–156.

Tomasello, M. (1999). *The cultural origins of human cognition.* Cambridge, MA: Harvard University Press.

Tomasello, M., & Barton, M. (1994). Learning words in non-ostensive context. *Developmental Psychology, 30,* 639–650.

Tomasello, M., & Farrar, M. J. (1986). Joint attention and early language. *Child Development, 57,* 1454–1463.

Tomasello, M., Kruger, A. C., & Ratner, H. H. (1993). Cultural learning. *Behavioral and Brain Sciences, 16,* 495–511.

Tomasello, M., Strosberg, R., & Akhtar, N. (1996). Eighteen-month-old children learn words in non-ostensive contexts. *Journal of Child Language, 23,* 157–176.

Tomie, J., & Whishaw, I. Q. (1990). New paradigms for tactile discrimination studies with the rat: Methods for simple, conditional, and configural discriminations. *Physiology and Behavior, 48,* 225–231.

Tomkins, S. S. (1962). *Affect, imagery, consciousness: Vol. 1. The positive emotions.* New York: Springer.

Trainor, L. J., & Heinmiller, B. M. (1998). The development of evaluative responses to music: Infants prefer to listen to consonance over dissonance. *Infant Behavior and Development, 21,* 77–88.

Trehub, S. E. (1993). Temporal auditory processing in infancy. *Annals of the New York Academy of Sciences, 682,* 137–149.

Trehub, S. E., & Schellenberg, E. G. (1995). Music: Its relevance to infants. *Annals of Child Development, 11,* 1–24.

Tremblay, R. E., Masse, L. C., Vitaro, F., & Dobkin, P. (1995). The impact of friends' deviant behavior on early onset of delinquency: Longitudinal data from 6 to 13 years of age. *Development and Psychopathology, 7,* 649–667.

Tremblay, R. E., Pihl, R., Vitaro, F., & Dobkin, P. L. (1994). Predicting early onset of male antisocial behavior from preschool behavior. *Archives of General Psychiatry, 51,* 732–739.

Trivers, R. (1972). Parental investment and sexual selection. In B. Campbell (Ed.), *Sexual selction and the descent of man 1871–1971* (pp. 136–179). New York: Aldine de Gruyter.

Trivers, R. L. (1983). The evolution of cooperation. In D. L. Bridgeman (Ed.), *The nature of prosocial development* (pp. 95–112). NY: Academic Press.

Tronick, E. Z., Thomas, R. B., & Daltabuit, M. (1994). The Quechua manta pouch: A caretaking practice for buffering the Peruvian infant against the multiple stressors of high altitude. *Child Development, 65*, 1005–1013.

Troy, M., & Sroufe, L.A. (1987). Victimization among preschoolers: Role of attachment relationship history. *Journal of the American Academy of Child and Adolescent Psychiatry, 26,* 166–172.

Tunmer, W. E., & Nesdale, A. R. (1985). Phonemic segmentation skill and beginning reading. *Journal of Educational Psychology, 77*, 417–427.

Turiel, E. (1978). Social regulation and domains of social concepts. In W. Damon (Ed.), *Social cognition: New directions for child development* (pp. 45–74). San Francisco: Jossey-Bass.

Turiel, E. (1987). Potential relations between the development of social reasoning and childhood aggression. In D. H. Crowell, I. M., Evans, & C. R. O'Donnell (Eds.), *Childhood aggression and violence: Sources of influence, prevention, and control* (pp. 95–114). New York: Plenum Press.

Turiel, E. (1998). The development of morality. In W. Damon (Series Ed.) and N. Eisenberg (Vol. Ed.), *Handbook of child psychology. Vol. 3. Social, emotional, and personality development* (pp. 863–932). New York: Wiley.

Turkheimer, E. (2000). Three laws of behavior genetics and what they mean. *Current Directions in Psychological Science, 9,* 160–164.

Turnbull, C. M. (1972). *The mountain people.* New York: Simon & Schuster.

Turner, P. J., & Gervai, J. (1995). A multidimensional study of gender typing in preschool children and their parents: Personality, attitudes, preferences, behavior, and cultural differences. *Developmental Psychology, 31*, 759–772.

Turner-Bowker, D. M. (1996). Gender stereotyped descriptions in children's picture books: Does "curious Jane" exist in the literature? *Sex Roles, 35*, 461–488.

Tversky, B., & Hemenway, D. (1984). Objects, parts, and categories. *Journal of Experimental Psychology: General, 113*, 169–193.

Twain, M. (1966). *Autobiography*. New York: Harper and Row.

Twenge, J. M., & Crocker, J. (2002). Race and self-esteem: Meta-analyses comparing Whites, Blacks, Hispanics, Asians, and American Indians and comment on Gray-Little and Hafdahl (2000). *Psychological Bulletin, 128*(3), 371–408.

Tyrka, A. R., Graber, J. A., & Brooks-Gunn, J. (2000). The development of disordered eating: Correlates and predictors of eating problems in the context of adolescence. In A. J. Sameroff, M. Lewis, et al. (Eds.), *Handbook of developmental psychopathology* (2nd ed., pp. 607–624). New York: Kluwer Academic/Plenum Press.

Uller, C., & Huntley-Fenner, G. (1995, March). Infant numerical representations. Paper presented at the Society for Research in Child Development Conference, Indianapolis.

Umana-Taylor, A., Diversi, M., & Fine, M. (2002). Ethnic identity and self-esteem among Latino adolescents: Distinctions among Latino populations. *Journal of Adolescent Research, 17,* 303–327.

Underwood, B., & Moore, B. (1982). Perspective-taking and altruism. *Psychological Bulletin, 91*, 143–173.

Unger, J. B., Simon, T. R., Newman, T. L., Montgomery, S. B., Kipke, M. D., & Albornoz, M. (1998). Early adolescent street youth: An overlooked population with unique problems and service needs. *Journal of Early Adolescence, 18*, 325–348.

Ungerer, J. A., Zelazo, P. R., Kearsley, R. B., & O'Leary, K. (1981). Developmental changes in the representation of objects in symbolic play from 18 to 34 months of age. *Child Development, 52,* 186–195.

UNICEF Statistics. (n.d.). Low birthweight. Retrieved July 12, 2002, from http://www.childinfo.org/eddb/lbw/index.htm

Urberg, K. A., Degirmencioglu, S. M., & Pilgrim, C. (1997). Close friend and group influence on adolescent cigarette smoking and alcohol use. *Developmental Psychology, 33*, 834–844.

Urberg, K. A., Degirmencioglu, S. M., Tolson, J. M., & Halliday-Scher, K. (1995). The structure of adolescent peer networks. *Developmental Psychology, 31*, 540–547.

U. S. Bureau of the Census. (1991). Fertility of American woman. *Current Population Reports*, Series P-20, No. 454, Washington, DC: U. S. Government Printing Office.

U. S. Bureau of the Census. (1992). *Marital status and living arrangements: March, 1992: Current population reports,* Series P-20, No. 468, Tables G. & 5. Washington, DC: U. S. Government Printing Office.

U. S. Bureau of the Census. (1998, March). *1998 Current population reports.* Washington, DC: U. S. Government Printing Office.

U. S. Census Bureau. (1998, October 29). *Marital status and living arrangements, March 1998 (update). Current population reports.* Washington, DC: U. S. Government Printing Office.

U. S. Bureau of the Census. (2001). *Statistical abstract of the United States* (121st ed.). Washington, DC: U. S. Government Printing Office.

U.S. Bureau of the Census (2002). Percent of people in poverty by definition of income and selected characteristics: 1998. Retrieved from: http://www.census.gov/hhes/poverty/prevdetailtabs.html.

U. S. Conference of Mayors. (1998*). A status report on hunger and homelessness in America's cities.* (Available from the U. S. Conference of Mayors, 1620 Eye St., NW, Washington DC 20006-4005.)

U. S. Department of Health and Human Services. (2001). *2001 federal poverty guidelines.* Retrieved July 16, 2001, from: http://aspe.hhs.gov/poverty/01poverty.htm

Uttal, D. H., Liu, L. L., & DeLoache, J. S. (1999). Taking a hard look at concreteness: Do real objects help children learn? In C. Tamis-LeMonda & L. Balter (Eds.), *Child psychology: A handbook of contemporary issues* (pp. 177–192). Hamden, CT: Garland.

Valdez-Menchaca, M. C., & Whitehurst, G. J. (1992). Accelerating language development through picture book reading: A systematic extension to Mexican day care. *Developmental Psychology, 28*, 1106–1114.

Valenzuela, M. (1997). Maternal sensitivity in a developing society: The context of urban poverty and infant chronic undernutrition. *Developmental Psychology, 33,* 845–855.

Valeski, T. N., & Stipek, D. J. (2001). Young children's feelings about school. *Child Development, 72,* 1198–1213.

Valleroy, L. A., Harris, J. R., & Way, P. O. (1990). The impact of HIV infection on child survival in the developing world. *AIDS*, *4*, 667–672.

van den Boom, D. C. (1994). The influence of temperament and mothering on attachment and exploration: An experimental manipulation of sensitive responsiveness among lower-class mothers with irritable infants. *Child Development, 65,* 1457–1477.

van den Boom, D. C. (1995). Do first-year intervention effects endure? Follow-up during toddlerhood of a sample of Dutch irritable infants. *Child Development, 66,* 1798–1816.

van den Boom, D. C., & Hoeksma, J. B. (1994). The effect of infant irritability on mother-infant interaction: A growth curve analysis. *Developmental Psychology, 30,* 581–590.

Van den Oord, E.J.C.G., Boomsma, D.I., & Verhulst, F.C. (2000). A study of genetic and environmental effects on the co-occurrence of problem behaviors in three-year-old twins. *Journal of Abnormal Psychology, 109,* 360–372.

van Geert, P. (1997). Que sera sera: Determinism and nonlinear dynamic model building in development. In A. Fogel, M. C. D. P. Lyra, & J. Valsiner (Eds.), *Dynamics and indeterminism in developmental and social processes* (pp. 13–38). Mahwah, NJ: Erlbaum.

van IJzendoorn, M. H. (1995). Adult attachment representations, parental responsiveness, and infant attachment: A meta-analysis on the predictive validity of the adult attachment interview. *Psychological Bulletin, 117,* 387–403.

van IJzendoorn, M. H. (1997). Attachment, emergent morality, and aggression: Toward a developmental socioemotional model of antisocial behaviour. *International Journal of Behavioral Development, 21,* 703–727.

van IJzendoorn, M. H., & De Wolff, M. S. (1997). In search of the absent father—Meta-analyses of infant-father attachment: A rejoinder to our discussants. *Child Development, 68,* 604–609.

van IJzendoorn, M. H., Juffer, F., & Duyvesteyn, M. G. C. (1995). Breaking the intergenerational cycle of insecure attachment: A review of the effects of the effects of attachment-based interventions on maternal sensitivity and infant security. *Journal of Child Psychology and Psychiatry, 36,* 225–248.

van IJzendoorn, M. H., & Kroonenberg, P. M. (1988). Cross-cultural patterns of attachment: A meta-analysis of the strange situation. *Child Development, 59,* 147–156.

van IJzendoorn, M. H., & Sagi, A. (1999). Cross-cultural patterns of attachment: Universal and contextual dimensions. In J. Cassidy & P. R. Shaver (Eds.), *Handbook of attachment: Theory, research, and clinical applications* (pp. 713–734). New York: Guilford Press.

Van Loosbroek, E., & Smitsman, A. W. (1990). Visual perception of numerosity in infancy. *Developmental Psychology, 26,* 916–922.

Vance, H. B., Hankins, N., & McGee, H. (1979). A preliminary study of Black and White differences on the revised Wechsler Intelligence Scale for Children. *Journal of Clinical Psychology, 35,* 815–819.

Vandell, D. L. (1987). Baby sister/baby brother: Reactions to the birth of a sibling and patterns of early sibling relations. *Journal of Children in Contemporary Society, 19,* 13–37.

Vasek, M. E. (1986). Lying as a skill: The development of deception in children. In R. W. Mitchell & N. S. Thompson (Eds.), *Deception: Perspectives on human and non-human deceit.* (pp. 271–292). New York: SUNY Press.

Vaughn, B. E., Goldberg, S., Atkinson, L., Marcovith, S., MacGregor, D., & Seifer, R. (1994). Quality of toddler-mother attachment in children with Down syndrome: Limits to interpretation of Strange Room behavior. *Child Development, 65,* 95–108.

Vaughn, C. (1996). *How life begins.* New York: Times Books.

Vellutino, F. R. (1991). Introduction to three studies on reading acquisition: Convergent findings on theoretical foundations of code-oriented versus whole-language approaches to reading instruction. *Journal of Educational Psychology, 83,* 437–443.

Vellutino, F. R., & Scanlon, D. M. (1987). Phonological coding, phonological awareness, and reading ability: Evidence from a longitudinal and experimental study. *Merrill-Palmer Quarterly, 33,* 321–363.

Vellutino, F. R., Scanlon, D. M., & Spearling, D. (1995). Semantic and phonological coding in poor and normal readers. *Journal of Experimental Child Psychology, 59,* 76–123.

Ventura, S. J., Martin, J. A., Curtin, S. C., & Mathews, T. J. (1997). Report of final natality statistics, 1995. *Monthly Vital Statistics Report, 45* (11, Suppl. 2). Hyattsville, MD: National Center for Health Statistics.

Verkuyten, M. (1990). Self-esteem and the evaluation of ethnic identity among Turkish and Dutch adolescents in the Netherlands. *Journal of Social Psychology, 130,* 285–297.

Verma, S. (1999). Socialization for survival: Developmental issues among working street children in India. *New Directions in Child Development, 85,* 5–18.

Vernon, P. A. (1993). Intelligence and neural efficiency. In D. K. Detterman (Ed.), *Current topics in human intelligence* (Vol. 3, pp. 171–187). Norwood, NJ: Ablex.

Verschueren, K., Marcoen, A., & Schoefs, V. (1996). The internal working model of the self, attachment, and competence in five-year-olds. *Child Development, 67,* 2493–2511.

Vikan, A., & Clausen, S. E. (1993). Freud, Piaget, or neither? Beliefs in controlling other by wishful thinking and magical behavior in young children. *Journal of Genetic Psychology, 154,* 297–314.

Vitaro, F., Brendgen, M., Pagani, L., Tremblay, R. E., & McDuff, P. (1999). Disruptive behavior, peer association, and conduct disorder: Testing the developmental links through early intervention. *Development and Psychopathology, 11,* 287–304.

Vitaro, F., Tremblay, R. E., Kerr, M., Pagani, L., & Bukowski, W. M. (1997). Disruptiveness, friends' characteristics, and delinquency in early adolescence: A test of two competing models of development. *Child Development, 68,* 676–689.

Vogel, G. (1996), School achievement: Asia and Europe top in world, but reasons are hard to find. *Science, 274,* 1296.

Vohr, B. R., & Garcia-Coll, C. T. (1988). Follow-up studies of high risk low-birthweight infants: Changing trends. In H. E. Fitzgerald, B. M. Lester, & M. W. Yogman (Eds.), *Theory and research in behavioral pediatrics* (Vol. 4). New York: Plenum Press.

Volling, B. L., & Belsky, J. (1991). Multiple determinants of father involvement during infancy in dual-earner and single-earner families. *Journal of Marriage and the Family, 53,* 461–474.

Volling, B. L., & Feagans, L. V. (1995). Infant day care and children's social competence. *Infant Behavior and Development, 18,* 177–188.

von Hofsten, C. (1979). Development of visually guided reaching: The approach phase. *Journal of Human Movement Studies, 5,* 160–178.

von Hofsten, C. (1980). Predictive reaching for moving objects by human infants. *Journal of Experimental Child Psychology, 30,* 369–382.

von Hofsten, C. (1982). Eye-hand coordination in the newborn. *Developmental Psychology, 18,* 450–461.

von Hofsten, C. (1991). Structuring of early reaching movements: A longitudinal study. *Journal of Motor Behavior, 23,* 280–292.

von Hofsten, C. & Spelke, E. S. (1985). Object perception and object-directed reaching in infancy. *Journal of Experimental Psychology: General, 114,* 198–212.

von Hofsten, C., Vishton, P., Spelke, E. S., Feng, Q., & Rosander, K. (1998). Predictive action in infancy: Tracking and reaching for moving objects. *Cognition, 67,* 255–285.

von Senden, M. (1960). *Space and sight. The perception of space and shape in the congenitally blind before and after operations.* Glencoe, IL: Free Press.

Vondra, J. I., Shaw, D. S., Swearingen, L., Cohen, M., & Owens, E. B. (2001). Attachment stability and emotional and behavioral regulation from infancy to preschool age. *Development and Psychopathology, 13*(1), 13–33.

Voyer, D., Voyer, S., & Bryden, M. P. (1995). Magnitude of sex differences in spatial abilities: A meta-analysis and consideration of critical variables. *Psychological Bulletin, 117,* 250–270.

Vraniak, D. (1994). Native Americans. In R. J. Sternberg (Ed.) *Encyclopedia of human intelligence* (pp. 747–754). New York: Macmillan.

Vygotsky, L. (1962). *Thought and language.* Cambridge, MA: MIT Press.

Vygotsky, L. S. (1978). *Mind in society: The development of higher mental processes.* Cambridge, MA: Harvard University Press. (Original works published 1930, 1933, 1935.)

Wadhwa, P. D. (1998). Prenatal stress and life-span development. In H. S. Friedman (Ed.), *Encyclopedia of mental health* (Vol. 3, pp. 265–280). San Diego, CA: Academic Press.

Wagner, R. K., Torgesen, J. K., Rashotte, C. A., Hecht, S. A., Barker, T. A., Burgess, S. R., et al. (1997). Changing relations between phonological processing abilities and word-level reading as children develop from beginning to skilled readers: A 5-year longitudinal study. *Developmental Psychology, 33,* 468–479.

Wainryb, C., & Turiel, E. (1995). Diversity of social development: Between and within cultures? In M. Killen & D. Hart (Eds.), *Morality in everyday life: Developmental perspectives* (pp. 283–313). Cambridge, England: Cambridge University Press.

Wakeley, A., Rivera, S., & Langer, J. (2000). Can young infants add and subtract? *Child Development, 71,* 1525–1534

Wakschlag, L. S., Gordon, R. A., Lahey, B. B., Loeber, R., Green, S. M., & Leventhal, B. L. (2001). Maternal age at first birth and boys' risk for conduct disorder. *Journal of Research on Adolescence, 10,* 417–441.

Walden, T. A., & Baxter, A. (1989). The effect of context and age on social referencing. *Child Development, 60,* 1511–1518.

Walden, T. A., & Field, T. M. (1990). Preschool children's social competence and production and discrimination of affective expressions. *British Journal of Developmental Psychology, 8,* 65–76.

Waldman, I. D. (1996). Aggressive boys' hostile perceptual and response biases: The role of attention and impulsivity. *Child Development, 67,* 1015–1033.

Walker, A. S. (1982). Intermodal perception of expressive behaviors by human infants. *Journal of Experimental Child Psychology, 33,* 514–535.

Walker, B. E., & Quarles, J. (1962). Palate development in mouse fetuses after tongue removal. *Archives of Oral Biology, 21,* 405–412.

Walker, K., Taylor, E., McElroy, A., Phillip, D.-A., & Wilson, M. N. (1995). Familial and ecological correlates of self-esteem in African American children. *New Directions in Child Development, 68,* 23–34.

Walker, L. J. (1980). Cognitive and perspective-taking prerequisites for moral development. *Child Development, 51,* 131–139.

Walker, L. J. (1984). Sex differences in the development of moral reasoning: A critical review. *Child Development, 55,* 677–691.

Walker, L. J. (1991). Sex differences in moral reasoning. In W. M. Kurtines & J. L. Gewirtz (Eds.), *Handbook of moral behavior and development: Vol. 2. Research* (pp. 333–364). Hillsdale, NJ: Erlbaum.

Walker-Andrews, A. S. (1997). Infants' perception of expressive behaviors: Differentiation of multimodal information. *Psychological Bulletin, 121,* 437–456.

Walker-Andrews, A. S., & Dickson, L. R. (1997). Infants' understanding of affect. In S. Hala (Ed.), *The development of social cognition* (pp. 161–186). West Sussex, England: Psychology Press.

Wall, J. A., Power, T. G., & Arbona, C. (1993). Susceptibility to antisocial peer pressure and its relation to acculturation in Mexican-American adolescents. *Journal of Adolescent Research, 8,* 403–418.

Wallerstein, J. S., & Blakeslee, S. (1989). *Second changes: Men, women and children a decade after divorce.* New York: Ticknor & Fields.

Wallman, J. (1992). *Aping language.* Cambridge, England: Cambridge University Press.

Walton, G. E., Bower, N. J., & Bower, T. G. (1992). Recognition of familiar faces by newborns. *Infant Behavior and Development, 15,* 265–269.

Wang, C-T., & Daro, D. (1997). *Current trends in child abuse reporting and fatalities: The results of the 1997 annual fifty state survey.* The Center on Child Abuse Prevention Research. (Working paper number 808.) Retrieved from: http://www.join-hands.com/welfare/1997castats.html.

Wang, D., Kato, N., Inaba, Y., Tango, T., Yoshida, Y., Kusaka, Y., et al. (2000). Physical and personality traits of preschool children in Fuzhou, China: Only child vs sibling. *Child: Care, Health and Development, 26,* 49–60.

Wark, G. R., & Krebs, D. L. (1996). Gender and dilemma differences in real-life moral judgment. *Developmental Psychology, 32,* 220–230.

Warren, S. L., Huston, L., Egeland, B., & Sroufe, L. A. (1997). Child and adolescent anxiety disorders and early attachment. *Journal of the American Academy of Child and Adolescent Psychiatry, 36,* 637–641.

Waterman, A. S., & Waterman, C. K. (1971). A longitudinal study of changes in ego identity status during the freshman year at college. *Developmental Psychology, 5,* 167–173.

Waters, E., & Cummings, E. M. (2000). A secure base from which to explore close relationships. *Child Development, 71,* 164–173.

Waters, E., Merrick, S., Treboux, D., Crowell, J., & Albersheim, L. (2000). Attachment security in infancy and early adulthood: A twenty-year longitudinal study. *Child Development, 71,* 684–689.

Waters, H.S. (1980). Class news: A single subject longitudinal study of prose production and schema formation during childhood. *Journal of Verbal Learning and Verbal Behavior, 19,* 152–167.

Waters, H. S. (1989, April). *Problem-solving at two: A year-long naturalistic study of two children.* Paper presented at the Society for Research in Child Development Conference, Kansas City, MO.

Watson, J., & Crick, F. (1953). A structure for Deoxyribose Nucleic Acid. *Nature, 171,* 737.

Watson, J. B. (1924). *Behaviorism.* New York: Norton.

Watson, J. B. (1928). *Psychological care of infant and child.* New York: Norton.

Watson, J. B., & Rayner, R. (1920). Conditioned emotional reactions. *Journal of Experimental Psychology, 3,* 1–14.

Watson, J. S., & Ramey, C. T. (1972). Reactions to response-contingency stimulation in early infancy. *Merrill-Palmer Quarterly, 18,* 219–227.

Watson-Gegeo, K. A., & Gegeo, D. W. (1986). Calling-out and repeating routines in Kwara'ae children's language socialization. In B. B. Schieffelin & E. Ochs (Eds.), *Language socialization across cultures* (pp. 17–50). *Studies in the social and cultural foundations of language, No. 3.* New York: Cambridge University Press.

Waxman, S. R. (1990). Linguistic biases and the establishment of conceptual hierarchies: Evidence from preschool children. *Cognitive Development, 5,* 123–150.

Waxman, S. R., & Hall, D. G. (1993). The development of a linkage between count nouns and object categories: Evidence from 15- to 21-month-old infants. *Child Development, 64,* 1224–1241.

Waxman, S. R., & Markow, D. B. (1995). Words as invitations to form categories: Evidence from 12- to 13-month-old infants. *Cognitive Psychology, 29,* 257–302.

Waxman, S. R., & Markow, D. B. (1998). Object properties and object kind: Twenty-one-month-old infants' extension of novel adjectives. *Child Development, 69,* 1313–1329.

Waxman, S. R., & Senghas, A. (1992). Relations among word meanings in early lexical development. *Developmental Psychology, 28,* 862–873.

Weber-Fox, C., & Neville, H. J. (1996). Maturational constraints on functional specializations for language processing: ERP and behavioral evidence in bilingual speakers. *Journal of Cognitive Neuroscience, 8,* 231–256.

Webster-Stratton, C. (1998). Preventing conduct problems in Head Start children: Strengthening parenting competencies. *Journal of Consulting and Clinical Psychology, 66,* 715–730.

Weems, C. F., Silverman, W. K., & La Greca, A. M. (2000). What do youth referred for anxiety problems worry about? Worry and its relation to anxiety and anxiety disorders in children and adolescents. *Journal of Abnormal Child Psychology, 28,* 63–72.

Weinberg, M. K., & Tronick, E. Z. (1994). Beyond the face: An empirical study of infant affective configurations of facial, vocal, gestural, and regulatory behaviors. *Child Development, 65,* 1503–1515.

Weir, R. H. (1962). *Language in the crib.* The Hague: Mouton.

Weiss, B., Dodge, K. A., Bates, J. E., & Pettit, G. S. (1992) Some consequences of early harsh discipline: Child aggression and a maladaptive social information processing style. *Child Development, 63,* 1321–1335.

Weist, R. M. (1989). Time concepts in language and thought: Filling the Piagetian void between two to five years. In I. Levin & D. Zakay (Eds.), *Time and human cognition: A life-span perspective* (pp. 63–118). Amsterdam: North-Holland.

Wellman, H. M. (1990). *Children's theories of mind.* Cambridge, MA: MIT Press.

Wellman, H. M., Cross, D., & Bartsch, K. (1987). Infant search and object permanence: A meta-analysis of the A-not-B error. *Monographs of the Society for Research in Child Development, 51*(3, Serial No. 214).

Wellman, H. M., & Gelman, S. (1998). Knowledge acquisition in foundational domains. In W. Damon (Series Ed.) & D. Kuhn & R. S. Siegler (Vol. Eds.), *Handbook of child psychology: Vol. 2: Cognition, Perception & Language.* (5th ed.). New York: Wiley.

Wellman, H. M., & Inagaki, K. (Eds.) (1997). The emergence of core domains of thought: Children's reasoning about physical, psychological, and biological phenomena. *New Directions for Child Development, No. 75.* San Francisco: Jossey-Bass.

Wellman, H. M., & Wooley, J. D. (1990). From simple desires to ordinary beliefs: The early development of everyday psychology. *Cognition, 35,* 245–275.

Wender, P. H. (1995). *Attention-deficit hyperactivity disorder in adults.* New York: Oxford University Press.

Wentzel, K. R., & Asher, S. R. (1995). The academic lives of neglected, rejected, popular, and controversial children. *Child Development, 66,* 754–773.

Wentzel, K. R., & Caldwell, K. (1997). Friendships, peer acceptance, and group membership: Relations to academic achievement in middle school. *Child Development, 68,* 1198–1209.

Werebe, M. J., & Baudonniere, P. (1991). Social pretend play among friends and familiar peers. *International Journal of Behavioral Development, 14,* 411–428.

Werker, J. F. (1989). Becoming a native listener. *American Scientist, 77,* 54–69.

Werker, J. F., & Lalonde, C. E. (1988). Cross-language speech perception: Initial capabilities and developmental change. *Developmental Psychology, 24,* 672–683.

Werker, J. F., Pegg, J. E., & McLeod, P. J. (1994). A cross-language investigation of infant preference for infant-directed communication. *Infant Behavior and Development, 17,* 323–333.

Werker, J. F., & Tees, R. C. (1984). Cross-language speech perception: Evidence for perceptual reorganization during the first year of life. *Infant Behavior and Development, 7,* 49–63.

Werner, E. E. (1989). Children of the Garden Island. *Scientific American, 260*(4), 106–111.

Werner, E. E. (1993). Risk, resilience, and recovery: Perspectives from the Kauai Longitudinal Study. *Development and Psychopathology, 5,* 503–515.

Wertheimer, M. (1961). Psychomotor coordination of auditory and visual space at birth. *Science, 134,* 1692.

Wessel, M. A., Cobb, J. C., Jackson, E. B., Harris, G. S., & Detwiler, A. C. (1954). Paroxysmal fussing in infancy, sometimes called "colic." *Pediatrics, 14,* 421–433.

West, M. J., & Rheingold, H. L. (1978). Infant stimulation of maternal instruction. *Infant Behavior and Development, 1,* 205–215.

Westinghouse Learning Center (1969). *The impact of Head Start: An evaluation of the effects of Head Start on children's cognitive and affective development.* Washington, DC: Clearinghouse for Federal Scientific and Technical Information.

Weston, D. R., Ivins, B., Zuckerman, B., Jones, C., & Lopez, R. (1989). Drug exposed babies: Research and clinical issues. *Zero-to-Three, 9,* 1–7.

White, B. L. (1985). *The first three years of life.* New York: Prentice-Hall.

White, J. L., Moffitt, T. E., Earls, F., Robins, L. & Silva, P. (1990). How early can we tell? Predictors of childhood conduct disorder and adolescent delinquency. *Criminology, 28,* 507–533.

White, M. I., & LeVine, R. A. (1986). What is an ii do (good child)? In H. Stevenson, H. Azuma, & K. Hakuta (Eds.), *Child development and education in Japan* (pp. 55–62). New York: W. H. Freeman.

Whitehurst, G. J., Epstein, N. J., Angell, A. L., Payne, A. C., Crone, D. A., & Fischel, J. E. (1994). Outcomes of an emergent literacy intervention in Head Start. *Journal of Educational Psychology, 86*, 542–555.

Whitesell, N. R., & Harter, S. (1996). The interpersonal context of emotion: Anger with close friends and classmates. *Child Development, 67*, 1345–1359.

Whiteside, M. F., & Becker, B. J. (2000). Parental factors and the young child's postdivorce adjustment; A meta-analysis with implications for parenting arrangements. *Journal of Family Psychology, 14*, 5–26.

Whiting, B. B., & Edwards, C. (1988). *Children of different worlds: The formation of social behavior.* Cambridge, MA: Harvard University Press.

Whiting, B. B., & Whiting, J. W. M. (1975). *Children of six cultures: A psychocultural analysis*. Cambridge, MA: Harvard University Press.

Whitney, M. P., & Thoman, E. B. (1994). Sleep in premature and full-term infants from 24-hour home recordings. *Infant Behavior and Development, 17*, 223–234.

Wichstrom, L. (1999). The emergence of gender difference in depressed mood during adolescence: The role of intensified gender socialization. *Developmental Psychology, 35*, 232–245.

Wideman, J. E. (1995). *Brothers and keepers*. New York: Vintage Books.

Wigfield, A., & Eccles, J. S. (1994). Children's competence beliefs, achievement values, and general self-esteem change across elementary and middle school. *Journal of Early Adolescence, 14*, 107–138.

Wiggers, M., & van Lieshout, C. F. M. (1985). Development of recognition of emotions: Children's reliance on situational and facial expressive cues. *Developmental Psychology, 21*, 338–349.

Wilk, S. L., Desmarais, L. B., & Sackett, P. R. (1995). Gravitation to jobs commensurate with ability: Longitudinal and cross-sectional tests. *Journal of Applied Psychology, 80*, 79–85.

Willatts, P. (1985). Adjustment of means-ends coordination and the representation of spatial relations in the production of search errors by infants. *British Journal of Developmental Psychology, 3*, 259–272.

Willatts, P. (1990). Development of problem solving strategies in infancy. In D. Bjorklund (Ed.), *Children's strategies: Contemporary views of cognitive development* (pp. 23–66). Hillsdale, NJ: Erlbaum.

Willats, P. (1999). Development of means-end behavior in young infants: Pulling a support to retrieve a distant object. *Developmental Psychology, 35*, 651–667.

Williams, B. R., Ponesse, J. S., Schachar, R. J., Logan, G. D., & Tannock, R. (1999). Development of inhibitory control across the life span. *Developmental Psychology, 35*, 205–213.

Williams, T. (Ed.). (1986). *The impact of television: A natural experiment in three communities*. Orlando, FL: Academic Press.

Willinger, M. (1995). SIDS prevention. *Pediatric Annals, 24*, 358–364.

Wilson, E. O. (1975). *Sociobiology: The new synthesis*. Cambridge, MA: Harvard University Press.

Wimmer, H., & Perner, J. (1983). Beliefs about beliefs: Representation and constraining function of wrong beliefs in young children's understanding of deception. *Cognition, 13*, 103–128.

Windle, M. (1992). A longitudinal study of stress buffering for adolescent problem behaviors. *Developmental Psychology, 28*, 522–530.

Windle, M. (1994). A study of friendship characteristics and problem behaviors among middle adolescents. *Child Development, 65*, 1764–1777.

Winner, E. (1996). *Gifted children: Myths and realities*. New York: Basic Books.

Wintre, M. G., & Vallance, D. D. (1994). A developmental sequence in the comprehension of emotions: Intensity, multiple emotions, and valence. *Developmental Psychology, 30*, 509–514.

Witelson, S. F. (1987). Neurobiological aspects of language in children. *Child Development, 58*, 653–688.

Witherington, D. C., Campos, J. J., & Hertenstein, M. J. (2001). Principles of emotion and its development in infancy. In G. Bremner & A. Fogel (Eds), *Blackwell handbook of infant development: Handbooks of developmental psychology* (pp. 427–464). Malden, MA: Blackwell Publishers.

Wittelson, S. F., & Swallow, J. A. (1988). Neuropsychological study of the development of spatial cognition. In J. Stiles-Davis, M. Kritchevsky, & U. Bellugi (Eds.), *Spatial cognition: Brain bases and development*. Mahwah, NJ: Erlbaum.

Wolchik, S. A., Ruehlman, L. S., Braver, S., & Sandler, I. N. (1989). Social support of children of divorce: Direct and stress buffering effects. *American Journal of Community Psychology, 17*, 485–501.

Wolf, D., Rygh, J., & Altshuler, J. (1984). Agency and experience: Actions and states in play narratives. In I. Bretherton (Ed.), *Symbiotic play* (pp. 195–217). New York: Academic Press.

Wolfe, S. M., Toro, P. A., & McCaskill, P. A. (1999). A comparison of homeless and matched housed adolescents on family environment variables. *Journal of Research on Adolescence, 9*, 53–66.

Wolfer, L. T., & Moen, P. (1996). Staying in school: Maternal employment and the timing of black and white daughters' school exit. *Journal of Family Issues, 17*, 540–560.

Wolff, P. (1987). *The development of behavioral states and expression of emotions in early infancy*. Chicago: University of Chicago Press.

Wolpert, L. (1991). *The triumph of the embryo*. Oxford, England: Oxford University Press.

Wood, C. C. (1976). Discriminability, response bias, and phoneme categories in discrimination of voice onset time. *Journal of the Acoustical Society of America*, 1381–1389.

Wood, D. (1986). Aspects of teaching and learning. In M. Richards & P. Light (Eds.), *Children of social worlds*. Cambridge, England: Polity Press.

Wood, D. J., Bruner, J. S., & Ross, G. (1976). The role of tutoring in problem-solving. *Journal of Child Psychology and Psychiatry, 17*, 89–100.

Wood, W., Wong, F. Y., & Chachere, G. (1991). Effects of media violence on viewers' aggression in unconstrained social interaction. *Psychological Bulletin, 109*, 371–383.

Woodward, A. L., & Hoyne, K. L. (1999). Infants' learning about words and sounds in relation to objects. *Child Development 70*, 65–77.

Woodward, A. L., & Markman, E. M. (1998). Early word learning. In D. Kuhn & R. S. Siegler (Eds.), *Handbook of child psychology: Vol. 2. Cognition, perception, and language* (5th ed., pp. 371–420). New York: Wiley.

Woodward, A. L., Markman, E. M., & Fitzsimmons, C. M. (1994). Rapid word learning in 13- and 18-month-olds. *Developmental Psychology, 30*, 553–566.

Woodward, L. J., & Fergusson, D. M. (1999). Childhood peer relationship problems and psychosocial adjustment in late adolescence. *Journal of Abnormal Child Psychology, 27*, 87–104.

Woolley, J. D. (1997). Thinking about fantasy: Are children fundamentally different thinkers and believers from adults? *Child Development, 68*, 991–1011.

Woolley, J. D., & Phelps, K. E. (1994). Young children's practical reasoning about imagination. *British Journal of Developmental Psychology, 12*, 53–67.

Wynn, K. (1992). Addition and subtraction by human infants. *Nature, 358*, 749–750.

Wynn, K. (1995). Infants possess a system of numerical knowledge. *Current Directions in Psychological Science, 4*, 172–177.

Xu, F., & Pinker, S. (1995). Weird past tense forms. *Journal of Child Language, 22*, 531–556.

Yamagata, K. (1997). Representational activity during mother-child interaction: The scribbling stage of drawing. *British Journal of Developmental Psychology, 15*, 355–366.

Yaniv, I., & Shatz, M. (1988). Children's understanding of perceptibility. In J. W. Astington, P. L. Harris, & D. R. Olson (Eds.), *Developing theories of mind* (pp. 93–107). New York: Cambridge University Press.

Yarrow, M. R., Scott, P. M., & Zahn-Waxler, C. (1973). Learning concern for others. *Developmental Psychology, 8*, 240–260.

Yates, M. & Youniss, J. (1996). A developmental perspective on community service in adolescence. *Social Development, 5*, 85–111.

Yau, J., & Smetana, J. G. (1996). Adolescent-parent conflict among Chinese adolescents in Hong Kong. *Child Development, 67*, 1262–1275.

Yeates, K. O., & Selman, R. L. (1989). Social competence in the schools: Toward an integrative developmental model for intervention. *Developmental Review, 9*, 64–100.

Yonas, A. (1981). Infants' responses to optical information for collision. In R. N. Aslin, J. Alberts, & M. Petersen (Eds.), *Development of perception: Psychobiological perspectives: The visual system.* New York: Academic Press.

Yonas, A., Arterberry, M. E., & Granrud, C. E. (1987). Space perception in infancy. In R. Vasta (Ed.), *Annals of child development* (pp. 1–34). Greenwich, CT: JAI Press.

Yonas, A., Cleaves, W. T., & Pettersen, L. (1978). Development of sensitivity to pictorial depth. *Science, 200,* 77–79.

Young, L. D., Suomi, S. J., Harlow, H. F., & McKinney, W. T. (1973). Early stress and later response to separation in rhesus monkeys. *American Journal of Psychiatry, 130*(4), 400–405.

Youngblade, L. M., & Belsky, J. (1992). Parent-child antecedents of 5-year-olds' close friendships: A longitudinal analysis. *Developmental Psychology, 28*, 700–713.

Youngblade, L. M., & Dunn, J. (1995). Individual differences in young children's pretend play with mother and siblings: Links to relationships and understanding of other people's feelings and beliefs. *Child Development, 66*, 1472–1492.

Youniss, J. (1980). *Parents and peers in social development: A Sullivan-Piaget perspective.* Chicago: University of Chicago Press.

Youniss, J. & Smollar, J. (1985). *Adolescents' relations with mothers, fathers, and friends.* Chicago: University of Chicago Press.

Youth Indicators. (2001). *Marriage and divorce rates.* Retrieved from: http://www.ed.gov/pubs/YouthIndicators/indtaP5.html.

Yuill, N., & Perner, J. (1988). Intentionality and knowledge in children's judgments of actor's responsibility and recipient's emotional reaction. *Developmental Psychology, 24*, 358–365.

Zahn-Waxler, C., Friedman, R. J., Cole, P. M., Mizuta, I., & Hiruma, N. (1996). Japanese and United States preschool children's responses to conflict and distress. *Child Development, 67,* 2462–2477.

Zahn-Waxler, C., & Kochanska, G. (1990). The origins of guilt. In R. Thompson (Ed.), *The 36th annual Nebraska symposium on motivation: Socioemotional development* (pp. 183–258). Lincoln, NE: University of Nebraska Press.

Zahn-Waxler, C., Radke-Yarrow, M., & King, R. A. (1979). Child rearing and children's prosocial initiations toward victims of distress. *Child Development, 50*, 319–330.

Zahn-Waxler, C., Radke-Yarrow, M., Wagner, E., & Chapman, M. (1992). Development of concern for others. *Developmental Psychology, 28*, 126–136.

Zahn-Waxler, C., & Robinson, J. (1995). Empathy and guilt: Early origins of feelings of responsibility. In J. P. Tangney & K. W. Fischer (Eds.), *Self-conscious emotions: The psychology of shame, guilt, embarrassment, and pride* (pp. 143–174). New York: Guilford Press.

Zahn-Waxler, C., Robinson, J., & Emde, R. N. (1992). The development of empathy in twins. *Developmental Psychology, 28*, 1038–1047.

Zametkin, A. J. (1995). Attention-deficit disorder: Born to be hyperactive? *Journal of the American Medical Association, 273*, 1871–1874.

Zawaiza, T. R., & Gerber, M. (1993). Effects of explicit instruction on math word-problem solving by community college students with learning disabilities. *Learning Disability Quarterly, 16*, 64–79.

Zelazo, P. D., Kearsley, R. B., & Stack, D. M. (1995). Mental representation for visual sequences: Increased speed of central processing from 22 to 32 months. *Intelligence, 20,* 41–63.

Zelazo, P. R., Zelazo, N. A., & Kolb, S. (1972). "Walking" in the newborn. *Science, 117,* 1058–1059.

Zeman, J., & Garber, J. (1996). Display rules for anger, sadness, and pain: It depends on who is watching. *Child Development, 67,* 957–973.

Zeman, J., & Shipman, K. (1996). Expression of negative affect: Reasons and methods. *Developmental Psychology, 32,* 842–849.

Zentall, S. S., & Ferkis, M. A. (1993). Mathematical problem solving for youth with ADHD, with and without learning disabilities. *Learning Disability Quarterly, 16*, 6–18.

Zentner, M. R., & Kagan, J. (1996). Perception of music by infants. *Nature, 383,* 29.

Zentner, M. R., & Kagan, J. (1998). Infants' perception of consonance and dissonance in music. *Infant Behavior and Development, 21,* 483–492.

Zeskind, P. S., & Barr, R. G. (1997). Acoustic characteristics of naturally occurring cries of infants with "colic." *Child Development, 68,* 394–403.

Zevalkink, J., Riksen-Walraven, J. M., & Van Lieshout, C. F. M. (1999). Attachment in the Indonesian caregiving context. *Social Development, 8*(1), 21–40.

Zhang, S. (1997). Investigation of behaviour problem of only child in kindergarten children in a Beijing urban area. *International Medical Journal, 4,* 117–118.

Zhou, Q. (2001). Parental socialization of children's emotion-related regulation in the People's Republic of China. Unpublished master thesis. Arizona State University, Tempe.

Zigler, E. F., & Styfco, S. J. (Eds.) (1993). *Head Start and beyond: A national plan for extended childhood intervention.* New Haven, CT: Yale University Press.

Zimmer, E. Z., Chao, C. R., Guy, G. P., Marks, F., & Fifer, W. P. (1993). Vibroacoustic stimulation evokes human fetal micturition. *Obstetrics and Gynecology, 81*(2), 178–180.

Zlotnick, C., Kronstadt, D., & Klee, L. (1998). Foster care children and family homelessness. *American Journal of Public Health, 88*, 1368–1370.

Zukow-Goldring, P. (1995). Sibling caregiving. In M. H. Bornstein (Ed.), *Handbook of parenting: Vol. 3: Status and social conditions of parenting* (pp. 177–208). Mahwah, NJ: Erlbaum.

NAME INDEX

SUBJECT INDEX

Locators in **bold** indicate additional display material.